FIFTH EDITION

Business

Ricky W. Griffin
Texas A&M University

Ronald J. Ebert
University of Missouri–Columbia

PRENTICE HALL
Upper Saddle River, New Jersey 07458

Senior Acquisitions Editor:	Donald J. Hull
Developmental Editor:	Elisa Adams
Editorial Assistant:	Paula D'Introno
Editor-in-Chief:	Natalie Anderson
Marketing Manager:	Debbie Clare
Production Editor:	John Roberts
Permissions Coordinator:	Monica Stipanov
Managing Editor:	Dee Josephson
Manufacturing Buyer:	Kenneth J. Clinton
Manufacturing Supervisor:	Arnold Vila
Manufacturing Manager:	Vincent Scelta
Senior Designer:	Cheryl Asherman
Design Manager:	Patricia Smythe
Interior Design:	Amanda Kavanaugh
Photo Research Supervisor:	Melinda Lee Reo
Image Permission Supervisor:	Kay Dellosa
Photo Researcher:	Melinda Alexander
Cover Design:	Amanda Kavanaugh
Composition:	UG

Griffin, Ricky W.
    Business / Ricky W. Griffin, Ronald J. Ebert.—5th ed.
        p. cm.
    Includes bibliographical references and index.
    ISBN 0-13-079611-5
    1. Industrial management—United States. 2. Business enterprises—
United States.   I. Ebert, Ronald J.   II. Title.
HD70.U5G73   1998
658—dc 21   98-19636
                                                                CIP

Prentice Hall International (UK) Limited, London
Prentice-Hall of Australia Pty. Limited, Sydney
Prentice-Hall Canada, Inc., Toronto
Prentice-Hall Hispanoamericana, S.A., Mexico
Prentice-Hall of India Private Limited, New Delhi
Prentice-Hall of Japan, Inc., Tokyo
Pearson Education Asia Pte. Ltd., Singapore
Editora Prentice-Hall do Brasil, Ltda., Rio de Janeiro

Printed in the United States of America

10 9 8 7 6 5 4 3 2

To Dustin

Live well and be happy
—(R.W.G.)

To Katy

A beloved companion
—(R.J.E.)

Overview

Contents

An unidentified Japanese executive recently said, "American and Japanese businesses are 90 percent the same, and different in all ways that matter." That's the way we see introduction to business textbooks. A quick and superficial review of the leading books might lead someone to conclude that they are all pretty much alike. After all, their basic outlines, frameworks, and sequence of chapters are all very similar to one another.

We believe that a more detailed and systematic review would highlight some very important and substantive differences. In short, we believe that this book is a superior introduction to the field of business. One reason for its superiority is the text itself. Indeed, as in previous editions, the fifth edition of *Business* has been developed and guided so as to have the following fundamental characteristics:

- Our book is *comprehensive*, providing a thorough survey of all the important facets of business.

- Our book is *accurate*, with all statements of fact based on research and/or actual managerial practice.

- Our book is *current*, with illustrative examples and cases from business situations that are still unfolding.

- Our book is *readable* so that students will enjoy the experience of reading this edition as much as they tell us they have liked earlier editions.

We believe that these qualities, a part of the book since its very first edition, are even more evident in this fifth edition. Indeed, *Business* continues to offer significant coverage of both traditional topics and newer ideas, and it continues to engage, inform, and enlighten the student reader in ways unmatched by other books.

We started work on this milestone edition by meeting with our publisher in Upper Saddle River, New Jersey, in the spring of 1997. We wanted to review every aspect and segment of the book and the support package, including reviewing each theme and approach that we had taken in the four previous editions to determine what had worked well and perhaps what hadn't. Through each of the four editions of *Business*, the supreme constant has been a belief that this book and support package will help students learn about, and perhaps launch a career in, business. We believe that this edition of *Business* is the best we have prepared yet for the beginning student of business and the professors who teach them.

The Fifth Edition Has a New Organization

This is a celebration of sorts. A textbook that makes it to its fifth edition has clearly established itself in the market. We are proud of the fact that hundreds of thousands of students have begun their careers with *Business*. One way that a textbook, or any successful product for that matter, succeeds in the long term is by close reevaluation on a regular basis. We have done this with *Business* over the years.

The fifth edition of *Business* has been reorganized based on reviewer feedback and our own observations of the market. *Business* is now 21 chapters organized in 6 parts with 2 appendices. This streamlined organization should make the material more manageable for a traditional semester and even for a quarter course.

Part One introduces the basics of the business system in the United States and includes chapters on two of the most contemporary influences in business today; the international business scene and ethics and social responsibility.

Part One: Introducing the Contemporary Business Environment
Chapter 1: Understanding the U.S. Business System
Chapter 2: Conducting Business in the United States
Chapter 3: Understanding the Global Context of Business
Chapter 4: Conducting Business Ethically and Responsibly

Part Two addresses the management side of business from a mostly macro view. In this part we discuss managing and organizing the business enterprise in two of the chapters. In another chapter we look closely at an increasingly important aspect of the U.S. business scene, entrepreneurship and small business.

Part Two: The Business of Managing
Chapter 5: Managing the Business Enterprise
Chapter 6: Organizing the Business Enterprise
Chapter 7: Understanding Entrepreneurship and Small Business

Part Three looks at the key element in any successful business, human resources. The three chapters in this part introduce students to the key elements of managing people. Topics addressed are motivation, leadership, group dynamics, and labor and management relations issues.

Part Three: Understanding People in Organizations
Chapter 8: Managing Human Resources
Chapter 9: Understanding Employee Motivation and Leadership
Chapter 10: Understanding Labor and Management Relations

Part Four covers a topic that is often fun for students—marketing. Typically this is fun for students because they can relate personally in some way to the topics covered. For example, in our experience, all students can identify with an advertisement of some type, usually a television commercial (so do we, for that matter!). The chapters in this part discuss topics such as consumer behavior and pricing, and promoting and distributing products.

Part Four: Understanding Principles of Marketing
Chapter 11: Understanding Marketing Processes and Consumer Behavior
Chapter 12: Developing and Pricing Products
Chapter 13: Promoting Products
Chapter 14: Distributing Products

Part Five gets at the way businesses manage operations and information. For the first time we have combined the topics of producing goods and producing services in one chapter. This was a difficult decision for us. We worked hard with the editorial staff to combine the best and essential ideas of these chapters into one cohesive and effective chapter. This part also examines managing for productivity and quality, accounting, and information systems.

Part Five: Managing Operations and Information
Chapter 15: Producing Services and Goods
Chapter 16: Managing for Productivity and Quality

Chapter 17: Managing Information Systems and Communication Technology
Chapter 18: Understanding Principles of Accounting

Part Six introduces the financial elements of business to the students. These can be tricky topics for beginning business students. We stress the fundamentals in these chapters with an even and consistent style. Our goal with these chapters is to address the key topics in a context that lets the students see application. Topics that we cover in this part are money and banking, securities, and financial and risk management.

Part Six: Understanding Financial Issues
Chapter 19: Understanding Money and Banking
Chapter 20: Understanding Securities and Investments
Chapter 21: Understanding Financial and Risk Management

In the appendices we cover two important topics, the legal aspects of business and insurance. Most reviewers of the fourth edition of *Business* told us they would not feel comfortable if these topics were excluded completely from the book, but that they are not necessary in the main table of contents. We know that you might differ with this; if so, let us know and we will reconsider for the sixth edition.

Appendix 1: Legal Environment and Business Law
Appendix 2: Insurance

More That's New— It's Your Business!

This new edition of *Business* has a completely new and student-centered theme. We call it "It's Your Business." This reflects our focus on the student and their success. "It's Your Business" is two things. First, it is the effort that went into this revision. Everything that we did in preparing this edition was done with the student in mind. We wanted to be accessible, clear and, maybe, fun! We wanted the student to grasp, understand, and do well in this course. So, "It's Your Business" is an approach dedicated to the students and stressing that business is something that touches every one of them in some way. It can be seen in everything from the new design of the text to the features in it. Second, "It's Your Business" is a set of new features that can be found in *every chapter in the book*. These features talk directly to the students and show them just how and why business is an important part of their lives. They cover an assortment of interesting and contemporary topics such as telecommuting (chapter 2), virtual teams (chapter 6), a job after college (chapter 8), on-line banking (chapter 19), and insurance for sport utility vehicles (appendix 2). See every chapter for the "It's Your Business" feature.

Web Vignettes—Another First

Business has been known for its many firsts. We were the first to provide an Annotated Instructor's Edition (1989), a laser disk (1991), an integrated Business Field Trip (Lawless Container Corporation in 1993 and Chaparral Steel Company in 1996), and a CD-ROM for students (*Enterprise* in 1996). The fifth edition of *Business* introduces the Web Vignette. Recognizing the explosion of information available on the World Wide Web, we felt compelled to integrate this dynamic technology in a major way. Part-opening Web Vignettes bring the Web right to the front of each major section of the book. The Web Vignettes discuss situations in companies or industries. The Web address of the principal subject is provided, as are additional Web sites and assignment and discussion questions. The Web Vignettes cover such topics as Beanie Babies, Southwest Airlines, NASCAR, and the year 2000 problem. See the table of contents for a complete listing of topics and page numbers.

It's Showtime! Showtime Networks Inc. Cases and Videos

In keeping with our tradition of integrating business information straight from the front lines, we worked with the managers and executives of one of the leading cable TV networks in the country, Showtime. During our visits with Showtime we gathered information and strategy that applies directly to all of the core areas of the introduction to business course. We wanted to be sure to create an environment where students can see the application of business concepts. Each of the six parts of *Business*, Fifth Edition, ends with a written case about a facet of the business at Showtime. To accompany this case, a videotape has been produced that can be shown in class. Many of the people interviewed and quoted in the text can be seen and heard in the video. We feel that the activities of Showtime will be of interest to the student.

The Total Support Package

Total support—that is the best way to describe the nature of the supplements and service that accompany *Business*, Fifth Edition. From the expected to the unexpected, from traditional to nontraditional, the supplements package has been designed to support the course experience in every way. For a set of the supplements or further information about them, just contact your Prentice Hall representative.

PHLIP, Prentice Hall's Learning on the Internet Partnership

This Internet supplement is by far the most successful and popular online textbook support Web site in the higher education textbook industry. PHLIP has generated over 4 million "hits" from faculty and students. Faculty can use PHLIP to integrate current events from business, search for related Web resources, or download supplements that are included on the site. There is also a faculty lounge where faculty can interact and exchange useful information. Students like the current events that illustrate text concepts. They also use the Ask the Tutor component for help from our faculty advisors. Surf over to PHLIP and explore it for yourself at http://www.phlip.marist.edu.

Business CD-ROM

Every copy of the textbook is packaged with a free student CD-ROM. The CD provides another way for the student to learn the principles of business. The CD contains interactive questions and comments written by Professor Tom Kaplan of Fairleigh Dickinson University. This information is supported by short video clips from the Showtime video series. We think that many students will be motivated to learn about business by using the CD.

Showtime Networks Inc. Video

To support the cases in the textbook about Showtime, we have produced a videotape that brings the sights and sounds of Showtime alive. More importantly, the video is another tool for the classroom that will help the students see the workings of business. Our goal with this and every video we produce is to illustrate business concepts. Audio and visual have proven to be an effective way to achieve this. The video is available free to adopters of *Business*, Fifth Edition.

Beginning Your Career Search

We know that students want to know just how they can fit into the business environment. We know they are interested in careers. This free book, by James S. O'Rourke IV of the University of Notre Dame, gives students a concise resource for resume preparation, interviewing, and overall career planning strategy. (ISBN 0-13-790312-X [free])

Study Guide

The study guide has been expertly prepared by veteran author Charles Beem of Bucks County Community College in Pennsylvania. Professor Beem has taught this course for many years and knows precisely what students need in a study guide to succeed. (ISBN 0-13-081552-7)

Instructor's Manual

This resource for professors has been prepared by James P. Hess of Ivy Tech State College in Indiana. The manual can be viewed as a resource and planning guide and will be helpful to both experienced and newer professors of the introduction to business course.

Test Bank and Prentice Hall Custom Test for Windows

Traditionally the best way to measure progress is to test the students. Professor Ed Blevins of Devry Institute of Technology in Texas has again written the test bank. It is fully updated and revised and contains more than 2,500 test questions. A unique element of the test bank is the crossword puzzles that reflect the content of each chapter.

The test bank is available in computer format on 3.5″ disks in Windows format. Based on the number-one state-of-the-art test generation software program, PH Custom Test has been developed by Engineering Software Associates (ESA). A key feature of the PH Custom Test is that you can customize the tests to meet the individual needs of your class. (ISBN 0-13-081555-1 [Test Bank], ISBN 0-13-081558-6 [PH Custom Test])

Overhead Transparencies and PowerPoint 4.0 Presentations

Athena Miklos has created a full set of 125 traditional overhead transparencies to accompany *Business*, Fifth Edition. These overheads are unique visuals and *not* picked up from inside the textbook. The visuals are also available in PowerPoint 4.0 on 3.5″ disks for technology-enabled classrooms.

Surfing for Success in Business 1998–99

This free and brief (about 70 pages) book is available to all adopters of *Business*, Fifth Edition. It concisely describes the workings of the Internet, provides some context by discussing the history of the Internet, and discusses navigating the Net. It also provides many Web addresses for Web sites that are relevant to business. This book is ideal for "value packs"—*Surfing* packaged with *Business*, Fifth Edition, at no additional charge. Ask your Prentice Hall representative how to order this package.

Threshold Competitor: A Management Simulation, Second Edition

Written by Philip H. Anderson of the University of St. Thomas and Timothy W. Scott of Mankato State University, *Threshold* is a Windows-based business management program that simulates the workings of small business. Working in groups, students interact with the program and make the decisions needed to run a small manufacturing business. *Threshold* is available for purchase at a modest price. (ISBN 0-13-675539-9)

The *New York Times* Contemporary View Program

Working with the *New York Times*, the editors at Prentice Hall have selected dozens of recent articles from the business section of the *New York Times* on topics that are directly relevant to the study of business. For example, when talking to students about management topics, it is useful to enlighten students by having them read about the management challenges that will be faced by CitiCorp and Travelers Group when they merge. Articles like this are exclusive to this newspaper supplement and it is free upon adoption of *Business*, Fifth Edition.

College Newslink

Now you can link up to the world news every day with Prentice Hall's College Newslink program. College Newslink is a unique educational service that brings today's news from the leading newspapers of the world to your computer via e-mail. Visit www.ssnewslink.com for a free trial.

Acknowledgments

Although only two names appear on the cover of this book, we could never have completed the fifth edition without the assistance of many fine individuals. Everyone who worked on the book was committed to making it the best that it could be. Quality and closeness to the customer are things that we read a lot about today. Both we and the people who worked with us took these concepts to heart in this book and made quality our watchword by listening to our users and trying to provide what they want.

First, we would like to thank all the professionals who took time from their busy schedules to review materials of *Business*, Fifth Edition, for us:

Ugur Yucelt
Penn State University

Elizabeth J. Wilson
Louisiana State University

Michael Cicero
Highline Community College

Mike Dougherty
Milwaukee Area Technical College

We also thank the reviewers of the previous editions:

Michael Baldigo
Sonoma State University

Betty Ann Kirk
Tallahassee Community College

Harvey Bronstein
Oakland Community College

Sofia B. Klopp
Palm Beach Community College

Gary Christiansen
North Iowa Area Community College

Kenneth J. Lacho
University of New Orleans

Pat Ellebracht
Northeast Missouri State University

John F. Mastriani
El Paso Community College

John Gubbay
Moraine Valley Community College

William E. Matthews
William Paterson College of New Jersey

Edward M. Henn
Broward Community College

Thomas J. Morrisey
Buffalo State College

David William Murphy
Madisonville Community College

Robert N. Stern
Cornell University

Scott Norwood
San Jose State University

Jane A. Treptow
Broward Community College

Joseph R. Novak
Blinn College

Janna P. Vice
Eastern Kentucky University

Constantine Petrides
Borough of Manhattan Community College

Philip A. Weatherford Ed.D
Embry-Riddle Aeronautical University

William D. Raffield
University of St. Thomas

Jerry E. Wheat
Indiana University Southeast

Richard Randall
Nassau Community College

Pamela J. Winslow
Berkeley College of Business

Betsy Ray
Indiana Business College

A number of other professionals also made substantive contributions to the text, ranging from draft material on specialized topics to suggested resource materials to proposals for cases and examples. In particular, we are greatly indebted to Elisa Adams and Judy Block for their inventive and indefatigable contributions in their capacity as professional writers and researchers.

The supplements package for *Business*, Fifth Edition, also benefited from the able contributions of several individuals, all under the direction of Don Hull, John Larkin, and Kristen Imperatore at Prentice Hall. We would like to thank these people for developing the finest set of instructional and learning materials for this field.

Meanwhile, a superb team of professionals at Prentice Hall made this book a pleasure to write. Authors often get the credit when a book is successful, but the success of this book must be shared with an outstanding group of people in New Jersey. Our editor, Don Hull, has been a true product champion and has improved both the book and the package in more ways than we can list, going all the way back to the first edition. John Roberts, the production editor, also made many truly outstanding contributions to the project.

We also want to acknowledge the contributions of the entire team at Prentice Hall Business Publishing, including James Boyd, Editorial Director; Natalie Anderson, Editor in Chief; Brian Kibby, Director of Marketing; Steve Deitmer, Director of Development; Debbie Clare, Marketing Manager; Paula D'Introno, Editorial Assistant; John Larkin, Assistant Editor; Kristen Imperatore, Assistant Editor; Bob Prokop, Marketing Assistant; Joanne Jay, Assistant Vice President and Director of Production and Manufacturing; Dee Josephson, Managing Editor; Carol Ann Peschke, copyeditor; Vincent Scelta, Manufacturing Manager; Arnold Vila, Manufacturing Supervisor; Kenneth J. Clinton, Manufacturing Buyer; Patricia Smythe, Design Manager; Cheryl Asherman, Senior Designer; Melinda Lee Reo, Photo Research Supervisor; Melinda Alexander, Photo Researcher; Kay Dellosa, Image Permission Supervisor; and Zina Arabia, Image Coordinator.

Our colleagues at Texas A&M University and the University of Missouri–Columbia also deserve recognition. Each of us has the good fortune to be a part of a community of scholars who enrich our lives and challenge our ideas. Without their intellectual stimulation and support, our work would suffer greatly. Phyllis Washburn, Dr. Griffin's staff assistant, deserves special mention for the myriad contributions she has made to this project as well.

Finally, our families. We take pride in the accomplishments of our wives, Glenda and Mary, and draw strength from the knowledge that they are there for us to lean on. And we take joy from our children, Ashley, Dustin, Matt, and Kristen. Sometimes in the late hours when we're ready for sleep but have to get one or two more pages written, looking at your pictures keeps us going. Thanks to all of you for making us what we are.

Ricky W. Griffin

Ronald J. Ebert

About the Authors

Ricky W. Griffin was born and raised in Corsicana, Texas. He received his B.B.A. from North Texas State University and his M.B.A. and Ph.D. from the University of Houston. He served on the faculty of the University of Missouri–Columbia from 1978 until 1981, when he joined the faculty at Texas A&M. In 1990, he was named the university's Lawrence E. Fouraker Professor of Business Administration. In 1997 he became the Head of the Department of Management in the Lowry Mays College and Graduate School of Business at Texas A&M.

Dr. Griffin's research interests include executive skill development, employee health and well-being, and dysfunctional behavior in organizations. He has done consulting in the areas of task design, employee motivation, and quality circles for such organizations as Baker-Hughes, Texas Instruments, Six Flags Corporation, Texas Commerce Bank, and AT&T. His research has won two Academy of Management Research Awards (both in the Organizational Behavior division) and one Texas A&M University Research Award.

Former president of the Southwest Division of the Academy of Management, Dr. Griffin also has served as the Director of the Center for Human Resource Management at Texas A&M. In addition to *Business*, he is the author or co-author of four books and more than 60 journal articles and book chapters.

Ronald J. Ebert is Professor of Management at the University of Missouri–Columbia. He received his B.S. in Industrial Engineering from the Ohio State University, his M.B.A. from the University of Dayton, and his D.B.A. from Indiana University, where he was a U.S. Steel Fellow. A member of and an active participant in the Academy of Management, the Institute of Management Sciences, the American Production and Inventory Control Society, and the Operations Management Association, Dr. Ebert has also served as the editor of the *Journal of Operations Management* and as Chair of the Production and Operations Management Division of the Academy of Management. In addition to *Business,* he is the co-author of three books: *Organizational Decision Processes, Production and Operations Management* (published in English, Spanish, and Chinese), and *Management.*

Dr. Ebert has held engineering and supervisory positions in quality management with the Frigidaire Division of General Motors Corporation. He has also done TQM and operations strategy consulting for the National Science Foundation, the United States Savings and Loan League, Kraft Foods, Oscar Mayer, Sola Optical USA, Inc., the City of Columbia, and the American Public Power Association. His research interests include manufacturing policy and strategy, engineering design processes in product development, statistical quality control, and subjective managerial judgements in strategy formulation.

Introducing the Contemporary
Business Environment

Want to make money fast? Drop everything and listen, because it's a deal you won't believe. No, we're not talking about a hot stock tip, an investment in commodities futures, or land in oil-well territory. This deal involves Bernie the St. Bernard, Nuts the Squirrel, Strut the Rooster, Web the Spider, and 141 more fist-size, plush beanbags called Beanie Babies.

Manufactured by Ty Inc., a privately held company in Oakbrook, Illinois, that specializes in stuffed animals, Beanie Babies have earned a fortune for the company and made staggering profits for tens of thousands of children and adults who trade them on secondary markets via the Internet. How Ty Inc. made this happen and how company executives handled the inevitable business problems along the way is a story worth telling.

An Idea Is Born

After graduating from college in 1962, Ty Warner, who would later found Ty Inc., began working for Dakin Inc., an Illinois-based stuffed animal manufacturer. He learned important lessons during his 18 years with the company, especially marketing lessons. "They taught me that it's better selling 40,000 accounts [to specialty gift shops] than it is five accounts" to mass-market retailers such as Toys R Us and Wal-Mart. "It's more difficult to do," said Warner, "but for the longevity of the company and the profit margins, it's the better of the two. [Beanie Babies] could be around for years just as long as I don't take the easy road and sell it to a mass merchant who's going to put it in bins."

Warner learned that in the stuffed animal business, affordable, high-quality merchandise is essential if you want children to spend their own money. Combining allowance, earnings, and gifts, children under 14 directly spend about $20 billion a year and influence adult spending to the tune of another $200 billion. When Warner began manufacturing Beanie Babies in 1993, he targeted this market.

Making the Business Work

The first task was manufacturing. To keep production costs down, Warner contracted with factories in China, where his Beanie Babies were sewn and stuffed with polyvinyl chloride pellets. He then sold his products to independent gift shops for roughly $3 each. Warner knew that an important benefit of working with these merchants was rapid cash flow because small retailers often pay cash on delivery or write a check within 15 days. "If we were to sell to Wal-Mart, we would not be paid in 30 days," said Warner, "and that would affect our financial situation."

When the Beanie Babies craze began in earnest in December 1995, Warner and a staff of about 100 clerks handled orders and shipments on what was quickly becoming an obsolete computer system. With as many as 100,000 calls a day coming into the company, Ty faced an information system crisis.

The original system was designed for use by a maximum of 100 order entry clerks and required 2 to 4 weeks from order to shipment. The system was also frustrating to learn and use, requiring order clerks to scroll through pages of forms for every customer and to enter every bit of information manually. Chris Johnson, Ty's director of management information systems, was in charge of finding a replacement system that would work right away. He was authorized to spend as much as needed, as long as he did it as fast as humanly possible.

After compressing system planning time from 6 months to 2 months, Johnson chose an information system designed for high-volume businesses. The system cut ordering steps, automated shipping information and billing, handled credit checks, generated separate invoices, balanced inventory with orders, and more. It was easy to use, as Johnson explains. Order clerks "have to be able to look up orders fast and click back and forth between windows. Customers need information on shipping fast, and the user interface needs to support that." Ty's new system promised to cut the time spent on many operations in half and to enter large chunks of data automatically.

Marketing Genius

The factor most responsible for the Beanie Babies craze is an innovative marketing strategy that relies on a basic economic principle: Provide stores with too few items to meet demand, stop production on individual items to produce permanent scarcity, and demand will increase as word spreads. By June 1997 Ty Inc. was limiting retailers to 36 pieces of each character per month, with only a single monthly order being accepted. The perception of scarcity and exclusivity was increased further by Warner's decision not to advertise on television.

The hardest part of the strategy involved the need for production restraint as demand increased. Although it would have been profitable in the short term to pump up production, Warner knew that Beanie Babies would last longer if there were a permanent scarcity. His plan worked, as Steve Josephson, owner of the Toy Box in Mamaroneck, New York explains: "I've been in the business 30 years and I've never seen an item like this."

A highly successful promotional relationship between Ty and McDonald's that broke all consumer response records helped increase the popularity of the toy. Offering customers one of 10 Teenie Beanie Babies with the purchase of a Happy Meal, McDonald's sold nearly 100 million meals in just 10 days, instead of the 35 days originally anticipated. In the process, Ty received about $45 million worth of free advertising for its full-size product.

Birth of a Secondary Market

With the Beanie Babies having a price tag of only $5, young children fueled demand as they made purchases with allowance money and convinced parents to buy on impulse. Children soon became avid collectors, and many owned the entire set.

With some items out of production and others nearly impossible to find at retail stores, Beanie Babies became collectibles and an active secondary market developed on the Internet. Ty Inc. encourages this market on its own Web site (Ty.com), which allows visitors to buy and sell and talk in chat rooms. Dozens of other Web sites have active marketplaces, where prices are set by supply and demand.

As prices rose, adults became the primary collectors of the most valuable items, including Peanut the Elephant (in royal blue), which recently sold for $2,200, Rex the Tyrannosaurus ($1,750), and Peking the Panda ($1,295). Although children are priced out of this market, they congregate at Web sites with offerings that start at about $10.

Will It Last?

Things are very good for Ty, at least for now. Sales increased tenfold in 1997 from about $26 million in 1996. Although there are cheaper competitors, none has achieved the levels of design and quality that make Beanie Babies a hot collectible. Those who produce knockoffs that are too close to Ty's designs are promptly sued by Warner. So far, three companies have been forced to recall their products and hand over profits to Warner.

Like the conductor of an orchestra, Warner has put together a business strategy that sings the tune of continued success. "Every time we make a shipment [retailers] want twice as many [Beanie Babies] as we can possible get to them," he said. "As long as kids keep fighting over the products and retailers are angry at us because they cannot get enough, I think those are good signs."

WEB LINKS

Beanie Baby Web sites abound, including the following. The information in these and other sites will help you answer the questions that follow:

Angel's Beanie Page   http://www.erols.com/angelisa/beanie.html

Barbies and Beanies: Your Unofficial Link to the   http://www.cyberstreet.com/users/coogan/main.htm
    World of Vintage Barbie Dolls and Beanie Babies

Beanie Babies: Buying Selling Trading   http://www.beaniepost.com/

Beanie Babies: Collectible Exchange   http://www.beaniex.com/

Twohogwild for Beanies   http://members.ad.com/twohogwild/4beanies.html

Ty Inc.: The Official Home of the Beanie Babies   http://www.ty.com

Wild About Beanies   http://www.wildaboutbeanies.com/

CASE QUESTIONS

1 How is Ty Inc.'s Beanie Baby business a good example of capitalism at work? Before you answer this question, visit Ty.com to learn how the company increases market demand in ways not mentioned in the case.

2 How is the business conducted at the various Web sites an example of capitalism at work? (Do not search Ty.com to answer this question.)

3 Warner's strategy is to control supply in order to increase demand. The case explained the benefits of this strategy. Can you think of possible problems?

4 Warner owns 100 percent of Ty Inc. Do you think it is easier or harder for a privately controlled corporation to accomplish such a daring business strategy? Explain your answer.

5 As described in this case, Warner and his staff faced information system and legal problems as the Beanie Baby business grew. Based on what you know about business, why do you think problem-solving is an important skill? Do you agree or disagree with the following statement: "Success in business depends on your ability to turn problems into opportunities."

6 Ty Inc. manufactures Beanie Babies in China. With product demand in primary and secondary markets linked to quality, what challenge does manufacturing abroad create for the company? Have you seen any comments on the Web expressing dissatisfaction with product quality?

7 Beanie Babies are a toy for young children, yet prices on the secondary market are out of children's reach. How do you feel about this from a business ethics point of view? Do children in Web chat rooms express frustration at not being able to afford retired or scarce Beanie Babies?

chapter 1

Understanding the U.S. business system

America Online meets supply and demand

It probably seemed like a good idea at the time. On December 1, 1996, America Online, already the country's largest Internet provider, with 7 million customers, changed its pricing strategy in a bid for growth. Instead of its regular per-hour charge, AOL announced it was offering new and existing customers a flat rate of $19.95 a month for unlimited access.

The trouble began almost at once. New customers flocked to AOL and old ones switched to the new pricing plan in droves. The number of daily on-line sessions surged, the average customer stayed on line 20 percent longer than before, and when the increased traffic began to result in busy signals, customers learned how to log on and stay on, using easy-to-get software to keep their on-line connections going even when they weren't using it, further clogging AOL's overloaded capacity. Internet access became increasingly difficult as AOL continued to promote its new

low price even while it struggled to keep up with increasing demand, and the electronic traffic jams began to spill over into local phone networks that handle voice calls.

> **" The real reason we have these problems is that the demand is so great. . . . And pricing for unlimited use is part of reaching a mainstream audience. "**
>
> —Steve Case,
> chairman of America Online

AOL scrambled to respond to angry customers frustrated by poor service. It first announced ambitious plans to spend $350 million to expand capacity and tried to placate customers for several weeks. But in early

1997, bruised by quick-thinking competitors and under pressure from several class-action suits filed against it, the company agreed to give customers millions of dollars in credits and refunds and temporarily curb its appetite for new subscribers. State attorneys general hailed the announcement as a milestone in consumer protection for the unfolding information age.

When the dust settled AOL had added about a million new subscribers and proven that flat-rate pricing in cyberspace is here to stay. Chairperson Steve Case said, "The real reason we have these problems is that the demand is so great. . . . And pricing for unlimited use is part of reaching a mainstream audience."

Supply and demand, competition and profitability, even social responsibility and the frontiers of the legal environment—the experience of AOL over 2 short months encompasses just a sampling of the main themes told over and over again in the annals of business enterprise in the United States. As you will see in this chapter, those forces are also the key factors in the U.S. market economy. You will also see that although the world's economic systems differ markedly, standards for evaluating success or failure are linked to a system's capacity to achieve certain basic goals.

By focusing on the learning objectives of this chapter, you will better understand the U.S. business system and the mechanisms by which it not only pursues its goals but permits businesses to pursue theirs. After reading this chapter, you should be able to

1 Define the nature of U.S. business and identify its main goals.

2 Describe different types of economic systems according to the means by which they control the factors of production.

3 Show how demand and supply affect resource distribution in the United States.

4 Identify the elements of private enterprise and explain the various degrees of competition in the U.S. economic system.

5 Explain the criteria for evaluating the success of an economic system in meeting its goals and show how the federal government attempts to manage the U.S. economy.

"Perhaps we could find a way to redefine 'profit.'"

The Concept of Business and the Concept of Profit

business
An organization that provides goods or services in order to earn profits

profits
The difference between a business's revenues and its expenses

economic system
A nation's system for allocating its resources among its citizens

What do you think of when you hear the word *business*? Does it conjure up images of huge corporations such as General Motors and IBM? Are you reminded of smaller firms such as your local supermarket? Or do you think of even smaller one-person operations such as the barbershop around the corner? Each of these organizations, of course, is a **business**—an organization that provides goods or services in order to earn profits. Indeed, the prospect of earning **profits**—the difference between a business's revenues and its expenses—is what encourages people to open and expand businesses. After all, profits reward owners for taking the risks involved in investing their money and time.

Today, businesses produce most of the goods and services we consume. They also employ most of the working people in the United States. Moreover, new forms of technology, service businesses, and international opportunities promise to keep production, consumption, and employment growing indefinitely.[1] In turn, profits from businesses are paid to millions of owners and stockholders. Taxes on business help support governments at all levels. In many cases, businesses also support charitable causes and provide community leadership.

In this chapter, we begin our introduction to business by looking at its role in both the U.S. economy and U.S. society. There are a variety of **economic systems** around the world. Once you understand something about the systems of most developed countries, you will better appreciate the workings of the U.S. system. As we will see, the effects of economic forces on businesses and the effects of businesses on the economy are dynamic—and sometimes volatile.

Global Economic Systems

Not surprisingly, a U.S. business operates differently from a business in, say, France or the People's Republic of China. And of course, businesses in these countries vary from those in Japan or Brazil. A major factor in these differences is the economic system of a firm's home country, in which it conducts most of its business. An economic system is a nation's system for allocating its resources among its citizens, both individuals and organizations. In this section we will show how economic systems differ according to the ownership or control of these resources, which are often called factors of production. We will also describe several kinds of economic systems.

Factors of Production

The key difference between economic systems is the different ways in which they manage the **factors of production**—that is, the basic resources that a country's businesses use to produce goods and services. These resources include labor, capital, entrepreneurs, and natural resources.[2]

Labor

The people who work for businesses provide labor. Sometimes called **human resources, labor** includes both the physical and mental contributions people make as they are engaged in economic production. For example, the Weyerhaeuser Company employs about 40,000 people. Not surprisingly, the operations of such a huge company require a widely skilled labor force, ranging from financial planners to loggers to truck drivers.

Capital

Obtaining and using material resources and labor requires **capital**—the funds needed to operate an enterprise. Capital is needed both to start a business and to keep it operating and growing. Weyerhaeuser requires millions of dollars every year to run its mills, pay its workers, and ship its wood products to customers. A major source of capital for most smaller businesses is personal investment by owners. Personal investment can be made by the individual entrepreneurs, by partners who start businesses together, or by investors who buy stock. Revenue from the sale of products is another important ongoing source of capital. Finally, many firms borrow funds from banks and other lending institutions.

Entrepreneurs

Weyerhaeuser Company can trace its roots back to 1858, when a young German immigrant named Frederick Weyerhaeuser opened a lumberyard in Illinois. Over the years his business prospered, and in 1900 he and 15 partners bought 900,000 acres of timbered land near Tacoma, Washington. Under Weyerhaeuser's leadership the firm grew and prospered, and today is one of the largest forest-products companies in the world. Many economic systems need and encourage **entrepreneurs** like Frederick Weyerhaeuser, who start new businesses and who make the decisions that expand small businesses into larger ones. These people embrace the opportunities and accept the risks inherent in creating and operating businesses.

Natural Resources

Natural resources are materials supplied by nature. The most common natural resources are land, water, mineral deposits, and trees. For example, Weyerhaeuser obviously relies on land and trees. But even firms that do not directly use natural resources are still likely to depend on them indirectly. Chemicals, for example, are the basis for the plastic resins that computer manufacturers use for keyboards. All companies need land on which to build factories and office buildings and to generate the electric power they need to operate.

Types of Economic Systems

Different types of economic systems manage the factors of production in different ways. In some systems, ownership is private; in others, the factors of production are owned by the government. Economic systems also differ in the ways decisions are made about production and allocation. A **planned economy**, for example, relies on a centralized government to control all or most factors of production and to make all or most production and allocation decisions. In market economies, individuals—producers and consumers—control production and allocation decisions through supply and demand. We will describe

---

factors of production
Resources used in the production of goods and services (natural resources, labor, capital, and entrepreneurs)

labor (or human resources)
The physical and mental capabilities of people as they contribute to economic production

capital
The funds needed to create and operate a business enterprise

entrepreneur
Person who starts a new business or makes the decisions that expand a small business

natural resources
Materials supplied by nature (such as land, water, mineral deposits, and trees)

planned economy
Economy that relies on a centralized government to control all or most factors of production and to make all or most production and allocation decisions

each of these economic types and then discuss the reality of the mixed market economy. We will also look closely at an important process in the development of the mixed market economy in more and more countries: privatization.

Planned Economies

The two most basic forms of planned economies are communism and socialism. As originally proposed by nineteenth-century German economist Karl Marx, communism is a system in which the government owns and operates all sources of production. Marx envisioned a society in which individuals would ultimately contribute according to their abilities and receive economic benefits according to their needs. He also expected government ownership of production factors to be only temporary: Once society had matured, government would wither away and the workers would gain direct ownership.

Most Eastern European countries and the former Soviet Union embraced communist systems until very recently. In the early 1990s, however, one country after another renounced communism as both an economic and a political system. Today, Cuba, North Korea, Vietnam, and the People's Republic of China are among the few nations with avowedly communist systems. Even in these countries, however, planned economic systems are making room for features of the free-enterprise system from the lowest to the highest levels.

For example, even though China is still governed according to communist doctrines, the nation's leaders are gradually opening its boundaries to foreign companies. Within the last few years, Motorola, Microsoft, and Sony have established major operations in China. Wal-Mart has opened discount stores there, and Coca-Cola is available on virtually any street corner. Thus, the free-enterprise system appears to be well on its way to becoming the standard way of doing business in the largest country in the world, a prospect that has virtually every international business eagerly awaiting opportunities there.

Market Economies

market
Mechanism for exchange between buyers and sellers of a particular good or service

A **market** is a mechanism for exchange between the buyers and sellers of a particular good or service. To understand how a **market economy** works, consider what happens when a customer goes to a fruit market to buy apples. While one vendor is selling apples for $1 per pound, another is charging $1.50. Both vendors are free to charge what they want, and customers are free to buy what they choose. If both vendors' apples are of the same quality, the customer will buy the cheaper ones. But if the $1.50 apples are fresher, the customer may buy them instead. In short, both buyers and sellers enjoy freedom of choice.

market economy
Economy in which individuals control production and allocation decisions through supply and demand

Capitalism

capitalism
Market economy that provides for private ownership of production and encourages entrepreneurship by offering profits as an incentive

Market economies, which are based on the principles of **capitalism**, rely on markets, not governments, to decide what, when, and for whom to produce. Capitalism provides for the private ownership of the factors of production. It also encourages entrepreneurship by offering profits as an incentive. Businesses can provide whatever goods and services and charge whatever prices they choose. Similarly, customers can choose how and where to spend their money.[3]

In market economies, profits motivate entrepreneurs to use resources efficiently and to produce the goods that consumers want. Businesses that produce inefficiently or fail to provide needed or desired products will not survive. At least that is the theory in "pure" market economies. Even in the United States, however, the government pays farmers billions of dollars per year to grow such grains as rice, cotton, and especially corn. Such income support programs are designed to help U.S. farmers keep prices low and thus compete against farmers elsewhere, who are subsidized even more generously. Not surprisingly, these programs have been controversial for a long time. Today, for example, although payments have dropped to $5.5 billion from $14 billion in 1987, critics still charge that they keep inefficient producers in business alongside efficient producers. They also argue that payments stimulate overproduction and thus drive down the prices that deserving commercial farmers could otherwise charge.[4]

Mixed Market Economies

In their pure theoretical forms, planned and market economies are often seen as two extremes or opposites. In reality, however, most countries rely on some form of **mixed market economy**—that is, a system featuring characteristics of both planned and market economies. For example, most countries of the former Eastern bloc are now adopting market mechanisms through a process called **privatization**—the process of converting government enterprises into privately owned companies.

In Hungary, for instance, privatization is being used to help reduce the country's $22-billion national debt. Among the industries now being privatized are the state-owned oil and telephone companies, all major banks, and the entire electricity and gas distribution industry. Successful privatization often requires the ingenuity of creative capitalists such as Peter Rona, a Hungarian who is a major financial backer of North American Bus

mixed market economy
Economic system featuring characteristics of both planned and market economies

privatization
Process of converting government enterprises into privately owned companies

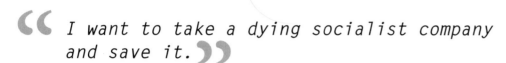

> ❝ *I want to take a dying socialist company and save it.* ❞
>
> —Peter Rona, Hungarian capitalist

Industries Ltd., a Hungarian company that manufactures buses for U.S. mass transit fleets in Miami, Baltimore, Buffalo, and Washington. After privatizing part of the state-owned bus company, Rona developed a plan to manufacture buses in both Hungary and Alabama, thereby meeting U.S. government requirements that 60 percent of the value of federally financed urban buses come from the United States. Although parts and partially assembled vehicle bodies are shipped back and forth from Budapest to Alabama, the company is more competitive than its U.S. business rivals, largely because of the low cost of Hungarian labor ($4 per hour) and Rona's perseverance. "I want to take a dying socialist

Global competitors can reach new U.S. markets as well, as did a Hungarian bus company whose vehicles now ply the streets of Portland, Oregon.

"Adopt-a-Highway" programs, such as the one for New York's Long Island Expressway, are one way in which a form of privatization has replaced state and municipal services. Groups or individuals agree to accept responsibility for maintaining the cleanliness of a specified section of the road, such as this area in the Queens section of New York City.

company and save it," says Rona, who left his native country after the Soviet-crushed uprising in 1956 and did not return until 1989.[5]

In the partially planned system often called **socialism**, the government owns and operates selected major industries. In such mixed market economies, the government may control banking, communication, transportation, and industries that produce such basic goods as oil and steel. Smaller businesses, such as clothing stores and restaurants, are privately owned. For example, many Western European countries, including England and France, allow free-market operations in most economic areas but maintain government control in others, such as health care. Government planners in Japan give special centrally planned assistance to new industries that are expected to grow.

Note that in the United States, regulation performs similar functions: The federal government regulates many aspects of business, including hiring practices, advertising, and waste disposal. Moreover, privatization is not entirely irrelevant in this country. Although the United States has no state-owned companies, privatization is nonetheless transforming the way many states and municipalities deliver key government services. For example, many cities contract with private companies to collect trash, process water bills, and handle park concessions and landscaping. Many states are successfully using "Adopt-a-Highway" programs in which civic groups and other organizations assume the responsibility for regularly cleaning up litter along a defined stretch of highway.

socialism
Planned economic system in which the government owns and operates only selected major sources of production

The U.S. Economic System

Understanding the complex nature of the U.S. economic system is essential to understanding the environment in which U.S. businesses operate. In this section, we will describe the workings of the U.S. market economy in more detail. Specifically, we will examine *markets*, the nature of *demand and supply*, *private enterprise*, and *degrees of competition*.

Markets, Demand, and Supply

A market economy consists of many different markets. For example, virtually every good or service has its own market. In each of these, businesses decide what to make, in what quantities, and what price to charge. Customers also make decisions: They decide what to buy and how much they are willing to pay. Billions of exchanges take place every day between businesses and individuals, between different businesses, and between individuals, businesses, and governments. Moreover, exchanges conducted under conditions in one place often have an impact on exchanges elsewhere.

The Natural Environment

Can Privatization Save Our Parks?

How successful is the 125-year-old government business of running our national parks? Since the creation of Yellowstone, the first national park, the system has grown to include 375 units across the country and has enclosed and protected some of the continent's most fragile and awe-inspiring sites. The number of visitors to such treasures as Yellowstone, the Grand Canyon, and Hawaii Volcanoes National Park continues to swell and is expected to top half a billion a year by 2010. But land development, pollution, underfunding, neglect, and vandalism are taking their toll in the battle to preserve the abundance and beauty of nature. Says Yellowstone's resource chief, John Varley, "We've crested: We can no longer offer the quality of experience we once did."

Money problems plague such sites as Gettysburg National Military Park in Pennsylvania, where priceless Civil War photographs, documents, and artifacts such as swords and uniforms are stored in rooms that lack temperature and humidity controls, sprinkler systems, and even security. Invading species, now unchecked, threaten the balance of ecosystems in a number of parks. At Great Smoky Mountains in Tennessee, for example, a tiny nonnative insect pest has destroyed an entire forest. Humans, too, are adding to the problem, with roads, factories, power plants, and even competing attractions such as nearby theme parks contributing pollutants to the once-pristine environment of the parks.

Although members of Congress lobby for—and sometimes get—controversial new parks that court local voters but drain the National Park Service's budget, annual appropriations for existing parks have declined some 12 percent in real dollars over the last 20 years. In response the National Park Service has raised entrance and parking fees, which range from $3 to $14, at nearly 100 parks and shut down some environmental monitoring and research services that could have enabled it to better track the condition of park wildlife, habitats, and historic sites.

> " *We've crested: We can no longer offer the quality of experience we once did.* "
>
> —John Varley, resource chief,
> Yellowstone National Park

Private sector partnerships with commercial sponsors are under consideration for some parks, along with park revenue bonds, similar to savings bonds. But even if sponsorship comes to pass, it seems likely that future visits to our nation's grandest environments will be noisy, crowded affairs, requiring advance reservations, high entrance fees, and the ability to cope with a busload of fellow visitors seeking fast-fading beauty and solitude.

▶ *POLITICS IN JOHANNESBURG + PRODUCTIVITY IN DETROIT.* The following events are not unrelated:

▶ In early April 1994, South Africa held the first all-race elections in the country's history.

▶ On April 28, 1994, the Ford Motor Co. joined General Motors and Chrysler in announcing first-quarter earnings that pointed to the automakers' best year since 1989.

▶ On April 29, 1994, the price of platinum futures—agreements to buy platinum at a future date—jumped by $7.70 per ounce on the New York Mercantile Exchange.

The connection? Investors on the New York exchange were unsure about the future policies of the new government in South Africa, which (with equally troubled Russia) produces most of the world's platinum. In other words, they were concerned about the platinum supply. Automakers require platinum in the manufacture of catalytic converters, so increased car sales—such as those being enjoyed by the United States' Big Three—trigger greater demand for platinum. According to the basic rules of demand and supply, there-

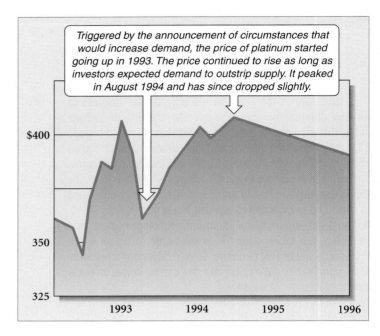

Figure 1.1 Price of Platinum, 1993–1996

Triggered by the announcement of circumstances that would increase demand, the price of platinum started going up in 1993. The price continued to rise as long as investors expected demand to outstrip supply. It peaked in August 1994 and has since dropped slightly.

demand
The willingness and ability of buyers to purchase a good or service

supply
The willingness and ability of producers to offer a good or service for sale

law of demand
Principle that buyers will purchase (demand) more of a product as its price drops and less as its price increases

law of supply
Principle that producers will offer (supply) more of a product for sale as its price rises and less as its price drops

demand and supply schedule
Assessment of the relationships between different levels of demand and supply at different price levels

demand curve
Graph showing how many units of a product will be demanded (bought) at different prices

supply curve
Graph showing how many units of a product will be supplied (offered for sale) at different prices

fore, the value and the price of platinum went up. Indeed, as you can see from Figure 1.1, the price of platinum rose between mid-1993 and August 1994, when it reached $410 an ounce. However, with the stabilization of the South African government, the price dropped back to $389 per ounce in June 1996.

The Laws of Demand and Supply

On all economic levels, decisions about what to buy and what to sell are determined primarily by the forces of demand and supply. **Demand** is the willingness and ability of buyers to purchase a product (a good or a service). **Supply** is the willingness and ability of producers to offer a good or service for sale. Generally speaking, demand and supply follow basic laws:

■ The **law of demand**: Buyers will purchase (demand) more of a product as its price drops and less of a product as its price increases.

■ The **law of supply**: Producers will offer (supply) more of a product for sale as its price rises and less as its price drops.

Demand and Supply Schedule. To appreciate these laws in action, consider the market for pizza in your town. If everyone in town is willing to pay $25 for a pizza (a high price), the town's only pizzeria will produce a large supply. But if everyone is willing to pay only $5 (a low price), the restaurant will make fewer pizzas. Through careful analysis, we can determine how many pizzas will be sold at different prices. These results, called a **demand and supply schedule**, are obtained from marketing research and other systematic studies of the market. Properly applied, they help managers better understand the relationships among different levels of demand and supply at different price levels.

Demand and Supply Curves. For example, the demand and supply schedule can be used to construct demand and supply curves for pizza in your town. A **demand curve** shows how many products—in this case, pizzas—will be demanded (bought) at different prices. A **supply curve** shows how many pizzas will be supplied (cooked) at different prices.

Figure 1.2 shows hypothetical demand and supply curves for pizzas. As you can see, demand increases as price decreases; supply increases as price increases. When the de-

Figure 1.2   Demand and Supply

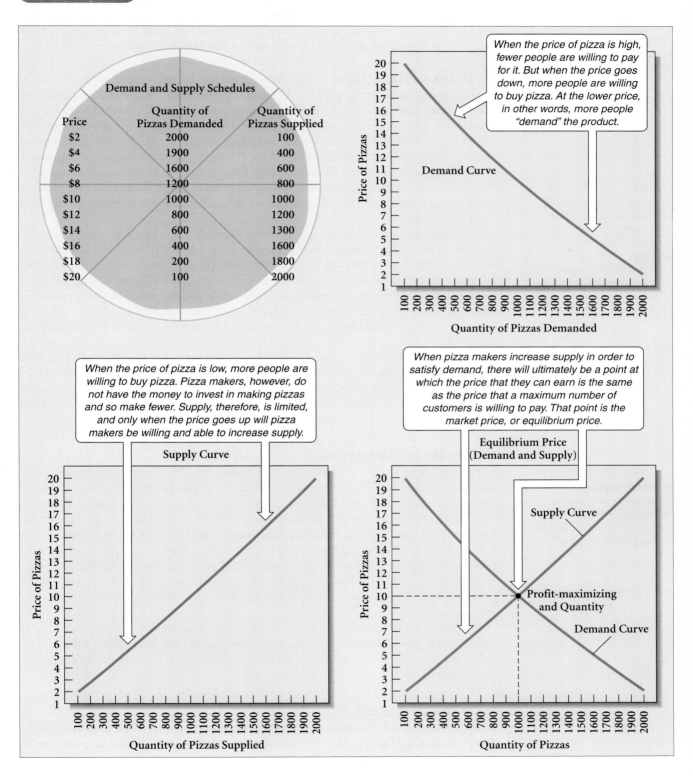

market price (or equilibrium price)
Profit-maximizing price at which the quantity of goods demanded and the quantity of goods supplied are equal

surplus
Situation in which quantity supplied exceeds quantity demanded

shortage
Situation in which quantity demanded exceeds quantity supplied

private enterprise
Economic system that allows individuals to pursue their own interests without undue government restriction

private property
The right to buy, own, use, and sell almost any form of property

mand and supply curves are plotted on the same graph, the point at which they intersect is the **market price** or **equilibrium price**: the price at which the quantity of goods demanded and the quantity of goods supplied are equal. Note in Figure 1.2 that the equilibrium price for pizzas in our example is $10. At this point, the quantity of pizzas demanded and the quantity of pizzas supplied are the same: 1,000 pizzas per week.

Surpluses and Shortages. What if the restaurant chooses to make some other number of pizzas? For example, what would happen if the owner tried to increase profits by making more pizzas to sell? Or what if the owner wanted to reduce overhead, cut back on store hours, and reduce the number of pizzas offered for sale? In either case, the result would be an inefficient use of resources and lower profits. For instance, if the restaurant supplies 1,200 pizzas and tries to sell them for $10 each, 200 pizzas will not be purchased. The demand schedule clearly shows that only 1,000 pizzas will be demanded at this price. The pizza maker will thus have a **surplus**—a situation in which the quantity supplied exceeds the quantity demanded. The restaurant will lose the money it spent making those extra 200 pizzas.

Conversely, if the pizzeria supplies only 800 pizzas, a **shortage** will result: The quantity demanded will be greater than the quantity supplied. The pizzeria will lose the extra money it could have made by producing 200 more pizzas. Even though consumers may pay more for pizzas because of the shortage, the restaurant will still earn lower profits than if it had made 1,000 pizzas. In addition, it will risk angering customers who cannot buy pizzas. To maximize profits, therefore, all businesses must constantly seek the right combination of price charged and quantity supplied. This right combination is found at the equilibrium point.

Of course, this simple example involves only one company, one product, and a few buyers. Obviously, the U.S. economy is far more complex. Thousands of companies sell hundreds of thousands of products to millions of buyers every day. In the end, however, the result is much the same: Companies try to supply the quantity and selection of goods that will earn them the largest profits.

Private Enterprise

In his book *The Wealth of Nations*, first published in 1776, Scottish economist Adam Smith argued that a society's interests are best served by **private enterprise**—a system that allows individuals to pursue their own interests without government restriction. Smith envisioned a system in which individual entrepreneurs sought their own self-interest. At the same time, the "invisible hand of competition" would lead businesses to produce the best products as efficiently as possible and to sell them at the lowest possible prices. After all, that strategy was the clearest route to successful profit making and fulfilled self-interest. In effect, then, each business would be working for the good of society as a whole. Society would benefit most from minimal interference with individuals' pursuit of economic self-interest.

Market economies are based on roughly the same concept of private enterprise. In both Smith's "pure" vision and the reality of contemporary practice, private enterprise requires the presence of four elements: private property rights, freedom of choice, profits, and competition.[6]

Private Property Rights

Smith maintained that the creation of wealth should be the concern of individuals, not the government. Thus, he argued that the ownership of the resources used to create wealth must be in the hands of individuals. Of course, individual ownership of property is part of everyday life in the United States. No doubt you or someone you know has bought and owned automobiles, homes, land, or stock. The right to hold **private property**—to buy, own, use, and sell almost any form of property—is one of the fundamental rights guaranteed by the U.S. Constitution.

Freedom of Choice

A related right is freedom of choice. You enjoy the right to sell your labor to any employer you choose. You can also choose which products you want to buy. Finally, freedom of choice means that producers can usually choose whom to hire and what to produce. For example, the U.S. government normally does not tell Sears what it can and cannot sell.

Profits

Naturally, a business that fails to make a profit will eventually close its doors. Indeed, many small businesses fail within the first 5 years.[7] But the lure of profits (and freedom) inevitably leads some people to give up the security of working for someone else and to assume the risks of entrepreneurship. Obviously, anticipated profits also play a large part in individuals' choices of the goods or services they will produce.

Competition

If profits motivate individuals to start businesses, competition motivates them to operate their businesses efficiently. **Competition** occurs when two or more businesses vie for the same resources or customers. For example, if you decide to buy a new pair of athletic shoes, you have a choice of several different stores in which to shop. After selecting a store, you may then choose between brands—say, Nike, Reebok, or Adidas. If you intend to buy only one pair of shoes, all these manufacturers are in competition with one another, as are all the shoe retailers in your area, from mass marketers such as Kmart to specialty outlets such as Foot Locker.

> **competition**
> Vying among businesses for the same resources or customers

To gain an advantage over its competitors, a business must produce its goods or services efficiently and must be able to sell them for prices that earn reasonable profits. To achieve these goals, it must convince customers that its products are either better or less expensive than those of competitors. In this sense, competition benefits society: It forces all competitive businesses to make their products better or cheaper. Naturally, a company that produces inferior, expensive products is sure to be forced out of business.

Degrees of Competition

Of course, not all industries are equally competitive. Economists have identified four basic degrees of competition within a private-enterprise system: pure competition, monopolistic competition, oligopoly, and monopoly. Table 1.1 summarizes the features of these four degrees of competition.

Table 1.1   Degrees of Competition

Characteristic	Pure Competition	Monopolistic Competition	Oligopoly	Monopoly
Example	Local farmer	Stationery store	Steel industry	Public utility
Number of competitors	Many	Many, but fewer than in pure competition	Few	None
Ease of entry into industry	Easy	Fairly easy	Difficult	Regulated by government
Similarity of goods or services offered by competing firms	Identical	Similar	Can be similar or different	No directly competing goods or services
Level of control over price by individual firms	None	Some	Some	Considerable

Pure Competition

pure competition
Market or industry
characterized by a very large
number of small firms
producing an identical
product

For **pure competition** to exist, two conditions must prevail:

- All firms in a given industry must be small.

- The number of firms in the industry must be large.

Under such conditions, no single firm is powerful enough to influence the price of its product or service in the marketplace.

In turn, these conditions reflect four important principles:

- The products offered by each firm are so similar that buyers view them as identical to those offered by other firms.

- Both buyers and sellers know the prices that others are paying and receiving in the marketplace.

- Because each firm is small, it is easy for any single firm to enter or leave the market.

- Going prices are set exclusively by supply and demand and accepted by both sellers and buyers.

Despite government price support programs such as those we described earlier, agriculture is a good example of pure competition in the U.S. economy. For example, the wheat produced on one farm is essentially the same as that produced on another. Both producers and buyers are well aware of prevailing market prices. Moreover, it is easy to start producing wheat and easy to stop when doing so is no longer profitable.

Monopolistic Competition

monopolistic competition
Market or industry
characterized by a large
number of buyers and a large
number of sellers trying to
differentiate products from
those of competitors

In **monopolistic competition**, there are fewer sellers than in pure competition. However, because there are still many buyers, sellers try to make their products at least appear to be different from those of competitors. Differentiating strategies include brand names (Tide and Cheer), design or styling (Ralph Lauren and Guess? jeans), and advertising (Coke and Pepsi). For example, in an effort to attract health-conscious consumers, the Kraft and General Foods divisions of Philip Morris are actively promoting such differentiated products as low-fat Breyers ice cream and Cool Whip, low-calorie Jell-O, and sugar-free Kool-Aid.

Monopolistically competitive businesses may be large or small. However, it is still easy for firms to enter or leave the market. For example, many small clothing stores compete successfully with large apparel retailers such as Liz Claiborne and The Limited. Product differentiation also gives sellers some control over the prices they charge. For instance, even though Sears shirts may have similar styling and other features, Ralph Lauren Polo shirts can be priced with little regard for the lower price of Sears shirts.

Oligopoly

oligopoly
Market or industry
characterized by a handful of
(generally very large) sellers
with the power to influence
the prices of their products

When an industry has only a handful of sellers, an **oligopoly** exists. As a general rule, these sellers are very large. The entry of new competitors is difficult because large capital investment is necessary. Consequently, oligopolistic industries—for instance, the automobile, rubber, airline, and steel industries—tend to stay that way. Thus only two companies, both among the biggest in the world, manufacture large commercial aircraft: Boeing (a U.S. company), and Airbus (a European consortium).

Not surprisingly, individual oligopolists have more control over their own strategies than do monopolistically competitive firms. At the same time, however, the actions of any one firm can significantly affect the sales of every other firm. For example, when one firm reduces prices or offers incentives to increase sales, the others usually protect their sales by doing the same. Likewise, when one firm raises prices, the others generally follow suit. Therefore, the prices of comparable products are usually quite similar. Whenever a major airline announces a new program of fare discounts, the others follow suit almost immediately. Just as quickly, when the fare discounts end for one airline, they usually end for all the others at the same time.

Because constant price competition—and instability—would reduce every seller's profits, oligopolistic firms commonly use product differentiation to attract customers. For example, the four major cereal makers—Kellogg, General Mills, General Foods, and Quaker Oats—control 90 percent of the U.S. cereal market. Each charges roughly the same prices for its cereals. Nevertheless, each continues to advertise that its cereals taste better or are more nutritious than the other brands. (Strategies for marketing consumer goods are discussed more fully in chapter 13.)

Another significant example of oligopolistic pricing is that used by OPEC (Organization of Petroleum Exporting Countries). This group of countries controls a significant share of the world's oil reserves. They cooperate with one another to restrict the amount of oil available for export and to maintain higher prices for that oil. On the other hand, two OPEC members, Venezuela and Nigeria, have recently begun to exceed the cartel's self-imposed limits on exports and, as a result, have caused worldwide prices to drop slightly.[8]

Monopoly

A **monopoly** exists when an industry or market has only one producer. Obviously, a sole supplier enjoys complete control over the prices of its products. Its only constraint is the fall of consumer demand in response to increased prices. In the United States, laws such as the Sherman Antitrust Act (1890) and the Clayton Act (1914) forbid many monopolies and regulate the prices charged by so-called **natural monopolies** (industries in which one company can most efficiently supply all the needed goods or services). For example, most local electric companies are natural monopolies because they can supply all the power needed in their local area. Duplicate facilities—such as two power plants, two sets of power lines, and so forth—would be wasteful.

monopoly
Market or industry in which there is only one producer, which can therefore set the prices of its products

natural monopoly
Industry in which one company can most efficiently supply all needed goods or services

Evaluating Economic Systems

Figures 1.3 through 1.8 display a variety of current economic indicators that can be used to highlight some key facts about the U.S. economy.[9] Using these data for reference points, we will explain more fully the key goals of the U.S. economic system and measure the success of that system in achieving its goals. We will conclude by describing government attempts to manage the U.S. economy in the interest of meeting national economic goals.

Economic Goals

Nearly every economic system has three broad goals: stability, full employment, and growth. Naturally, different systems place different emphasis on each of these goals and take different approaches to achieving them.

Stability

In economic terms, **stability** is the condition in which the money available in an economy and the goods produced in that economy remain about the same. In other words, there are enough desirable products to satisfy consumer demand, and consumers have enough money, in the aggregate, to buy what they need and want. When conditions are stable, therefore, prices for consumer goods, interest rates, and wages paid to workers change very little. Stability helps maintain predictable conditions in which managers, consumers, and workers can analyze the business environment, project goals, and assess performance.

Inflation.   The biggest threat to stability is **inflation**: a period of widespread price increases throughout an economic system. Typically, inflation has an impact on virtually all

stability
Condition in which the balance between the money available in an economy and the goods produced in it remains about the same

inflation
Period of widespread price increases throughout an economic system

In the years immediately following the nation's defeat in World War I, the German government adopted a policy of closing budget deficits by issuing more and more currency. Combined with other factors, this policy precipitated a disastrous inflationary spiral. Relative to the dollar, the world's strongest postwar currency, the German mark began an astounding freefall. From a value of 8.9 marks to the dollar in January 1919, it had dropped to 191.8 to 1 by January 1922. Thereafter, the numbers approach the unfathomable. Between June and October 1922, the value of the mark in relation to the dollar went from 350 to 4,500 to 1, and by January 1923, it had reached 18,000 to 1. In November 1923, the mark reached the astronomical low point of 4.2 trillion to 1 dollar. Banking transactions were conducted by cartfuls, but virtually all meaningful exchanges were reduced to barter (trading of durable goods in kind).

the goods and services that the system produces. For example, inflation explains why a pair of Levi's jeans that costs $35 today cost only $29 ten years ago and only $18 twenty years ago. For the last several years, inflation rates in the United States have hovered around 4 percent per year, finally dropping below 3 percent in 1994. Recent annual rates have ranged from 2.6 to 2.9 percent.

Over the course of this century, inflation in the United States has varied dramatically. For example, prices rose sharply before the Great Depression and then plunged headlong. Immediately after the Depression, they began to rise steadily again, punctuated by brief periods of deflation. This same pattern characterized economic activity in the entire industrialized world in the years just before World War II. In the period immediately following the war, the United States experienced several decades of constant inflation, with steep increases often exceeding 10 percent per year in the late 1970s and early 1980s. Since then, however, inflation rates have declined.

Figure 1.3 shows inflation rates in the United States since 1960 by tracing the average annual increase in producer prices. At current levels, prices double approximately every 19 years. What does this figure mean in real terms for consumers? Among other things, it means that when they enter college, your children will pay twice what you are now paying for tuition, fees, textbooks, clothing, and housing.

Figure 1.3   Inflation Trends in the United States

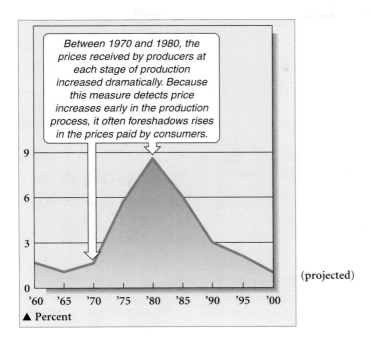

Between 1970 and 1980, the prices received by producers at each stage of production increased dramatically. Because this measure detects price increases early in the production process, it often foreshadows rises in the prices paid by consumers.

However, inflation is not necessarily or entirely bad. Stability can degenerate into stagnation and contribute to a decline in the development and marketing of new products. After all, when there are enough products to buy at reasonable prices and enough money with which to buy them, innovation and growth in new areas are not urgent business priorities. For the same reason, the onset of inflation is often a sign of economic growth. When businesses see that they can charge higher prices, they may hire new workers, invest more money in advertising, and introduce new products. In addition, new businesses open to take advantage of perceived prosperity. At this point, of course, a damaging inflationary trend may set in: Workers may start demanding higher wages to pay for more expensive products, and because higher wages mean lower profits, sellers may raise prices even more. Inflation can be curtailed both naturally and artificially. For example, rates of increase may slow either because of an economic slump, such as the recession that hit the United States in the late 1980s, or through government intervention (see Appendix 1).

Recession and Depression.   Inflation is not the only threat to economic stability. Suppose that a major factory in your home town closed. Hundreds or even thousands of workers would lose their jobs. If other companies in the area do not have jobs for them, these unemployed people will reduce their spending. Other local businesses will thus suffer drops in sales and perhaps cut their own work forces. The resulting **recession**, characterized by decreases in employment, income, and production, may spread across the city, the state, or even the nation. A particularly severe and long-lasting recession, such as the one that affected much of the world in the 1930s, is called a **depression**.

Full Employment

Although there is some disagreement about the meaning of the term *full employment*, the concept remains a goal of most economic systems. Strictly speaking, full employment means that everyone who wants to work has an opportunity to do so. In reality, full employment is impossible: There will always be people looking for work.

recession
Period characterized by decreases in employment, income, and production

depression
Particularly severe and long-lasting recession

It's Your Business

Wages Are Rising, But Whose? Will Yours?

How much money do you expect to make next year? In the spring of 1997 *Fortune* magazine announced that "These *Are* the Good Old Days" for the U.S. economy. Citing improved job prospects, the lowest unemployment rate in 25 years, booming financial markets, and the disappearance of inflation, the article called the moment "the best economy" the United States had ever enjoyed. Around the same time *Business Week* reported that most of that employment growth had benefited groups with historically high jobless rates in the past: black teenagers, Hispanics, female heads of households, and people over 55. In defiance of popular wisdom, productivity didn't fall when these workers were hired.

But despite this rosy picture, some social scientists are still worried about data that show a disturbing trend: Workers at the low end of the pay scale are much more likely to stay there than ever before. Professionals and highly skilled college graduates seem to be the ones getting the biggest bene-fit from the general increase in wages and productivity. A number of long-term studies have followed people such as Keith Mahone of Baltimore, who has worked at a succession of jobs in his 37 years and still makes close to the minimum wage. "These low-wage jobs trap you and take away your hope," Mahone says. "It's hell to fight your way out."

> " *These low-wage jobs trap you and take away your hope. It's hell to fight your way out.* "
>
> —Keith Mahone of Baltimore

Some fear that the United States is developing a class society unlike any seen in its history. Food banks serve more meals than ever before, often to regular clients who are working but chronically poor. What could happen if our society became increasingly stratified? "You'd expect our democratic identity to diminish," predicts Carey McWilliams, professor of political science at Rutgers University.

Unemployment

unemployment
Level of joblessness among people actively seeking work

Unemployment can be defined as the level of joblessness among people actively seeking work. There are four different forms of unemployment:

- *Frictional unemployment* affects people who are out of work temporarily while looking for new jobs. This category includes the skilled engineer who has just left her job at Texas Instruments or Motorola but who will soon find a new job.

- *Seasonal unemployment* affects people who are out of work because of the seasonal nature of their jobs. In most areas, for example, farm and construction laborers do not work much during the winter.

- *Structural unemployment* strikes people who lack the skills needed to perform available jobs. A steelworker laid off in a town looking for computer programmers falls into this category.

- *Cyclical unemployment* occurs when reduced economic activity puts people out of work. In recent years, for instance, many U.S. firms have been forced to reduce costs, sometimes by laying off employees, in order to compete with foreign firms. This trend was heightened during the recession of 1991–1992, when many businesses slashed prices (and sometimes their work forces) just to stay in business.

Employment rates are an important element in the health of a nation's economy. For example, high unemployment suggests that businesses are performing poorly, low unem-

Figure 1.4 The Changing U.S. Labor Force

ployment that business is better. The rate of unemployment in the United States has varied widely during the twentieth century. As with inflation, major fluctuations occurred during the Great Depression, which began in 1929 and lasted through most of the 1930s. Since the end of World War II, unemployment has generally varied between 5 and 10 percent.

Because full employment is essentially impossible, the real goal of both the economic system and public policy is minimized unemployment. Admittedly, economists and politicians have been unable to agree on an acceptable level of unemployment. However, all agree that high unemployment wastes talent and drains resources—much of which, ironically, must be allocated to unemployment-related assistance programs. The costs of unemployment insurance and other forms of welfare increase with higher levels of unemployment, which, in turn, forces taxes higher.

Finally, as Figure 1.4 suggests, the composition of the U.S. labor force is changing. One major element of this change is the fact that the potential work force is becoming better educated. In 1960, for example, less than 8 percent of the population over the age of 25 had spent 4 years or more in college. Now, however, well over 20 percent of that same population segment has 4 or more years of higher education.[10] Naturally, a more highly educated work force boasts a greater mix of skills, greater mobility, and more flexibility. Because of this significant change in its composition, raw unemployment data for the current work force may not be directly comparable to the same data from earlier periods.

Growth

Perhaps the most fundamental goal of most economic systems is **growth**: an increase in the amount of goods and services produced by a nation's resources. In theory, we all want the whole system to expand and provide more businesses, more jobs, and more wealth for everyone. In practice, however, it is difficult to achieve growth without triggering inflation or other elements of instability. On the other hand, an extended period without growth may eventually result in economic decline: business shutdowns, lost jobs, a decrease in overall wealth, and a lower standard of living for everyone.

growth
Increase in the amount of goods and services produced by a nation's resources

Measuring Economic Performance

To judge the success of an economic system in meeting its goals, economists use one or more of five measures: gross national and gross domestic product, productivity, balance of trade, and national debt.

This Subaru-Isuzu plant in Lafayette, Indiana, employs 1,700 local residents to make 60,000 cars and 60,000 trucks annually. The local payroll is $39 million per year. The plant's payroll, the value of the 120,000 vehicles manufactured there, and the profits earned by its Japanese owners are produced domestically and therefore counted in the U.S. gross domestic product.

Gross National Product and Gross Domestic Product

If we add the total value of all the goods and services produced by an economic system in a 1-year period, the sum is that country's **gross national product**, or **GNP**. GNP is a useful indicator of economic growth because it allows us to track an economy's performance over time. The measure of an economy can be affected by inflation as well as other factors affecting the value of its currency. For example, if an economic system has a 5-percent decline in goods produced but experiences a 10-percent increase in inflation, its GNP will go up 5 percent. Changes in the value of a nation's currency relative to those of other countries also distort the value of imports and exports, and thus GNP. To control the effects of such factors, experts compare economies according to an adjusted figure called the **real gross national product**: the gross national product adjusted for inflation and changes in the value of a country's currency.

The United States has the highest real GNP of any industrial nation in the world. For example, real GNP per capita in the United States is almost $21,000. By comparison, real GNP per capita in Japan is only slightly over $14,000. Other countries with high real GNP per capita include Canada (almost $19,000), Norway (almost $17,000), and Germany (almost $15,000). But the recent growth in international trade has made GNP a less valid indicator of economic performance than was true in the past. This stems from the fact that GNP includes a nation's output *regardless of where the factors of production are located.*

To more accurately reflect economic performance in today's global environment, many experts prefer to use **gross domestic product**, or **GDP**. Like GNP, GDP measures a nation's annual output. However, the profits earned by a U.S. company abroad are included in GNP, but *not* in GDP. Why? Because the output is not produced domestically (that is, in the United States). Conversely, goods and services produced by foreign workers inside the United States, as well as profits earned by foreign companies operating here, are counted in the U.S. GDP because they are produced domestically. Currently, U.S. GDP is about $6.7 trillion, (about $12 billion higher than GNP).[11]

Productivity

As a measure of economic growth, **productivity** compares what a system produces with the resources needed to produce it. The principle may be easier to understand if we apply the same measure on a smaller scale: If Xerox can produce a copier for

---

gross national product (GNP)
Total value of all the goods and services produced by an economic system in a 1-year period

real gross national product
Gross national product adjusted for inflation and changes in the value of a country's currency

gross domestic product (GDP)
Total value of all the goods and services consumed by one nation in a 1-year period

productivity
Measure of economic growth that compares how much a system produces with the resources needed to produce it

Figure 1.5 Manufacturing Productivity in the United States

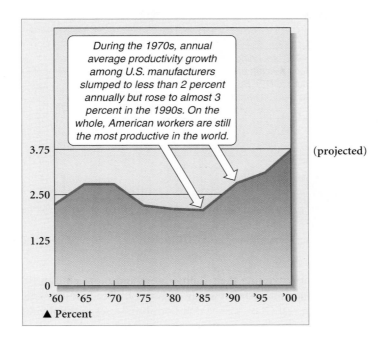

During the 1970s, annual average productivity growth among U.S. manufacturers slumped to less than 2 percent annually but rose to almost 3 percent in the 1990s. On the whole, American workers are still the most productive in the world.

$1,000 but Canon needs $1,200 to make a comparable product, Xerox is being more productive.

U.S. workers are among the most productive in the world.[12] For instance, Figure 1.5 shows manufacturing productivity growth since 1960 in terms of annual average percentage of increase. As you can see, that growth slumped during the 1970s but began to rise again in the mid-1980s. In recent years, however, other countries have made even greater strides in productivity growth.[13] For example, annual increases in productivity in Taiwan have just about doubled gains made in the United States over the past 10 years.

Figures 1.6 and 1.7 also show two other aspects of the U.S. economy that affect productivity. First, if we calculate output per dollar of equipment and plants, we see that U.S.

Figure 1.6 Capital Investment in the United States

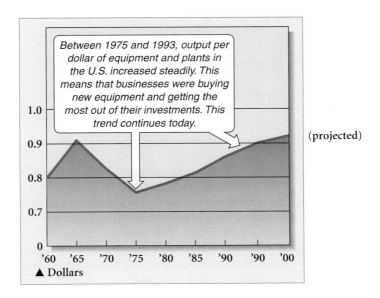

Between 1975 and 1993, output per dollar of equipment and plants in the U.S. increased steadily. This means that businesses were buying new equipment and getting the most out of their investments. This trend continues today.

Figure 1.7 Technology Spending in the United States

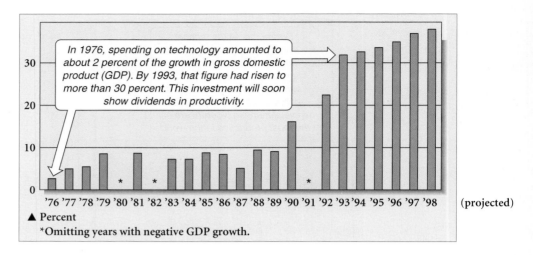

In 1976, spending on technology amounted to about 2 percent of the growth in gross domestic product (GDP). By 1993, that figure had risen to more than 30 percent. This investment will soon show dividends in productivity.

'76 '77 '78 '79 '80 '81 '82 '83 '84 '85 '86 '87 '88 '89 '90 '91 '92 '93 '94 '95 '96 '97 '98 (projected)

▲ Percent
*Omitting years with negative GDP growth.

businesses are investing their capital more and more efficiently. That is, they are buying new equipment and using it wisely (Figure 1.6). Second, if we calculate spending as a share of growth in real GDP, we see that both businesses and individuals have dramatically increased spending on information and multimedia equipment and technology (Figure 1.7). As the information revolution picks up steam, this investment should also begin to pay big dividends in productivity. In chapter 16 we will take a more detailed look at the importance—and specific features—of productivity.

Balance of Trade

Balance of trade is the difference between a country's exports to and imports from other countries. A positive balance of trade is generally considered favorable because new money flows into a country from the sales of its exports. A negative balance means that money is flowing out to pay for imports. During the 1980s, the United States suffered a large negative balance of trade. Things have improved during the 1990s, however, thanks largely to high foreign demand for U.S. services.[14] For example, at the end of 1996 the United States had a negative balance of merchandise trade of $191.2 billion, but a positive balance of service trade of $80.2 billion. As Figure 1.8 shows, international trade is becoming an increasingly important part of the U.S. economy if we measure exports plus imports as a share of GDP. Thus, makers of economic and public policy pay closer attention to such economic indicators as balance of trade.

National Debt

Like a business, the government takes in revenues (primarily in the form of taxes) and has expenses (military spending, social programs, and so forth). For the last several years, the United States has been running a **budget deficit**: It has been spending more money than it has been taking in. This deficit has created a huge **national debt**—the amount of money that the United States owes its creditors.

The current national debt exceeds $5.5 trillion. Because this high level of debt results in higher interest rates throughout the economy, it limits growth. One of the campaign promises that propelled President Clinton to the White House was a commitment to reduce the size of the national debt. Unfortunately, doing so has proven to be difficult. To reduce the budget deficit, the United States will have to raise taxes or reduce spending. Unfortunately, neither of these is a popular option: No one is happy about the prospect of paying more taxes, and the prospect of spending cuts in virtually any area (the military, social programs, environmental protection, the prison system, education, or transportation) brings outcries from so many special-interest groups that policy makers have long been reluctant to take the political risks involved.

budget deficit
Situation in which a government body spends more money in 1 year than it takes in

national debt
Total amount that a nation owes its creditors

Figure 1.8 Expanding International Trade in the United States

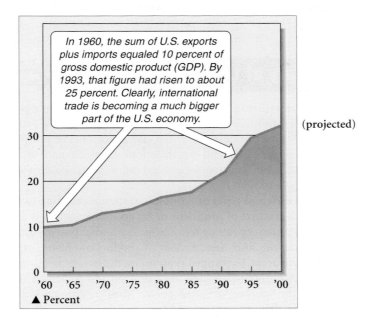

In 1960, the sum of U.S. exports plus imports equaled 10 percent of gross domestic product (GDP). By 1993, that figure had risen to about 25 percent. Clearly, international trade is becoming a much bigger part of the U.S. economy.

(projected)

▲ Percent

Managing the U.S. Economy

The government manages the collection and spending of its revenues through **fiscal policies**. Tax increases, for instance, can function as fiscal policy to increase revenues. President Clinton's income tax increase in 1993, for example, generated an estimated $50 billion in additional revenues. Similarly, budget cuts (for example, closing military bases) function as fiscal policy when spending is decreased. Such policies can have a direct impact on inflation, growth, and employment.

The government also acts to manage the U.S. economic system through two sets of policies. **Monetary policies** focus on controlling the size of the nation's money supply. Working primarily through the Federal Reserve System (the nation's central bank), the

fiscal policies
Government economic policies centered on how the government collects and spends its revenues

monetary policies
Government economic policies that focus on controlling the size of a nation's money supply

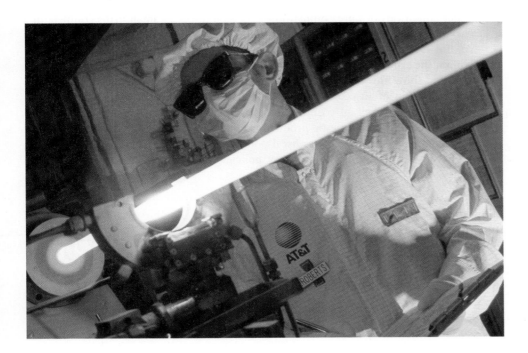

The Information Superhighway is actually constructed of vast fiber-optic networks such as those being built at AT&T Bell Laboratories. "Information technologies," says Bell Labs president John S. Mayor, "are the most powerful forces ever generated to make things cost-effective."

government can influence the ability and willingness of banks throughout the country to lend money. It can also influence the supply of money by prompting interest rates to go up or down. A primary goal in recent years, for example, has been to adjust interest rates so that inflation is kept at a manageable level.

Summary of Learning Objectives

1   **Define the nature of U.S. business and identify its main goals**. Businesses are organizations that produce or sell goods or services to make a profit. Profits are the difference between a business's revenues and expenses. The prospect of earning profits encourages individuals and organizations to open and to expand businesses. The benefits of business activities also extend to wages paid to workers and to taxes that support government functions.

2   **Describe different types of economic systems according to the means by which they control the factors of production**. An economic system is a nation's system for allocating its resources among its citizens. Economic systems differ in terms of who owns or controls the four basic factors of production: labor, capital, entrepreneurs, and natural resources. In planned economies, the government controls all or most factors. In market economies, which are based on the principles of capitalism, individuals control the factors of production. Most countries today have mixed market economies that are dominated by one of these systems but include elements of the other. The process of privatization is an important means by which many of the world's planned economies are moving toward mixed market systems.

3   **Show how demand and supply affect resource distribution in the United States**. The U.S. economy is strongly influenced by markets, demand, and supply. Demand is the willingness and ability of buyers to purchase a good or service. Supply is the willingness and ability of producers to offer goods or services for sale. Demand and supply work together to set a market or equilibrium price: the price at which the quantity of goods demanded and the quantity of goods supplied are equal.

4   **Identify the elements of private enterprise and explain the various degrees of competition in the U.S. economic system**. The U.S. economy is founded on the principles of private enterprise: private property rights, freedom of choice, profits, and competition. Degrees of competition vary because not all industries are equally competitive. Under conditions of pure competition, a large number of small firms compete in a market governed entirely by demand and supply. In an oligopoly, there is only a handful of sellers. A monopoly exists when there is only one seller.

5   **Explain the criteria for evaluating the success of an economic system in meeting its goals and show how the federal government attempts to manage the U.S. economy**. The basic goals of an economic system are stability, full employment, and growth. Measures of how well an economy has accomplished these goals include gross national product, gross domestic product, productivity, balance of trade, and national debt. The U.S. government uses fiscal policies to manage the effects of its spending and revenue collection and monetary policies to control the size of the nation's money supply.

Questions and Exercises

Questions for Review

1   What are the factors of production? Is one more important than the others? If so, which one? Why?

2   What is GDP? Real GDP? What do they measure?

3 Explain the differences between the four degrees of competition and give an example of each. (Do not use the examples given in the text.)

4 Why is inflation both good and bad? How does the government try to control it?

Questions for Analysis

5 Select a local business and show how it uses the basic factors of production. Now show how they are used by your college or university. What are the similarities and differences?

6 In recent years, many countries have moved from planned economies to market economies. Why do you think this has occurred? Can you envision a situation that would cause a resurgence of planned economies?

7 Identify a situation in which excess supply of a product led to decreased prices. Identify a situation in which a shortage led to increased prices. What eventually happened in each case? Why?

Application Exercises

8 Choose a locally owned and operated business. Interview the owner to find out how the business uses the factors of production and identify its sources for acquiring them.

9 Visit a local shopping mall or shopping area. List each store that you see and determine what degree of competition it faces in the immediate environment. For example, if there is only one store in the mall that sells shoes, that store represents a monopoly. Note the businesses with direct competitors (i.e., two jewelry stores) and describe how they compete with one another.

10 Go to the library or the Internet and research 10 different industries. Classify each according to degree of competition.

Building Your Business Skills

This exercise enhances the following SCANS workplace competencies: demonstrating basic skills, demonstrating thinking skills, exhibiting interpersonal skills, and working with information.

Goal   To encourage students to analyze the business challenges in moving from a planned to a market economy.

Situation   An entrepreneur in Moscow wants to start a new business selling women's clothing. However, he is still adapting to the country's new economic and social environment, which is encouraging the development of free enterprise. As a result, he is uncertain how various economic factors will influence his chance for business success.

Method   Divide into groups of four or five people. The mission of each group is to brainstorm the entrepreneur's situation. In your discussion, analyze how each of the following factors is likely to influence business success. Remember to place yourself in the shoes of an entrepreneur whose country was communist until recently:

- Availability of startup capital
- Availability of the raw materials needed in manufacturing
- Availability of manufacturers skilled in clothing production
- Adequacy of transportation network to move raw materials, supplies, and finished garments
- Availability of skilled retail employees

- Availability of bankers and other lenders who are willing to participate in continuing financing
- The nature of government regulations of business
- Consumer buying habits, attitudes, and tastes
- Retailing environment and existing competition

After your brainstorming session, work with group members to research the new market economies in Russia and other Eastern European countries. What do current articles in publications such as *Business Week*, *Fortune*, the *Wall Street Journal*, and the *New York Times* tell you about the situation struggling entrepreneurs face?

Follow-Up Questions

1 Based on what you learned in this exercise, how does a planned economy differ from a market economy?
2 What do you think are the biggest stumbling blocks in moving from a planned to a market economy?
3 How did the conclusions you developed in your brainstorming session differ from what you learned in your research?
4 In the course of business, the entrepreneur will deal with creditors, suppliers, employees, government officials, consumers, and others. In what ways do the entrepreneur's relationships with each group in a market economy differ from those in a planned economy?

Dinner and a Movie? Just Click Here

How appealing is the chance to earn just 1 percent of the revenue generated by local newspaper ads? What if that translates into $345 million a year?

That enormous target is the goal of a new industry springing up in cyberspace: on-line city guides. These new Web sites, which *Business Week* dubs "yourtown.com," list hundreds of information items for local residents including restaurant guides (complete with photos and menus), maps, movie clocks, upcoming sports events down to Little League games, arts and entertainment guides with theater floor plans, and even current traffic conditions and the location of the nearest dry cleaner. More than just a source of information, these interactive sites allow residents to order tickets and make reservations as well. The unlimited space available on the Web and the easy search and cross-reference capabilities make such local guides a perfect Internet application.

Dozens of city guides exist already, started by Internet pioneers such as Yahoo! Local phone companies have joined them, along with Microsoft Corp. (www.sidewalk.com) and America Online (www.digital-city.com) in a joint venture with Tribune Co. CitySearch (www.city-search.com), an early entrant in the market, now plans to triple the number of cities it serves. Time Warner Inc. is putting together an ambitious service with local TV stations contributing programming and saleable airtime to its CityWeb in exchange for access to CNN. Even the networks are getting into the act; NBC's entry is in the planning stages.

The new services offer consumers convenience, timeliness, and visual appeal. So who loses? The biggest threat is to traditional carriers of local, and particularly classified, advertising: community newspapers and local TV and radio stations. The sheer size and spending power of the Internet firms and phone companies getting into the market give them almost unlimited resources for staffing, research, and product development that tiny local firms just can't match. Microsoft alone plans to spend hundreds of millions of dollars on its Internet media business over the next few years and will use cross-promotions and joint ventures to expand its reach. Unlike smaller, traditional local media such as newspapers, it can afford to lose money on the startup.

Industry analysts see room for everyone in the lucrative market, though, and hundreds of newspapers are rushing on-line themselves, teaming up with each other and with Internet firms to keep their slice of the pie.

Questions

1 How should local newspapers respond to the competition from on-line city guides?
2 What additional services could city guides offer in your community?
3 What are some potential disadvantages of the on-line guides, and how can traditional media counter them?

Connecting to the Web

The following Web sites will give you additional information and points of view about topics covered in this chapter. Many sites lead to other related Internet locations, so approach this list with the spirit of an explorer.

ADAM SMITH INSTITUTE

http://www.cyberpoint.co.uk/asi/

The free-market, limited-government ideals embraced by eighteenth-century economist Adam Smith underpin the Adam Smith Institute, an independent economic policy institute based in Great Britain that promotes market-based economic reform. This site will introduce you to key economic issues of vital interest to ASI, including privatization, employment, and the environment, and provide bibliographies for each topic.

ANTITRUST POLICY

http://www.antitrust.org/

This on-line site provides a wealth of information on issues related to antitrust cases and current legislation. Among the specific topics explored are mergers, price fixing, and vertical restraints.

BOARD OF GOVERNORS OF THE FEDERAL RESERVE

http://www.bog.frb.fed.us/

This site provides background and current information about the Federal Reserve System's role in the U.S. economy. A visit to the site will introduce you to how the Federal Reserve regulates monetary and fiscal policy. The site also provides current economic data that are part of various federal publications, reports to Congress, and domestic and international research.

CAPITALISM: FREQUENTLY ASKED QUESTIONS

http://www.ocf.berkeley.edu/~shadab/

If you have questions about what capitalism is, how it works in a democracy, and how other economic systems compare to it, this site will provide the theoretical and practical answers. Don't look for balance: The site developer is an unabashed fan of capitalism and does all he can to convince through information and opinion.

EVERYONE LOVES ECONOMICS BY E-MAIL

http://www.dezines.com/web/econ/index.html

This free service will e-mail you current economic statistics on a biweekly basis, including the consumer price index, producer price index, unemployment rate, gross domestic product, civilian labor force, trade deficit, retail sales, average hourly earnings, manufacturing inventories, and new orders for durable goods.

THE GREAT LAKES ECONOMY

http://www.great-lakes.net/econ/econ.html

This site zeroes in on the economy of the Great Lakes states. You'll find specific region-related information on economic development, employment, and workforce development and trade. The site also offers a direct link to regional economic studies from the Federal Reserve Bank of Chicago.

MARXISM PAGE

http://www.anu.edu.au/polsci/marx/

Although the Soviet Union is dead and buried, Marxist communism is alive and well on this Web site. If you are interested in researching planned economies, you'll find such Marxist classics as the *Communist Manifesto*, as well as a primer on Marxist politics.

NATIONAL CENTER FOR POLICY ANALYSIS/NCPA PRIVATIZATION ISSUES

http://www.public-policy.org/~ncpa/pd/private/privat.html

Privatization is one of the cornerstone policies of the National Center for Policy Analysis, a lobbying organization that seeks to shift control of key economic resources from the public to the private sector. This site explores different facets of the privatization issue.

STAT-USA/INTERNET

http://domino/stat-usa.gov/

Run by the U.S. Department of Commerce, this site provides access to trade, business, and economic data for U.S. and international economies. Stat-USA gathers and consolidates data from more than 40 government agencies and disseminates this information on-line.

U.S. DEPARTMENT OF LABOR

http://www.dol.gov/

Included in this Web site are extensive employment and unemployment data from the Department of Labor's Bureau of Labor Statistics.

chapter 2

Conducting business in the United States

When gorillas dance

In July 1997 American Express and Microsoft, two of the largest corporations in the world, announced the result of their year-long joint effort to create an on-line travel reservation system. Called AXI, the system is designed for sale to companies that want to give their employees the means to make their own air, hotel, and car rental arrangements from their laptop or PC.

AXI is expected to appeal to firms interested in controlling their travel costs, which makes for a broad market indeed. Unlike Web sites designed for consumer travel needs, the new corporate system offers a number of special features that help employees adhere to corporate travel policies such as company-negotiated rates, prompts for preferred suppliers, and the ability to track travel information. It also provides a wealth of information about hotels and destinations.

AXI was developed in a special one-time alliance between American Express and Microsoft that was designed to allow the firms to develop the product jointly. Both companies dominate their markets. Although this is its first entry into the already growing on-line travel business, American Express is considered the largest travel agency in the United States, and Microsoft's enormous software development resources have recently been redirected solely at the Internet, where chairperson Bill Gates hopes to repeat his firm's well-publicized success in the PC operating software arena.

> **"** *Any time two gorillas get up to dance, you've got to get out of the way.* **"**
>
> —Ivan Michael Schaeffer, president,
> Woodside Travel Trust

Both stand to gain from their joint venture, a strategic alliance of the kind more and more companies are forming to temporarily pool their strengths with those of other, unrelated firms. Sometimes called virtual corporations, such partnerships bring combined marketing and research savvy to bear in many markets. It's not likely, though, that many of them will marry firms with the clout that American Express and Microsoft can wield. As one travel industry analyst said of the AXI creators, "Any time two gorillas get up to dance, you've got to get out of the way."

Creative solutions to business challenges are becoming more common as firms struggle to remain competitive in rapidly changing markets, or, as in American Express's case, to enter new ones.

In this chapter we will examine the business structures that are open to both large and small businesses. By focusing on the learning objectives of this chapter, you will better understand the structural options open to U.S. businesses.

After reading this chapter, you should be able to

1 Trace the history of business in the United States.

2 Identify the major *forms of business ownership*.

3 Describe *sole proprietorships* and *partnerships* and explain the advantages and disadvantages of each.

4 Describe *corporations* and explain their advantages and disadvantages.

5 Describe the basic issues involved in creating and managing a corporation.

6 Identify recent trends and issues in corporate ownership.

A Short History of Business in the United States

The contemporary landscape of U.S. business ownership has evolved over the course of many decades. Specifically, a look at the history of U.S. business shows a steady development from sole proprietorships to today's intricate corporate structures. We can gain a more detailed understanding of this development by tracing its history.

The Colonial Period

The British colonists who arrived in North America in the seventeenth century had two choices: farm or starve. Given a favorable climate and an abundance of land, they soon began to produce more food, lumber, and other raw materials than they needed for their survival. Eventually, they became an integral part of the British trade network, typically selling farm products and raw materials to Great Britain and buying manufactured British goods.

Gradually, however, colonial producers began to realize that they were not receiving fair value for their products. Moreover, the British government was beginning to tax all shipments of goods between the colonies and Great Britain. Their sense of economic injustice eventually played a major role in the colonists' decision to fight for independence.

After the American Revolution, the newly emergent United States began to expand its own economy and to seek new trading partners abroad. Growth promoted economic prosperity in a variety of ways. Some farmers, for example, expanded operations so as to produce more products for sale in domestic and international markets. Others abandoned farming altogether and established small manufacturing enterprises. Although these first manufacturers originally played only a minor role in the economy, that role would soon change dramatically.

The Factory System and the Industrial Revolution

With the coming of the Industrial Revolution in the middle of the eighteenth century, a manufacturing revolution was made possible by advances in technology and by the development of the factory system. Replacing hundreds of cottage workers who had turned out one item at a time, the factory system brought together in one place the materials and workers required to produce items in large quantities and the new machines needed for mass production.

In turn, mass production reduced duplication of equipment and allowed firms to purchase raw materials at better prices by buying in large lots. Even more important, it encouraged specialization of labor. Mass production replaced a system of highly skilled craftspeople who performed all the different tasks required to make a single item. Instead, a series of semiskilled workers, each trained to perform only one task and supported by specialized machines and tools, greatly increased output.

Laissez-Faire and the Entrepreneurial Era

Despite a number of early problems during the nineteenth century, the U.S. banking system began providing domestic businesses with some independence from European capital markets. In addition, improvements in transportation—the opening of the Erie Canal in the 1820s, steamboat navigation on major rivers, and the development of the railroads—soon made it not only possible, but economical to move products to distant markets.

Another significant feature of the times was the rise of the entrepreneur on a grand scale. Like businesses in many other nations in the nineteenth century, U.S. business embraced the philosophy of laissez-faire—the principle that the government should not interfere in the economy but should instead let business function without regulation and ac-

Founders and their guests celebrate the birth of U.S. Steel in 1901. When it was born out of a merger of competing steel companies, U.S. Steel inherited 65 percent of the nation's steel-producing capacity; a little over a decade later, the firm's gross income was greater than that of the U.S. Treasury. Today, it is known as USX and is mainly in the oil business.

cording to its own "natural" laws. Risk taking and entrepreneurship became hallmarks of aggressive practices that created some of the biggest companies in the country—indeed, the world. During the last half of the 1800s, for instance, Andrew Carnegie founded U.S. Steel and Andrew Mellon created the Aluminum Company of America (Alcoa). At the same time, J. P. Morgan's Morgan Guarantee and Trust came to dominate the U.S. financial system, and John D. Rockefeller's Standard Oil controlled—in fact, monopolized— the petroleum industry.

The rise of such giant enterprises increased the national standard of living and made the United States a world power. But the size and economic power of such firms made it difficult, if not impossible, for competitors to enter their markets. Complete market control became a watchword in many industries, with many major corporations opting to collude rather than compete. Price fixing and other forms of market manipulation became common business practices, with captains of industry often behaving as robber barons. Reacting against unethical practices and the unregulated struggle for dominance, critics in many quarters began calling for corrective action and, ultimately, for antitrust laws and the breakup of monopolies.

Among other important laws, two—the Sherman Antitrust Act of 1890 and the Clayton Act of 1914—were passed specifically to limit the control a single business could gain in any given market. Other laws passed during this era sought to regulate a variety of employment and advertising practices, and still others attempted to regulate the ways in which businesses could handle their financial affairs. (Appendix 1 provides more information about the legal environment of business, much of which has its roots in this era.)

The Production Era

The concepts of specialization and mass production that originated in the Industrial Revolution were further refined in the early twentieth century. At this time, many analysts of business organizations sought to focus management's attention on the production process. Especially among the theorists of so-called scientific management, increased efficiency through the "one best way" to accomplish production tasks became a major goal of management. Developed during the early 1900s, scientific management focused on maximizing output by developing the most efficient and productive ways for workers to perform carefully designed tasks.

production era
Period during the early twentieth century in which U.S. business focused almost primarily on improving productivity and manufacturing efficiency

Scientific management was given further impetus when, in 1913, Henry Ford introduced the moving assembly line and ushered in the **production era**. The focus was largely on manufacturing efficiency: By adopting fixed workstations, increasing task specialization, and moving the work to the worker, Ford increased productivity and lowered prices. In so doing, he made the automobile affordable for the average person.

Both the growth of corporations and improved assembly-line output came at the expense of worker freedom. For one thing, the dominance of big firms made it harder for individuals to go into business for themselves. In some cases, employer-run company towns gave people little freedom of choice, either in selecting an employer or in choosing what products to buy. If some balance were to be restored in the overall system, two elements within it had to grow in power: government and organized labor. Thus the production era saw the rise of labor unions and the practice of collective bargaining (see chapter 10). In addition, the Great Depression of the 1930s and World War II prompted the government to intervene in the economic system on a previously unforeseen scale. Today, business, government, and labor are often referred to by economists and politicians as the three countervailing powers in society: Although all are big and all are strong, none completely dominates the others.

The Marketing Era

After World War II, the demand for consumer goods that had been frustrated by wartime shortages fueled the U.S. economy for some time. Despite brief periodic recessions, the 1950s and 1960s were prosperous times. Production continued to increase, technology advanced, and the standard of living rose. During this era, a new philosophy of business came of age: the **marketing concept**. Previously, business had been essentially production- and sales-oriented: Businesses tended to produce what other businesses produced, what they thought customers wanted, or simply what owners wanted to produce. Henry Ford, for example, is supposed to have said that his customers could buy his cars in whatever color they wanted—as long as it was black.

marketing concept
Philosophy that in order to be profitable, a business must focus on identifying and satisfying consumer wants

According to the marketing concept, however, business starts with the customer. Producers of goods and services begin by determining what customers want and then provide it. The most successful practitioners of the marketing concept are companies such as Procter & Gamble and Anheuser-Busch. Such firms allow consumers to choose what best suits their needs by offering an array of products within a given market (toothpaste or beer, for example).

The Global Era

The 1980s saw the continuation of technological advances in production, computer technology, information systems, and communications capabilities. They also saw the emergence of a truly global economy. U.S. consumers now drive cars made in Japan, wear sweaters made in Italy, and turn on CD players made in Taiwan. Elsewhere around the world, people drive Fords, drink Pepsi, wear Levi's jeans, use IBM computers, and watch Disney movies and television shows.

As we discuss in more detail in chapter 3, globalization has become a fact of life for most businesses today. Improved communication and transportation, combined with more efficient international methods for financing, producing, distributing, and marketing products and services, have combined to open distant marketplaces to businesses as never before.

Admittedly, many U.S. businesses have been hurt by foreign competition. Many others, however, have profited from new foreign markets. In addition, international competition has forced many U.S. businesses to work harder than ever to cut costs, increase efficiency, and improve quality. A variety of important trends, opportunities, and challenges in the new global era are explored throughout this book.

The Workplace Environment

Coping with Foreign Competition: How Do Foreigners Do It?

Workers in the United States sometimes feel their jobs are threatened by cheap labor abroad, and consumers are constantly urged to "buy American" to keep jobs at home. Yet in many industrialized countries around the world, foreign workers have the same fears. Freer trade among nations and the continued globalization of many industries have hurt workers in Germany, France, Italy, Japan, and elsewhere. The difference is in how their governments cope.

Rather than making the sometimes dramatic corporate layoffs common in the last few years in the United States, companies in Europe and Japan are trying to protect jobs in the interests of economic stability. Even though Germany's growth is slow and its unemployment rate is nearly 11 percent thanks to the loss of jobs abroad, its citizens cling to its generous social safety net and scorn the U.S. remedies of deregulation and layoffs. Japan is downsizing by attrition only, and its corporate CEOs, who already make less than their U.S. counterparts, are taking pay cuts rather than lay off even unproductive workers. Although its public

deficit may remain too high for it to qualify for acceptance into a European monetary union, France struggles to maintain its welfare state to cope with 12 percent unemployment. "In Europe, the hard line doesn't work," says Giuseppe Roma, who directs a corporate think tank called Censis in Rome.

> ❝*In Europe, the hard line doesn't work.*❞
>
> —Giuseppe Roma, director, Censis

Will the United States continue to rely on cutting labor costs to the bone? Will the other industrialized nations succeed in taking a slower route to low-cost production? What can we learn from each other? We may be well into the twenty-first century before we can say for sure who was right, but some experts believe that no matter what happens, the differences in approach will remain.

Types of Business Organizations

Whether they run small agricultural enterprises or large manufacturing concerns, all business owners must decide which form of legal organization best suits their goals: *sole proprietorship, partnership, corporation,* or *cooperative.* Because this choice affects a host of managerial and financial issues, few decisions are more critical. In choosing a form of organization, entrepreneurs must consider their own preferences, their immediate and long-range needs, and the advantages and disadvantages of each form.

Sole Proprietorships

The very first legal form of business organization, the **sole proprietorship,** is owned and usually operated by one person who is responsible for its debts. Today, about 74 percent of all businesses in the United States are sole proprietorships.[1] However, they account for only about 6 percent of the country's total business revenues.

Although a sole proprietorship is usually small, it may be as large as a steel mill or a department store. Moreover, many of today's largest companies started out as sole proprietorships. Sears, Roebuck and Co., for example, was originally a one-man enterprise owned and operated by Richard Sears, who had started the R. W. Sears Watch Co. in 1886. (Alvah Roebuck, who had answered an advertisement for a watchmaker in 1887, joined Sears to form a partnership in 1893.)

sole proprietorship
Business owned and usually operated by one person, who is responsible for all of its debts

Advantages of Sole Proprietorships

Freedom is perhaps the most important benefit of sole proprietorships. Because they own their businesses completely, sole proprietors answer to no one but themselves. Moreover, they enjoy a certain degree of privacy because they need not report information about their operations to anyone. Finally, they alone reap the rewards of success or suffer the penalties of failure.

Furthermore, sole proprietorships are simple to form. Sometimes, a proprietor can go into business simply by putting a sign on the door. Naturally, the simplicity of legal setup procedures makes this form of organization appealing to self-starters and independent spirits. Sole proprietorships are also easy to dissolve. In fact, many proprietorships are organized for short life spans. For example, rock concerts and one-time athletic events are often organized as sole proprietorships and then dissolved when the events are over.

Low startup costs also make sole proprietorships attractive. Because some sole proprietorships must register only with state governments (to ensure that no other business bears the same name), legal fees are usually low. However, some proprietorships, such as restaurants, beauty salons, florist shops, and pet shops, must be licensed.

Finally, a particularly appealing feature of sole proprietorships is the tax benefits extended to new businesses that are likely to suffer losses in their early stages. Tax laws generally permit sole proprietors to treat sales revenues and operating expenses as part of their personal finances. They can thus cut their taxes by deducting business losses from income earned elsewhere (that is, from personal sources other than the business). Because most new businesses lose money in the early stages of operation, tax incentives are quite helpful to entrepreneurs.

Disadvantages of Sole Proprietorships

unlimited liability
Legal principle holding owners responsible for paying off all the debts of a business

A major drawback of sole proprietorships is **unlimited liability**: A sole proprietor is personally liable for all debts incurred by the business. In other words, if the business fails to generate enough cash, bills must be paid out of the proprietor's own pocket. If bills are not paid, creditors can claim many of the proprietor's personal possessions, including home, furniture, and automobiles. Another disadvantage is lack of continuity: A sole proprietorship legally dissolves when the owner dies. Although the business can be reorganized if a successor is prepared to take over, executors or heirs must otherwise sell the assets of the business.

Finally, a sole proprietorship depends on the resources of a single individual. If the proprietor is a skillful manager with ample resources, this limitation is not a problem. In many cases, however, owners' managerial and financial limitations put limits on their organizations. Sole proprietors often find it hard to borrow money, not only to start up but also to expand. Many commercial bankers fear that they will not be able to recover loans when sole proprietors become disabled or insolvent. Often, therefore, would-be proprietors must rely for startup funds on personal savings or family loans.

Partnerships

general partnership
Business with two or more owners, who share in both the operation of the firm and financial responsibility for its debts

The most common type of partnership, the **general partnership**, is simply a sole proprietorship multiplied by the number of partner-owners. There is no legal limit to the number of parties who may form a general partnership. Moreover, partners may invest equal or unequal sums of money and may earn profits that bear no relation to their investments. In other words, a partner with no financial investment in a two-person partnership could receive 50 percent or more of the profits. Bill Trainer and Harvey Woodman, for example, opened an automatic car wash in Houston called Shinin' Bright. Woodman put up most of the funds, and Trainer provided the expertise needed to manage the business. They agreed to split the profits equally for the first 3 years. Trainer then had the option to invest some of his profits in return for a larger share.

Partnerships are often extensions of sole proprietorships. The original owner may want to expand, or the business may have grown too big for one person to handle. Richard

The "Big Store" actually began as a sole proprietorship in a railroad station in North Redwood, Minnesota, from which the Sears Watch Co. began operations in 1886. In 1893, founder Richard Sears joined with fellow entrepreneur Alvah Roebuck to create Sears, Roebuck and Co. Roebuck sold out his one-third interest in 1897 for $25,000, and Sears took on a new partner named Julius Rosenwald. In 1900, gross sales under Sears and Rosenwald reached $10 million and topped $50 million in 1907. The company issued common and preferred stock on the open market for the first time in 1905 and has been publicly owned ever since.

Sears sold his watch business and, 2 years later, formed a mail-order catalog business. When his new business grew so large that he could no longer run it by himself, he invited former business associate Alvah Roebuck to join him as a partner. Many professional organizations, such as legal, architectural, and accounting firms, are also organized as partnerships.

Advantages of Partnerships

The most striking advantage of general partnerships is their ability to grow with the addition of new talent and money. Because lending institutions prefer to make loans to enterprises that are not dependent on single individuals, partnerships also find it easier to borrow money than do sole proprietorships. Moreover, most partnerships have access to the resources of more than one individual. Thus, when they needed money to fund an expansion program, Sears and Roebuck invited new partners to join them by investing in the company.

Like a sole proprietorship, a partnership can be organized by meeting only a few legal requirements. Even so, all partnerships must begin with an agreement of some kind. All but two states subscribe to the Revised Uniform Limited Partnership Act. This statute describes a written certificate that requires the filing of specific information about the business and its partners. Partners may also agree to bind themselves in ways not specified by the certificate.[2] In any case, a partnership agreement should answer questions such as the following:

- Who invested what sums of money?

- Who will receive what share of the profits?

- Who does what and who reports to whom?

■ How may the partnership be dissolved? In the event of dissolution, how will assets be distributed?

■ How will surviving partners be protected from claims made by a deceased partner's heirs?

Although it helps to clarify matters for the partners themselves, the partnership agreement is strictly a private document; no laws require partners to file their agreements with any government agency. Nor are partnerships regarded as legal entities; in the eyes of the law, a partnership is just two or more people working together. Because partnerships have no independent legal standing, the Internal Revenue Service taxes partners as individuals.

Disadvantages of Partnerships

For general partnerships, as for sole proprietorships, unlimited liability is the greatest drawback: By law, each partner may be liable for all debts incurred in the name of the partnership. If any partner incurs a business debt (with or without the knowledge of the other partners), all partners may still be held liable.

For example, shortly after Trainer and Woodman's car wash opened, their equipment severely damaged a customized van. The owner sued for damages. Because the business was just getting started and had no financial reserves, Trainer and Woodman were faced with the prospect of covering the costs from their own pockets. Unfortunately, Trainer lacked the personal funds to cover his share. To keep the business afloat, Woodman agreed to lend Trainer the money for his half of the business expense.

Partnerships also share with sole proprietorships the potential lack of continuity: When one partner dies or leaves it, the original partnership dissolves, even if one or more of the other partners want it to continue. The dissolving of a partnership need not cause a loss of sales revenues: Surviving partners may form a new partnership to retain the old firm's business.

A related disadvantage is the difficulty of transferring ownership. No partner may sell out without the consent of the others. Moreover, a partner who wants to retire or to transfer interest to a son or daughter must have the other partners' consent. Thus, the life of a partnership depends on the ability of retiring partners to find buyers who are compatible with current partners. Failure to do so may end a partnership. Of course, remaining partners may also buy out a retiring partner.

Finally, a partnership provides little or no guidance for resolving internal conflicts. Suppose that one partner wants to expand the business rapidly and the other wants it to grow cautiously. If the partnership agreement grants equal power, it may be difficult for the two partners to resolve the dispute. Conflicts can involve disagreements ranging from the company smoking policy to key managerial practices. Quite simply, it is sometimes impossible to resolve disagreements.

Alternatives to General Partnerships

Because of these disadvantages, general partnerships are among the least popular legal forms of business. In the United States today, roughly 1.7 million partnerships generate less than 4 percent of total sales revenues.[3] To resolve some of the problems inherent in general partnerships, especially unlimited liability, some partners have tried other types of agreements. The **limited partnership**, for example, allows for both limited partners and a general partner. **Limited partners** invest money without being liable for debts incurred by general partners. If the business fails, limited partners are liable only to the extent of their investment. However, limited partners cannot take active roles in business operations.

By law, a limited partnership must have at least one general (or active) partner, mostly for liability purposes. The **general partner** is usually the person who runs the business and bears the responsibility for its survival and growth. Until recently, limited partnerships were quite popular as tax shelters (investments for reducing personal tax liabilities). However, when changes in the 1986 and 1987 tax laws reduced these advantages, the appeal of the limited partnership declined.

---

limited partnership
Type of partnership consisting of limited partners and an active or managing partner

limited partner
Partner who does not share in a firm's management and is liable for its debts only to the limit of his or her investment

general partner
Partner who actively manages a firm and who has unlimited liability for its debts

Meanwhile, a variation on the limited partnership, the **master limited partnership** (**MLP**), is growing in popularity. Under this arrangement, an organization sells shares (partnership interests) to investors on public markets such as the New York Stock Exchange. Investors are paid back out of profits. The master partner retains at least 50-percent ownership and runs the business; the minority partners have no management voice. (The master partner differs from a general partner, who has no such minimum ownership restriction.) However, the master partner must provide minority partners with detailed operating and financial data on a regular basis. In 1986, for example, the Boston Celtics basketball team restructured as a master limited partnership. In that year, owners offered for public sale 2.6 million shares of the MLP. The offer attracted $119 million in investment capital for the three principal owners, who had originally invested a total of $19 million.[4]

master limited partnership
Form of organization that sells shares to investors who receive profits and pay taxes on individual income from profits

Corporations

There are almost 3.5 million corporations in the United States. As you can see from Figure 2.1, although they account for about 20 percent of all U.S. businesses, they generate about 70 percent of all sales revenues.[5] Almost all larger businesses use this form, and corporations dominate the global business landscape. For example, General Motors, the world's largest industrial firm, had revenues in 1997 that approached $170 billion, with total profits of almost $7 billion. North American Operations had total *profits* in 1994 of $690 million. Even "smaller" large corporations post huge sales figures. For example, Bethlehem Steel is only the 300th largest corporation in the United States, but it still has annual sales of almost $5 billion. Given the size and influence of this form of ownership, we will devote a great deal of attention to various aspects of corporations.

The Corporate Entity

When you think of corporations, you probably think of giant businesses such as General Motors and IBM. Indeed, the very word *corporation* inspires images of size and power. In reality, however, the tiny corner newsstand has as much right to incorporate as a giant automaker. Moreover, the incorporated newsstand and GM would share the characteristics of all corporations: legal status as separate entities, property rights and obligations, and indefinite life spans.

Figure 2.1 Corporations: Business and Revenues

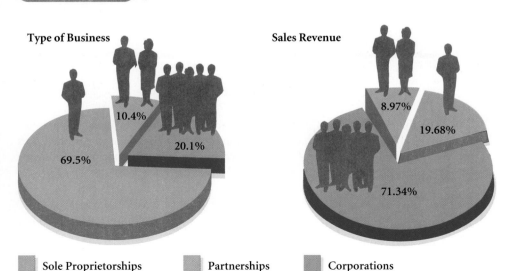

Type of Business
10.4%
20.1%
69.5%

Sales Revenue
8.97%
19.68%
71.34%

Sole Proprietorships Partnerships Corporations

It's Your Business

Working At Home: Is It for You?

Taking a conference call in your pajamas may not be your idea of getting ahead at the office. But it might be just the ticket to getting ahead from home.

Working at home, or telecommuting, has entered the mainstream of U.S. business life. (It's even the theme of several TV commercials.) Long debated and at first slow to spread, the option to hold down a regular job without making regular appearances at the office seems to finally be catching on. E-mail, intranets, and inexpensive fax and copy equipment are helping to support the trend, along with the increase in personal computers and the acceptance of flextime. According to the American Management Association, telecommuting is one of the fastest-growing uses of the Internet, and its share of Net traffic is expected to increase nearly 200 percent by the year 2000.

> **❝** I love [telecommuting]. It's easier for me to meet my personal needs, too. **❞**

—Jenny Nelson, engineering team leader, AT&T

Researchers estimate that there are somewhere between 10 and 14 million telecommuters in the United States, most of whom stick with the arrangement for 6 to 18 months, and at least two-thirds of Fortune 500 companies are believed to employ them. (The number is difficult to measure precisely because definitions of telecommuting differ widely and because few such arrangements are made for the long term.) Some workers are full-time telecommuters; others work at home one or more days a week. In some firms, such as IBM, telecommuting employees share office space with others when they do come in. When they don't come in, studies show, many people, including managers who traditionally spend most of their workday with others, feel their productivity increases 5 to 20 percent at home because there are fewer interruptions and distractions.

Working at home (as opposed to running your own business from home) can reduce stress and enhance the quality of family life. "I love it. It's easier for me to meet my personal needs, too," says Jenny Nelson, an engineering team leader for AT&T who has telecommuted 2 or 3 days a week for eight years. A 1993 study done for the Small Business Administration suggests that rather than being overlooked by their absence, telecommuters still get promoted, in fact at greater rates than in-house employees.

But there are some disadvantages. Telecommuting seems to work best in companies where the rules are well thought out beforehand and clearly understood by everyone, and where they include provisions for ensuring that at-home workers keep in touch with coworkers. For lack of one or more of these safeguards, it's estimated that one of every five telecommuting arrangements fails.

But if you are in the right kind of job (easily portable and easily measurable white collar work with a lot of independent tasks), have the right mindset (experience, a better-than-average performance history, and self-motivation are crucial), and have the support of your immediate manager and upper management, telecommuting might very well be in your future.

---

corporation
Business that is legally considered an entity separate from its owners and is liable for its own debts; owners' liability extends to the limits of their investments

In 1819, the U.S. Supreme Court defined a **corporation** as "an artificial being, invisible, intangible, and existing only in contemplation of the law." By these words, the Court defined the corporation as a legal person. Thus corporations may perform the following activities:

- Sue and be sued

- Buy, hold, and sell property

- Make and sell products to consumers

- Commit crimes and be tried and punished for them

Public and Private Corporations

Corporations may be either public or private. The stock of a **public corporation** is widely held and available for sale to the general public. For example, anyone who has the money can buy shares of Caterpillar, Digital Equipment, or Time Warner. The stock of a **private corporation**, on the other hand, is held by only a few people and is not available for sale to the general public. The controlling group of stockholders may be a family, a management group, or even the firm's employees. Gallo Wine, Levi Strauss, and United Parcel Service are all private corporations. Because few investors will buy unknown stocks, most new corporations start out as private corporations. As the corporation grows and investors see evidence of success, it may issue shares to the public as a way to raise additional money. For example, Netscape Communications publicly issued stock for the first time in 1995. The firm quickly sold 81 million shares and raised over a billion dollars for new product development and expansion.

Advantages of Incorporation

The biggest advantage of regular corporations is **limited liability**: The liability of investors is limited to their personal investments in the corporation. In the event of failure, the courts may seize and sell a corporation's assets but cannot touch the personal possessions of investors. For example, if you invest $1,000 in a corporation that goes bankrupt, you may lose your $1,000, but no more. In other words, $1,000 is the extent of your liability.

Another corporate advantage is continuity. Because it has a legal life independent of its founders and owners, a corporation can, at least in theory, go on forever. Shares of stock, for example, may be sold or passed on from generation to generation. Moreover, most corporations also benefit from the continuity provided by professional management.

Finally, corporations have advantages in raising money. By selling more stock, for instance, they can expand the number of investors and the amount of available funds. Continuity and the legal protections afforded to corporations also tend to make lenders more willing to grant loans.

Disadvantages of Incorporation

One of the corporation's chief attractions is ease of transferring ownership. However, this same feature can also complicate the lives of managers. Consider, for example, the recent travails of several California-based bank corporations. A few years ago one bank, First Interstate, tried to gain control of one of its largest competitors, Bank of America, by buying its shares on the open market. First Interstate was unable to acquire enough shares of its rival to gain control over it and ended up having to sell its shares at a big loss. In its weakened financial state, First Interstate then became a target itself and was purchased by a third bank corporation, Wells Fargo & Company. But so far, at least, this corporate marriage has not paid dividends for Wells Fargo because its costs in integrating the two companies have been far greater than anticipated.

Corporations can take steps that make it more difficult to be taken over by another corporation. The most common strategy is called the poison pill. Generally speaking, a poison pill is a defensive tactic designed to make a company less attractive to hostile investors. The "pill" is "poison" because it also decreases the value of the company. For example, the board might adopt a policy that in the event of a takeover all current stockholders will receive an extremely large dividend. Other popular tactics for avoiding a takeover include selling valuable assets and taking on added debt. For example, Hilton recently made a bid to acquire ITT Corp., owner of Sheraton Hotels. ITT countered by selling several of its most profitable Sheraton properties.

Among other disadvantages of incorporation is the cost. Not surprisingly, forming a corporation is more expensive than forming a sole proprietorship or a partnership. For one thing, corporations are heavily regulated, and incorporation entails meeting the complex legal requirements of the state in which the firm is chartered. Nonetheless, some states provide much better environments in which to charter corporations than others.

public corporation
Corporation whose stock is widely held and available for sale to the general public

private corporation
Corporation whose stock is held by only a few people and is not available for sale to the general public

limited liability
Legal principle holding investors liable for a firm's debts only to the limits of their personal investments in it

Table 2.1 Comparative Summary: Three Forms of Business

Business Form	Liability	Continuity	Management	Sources of Investment
Proprietorship	Personal, unlimited	Ends with death or decision of owner	Personal, unrestricted	Personal
General Partnership	Personal, unlimited	Ends with death or decision of any partner	Unrestricted or depends on partnership agreement	Personal by partner(s)
Corporation	Capital invested	As stated in charter, perpetual or for specified period of years	Under control of board of directors, which is selected by stockholders	Purchase of stock

For this reason, businesses often take out charters and maintain small headquarters facilities in one state while conducting most of their business in others. With its low corporate tax rate, for instance, Delaware is home to more corporations than any other state.

double taxation
Situation in which taxes may be payable both by a corporation on its profits and by shareholders on dividend incomes

Double Taxation The greatest potential drawback to corporate organization, however, is **double taxation**. First, a regular corporation must pay income taxes on company profits. In addition, stockholders must pay taxes on income returned by their investments in the corporation. Consider Electronic Data systems, or EDS. In 1995 the firm had to pay federal income tax on $939 million in profits. But the firm also paid a dividend of 52 cents per share that year, so each shareholder also had to pay personal income tax on the total dividend they received from EDS. Thus, the profits earned by EDS are essentially taxed twice, once at the corporate level and again at the level of its individual owners. In contrast, because profits are treated as owners' personal income, sole proprietorships and partnerships are taxed only once.

Table 2.1 summarizes and compares the most important differences among three major business forms.

Cooperatives

cooperative
Form of organization in which a group of sole proprietorships or partnerships agrees to work together for common benefits

Sometimes, groups of sole proprietorships or partnerships agree to work together for their common benefit by forming **cooperatives**. Although cooperatives make up only a minor segment of the U.S. economy, their role is still quite important in agriculture. In a sense, a cooperative combines the freedom of the sole proprietorship with the financial power of a corporation. Cooperatives give their members greater production power, greater marketing power, or both. On the other hand, the cooperative is by nature limited to serving the specific needs of its members.

One well-known cooperative is Ocean Spray, a juice producers' cooperative that includes 700 cranberry growers and 100 citrus growers around the country. The cooperative structure allows members to buy things such as fertilizer in bulk, negotiate shipping contracts, and develop a nationwide marketing campaign, just like one big company. Instead of distributing a share of the profits to stockholders, cooperatives divide all profits among their members. Other big cooperatives in the United States include Riceland and Blue Diamond Growers. Of course, other countries also have cooperatives. In fact, almost all Japanese farmers belong to Nokyo, one of the largest cooperatives in the world.

Creating and Managing a Corporation

Not surprisingly, creating a corporation can be complicated. In addition, once the corporate entity has come into existence, it must be managed by people who understand the complex principles of **corporate governance**, or the roles of shareholders, directors, and other managers in corporate decision making.

   In this section, we will describe the steps in creating a corporation. We will then discuss the principles of stock ownership and stockholders' rights and describe the role of boards of directors. Finally, we will examine some of the most important trends in corporate ownership.

corporate governance
Roles of shareholders, directors, and other managers in corporate decision making

Creating a Corporation

In its simplest form, the process of creating a corporation consists of three basic steps:

1 *Consult an attorney.* Although it is possible to establish a corporation without legal guidance, most people soon realize that the process involves, among other things, satisfying various government rules and regulations.

2 *Select a state in which to incorporate.* As we noted earlier, many companies choose Delaware for tax purposes. However, it usually makes sense for a smaller company to incorporate in the state in which it will conduct most of its business.

3 *File articles of incorporation and corporate bylaws.* **Articles of incorporation** specify such information as the firm's name and address, its purpose, the amount of stock it intends to issue, and other legally required information. **Bylaws** detail methods for electing directors and define terms and basic responsibilities. They also describe the process of issuing new stock and address such issues as stock ownership and stockholders' rights.

articles of incorporation
Document detailing the corporate governance of a company, including its name and address, its purpose, and the amount of stock it intends to issue

bylaws
Document detailing corporate rules and regulations, including election and responsibilities of directors and procedures for issuing new stock

Corporate Governance

Corporate governance, which is specified for each firm by its bylaws, involves three distinct bodies. Stockholders are the real owners of a corporation—investors who buy shares of ownership. The board of directors is a group of people elected by stockholders to oversee the management of the corporation. Corporate officers are top managers hired by the board to run the corporation on a day-to-day basis.

Stock Ownership and Stockholders' Rights

Corporations sell shares in the business—**stock**—to investors, who then become **stockholders**, or **shareholders**. Profits are distributed among stockholders in the form of dividends, and corporate managers serve at their discretion. Stockholders, then, are the owners of a corporation.

stock
A share of ownership in a corporation

stockholder (or **shareholder**)
An owner of shares of stock in a corporation

Preferred and Common Stock

Corporate stock may be either preferred or common. **Preferred stock** guarantees holders fixed dividends, much like the interest paid on savings accounts. Preferred stockholders are so called because they have preference, or priority, over common stockholders when dividends are distributed and, if a business liquidates, when the value of assets is distributed. Although many major corporations issue preferred stock, few small corporations do.

   Common stock, however, must be issued by every corporation, big or small. It usually pays dividends only if the corporation makes a profit. Dividends on both common and preferred stock are paid on a per-share basis. Thus, a stockholder with 10 shares re-

preferred stock
Stock that guarantees its holders fixed dividends and priority claims over assets but no corporate voting rights

common stock
Stock that guarantees corporate voting rights but last claims over assets

ceives 10 times the dividend paid to a stockholder with one. Holders of common stock have the last claims to any of the company's assets if it folds.

Another difference involves voting rights. Preferred stockholders generally have no voting rights. Common stockholders always have voting rights, with each share of stock carrying one vote. Investors who cannot attend a stockholders' meeting may delegate their voting shares to someone who will attend. This procedure, called voting by **proxy**, is the way almost all individual investors vote.

However, ownership of common stock does not automatically give an individual the right to act for the corporation or to share in its management. The only way that most stockholders can influence the running of a corporation is by casting their annual votes for the board of directors. In reality, however, any given individual usually has very little influence over the affairs of a large corporation. For example, although General Motors boasts more than 1 million stockholders, only a handful have enough votes to affect the way GM is actually run.

Boards of Directors

By law, the governing body of a corporation is its **board of directors**. Boards communicate with stockholders and other potential investors through such channels as the annual report, a summary of the company's financial health. Directors also set policy on dividends, major spending, and executive salaries and benefits. They are legally responsible for corporate actions and are increasingly being held liable for their actions.

Board Makeup   Although requirements differ, most states require that there be at least three directors and one board meeting per year. Large corporations tend to have as many as 20 or 30 directors. Smaller corporations often have no more than five. Usually, directors are people with personal or professional ties to the corporation, such as family members, lawyers, and accountants.

Many boards have both outside and inside directors. Inside directors are top managers who have primary responsibility for the corporation. Outside directors are typically attorneys, accountants, university officials, and executives from other firms. However, all directors share the same basic responsibility: to ensure that the corporation is managed in the best interests of the stockholders.

On the other hand, managers and boards argue that the risk of conflicts is actually slight. They also contend that affiliated members contribute valuable insights at bargain prices. Nevertheless, a general movement to diminish insider influence is gaining momentum: lawsuits. In one recent year alone, 713 claims were filed against directors and officers at about 300 U.S. companies. The cost of defending such suits is increasing, and claim payments are up by 53 percent. Moreover, shareholders win about 80 percent of the time.[6]

As a result of such expensive problems, some institutional investors now recommend that boards and their committees have majorities of independent members. Many companies, such as Time Warner, General Motors, and the Walt Disney Co., have already set up policies to lessen the likelihood of conflict-of-interest charges.

Officers   Although board members oversee the corporation's operation, most of them do not participate in day-to-day management. Rather, they hire a team of managers to run the firm. As we have already seen, this team, called officers, is usually headed by the firm's **chief executive officer**, or **CEO**, who is responsible for the firm's overall performance. Other officers typically include a president, who is responsible for internal management, and vice presidents, who oversee various functional areas such as marketing and operations. Some officers may also be elected to serve on the board, and in some cases, a single person plays multiple roles. For example, one person might serve as board chairperson, CEO, and president. In most cases, however, a different person fills each slot.

proxy
Authorization granted by a shareholder for someone else to vote his or her shares

board of directors
Governing body of a corporation, which reports to its shareholders and delegates power to run its day-to-day operations

chief executive officer (CEO)
Top manager hired by the board of directors to run a corporation

"Divide and conquer. Then, a merger."

Special Issues in Corporate Ownership

In recent years, several special issues have arisen or grown in importance in corporate ownership. The most important of these trends are mergers and acquisitions (including corporate alliances), multinational corporations, joint ventures, employee stock ownership plans, and institutional ownership.

Mergers and Acquisitions

A **merger** occurs when two firms combine to create a new company. In an **acquisition**, one firm buys another outright. Although mergers and acquisitions are not new, they increased in both frequency and importance in the United States during the 1980s. In the 1990s, they remain an important form of corporate strategy. They allow firms to increase product lines, expand operations, go international, and create new enterprises in conjunction with other organizations. Mergers usually take one of three forms:

■ A *horizontal merger* occurs between two companies in the same industry. For example, Boeing and McDonnell Douglas, the two largest commercial aircraft manufacturers in the United States, recently merged to create one new, exceptionally large company. Other recent examples include Daimler-Benz–Chrysler and Norwest–Wells Fargo.

■ When one of the companies is a supplier to or customer of the other, the venture is called a *vertical merger*. For example, when IBM bought Lotus Development Corporation a few years ago, its goal was to acquire its own software development company as a way of reducing its dependence on Microsoft.

■ Finally, when the companies are unrelated, the acquisition is called a *conglomerate merger*. In August 1994, for instance, ITT Corp., which already had interests in insurance, financial services, hotels, and other areas, joined with Cablevision Systems Inc. to purchase Madison Square Garden, a sports entertainment company that includes two professional sports franchises among its holdings.

A merger or acquisition can take place in one of several different ways. The process usually starts when one firm announces that it wants to buy another for a specified price. After some negotiation, the owners or board of the second company agree to the sale and the firm is soon taken over by the buyer. Sometimes, a firm may realize that it is a likely takeover target and cannot forestall the inevitable. It may therefore seek out a favorable buyer and, in effect, ask to be acquired. In both of these two scenarios, the acquisition is called a friendly takeover because the acquired company welcomes the merger.

merger
The union of two corporations to form a new corporation

acquisition
The purchase of one company by another

Sometimes, however, takeover targets resist. In such a case, a firm may wish to remain independent, or it may regard a purchase offer as too low or a potential buyer as a poor match. The would-be buyer, however, may persist. For instance, it may offer to buy the target firm's stock on the open market, usually at a premium price. If it can acquire a sufficient quantity of stock, it will gain control of the target company despite the resistance of the target firm's management. In this case, the acquisition is called a hostile takeover.

After successful mergers or acquisitions, whether friendly or hostile, one of three things can happen:

- *The acquired company continues to operate as a separate entity.* For example, Royal Caribbean Cruise Lines recently bought Celebrity Cruise Lines but announced that it intended to maintain the two operations as separate businesses.

- *The acquired business is absorbed by the buyer and simply disappear.* When Wells Fargo & Company bought First Interstate (as described earlier), all First Interstate offices and branches were either renamed Wells Fargo & Company or closed. Within a few months, no trace of First Interstate remained.

- *The two companies may form a new company.* For example, when the Northrop Corporation successfully acquired the Grumman Corporation, the new entity was renamed Northrop Grumman. Similarly, after North Carolina National Bank (NCNB) acquired several other large banks, it renamed itself NationsBank to more accurately reflect its national stature and competitiveness.

Divestitures and Spin-Offs

Sometime a corporation adopts the opposite strategy in that it decides to take a part of its existing business operations and either sell it to another corporation or else set it up as a new independent corporation. Several reasons might motivate such a step.

For example, a firm might decide that it needs to focus more specifically on its core businesses. Unilever, a large European consumer products company, recently did this. The firm makes such well-known products as Close-Up toothpaste, Dove soap, Vaseline lotions, and Q-tips. The company also owned several specialty chemical businesses which had been set up to make ingredients for its consumer products. The firm decided that it needed to focus more on the consumer products themselves and sold the chemical businesses to ICI, a European chemical giant. Such a sale is called a **divestiture**.

In other cases a firm might decide to sell part of itself in order to raise capital. Kmart has had to resort to this strategy. It sold its profitable book store operations, including Borders and Waldenbooks, to raise money to expand its discount chain. But the actual sale was a new stock offering in a newly created corporation comprising the book store chains. Such a sale is known as a **spin-off**.

divestiture
The selling of one or more business units by a corporation

spin-off
Taking one or more business units from an existing corporation and setting it up as a new, independent corporation.

General Mills joined with Nestlé in 1989 to dramatically expand its international cereal business. Cereal Partners Worldwide (CPW) now features more than 40 distinctive cereal brands, including such familiar General Mills cereals as Honey Nut Cheerios and such Nestlé brands as Chocopic. With sales in more than 60 countries, CPW has quickly become the second largest cereal company outside North America.

Joint Ventures

In a strategic alliance, two or more organizations collaborate on an enterprise. When the partners share ownership stakes in the enterprise, it is called a **joint venture**. The number of joint ventures has increased rapidly in recent years on both domestic and international fronts. In 1995, for example, the U.S. telecommunications firm MCI Communications Corp. entered into a joint venture with News Corp., a British-based media giant. The new venture intends to produce and distribute various communication products internationally, including movies "on demand" sent to consumers' TV sets and high-speed information services delivered to PCs of business clients. MCI and News Corp. suggest that the new joint venture company will ultimately be in a position to deliver home shopping by satellite and *The Simpsons* over the Internet.

joint venture (or **strategic alliance**) Collaboration between two or more organizations on an enterprise

Employee Stock Ownership Plans

Still another development in corporate ownership is the **employee stock ownership plan**, or **ESOP**. As the term suggests, this is a plan wherein employees own a significant share of the corporation through what are essentially trusts established on behalf of the employees. The company first secures a loan with which it buys shares of its own stock on the open market. A portion of future corporate profits is used to guarantee and eventually repay the loan. Employees gradually receive ownership of the stock, usually on the basis of seniority. Because it is being used to secure the original loan, they do not receive immediate possession of the stock, but they do take immediate control of its voting rights. Current estimates suggest that there are now almost 10,000 ESOPs in the United States. The growth rate in new ESOPs has slowed a bit in recent years, but they still are an important part of corporate ownership patterns in the United States.

employee stock ownership plan (ESOP) Arrangement in which a corporation holds its own stock in trust for its employees, who gradually receive ownership of the stock and control its voting rights

Institutional Ownership

Most individual investors do not own enough stock to exert any influence on the management of big corporations. In recent years, however, more and more stock has been purchased by **institutional investors**. Because they control enormous resources, these investors—especially mutual and pension funds—can buy huge blocks of stock. For example, the national teachers' retirement system (TIAA-CREF) has assets of over $95 billion and invests over one-third of that amount in stocks.

institutional investors Large investors, such as mutual funds and pension funds, that purchase large blocks of corporate stock

Indeed, institutional investors now own almost 40 percent of all the stock in the United States. An important trend in recent years is increased involvement by such investors in the companies that they partially own. TIAA-CREF, for example, now recommends standards for the makeup of company boards: They should have a majority of independent directors, and committees should be composed entirely of unaffiliated outsiders. Investor influence was important when PepsiCo decided to spin off its restaurant businesses—KFC, Taco Bell, and Pizza Hut—into a new corporation in 1997. Several large institutional investors had become unhappy with the firm's performance relative to Coca-Cola and pressured the board to take action. The board's response was to sell off these businesses in order to allow management to focus more attention on the firm's core soft drink business.

Summary of Learning Objectives

1 **Trace the history of business in the United States**. Modern U.S. business structures reflect a pattern of development over centuries. Throughout much of the colonial period, sole proprietors supplied raw materials to English manufacturers. The rise of the factory system during the Industrial Revolution brought with it mass production and specialization of labor. During the entrepreneurial era in the nineteenth century, huge corporations—and monopolies—emerged. During the production era of the early twentieth century, companies grew by emphasizing output and production. During the marketing era of the mid-1900s, businesses began focusing on sales staff, advertis-

ing, and the need to produce what consumers wanted. The most recent development has been toward a global perspective.

2 **Identify the major forms of business ownership.** The most common forms of business ownership are the sole proprietorship, the partnership, the cooperative, and the regular corporation. Each form has several advantages and disadvantages. The form under which a business chooses to organize is crucial because it affects both long-term strategy and day-to-day decision making. In addition to advantages and disadvantages, entrepreneurs must consider their preferences and long-range requirements.

3 **Describe sole proprietorships and partnerships and explain the advantages and disadvantages of each.** Sole proprietorships, the most common form of business, consist of one person doing business. Although sole proprietorships offer freedom and privacy and are easy to form, they lack continuity and present certain financial risks. For one thing, they feature unlimited liability: The sole proprietor is liable for all debts incurred by the business. General partnerships are proprietorships with multiple owners. Limited partnerships allow for limited partners who can invest without being liable for debts incurred by general or active partners. In master limited partnerships, master partners can sell shares and pay profits to investors. Partnerships have access to a larger talent pool and more investment money than do sole proprietorships but may be dissolved if conflicts between partners cannot be settled.

4 **Describe corporations and explain their advantages and disadvantages.** Corporations are independent legal entities that are usually run by professional managers. The corporate form is used by most large businesses because it offers continuity and opportunities for raising money. It also features financial protection through limited liability: The liability of investors is limited to their personal investments. However, the corporation is a complex legal entity subject to double taxation. In addition to taxes paid on corporate profits, investors must pay taxes on earned income. The stock of public corporations is sold widely to the general public; the stock of private corporations is held by a few investors and is unavailable for sale to the public.

5 **Describe the basic issues involved in creating and managing a corporation.** Creating a corporation generally requires legal assistance to file articles of incorporation and corporate bylaws and to comply with government regulations. Managers must understand stockholders' rights as well as the rights and duties of the board of directors.

6 **Identify recent trends and issues in corporate ownership.** Recent trends in corporate ownership include mergers (when two companies combine to create a new one) and acquisitions (when one company buys another outright), multinational corporations (which conduct activities on an international scale), joint ventures or strategic alliances (in which two or more organizations collaborate on an enterprise), employee stock ownership plans (ESOPs by which employees buy large shares of their employer companies), and institutional ownership of corporations (by groups such as mutual and pension funds).

Study Questions and Exercises

Questions for Review

1 Why is it important to understand the history of U.S. business?
2 Compare the advantages and disadvantages of the major forms of business ownership.
3 What are the primary benefits and drawbacks to serving as a general partner in a limited partnership?
4 Why might a corporation choose to remain private? Why might a private corporation choose to go public?
5 Why have joint ventures become more common in recent years?

Questions for Analysis

6 How can you, as a prospective manager, better prepare yourself now for the challenges you will face in the next 20 years?

7 What basic steps must be taken to incorporate a business in your state?

8 Go to the library or the Internet and research a recent merger or acquisition. What factors led to the arrangement? What circumstances characterized the process of completing the arrangement? Were they friendly or unfriendly?

Application Exercises

9 Interview the owner-manager of a sole proprietorship or a general partnership. What characteristics of that business form led the owner to choose it? Does he or she ever contemplate changing the form of the business?

10 Interview the owner of or principal stockholder in a corporation. What characteristics of that business form led the individual to choose it?

Building Your Business Skills

This exercise enhances the following SCANS workplace competencies: demonstrating basic skills, demonstrating thinking skills, exhibiting interpersonal skills, and working with information.

Goal   To help students analyze the implications of corporate acquisitions and mergers on individual stockholders.

Situation   You own 500 shares of Widget International (WI). Although you like the company's products, you are disappointed with the stock price. Analysts agree with you and warn that the company must drastically cut expenses or risk a takeover. Management begins to trim budgets, but its efforts are seen as too little too late. With the stock price continuing to drop, XYZ Corporation offers to buy WI. After successful negotiations, XYZ is set to acquire WI on January 1. When this happens, your 500 shares of WI will be converted into XYZ Corporation stock.

Method   Working in groups of four or five, analyze how this acquisition may affect your stock holdings. Research a similar corporate merger that took place in the past year as you consider the following factors:

- The nature of the acquiring company.
- The fit between the products or services of the two companies.
- The fiscal health of the acquiring company, as reflected in its own stock price.
- The stock market's long-term reaction to the acquisition. Does the market think it is a good move?
- Changes in corporate leadership as a result of the acquisition.
- Changes in the way the acquired company's products are produced and marketed.
- Announced budgetary changes.

Follow-Up Questions

1 After one company acquires another, what factors are likely to influence the stock market so that the stock price rises?

2 After one company acquires another, what factors are likely to influence the stock market so that the stock price drops?

3 Did your research identify any factors that are likely to trigger a corporate takeover?

4 In an acquisition, who is likely to be named CEO (the person in charge of the acquired or acquiring company)? Who is likely to be named CEO in a merger of equals? What factors are likely to influence this decision?

5 How is the board of directors likely to change as a result of an acquisition? A merger?

Business Case 2

The Gee Whiz Company Stumbles

Silicon Graphics Inc. (SGI) was a hot company in 1995. Its cutting-edge computers and workstations produced dazzlingly realistic 3-D graphics that showed up everywhere from Nintendo games to blockbuster movies such as *Jurassic Park* and *The Terminator,* and Wall Street was calling the firm "the new Apple." Its executives were flying high and the firm quickly grabbed 14 percent of the nearly $13-billion workstation market.

A mere 2 years later, the company was posting enormous losses ($35 million in the first half of 1997 alone) and its stock value had dropped over 50 percent. SGI's CEO, Ed Mc-Cracken, publicly admitted, "If we can't produce good quarters, we're not going to have a future."

What happened?

Observers list a catalogue of just about everything that can go wrong at a high-tech, high-pressure firm. Cofounder Jim Clark left the firm to start a new venture that came to be known as Netscape. McCracken joined President Clinton's National Information Infrastructure Advisory Council, putting the company in the hands of Chief Operating Officer Tom Jermoluk. With an aggressive management style and with Mc-Cracken's backing, Jermoluk launched a feverish and ultimately ill-fated campaign to achieve 50 percent growth for SGI, most of it to come from the highly speculative

market for interactive TV. That meant the company had to turn its back on the Internet, where competitors such as Sun Microsystems began to make their fortunes.

> **"If we can't produce good quarters, we're not going to have a future."**
>
> —Ed McCracken, CEO, Silicon Graphics

Basics such as inventory management and quality control started to slide. At one point SGI was shipping 80 percent of its sales in the last month of the quarter, and replacement microprocessors for flawed computers shipped around the world set the firm back a whopping $10 million. New SGI chips subcontracted to suppliers NEC and Toshiba were delivered late, leaving SGI with product shortages. Jermoluk, who was building a reputation for partying hard, resigned to head a startup firm (@Home Corp., a cable Net service). Turnover among top executives doubled. McCracken divorced and openly began a relationship with a fellow employee. Then in 1996 SGI ran afoul of the Justice and Commerce Departments by unwittingly selling four supercomputers to a Russian factory that designs nuclear warheads.

SGI hasn't given up, however. The firm has purchased supercomputer maker Cray Research Inc., making it to the top seller of high-speed computing, and plans to continue battling competitors IBM, Sun Microsystems, and Hewlett-Packard in the lucrative workstation market. The Jet Propulsion Laboratory in Pasadena is processing Mars data from the Pathfinder mission with SGI equipment, and *The Lost World,* sequel to *Jurassic Park,* was made with SGI computers. McCracken is still at the helm and hopes for a comeback.

Questions

1. What key lessons about doing business can be learned from the story of Silicon Graphics? Which of these lessons can be applied outside the computer industry?
2. What evidence indicates that SGI may have lost its market focus after 1995?
3. What mistakes might have been avoided?
4. How should McCracken ensure the future of SGI?

Connecting to the Web

The following Web sites will give you additional information and points of view about topics covered in this chapter. Many sites lead to other related Internet locations, so approach this list with the spirit of an explorer.

CHASE MANHATTAN BANK

http://www.chasemanhattan.com/

Chase Manhattan became the largest U.S. bank as a result of its horizontal merger with Chemical Bank. Visit this site for continuing information on merger impact.

DOING BUSINESS IN FRANCE: STRUCTURE OF BUSINESS

http://www.business-in-europe.com/gb/telechrge/structure.htm.

Compare the structure of U.S. businesses with the structure of businesses in France. This site, prepared by the consulting firm Ernst & Young France, lists business entities in France. You can download a free *Doing Business in France* guide for more information about French business structures.

FORD WORLDWIDE CONNECTION: HISTORICAL LIBRARY

http://www.ford.com/archive/

Click on this site for the Ford Motor Company's look at its own history, including Henry Ford's invention of the moving assembly line for the Model T and Model A.

GE HOME PAGE

http://www.ge.com/

General Electric is a public corporation. This Web site includes the corporate annual report, which GE and all corporations are required to issue.

HISTORY OF SEARS

http://www.sears.com/company/pubaff/history1.htm

This site describes the growth of Sears, Roebuck and Co. from a sole proprietorship to one of the world's largest corporations.

HOME OFFICE ASSOCIATION OF AMERICA

http://www.hoaa.com/

This site is dedicated to the millions of full- and part-time home-based workers and telecommuters. Click on "Home Office Related Resources" for a comprehensive list of Web sites, including some that focus on the structure of small business.

THE NATIONAL CENTER FOR EMPLOYEE OWNERSHIP

http://www.nceo.org/

Click on this Web site for information on employee stock ownership plans, employee stock options, and other forms of employee ownership.

NORTHROP GRUMMAN CORPORATION

http://www.northgrum.com/

This is the Web site of the Northrop Grumman Corporation. Click here to learn about Northrop's acquisition of Grumman in 1994 and the 1997 merger of Northrop Grumman and Lockheed Martin.

RHODE ISLAND HISTORY BOOKSTORE

http://www.aclock.com/history/

The American Industrial Revolution began in Rhode Island. Visit this site for a catalog of books on this and other topics.

RICELAND FOODS INC.

http://www.riceland.com/

This site introduces you to the Riceland Foods farmer-owned marketing cooperative, the world's largest miller and marketer of rice and other agricultural products.

chapter 3

Understanding the **global context** of business

Coke is it—or it soon will be

Many U.S. companies are seeking entry into new markets for their products around the world. Perhaps no market excites as much interest as China, with its 1.2 billion consumers to whom many Western products are still a novelty. For Coca-Cola, in fact, "the per capita consumption is so low and the population so high, the opportunity is incredible," says industry analyst Roy D. Burry. The soft drink giant, which already gets about 70 percent of its sales abroad, is now braving a number of challenges to take advantage of that opportunity.

China's undeveloped manufacturing and transportation infrastructure and its complex regulations make distribution difficult. Political backlash routinely threatens Coke and all U.S. consumer products in Asia. Hiring local labor often requires extensive searches and training. And many storekeepers simply lack the electricity needed to run the big coolers Coca-Cola would like to fill. But the firm's managers see unlimited promise and, indeed, a one-time-only chance to dominate the market where Pepsi is prepared to compete hard. They expect soft drink sales in China to double every 3 years indefinitely. When you consider that per capita consumption of Coke is already 343 servings a year in the United States (that's nearly a Coke a day for every American man, woman, and child), China's 5 servings per person per year leaves a lot of room for growth. Wall Street seems to agree with this assessment; Coke's stock rose 44 percent in 1995.

So Coke will be investing about $2 billion over the next few years to build bottling plants and distribution systems in China, to buy refrigerators and trucks, to upgrade wiring in stores, and to give out millions of samples. The company has even promised the government that it will help local farmers by producing a new fruit drink. Coca-Cola has worked hard for the 49 percent growth it has already enjoyed in China for the past 10 years, and the firm's managers are betting there is much more growth to come.

In a climate of growing international activity, the study and practice of basic business management has in many ways become the study and practice of international business. By focusing on the learning objectives of this chapter, you will better understand the dynamics of international business management.

After reading this chapter, you should be able to

1 Identify the major world marketplaces and explain how different forms of competitive advantage, import-export balances, exchange rates, and foreign competition determine how countries and businesses respond to the international environment.

2 Discuss the factors involved in deciding to do business internationally and in selecting the appropriate levels of international involvement and international organizational structure.

3 Describe some of the ways in which social, cultural, economic, legal, and political differences among nations affect international business.

The Rise of International Business

The total volume of world trade today is immense—around $7 trillion each year. Foreign investment in the United States alone is approaching $1 trillion, and direct investment abroad by U.S. firms has already passed the $1 trillion mark. As more and more firms engage in international business, the world economy is fast becoming a single interdependent system in a process called **globalization**. Even so, we often take for granted the diversity of goods and services available today as a result of international trade. Your television set, your shoes, and even the roast lamb on your dinner table all may be U.S. **imports**, made or grown abroad but sold in this country. At the same time, the success of many U.S. firms depends in large part on **exports**, made or grown here and shipped for sale abroad.

The Contemporary Global Economy

"There is no more mystical sense in which we have a global economy," says MIT professor of economics Paul Krugman, who has identified five very basic facets of a truly global economy:

- An international trade in goods
- A lesser international trade in services
- An international movement of labor
- An international flow of money
- An international flow of information

Surprisingly, reports Krugman, what we now think of as an extremely active global economy is not as unprecedented as we might think. For instance, recall our discussion of gross domestic product in Chapter 1. In 1880, Krugman points out, U.S. imports were 8 percent of GDP. Today, they are only 11 percent. In other words, actual trade of products is not much more active than it was in the nineteenth century. What about the movement of money from country to country, a phenomenon known as capital mobility? Except for some new forms of exchange, observes Krugman, it is about the same as it was in 1914. At that time, moreover, England's trade surplus—4 percent of GDP—was the same as the surplus enjoyed by Japan during the peak decade of the 1980s.

What factors typify the global economy in the mid-1990s? Krugman points to vastly expanding growth in the exchange of information and the trade in services:

▶ In Cambridge, Massachusetts, Montague Corp. designs a unique product: folding mountain bikes. Montague manufactures most of its bikes in Taiwan and sells them in Europe. A key facet of the company's operations is transmitting design specifications among three continents, sometimes on a daily basis. The process works and the small firm survives, largely because fax machine technology is available.

▶ Molloy Electric is a small firm that services electric motors in Sioux Falls, South Dakota. Owner Garry Jacobson has observed that more and more customers are bringing in products powered by unreliable foreign-made motors. "Either they bring them in or they just throw them away, which costs us," says Jacobson, who thus acknowledges the impact of the global economy on his small part of the business world.

Note that Molloy Electric's service is not even tradable—it cannot be directly exchanged for another product on the international market. In fact, such is the case with about 85 percent of all U.S. services (restaurants, retailing, and the like). In effect, then, the shift to the service economy seems to work against the development of a global economy. That situation, predicts Krugman, will change; witness the experience of Molloy Electric, which has already made contact with the manufacturing operations of China and other countries. The conclusion to be drawn from the experiences of firms such as Molloy Elec-

globalization
Process by which the world economy is becoming a single interdependent system

import
Product made or grown abroad but sold domestically

export
Product made or grown domestically but shipped and sold abroad

tric and Montague Corp. is twofold: Information technology will be the centerpiece of the new global economy, and the growth in the service sector will help to fuel its development.[1]

In this section, we will examine some of the key factors that have shaped—and are shaping—the global business environment of the 1990s. First, we will identify and describe the major world marketplaces. Then we will discuss some important factors that determine the ways in which both nations and their businesses respond to the international environment: the roles of different forms of competitive advantage, of import-export balances, and of exchange rates.[2]

Major World Marketplaces

The contemporary world economy revolves around three major marketplaces: North America, Western Europe, and the Pacific Rim. Obviously, business is not conducted solely in these markets. The World Bank notes, for example, that 77 percent of the world's people live in so-called developing areas. Economies in those areas are expanding 5 percent to 6 percent annually. There are 300 million consumers in Eastern Europe and another 300 million in South America. In India alone, estimates of the size of the middle class run from 100 million to 300 million.[3]

North America

The United States dominates the North American business region. It is the single largest marketplace and enjoys the most stable and sound economy in the world. Many U.S. firms, such as General Motors and Procter & Gamble, have had successful Canadian operations for years, and Canadian firms such as Northern Telecom and Alcan Aluminum are major international competitors.

Mexico has also become a major manufacturing center, especially along the U.S. border, where cheap labor and low transportation costs have encouraged many firms, from the United States and other countries, to build plants on the Mexican side. Both Chrysler and General Motors, for instance, are building new assembly plants, as are suppliers such as Rockwell International Corp. Nissan opened an engine and transmission plant in 1983 and a car-making plant in 1992. In addition to suppliers, Nissan has also attracted nonauto companies to the area, including Xerox and Texas Instruments. Mexican forecasters expect 200,000 workers to be in the automobile industry by 1998.

Meanwhile, retailers in areas such as Laredo, Texas, who have long offered Mexican shoppers lower prices and greater selections of brand-name products, now find themselves competing not only with more competitive Mexican merchants but with American retailers such as Wal-Mart and Sears, both of whom have opened large outlets in Monterrey, a nearby industrial city in northern Mexico. In any case, commerce between the United States and Mexico is growing rapidly. As you can see from Figure 3.1, which com-

Figure 3.1 U.S. and Texas Exports to Mexico, 1988–1997

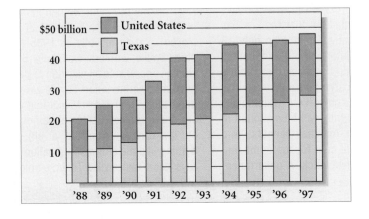

pares the increase in U.S. and Texas exports to Mexico since 1988, so is commerce between Mexico and the state of Texas. In fact, Texas—and even the city of Dallas—have developed what amount to foreign policies in order to encourage this trend. The states of Texas and Nuevo León, for example, have joint trade and research missions and have already launched a project called Two Nation Vacation/Vacaciones en Dos Naciones.[4]

Western Europe

Europe is often divided into two regions. Western Europe, dominated by Germany, the United Kingdom, France, and Italy, has been a mature but fragmented marketplace for years. The evolution of the European Union in 1992 into a unified marketplace has further increased the importance of this marketplace. Major international firms such as Unilever, Renault, Royal Dutch Shell, Michelin, Siemens, and Nestlé are all headquartered in this region.

Eastern Europe, which was until recently primarily communist, has also gained in importance, both as a marketplace and as a producer. In May 1994, for example, Albania became the 197th country in which Coca-Cola is produced, as Coke opened a new $10-million bottling plant outside the capital city of Tirana. Meanwhile, Kellogg has opened a new plant in Riga, capital of the former Soviet republic of Latvia. Kellogg has also launched a vigorous campaign of television ads and in-store demonstrations to capitalize on one of the world's few remaining cereal frontiers.[5]

The Workplace Environment

A Kind of Equality Arrives in Japan

It may not reassure them to know it, but the Japanese women who are making their way into the mainstream of Japan's traditionally male jobs now face the same issue U.S. women already contend with: the clash between their belief in equality and the effect their work has on their families and themselves.

The second-class status of women is more deeply institutionalized in Japan than in the West. For example, in addition to cultural pressures that led women to quit their (usually menial) jobs when they married or became pregnant, until recently a law prevented women from working between 10 P.M. and 5 A.M., so they could not hold high-paying jobs in factories where job rotation (a week of days and a week of nights) is the norm. Now that the law has been lifted, Nissan's Oppama plant still employs only 18 women among its 2,200 workers, although other industries such as electronics have higher ratios because they require "delicate" work. But some women aren't sure they want to follow in the footsteps of their male coworkers, traditionally overworked on the job. Some fear they will be exploited in part-time jobs with low pay and minimal benefits. And some are concerned about who will care for the home and family if both parents are on the fast track. A government study found that Japanese men devote less than half an hour a day to housework and child care, even when their wives work.

> ❝ *It is improving, but it's nothing like the anti-discrimination law in the United States.* ❞

—Kaori Takizawa, a Tokyo employment lawyer.

At the moment, women in Japan make up 40 percent of the workforce (nearly half of all Japanese women are employed). Yet as recently as 1995 the average wage for full-time female workers was only 60 percent of men's and women represented less than 9 percent of all managers. A new antidiscrimination law requires firms to provide equal opportunity (the old law required them merely to try to do so) and promises violators' names will be made public (the old law carried no penalty at all). "It is improving, but it's nothing like the anti-discrimination law in the United States," says Kaori Takizawa, a Tokyo employment lawyer.

The Pacific Rim

The Pacific Rim consists of Japan, the People's Republic of China, Thailand, Malaysia, Singapore, Indonesia, South Korea, Taiwan, Hong Kong, the Philippines, and Australia. Fueled by strong entries in the automobile, electronics, and banking industries, the economies of these countries grew rapidly in the 1970s and 1980s. Today the Pacific Rim is an important force in the world economy and a major source of competition for North American firms. Japan, led by companies such as Toyota, Toshiba, and Nippon Steel, dominates the region. In addition, South Korea (with such firms as Samsung and Hyundai), Taiwan (owner of Chinese Petroleum and manufacturing home of many foreign firms), and Hong Kong (a major financial center) are also successful players in the international economy. China, the most densely populated country in the world, continues to emerge as an important market in its own right. In fact, the International Monetary Fund concluded in 1993 that the Chinese economy is now the world's third largest, behind the United States and only slightly behind Japan.[6]

Forms of Competitive Advantage

No country can produce all the goods and services that its people need. Thus, countries tend to export the things that they can produce better or less expensively than other countries. The proceeds are then used to import things that they cannot produce effectively. However, this very general principle does not fully explain why nations export and import what they do. Such decisions hinge, among other things, on whether a country enjoys an absolute or a comparative advantage in the production of different goods and services.[7]

An **absolute advantage** exists when a country can produce something more cheaply than any other country can. Saudi oil and Canadian timber approximate absolute advantage, but examples of true absolute advantage are rare. In reality, "absolute" advantages

absolute advantage
A nation's ability to produce something more cheaply than any other country can

When Korean automaker Daewoo Group purchased this truck-making plant in Lublin, Poland, in 1995, it was a ramshackle collection of 14 overstaffed buildings with broken windows and 20-year-old equipment. Even today, molten steel for molding parts is poured by hand, and there is no computer system for keeping track of parts. Daewoo intends to change this state of affairs. Whereas demand for new cars is slowing in Western Europe, it's jumping in Central Europe, where Poland enjoys the largest economy. Says Daewoo founder and CEO Kim Woo-Chong: "We have to move into big potential markets where few competitors have gone."

are always relative. Brazil, for instance, produces about one-third of the world's coffee. However, because its high-quality coffees are preferred by American consumers, the impact of Brazil's production is widely felt. For example, a severe frost in the winter of 1994 destroyed perhaps 45 percent of the 1995–1996 harvest. First, commodities prices—prices paid by producers, roasters, and speculators—jumped to their highest levels in 10 years. Then, the three largest U.S. coffee producers—Procter & Gamble, Kraft, and Nestlé—raised retail prices by 45 percent. With the threat to worldwide supplies, prices for lower-quality African coffees also went up. Not surprisingly, forecasters predict that the prices paid by American consumers will continue to reflect the damage to the 1995–1996 Brazilian crop.[8]

comparative advantage
A nation's ability to produce some products more cheaply or better than others

A country has a **comparative advantage** in goods that it can make more cheaply or better than other goods. For example, if businesses in a country can make computers more cheaply than automobiles, then computers represent a comparative advantage for its firms. The United States has comparative advantages in the computer industry (because of technological sophistication) and in farming (because of fertile land and a temperate climate). South Korea has a comparative advantage in electronics manufacturing because of efficient operations and cheap labor. Thus, U.S. firms export computers and grain to South Korea, from whom U.S. firms import VCRs and stereos.

Import-Export Balances

The advantages of international trade are obvious. However, trading with other nations can pose problems if a country's imports and exports do not strike an acceptable balance. In deciding whether an overall balance exists, economists use two measures: balance of trade and balance of payments.

Balance of Trade

balance of trade
Total economic value of all products that a country imports minus the total economic value of all products that it exports

A nation's **balance of trade** is the total economic value of all products it imports minus the total economic value of all products that it exports. Small trade imbalances are quite common and generally unimportant. Large imbalances, however, are another matter. In 1996, for example, the United States imported $960 billion worth of goods and services while exporting only $849 billion. Thus, the U.S. trade balance in 1996 was a negative $111 billion. But the U.S. trade imbalance has been declining in recent years and experts predict this trend will continue.

trade deficit
Situation in which a country's imports exceed its exports, creating a negative balance of trade

Trade Deficits and Surpluses   When a country's imports exceed its exports—that is, when it has a negative balance of trade—it suffers a **trade deficit**. In short, more money is flowing out than flowing in. A positive balance of trade occurs when a country's exports exceed its imports and it enjoys a **trade surplus**: More money is flowing in than flowing out.

trade surplus
Situation in which a country's exports exceed its imports, creating a positive balance of trade

For years, Japan has enjoyed consistently large surpluses. Today, Japan exports about 15 percent of everything it makes while importing goods and services equal to only about 5 percent of what it makes at home. The resulting surplus is several billion dollars each year. At the same time, just as the U.S. trade deficit has been declining, so has the Japanese surplus. Higher domestic costs, shifts in currency exchange rates, a worldwide economic slowdown, and greater international competition have all combined to cut Japan's trade surplus by reducing the flow of its exports.

Balance of Payments

balance of payments
Flow of all money into and out of a country

Balance of payments refers to the flow of money into or out of a country. The money that a nation pays for imports and receives for exports—that is, its balance of trade—makes up much of its balance of payments. But other financial exchanges also enter in. For example, money spent by tourists, money spent on foreign aid programs, and money spent and received in the buying and selling of currency in international money markets all affect the balance of payments.

For many years the United States enjoyed a positive balance of payments (more inflows than outflows); more recently, the balance has been negative. That trend is gradually reversing itself, however, and many economists soon expect a positive balance of payments. Naturally, some U.S. industries have positive balances and others have negative balances. For example, U.S. firms such as Dow Chemical and Monsanto are among the world leaders in chemical exports. The cigarette, truck, and industrial machinery industries also enjoy positive balances; the United States is exporting more than it is importing in these industries. Conversely, the metalworking machinery, electricity, airplane part, and auto industries are suffering negative balances because the United States is importing more than it is exporting.

Exchange Rates

The balance of imports and exports between two countries is affected by the exchange rate differences in their currencies. An **exchange rate** is the rate at which the currency of one nation can be exchanged for that of another. In early 1998, for example, one U.S. dollar was worth (that is, would buy the same value of goods as) about six French francs. The exchange rate, then, was 6 to 1.

At the end of World War II, the major nations of the world agreed to establish fixed exchange rates: The value of any country's currency relative to that of another country would remain constant. Gradually, however, this system proved impractical. Today, floating exchange rates are the norm. The value of one country's currency relative to that of another varies with market conditions. For example, when many French citizens want to spend francs to buy U.S. dollars (or goods), the value of the dollar relative to the franc goes up or gets stronger; demand for it is high. Therefore, the value of the dollar goes up with the demand for U.S. goods. In reality, exchange rates fluctuate by very small degrees on a daily basis. More significant variations usually occur over a longer period of time.

Fluctuation in exchange rates can have an important impact on the balance of trade. Suppose that you want to buy some French wines priced at 50 francs per bottle. At an exchange rate of 10 francs to the dollar, a bottle will cost you $5.00 (50 ÷ 10 = 5). But what if the franc is stronger? At an exchange rate of only 5 francs to the dollar, that same bottle of wine would cost you $10.00 (50 ÷ 5 = 10).

Of course, rate changes would affect more than wine. If the dollar were stronger in relation to the franc, the prices of all U.S.-made products would rise in France and the prices of all French-made products would fall in the United States. The French, therefore, would buy fewer U.S.-made products. Meanwhile, U.S. residents would be prompted to spend more valuable dollars on French-made products. The result could conceivably be a U.S. trade deficit with France.

▶ *OLDSMOBILE PRACTICES EXCHANGE RATE COMPETITION.* Companies conducting international operations must watch exchange rate fluctuations closely because such changes affect overseas demand for their products. In the summer of 1993, for example, Oldsmobile began running television ads with the tag line, "It's the exchange rate, you simpleton." At the time, the Japanese yen was strong: The U.S. dollar purchased fewer yen and fewer of the products for which Japanese manufacturers paid in yen. The price of Japanese products, including Japanese cars, was higher, and Oldsmobile was capitalizing on that fact.[9]

During this period, Japanese automakers had suffered their biggest loss of market share in over a decade. Because of the exchange rate, the reason was largely price: Models made by Toyota, Honda, and Nissan cost about $3,300 more than comparably equipped American-made cars. In Europe, meanwhile, several countries, including Sweden, had opted to make their products more price-competitive by devaluing their currencies. In 1993, U.S. sales of Swedish-made Volvos increased, with Volvo passing Volkswagen as the year's biggest-selling European automaker in the United States.[10]

As you can see from Figure 3.2, there has been a clear correlation between the exchange rate of the U.S. dollar and total U.S. exports in the period 1978–1993. With the 1978

exchange rate
Rate at which the currency of one nation can be exchanged for that of another

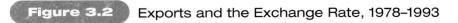

Figure 3.2 Exports and the Exchange Rate, 1978–1993

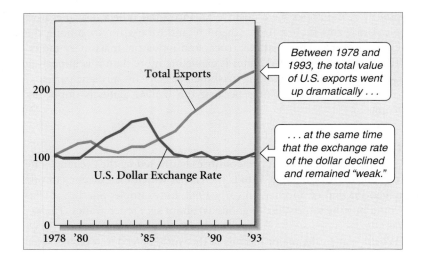

> Between 1978 and 1993, the total value of U.S. exports went up dramatically . . .

> . . . at the same time that the exchange rate of the dollar declined and remained "weak."

dollar indexed at a value of 100, the graph shows that the value of the dollar has declined and then leveled off since the mid-1980s. During that period, the volume of exports has climbed dramatically—121 percent since 1978. Note, too, that the rise in the dollar's value from the early to mid-1980s had a dampening effect on the growth in exports. It is important to remember, however, that the exchange rate is by no means the sole factor in the export boom; more precisely, it is a key factor in a set of advantageous economic conditions. Even more important has been the overall globalization of U.S. business in the last two decades.[11]

The Deficit, in Theory However, the theoretical relationship between the exchange rate and the balance of trade does not always hold. As you can see from Figure 3.3, which traces the deficit on a monthly basis for 18 months, the U.S. trade deficit decreased from $10.5 billion to $8.1 billion from January 1995 to June 1996. Also note the steep decline between May and June 1996: $2.4 billion. Why this dropoff? Part of the answer is revealed in Figure 3.4. Although exports decreased, the decline was quite small: a mere $200 million (to $69.71 billion). At the same time, however, imports decreased by a whopping $2.6 billion (to $77.82 billion). That difference—$2.4 billion—is the balance-of-trade surplus for the month.

Figure 3.3 U.S. Trade Deficit, January 1995–June 1996

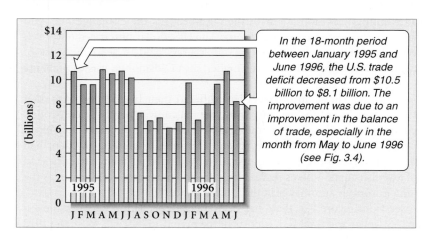

> In the 18-month period between January 1995 and June 1996, the U.S. trade deficit decreased from $10.5 billion to $8.1 billion. The improvement was due to an improvement in the balance of trade, especially in the month from May to June 1996 (see Fig. 3.4).

Figure 3.4   U.S. Imports and Exports, January 1995–June 1996

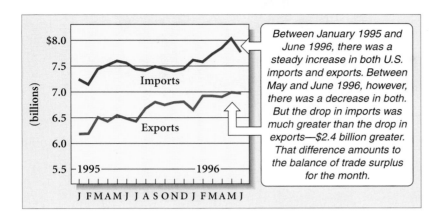

Between January 1995 and June 1996, there was a steady increase in both U.S. imports and exports. Between May and June 1996, however, there was a decrease in both. But the drop in imports was much greater than the drop in exports—$2.4 billion greater. That difference amounts to the balance of trade surplus for the month.

International Business Management

Wherever a firm is located, its success depends largely on how well it is managed. International business is so challenging because the basic management responsibilities—planning, organizing, directing, and controlling—are much more difficult to carry out when a business operates in several markets scattered around the globe.

It is not surprising, then, that the annals of business abound in legends about managers who made foolish decisions because they failed to familiarize themselves with the foreign markets in which they had hoped to do business. Estée Lauder, for example, launched an Italian cosmetics line with a picture of a model holding some flowers. The approach was conventional and seemingly harmless. Unfortunately, the flowers chosen were the kind traditionally used at Italian funerals—hardly the image that Lauder intended to communicate. Another U.S. firm introduced a cooking oil into South America with a Spanish name that translated as "jackass oil." Because of such legendary misadventures, before Marriott opens a hotel in a foreign country, it sends a team of managers to conduct exhaustive studies of every facet of the economy, business system, and culture.

Planning difficulties are compounded by difficulties in organizing, directing, and controlling. For example, an organizational structure that works well in one country may fail in others. Management techniques that lead to high worker productivity in the United States may offend workers in Japan or the United Kingdom. Accounting and other control systems are well developed in U.S. firms but may be unsophisticated or even nonexistent in developing nations.

Managing means making decisions, and in this section we will examine in some depth the three most basic decisions that a company's management must make when faced with the prospect of globalization. Naturally, the first decision is whether to go international at all. Once that decision has been made, managers must decide on the company's level of international involvement and on the organizational structure that will best meet its global needs.

Going International

The world economy is becoming globalized, and more and more firms are conducting international operations. However, this route is not appropriate for every company. For example, companies that buy and sell fresh produce and fish may find it most profitable to confine their activities to limited geographic areas: Storage and transport costs may be too high to make international operations worthwhile.

"Look, everyone here loves vanilla, right? So let's start there."

As Figure 3.5 shows, several factors enter into the decision to go international. One overriding factor is the business climate of other nations. Even experienced firms have encountered cultural, legal, and economic roadblocks. (These problems are discussed in more detail later in this chapter.) In considering international expansion, a company should also consider at least two other questions: Is there a demand for its products abroad? If so, must those products be adapted for international consumption?

Gauging International Demand

Obviously, products that are embraced as vital in one country may be useless in another. Snowmobiles are not only popular for transportation and recreation in Canada and the northern United States but actually revolutionized reindeer herding in Lapland. Naturally, there would be no demand at all in Central America. Although this is an extreme example, the point is quite basic to the decision to go international: Foreign demand for a company's product may be greater than, the same as, or weaker than domestic demand. Market research or the prior market entry of competitors may indicate that there is an international demand for a firm's products.

Figure 3.5 Going International

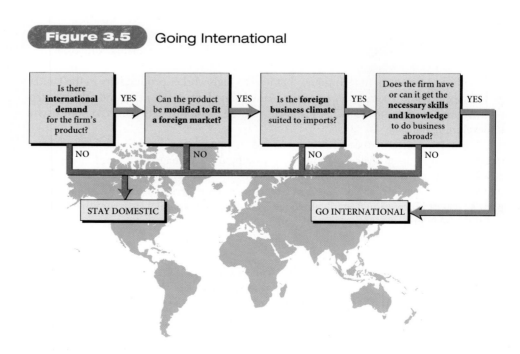

▶ *THE POP-CULTURE EMPIRE.* One very large category of U.S. products that travels well is U.S. popular culture. Of the world's 100 most popular movies in 1993, for instance, 88 were from the United States (no foreign film placed higher than 27th). Billions of dollars are also involved in popular music, television shows, books, and even street fashions. Teenagers in Rome and Beirut, for instance, sport U.S. baseball caps as part of their popular street dress; Super Mario Brothers is advertised on billboards in Bangkok, Thailand, and Bart Simpson piñatas are sold at bazaars in Mexico City. Vintage Levis from the 1950s and 1960s sell for as much as $3,000 in countries from Finland to Australia.

The images conjured by thoughts of such cross-cultural products are often amusing, but they also draw attention to some serious issues. Is U.S. popular culture so popular because it is energetic, democratic entertainment? Because it is creating virtually a new international language? Or is it merely a byproduct of military and economic imperialism? Defenders of foreign cultures have charged—often on seemingly good evidence—that American popular culture displays insensitivity to local cultures and even threatens traditional local values. Other critics point to crudity and pervasive themes of aggression and brutality. U.S. producers respond by arguing that U.S. popular culture fares so well because of aggressive marketing. They also contend that it is a successful commodity because it caters to multicultural demand in a global marketplace that is more often characterized by real hatred and violence.[12]

Adapting to Customer Needs

If there is international demand for its product, a firm must consider whether and how to adapt that product to meet the special demands of foreign customers. Consider the experience of General Motors in marketing the same product to buyers in two very different developing countries.

In Mexico, GM's Chevrolet division sells a Spanish-made subcompact called the Joy. Chevy prices the Joy $1,500 to $2,000 more than Volkswagen's original Beetle, which still sells well in Mexico. GM has upped its price because it has found that in a country where 60 percent of the population is under 25, there is a huge market of younger buyers who will pay for stylish, more powerful vehicles.

In the Czech Republic, however, GM markets the same car, known as the Opel Corsa, to potential buyers in their thirties. "Here," says GM's director of sales for Central Europe, "younger buyers can't even afford bicycles."[13]

When they think of importing and exporting, many people think of products such as cars and stereos. But another important export by U.S. companies is movies. Because of the high production values that characterize most films and their cultural association with the United States, U.S. films often find big markets in other countries. For example, when Titanic opened in London in March 1998, several thousand people lined up hours in advance to buy tickets. Even markets such as Turkey, shown here, can add big profits to a film's bottom line.

Obviously, in many cases what works in one country will not work in others. The product in question hardly needs to be as complex as a five-speed subcompact such as the Joy/Corsa. Consider plugs for electrical sockets. Because of different shapes and voltage, a plug that works in the United States will not work in England. Nor will British plugs fit French outlets any more than Italian plugs will fit Japanese outlets. A manufacturer cannot simply export the same plugs to every market around the globe. It must modify them to meet the standards of different countries.

Levels of Involvement

After a firm decides to go international, it must decide on the level of its international involvement. At least three levels of involvement are possible: The firm may act as an exporter or importer, organize as an international firm, or operate as a multinational firm.[14] Most of the world's largest industrial firms are multinationals.

Exporters and Importers

exporter
Firm that distributes and sells products to one or more foreign countries

importer
Firm that buys products in foreign markets and then imports them for resale in its home country

An **exporter** is a firm that makes products in one country and then distributes and sells them in others. An **importer** buys products in foreign markets and then imports them for resale in its home country. Exporters and importers tend to conduct most of their business in their home nations. Both enterprises entail the lowest level of involvement in international operations and are excellent ways to learn the fine points of global business. Many large firms began international operations as exporters. IBM and Coca-Cola, among others, exported to Europe for several years before building manufacturing facilities there.

The Exporting Boom   Here are some facts about recent exporting activities in the United States:

- From 1986 to 1992, exports of private services such as investment banking and real estate grew 14 percent annually; since 1990, service exports to Eastern Europe have increased by 25 percent.

- Between 1991 and 1993, exports of consumer goods to Latin America rose by 46 percent.

- In 1993, sales of capital goods—factories and industrial equipment—to Asia increased by 19 percent.

- Between 1986 and 1993, the number of jobs supported by exporting rose from 6.7 million to 10.5 million.

- In June 1994, the total of exported U.S. goods and services hit a record high of $58.2 billion.

Since 1986, exports have been growing four times as fast as the gross domestic product. At that rate, exports in two decades would equal 37 percent of GDP. Says one Wall Street economist, "We are now—far more than we ever have been—an export economy."[15]

The top 50 U.S. exporters—giant firms such as General Motors, Boeing, Motorola, and Philip Morris—had export sales of more than $1.8 billion in 1997. However, experts point out that such companies are joined in the export boom by U.S. businesses of almost every size and shape. For example, small companies—so-called mini-nationals—are increasingly visible among global market entrants. They are armed with the latest advances in long-distance communication technology and, more importantly, have access to numerous new markets.

International Firms

international firm
Firm that conducts a significant portion of its business in foreign countries

As firms gain experience and success as exporters and importers, they may grow to the next level of involvement. An **international firm** conducts a significant portion of its business in foreign countries. Increasingly, international firms also maintain manufacturing facilities overseas. Kmart, for instance, is an international firm. Most of the retailer's stores are in the United States, but it has also opened stores in Canada, the Czech Republic, Slovakia, and Mexico. It has also bought an ownership interest in an Australian retailer and a department store chain in Prague. In addition, Kmart also imports a substantial portion of its merchandise from other countries.

Although an international firm may be large and influential in the global economy, it remains basically a domestic firm with international operations; its central concern is the domestic market in its home country. For instance, Kmart still earns over 90 percent of its revenues from U.S. sales. Product and manufacturing decisions typically reflect this concern. Burlington Industries, Toys Я Us, and BMW are also international firms.

Multinational Firms

Multinational firms do not ordinarily think of themselves as having specific domestic and international divisions. Rather, planning and decision making are geared to international markets. Headquarters locations are almost irrelevant. Royal Dutch Shell, Nestlé, IBM, and Ford are well-known multinational firms. International Paper Co. used acquisitions such as the Dutch paper distribution company Scaldia Papier BV to establish itself as a multinational firm. International Paper is now the worldwide leader in the paper industry and realizes a substantial percentage of its annual earnings from exporting the goods of its European operations.

multinational firm
Firm that designs, produces, and markets products in many nations

The British firm Imperial Chemical Industries is also a truly multinational firm. It is one of the 50 largest industrial firms in the world, with nine major business units, four of which are headquartered outside of Britain. Until 1982, all 16 of its directors were British; today, the board includes one Canadian, one Japanese, one German, and two U.S. executives. ICI has major operations in 25 different countries, and rather than managing businesses that are located and active within given countries, ICI managers are now in charge of business units that compete around the world.[16]

International Organizational Structures

Different levels of involvement in international business require different kinds of organizational structure. For example, a structure that would help coordinate an exporter's activities would be inadequate for the activities of a multinational firm. In this section, we will consider the spectrum of international organizational strategies, including independent agents, licensing arrangements, branch offices, strategic alliances, direct investment, and global business.

Independent Agents

An **independent agent** is a foreign individual or organization who agrees to represent an exporter's interests in foreign markets. Independent agents often act as sales representatives: They sell the exporter's products, collect payment, and make sure that customers are satisfied. They often represent several firms at once and usually do not specialize in any one product or market. Levi Strauss uses agents to market clothing products in many smaller countries in Africa, Asia, and South America.

independent agent
Foreign individual or organization who agrees to represent an exporter's interests

The use of independent agents has several advantages:

■ It is easy for companies starting international operations to locate agents, develop sales agreements, and begin exporting.

■ Agents supply exporters with readily available knowledge about foreign sales environments.

■ The risks are small: If a company finds that it is not being fairly represented, it can usually sever its relationship at minimal cost.

■ Because agents are compensated on the basis of sales, little capital and financial resources are placed at risk.

licensing arrangement
Arrangement in which firms choose foreign individuals or organizations to manufacture or market their products in another country

royalty
Payment made to a license granter from a licensee in return for the rights to market the licenser's product

Licensing Arrangements

Companies seeking more substantial involvement in international business may opt for **licensing arrangements**: Firms give individuals or companies in a foreign country exclusive rights to manufacture or market their products in that market. In return, the exporter typically receives a fee plus ongoing payments called royalties. **Royalties** are usually calculated as a percentage of the license holder's sales.

A major disadvantage of using license holders is the length of time stipulated in most agreements. For example, to attract high-quality license holders, exporters must typically grant exclusive rights for some period of time. This arrangement is fine if the license holder is effective. However, even if the license holder fails to represent the firm well, the arrangement can be hard to dissolve.

Licensing arrangements have two major advantages:

- License holders are often larger, better-known companies than independent agents. Unlike agents, they usually depend on a specific licensed product for most of their revenues. As a result, they are often better representatives of an exporter's products.

- Licensing arrangements, like those with independent agents, are inexpensive and easy to develop. License holders save exporters the expense of researching foreign markets and cultures. Exporters can rely on the license holders' experience and expertise in these matters.

branch office
Foreign office set up by an international or multinational firm

Branch Offices

Instead of developing relationships with foreign companies or independent agents, a firm may simply send some of its own managers to overseas **branch offices**. Naturally, a company has more direct control over branch managers than over agents or license holders. Branch offices also give a company a much more visible public presence in foreign countries. Potential customers tend to feel more secure when a business has branch offices in their country.

Branch offices require firms to develop a deep understanding of the markets and cultures to which they are selling. Thus, a company that opens a foreign branch office may take longer to establish its business than would an exporter that relies on independent agents or license holders who already know the marketplace. Some companies therefore opt for both branch offices and licensing arrangements; whereas the license holder provides access to the local business community, the branch office maintains the firm's control over its license holders.

strategic alliance (or **joint venture**)
Arrangement in which a company finds a foreign partner to contribute approximately equal amounts of resources and capital to a new business in the partner's country

Strategic Alliances

In a strategic alliance, a company finds a partner in the country in which it would like to conduct business. Each party agrees to invest roughly equal amounts of resources and capital into a new business. This new business—the alliance—is then owned by the partners, who divide its profits. Such alliances are sometimes called **joint ventures**. As we saw in chapter 2, however, the term *strategic alliance* has arisen because of the increasingly important role such partnerships now play in the larger organizational strategies of many major companies.

The number of strategic alliances among major companies has increased significantly over the last decade and is likely to grow even more in the years ahead.[17] In fact, laws in many countries—Mexico, India, and China among them—make alliances virtually the only way to do international business within their borders. For instance, Mexico requires that all foreign firms investing there have local partners.

In addition to easing the way into new markets, alliances give firms greater control over their foreign activities than do independent agents and licensing arrangements. (At the same time, of course, all partners in an alliance retain some say in its decisions.) Perhaps most important, however, alliances allow firms to benefit from the knowledge and expertise of their foreign partners. The importance of such knowledge in Japan, for instance, has prompted all but a handful of U.S. companies to do business there through al-

An International Partnership Brings Space Shuttle's Fuel to Earth

A dynamic partnership between German automaker Daimler-Benz, Ford Motor Company of the United States, and Canadian fuel-cell maker Ballard Power Systems wants to bring you a new way to power your car: a low-polluting fuel cell like the one that runs the space shuttle. In 1997, just before Ford joined the partnership, Daimler announced that by the year 2004 it hopes to sell 100,000 new cars that use hydrogen to make electric power without combustion.

Daimler and Ford may be in the lead, but it is not the only auto manufacturers trying to perfect the new fuel. The U.S. Department of Energy says the future for fuel cells now is brighter than ever, and several major firms are in the race to market, including Toyota (which already markets a hybrid car powered by electricity and gasoline), General Motors, Honda, Nissan, and Volkswagen. Among the challenges to be overcome is the building of a network of new filling stations, no small feat at an estimated cost of $200 billion. Moving downward in the future are the cost of fuel cells and their size; they are currently several times too large for the engine compartment of a Mercedes A-class, and in a recent road test in Frankfurt, Germany, the hydrogen-converting part of the cell took up the entire back seat of the car. Ferdinand Panik, Daimler-Benz senior vice president, said of the ride, "Frankly, it was terrible."

> **"[Ballard] may have the Holy Grail. The innovation we have seen from them over the last five years has just blown us away."**
>
> —Roland Hwang of the Union of Concerned Scientists in Berkeley, CA.

But fuel-cell cars are expected to outperform today's battery-powered electric cars, coming to full power almost instantly, accelerating fast, and offering almost unlimited range. In the effort to build an environmentally friendlier car, Ballard's innovation has put it out in front, and even scientists have taken note. "They may have the Holy Grail," says Roland Hwang of the Union of Concerned Scientists in Berkeley, CA. "The innovation we have seen from them over the last five years has just blown us away."

By the way, if you think a Mercedes is too pricey for you, Toyota already has a prototype on the road.

liances. For example, Petrofsky's International, a St. Louis maker of frozen bagel dough, encountered trouble with health officials when it first tried to market its product in Japan: Food inspectors objected to the fact that yeast—an absolutely essential ingredient—was an "active bacteria." Petrofsky thus entered an alliance with Itochu, a giant Japanese importer who managed to get the product certified.[18]

Direct Investment

Direct investment means buying or establishing tangible assets in another country. For example, Toyota has already made significant investments in the United States by building a major manufacturing plant in Georgetown, Kentucky, which opened in 1988. Two German auto makers, Mercedes-Benz and BMW, have made similar investments, BMW in Spartanburg, South Carolina, and Mercedes in Tuscaloosa, Alabama.[19]

Although branch offices can be considered a form of direct investment, the term *direct investment* usually refers to arrangements that are much more substantial. Instead of just a few localized company representatives, direct investment usually involves opening a manufacturing plant or a research and development unit. In other words, direct investment may involve the commitment of hundreds of managers and millions of dollars in capital.

direct investment Arrangement in which a firm buys or establishes tangible assets in another country

▶ *THE UNITED STATES AS A DIRECT INVESTOR.* Exxon, for example, has spent $1 billion to expand an oil refinery in Thailand, where it also opens 40 new service stations every year. Texas Instruments recently invested $1.2 billion to build calculator and semiconductor plants in Italy. General Electric has invested $2.5 billion in an Indonesian power plant. In China, drug maker Merck has opened a new factory to manufacture a vaccine for hepatitis B, and AT&T has entered a joint venture to make fiber-optic cable with a Chinese partner. Allied-Lyons, the parent firm of Baskin-Robbins, has opened China's first ice cream parlor.[20]

U.S. companies now employ 5.4 million people abroad, 80 percent of them in manufacturing U.S. products in foreign plants. Indeed, foreign investment by U.S. firms is growing at twice the rate of exports. Why are U.S. companies making their products overseas instead of exporting them? "If you are going to be really important in the world market," answers one analyst at the National Bureau of Economic Research, "you are going to grow by producing in many countries, and not by exporting, which has its limits." The Gillette Co., for example, increased production of its Sensor XL razor blade cartridge in 1992 not by expanding its Boston plant, but by expanding its facility in Berlin, Germany. Quite simply, the demand for the product is much greater in Europe, and Gillette wants to keep its manufacturing operations close to its markets. Gillette now has 62 factories in 28 countries, each of which is run as a regional company in competition with other local producers. This strategy produces higher returns than exporting blades to the European market. Production costs are lower at plants in Poland, Russia, and China than in the United States. In Germany, on the other hand, they are higher. Gillette is in Germany for what one official calls "insurance" to hedge against labor, technical, or supply disruptions at more distant plants.[21]

In a sense, direct investment makes a firm a "corporate citizen" of a foreign country. Because they are members of local business communities, companies that have made direct investments may gain access to resources unavailable to exporters or multinational firms. Such resources include the ability to bid on government projects, tax advantages, and exemption from certain regulations and laws.

Although the benefits of direct investment can be great, so can the risks. For example, a firm that makes direct investments abroad is placing its assets at risk, especially if the economic or political environment of the foreign country is unstable. An interesting case is South Africa, which has taken historic steps to shed a history of violent racial turmoil and global ostracism and to reorganize its political, economic, and social structures. Both white and black South African leaders have made pleas for Western investment in the country, but most firms have been cautious. In 1993 Digital Equipment Corp. announced plans to open a branch office, and British-owned Pillsbury Co. entered into a joint venture with a South African firm, Foodcorp, to modernize processing plants and distribute food products. However, such commitments fall short of direct investment. Many companies worry about the potential problems of an impoverished majority and a labor force that is quite militant after many years of repression. So far, most investors have tried to minimize their risks by investing only in well-established companies.[22]

Global Business

As the case of South Africa shows, multinational firms often use whatever approach seems best suited to a particular situation in their search for worldwide business opportunities. In some cases, they opt for independent agents; in others, they prefer licensing arrangements, strategic alliances, or direct investments.

For example, fewer than 5,000 of Nestlé Food Corp.'s 200,000 employees are stationed in its home country of Switzerland. The giant food products company has manufacturing facilities in 50 countries and owns suppliers and distributors around the globe. Nestlé markets products worldwide by taking advantage of all possible levels of international involvement. In 1991, for instance, Nestlé entered a strategic alliance with the U.S. food products company General Mills to create a new company called Cereal Partners Worldwide. General Mills initiated the joint venture with a European partner in an effort to cut into Kellogg's commanding lead in ready-to-eat cereals. For its part, Nestlé sees the venture as an opportunity to affirm its leadership in the $550 billion European food industry.

Barriers to International Trade

Whether a business is truly multinational or sells to just a few foreign markets, a number of factors will affect its international operations. Its success in foreign markets will be determined largely by the ways in which it responds to social, economic, and political barriers to international trade.

Social and Cultural Differences

▶ In 1991, American baby-food maker Gerber spent $25 million to buy a juice-making plant in southern Poland. The price was right, and the strategy seemed sound: There were no competitors to counter Gerber quality, and U.S. consumption of baby food had dropped almost 30 percent in two decades. Ultimately, however, it took over 2 years before the Polish venture began to pay off. Sanitary conditions had to be improved, for example, and Polish workers had to be taught not to smoke around production lines. Even more important was overcoming the resistance of Polish mothers. "It's taken us a little longer to learn these things than we would have liked," admits CEO Alfred Piergallini.[23]

As Gerber's experience shows, any firm planning to conduct business in another country must understand the differences between its host's society and culture and those of its own home country. Some differences are fairly obvious. For example, companies must take language factors into account when making adjustments in packaging, signs, and logos. Pepsi-Cola, of course, is exactly the same product whether it is sold in Seattle or Moscow, except for the lettering on the bottle. Less "universal" products, however, face a variety of conditions that require them to adjust their practices. In Thailand, for example, Kentucky Fried Chicken stores thrive on menus, ingredients, and hours of operation that are adjusted to suit Thai culture.

Sometimes, even the physical stature of different people must be considered. For example, average Japanese and French consumers are slimmer and shorter than their U.S. counterparts—an important consideration if you intend to sell clothes in these markets. Differences in the average ages in the local population can also have ramifications. Countries with growing populations (such as South Korea) tend to have a high percentage of young people. Thus, electronics and fashionable clothing sell well. Countries with stable or declining populations (such as Sweden) tend to have more older people. Generic pharmaceuticals are successful in such markets.

In addition to these obvious differences, a wide range of subtle value differences can affect international operations. For example, many Europeans shop daily. To U.S. consumers accustomed to weekly supermarket trips, the European pattern may seem like a waste of time. For Europeans, however, shopping is not just buying food; it is also an outlet for meeting friends and exchanging political views.

Consider the implications of this cultural difference for U.S. firms selling food products in European markets. First, large supermarkets such as those that dot the U.S. landscape have no place in Europe. Second, people who shop daily do not need large refrigerators and freezers. Finally, Europeans buy different kinds of foods. In the United States, for example, prepared and frozen foods are important. Europeans, on the other hand, prefer to buy fresh ingredients and prepare meals from scratch. However, because some of these differences are gradually disappearing, both foreign and European-based firms must be on the lookout for new opportunities.

Economic Differences

Although cultural differences are often subtle, economic differences can be fairly pronounced. In dealing with mixed economies such as those of France and Sweden, for example, firms must be aware of when and to what extent the government is involved in a given industry. The French government, for instance, is heavily involved in all aspects of airplane design and manufacturing.

▶ ***SCALING THE GREAT WALL OF CHINESE BUSINESS.*** Similarly, a foreign firm doing business in a planned economy must understand the unfamiliar relationship of government to business, including a host of idiosyncratic practices. Take the case of General Motors, which entered a $100-million joint venture to build pickup trucks in China. First, GM found itself faced with an economic system that favored state-owned companies over foreign investors. For example, its Chinese suppliers passed on inflation-based price increases for steel and energy, but GM could not pass increases on to Chinese consumers. With subsidized state-owned automakers charging considerably less per truck, GM has had no choice but to hold its own prices—and lose money on each sale. A large portion of the sticker price on each GM vehicle goes to government fees and taxes.

General Motors also discovered that the Chinese system not only subsidizes unprofitable state-owned factories but also has no commercial code or independent courts to settle disputes. China's home-field ground rules also prevent profitable companies such as Gillette and Coca-Cola from sending money back to the United States and from importing their own equipment.

Despite such problems, however, some companies have had successful experiences in China. For example, when Motorola opened a factory to manufacture paging devices, it planned to export most of the pagers because it forecast limited internal demand. In a pleasant surprise, Motorola was forced to reassess the Chinese market after repeatedly selling out its weekly output of 10,000 units. This experience helped convince Motorola to build a $120-million plant in the northern port city of Tianjin, where it will manufacture pagers, simple integrated circuits, and cellular phones. As part of the largest manufacturing venture in China, it will also involve Chinese technicians in the production process. Chinese designers and engineers will play key roles in creating an operation that integrates manufacturing, sales, research, and development.[24]

Legal and Political Differences

Governments can affect international business activities in many ways. For example, they can set conditions for doing business within their borders or even prohibit doing business altogether. They can control the flow of capital and use tax legislation to discourage or encourage international activity in a given industry. In the extreme, they can even confiscate the property of foreign-owned companies. In this section, we will discuss some of the more common legal and political issues in international business: quotas, tariffs, and subsidies, local content laws, and business practice laws.

Quotas, Tariffs, and Subsidies

Even free-market economies often establish some system of quotas or tariffs that affects the prices and quantities of foreign-made products. A **quota** restricts the total number of products of a certain type that can be imported into a country; by reducing the supply, the quota thus raises the prices of those imports. For example, Belgian ice cream makers can ship no more than 922,315 kilograms of ice cream into the United States each year. Such figures are often determined by treaties. Moreover, better terms are often given to friendly trading partners and typically adjusted to protect domestic producers.

The ultimate form of quota is an **embargo**: a government order forbidding exportation or importation of a particular product, or even all the products, from a particular country. For example, many countries control bacteria and disease by banning certain agricultural products. The United States has a blanket embargo against Cuba and Iraq. On the other hand, the Clinton administration announced in November 1993 that it would lift a long-standing embargo against China and permit Cray Research Inc. to sell the Chinese government an $8 million supercomputer. Seeking to secure a share of China's huge market for industrial goods, the government also lifted a ban on components for nuclear power plants. The latter agreement could be worth billions of dollars to General Electric, which has already made inroads into the Chinese market for such components.[25]

A **tariff** is a tax on imported products. Tariffs directly affect prices by raising the price of imports. Consumers pay not only for the products but also for tariff fees. Tariffs may take two forms. Revenue tariffs are imposed strictly to raise money for governments. However, most tariffs are protectionist tariffs meant to discourage the import of particular

quota
Restriction on the number of products of a certain type that can be imported into a country

embargo
Government order banning exportation or importation of a particular product or all the products from a particular country

tariff
Tax levied on imported products

In their efforts to punish certain regimes of the Middle East—Iran, Iraq, and Libya—U.S. policy makers are encountering some cold, hard economic facts. Iraq's oil reserves, for example, are second only to those of Saudi Arabia; oil fields like this one in Iran make it the world's third largest exporter. In addition, oil companies headquartered in other countries—notably Russia and France—are putting pressure on U.S. competitors by striking deals with Middle East producers. In 1995, for example, Conoco Inc. struck a $1-billion deal with Iran that it claims is legal despite the U.S. government embargo.

products. For example, firms that import ironing board covers into the United States pay a tariff of 7 percent of the price of the product. Firms that import women's athletic shoes pay a flat rate of 90 cents per pair plus 20 percent of the price of the shoes. Again, each of these figures is set through a complicated process designed to put foreign and domestic firms on reasonably even competitive ground.

A **subsidy** is a government payment to help a domestic business compete with foreign firms. Subsidies are really indirect tariffs: They lower prices of domestic goods rather than raise prices of foreign goods. For instance, many European governments subsidize farmers to help them compete with U.S. grain imports.

Quotas and tariffs are imposed for a variety of reasons. For example, the U.S. government aids domestic automakers by restricting the number of Japanese automobiles that can be imported into this country. Conversely, national security concerns have prompted the United States to limit the extent to which certain forms of technology can be exported to other countries (for example, computer and nuclear technology to China). The recent relaxation of controls on the licensing of technology has contributed to the export boom we described earlier in this chapter. Of course, the United States is not the only country that uses tariffs and quotas. Italy, for example, imposes high tariffs on imported electronic goods to protect domestic firms. A Sony Walkman thus costs almost $150 in Italy, and CD players are prohibitively expensive.

The protectionism debate. In the United States as elsewhere, **protectionism**—the practice of protecting domestic business at the expense of free-market competition—has long been controversial. Supporters argue that tariffs and quotas protect domestic firms and jobs and shelter new industries until they are able to compete internationally. They also argue that the United States needs such measures to counter those of other nations. Other advocates justify protectionism in the name of national security: A nation must be able to produce the goods needed for its survival in the event of war, and advanced technology should not be sold to potential enemies. Thus, the U.S. government requires the U.S. Air Force to buy all its planes from U.S. manufacturers.

Critics cite protectionism as a source of friction between nations. They also charge that it drives up prices by reducing competition. In addition, they maintain that although jobs in some industries would indeed be lost, jobs in others—for example, electronics and automobiles—would expand if all nations abandoned protectionist tactics.

subsidy
Government payment to help a domestic business compete with foreign firms

protectionism
Practice of protecting domestic business at the expense of free-market competition

local content law
Law requiring that products sold in a particular country be at least partly made there

Local Content Laws

Many countries, including the United States, have **local content laws:** requirements that products sold in a particular country be at least partly made there. Typically, firms seeking to do business in a country must either invest there directly or take on a domestic partner. In this way, some of the profits from doing business in a foreign country stay there rather than flowing out to another nation. In some cases, the partnership arrangement is optional but wise. In Mexico, for instance, Radio Shack de Mexico is a joint venture owned by Tandy Corp. (49 percent) and Mexico's Grupo Gigante (51 percent).

Business Practice Laws

Even with this arrangement, however, Tandy reports problems, especially in importing merchandise across the Mexican border. Consider, too, the recent experience of Wal-Mart officials in Mexico City:

▶ One day in June 1994, a troop of government inspectors swooped down on Wal-Mart's brand-new Supercenter in the Mexican capital. Citing Mexican regulations, they reminded Wal-Mart managers that each of the store's 80,000 products must be labeled in Spanish. Labels must also indicate country of origin and provide instructions for use. Where necessary, they must display import permit numbers. Charging 11,700 violations, inspectors ordered the store closed for 72 hours while Wal-Mart rectified oversights. The store appealed to the U.S. ambassador, who managed to have the order lifted after only 24 hours.

business practice laws
Laws or regulations that legalize in one country practices that are illegal in another

cartel
Association of producers whose purpose is to control supply and prices

dumping
Practice of selling a product abroad for less than the comparable price charged at home

Wal-Mart and other American companies that have recently entered Mexico have reported a wealth of problems in complying with stringent and often changing regulations and other bureaucratic obstacles.[26] Such practices fall under the heading of the host country's **business practice laws**. Sometimes, a legal—even an accepted—business practice in one country is illegal in another. For example, in some South American countries it is occasionally legal to bribe both other businesses and government officials. The formation of **cartels**—associations of producers to control supply and prices—has given tremendous power to some nations, such as those belonging to the Oil Producing and Exporting Countries (OPEC). U.S. law forbids both bribery and cartels.

Dumping. Many (but not all) countries forbid **dumping**: selling a product abroad for less than the comparable price charged at home. U.S. antidumping legislation is contained in the Trade Agreements Act of 1979. This statute sets tests for determining two conditions:

■ Products are being priced at less than fair value.

■ The result unfairly harms domestic industry.

In a 1987 case with a twist, Carus Chemical Co. of the United States charged that two importers were dumping a compound used in disinfectants on the U.S. market at 40 percent less than the price of the domestic product. The importers responded that because the compound was produced in a nonmarket nation—China—it was impossible to tell whether it was being marketed at below fair domestic (that is, Chinese) value. A U.S. Court of Appeals referred to established value on the U.S. and European markets and ruled in favor of Carus.[27]

Summary of Learning Objectives

1 **Identify the major world marketplaces and explain how different forms of competitive advantage, import-export balances, exchange rates, and foreign competition determine how countries and businesses respond to the international environment.** The three major marketplaces for international business are North America,

Western Europe, and the Pacific Rim. Goods and services are imported and exported from these areas to meet the needs of consumers worldwide.

Among the elements critical to international business are the different forms of competitive advantage. With an absolute advantage, a country engages in international trade because it can produce a product more efficiently than any other nation. But more often, countries trade because they enjoy comparative advantages: They can produce some items more efficiently than they can produce other items. The import-export balance, including the balance of trade and the balance of payments, and exchange rate differences in national currencies affect the international economic environment and are important elements of international business.

2 **Discuss the factors involved in deciding to do business internationally and in selecting the appropriate levels of international involvement and international organizational structure.** In deciding whether to do business internationally, a firm must determine whether a market for its product exists abroad, and if so, whether the firm has the skills and knowledge to manage such a business. It must also assess the business climates of other nations to make sure that they are conducive to international operations.

A firm must also decide on its level of international involvement: It can choose to be an exporter or importer, to organize as an international firm, or to operate as a multinational firm. This choice will influence the organizational structure of its international operations, specifically, its use of independent agents, licensing arrangements, branch offices, strategic alliances, direct investment, and global business.

3 **Describe some of the ways in which social, cultural, economic, legal, and political differences among nations affect international business.** Social and cultural differences that can serve as barriers to trade include language, social values, and traditional buying patterns. Differences in economic systems may force businesses to establish close relationships with foreign governments before they are permitted to do business abroad. Quotas, tariffs, subsidies, and local content laws offer protection to local industries. Differences in business practice laws can make the normal business practices of one nation illegal in another.

Study Questions and Exercises

Questions for Review

1 How does a nation's balance of trade differ from its balance of payments?
2 What are the three possible levels of involvement in international business? Give examples of each.
3 How does the economic system of a country affect the decisions of outside firms interested in doing business there?
4 What aspects of the culture in your state or region would be of particular interest to a foreign firm considering doing business there?

Questions for Analysis

5 Make a list of all the major items in your bedroom, including furnishings. Now try to identify the country in which each item was made. Offer possible reasons why a given nation might have a comparative advantage in producing a given good.
6 Suppose that you are the manager of a small firm seeking to enter the international arena. What basic information would you need about a particular market you are thinking of entering?
7 Do you support protectionist tariffs for the United States? If so, in what instances and for what reasons? If not, why not?
8 How well does the European Union seem to be working as a vehicle for promoting trade among its member nations?

Application Exercises

9   Interview the manager of a local firm that does at least some business internationally. Identify reasons why the company decided to go international. Describe the level of the firm's international involvement and the organizational structures it uses for its international operations.

10   Select a product familiar to you. Using library reference works to gain some insight into the culture of India, identify the problems that might arise in trying to market this product to Indian consumers.

Building Your Business Skills

This exercise enhances the following SCANS workplace competencies: demonstrating basic skills, demonstrating thinking skills, exhibiting interpersonal skills, and working with information.

Goal   To encourage students to understand that in a global workplace, local cultural differences can affect career success.

Situation   Imagine that you have just been offered a promotion to your company's Mexico City office. The job involves supervising a staff of 100 and conducting business with a host of government officials and suppliers. You are hesitant to take the offer for two reasons:

- You are concerned that your nonstop, direct work style, which worked so well for you in the United States, will not be effective in Mexico.
- You are concerned that as a woman, you may not be treated as fairly as your male counterparts.

Your boss needs an answer by the end of the month, but you are in a quandary over what to do. You realize that in order to make the best decision for yourself and your company you have to learn more about the Mexican business culture. Although you have spent some time in Mexico and speak fluent Spanish, you still feel very much like an outsider.

Method   **Step 1:**   Working together with four or five students, place yourself in the position of this up-and-coming manager. Then go to the library and research the following topics:

- The nature of the Mexican culture.
- The specific expectations for business behavior: In general, what is the accepted pace of work? What is the relationship between personal trust and business success? Is the culture formal or informal? How important is business etiquette?
- The treatment of women in the workplace.

Step 2:   Based on your findings, what can the company do to help this executive succeed if she takes the assignment? Analyze the value of the following sources of help:

- Reading books and other written materials on doing business in Mexico
- Attending a cross-cultural workshop
- Spending time in Mexico City studying the culture first-hand

Follow-Up Questions

1   Based on your research, would you recommend that the woman take the job?
2   What are the most serious cultural problems she is likely to face?
3   List three cultural differences between the U.S. and Mexican cultures that are likely to create workplace challenges.
4   Why would a direct, down-to-business work style be unlikely to succeed in Mexico?

Business Case 3

Toyota Expands Its Reach

Despite its occasionally ho-hum products, Toyota's high quality and efficiency have seen the company through the ups and downs of the global auto industry in the 1980s and 1990s. Now, however, the Japanese firm's president, Hiroshi Okuda, is determined to take the lead once and for all.

Okuda will oversee the most aggressive overseas expansion ever in the auto industry, a $13.5-billion expansion program to run through the year 2000. By investing in production capacity in North America, Japan, China, Thailand, England, France, and the Philippines, Okuda wants to gain the ability to customize cars for local customers' tastes. In North America alone, Toyota plans to increase capacity in its Georgetown, Kentucky plant by almost a third to 500,000 vehicles and to open a new plant in Evansville, Indiana for the production of 100,000 pickup trucks with improved design features. Production of Corollas in Ontario will double to 200,000 units. Similar expansion is set to occur abroad.

Okuda has positioned the firm to play both sides of the foreign exchange seesaw. When the yen is weak Toyota exports more cars, and when it is strong the automaker will stock up on parts that it pays for in dollars. Toyota's president has cut the firm's already legendary low costs even further and plans to continue cutting at the ambitious rate of $800 million a year. He has driven the design process into high gear to get new models out in record time (15 months from concept to production) and engineered Toyota's entry into the minivan market with the new Sienna, to be produced in Kentucky. Since his appointment in 1995, sales have risen worldwide (by almost 33 percent in the United States, where the Camry is close to becoming the best-selling car) and the company's stock price has climbed 80 percent.

Problems Okuda still faces include Toyota's less than stellar reputation for customer service (only 42 percent of customers buy another Toyota, compared to 62 percent for GM), and stiff competition at home from Honda. Okuda also wants to make his company more multinational in its outlook by hiring more foreign designers, eliminating management layers, speeding up the decision-making process, tying pay to performance rather than seniority, and even selling cars over the Internet. Between his industry rivals and the entrenched traditional culture he faces in the boardroom, Okuda is likely to have his hands full.

Questions

1 In what ways does Toyota depend on the U.S. market for success?

2 How is Okuda wooing the U.S. customer?

3 What else do you think Toyota can do to succeed with its expansion plan?

| 77

Connecting to the Web

The following Web sites will give you additional information and points of view about topics covered in this chapter. Many sites lead to other related Internet locations, so approach this list with the spirit of an explorer.

FORD WORLDWIDE CONNECTION

http://www.ford.com/global/

Click on the Ford Motor Company's presence in 78 locations throughout the world to learn how important global commerce is to Ford.

FREE BUSINESS IN EUROPE GUIDES TO DOWNLOAD

http://www.business-in-europe.com/gb/telechrge/centre.html

Click on this site for free downloadable guides that include excerpts from "Doing Business in France," a publication of the Ernst & Young consulting firm. Included in the guides is information on the structure of business entities, foreign investment, the labor force, and taxation.

GLOBAL CONTACT INCORPORATED

http://www.globalcontact.com/

The Global Contact Web site helps companies locate products and services worldwide. Included in the site is an online database that includes a NAFTA register.

GLOBAL WINDOW: THE GUIDE TO BUSINESS SUCCESS: JAPAN

http:www.anderson.ucla.edu/research/japan/

Developed and maintained by the Anderson School at the University of California, Los Angeles, this site is a useful introduction to doing business in Japan. Click on the site and you'll learn about the Japanese people and culture and Japanese business practices. Included are tips for the business traveler.

McDONALD'S

http://www.mcdonalds.com

This site will introduce you to McDonald's worldwide presence. Click on McDonald's Japan if you speak Japanese and have a computer that can process the Japanese alphabet.

MERCEDES BENZ

http://www.mercedes-benz.com

Search the Mercedes-Benz home page for information about the M-class plant in Tuscaloosa, Alabama.

NATIONAL BUREAU OF ECONOMIC RESEARCH: INTERNATIONAL STUDIES PROGRAM

http://www.nber.org/programs/international.html

The mission of the NBER is to produce and disseminate unbiased economic research. The bureau's international studies program analyzes issues involving international trade and exchange rates. Visit this site for a close look at various research reports.

STAT-USA/INTERNET: EXPORT AND INTERNATIONAL TRADE

http://www.stat-usa.gov/BEN/subject/trade.html

This specialized section of the U.S. Department of Commerce's Stat-USA Web site is designed to help U.S. and foreign exporters. Included are a national trade data bank, trade leads, market research reports, company indexes, general country information, and export/import statistics.

UNITED STATES COUNCIL FOR INTERNATIONAL BUSINESS

http://www.imex.com/uscib/index.html

The goal of the United States Council for International Business, an organization sponsored by more than 300 multinational companies, is to promote an open system of world trade, investment, and finance. Click on this site for information on how the USCIB serves the American business community.

WORLD TRADE ORGANIZATION

http://www.wto.org/

The Word Trade Organization, an international organization with 132 member countries, specializes in promoting trade. Its purpose is to help trade flow smoothly, to settle trade disputes between nations, and to organize trade negotiations. Click on this site for information on the WTO's relationship to GATT.

chapter 4

Conducting business **ethically** and responsibly

Denny's tries an about-face

As recently as 1994, Denny's Inc., a nationwide restaurant chain, was reeling from a series of discrimination suits and complaints and waking up to the realization that cultural changes it had long ignored were exposing it as an ugly relic of racism. Besides having a loose management policy that tolerated blatant discrimination in its 512 franchises, the firm was revealed to have no nonwhite directors or officers and only one black franchise holder. Black customers were routinely given poor service or no service, and some stores even maintained a policy of closing when there were "too many" blacks in the restaurant.

An independent civil rights monitor was appointed as part of the settlement of the suits. Although the parent company, Flagstar Companies, Inc., denied that any of the abuses were sanctioned by its management, it took quick steps to remedy the situation. A massive overhaul of the company's culture was begun with the blunt warning, "If you discriminate, you're

history." Eight of its 12 top executives, all white males, left the firm, and among their replacements were a Hispanic man, a black woman, and two white women.

A new top management position was created to direct diversity in hiring and purchasing. Store managers' bonuses were tied to meeting diversity hiring and promotion goals, and mandatory diversity training programs were set up for the entire staff. Management training programs have begun for minorities to encourage them to become Denny's franchisees, and all job applicants are screened for racial bias. Blacks now own 27 Denny's franchises.

To give him more direct control over the way individual restaurants are run, Flagstar's CEO Jim Adamson reduced the corporate hierarchy, filled 17 percent of management jobs with blacks, and brought minority purchasing contracts to $80 million, substantially ahead of the goal set in a 1993 agreement with the National Association for the Advancement of Colored People (NAACP). The NAACP awarded him its 1996 Corporate CEO Achievement Award.

An apparent step backward occurred in April 1997 when several Asian students were assaulted in a

Denny's employees with franchise owner Charles Davis.

Denny's parking lot in Syracuse, New York after being denied service inside. It appeared that the staff had not received the required diversity training.

> ## *If you discriminate, you're history.*
>
> —Denny's company policy

Although some critics feel the company can go farther still (and it is struggling to show a profit), new franchise owner Jerome Edmondson says, "I was skeptical about Denny's at first. But after a few months I knew this company was really committed to helping minorities."

Ethics in the workplace are becoming increasingly important as we move into an era of intense competition not only for public and consumer support but also for the support of employees and stockholders. By focusing on the learning objectives of this chapter, you will see why many companies have policies on business ethics and social responsibility. These are developed to help indicate how both managers and employees should act with regard to the environment, customers, fellow employees, and investors. After reading this chapter, you should be able to

1 Explain how people develop their personal codes of ethics and why ethics are important in the workplace.

2 Distinguish social responsibility from ethics and trace the evolution of social responsibility in U.S. business.

3 Show how the concept of social responsibility applies both to environmental issues and to a firm's relationships with customers, employees, and investors.

4 Identify three general approaches to social responsibility and describe the four steps that a firm must take to implement a social responsibility program.

5 Explain how issues of social responsibility and ethics affect small businesses.

In this chapter we will look at the issues of individual ethics in business and the social responsibility of business as a whole. Remember that these issues were not always considered important in business philosophy or practice. Today, however, the ethical implications of business practices are very much in the spotlight. Managers must confront a variety of ethical problems, and companies must address many issues of social responsibility.

Ethics in the Workplace

ethics
Beliefs about what is right and wrong or good and bad in actions that affect others

ethical behavior
Behavior conforming to generally accepted social norms concerning beneficial and harmful actions

unethical behavior
Behavior that violates generally accepted social norms concerning beneficial and harmful actions

business ethics
Beliefs about acceptable and unacceptable business practices

Just what is ethical behavior? **Ethics** are beliefs about what is right and wrong or good and bad. An individual's personal values and morals and the social context in which it occurs determine whether a particular behavior is seen as being ethical or unethical. That is, **ethical behavior** is behavior that conforms to individual beliefs and social norms about what is right and good, whereas **unethical behavior** is behavior that individual beliefs and social norms define as being wrong and bad. *Business ethics* is a term often used to refer to ethical or unethical behaviors by a manager or employee of an organization.

For example, a fire recently devastated Malden Mills, the company that makes Polartec fleece, a popular insulating fabric used in cold weather clothes by such brands as L.L. Bean, Patagonia, and Eddie Bauer. The "rational" decision for Aaron Feuerstein, the firm's owner, would have been to use his insurance proceeds and build a new factory overseas, where he could obtain labor at a much lower cost than in suburban Boston, site of the burned plant. But Feuerstein felt that such a step would be unethical. As a result, he not only rebuilt his factory on its old site, but he also kept his entire workforce on the payroll while the company's operations were shut down! This behavior clearly reflects a high degree of business ethics.[1]

Because ethics are based on both individual beliefs and social concepts, they vary from person to person, from situation to situation, and from culture to culture. Social standards, for example, tend to be broad enough to support certain differences in beliefs. Without violating the general standards of the culture, therefore, individuals may develop personal codes of ethics that reflect a fairly wide range of attitudes and beliefs. Thus, what constitutes ethical and unethical behavior is determined partly by the individual and partly by culture.

Company Policies and Business Ethics

Within the workplace, the company itself becomes an additional factor in influencing individual ethical behavior. As unethical and even illegal activities by both managers and employees have plagued more and more companies, many have taken steps to encourage ethical behavior in the workplace.[2] For example, many firms establish codes of conduct and develop clear ethical positions on how the firm and its employees will conduct its business.

Perhaps the single most effective step that a company can take is to demonstrate top management support. For example, like many companies Texas Instruments has an ethics booklet that it routinely distributes to all its employees. But the firm also has an ethics department staffed by managers whose responsibility it is to ensure that the firm's managers adhere to its ethics policies and to act as a sounding board for anyone in the firm faced with an ethical dilemma. Conversely, the effects of management leadership in the opposite direction were evident when a scandal at a plutonium processing plant raised serious questions about Rockwell International's ability to maintain appropriate safety controls over supplies of plutonium, a vital ingredient in nuclear technology. Top managers at Rockwell, an industrial manufacturer based in California, not only denied wrongdoing but refused to investigate the charges. Not surprisingly, that response helped to focus criticism even more sharply on procedural shortcomings at the plant, which eventually lost several lucrative government contracts.

Demonstrating Commitment

An excellent and now classic illustration of the power of ethical commitment involves Johnson & Johnson. In 1982 capsules of the company's Tylenol pain reliever were found to be laced with cyanide. Managers at J&J quickly recalled all Tylenol bottles still on retailers' shelves and then went public with candid information throughout the crisis. Its ethical choices proved to be a crucial factor in J&J's campaign to rescue its product: Both the firm and the brand bounced back much more quickly than most observers had thought possible. A more recent example took place in England. Government reports linking beef products tainted by "mad cow disease" and fatal illnesses prompted fast food giants such as McDonald's and Burger King to quickly suspend sales of all British beef products. In addition to demonstrating an attitude of honesty and openness, firms can take specific steps to formalize the commitment to ethical practices. Three options are adopting written codes, instituting ethics programs, and developing ethics orientations.

Adopting Written Codes. Many companies—including J&J, McDonald's, and Burger King—have adopted written codes of ethics that formally acknowledge their intent to do business in an ethical manner. Indeed, the number of such companies has risen dramatically in the last three decades. In 1968, for example, polls revealed that 32 percent of the companies surveyed maintained ethical codes. A mere 2 years later, the number was 75 percent. Today, over 90 percent of all Fortune 500 firms have such codes.[3] These codes serve one or more of the following functions:

- They increase public confidence in the firm.
- They lessen the potential for government regulation by indicating a commitment to self-control.
- They improve internal operations by providing a consistent blueprint for acceptable conduct.
- They prescribe a response when unethical behavior does occur.

Figure 4.1 shows the code of ethics adopted by Whirlpool Corp.

Instituting Ethics Programs. Cases such as the one involving J&J suggest that ethical responses can be learned through experience. However, a related question remains to be considered: Can business ethics be taught, either in the workplace or in schools? Not surprisingly, business schools have become important players in the debate about ethics education. Most analysts agree that even though business schools must address the issue of ethics in the workplace, companies must take the chief responsibility for educating employees. In fact, more and more firms are doing so.

For example, Bruce Klatsky, CEO of Phillips–Van Heusen Corporation, is a strong believer in business ethics. He personally belongs to several organizations that promote the humane treatment of workers in foreign factories. To instill his beliefs in his own company, he also requires that all new Phillips employees attend an ethics training program. He also encourages senior managers to periodically participate in new ethics seminars the company develops.[4]

Developing an Ethics Orientation. Formulating a code of ethics is not an easy task, but analysts and top-level managers agree that it can and must be done. As Johnson & Johnson chairperson James Burke puts it, "Ethical behavior has always been very good business." For one thing, the costs of ethical behavior are far lower than those of questionable activity.

> **Figure 4.1** The Whirlpool Code of Ethics

ETHICS AS A PRACTICAL MATTER

A message from
David R. Whitwam
Chairman of the
Board

The question of ethics in business conduct has become one of the most serious challenges to the business community in modern times.

At Whirlpool, we share with millions of other Americans a deep concern over recent revelations of unethical and often illegal conduct on the part of some of this nation's most prominent business people and corporations.

The purpose of this message is not to pass judgement on any of these occurrences; each must and will be judged on its own merits by those charged with that responsibility.

Rather this message is intended to place firmly on record the position of Whirlpool Corporation regarding business ethics and the conduct of every Whirlpool employee. It represents an irrevocable commitment to our customers and stockholders that our actions will be governed by the highest personal and professional standards in all activities relating to the operation of this business.

Over the years, circumstances have prompted us to develop a number of specific policies dealing with such critical elements of ethical business practice as **conflicts of interest, gifts, political activities, entertainment, and substantiation of claims.**

We also have a basic statement of ethics which places the ultimate responsibility for ethical behavior precisely where it belongs in any organization . . . on the shoulders of the person in charge:

> "No employee of this company will ever be called upon to do anything in the line of duty that is morally, ethically or legally wrong.
>
> Furthermore, if in the operation of this complex enterprise, an employee should

Experts in business ethics have thus made some basic recommendations for firms seeking to develop ethics-oriented programs. Following are some of the most important:

- Vague statements are useless. In outlining both possible problems and appropriate responses, ethical codes must be as specific as possible.

- Companies should monitor conformance with ethical codes as often and as vigorously as they do with financial regulations. While recognizing a manager's responsibility for economically satisfactory outcomes, an auditor should not tolerate severe deviations from the ethical code.

- Employees must be held accountable for their actions. Compliance with key aspects of the ethical code should be a condition of employment. Employees who violate restrictions should be warned, demoted, or fired.

- Experience shows that when managers are rewarded only for profitability, they tend to ignore ethics. They should be rewarded for conforming to ethical standards.

- Managers may be uncertain about proper ethical behavior in some situations, especially those that arise suddenly. Because the consensus has a higher chance of being ethically correct, managers should be encouraged to discuss such situations with colleagues and employees.[5]

Figure 4.1   The Whirlpool Code of Ethics (continued)

come upon circumstances of which he or she cannot be personally proud, it should be that person's duty to bring it to the attention of top management if unable to correct the matter in any other way."

Every Whirlpool manager carries the dual responsibility implicit in this policy statement, including the chairman of the board.

Our written policies deal with nearly all facets of business experience. We review, revise and recommunicate them to our managers on a regular basis . . . and we see that our managers carry on the communication throughout the company.

But as a practical matter, there is no way to assure ethical behavior with written policies or policy statements.

In the final analysis, "ethical behavior" must be an integral part of the organization, a way of life that is deeply ingrained in the collective corporate body.

I believe this condition exists at Whirlpool, and that it constitutes our greatest single assurance that this company's employees will conduct the affairs of this business in a manner consistent with the highest standards of ethical behavior.

At Whirlpool we have certain ways of doing things. They are commonly accepted practices, enforced not by edict, but rather by a mutual conviction that they will, in the long term, work in the best interest of our customers, our stockholders, the company and all its employees.

In any business enterprise, ethical behavior must be a tradition, a way of conducting one's affairs that is passed on from generation to generation of employees at all levels of the organization. It is the responsibility of management, starting at the very top, to both set the example by personal conduct and create an environment that not only encourages and rewards ethical behavior, but which also makes anything less totally unacceptable.

I believe this has been achieved at Whirlpool. The men who founded this company back in 1911 were individuals possessed of great integrity and honor. They fostered a tradition of ethical conduct in their business practices, and they perpetuated that tradition through careful selection of the people who would one day fall heir to leadership of the company.

The system works. Time and time again I have witnessed its efficacy. It shows no hospitality whatsoever to those not willing to abide by its standards, and unerringly identifies and purges them.

Unfortunately, the system is not auto- matically self-sustaining. It must be constantly reaffirmed by each new generation of leaders. In the position I now occupy, I view this as one of my most important responsibilities.

As this company grows, and as the pressures upon it increase, maintaining our tradition of ethical conduct becomes an increasingly difficult task. But I am confident it will be maintained, because it is necessary for continued growth, profitability and success.

Sincerely,

David R. Whitwam

Social Responsibility

Ethics affect individual behavior in the workplace. **Social responsibility**, however, is the way in which a business behaves toward other groups and individuals in its social environ- ment: customers, other businesses, employees, and investors. In effect, social responsibil- ity is an attempt to balance different commitments. For example, to behave responsibly toward investors, a company must try to maximize profits. But it also has a responsibility toward its customers to market safe products, which may raise production costs and lower profits. Not surprisingly, firms sometimes act irresponsibly toward customers because of their zeal to please investors.

For example, Jacques Robinson, CEO of cordless phone maker Cincinnati Microwave, Inc. recently announced that substantial losses by the firm were attributable to a worldwide parts shortage—a one-time problem, he contended, that was beyond the firm's control. But critics charged that the real problem was poor relationships between the firm and its suppli- ers. They also charged that he was using the parts shortage explanation to cover up more sig- nificant problems at the firm and to hide the fact that optimistic sales figures he had been using for investors were far greater than those developed by his own marketing experts.[6]

Much like an individual's personal code of ethics, an organization's sense of social responsibility is influenced by many factors. To a large extent, of course, social responsi-

social responsibility
The attempt of a business to balance its commitments to groups and individuals in its environment, including customers, other businesses, employees, and investors

Many companies today move production to foreign markets to take advantage of lower labor costs. For example, one reason that BMW and Mercedes have built factories in the United States is because U.S. wages are about half of what German firms must pay at home. But sometimes companies appear to go too far. Nike, for example, has been criticized because many of its workers in Southeast Asia are paid what appear to be especially low wages and often work in poor conditions. Nike, in turn, usually points out that its foreign wages and working conditions are superior to those available to those workers in other jobs.

bility reflects the ethics of the individuals employed by a firm, especially its top management. But social responsibility can also be encouraged—even enforced—from outside, whether by government agencies or by consumers. Finally, a firm's behavior is also shaped by the demands of investors and by the behavior of other firms in the same country and same industry.

The Evolution of Social Responsibility

Both U.S. society and U.S. business have changed dramatically in the last two centuries. Not surprisingly, so have views about social responsibility. Many scholars identify at least three different phases in the evolution of social responsibility.[7]

The Entrepreneurial Era

The first phase corresponds to the era in the late nineteenth century that was characterized by the entrepreneurial spirit and the laissez-faire philosophy. The enormous empires of men such as John D. Rockefeller, J. P. Morgan, and Cornelius Vanderbilt exercised tremendous economic power, but abuses of power inevitably led to public backlash. During this era of labor strife and predatory business practices, both individual citizens and the government first became concerned about unbridled business activity. This concern was translated into the nation's first laws regulating basic business practices.

The Great Depression

The second major phase in the evolution of social responsibility occurred during the Great Depression. In the 1930s, many people blamed the failure of businesses and banks and the widespread loss of jobs on a general climate of business greed and lack of restraint. Out of the economic turmoil emerged new laws that described an expanded role for business in protecting and enhancing the general welfare of society.

How Ethical Are You?

A recent study conducted for the Ethics Officers Association and the American Society of Chartered Life Underwriters uncovered acknowledgment of at least one act of unethical or illegal behavior in the last year among about half the respondents. Covering 1,300 workers in all kinds of businesses, the

> ❝Just because you have a high-minded statement of principles or send a certain percentage of your profits to save rain forests doesn't mean you have the internal controls to prevent ethics problems. ❞
>
> —Ed Petrie, executive director of the Ethics Officers Association

survey prompted Ed Petrie, executive director of the Ethics Officers Association, to say, "Just because you have a high-minded statement of principles or send a certain percentage of your profits to save rain forests doesn't mean you have the internal controls to prevent ethics problems." The moral of the story? Ethics begin at home.

Here are some of the results of the study. The most basic reason for their behavior, respondents said, was pressures of the workplace.

The percentage of respondents who said they engaged in these unethical activities during the past year was as follows:

Cut corners on quality control	16%
Covered up incidents	14
Abused or lied about sick days	11
Lied to or deceived customers	9
Put inappropriate pressure on others	7
Falsified numbers or reports	6
Dismissed or demoted employees unfairly	6
Lied to or deceived superiors on serious matters	5
Withheld important information	5
Misused or stole company property	4
Engaged in or overlooked environmental infractions	4
Took credit for someone's work or idea	4
Discriminated against a coworker	4
Abused drugs or alcohol	4
Engaged in copyright or software infringement	3
Lied to or deceived subordinates on serious matters	3
Overlooked, paid, or accepted bribes	3
Had extramarital affair with business associate	3
Abused an expense account	2
Abused or leaked proprietary information	2
Forged name without person's knowledge	2
Accepted inappropriate gifts or services	1
Filed false regulatory or government reports	1
Engaged in insider trading	1

The Era of Social Activism

The third major phase began with the social unrest of the 1960s and 1970s, when business was often characterized as a negative social force. Some critics even charged that defense contractors had promoted the Vietnam War to spur profits. Eventually, increased activism prompted increased government regulation in a variety of areas: Health warnings, for example, were placed on cigarettes, and stricter environmental protection laws were enacted.

Contemporary Social Consciousness

Some observers today suggest that we are entering a fourth era of social responsibility. In this era, they say, an increased awareness of the global economy and heightened campaigning on the part of environmentalists and other activists have combined to make many businesses more sensitive to their social responsibilities.

Firms in numerous other industries have also integrated socially conscious thinking into their production plans and marketing efforts. The production of environmentally safe products, for example, has become a potential boom area, as many companies introduce products designed to be environmentally friendly. Sales of vegetable-based cleaning products, recycled-paper products, and all-natural toiletries are on the rise. Procter & Gamble's Downy fabric softener concentrate is sold in paper packages and reconstituted in plastic bottles already owned by consumers. Paper maker Union Camp Corp. now removes the ink from discarded paper so that recycled fibers can go into new paper; the company has also replaced chlorine (a toxic water pollutant) with ozone in the bleaching line at its riverside plant in Franklin, Virginia.[8] Volkswagen and BMW are designing cars whose parts will be completely recyclable.

Areas of Social Responsibility

When defining its sense of social responsibility, a firm typically confronts four areas of concern: the environment, its customers, its employees, and its investors.

Responsibility Toward the Environment

Controlling pollution—the transmission of harmful substances into the environment—is a significant challenge to contemporary business. Although noise pollution is now attracting increased concern, air, water, and land pollution remain the greatest problems facing governments and businesses. In the following sections, we will focus on the nature of the problems in these areas as well as some of the current efforts to address them.

Air Pollution

Air pollution results when several factors converge to lower air quality. Carbon monoxide emitted by automobiles contributes to air pollution, as do smoke and other chemicals from manufacturing plants. Air quality is usually worst in certain geographic locations, such as the Denver area and the Los Angeles basin, where pollutants tend to get trapped in the atmosphere.

Legislation has gone a long way toward controlling air pollution. Under new laws, for example, many companies must now install special devices to limit the pollutants that they expel into the air. Such efforts are not without costs. In addition, air pollution is also compounded by problems such as acid rain, which occurs when sulphur is pumped into the atmosphere, mixes with natural moisture, and falls to the ground as rain. Much of the damage to forests and streams in the eastern United States and Canada has been attributed to acid rain originating in sulphur from manufacturing and power plants in the midwestern United States.

Acid rain poses a clearly definable dilemma in the social responsibility of businesses. Current sulphur-reduction technologies, for example, are so costly that installing them

Air pollution tends to get trapped in the air over large cities such as Los Angeles, pictured here. Legislation calls for companies to control the amount of pollutants they expel into the air, the water, and the land, but such efforts are costly for many firms, sometimes prohibitively so. Finding the right balance between desired environmental benefits, such as cleaner air, and inevitable costs, which must sometimes reduce profit or be passed along to the customer through higher prices, is a task in which firms are guided by the strength of their social responsibility.

would force many businesses to close. Closure would cause major financial hardships for investors and laid-off employees, as well as the loss of crucial services for the Midwest and the United States as a whole. At the same time, however, acid rain jeopardizes the livelihoods and environments of people in Canada and the northeastern United States. The challenge, then, is to find ways of reducing sulphur emissions without incurring unsupportable costs. The same challenge faces government and business in their efforts to reduce other forms of pollution.

Water Pollution

Water becomes polluted primarily from chemical and waste dumping. For years, both businesses and cities dumped waste into rivers, streams, and lakes with little regard for the consequences. Cleveland's Cuyahoga River was once so polluted that it burst into flames one hot summer day. After an oil spill in 1994, a Houston shipping channel burned for days.

Thanks to new legislation and increased awareness, water quality in many areas of the United States is improving. The Cuyahoga now boasts fish and is even used for recreation. Laws forbidding phosphates (an ingredient found in many detergents) in New York and Florida have helped to make Lake Erie and other major waters safe for fishing and swimming again. Both the Passaic River in New Jersey and the Hudson River in New York are much cleaner now than they were just a few years ago.

However, the problem is far from solved. In 1993 Texaco was sued by native Indian residents for dumping 3,000 gallons of oil daily into lagoons in the rainforest of Ecuador. New York City still dumps 200 million gallons of raw sewage into nearby water sources every day, and ocean dumping of sewage sludge remains a major problem. And in many less-developed nations businesses still routinely dump waste byproducts into lakes, rivers, and streams.

Land Pollution

There are two key problems in land pollution. The first is how to restore the quality of land that has already been damaged. Land and water damaged by toxic waste, for example, must be cleaned up for the simple reason that we still need to use them. The second problem is how to prevent future contamination. New forms of solid waste disposal are one response to these problems. Combustible wastes, for example, can now be separated and used as fuels in industrial boilers; decomposition can be accelerated by exposing waste matter to certain microorganisms.

Land can also be damaged in ways other than pollution. Strip mining and deforestation, for example, can cause major damage. Major public relations battles have been fought for years over logging rights and restrictions in the Pacific Northwest. Connecticut-based Champion International Corp., a logging company and paper maker, recently announced plans to pull out of Montana, leaving behind not only 1,000 square miles of overlogged landscape but several hundred unemployed workers. The firm's decision to sell almost 900,000 acres to another logging company renewed charges in Montana that the state's resources had long been exploited and devastated by out-of-state corporate raiders.[9] And the controversies associated with developing the rainforest regions in South America have attracted international attention.

Toxic Waste Disposal. An especially controversial problem in land pollution is toxic waste disposal. Toxic wastes are dangerous chemical or radioactive byproducts of manufacturing processes. Altogether, U.S. manufacturers produce between 40 and 60 million tons of such material each year. As a rule, toxic waste can be neither destroyed nor processed into harmless material; it must be stored. Of course, very few people want toxic waste storage sites in their backyards.

Recycling. At the same time, at least one new industry has arisen from increased consciousness about land pollution. Recycling, which is the reconversion of waste materials into useful products, has become a priority not only for municipal and state governments but also for many companies engaged in high-waste activities. At Union Camp's Virginia paper plant, for example, one executive explains the firm's commitment to recycling as a market-oriented strategy: "Customers," he says, "want recycled products. There is a growing awareness that waste is a form of pollution, and that will keep demand for recycled paper high."

> ❝ *There is a growing awareness that waste is a form of pollution.* ❞
>
> —Charles H. Greiner, Jr., vice president, Union Carbide Corp.

Over the past 25 years, recycling enterprises have established a solid industry. First, commitments by manufacturers to build plants using recycled products has increased capacity. Figure 4.2, for example, shows the announced additional capacity of recycled paper mills in the United States through 1996: for office paper alone, an increase of nearly 4 million tons in 1995–1996, as opposed to an increase of just 700,000 tons in 1993–1994.

Second, economic recovery has increased the demand for—and the price of—raw materials. For example, old corrugated boxes, which sold for $35 per ton in September 1993, recently soared to $110 per ton. Even international events have had an impact on the demand for recycled raw material in the United States: Because China recently had a poor cotton harvest, Chinese textile makers began to offer a premium price to U.S. recyclers for old soda bottles, which can be converted into synthetic fibers.[10]

Environmental Protection Agency (EPA)
Federal agency established to protect and encourage the conservation of natural resources

The EPA Superfund. In 1980 Congress created the so-called Superfund to help clean up heavily polluted land. The **Environmental Protection Agency (EPA)**, an independent federal agency charged with protecting resources and encouraging conservation, administers the program under which chemical and oil companies pay a special tax that goes to restoring polluted land to its natural state. Unfortunately, although some Superfund money has been used to locate problems, little has been spent on actual cleanup. For example, the EPA has identified more than 350,000 sites with leaking underground storage tanks. The projected cost of cleanup stands at $80 billion to $120 billion.

Figure 4.2 Capacity of Recycled Paper Mills, 1993–1996

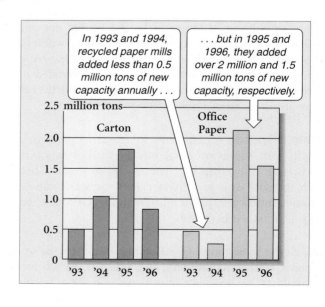

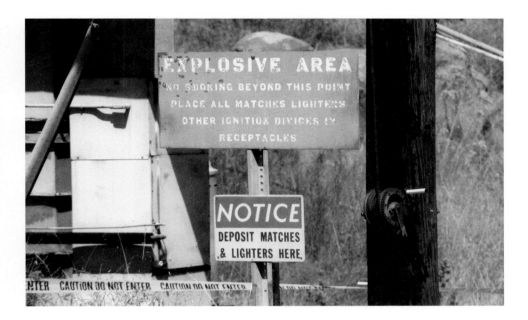

In 1992, the State of California fined Rockwell International Corp. $650,000 for burning toxic solvents in open barrels at its jet engine plant in Santa Susana. In the same year, Rockwell paid $18.5 million in federal fines for illegally storing nuclear waste at its nuclear weapons plant in Rocky Flats, Colorado. Rockwell contends that its record has improved, and in fact it won an Environmental Protection Agency award for reducing toxic emissions in 1995.

To enhance its effectiveness, President Clinton has proposed revisions in the Superfund law. If passed, his revisions would make the Superfund more flexible in its cleanup requirements at identified sites. Currently, for example, the law usually assumes that every polluted landfill will ultimately be used for residential development, where the risk of exposure would be great; each site must be restored accordingly. The revised law would acknowledge different levels of "clean": Less restoration would be required at commercially developed property—say, parking lots—where the risk is lower. However, the plan would retain at least one feature that environmental organizations deem important: The Superfund liability system requires firms to pay for cleaning up any pollution to which they contributed, even if they are not solely responsible.[11]

Responsibility
Toward Customers

A company that does not act responsibly toward its customers will ultimately lose their business. Moreover, the government actively controls what businesses can and cannot do regarding consumers. The Federal Trade Commission, for example, regulates advertising and pricing practices. The Food and Drug Administration enforces guidelines for labeling food products.

Unethical and irresponsible business practices toward customers can result in government fines and penalties. In the fall of 1993, for example, C. R. Bard Inc., one of the world's largest makers of medical devices, pleaded guilty to charges of fraud and other infractions for selling untested heart catheters. The chairman, CEO, and five other executives were indicted on 393 federal counts, and the firm agreed to pay $61 million in criminal fines and civil damages.[12]

Social responsibility toward customers generally falls into two categories:

■ Providing high-quality products

■ Pricing products fairly

Naturally, firms differ as much in their level of concern about responsibility to customers as in their approaches to environmental responsibility. Yet unlike environmental problems, many customer problems do not require expensive solutions. In fact, most problems can be avoided if companies simply heed laws regarding consumer rights and regulated practices.

Consumer Rights

consumerism
Form of social activism dedicated to protecting the rights of consumers in their dealings with businesses

Much of the current interest in business responsibility toward customers can be traced to the rise of **consumerism:** social activism dedicated to protecting the rights of consumers in their dealings with businesses. The first formal declaration of consumer rights protection came in the early 1960s, when President John F. Kennedy identified four basic consumer rights. These rights are now backed by numerous federal and state laws:

■ Consumers have a right to safe products.

■ Consumers have a right to be informed about all relevant aspects of a product.

■ Consumers have a right to be heard.

■ Consumers have a right to choose what they buy.

Unfair Pricing

collusion
Illegal agreement between two or more companies to commit a wrongful act

Interfering with competition can also take the form of illegal pricing practices. **Collusion** occurs when two or more firms agree to collaborate on such wrongful acts as price fixing. A few years ago two major airlines were found guilty of discussing and agreeing on price increases so that each airline would announce higher fares at the same time, thus not putting either at a competitive disadvantage. More recently, several hospitals in Danbury, Connecticut, and St. Joseph, Missouri, were charged with price fixing. In each case, the charges involved illegal agreements between hospitals and local physicians as to what prices physicians would charge for various hospital services. There were also agreements

The Workplace Environment

The Harder Side of Sears

When a father in financial difficulties pleads with a judge for help in keeping a prized possession to pacify his children, the judge discovers that a local merchant has unlawfully collected payments on debts that were legally canceled. Is this the plot of a Charles Dickens novel?

❝*There's not a dollar's worth of profit worth having if it compromises your integrity.***❞**

—Arthur C. Martinez, CEO, Sears, Roebuck & Co.

No, it's the true story of the latest scandal to rock Sears, Roebuck & Company. In this case and others like it, Sears has signed contracts with bankrupt debtors to collect on debts and then failed to file the contracts with the bankruptcy court for review. Since 1992 the firm has collected up to $160 million to which it may not have been entitled.

CEO Arthur C. Martinez quickly offered refunds, debt relief, and cash payments to tens of thousands of formerly bankrupt consumers who had been victims of the lapse. "There's not a dollar's worth of profit worth having if it compromises your integrity," he said. But industry observers are even more curious about how Martinez will deal with the culprits, if there are any.

Blame has already fallen on the firm's legal department for dispensing faulty advice, but some insiders feel it belongs higher up, with the management of the credit operations. Martinez will have to determine whether the corporate culture and its compensation system influenced well-meaning employees to act unwisely, or whether the illegal behavior was knowing and deliberate. David Messick, professor of ethics at the Kellogg Graduate School of Management at Northwestern University, defines Martinez' difficult task in this way: "You want to root out immoral activity because it's wrong and it's bad for business. On the other hand, you need room for honest errors."

Time will tell how Martinez will decide, and what this latest trouble means for Sears and its embattled ethics policies.

by which doctors would perform a specified percentage of their outpatient services (such as radiology and minor surgery) in the hospitals. As a result of these agreements, managed care companies were unable to enter the markets because virtually all of the local doctors were affiliated with the hospitals.[13]

Under some circumstances, firms can also come under attack for price gouging: responding to increased demand with overly steep (and often unwarranted) price increases. For example, when BMW introduced its sporty Z3 Roadster, it announced that only a limited number would be produced each year. Because the car was an immediate hit, Z3s were in very short supply. As a result, some unscrupulous BMW dealers began to tack on additional dealer markups of several thousands of dollars over the sticker price the manufacturer has set for the car.

Ethics in Advertising

In recent years, there has also been increased attention on ethics in both advertising and product information. Several years ago, for example, many firms began promoting food products touted as being "light," presumably to announce that they were low in calories or saturated fat. The FDA confirmed that many such products were in fact lower in saturated fat than the same products in their "nonlight" versions; often, however, they still contained high levels of fat and calories, and certainly did not qualify as health food. As a result, many products were forced to drop "light" labeling; others added notices to the consumer that they were not truly low-fat products. Similarly, food producers are now required to use a standardized format for presenting ingredients on product packages.

Critics also charge that many companies are too aggressive in how they advertise and market their products to children. Saturday morning cartoons are filled with animated commercials, for example, that many young viewers might not distinguish from the program. Merchandising tie-ins, licensed characters, and brand names are continuously flashed before the eyes of children on television, movies, radio programs, magazines, and billboards. The average child of 7 sees approximately 20,000 television commercials a year.[14]

Responsibility
Toward Employees

In chapter 8 we will see how a number of human resource management activities are essential to a smoothly functioning business. These activities—recruiting, hiring, training, promoting, and compensating—are also the basis for social responsibility toward employees. A company that provides its employees with equal opportunities for rewards and advancement without regard to race, sex, or other irrelevant factors is meeting its social responsibilities. Firms that ignore these responsibilities run the risk of losing productive, highly motivated employees. They also leave themselves open to lawsuits.

Some progressive companies go well beyond legal requirements. AT&T, for example, actively hires and trains the so-called hard-core unemployed: people with little education, training, and history of employment. The National Alliance of Business, a joint business and government program to train the hard-core unemployed, has helped to find work for over 4 million people who could not get jobs on their own.

In addition to their responsibility to employees as company resources, firms have a responsibility to employees as people who are more productive when their needs are met. For example, firms that accept this responsibility ensure that the workplace is safe, both physically and socially. They will no more tolerate an abusive manager or one who sexually harasses employees than they would a gas leak.

One related area that has recently received considerable media attention involves the treatment of foreign workers by U.S. companies. Many firms such as Nike, Reebok, and Levi Strauss have contracts with factories in other countries to manufacture shoes and other apparel for prices far lower than the firms could make these same products in the United States because of the substantially lower wage rates in those countries. However, these factory owners sometimes pay their workers wages that are so low as to constitute near-slavery. And they also have been known to mistreat workers, employ young children, and maintain unsafe work areas.[15]

Ethical Commitments: The Case of Whistle-Blowers. Finally, respecting employees as people means respecting their behavior as ethically responsible individuals. Too often, however, people who try to act ethically on the job find themselves in trouble with their employers. This problem is especially true for **whistle-blowers**: employees who detect and try to put an end to a company's unethical, illegal, or socially irresponsible actions by publicizing them.

whistle-blower
Employee who detects and tries to put an end to a company's unethical, illegal, or socially irresponsible actions by publicizing them

In a socially responsible company, whistle-blowers can confidently report findings to higher-level managers, who can be expected to take action. Unfortunately, many whistle-blowers find management unwilling to listen—or worse. Whistle-blowers at Beech-Nut, Citicorp, and General Dynamics have all reported a lack of interest by managers about charges of company misconduct. In extreme circumstances, whistle-blowers may find themselves demoted or fired.

The current whistle-blower law stems from the False Claims Act of 1863, which was designed to prevent contractors from selling defective supplies to the Union Army during the Civil War. With 1986 revisions to the law, the government can recover triple damages from fraudulent contractors. Since then, almost 1,000 suits have been filed. The government has intervened to prosecute in about 100 of those suits and collected $750 million from convicted firms. Because more cases are being filed and larger amounts of fraudulent funds are coming to light, that figure will soon top $1 billion. Whistle-blowers receive 15 to 25 percent of what the government collects. If the Justice Department does not intervene, a whistle-blower can still proceed with a civil suit. In that case, the whistle-blower receives 25 to 30 percent of any money recovered.[16] More than 700 civil suits were filed by whistle-blowers between 1986 and 1994. In one, a former vice president for finance at United Technologies received 15 percent of a $150 million settlement ($22.5 million).

Responsibility Toward Investors

Because shareholders are the owners of a company, it may sound odd to say that a firm can act irresponsibly toward its investors. However, managers can abuse their responsibilities to investors in a number of ways. In such cases, the ultimate losers are indeed the owners, who do not receive their due earnings or dividends. Companies can also act irresponsibly toward investors by misrepresenting company resources.

Improper Financial Management

Occasionally, organizations or their officers are guilty of blatant financial mismanagement, or even fraud. For example, until recently Lars Bildman served as CEO of Astra USA, the U.S. division of a large Swedish drug maker. He was recently charged with, among other offenses, redecorating his home and having the charges billed to the company, taking other managers on private company-sponsored cruises accompanied by prostitutes, and using company funds to buy art for his personal collection.[17]

Check Kiting

check kiting
Illegal practice of writing checks against money that has not yet been credited at the bank on which checks are drawn

Some practices are specifically illegal. **Check kiting**, for instance, involves writing a check against money that has not yet arrived at the bank on which it is drawn. E. F. Hutton and Co., for instance, was convicted of violating kiting laws on a massive scale: In a carefully planned scheme, company managers were able to use as much as $250 million every day that did not belong to the firm. How did the scheme work? Managers would deposit customer checks totaling $1 million, for example, into the company account. Knowing that the bank would not collect some percentage of the total deposit for several days, they nevertheless wrote checks against the total $1 million.

Insider Trading

Insider trading occurs when someone uses confidential information to gain from the purchase or sale of stocks. One highly publicized case featured noted Wall Street trader Ivan Boesky. An acquaintance of Boesky's, Dennis Levine, worked for Drexel Burnham Lambert, an investment banking firm. When Levine heard of an upcoming merger or acquisition, he passed the information along to Boesky. Boesky then bought and sold the appropriate stocks at times calculated to generate huge profits that he split with Levine. In one especially profitable instance, Boesky used Levine's information about Nestlé's plans to buy Carnation stock to earn over $28 million in profits.[18]

insider trading
Use of confidential information to gain from the purchase or sale of stocks

Misrepresentation of Finances

Certain behavior regarding financial representation is also illegal. In maintaining and reporting its financial status, every corporation must conform to generally accepted accounting practices (GAAP) (see chapter 18). Sometimes, however, managers project profits far in excess of what they actually expect to earn. When the truth comes out, investors

In February 1987, investment banker Dennis Levine (top) was sentenced for securities fraud, tax evasion, and perjury. In April 1987, Wall Street trader Ivan Boesky (bottom left) pleaded guilty to securities law violations. Levine, who was given 2 years in prison and fined $362,000, agreed to help investigators snag Boesky. Meanwhile, Boesky, although fined $100 million, served less than 2 years in prison because he helped investigators bring indictments against the investment banking firm of Drexel Burnham Lambert and Drexel banker Michael Milken (bottom right). In April 1990, Milken pleaded guilty to charges of conspiracy and securities fraud; he was sentenced to 10 years in prison and fined $200 million, and he agreed to pay $400 million to settle a civil suit brought by the Securities and Exchange Commission. In December 1988, Drexel agreed to pay $650 million in criminal fines. The Federal Deposit Insurance Corp. later cited Milken and Drexel for another $12 billion in damages for pillaging the savings and loan industry. In February 1990, Drexel filed for brankruptcy.

are disappointed. For example, Jacques Robinson, the CEO of Cincinnati Microwave, has been accused of misrepresenting the finances of his firm in order to boost the price of the firm's shares.

Implementing Social Responsibility Programs

Thus far, we have discussed social responsibility as if there were some agreement on how organizations should behave. In fact, there are dramatic differences of opinion concerning the role of social responsibility as a business goal. For excample, some people oppose any business activity that threatens profits. At the opposite extreme are those who argue that social responsibility must take precedence over profits.

Even businesspeople who agree on the importance of social responsibility cite different reasons for their views. For example, some skeptics of business-sponsored social projects fear that if businesses become too active, they will gain too much control over the ways in which those projects are addressed by society as a whole. These critics point to the influence many businesses have been able to exert on the government agencies that are supposed to regulate their industries. Other critics claim that business organizations lack the expertise needed to address social issues. They argue that technical experts, not businesses, should decide how to clean up polluted rivers, for example.

On the other hand, proponents of socially responsible business believe that corporations are citizens and should therefore help to improve the lives of fellow citizens. Still others point to the vast resources controlled by businesses and note that they help to create many of the problems that social programs are designed to alleviate.

Approaches to Social Responsibility

Given these differences of opinion, it is little wonder that corporations have adopted a variety of approaches to social responsibility. In this section we will describe the three most common: the social obligation, social reaction, and social response approaches.

Social Obligation Approach

social obligation approach Approach to social responsibility by which a company meets only minimum legal requirements in its commitments to groups and individuals in its social environment

The **social obligation approach**, a fairly conservative concept, is consistent with the argument that profits should not be spent on social programs. From this posture, companies tend to meet the minimum requirements of government regulation and standard business practices, but nothing more. Alcohol makers and tobacco companies exemplify this approach. They attach health warnings on their packaging and limit their advertising as specifically ordered by the government. But in countries that lack such controls, U.S. tobacco companies advertise heavily and make no mention of the negative effects of smoking.

Social Reaction Approach

social reaction approach Approach to social responsibility by which a company, if specifically asked to do so, exceeds legal minimums in its commitments to groups and individuals in its social environment

An intermediate level of social responsibility is found in the **social reaction approach**. Firms taking this stance go beyond the bare minimum, usually if they are specifically asked to do so. For example, many companies match employee contributions to company-approved causes. Others sponsor various community activities. As a rule, however, someone must first ask.

Social Response Approach

social response approach Approach to social responsibility by which a company actively seeks opportunities to contribute to the well-being of groups and individuals in its social environment

Firms that adopt the most liberal approach to social responsibility, the **social response approach**, actively seek opportunities to contribute to social projects. McDonald's, for example, established Ronald McDonald Houses to provide lodging for families of children hospitalized away from home. Sears and General Electric support artists and performers.

Table 4.1 Top Corporate Givers, 1995 (in Millions)

IBM	$92.7*
Microsoft Corp.	73.2*
Johnson & Johnson	72.8
Eli Lilly and Co.	71.9
Hewlett-Packard Co.	71.2†
General Motors Corp.	69.2
Philip Morris Cos. Inc.	68.0
Pfizer Inc.	60.4
Bristol-Myers Squibb Co.	56.0
Exxon Corp.	55.4

* Fiscal year ending June 30, 1996. †Fiscal year ending October 31, 1995.

Such efforts are clearly beyond the normal response to requests for contributions. Many firms also make substantial contributions to various social causes. Table 4.1 lists the 10 top corporate givers. For example, note in the table that IBM recently gave $92.7 million to charity.

Managing Social Responsibility Programs

Making a company socially responsible in the full sense of the social response approach requires a carefully organized and managed program. In particular, managers must take steps to foster a companywide sense of social responsibility. Figure 4.3 summarizes those steps.

Social responsibility must start at the top: Without the support of top management, no program can succeed. Thus, top management must take a strong stand on social responsibility and develop a policy statement outlining that commitment.

Next, a committee of top managers must develop a plan detailing the level of management support. Some companies set aside percentages of profits for social programs. Levi Strauss, for example, earmarks 2.4 percent of pretax earnings for worthy projects.

Figure 4.3 Establishing a Social Responsibility Program

- Social Responsibility
- Social Audit
- Appointment of a Director
- Strategic Planning
- Top-Management Support

Managers must also set specific priorities. For instance, should the firm train the hard-core unemployed or support the arts?

Third, one executive must be put in charge of the firm's agenda. Whether the role is created as a separate job or added to an existing one, the selected individual must monitor the program and ensure that its implementation is consistent with the firm's policy statement and strategic plan.

social audit

Systematic analysis of a firm's success in using funds earmarked for meeting its social responsibility goals

Finally, the organization must conduct occasional **social audits**: systematic analyses of its success in using funds that it has earmarked for its social responsibility goals. Consider the case of a company whose strategic plan calls for spending $100,000 to train 200 hard-core unemployed people and subsequently to place 180 of them in jobs. If at the end of 1 year the firm has spent $98,000, trained 210 people, and filled 175 jobs, a social audit will confirm the program's success. But if the program has cost $150,000, trained only 90 people, and placed only 10 of them, the audit will reveal the program's failure. A failure should signal a rethinking of the program's implementation or priorities.

Social Responsibility and the Small Business

As the owner of a garden supply store, how would you respond to a building inspector's suggestion that a cash payment will speed up your application for a building permit? As the manager of a liquor store, would you call the police, refuse to sell, or sell to a customer whose identification card looks forged? As the owner of a small laboratory, would you call the state board of health to make sure that it has licensed the company with which you want to contract to dispose of medical waste? Who will really be harmed if a small firm pads its income statement to help it get a much-needed bank loan?

Most of the examples in this chapter illustrate big-business responses to ethical and social responsibility issues. However, examples such as these show quite clearly that small businesses must answer many of the same questions. Differences are primarily differences of scale.

At the same time, these are largely questions of individual ethics. What about questions of social responsibility? Can a small business afford a social agenda? Should it sponsor Little League baseball teams, make donations to the United Fund, and buy lightbulbs

The small business can demonstrate its responsibility toward the local community in a variety of ways, such as sponsoring a Little League baesball team. In fact, one recent study concluded that "companies that increased their community involvement were more likely to show an improved financial picture than those that did not increase their community involvement."

from the Lion's Club? Do joining the Chamber of Commerce and supporting the Better Business Bureau cost too much? Clearly, ethics and social responsibility are decisions faced by all managers in all organizations, regardless of rank or size. One key to business success is to decide in advance how to respond to the issues that underlie all ethical and social responsibility questions.

Summary of Learning Objectives

1 **Explain how people develop their personal codes of ethics and why ethics are important in the workplace.** Individual codes of ethics are derived from social standards of right and wrong. Ethical behavior is behavior conforming to generally accepted social norms concerning beneficial and harmful actions. Because ethics affect the behavior of individuals on behalf of the companies that employ them, many firms are adopting formal statements of ethics. Unethical behavior can result in loss of business, in fines, and even in imprisonment.

2 **Distinguish social responsibility from ethics and trace the evolution of social responsibility in U.S. business.** Social responsibility is an organization's response to social needs. Until the second half of the nineteenth century, businesses often paid little attention to these needs. Since then, however, both public pressure and government regulation, especially as a product of the Great Depression of the 1930s and the social activism of the 1960s and 1970s, have forced businesses to consider the public welfare, at least to some degree. A trend toward increased social consciousness, including a heightened sense of environmental activism, has recently emerged.

3 **Show how the concept of social responsibility applies both to environmental issues and to a firm's relationships with customers, employees, and investors.** Social responsibility toward the environment requires firms to minimize pollution of air, water, and land. Social responsibility toward customers requires firms to provide high-quality products, price products fairly, and respect consumers' rights. Social responsibility toward employees requires firms to respect workers both as resources and as people who are more productive when their needs are met. Social responsibility toward investors requires firms to manage their resources and to represent their financial status honestly.

4 **Identify three general approaches to social responsibility and describe the four steps a firm must take to implement a social responsibility program.** The social obligation approach emphasizes compliance with legal minimum requirements. Companies adopting the social reaction approach go beyond minimum activities, if asked. The social response approach commits a company to contributing to socially concerned projects. Implementing a social responsibility program entails four steps: drafting a policy statement with the support of top management, developing a detailed plan, appointing a director to implement the plan, and conducting social audits to monitor results.

5 **Explain how issues of social responsibility and ethics affect small businesses.** Managers and employees of small businesses face many of the same ethical questions as their counterparts at larger firms. Small businesses must confront the same areas of social responsibility and decide on an approach to social responsibility. The differences are primarily differences of scale.

Questions and Exercises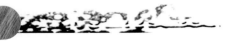

Questions for Review

1 What is the essential factor in any ethical decision?
2 What are the major areas of social responsibility with which businesses should be concerned?

3 List the four rights of consumers that were proposed during the Kennedy administration and eventually formalized by state and federal law.

4 What are the three basic approaches to social responsibility?

Questions for Analysis

5 In what ways do you think your personal code of ethics might clash with the operations of some companies? Why? How might you try to resolve these differences?

6 What kind of wrongdoing would most likely prompt you to be a whistle-blower? What kind of wrongdoing would least likely? Why?

7 In your opinion, which area of social responsibility is most important? Why? Are there areas other than those noted in the chapter that you consider important?

8 Identify some specific ethical or social responsibility issues that might be faced by small business managers and employees in each of the following areas: environment, customers, employees, and investors.

Application Exercises

9 Develop and put in writing a code of ethics for use in the classroom. Your document should include guidelines for students, instructors, and administrators.

10 Using newspapers, magazines, and other business references, identify and describe at least three companies that take a social obligation approach to social responsibility, three that take a social reaction approach, and three that take a social response approach.

Building Your Business Skills

This exercise enhances the following SCANS workplace competencies: demonstrating basic skills, demonstrating thinking skills, exhibiting interpersonal skills, and working with information.

Goal   To encourage students to place themselves in the position of a manager who is forced to make a decision with ethical and financial consequences.

Situation   Imagine that you are a manager in a meat processing plant. As part of the normal routine, the meat is tested for bacteria, and U.S. Department of Agriculture inspectors monitor the results. The results from the morning's test show that the meat contains high levels of *E. coli*, a bacteria that can sicken and even kill unsuspecting consumers. Based on information you alone have, you are concerned that these results may be the tip of the iceberg and that all the meat your company has recently distributed to restaurants and retailers may also be contaminated. Reporting your concerns means that your company may be forced to close. Not reporting them means that thousands of people may get sick. With an inspection report due later today, you have to decide what to do.

Method   **Step 1:** Working with four other students, brainstorm the ethical implications of the decision. Among the factors to consider are

- Your responsibility to the public.
- Your responsibility to company employees (if your suspicion of widespread contamination is correct, every employee may be out of work).
- Your responsibility to stockholders (if your suspicions are made public, the stock price may plummet).
- Your legal responsibility to disclose a public health hazard to Department of Agriculture inspectors (library research may be necessary to determine this).
- Your responsibility to yourself (you have no way of knowing whether disclosing this type of information will help or hurt your career).

Step 2: Make a decision. Then, working with group members, write a memo to your manager describing the problem. Decide whether you will limit your comments to your concerns about the small batch of contaminated meat or whether you will broaden your comments to include the possibility of massive contamination.

Follow-Up Questions

1 Did your memo focus only on what you knew for certain or did you include your broader suspicions? Explain the ethical reasons for your approach.
2 Is it necessary to share your concerns of widespread contamination with other plant managers before you send the memo? Should the memo come from them as well as you?
3 Do you consider the situation a crisis? If so, how does it affect the way you respond?
4 How do you balance your ethical obligations to customers with your ethical obligations to employees and stockholders?
5 What role did legal consequences play in your decision?
6 What role did your personal career concerns play in the decision?

Business Case 4

The Case Against Recycling

Most of us cherish the belief that recycling is a good thing. It's good for the environment, it's good for the economy, it's even good for the soul (we feel better doing "the right thing"). But writer John Tierney suggests that we rethink our notions of what recycling really accomplishes and cites the following data:

- The supposed shortage of landfill space to bury unrecycled garbage in the late 1980s was a false alarm; landfills are scarce in only a few places, mostly around Northeastern cities.
- Paper, cardboard, and other organic materials, although biodegradable, remain intact in airless landfills, whereas plastic packaging, which is cheaper and uses less energy to produce, preserves food better and, after use, takes up less landfill space.
- Mandatory recycling programs cost communities money for collection, administration, public relations campaigns, and equipment and personnel—sometimes three times as much as for collecting garbage.
- The costs of natural resources, even nonrenewable ones, are de-

clining, making it wasteful to spend money on saving them.
- Some recycling processes, such as those for paper, create more pollution than the original production processes (5,000 extra gallons of waste water for each ton of recycled newsprint, for example).
- Regulations force firms to buy recycled materials they can't use, but landfills in the South and Midwest are eager to bury garbage from paying customers, whose money can be used to improve local services such as schools and libraries.

Tierney claims many experts and public officials now recognize that putting garbage in landfills is a good solution for the present as well as for the future. He quotes a Gonzaga University economist who estimates that if the United States continues to generate garbage at the present rate for the next 1,000 years, a landfill 100 yards deep to hold it all would be a mere 35 miles square.

A federally funded study by the Solid Waste Association of North America found that recycling increased the cost of garbage in five of the six U.S. communities it analyzed (in the sixth, recycling was cheaper

by only .1 percent), and similar results have been found in Europe. Tierney calls recycling "the most wasteful activity in modern America: a waste of time and money, a waste of human and natural resources." He advocates a "pay as you throw" system, already adopted in some cities such as Minneapolis, San Francisco, and Seattle, that charges people directly for their disposable garbage by weight or by volume. Given as economic incentive, Tierney says, people will automatically be motivated to use less, to reduce waste and—when it makes sense—to recycle.

Questions

1. Do you think it is ethically responsible to recycle? Why or why not?
2. What role do you think the government should play in mandating recycling programs?
3. Tierney claims there is little market for recyclables. How could firms make better use of recycled materials? Who do you think should bear the costs, if any?
4. What are the recycling regulations for businesses in your community? Do you think they are reasonable? Why or why not?

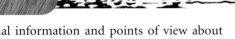

Connecting to the Web

The following Web sites will give you additional information and points of view about topics covered in this chapter. Many sites lead to other related Internet locations, so approach this list with the spirit of an explorer.

THE BETTER BUSINESS BUREAU

http://www.bbb.org/

The mission of the Better Business Bureau is to work with businesses and consumers to maintain an ethical marketplace. Included in the Bureau's on-line site are business report databases, a mechanism for dispute resolution, and consumer warnings. You will learn about the BBBOnLine Program, which is designed to build consumer confidence in the on-line marketplace.

CORPORATE ENVIRONMENTAL STRATEGY: THE JOURNAL OF ENVIRONMENTAL LEADERSHIP

http://www.rpi.edu/dept/mgmt/SOM.pages/EMP/ces.html

This quarterly journal helps business executives connect sound business strategy with strategic environmental management. Using a case study approach, journal articles discuss how companies can be both profitable and environmentally responsible. Members of the journal's board of directors include executives from such major companies as AT&T and Eastman Kodak.

ETHICS AT TEXAS INSTRUMENTS

http://www.ti.com/corp/docs/ethics/home.htm

Texas Instruments' commitment to workplace ethics is demonstrated here. The site includes a history of TI's ethical policies and programs as well as specific ethics-related documents. Students will find TI's Ethics Quick Test particularly interesting because it is so simple and direct.

THE GOLDMAN ENVIRONMENTAL PRIZE

http://www.goldmanprize.org/goldman/

The Goldman Environmental Foundation of San Francisco awards $75,000 annually to six environmental heroes from around the world. Click on this page to learn who these grassroots heroes are. In 1997 the foundation also gave $1-million grants to three environmental organizations, including the Earth Island Institute, which in its promotion of safe commercial fishing practices saved over 500,000 dolphins.

JOHNSON & JOHNSON

http://www.johnsonandjohnson.com

Johnson & Johnson's commitment to corporate ethics began with the 1943 publication of the first Johnson & Johnson credo, which put customers first. Click on this Web site for information about how the Johnson & Johnson credo guides corporate social responsibility and environmental programs.

McDONALD'S: OUR COMMUNITY/ADULT

http://www.mcdonalds.com/a_community/

This site introduces the social responsibility action programs of the McDonald's Corporation, including the Ronald McDonald House charities. Corporate scholarships and community and educational programs that are part of the legacy of McDonald's founder Ray Kroc are also presented.

NAACP

http://www.naacp.org

The Web site of the National Association for the Advancement of Colored People includes information about programs to fight racial discrimination in the workplace.

U.S. ENVIRONMENTAL PROTECTION AGENCY

http://www.epa.gov/

The Web site of the Environmental Protection Agency will introduce you to the functions of this federal agency and, specifically, to information on the EPA Superfund.

U.S. FEDERAL TRADE COMMISSION

http://www.ftc.gov/

Click on this site to learn how the Federal Trade Commission works to protect consumers in a competitive marketplace by enforcing a variety of federal antitrust and consumer protection laws.

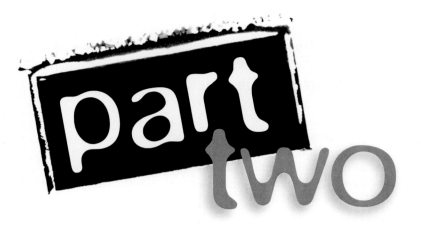

part two

The Business of Managing

Songwriters tell us that love is better the second time around, but they don't say a word about business ownership. Is success sweeter, more satisfying, more pleasurable when you build a company, sell it, then buy it back to build it again? There aren't many people with the first-hand experience to answer this question, but one who qualifies is entrepreneur Stephen Bernard. In 17 years, Bernard founded, sold, then repurchased Massachusetts-based Cape Cod Potato Chips. His story is one of an unsinkable entrepreneurial spirit and keen management know-how.

Step 1: Build the Business

Since he was a kid, Bernard dreamed of running a food company, and potato chips seemed like a product in search of invention. Whatever the manufacturer, all chips tasted the same to Bernard. Whether they were plain, ruffled, or coated with sour cream or barbecue flavoring, they had a mass produced taste, look, and feel.

Sensing opportunity, Bernard began experimenting with a dough fryer and potato slices until he hit on an all-natural chip that looked homemade, tasted rich, and was different from everything on the market. "Most commercial potato chips are continuously processed so the temperature and other conditions remain constant," he explained. "What we figured out is that doing them as a batch in a single container causes the temperature to drop as soon as they go into the oil, and then it comes back up slowly. This gives the chips their unique texture."

Believing that his chips would create a new premium-quality marketing niche, Bernard and his wife mortgaged their home and invested about $25,000 to start the Cape Cod Potato Chip Company. Operating out of a tiny storefront in Hyannis, Massachusetts, they ran a 100-hour a week mom-and-pop operation, making, packaging, and selling the chips to local retailers. Tourists who sampled the brand were quickly hooked and demanded that retailers stock the product.

As is often the case, luck played a role in building the company. When, in 1981, a driver lost control of his car and crashed through Cape Cod's storefront window, the accident brought enough insurance money to carry the company through a slow winter season. (Luck was also on the driver's side; he survived.) It also brought front-page media attention that got retailers interested. Said Bernard, "everything came together over the next few weeks" as new retailers tried, then stocked the product. "We never looked back." By 1985 the company was in a 20,000-square-foot plant and had grown into a profitable $10-million enterprise.

Believing that his chips would speak for themselves, Bernard's chief marketing tool was product sampling instead of expensive advertising. The product's distinctive taste and simplicity created immediate consumer loyalty and convinced retailers to waive shelf space stocking fees. Said Boston food broker Gus Lordi, "There are damn few products that have that kind of discernible difference" and that can make it without advertising.

A bag of Cape Cod Chips costs between 20 and 30 cents more than other brands, but consumers were willing to pay more for a specialty product with an unmatched taste. Instead of competing head-to-head with industry giant Frito-Lay, Bernard went after a business niche that gave consumers the quality they wanted but that did not try to capture a large market share. Like the microbrewers who would later redefine the beer industry, he took a premium product approach that identified a small but profitable, market segment. Harvard Business School professor Ray A. Goldberg explains: Bernard "was catering to individual tastes long before beer companies were talking about micromanaging and micromarketing. He woke up a sleepy industry where people weren't being as creative as they could be, because they didn't feel they had to be."

Step 2: Sell the Business

Cape Cod's extraordinary success forced Bernard to think about expanding to other states, a risky move that would require an infusion of capital. Before he could decide what to do, he received a call from Anheuser-Busch. A company known primarily for beer, Anheuser was creating a new snack division, Eagle Snacks, to compete with PepsiCo's Frito-Lay. By purchasing regional snack companies with excellent track records, Anheuser was developing a line of premium niche products, and Cape Cod seemed a natural fit.

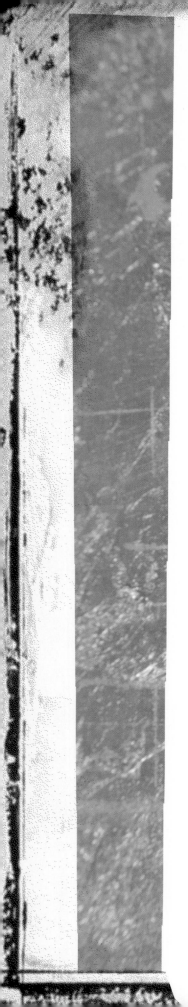

Bernard received an offer he couldn't refuse and sold his company for a reported $7 million. As part of the deal, he agreed to stay on as president. Within 5 years, sales hit $40 million, and Cape Cod Chips could be found throughout the United States and in Canada. Despite this success, Cape Cod's specialty status was a mismatch with Anheuser-Busch. "It became just another part of a much bigger effort, and they lost focus on Cape Cod," explained Bernard.

Anheuser's commitment to Eagle also waned as the corporation realized that Frito-Lay's grip on the $5 billion salty-snack market was hard to break. Whereas Eagle held a mere 10 percent of the market, Frito-Lay controlled 50 percent. These statistics convinced Anheuser to pull back on its support for Cape Cod, and by 1995 annual sales dropped to $12 million. By early 1996, Cape Cod Potato Chips were no more, and the product capacity of Eagle Snacks had been sold to Frito-Lay.

Step 3: Buy Back the Business

Bernard could have walked away (he had already started another food-related company and had profited handsomely from Cape Cod's sale), but Cape Cod meant more to him than dollars and cents. It was a company he and his wife had created and nurtured; it was their business home. So with the help of venture capitalists, he bought back the company for $2 million less than he had received from Anheuser. Bernard describes what happened as "an emotional experience." He explains: "When I entered the factory and told 100 employees that we were back and their jobs were safe, they began to cheer and my knees began to shake."

His next job was rebuilding. He had to get Cape Cod Potato Chips back on store shelves as soon as possible in order to maintain consumer loyalty. Bernard's marketing team connected first with New England retailers, who had supported the brand from the beginning. These "retailers were tremendously supportive upon hearing that the brand was coming back," said Tony Cusano, Cape Cod's vice president of sales. Within 3 months, the chips were in 3,000 New England stores.

The right marketing strategy was critical to a successful comeback, but lacking Anheuser-Busch's deep pockets, the company had limited resources for advertising. As a result, marketing director Nicole Bernard returned to product sampling, and in 1996 gave away 400,000 1-oz. bags throughout New England. "We really believe in our product," said Nicole Bernard, who is also the boss's daughter. "Once we can get a customer to try it, the retention rate is high. We look at sampling as a way to create a purchase."

With success in New England, managers saw sales opportunities up and down the East Coast and in the midwest and California. With store shelf space formerly held by Eagle Snack products up for grabs, they knew that a premium potato chip would attract interest. Within months, Cape Cod was aligned with 60 master distributors and was in 5,000 supermarket outlets.

Three new products introduced in 1997 fueled the comeback: Golden and Dark Russet Chips and 40 percent Reduced Fat Chips. Each product is cooked in the small batch method in order to maximize quality. According to Bernard, the method enables the company "to closely monitor the individual needs of each type of potato chip."

1997 was a good year for Cape Cod Potato Chips. Through his entrepreneurial pluck and management talent, Stephen Bernard turned his company around, moving from $6 million in sales in 1996 to nearly $30 million in 1997. "Our focus is to get about 3 percent of the [overall] business, wherever the business is," he said. Potato chips are a multibillion-dollar market, so 3 percent would be terrific."

Snack food, small business, and management Web sites abound, including the following. The information in these and other sites will help you answer the questions that follow.

American Management Association	http://www.amanet.org/
Cape Cod Potato Chips	http://www.capecodchips.com
Dun & Bradstreet's Small Business Services	http://www.dnb.com/sbs/hmenu.htm
Entrepreneur Magazine: The Online Small Business Authority	http://www.entrepreneurmag.com/
Frito-Lay	http://www.fritolay.com
Hopnotes.com: Home of Anheuser-Busch's Specialty Beers	http://www.hopnotes.com/
Online Women's Business Center: Finance Center	http://www.onlinewbc.org/docs/finance/index.html
Small Business Administration	http://www.sba.gov/

CASE QUESTIONS

1 Imagine that Stephen Bernard is about to write a mission statement for Cape Cod Potato Chips and that you are his advisor. Draft a statement that reflects the company's product and marketing objectives.

2 Which of Stephen Bernard's management skills do you think contribute most to his success? Why?

3 Does it surprise you that Cape Cod, rather than Frito-Lay, developed the batch processing method that makes Cape Cod Chips distinctive? Link your answer to the role small businesses play in creating innovative products. (Visit the Cape Cod, Frito-Lay, and *Entrepreneur* Magazine Web sites for helpful information.)

4 Does it surprise you that Bernard's startup company needed the insurance money from an automobile accident to make ends meet? Support your answer with information you gather from the Online Women's Business Center and SBA Web sites.

5 Would you characterize Stephen Bernard as a small business owner or an entrepreneur? Explain your answer by searching the Web site of *Entrepreneur* Magazine for others with Bernard's characteristics.

6 Analyze Hopnotes.com: Home of Anheuser Busch's Specialty Beers. Why do you think Anheuser-Busch is able to market specialty beers, but not a specialty potato chip?

7 What kind of SBA assistance would have helped Stephen Bernard when he first opened his company? What kind of SBA assistance did he need when he bought back the company? Search the SBA's Web site for information.

8 Although Bernard is operating a small company, he has built a business organization around employees who perform specialized functions. Why is departmentalization crucial to the success of a small company such as Cape Cod?

chapter 5

Managing
the business
enterprise

Delta clips its own wings

In an effort to make Delta Airlines profitable again, its Board of Directors and CEO Ronald Allen may have gone too far. Just as the firm announced record profits and the achievement of its ambitious cost-cutting goals, Delta found itself suddenly leaderless and its employees disillusioned.

What went wrong? In the attempt to save the targeted $2 billion, Delta cut employee benefits such as vacations and health benefits. Though neither severe nor unique, these changes damaged employee morale. Says airline industry analyst Samuel C. Buttrick, "They certainly put a big dent in Delta's corporate culture. . . . Morale fell a lot further than costs did."

Delta also underestimated the speed with which electronic ticketing would catch on, and was one of the last airlines to introduce improved reservation technology. Instead, Delta promoted 4-year research effort that preceded the repainting of its planes. Early cost-saving measures were easy (such as hiring students to process reservations more cheaply, replacing linen napkins on board with paper ones, and cutting the commission paid to travel agents), but Delta continued to prune past the point where the savings outweighed the costs. Customer service suffered when baggage handlers were let go and meals were eliminated from flights. Expensive severance packages offered to senior employees cost the company money and valuable experience.

Lack of flexibility and the unwillingness of the long-tenured board to change Delta's strategy contributed to its short-sightedness. In July 1997, the board declined to renew CEO Allen's contract. But having appointed him to all three of the company's

top posts (chairman, CEO, and president), it had no immediate successor available.

Goals, strategy, and skills were all at work at Delta, but as in every management situation, they alone are not enough. Flexibility, planning, and sensitivity to the cor-

porate culture are vital in steering a firm through the process of change. By focusing on the learning objectives of this chapter, you will better understand the nature of managing, the meaning of corporate culture, and the range of skills managers need if they are to work effectively. After reading this chapter, you should be able to

1 Explain the importance of setting goals and formulating strategies as the starting points of effective management.

2 Describe the four activities that constitute the management process.

3 Identify types of managers by level and area.

4 Describe the five basic management skills.

5 Describe the development and explain the importance of corporate culture.

Although our focus here is on managers in business settings, remember that the principles of management apply to all kinds of organizations. Managers work in charities, churches, social organizations, educational institutions, and governments. The head of the Red Cross, the Prime Minister of Canada, the dean of your college, and the president of the United States are just as much managers as are the CEO of Delta, the manager of your local Wal-Mart store, and the vice president of marketing at IBM. Managers bring to small organizations the same kinds of skills—the ability to make a variety of decisions and to respond to a variety of challenges—as they bring to large organizations.

Regardless of the nature and size of an organization, managers are among its most important resources. For example, consider recent events regarding three of the most visible managers in U.S. business:

▶ After several years of phenomenal growth, Compaq Computer's sales stalled in 1991. The firm's board of directors ousted founder and CEO Rod Canion and replaced him with German-born and -educated Eckhard Pfeiffer. Pfeiffer had gone to work for Texas Instruments (TI) in 1964 and, at the age of 32, eventually became the firm's youngest vice president. Canion had hired Pfeiffer away from TI in 1983 to set up Compaq's European operation. After replacing his mentor in 1991, Pfeiffer quickly changed the firm from a bureaucratic, engineering-oriented operation into a flexible, sales-oriented company. By 1994 Compaq had regained its form and by 1997 had grown to become the largest PC maker in the world (Fig. 5.1).[1]

▶ When she was appointed CEO of Mattel in early 1997, Jill Barad became only the second woman to hold the top spot in a Fortune 500 firm. Barad had joined Mattel as a product manager in 1981. Over the next few years, she developed a reputation as a tough, no-nonsense manager. Her biggest contribution to the firm came when she took over the Barbie product line. Barad immediately began to identify new markets and product extensions, and today Barbie products account for more than 40 percent of Mattel's revenues. Barad was appointed to the firm's board of directors in 1991 and named president in 1992. Now that she's CEO, she plans to continue Mattel's aggressive international expansion, which she sees as the key to future growth.[2]

Figure 5.1   Compaq Performance, 1991–1997

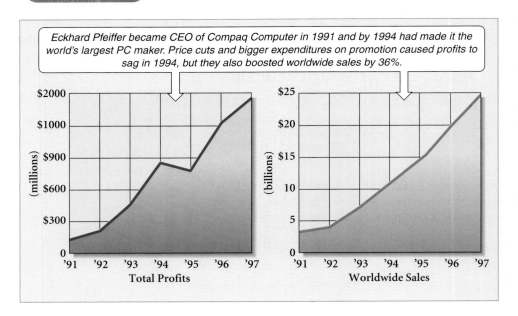

Eckhard Pfeiffer became CEO of Compaq Computer in 1991 and by 1994 had made it the world's largest PC maker. Price cuts and bigger expenditures on promotion caused profits to sag in 1994, but they also boosted worldwide sales by 36%.

Jill Barad joined Mattel as a product manager in 1981. The next year, she took over Barbie—a dormant brand with $238 million in annual sales. Barad reincarnated her as Doctor Barbie, Business Executive Barbie, and a host of other career women. In 1996 sales of Barbie dolls and wardrobes reached $1.7 billion. When Barad became CEO of Mattel in 1997, she became one of only two women chief executives of a Fortune 500 company.

▶ In 1994, Continental Airlines was headed nowhere. The company was saddled with enormous debt, high costs, declining revenues, low employee morale, and one of the poorest images in its industry. That's when Boeing executive Gordon Bethune was brought in to turn things around. Within months, Bethune had revamped the firm's reward system, overhauled its basic operational systems, and figured out dozens of ways to cut costs. As employees started to respond to companywide changes, Continental began to take off. Within a year, the firm was enjoying its highest profits ever, and the carrier was subsequently rated by J. D. Powers as having among the highest levels of customer satisfaction in the industry. Indeed, some experts see the results of Bethune's performance as one of the greatest corporate turnarounds in U.S. business history, especially after Continental became the first airline to win the Powers award two consecutive years.[3]

Clearly, people like Eckhard Pfeiffer, Jill Barad, and Gordon Bethune are considered special in the business world. What do they do that sets them apart so conspicuously? In this chapter we will describe the management process and the skills managers must develop to perform their functions in organizations. You will then have a better feel for why organizations value managers so highly.

Setting Goals and Formulating Strategy

The starting point in effective management is setting **goals**: objectives that a business hopes (and plans) to achieve. Every business needs goals, and we will begin by discussing the basic aspects of organizational goal setting. Remember, however, that deciding what it intends to do is only the first step for an organization: Managers must also make decisions about actions that will and will not achieve company goals. Naturally, those decisions cannot be made on a problem-by-problem basis or merely to meet needs as they arise. At

goal
Objective that a business plans to achieve

most companies, a broad program underlies those decisions. That program is called strategy, and we will complete this section by detailing the basic steps in strategy formulation.

Setting Business Goals

Goals are performance targets: the means by which organizations and their managers measure success or failure at every level. For instance, Compaq Computer was perceived as failing not because it was generating negative balances, but because it was failing to meet goals for profits and growth. In this section we will identify the main purposes for which organizations establish goals, classify the basic levels of business goals, and describe the process by which goals are commonly set.

Purposes of Goal-Setting

An organization functions systematically because it sets goals and plans accordingly. Indeed, an organization functions because it commits its resources on all levels to achieving its goals. Specifically, we can identify four main purposes in organizational goal-setting:

- Goal-setting provides direction and guidance for managers at all levels. If managers know precisely where the company is headed, there is less potential for error in the different units of the company. For example, 3M has a stated goal of earning 20 percent of its profits from sales of products less than 5 years old. 3M managers know that they must emphasize research and development and promote creativity and innovation.

- Goal-setting helps firms allocate resources. Areas that are expected to grow, for example, will get first priority. Thus, 3M allocates more resources to new projects with large sales potential than to mature products with established but stagnant sales potential.

- Goal-setting helps to define corporate culture. General Electric's goal, for instance, is to push each of its divisions to number one or number two in its industry. The result is a competitive, often stressful environment and a culture that rewards success and has little tolerance for failure.[4]

- Goal-setting helps managers assess performance. If a unit sets a goal of increasing sales by 10 percent in a given year, managers in that unit who attain or exceed the goal can be rewarded. Units failing to reach the goal will also be compensated accordingly.

The success of 3M Corp.'s Scotch-Brite Never Rust soap pads is an object lesson in setting goals and allocating resources. "We couldn't hit our growth targets without stepping up new products," explains CEO L. D. DeSimone, who demanded in 1991 that the company move much more quickly to bring new products from prototype to production. As a result, Never Rust (which won't rust or splinter because it's made from recycled plastic bottles) was the fastest product introduction in 3M history: Ground was broken on a brand-new plant in March 1992 and the product was launched by March 1993.

Kinds of Goals

Goals differ from company to company, depending on the firm's purpose and mission. Every enterprise, of course, has a purpose—a reason for being. Businesses seek profits, universities work to discover and transmit new knowledge, and government agencies exist to set and enforce public policy. At the same time, every enterprise also has a mission and a **mission statement**: a statement of how it will achieve its purpose in the environment in which it conducts its business. A company's purpose is usually fairly easy to identify. Reebok, for example, attempts to make a profit by making and selling athletic shoes and related merchandise. Compaq expresses the same purpose in selling computers and computer technology. On the other hand, the demands of change force many companies to rethink their missions, and thus their statements of what they are and what they do. (We will discuss more fully the problems in managing change later in this chapter.)

At many companies, top management draws up and circulates detailed mission statements. Because such a statement reflects a company's understanding of its activities as a marketer, it is not easily described. For example, consider the similarities and differences between Timex and Rolex. Although both firms share a common purpose—to sell watches at a profit—they have very different missions. Timex sells low-cost, reliable watches in outlets ranging from department stores to corner drugstores. Rolex, on the other hand, sells high-quality, high-priced fashion watches through selected jewelry stores.

Regardless of a company's purpose and mission, however, every firm needs long-term, intermediate, and short-term goals:

- **Long-term goals** relate to extended periods of time, typically 5 years or more. American Express, for example, might set a long-term goal of doubling the number of participating merchants during the next 10 years. Similarly, Kodak might adopt a long-term goal of increasing its share of the 35-mm film market by 10 percent during the next 8 years.

- **Intermediate goals** are set for a period of 1 to 5 years. Companies usually have intermediate goals in several areas. For example, the marketing department's goal might be to increase sales by 3 percent in 2 years. The production department might want to decrease expenses by 6 percent in 4 years. Human resources might seek to cut turnover by 10 percent in 2 years. Finance might aim for a 3-percent increase in return on investment in 3 years. In 1996 Compaq Computer announced a goal of becoming one of the three largest computer companies in the world by the year 2000.

- Like intermediate goals, **short-term goals**, which are set for perhaps 1 year, are developed for several different areas. Increasing sales by 2 percent this year, cutting costs by 1 percent next quarter, and reducing turnover by 4 percent over the next 6 months are all short-term goals.

Formulating Strategy

Planning, then, is often concerned with the nuts and bolts of setting goals, choosing tactics, and establishing schedules. Strategy, on the other hand, tends to be a little wider in scope. It is by definition a broad program that describes what an organization intends to do. It also includes the organization's responsiveness to new challenges and new needs. **Strategy formulation** involves three basic steps:[5]

1 Setting strategic goals

2 Analyzing the organization and its environment

3 Matching the organization and its environment

Setting Strategic Goals

Strategic goals are long-term goals derived directly from the firm's mission statement. For example, one of the first things Gordon Bethune did at Continental was to critically assess the firm's deteriorating performance and set new strategic goals for enhancing both quan-

mission statement
Organization's statement of how it will achieve its purpose in the environment in which it conducts its business

long-term goals
Goals set for extended periods of time, typically 5 years or more into the future

intermediate goals
Goals set for a period of 1 to 5 years into the future

short-term goals
Goals set for the very near future, typically less than 1 year

strategy formulation
Creation of a broad program for defining and meeting an organization's goals

strategic goals
Long-term goals derived directly from a firm's mission statement

titative targets (such as on-time performance, seat use, profitability, and growth) and qualitative targets (such as employee morale and firm reputation).

Analyzing the Organization and Its Environment

environmental analysis
Process of scanning the business environment for threats and opportunities

Environmental analysis involves scanning the environment for threats and opportunities. Obviously, changing consumer tastes and hostile takeover offers are threats, as are new government regulations. Even more important threats come from new products and new competitors. At Continental, Gordon Bethune saw significant growth opportunities at the airline's hubs in Houston, Cleveland, and Newark. He also realized that air traffic was increasing, and that Continental's competitors had high labor costs.

organizational analysis
Process of analyzing a firm's strengths and weaknesses

In addition to environmental analysis—that is, analysis of external factors—managers also must examine internal factors. Thus, the purpose of **organizational analysis** is to better understand a company's strengths and weaknesses. Strengths might include surplus cash, a dedicated work force, an ample supply of managerial talent, technical expertise, or little competition. The absence of any of these strengths could be an important weakness. Bethune recognized that Continental had low labor costs and a talented (albeit unmotivated) work force.

Matching the Organization and Its Environment

The final step in strategy formulation is matching environmental threats and opportunities against corporate strengths and weaknesses. The matching process is the heart of strategy formulation: More than any other facet of strategy, matching companies with their environments is fundamental in planning and conducting business.[6] Gordon Bethune began to offer financial incentives to Continental employees tied to improving such quantitative measures as on-time performance. This resulted in improvements in the quantitative measures as well as a boost in employee motivation and commitment to the organization: Employees realized that their hard work would be recognized and rewarded.

Over the long term, this process may also determine whether a firm typically takes risks or behaves more conservatively. Either strategy can be successful. For example, Dial

In addition to a poorly motivated work force, the organization analysis conducted by Gordon Bethune, who became CEO of Continental Airlines Inc. in 1994, revealed that "we had a crappy product and were trying to discount ourselves into profitability." Bethune thus turned his attention to improving operations. Between 1995 and 1996, Continental went from tenth to third in on-time service among the top ten carriers. It went from tenth to second in baggage handling, and customer complaints dropped 60 percent. Since 1996, Continental has remained at or near the top of the industry by all major indicators of performance.

Corp., best known as the maker of such products as Dial soap, Purex detergent, and Armour canned meats, is a conservative company. Rather than spend heavily on research and development or marketing, Dial lets competitors lead the way and then follows with similar, or "me-too," products. In 1991, for example, Dial's Purex brand followed Procter & Gamble's Tide concentrated powder to market by a year, at a one-third lower price. Dial thus remains content to rely on small profit margins and an amalgam of slow-growth businesses. It has also enjoyed 28 consecutive quarters of increased operating income.[7]

A Hierarchy of Plans

Plans can be viewed on three levels: strategic, tactical, and operational. Each level reflects plans for which managers at that level are responsible. These levels constitute a hierarchy because implementing plans is practical only when there is a logical flow from one level to the next.

- **Strategic plans** reflect decisions about resource allocations, company priorities, and the steps needed to meet strategic goals. They are usually set by the board of directors and top management. Procter & Gamble's decision that viable products must be number one or number two within their respective categories is a matter of strategic planning.

- **Tactical plans** are shorter-range plans for implementing specific aspects of the company's strategic plans. They typically involve upper and middle management. Coca-Cola's decision to increase sales in Europe by building European bottling facilities is an example of tactical planning.

- Developed by middle and lower-level managers, **operational plans** set short-term targets for daily, weekly, or monthly performance. For example, McDonald's establishes operational plans when it explains to franchisees precisely how Big Macs are to be cooked, warmed, and served.

strategic plans
Plans reflecting decisions about resource allocations, company priorities, and steps needed to meet strategic goals

tactical plans
Generally short-range plans concerned with implementing specific aspects of a company's strategic plans

operational plans
Plans setting short-term targets for daily, weekly, or monthly performance

Contingency Planning and Crisis Management

In 1994 the Walt Disney Company announced plans to launch a cruise line replete with familiar Disney characters and themes. The first sailing was scheduled for early in 1998, and the company began to book reservations a year in advance. However, the shipyard constructing Disney's first ship notified the company in October 1997 that it was behind schedule and that the ship would be delivered several weeks late. When similar problems befall other cruise lines, they can offer to rebook passengers on alternative itineraries. But because Disney had no other ship, it had no choice but to refund the money it had collected as prebooking deposits for its first 15 cruises. The 20,000 displaced customers were offered big discounts if they rebooked on a later cruise. However, many of them could not rearrange their schedules and requested full refunds. Moreover, quite a few blamed Disney for their problem, and a few expressed outrage at what they saw as poor planning by the entertainment giant.[8]

Because things change, often with little warning, most managers recognize that even the best-laid plans sometimes become impractical. Two common methods of dealing with the unknown and unforeseen are contingency planning and crisis management.

Contingency Planning

Contingency planning recognizes the need to find solutions to specific aspects of a problem. By its very nature, a contingency plan is a hedge against changes that *might* occur. **Contingency planning**, then, is a planning for change: It seeks to identify in advance important aspects of a business or its market that might change. It also identifies the ways in which a company will respond to changes. Today, many companies use computer programs for contingency planning.

For example, suppose that a company develops a plan to create a new division. It expects sales to increase at an annual rate of 10 percent for the next 5 years and develops a

contingency planning
Identifying aspects of a business or its environment that might entail changes in strategy

marketing strategy for maintaining that level. But suppose that sales have increased by only 5 percent by the end of the first year. Does the firm abandon the venture, invest more in advertising, or wait to see what happens in the second year? Any of these alternatives is possible. Regardless of the firm's choice, however, its efforts will be more efficient if managers decide in advance what to do in case sales fall below planned levels. Contingency planning helps them do exactly that.

Crisis Management

crisis management
An organization's methods for dealing with emergencies

A crisis is an unexpected emergency requiring immediate response. **Crisis management** involves an organization's methods for dealing with emergencies. For example, when the oil tanker *Exxon Valdez* spilled millions of gallons of oil off the coast of Alaska in March 1989, Exxon went into a crisis management mode (albeit more slowly than some critics would have liked). Likewise, the October 1989 earthquake that left thousands in the San Francisco area without electricity prompted an emergency response from Pacific Gas & Electric.

A highly publicized case of effective crisis management involved Johnson & Johnson's nonaspirin pain reliever Tylenol. J&J has been widely praised for its response to two incidents in which Tylenol capsules were found to be tainted with cyanide. As soon as the company learned of the poisonings, it removed all Tylenol capsules from grocery and drugstore shelves. J&J management also made itself available to the media and embarked on an education program to inform the public of the steps it had taken to correct the problem. Most experts credit J&J's skilled handling of the crisis with saving an extremely valuable product from extinction.

Designed to help employees cope under extreme or unpredictable circumstances, good crisis plans typically outline who will be in charge in different kinds of situations, how the organization will respond, and so forth. In addition, they usually lay out plans for assembling and deploying crisis management teams. Current estimates suggest that roughly half of the firms in the United States have crisis management plans.

The Management Process

management
Process of planning, organizing, directing, and controlling an organization's resources in order to achieve its goals

Management is the process of planning, organizing, directing, and controlling an organization's financial, physical, human, and information resources to achieve its goals. As managers, Eckhard Pfeiffer, Jill Barad, and Gordon Bethune oversee the use of all these resources. Moreover, all aspects of a manager's job are interrelated. In fact, any given manager is likely to be engaged in each of these activities during the course of any given day.

Planning

planning
Management process of determining what an organization needs to do and how best to get it done

Determining what the organization needs to do and how best to get it done requires **planning**. Generally speaking, planning has three components. As we have seen, it begins when managers determine the firm's goals. Next, they develop a comprehensive strategy for achieving those goals. After a strategy is developed, they design tactical and operational plans for implementing it.

For example, now that Continental has completed its turnaround, Gordon Bethune is turning his attention to new growth opportunities. Consequently, the firm is investing in a major renovation of its terminal in Houston, expanding its international routes into Germany and South America, and actively seeking strategic alliances with other major airlines.

Organizing

organizing
Management process of determining how best to arrange an organization's resources and activities into a coherent structure

The second major function of management is organizing. **Organizing** means determining the best way to arrange a business's resources and activities into a coherent structure. Eckhard Pfeiffer believed that Compaq was too bureaucratic: It had too many rules and regulations and too much paperwork, and decisions were made far too slowly. For example, all

The Natural Environment

Scandic Hotels Turn Green—And Profitable

Pulling one of Europe's largest hotel chains from the edge of failure was no easy task, even for a skilled manager with a string of successful turnarounds to his credit. But Scandic Hotel's new CEO, Roland Nilsson, succeeded by blending the same noteworthy goals he has pursued in Sweden's industries for the last 20 years.

Chief among those goals was establishing a new customer focus, with decentralized management and environmentally responsible corporate values. Nilsson started redirecting the 100-hotel chain toward these goals by transferring all management responsibility to the hotel managers, so that each unit now functions as a separate company. He also built an extensive industry database so managers can benchmark their performance against those of peers and competitors. A third key move was to institute ongoing courses in company culture and values, world cultures, sales and marketing techniques, and management strategy.

But the initiative that made Scandic renowned as one of the world's greenest hotel chains was Nilsson's specifically environmental measures, which now number over 1,500. With the help of an environmental firm called the Natural Step, Scandic has created a 97 percent recyclable hotel room that drastically reduced its reliance on the use of plastic and metal. Already 2,500 of its existing rooms have been converted to the new model, and the plan is to convert the remaining 17,000 rooms at a rate of 1,500 a year.

What are the results of Scandic's new focus on customers and the environment? After posting millions of dollars in losses, the new Scandic is growing at the rate of 30 to 40 percent a year, dominating the mid to upscale market in its region. Revenues and profits are soaring.

of the firm's research and development, manufacturing, and marketing were done in large corporate-level departments. Because they had grown so large, they also had become unwieldy and slow. Pfeiffer broke the company down into several small business groups and gave each one the responsibility for its own R&D, manufacturing, and marketing. This made each one much more flexible and responsive. (We will explore organizing further in chapter 6.)

"I hereby empower you, Ambrose T. Wilkins, to water my plants. And let's hear no more talk about how I never delegate authority."

Directing

directing
Management process of guiding and motivating employees to meet an organization's objectives

By definition, managers have the power to give orders and demand results. **Directing**, however, requires more complex activities: In directing, a manager works to guide and motivate employees to meet the firm's objectives. Shortly after reorganizing Compaq, Eckhard Pfeiffer informed the company's engineers that he wanted them to cut product costs, shorten the lead time required to get new products to market, and boost product quality—all at the same time. He also told them that they could decide how to best meet these expectations. As a result, the engineers accepted his challenge, became energized and focused, and worked hard to show Pfeiffer that they could do it. Not only did they meet his expectations, they actually exceeded them.

Controlling

controlling
Management process of monitoring an organization's performance to ensure that it is meeting its goals

Controlling is the process of monitoring a firm's performance to make sure that it is meeting its goals. Obviously, each of the new CEOs profiled at the outset of this chapter must pay close attention to costs and performance. When a firm is small, monitoring costs is especially important. The same task faces managers at the largest firms. For example, when Jill Barad took over at Mattel, she concluded that profit margins on several of the firm's products were too small. As a result, she challenged her operation managers to figure out exactly how to cut costs on each product. Barad also gave them precise cost reduction targets and deadlines for meeting those targets.

Figure 5.2 illustrates the control process, which begins when management establishes standards, often for financial performance. For example, if a company wants to increase sales by 20 percent over the next 10 years, an appropriate standard might be an increase of 2 percent each year.

Figure 5.2 The Control Process

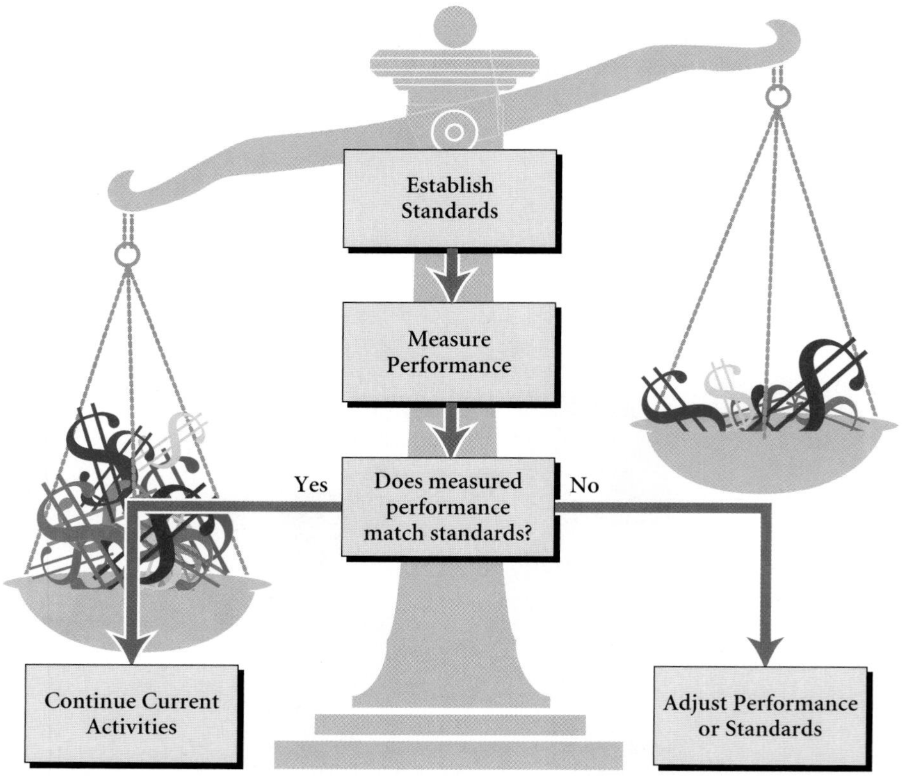

Managers then measure actual performance against standards. If the two figures agree, the organization continues along its present course. If they vary significantly, however, one or the other needs adjustment. For instance, if sales have increased 2.1 percent at the end of the first year, things are probably fine. If sales have dropped 1 percent, some revision in plans may be needed; perhaps the original goal should be lowered or more money should be spent on advertising.

Types of Managers

Although all managers plan, organize, direct, and control, not all managers have the same degree of responsibility for these activities. Thus it is helpful to classify managers according to levels and areas of responsibility.

Levels of Management

The three basic levels of management are top, middle, and first-line. Not surprisingly, most firms have more middle managers than top managers and more first-line managers than middle managers. Both the power of managers and the complexity of their duties increase as they move up the ladder.

Top Managers

Like Eckhard Pfeiffer, Jill Barad, and Gordon Bethune, the fairly small number of executives who guide the fortunes of most companies are **top managers**. Common titles include *president, vice president, treasurer, chief executive officer (CEO)*, and *chief financial officer (CFO)*. Top managers are responsible for the overall performance and effectiveness of the firm. They set general policies, formulate strategies, approve all significant decisions, and represent the company in dealings with other firms and with government bodies.

top managers
Managers responsible to the board of directors and stockholders for a firm's overall performance and effectiveness

Middle Managers

Middle managers occupy positions of considerable autonomy and importance. Titles such as *plant manager, operations manager*, and *division manager* designate middle-management slots. In general, **middle managers** are responsible for implementing the strategies, policies, and decisions made by top managers. For example, if top management decides to bring out a new product in 12 months or to cut costs by 5 percent in the next quarter, middle management must decide how these goals will be met. The managers at a Compaq computer factory, Continental's reservation system, and Mattel's advertising department are all middle managers.

middle managers
Managers responsible for implementing the strategies, policies, and decisions made by top managers

First-Line Managers

First-line managers hold titles such as *supervisor, office manager*, and *group leader*. Although they spend most of their time working with and supervising the employees who report to them, their activities are not limited to that arena. At a building site, for example, the project manager not only ensures that workers are carrying out construction as specified by the architect, but also interacts extensively with material suppliers, community officials, and middle- and upper-level managers at the home office. The flight service manager on a Continental flight is a first-line manager.

first-line managers
Managers responsible for supervising the work of employees

Areas of Management

In any large company, top, middle, and first-line managers work in a variety of areas, including human resources, operations, marketing, information, and finance. For the most part, these areas correspond to the managerial skills described later in this chapter and to the wide range of business principles and activities discussed in the rest of this book.

Human Resource Managers

Most companies have human resource managers to hire and train employees, evaluate performance, and determine compensation. At large firms, separate departments deal with recruiting and hiring, wage and salary levels, and labor relations. A smaller firm may have a single department—even a single person—responsible for all human resource activities. (Some key issues in human resource management are discussed in part three.)

Operation Managers

As we will see in Chapter 15, the term *operations* refers to the systems by which a firm produces goods and services. Among other duties, operation managers are responsible for production, inventory, and quality control. Manufacturing companies such as Texas Instruments, Ford, and Caterpillar have a strong need for operation managers at many levels. Such firms typically have a vice president for operations (top), plant managers (middle), and production supervisors (first-line). In recent years, sound operation management practices have become increasingly important to a variety of service organizations. (Operation management is examined more fully in part five.)

Marketing Managers

As we will see in chapter 11, marketing encompasses the development, pricing, promotion, and distribution of goods and services. Marketing managers are responsible for getting products from producers to consumers. Marketing is especially important for firms dealing in consumer products, such as Procter & Gamble, Coca-Cola, and Levi Strauss. Such firms often have large numbers of marketing managers at several levels. For example, a large consumer products firm is likely to have a vice president for marketing (top), several regional marketing managers (middle), and several district sales managers (first-line). (We will discuss the different areas of marketing in part four.)

Information Managers

Occupying a fairly new managerial position in many firms, information managers design and implement systems to gather, organize, and distribute information. Dramatic increases in both the amount of available information and the ability to manage it have led to the emergence of this important function.

Although there are few now, the ranks of information managers are growing at all levels. Some firms, such as Firestone and Federal Express, have a top management position called a chief information officer. Middle managers help design information systems for divisions or plants. Computer system managers within smaller businesses are usually first-line managers. (Information management is discussed in more detail in chapter 17.)

Financial Managers

Nearly every company has financial managers to plan and oversee its accounting functions and financial resources. Levels of financial management may include a vice president for finance (top), a division controller (middle), and an accounting supervisor (first-line). Some institutions—NationsBank and Prudential, for example—have made effective financial management the company's reason for being. (Financial management is treated in more detail in part six.)

Other Managers

Some firms also employ other specialized managers. For example, many companies have public relations managers. Chemical and pharmaceutical companies such as Monsanto and Merck have research and development managers. The range of possibilities is very broad, and the areas of management are limited only by the needs and imagination of the firm.

Basic Management Skills

Although the range of managerial positions is almost limitless, the success people enjoy in those positions is often limited by their skills and abilities. Effective managers must develop technical, human relations, conceptual, decision-making, and time management skills.

Technical Skills

The skills needed to perform specialized tasks are called **technical skills**. A secretary's ability to type, an animator's ability to draw, and an accountant's ability to audit a company's records are all technical skills. People develop technical skills through a combination of education and experience. Technical skills are especially important for first-line managers. Most of them spend considerable time helping employees solve work-related problems, training them in more efficient procedures, and monitoring performance. Gordon Bethune acquired his technical skills by first serving as a pilot in the U.S. Navy and then working for Boeing in its aircraft design division.

technical skills
Skills needed to perform specialized tasks

Human Relations Skills

A few years ago, Hyatt Hotels checked 379 corporate employees into the chain's 98 hotels. They were not treated as guests; rather, they were asked to make beds, carry luggage, and perform the other tasks necessary to make a big hotel function. Top management at Hyatt believes that learning more about the work of lower-level employees will allow executives to understand them better as human beings (and co-workers).

The Hyatt experiment was designed to test and improve the **human relations skills** of upper-level managers—that is, skills in understanding and getting along with other people. A manager with poor human relations skills may experience conflict with subordinates, cause valuable employees to quit or transfer, and contribute to poor morale.

Human relations skills are important at all levels, but they may be most important for middle managers, who must often act as bridges between top managers, first-line managers, and managers from other areas of the organization. Among their human relations skills, managers should possess good communication skills. Many managers have found that being able to understand others—and to get them to understand in return—can go far toward maintaining good relations in an organization.

human relations skills
Skills in understanding and getting along with other people

Conceptual Skills

Conceptual skills refer to a person's ability to think in the abstract, to diagnose and analyze different situations, and to see beyond the present situation. Conceptual skills help individuals recognize new market opportunities and threats. They can also help managers analyze the probable outcomes of their decisions. Naturally, the need for conceptual skills differs at various management levels: Top managers depend the most on conceptual skills, first-line managers the least. Although the purposes and everyday needs of various jobs are different, conceptual skills are rarely irrelevant to any job-related activity.

conceptual skills
Abilities to think in the abstract, diagnose and analyze different situations, and see beyond the present situation

Decision-Making Skills

Decision-making skills include the ability to define problems and to select the best course of action. Figure 5.3 illustrates the basic steps in decision making.

decision-making skills
Skills in defining problems and selecting the best courses of action

1 Define the problem, gather facts, and identify alternative solutions. For example, a new management team at Schwinn recently realized that their predecessors had made some serious errors, including assuming that mountain bikes were just a fad. The opposite proved to be true, and Schwinn's share of the bicycle market had dropped significantly.

2 Evaluate each alternative and select the best one. Managers at Schwinn acknowledged that they had to take corrective action. They discussed such options as buying an existing mountain bike producer, launching their own line of mountain bikes, or refocusing their existing product line to appeal more to mountain bikers. After considerable discussion, they decided to develop their own line of mountain bikes.

Figure 5.3 The Decision-Making Process

3 Implement the chosen alternative, periodically following up and evaluating the effectiveness of that choice. Today Schwinn appears to be back on track. Sales and profits have increased steadily in recent times and the firm's new products are gaining the attention and acceptance of top mountain bike racers.

Time Management Skills

time management skills
Skills associated with the productive use of time

Time management skills refer to the productive use that managers make of their time. In one recent year, for example, Compaq Computer CEO Eckhard Pfeiffer was paid $4,250,000 in salary and bonus.[9] Assuming that he worked 50 hours a week and took 2 weeks of vacation, Pfeiffer earned $1,700 an hour—about $28 per minute. Any time he might have wasted clearly represents a major cost to Compaq and its shareholders. Of course, most managers receive much smaller salaries than Pfeiffer. However, their time is still quite valuable, and poor use of it still translates into costs and wasted productivity.

To manage time effectively, managers must address four leading causes of wasted time:

■ *Paperwork*. Some managers spend too much time deciding what to do with letters and reports. In fact, most documents of this sort are routine and can be handled quickly. Of course, managers must learn to recognize documents that do require more attention.

■ *E-mail*. Electronic mail has become an important method of communication for managers in recent years. Some estimates place the number of e-mails the average manager receives each day between 170 and 180. Although this mode of communication can improve efficiency, it can also contribute to wasted time and effort.

■ *Phone calls*. Experts estimate that managers are interrupted by the telephone every 5 minutes. To manage this time more effectively, they suggest having a secretary screen all calls and set aside a certain block of time each day to return the important ones.

■ *Meetings*. Many managers spend as much as 4 hours a day in meetings. To help keep this time productive, the person handling the meeting should specify a clear agenda, start on time, keep everyone focused on the agenda, and end on time.[10]

Management Skills for the 1990s

Tomorrow's managers face major challenges as they prepare for the twenty-first century. Obviously, many changes and challenges could be identified. Here, however, we will touch upon just two of the most significant: global management and technology.

Global Management

Clearly, tomorrow's managers must equip themselves with the special tools, techniques, and skills necessary to compete in a global environment. They will need to develop insights into foreign markets, cultural differences, and the motives and practices of foreign rivals.

On a more practical level, businesses will need more managers who are capable of understanding international operations. In the past, most U.S. businesses hired local managers to run their operations in the various countries where they set up shop. More recently, however, a trend has emerged to transfer U.S. managers to foreign locations. For one thing, this practice helps firms better transfer their corporate cultures to foreign operations. In addition, foreign assignments help managers become better prepared for international competition as they advance in the organization. For example, General Motors now has over 500 U.S. managers in foreign posts.

Management and Technology

Another significant issue facing tomorrow's managers is technology, especially as it relates to communication. Of course, managers have always had to deal with information. In today's world, however, the amount of available information has reached staggering proportions. In the United States alone there are an estimated 150 million electronic mailboxes. New forms of technology have added to a manager's ability to process information while simultaneously making it even more important that he or she organize and apply an ever-increasing wealth of input.

Technology has also begun to change the way in which the interaction of managers shapes corporate structures. Computer networking, for example, exists because it is no longer too expensive to put a computer on virtually every desk in the company. In turn, this elaborate network controls the flow of the firm's lifeblood: information. It no longer flows strictly up and down through hierarchies: It flows to everybody at once. As a result, decisions are made more quickly, and more people are directly involved. With e-mail, teleconferencing, and other forms of communication, neither time nor distance—nor such corporate boundaries as departments and divisions—can prevent people from working more closely together. More than ever, bureaucracies are breaking down; planning, decision-making, and other activities are beginning to benefit from group-building and teamwork.

> ❝*E-mail is a major cultural event—it changes the way you run the organization.*❞
>
> —Bill Raduchel, chief information officer of Sun Microsystems

This is why Bill Raduchel, chief information officer of Sun Microsystems, goes so far as to say that "E-mail is a major cultural event—it changes the way you run the organization."[11]

Management and the Corporate Culture

Another important part of managing an organization is creating and maintaining an appropriate and viable corporate culture. Just as every individual has a unique personality each company has a unique identity, or **corporate culture**: the shared experiences, stories, beliefs, and norms that characterize an organization.[12]

Consider the case of Hyperion Software Corporation. Employees in the ultracompetitive software industry often enjoy working long hours on flexible schedules. They also enjoy a casual lifestyle that allows them to intermingle their work and private lives, and often are motivated by their actual work rather than their salaries. In order to attract and

corporate culture
The shared experiences, stories, beliefs, and norms that characterize an organization

The success of Hyperion Software Corp. depends on its ability to create new lines of financial management software. To do this, it must attract the best software designers to its Fairfield County, Connecticut, headquarters, which is a long way from such desirable locations as Boston and Silicon Valley. For Hyperion, the solution to this problem has been providing the right atmosphere in a relaxed workplace. "We don't care how you look or dress," says CFO Lucy Ricciardi. "We're looking for people who are geniuses at writing software."

retain qualified people, Hyperion has created a unique workplace at its Stamford, Connecticut, headquarters. Each wing of the building has its own kitchen stocked with snacks and drinks. There is also a gym on the premises and a meandering nature trail through the firm's 38-acre campuslike setting. And there's even a pool table outside the cafeteria open to everyone.[13] This contrasts markedly with the corporate culture at large, old-line firms such as Exxon. Employees there still dress very formally, work a rigid 8-to-5 schedule, and follow established chains of command and rules of order.

A strong corporate culture serves several purposes:

■ It directs employees' efforts and helps everyone work toward the same goals.

■ It helps newcomers learn accepted behaviors.

■ Its gives each organization its own identity, just as personalities give identity to people.

Communicating the Culture and Managing Change

Clearly, corporate culture influences management philosophy, style, and behavior. Managers must carefully consider the kind of culture they want for their organization. Then they must work to nourish it by communicating it to everyone who works there. Wal-Mart, for example, is acutely conscious of the need to spread the message of its culture as it opens new stores in new areas. One of the company's methods is regularly assigning veteran managers to lead employees in new territories.[14]

Communicating the Culture

To use its culture to a firm's advantage, managers must accomplish several tasks, all of which hinge on effective communication:

■ Managers themselves must have a clear understanding of the culture.

■ Managers must transmit the culture to others in the organization. Communication is thus one of the aims in training and orienting newcomers. A clear and meaningful statement of the organization's mission is also a valuable communication tool.

■ Managers can maintain the culture by rewarding and promoting those who understand it and who work toward maintaining it.

Dilbert Goes Establishment

Once merely a hapless office worker who won the hearts of underlings everywhere, cartoon character Dilbert has leaped into the hallowed halls of corporate America. A master of deadpan irony, the lowly champion of the office underdog has gone from almost a cult figure with his own Web site (www.unitedmedia.com) to a fixture in corporate culture, handing down management messages about ethics, quality, and problem solving.

A Boston corporate communication consultant bought the rights to use Dilbert's image in both existing comic strips and new scenarios. Since then, the straight-shooting cubicle hero has gone to work for Xerox, Lockheed Martin, and Honda. His résumé as a corporate consultant includes hitches at small hi-tech firms and at offices of the Fortune 500.

Dilbert's creator, Scott Adams, has had plenty of corporate experience of his own: Until 1995, long after his comic strip became a hit, he was a full-time manager at Pacific Bell. Among the insights he gained was his belief that corporate culture is more evident in the little things, such as letting an employee extend a business trip over a weekend, than in profound messages and high-flown mottoes.

> *If . . . the people I'm lampooning give me money, and I continue lampooning them, that to me is a bit like performance art.*
>
> —Scott Adams, creator of Dilbert

Has Dilbert's creator sold out? "I'm always attracted to irony," Adams says. "And if in fact the people I'm lampooning give me money, and I continue lampooning them, that to me is a bit like performance art."

Managing Change

Not surprisingly, organizations must sometimes change their cultures. In such cases, of course, they must also communicate the nature of the change to employees and customers. According to the CEOs of several companies that have undergone radical change in the last decade or so, the process usually goes through three stages:

1 At the highest level, analysis of the company's environment highlights extensive change as the most effective response to its problems. This period is typically characterized by conflict and resistance.

2 Leaders, and then employees, begin to formulate a shared vision of a new company. Whatever that vision, it must include renewed focus on the activities of competitors and the needs of customers.

3 The firm sets up new systems for appraising and compensating employees who enforce its new values. The purpose is to give the new culture solid shape from within.

Summary of Learning Objectives

1 **Explain the importance of setting goals and formulating strategies as the starting points of effective management.** Goals—the performance targets of an organization—can be long term, intermediate, or short term. They provide direction for managers, help managers decide how to allocate limited resources, define the corporate culture, and help managers assess performance. Strategies—the methods a company uses to meet its stated goals—involve three major activities: setting strategic goals, analyzing the organization and its environment, and matching the organization and its environment. These strategies are translated into strategic, tactical, and operational plans. To deal with crises or major environmental changes, companies develop contingency plans and plans for crisis management.

2 **Describe the four activities that constitute the management process.** Management is the process of planning, organizing, directing, and controlling an organization's financial, physical, human, and information resources to achieve the organization's goals. Planning means determining what the company needs to do and how best to get it done. Organizing means determining how best to arrange a business's resources and the necessary jobs into an overall structure. Directing means guiding and motivating employees to meet the firm's objectives. Controlling means monitoring the firm's performance to ensure that it is meeting its goals.

3 **Identify types of managers by level and area.** Managers can be differentiated in two ways: by level and by area. By level, top managers set policies, formulate strategies, and approve decisions. Middle managers implement strategies, policies, and decisions. First-line managers usually work with and directly supervise employees. Areas of management include human resources, operations, marketing, information, and finance. Managers at all levels may be found in every area of a company.

4 **Describe the five basic management skills.** Most managers agree that five basic management skills are necessary for success. Technical skills are associated with performing specialized tasks ranging from typing to auditing. Human relations skills are associated with understanding and getting along with other people. Conceptual skills are the abilities to think in the abstract, diagnose and analyze different situations, and see beyond present circumstances. Decision-making skills allow managers to define problems and to select the best course of action. Time management skills refer to the productive use managers make of their time.

5 **Describe the development and explain the importance of corporate culture.** A strong, well-defined culture can help a business reach its goals and can influence management styles. Corporate culture is determined by several factors, including the values of top management, the organization's history, stories and legends, and shared experiences. If carefully communicated and flexible enough to accommodate change, corporate culture can be managed for the betterment of the organization.

Questions and Exercises

Questions for Review

1 What are the four main purposes of setting goals in an organization?
2 Identify and explain the three basic steps in strategy formulation.
3 Relate the five basic management skills to the four activities in the management process. For example, which skills are most important in leading?
4 What is corporate culture? How is it formed? How is it sustained?

Questions for Analysis

5 Select any group of which you are a member: your company, your family, or a club or organization, for example. Explain how planning, organizing, directing, and controlling are practiced in that group.

6 Identify managers by level and area at your school, college, or university.

7 In what kind of company would the technical skills of top managers be more important than human relations or conceptual skills? Are there organizations in which conceptual skills are not important?

8 How well do you manage your own time? What activities or habits waste your time?

Application Exercises

9 Interview the manager at any level of a local company. Identify that manager's job according to level and area. Show how planning, organizing, directing, and controlling are part of this person's job. Inquire about the manager's education and work experience. Which management skills are most important for this manager's job?

10 Compare the corporate cultures of two businesses in your community. Be sure to choose two companies in the same industry (for example, a Sears department store and a Wal-Mart discount store).

Building Your Business Skills

This exercise enhances the following SCANS workplace competencies: demonstrating basic skills, demonstrating thinking skills, exhibiting interpersonal skills, and working with information.

Goal To encourage students to use management skills to make important business decisions.

Situation With 5 years of experience working in the corporate offices of one of the country's largest booksellers, you have just been assigned to be part of the team to develop a new chain of specialty bookstores. The idea behind the chain is that people want smaller bookstores that emphasize customer service, amenities, and product knowledge. They are tired of stores the size of supermarkets and clerks who know little about the books they sell. Your job is to work with team members to make key management decisions.

Method **Step 1:** Working with four or five classmates, do library research on the bookselling business and particularly on the strengths and weaknesses of independent bookstores. Use what you learn to focus on the following factors. Brainstorm with team members to analyze the following issues:

- *The best markets for these stores.* Would specialized bookstores be likely to succeed in university towns, large cities, suburbs, or other areas?
- *The customer base.* Define your market in terms of socioeconomic status and educational level.
- *The best competitive environment.* Should you target locations that already have mega-booksellers or sites without them?

Step 2: Begin to define the business venture through the following management steps:

- Write a mission statement that defines your business purpose and strategy for achieving it.
- Define long-term and short-term goals by determining the markets you want to enter, the number of stores you want to open during the first year

and within 5 years, the kind of books you want to stock, the ambiance and size of each store, and employees characteristics.

- Define how to differentiate your stores from the competition. For example, will you have a children's corner with a daily storytelling hour? Will you highlight prize-winning community interest books? Will you have a book-ordering service that guarantees that customers receive requested books within 72 hours? Will your choose employees who are dedicated to customer service?

Follow-Up Questions

1 Why is an environmental analysis particularly important to the success of your venture?

2 Mega-booksellers are now on-line, including Amazon.com and Barnes & Noble. How is online commerce likely to affect your business?

3 Considering the competitive environment, do you think your venture will succeed? Why or why not?

4 Of all the management decisions you make, which do you consider the most important to the success of the business?

5 If the venture succeeds, what do you think the corporate culture will be like in 5 years?

Business Case 5

The Glass Ceiling: Scratched but Unbroken

The last 10 years have seen an enormous influx of women into the work force (60 percent of all women in the United States now work outside the home). Their arrival has transformed many aspects of society, from wage structures to education, day care, and corporate culture.

But one area where most observers agree the change is slight is in the ranks of upper management, which remain largely male (and mostly white). Below them is the so-called glass ceiling through which women who aspire to top management roles can look but not pass. Some firms have undertaken specific diversity measures aimed at giving women the training and opportunity to advance. For example, Avon Products gives its managers awards for promoting women. "Women are in the pipeline in droves," says Avon's CEO Jim Preston. Colgate-Palmolive mandates 2 days of diversity training for all employees and cross-trains women it believes have management potential. Coopers & Lybrand has set a goal that by the year 2000, 30 percent of its new partners will be women. Mentoring programs that team women with older and more experienced executives and bonuses tied to diversity goals are just two of its strategies.

Dow Chemical and Hoechst Celanese have promoting goals. Dow wants to promote as many women as men; Hoechst wants hires and promotions to match the demographics of its college recruiting pool. Motorola researched census data to set its diversity goals and asks its managers to identify specific women and minorities for career development and possible succession to top posts. Motorola vice president Robert Gutman says, "We see the handwriting on the wall, and we have to get ready."

Although some of these firms boast impressive results, with women holding more (and more senior) management positions, according to some research the overall picture shows women in only 10 percent of top jobs at the country's top 500 firms. The higher up the management hierarchy, the fewer women. Some firms, such as Walt Disney, Whirlpool and Exxon, have no women corporate officers at all. Some managers apparently fear a backlash from white male managers who will resent the opportunities and training offered to women. And some women appear to have simply given up, abandoning corporate careers to work at smaller firms, to work for themselves, or to raise families. For the moment, the glass ceiling appears to be scratched but intact.

Questions

1 Which strategies—quotas, bonuses, mentoring, succession planning—do you think offer the greatest promise for companies seeking to diversify their top management ranks? Which best meets the needs of women? Minorities?

2 What difficulties might firms face in instituting one or more of these strategies? How might they be overcome?

3 How can companies prevent or deal with a possible backlash against the promotion of women and minorities?

4 Do you think it is appropriate for firms to ask top management specifically to identify women among the candidates for all management jobs, as Motorola does? Defend your answer, then prepare a counterargument.

Connecting to the Web

The following Web sites will give you additional information and points of view about topics covered in this chapter. Many sites lead to other related Internet locations, so approach this list with the spirit of an explorer.

AMERICAN MANAGEMENT ASSOCIATION INTERNATIONAL

http://www.amanet.org/

As the world's leading membership-based management development and training organization, the American Management Association offers a variety of goods and services via the Internet. Among these are seminars, books, courses, a newsletter, and conferences.

BARBIE SOFTWARE FOR GIRLS

http://www.mattelmedia.com/barbie/index.html

Click on this Web site for a look at Barbie CD-ROMs, another extension of the Barbie line, which has grown dramatically under the management of Mattel CEO Jill Barad. Here you'll find such Barbie CD-ROMs as *Ocean Discovery, Fashion Designer*, and *Storymaker.*

COMPAQ ONLINE: CAREER OPPORTUNITIES

http://compaq.monster.com/pf/search/USsearch.htm

Click on this Web page to learn about managerial jobs at Compaq. On a recent visit to the listing of administrative jobs, we found opportunities for a manager of business planning, a manager of training and professional development, and a finance manager.

CONTINENTAL AIRLINES: A MESSAGE FROM GORDON BETHUNE

http://www.flycontinental.com/corporate/ceomessage.html

The message from Continental chairperson and CEO Gordon Bethune reveals some key management decisions that will affect the airline's future. The site will also link you to a company profile and information on alliance partners.

DELTA SKYLINKS RESERVATION DESK

http://www.delta-air.com/res/

Although Delta came late to electronic ticketing (see the chapter's opening story), this technology is now an important part of the airline's reservation system. Visit this site for a look at what this system is and how it works.

THE DILBERT ZONE

http://www.unitedmedia.com/comics/dilbert/

The Dilbert comic strips you will find on this site provide a different look at work in America.

INSIDE MOTOROLA

http://www.mot.com/General/inside.html

Search this Web site for a look at management in action at Motorola. Included are descriptions of Motorola's seven business units and the corporate leadership development program. This program trains employees from Latin America, Europe, the Middle East, Africa, Asia, and the Pacific in key management areas.

THE TIDE CLOTHESLINE

http://www.tide.com/

Procter & Gamble's strategic goal to market products that are at the top of the product category is reflected in the Web page P&G constructed for market leader Tide.

WELCOME TO THE SCHWINN ADULT BIKE CATALOG

http://www.schwinn.com/catalog_index.html

Schwinn's online catalog for adults reflects management's decision to focus on the sale of mountain bikes.

YANKELOVICH PARTNERS

http://www.yankelovich.com/

Yankelovich Partners, one of the world's premier marketing research and consulting organizations, list jobs for marketing and other managers in its Norwalk, Connecticut, headquarters and five satellite offices.

chapter 6

Organizing
the business
enterprise

Firms find strength in related diversification

Once upon a time the term *conglomerate* meant a company consisting of a grab-bag of businesses, loosely organized under a single top manager and board of directors. Purchased for their profit potential, these businesses might have little or no relation to each other. In the 1970s, for instance, Textron was manufacturing everything from weapons to office supplies. The guiding principle for conglomerate acquisitions seemed to be to get into any business as long as it was profitable.

Today, however, a new strategy prevails. Conglomerates have streamlined themselves, shedding unrelated businesses and focusing on a few core markets within which they aim to be leaders. It is as if they are expanding by deepening, not broadening,

their reach. Textron, for instance, has eliminated its insurance, consumer products, and military contracting companies. It now concentrates on the manufacture of aircraft, automotive parts, and industrial products and equipment and on consumer and commercial finance. Within these areas Textron can still diversify, thus retaining one of the most notable advantages of the old-style conglomerate. After all, as Lawrence Bossidy, chairperson of Allied Signal, another conglomerate, asks, "Why give up a nice spread of risk to become dependent on just one market?"

Other conglomerate firms that have successfully refined their focus include GE, W.R. Grace, Rockwell International, Corning, ITT, and Westinghouse Electric. Their management would probably agree with Allied Signal's Bossidy, who said, "We had too many businesses before. Now, I can get involved in all the management reviews, and I can keep a clear focus on where we want to be, not just where we are."

Corning Incorporated, maker of this liquid crystal display, is one of many conglomerate firms to refine its business focus recently.

Conglomerates may represent an extreme answer to the question of how a company should organize itself. But as one analyst says, "Being No. 1 in every market is a great organizing theme, and if you can stick to that strategy you can be as diverse as you want."

> **Why give up a nice spread of risk to become dependent on just one market?**
>
> —Lawrence Bossidy, chairperson of Allied Signal

By focusing on the learning objectives of this chapter, you will better understand the importance of business organization and the ways in which both formal and informal aspects of its structure affect the decisions that a business makes. After reading this chapter, you should be able to

1 Discuss the elements that influence a firm's organizational structure.

2 Describe specialization and departmentalization as the building blocks of organizational structure.

3 Distinguish between responsibility and authority, delegation and accountability, and explain the differences in decision making in centralized and decentralized organizations.

4 Explain the differences among functional, divisional, matrix, and international organization structures.

5 Describe the informal organization and discuss intrapreneuring.

What Is Organizational Structure?

What do we mean by the term *organizational structure*? Consider a simple analogy. In some ways, a business is like an automobile. All cars have engines, four wheels, fenders, and other structural components. They all have passenger compartments, storage areas, and various operating systems (fuel, braking, climate control). Although each component has a distinct purpose, it must also work in accord with the others. In addition, although the ways they look and fit may vary widely, even automobiles made by competing firms have the same basic components. Similarly, all businesses have common structural and operating components, each composed of a series of jobs to be done and each with a specific overall purpose. From company to company, these components look different and fit together differently. Nevertheless, in every organization components have the same fundamental purpose: Each must perform its own function while working in concert with the others.

In other words, although all organizations feature the same basic elements, each must develop its own most appropriate structure. What works for Texas Instruments will not work for Exxon or the U.S. Department of Justice. The structure of the American Red Cross will probably not work for Union Carbide or the University of Minnesota. We will define **organizational structure** as the specification of the jobs to be done within an organization and the ways in which those jobs relate to one another.

Determinants of Organization

How is an organization's structure determined? Does it just happen by chance, or is there some logic that managers use to create structure? Does it develop by some combination of circumstance and strategy? The ideal answer is that managers carefully assess a variety of important factors as they plan for and then create a structure that will allow their organization to function efficiently.

Indeed, many elements work together to determine an organization's structure. Chief among these are the organization's purpose, mission, and strategy. A dynamic and rapidly growing enterprise achieved that position because of its purpose and successful strategies for achieving it. Such a firm needs a structure that contributes to flexibility and growth. Meanwhile, a stable organization with only modest growth will naturally function best with a different structure.

Size, technology, and changes in environmental circumstances also affect structure. A large manufacturer operating in a strongly competitive environment—say, Boeing or Hewlett-Packard—requires a far different structure from a local barbershop or video store. Moreover, even after a structure has been created, it is rarely free from tinkering, or even outright re-creation. Indeed, most organizations change their structures on an almost continuing basis.

Compaq Computer, for example, has changed its structure several times in the last few years. A combination of the firm's phenomenal growth rate in its core business, its diversification into related businesses, and the acquisition of Tandem Computers has caused the firm to outgrow its structure repeatedly. As a result, new divisions are created, moved, and eliminated almost constantly.

Chain of Command

Most businesses prepare **organization charts** to clarify structure and to show employees where they fit into a firm's operations. Figure 6.1 is an organization chart for Contemporary Landscape Services Inc., a small but thriving business in Bryan, Texas. Each box in the chart represents a job. The solid lines define the **chain of command** or reporting relationships within the company. For example, the retail shop, nursery, and landscape operation managers all report to the owner and president, Mark Ferguson. Within the landscape op-

organizational structure
Specification of the jobs to be done within an organization and the ways in which they relate to one another

organization chart
Diagram depicting a company's structure and showing employees where they fit into its operations

chain of command
Reporting relationships within a company

Figure 6.1 The Organization Chart: Contemporary Landscape Services Inc.

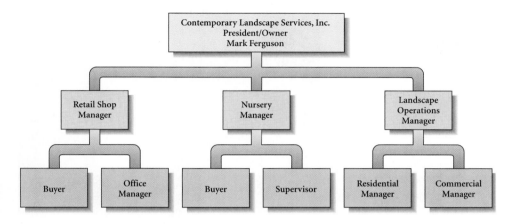

eration is one manager for residential accounts and another for commercial accounts. Similarly, there are other managers in the retail shop and the nursery.

The organization charts of large firms are far more complex and include individuals at many more levels than those shown in Figure 6.1. Indeed, size prevents many large firms from drawing charts that include all their managers. Typically, they create one organization chart showing overall corporate structure and separate charts for each division.

The Building Blocks of Organizational Structure

The first step in developing the structure of any business, large or small, involves two activities:

■ Specialization: determining who will do what

■ Departmentalization: determining how people performing certain tasks can best be grouped together

These two activities are the basic building blocks of all business organizations.[1]

Specialization

The process of identifying the specific jobs that need to be done and designating the people who will perform them leads to **job specialization**. In a sense, all organizations have only one major job, such as making computers (like Compaq), selling finished goods to consumers (like Wal-Mart), or providing transportation services (like Continental Airlines). Usually, of course, the job is more complex. For example, consider the job of Continental Airlines. Managers have taken this overall job and broken it down into smaller, more specialized jobs. Consequently, some employees schedule flights, some maintain airplanes, some sell tickets, some collect tickets at airports, some fly airplanes, some load and unload luggage, and still others attend to passenger needs, safety, and comfort during flights. When the overall job can be broken down in this fashion, the firm can hire people with specialized skills to perform each individual job, those people can be further trained to improve their proficiency even more, and employees can better coordinate their work with the work done by others. Specialization also tends to be a natural byproduct of organizational growth.

For example, in a very small organization, the owner may perform every job. As the firm grows, however, so does the need to specialize jobs so that others can perform them.

job specialization
The process of identifying the specific jobs that need to be done and designating the people who will perform them

Whether they are produced manually or digitally, the drawings that make up a full-length Walt Disney cartoon are the result of highly coordinated job specialization. A lead animator, for example, may provide a rough pencil sketch that is then refined by one or more artists. Other teams scan clean drawings into a computer and color them according to a plan devised by the art director. Finally, to achieve hand-drawn movement, a team of so-called in-betweeners completes all the drawings needed to give fluid motion to one or two key frames drawn by the lead animator.

To see how specialization can evolve in an organization, consider the case of Walt Disney and the company he founded in 1923. In those early years he and his brother, Roy, did everything. For example, as they created the first animated feature, *Steamboat Willy*, Walt and Roy developed the story, drew the images, transferred these images to film, provided the voices for the characters, printed the advertising posters, and then went out and sold the film to movie theaters. But as the business grew Walt had to turn over various tasks to others as he found it necessary to devote more time to business issues. By the time the first full-length animated movie, *Snow White*, was made Walt had stopped animating altogether. And in the Disney Studio today, a single animator may specialize solely in drawing the face of a single character throughout an entire feature. Another job is to concentrate solely on erasing stray pencil marks in finished drawings. Yet another job might be to apply shades of a single color throughout the animated feature, with other animators adding different colors.

Job specialization, then, is a natural part of organizational growth. Obviously, it has certain advantages. For example, specialized jobs are learned more easily and can be performed more efficiently than nonspecialized jobs, and it is also easier to replace people who leave an organization. On the other hand, jobs at lower levels of the organization are especially susceptible to overspecialization. If such jobs become too narrowly defined, employees may become bored and careless, derive less satisfaction from their jobs, and lose sight of their roles in the organization.

Departmentalization

After jobs are specialized, they must be grouped into logical units. This process is called **departmentalization**. Departmentalized companies benefit from the division of activities. Control and coordination are clearer, and top managers can see more easily how various units are performing.

For example, departmentalization allows the firm to treat a department as a **profit center**: a separate unit responsible for its own costs and profits. For example, Sears can calculate the profits it generates from men's clothing, appliances, home furnishings, and every other department within a given store. Managers can then use this information in making decisions about advertising and promotional events, space allocation, and so forth.

departmentalization
Process of grouping jobs into logical units

profit center
Separate company unit responsible for its own costs and profits

Of course, managers do not just group jobs randomly. Rather, they group them logically, according to some common thread or purpose. In general, departmentalization may occur along customer, product, process, geographic, or functional lines (or any combination of these).

Customer Departmentalization

Stores such as Sears and Macy's are divided into departments: a men's department, a women's department, a luggage department, and so on. Each department targets a specific customer category (men, women, people who want to buy luggage). Thus, the customer provides the logic for grouping jobs. **Customer departmentalization** makes shopping easier by providing identifiable store segments. Thus, a customer shopping for a baby's playpen can bypass lawn and garden supplies and head straight for children's furniture. Stores can also group products in locations designated for deliveries, special sales, and other service-oriented purposes. In general, the store is more efficient and customers get better service.

customer departmentalization Departmentalization according to types of customers likely to buy a given product

Product Departmentalization

Manufacturers often opt for **product departmentalization**, dividing an organization according to the specific product or service being created. A bank, for example, may handle consumer loans in one department and commercial loans in another. On a larger scale, 3M Corp., which makes both consumer and industrial products, operates different divisions for Post-it tape flags, Scotch-Brite scrub sponges, and the Sarns 9000 perfusion system for open-heart surgery.

product departmentalization Departmentalization according to specific products being created

Process Departmentalization

Other manufacturers favor **process departmentalization**, in which the organization is divided according to production processes. This principle is logical for the pickle maker Vlasic, which has separate departments to transform cucumbers into fresh-packed pickles, pickles cured in brine, and relishes. Cucumbers destined to become fresh-packed pickles must be packed into jars immediately, covered with a solution of water and vinegar, and prepared for sale. Those slated for brined pickles must be aged in brine solution before packing. Relish cucumbers must be minced and combined with a host of other ingredients. Each process requires different equipment and worker skills.

process departmentalization Departmentalization according to production process used to create a good or service

Geographic Departmentalization

Some firms are divided according to the areas of the country—or even the world—that they serve. Levi Strauss, for instance, has one division for the United States, one for European markets, and another for the rest of the world. In the United States itself, **geographic departmentalization** is common among utilities. Thus, Pacific Power and Light is organized as four geographic departments: Southwestern, Columbia Basin, Mid-Oregon, and Wyoming.

geographic departmentalization Departmentalization according to areas served by a business

Functional Departmentalization

Finally, many service and manufacturing companies develop departments according to a group's functions or activities, a form of organization known as **functional departmentalization**. Such firms typically have production, marketing and sales, human resource, and accounting and finance departments. Departments may be further subdivided. For example, the marketing department might be divided geographically or into separate staffs for research and advertising.

functional departmentalization Departmentalization according to groups' functions or activities

Because different forms of departmentalization have different advantages, larger companies tend to adopt different types of departmentalization for various levels. For example, the company illustrated in Figure 6.2 uses functional departmentalization at the top level. At the middle level, production is divided along geographic lines. At a lower level, marketing is departmentalized by product group.

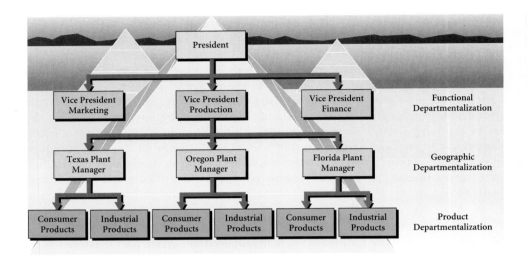

Figure 6.2 Multiple Forms of Departmentalization

Establishing the Decision-Making Hierarchy

After jobs have been appropriately specialized and grouped into manageable departments, the next step in organizing is to establish the decision-making hierarchy. That is, managers must explicitly define reporting relationships among positions so everyone will know who has responsibility for various decisions and operations. Thus, the goal is to figure out how to structure and stabilize the organizational framework so that everyone works together to achieve common goals. Companies vary greatly in the ways in which they handle the delegation of tasks, responsibility, and authority.

A major question that must be asked about any organization is Who makes which decisions? The answer almost never focuses on an individual or even on a small group. The more accurate answer usually refers to the decision-making hierarchy. Generally speaking, the development of this hierarchy results from a three-step process:

1 Assigning tasks: determining who can make decisions and specifying how they should be made

2 Performing tasks: implementing decisions that have been made

3 Distributing authority: determining whether the organization is to be centralized or decentralized

For example, when John F. (Jack) Smith, Jr., became CEO of General Motors in late 1992, he immediately undertook the reorganization of a company that had long been acknowledged as unwieldy. Within a year, he had compressed a convoluted divisional structure into a single unit called North American Operations. A special NAO Strategy Board was formed to speed decision making. Corporate staff was cut from 13,500 to 2,500. Non-core businesses worth $2 billion in annual sales were sold, and those worth another $3 billion were put on the block.[2] These changes were all focused on the same goal: modifying GM's decision-making hierarchy in ways that were preferred by Smith.

Assigning Tasks: Responsibility and Authority

The question of who is supposed to do what and who is entitled to do what in an organization are complex. In any company with more than one person, individuals must work out agreements about responsibilities and authority. **Responsibility** is the duty to perform

responsibility
Duty to perform an assigned task

an assigned task. **Authority** is the power to make the decisions necessary to complete the task.

For example, imagine a mid-level buyer for Macy's department store who encounters an unexpected opportunity to make a large purchase at an extremely good price. But let's assume that an immediate decision is absolutely necessary—a decision that this buyer has no authority to place without confirmation from above. In this case, the problem resides in a contradiction in company policy regarding delegation and authority. Obviously, our buyer needs both: He or she is responsible for purchasing the clothes that will be sold in the upcoming season and must therefore have the authority to make the needed purchases.

Performing Tasks: Delegation and Accountability

Trouble occurs when appropriate levels of responsibility and authority are not clearly spelled out in the working relationships between managers and subordinates. Here, the issues become those of delegation and accountability. **Delegation** begins when a manager assigns a task to a subordinate. **Accountability** falls to the subordinate, who must then complete the task. If the subordinate does not perform the assigned task properly and promptly, he or she may be subject to reprimand or other punishment, including dismissal.

Of course, subordinates sometimes fail to complete tasks because managers have not delegated the necessary authority. Employees may then face a dilemma: They cannot do what they are supposed to do because of a boss who will nevertheless hold them accountable. When Harold Geneen ran ITT Corp., his top managers often complained that he expected them to make important decisions but failed to give them the power to carry them out. Thus, they occasionally launched new ventures or announced new programs only to discover later that Geneen would not approve the plan.

Distributing Authority: Centralization and Decentralization

Delegation involves a specific relationship between managers and subordinates. Most businesses must also make decisions about general patterns of authority throughout the company. This pattern may be largely centralized or decentralized (or, usually, somewhere in between).

In a **centralized organization**, most decision-making authority is held by upper-level managers. Most lower-level decisions must be approved by upper management before they can be implemented. McDonald's, for example, practices centralization as a way to maintain standardization. At Dillard's Department Stores, a $2.7-billion family-run chain based in Little Rock, Arkansas, family management still insists on tight cost controls and the centralized administration of everything from payroll to buying. Indeed, owner-operated companies often have presidents or CEOs who make most of their decisions. Centralized authority is also typical of small businesses.

As a company gets larger, however, more and more decisions must be made. Thus, there is a tendency to adopt a more decentralized pattern. In a **decentralized organization**, much decision-making authority is delegated to levels of management at various points below the top. The purpose of decentralization is to make a company more responsive to its environment by breaking it into more manageable units, ranging from product lines to independent businesses. Reducing top-heavy bureaucracies is also a common goal.

Span of Control

The distribution of authority in an organization also affects the number of people who work for any individual manager. The number of people managed by one supervisor is called the manager's **span of control** and depends on many factors. Employees' abilities and the supervisor's managerial skills help determine whether span of control is wide or

authority
Power to make the decisions necessary to complete a task

delegation
Assignment of a task, responsibility, or authority by a manager to a subordinate

accountability
Liability of subordinates for accomplishing tasks assigned by managers

centralized organization
Organization in which most decision-making authority is held by upper-level management

decentralized organization
Organization in which a great deal of decision-making authority is delegated to levels of management at points below the top

span of control
Number of people supervised by one manager

The Workplace Environment

How Is Your Doctor's Stock Today?

The last few years have brought enormous changes to the medical profession and the way it delivers care. Doctors still control nearly 80 percent of all health care spending, however, and the weight of those millions of dollars means that the way physicians organize themselves in the future could have a profound effect on the health care industry.

Ten years ago most doctors were self-employed professionals in individual practice. Today nearly three-quarters of the 527,000 practicing physicians in the United States belong to a group practice, and the trend is accelerating. Although group practices are believed to provide better care, the move to unite may also be a defensive one. Seventy-five percent of all workers are enrolled in managed-care plans, whose main goal is to cut employers' medical costs for insured employees. Doctors are therefore looking for ways to protect their incomes, and one advantage of group practices is that they are rapidly being bought up by larger firms called physician practice management (PPM) companies. These firms unite doctors by the thousands and give them power in their dealings with health maintenance organizations (HMOs), employers, and insurance companies.

In the new organization the doctors are technically the employees of the PPM, which buys the physical assets of the practice and manages its business affairs, but leaves all medical policy and personnel decisions in the doctors' hands.

As beneficial for doctors as such an arrangement may seem, one recent development has some physicians worried. A number of PPMs have gone public, selling shares of ownership on the stock exchange. That raises the question of whether the best interests of the medical practice's patients will be brought into conflict with the shareholders' desire for profit. Says Dr. Jason Rosenbluth, a doctor who became a medical industry analyst, "I'm convinced that PPM is not only here to stay—it will become the new center of the health-care universe."

> **❝** *I'm convinced that PPM is not only here to stay—it will become the new center of the health-care universe.* **❞**
>
> —Dr. Jason Rosenbluth, medical industry analyst

Will that be bad or good for the medical profession and for its patients? Given the current rate of change in the medical profession, only time will tell.

narrow. So do the similarity and simplicity of tasks performed under the manager's supervision and the extent to which they are interrelated.

When several employees perform either the same simple task or a group of interrelated tasks, a wide span of control is possible and often desirable. For instance, because all the jobs are routine, one supervisor may well control a whole assembly line. Moreover, each task depends on another: If one station stops, everyone stops. Having one supervisor ensures that all stations receive equal attention and function equally well.

In contrast, when jobs are more diversified or prone to change, a narrow span of control is preferable. For example, the fully automated Kellogg plant in Battle Creek, Michigan, produces breakfast cereals. While some machines process and mix ingredients, others sort and package. Although workers are highly skilled operators of their particular machines, each machine is quite different. In this kind of setup, the complexities of each machine and the advanced skills needed by each operator mean that one supervisor can oversee only a small number of employees.

Three Forms of Authority

Whatever type of structure a company develops, it must decide who will have authority over whom. As people are delegated responsibility and authority in a firm, a complex web of interactions develop. These interactions may take one of three forms of authority: line,

Since February 1995, when Shirley Halperin launched Smug *as an alternative-music magazine, her circulation has grown from 5,000 to 20,000.* Smug, *like many small businesses, is still a highly centralized organization. Halperin herself selects and arranges stories, writes and edits copy, sells ads, hires staff, shoots some photos, oversees printing, and even delivers stacks of magazines around Manhattan. Most of her employees work for bylines, photo credits, and free concert tickets. She pays an advertising director a 20-percent commission and draws $2,000 a month for herself, $640 of which goes toward rent for both Halperin and her business.*

staff, and committee or team. In reality, like departmentalization, all three forms may be found in a given company, especially a large one.

Line Authority

Line authority is authority that flows up and down the chain of command. Most companies rely heavily on **line departments**: departments directly linked to the production and sales of specific products. For example, Clark Equipment Corp. has a division that produces forklifts and small earth movers. In this division, line departments include purchasing, material handling, fabrication, painting, and assembly (all of which are directly linked to production) along with sales and distribution (both of which are directly linked to sales).

Each line department is essential to an organization's success. Line employees are the "doers" and producers in a company. If any line department fails to complete its task, the company cannot sell and deliver finished goods. Thus, the authority delegated to line departments is important: A bad decision by the manager in one department can hold up production for an entire plant. For example, say that the painting department manager at Clark Equipment changes a paint application on a batch of forklifts, which then show signs of peeling paint. The batch will have to be repainted (and perhaps partially reassembled) before the machines can be shipped.

Staff Authority

Most companies also rely on staff authority. **Staff authority** is based on special expertise and usually involves counseling and advising line managers. Common **staff members** include specialists in areas such as law, accounting, and human resource management. A corporate attorney, for example, may be asked to advise the marketing department as it prepares a new contract with the firm's advertising agency. However, the legal staff does not actually make decisions that affect how the marketing department does its job. Staff members therefore aid line departments in making decisions but do not have the authority to make final decisions.

Suppose, for example, that the fabrication department at Clark Equipment has an employee with a drinking problem. The manager of the department could consult a human resource staff expert for advice on handling the situation. The staff expert might

line authority
Organizational structure in which authority flows in a direct chain of command from the top of the company to the bottom

line department
Department directly linked to the production and sales of a specific product

staff authority
Authority based on expertise that usually involves advising line managers

staff members
Advisers and counselors who aid line departments in making decisions but do not have the authority to make final decisions

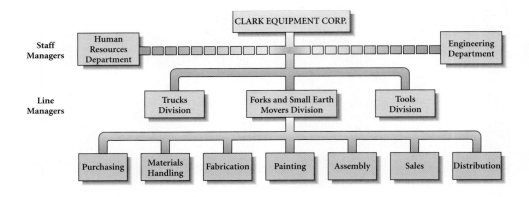

Figure 6.3 Line and Staff Organization: Clark Equipment Corp.

suggest that the worker stay on the job but enter a counseling program. But if the line manager decides that the job is too dangerous to be handled by a person whose judgment is impaired by alcohol, that decision will most likely prevail.

Typically, the separation between line authority and staff responsibility is clearly delineated. As Figure 6.3 shows, this separation is usually shown in organization charts by solid lines (line authority) and dotted lines (staff responsibility). It may help to understand this separation by remembering that whereas staff members generally provide services to management, line managers are directly involved in producing the firm's products.

Committee and Team Authority

Recently, more organizations have started to use **committee and team authority**: authority granted to committees or work teams that play central roles in the firm's daily operations. For example, a committee may consist of top managers from several major areas. If the work

committee and team authority
Authority granted to committees or work teams involved in a firm's daily operations

Westley Bingess works for BlueJacket Ship Crafters, a maker of mail-order model ship kits located in Searsport, Maine. Bingess has only nine colleagues at BlueJacket, who are divided into five different teams that handle areas such as production scheduling. Everyone serves on three or four teams. Since 1993 BlueJacket's owners have also introduced performance bonuses and self-scheduling and begun sharing financial information.

Hi-Tech Teamwork Pays Off

Work teams are among the newest tools of the most efficient and flexible firms competing today. Because you might find yourself serving as a member of a work team in the near future, consider the case of an expert at devising and managing such teams, the cofounder of an innovative hi-tech company called VeriFone, Inc. William R. Pape is a firm believer in harnessing the power of technology; with his bruising schedule of international travel, he keeps in touch with operations at home by a constant stream of e-mail via his laptop computer.

It's not surprising, therefore, that Pape would also champion a new kind of team: the virtual team. Virtual teams are made up of coworkers who may be separated by miles and even time zones but who band together to get a specific job done. Pape offers a favorite example: A VeriFone sales rep in Athens needed help closing a sale that revolved around a new banking technology that few people in Greece were familiar with. Under pressure at the end of the business day to come up with support for the product by morning, the rep e-mailed the entire worldwide staff of VeriFone's sales, marketing, and technical support departments for help. An international marketing staff member in San Francisco (6:30 A.M.) contacted two colleagues in Atlanta (9:30 A.M.) and Hong Kong (10:30 P.M.). Together the U.S. employees drafted a strategy for the Athens rep and used the company's wide area network to pass it on to the Hong Kong team member for fine tuning first thing in the morning. When the Greek sales rep retrieved the virtual team's presentation from his laptop at the customer's office at 8:00 A.M., VeriFone's speedy response and convincing product support won him the order.

> *E-mail . . . is great for sharing information, but it's a terrible tool for arguing.*
>
> —William R. Pape, CEO of VeriFone, Inc.

Pape offers the following guidelines for making virtual teams successful:

1. Define the purpose of the team and put it in writing.

2. Recruit members carefully for their experience and range of views. Three to seven people from different work shifts or time zones can work through more than one work period, and smaller teams are more efficient than larger ones.

3. Determine how long the team will exist. Virtual teams can work on short-term tasks, longer-term problem-solving assignments, process improvements, or long-term operational goals.

4. Choose the technology wisely. VeriFone teams rely on beepers, cellular phones, voice mail, fax, e-mail, conference calls, and videoconferencing. All of these are useful. But there are subtleties to keep in mind, too. Says Pape, "E-mail, for instance, is great for sharing information, but it's a terrible tool for arguing."

of the committee is especially important, and if the committee will be working together for an extended time, the organization may even grant it special authority as a decision-making body that goes beyond the individual authority possessed by each of its members.

At the operating level, many firms today are also using work teams: groups of operating employees empowered to plan and organize their own work and to perform that work with a minimum of supervision. As with permanent committees, the organization will usually find it beneficial to grant special authority to work teams so that they may function more effectively.

Basic Forms of Organizational Structure

There are an infinite number of ways in which organizations can structure themselves—according to specialization, for example, or departmentalization or the decision-making hierarchy. Nevertheless, it is possible to identify four basic forms of organizational structure that reflect the general trends followed by most firms: functional, divisional, matrix, and international.

Functional Organizations

functional organization
Form of business organization in which authority is determined by the relationships between group functions and activities

Functional organization is the approach to organizational structure used by most small to medium-sized firms. Such organizations are usually structured around basic business functions (marketing, operations, finance, and so forth). Thus, there is a marketing department, an operation department, and a finance department. The benefits of this approach include specialization within functional areas and smoother coordination among them. Experts with specialized training, for example, are hired to work in the marketing department, which handles all marketing for the firm.

In large firms, coordination among functional departments becomes more complicated. Moreover, functional organization also fosters centralization (which may or may not be desirable) and makes accountability more difficult. As organizations grow, therefore, they tend to shed this form and move toward one of the other three structures.

Divisional Organization

divisional organization
Organizational structure in which corporate divisions operate as autonomous businesses under the larger corporate umbrella

division
Department that resembles a separate business in producing and marketing its own products

A **divisional organization** relies on product departmentalization: The firm creates product-based **divisions**, each of which may be managed as a separate enterprise. Organizations using this approach are typically structured around several divisions, which resemble separate businesses in that they produce and market their own products. The head of each division may be a corporate vice president or, if the organization is large, a divisional president. In addition, each division usually has its own identity and operates as an autonomous business under the larger corporate umbrella.

Aircraft-engine maker Pratt & Whitney, United Technologies Corp.'s largest division, has lost $1.3 billion and laid off 23,000 employees since 1991. On the other hand, the fortunes of UTC's smaller units— Carrier air conditioning, Otis Elevator, and Sikorsky helicopter—have been revived by new manufacturing techniques and lighter payrolls. "This company is really two companies," observes CEO Robert F. Daniell. "The other part is doing quite well." At Sikorsky, for example, more efficient worker teams that now assemble products from start to finish are busy filling a $1-billion order for 95 helicopters from Turkey, and UTC's smaller divisions have more than picked up the slack from P&W.

▶ Consider United Technologies Corp., which is located in Hartford, Connecticut. Its divisions include Pratt & Whitney, an aircraft engine maker; Carrier Corp., which makes air conditioners; Otis Elevator Co.; and Flight Systems, which includes the Sikorsky helicopter. In the 1980s, UTC sold off such unrelated companies as a trout farm and a dumpster manufacturer. Since then, however, UTC's largest division, Pratt & Whitney, has been hurt by airline and military cutbacks and is currently the biggest drain on its profits. Smaller units, however, are performing well, largely because UTC has succeeded in developing new products, modernizing its manufacturing techniques, and finding new overseas markets. UTC is a good example of a divisionalized company that struggled into the 1980s but has begun to recover by focusing on the related businesses that it houses under a single organizational roof.[3]

Like UTC, divisionalized companies are free to buy, sell, create, and disband divisions without disrupting the rest of their operations. Divisions can maintain healthy competition among themselves by sponsoring separate advertising campaigns, fostering different corporate identities, and so forth. They can also share certain corporate-level resources (such as marketing research data). Of course, if too much control is delegated to divisional managers, corporate managers may lose touch with daily operations. Competition between divisions has also been known to become disruptive, and efforts in one division may be duplicated by those of another.

Matrix Organization

In a **matrix structure**, teams are formed in which individuals report to two or more managers, usually including a line manager and a staff manager. This structure was pioneered by the National Aeronautics and Space Administration (NASA) for use in developing specific programs. It is a highly flexible form that is readily adaptable to changing circumstances. Matrix structures rely heavily on committee and team authority.

In some companies, matrix organization is a temporary measure, installed to complete a specific project and affecting only one part of the firm. In these firms, the end of the project usually means the end of the matrix—either a breakup of the team or a restructuring to fit it into the company's existing line and staff structure. For example, IBM used a matrix organization to put together the original PC but then disbanded the team and returned members to the line and staff structure when the PC succeeded. Elsewhere, the matrix organization is a semipermanent fixture.

▶ ***THERMOS WARMS TO TEAMWORK.*** For example, at Thermos, the well-known maker of insulated bottles, lunchboxes, and barbecue grills, interdisciplinary teams have largely replaced functions—marketing, engineering, and so forth—as the company's basic organizational principle. Japanese-owned Thermos now employs teams in all its product lines because of the success of its first experiment in matrix organization.

Growth at Thermos had slowed because its products were becoming commodities: mass-produced lookalikes bought by consumers with little regard to differences in brand or quality. What the company needed most of all was innovative products. A product development team of six managers from different disciplines, such as marketing, manufacturing, and finance, was assembled. Team members abandoned their focus on separate functions in favor of a concentration on their target market—in this case, users of barbecue grills. Several more team members came from the industrial design firm of Fitch Inc., adding outside perspectives on design and market research.

Most important, therefore, was the shift in focus from product to consumer, and the team spent much of its time in the field learning about customers' cookout needs. The result was the Thermos Thermal Electric Grill, which uses entirely new technology to give food a barbecued taste while burning cleaner than gas or charcoal. The new grill, which also eliminates heavy propane tanks and messy cleanup, has already won numerous design awards and is expected to raise Thermos's market share for electric grills from 2 percent to 20 percent over the next few years. "We need to reinvent our product lines," admits Thermos CEO Monte Peterson, "and teamwork is doing it for us."[4]

matrix structure
Organizational structure in which teams are formed and team members report to two or more managers

After an initial meeting in 1990, members of Thermos Lifestyle team hit the road, holding focus groups, visiting homes, and videotaping family gatherings to find out what consumers wanted in a barbecue grill. Back at headquarters after field research was complete, they hammered out a consensus on what the new grill should look like and do. Members from engineering, meanwhile, worked at improving electric grill technology and making sure that new designs were economically feasible. Designers worked out features that would add value and differentiate the new product. The first batch rolled off the line in 1992, and those grills were given to fellow employees for testing. When tests proved successful, the new Thermos Thermal Electric Grill was finally rolled out nationally.

Advantages and Disadvantages

Matrix organizations are particularly appealing to firms that want to speed up the decision-making process. They are also ideal for companies that want to engage in time-based competition. Like those at Thermos, the project teams created in the matrix typically help the organization develop and implement new ideas quickly.

A matrix organization is not without its problems:

■ First, a team is often only a temporary group meant to carry out a single-use plan. When the project is completed, the team is disbanded. Thus, matrix organization may not allow long-term working relationships to develop.

■ A second problem is the use of multiple managers for one employee. For example, if your project manager demands that you work on one aspect of a proposal while the department manager wants you to work on another, you must resolve the conflict between your two immediate supervisors.

■ A third problem, which is related to the number of managers per employee, is authority. Employees in matrix organizations do not always know which of their managers has authority in a given area. In some cases, they do not know which manager will evaluate performance or the manager to whom they will be accountable.

International Organization

international organizational structures
Approaches to organizational structure developed in response to the need to manufacture, purchase, and sell in global markets

As we saw in chapter 3, many businesses today manufacture, purchase, and sell in the world market. Thus, a number of different **international organizational structures** have emerged. Moreover, as competition on a global scale becomes more complex, companies often find that they must experiment with the ways in which they compete.

For example, Club Méditerranée, an international French-based firm that provides vacation sites (called villages) around the world, originally functioned as a matrix organization: Each village manager reported both to a country manager and to a number of different directors. Directors worked out of company headquarters, and each director had primary responsibility for some facet of Club Med operations and marketing. However, this structure proved less than satisfactory. Club Med prides itself on providing village arrangements that reflect various local atmospheres—a difficult feat for directors to achieve from remote locations. To resolve this problem, the company adopted a different form of organization. A major component of the new structure involved sending operations and marketing staff to specific geographic regions.

For similar reasons, other firms have developed a wide range of approaches to international organizational structure. Whirlpool, for example, purchased the appliance division of the Dutch electronics giant N.V. Philips and as part of its international organization structure now makes the cooling coils for its refrigerators at its new plant in Trento, Italy.[5] Other companies, such as Levi Strauss, handle all international operations through separate international divisions. Still others concentrate production in low-cost areas and then distribute and market globally. Some firms, such as Britain's Pearson PLC (which runs such diverse businesses as publishing, investment banking, and Madame Tussaud's Wax Museum), allow each of their businesses to function autonomously within local markets.

Finally, some companies adopt a truly global structure in which they acquire resources (including capital), produce goods and services, engage in research and development, and sell products in whatever local market is appropriate, without any consideration of national boundaries. General Electric uses a global structure for many of its businesses and has also managed to graft other forms of organization onto its global operations. For its $3-billion lighting business, for example, GE has created a matrix-type team of 9 to 12 senior managers. Team members have multiple competencies rather than narrow specialties, and the team itself is multidisciplinary—that is, it cuts across functions. From new product design to equipment redesign, the matrix team oversees about 100 programs and processes located all around the world.[6]

Informal Organization

Much of our discussion thus far has focused on the organization's formal structure—its official arrangement of jobs and job relationships. In reality, however, all organizations also have another dimension: an **informal organization** within which people do their jobs in different ways and interact with other people in ways that do not follow formal lines of communication.

informal organization
Network, unrelated to the firm's formal authority structure, of everyday social interactions among company employees

Formal Versus Informal Organizational Systems

The formal organization of a business is the part that can be seen and represented in chart form. However, the entire structure of a company is by no means limited to the organization chart and the formal assignment of authority. Often, the informal organization—everyday social interactions among employees that transcend formal jobs and job interrelationships—effectively alters a company's formal structure. Indeed, this level of organization is sometimes just as powerful as, if not more powerful than, the formal structure.

In their milestone book *In Search of Excellence*, Thomas Peters and Robert Waterman report that many successful companies support and encourage informal organization just as much as they support formal structure.[7] For example, 3M sponsors clubs for 12 or more employees to enhance communication and interaction across departments. Other companies have rearranged offices and other facilities to make them more conducive to informal interaction. For instance, Citibank once moved two departments to the same floor to encourage intermingling of employees. In its brand-new headquarters not far from the White House, MCI still has no doors on its offices—the better to grease the flow of ideas. These and other companies believe that informal interaction among employees stimulates the kind of discussions and group processes that can help solve organizational problems.[8]

On the negative side, the informal organization can reinforce office politics that put the interests of individuals ahead of those of the firm. Likewise, a great deal of harm can be caused by distorted or inaccurate information when it is communicated without management input or review. For example, if the informal organization is highlighting false information about impending layoffs, valuable employees may act quickly (and unnecessarily) to seek other employment.

The compact battery-operated copier is the brainchild of Denis Stemmle (center), a 25-year veteran of Xerox who had presented his idea to his bosses for 5 straight years before it was finally brought to market by QuadMark Ltd. Through Xerox Technology Ventures (XTV), Xerox funds intrapreneurial companies such as QuadMark, in large part to retain the technological creativity that is born within the company but often matures elsewhere when the giant parent firm overlooks it. XTV, admits Xerox Chairman Paul Allaire, "is a hedge against repeating missteps of the past."

Intrapreneuring

Sometimes organizations actually take steps to encourage the informal organization. They do so for a variety of reasons. We have already touched upon two of them. First, most experienced managers recognize that the informal organization exists whether they want it or not. Second, many managers know how to use it to reinforce the formal organization. Perhaps more important, however, the energy of informal organization can be harnessed to improve productivity.

Firms, such as Compaq Computer, Rubbermaid, 3M, and Xerox are supporting a process called **intrapreneuring**: creating and maintaining the innovation and flexibility of a small business environment within the confines of a large, bureaucratic structure. The concept is basically sound. Historically, most innovations have come from individuals in small businesses (see chapter 8). As businesses increase in size, however, innovation and creativity tend to become casualties in the battle for more sales and profits. In some large companies, new ideas are even discouraged, and champions of innovation have been stalled in mid-career. Compaq is an excellent example of how this works. The firm has one major division called the New Business Group. Whenever a manager or engineering has an idea for a new product or product application, he or she takes it to the New Business Group and "sells" it. The managers in the group itself are then encouraged to help the innovator develop the idea for field testing. If the product takes off and does well, it is then spun off into its own new business group or division. If it doesn't do as well, it may still be maintained as part of the New Business Group, or phased out altogether.

intrapreneuring
Process of creating and maintaining the innovation and flexibility of a small business environment within the confines of a large organization

Summary of Learning Objectives

1 **Discuss the elements that influence a firm's organizational structure.** Every business needs structure to operate. Its organizational structure varies according to a firm's mission, purpose, and strategy. Size, technology, and changes in environmental circumstances also influence structure. In general, although all organizations have the same basic elements, each develops the specific structure that contributes to the most efficient operations.

2 **Describe specialization and departmentalization as the building blocks of organizational structure.** The building blocks of organizational structure are job specialization and departmentalization. As a firm grows, it usually has a greater need for people to perform specialized tasks (specialization). It also has a greater need to group types of work into logical units (departmentalization). Common forms of departmentalization are customer, product, process, geographic, and functional. Large businesses often use more than one form of departmentalization. Process organization (as opposed to process departmentalization) means organizing according to units or teams responsible for the various processes involved in getting products to consumers.

3 **Distinguish between responsibility and authority, delegation and accountability, and explain the differences in decision making in centralized and decentralized organizations.** Responsibility is the duty to perform a task; authority is the power to make the decisions necessary to complete tasks. Delegation begins when a manager assigns a task to a subordinate; accountability means that the subordinate must complete the task. *Span of control* refers to the number of people who work for any individual manager: The more people supervised, the wider the span of control. Wide spans are usually desirable when employees perform simple or unrelated tasks; when jobs are diversified or prone to change, a narrower span is generally preferable.

In a centralized organization, only a few individuals in top management have real decision-making authority. In a decentralized organization, much authority is delegated to lower-level management. In areas where both line and line and staff systems are involved, line departments generally have authority to make decisions while staff departments have a responsibility to advise. A new concept, committee and team authority empowers committees or work teams involved in a firm's daily operations.

4 **Explain the differences among functional, divisional, matrix, and international organization structures.** In a functional organization, authority is usually distributed among such basic functions as marketing and finance. In a divisional organization, the various divisions of a larger company, which may be related or unrelated, operate in an autonomous fashion. In matrix organizations, in which individuals report to more than one manager, a company creates teams to address specific problems or to complete specific projects. A company that has divisions in many countries may require an additional level of international organization to coordinate those operations.

5 **Describe the informal organization and discuss intrapreneuring.** The informal organization consists of the everyday social interactions among employees that transcend formal jobs and job interrelationships. To foster the innovation and flexibility of a small business within the big-business environment, some large companies also encourage intrapreneuring, creating and maintaining the innovation and flexibility of a small business environment within the confines of a large, bureaucratic structure.

Questions and Exercises

Questions for Review

1 What is an organization chart? What purpose does it serve?
2 Explain the significance of size as it relates to organizational structure. Describe the changes that are likely to occur as an organization grows.
3 What is the difference between responsibility and authority?
4 Why is process organization an innovative approach to organizational structure?
5 Why is a company's informal organization important?

Questions for Analysis

6 Draw up an organization chart for your college or university.
7 Describe a hypothetical organizational structure for a small printing firm. Describe changes that might be necessary as the business grows.
8 Compare the matrix and divisional approaches to organizational structure.

Application Exercises

9 Interview the manager of a local service business (say, a fast-food restaurant). What types of tasks does this manager typically delegate? Is the appropriate authority also delegated in each case?

10 Using books, magazines, or personal interviews, identify an individual who has succeeded as an intrapreneur. In what ways did the structure of the intrapreneur's company help this individual succeed? In what ways did the structure pose problems?

Building Your Business Skills

This exercise enhances the following SCANS workplace competencies: demonstrating basic skills, demonstrating thinking skills, exhibiting interpersonal skills, working with information, and applying systems knowledge.

Goal   To encourage students to see the relationship between organizational structure and a company's ability to attract and keep valued employees.

Situation   You're the founder of a small but growing high-technology company that is developing new computer software. With your current workload and new contracts in the pipeline, your business is thriving, except for one problem: You can't find computer programmers for product development. Worse yet, current staff members are being lured away by other high-tech firms that offer fat salaries, fatter bonuses, and better working conditions. After a particularly discouraging head-hunter raid that captured three valued workers, you schedule a meeting with your director of human resources to plan organizational changes that will encourage worker loyalty. You already pay top dollar, but the continuing exodus tells you that programmers are looking for something more.

Method   Working with three or four classmates, identify how specific organizational changes might improve the working environment and encourage employee loyalty. As you analyze the following factors, ask yourself this question: "If I were a programmer, what organizational changes would encourage me to stay?"

- *Level of job specialization:* With many programmers describing their jobs as tedious because of the focus on detail in a narrow work area, what changes, if any, would you make in job specialization? Right now, few programmers in the company have any say in product design.
- *Decision-making hierarchy:* What decision-making authority would encourage people to stay? Is expanding worker authority likely to work better in a centralized or decentralized organization?
- *Team authority:* Can team empowerment make a difference? Taking the point of view of the worker, describe the ideal team.
- *Intrapreneuring:* What can your company do to encourage and reward innovation?

Follow-Up Questions

1 With the average computer programmer earning nearly $67,000 in 1996 and with all competitive firms paying top dollar, why may organizational issues be critical in determining employee loyalty?

2 If you were a programmer, what organizational factors would make a difference to you? Why?

3 As the company founder, how willing would you be to make major organizational changes in light of the shortage of qualified programmers?

Pepsico Sends Its Restaurants Out into the Cold

Has America's love affair with fast food finally come to an end? Management of a new company may soon find out. When the Pepsico conglomerate recently decided to spin off Pizza Hut, KFC, and Taco Bell into a separate new corporation called Tricon Global Restaurants, Inc., the announcement came at a time when the restaurant business, after booming for years, was beginning to taper off as the public's appetite for fast food started to dull. Price wars had done little to restore the big food chains to their once-dominant positions, and Pepsico decided to spin its three holdings off and see whether they could survive on their own.

Andrall Pearson, who had been a past president of Pepsico, was appointed to run the new firm, which would be second only to McDonald's in terms of revenues. "I'm not presiding over their departure," he said of the three restaurant chains, "I'm presiding over their rebirth."

Their rebirth may be a difficult delivery, particularly for Pizza Hut, which unlike Taco Bell and KFC has experienced declining sales in the preceding years. Pizza Hut was having trouble positioning itself in the pizza market, where local independent eateries are still very strong, and most of its success came from products such as stuffed crust pizza. A complete revamping of Pizza Hut's menu is already under way, and one of the benefits of the spinoff from Pepsico is management's greater flexibility to make rapid changes if new products prove more or less popular than expected.

Central to the new strategy is expansion, despite concern of many analysts that the fast-food market has saturated urban and suburban locations alike. All three restaurants will grow in the United States but even more so abroad, and unprofitable units at home will be offered for sale to franchisees, bringing in needed cash. More than 700 unprofitable Pizza Hut outlets are scheduled to be closed. KFC already gets more than half its business overseas, where the fast-food market is estimated to be worth $62 billion in sales every year. The number of locations where Taco Bell and KFC are both available, known as "two-in-ones," will also be increased.

Heavy marketing campaigns will attempt to generate business in historically slow times. For instance, KFC and Pizza Hut do well at dinner time, so Tricon will spend on advertising to the lunch-hour crowd. At Taco Bell, where about half the business already comes from lunches, the firm will promote its dinner business.

How does the rest of the fast-food market feel about the changes planned for the three chains? A spokesman for Wendy's International said, "They are certainly formidable competitors, but our approach won't change because they have new owners."

Questions

1 What additional strategies might Tricon use to increase off-hours business at each of its restaurants? Why do you think price wars among fast-food restaurants have failed as a strategy to increase market share?

2 To what extent do you think Tricon's independence from Pepsico will help its management face the challenge ahead? Will there be any downside to the change?

3 Do you think there is room for growth in the U.S. fast-food business today? Why or why not?

4 What factors in the international market might account for the growth Tricon expects in the fast-food business overseas? What strategies might help Tricon succeed in that market?

Connecting to the Web

The following Web sites will give you additional information and points of view about topics covered in this chapter. Many sites lead to other related Internet locations, so approach this list with the spirit of an explorer.

DILLARD'S: ABOUT OUR COMPANY

http://www.azstarnet.com/dillards/mr_dillard/mr_dillard.htm

Dillard's tradition of tight controls and a centralized organization began 60 years ago when company founder William Dillard started his first department store. Visit Dillard's Web site to learn more about this tradition, which has passed from one family member to the next.

FORD MOTOR COMPANY

http://www.ford.com/careercenter/

Visit the Career Center at Ford for a look at current job opportunities. Job postings are found in nine specialized areas: manufacturing, finance, purchasing, marketing and sales, product engineering, human resources, process leadership/systems, Ford Credit, and real estate.

GENERAL MOTORS/NORTH AMERICAN OPERATIONS

http://www.gm.com/about/info/overview/gmnao.html

The products produced by General Motor's North American Operations are described on this Web site.

THE HOME DEPOT

http://www.homedepot.com/

Home Depot is divided into departments according to customers' shopping needs (for example, plumbing, electrical, paint, carpentry, and gardening). Visit Home Depot's Web site to learn more about its warehouse stores.

NASA ORGANIZATIONS

http://www.nasa.gov/nasaorgs/index.html

The National Aeronotics and Space Administration has used a matrix organization to develop many of the specific programs described on this site.

PINCHOT & COMPANY

http://www.pinchot.com/

The mission of Pinchot & Company is to increase innovation and productivity within organizations. Visit this site to learn how Pinchot promotes intrapreneurship.

RUBBERMAID

http://www.rubbermaid.com/

Visit this Web site to see how innovation is part of Rubbermaid's internal organizational vision.

UNITED TECHNOLOGIES CORPORATION: WHO WE ARE

http://www.utc.com/whowe.html

Visit this Web site for a description of United Technology's divisional structure, which includes Pratt & Whitney aircraft engines, Otis elevators, Carrier heating and cooling, Sikorsky helicopters, Hamilton Standard aerospace systems, and United Technologies Automotive Components and Systems.

WELCOME TO VERIFONE, INC.

http://www.verifone.com/

Visit the VeriFone Web site for a glimpse of the company's international deals, all of which require well-oiled virtual teams.

XEROX: THE DOCUMENT COMPANY

http://www.xerox.com/

See the Xerox headlines on this Web site for news of innovative business advances that have been encouraged, in part, through intrapreneuring.

chapter 7

Understanding **entrepreneurship** and the small business

Advice for nonprofits: "think like an entrepreneur"

In the world of nonprofit organizations, money has always been hard to come by. In recent years, though, with federal and state funding on a steady decline and many social problems on the rise, managing a nonprofit organization has become an exercise in ingenuity. Most charitable and social organizations are facing an uncomfortable future of having to do more with less.

One new development is promising, however: the birth of an entrepreneurial spirit among the next generation of nonprofit managers. To try to find new sources of money for social needs such as hunger and poverty, and to become less dependent on unpredictable sources such as foundation and government grants, many nonprofits are turning to the management techniques of small-business and entrepreneurial firms. Some charities are even running small for-profit firms to create their own source of funds for

social services. "At least half the nonprofit executives in this country now understand that they have to do something different," says Jerr Boschee, director of the National Center for Social Entrepreneurs. "Probably the best 2% to 3% of them understand what needs to be done and have the guts to actually try it."

Melissa Bradley is a good example of the new nonprofit entrepreneur. After selling her first successful business at the age of 23, she started the Entrepreneurial Development Institute (TEDI) to teach at-risk kids in Washington, DC. Unable to charge her students anything, Bradley got a quick education in nonprofit tax and accounting matters but decided to run TEDI just like a business. One of her innovations is selling "community stock" to shareholders in the new firm.

This kind of hybrid organization is breaking down the barriers between business and charitable organizations, promising steadier income for nonprofits and changing the way they view profits and assets. According to Jed Emerson, who has written a book of case studies called *The New Social Entrepreneurs*, "People are talking not about charitable contributions but how to add economic value to the interaction between nonprofits and the communities in which they work."

Entrepreneur Melissa Bradley

Their hoped-for financial independence from government and foundation grants allows nonprofits to promise accountability to their clients, putting an end to the exploitation of their needs in the pursuit of sympathy and dollars. And new social entrepreneurs such as Melissa Bradley feel that accountability is what puts the focus back on their clients, where it belongs.

> **People are talking not about charitable contributions but how to add economic value to the interaction between nonprofits and the communities in which they work.**
>
> — Jed Emerson, author of *The New Social Entrepreneurs*

Social problems are the focus of much attention today, and the application of so many entrepreneurial techniques and so much talent promises results for today and beyond. What sets entrepreneurships and small businesses apart? By focusing on the objectives of this chapter, you will learn what small businesses are and why they are so important to the U.S. economy. After reading this chapter, you should be able to

1 Define *small business* and explain its importance to the U.S. economy.

2 Explain which types of small business best lend themselves to success.

3 Define *entrepreneurship* and describe some basic entrepreneurial characteristics.

4 Describe the startup decisions made by small businesses and identify sources of financial aid and management advice available to such enterprises.

5 Identify the advantages and disadvantages of franchising.

What Is a Small Business?

small business
Independently owned and managed business that does not dominate its market

Small Business Administration (SBA)
Federal agency charged with assisting small businesses

The term *small business* defies easy definition. Clearly, locally owned and operated groceries, video stores, and restaurants are small businesses, and giant corporations such as Sony, Caterpillar, and Eastman Kodak are big businesses. Between these two extremes fall thousands of companies that cannot be easily categorized.

The U.S. Department of Commerce considers a business small if it has fewer than 500 employees. But the U.S. **Small Business Administration (SBA)**, a government assistance agency for small businesses, regards some companies with 1,500 employees as small. The SBA bases its definition on two factors: number of employees and total annual sales. For example, manufacturers are defined as small according to the first criterion and grocery stores according to the second. Thus, although an independent grocery store with $13 million in sales may sound large, the SBA still sees it as a small business when its revenues are compared to those of truly large food retailers.

Because it is difficult to define a small business in numerical terms, we will define a small business as one that is independently owned and managed and does not dominate its market. A small business, then, cannot be part of another business: Operators must be their own bosses, free to run their businesses as they please. In addition, the small business must have little influence in its market. For example, although Compaq Computer was certainly a small business when it was founded in 1984, it is now a dominant company in the personal computer market. Like so many enterprises, Compaq was a small business once but certainly is no longer.

The federal government plays a significant role in the formation and operation of small business in the United States. On the whole, this interest in the role and well-being of small business derives from the importance of such businesses to the overall economy. (As we will see later in this chapter, the U.S. government sponsors numerous assistance programs for small businesses.) In this section, we will discuss the role and importance of small business in the U.S. economy and then describe the major types of small businesses in the United States.

The Importance of Small Business in the U.S. Economy

As Figure 7.1 shows, most U.S. businesses employ fewer than 100 people, and most U.S. workers are employed by small firms. For example, Figure 7.1(a) shows that approximately 87.5 percent of all U.S. businesses employ 20 or fewer people; another 10.4 percent employ between 20 and 99 people. Figure 7.1(b) shows that 26.7 percent of all U.S. workers are employed by firms with fewer than 20 people; another 29.2 percent work in firms that employ between 20 and 99 people. The vast majority of these companies are owner-operated.

On the basis of numbers alone, then, small business is a strong presence in the economy. This is true in virtually all the world's mature economies. In Germany, for example, companies with fewer than 500 employees produce two-thirds of the nation's gross national product, train nine out of ten apprentices, and employ four out of every five workers. Small businesses also play major roles in the economies of Italy, France, and Brazil. In addition, experts agree that small businesses will be quite important in the emerging economies of countries such as Russia and Vietnam.[1]

The contribution of small business can be measured in terms of its effects on key aspects of an economic system. In the United States, these aspects include job creation, innovation, and importance to big business.

Job Creation

In the early 1980s, business consultant David Birch of the Massachusetts Institute of Technology proposed that small businesses create 8 out of every 10 new jobs in the United States. Birch's argument touched off considerable interest in the fostering of small business as a matter of public policy. As we will see, those numbers are no longer regarded as very accurate. The fact remains, however, that small business—especially in certain industries—is an important source of new (and often well-paid) jobs in this country.

Figure 7.1 The Importance of Small Business in the United States

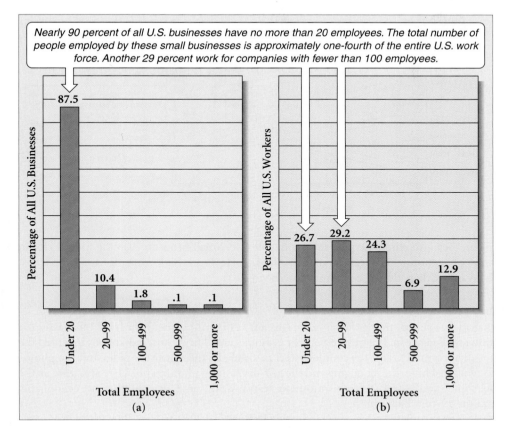

Nearly 90 percent of all U.S. businesses have no more than 20 employees. The total number of people employed by these small businesses is approximately one-fourth of the entire U.S. work force. Another 29 percent work for companies with fewer than 100 employees.

New jobs are also being created by small firms specializing in international business. For example, Bob Knosp operates a small business in Bellevue, Washington, that makes computerized sign-making systems. Knosp gets over half his sales from abroad and has dedicated almost 75 percent of his work force to handling international sales.

Adjusting the Myth: The Big Business Job Machine. Although small businesses certainly create many new jobs each year, the importance of big businesses in job creation should not be overlooked.[2] The large-scale layoffs and cutbacks of the late 1980s and early 1990s contributed to an impression that jobs in all big businesses were on the decline. In reality, however, many large businesses have also been creating thousands of new jobs every year. Figure 7.2 details the increase in jobs at eight large U.S. companies between 1992 and 1994. As you can see, Wal-Mart alone created 182,000 new jobs during that period. Moreover, the other firms on the list occupy the spectrum of business areas from manufacturing to service.

At least one message is clear: Business success, more than business size, accounts for most new job creation. In 1993, for example, while struggling retail chains such as Sears and Woolworth eliminated 80,000 jobs, Wal-Mart more than made up the difference by adding 85,000. Other successful chains, including Home Depot, Toys Я Us, Federated Department Stores, and Dayton Hudson, not only added 400,000 retailing jobs in the 1990s but also announced expansion plans that will add thousands more. Furthermore, many high-tech giants such as Dell, Compaq, and Microsoft continue to add jobs at a constant pace.

"Size isn't the issue," reports MIT economist Frank Levy. "The issue is which firms are adding jobs." Jobs are created by companies of all sizes, all of which hire workers and all of which lay them off. Admittedly, recent studies by Levy and others show that, relative to their total employment, small firms hire at twice the rate as large ones. By the same

Figure 7.2 Big Business and Job Creation

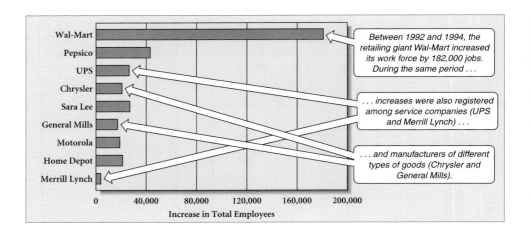

token, they also eliminate jobs at a far higher rate. Small firms are also the first to hire in times of economic recovery, large firms the last. However, big companies are also the last to lay off workers during economic downswings.

Innovation

History has shown that major innovations are as likely to come from small businesses (or individuals) as from big businesses. For example, small firms and individuals invented the personal computer and the stainless-steel razor blade, the transistor radio and the photocopying machine, the jet engine and the self-developing photograph. They also gave us the helicopter and power steering, automatic transmissions and air conditioning, cellophane, and the 19-cent ballpoint pen.

Not surprisingly, history is repeating itself infinitely more rapidly in the age of computers and high-tech communication. Since it was founded in 1983, for example, Maxim Integrated Products has introduced more than 600 semiconductor chips for use in computers, telecommunications, and high-tech instruments. Maxim, which is located in Sunnyvale, California, specializes in the analog semiconductors needed to control such com-

Barely more than a decade old, Maxim Integrated Products is already recognized as an industry leader in designing analog chips for such portable devices as laptop computers and cellular phones. The analog chip market is worth $10 billion per year, and Maxim targets the $2-billion-a-year high-performance segment. The company has found that this end of the market is highly profitable for the handful of U.S. specialty producers who have discovered a worldwide market for high-performance, high-margin products.

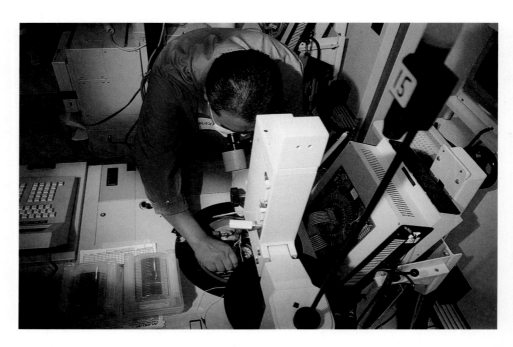

puterized functions as temperature, pressure, and sound. About half the company's revenues come from Europe and Asia.[3]

Importance to Big Business

Most of the products made by big manufacturers are sold to consumers by small businesses. For example, the majority of dealerships selling Fords, Chevrolets, Toyotas, and Volvos are independently owned and operated. Moreover, small businesses provide big businesses with many of the services, supplies, and raw materials they need. In Poway, California, for example, Norris Communications makes the EarPhone, a device designed by inventor Elwood G. "Woody" Norris to pick up the wearer's voice through the vibrations of bones in the skull. Because the EarPhone is a peanut-sized apparatus that combines a speaker and a microphone, Apple Computer includes it in a hardware/software package that permits a Macintosh PC to dial phone calls, play voice mail, and send faxes.[4]

As suppliers, small businesses are almost always less expensive than large firms when goods or services have small sales, require close personal contact between seller and customer, or—as in the case of the EarPhone—must meet buyers' unique needs or specifications.[5]

Popular Forms of Small Business Enterprise

Small businesses are more common in some industries than in others. The five major small business industry groups are services, retailing, wholesaling, agriculture, and manufacturing. Obviously, each group differs in its requirements for employees, money, materials, and machines. Remember: The more resources an industry requires, the harder it is to start a business and the less likely that the industry is dominated by small firms. Remember, too, that *small* is a relative term: The criteria (number of employees and total annual sales) differ from industry to industry and are often meaningful only when compared to businesses that are truly large.

Finally, remember that, as a general rule, manufacturing businesses are the hardest to start and service businesses the easiest. To make sewing machines, for example, a manufacturer must invest not only in people but also in raw materials and machines. It must also develop a distribution network and advertise heavily. To prepare tax forms, however, an entrepreneur need invest only in an education and a few office supplies and reference books. The business can be run out of a storefront or a home.

Services

Partly because they require few resources, service businesses are the largest and fastest-growing segment of small business enterprise. In addition, no other industry group offers a higher return on time invested. Finally, services appeal to the talent for innovation typified by many small enterprises.

Small business services range from shoeshine parlors to car rental agencies, from marriage counseling to computer software, from accounting and management consulting to professional dog walking. In Cambridge, Massachusetts, Marcia J. Radosevich started HPR Inc., a health care consultancy firm that assists health maintenance organizations (HMOs) spot medical claims that do not comply with company standards. HPR also offers a program that determines when patients are receiving insufficient care. In Atlantic Highlands, New Jersey, Maben Smith has started a business that provides information about small and mid-size businesses. Business Opportunities Online is an electronic database that provides listings for basic transactions (buying, selling, and even the criteria used by about 500 potential investors). It also collects information on about 500 franchisers and 350 professional consultants.[6]

Retailing

A retail business sells directly to consumers products manufactured by other firms. There are hundreds of different kinds of retailers, ranging from wig shops and frozen yogurt stands to automobile dealerships and department stores. Usually, however, small busi-

Small businesses often do very well in retailing. For example, Starbucks started as a small-time operation, but today it has grown into an internationally recognized brand with dozens of new stores opening every year. The firm's commitment to quality and keen understanding of its customers have made Starbucks the dominant firm in its market.

nesspeople favor specialty shops—say, big men's clothing or gourmet coffees—that let them focus limited resources on narrow market segments.

For example, Harold Schultz got his start when he took a job with a small coffee bean mail-order distributor in Seattle. When the three partners who owned the business decided to sell it, Schultz stepped in and bought the business. He believed that mail-order distribution had limited growth opportunities and decided to enter retailing instead. He began opening Starbucks coffee shops in select locations, and the business began to take off. Today, Schultz owns a multi–million-dollar enterprise and is opening a new Starbucks somewhere in the world virtually every day.

Wholesaling

As with services and retailing, small businesspeople dominate wholesaling. A wholesale business buys products from manufacturers or other producers and then sells them to retailers. Wholesalers usually buy goods in bulk and store them in quantities and places convenient for retailers. For a given volume of business, therefore, they need fewer employees than do manufacturers, retailers, or service providers.

They also serve fewer customers than other providers—usually customers who repeatedly order large volumes of goods. For example, wholesalers in the grocery industry buy packaged food in bulk from companies such as Del Monte and Campbell's and then sell it to both large grocery chains and smaller independent grocers. Like retailing, the wholesaling industry has also been affected by the increase in consumer demand for specialty products, a trend that has fueled the growth of firms such as Central Garden & Pet, a warehousing firm located in Lafayette, California. Central began by stocking and distributing garden and pool supplies made by firms such as Ortho and Monsanto. In 1991 it bought out a distributor of pet supplies and diversified. Now, in addition to pesticides, gopher traps, and garden hoses, Central stocks shelves and manages inventory for pet supply retailers—the fastest-growing facet of its business.[7]

Manufacturing

More than any other industry group, manufacturing lends itself to big business—and for good reason. Because of the investment normally required in equipment, energy, and raw materials, a good deal of money is usually needed to start a manufacturing business. Automobile manufacturing, for example, calls for billions of dollars of investment and thousands of workers before the first automobile rolls off the assembly line. Obviously, such requirements shut out most individuals. Although Henry Ford began with $28,000, it has been a long time since anyone started a U.S. car company from scratch.

This is not to say that there are no small businesspeople who do well in manufacturing. Indeed, it is not uncommon for them to outdo big business in such innovative industries as chemistry, electronics, toys, and computer software. For example, entrepreneur Bill Gates started Microsoft Corp. in 1975. In 1980, he had 125 employees. Microsoft now employs over 22,000 people, and Gates is widely counted the richest man in the United States and one of the richest in the world. As we already noted, Dell Computer and Compaq Computer also started as small businesses and have grown to become major players in the personal computer industry.

Entrepreneurship

In the previous section, we discussed each of the popular forms of small business. We also described a couple of firms that started small and grew larger (sometimes much larger). In each of these cases, growth was spurred by the imagination and skill of the entrepreneurs who operated those companies. Although the concepts of entrepreneurship and small business are closely related, in this section we will begin by discussing some important, though often subtle, differences between them. Then we will describe some of the key characteristics of entrepreneurial personalities and activities.

The Workplace Environment

Go Home and Stay There

What makes a successful entrepreneur? That depends on your definition of success. For Michael Bryant, whose one-person consulting firm is called Career Transitions Services, success means having control over the business ebb and flow and keeping to a 4-day workweek. By those standards, Bryant is a complete success, although he'll never be rich or famous.

A career and employment consultant, Bryant has been running his own business out of his home in Baltimore since 1981. He gets as much pleasure from his "life's calling," helping other people find the right career for them, as he does from spending nonworking time at home with his three children. "I love the life I've created," he says.

His success is also due to genuine hard work and diligence. From an early business failure Bryant learned that earning a living had to be his most critical goal. Although he jokes about holding staff meetings ("no one is ever late") and uses the simplest bookkeeping procedures, he pays close attention to his business's finances. He has four main sources of revenue: individual clients, consulting jobs, speeches and

workshops, and corporate outplacement. Although his corporate clients bring in more than 80 percent of his revenues in a typical month, most of his new business comes from leads generated by his speeches, articles, and workshops. Knowing that has helped him allocate his time and energy so as to maintain his present income and keep new clients coming in.

> **"** *I love the life I've created.* **"**
>
> —Michael Bryant, sole proprietor of Career Transitions Services

With this kind of understanding of his business, Bryant can turn to setting monthly revenue goals for himself—and giving himself rewards such as a new camera, a CD-ROM player for his kids, and even some time off. No wonder his idea of a great day is to go to work in the morning and stay there all day.

The Distinction Between Entrepreneurship and Small Business

entrepreneur
Businessperson who accepts both the risks and the opportunities involved in creating and operating a new business venture

Many small businesspeople like to think of themselves as **entrepreneurs**—people who assume the risk of business ownership with a primary goal of growth and expansion. In reality, however, a person may be a small businessperson only, an entrepreneur only, or both. Consider a person who starts a small pizza parlor with no plans other than to earn enough money from the restaurant to lead a comfortable life. That person is clearly a small businessperson. With no plans to grow and expand, he is not really an entrepreneur. On the other hand, an entrepreneur starts with one pizza parlor and fulfills the ambition of turning it into a national chain to rival Domino's or Little Caesar's. Although this person may have started as a small businessperson, the growth of the firm resulted from entrepreneurial vision and activity.

Entrepreneurial Characteristics

In general, most successful entrepreneurs have characteristics that set them apart from most other businesspeople (for example, resourcefulness and a concern for good, often personal, customer relations). Most successful entrepreneurs also have a strong desire to be their own bosses. Many express a need to "gain control over my life" or "build for the family" and believe that building successful businesses will help them do it. They can also handle ambiguity, not knowing what tomorrow holds.[8]

Success and Failure in Small Business

For every Henry Ford, Walt Disney, or Bill Gates—people who transformed small businesses into major corporations—there are many small businesspeople and entrepreneurs who fail. Figure 7.3 illustrates recent trends in new business startups and failures. As you can see, new business startups exceeded 800,000 a year in 1994. Although failures have declined recently, almost 100,000 firms fail each year. In this section, we will look first at a few key trends in small business startups. Then we will examine some of the main reasons for success and failure in small business undertakings.

Figure 7.3 Startups: Success and Failure

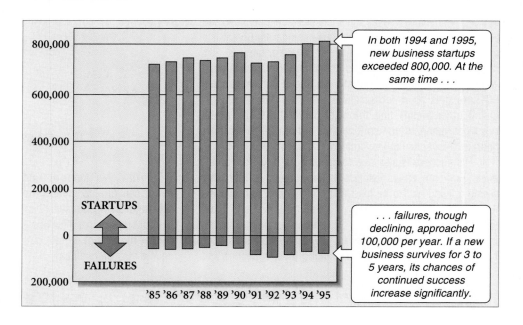

In both 1994 and 1995, new business startups exceeded 800,000. At the same time . . .

. . . failures, though declining, approached 100,000 per year. If a new business survives for 3 to 5 years, its chances of continued success increase significantly.

Trends in Small Business Startups

Thousands of new businesses are started in the United States every year. Several factors account for this trend, and in this section we will focus on four of them: entrepreneurs who cross over from big business, increased opportunities for minorities and women, new opportunities in global enterprise, and improved rates of survival among small businesses.

Crossovers from Big Business

It is interesting to note that, more and more, businesses are being started by people who have opted to leave big corporations and put their experience and know-how to work for themselves.

For example, Ely Callaway left Burlington Industries Inc. after 17 years to found Callaway Golf Co. Callaway developed the Big Bertha Metal Wood driver and a set of equally innovative irons that now enjoy the highest dollar sales of any golf clubs in the United States. Callaway credits his years at Burlington for making him the manager he is today: "I'd rather learn how to ride a bike on somebody else's bicycle," he says, "than on my own."[9]

Opportunities for Minorities and Women

In addition to big business expatriates, more small businesses are being started by minorities. Black-owned businesses, for example, are increasing two and one-half times faster than all other types of startups. T. J. Walker and Carl Jones operate Threads 4 Life, a California-based fashion firm that makes and markets hip, inner-city designs—colorful T-shirts and outsized pants—aimed at young blacks. Walker and Jones realize that, in addition to expressing themselves through street dress, young blacks set broader trends in fashion. Their marketing message therefore has a distinctly multicultural tone. Sixty percent of their clothes are sold to white suburban teens, and they also sell well in Europe and Asia.[10]

The number of women entrepreneurs is also growing rapidly. According to the National Foundation for Women Business Owners, almost a third of all U.S. firms with fewer than 500 employees—some 7.7 million enterprises—are owned or controlled by women. Figure 7.4 shows rates of increase in various industries between 1987 and 1996; the increase in the number of women-owned companies cuts across the business spectrum.

For example, when Hillary Sterba and Nancy Novinc were laid off by Cleveland Twist Drill Co., they decided to pool 26 years of experience and contacts. They started

Figure 7.4   Growth Among Women-Owned Firms in the United States, 1987–1996

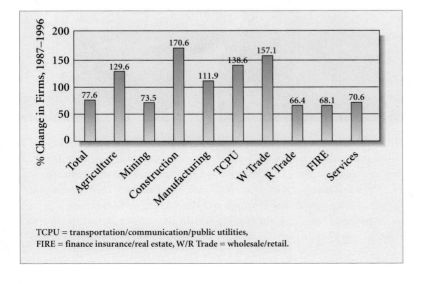

TCPU = transportation/communication/public utilities,
FIRE = finance insurance/real estate, W/R Trade = wholesale/retail.

S&N Engineering Services, which is now a successful competitor in the male-dominated field of tool engineering.[11] Similarly, Brenda French started a small scarf-making operation in a spare bedroom of her home. By using the newest technology as it became available, French's business now generates $5 million a year in sales.

Global Opportunities

Many entrepreneurs today are also finding new opportunities in foreign markets. For example, Michael Giles left a lucrative IBM job to start a new venture in South Africa. Giles saw that the country's black townships had few laundromats. One area, for example, had only four laundromats for 4.5 million people. Using a loan from the U.S. Overseas Private Investment Corp., he launched a chain of 108 coin-operated laundromats throughout the region's black townships. Other entrepreneurs have launched startup newspapers, accounting firms, and communication companies throughout the world, especially in Eastern Europe.[12]

Better Survival Rates

Finally, more people are encouraged to test their skills as entrepreneurs because the failure rate among small businesses has been declining in recent years. During the 1960s and 1970s, for example, less than half of all new startups survived more than 18 months; only one in five lasted 10 years. Now, however, new businesses have a better chance of surviving. Of new businesses started in the 1980s, for instance, over 77 percent remained in operation for at least 3 years. Today, the SBA estimates that at least 40 percent of all new businesses can expect to survive for 6 years.

When CEO Brenda French founded French Rags, a small scarf-making business, in 1978, her basic goal—and challenge—was to produce custom-made knitwear to be sold directly to customers. In addition to a sell-at-home distribution scheme, the means to meeting this challenge was technology. From Silicon Graphics, French first acquired a workstation for designing knitwear. Then partner, Milé Rasic designed a software program for producing templates and loading yarn for fast and easy switching from garment to garment. New machines duplicate hand-knit quality with mass-production speed, and items that used to take a skilled craftsperson a day and a half can now be produced in less than an hour.

Location, Location, Location

So you want to be an entrepreneur? You may be interested in knowing what are considered the best areas in the United States for setting up shop.

In a recent survey of the state of small business, *Inc.* magazine identified four outstanding metropolitan areas for entrepreneurs. The criteria were the right work force, undervalued (that is, cheap) resources, a hungry market, intellectual capital, coaching and contacts, lack of distractions, small business organizations, capital, and a positive business culture. The four cities that scored high on most of these attributes were

■ Fort Myers, FL, "the boomtown." Rapid population growth is creating new markets for goods and services.

■ Raleigh-Durham, NC, "the science city." Many industrial parks and three major universities provide an orderly business culture conducive to hi-tech firms.

■ Houston, TX, "the reinvented district." The city is back on the upswing, and "the best place in the country to do business, even if no one on the outside knows it," according to Houston motel owner Don Wang.

■ Culver City, CA, "the networked neighborhood." Thanks to its proximity to film and video centers such as Venice, Santa Monica, and Hollywood, many companies here can maintain ties to the lucrative entertainment industry.

If none of these locales appeal to you, try the 10 metropolitan areas with the greatest number of business start-ups per 100 people: Anchorage, AK, Boulder-Longmont, CO, Austin–San Marcos, TX, Houston, TX, Denver, CO, Colorado Springs, CO, Las Vegas, NV, Dallas, TX, Boise City, ID, and Provo-Orem, UT.

Houston may be your best bet—it's the only city to appear on both lists.

Reasons for Failure

Unfortunately, 60 percent of all new businesses will not celebrate a sixth anniversary. Why do some succeed and others fail? Although there is no set pattern, there are some common causes of both failure and success.

Four general factors contribute to small business failure:

■ Managerial incompetence or inexperience. If managers do not know how to make basic business decisions, they are unlikely to be successful in the long run.

■ Neglect. Starting a small business requires an overwhelming time commitment.

■ Weak control systems. If control systems do not signal impending problems, managers may be in serious trouble before more visible difficulties alert them.

■ Insufficient capital. A new business should have enough capital to operate at least 6 months without earning a profit.

Reasons for Success

Similarly, four basic factors are typically cited to explain small business success:

■ Hard work, drive, and dedication. Small business owners must be committed to succeeding and be willing to put in the time and effort to make it happen.

■ Market demand for the products or services being provided. Careful analysis of market conditions can help small businesspeople assess the probable reception of their products in the marketplace.

■ Managerial competence. Successful small businesspeople may acquire competence through training or experience, or by using the expertise of others.

■ Luck. Luck also plays a role in the success of some firms. For example, after Alan McKim started Clean Harbors, an environmental cleanup firm based in New England, he struggled to keep his business afloat. Then the U.S. government committed $1.6 billion to toxic waste cleanup, McKim's specialty. He was able to get several large government contracts and put his business on solid financial footing. Had the government fund not been created at just the right time, McKim may have failed.

Starting and Operating the Small Business

Several other factors contribute to the success of a small business. In particular, most successful entrepreneurs make the right decisions when they start their businesses. For example, they must decide precisely how to get into business. Should they buy an existing business or build from the ground up? In addition, would-be entrepreneurs must find appropriate sources of financing and decide when to seek the advice of experts.

Starting the Small Business

An old Chinese saying notes that a journey of a thousand miles begins with a single step. This is also true of a new business. The first step is the individual's commitment to becoming a small businessperson. Next is choosing the good or service to be offered, a process that means investigating one's chosen industry and market. Making this choice also requires would-be entrepreneurs to assess not only industry trends but also their own skills. Like the managers of big businesses, small businesspeople must also be sure that they understand the true nature of their businesses.

Buying Out an Existing Business

After choosing a product and making sure that the choice fits his or her skills and interests, an entrepreneur must decide whether to buy an existing business or to start from scratch. Consultants often recommend the first approach. Quite simply, the odds are better: If successful, an existing business has already proved its ability to draw customers at a profit. It has established working relationships with lenders, suppliers, and the community. Moreover, the track record of an existing business gives potential buyers a much clearer picture of what to expect than any estimate of a new business's prospects. Around 30 percent of the new businesses started in the past decade were bought from someone else.

Starting from Scratch

Some people seek the satisfaction that comes from planting an idea, nurturing it, and making it grow into a strong and sturdy business. There are also practical reasons to start a business from scratch. A new business does not suffer the ill effects of a prior owner's errors. The startup owner is also free to choose lenders, equipment, inventories, locations, suppliers, and workers, unbound by a predecessor's commitments and policies. Of the new businesses begun in the past decade, 64 percent were started from scratch. (The remaining 6 percent of all new businesses were inherited or created when one partner bought out another.)

▶ **INTUIT QUICKENS THE PACE IN SOFTWARE SALES.** One conspicuous startup success is a company called Intuit. The enterprise was born when Scott Cook, a former Procter & Gamble brand manager, realized that most people hate to balance their checkbooks and otherwise handle their household accounting chores. Convinced that the solution was computerization, Cook teamed up with a college computer major named Tom Proulx. Together, they started Intuit and developed a personal finance software program called Quicken.

The early years were a struggle; the partners sometimes failed to make payroll. Skeptics denounced the Intuit idea as "stupid," and Cook recalls "the honor of getting turned down by some of the finest venture-capital firms in the country." A more serious problem was competition: There were already more than two dozen similar software packages on the market. After 2 years of modest growth, Cook and Proulx decided to invest their last $100,000 in direct response advertising in computer magazines. When their ads appealed to small business owners, Quicken sales caught fire, and by 1990 Intuit's revenues had reached $33 million.

Ultimately, a combination of entrepreneurship, a hit product, and solid management paid off in a big way. Moreover, events in a once-hostile competitive environment also transpired in Intuit's favor. Personal finance software caught on, and sales of all titles tripled between 1991 and 1993. By 1994, some 6 million people were using Quicken; in 1993 alone, Intuit sold 1.5 million copies of the $39 program. As Cook sees it, Quicken succeeded because of its simplicity. "People don't buy technology," he believes. "They don't say 'Fill' er up. I'll take 10 gallons of technology.' They buy what technology does for them." Users seem to agree: "It almost makes bill paying fun," reports one. "I haven't fired my accountant, but it's given me reports that make my accountant less expensive."

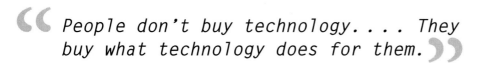

People don't buy technology. . . . They buy what technology does for them.

—Scott Cook, cofounder of Intuit

Obviously, stories such as Cook and Proulx's are the exceptions. For one thing, the risks of starting a business from scratch are greater than those of buying an existing firm. Founders of new businesses can only make predictions and projections about their prospects. Success or failure thus depends heavily on identifying a genuine business opportunity—a product for which many customers will pay well that is currently unavailable to them. To find openings, entrepreneurs must study their markets and answer the following questions:

- Who are my customers?

- Where are they?

- At what price will they buy my product?

- In what quantities will they buy?

- Who are my competitors?

- How will my product differ from those of my competitors?

Finding answers to these questions is a difficult task even for large, well-established firms. Where can the small businessperson get the necessary information? Other sources of assistance are discussed later in this chapter, but we will briefly describe three of the most accessible here:

- The best way to gain knowledge about a market is to work in it before going into business in it. For example, if you once worked in a bookstore and now plan to open one of your own, you probably already have some idea about the kinds of books people request and buy.

- A quick scan of the Yellow Pages will reveal many potential competitors, as will advertisements in trade journals. Personal visits to these establishments can give you insights into their strengths and weaknesses.

- Studying magazines and books aimed specifically at small businesses can also be of help, as can hiring professionals to survey the market for you.

Financing the Small Business

Although the choice of how to start is obviously important, it is meaningless unless a small businessperson can obtain the money to set up shop. As Figure 7.5 shows, a wide variety of monetary resources, ranging from private to government sources, is available. Notice that lending institutions are more likely to help finance the purchase of an existing business than a new business because the risks are better understood. Individuals starting up new businesses must rely more on their personal resources.

According to a study by the National Federation of Independent Business, an owner's personal resources, not loans, are the most important source of money. Including money borrowed from friends and relatives, personal resources account for over two-thirds of all money invested in new small businesses and one-half of that invested in the purchase of existing businesses.

Although banks, independent investors, and government loans all provide much smaller portions of startup funds than the personal resources of owners, they are important in many cases. However, getting money from these sources requires some extra effort. Banks and private investors usually want to see formal business plans—that is, detailed outlines of proposed businesses and markets, owners' backgrounds, and other sources of funding. Government loans have strict eligibility guidelines.

Small Business Investment Companies

Small business investment companies (SBICs) take a more balanced approach in their choices than do **venture capital firms**, which seek profits from investments in companies with potential for rapid growth. Created by the Small Business Investment Act of 1958, SBICs are federally licensed to borrow money from the SBA and to invest it in or lend it to small businesses. They are themselves investments for their shareholders. Past beneficiaries of SBIC capital include Apple Computer, Intel, and Federal Express. In addition, the government has recently begun to sponsor **minority enterprise small business investment companies** (MESBICs). As the name suggests, MESBICs specialize in financing businesses that are owned and operated by minorities.[13]

small business investment company (SBIC) Federally licensed company that borrows money from the SBA to invest in or make loans to small businesses

venture capital firm Group of small investors that invests money in companies with rapid growth potential

minority enterprise small business investment company (MESBIC) Federally sponsored company that specializes in financing minority-owned and -operated businesses

Figure 7.5 Financing the Small Business

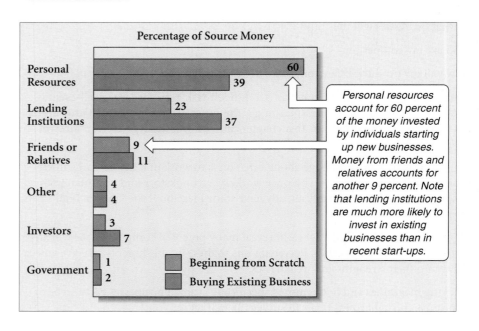

Foreign Investors

Another fairly new (but growing) source of funds is foreign investors. Several Japanese firms, for example, have established venture capital operations for investing in small U.S. businesses. Like venture capital firms, foreign investors usually seek high-growth ventures because they have the highest potential return. Japanese venture capitalists are currently investing almost $500 million a year in small U.S. companies.

SBA Financial Programs

Since its founding in 1953, the SBA has offered more than 20 financing programs to small businesses that meet standards in size and independence. Eligible firms must also be unable to get private financing at reasonable terms. Because of these and other restrictions, SBA loans have never been a major source of small business financing. In addition, budget cutbacks at the SBA have reduced the number of firms benefiting from loans. Several SBA programs currently offer funds to qualified applicants:

■ Under the SBA's **guaranteed loans program**, small businesses can borrow from commercial lenders. The SBA guarantees to repay 75 to 85 percent of the loan amount, not to exceed $750,000. Under a related program, companies engaged in international trade can borrow up to $1.25 million. Such loans may be made for as long as 15 years. Most SBA lending activity flows through this program.[14]

■ Sometimes both the desired bank and SBA-guaranteed loans are unavailable (perhaps because the business cannot meet stringent requirements). In such cases, the SBA may help finance the entrepreneur through its **immediate participation loans program**. Under this arrangement, the SBA and the bank each put up a share of the money, with the SBA's share not to exceed $150,000.

■ Under the **local development companies (LDCs) program**, the SBA works with a corporation (either for-profit or nonprofit) founded by local citizens who want to boost the local economy. The SBA can lend up to $500,000 for each small business to be helped by an LDC.

Sources of Management Advice

Financing is not the only area in which small businesses need help. Until World War II, for example, the business world involved few regulations, few taxes, few records, few big competitors, and no computers. Since then, simplicity has given way to complexity: Today, few entrepreneurs are equipped with all the business skills they need to survive.

Small businesspeople can no longer be their own troubleshooters, lawyers, bookkeepers, financiers, and tax experts. For these jobs, they rely on professional help. But to survive and grow, small businesses also need advice regarding management. This advice is usually available from four sources: advisory boards, management consultants, the SBA, and a process called networking.

Advisory Boards

All companies, even those that do not legally need boards of directors, can benefit from the problem-solving abilities of advisory boards. Thus, some small businesses create boards to provide advice and assistance. For example, an advisory board might help an entrepreneur determine the best way to finance a plant expansion or to start exporting products to foreign markets.

Management Consultants

Opinions vary widely about the value of **management consultants**: experts who charge fees to help managers solve problems. They often specialize in one area, such as international business, small business, or manufacturing. Thus, they can bring objective and trained eyes to problems and provide logical recommendations. However, they can be quite expensive. Some consultants charge $1,000 or more for one day of assistance.

guaranteed loans program
Program in which the SBA guarantees to repay 75 to 85 percent of small business commercial loans up to $750,000

immediate participation loans program
Program in which small businesses are lent funds put up jointly by banks and the SBA

local development companies (LDCs) program
Program in which the SBA works with local for-profit or nonprofit organizations seeking to boost a community's economy

management consultant
Independent outside specialist hired to help managers solve business problems

Like other professionals, consultants should be chosen with care. They can be found through major corporations who have used their services and who can provide references and reports on their work. Not surprisingly, they are most effective when the client helps (for instance, by providing schedules and written proposals for work to be done).[15]

The Small Business Administration

Even more important than its financing role is the SBA's role in helping small business-people improve their management skills. It is easy for entrepreneurs to spend money; SBA programs are designed to show them how to spend it wisely. The SBA offers small businesses four major management counseling programs at virtually no cost:

- A small businessperson who needs help in starting a new business can get it free through the **Service Corps of Retired Executives (SCORE)**. All SCORE members are retired executives, and all are volunteers. Under this program, the SBA tries to match the expert to the need. For example, if a small businessperson needs help putting together a marketing plan, the SBA will send a SCORE counselor with marketing expertise.

- Like SCORE, the **Active Corps of Executives (ACE)** program is designed to help small businesses that cannot afford consultants. The SBA recruits ACE volunteers from virtually every industry. All ACE volunteers are currently involved in successful activities, mostly as small businesspeople themselves. Together, SCORE and ACE have more than 12,000 counselors working out of 350 chapters throughout the United States. They provide assistance to some 140,000 small businesses each year.

- The talents and skills of students and instructors at colleges and universities are fundamental to the **Small Business Institute (SBI)**. Under the guidance of seasoned professors of business administration, students seeking advanced degrees work closely with small businesspeople to help solve specific problems, such as sagging sales or rising costs. Students earn credit toward their degrees, with their grades depending on how well they handle a client's problems. Several hundred colleges and universities counsel thousands of small businesspeople through this program every year.

- The newest of the SBA's management counseling projects is its **Small Business Development Center (SBDC)** program. Begun in 1976, SBDCs are designed to consolidate information from various disciplines and institutions, including technical and professional schools. Then they make this knowledge available to new and existing small businesses. In 1995, universities in 45 states took part in the program.

Networking

More and more, small businesspeople are discovering the value of **networking**: meeting regularly with one another to discuss common problems and opportunities and, perhaps most important, pool resources. Businesspeople have long joined organizations such as the local Chamber of Commerce and the National Federation of Independent Businesses (NFIB) to make such contacts.

Today, organizations are springing up all over the United States to facilitate small business networking. One such organization, the Council of Smaller Enterprises of Cleveland, boasts a total membership of more than 9,000 small businesspeople, the largest number in the country. This organization offers its members not only networking possibilities but also educational programs and services tailored to their needs. In a typical year, its 85 educational programs draw more than 8,500 small businesspeople.

In particular, women and minorities have found networking to be an effective problem-solving tool. For example, the Chief Executive Roundtable, a group of women business owners from across the United States, meets in a different major city every month to discuss and solve business problems. Topics range from dealing with late-paying customers to conflicts between partners over financing expansion. Sponsored by the New York–based American Women's Economic Development Corp., the Roundtable's members own and operate companies with annual sales of $1 million to $10 million.[16]

Service Corps of Retired Executives (SCORE) SBA program in which retired executives work with small businesses on a volunteer basis

Active Corps of Executives (ACE) SBA program in which currently employed executives work with small businesses on a volunteer basis

Small Business Institute (SBI) SBA program in which college and university students and instructors work with small businesspeople to help solve specific problems

Small Business Development Center (SBDC) SBA program designed to consolidate information from various disciplines and to make it available to small businesses

networking Interactions among businesspeople for the purpose of discussing mutual problems and opportunities and perhaps pooling resources

Franchising

▶ When Louis Minella left his job as a store planner for Sears, he did the same thing as thousands of other managers who have voluntarily left—or been forced out of—big companies: After 31 years in the corporate world, Minella decided join the ranks of more than a half million small business owners who run their own franchise stores. "It was time to do something different," says Minella, who adds, "I'm in reality now."

Minella chose Mail Boxes Inc., a San Diego–based company that serves at-home businesses, mobile workers, and large corporate accounts. For an up-front fee and a percentage of gross sales, Minella received rights to the Mail Boxes name, advertising support, and access to a variety of national accounts, such as Xerox and Panasonic, whose employees can contract to use his facility as a branch office for postal services such as mailing, shipping, and faxing. To succeed in his new undertaking, then, Louis Minella had to master such nuts-and-bolts skills as sending faxes, making photocopies, and operating a cash register. Not everyone can make the transition, but Mail Boxes happens to be one franchiser that thinks corporate refugees are the best bet. They "tend to be better business people," says President Tony DeSio, who appreciates the fact that they perform the management basics, such as "checking their pricing and making sure costs are being controlled."[17]

As many people like Louis Minella have discovered, franchising agreements are an accessible doorway to entrepreneurship. A **franchise** is an arrangement that permits the franchisee (buyer) to sell the product of the franchiser (seller, or parent company). Franchisees can thus benefit from the selling corporation's experience and expertise. They can also consult the franchiser for managerial and financial help.

For example, the franchiser may supply financing. It may pick the store location, negotiate the lease, design the store, and purchase necessary equipment. It may train the first set of employees and managers and provide standardized policies and procedures. Once the business is open, the franchiser may offer savings by allowing it to purchase from a central location. Marketing strategy (especially advertising) may also be handled by the franchiser. Finally, franchisees may benefit from continued management counseling. In short, franchisees receive—that is, invest in—not only their own ready-made businesses but expert help in running them.

franchise
Arrangement in which a buyer (franchisee) purchases the right to sell the good or service of the seller (franchiser)

Advantages and Disadvantages of Franchising

Franchises offer many advantages to both sellers and buyers. For example, franchisers benefit from the ability to grow rapidly by using the investment money provided by franchisees. This strategy has enabled giant franchisers such as McDonald's and Baskin-Robbins to mushroom into billion-dollar concerns in a brief time.

For the franchisee, the arrangement combines the incentive of owning a business with the advantage of access to big business management skills. Unlike the person who starts from scratch, the franchisee does not have to build a business step by step. Instead, the business is established virtually overnight. Moreover, because each franchise outlet is probably a carbon copy of every other outlet, the chances of failure are reduced. According to the U.S. Department of Commerce, only 5 percent of all franchises in the country were discontinued in 1990.

Of course there are disadvantages as well. Perhaps the most significant is the startup cost. Franchise prices vary widely. Fantastic Sam's hair salon franchise fees are $25,000, but a Gingiss Formalwear franchise can run as high as $100,000. Extremely profitable or hard-to-get franchises are even more expensive. A McDonald's franchise costs $650,000 to $750,000, and a professional sports team can cost several million dollars. Franchisees may also have continued obligations to contribute percentages of sales to parent corporations.

Buying a franchise also entails less tangible costs. For one thing, the small businessperson sacrifices some independence. A McDonald's franchisee cannot change the way hamburgers or milkshakes are made. Nor can franchisees create individual identities in their communities; for all practical purposes, the McDonald's owner is anonymous. In addition, many franchise agreements are difficult to terminate.

Finally, although franchises minimize risks, they do not guarantee success. Many franchisees have seen their investments—and their dreams—disappear because of poor locations, rising costs, or lack of continued franchiser commitment. Moreover, figures on failure rates are artificially low because they do not include failing franchisees bought out by their franchising parent companies. An additional risk is that the chain itself could collapse. In any given year, dozens—sometimes hundreds—of franchisers close shop or stop selling franchises.

Summary of Learning Objectives

1 **Define *small business* and explain its importance to the U.S. economy.** A small business is independently owned and managed and does not dominate its market. Small businesses are crucial to the economy because they create new jobs, foster entrepreneurship and innovation, and supply goods and services needed by larger businesses.

2 **Explain which types of small business best lend themselves to success.** Services are the easiest operations for small businesspeople to start because they require low levels of resources. They also offer high returns on investment and tend to foster innovation. Retailing and wholesaling are more difficult because they usually require some experience, but they are still attractive to many entrepreneurs. New technology and management techniques are making agriculture profitable once again for small farmers. As the most resource-intensive area of the economy, manufacturing is the area least dominated by small firms.

3 **Define *entrepreneurship* and describe some basic entrepreneurial characteristics.** Entrepreneurs are small businesspeople who assume the risk of business ownership. Unlike many businesspeople, they seek growth and expansion as their primary goal. Most successful entrepreneurs share a strong desire to be their own bosses and believe that building businesses will help them gain control over their lives and build for their families. Many also enjoy taking risks and committing themselves to the necessary time and work. Finally, most report that freedom and creative expression are important factors in the decision to own and operate their own businesses.

4 **Describe the startup decisions made by small businesses and identify sources of financial aid and management advice available to such enterprises.** In deciding to go into business, the entrepreneur must choose between buying an existing business and starting from scratch. There are practical advantages and disadvantages to both approaches. A successful existing business has working relationships with other businesses and has already proved its ability to make a profit. New businesses, on the other hand, allow owners to plan and work with clean slates, but it is hard to make projections about the business's prospects.

Although small businesspeople generally draw heavily on their own resources for financing, they can get financial aid from venture capital firms, which seek profits from investments in companies with rapid growth potential. The Small Business Administration (SBA) also sponsors a variety of loan programs, including small business investment companies. Finally, foreign firms and other nonbank lenders make funds available under various circumstances. Management advice is available from advisory boards, management consultants, the SBA, and the practice of networking (meeting regularly with people in related businesses to discuss problems and opportunities).

5 **Identify the advantages and disadvantages of franchising.** Franchising has become a popular form of small business ownership because the franchiser (parent company) supplies financial, managerial, and marketing assistance to the franchisee, who buys the right to sell the franchiser's product. Franchising also enables small businesses to

grow rapidly. Finally, the risks in franchising are lower than those in starting a new business from scratch. However, the costs of purchasing a franchise can be quite high, and the franchisee sacrifices independence and creativity. In addition, franchises are no guarantee of success.

Questions and Exercises

Questions for Review

1 Why are small businesses important to the U.S. economy?
2 What key factors typically contribute to the success and failure of small businesses?
3 Identify the primary sources of funding for small businesses and rank them in order of importance.
4 From the standpoint of the franchisee, what are the primary advantages and disadvantages of most franchise arrangements?

Questions for Analysis

5 If you were going to open a small business, what type would it be? Why?
6 Do you think you would be a successful entrepreneur? Why or why not?
7 Would you prefer to buy an existing business or start your own business from scratch? Why?
8 Would you prefer to open an independent business or enter a franchise agreement? Why?

Application Exercises

9 Select a small local firm that has gone out of business recently. Identify as many factors as you can that led to the company's failure.
10 At the library, research the role of small business in another country.

Building Your Business Skills

This exercise enhances the following SCANS workplace competencies: demonstrating basic skills, demonstrating thinking skills, exhibiting interpersonal skills, and working with information.

Goal To encourage students to define the opportunities and problems for small companies doing business on the Internet.

Situation Suppose you and two partners own a gift basket store, specializing in special-occasion baskets for individual and corporate clients. You're doing well in your community, but feel that there may be opportunity for growth through a virtual storefront on the Internet.

Method **Step 1:** Come together with two other students and assume the role of business partners. Start by researching Internet businesses. Look at books and article at the library, and contact the following Web sites for help:
  • Small Business Administration: http://www.sba.gov/
  • IBM Small Business Center: http://www.businesscenter.ibm.com/
  • Apple Small Business Home Page: http://www.smallbusiness.apple.com/

These sites may lead you to other sites, so keep an open mind.

Step 2: Based on your research, determine the importance of the following small business issues:
  • An analysis of changing company finances as a result of expansion onto the Internet

- An analysis of your new competitive marketplace (the world) and how it affects your current marketing approach, which focuses on your local community
- Identification of sources of management advice as the expansion proceeds
- The role of technology consultants in launching and maintaining the Web site
- Customer service policies in your virtual environment

Follow-Up Questions

1 Do you think your business would be successful on the Internet? Why or why not?
2 Based on your analysis, how will Internet expansion affect your current business practices? What specific changes are you likely to make?
3 Do you think that operating a virtual storefront will be harder or easier than doing business in your local community? Explain your answer.

Vincent Yost has what he thinks is a great new product, a "smart" parking meter. The trouble is, he can't get anyone to buy it.

The new meter can sense when a car has pulled away, and it automatically resets the time to zero when that happens, eliminating the occasional free-parking bonus for drivers but offering cities the opportunity to increase parking meter revenues. The meter also counts coins automatically, which cuts down on theft of receipts by employees, a common problem for municipal parking departments. In addition to the difficulty of selling to city governments, which typically move on such purchases with glacial slowness and deliberation, Yost faces several other concerns.

First, his product is sure to be unpopular with voters, which understandably gives politicians pause. Second, it is quite expensive—about $400 compared to about $150 for competitors' electronic models. Yost offers a leasing program and promises that the product will pay for itself, but so far there are no takers. Part of his high cost arises from his decision to outsource the manufacture of the meter's coin-handling mechanism, for which he pays top dollar. In addition, the meter had some early glitches getting enough power out of its batteries. Yost says these problems have been fixed.

On the plus side, the time seems to be right for cities to make the next big leap in parking meter technology. For one thing, Yost's new meter can help cut labor costs by replacing expensive researchers and consultants with hand-held remote units that provide the same kind of data on motorists' parking habits. It's expected that in the next 10 years about 90 percent of the nation's 5 million parking meters will be electronic instead of mechanical. Yost, who has only four technical employees and does his own typing, would like a piece of that market, but he may not have enough time left to wait for it to come. The competition will be catching up with him soon, and to keep the company financed, Yost has been selling shares of the firm to some of his suppliers. He is now in danger of losing his majority voting position. "I didn't anticipate this," he says.

Questions

1. Can Yost improve the appeal of his product to the public and thereby to the politicians who control city budgets?
2. Do you think Yost is doing everything he can to contain costs? Why or why not?
3. Yost currently allows potential customers to do field testing of the meter, which takes them several months, and he lets the cities keep any revenue the meters generate in the tests. Is this strategy in his company's best interest? Why or why not?
4. Yost has so far made one sale, to the town of New Hope, PA, which bought 58 meters. Given that politicians are reluctant to be innovators, how might Yost use the sale to leverage other sales?
5. City budgets are annual, and when Yost misses a budget he loses an entire year. How might he lessen the impact of such a loss? Are there any ways in which he can try to shorten the selling process?

Connecting to the Web

The following Web sites will give you additional information and points of view about topics covered in this chapter. Many sites lead to other related Internet locations, so approach this list with the spirit of an explorer.

APPLE SMALL BUSINESS HOME PAGE

http://www.smallbusiness.apple.com/

This site is a valuable resource for small business owners. It features expert advice, discussion areas, and information on Apple products.

DUN & BRADSTREET'S SMALL BUSINESS SERVICES

http://www.dnb.com/sbs/hmenu.htm

This site includes practical tips on how to manage a small business. Among the issues explored are coping with regulations and paperwork, as well as time and financial management.

ENTREPRENEUR MAGAZINE: THE ONLINE SMALL BUSINESS AUTHORITY

http://www.entrepreneurmag.com/

Visit this site for articles on entrepreneurship and small business from the print version of *Entrepreneur* magazine.

HOME BUSINESS BOOKSTORE

http://www.homebusiness.com/bookstore

This online bookstore specializes in books and tapes about small and home businesses.

HOME OFFICE ASSOCIATION OF AMERICA

http://www.hoaa.com/

The Home Office Association of America serves the needs of millions of full-time home-based professionals, including telecommuters. Click on this site for the organization's online newsletter, membership services, and information on related sites.

IBM SMALL BUSINESS CENTER

http://www.businesscenter.ibm.com/

This specialized IBM Web site is designed for small business owners who are interested in small business information and IBM product information.

INTERNATIONAL FRANCISE ASSOCIATION (IFA)

http://www.franchise.org/

The International Franchise Association is dedicated to promoting the business environment for franchising. Visit this site for information about IFA activities and the resources it offers current and prospective franchisees and franchisers.

MINORITY BUSINESS DEVELOPMENT AGENCY (MBDA)

http://www.mbda.gov/textonly/intro.html

The mission of the federal Minority Business Development Agency is to foster the creation, growth, and expansion of minority-owned businesses in the United States. Visit this site to learn about specific assistance for minority business owners.

NATIONAL FOUNDATION FOR WOMEN BUSINESS OWNERS (NFWBO)

http://www.nfwbo.org

NFWBO provides original research to document the economic and social contributions of women-owned businesses and leadership development for women who own and lead growing enterprises.

SBA: SMALL BUSINESS ADMINISTRATION

http://www.sba.gov/

Packed with valuable information, this home page should be every small business owner's home base. Included is information on starting and expanding small businesses, small business financing, disaster assistance, pertinent legislation and regulations, and leads to additional resources.

SCORE: SERVICE CORPS OF RETIRED EXECUTIVES

http://www.score.org/

With chapters in every state, the Service Corps of Retired Executives works with the Small Business Administration to promote the formation, growth, and success of small businesses. Visit this site for information about SCORE's mentoring services.

part three

Understanding
People
in Organizations

What could be more serious than running an airline? Meeting schedules, maintaining equipment, tracking baggage, training staff, dealing with federal and
state regulations, and keeping customers happy are
ingredients for stress—or so it would seem. Then why
does Herb Kelleher, cofounder and chief executive of
Southwest Airlines, encourage his 25,000 employees
to outsmile and outjoke the competition? Because
Kelleher believes that a workplace that is fun is also a
workplace with high productivity. And that means that
Southwest can charge less and earn more.

Figures don't lie: Operating costs at Southwest are 7.5 cents per seat per mile, and the per mile operating costs of other airlines are 2 cents higher. Southwest's profit margin is more than 6 percent, but other airlines earn about a third less. The result: Southwest has become the nation's most consistently profitable, rapidly growing airline.

Fun + Empowerment + Respect = High Productivity

The employee productivity that made Southwest the nation's fifth largest airline is a sight to behold: Whereas it takes other airlines a full 45 minutes to service arriving planes and get them back in the air, Southwest does it in just 20 minutes. In what can best be described as a whirlwind of activity, employees fuel the plane, load and unload passengers and bags, and restock refreshments (Southwest doesn't serve meals). Everyone pitches in, including pilots, who can be seen picking up trash along with the ground crew. These break-the-sound-barrier turnarounds enable Southwest's fleet of 250 planes to do the job of 300.

Employees work their tails off largely because of the corporate culture Herb Kelleher created—a culture based on respect for the individual, empowerment, and just plain fun. A case in point is Marilyn, a flight attendant, who takes the mike as her plane backs away from the Houston terminal.

"Could y'all lean in a little toward the center aisle, please?' she chirps in an irresistible Southern drawl. "Just a bit, please," she says. "That's it. No, the other way, sir. Thanks." Baffled passengers comply, but have no idea why until Marilyn hits the punch line: "You see, the pilot has to pull out of this space here, and he needs to be able to check the rearview mirrors." When the laughter subsides, Marilyn begins the standard safety speech. An environment that respects individuals enough to encourage this kind of unique self-expression has helped make Southwest the number one company in *Fortune* Magazine's list of the 100 best companies to work for in America.

Employees Come First

Kelleher believes that his employees are his prime business advantage. Competitors "can imitate the airplanes. They can imitate our ticket counters and all the other hardware," he said. "But they can't duplicate the people of Southwest and their attitudes. . . . It used to be a business conundrum: 'Who comes first? The employees, customers, or shareholders?' That's never been an issue to me. The employees come first. If they're happy, satisfied, dedicated, and energetic, they'll take real good care of the customers. When the customers are happy, they come back. And that makes the shareholders happy."

Of the 150,000 résumés Southwest receives a year, it hires just 5,000 people. Those who make the cut are chosen mainly for their can-do attitude, their desire to color outside the lines, and their sense of humor. New employees are trained at Southwest's University for People, where they are encouraged to reach their personal best and to do whatever they are doing better, faster, and cheaper.

Employees are rewarded for taking initiative and making decisions that are sound for the situation. They are trained to look beyond the obvious through a cross-training program that gives them the big picture of company operations. When pilots help skycaps and reservationists work with baggage handlers, they begin to take ownership of total operations and find ways to make a difference. Kelleher realizes that mistakes are inevitable when people take responsibility, but punishment is not part of this human resource plan. His focus is on learning and doing better the next time.

In return for dedicated service, employees receive impressive benefits:

- *Job security:* Southwest has never furloughed anyone in 27 years.

- *Opportunities for personal career growth:* Stability brings steady promotions that depend on skill, experience, and attitude.

- *Perks:* Employees with perfect attendance for 3 months receive two free space-available airline tickets to anywhere Southwest travels.

- *Compensation:* Southwest is a union company (more than 8 out of 10 employees are union members) with union wages that are negotiated for the entire airline industry. Kelleher sweetens the compensation pot through a generous profit-sharing plan that invests in Southwest stock. Southwest's superior stock market performance has made millionaires out of many long-time employees.

- *Social gatherings:* Motivation in the form of fun can be found at Christmas parties in July, chili cook-offs, and outlandish Halloween bashes.

"It All Starts with Herb"

Herb Kelleher's leadership style has a lot to do with the success of Southwest. "It all starts with Herb," said pilot Sonny Childers. "I've seen Herb hand out peanuts on flights. He'll go out the Wednesday before Thanksgiving and load bags onto planes. We know he'd never ask us to do anything he wouldn't do himself."

And then there's the fun. "He is a true party animal who is always the last one standing," says director of employment Sherry Phelps. Kelleher takes several trips a month, and he can be found handing out peanuts and cracking jokes with passengers and crew. He has also been known to visit mechanics on the night shift wearing a feather boa and floppy hat.

Is Kelleher's fun leadership style important to productivity and profits? Absolutely, says Robert Levering, coauthor of *The 100 Best Companies to Work for in America*. "The fact is that in companies that are truly fun, [fun] is a separate objective. People explicitly say this is what we want to do here: We want to have fun. After all, what's life for and what's work for?"

The Challenge Ahead

Since its first flight in June 1971, Southwest Airlines has expanded from its home base in Dallas to Louisiana, New Mexico, Oklahoma, Arizona, California, the Midwest, Florida, Rhode Island, Alabama, and Maryland, and it now flies coast-to-coast with one stopover. Kelleher's next expansion target is expected to be the New York region. As Southwest expands, passengers follow in search of low-cost, efficient transportation.

Perhaps the greatest challenge facing Kelleher is maintaining the corporate culture as the company grows. Is it likely that Southwest will find employees in the Northeast who can embrace the company's core values? More pointedly, can Southwest turn the legendary New York what-are-you-bothering-me-for scowl into a helpful smile? Kelleher is hopeful. "There are people everywhere who fit into the Southwest culture," he said.

Kelleher also believes that from management's point of view, bigger does not necessarily mean different. "You should not get yourself into a rigid frame of mind where you say, 'By virtue of the fact that we're bigger, we have to function differently,' and give up all the advantages that the smaller, more entrepreneurial company has. We've tried to reduce the bureaucracy and avoid the hierarchy as much as we can," said Kelleher. We want people to continue to "deal with each other person-to-person and informally instead of through a formalized network of communication." As managers, "we never think that [we] get too big to have a personal relationship with the people of Southwest Airlines."

Along with Southwest Airlines, the January 12, 1998, issue of Fortune Magazine lists the following companies as among the 100 best companies to work for in the United States. Visit their Web sites and see what you learn about their attitude toward employees. The information in these sites will help you answer the questions that follow.

Corning	http://www.corning.com/
Deloitte & Touche	http://www.dttus.com/us/home.htm
Microsoft Job Search	http://www.microsoft.com/jobs/visit.htm
Smucker's	http://www.smucker.com/
Southwest Airlines	http://www.southwest.com/
TDIndustries	http://www.tdindustries.com/

CASE QUESTIONS

1 As a motivational factor, how important is fun likely to be in your personal job choice? Do you think it will be more or less important than good pay and benefits?

2 Why is Southwest's no-furlough policy so important to employee morale?

3 Do you think that Herb Kelleher believes in theory X or theory Y? Explain your answer. Explain why you think Corning, Deloitte & Touch, Microsoft, Smucker's, and TDIndustries are theory Y organizations.

4 Based on the information in this case and on Southwest Airlines' Web site, how does Herzberg's two-factor theory apply to employees at Southwest?

5 Why is empowerment such an important motivational factor at Southwest? What evidence do you see at the other Web sites that employees have a voice in the management of their jobs and the company?

6 How would you describe Herb Kelleher's leadership style? Do you consider Kelleher a year-2000 leader? Explain your answer.

chapter 8

Managing human resources

Diversity reigns

Brian Dickinson is a well-known and well-respected newspaper reporter for the Providence *Journal-Bulletin* in Rhode Island. He has rarely missed a deadline in his nearly 35 years in the business, and he normally puts in 8 to 9 hours of writing a day, 7 days a week.

Dickinson is also profoundly disabled by amyotrophic lateral sclerosis (ALS), unable to speak, swallow, move arms or legs, use his fingers, or turn his head. But with the help of the new technology of the Eyegaze computer from LC Technologies, he produces a steady flow of work including columns, book reviews, and letters and e-mail to his family.

Better known as Lou Gehrig's disease, ALS is an incurable and often fatal degenerative ailment that paralyzes the muscles. Dickinson's symptoms first appeared in 1992, and when he became too ill to type he first used a voice-recognition device known as a Dragon Dictate. When his speech failed, he used a specially

adapted computer on which he typed with the one finger he could still command. Finally, in 1995, he turned to Eyegaze, a $20,000 system that tracks the user's glance with an infrared beam. As Dickinson looks at his computer screen, which is covered by a grid of characters, he selects them one by one by shifting his pupils to the letters he needs. Although it is fatiguing, it is now the only means by which his words and sentences can appear on the screen, where he then engages in his customary editing and polishing. He also communicates with visitors via the screen.

"Having ALS has freed me to take risks with style—plus I have an indulgent editor," he recently told a reporter from the *New York Times*. With a little help from technology, the *Journal-Bulletin's* readers can continue to enjoy Dickinson's comic and sometimes biting style, flavored by the experiences of his pre-ALS career, spent in traveling widely to report on world and national political news. Of Labor Day he recently wrote, "If the purpose is to recognize us all for toiling

Newspaper columnist Brian Dickinson

all summer, the term 'Labor Day' is a howler. No one works any harder in summer than he absolutely must."

Having ALS has freed me to take risks with style—plus I have an indulgent editor.

—Newspaper writer Brian Dickinson

This chapter discusses the nature of benefits in response to changing employee needs and changes in a company's external environment. By focusing on the learning objectives, you will better understand some of the formal systems that companies use to manage their employees. After reading this chapter, you should be able to

1 Define *human resource management* and explain how managers plan for human resources.

2 Identify the steps involved in staffing a company.

3 Explain how organizations can develop workers' skills and manage workers who do not perform well.

4 Discuss the importance of wages and salaries, incentives, and benefit programs in attracting and keeping skilled workers.

5 Describe some of the key legal and ethical issues involved in hiring, compensating, and managing workers in today's workplace.

6 Discuss work-force diversity and the contingent work force as important changes in the contemporary workplace.

The Foundations of Human Resource Management

human resource management
Development and administration of programs to enhance the quality and performance of a company's work force

human resource managers
Managers responsible for hiring, training, evaluating, and compensating employees

job relatedness
Principle that all employment decisions should be based on the requirements of the jobs in question

person-job matching
Process of matching the right person to the right job

job analysis
Evaluation of the duties and qualities required by a job

job description
Outline of the objectives, tasks, and responsibilities of a job

job specification
Description of the skills, education, and experience required by a job

Human resource management is the development and administration of programs to enhance the quality and performance of people working in an organization. **Human resource managers**, sometimes called personnel managers, are employed by all but the smallest firms. They recruit, train, and develop employees and set up evaluation, compensation, and benefit programs. In reality, however, all managers deal with human resources: Managers of accounting, finance, and marketing departments, for example, help select and train workers and evaluate their performance.[1] In this respect, two main concerns of all managers are job relatedness and person-job matching.

Job Relatedness and Person-Job Matching

Job relatedness, the foundation of effective human resource management, requires that all employment decisions be based on the requirements of a position; that is, the criteria used in hiring, evaluating, promoting, and rewarding people must be tied directly to the jobs being performed. For example, a policy that all office managers must be female would violate job relatedness because gender is irrelevant to the job. On the other hand, hiring only young females to model clothing designed for teenage girls is a job-related practice and thus reflects sound human resource management.

Central to the principle of job relatedness is **person-job matching**: the process of matching the right person to the right job. Good human resource managers match people's skills, interests, and temperaments with the requirements of their jobs. When people and jobs are well matched, the company benefits from high performance and employee satisfaction, high retention of effective workers, and low absenteeism.

Planning for Human Resources

Like planning for future equipment, planning for future human resource needs is crucial in any organization. The basis for human resource planning, in turn, is job analysis. **Job analysis** is an evaluation of the duties required by a particular job and the qualities required to perform it. For simple, repetitive jobs, managers may ask workers to create checklists of all the duties they perform and the importance of each. In analyzing more complex jobs, they may also hold interviews to determine jobholders' exact duties. Managers may also observe workers to record the nature of their duties.

From the job analysis, a manager develops a **job description**: a statement outlining the objectives, tasks, and responsibilities of a job. It also describes the conditions under which the job will be done, the ways in which it relates to other positions, and the skills needed to perform it. Managers also draw up **job specifications**, which describe the skills, education, and experience required by a job.

Together, job analyses and descriptions serve as tools for filling specific positions, as guides in establishing training programs, and as comparative guidelines for setting wages. Most importantly, by objectively defining requirements, they allow managers to make employment decisions based on job relatedness.

Staffing the Organization

Once managers have decided what positions they need to fill, they must find and hire qualified people. Staffing the organization is one of the most complex and important tasks of good human resource management. In this section we will describe both the process of acquiring staff from outside the company (external staffing) and the process of promoting staff from within (internal staffing).

"Well, this is a reassuring note, Mr. Bonwell: 'No dolphins were killed in the preparation of this résumé.'"

External Staffing

A new firm has little choice but to hire people from the outside. Established firms may also hire outsiders for a variety of reasons: to fill positions for which there are no good internal candidates, to accommodate growth, or to attract fresh ideas. External staffing involves recruitment and selection.

Recruitment

The first step in hiring new workers is to recruit a pool of applicants who are interested in and qualified for available positions. Successful recruiting focuses only on the most basic qualifications of a job. For example, a recruitment ad for a financial analyst might specify applicants with degrees in finance. Requiring a degree from a particular school, however, would unduly restrict applicants.

Recruiters often visit high schools, vocational schools, colleges, and universities. In some cases, labor agreements stipulate that new employees be hired from union membership rolls. Many companies advertise in newspapers or trade publications or seek the help of employment agencies. In addition, unsolicited letters and résumés from job seekers can help identify the right person for a job.

Recruiters have faced a difficult job in recent years as unemployment has continued to drop. Indeed, in early 1998 unemployment had dropped to a 23-year low of 4.6 percent. As a result, recruiters at firms such as Sprint, PeopleSoft, and Cognex had started to stress how much fun it was to work at their companies and to reinforce this message with ice cream socials, karaoke contests, softball leagues, and free movie nights.[2]

Selection

Once recruiting efforts have attracted job applicants, managers must evaluate each individual and select the best candidate. Figure 8.1 places testing procedures among the stages and possible outcomes of a typical selection process: applications or résumés, screening interviews, ability and aptitude tests, on-site interviews, reference checks, and medical and drug tests. Each organization develops its own mix of selection techniques and may use them in any order.

- *Applications or résumés.* A job application is a standardized form that asks the applicant for such information as background, experience, and education. A résumé is a prepared statement of the applicant's qualifications and career goals.

- *Screening interviews.* Companies often find themselves with several applications or résumés for every job opening. Managers thus narrow the field, first on the basis of applications and then by holding screening interviews to eliminate clearly unqualified applicants. Then they interview qualified applicants in greater depth.

Is There a Job for You After College?

What does the world of work hold in store for you? That depends in large measure on who you are.

If you've enjoyed your studies in English and history, for instance, you'll be glad to know that in a recent survey by Hobart and William Smith Colleges in New York State, a majority of CEOs said the liberal arts are essential for developing critical thinking and problem-solving skills. If you thought college was for acquiring specific work skills, only 37 percent of the CEOs in the survey agree with you.

If you plan to start your career as a secretary, be aware that this job is undergoing fundamental changes. In offices where secretaries have not already been eliminated (along with the middle managers to whom they once reported), the traditional clerical role is now unrecognizable. Most bosses handle their own correspondence and meeting and travel plans, thanks to e-mail and the Internet, so secretaries are increasingly taking on higher-level tasks such as drafting contracts, compiling spreadsheets, and handling customer service problems. Those willing to expand their horizons should do well.

Do you like to draw? Starting salaries for Hollywood animators can run as high as $40,000, and they climb fast. Forbes magazine reports that in 1996 about 14,000 young animators graduated from U.S. art schools and 34,000 jobs opened up. Graduates of a new training program at Rowland High School in southern California are among the beneficiaries of the burgeoning cartoon industry. Creativity, not technology, is stressed both in the regular day curriculum and at Rowland's innovative night school for adults.

If you're a woman interested in law enforcement, note that some states and cities are working hard to reach fair standards for female applicants. Although most small suburban police departments are still deeply traditional, and some are reluctant even to recruit women, among the nation's largest forces about 15 percent of the officers are female, five times as many as a generation ago. In New Haven, Connecticut, where there are 66 women officers (up from a handful only 7 years ago), director of training

Kay Codish says, "Women are not going out of their way to seek nontraditional jobs, so you have to go after them." The job is still among the world's toughest, but Sgt. Wendy Galloway of the New Jersey State Police says women are welcome. "If you put the message out, they'll come," she says.

Degrees in sports management are also on the rise. Two hundred U.S. colleges and universities, 10 times as many in 1985, now offer undergraduate courses in sports management, and some have advanced degree programs. At some schools you can also combine an MBA in sports management with a law degree. Based on the explosion of media sports coverage and the huge profits being made in both professional and amateur sports, comparable growth is expected in job areas such as team management, sponsorship, representation of sports figures, public relations, labor relations, apparel licensing and advertising, and organizing events and managing arenas. Although competition for such jobs can be fierce and starting salaries are low, many students will probably agree with David R. Shipitofsky, a senior at Seton Hall University in New Jersey, who says, "I love sports. And how many jobs are there that you can talk about last night's game without getting in trouble with the boss?"

> *Women are not going out of their way to seek nontraditional jobs, so you have to go after them.*
>
> —New Haven Police Department Director of Training Kay Codish

Finally, if you've set your sights on a traditional MBA, take heart. MBA recruitment is way up, and salaries and compensation are competitive. Base starting salaries range from $75,000 to $150,000, and "this is definitely a students' market," according to Andrew Adams, Wharton's director of career placement. But money isn't all today's MBAs are looking for. A recent study of nearly 1,800 MBA students in the United States and Canada found that 68 percent agree with the statement, "My family will always be more important than my career."

Figure 8.1 Sample Selection System

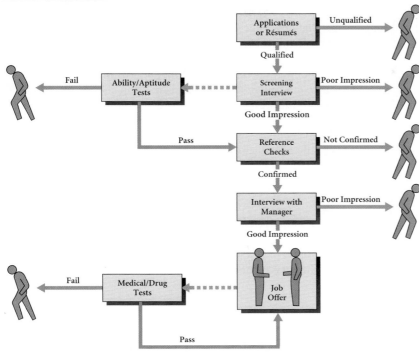

- *Ability and aptitude tests.* For some positions, ability or aptitude tests may be given. Such tests must meet two conditions. First, they must be job-related and the test must indicate clearly that top scorers are more likely to perform well in the specified job.

- *Physical exams and tests.* After applicants have been interviewed and their references checked (usually to verify employment and salary history), the manager will make a hiring decision. Before an offer is made, however, some companies require physical exams. These tests are designed to protect the employer under certain circumstances (for example, if a job involves lifting heavy boxes). Such tests reveal preexisting injuries and help the company determine whether a prospective employee is physically able to do required work. In addition, although they remain quite controversial, some organizations rely heavily on drug tests for new employees.[3]

The Workplace Environment

Increasingly, many firms are also stressing skills related to teamwork in selecting new employees. Southwest Airlines, Procter & Gamble, and Merck, for example, all use current employees, in addition to managers, to interview applicants. These employees strive to determine how well applicants will fit into the company's culture and how well they will get along with other people in the firm.[4]

Internal Staffing: Promotions

Many organizations prefer to hire from within. That is, they prefer whenever possible to promote or transfer existing employees to fill openings. Systems for promoting employees usually take one of two forms:

- In **closed promotion systems**, managers decide which workers will be considered for promotions. Decisions are usually made informally (and often subjectively) and tend to rely on the recommendations of immediate supervisors.

- In **open promotion systems**, available jobs and requirements are posted. Employees who feel that they have the necessary qualifications fill out applications, take tests, and interview with managers.

closed promotion system
System by which managers, often informally, decide which workers are considered for promotions

open promotion system
System by which employees apply, test, and interview for available jobs whose requirements are posted

Seniority

Some promotions are determined, at least in part, by seniority: Employees with more years of service receive priority in promotions. This pattern is a standard feature of many union contracts and ensures that experienced employees are promoted. Of course, it does not guarantee that they will be the most competent candidates.

Initially, courts were receptive to challenges against seniority systems. They tended to agree that such agreements perpetuated long-standing patterns of discrimination and often ruled in favor of groups and individuals who had traditionally been victimized by discrimination. Since about 1977, however, they have tended to uphold seniority clauses in labor contracts. For example, they have upheld last-hired-first-fired provisions and systems that benefit workers—usually male—who have long held higher-paying positions to which other employees have only recently had access.

Developing the Work Force

After a company has hired new employees, it must acquaint them with the firm and their new jobs. Managers also take steps to train employees and further develop necessary job skills. In addition, every firm has some system for performance appraisal and feedback. Unfortunately, the results of these assessments sometimes require procedures for demoting or terminating employees.

Orientation

The purpose of orientation is to help employees learn about and fit into the company. This process can focus on simple things, such as work hours, parking priorities, and pay schedules. People may simply watch films, read manuals, and be introduced to co-workers. They may also learn the details of the firm's promotion, smoking, and sexual harassment policies.

Training and Development

At many companies, both old and new employees periodically receive additional training. Such training may be designed to overcome on-the-job shortcomings or to give employees the chance to acquire new skills. Similarly, managers may attend seminars designed to prepare them for higher-level responsibilities. The most common procedures are on-the-job training, off-the-job training, and management development programs.

On-the-Job Training

on-the-job training
Training, sometimes informal, conducted while an employee is at work

As its name suggests, **on-the-job training** occurs while the employee is at work. Much of this training is informal, as when one employee shows another how to use the photocopier. In other cases, it is quite formal. For example, a trainer may teach secretaries how to operate a new e-mail system from their workstations. Although distractions sometimes make on-the-job training difficult, it does have two advantages: It occurs in the real job setting, and it can be conducted over an extended period of time. Chaparral Steel, for example, requires all of its new employees to complete a 3½-year training program in which one major component is on-the-job training in a variety of job-related skills.

Off-the-Job Training

off-the-job-training
Training conducted in a controlled environment away from the work site

vestibule training
Off-the-job training conducted in a simulated environment

Off-the-job training takes place at locations away from the work site. This approach offers a controlled environment and allows focused study without interruptions. For example, the petroleum equipment manufacturer Baker-Hughes uses classroom-based programs to teach new methods of quality control. Chaparral Steel's training program includes 4 hours a week of classroom training in areas such as basic math and grammar. Other firms use **vestibule training**, in simulated work environments, to make off-the-job training more realistic. American Airlines, for example, trains flight attendants through vestibule training, and AT&T uses it to train telephone operators.

Management Development

Unlike job training, which focuses on technical skills, **management development programs** enhance conceptual, analytical, and problem-solving skills. Some programs are run on-site by managers or specialists, and others are conducted on university campuses or other educational centers. Harvard, Stanford, Michigan, and Northwestern are among the business schools most respected for their executive development programs.[5] Most large companies have development programs, and a well-conceived strategy for developing managerial talent is essential if an organization is to prosper.

management development program
Program designed to enhance the conceptual, analytical, and problem-solving skills of management personnel

Networking and Mentoring

In addition, some management development also takes place informally, often through processes known as networking and mentoring. *Networking* refers to informal interactions among managers for the purpose of discussing mutual problems, solutions, and opportunities. Networking takes place in a variety of settings, both inside and outside the office (for example, at conventions and conferences, meetings, business lunches, and social gatherings).

A **mentor** is an older, more experienced manager who sponsors and teaches younger, less experienced managers. The mentoring process helps younger managers learn the ropes and benefit from the experiences, insights, and successes (and failures) of senior executives. Networking and mentoring may be especially useful for female and minority managers; these people may have fewer role models and may be more likely to benefit from greater interaction with experienced managers.

mentor
Experienced manager who sponsors and teaches younger, less experienced managers

Performance Appraisal

In some small companies, **performance appraisal** takes place when the owner tells an employee, "You're doing a good job." In larger firms, performance appraisals are designed to show more precisely how well workers are doing their jobs. Typically, the appraisal process involves a written assessment issued on a regular basis. As a rule, however, the written evaluation is only one part of a multistep process.

The appraisal process begins when a manager defines performance standards for an employee. The manager then observes the employee's performance. If the standards are clear, the manager should have little difficulty comparing expectations with performance. For some jobs, a rating scale like the abbreviated one in Figure 8.2 is useful in providing a basis for comparisons. In addition to scales for initiative, punctuality, and cleanliness, a complete form will include several other scales directly related to performance. Comparisons drawn from such scales form the basis for written appraisals and for decisions about raises, promotions, demotions, and firings. The process is completed when manager and employee meet to discuss the appraisal.

performance appraisal
Evaluation, often in writing, of an employee's job performance

Formal Appraisals

When performance expectations are based on job requirements, formal appraisals offer many benefits to both company and worker. The firm is protected from lawsuits charging unfair treatment. It also has an objective basis on which to compare employees for promotions and to identify those who need training. Workers benefit from clear job-related goals and feedback. Not surprisingly, they often feel that such systems are fairer than subjective evaluations.

Demotion and Separation

Written appraisals are especially important when a company must dismiss or demote employees. Most companies have step-by-step processes for dismissal. The first step might be a verbal warning about a particular problem (poor performance or attendance, for example). Many companies also require managers to give employees written warnings. The problem might be discussed at the employee's formal appraisal. At that time, the manager will indicate specific changes that the employee must make to keep his or her job. While

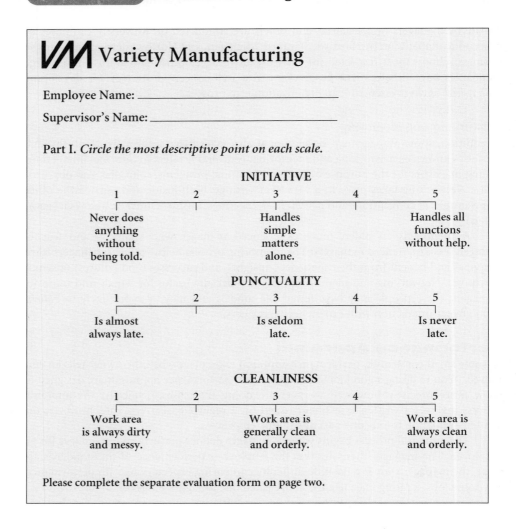

Figure 8.2   Performance Rating Scale

> **V/M** Variety Manufacturing
>
> Employee Name: _____
>
> Supervisor's Name: _____
>
> Part I. *Circle the most descriptive point on each scale.*
>
> ### INITIATIVE
>
> 1   2   3   4   5
>
> Never does   Handles   Handles all
> anything   simple   functions
> without   matters   without help.
> being told.   alone.
>
> ### PUNCTUALITY
>
> 1   2   3   4   5
>
> Is almost   Is seldom   Is never
> always late.   late.   late.
>
> ### CLEANLINESS
>
> 1   2   3   4   5
>
> Work area   Work area is   Work area is
> is always dirty   generally clean   always clean
> and messy.   and orderly.   and orderly.
>
> Please complete the separate evaluation form on page two.

protecting the company, this system also lets the employee know that his or her job is in jeopardy and offers a chance to improve performance.

Disciplinary Action and Demotion

If the problem persists, a manager may resort to stronger measures. **Disciplinary action**, such as suspension, is usually taken when an employee's behavior is dangerous or disruptive. For example, someone who screams at a fellow worker might be sent home to cool off. **Demotion** involves moving an employee to a lower-level position, usually at reduced pay. For instance, a sales manager who continues to perform poorly may be demoted to sales representative. Alternatively, the individual may be transferred to a new work setting. Rather than demoting the sales manager, for example, the organization might transfer the person to a smaller region or to a less desirable territory.

Separation

In extreme cases, outright **separation**, or **termination**, may be the only recourse. For example, the sales manager's performance may be so poor that the firm has no recourse but firing. Although firings are never pleasant, managers of companies with sound human resource policies can take some solace in knowing that by the time a dismissal takes place, the employee is usually expecting it.

disciplinary action
Action taken by management in response to employee behavior that is considered dangerous or disruptive

demotion
Action, such as removal to a lower position, taken by management in response to an employee's poor performance

separation (or termination)
Dismissal of an employee, usually for unacceptably poor performance

Cutbacks and Downsizing

When an organization is eliminating many jobs, it must develop a plan for deciding who will be terminated. Among operating employees, those with the least seniority or weakest performance records will probably be the first to go. Older managers and other professionals (staff specialists, for example) may be offered early retirement, usually with the option of retiring with full (or almost full) benefits before normal retirement age. For example, when General Motors embarked on a plan to reduce its work force, it used a program of carefully planned early retirement to eliminate over 16,000 hourly workers.

This process is called **downsizing**: consolidating internal operations to make them more flexible and productive. In 1993, in a study conducted by the Families and Work Institute, 42 percent of all workers reported that their companies were in the process of downsizing. Indeed, during 1997 alone, International Paper laid off 9,000 workers, Stanley Works and Fruit of the Loom 5,000 each, Whirlpool 4,700, and Food Lion 3,100. The reasons for these cutbacks varied. International Paper was cutting costs and consolidating operations. Food Lion's cuts came from store closures in Texas and Oklahoma. And Fruit of the Loom was moving jobs to foreign countries where wages are lower.[6]

Strategies for downsizing and cost cutting vary widely. Naturally, the impact of such a strategy will vary from company to company, as will its effect on each company's work force.

▶ Analysts have expressed particular interest in the outcome of a cutback plan at Xerox. On the day the firm announced its plan, investors responded favorably and stock value rose significantly. However, critics pointed out that Xerox was a financially sound company in part because it had carefully formed strong relationships among managers and workers. At Xerox, factory workers are encouraged to look for quality problems and to serve on product development teams with engineers and marketing and sales managers. Observers wonder whether such effective arrangements will survive cutbacks and restructuring.

downsizing
Process of consolidating internal operations to make a firm more flexible and productive

Compensation and Benefits

People do not work for free. Providing workers with appropriate compensation for their time and talents is thus another important part of human resource management. Most workers today also expect certain benefits from their employers. Indeed, a major factor in retaining skilled workers is a company's **compensation system**: the total package that it offers employees in return for their labor.

Although wages and salaries are key parts of all compensation systems, most also include incentives and employee benefits programs. We will discuss these and other types of employee benefits in this section. Remember, however, that finding the right combination of compensation elements is always complicated by the need to make employees feel valued while holding down company costs. Thus, compensation systems differ widely, depending on the nature of the industry, the company, and the types of workers involved.

compensation system
Total package offered by a company to employees in return for their labor

Wages and Salaries

Wages and salaries are the dollar amounts paid to employees for their labor. **Wages** are paid for time worked. For example, workers who are paid by the hour receive wages. A **salary** is paid for discharging the responsibilities of a job. A salaried executive earning $100,000 per year is paid to achieve results even if that means working 5 hours one day and 15 the next. Salaries are usually expressed as an amount paid per year.

In setting wage and salary levels, a company may start by looking at its competitors' levels. A firm that pays less than its rivals knows that it runs the risk of losing valuable personnel. Conversely, to attract top employees, some companies pay more than their rivals. M&M/Mars, for example, pays managerial salaries about 10 percent above the average in the candy and snack food industry.

wages
Compensation in the form of money paid for time worked

salary
Compensation in the form of money paid for discharging the responsibilities of a job

The Workplace Environment

Downsizing Pros and Cons

The 1990s were all about downsizing, the practice of laying off large numbers of staff in the search for efficiency and profitability. More than 17 million workers were laid off between 1988 and 1995, although about 28 million jobs were added back to the economy.

Two economists at the Federal Reserve Bank in Dallas, W. Michael Cox and Richard Alin, reported on the 10 largest downsizers of the 1990–1995 period, which include Digital Equipment, McDonnell Douglas, General Electric, and Kmart. Collective output (sales adjusted for inflation) declined by almost 10 percent. On the other hand, productivity per worker rose nearly 28 percent, compared with a gain of 1.5 percent in the rest of the economy. Says Cox, "Most of the companies emerged from the downsizing more competitive than before and thus were able to provide greater security to their workers." The cost? 850,000 workers.

Yet negative outcomes prevailed at many firms. Devastatingly low morale, increased disability claims and suits for wrongful discharge, and general mistrust of management plague many companies. A study done at the Wharton School examined data on several thousand firms and found that downsizing had little or no effect on earnings or stock market performance. Far more effective were leveraged buyouts and portfolio restructuring.

There is some evidence that consistent focus on creating value for shareholders, which includes paring un-

needed workers, actually increases jobs in the long run. "Stronger, leaner companies are able to compete in the world market more effectively, and that ultimately draws jobs back to those companies." That's the opinion of Thomas Copland, a director of McKinsey and Co., a management consulting firm that studied 20 years of data on 1,000 companies in the United States, Canada, Germany, Holland, Belgium, and France. The study revealed that, unlike those in the United States and Canada, the European firms lost jobs in the log term because their return to shareholders fell between 1970 and 1990.

> " *Stronger, leaner companies are able to compete in the world market more effectively, and that ultimately draws jobs back to those companies.* "
>
> —Thomas Copland,
> a director of McKinsey and Co.

Although long-run growth is a pleasant prospect for shareholders, the short-term loss of jobs and income has left many employees and their families struggling in the aftermath of downsizing.

A firm must also decide how its internal wage and salary levels will compare for different jobs. For example, Sears must determine the relative salaries of store managers, buyers, and advertising managers. In turn, managers must decide how much to pay individual workers within the company's wage and salary structure. Although two employees may do exactly the same job, the employee with more experience may earn more. Moreover, some union contracts specify differential wages based on experience.

Incentive Programs

Naturally, employees feel better about their companies when they believe that they are being fairly compensated. However, both studies and experience have shown that beyond a certain point, more money will not produce better performance. Indeed, neither across-the-board nor cost-of-living wage increases cause people to work harder. Money motivates employees only if it is tied directly to performance. The most common method of establishing this link is the use of **incentive programs**: special pay programs designed to motivate high performance. Some programs are available to individuals, whereas others are distributed on a companywide basis.

incentive program
Special compensation program designed to motivate high performance

Individual Incentives

A sales bonus is a typical incentive: Employees receive **bonuses**—special payments above their salaries—when they sell a certain number or certain dollar amount of goods for the year. Employees who fail to reach this goal earn no bonuses. **Merit salary systems** link raises to performance levels in nonsales jobs. For example, many baseball players have contract clauses that pay them bonuses for hitting over .300, making the All-Star team, or being named Most Valuable Player. Executives commonly receive stock options as incentives. Disney CEO Michael Eisner, for example, can buy several thousand shares of company stock each year at a predetermined price. If his managerial talent leads to higher profits and stock prices, he can buy the stock at a price lower than the market value for which, in theory, he is largely responsible. He is then free to sell them at market price, keeping the profits for himself.

A newer incentive plan is called **pay for performance**, or **variable pay**. In essence, middle managers are rewarded for especially productive output—that is, for producing earnings that significantly exceed the cost of bonuses. Such incentives have long been common among top-level executives and factory workers, but variable pay goes to middle managers on the basis of companywide performance, business unit performance, personal record, or all three factors.

Since 1988 the number of U.S. companies with variable pay programs has jumped from 47 to 68 percent. Eligible managers must often forgo merit or "entitlement" raises (increases for staying on and reporting to work every day), but many firms say that variable pay is a better motivator because the range between generous and mediocre merit raises is usually quite small anyway. Merit raises also increase fixed costs: They are added to base pay and increase the base pay used to determine the retirement benefits that the company must pay out.[7]

Companywide Incentives

Some incentive programs apply to all the employees in a firm. Under **profit-sharing plans**, for example, profits earned above a certain level are distributed to employees. Conversely, **gain-sharing plans** distribute bonuses to employees when a company's costs are reduced through greater work efficiency. **Pay-for-knowledge plans** encourage workers to learn new skills and to become proficient at different jobs. They receive additional pay for each new skill or job that they master.

Benefits Programs

A growing part of nearly every firm's compensation system is its benefits program. **Benefits**—compensation other than wages and salaries offered by a firm to its workers—make up a large percentage of most compensation budgets. Most companies are required by law to provide social security retirement benefits and **worker's compensation insurance** (insurance for compensating workers injured on the job). Most businesses also voluntarily provide health, life, and disability insurance. Many also allow employees to use payroll deductions to buy stock at discounted prices. Another common benefit is paid time off for vacations and holidays. Counseling services for employees with alcohol, drug, or emotional problems are also becoming more common.[8]

Retirement Plans

Retirement plans are also an important—and sometimes controversial—benefit that is available to many employees. Most company-sponsored retirement plans are set up to pay pensions to workers when they retire. In some cases, the company contributes all the money to the pension fund. In others, contributions are made by both the company and employees. Currently, about 60 percent of U.S. workers are covered by pension plans of some kind.

During the 1960s, a few company-controlled pension plans lost money due to poor investments by fund managers. To protect members from such losses, Congress passed the

---

bonus
Individual performance incentive in the form of a special payment above the employee's salary

merit salary system
Incentive program linking compensation to performance in nonsales jobs

pay for performance (or variable pay)
Individual incentive that rewards a manager for especially productive output

profit-sharing plan
Incentive program for giving employees company profits above a certain level

gain-sharing plan
Incentive program for distributing bonuses to employees whose performances improve productivity

pay-for-knowledge plan
Incentive program to encourage employees to learn new skills or become proficient at different jobs

benefits
Compensation other than wages and salaries

worker's compensation insurance
Legally required insurance for compensating workers injured on the job

John A. Doherty runs a Nucor Steel mill in Norfolk, Nebraska. In one good year, bonuses totaling $120,000 almost doubled his salary. The catch: Doherty's bonus is tied to companywide performance—that is, to the achievements of other Nucor plant managers. Every year, therefore, plant managers and top Nucor executives get together to exchange sometimes blunt criticisms. "These bonuses aren't entitlements," explains Doherty. "We're running our own businesses, and we'd better perform."

Employee Retirement Income Security Act (ERISA)
Federal law regulating private pension plans

Employee Retirement Income Security Act (ERISA) in 1974. First, the law established investment guidelines to protect pension funds. Managers are prohibited from making certain types of transactions, and companies are liable for negligent handling of funds. ERISA also set guidelines for protection of underfunded plans and established the Pension Guaranty Corp. to insure employees if an employer goes bankrupt.

Finally, ERISA set guidelines in two basic areas:

■ *Vesting* refers to workers' rights to participate in plans and receive funds.

■ *Portability* refers to workers' rights to transfer pension fund assets when they leave their employers.

Recently, the issue of portability has become an area of increasing debate. Currently, covered employees who resign or are fired will lose some or even all of the benefits they have earned. Critics argue that under such circumstances, accumulated pension assets should be fully portable—that is, employees should be able to take them to their new employers. Unfortunately, most pension plans are carefully designed to fit the unique needs of the companies that sponsor them. It would thus be difficult to determine how benefits structured by one employer should translate into benefits structured by another.

Containing the Costs of Benefits

As the range of benefits has grown, so has concern about containing their costs. Many companies are experimenting with cost-cutting plans under which they can still attract and retain valuable employees. One approach is the **cafeteria benefit plan**: A certain dollar amount of benefits per employee is set aside so that each employee can choose from a variety of alternatives. A recent variation on cafeteria plans permits employees to choose whether their portion of benefits comes from their salaries before or after taxes are computed. For most individuals, the right choice results in real tax savings because benefits themselves are not taxed. Thus, people can lower their taxable incomes by paying for some of their benefits before the calculation of taxes. These and other variations are all intended to accomplish the same goal: to give employees some flexibility in tailoring benefit packages that best fit their personal needs.

Another area of increasing concern is health care costs. Medical procedures that once cost several hundred dollars now cost several thousand. Medical expenses have in-

cafeteria benefit plan
Benefit plan that sets limits on benefits per employee, each of whom may choose from a variety of alternative benefits

creased insurance premiums, which in turn have increased the cost to employers of maintaining benefits plans.

Many employers are looking for new ways to cut those costs. One increasingly popular approach is for organizations to create their own networks of health care providers. These providers agree to charge lower fees for services rendered to employees of member organizations. In return, they enjoy established relationships with large employers, and thus more clients and patients. Because they must make lower reimbursement payments, insurers also charge less to cover the employees of network members. One variation on the formula has been successful at Alcon Laboratories. Alcon asked its employees to nominate their own personal physicians for the network and then negotiated reduced fees with those physicians. The result was a cost savings of over $1 million per year for the employer.

Legal and Ethical Issues in Managing People

It should be obvious by now that in the course of performing their jobs, human resource managers are confronted by a number of legal issues, which often have ethical implications as well. In this section, we will discuss some of the basic principles that underlie human resource policies in U.S. business: equal employment opportunity, equal pay and comparable worth, occupational safety and health, and the doctrine of employment at will.

Equal Employment Opportunity

For many years, white males dominated U.S. business, especially at the managerial and professional levels. In recent years, however, this situation has begun to change, partly as a result of changes in the legal environment. Title VII of the 1964 Civil Rights Act was the first major law to prohibit discrimination and paved the way for over three decades of change. This act also created the Equal Employment Opportunity Commission (EEOC), which is responsible for enforcing its provisions. Today, numerous federal and state laws, federal guidelines, presidential executive orders, and judicial decisions mandate **equal employment opportunity**: nondiscrimination in employment on the basis of race, color, creed, sex, or national origin.

Under the Equal Employment Opportunity Act of 1992, the EEOC can file civil suits in federal court on behalf of individuals who claim that their rights have been violated. Remedies include reinstatement, back pay, and compensation for the victim's suffering. Because litigation can last for years, settlements can be huge. Recent awards include $2.3 million in back pay to three older employees of Federated Department Stores, $42.5 million to female and minority employees at General Motors, and $52.5 million to female employees at Northwest Airlines.[9]

equal employment opportunity
Legally mandated nondiscrimination in employment on the basis of race, creed, sex, or national origin

Sexual Harassment
Sexual harassment is a form of employer or management behavior that falls under the category of employment discrimination. Do you know which of the following behaviors legally constitutes sexual harassment?

- Demanding that a subordinate have sexual relations in order to keep a job or get a promotion

- Repeatedly asking a co-worker or subordinate for a date, despite past refusals

- Touching a co-worker's buttocks

- Telling off-color jokes

- Addressing a female employee as "sweetheart"

- Displaying nude pictures in the office

■ Wearing a button that proclaims "Keep 'em barefoot and pregnant"

■ Making sexual overtures to a willing co-worker in the presence of another unwilling co-worker

Nearly everyone today recognizes that demanding sexual relations in return for job security constitutes sexual harassment. Nonetheless, the 1991 Supreme Court confirmation hearings of Clarence Thomas showed, among other things, that many people do not understand the nature and breadth of behaviors that constitute harassment.

The law is abundantly clear. Under the terms of the Equal Opportunity Act, all of the behaviors listed above are forms of sexual harassment. In fact, any "'unwelcome' sexual attention, whether verbal or physical, that affects an employee's job conditions or creates a 'hostile' working environment" constitutes sexual harassment. When does acceptable behavior become unacceptable? The U.S. Supreme Court ruled in 1986 that behavior may be judged on the basis of what would offend a "reasonable woman." (Although the situation may change as more women enter positions of authority, and the hit movie *Disclosure* notwithstanding, only a handful of cases have so far involved allegations by men.)

In November 1993, the Court expanded its 1986 ruling and issued an even broader definition of sexual harassment in the workplace: The law is violated when "the environment would be reasonably perceived, and is perceived, as hostile or abusive." Furthermore, the court ruled that the victim's job performance does not have to suffer for a behavior to constitute harassment. The plaintiff, wrote Justice Ruth Ginsburg, "need not prove that his or her tangible productivity has declined as a result of the harassment." The law, concurred Justice Sandra Day O'Connor, "comes into play before the harassing conduct leads to a nervous breakdown."

Today, most large corporations provide their employees with detailed information regarding what kinds of behavior are and are not acceptable. They also publish standard procedures for receiving and investigating reports of harassment. Others, such as Du Pont and Corning, go even further. Both of these firms require all employees to attend seminars in which participants role-play potential harassment situations.

A newly emerging emphasis on a harassment-free workplace, plus the willingness to discipline offenders, reflects a number of trends in modern business. For example, grow-

When the EEOC filed sexual harassment charges at Mitsubishi Motors' Normal, Illinois, factory in April 1996, Jesse Jackson's Operation PUSH joined with the National Organization for Women to picket such sites as the carmaker's Illinois dealerships. Although the boycott itself had limited impact, automotive dealers and retailers of other Mitsubishi products wanted the parent company to resolve the issue. Matters only got worse, they claimed, when Mitsubishi instead sent 3,000 workers from the Normal plant to protest outside the EEOC's Chicago office.

ing public outrage over sexual harassment, coupled with rising numbers of women in the work force, has had a significant impact. Any company that does not vigorously pursue all employee complaints of harassment may find itself being sued and paying huge settlements.

However, money is not always the prime consideration: Many firms are concerned about harassment because it affects morale and productivity. In fact, Corning launched its drive against harassment when it discovered that it was losing 16.2 percent of its salaried women each year. Many exiting employees cited an uncomfortable sexual atmosphere as a reason for leaving. Today, Corning loses only slightly more salaried women than salaried men.[10]

Affirmative Action

Various executive orders spanning more than two decades have also required many organizations to engage in affirmative action. Executive Order 11246, for example, mandates **affirmative action programs** to recruit qualified or qualifiable employees from racial, gender, and ethnic groups that are underrepresented in an organization. All organizations receiving over $100,000 per year in government contracts must have written affirmative action plans. Many other businesses practice affirmative action on a voluntary basis.

Legislation passed in 1991 reinforces the legal basis of affirmative action but specifically forbids organizations to set hiring quotas that might result in **reverse discrimination**. This practice can occur when an organization concentrates so much on hiring from some groups that others suffer discrimination.

Equal Pay and Comparable Worth

A special area of equal employment, employment opportunities for women, has given rise to one of the most controversial issues in compensation today. The Equal Pay Act of 1963 specifically forbids sex discrimination in pay: No company can legally pay men and women of equal experience differently for work performed under similar conditions that requires equal skill, effort, and responsibility. Differing job titles alone cannot justify pay differences. Thus, if a woman whose job title is *senior secretary* performs essentially the same job as a man whose title is *administrative assistant*, the two must have the same pay scale. As a result of the Equal Pay Act, many women have sued and received back pay and other adjustments from employers who have discriminated on the basis of pay.

The Glass Ceiling

Despite the Equal Pay Act, however, statistics show that women still earn less than men for performing similar jobs. Only in the last 20 or so years have large numbers of women sought professional careers. Thus, most women typically have less work experience than do men of the same age. A related issue is the glass ceiling phenomenon, so called because there still seems to be an invisible but very real barrier over their heads that keeps not only women but also minorities from advancing to higher levels in U.S. organizations.

In a series of hearings held between 1991 and 1994, a Congressional panel called the Glass Ceiling Commission gathered information and opinion for a report on the lack of progress in advancement by women and minorities. Findings show that despite the Civil Rights Act and women's rights activism, women make up one-half the nation's work force but only 3 to 6 percent of its corporate officials. Minorities make up only 1 percent. Labor Secretary Robert B. Reich revealed that the federal government's managerial structure is also seriously skewed. Although minorities fill 28 percent of all federal jobs, they occupy only 8 percent of upper-level positions. Women make up 44 percent of the work force but hold only 13 percent of the top jobs. "In Washington sometimes," concluded Reich, "the only architectural feature as prominent as the Capitol Dome is the glass ceiling." Most analysts cite lack of

affirmative action program
Legally mandated program for recruiting qualified employees belonging to racial, gender, or ethnic groups who are underrepresented in an organization

reverse discrimination
Practice of discriminating against well-represented groups by overhiring members of underrepresented groups

Table 8.1 Women in Selected Occupational Categories

Occupational Category	Percentage of Women
Engineers	7.3
Lawyers and judges	19.5
Librarians	85.4
Physicians	20.0
Dentists	9.3
Registered nurses	94.6
Elementary, secondary teachers	72.9
Managers, administrators	44.7
Sales workers, retail, and personal service	68.6
Secretaries, stenographers, and typists	98.2
Precision production, craft, and repair	8.7
Transportation and material moving	9.0
Food service workers	61.6
Private household (maids, servants)	96.3

resources and unaggressive enforcement of existing laws as a primary reason why so little progress has been made in the three decades since passage of the Civil Rights Act of 1964.[11]

Progress Toward Comparable Worth

Many experts agree that subtle and perhaps even unconscious discrimination still exists in many organizations. To combat this discrimination, some analysts have called for a policy of **comparable worth**: Women would receive the same wage for traditionally "female" jobs (such as secretary) as men do for traditional "male" jobs of the same worth to the company (say, mechanic).

comparable worth
Principle that women should receive the same pay for traditionally "female" jobs of the same worth to a company as traditionally "male" jobs

Both government statistics and working women confirm the suspicions of experts about lingering discrimination. For instance, figures show that women still earn substantially less than men. Part of this differential results from the fact that women are still concentrated in occupational categories that are traditionally low-paying, especially nursing, teaching, secretarial, and retail sales (see Table 8.1).

Moreover, women continue to report bias in working conditions. One recent survey by the Women's Bureau of the Department of Labor reported the following findings:

- 60 percent of women said they had little or no chance of advancement.

- 14 percent of white women and 26 percent of minority women reported losing jobs or promotions because of sex or race.

- Almost 25 percent said they had no pension plans, and 14 percent had no sick leave.

- 43 percent of part-time workers had no health insurance (compared to 18 percent of the general population).

Figure 8.3 divides respondents into salary ranks and show the percentages of women reporting satisfaction on three measures of compensation and benefits. Even Labor Department administrators were surprised by the emphasis on discrimination and equal pay. "The popular wisdom," says Karen Nussbaum, director of the Women's Bureau, "had been that we don't talk about things that way anymore, but clearly that is the way women talk about it." (The report acknowledged that many of the problems described by women also applied to men.)[12]

Figure 8.3 Women Reporting Satisfaction with Three Measures of Compensation

Salary	Flexible Hours	Good Pay	Good Benefits
Under $10,000	62%	24%	11%
10–25,000	35	31	36
25–50,000	34	42	37
Over 50,000	41	68	39

Occupational Safety and Health

Issues of worker safety on the job have also been addressed through legislation. The Occupational Safety and Health Act of 1970, which created the **Occupational Safety and Health Administration (OSHA)**, is the most far-reaching piece of legislation in this area. The act covers all firms with one or more employees.

OSHA sets numerous guidelines in two general areas. First, it protects employee safety by eliminating unsafe working conditions, such as dangerous machinery and unsafe ladders and scaffolding, that might lead to accidents. Second, it protects the health of workers from long-term exposure to health hazards ranging from excessive noise to cancer-causing chemicals.

OSHA inspectors can investigate any complaint filed by a worker. They also spot-check companies in particularly hazardous industries. Plants failing to meet safety or health standards can be fined. For example, fines for alleged violations have been proposed by OSHA against ConAgra ($1.1 million for various violations, one resulting in a worker's death), Chrysler ($1.5 million for overexposure to lead and arsenic), and meat-packer John Morrell & Co. ($4.3 million for injuries related to repetitive motion tasks).[13] Repeated or extreme violations can even lead to shutdowns.

Employment at Will

Employment at will is the principle that organizations should be able to retain or dismiss workers at their discretion. Most managers believe that although they should follow legal guidelines in hiring, they should also be free, when justified, to fire employees without worrying about the legal consequences.

In recent years, however, the courts have become increasingly involved in employment-at-will disputes. Indeed, it is becoming fairly common for people to sue former employers on the grounds that they were dismissed unfairly. Although laws prohibit organizations from firing employees for some specified reasons, such as joining unions or reporting safety violations, the courts have extended protection in some cases on the simple basis of fairness. In one case, for example, a worker who was fired because he refused a transfer to another city was reinstated, with back pay, when the court ruled the dismissal unfair.

New Challenges in the Changing Workplace

As we have seen throughout this chapter, human resource managers face a number of ongoing challenges in their efforts to keep their organizations staffed with effective work forces. To complicate matters, new challenges arise as the economic and social environments of business change. More specifically, today's human resource managers must deal with work forces that are increasingly diverse and contingent.

Occupational Safety and Health Administration (OSHA)
Federal agency that sets and enforces guidelines for protecting workers from unsafe conditions and potential health hazards in the workplace

employment at will
Principle, increasingly modified by legislation and judicial decision, that organizations should be able to retain or dismiss employees at their discretion

Managing Work-Force Diversity

work-force diversity
Range of workers' attitudes, values, and behaviors that differ by gender, race, and ethnicity

An extremely important set of human resource challenges centers on **work-force diversity**: the range of workers' attitudes, values, beliefs, and behaviors that differ by gender, race, and ethnicity. The diverse work force is also characterized by individuals of different ages and physical abilities. In the past, organizations tended to work toward homogenizing their work forces, getting everyone to think and behave in similar ways. Partly as a result of affirmative action efforts, however, many U.S. organizations are now creating work forces that are more diverse, embracing more women, more ethnic minorities, and more foreign-born employees than ever before.

Figures 8.4 and 8.5 help put the changing U.S. work force into perspective. Figure 8.4 shows changes in the percentages of different groups of workers—white males, white females, blacks, Hispanics, and Asians and others—in the total work force in the years 1980, 1993, and (as projected) 2005. Figure 8.5 shows the same changes among managerial and professional workers in the decade between 1983 and 1993. The first picture is one of increasing diversity over the past decade. The second is one of a slower but steady trend toward diversity: By 2005, says the Labor Department, half of all workers entering the labor force will be women and more than one-third will be blacks, Hispanics, Asian Americans, and others.[14]

Diversity as a Competitive Advantage

Today, organizations are recognizing not only that they should treat everyone equitably, but also that they should acknowledge the individuality of each person they employ. They are also recognizing that diversity can be a competitive advantage. For example, by hiring the best people available from every single group rather than hiring from just one or a few groups, a firm can develop a higher-quality labor force. Similarly, a diverse work force can bring a wider array of information to bear on problems and can provide insights on marketing products to a wider range of consumers. Says the head of work-force diversity at IBM: "We think it is important for our customers to look inside and see people like them. If they can't . . . the prospect of them becoming or staying our customers declines."

Levi Strauss adhered to this principle when it revised ads for 501 jeans. The original "501 Blues" spots aimed at and attracted hip, independent youngsters—mostly white. They did not appeal to Hispanics. Why not? Levi's own Hispanic employees provided an answer. The characters in the ads were depicted as hip and carefree, but they were always solitary figures. Because Hispanic culture places a higher value on day-to-day contact with friends and family, Levi's was advised to create ads that stressed camaraderie. Because Hispanics buy 50 percent more jeans than the average consumer, the company heeded the advice of its own employees and has been a much more successful marketer to Hispanic buyers.[15]

Admittedly, not all U.S. companies have worked equally hard to adjust their thinking and diversify their work forces. In fact, experts estimate that a mere 3 to 5 percent of

Figure 8.4 Diversity: Total Work Force, 1980–2005

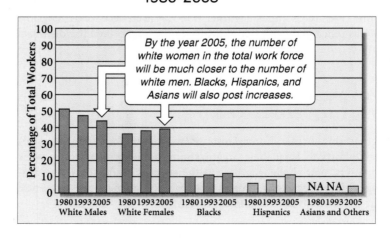

Figure 8.5 Diversity: Managerial and Professional Workers, 1983–1993

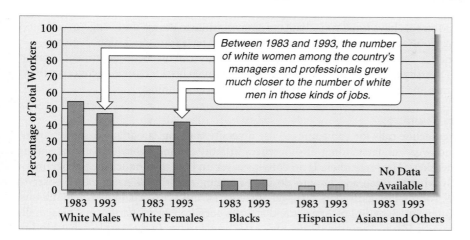

Between 1983 and 1993, the number of white women among the country's managers and professionals grew much closer to the number of white men in those kinds of jobs.

U.S. corporations are diversifying with any effect. In a recent survey of executives at 1,405 participating firms, only 5 percent believed that they were doing a "very good job" of diversifying their human resources. Many others, however, have instituted—and, more importantly, maintained—diversity programs. The experience of these companies (including IBM, Xerox, Avon, AT&T, Burger King, Levi Strauss, and Hoechst Celanese) has made it possible to draw up some general guidelines for a successful work-force diversity program:[16]

- *Make diversity a specific management goal.* For example, Hoechst Celanese, a giant chemical company, has a very specific diversity target: It wants a minimum of 34 percent representation of women and minorities at all levels by 2001. That figure is drawn from the pool of people—graduates with appropriate degrees at colleges where Hoechst recruits-who will ultimately make up the firm's work force.

- *Analyze compensation scales and be scrupulously fair in tracking individual careers.* At Hoechst and other companies, compensation reviews, called salary equity reviews, are conducted to spot pay disparities that are not related to performance or seniority. Many firms also have programs to identify high-potential employees and assist them in moving up through the ranks.

- *Continue to focus on diversity in the midst of downsizing.* Because many women and minorities are steered into low-level jobs, they are among the first to go when cutbacks are made. It is important, then, that firms reaffirm diversity commitments when downsizing. For example, AT&T monitors reduction on a department-by-department basis and rewards managers who come up with creative ways of saving the jobs of valued workers—whites as well as minorities. Another program grants valued employees 2-year leaves of absence with full benefits coverage and assurance of reemployment at the same level if such a job is available.

- *Contribute to the supply of diverse workers.* Many firms recruit not merely at Ivy League schools but on college campuses with diverse student bodies. In Jersey City, New Jersey, Merrill Lynch helps high school students prepare for relevant careers by contributing computers and financial services software, and the training needed to use them. Merrill Lynch and Hoechst both maintain scholarship programs, as do numerous other firms.

- *Celebrate diversity.* IBM's Systems Storage Division is located in San Jose, California, a city where 33 languages are spoken. Each year, employees dress in ethnic costumes and bring in ethnic dishes for a company-sponsored diversity-day festival.

■ *Respond to the concerns of white males.* Both moral and legal problems may arise when managers must choose between equally qualified candidates, one of them a white male, the other a female or a male minority member. Many companies have thus taken steps to help resolve problems, ensure fairness, and avoid white-male backlash. Both AT&T and Motorola have hired consultants to counsel white males on the changing workplace. CoreStates Financial Corp. and Du Pont Co. have sponsored support groups. Rochester Telephone Co. has eliminated its minority-run diversity department in favor of a Diversity Council empowered to deal with a much broader range of concerns than just race and gender, including job sharing and career planning.

Diversity Training

diversity training
Programs designed to improve employees' understanding of differences in co-workers' attitudes and behaviors

Another guideline calls for companies to use **diversity training**: programs designed to improve employees' understanding of differences in attitudes and behavior patterns among their co-workers. However, there is no consensus yet on how to conduct such programs—on exactly what to teach and how to do it. "Changing a culture is never easy," observes Nathaniel Thompkins, a diversity manager at Baxter Healthcare Corp. in Deerfield, Illinois. At First Interstate Bank in Los Angeles and at Sears corporate headquarters in Chicago, diversity trainers like to begin by discussing "safer" stereotypes (for example, what kind of people are more likely to be bad drivers). At Baxter, Thompkins prefers a much more direct approach: He might challenge employees to reveal their positions on such issues as abortion or ask them such questions as "Why are you afraid of black people?"

Not surprisingly, says Thompkins, there are sometimes repercussions to such an approach. Indeed, some recent studies have shown that focusing strictly on such issues as race and gender can arouse deep feelings and be almost as divisive as ignoring negative stereotyping in the first place. Other studies suggest that too many training programs are limited to correcting affirmative action problems: Backlash occurs when participants appear to be either "winners" (say, black women) or "losers" (white men) as a result of the process.

Many companies therefore try to go beyond mere awareness training. Du Pont, for example, offers a course for managers on how to seek and use more diverse input before making decisions. Sears offers what it calls diversity-friendly programs: bus service for workers who must commute from the inner city to the suburbs and leaves of absence for foreign-born employees to visit families still living overseas.[17] Finally, one consultant emphasizes that it is extremely important to integrate training into daily routines: "Diversity training," he says, "is like hearing a good sermon on Sunday. You must practice what you heard during the week."[18]

Ernest Drew, CEO of chemical giant Hoechst Celanese (shown here with a group of students), remembers a 1990 conference of the company's top 125 officers (most of them white males). Attendees were split into problem-solving teams and asked to address the impact of corporate culture on the company's business activities. Some groups were all male; others were mixed by race and gender. His eyes, says Drew, were opened wide: "It was so obvious that the diverse teams had the broader solutions. They had ideas I hadn't even thought of. For the first time, we realized that diversity is a strength as it relates to problem solving."

The Contingency Work Force

Can you identify the largest private employer in the United States? Is it General Motors? Exxon? IBM? Actually, it is not a manufacturing company at all. Manpower Inc., the nation's largest supplier of temporary workers, has a payroll of over 600,000. (This is more than GM and IBM combined.) Firms such as Manpower are products of some fairly dramatic changes in the U.S. work force.[19] For decades, businesses in all industries added new employees with regularity. In the 1980s and 1990s, however, cutbacks and retrenchments caused many human resource managers to rethink their staffing philosophies. Rather than hiring permanent employees to fill all new jobs, many firms now use **contingent workers**: employees hired to supplement an organization's permanent work force. They include part-time employees, freelancers, subcontractors, and temporary workers. Figure 8.6 illustrates recent trends among contingent workers.

contingent worker
Employee hired to supplement an organization's permanent work force

By most accounts, the number of contingent workers is on the rise. Figure 8.6 shows the increase in daily temporary workers, or temps, between 1980 and 1993.[20] According to a poll conducted by the research firm Clark Martire & Bartolomeo, 44 percent of Fortune 500 CEOs said that they use more temps than they did 5 years ago; only 13 percent said they used fewer. Moreover, 44 percent indicated that they would be using more in the future. "Any worker still expecting to hold one job from cradle to grave," says Sara Lee CEO John Bryan, "will need to adjust his thinking."

As these numbers indicate, more and more organizations are starting to use small cores of permanent employees, with another group of contingency workers who move in and out of the organization as needed. The main appeal of this approach is maximum flexibility: Managers do not have to worry about hiring people today and then laying off the same workers during slack periods. Nor do companies pay benefits to contingent workers.

Of course, there are also drawbacks. For one thing, many contingent workers have not joined this segment of the work force by choice; they would much prefer the security of a permanent job. Not surprisingly, they usually display less loyalty and dedication than do permanent employees. According to many observers, productivity thus suffers.

Nevertheless, 1.6 million people now work for agencies such as Manpower—up 240 percent in the last 10 years. In addition to large agencies such as Manpower and Kelly Ser-

Figure 8.6 The Contingent Work Force, 1980–1993

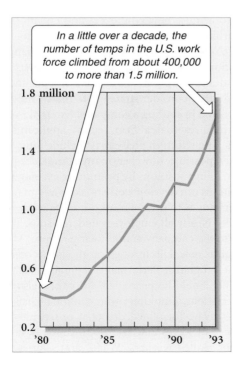

In a little over a decade, the number of temps in the U.S. work force climbed from about 400,000 to more than 1.5 million.

Although most temp workers would prefer permanent jobs, some—especially those who are young—find that low-commitment work lets them sample a variety of jobs and explore career opportunities. This is the attitude of 23-year-old Jillian Perlberger, who earns $16 an hour in the secretarial pools at New York law firms. Temping, says one veteran, can be "wonderful, exhilarating, rewarding, and exciting. And it is also horrible, demeaning, thankless, and boring."

vices, there is a growing number of specialty suppliers. LabForce, for example, places scientists in temporary jobs; Attorneys per Diem furnishes lawyers on an as-needed basis. Both large and small, most of these firms have come into existence since 1983. Between 1983 and 1993, 20 percent of the 18 million jobs created in the United States were temporary or part-time. Some analysts predict that by the year 2000, one-half of all U.S. workers will be among the contingency workers supplied by such agencies.

Summary of Learning Objectives

1 **Define** *human resource management* **and explain how managers plan for human resources.** Human resource management is the development, administration, and evaluation of programs to acquire new employees and enhance the quality and performance of people working in an organization. Planning for human resource needs entails several steps. Conducting a job analysis enables managers to create detailed, accurate job descriptions and specifications. After analysis is complete, managers must forecast demand and supply for both the numbers and types of workers they will need. Only then do they consider strategies to match supply with demand.

2 **Identify the steps involved in staffing a company.** External staffing—hiring from outside the company—requires that a firm recruit applicants and then select from among the applicants. The selection phase may include interviewing, testing, and reference checking. When possible, however, many companies prefer the practice of internal staffing (that is, filling positions by promoting existing personnel).

3 **Explain how organizations can develop workers' skills and manage workers who do not perform well.** If a company is to get the most out of its workers, it must develop those workers and their skills. Nearly all employees undergo some initial orientation process that introduces them to the company and to their new jobs. Many employees are given the opportunity to acquire new skills through on-the-job or off-the-job training or management development programs. Performance appraisals help managers decide who needs training and who should be promoted. Appraisals also tell employees how well they are meeting expectations. Employees who continually fail to meet performance or behavior expectations may be disciplined, demoted, or separated (terminated).

4 **Discuss the importance of wages and salaries, incentives, and benefits programs in attracting and keeping skilled workers.** Wages and salaries, incentives, and benefit

packages may all be parts of a company's compensation program. By paying its workers as well as or better than competitors do, a business can attract and keep qualified personnel. Incentive programs (for example, bonuses, gain sharing, profit sharing, and pay for knowledge) can also motivate personnel to work more productively. Although benefits programs may increase employee satisfaction, they are a major expense to business today.

5 **Describe some of the key legal and ethical issues involved in hiring, compensating, and managing workers in today's workplace.** In hiring, compensating, and managing workers, managers must obey a variety of federal laws. Equal employment opportunity and equal pay laws forbid discrimination other than action based on legitimate job requirements. The concept of comparable worth holds that different jobs requiring equal levels of training and skill should pay the same. Firms are also required to provide employees with safe working environments, as set down by the guidelines of the Occupational Safety and Health Administration. Managers must also consider employment-at-will issues (that is, limitations on their rights to hire and fire at their own discretion).

6 **Discuss work-force diversity and the contingent work force as important changes in the contemporary workplace.** Work-force diversity refers to the range of workers' attitudes, values, beliefs, and behaviors that differ by gender, race, ethnicity, age, and physical ability. Today, many U.S. businesses are working to create work forces that reflect the growing diversity of the population as it enters the labor pool. Although many firms see the diverse work force as a competitive advantage, not all are equally successful in or eager about implementing diversity programs. Diversity training consists of programs to improve employees' understanding of differences among their co-workers.

Contingent workers are temporary and part-time employees hired to supplement an organization's permanent work force. Their numbers have grown significantly since the early 1980s and are expected to rise further. The practice of hiring contingent workers is gaining in popularity because it gives managers more flexibility and because temps are usually not covered by employers' benefit programs.

Questions and Exercises

Questions for Review

1 What are the advantages and disadvantages of internal and external staffing? Under what circumstances is each more appropriate?
2 Why is the formal training of workers so important to most employers? Why not just let people learn about their jobs as they perform them?
3 What different forms of compensation do firms typically use to attract and keep productive workers?
4 What is the glass ceiling? Do you think it will be a less important issue in the future?

Questions for Analysis

5 What are your views on drug testing in the workplace? What would you do if your employer asked you to submit to a drug test?
6 Have you or anyone you know ever suffered discrimination in a hiring decision? Did you or that person do anything about it?
7 Would you consider a career in human resource management? What do you think would be the most difficult aspect of the job?
8 How much will benefit considerations affect your choice of an employer after graduation?

Application Exercises

9 Interview a human resource manager at a local company. Focus on a position for which the firm is currently recruiting applicants and identify the steps in the selection process.
10 Identify some journals in your library that might be useful to a human resource manager. What topics have been covered in recent features and cover stories?

Building Your Business Skills

This exercise enhances the following SCANS workplace competencies: demonstrating basic skills, demonstrating thinking skills, exhibiting interpersonal skills, and working with information.

Goal
To encourage students to develop mechanisms for increasing the cohesiveness of a large, diverse work force.

Situation
As the director of human resources at one of the country's leading banks, you realize that business success depends, in large part, on how effectively the firm's 40,000 employees work together. You convince the CEO and management committee that active steps are needed to make diversity a day-to-day corporate value.

Method
Work with three other students to translate the guidelines presented in this chapter into elements of a workable diversity program that fits the unique needs of your company:

- *Make diversity a specific management goal:* Write a short (one- to four-sentence) mission statement making diversity a corporate goal. The statement should link diversity with competitive success in an increasingly diverse marketplace.
- *Analyze compensation scales and be scrupulously fair in tracking individual careers:* Two years ago, your company merged with another bank, with the result that compensation for the same work varies widely, depending on the original employer. This is particularly problematic because the other firm tended to pay staff workers, many of whom are women and minorities, less than your firm does. Describe how you would correct this disparity, recognizing that it is impossible for a company to equalize everyone's pay at one time and that it is also unfair to freeze, for several years, the compensation of workers who have a higher wage base.
- *Continue to focus on diversity in the midst of downsizing:* With stock analysts criticizing the "fat" in the newly merged firm, the company must cut costs by eliminating 3,000 jobs. Describe the specific steps you would take to ensure that women and minorities do not lose their jobs at a disproportionately high rate.
- *Contribute to the diversity of the work force:* Briefly describe the criteria you would use to award scholarships to needy students. Would you award scholarships to young women who show promise in math and science, despite their economic backgrounds?
- *Celebrate diversity:* Write a one-page memo describing the activities planned during your company's Diversity Day.
- *Respond to the concerns of white males:* Make a list of five ways to increase the comfort of white males to prevent a diversity backlash. You may decide, for example, that men as well as women may be subject to sexual harassment and that appropriate actions will be taken against any man or woman who commits an act of harassment.

Follow-Up Questions

1 Which of these measures do you consider to be most important to the success of your corporate diversity program? Why?
2 After these measures are taken, do you think diversity training is necessary? If you do, describe the objectives of the training.
3 Can you think of any downside to emphasizing diversity?

It May Be Obnoxious, but Is It Illegal?

In 1990 the Equal Employment Opportunity Commission (EEOC) heard 6,127 cases alleging sexual harassment in the workplace. In 1996, it heard *15,342*.

That surge may represent an increased awareness of sexual behavior and a growing intolerance of it by female employees. However, the EEOC's decisions are still largely in favor of defendants in harassment suits; the number of cases resolved in favor of the plaintiff remained between 2,000 and 3,000 throughout the 1990–1996 period. Yet the rising number of cases also reflects attempts to broaden the application of the employment discrimination law known as Title VII of the Civil Rights Act of 1964. How far the law can stretch has yet to be determined. "There are a growing number of cases involving what the courts may deem boorish, but not actionable, behavior," according to Jay Waks of Kaye, Scholer, Fierman, Hays, and Handler, a New York firm that represents employers.

Here is a sampling of such cases:

- Charles Hardy of Nashville's Forklift Systems, Inc., never touched the woman who is suing him but often asked her to take coins from his pants pocket and would berate her publicly, saying, for example, "You're a woman, what do you know?" The woman, Teresa Harris, won her 1993 case against Hardy on appeal when the Supreme Court overturned a lower court's decision.

- Tim Zaring of Zaring Homes, a Cincinnati firm, was acquitted on appeal in a suit alleging that he made frequent sexually suggestive remarks in meetings and told plaintiff Debra Black that she was "paid great for a woman." The appeals judge wrote that while Zaring's behavior was unpleasant, "Title VII was not designed to purge the workplace of vulgarity."

- Peter Arnell, an ad agency executive in New York, has been accused of using foul and abusive language in criticizing female employees for their performance of routine tasks. Their suit claims his behavior targeted them as females and ended only when they left or were fired. One plaintiff stated, "Mr. Arnell constantly referred to my sex and on numerous occasions called me a 'stupid [expletive deleted] woman.'... His abusive behavior often brought me to tears." The case asserts sexual harassment and is still pending.

Commenting on the Arnell case, Jocelyn Frye, a lawyer for the Woman's Legal Defense Fund, said, "People have started to look at Title VII for a broad range of conduct. This is a perfect example of how an employee can bring actions against an employer, who may have just seemed like a bad guy but once he started injecting gender found out his behavior was prohibited."

Questions

1 The Arnell case will be defended on the grounds that words Arnell used, such as *stupid*, *useless*, *worthless*, and *incompetent*, are nonactionable opinions rather that facts and are protected by free speech, and that Arnell's conduct, though rude, is not illegal. Review the wording of Title VII and determine whether you think this defense is a good one. What counterargument is the plaintiff likely to bring?

2 Should the law protect women (and men) from behavior that, though not explicitly sexual, is still offensive or demeaning?

3 What alternative actions might women like the plaintiffs in these cases pursue? Do your suggestions have the same impact on the defendant as a lawsuit? On the plaintiff?

4 How can managers distinguish between frivolous suits and valid ones? What actions can they take to prevent workplace behavior from reaching the point of legal action without abridging free speech?

Connecting to the Web

The following Web sites will give you additional information and points of view about topics covered in this chapter. Many sites lead to other related Internet locations, so approach this list with the spirit of an explorer.

BUREAU OF LABOR STATISTICS

http://www.bls.gov/

Visit the site of the U.S. Bureau of Labor Statistics for economic data, including wages and benefits for the country as a whole and specific regions. The site also presents BLS surveys and publications.

THE BUSINESS JOB FINDER

http://www.cob.ohio-state.edu/dept/fin/osujobs.htm

Developed and maintained by the Fisher College of Business at Ohio State University, this site introduces recent college graduates to career opportunities in business. The site contains valuable links to other on-line career sites.

CAREER MAGAZINE

http://www.careermag.com/

The on-line version of *Career* magazine includes articles on scannable résumés, industry trade shows, and recruiting on campus. You'll also find a résumé bank and a directory of job recruiters and consultants.

CHASE CAREER OPPORTUNITIES: YOUR CAREER AT CHASE

http://www.chase.com/careers/yrcareer.html

As the largest bank in the country, the Chase Manhattan Bank needs employees at all levels with different skills and expertise. Visit this site for on-line job postings and to learn how to submit a résumé via the Internet, mail, or fax.

DIVERSITY @ IBM

http://www.empl.ibm.com/diverse/divhome.htm

IBM's commitment to workplace diversity is evident on this Web page, where you'll meet a diverse range of IBM people and learn about IBM's commitment to equal employment opportunity, affirmative action, and work/life programs.

EQUAL EMPLOYMENT OPPORTUNITY COMMISSION

http://www.eeoc.gov/

The Web site for the U.S. Equal Employment Opportunity Commission provides background information on employment discrimination and the mechanism for filing a discrimination charge with the EEOC.

OCCUPATIONAL SAFETY AND HEALTH ADMINISTRATION (OSHA)

http://www.osha.gov/

Visit the OSHA home page for OSHA guidelines as they affect employers and employees.

SPRINT CAREER OPPORTUNITIES

http://www.sprint.com/hr/index.html

Here you'll learn about "some Very Cool career opportunities" at Sprint as well as information on benefits and training.

U.S. DEPARTMENT OF LABOR: WOMEN'S BUREAU

http://www.dol.gov/dol/wb/

The Women's Bureau of the U.S. Department of Labor is the only unit in the federal government exclusively concerned with serving and promoting the interests of working women. Visit this site to learn what the bureau does, including alerting women about their rights in the workplace, proposing policies and legislation that benefit working women, conducting research on women's issues, and reporting findings to the president, Congress, and the public.

WHARTON SCHOOL AT THE UNIVERSITY OF PENNSYLVANIA: CAREER DEVELOPMENT AND PLACEMENT

http://www.cdp.wharton.upenn.edu/index~1.htm

Among the features on this site is a salary calculator, which allows you to compare the cost of living in hundreds of U.S. and international cities to learn the real value of wage offers. There are also networking opportunities on the business school home page.

chapter 9

Understanding employee **motivation** and leadership

An unusual group owns this firm

In some industries, employee ownership is common. Among its virtues is its value in motivating employee-owners to do their best for the company because they have more at stake than ordinary workers. But employee ownership is still highly unusual in agriculture. In fact, according to the *New York Times*, only one U.S. firm offers employees a share of ownership, and what makes it more unusual is that the employees are migrant workers. McKay Nursery Co. in Waterloo, Wisconsin, began giving its employees shares of stock in the 1960s and has grown to be 100 percent employee owned.

Motivated at first by the need to attract workers to the kind of hard and dirty labor the nursery business requires, the policy has come to be an integral part of the firm's compensation plan. Migrant Mexican workers make up most of the work force, and many of them are seasonal employees. Their base wages are near the legal minimum, and some workers of long standing are still making less than $10 an hour. But more than 90

percent of McKay's seasonal employees return to work there year after year, drawn by the employee stock ownership plan, the advancement opportunities, and other benefits.

About 60 workers are year-round employees. Another 60 are employed 8 months of the year, enough to qualify for bonus payments in the form of stock or cash. These payments can range from 20 to 25 percent of wages, or about $2,000 a year for even the lowest-paid worker. Griff Mason, the firm's president, estimates that accumulated payments could total at least $100,000 over 30 years. Mason himself began as an apprentice at McKay's more than 30 years ago.

The company's stock is not traded publicly, and McKay's will not disclose its price except to say that it has appreciated. When an employee retires, he or she is required to sell the shares back to the company. Although it may limit the value of the stock, the policy is allowing Juanita Gomez, a full-time worker, to retire at 55. "I never expected to see this when I started," she said.

McKay's has succeeded in drawing needed workers to Wisconsin from Texas and California, where most migrant laborers live and work. Some of its workers

Griff Mason, president, with employee-owners of McKay's Nursery

think it could offer even more benefits, such as dental coverage and paid vacations. But the stock distributions have helped reduce turnover and training costs, which is crucial for profitability in the labor-intensive nursery business.

An added benefit, according to Mason, is the emphasis that employee ownership places on continuous improvement. "It's an excuse for changing the culture to get more bottom-up participation," he says. And the results are apparent even to outsiders. "I've never heard of giving stock to migrants," says a representative of the United Farm Workers Union pension plan administrators. "I think it's fantastic."

> **[Employee ownership is] an excuse for changing the culture to get more bottom-up participation.**
>
> —Griff Mason,
> president of McKay Nursery Co.

Although there are many ways to lead and motivate employees, and employee ownership is just one, there is no doubt that leadership and motivation go hand in hand. By focusing on the learning objectives of this chapter, you will better understand why employee morale and job satisfaction are important to all types of business organizations. You will also understand the role of leadership in motivating employees or team members to high levels of achievement. After reading this chapter, you should be able to

1 Discuss the importance of job satisfaction and employee morale and summarize their roles in human relations in the workplace.

2 Identify and summarize the most important theories of employee motivation.

3 Describe some of the strategies used by organizations to improve job satisfaction and employee motivation.

4 Discuss different managerial styles of leadership and their impact on human relations in the workplace.

Human Relations in the Workplace

human relations
Interactions between employers and employees and their attitudes toward one another

The foundation of good **human relations**—the interactions between employers and employees and their attitudes toward one another—is a satisfied work force. Although most people have a general idea of what job satisfaction is, both job satisfaction and high morale can be elusive in the workplace. Because they are critical to an organization's success, we will begin our discussion by explaining their importance.

The Importance of Satisfaction and Morale

job satisfaction
Degree of enjoyment that people derive from their jobs

morale
Overall attitude employees have toward their workplace

Broadly speaking, **job satisfaction** is the degree of enjoyment people derive from performing their jobs. Quite simply, if people enjoy their work, they are satisfied; if they do not enjoy their work, they are dissatisfied. In turn, satisfied employees are likely to have high **morale**: the overall attitude employees have toward their workplace. It reflects the degree to which they perceive that their needs are being met by their jobs. Morale is determined by a variety of factors, including job satisfaction and satisfaction with such things as pay, benefits, co-workers, and promotion opportunities.

Companies can improve employee morale and job satisfaction in a variety of ways. Some large firms have instituted companywide programs designed specifically to address employees' needs. Some, such as Dow Chemical and Hewlett-Packard, sponsor special career-training programs for young students. These programs benefit both students and the sponsors, who ultimately benefit from a more educated, skilled, and committed work force. Managers at Hyatt Hotels report that conducting frequent surveys of employee attitudes, soliciting employee input, and, most importantly, acting on that input gives their company an edge in recruiting and retaining productive workers. Meanwhile, small business managers realize that the personal touch can reap big benefits in employee morale and even devotion. About once a month, for instance, Anita Roddick of Body Shop cosmetics stores hosts a 3-day party at her home in Scotland, where she, her husband, and about 20 franchise owners and employees "all cook together, talk, dance, and play music."[1]

Hewlett-Packard's decentralized structure gives individual business units considerable autonomy to define and pursue business opportunities. This approach combines the advantages of a fast-moving startup business with the depth and breadth of a global, diversified organization and contributes to high morale and worker satisfaction.

When workers are satisfied and morale is high, the organization benefits in many ways. Compared with dissatisfied workers, for example, satisfied employees are more committed and loyal. Such employees are more likely to work hard and to make useful contributions to the organization. In addition, they tend to have fewer grievances and engage in fewer negative behaviors (complaining, deliberately slowing their work pace, and so forth) than dissatisfied counterparts. Finally, satisfied workers tend not only to come to work every day but to remain with the organization. By promoting satisfaction and morale, then, management is working to ensure more efficient operations.[2]

Conversely, the costs of dissatisfaction and poor morale are high. Dissatisfied workers are far more likely to be absent for minor illnesses, personal reasons, or a general disinclination to go to work. Low morale may also result in high turnover (the ratio of newly hired to currently employed workers). In turn, high levels of turnover have many negative consequences, including the disruption of production schedules, high retraining costs, and decreased productivity.

Recent Trends in Managing Satisfaction and Morale

Achieving high levels of job satisfaction and morale seems like a reasonable organizational goal. Although many organizations work to meet it, some do not. Moreover, some that have tried have been unsuccessful. Reacting in large part to massive worker layoffs and downsizing programs, many workers in the late 1980s and early 1990s reported feeling unhappy with their work and concerned about their futures. More recently, however, downsizing programs have been completed, displaced workers have found new jobs, and job security has become a little more stable. Consequently, survey results suggest that satisfaction and morale in the United States have started to improve after several years of decline. Indeed, one recent survey found that most workers expressed positive attitudes about many different aspects of their work. The results compare very favorably with similar surveys of Canadian, Mexican, British, Japanese, and German workers.[3]

However, cutbacks and layoffs still continue in some organizations. For example, Nabisco recently announced plans to cut 4,200 jobs as Conagra, another giant food products company, slashed 6,500 jobs. Apple Computer laid off 1,300 workers, and in one of the largest and most widely publicized downsizing programs, AT&T cut 40,000 jobs (2,000 in a single day).[4] Thus, although many workers are more satisfied today, they do not feel secure. Even if they are satisfied with their own jobs, many know other people— friends, relatives, or neighbors—who are losing their jobs. Others see similarities between their own employers and other firms that are downsizing. Still others experience drastically reduced morale in jobs they still hold.

> **❝***I have a job, but I don't feel like I won the lottery. I was an AT&T man, but I don't feel like that anymore.***❞**
>
> —AT&T employee who survived downsizing job cuts[5]

▶ In January 1996 AT&T announced the cutting of 40,000 jobs over a 3-year period. AT&T's action was part of the fallout from a so-called job creation bill that, in theory, would create 3.6 million new jobs. The idea is to make local phone companies, long-distance carriers, and cable TV operators more competitive by allowing them to enter each others' businesses. The tradeoff: They must learn to live without the regulations that have always protected them from competition. According to officials such as those at AT&T, companies must drop the excess baggage—including payrolls bulging with too many traditional telecommunication jobs—that they've been carrying around for years. "I have a job," admits one AT&T employee who survived the company's cuts, "but I don't feel like I won the lottery. I was an AT&T man, but I don't feel like that anymore."

Experts agree that a firm's best response is announcing and implementing a solid plan for future growth. Obviously, management can also reassure employees by finding ways to avoid laying them off. Between 1990 and 1993, for example, Hewlett-Packard managed to reduce operating costs by over 7 percent without laying off a single worker. Analysts also suggest that when they can no longer provide job security, companies should assist employees in rethinking the nature of their roles in alternative organizational systems.

Many workers are dissatisfied with basic facets of their work lives, such as compensation. For example, some do not think that pay is fairly distributed within their firms. Others believe that they are underpaid compared with people in other companies. Meanwhile, a large majority of nonmanagement employees doubt that pay increases are directly linked to performance.

Another problem is cynicism about quality of operations and opportunities and requirements for advancement. For example, one recent study of middle managers found them to be less satisfied with these aspects of their work than they were just a few years ago.[6] Because middle managers are typically responsible for areas such as product development, marketing, and finance, this trend does not bode well for the future of U.S. businesses.

Motivation in the Workplace

Although job satisfaction and morale are important, employee motivation is even more critical to a firm's success. As we saw in chapter 5, motivation is one part of the managerial function of directing. Broadly defined, **motivation** is the set of forces that cause people to behave in certain ways. For example, whereas one worker may be motivated to work hard to produce as much as possible, another may be motivated to do just enough to get by. Managers must understand these differences in behavior and the reasons for them.

Over the years, therefore, a steady progression of theories and studies has attempted to address these issues. In this section we will survey the major studies and theories of employee motivation. In particular, we will focus on three approaches to human relations in the workplace that reflect a basic chronology of thinking in the area: classical theory and scientific management, behavior theory, and contemporary motivational theories.

Classical Theory and Scientific Management

According to the **classical theory of motivation**, workers are motivated solely by money. In his seminal book *The Principles of Scientific Management* (1911), industrial engineer Frederick Taylor proposed a way for both companies and workers to benefit from this widely accepted view of life in the workplace.[7] If workers are motivated by money, Taylor reasoned, then paying them more would prompt them to produce more. Meanwhile, the firm that analyzed jobs and found better ways to perform them would be able to produce goods more cheaply, make higher profits, and thus pay—and motivate—workers better than its competitors.

Taylor's approach is known as **scientific management**. His ideas captured the imagination of many managers in the early twentieth century. Soon, plants across the United States were hiring experts to perform **time-and-motion studies**: Industrial-engineering techniques were applied to each facet of a job in order to determine how to perform it most efficiently. These studies were the first scientific attempts to break down jobs into easily repeated components and to devise more efficient tools and machines for performing them.[8]

motivation
The set of forces that cause people to behave in certain ways

classical theory of motivation
Theory holding that workers are motivated solely by money

scientific management
Theory of management that uses scientific analysis of individual jobs to increase productivity and efficiency

time-and-motion studies
Scientific management studies using industrial engineering techniques to analyze each facet of a job in order to determine how to perform it most efficiently

Behavior Theory: The Hawthorne Studies

In 1925 a group of Harvard researchers began a study at the Hawthorne Works of Western Electric outside Chicago. With an eye to increasing productivity, they wanted to examine the relationship between changes in the physical environment and worker output.

The results of the experiment were unexpected and confusing. Not surprisingly, increased lighting levels improved productivity. For some reason, however, so did lower lighting levels. Moreover, against all expectations, increased pay failed to increase productivity. Gradually, the researchers pieced together the puzzle. The explanation lay in the workers' response to the attention they were receiving: The researchers concluded that productivity rose in response to almost any management action that workers interpreted as special attention.[9] This finding, known widely today as the **Hawthorne effect**, had a major influence on human relations theory, although in many cases it amounted simply to convincing managers that they should pay more attention to employees.

Hawthorne effect
Tendency for productivity to increase when workers believe they are receiving special attention from management

Contemporary Motivational Theories

Following the Hawthorne studies, managers and researchers alike focused more attention on the importance of good human relations in motivating employee performance. Stressing the factors that cause, focus, and sustain workers' behavior, most motivation theorists are concerned with the ways in which management thinks about and treats employees. The major motivation theories include the human resources model, the hierarchy of needs model, two-factor theory, expectancy theory, equity theory, and goal-setting theory.

Human Resources Model: Theories X and Y

In an important study, behavioral scientist Douglas McGregor concluded that managers had radically different beliefs about how best to use the human resources at a firm's disposal. He classified these beliefs into sets of assumptions that he labeled Theory X and Theory Y.[10] The basic differences between these two theories are highlighted in Table 9.1.

In the account reconcilement department of First Tennessee Bank's Alcoa branch, Constance Wembley balances work and family needs by doing her own scheduling and, if necessary, bringing her daughter into the office when she has to put in overtime. First Tennessee Bank also offers job-sharing and on-site child care. The rationale is that if family concerns affect productivity, helping to ease those concerns improves overall results.

Table 9.1 Theory X and Theory Y

Theory X	Theory Y
People are lazy.	People are energetic.
People lack ambition and dislike responsibility.	People are ambitious and seek responsibility.
People are self-centered.	People can be selfless.
People resist change.	People want to contribute to business growth and change.
People are gullible and not very bright.	People are intelligent.

Theory X
Theory of motivation holding that people are naturally irresponsible and uncooperative

Theory Y
Theory of motivation holding that people are naturally responsible and growth-oriented, self-motivated, and interested in being productive

hierarchy of human needs model
Theory of motivation describing five levels of human needs and arguing that basic needs must be fulfilled before people work to satisfy higher-level needs

Managers who subscribe to **Theory X** tend to believe that people are naturally lazy and uncooperative and must therefore be punished or rewarded to be made productive. Managers who incline to **Theory Y** tend to believe that people are naturally energetic, growth-oriented, self-motivated, and interested in being productive.

McGregor generally favored Theory Y beliefs. He argued that Theory Y managers are more likely to have satisfied, motivated employees. Of course, Theory X and Y distinctions are somewhat simplistic and offer little concrete basis for action. Their value lies primarily in their ability to highlight and classify the behavior of managers in light of their attitudes toward employees.

Maslow's Hierarchy of Needs Model

Psychologist Abraham Maslow's **hierarchy of human needs model** proposed that people have a number of different needs that they attempt to satisfy in their work. He classified these needs into five basic types and suggested that they are arranged in the hierarchy of importance shown in Figure 9.1. According to Maslow, needs are hierarchical because lower-level needs must be met before a person will try to satisfy those on a higher level.[11]

- Physiological needs are necessary to survival and include food, water, shelter, and sleep. Businesses address these needs by providing comfortable working environments and salaries sufficient to buy food and shelter.

- Security needs include the needs for stability and protection from the unknown. Many employers thus offer pension plans and job security.

- Social needs include the needs for friendship and companionship. Making friends at work can help to satisfy social needs, as can the feeling that you belong in a company.

- Esteem needs include the need for status and recognition as well as the need for self-respect. Respected job titles and large offices are among the things that businesses can provide to address these needs.

- Finally, self-actualization needs are needs for self-fulfillment. They include the needs to grow and develop one's capabilities and to achieve new and meaningful goals. Challenging job assignments can help satisfy these needs.

According to Maslow, once one set of needs has been satisfied, it ceases to motivate behavior. This is the sense in which the hierarchical nature of lower- and higher-level needs affects employee motivation and satisfaction. For example, if you feel secure in your job, a new pension plan will probably be less important to you than the chance to make new friends and join an informal network among your co-workers. However, if a lower-level need suddenly becomes unfulfilled, most people immediately refocus on that lower level. Suppose, for example, that you are seeking to meet your esteem needs by working as a divisional manager at a major company. If you learn that your division—and conse-

Figure 9.1 Maslow's Hierarchy of Needs

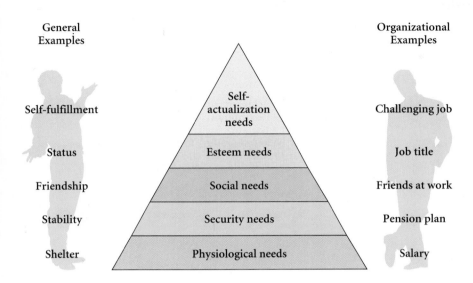

quently your job—may be eliminated, you might very well find the promise of job security at a new firm as motivating as a promotion once would have been at your old company.

Maslow's theory recognizes that because different people have different needs, they are motivated by different things. Unfortunately, it provides few specific guidelines for action in the workplace. Furthermore, research has found that the hierarchy varies widely, not only for different people but across different cultures.

Two-Factor Theory

After studying a group of accountants and engineers, psychologist Frederick Herzberg concluded that job satisfaction and dissatisfaction depend on two factors: hygiene factors, such as working conditions, and motivation factors, such as recognition for a job well done.[12]

According to the **two-factor theory**, hygiene factors affect motivation and satisfaction only if they are absent or fail to meet expectations. For example, workers will be dissatisfied if they believe that they have poor working conditions. If working conditions are improved, however, they will not necessarily become satisfied; they will simply be less dissatisfied. On the other hand, if workers receive no recognition for successful work, they may be neither dissatisfied nor satisfied. If recognition is provided, they will probably become more satisfied.

Figure 9.2 illustrates the two-factor theory. Note that motivation factors lie along a continuum from satisfaction to no satisfaction. Hygiene factors, on the other hand, are likely to produce feelings that lie on a continuum from dissatisfaction to no dissatisfaction. Whereas motivation factors are directly related to the work that employees perform, hygiene factors refer to the environment in which they perform it.

This theory suggests that managers should follow a two-step approach to enhancing motivation. First, they must ensure that hygiene factors—working conditions, clearly stated policies—are acceptable. This practice will result in an absence of dissatisfaction. Then they must offer motivation factors—recognition, added responsibility—as means of improving satisfaction and motivation.

Research suggests that although two-factor theory works in some professional settings, it is not as effective in clerical and manufacturing settings. (Herzberg's research was limited to accountants and engineers.) In addition, one person's hygiene factor may be another person's motivation factor. For example, if money represents nothing more than pay for time worked, it may be a hygiene factor for one person. For another person, however, money may be a motivation factor because it represents recognition and achievement.

two-factor theory
Theory of motivation holding that job satisfaction depends on two types of factors: hygiene and motivating

Figure 9.2 The Two-Factor Theory of Motivation

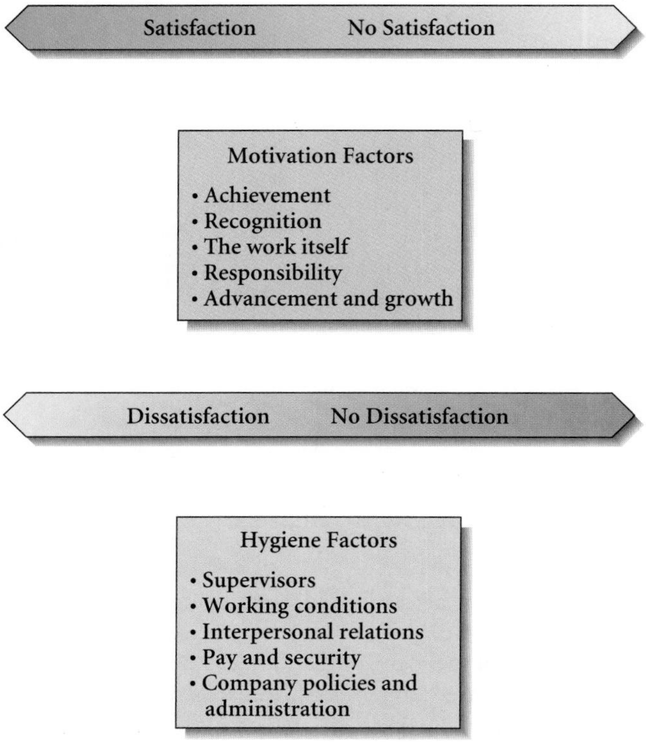

Satisfaction   No Satisfaction

Motivation Factors

- Achievement
- Recognition
- The work itself
- Responsibility
- Advancement and growth

Dissatisfaction   No Dissatisfaction

Hygiene Factors

- Supervisors
- Working conditions
- Interpersonal relations
- Pay and security
- Company policies and administration

Expectancy Theory

expectancy theory
Theory of motivation holding that people are motivated to work toward rewards that they want and that they believe they have a reasonable chance of obtaining

Expectancy theory suggests that people are motivated to work toward rewards that they want and that they believe they have a reasonable chance, or expectancy, of obtaining.[13] A reward that seems out of reach, for example, is likely to be undesirable even if it is intrinsically positive. Consider the case of an assistant department manager who learns that a division manager has retired and that the firm is looking for a replacement. Even though she wants the job, she does not apply for it because she doubts that she would be selected. She also learns that the firm is looking for a production manager on a later shift. She thinks that she could get this job but does not apply because she does not want to change shifts. Finally, she learns of an opening one level higher—full department manager—in her own division. She may well apply for this job because she both wants it and thinks that she has a good chance of getting it.

Expectancy theory also helps to explain why some people do not work as hard as they can when their salaries are based purely on seniority: Because they are paid the same whether they work very hard or just hard enough to get by, there is no financial incentive for them to work harder. In other words, they ask themselves, "If I work harder, will I get a pay raise?" and conclude that the answer is no. Similarly, if hard work will result in one or more undesirable outcomes—say, a transfer to another location or a promotion to a job that requires travel—employees will not be motivated to work hard.

Equity Theory

equity theory
Theory of motivation holding that people evaluate their treatment by employers relative to the treatment of others

Equity theory focuses on social comparisons: people evaluating their treatment by the organization relative to the treatment of others. This approach holds that people begin by analyzing what they contribute to their jobs (time, effort, education, experience, and so forth) relative to what they get in return (salary, benefits, recognition, security). The result is a ratio of contribution to return. Then they compare their own ratios to those of other employees. Depending on their assessments, they experience feelings of equity or inequity.[14]

For example, suppose a new college graduate gets a starting job at a large manufacturing firm. His starting salary is $35,000 per year, he gets a compact company car, and he shares an office with another new employee. If he later learns that another new employee has received the same salary, car, and office arrangement, he will feel equitably treated. However, if the other newcomer has received $40,000, a full-size company car, and a private office, he may feel inequity.

Note that for an individual to feel equitably treated, the two ratios do not have to be the same—they need only be fair. Let's assume, for instance, that our new employee has a bachelor's degree and 2 years' work experience. Perhaps he learns that the other new employee has an advanced degree and 10 years' experience. After first feeling inequity, our new employee may now conclude that the person with whom he compared himself is actually contributing more to the organization. He or she is equitably entitled, therefore, to receive more in return.

When people feel that they are being inequitably treated, they may do various things to restore fairness. For example, they may ask for raises, reduce their efforts, work shorter hours, or just complain to their bosses. They may also rationalize ("Management succumbed to pressure to promote an Asian American"), find different people with whom to compare themselves, or leave their jobs altogether.

Virtually perfect examples of equity theory at work can be found in professional sports. Each year, for example, rookies, sometimes fresh out of college, are often signed to lucrative contracts. Before the ink is dry, veteran players start grumbling about raises or revised contracts.

Strategies for Enhancing Job Satisfaction and Motivation

Determining what provides job satisfaction and motivates workers is only one part of human resource management. The other part is applying that knowledge. Experts have suggested—and many companies have implemented—a wide range of programs designed to make jobs more interesting and rewarding and to make the work environment more pleasant.

Reinforcement/Behavior Modification Theory

Many companies try to control workers' behavior through systematic rewards and punishments for specific behaviors. In other words, they first try to define the specific behaviors that they want their employees to exhibit (working hard, being courteous to customers, stressing quality) and the specific behaviors that they want to eliminate (wasting time, being rude to customers, ignoring quality). Then they try to shape employee behavior by linking reinforcement with desired behaviors and punishment with undesired behaviors.

Reinforcement is used when a company pays piecework rewards—that is, when workers are paid for each piece or product completed. In reinforcement strategies, rewards are all the positive things that people get for working: pay, praise, promotions, job security, and so forth. When rewards are tied directly to performance, they serve as positive reinforcement. For example, paying large cash bonuses to salespeople who exceed quotas prompts them to work even harder during the next selling period. Thus, John Deere has recently adopted a new reward system based on positive reinforcement: The firm now gives pay increases when its workers complete college courses and demonstrate mastery of new job skills.[15]

Punishment is designed to change behavior by presenting people with unpleasant consequences if they fail to change in desirable ways. Employees who are repeatedly late to

reinforcement
Theory that behavior can be encouraged or discouraged by means of rewards or punishments, respectively

work, for example, may be suspended or have their pay docked. Similarly, when the National Basketball Association (NBA) recently suspended a player for choking and threatening his coach, the organization was seeking to change his behavior while sending a message to other players that violence would not be tolerated.

Extensive rewards work best when people are learning new behavior, new skills, or new jobs. As workers become more adept, rewards can be used less often. Because such actions contribute to positive employer-employee relationships, managers generally prefer giving rewards and placing positive value on performance. Conversely, most managers dislike meting out punishment, partly because workers may respond with anger, resentment, hostility, or even retaliation. To reduce this risk, many managers couple punishment with reward for good behavior.

Generally speaking, studies show that rewards are more likely than punishments to motivate and increase job satisfaction. However, there are some limitations on using rewards to shape behavior. They usually work only if employees

■ Believe that they can perform better by making an effort

■ Believe that they will receive rewards for performing better

■ Want the rewards that the company has to offer

Management by Objectives

management by objectives (MBO)
Set of procedures involving both managers and subordinates in setting goals and evaluating progress

Management by objectives (MBO) is a system of collaborative goal-setting that extends from the top of an organization to the bottom. As a technique for managing the planning process, MBO is concerned mainly with helping managers implement and carry out their plans.[16] As you can see from Figure 9.3, however, MBO involves both managers and subordinates in setting goals and evaluating progress. Once the program is set up, the first step is establishing overall organizational goals. These goals will ultimately be evaluated to determine the success of the program. At the same time, however, collaborative activity—communicating, meeting, controlling, and so forth—is the key to MBO. Therefore, it can also serve as a program for improving satisfaction and motivation.

Indeed, according to many experts, motivational impact is the biggest advantage of MBO. When employees sit down with managers to set upcoming goals, they learn more about companywide objectives, come to feel that they are an important part of a team, and see how they can improve companywide performance by reaching their own goals. If an MBO system is used properly, employees should leave meetings not only with an understanding of the value of their contributions, but with fair rewards for their performances. They should also accept and be committed to the moderately difficult and specific goals that they have helped set for themselves.

Of course, MBO also has its limits. One major disadvantage is the time it takes to implement MBO strategies at every level of an organization. First, for example, midlevel managers must meet with their own bosses to set goals. Next, they must meet with each of their

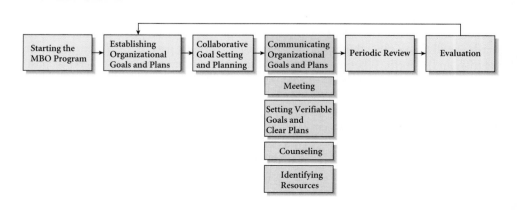

Figure 9.3 Management by Objectives

subordinates to help them set mutually acceptable goals. Moreover, the paperwork necessary to record, document, and keep track of all these goals can be formidable. Because people also tend to focus on the specific time periods defined by the MBO system, they may lose sight of longer-term issues, challenges, and opportunities. Finally, as with most approaches, a poorly administered MBO program can actually hurt morale and motivation.

Participative Management and Empowerment

In **participative management and empowerment**, employees are given a voice in how they do their jobs and how the company is managed; they become empowered to take greater responsibility for their own performance. Not surprisingly, participation and empowerment make employees feel more committed to organizational goals that they have helped to shape.

Participation and empowerment can be used in large firms or small firms, with both managers and operating employees. For example, managers at General Electric who once needed higher-level approval for any expenditure over $5,000 now have the autonomy to make their own expense decisions up to as much as $50,000. At Adam Hat Co., a small firm that makes men's dress, military, and cowboy hats, workers who previously had to report all product defects to supervisors now have the freedom to correct problems themselves or even return products to the workers responsible for them.

participative management and empowerment
Method of increasing job satisfaction by giving employees a voice in the management of their jobs and the company

Team Management

At one level, employees may be given decision-making responsibility for certain narrow activities, such as when to take lunch breaks or how to divide assignments with co-workers. On a broader level, employees are also being consulted on decisions such as production scheduling, work procedures and schedules, and the hiring of new employees.

To make its continuous improvement program work, the Freudenberg-NOK auto parts factory has implemented a number of team-oriented policies. Top management is committed to providing teams with resources and authority needed to make changes. To encourage a variety of ideas, teams are composed of individuals from diverse company backgrounds, and a no-layoff pledge ensures that workers will speak their minds without fear of losing their jobs. Finally, action is preferred over theory: Small but immediate and measurable improvements, for instance, are more desirable than ideas for the long-term high-tech revamping of operations.

Although some employees thrive in participative programs, they are not for everyone. Many people are frustrated by responsibilities that they are not equipped to handle. Moreover, participative programs may actually result in dissatisfied employees if workers see the invitation to participate as more symbolic than substantive. One key, say most experts, is to invite participation only to the extent that employees want to have input and only if participation will have real value for an organization.[17] Equally important, they say, is commitment from top management. Similarly, the line of responsibility between workers and their managers must be made very clear.

▶ When General Electric's medical systems division needed software for two new ultrasound devices, it assigned two teams of engineers: One team consisted of 13 designers in Hino, Japan, the other of 30 Americans in Waukesha, Wisconsin. The U.S. team had expertise in software design, the Japanese experience in marketing ultrasound products in Asia. The idea was for the two groups to complement each other. However, each team reported to a different manager in its own country, and the results for 2 years were predictable. Local managers focused on features that appealed to their respective markets. In other areas, duplication wasted time and money. Finally, GE assigned both teams to a single general manager with direct access to top management. The project is still in operation, with communication improved and a collaborative sensibility more in evidence.[18]

Job Enrichment and Job Redesign

MBO programs and empowerment can work in a variety of settings, but job enrichment and job redesign programs are generally used to increase satisfaction in jobs significantly lacking in motivating factors.

Job Enrichment Programs

job enrichment
Method of increasing job satisfaction by adding one or more motivating factors to job activities

Job enrichment is designed to add one or more motivating factors to job activities. For example, job rotation programs expand growth opportunities by rotating employees through various positions in the same firm. Workers thus gain not only new skills but broader overviews of their work and their organization. Other programs focus on increasing responsibility or recognition. At Continental Airlines, for example, flight attendants now have more control over their own scheduling. The jobs of flight service managers were enriched when they were given more responsibility and authority for assigning tasks to flight crew members.

Job Redesign Programs

job redesign
Method of increasing job satisfaction by creating a more satisfactory fit between workers and their jobs

Job redesign acknowledges that different people want different things from their jobs. By restructuring work to achieve a more satisfactory fit between workers and their jobs, job redesign can motivate people with strong needs for career growth or achievement.[19] Job redesign is usually implemented in one of three ways: through combining tasks, forming natural work groups, or establishing client relationships.

Combining Tasks. Combining tasks means enlarging jobs and increasing their variety to make employees feel that their work is more meaningful than before. In turn, employees become more motivated. For example, the job done by a programmer who maintains computer systems might be redesigned to include some system design and system development work. While developing additional skills, the programmer also gets involved in the overall system package.

Forming Natural Work Groups. People who do different jobs on the same projects are candidates for natural work groups. These groups are formed to help employees see the place and importance of their jobs in the total structure of the firm. They are valuable to management because the people working on a project are usually the most knowledgeable about it, and thus the most capable problem solvers.

To understand how natural work groups affect motivation, consider a group of employees, each of whom performs one small part of the task of assembling radios. One person sees his job as attaching red wires, and another sees hers as attaching control knobs. Both jobs could be redesigned and the group permitted to decide who does what and in what order. Under this arrangement, the workers could exchange jobs and plan their own work schedules. They would thus be far more likely to see themselves as parts of a team that assembles radios instead of automatons who do the same repetitive jobs every day.

Establishing Client Relationships. Establishing client relationships means letting employees interact with customers. This approach increases job variety. It gives workers both a greater sense of control and more feedback about performance than they get when their jobs are not highly interactive.

For example, software writers at Microsoft watch test users work with programs and discuss problems with them directly rather than receive feedback from third-party researchers. In Fargo, North Dakota, Great Plains Software has employee turnover of less than 7 percent, compared with an average 15 to 20 percent in the software industry. The company recruits and rewards in large part according to the candidates' customer service skills and their experience with customer needs and complaints.[20]

Modified Work Schedules

As another way of increasing job satisfaction, many companies are experimenting with modified work schedules: different approaches to working hours and the work week. The two most common forms of modified scheduling are work-share programs and flextime programs, including alternative workplace strategies.

"Keeping customers always seemed like common sense to me," explains Doug Bergum (left), CEO of Great Plains Software. Bergum not only maintains personal contact wherever possible with customers such as lumberyard owner Peter Simonson, but also has compiled detailed profiles of 45,000 clients. Great Plains programs actually require users to contact the company after 50 transactions, whereupon they automatically receive personalized attention from specially trained consultants. In 1993, Great Plains induced an unheard-of 42 percent of users to update from one program to its newer version. When the new version proved to be flawed, Bergum personally mailed new disks to every buyer and offered cash compensation to anyone whose business had suffered.

Work and Family: Can They Coexist?

The eternal balancing act between work and family seems ever more in the spotlight these days, as technology makes it possible for employees to keep in touch electronically and shorten their time in the office. But are managers letting workers take advantage of telecommuting, networking, and e-mail to enrich their home life and take care of children and elderly parents?

Despite some notable successes at firms such as MBNA America, Motorola, Hewlett-Packard, DuPont, and Eddie Bauer, corporate workers say they are still struggling to keep their lives in balance, often with little help from the office. Some programs merely pay lip service to family needs; others give with one hand and take away with the others. Said one worker in a letter to *Business Week*, "I may have flexibility to accommodate family needs . . . but I'm home working until midnight to get my job done."

What are the issues, and how do firms stack up? Business publications such as the *Wall Street Journal, Fortune*, and *Working Mother* often ask. *Business Week* has conducted two broad surveys of family and corporate life, in 1996 and 1997, and each year disillusioned employees sent letters along with their questionnaires, voicing complaints about the difficulties of putting in sufficient "face time" in the office while trying to keep things aloft at home. "My company is relatively understanding (I think)," said one. "My department is actively hostile."

Some firms offer everything from on-site day care, summer camps, flexible hours, facilities for nursing mothers, and referrals for elder care to job sharing, fitness centers, adoption benefits, and even pet care. But for every success story there is a complaint about unfair application of standards, deferred promotion or recognition, and lack of management commitment to family-friendly programs. Things like meetings on Father's Day, last minute demands for travel, and unrealistically long work hours (explicit or implied) continue to place stress on many workers.

Some firms do see the problem. Says Randall Tobias, CEO of family-friendly Eli Lilly Co., "Historically we looked at whose cars were in the parking lot at 7 P.M. and we made the assumption that they belonged to the corporate heroes hard at work. In truth some of those people were probably poorly organized or spending time on the wrong things. . . . I'm not sure a lot of corporate America understands."

> *Historically we looked at whose cars were in the parking lot at 7 P.M., and we made the assumption that they belonged to the corporate heroes hard at work. In truth some of those people were probably poorly organized or spending time on the wrong things.*
>
> —Randall Tobias, CEO of Eli Lilly Co.

Family benefits seem to transcend gender, age, and seniority. Women with children made up less than 25 percent of *Business Week*'s respondents in the 1997 survey, and the most dissatisfied employees were those who care for elderly parents. Even childless employees found issues; some feel that family benefits, however they may meet parents' needs, take resources away from other employees.

But it seems clear that the dilemma is here to stay. The median income of families rose only 6.7 percent (adjusted for inflation) between 1979 and 1994, and that includes the income of women, who doubled their hours at work in that period. Their contribution to families' standard of living "is not pin money," say Kathy Newman, a Harvard professor of public policy. "It's not fulfillment of stated ambitions. This is driving economic necessity."

Work-Share Programs

work sharing (or job sharing)
Method of increasing job satisfaction by allowing two or more people to share a single full-time job

At Steelcase Inc., the country's largest maker of office furnishings, two very talented women in the marketing division both wanted to work only part-time. The solution: They now share a single full-time job. With each working 2½ days a week, both got their wishes and the job gets done (and done well). In another situation, one person might work mornings and the other afternoons. The practice is known as **work sharing** (or **job sharing**), and it has, according to at least one Steelcase employee, "brought sanity back to our lives."

❝ *Job sharing has brought sanity back to our lives.* ❞

—Steelcase employee

Short-run work-share programs can help ease experienced workers into retirement while training their replacements. They can also allow students to combine academics with practical experience. As at Steelcase, long-run programs have proved a boon to people who want only part-time work. At American Airlines, for example, five part-time employees often share one reservationist's job, each working 1 day a week. They each earn some income, remain in the job market, and enjoy limited travel benefits. Meanwhile, American saves on insurance and retirement benefits and keeps trained employees.

Job sharing usually benefits both employees and employers. Employees tend to appreciate the organization's attention to their personal needs. At the same time, the company can reduce turnover and save on the cost of benefits. On the negative side, job-share employees generally receive fewer benefits than their full-time counterparts and may be the first to be laid off when cutbacks are necessary.

Flextime Programs and Alternative Workplace Strategies

Flextime programs allow people to choose their working hours by adjusting a standard work schedule on a daily or weekly basis. Of course, there are limits. The Steelcase program, for instance, requires all employees to work certain core hours. This practice allows everyone to reach co-workers at a specified time of day. But employees can decide whether to make up the rest of the standard 8-hour day by coming in and leaving early (say, by working 6:00 A.M. to 2:00 P.M. or 7:00 A.M. to 3:00 P.M.) or late (9:00 A.M. to 5:00 P.M. or 10:00 A.M. to 6:00 P.M.).

Figure 9.4 shows a hypothetical flextime system that could be used by three different people. The office is open from 6:00 A.M. until 7:00 P.M. Core time is 9:00 A.M. to 11:00

flextime programs
Method of increasing job satisfaction by allowing workers to adjust work schedules on a daily or weekly basis

---

Figure 9.4 Sample Flextime Schedule

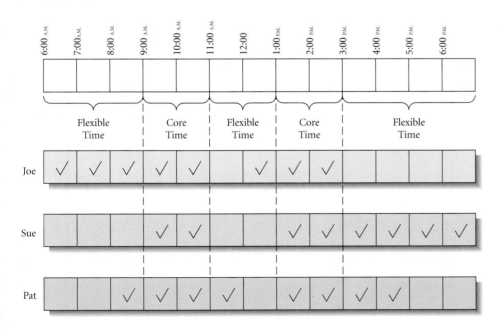

A.M. and 1:00 P.M. to 3:00 P.M. Joe, an early riser, comes in at 6:00, takes an hour for lunch between 11:00 and noon, and finishes his day by 3:00. Sue, a working mother, prefers a later day: She comes in at 9:00, takes a long lunch from 11:00 to 1:00, and then works until 7:00. Pat works a more traditional 8:00 to 5:00 schedule.

In one variation, companies may also allow employees to choose 4 of 5 or 6 days on which to work each week. Some may choose Monday through Thursday, others Tuesday through Friday; still others may work Monday–Tuesday and Thursday–Friday and take Wednesday off. By working 10 hours over 4 workdays, employees still complete 40-hour weeks.

Telecommuting and Virtual Offices

telecommuting
Form of flextime that allows people to perform some or all of a job away from standard office settings

Tammy Aultman sells computer systems for Hewlett-Packard, which is located in Mountain View, California. Aultman accepted the job even though she lives in Laguna Hills, 350 miles away. Her solution: She outfitted a room in her home with a personal computer and a fax machine and now works comfortably out of Laguna Hills. As you can see from Figure 9.5, there has been a dramatic increase in the number of stay-at-home workers. Indeed, Aultman is one of a rapidly growing number of U.S. workers who do a significant portion of their work by a new version of flextime known as **telecommuting**: performing some or all of a job away from standard office settings.

Among salaried employees, the telecommuter work force grew by 21.5 percent in 1994, to 7.6 million. By the year 2000, that number may be 25 million (although ways of defining telecommuting vary widely). The key to telecommuting is technology: The availability of networked computers, fax machines, cellular telephones, and overnight delivery services makes it possible for many professionals to work at home or while traveling. Many of these workers have traded in traditional careers for the benefits of working out of their homes, and telecommuting is playing a larger role in increasingly cost-conscious firms. At IBM, for instance, "shared work spaces" consist of one desk for every six or eight employees. About 5,000 IBM employees now work under this system. Most of them work at home, in their cars, or at customer sites. AT&T, meanwhile, has eliminated office space

Figure 9.5 Number of Telecommuters, 1987–2000

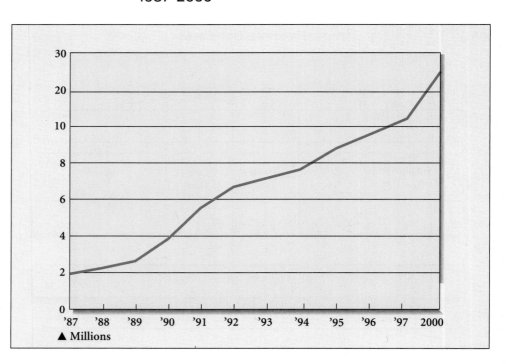

▲ Millions

for about 7,000 salespeople. They have been given notebook computers and cellular phones and permitted to set up virtual offices just about anywhere they want. "For every $1 we invested in technology," reports one upper-level manager, "we've saved $2 in real estate."

In addition to real estate savings, companies are coming to realize that the traditional office is not necessarily a very productive place. In Chicago, for instance, regional telephone company Ameritech Corp. has found that work-at-home employees handle 20 percent more customer service calls than their in-office counterparts.[21]

Other companies have experimented with so-called virtual offices: They have redesigned conventional office space to accommodate jobs and schedules that are far less dependent on assigned spaces and personal apparatus. At the advertising firm Chiat Day Mojo in Venice, California, only about one-third of the salaried work force is in the office on any given day. The office building itself features informal work carrels or nooks and open areas available to every employee. "The work environment," explains director of operations Adelaide Horton, "was designed around the concept that one's best thinking isn't necessarily done at a desk or in an office. Sometimes it's done in a conference room with other people. Other times it's done on a ski slope or driving to a client's office."[22]

Advantages and Disadvantages of Modified Schedules and Alternative Workplaces

Flextime gives employees more freedom in their professional and personal lives. It allows workers to plan around the work schedules of spouses and the school schedules of young children. Studies show that the increased sense of freedom and control reduces stress and thus improves individual productivity.

Companies also benefit in other ways. In urban areas, for example, such programs can reduce traffic congestion and similar problems that contribute to stress and lost work time. Furthermore, employers benefit from higher levels of commitment and job satisfaction. John Hancock Insurance, Atlantic Richfield, and Metropolitan Life are among the major American corporations that have successfully adopted some form of flextime.

On the other hand, flextime sometimes complicates coordination because people are working different schedules. In the schedules shown in Figure 9.4, for instance, Sue may need some important information from Joe at 4:30 P.M. But because Joe is working an earlier schedule, he leaves for the day at 3:00. In addition, if workers are paid by the hour,

Nancy Allen (left) is head of human resources at the advertising firm Chiat Day Mojo, which prides itself on the interplay of creativity and productivity in its office design. Appropriated from carnival rides, for instance, colorful Tilt-a-Whirls now function as office furniture with built-in privacy. "I'm not tethered to a specific work area," says Allen. "As long as I get everything done, that's what counts. Ultimately, my productivity is greater and my job-satisfaction level is higher."

flextime may make it difficult for employers to keep accurate records of when they are actually working.

As for telecommuting and virtual offices, although they may be the wave of the future, they may not be for everyone. For example, consultant Gil Gordon points out that telecommuters are attracted to the ideas of "not having to shave and put on make-up or go through traffic, and sitting in their blue jeans all day." However, he suggests that would-be telecommuters ask themselves a number of other questions: "Can I manage deadlines? What will it be like to be away from the social context of the office five days a week? Can I renegotiate the rules of the family, so my spouse doesn't come home every night expecting me to have a four-course meal on the table?" One study has shown that even though telecommuters may be producing results, those with strong advancement ambitions may miss networking and rubbing elbows with management on a day-to-day basis.

Another obstacle to establishing a telecommuting program is convincing management that it can be beneficial for all involved. Telecommuters may have to fight the perception, from both bosses and co-workers, that if they are not being supervised, they are not working. Managers, admits one experienced consultant, "usually have to be dragged kicking and screaming into this. They always ask, 'How can I tell if someone is working when I can't see them?'" By the same token, he adds, "that's based on the erroneous assumption that if you can see them they are working." Most experts agree that reeducation and constant communication are requirements of a successful telecommuting arrangement. Both managers and employees must determine expectations in advance.[23]

Managerial Styles and Leadership

In trying to enhance morale, job satisfaction, and motivation, managers can use many different styles of leadership. **Leadership** is the process of motivating others to work to meet specific objectives. Leading is also one of the key aspects of a manager's job and an important component of the directing function.

leadership
Process of motivating others to work to meet specific objectives

▶ *OVERHAULING THE CULTURE AT GM.* Consider the experience of Jack Smith, whose leadership abilities were put to the test shortly after he became CEO of General Motors in November 1992. After losing $23.5 billion in 1991—the largest single-year net loss in U.S. corporate history—GM brought in Smith to turn things around. One of Smith's first moves as CEO was to close the executive dining room on the fourteenth floor of the com-

"It's a vice-president thing, Berger. You wouldn't understand."

pany's corporate headquarters in Detroit. The dining room, a symbol of privilege and elitism that had survived war, recession, and even the invasion of Japanese imports, could not survive Smith's determination to make GM more democratic. Symbols count, observes GM executive vice president William E. Hound: "Before," recalls Hoglund, "the big shooters went to the fourteenth floor, and the little people went somewhere else. [This] is a tiny step toward a company that moves and is responsive."

Since taking over GM, Smith has focused on five goals: developing a new product plan, reducing materials costs, aligning production capacity with demand, reducing the work force, and improving quality while reducing warranty expenses. Success in meeting these goals is important to everyone at GM, and Smith has introduced a management style that favors participation, delegation, and openness. Smith's style is also one of self-effacement, and close associates explain that he has been reluctant to take personal credit for improving GM's fortunes because he regards himself as part of a team.

Observers also attribute at least part of Jack Smith's success at GM to his concern for his work force. He believes in open communication, even with the United Auto Workers Union, whose top leaders have often locked horns with GM. After a recent meeting, for example, the leaders of several hundred UAW locals expressed approval of Smith's democratic approach even though they remained aware that tough times were still ahead. "He didn't use $600 words, and he was frank," reported Dick Long, president of UAW Local 653 in Pontiac, Michigan. "It's just refreshing."[24]

David E. Cole, director of the Office for the Study of Automotive Transportation at the University of Michigan, summarizes the leadership style Jack Smith has displayed at GM: "One of Smith's greatest attributes," says Cole, "is that he relies on people around him. He knows what he doesn't know, and a lot of people who are executives don't. He's not into picking car designs or second-guessing engineers. He's a good listener, but he's not afraid of making decisions." In this section, we will begin by describing some of the basic features of and differences in managerial styles and then focus on an approach to managing and leading that, like Jack Smith's, understands those jobs as responses to a variety of complex situations.

Managerial Styles

Early theories of leadership tried to identify specific traits associated with strong leaders. For example, physical appearance, intelligence, and public speaking skills were once thought to be leadership traits. Indeed, it was once believed that taller people made better leaders than shorter people. The trait approach proved to be a poor predictor of leadership potential. Ultimately, attention shifted from managers' traits to their behaviors, or **managerial styles**: patterns of behavior that a manager exhibits in dealing with subordinates. Managerial styles run the gamut from autocratic to democratic to free-rein. Naturally, most managers do not conform clearly to any one style. But these three major types of styles involve very different kinds of responses to human relations problems. Under different circumstances, any given one, or any combination, may prove appropriate:

- Managers who adopt an **autocratic style** generally issue orders and expect them to be obeyed without question. The military commander prefers and usually needs the autocratic style on the battlefield. Because no one else is consulted, the autocratic style allows for rapid decision making. It may therefore be useful in situations testing a firm's effectiveness as a time-based competitor.

- Managers who adopt a **democratic style** generally ask for input from subordinates before making decisions but retain final decision-making power. For example, the manager of a technical group may ask other group members to interview and offer opinions about job applicants. However, the manager will ultimately make the hiring decision.

- Managers who adopt a **free-rein style** typically serve as advisers to subordinates, who are allowed to make decisions. The chairperson of a volunteer committee to raise funds for a new library may find a free-rein style most effective.

managerial style
Pattern of behavior that a manager exhibits in dealing with subordinates

autocratic style
Managerial style in which managers generally issue orders and expect them to be obeyed without question

democratic style
Managerial style in which managers generally ask for input from subordinates but retain final decision-making power

free-rein style
Managerial style in which managers typically serve as advisers to subordinates, who are allowed to make decisions

The Workplace Environment

Power Gets a New Look

Is the face of leadership changing? Or do the corner office, secretary, limo, and expensive decor still define the wielder of corporate power?

Some commentators see these visible signs of power fading in the era of laptops and casual Friday. Today's managers and even CEOs are more likely to opt for a simple cubicle, no window, and no secretary. Regardless of the source of their power, its image has altered, perhaps permanently.

One reason is that workers are better educated and more willing to question leadership. Casual attire, even if worn only on Fridays, has lowered barriers still more. Empowerment, the management philosophy that pushes decision-making authority down through the organization to workers on the front lines, channels power away from the top. Flattened hierarchies have less concentrated power to begin with, and networking, teams, and cross-functional collaboration diffuse power as well. If anywhere, power today seems to reside more with the technologically proficient than with the merely well paid.

Some prime examples of the new look of power:

- Intel CEO Andy Grove works out of a low-walled cubicle.
- Citibank chief John Reed rides the New York subway to work.
- Microsoft Bill Gates answers his own e-mail (and he types it himself).
- Lowe's CEO Robert Tillman says, "It pleases me that everybody calls me Bob."

 *People don't need to see me in big fancy office to know that I'm the CEO.*

—Jim Hackett, CEO of Steelcase Inc.

More and more top executives seem to agree with Steelcase's Jim Hackett, who says, "People don't need to see me in big fancy office to know that I'm the CEO." Yes, power has changed.

According to many observers, the free-rein style of leadership is currently giving rise to an approach that emphasizes broad-based employee input into decision making and the fostering of work environments in which employees increasingly determine what needs to be done and how.

Regardless of theories about the ways in which leaders ought to lead, the effectiveness of any leadership style depends largely on the desire of subordinates to share input or to exercise creativity. Whereas some people are frustrated, others prefer autocratic managers because they do not want a voice in making decisions. The democratic approach, meanwhile, can be disconcerting both to people who want decision-making responsibility and to those who do not. A free-rein style lends itself to employee creativity, and thus to creative solutions to pressing problems. This style also appeals to employees who like to plan their own work. However, not all subordinates have the necessary background or skills to make creative decisions. Others are not sufficiently motivated to work without supervision.

The Contingency Approach to Leadership

Because each managerial style has both strengths and weaknesses, most managers vary their responses to different situations. Flexibility has not always characterized managerial style or responsiveness. For most of the twentieth century, in fact, managers tended to believe that all problems yielded to preconceived, pretested solutions: If raising pay reduced turnover in one plant, for example, it followed that the same tactic would work equally well in another.

More recently, however, managers have begun to adopt a **contingency approach** to managerial style: They have started to view appropriate managerial behavior in any situation as dependent, or contingent, on the elements unique to that situation. This change in outlook has resulted largely from an increasing appreciation of the complexity of managerial problems and solutions. For example, pay raises may reduce turnover when workers have been badly underpaid. However, they will have little effect when workers feel adequately paid but ill-treated by management. This approach also recommends that training managers in human relations skills may be crucial to solving the problem in the second case.

The contingency approach also acknowledges that people in different cultures behave differently and expect different things from their managers. A certain managerial style, therefore, is more likely to be successful in some countries than in others. For example, Japanese workers generally expect managers to be highly participative and to give them input in decision making. In contrast, many South American workers actually balk at participation and want take-charge leaders. The basic idea, then, is that managers will be more effective when they adapt their styles to the contingencies of the situations they face.[25]

contingency approach
Approach to managerial style holding that the appropriate behavior in any situation is contingent on the unique elements of that situation

Motivation and Leadership in the 1990s

Motivation and leadership remain critically important areas of organizational behavior. As times change, however, so do the ways that managers motivate and lead their employees.

From the motivational side, today's employees want rewards that are often very different from those that earlier generations desired. Money, for example, is clearly no longer the prime motivator for most people. In addition, because businesses today cannot offer the degree of job security that many workers want, motivating employees to strive toward higher levels of performance requires skillful attention from managers.

Finally, as we saw in chapter 8, the diversity inherent in today's work force makes motivating behavior more complex for managers. The reasons for which people work reflect more goals than ever before, and the diverse lifestyles of workers mean that managers must first pay closer attention to what their employees expect to get for their efforts and then try to link rewards with job performance.

Today's leaders are also finding it necessary to change their own behavior. As organizations become flatter and workers more empowered, managers naturally find it less acceptable to use the autocractic approach to leadership. Instead, many are becoming more democratic, functioning more as coaches than bosses. Just as an athletic coach teaches athletes how to play and then steps back to let them take the field, many leaders now try to provide workers with the skills and resources to perform at their best before backing off to let them do their work with less supervision.

Summary of Learning Objectives

1 **Discuss the importance of job satisfaction and employee morale and summarize their roles in human relations in the workplace.** Good human relations—the interactions between employers and employees and their attitudes toward one another—are important to business because they lead to high levels of job satisfaction (the degree of enjoyment that workers derive from their jobs) and morale (workers' overall attitude toward their workplace). Satisfied employees generally exhibit lower levels of absenteeism and turnover; they also have fewer grievances and engage in fewer negative behaviors.

2 **Identify and summarize the most important theories of employee motivation.** Views of employee motivation have changed dramatically over the years. The classical theory holds that people are motivated solely by money. Scientific management tried to analyze jobs and increase production by finding better ways to perform tasks. The Hawthorne studies were the first to demonstrate the importance of making workers feel that attention is being paid to their needs. The human resources model identifies

two kinds of managers: Theory X managers, who believe that people are inherently uncooperative and must be constantly reinforced, and Theory Y managers, who believe that people are naturally responsible and motivated to be productive.

Maslow's hierarchy of needs model proposes that people have a number of different needs (ranging from physiological to self-actualization) that they attempt to satisfy in their work. People must fulfill lower-level needs before seeking to fulfill higher-level needs. The two-factor theory suggests that if basic hygiene factors are not met, workers will be dissatisfied; only by increasing more complex motivation factors can companies increase employees' performance.

Expectancy theory holds that people will work hard if they believe that their efforts will lead to desired rewards. Equity theory says that motivation depends on the way employees evaluate their treatment by an organization relative to its treatment of other workers. Management by objectives focuses on the motivational impact of goals that are established by both supervisors and workers.

3 **Describe some of the strategies used by organizations to improve job satisfaction and employee motivation.** Managers can use several strategies to increase employee satisfaction and motivation. The principle of reinforcement, or behavior modification theory, holds that reward and punishment can control behavior. Rewards are positive reinforcement when they are tied directly to desired or improved performance. Punishment (using unpleasant consequences to change undesirable behavior) is generally less effective.

Management by objectives (a system of collaborative goal-setting) and participative management and empowerment (techniques for giving employees a voice in management decisions) can improve human relations by making employees feel like part of a team. Job enrichment, job redesign, and modified work schedules (including work-share programs, flextime, and alternative workplace strategies) can enhance job satisfaction by adding motivation factors to jobs in which they are normally lacking.

4 **Discuss different managerial styles of leadership and their impact on human relations in the workplace.** Effective leadership—the process of motivating others to meet specific objectives—is an important determinant of employee satisfaction and motivation. Generally speaking, managers practice one of three basic managerial styles. Autocratic managers generally issue orders that they expect to be obeyed. Democratic managers generally seek subordinates' input into decisions. Free-rein managers are more likely to advise than to make decisions. The contingency approach to leadership views appropriate managerial behavior in any situation as dependent on the elements of that situation. Managers thus need to assess situations carefully, especially to determine the desire of subordinates to share input or exercise creativity.

Questions and Exercises

Questions for Review

1 Do you think most people are satisfied or dissatisfied with their work? Why are they mainly satisfied or dissatisfied?

2 Compare Maslow's hierarchy of needs with the two-factor theory of motivation.

3 How can participative management programs enhance employee satisfaction and motivation?

4 What managerial style do you think best describes your own general approach to leadership?

Questions for Analysis

5 Some evidence suggests that people fresh out of college show high levels of job satisfaction. Levels drop dramatically as they reach their late twenties, only to increase gradually once again as they get older. What might account for this pattern?

6 As a manager, under what sort of circumstances might you apply each of the theories of motivation discussed in this chapter? Which would be easiest to use? Which would be hardest? Why?

7 Suppose you realize one day that you are essentially dissatisfied with your job. Short of quitting, what might you do to improve your situation?

8 List five noteworthy U.S. managers whom you think would also qualify as great leaders.

Application Exercises

9 At the library, research the manager or owner of a company in the early twentieth century and the manager or owner of a company in the 1990s. Compare the two in terms of their times, leadership styles, and views of employee motivation.

10 Interview the manager of a local manufacturing company. Identify as many different strategies for enhancing job satisfaction at that company as you can.

Building Your Business Skills

This exercise enhances the following SCANS workplace competencies: demonstrating basic skills, demonstrating thinking skills, exhibiting interpersonal skills, and working with information.

Goal To encourage students to consider whether they could become successful telecommuters and to analyze the advantages and disadvantages of telecommuting.

Situation You've worked for the same company for 3 years. Although you're satisfied with your job, your work schedule is a real problem. Your commute, by car, normally takes an hour, but if weather or traffic conditions are bad, the time can double. Life is too short for this, you tell yourself, and you are determined to try telecommuting. Your boss is willing, but you're still not sure whether it's the right decision for your personal life or your career.

Method **Step 1:** Working alone, take the following test to judge whether you are a good candidate for telecommuting. Many of the answers require work experience, so you may have to ask a friend or family member for some on-the-job insights. Record your answers so you can share them with others:

1 Do you have the right personality for telecommuting?
   - Are you self-disciplined enough to work alone?
   - Are you a self-starter?
   - Would being isolated from other workers bother you?
   - Are you an effective time manager?
   - Can you block out distractions and chores (e.g., cooking dinner, watching TV)?

2 What are the characteristics of an ideal telecommuting job? How do you think the following factors would affect your success? (If you are a full-time student, answer these questions based on the work you expect to do.)
   - Do you interact with others all day or is most of your work independent?
   - Are your work materials portable? Can you move them easily from office to home?
   - Is most of your work computer or telephone based? Can you transmit your work electronically?

3 Do you understand the career risks of telecommuting, and are you willing to make adjustments for them?
   - Why do you think it is important for telecommuters to keep a high profile at work?

- List three ways to maintain your visibility.
- Do you think it is important to continue to socialize with co-workers?

4   Are your working conditions right for telecommuting?

- How would you describe an appropriate at-home work space?
- What equipment would you need to set up a virtual office? Do you have a computer? Are you connected to the Internet? Do you have voice mail, a fax, and multiple phone lines to handle your various messages?
- If you have children, what child care arrangements would you require?

Step 2: Come together with three or four other students to share and compare your answers. Based on your comparative analysis, can you identify critical differences in the way people view their suitability for telecommuting and the advantages and disadvantages of working in a virtual office?

Follow-Up Questions

1   What are the major advantages of telecommuting?
2   What are the major disadvantages?
3   How can a manager make telecommuting success more likely? How can he or she make it more difficult?
4   Many workers are struggling to achieve a work/life balance. Based on your responses and the responses of your classmates, is telecommuting a viable solution?

Levi Strauss & Co. is not only the world's leading maker of branded clothing and one of Fortune magazine's most admired companies. It is also a leader in creating a supportive work environment based on worker loyalty and trust.

The average length of service at the legendary blue jeans maker is more than 10 years, and management turnover at its headquarters in San Francisco is a mere 1.5 percent a year. Pay and bonuses are generous, and Levi's stock has risen with its fortunes, from $2.53 in 1984 to $265 in 1996, a record most firms would envy. This is the firm that's paying children in Bangladesh to stay in school full time until they are old enough to reclaim the guaranteed jobs in Levi factories that await them when they turn 14. Under the leadership of CEO Robert Haas, whose great-great-grand-uncle started the firm, Levi's seems to have figured out how to be ethical and make money at the same time.

Employee motivation has been high during Haas' tenure, sustained by his vision of the firm. "I believe that if you create an environment that your people identify with, that is responsive to their sense of values, justice, fairness, ethics, compassion, and appreciation, they will help you be successful. There's no guarantee, but I will stake all my chips on this vision."

The company sets great store in its Aspirations Statement, which invokes teamwork, trust, diversity, recognition, and ethics, and is backed by required courses in leadership, diversity and ethical decision-making. Employees are assured that these values are real. Managers' bonuses, which can be as much as twice their salaries, depend directly on how well they achieve "aspirational behavior," as judged by their subordinates and others. To compensate for ending its ESOP plan, Levi's has conscientiously promised an extra year's pay to each of its 37,000 employees if cash flow goals for 1997–2001 are met. Says Clive Smith, who works at the new plant in Cape Town, South Africa, "When we tell people what it's like working here, they think we're lying. . . . You'll have to fish the cops to get me out of here."

Yet the company is dealing with a possible threat to its sterling employee relations: a stunning layoff affecting 1,000 jobs was announced in 1997. Partly the result of debt incurred in a massive buyback of company stock in 1996, the layoffs seem to go against everything the company had stood for in its dealings with employees, although job security was never promised. Ironically, another contributing factor to the loss of jobs was an expensive plan to improve Levi's service to retailers that depended on developing new computer systems and software, not the firm's core business. The effort failed.

About 250 of the layoffs will occur by attrition through early retirement. The remainder constitute about 2 percent of the total workforce, a small reduction in force by today's standards, but perhaps enough to shake the firm's normally stable relations with its workers.

> ❝ *When we tell people what it's like working here, they think we're lying. . . . You'll have to fish the cops to get me out of here.* ❞
>
> —Clive Smith, employee at Levi's plant in Cape Town, South Africa

Questions

1 How can Levi's minimize the damage its uncharacteristic actions might cause to employee morale and motivation? What specific strategies should management use?

2 CEO Haas has accepted responsibility for the situation that created the need for layoffs and plans to adhere to the firm's aspirational values. How can he use his position to focus employees on the positive aspects of working for Levi's?

3 Levi's president Peter Jacobi sees the company's unusual commitment to teamwork and trust as "a business strategy, pure and simple." Do you agree? Why or why not?

4 Jacobi also says "We're not in business to create world peace." Can you think of any downside to the aspirational approach?

5 Do you think you would be satisfied working at Levi's? Why or why not?

Connecting to the Web

The following Web sites will give you additional information and points of view about topics covered in this chapter. Many sites lead to other related Internet locations, so approach this list with the spirit of an explorer.

AMERICAN MANAGEMENT ASSOCIATION INTERNATIONAL

http://www.amanet.org

The American Management Association International, the world's leading membership-based development and training organization, offers seminars, training, conferences and special events, and research reports about a variety of management issues, including motivation and leadership.

THE BODY SHOP

http://www.bodyshop.com/

The high morale at the Body Shop International is linked to owner Anita Roddick's commitment to social causes. Visit this site for a look at the company values that help motivate employees and customers.

EDDIE BAUER: BENEFITS

http://www.eddiebauer.com/eb/EBhq/frame_benefits.asp

Eddie Bauer's emphasis on Work/Life Benefits is featured on this Web page. The site lists the ways in which the company helps employees balance the often conflicting demands of work and family.

JOHN DEERE

http://www.deere.com

Visit this Web site for a look at employment at John Deere and how the company defines itself as a good place to work.

MOTOROLA: MOTOROLA LIFE

http://www.mot.com/Employment/motlife/motlife.htm

Motorola's reputation as a company that values and empowers employees is reflected on this Web page. Visit this site and you will learn about empowered teams, continuing education, work/family strategies, and more.

NORTHERN LIGHT SEARCH

http://www.nlsearch.com/

Northern Light is a search service linked to the American Management Association's Web site that provides researchers with high-caliber information based on Internet and special collection results. Information is organized into content folders for easy access.

RESOURCES FOR EMPLOYER AND EMPLOYEE

http://www.employer-employee.com/

Written by an employee assistance counselor, this Web site is designed to help employers and employees handle workplace problems. Among the issues examined on a recent visit to this site are employee motivation, workplace procrastination, and sexual harassment.

SLOAN MANAGEMENT REVIEW

http://web.mit.edu/smr-online/

Published by the Sloan School of Business at the Massachusetts Institute of Technology, the Sloan Management Review is intended for professional managers and management students and includes articles on motivation, teams, leadership, and many other management topics. The current journal is available on-line.

TRAINING FORUM: THE ON-LINE RESOURCE FOR PREMIUM TRAINING INFORMATION

http://www.trainingforum.com/

With links to thousands of professional associations, speakers, and events, this site is a comprehensive resource for managers and management students. Use this site to search for information on various management topics.

WELCOME TO STEELCASE

http://www.steelcase.com/

Visit this site for Steelcase's human resources philosophy, which, in part, reads, "Our relationships are conducted in a spirit of partnership, and we balance the needs of the business with those of our employees and their families." Job sharing fits comfortably within this philosophy and is a practice Steelcase uses to help employees maintain a work–family life balance.

chapter 10

Understanding **labor** and management relations

Union takes up her cause

Who wouldn't jump at the chance for promotion? That's what Patricia Jones did when her employer, Albertson's Inc., offered to make the grocery checkout clerk a customer service supervisor. Jones got no raise, and she still worked the register at the Albertson's grocery store near Los Angeles, as she had done for 15 years. But she expected to gain valuable experience and new skills.

That's not how Albertson's saw her new job, however. Jones was supposed to do the additional work after hours without pay, and she did so for the next 4 years. "I asked about it all the time," she says of the 4 or 5 hours of free time she gave the firm every week. "They just said I had to work it out."

As union steward for the United Food and Commercial Workers (UFCW), Jones soon found out she was

not alone. The union has since received more than 4,500 employee complaints about "off the clock" labor at Albertson's, about 2,000 of which it has substantiated. A survey by a firm hired by the union found that about a third of Albertson's 85,000 workers had occasionally worked without pay. Jones returned to the position of cashier in 1996 and is represented in a class-action lawsuit the union is bringing against the food chain, alleging that it regularly requires employees to work without compensation. If successful, the suit could cost the Idaho-based chain $200 million in back pay and damages and might change work rules radically enough to lower Albertson's higher-than-average profit margins.

What is unusual about the suit is that the union is bringing the action itself, instead of depending on government agencies to do so. It has filed in California, Florida, and Washington and plans actions in other states as well. Albertson's has protested that the union's own grievance process should be followed

first, but the Labor Department has come out in support of the UFCW.

> *I asked about it all the time. They just said I had to work it out.*
>
> —Patricia Jones, Albertson's clerk, commenting on the unpaid extra hours she worked after being promoted

Many of the issues raised by the lawsuit against Albertson's highlight the importance of key principles in contemporary labor-management relations. By focusing on the learning objectives of this chapter, you will better understand the formation of unions as a result of workers' fundamental concerns about workplace conditions, the legal and regulatory basis for labor-management relations, and the working of the collective bargaining process. After reading this chapter, you should be able to

1 Explain why workers unionize.

2 Trace the evolution and discuss the future of unionism in the United States.

3 Describe the major laws governing labor-management relations.

4 Describe the union certification and decertification processes.

5 Identify the steps in the collective bargaining process.

Why Do Workers Unionize?

Over 2,000 years ago, the Greek poet Homer wrote, "There is a strength in the union even of very sorry men." There were no labor unions in Homer's time, but his comment is a particularly effective expression of the rationale for unions. A labor union is a group of individuals working together to achieve shared job-related goals, such as higher pay, shorter working hours, greater benefits, or better working conditions.[1]

Labor unions grew in popularity in the United States in the nineteenth and early twentieth centuries. The labor movement was born with the Industrial Revolution, which also gave birth to a factory-based production system that carried with it enormous economic benefits. Job specialization and mass production allowed businesses to create ever greater quantities of goods at ever lower costs.

But there was also a dark side to this era. Workers became more dependent on their factory jobs. Eager for greater profits, some owners treated their workers like other raw materials: resources to be deployed with little or no regard for the individual worker's well-being. Many businesses forced employees to work long hours; 60-hour weeks were common, and some workers were routinely forced to work 12 to 16 hours a day. With no minimum-wage laws or other controls, pay was also minimal and safety standards virtually nonexistent. Workers enjoyed no job security and received few benefits. Many companies, especially textile mills, employed large numbers of children at poverty wages. If people complained, nothing prevented employers from firing and replacing them at will.

Collective Bargaining

collective bargaining
Process by which labor and management negotiate conditions of employment for union-represented workers

Unions appeared and ultimately prospered because they constituted a solution to the worker's most serious problem: They forced management to listen to the complaints of all their workers rather than to just the few who were brave (or foolish) enough to speak out. The power of unions, then, comes from collective action. **Collective bargaining** is the process by which union leaders and managers negotiate common terms and conditions of employment for the workers represented by unions. Although collective bargaining does not often occur in small businesses, many midsize and larger businesses must engage in the process, which we will discuss in more detail in this chapter.

The Evolution of Unionism in the United States

As we discuss the growth—and more recent decline—of unionism in this section, it is important to remember that the influence of labor unions goes far beyond their membership. For example, many nonunion members have benefited from the improved working conditions won by unions. Union gains often set standards for entire industries, and some organizations make workplace improvements just to keep unions out.[2]

Early Unions

craft union
Union representing workers whose common interest is a specific job

Labor unions grew up with the United States. Indeed, the earliest formal organizations of U.S. workers appeared during the Revolutionary War. These early organizations were **craft unions**: Each limited itself to representing workers whose common interest was a specific skilled job, and each sought to promote the economic welfare of the skilled craftspeople who made up its membership.

For example, the Federal Society of Journeymen Cordwainers, formed in Philadelphia in 1794, strove to better the pay and working conditions of shoemakers. The Cordwainers was also one of the first unions to encounter legal roadblocks to collective action. When the union struck for higher wages in 1806, the court ruled in favor of employers, who claimed that unions were illegal "combinations" conspiring to restrain trade. The court's ruling applied the common law conspiracy doctrine: the principle that the public interest was harmed when two or more people conspired to do something jointly. Unions continued to organize, but for the next four decades they found it extremely difficult to take action in the face of the conspiracy doctrine.

Early National Unions

The founding of the National Trades Union in New York in 1834 marked the appearance of labor organizations with national, rather than local or regional, memberships. Among other things, the NTU battled for shorter workdays, persuading president Martin Van Buren to reduce the workday for all workers at federal public works from 12 to 10 hours. However, when an economic depression in 1837 led to job shortages, many workers sought to keep their jobs by abandoning the NTU, and its subsequent collapse weakened the entire U.S. labor movement. Indeed, this episode typified a trend in union fortunes that persists to this day: the tendency for union strength to decline during hard economic times.

In 1842, however, another court case aided the union cause by weakening the conspiracy doctrine. When the Journeymen Bootmakers Society of Boston agreed to refuse work from any employer hiring nonunion labor, employers went to court. This time, the Massachusetts Supreme Court ruled that neither the union's action (refusing to work) nor its purpose (getting nonunion workers to join a union) was illegal.

The 1850s and 1860s witnessed the emergence of several new trade organizations, such as the National Typographical Union (1852), the United Cigarmakers (1856), and the Iron Molders (1859). Toward the end of the nineteenth century there were 30 national unions with a total membership of about 300,000 in the United States. Again, however, membership eroded substantially when the country was hit by another economic depression in 1893.

The Knights of Labor

A milestone in the history of U.S. labor occurred with the formation of the Knights of Labor in 1869. Like earlier unions, the Knights began as a craft union. Soon, however, the organization set larger goals for itself: In a drive to organize any workers who were interested in its representation, the Knights expanded to encompass workers in numerous fields (noteworthy exceptions were lawyers, bankers, and bartenders). The Knights was also the first union that actively sought women and blacks as members, and one of the few unions that have ever focused on political lobbying rather than collective bargaining as a means of reaching its goals.

In 1886, the McCormick Harvester Co. in Chicago locked out 1,400 unionized workers and hired strikebreakers. Fired on by police, workers retreated to the area known as the Haymarket to conduct a protest meeting. At first, the meeting was peaceful. Then, however, 70 policemen were injured when a bomb exploded, and the notorious Haymarket riot erupted. Ultimately, "labor agitators" were blamed for the violence, and four anarchists were hanged for conspiring to commit murder. In reality, the role of radicals was exaggerated by unsympathetic newspapers and employer propaganda.

The Knights championed such traditional union issues as better working conditions, campaigning especially for the 8-hour day and the abolition of child labor. At the same time, however, the union also hoped to achieve a broad range of social goals. Chief among these were such liberal, or reformist, objectives as worker ownership of factories and free public land for those who wished to farm.

These same goals also attracted to the labor movement a variety of radicals and other political reformers, many of whom came in the waves of European immigrants who had begun arriving a few decades earlier. Their activities were directed against what they saw as the oppressive nature of the industrial capitalist system, and their tactics did not necessarily reflect the typical strategies of the labor unions. Spurred by a severe depression in 1873, for example, a series of violent labor actions characterized labor-management relations from the mid-to late 1870s. Demonstrators and locked-out strikers blockaded factories, battled strikebreakers in the streets of major cities, and exchanged fire with municipal police, state militia, and armed private agents. Assassinations and bombings led to the trial and execution of "anarchists" and "labor agitators."

However, much of the violence in this period came in direct response to the extraordinary pressures of the depression. Most American laborers were conservative by nature and sought the stability of organizations such as the Knights of Labor. Under the leadership of Terence V. Powderly, the Knights grew to include roughly 700,000 members by the mid-1880s. The union was never successful, however, at increasing the number of skilled workers among its members. In addition, it was weakened by internal disagreements about social goals and outside charges of union violence. By the turn of the century, Knights had disbanded.

The Emergence of the Major Unions

With its focus on the social welfare of unskilled workers, the Knights of Labor tended to forget that its economic strength lay with its skilled craft workers. As a result, many of these workers soon began to look for organizations that would better represent their interests: namely, unions whose primary concern was to improve wages, hours, and working conditions.

The AFL

American Federation of Labor (AFL)
Group of craft unions formed in 1866 to stress collective bargaining, economic action, and a pragmatic approach to union-management relations

Many workers disenchanted with the social agenda of the Knights of Labor found a home in the **American Federation of Labor (AFL)**. Made up of craft unions, the AFL was formed in 1886 by Samuel Gompers and other veteran organizers. Unlike the Knights of Labor, the AFL stressed no broad, idealistic legislative or political program. Gompers himself saw the labor union as an integral component, not the inherent enemy, of the capitalist system: "As we get a 25-cents-a-day wage increase," he argued, the process "brings us nearer the time when a greater degree of social justice and fair dealing will obtain among men." The enduring importance of the AFL lies in the fact that it established a solid organizational basis for collective bargaining, economic action, and a pragmatic approach to union-management relations.

The AFL grew rapidly in the early decades of the twentieth century, and by the end of World War I, membership had reached more than 5 million. The 1920s proved difficult for the AFL, as increased employer resistance to unions contributed to a steady decline in membership. By 1929, membership had dropped to 3.4 million.

The Great Depression of the 1930s witnessed further decline. By 1933, membership stood at just 2.9 million. In the same year, however, newly elected President Franklin D. Roosevelt introduced the nation to the New Deal, a far-reaching program aimed at stimulating the U.S. economy and creating jobs. The New Deal inspired an era of recovery for organized labor. Moreover, as we will see later in this chapter, the New Deal Congress passed a series of laws that made it easier for workers to organize.

The CIO

By the mid-1930s, the advent of mass production had significantly increased the demand for semiskilled workers in the automobile, steel, and mining industries. The AFL, while continuing to grow throughout the 1930s, remained open only to skilled craftspeople. In fact, most AFL leaders opposed **industrial unionism**—the organizing of employees by industry rather than by skill or occupation. When a 1935 convention of AFL unions confirmed this stance, dissident leaders, including John L. Lewis of the United Mine Workers, objected bitterly. Ultimately, the AFL expelled 32 national unions, which in 1938 banded together to form the **Congress of Industrial Organizations (CIO)**.

Soon, the CIO had organized the auto, steel, mining, meatpacking, paper, textile, and electrical industries. By the early 1940s, CIO unions claimed close to 5 million of the slightly more than 10 million unionized U.S. workers. Not surprisingly, the AFL soon abandoned rigid craft unionism and began to charter industrial unions.

The AFL-CIO

Union membership continued to increase during World War II, reaching more than 14 million by the end of the war. However, a series of postwar strikes led Congress to curtail the power of unions. Partly in response to this change, and partly in response to growing conflicts within their ranks, leaders of the AFL and the CIO began merger negotiations. These meetings culminated in the 1955 formation of the AFL-CIO, with a total membership of 15 million. At the same time, organized labor reached its membership zenith, claiming almost 35 percent of the nonfarm work force.

Today, in addition to lobbying for pro-union issues, the AFL-CIO settles jurisdictional disputes between unions. Remember, however, that the AFL-CIO is not a union itself. Rather, it is a federation of 86 individual unions that belong to various trade or industrial departments (such as building trades, maritime trades, and public employees). The United Food and Commercial Workers is a union, as are the International Brotherhood of Teamsters and the National Education Association.

The five largest unions in the United States now count 7 million members, or 42 percent of all organized workers. In a similar trend, there are also fewer unions than there used to be. For example, whereas the AFL-CIO had 146 affiliates in 1955, it now has only 86. Since 1955, there have been 92 mergers between unions, almost 50 percent occurring between 1974 and 1984. Finally, although overall union membership has been declining, unionization among public employees has grown steadily, even dramatically. In 1956, for instance, only 12 percent of public employees were organized; today, that figure is 37 percent (compared to 11 percent of all workers in the private sector). Between 1960 and 1990, the American Federation of State, County, and Municipal Employees grew from 185,000 members to 1.2 million. During the 1960s and 1970s, both the National Education Association and the rival American Federation of Teachers posted huge gains in membership.[3]

Unionism Today

Figure 10.1 shows trends in union membership as a percentage of the work force between 1977 and 1996. Since the mid-1950s, unions have experienced increasing difficulties in attracting members. Even as late as 1977, however, over 26 percent of U.S. wage and salary employees (both private and public) still belonged to unions. Today, as you can see, less than 15 percent of those workers are union members. If government employees are not counted, unions represent only around 11 percent of private industry employees, and some experts suggest that this figure could drop to 4 or 5 percent by the turn of the century.[4]

Moreover, workers at many plants are increasingly rejecting attempts to unionize. In the 1940s, 1950s, and 1960s, unions routinely won most certification elections in which

industrial unionism
Organizing of workers by industry rather than skill or occupation

Congress of Industrial Organizations (CIO)
Group of industrial unions formed in 1938 that rapidly organized the auto, steel, mining, meatpacking, paper, textile, and electrical industries

Figure 10.1 Union Membership as a Percentage of the Work Force

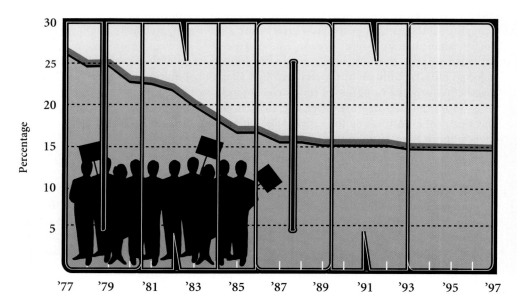

workers voted whether or not to unionize. In recent years, they have been winning only about 45 percent of those elections.

▶ **THE FABRIC OF LIFE IN THE TEXTILE BELT.** One area in which unions are countering that trend is the textile industry in the southeastern United States. According to Bruce Raynor, southern regional director of the Amalgamated Clothing and Textile Workers Union, labor in the South won 13 of 14 elections to unionize in 1993, 7 more than in 1992. Another big win, the fourth union victory in the South in 1994, came at Tultex Corp.'s Martinsville, Virginia, plant. Not since the J. P. Stevens Co. plant in North Carolina was organized 20 years ago has the Textile Workers Union gained such a big victory for organized labor. Tultex, a 57-year-old activewear company, had been targeted for organization for years. A near-miss effort by the Textile Workers in 1990 was occasioned by plantwide modernization and streamlining. By most accounts, the 1994 campaign was an unfriendly affair, long fought and hard won by a vote of 1,321 to 710.

At issue were changes in the employer's salary and benefits policy: namely, wage cuts and an end to company contributions to the employees' retirement plan. Union campaign director Ernest Bennett charged that workers were angry not only because of lost compensation (almost $6,000 a year, on average) but also because they were given no say in the changes. "There is more anger and frustration right now than I've seen in 15 or 16 years of organizing," he said. "The pie is shrinking and people aren't being consulted."

For its part, Tultex was responding to shrinking demand and shrinking profits. The cuts were necessary, says the company, because orders were down across the board. Moreover, say Tultex officials, their changes brought the company more in line with competitors' wage and bonus structures. For example, a profit-sharing plan was introduced to replace the annual Christmas bonus. The new plan, argued a Tultex spokesperson, "fits in with our strategy that we all have a stake in the company" and could be even more lucrative for employees. Organizers pointed out that this would be the case only if Tultex were to return to a level of profitability that it had not reached for some time. Employees contended that the company's focus on a mutual stake in the organization was misplaced: "Everything is focused on customers and stockholders, not on employees," explains one worker. "That was their downfall."[5]

Factors in Declining Union Power

Despite occasional successes, union fortunes have been in decline for the past 40 years. In this section, we will first survey some of the key factors that have contributed to this reduction of union power. Then we will take a brief look at the future of American labor unions. Finally, in order to better explain the role of unions not only in such processes as collective bargaining but also in the daily life of the unionized work force, we will describe the typical structure of the contemporary labor union.

Several factors have contributed to the downward slide in union fortunes. Following are three of the most important:

- *Composition of the work force.* Traditionally, union members have been white men in blue-collar jobs. However, today's work force is increasingly composed of women and minorities. With a much weaker tradition of union affiliation, members of those groups are less likely to join unions when they enter the work force.

- *Antiunionization strategies.* Many nonunionized industries have developed strategies for avoiding unionization. For example, some companies have introduced new employee relations programs to keep facilities union free. Other employers have launched carefully managed campaigns to persuade workers to reject unions. Some firms have even relocated to states or countries in which unions are unpopular or difficult to install.[6]

- *Negotiated concessions.* Growing international competition in certain industries has led employers to demand unprecedented concessions. As a result, givebacks, or sacrifices of previously won rights and terms, have become common.

As a result of such trends, many experts have observed that in the 1980s and 1990s, unions have altered the focus of the demands that they make at the bargaining table. In recent talks, for example, the United Automobile Workers has shifted its emphasis away from higher wages. Instead, the union now is fighting to prevent wage cuts, preserve health benefits, improve job security, and secure larger pensions.[7]

Even as unions refocus, however, many experts point to declining union power at U.S. bargaining tables. Moreover, they point to weakened union power as a key factor in certain trends in the U.S. workplace, especially outside such traditional union strongholds as the auto industry. Through the 1980s, for example, the number of workers with employer-paid pension funds dropped by 6 percent; the number of those with health plans dropped by 7 percent.[8] In this section we will focus on three of the most important factors in the decline of contemporary union influence: the changing composition of the work force, the development by employers of effective anti-union strategies, and the advent and increase of union concessions at the bargaining table.

The Future of Unions

Despite setbacks, however, labor unions remain a major factor in the U.S. business world. The 86 labor organizations in the AFL-CIO, as well as independent major unions such as the Teamsters and the National Education Association, still play a major role in U.S. business.

Moreover, some unions still wield considerable power, especially in traditional strongholds in goods-producing industries. In March 1996, for example, 3,200 members of the United Automobile Workers struck General Motors' brake parts plant in Dayton, Ohio. The strike was prompted by GM's decision to buy certain parts from outside suppliers. Managers at GM argued that they could buy parts from nonunionized suppliers more cheaply than they could manufacture them, largely because the GM plant was paying higher, union-mandated wages. The UAW, meanwhile, was concerned that GM's decision threatened union jobs. Within 2 weeks, three-quarters of all GM plants had been shut down because of the parts shortage resulting from the strike at a single factory. When the strike was finally settled 17 days later, GM announced that its effects would include a 50-percent drop in anticipated profits for the first quarter of 1996.[9]

It's Your Business

Is Union Membership in Your Future?

By any measure, union membership is down in the United States. From a peak of 35 percent in 1953, it has sunk to just 15 percent of wage and salaried workers, and in the private sector only 10 percent are union workers. Only in the public sector are the numbers up. There, among government workers, unionization is at 38 percent, and public employees now make up 42 percent of U.S. union membership.

The general decline is leading unions on a drive to add new members. The Service Employees' International Union (SEIU) is working hard to convince health care and service employees to add their numbers to the country's fastest-growing union. Although health care employers and other service firms have long resisted unionization, SEIU president Andy Stern has a track record of success in recruiting low-wage workers. Alliances with local churches and communities groups have led to such attention-getting tactics as mass protests and civil disobedience. "Nonunion workers are ready to join unions," says Stern. "The question is whether unions are ready to reach out to them."

AFL-CIO president John Sweeny is using the same tactics, which he pioneered during his own tenure at SEIU, where he preceded Stern. He hopes to add to the ranks of the AFL-CIO and its 78 member unions with a massive drive for membership, particularly among minorities and women, and he backs his hopes with an impressive third of the union's budget.

The United Farm Workers (UFW) has added thousands of new members, as did the Teamster's Union in an aggres-sive campaign for unionization at firms that had held off for unions for decades. Union leaders in the steel, auto, and building trades are gearing up as well. They are counting on downsizing, loss of job security, and wage stagnation to motivate new members to join.

What the unions have to combat are the globalization of business, the growth of services (where union membership has traditionally been low), and the pressure on businesses to keep prices down in today's highly competitive markets. Unionization costs firms money in pay and benefits, which are typically 20 percent higher for union members, and one way they may choose to deal with such increases when they can't raise prices is to post lower profits and smaller stock gains. Whether they are willing to do so is an open question at the moment.

> " *Nonunion workers are ready to join unions. The question is whether unions are ready to reach out to them.* "
>
> —Andy Stern, president of the Service Employees' International Union

Although union membership in 1996 slipped by 100,000 workers, September 1997 saw the biggest union organizing election in the private sector in years, when nearly 10,000 reservation and ticket agents at US Airways voted to join the Communications Workers of America. Labor leaders saw the victory as doubly significant, not only for the sheer number of workers involved but also for the fact that they represent one of labor's most difficult targets: white-collar workers.

Odds are, almost anywhere you may work, union leaders will be looking your way.

Labor and management in some industries, notably airlines and steel, are beginning to favor contracts that establish formal mechanisms for greater worker input into management decisions. Inland Steel, for instance, recently granted its major union the right to name a member to the board of directors; union officers can also attend executive meetings.[10]

However, the big question remains: Will unions dwindle in power and perhaps disappear, or can they evolve, survive to face new challenges, and play a new role in U.S. business? They will probably evolve to take on new roles and responsibilities. As we have already seen, more and more unions are asking for—and often getting—voices in management. In 1980, for example, as a part of the Chrysler bailout, UAW president Dou-

"Actually, Tommy, we're just about full-blooded management, except for your grandfather on your mom's side, who was one-quarter labor."

glas Fraser became the first labor official appointed to the board of directors of a major corporation. Several other companies have since followed suit.

By the same token, unions are increasingly aware that they must cooperate with employers if both are to survive. Critics of unions contend that excessive wage rates won through years of strikes and hard-nosed negotiation are partly to blame for the demise of large employers such as Eastern Airlines. Others argue that excessively tight work rules limit the productivity of businesses in many industries. More often, however, unions are working with organizations to create effective partnerships in which managers and workers share the same goals: profitability, growth, and effectiveness with equitable rewards for everyone.

▶ **STEELING FOR CHANGE AT LTV.** Similarly, a combined management-labor steering committee is now responsible for new technology at LTV Corp., a large steelmaker based in Cleveland. In fact, LTV has committed itself to the principle of management-labor co-operation and participatory management in its basic production activities. At the company's L-S Electro-Galvanizing plant, for instance, production workers are hired by a committee composed entirely of unionized employees. The whole operation is run by self-managing worker teams.

What did the union concede in return for this system of participatory management? Most important, it granted management less stringent union work rules and more flexibility in job classifications. Thus, even though L-S workers are represented by Local 9126 of the United Steelworkers of America, there are no job classifications at the factory. Instead, LTV offers better wages to workers who cross-train in order to become skilled in a variety of jobs. Successful training is certified by committees of workers, which then pay out raises. With overtime, a multiskilled LTV worker can earn $50,000 a year.

According to Edgar L. Ball, a former official with the United Steelworkers, the system at LTV is promising because it has largely moved beyond the long-standing premise of management-labor relations: "I had thought for a long time," says Ball, "that the way we conducted relations was crazy. . . . We are set up by law to fight. We had to fight to get the union, then we had to fight to get a contract. Labor laws just set the rules for the fighting."[11]

Jack Parton, a Steelworkers negotiator who worked on the contracts at both Inland and LTV, agrees: "We ain't going to survive by fighting every three years," he concedes. LTV chief executive David H. Hoag also sounds a conciliatory note: "There's definitely a place in American society for unions," he admits. Many managers do not share Hoag's relaxed view of their traditional adversaries. Nor do many labor leaders, who point out that they still have work to do. In particular, they want to regain some of the ground they lost in the 1980s.[12]

> **" We ain't going to survive by fighting every three years. "**
>
> —Jack Parton, a Steelworkers negotiator

At the same time, corporate cost-cutting has given unions new ammunition, enabling them to appeal to the many workers who have been laid off, suffered reduced wages, or lost job security. For example, automation has reduced the number of jobs in manufacturing and has begun to do the same in other areas, such as communication. In November 1994, for example, Pennsylvania members of the Communications Workers of America protested plans by Bell Atlantic Corp. to cut 1,500 regional jobs by wearing T-shirts depicting workers as roadkill on the information superhighway. Unamused, Bell Atlantic docked the protesters two days' pay. Other local unions have already agreed to meet productivity goals in return for 1-year guarantees of job security at Bell Atlantic.[13]

Finally, unions, like multinational employers, are now beginning to devise strategies that cross borders. For example, during the debate over the North American Free Trade Agreement (see chapter 3), U.S. unions not only protested the possibility of American jobs lost to Mexico but worked to support Mexican union organizers. When Campbell Soup Co. responded to the demands of U.S. tomato pickers for higher wages by threatening to move some of its midwestern operations to Mexico, the Farm Labor Organizing Committee helped Mexican counterparts win higher wages. Such strategies not only support Mexican union efforts but also discourage U.S. companies from fleeing to Mexico in search of lower wage scales.[14]

Ultimately, however, unions must deal with the attitude of workers toward the kind of representation that unions afford them in today's workplace. In December 1994, a study conducted by a presidential labor commission revealed some interesting findings. For example, 90 percent of unionized workers said that they wanted to keep their unions. One-third of nonunion workers said that they would vote yes on union representation, though not in the face of management opposition.

Then all workers were given a choice between two types of representative groups: a group with no power but with management cooperation and a group that (like unions) had power but was opposed by management. Workers chose the first and weaker form of representation by a 3-to-1 margin. Why? Because management was too powerful, said 73 percent of the workers surveyed. They believe that labor representation can get input on such matters as wages, working conditions, and production goals only if management truly cooperates. In other words, although workers do indeed want independence and decision-making power, they are not sure that traditional union representation permits them to speak up without fear of jeopardizing their jobs.[15]

Contemporary Union Structure

Just as each organization has its own unique structure, each union creates a structure that best serves its own needs. As Figure 10.2 shows, however, a general structure characterizes most national and international unions. A major function of unions is to provide service and support to both members and local affiliates. Most of these services are carried out by the types of specialized departments shown in Figure 10.2. In other unions, departments serve specific employment groups. The Machinists' Union, for instance, has departments for automotive, railroad, and airline workers.[16]

Figure 10.2 Organization of a Large National Union

Locals

At the same time, most national unions are composed of **local unions (locals)**, which are organized at the level of a single company, plant, or small geographic region. The functions of these locals vary, depending not only on governance arrangements but also on bargaining patterns in particular industries. Some local unions bargain directly with management regarding wages, hours, and other terms of employment. Many local unions are also active in disciplining members for violations of contract standards and in pressing management to consider worker complaints. Local unions also serve as grass-roots bases for union political activities, registering voters and getting them out to vote on election day.

local union (local)
Union organized at the level of a single company, plant, or small geographic region

Officers and Functions

Each department or unit represented at the local level elects a **shop steward**: a regular employee who acts as a liaison between union members and supervisors. For example, if a worker has a grievance, he or she takes it to the steward, who tries to resolve the problem with the supervisor. If the local is very large, the union might hire a full-time **business agent** (or **business representative**) to play the same role.

Within a given union, the main governing bodies are the national union (or international union when members come from more than one country) and its officers. Among their other duties, national and international unions charter local affiliates and establish general standards of conduct and procedures for local operations. For example, they set dues assessments, arrange for the election of local officers, sanction strikes, and provide guidance in the collective bargaining process. Many national unions also engage in a variety of political activities, such as lobbying. They may also help coordinate organizing efforts and establish education programs.

Given the magnitude of their efforts, it is little wonder that unions often take on many of the same characteristics as the companies for which their members work. For example, almost all large unions have full-time administrators, formal organizational structures (see Figure 10.2), goals and strategic plans, and so forth. Because of their size, power, and importance, Congress has passed numerous laws to govern union activities. It is to these laws that we now turn our attention.

shop steward
Union employee who acts as liaison between union members and supervisors

business agent (or business representative)
Full-time official who acts as liaison between members of a large union and their supervisors

Laws Governing Labor-Management Relations

Like almost every other aspect of labor-management relations today, the process of unionizing workers is governed by numerous laws, administrative interpretations, and judicial decisions. In fact, the growth and decline of unionism in the United States can be traced by following the history of labor laws.

For the first 150 years of U.S. independence, workers were judged to have little legal right to organize. Indeed, interpretation of the 1890 Sherman Antitrust Act classified labor unions as monopolies, thus making them illegal. During the first 30 years of the twentieth century, however, social activism and turmoil in the labor force changed the landscape of U.S. labor relations.

The Major Labor Laws

Five major federal laws, all enacted between 1932 and 1959, lay the groundwork for all the rules, regulations, and judicial decisions governing union activity in the United States. A number of more recent laws have dealt with specific groups and specific issues.

Norris-LaGuardia Act

During the 1930s, labor leaders finally persuaded lawmakers that the legal environment discriminated against the collective efforts of workers to improve working conditions. Legislators responded with the **Norris-LaGuardia Act** in 1932. This act imposed severe limitations on the ability of the courts to issue injunctions prohibiting certain union activities, including strikes. Norris-LaGuardia also outlawed **yellow-dog contracts**: requirements that workers state that they did not belong to and would not join a union.

National Labor Relations (Wagner) Act

In 1935 Congress passed the **National Labor Relations Act** (also called the **Wagner Act**), which is the cornerstone of contemporary labor relations law. This act put labor unions on a more equal footing with management in terms of the rights of employees to organize and bargain. For example,

- It gave most workers the right to form unions, bargain collectively, and engage in group activities (such as strikes) to reach their goals.

- It forced employers to bargain with duly elected union leaders and prohibited employer practices that unjustly restrict employees' rights (for example, discriminating against union members in hiring, promoting, and firing).

The Wagner Act also established the **National Labor Relations Board (NLRB)** to administer its provisions. Today, the NLRB administers virtually all labor law in this country. For example, it determines the appropriate unit for conducting bargaining at any workplace. The NLRB also oversees most of the elections held by employees to determine whether they will be represented by particular unions. For instance, it decides who is eligible to vote and who will be covered by bargaining agreements once they have been reached.

Fair Labor Standards Act

Enacted in 1938, the **Fair Labor Standards Act** addressed issues of minimum wages and maximum work hours:

- It set a minimum wage (originally $.25 an hour) to be paid to workers. The minimum wage has been increased many times since 1938 and now stands at $5.15 per hour.

- It set a maximum number of hours for the workweek, initially 44 hours per week, later 40 hours.

- It mandated time-and-a-half pay for those who worked beyond the legally stipulated number of hours.

- It outlawed child labor.

Taft-Hartley Act

Supported by the Norris-LaGuardia, Wagner, and Fair Labor Standards Acts, organized labor eventually grew into a powerful political and economic force. But a series of disruptive strikes in the immediate post–World War II years turned public opinion against

Norris-LaGuardia Act
Federal law (1932) limiting the ability of courts to issue injunctions prohibiting certain union activities

yellow-dog contract
Illegal contract clause requiring workers to begin and continue employment without union affiliation

National Labor Relations Act (Wagner Act)
Federal law (1935) protecting the rights of workers to form unions, bargain collectively, and engage in strikes to achieve their goals

National Labor Relations Board (NLRB)
Federal agency established by the National Labor Relations Act to enforce its provisions

Fair Labor Standards Act
Federal law (1938) setting minimum wage and maximum number of hours in the workweek

unions. Inconvenienced by strikes and the resulting shortages of goods and services, the public became openly critical of unions and pressured the government to take action. Congress responded by passing the **Labor-Management Relations Act** (more commonly known as the **Taft-Hartley Act**) in 1947.

Unfair and Illegal Union Practices. The Taft-Hartley Act defined certain union practices as unfair and illegal. For example, it prohibited such practices as featherbedding (requiring extra workers solely in order to provide more jobs) and refusing to bargain in good faith. It also generally forbade the **closed shop**: a workplace in which only workers already belonging to a union may be hired by an employer. Instead, Taft-Hartley promoted open shops by allowing states to enact **right-to-work laws**. Such laws prohibit both union shops and agency shops, thus making it illegal to require union membership as a condition of employment. A **union shop** requires employees to join a union within a specified period after being hired. An **agency shop** requires employees to pay union fees even if they choose not to join. To date, 20 states, mostly in the South and the Southwest, have enacted right-to-work laws.

Injunctions and Cooling-Off Periods. Passed in the wake of crippling strikes in the steel industry, the Taft-Hartley Act also established procedures for resolving any strike deemed to pose a national emergency. Initially, the concept of national emergency was broadly interpreted. For example, virtually any large company could claim that a strike was doing irreparable harm to its financial base and that the nation's economy would be harmed if workers were not forced back to their jobs.

Today, however, the courts use a more precise definition of national emergency. For example, a strike must affect a whole industry or most of it. Similarly, the use of Taft-Hartley is more restrictive. Now the president may request an injunction requiring that workers restrain from striking for 60 days. During this cooling-off period, labor and management must try to resolve their differences.

Enforced Resolution. If differences are not resolved during the cooling-off period, the injunction may be extended for another 20 days. During this period, employees must vote, in a secret ballot election, on whether to accept or reject the employer's latest offer. If they accept the offer, the threat of strike is ended and the contract signed. If they do not accept the offer, the president reports to Congress and the workers may either be forced back to work under threat of criminal action or fired and replaced by nonunion employees. Presidential intervention has been invoked only 35 times since Taft-Hartley was passed.

Landrum-Griffin Act

The National Labor Relations Act was further amended by the **Landrum-Griffin Act** in 1959. Officially titled the **Labor-Management Reporting and Disclosure Act**, this law resulted from congressional hearings that revealed unethical, illegal, and undemocratic union practices. The act thus imposed regulations on internal union procedures:

- ■ It required the election of national union leaders at least once every 5 years.

- ■ It gave union members the right to participate in various union affairs.

- ■ It required unions to file annual financial disclosure statements with the Department of Labor.

Other Laws

The labor relations environment cannot be fully described without mention of a few other laws. In particular, two acts affect federal employees, most of whom are not covered by other statutes:

- ■ The Postal Reorganization Act of 1970 gives postal workers the right to form unions and bargain collectively but does not extend the right to strike.

Labor-Management Relations Act (Taft-Hartley Act) Federal law (1947) defining certain union practices as unfair and illegal

closed shop Workplace in which an employer may hire only workers already belonging to a union

right-to-work laws Statutes making it illegal to require union membership as a condition of employment

union shop Workplace in which workers must join a union within a specified period after being hired

agency shop Workplace in which workers must pay union dues even if they do not join

Labor-Management Reporting and Disclosure Act (Landrum-Griffin Act) Federal law (1959) imposing regulations on internal union procedures, including elections of national leaders and filing of financial disclosure statements

■ The Federal Service Labor-Management Relations Statute (Title VII of the Civil Service Reform Act of 1978) gives other federal employees the same rights. This statute also prohibits strikes and bars bargaining over economic items such as pay and benefits (which are established by the U.S. Civil Service).

A third measure, the Worker Adjustment and Retraining Notification Act of 1988 (WARN), stipulates that companies employing more than 100 people must give workers at least 60 days' notification of a shutdown or mass layoff. More popularly known as the Plant-Closing Notification Act, this law also created a fund to provide new training, assistance with relocation expenses, and career counseling services for affected workers.

Labor unions have also been instrumental in securing legislation extending other employee rights. Most notably, they played a key role in the enactment of the Civil Rights Act of 1964, which (as we saw in chapter 9) prohibits employment discrimination on the basis of race, sex, religion, and national origin.

How Unions are Organized and Certified

Many of the laws described above address the issue of union certification. Figure 10.3 illustrates a simplified version of this process. First, there must be some interest among workers in having a union. Sometimes this interest comes from dissatisfied employees; sometimes it is stirred by professional organizers sent by unions themselves. For example, the United Auto Workers has for years dispatched organizers to promote interest among workers at the Honda plant in Marysville, Ohio. To date, they have had no success in Marysville or in Smyrna, Tennessee, where Nissan built its major American plant.[17]

bargaining unit
Designated group of employees who will be represented by a union

1 *Defining the bargaining unit.* Interested organizers start by asking the NLRB to define the **bargaining unit**: the group of employees who will be represented by the union. For instance, a bargaining unit might be all nonmanagement employees in an organization or all electrical workers at a certain plant.

2 *Gaining authorization.* Organizers must then get 30 percent of the eligible workers within the bargaining unit to sign authorization cards requesting a certification election. If less than 30 percent of the workers want an election, the process ends.

3 *Conducting an election.* If the required number of signatures is obtained, the organizers petition the NLRB to conduct the election. The NLRB then holds a secret ballot election. If a simple majority of those voting approves the certification, the union becomes the official bargaining agent of eligible employees. If a majority fails to approve certification, the process ends and an election cannot be called again for at least 1 year.

Decertification

Unions are not necessarily permanent fixtures in a workplace, and if conditions warrant, a union may be decertified. For example, workers may become disenchanted with a union and may even feel that they are being hurt by its presence. They may believe that management is trying to be cooperative while the union is refusing to negotiate in good faith.

Decertification requires two conditions:

■ The union must have served the unit as its official bargaining agent for at least 1 year.

■ There must be no labor contract currently in effect.

If these conditions are met, employees or their representatives can solicit signatures on decertification cards. If 30 percent of the employees in the unit sign, the NLRB conducts a decertification election. If a majority of those voting favor decertification, the union is removed as the unit's official bargaining agent. Following decertification, a new election cannot be requested for at least 1 year.

Figure 10.3 Certifying a Labor Union

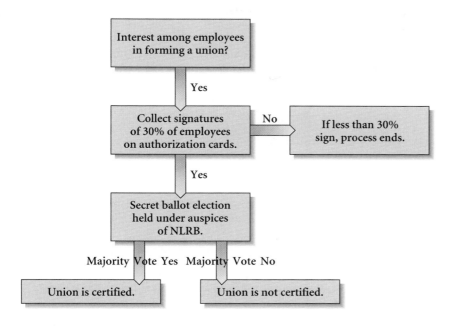

Collective Bargaining

When a union has been legally certified, it assumes the role of official bargaining agent for the workers whom it represents. Collective bargaining is an ongoing process involving both the drafting and the administering of the terms of a labor contract.

Reaching Agreement on Contract Terms

The collective bargaining process begins when the union is recognized as the exclusive negotiator for its members. The bargaining cycle itself begins when union leaders meet with management representatives to agree on a contract. By law, both parties must sit down at the bargaining table and negotiate in good faith.

When each side has presented its demands, sessions focus on identifying the bargaining zone.[18] The process is shown in Figure 10.4. For example, although an employer

Figure 10.4 The Bargaining Zone

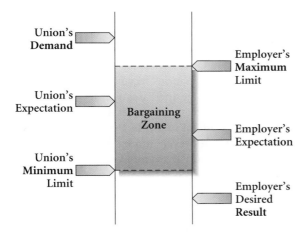

may initially offer no pay raise, it may expect to grant a raise of up to 6 percent. Likewise, the union may initially demand a 10-percent pay raise while expecting to accept a raise as low as 4 percent. The bargaining zone, then, is a raise between 4 and 6 percent. Ideally, some compromise is reached between these levels and the new agreement submitted for a ratification vote by union membership.

Sometimes, this process goes quite smoothly. At other times, however, the two sides cannot—or will not—agree. The speed and ease with which such an impasse is resolved depend in part on the nature of the contract issues, the willingness of each side to use certain tactics, and the prospects for mediation or arbitration.

Contract Issues

The labor contract itself can address an array of different issues. Most of these concern demands that unions make on behalf of their members. In this section we will survey the categories of issues that are typically most important to union negotiators: compensation, benefits, and job security. Although few issues covered in a labor contract are company sponsored, we will also describe the kinds of management rights that are negotiated in most bargaining agreements.

First, note that bargaining items generally fall into two categories:

■ Mandatory items are matters over which both parties must negotiate if either wants to. This category includes wages, working hours, and benefits.

■ Permissive items may be negotiated if both parties agree. A union demand for veto power over the promotion of managerial personnel would be a permissive bargaining item.

Illegal items may not be brought to the table by either party. A management demand for a nonstrike clause would be an illegal item.

Compensation

The most common issue is compensation. One aspect of compensation is current wages. Obviously, unions generally want their employees to earn higher wages and try to convince management to raise hourly wages for all or some employees.

cost-of-living adjustment (COLA)
Labor contract clause tying future raises to changes in consumer purchasing power

Of equal concern to unions is future compensation: wage rates to be paid during subsequent years of the contract. One common tool for securing wage increases is a **cost-of-living adjustment (COLA)**. Most COLA clauses tie future raises to the consumer price index, a government statistic that reflects changes in consumer purchasing power. The premise is that as the CPI increases by a specified amount during a given period of time, wages will automatically be increased. Almost half of all labor contracts today include COLA clauses.

wage reopener clause
Clause allowing wage rates to be renegotiated during the life of a labor contract

Wage reopener clauses are now included in almost 10 percent of all labor contracts. Such a clause allows wage rates to be renegotiated at preset times during the life of the contract. For example, a union might be uncomfortable with a long-term contract based solely on COLA wage increases. A long-term agreement might be more acceptable, however, if management agrees to renegotiate wages every 2 years.

giveback clause
Labor contract clause by which a union agrees to give up wage increases won in earlier contracts

A fairly recent trend in labor contracts has been the inclusion of **giveback clauses**. For example, many large organizations faced with tough competition in the 1980s convinced unions to give back wage increases granted in earlier contracts. Some unions made concessions in order to help businesses avoid bankruptcy. Thus, pilots at American Airlines took a 10-percent cut in pay in 1990 in order to help their employer remain competitive. More recently, however, unions have been more insistent on tying givebacks to employer concessions. For example, some negotiators now insist that concessions be returned if the company is sold. American Airlines pilots are now arguing that because the company has returned to profitability, their previous wage rates should be restored.

Benefits

Employee benefits are also an important component in most labor contracts. Unions typically want employers to pay all or most of the costs of insurance for employees. Other benefits commonly addressed during negotiations include retirement benefits, paid holidays, and working conditions.

▶   In 1990 General Motors actually negotiated a program with the United Automobile Workers whereby employees were paid to stay home: CEO Robert Stempel figured that the program was cheaper than continuing to run the plants at which they were employed. Thus, when GM closed down its Chevrolet plant in Los Angeles, 1,200 workers were guaranteed 3 years' worth of paychecks unless they accepted temporary jobs, moved to other GM facilities, or retired. Very few have found those options attractive, and in its first 3 years, the giveaway program cost GM more than $3 billion. In the fall of 1993, meanwhile, Ford Motor Co. agreed to a similar deal with the UAW. However, Ford had already closed most of its unprofitable plants. Then it was GM's turn to negotiate a new contract with the UAW. Because it could not break the pattern set by the Ford agreement, GM was forced to commit another $4 billion to the giveaway program, despite having cut its work force by tens of thousands.[19]

Job Security

Nevertheless, the UAW's top priority in its most recent negotiations with U.S. automakers has been job security, an increasingly important agenda item in many bargaining sessions today. In some cases, demands for job security entail the promise that a company not move to another location. In others, the contract may dictate that if the work force is reduced, seniority will be used to determine which employees lose their jobs.

Other Union Issues

Other possible issues might include such things as working hours, overtime policies, rest period arrangements, differential pay plans for shift employees, the use of temporary workers, grievance procedures, and allowable union activities (dues collection, union bulletin boards, and so forth).

For example, Local 95 of the UAW in Janesville, Wisconsin, negotiated a contract with General Motors that provided a work week of four 10 hour days with 3 days off. If the company felt it was needed, it could add a fifth 10-hour day. Problems arose when the fifth workday became the rule rather than the exception. Admittedly, workers who received $18.50 an hour got $27.75 for overtime hours and $37 an hour on Sundays and holidays. After 7 years, however, GM employees had grown so tired of 50-hour weeks that they threatened to strike if GM did not hire more workers.

"People don't just want the money," explains one assembly line worker. "They want time with their families." "We need more help in that place," says another, and the union argues that GM is forcing so much overtime because it is still cheaper than hiring permanent new workers. Local president Michael Marks also resents what he regards as pressure tactics on GM's part: "They'll say: 'You know, we've got customers and they need our product. They could go buy product somewhere else.' You can lean on people that way."[20]

Management Rights

Management wants as much control as possible over hiring policies, work assignments, and so forth. Unions, meanwhile, often try to limit management rights by specifying hiring, assignment, and other policies. At a Chrysler plant in Detroit, for example, the contract stipulates that three workers are needed to change fuses in robots: a machinist to open the robot, an electrician to change the fuse, and a supervisor to oversee the process. As in this case, contracts often bar workers in one job category from performing work that falls in the domain of another. Unions try to secure jobs by defining as many different categories as possible (the Chrysler plant has over 100). Of course, management resists the practice, which limits flexibility and makes it difficult to reassign workers.

The Workplace Environment

Union as Management Consultant: It Worked

With their current big push for new membership, unions are also working hard to make themselves attractive to management. One notable effort is the alliance formed by the International Association of Machinists (IAM) and the Aluminum Co. of America, which makes packaging equipment. In 1994 the union, which represents 170 of 500 workers at the plant, approached manager David Groetsch and offered to help create a high-performance work system. "If someone from Andersen Consulting had said: 'We can improve product delivery, customer satisfaction, and profitability—hire me,' I would have yawned," said Groetsch. "But when the union walked in and said all that, it got my attention."

Three managers from the firm's Denver plant went to a week-long course at the union's school in Maryland. They studied labor-management partnerships and productivity boosters, all in the context of protecting jobs. After the course IAM sent its own experts back to Denver to create management teams drawing from manufacturing, marketing, and other units. The teams were then trained in joint decision making.

There are no hard data on whether efficiency improved as a result of the effort, but shop floor relations already have, says Groetsch. Other unions in the construction, steel, and needle trades are taking the same road, reasoning that cooperation and mutual effort are better for their own interests in the long run. After all, if the employer is healthy and competitive, jobs and pay are that much more secure.

> " If someone from Andersen Consulting had said: 'We can improve product delivery, customer satisfaction, and profitability—hire me,' I would have yawned. But when the union walked in and said all that, it got my attention. "

—David Groetsch, plant manager, Aluminum Company of America

When Bargaining Fails

An impasse occurs when, after a series of bargaining sessions, management and labor have failed to agree on a new contract or a contract to replace an agreement that is about to expire. Although it is generally agreed that both parties suffer when an impasse is reached and action is taken, each side can use several tactics to support its cause until the impasse is resolved.

Union Tactics

When their demands are not met, unions may bring a variety of tactics to the bargaining table. Chief among these is the strike, which may be supported by pickets, boycotts, or both.

The Strike.   A **strike** occurs when employees temporarily walk off the job and refuse to work. Most strikes in the United States are **economic strikes**, triggered by stalemates over mandatory bargaining items, including such noneconomic issues as working hours. For example, employees at United Parcel Service (UPS) staged a strike in 1997. They wanted higher wages and for the firm to transform some of the many temporary and part-time jobs it had been creating into permanent and full-time jobs. The strikers returned to work only when company management agreed to boost wages and create several thousand new jobs.

Not all strikes are legal. **Sympathy strikes** (also called **secondary strikes**), which occur when one union strikes in sympathy with action initiated by another, may violate the sympathetic union's contract. **Wildcat strikes**—strikes unauthorized by the union

strike
Labor action in which employees temporarily walk off the job and refuse to work

economic strike
Strike usually triggered by stalemate over one or more mandatory bargaining items

sympathy strike (or secondary strike)
Strike in which one union strikes to support action initiated by another

wildcat strike
Strike that is unauthorized by the strikers' union

Unions occasionally resort to strikes in a list-ditch effort to get management to agree with their contract demands. For example, the Teamsters strike against UPS in 1997 lasted only a few days, but when the company realized how much business it was losing to rivals such as Federal Express it quickly gave in and offered striking workers most of what they had been seeking. At the same time, however, these workers also risked losing their jobs if the company had not capitulated and had hired replacement workers.

that occur during the life of a contract—deprive strikers of their status as employees and thus of the protection of national labor law.

Other Labor Actions.   To support a strike, a union faced with an impasse has recourse to additional legal activities:

- In **picketing**, workers march at the entrance to the employer's facility with signs explaining their reasons for striking.

- A **boycott** occurs when union members agree not to buy the products of a targeted employer. Workers may also urge consumers to boycott the firm's products. Employees of the Coors Brewing Co. led a boycott of that company's products for several months in the mid-1980s.

- Another alternative to striking is a work **slowdown**. Instead of striking, workers perform their jobs at a much slower pace than normal. A variation is the sickout, during which large numbers of workers call in sick.

Management Tactics

Like workers, management can respond forcefully to an impasse:

- **Lockouts** occur when employers deny employees access to the workplace. Lockouts are illegal if they are used as offensive weapons to give management a bargaining advantage. However, they are legal if management has a legitimate business need (for instance, avoiding a buildup of perishable inventory). Although rare today, lockouts were used by baseball team owners in 1990 (without success).

- A firm can also hire temporary or permanent replacements called **strikebreakers**. However, the law forbids the permanent replacement of workers who strike because of unfair practices. In some cases, an employer can also obtain legal injunctions that either prohibit workers from striking or prohibit a union from interfering with its efforts to use replacement workers.

Mediation and Arbitration

Rather than wield these often unpleasant weapons against one another, labor and management can agree to call in a third party to help resolve the dispute:

- In **mediation**, the neutral third party (the mediator) can advise, but cannot impose a settlement on the other parties.

picketing
Labor action in which workers publicize their grievances at the entrance to an employer's facility

boycott
Labor action in which workers refuse to buy the products of a targeted employer

slowdown
Labor action in which workers perform jobs at a slower than normal pace

lockout
Management tactic whereby workers are denied access to the employer's workplace

strikebreaker
Worker hired as permanent or temporary replacement for a striking employee

mediation
Method of resolving a labor dispute in which a third party suggests, but does not impose, a settlement

voluntary arbitration
Method of resolving a labor dispute in which both parties agree to submit to the judgment of a neutral party

compulsory arbitration
Method of resolving a labor dispute in which both parties are legally required to accept the judgment of a neutral party

- In **voluntary arbitration**, the neutral third party (the arbitrator) dictates a settlement between the two sides, who have agreed to submit to outside judgment.

- In some cases, arbitration is legally required to settle bargaining disputes. **Compulsory arbitration** is used to settle disputes between the government and public employees such as firefighters and police officers.

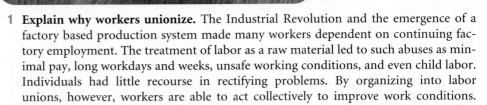

Summary of Learning Objectives

1 **Explain why workers unionize.** The Industrial Revolution and the emergence of a factory based production system made many workers dependent on continuing factory employment. The treatment of labor as a raw material led to such abuses as minimal pay, long workdays and weeks, unsafe working conditions, and even child labor. Individuals had little recourse in rectifying problems. By organizing into labor unions, however, workers are able to act collectively to improve work conditions. Most important, acting as a group, they can engage in collective bargaining for higher wages, greater benefits, or better working conditions.

2 **Trace the evolution and discuss the future of unionism in the United States.** The earliest unions in the United States were local craft unions of specialized workers. Important early national unions included the National Trades Union, the Knights of Labor, the American Federation of Labor (AFL), and the Congress of Industrial Organizations (the CIO), the first U.S. industrial union. The last two merged in 1955 to form the AFL-CIO. Although their membership has slipped in recent years, unions remain an important force in U.S. business and political life and have gained better pay and working conditions for all workers, unionized and nonunionized.

   The future of unionism in the United States is uncertain. Union membership has declined in recent years, but recent cutbacks in many industries, combined with what some see as excessive executive compensation, may prompt a resurgence in unionism. It seems clear, though, that unions are increasingly realizing that they must cooperate with employers if they are to survive.

3 **Describe the major laws governing labor-management relations.** Several significant laws affect labor-management relations. The Norris-LaGuardia Act and the National Labor Relations (Wagner) Act limited the ability of employers to keep unions out of the workplace. The Fair Labor Standards Act established a minimum wage and outlawed child labor. But the Taft-Hartley Act and the Landrum-Griffin Act limited the power of unions and provided for the settlement of strikes in key industries. Other important laws include the Postal Reorganization Act of 1970, the Federal Service Labor-Management Relations Statute, the Civil Rights Act of 1964, and the Plant-Closing Notification Act.

4 **Describe the union certification and decertification processes.** Successful unionization requires first of all an interest among workers in forming a union. Those interested in forming the union begin by defining the bargaining unit. Organizers must then get 30 percent of the eligible workers in the bargaining unit to sign authorization cards requesting a union certification election. The National Labor Relations Board then sends representatives to the organization and holds a secret ballot election. If a majority of those voting approve the union certification, the union becomes the official bargaining agent of eligible employees. To decertify a union, 30 percent of eligible employees must sign decertification authorization cards. The NLRB will then conduct a decertification election. For the union to be decertified, a majority of those voting must favor the decertification.

5 **Identify the steps in the collective bargaining process.** Once certified, the union engages in collective bargaining with the organization. The initial step in collective bargaining is reaching agreement on a labor contract. Contract demands usually involve wages, job security, or management rights.

Both labor and management have several tactics that can be used against the other if negotiations break down. Unions may attempt a strike or a boycott of the firm or may engage in a slowdown. Companies may hire replacement workers (strikebreakers) or lock out all workers. In extreme cases, mediation or arbitration may be used to settle disputes. Once a contract has been agreed on, union and management representatives continue to interact to settle worker grievances and interpret the contract.

Questions and Exercises

Questions for Review

1 Why do workers in some companies unionize whereas workers in others do not?
2 Why did the AFL succeed whereas the Knights of Labor failed?
3 Compare the effects of the Norris-LaGuardia and Wagner Acts with the effects of the Taft-Hartley and Landrum-Griffin Acts. What circumstances of the times led to the passage of such different laws?
4 What steps must be taken to certify a union?
5 What circumstances might cause union membership to rise again in the future?

Questions for Analysis

6 Workers at Ford, GM, and Chrysler are represented by the United Auto Workers (UAW). However, the UAW has been unsuccessful in its attempts to unionize U.S. workers employed at Toyota, Nissan, and Honda plants in the United States. Why do you think this is so?
7 Suppose you are a manager in a nonunionized company. You have just found out that some of your workers are talking about forming a union. What would you do?
8 Do you think unions serve a useful purpose today? Under what circumstances would you be willing to join a union?

Application Exercises

9 Interview the managers of two local companies, one unionized and one nonunionized. Compare the wage and salary levels, benefits, and working conditions of employees at the two firms.
10 With your instructor playing the role of a manager and a student playing the role of a union organizer, role-play the processes involved in attempting to form a union.

Building Your Business Skills

This exercise enhances the following SCANS workplace competencies: demonstrating basic skills, demonstrating thinking skills, exhibiting interpersonal skills, and working with information.

Goal   To encourage students to understand why some companies unionize and others do not.

Situation   You've been working for the same nonunion company for 5 years. Although there are problems in the company, you like your job and have confidence in your ability to get ahead. Recently, you've heard rumblings that a large group of workers want to call for a union election. You're not sure how you feel about this because none of your friends or family are union members.

Method   **Step 1:** Come together with three other "co-workers" who have the same questions as you do. Each person should target four companies to learn their union status. Avoid small businesses; choose large corporations such as General Motors, Intel, and Sears. As you investigate, answer the following questions:

- Is the company unionized?
- Is every worker in the company unionized or just selected groups of workers? Describe the groups.
- If a company is unionized, what is the union's history in that company?
- If a company is unionized, what are the main labor-management issues?
- If a company is unionized, how would you describe the current status of labor-management relations? For example, is it cordial or strained?
- If a company is not unionized, what factors are responsible for its nonunion status?

To learn the answers to these questions, contact the company, read corporate annual reports, search the company's Web site, contact union representatives, or do research on a computerized database.

Step 2: Go to the Web site of the AFL-CIO (http://www.aflcio.org/) to learn more about the current status of the union movement. Then, with your co-workers, write a short report about the advantages of union membership.

Step 3: Research the disadvantages of unionization. A key issue to address is whether unions make it harder for companies to compete in the global marketplace.

Follow-Up Questions

1 Based on everything you learned, are you sympathetic to the union movement? Would you want to be a union member?
2 Are the union members you spoke with satisfied or dissatisfied with their union's efforts to achieve better working conditions, higher wages, and improved benefits?
3 What is the union's role when layoffs occur?
4 Based on what you learned, do you think the union movement will stumble or thrive in the years ahead?

A Tale of Two Cities

Union contracts expired in the symphony halls of two major U.S. cities in 1997, but in only one of those cities did the orchestra reach an agreement with management and go back to work. In the other city there is no longer an orchestra. What happened?

The Chicago Symphony Orchestra's 3-year contract expired on the eve of its new season and the opening of its newly renovated Orchestra Hall, part of the multi–million-dollar Symphony Center project in Chicago. Most of the issues between the musicians and the orchestra management were resolved easily, but the differences over pensions and salaries threatened to mar the long-awaited season with a strike by the orchestra's 105 members. "To withhold our services for what management feels is the opening night of the next century is something we'd have to weigh very heavily," said Ed Ward, president of the Chicago Federation of Musicians at the time.

However, management's pockets proved very deep. The strike was averted by a new agreement that brought the musicians' salaries to $1,575 per week in the first year (a 4.3 percent increase) and $1,700/week in the third year, making Chicago's players the highest-paid orchestra members in the United States. Pensions were increased by $5,000 to $53,000.

In Sacramento, California, however, the orchestra operated on a smaller budget. Its profits had been tiny since the 1980s, and there were

few corporate backers. In 1986 the orchestra began losing money every year, and after a bankruptcy filing and reorganization (in 1992 and 1993, respectively), the 76-member orchestra had a new 3-year collective bargaining agreement that promised continual salary increases and a longer season (which increased operating costs).

In 1994 management took a pay cut and asked the orchestra for a pay freeze. By 1996, however, the symphony was bankrupt again. Local businesses pledged $1 million to keep it going if it could balance its budget first. That in turn meant a 25 percent salary cut for the musicians, and they overwhelmingly voted it down. "You can't turn us into nonprofessionals," said violinist and union steward Elizabeth Glattly.

So the orchestra was disbanded and its assets were sold. "If we'd only had flexibility from the musicians,"

> ## You can't turn us into nonprofessionals,
>
> —Sacramento orchestra violinist and union steward Elizabeth Glattly

said director Lynn Osmond, "we could have made it work."

Questions

1. Do you think the Sacramento musicians could have been persuaded to take a 25 percent pay cut in order to save the orchestra? Would you have made such a sacrifice?

2. Chicago's market for orchestral music is bigger than Sacramento's. How do you think that

> ## If we'd only had flexibility from the musicians, we could have made it work.
>
> —Sacramento orchestra director Lynn Osmond

influenced the outcome of the Chicago orchestra's strike threat?

3. What elements did the two situations have in common? What were the key differences between the two situations in terms of management's ability to meet the union's demands?

4. What strategies did each of the unions use? What might they have learned from each other?

Connecting to the Web

The following Web sites will give you additional information and points of view about topics covered in this chapter. Many sites lead to other related Internet locations, so approach this list with the spirit of an explorer.

AFL-CIO

http://www.aflcio.org/

Visit the AFL-CIO home page for information on such issues as union-related legislation and news, union membership, working women, and working conditions. The site also lists the unions affiliated with the AFL-CIO.

AMERICAN FEDERATION OF STATE, CITY, AND MUNICIPAL EMPLOYEES

http://www.afscme.org/

With 4 out of every 10 union members now in the public, rather than the private sector, this Web site provides important information about the issues facing union members today.

AMERICAN FEDERATION OF TEACHERS

http://www.aft.org/index.htm

The nation's schoolteachers are unionized under the American Federation of Teachers. Visit the site for a glimpse of the issues and problems the union considers important and to read the AFT's weekly online newsletter.

BROADCASTING ENTERTAINMENT, CINEMATOGRAPH, AND THEATRE UNION (UK)

http://www.bectu.org.uk/

Visit this Web page for a look at a union in the United Kingdom. The Broadcasting Entertainment, Cinematograph, and Theatre Union is an independent trade union for 32,000 nonperformance workers in broadcasting, film, theater, entertainment, leisure, and allied industries.

CORPORATE WATCH

http://www.corpwatch.org/home.html

Corporate Watch is a self-designated watchdog over the actions of transnational corporations that affect the environment and human rights. The organization's stated agenda is to force corporations to correct unacceptable conditions.

GEORGE MEANY CENTER FOR LABOR STUDIES

http://www.georgemeany.org/

The George Meany Center for Labor Studies, the college of the union movement, is a national center to educate union activists. Courses include organizing, negotiating, union building, and leadership development. Visit this site for detailed information on the Center's mission and course offerings.

THE LABOR PROJECT FOR WORKING FAMILIES

http://violet.berkeley.edu/~iir/workfam/home.html

Founded in 1992, the Labor Project for Working Families works with unions to develop family policies at the workplace through collective bargaining agreements. These policies include family leave, flexible hours (part time, job sharing, flextime, telecommuting), dependent care, sick time for families, and domestic partner benefits. The organization works with unions to negotiate union contracts that reflect the needs of working families.

NATIONAL LABOR RELATIONS BOARD

http://www.nlrb.gov/

Created in 1935, the Federal National Labor Relations Board administers and enforces the National Labor Relations Act by conducting secret ballots to determine union representation and investigating and repairing unfair labor practices. Visit this Web site to learn how the NLRB works and the issues it currently faces.

THE SCHOOL OF INDUSTRIAL AND LABOR RELATIONS AT CORNELL UNIVERSITY

http://www.ilr.cornell.edu/texthome.html

One of the country's most important educational centers for industrial and labor relations is located at Cornell University. Visit this site for a description of the program and course offerings and full-text documents available through electronic archives.

UNION RESOURCE NETWORK

http://www.unions.org/

The Union Resource Network is the most complete list of union Web sites on the Internet. Its mission is to bring the labor community together, to promote American-made products globally, and to link labor unions to the world's work force.

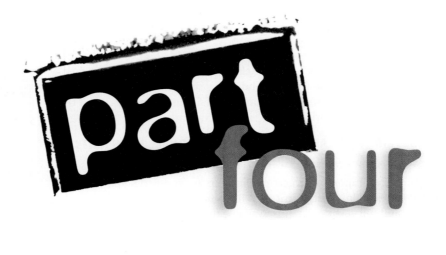

part four

Understanding Principles of Marketing

There is nothing subtle about the kind of auto racing that takes place on the NASCAR (National Association for Stock Car Auto Racing) racing circuit. It is fast, furious, and demanding of drivers, their cars, and the products drivers depend on to win. Speeds topping 200 miles an hour, daredevil maneuvers with little margin for error, and grueling conditions attract fans.

When a car wins an important race, the companies that sponsor it are winners too because all America is watching—or so it seems. With an astounding 25 percent of the American public describing itself as racing enthusiasts, auto racing is America's number-one spectator sport. It is not surprising, therefore, that companies such as Kellogg, Kodak, Texaco, and even the Cartoon Network make motorsport sponsorship an important element in their marketing plan. The NASCAR racing circuit alone attracts more than one-third of the nation's 100 leading advertisers. In 1997, corporate sponsorships totaled $441 million, up from $405 million in 1996.

Advertising Value Through Impression Value

Underpinning the success of motorsport sponsorships is advertising value. This value is linked to repeated brand impressions: Put a recognizable corporate or product emblem in front of consumers again and again, and do it in the exciting, compelling environment of auto racing, and consumers will remember the company and products in a positive way.

Thus, every time a Texaco/Havoline Motor Oil–sponsored car comes around the track at a major NASCAR race, and the Texaco star is seen by millions of fans in the stadium and around the world, these impressions have measurable marketing value. Similarly, every time the Texaco/Havoline brand is mentioned on radio, in newspaper and magazine articles, in track signage, and even on the clothing worn by drivers and fans, the impact translates into advertising value. And every time Michael Andretti, Shelly Anderson, and other drivers make public appearances for Texaco/Havoline, the result is positive advertising impressions.

Companies determine the value of these impressions by calculating how many times viewers get a 1-second impression of a specific brand name. The aggregate number of these impressions is considered to be worth half as much as the advertising value of commercial spots, which directly tell a brand's story. Impact comes because impressions are so numerous. Thus, when Valvoline motor oil writes a $6-million check to sponsor a team, it can expect more than $30 million in impression-based advertising.

Targeting Key Audiences

Participating companies target their marketing efforts at racing enthusiasts, who are known for their loyalty. Research has shown that more than 70 percent of NASCAR fans make a conscious effort to buy sponsors' products, as compared with only 36 percent of pro football fans. Thus, when the Goodyear logo appears on a car, fans associate it with the sport they love and are more likely to buy Goodyear tires.

Research has shown that more than seven out of ten NASCAR fans are between 25 and 54 years old (the prime buying years) have full-time jobs, and own a home. Nearly 50 percent earn more than $40,000 annually and nearly 30 percent are professionals and managers. And despite auto racing's reputation as a male bastion, nearly 4 out of 10 fans are women.

These demographics and fan loyalty are bringing new sponsors to auto racing. Although the sport traditionally attracted oil companies (Texaco), tire makers (Goodyear), auto parts manufacturers (Raybestos brakes), cigarette brands (Winston), and beer manufacturers (Budweiser), today's cars may also carry emblems from McDonald's, Tide, The Family Channel, and Coca-Cola. These companies seek the stadium and media exposure and increasing brand awareness associated with auto racing. Many promote their motorsport connections on the World Wide Web.

The Publicity Value of Auto Racing

Racing generates millions of dollars in free publicity. As droves of reporters from around the world cover major races, sponsor names are mentioned again and again. The broadcast and print coverage that results brings a sponsor's message to millions of consumers worldwide. Only 60,000 people may be at the track, but millions more watch the races at home in real time and during rebroadcasts. As we saw earlier, the impression value of this coverage adds up to millions of dollars in advertising benefits. Print coverage also reaches millions. A single article in *Sports Illustrated* on a race car team may reach nearly 8 million readers.

Forging Business Alliances

Motorsport programs target trade customers, including wholesalers, as well as the general public. To positively influence this audience, companies run hospitality programs in which trade customers are escorted to and from the track, treated to meals before the races, and introduced to drivers. This VIP treatment builds relationships that lead to sales. Rather than spending 15 minutes making a sales presentation in a purchasing agent's office, sales personnel have the opportunity to spend hours with a purchasing agent before a race. By the end of the day, trade customers feel part of a team and leave the track infected with the company's esprit de corps.

Trade customers are particularly impressed by racing's demanding product-testing environment. Steve Myers, director of racing tire sales and marketing for Goodyear, explains: "There's no environment that tests [products better] than racing. If you can develop a product that will withstand the environment and is successful in it, it is very easy to transfer information and produce a better passenger tire for a sedan, a sports car, a luxury vehicle, or a sports utility vehicle."

The success of many motorsport programs is also linked to business alliances with other companies involved with motorsports. For example, Texaco has alliances with such retailing giants as Target, Kmart, and Western Auto. By virtue of these partnerships, Texaco lubricant products are featured on store shelves. In the case of Western Auto and Western Auto's Parts America, both subsidiaries of Sears, Roebuck and Co., this distribution link opened nearly 1,500 stores nationwide to Texaco brands. These major retailers are convinced that appealing to racing enthusiasts makes good business sense.

The most effective motorsport marketing programs connect all the pieces of the marketing puzzle so that the message, impact, and timing of every piece support the message, impact, and timing of every other piece. Companies that sponsor winning teams attract consumers and trade customers through advertising, publicity, sales promotions, and even clothing lines that showcase products. "Race on Sunday. Sell on Monday." is a slogan that works well for sponsors. With annual sponsorships expected to grow as much as 10 percent a year, the marketing formula seems to be catching on.

WEB LINKS

Among the companies and products mentioned in this case, the following have Web sites that highlight motorsports programs. The information in these sites will help you answer the questions that follow.

Budweiser	http://www.budweiser.com/comp.html
Goodyear Racing	http://www.goodyear.com/aboutracing/index.html
Kodak: NASCAR Section	http://www.kodak.com/ciHome/nascar/nascar.shtml
McDonald's Motor Sports	http://www.mcdonalds.com/a_sports/motor_sports/
NASCAR Online: Home Page	http://www.nascar.com/
People Who Know Use Valvoline	http://www.valvoline.com/
Raybestos Racing	http://www.raybestosracing.com/index.htm
Texaco/Havoline: Racing Guide	http://www.texaco.com/tic/racing.htm
Tide Racing	http://www.tide.com/tideRacing/index.html
Welcome to Kellogg's Racing	http://www.kelloggs.com/nascar/njs/index.html
Welcome to Target Team	http://beepbeep.target.com/
Western Auto: Motorsports WAPA Racing	http://www.westernauto.com/motorsports/

CASE QUESTIONS

1 Imagine you are a member of the marketing team of a company specializing in auto supplies. What are the primary goals of your motorsports program? (See Web sites for Texaco, Valvoline, Goodyear, Raybestos, and other auto-related companies.)

2 Imagine you are a member of the marketing team of a consumer products company (nonautomotive). What are the primary goals of your motorsports program? (See Web sites for McDonald's, Kellogg's, Tide, and other consumer products companies.)

3 Why is it a natural marketing fit for companies such as Valvoline, Goodyear, McDonald's, and Kodak to target racing enthusiasts? In your answer, refer to demographic, psychographic, and product use variables that make racing enthusiasts an ideal market.

4 What is the role of brand loyalty in this market, and how are companies trying to influence it through their motorsports program? Be specific in your answer as you refer to company Web sites.

5 Why are Texaco's alliances with retailers such a vital part of its marketing strategy? Relate these alliances to Texaco's need for an effective distribution network.

6 Sponsors place a great deal of emphasis on impression value. How do impressions affect advertising, sales promotion, publicity, and distribution?

7 Many companies sell racing-related products, including clothing and toys (see Web sites for specific offerings). What role do these items play in a marketing program?

chapter 11

Understanding
marketing
processes and
consumer
behavior

What do girls really want?

It's no secret among advertisers that children control an enormous proportion of consumer spending in the United States. There are about 40 million American children under 12, and they directly spend about $17 billion a year in gift money and allowances. It's also estimated that they influence an additional $172 billion spent by their parents.

That kind of market power is bound to draw the attention of makers of computer software, particularly those firms that want to sell computer games to young girls. Thanks to some recent market research, the last few years have seen an extraordinary increase in the number and the success of such games. Some research indicates that the age at which a child begins to play interactive videogames is more important than gender in influencing whether the child goes on to play regularly. True or not, as Brenda Laurel of Purple Moon discovered, boys and girls do show wide differences in their computer game preferences.

While working at Interval Research Co. in California, Brenda spent the years between 1992 and 1995 researching those gender differences. She says, "The problem we were trying to explore was, 'Why is it that girls don't play computer games, and what would it take to get them to put their hands on a computer and establish some sense of comfort with it?'" Brenda put her findings into action via Purple Moon, a spinoff of Interval Research that creates and markets adventure software for girls 8–12. Purple Moon's first two titles, *Rockett's New School* and *Secret Paths in the Forest*, quickly made their way into the top 20 best-selling children's software titles for 1997.

Together these two games represent Brenda's conclusion that most girls in the target age bracket were simply bored by the violent games marketed to boys; they wanted characters about whom they could make up stories and whom they could use to define and explore relationships. Boys were more interested in status, achieved by winning in competition. These consumer research results echo play-behavior patterns that social scientists have convincingly documented in their own research and confirm beliefs held by makers of other computer programs for children. They may also in part explain the success of the number-one children's title

for 1997, Mattell's *Barbie Fashion Designer*. (Other Barbie programs were ranked second, sixth, and ninth that year.)

“ Why is it that girls don't play computer games, and what would it take to get them to put their hands on a computer and establish some sense of comfort with it? **”**

—Brenda Laurel of Purple Moon

Taking their success a step further along a path already well trod by other successful marketers of children's products, Purple Moon also sells Rockett dolls and Secret Path toys. There's even a tie-in to Bonne Belle's popular Lip Smacker lip gloss, which offers a link to Purple Moon on its Web site.

The enormous focus on spending by and for children in the United States today is just one aspect of marketing in the 1990s. Understanding and keeping in touch with its market, as Purple Moon does, is one key to success. By focusing on the learning objectives in this chapter, you will discover some of the other powerful marketing tools that can make the difference between success and disaster.

After reading this chapter, you should be able to

1 Define *marketing.*

2 Describe the five forces that constitute the external marketing environment.

3 Explain market segmentation and show how it is used in target marketing.

4 Explain the purpose and value of market research.

5 Describe the key factors that influence the consumer buying process.

6 Discuss the three categories of organizational markets and explain how organizational buying behavior differs from consumer buying behavior.

As you read this chapter, remember that without a clear understanding of the market and a careful marketing strategy, Purple Moon's new ventures for children may have remained nothing more than a concept. A good idea is necessary for business success, but it is rarely sufficient. Good marketing must also be part of the equation.

What Is Marketing?

What do you think of when you think of marketing? Most people usually think of advertising for detergent, soft drinks, and other products. But marketing encompasses a much wider range of activities. The American Marketing Association has formally defined **marketing** as the process of planning and executing the conception, pricing, promotion, and distribution of ideas, goods, and services to create exchanges that satisfy individual and organizational objectives.[1]

In this section we will discuss the multifaceted activity of marketing by exploring most of the major terms of this definition. We will then explore the marketing environment and the development of marketing strategy. In particular, we will focus on the four major marketing activities: developing, pricing, promoting, and placing products.

Marketing: Goods, Services, and Ideas

The marketing of tangible goods is obvious in everyday life. For instance, you walk into a department store and a woman with a clipboard asks whether you would like to try a new cologne. A pharmaceutical company proclaims the virtues of its new cold medicine. Your local auto dealer offers an economy car at an economy price. The cologne, the cold medicine, and the car are all **consumer goods**: products that you, the consumer, may buy for personal use. Firms that sell products to consumers for personal consumption are engaged in consumer marketing.

Marketing also applies to **industrial goods**: products that are used by companies to produce other products. Conveyors, surgical instruments, and earth movers are all industrial goods, as are components and raw materials such as transistors, integrated circuits, coal, steel, and unformed plastic. Firms that sell their products to other manufacturers are engaged in industrial marketing.

Marketing techniques can also be applied to **services**: intangible products, such as time or expertise or some activity, that can be purchased. Service marketing has become a major area of growth in the U.S. economy. Insurance companies, airlines, investment counselors, health clinics, security guards, janitors, public accountants, and exterminators all engage in service marketing, either to individuals or to other companies.

Finally, marketing can be applied to ideas. For example, television advertising and other promotional activities have made environmental awareness a popular movement for recycling and preserving natural resources. Other advertisements increasingly stress another modern idea: the opportunities for establishing a business in the home rather than in the traditional outside workplace.

Relationship Marketing

Although marketing often focuses on single transactions for products, services, or ideas, a longer-term perspective has become equally important for successful marketing. Rather than emphasizing a single transaction, **relationship marketing** emphasizes lasting relationships with customers and suppliers. Not surprisingly, stronger relationships, including stronger economic and social ties, can result in greater long-term satisfaction and retention of customers. Commercial banks, for example, feature "loyalty banking" programs that offer financial incentives to encourage longer-lasting relationships: Customers who purchase more of the bank's products—checking accounts, savings accounts, and loans—accumulate credits toward free or reduced-price services, such as free travelers' checks or lower interest rates. Harley-Davidson offers social incentives through the Harley Owners

marketing
The process of planning and executing the conception, pricing, promotion, and distribution of ideas, goods, and services to create exchanges that satisfy individual and organizational objectives

consumer goods
Products purchased by consumers for personal use

industrial goods
Products purchased by companies to produce other products

services
Intangible products, such as time, expertise, or some activity, that can be purchased

relationship marketing
Strategy that emphasizes lasting relationships with customers and suppliers

Group (H.O.G.), the largest motorcycle club in the world, with nearly 300,000 members and approximately 900 dealer-sponsored chapters worldwide. H.O.G., explain Harley marketers, "is dedicated to building customers for life. H.O.G. fosters long-term commitments to the sport of motorcycling by providing opportunities for our customers to bond with other riders and develop long-term friendships."[2]

The Marketing Environment

Marketing plans, decisions, and strategies are not determined unilaterally by any business, not even by ones as experienced and influential as Coca-Cola and Procter & Gamble. Rather, they are strongly influenced by powerful outside forces. As you can see in Figure 11.1, any marketing program must recognize the outside factors that make up a company's **external environment**. In this section we will describe five of these environmental factors: the political/legal, social/cultural, technological, economic, and competitive environments.

external environment
Outside factors that influence marketing programs by posing opportunities or threats

Political and Legal Environment

Political activities, both foreign and domestic, have profound effects on business. For example, Congressional hearings on tobacco, budgetary decisions on national defense expenditures, and enactment of the Clean Air Act have substantially determined the destinies of entire industries.

To help shape their companies' futures, marketing managers try to maintain favorable political/legal environments in several ways. For example, to gain public support for their products and activities, marketing uses advertising campaigns for public awareness on issues of local, regional, or national import. They also contribute to political candidates (although there are legal restrictions on how much they can contribute). Often, they support the activities of the PACs, or political action committees, maintained by their respective industries. Such activities sometimes result in favorable laws and regulations and may even open new international business opportunities.

Figure 11.1 The External Marketing Environment

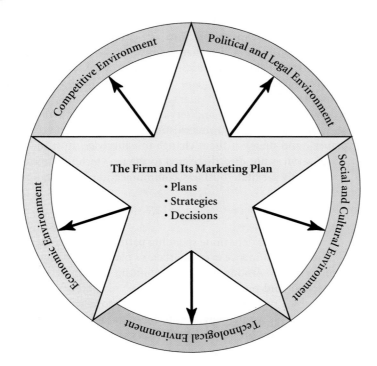

In addition, marketers must deal with a host of regulations that can influence marketing decisions every day. For example, consider the way current regulations affect just three of the many marketing activities we will describe in this section of the book:

- The Consumer Goods Pricing Act (1975) prohibits price collusion among companies engaging in interstate commerce.

- The Telephone Consumer Protection Act (1991) places restrictions on ways that companies can use telephone solicitations.

- The Child Safety Protection Act (1995) requires labels to identify toys that are choking hazards.

Social and Cultural Environment

More women are entering the work force, the number of single-parent families is increasing, food preferences and physical activities reflect the growing concern for healthful lifestyles, violent crimes are on the increase, and the recognition of cultural diversity continues to grow. These and other issues reflect the values, beliefs, and ideas that form the fabric of U.S. society. Obviously, these broad attitudes toward issues have direct effects on business. Today, for example, as we continue to insist on a greener America, we have seen a mandated reduction in the use of freon in air conditioners and increased reliance on recycling materials in the goods we consume.

By the same token, the need to recognize social values stimulates marketers to take fresh looks at the ways they develop and promote new products for both consumers and industrial customers. For example, there are now more than 5 million female golfers spending nearly $170 million on equipment, most of which, up to now, has been copied from men's gear. Responding to this lifestyle value, Spalding has introduced a line of golf gear designed specifically for women. Naturally, such equipment has entailed new methods for advertising, promoting, and distributing products to meet the emerging preferences of women golfers.[3]

Technological Environment

Consider the technique of DNA identification. Just about everyone is aware of its availability to law enforcement officials. However, it is also the focal point of a new industry that involves biological science and laboratory analysis and instrumentation as well as criminology. DNA identification, then, is a product; it involves marketing decisions such as pricing and promotion. This has been the case with thousands of technological breakthroughs in such fields as genetics, electronics, aeronautics, medicine, information sciences, communication systems, and transportation.

New technologies affect marketing in several ways. Obviously, they create new goods (say, the satellite dish) and services (home television and Web-based shopping). Of course, new products make some existing products obsolete (compact disks are replacing audiotapes), and many of them change our lifestyles. In turn, they often stimulate new goods and services not directly related to the new technology itself. For example, cellular phones not only facilitate business communication but free up time for recreation and leisure.

Economic Environment

Economic conditions determine spending patterns by consumers, businesses, and governments. Thus, they influence every marketer's plans for product offerings, pricing, and promotional strategies. Among the more significant economic variables are inflation, interest rates, recession, and recovery. In other words, marketers must monitor the general business cycle, which typically features a pattern of prosperity, recession, and recovery (return to prosperity). Not surprisingly, consumer spending increases as consumer confidence in economic conditions grows during periods of prosperity. Conversely it decreases during low-growth periods, when unemployment rises and purchasing power declines.

Traditionally, analysis of economic conditions focused on the national economy and government policies for controlling it. Increasingly, however, as nations form more and more economic connections, the global economy is becoming more prominent in the thinking of marketers everywhere. With pacts such as the 1993 North American Free Trade Agreement (NAFTA) and the 1994 General Agreement on Tariffs and Trade (GATT) now in place, global economic conditions—indeed, conditions from nation to nation—will directly influence the economic fortunes of all trading partners (see chapter 3). Certainly, marketers must now consider this new and perhaps unpredictable economic variable in developing both domestic and foreign marketing strategies.

Competitive Environment

In a competitive environment, marketers must convince buyers that they should purchase their products rather than those of some other seller. In a broad sense, because both consumers and commercial buyers have limited resources to spend, every dollar spent to buy one product is no longer available for other purchases. Each marketing program, therefore, seeks to make its product the most attractive; theoretically, a failed program loses the buyer's dollar forever (or at least until it is time for the next purchase decision).

By studying the competition, marketers determine how best to position their own products for three specific types of competition:

- **Substitute products** are different from those of competitors but can fulfill the same need. For example, your cholesterol level may be controlled with a physical fitness program or a drug regimen; the fitness program and the drugs compete as substitute products.

- **Brand competition** occurs between similar products, such as the auditing services provided by large accounting firms such as Ernst & Young and KPMG Peat Marwick. The competition is based on buyers' perceptions of the benefits of products offered by particular companies.

- **International competition** matches the products of domestic marketers against those of foreign competitors (say, a flight on Swissair versus Delta Airlines). The intensity of international competition has been heightened by the formation of alliances such as the European Community and NAFTA.

Planning and Executing Marketing Strategy

As a business activity, marketing requires management. Although many individuals contribute to the marketing of a product, a company's **marketing managers** are typically responsible for planning and implementing all the marketing activities that result in the transfer of goods or services to its customers. These activities culminate in the **marketing plan**: a detailed and focused strategy for gearing the marketing efforts to meet consumer needs and wants. Therefore, marketing actually begins when a company identifies a consumer need and develops a product to meet it. One way of identifying those needs—market research—is explored later in this chapter. Here, however, we will begin by noting two important aspects of the larger marketing process: developing the marketing plan and setting marketing goals.

Developing the Marketing Plan

First, marketing managers must realize that planning takes time. Indeed, the planning process may begin years before a product becomes available for sale. Some firms expect to gain market advantage by speeding up new product introductions.

▶ Lockheed-Martin Corporation, for example, is establishing a computer-linked design environment with two major shipbuilders—Ingalls Shipbuilding and Newport News Shipbuilding & Dry Dock Company—in a bid for a $300-million Navy ship deal. Once the electronic network has been established, the firms expect to develop new ships by

substitute product
Product that is different from those of competitors but can fulfill the same need

brand competition
Competitive marketing that appeals to consumer perceptions of similar products

international competition
Competitive marketing of domestic against foreign products

marketing manager
Manager who plans and implements the marketing activities that result in the transfer of products from producer to consumer

marketing plan
Detailed and focused strategy for gearing marketing efforts to meet consumer needs and wants

including their customers and some 200 suppliers via secure Internet links. This data-sharing environment will allow transfer of design, data on product features, project management, and financial data for pricing. The objective of the network is to increase communication among the three partners so, by acting together, they can design better new ships in one-third the time and at one-half the cost of competitors.[4]

Setting Goals for Performance

Next, marketing managers must set goals and then establish ways to evaluate performance.

▶   Barnes & Noble (B&N), the world's largest bookseller, had 112 superstores in 1994 and planned to open a stream of additional outlets. By 1997 it had grown to 439 super-stores displaying up to 175,000 titles in an atmosphere especially conducive to browsing. It takes about 4 years for a new superstore to become as productive as older stores, and the performance of individual store managers is evaluated against sales goals set on a store-by-store basis. At the same time, B&N was planning to expand into a new distribution channel: online book retailing with a global reach. Finally, in 1997 B&N launched its own Web site (http://www.barnesandnoble.com) and also became the exclusive bookseller in America Online's (AOL) Marketplace. B&N's planning efforts are paying off, enabling it to display, sell, and distribute more than 400,000 titles at greater discounts than offered by any other online or retail bookstore (30 percent off hardcovers and 20 percent off paperbacks).[5]

The Marketing Mix

marketing mix
The combination of product, pricing, promotion, and distribution (place) strategies used to market products

In planning and implementing strategies, marketing managers rely on four basic components. These elements, often called the "Four P's" of marketing, constitute the **marketing mix**. In this section we will describe each of the following activities:

- ■ Product
- ■ Pricing
- ■ Promotion
- ■ Place

Product

product
Good, service, or idea that is marketed to fill consumer needs and wants

Marketing begins with a **product**: a good, service, or idea designed to fill a consumer need. Conceiving and developing new products is a constant challenge for marketers, who must always consider the factor of change. For example, marketers must consider changing technology, changing consumer wants and needs, and changing economic conditions.

Meeting consumer needs often means changing existing products. In the clothing industry, for example, manufacturers must be alert to changes in fashion, which often occur rapidly and unpredictably. This is also true in electronics technology, where there are constant advances in electronics equipment.

▶   Zebra Technologies Corp., for example, long enjoyed a reputation for manufacturing high-quality, top-of-the-line printers used by other companies for bar code labeling. Zebra also saw sales potential in the low-end market but did not want to market a product that would tarnish its reputation or divert sales from its existing printers. Zebra thus developed a no-frills version, the new Stripes printer, to complement its faster, more versatile, more expensive model. Stripes was an immediate market success in its own right, boosting sales by 47 percent in the first year, and did not compete with Zebra's high-end model. Because of Stripes' continued growth, Zebra recently announced the formation of the personal printer division, a new business unit focusing on low-cost desktop bar code printers.[6]

Companies may also develop new products and enter markets in which they have not previously competed. For example, Daka International had an established winner with its Fuddruckers restaurants, which claim to make the world's greatest hamburger. Then Daka expanded into the food service business and now runs cafeterias and concession

This employee is examining printouts from Zebra Technologies' production line. In developing a new bar code printer, Zebra had to stress two elements of the marketing mix. First, because its main goal was a larger share of the lower end of the market, Zebra had to build a machine that would price for $500 less than its high-end model. Second, the new product had to be differentiated from the faster, more flexible model, without sacrificing the company's widely recognized level of quality. The result: The new Stripes printer is a high-quality printer minus a few top-of-the-line features. Moreover, because it cannot be upgraded, it cannot compete with Zebra's existing product.

stands at more than 710 hospitals, schools and universities, and corporations. With customers such as the Smithsonian Institution and the University of Florida, revenues from its food service business have grown to 65 percent of Daka's total revenues, making Daka one of the 10 largest U.S. food service management services.[7]

Product Differentiation

Often, producers develop new or improved products for the sake of distinguishing them in the marketplace. **Product differentiation** is the creation of a product or product image that differs enough from existing products to attract consumers. For example, the popularity of Campbell's Soups is based, in part, on successful differentiation. In 1995 the company changed the packaging and ingredient mix for some of its classic soup lines, updating the time-honored red-and-white label with color pictures of what's inside. The label for condensed chicken noodle soup added a prominent announcement: "Now! 33% more chicken meat." In an even riskier move, Campbell's famous slogan was changed from "M'm-m'm good" to "M'm-m'm better." The reasoning behind these changes? According to Marty Thrasher, president of Campbell's U.S. soup business, "We needed to get noticed in a new way, and we needed to break through," and renewing the emphasis on the company's differentiated product line seemed to be the most logical strategy.[8]

product differentiation
Creation of a product or product image that differs enough from existing products to attract consumers

> ❝ *We needed to get noticed in a new way, and we needed to get through.* ❞
>
> —Marty Thrasher, president of Campbell Soup's U.S. operations

Product differentiation does not always mean changing a product's function. When successful, however, it always entails a change in the way customers respond to the product. For example, early kitchen and laundry appliances were available only in white. Frigidaire capitalized on this situation by offering comparably priced, equally efficient appliances in colors.

Services can also be sources of differentiation. For example, United Airlines is offering upscale meals to differentiate their coach class service from that of other airlines. United, inspired by a culinary expert, touts a classic regional cuisine along with a special blend of Starbuck's coffee as a step above the competition.

Pricing

Pricing a product—selecting the most appropriate price at which to sell it—is often a balancing act. On one hand, prices must support a variety of costs: the organization's operating, administrative, and research costs as well as marketing costs, such as advertising and sales salaries. On the other hand, prices cannot be so high that consumers turn to competing products. Obviously, successful pricing means finding a profitable middle ground between these two requirements. For Dell Computer, for instance, price is a competitive weapon: Dell's extraordinary growth stems from selling its computers at prices lower than its competitors can offer. Rock-bottom prices are possible by selling directly to customers (90 percent of which are other businesses and organizations), and Dell builds the PCs only after they've received the customer's order.[9]

However, both low- and high-price strategies can be effective in different situations. Low prices generally lead to larger sales volumes. Although high prices usually limit market size, they also increase profits per unit. Moreover, high prices may even attract customers by implying that a product is of especially high quality. We will discuss pricing in more detail in chapter 12.

Promotion

The most visible component of the marketing mix is promotion, which refers to techniques for communicating information about products. We will describe promotional activities more fully in chapter 13. Here, we will briefly describe the most important promotional tools: advertising, personal selling, sales promotions, and public relations.

Advertising.   Advertising is any form of paid nonpersonal communication used by an identified sponsor to persuade or inform certain audiences about a product. For example, Norrell Corporation, a provider of work force services and staffing for other companies, reaches its customer audience by advertising its services in *Fortune* magazine and on the Internet (www.Norrell.com). Advertising typically uses all types of broadcast, print, and electronic media, such as television, radio, magazines, newspapers, and billboards.

Personal Selling.   Many products, such as insurance, clothing, and stereo equipment, are best promoted through personal selling, or person-to-person sales. However, industrial goods receive the bulk of personal selling. When companies buy from other companies, purchasing agents and others who need technical and detailed information are usually referred to the selling company's sales representatives.

Sales Promotions.   Inexpensive items are often marketed through sales promotions, which involve one-time direct inducements to buyers. Premiums (usually free gifts), trading stamps, coupons, and package inserts are all sales promotions meant to tempt consumers to buy products. Circuit City, for instance, uses sales promotions when it offers free software with computer purchases. Free samples, exhibits, and trade shows allow buyers to try products or to talk with company representatives.

Public Relations.   Finally, public relations includes all communication efforts directed at building good will among various groups in the population. It seeks to build favorable attitudes toward the organization and its products. Ronald McDonald Houses are a famous example of public relations. Other familiar public relations efforts include sponsorships of public television programming, local sports teams, and scholarship contests.

Drug Companies Go Right to the Source—And It's You

Most products are chosen by the people who ultimately use them. But there are exceptions: Parents choose furniture for their children, for example, and your professor chose this textbook. Doctors choose your medicine—or do they?

A new trend in drug advertising got a big boost recently when the Food and Drug Administration issued new guidelines covering radio and television ads for prescription drugs. The rule allows advertisers to state the benefits in their ads but offer only a summary of the risks—or just include a toll-free number or Internet address for more information.

Whether the rule is a benefit to consumers or "a setup for misleading people," as the Public Citizen's Health Re-

search Group fears, will become clearer over time. For the moment, however, it's apparent that drug companies have moved another step closer to their ultimate market, the consumer. Prescription remedies for a number of ailments from depression to AIDS are increasingly being promoted directly to patients in mass media campaigns running into the millions of dollars. In fact, pharmaceutical companies spent almost $600 million in 1996 advertising directly to patients, twice as much as the year before, making prescription drugs one of the fastest-growing categories in the advertising industry.

Doctors are still prime targets, and at least one telecommunications company is working on an interactive videoconferencing system to bring drug salespeople into doctors' offices without the expense of a personal visit. There's also plenty of evidence that patients' requests for specific drugs are heeded by doctors: A 1995 study of physicians found an amazing 99 percent would prescribe or consider a specific drug requested by a patient.

Publicity also refers to a firm's efforts to communicate to the public, usually through mass media. However, publicity is not paid for by the firm, nor does the firm control its content. Therefore, publicity can sometimes hurt a business. For example, Columbia/HCA Healthcare Corporation received substantial negative publicity when the media reported lawsuits filed against the company under federal whistle-blower laws. The lawsuits contended that the company engaged in schemes to defraud national health care programs such as Medicare. News articles cited federal investigations of Columbia's operations intended to discover whether the firm systematically overcharged government health insurance programs for services ranging from blood tests to hospital stays to home health care. After the negative publicity, Columbia's stock value fell more than 25 percent below its previous high for the year in trading on the New York Stock Exchange.[10]

Place (Distribution)

In the marketing mix, *place* refers to **distribution**. Placing a product in the proper outlet (say, a retail store) requires decisions about a number of distribution activities, all of which are concerned with getting the product from the producer to the consumer. For example, transportation options include railroad, truck, air freight, and pipelines. Decisions about warehousing and inventory control are also distribution decisions.

In addition, firms must make decisions about the channels through which they distribute their products. For instance, many manufacturers sell to other companies, which, in turn, distribute the goods to retailers. For example, Del Monte produces canned foods that it sells to Evco Wholesale Foods and other distributors, who then sell the food to grocery stores. Other companies sell directly to major retailers such as Sears, Wal-Mart, Kmart, and Safeway. Still others sell directly to final consumers. We will explain distribution decisions further in chapter 14.

distribution
Part of the marketing mix concerned with getting products from producers to consumers

Target Marketing and Market Segmentation

Marketers recognized long ago that products and services cannot be all things to all people. Buyers have different tastes, interests, goals, lifestyles, and so on. The emergence of the marketing concept and the recognition of consumer needs and wants led marketers to think in terms of target marketing. **Target markets** are groups of people with similar wants and needs. For most large companies, selecting target markets is the first step in the marketing strategy.

target market
Group of people who have similar wants and needs and who can be expected to show interest in the same products

market segmentation
Process of dividing a market into categories of customer types

Target marketing clearly requires **market segmentation**: dividing a market into categories of customer types or segments. Once they have identified market segments, companies may adopt a variety of strategies. Some firms try to market products to more than one segment of the population. For example, General Motors offers compact cars, vans, trucks, luxury cars, and sports cars with various features and at various price levels. GM's strategy is to provide an automobile for nearly every segment of the market.

In contrast, some businesses appeal to the optimal number of market segments by offering fewer products. *Reader's Digest* is an example of a single product that reaches several market segments (and is currently seeking to broaden its range). The *Digest*'s total audience of more than 50 million includes a young-adult segment (25 percent of its readership), another of computer owners (45 percent), a smaller segment of brides-to-be (3 percent), and a segment consisting of professionals and managers (17 percent). To increase its readership, the magazine is trying to reach more young people by experimenting with new advertisements, integrating more photographs and contemporary graphics, and incorporating highly visible biographies and photos of the *Digest*'s prominent contributing writers, many of whom are popular among a somewhat younger audience, namely, families with parents under 50. This strategy, according to publisher Gary G. Coleman, means reaching "misperceivers"—people who do not know what a typical issue of *Reader's Digest* currently offers. "It's very much on our radar screen," says Coleman, "to say, 'Let's do something about the people who really don't understand us.' So we're making painstaking efforts to listen to America. We must get a handle on what their thoughts are."[11]

> " *We're making painstaking efforts to listen to America. We must get a handle on what their thoughts are.* "
>
> —Gary G. Coleman, publisher of *Reader's Digest*

Table 11.1 shows how the radio market might be segmented by a marketer of home electronic equipment. Note that segmentation is a strategy for analyzing consumers, not products. For example, the analysis in Table 11.1 identifies consumer types such as joggers, commuters, and travelers. Only indirectly, then, does it focus on the uses of the product itself. In marketing, the process of fixing, adapting, and communicating the nature of the product itself is called positioning.[12]

Identifying Market Segments

By definition, the members of a market segment must share some common traits that will affect their purchasing decisions. In identifying market segments, researchers look at a number of different influences on consumer behavior. Four of the most important are geographic, demographic, psychographic, and product use variables.

Geographic Variables

In many cases, buying decisions are affected by the places that people call home. The heavy rainfall in Washington State, for instance, invites inhabitants to purchase more umbrellas than people living in the Sunbelt do. Urban residents have little use for four-wheel-

Table 11.1 Possible Segmentation of the Radio Market

Segmentation By	Product/Target Market
Age	Inexpensive, unbreakable, portable models for young children
	Inexpensive equipment, possibly portable, for teens
	Moderate to expensive equipment for adults
Consumer attitude	Sophisticated components for audio buffs
	All-in-one units in furniture cabinets for those concerned with room appearance
Product use	Miniature models for joggers and commuters
	Boom box portables for taking outdoors
	Car stereo systems for traveling
	Components and all-in-one units for home use
Location	Battery-powered models for use where electricity is unavailable
	110-volt current for North American users
	220-volt current for other users

drive vehicles, and sailboats sell better along the coasts than in the Midwest. **Geographic variables** are the geographical units, from countries to neighborhoods, that may be considered in developing a segmentation strategy.

These patterns affect decisions about the marketing mix for a huge range of products. For example, consider a project to market down-filled parkas in rural Minnesota. Demand will be high and price competition intense; local newspaper advertising may be very effective, and the best retail location may be one that is easily reached from several small towns. Marketing the same parkas in downtown Honolulu would be considerably more challenging.

Although the marketability of some products is geographically sensitive, others benefit from nearly universal acceptance. Coca-Cola, for example, derives 79 percent of its income from international sales. Coke is the market leader in Great Britain, Germany, Japan, Brazil, and Spain. Meanwhile, Pepsi's international sales equal only about 5 percent of Coke's. In fact, Coke's chief competitor in most countries is some local soft drink, not Pepsi, which earns 80 percent of its income at home.[13]

Clearly, marketers must keep track of changes in geographic patterns. The U.S. population, for instance, has been moving south and west for the past few decades. Revitalization of urban areas has also led to marketing changes, particularly in deciding where to locate stores.

Demographic Variables

Demographic variables describe populations, including such traits as age, income, gender, ethnic background, marital status, race, religion, and social class. Table 11.2 lists some possible demographic breakdowns in the market as a whole. Depending on the marketer's purpose, a targeted segment could be a single classification (aged 20–34) or a combination of categories (aged 20–34, married with children, earning $25,000–$34,999). For example, in its attempts to reach younger readers (the median age of its readers was 47 in 1996), *Reader's Digest* targets advertising at specific demographic groups, especially families with parents under the age of 50 who have children at home and households with incomes of more than $75,000.[14]

Naturally, demographics affect marketing decisions. For example, a number of general consumption characteristics can be attributed to certain age groups (18–25, 26–35,

geographic variables
Geographic units that may be considered in developing a segmentation strategy

demographic variables
Characteristics of populations that may be considered in developing a segmentation strategy

Table 11.2   Demographic Variables

Age	Under 5, 5–11, 12–19, 20–34, 35–49, 50–64, 65+
Education	Grade school or less, some high school, graduated high school, some college, college degree, advanced degree
Family life cycle	Young single, young married without children, young married with children, older married with children under 18, older married without children under 18, older single, other
Family size	1, 2–3, 4–5, 6+
Income	Under $9,000, $9,000–14,999, $15,000–24,999, $25,000–34,999, $35,000–45,000, over $45,000
Nationality	Including African, American, Asian, British, Eastern European, French, German, Irish, Italian, Latin American, Middle Eastern, and Scandinavian
Race	Including American Indian, Asian, black, and white
Religion	Including Buddhist, Catholic, Hindu, Jewish, Muslim, and Protestant
Sex	Male, female

36–45, and so on). Marketers can thus divide markets into age groups as they develop specific marketing plans. For example, the Chicago Bicycle Co. has developed a new line of high-end "cruiser" bicycles for the recreational cyclist in the 40-and-over group, whose members want a comfortable ride and minimum maintenance without the complications of mountain bikes (complex speed-shifting and braking devices). Avoiding fancy technology, the cruiser offers a soft ride with minimal maintenance. At the same time, it is aimed at cyclists with incomes sufficient to afford the nearly $1,000 price tag.[15]

In addition, marketers can use demographics to identify trends that might shape future spending patterns. Nursing care and funeral service companies, for example, are expanding offerings in response to projected changes in the U.S. population in the years 1995 to 2005. Those changes are shown in Figure 11.2. Whereas the number of people between ages 30 and 39 is expected to drop, the number of those over 75 will increase by more than 20 percent. So-called death care companies, such as Stewart Enterprises and Service Corp. International, are preparing for the upturn by acquiring additional cemetery and funeral homes that give customers one-stop shopping.

Figure 11.2   Changes in the U.S. Population, 1995–2005

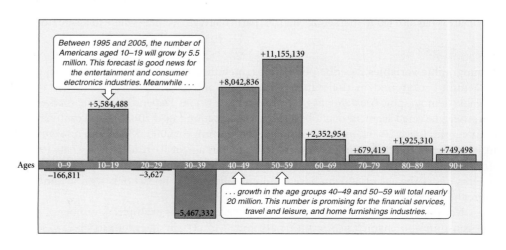

Similar data indicate that the fastest-growing segment of the United States' population during the next decade will be aging baby boomers in the age group 45 to 60. "You can see the trends working through the population," observes an economist at Merrill Lynch. "Fifteen years ago, openings at ski resorts and tennis courts were hard to come by. Now it's tee times at golf clubs." The resulting growth trends will be reflected in such industries as investment services, where boomers will be placing more of their savings in order to prepare for retirement. Similarly, mutual funds, financial services, insurance, and brokerage firms are expected to see greater demand for their products among this massive age group.[16]

> ❝ *Fifteen years ago, openings at ski resorts and tennis courts were hard to come by. Now it's tee times at golf clubs.* ❞
>
> —Donald Straszheim, Merrill Lynch economist

▶ **GLOBAL TEENS: THE DREAM SEGMENT?** At the other end of the age spectrum is the group known as teenagers. To the delight of marketers, today's teenagers are big spenders. In fact, they are spending more than teenagers ever have: The 29 million 12- to 19-year-olds in the United States made $109 billion in purchases in 1995, up from $99 billion in 1994.

In demographic terms, America's teen population started growing in 1992, following a 15-year period of stagnation and decline called the Baby Bust. The U.S. Census Bureau now predicts that this segment will grow twice as fast as the overall population, and when the growth wave peaks in 2010, there will be about 35 million teens. On a worldwide basis, the teenage population has grown to nearly 1 billion. This statistic, combined with the spending power, attitudes, and interests shared by today's teens, means that many companies are learning as much as they can about teenage buying habits.

What do marketers already know about today's teenagers? According to a recent survey of 25,000 adolescents in 41 countries, teenagers are comfortable enough with computers to be the primary force behind family technology purchases. They are also passionate about sports (especially basketball and soccer), watch about 6 hours of television a day, and love MTV and music videos. Companies such as Levi Strauss and Procter & Gamble recognize MTV's extraordinary power in the teen market and consider it a perfect vehicle for reaching teens worldwide.

As for what they buy, apparel and related items (including athletic shoes) lead the way in attracting over $6 billion in annual sales. A survey conducted by Teenage Research Unlimited, a marketing research firm, reveals some additional facts about teenage spending:

- With the increase in single-parent and dual-income families, teenagers are playing a larger role than ever in household purchases. With 83 percent of all teens shopping for at least some family groceries, food manufacturers are now designing packages with teens in mind. According to Audrey Guskey, a Duquesne University marketing expert, "the packaging of supermarket products is being made brighter to catch the eye of young shoppers."

- Teens are attracted to expensive brands, including Tommy Hilfiger and Calvin Klein. Calvin Klein's success in this market was boosted by his controversial 1995 ads showing teenagers in provocative poses. Although many adults considered the ads pornographic, teens liked them and paid greater attention to the Calvin Klein brand.

- With 42 percent of all surveyed teens calling Nike a "cool" brand, no company comes close to Nike's brand recognition.

- Teens pay for their purchases with their allowances and with the money they earn doing part-time work. With half of all 16- to 19-year-olds holding jobs, teens average an astounding $64 a week in income. Most teens spend 84 percent of their money right away on food, movies, and compact disks. They hoard their meager savings only until they can afford to buy such big-ticket items as sound systems and rock concert tickets.

Companies that want to get in sync with teen tastes are conducting even more extensive market research to better understand what 13- to 19-year-olds want and need. For example, BSB Worldwide, a New York–based advertising agency, videotaped teenagers' bedrooms in 25 countries. Researchers reported remarkable similarities in what they found: Nike shoes, and Levi's jeans and Sega video games. Not surprisingly, marketing programs at companies in these industries reflect an intense interest in young people. For example, Reebok is trying to capitalize on teens' interest in sports, especially soccer. The company recently rolled out a line of soccer gear, with ads in Latin America and Europe featuring local soccer stars.

Marketers are also monitoring teen trendsetters to stay on the cutting edge of changing fashions. Corporate scouts are following teen trendsetters to rock concerts, clubs, and restaurants in an effort to spot products that are likely to sell to more mainstream buyers. "Now," admits one product director at Reebok, "we're watching kids, whereas we used to watch designers." According to Sputnik Inc., a New York–based market research company that specializes in the buying habits of teen trendsetters, the following trends are now considered cool:

- Girls in dominatrix clothing

- Bright skeleton prints

- Comic graphic T-shirts

- Reflective trim on field-sports shoes

- Hair sectioned into little wrapped ponytails that look like rockets projecting from the head

- Guys in vinyl skirts

- See-through track shoes

- Suspenders with African-print shirts

- Military shoes, traditional Oxfords, mixed with Muslim Malcolm X look

- Skinny ties, white shirts, basic black pants and jackets

> ❝ *Now we're watching kids, whereas we used to watch designers.* ❞
>
> —Ruth A. Davis, product director at Reebok International

Although marketers are increasingly targeting cutting-edge teen fashions, there is danger in assuming that all teens will embrace every trend. Although the trendiest teens, according to one market researcher, may "experiment with ten trends, only one will cross over" to a mainstream market.[17]

Psychographic Variables

psychographic variables
Consumer characteristics, such as lifestyles, opinions, interests, and attitudes, that may be considered in developing a segmentation strategy

Members of a market can also be segmented according to such **psychographic variables** as lifestyles, opinions, interests, and attitudes. One company that has combined demographic and psychographic variables to get a better picture of its market is Starbucks Coffee Co., which has expanded its original coffee bean shops into coffee bars. Among the trends observed by Starbucks, for example, is the nationwide push for sobriety: Young urbanites out for a night on the town are often looking for an alternative to alcohol. Moreover, Starbucks fans enjoy the stylish coffee bars with lattes, mochas, and espresso drinks prepared by skilled baristas.[18]

Psychographics are particularly important to marketers because, unlike demographics and geographics, they can sometimes be changed by marketing efforts. For example, many companies have succeeded in changing at least some consumers' opinions by running ads highlighting products that have been improved directly in response to consumer desires. For example, many companies in Poland have succeeded in overcoming consumer resistance by promoting the safety and desirability of using credit rather than depending solely on cash for family purchases. One result of such changing attitudes is a booming economy and the emergence of a growing and robust middle class. The increasing number of Polish households owning televisions, appliances, automobiles, and houses is fueling the status of Poland's middle class as the most stable in the former Soviet bloc.[19]

Product Use Variables

Product use variables include the ways in which consumers use a product, their brand loyalty to it, and their reasons for purchasing it. A women's shoemaker, for example, might identify three segments: wearers of athletic, casual, and dress shoes. Each market segment is looking for different benefits in a shoe. A woman buying an athletic shoe, for instance, may not care much about its appearance but will care a great deal about arch support, sturdiness, and traction in the sole. A woman buying a casual shoe will want it to look good and feel comfortable. A woman buying a dress shoe may require a specific color or style and may even accept some discomfort in a fragile shoe.

Of course, some products are designed for a combination of segmenting variables. Ryka Inc., for instance, targets its specialized shoes demographically (to women), by product use (for athletics), and psychographically (women who take aerobics classes regularly) all in one product.

product use variables
Consumer characteristics based on the ways in which a product is used, the brand loyalty it enjoys, and the reasons for which it is purchased

Market Research

Although segmentation can never be a perfect process, accuracy and effectiveness can be greatly improved through **market research**: the study of what buyers need and how best to meet those needs. Market research can support any element in the marketing mix. For example, one marketer might study consumer response to an experimental paint formula (new product). Another might explore the response of potential buyers to a price reduction (new price) on calculators. Still a third might check audience response to a proposed advertising campaign with a humorous theme (new promotion). Marketers can also try to learn whether customers are more likely to purchase a given product in a specialty shop or a discount store (new place).

Moreover, the importance of selling products in today's international markets is expanding the role of market research into new areas. For example, when companies decide to sell their goods or services in other countries, they must decide whether to standardize products or to specialize them for new markets.

market research
The study of consumer needs and wants and the ways in which sellers can best meet them

▶ Consider the case of Honda Motor Co. Ltd, which traditionally had its new product research and development centralized at Honda R&D Ltd. in Japan, with a desire for a single global design. Now, however, international differences in customers' desires are requiring a whole new way of doing business for Honda: The company has turned over more of its decision-making to its regional R&D operations in response to massive new product demands worldwide. North America is expected to need 10 new models for the years 1997–1999, Europe needs 7, Japan 15. The greater regional independence is reflected in the '97 Acura CL, which is aimed at the U.S. consumer and was developed and engineered in the United States. Honda sales are also growing in Latin America, but the market is not yet big enough to justify an independent product design center, so its designs are done by Honda Research of America in the United States. Honda also plans to expand into India and Vietnam.[20]

At Honda, the moral of the story is clear: Before committing itself to the large costs of marketing specialized versions of its products, or before adopting just one global product, a company is wise to undertake market research to find out which choice best meets its customers' desires in various regions.

The Research Process

Market research can occur at almost any point in a product's existence. Most commonly, however, it is used when developing new or altered products. These are the five basic steps in performing market research:

1 *Study the current situation.* What is the need and what is currently being done to meet it? Such a study should note how well a firm is currently meeting the need that has been identified.

2 *Select a research method.* Marketers have a wide range of methods available. In choosing one, they must bear in mind the effectiveness and costs of different methods.

3 *Collect data.* There are two types of research data. **Secondary data** are already available as a result of previous research. For example, the *Statistical Abstract of the United States* offers data on geographic and demographic variables. Using secondary data can save time, effort, and money. When secondary data are unavailable or inadequate, however, **primary data** (new data from research performed by a firm or its agents) must be obtained.

4 *Analyze the data.* Data are of no use until they have been organized into information.

5 *Prepare a report.* This report should include a summation of the study's methodology and findings. It should also identify alternative solutions and (where appropriate) make recommendations for the best course of action.

Research Methods

The success of a market research study often depends on the appropriateness of the method used. The four basic methods of market research are observation, surveys, focus groups, and experimentation.

Observation

Probably the oldest form of market research is simple **observation**. Perhaps the owner of a toy store notices that customers are buying red wagons instead of green ones. When the retailer reorders more red wagons, the manufacturer's records show high sales of red wagons, and marketing concludes that customers want red wagons. Today, computerized systems allow marketers to observe consumer preferences rapidly and with incredible accuracy. For example, electronic supermarket scanners allow managers to see what is and is not selling without having to check shelves. Observation is also inexpensive, often drawing on data that must be collected for some other reason, such as reordering.

Surveys

Sometimes, however, marketers must go a step further and ask questions about marketing ideas or product performance. One way to get answers is by conducting **surveys**. The heart of any survey is a questionnaire that is either mailed to individuals or used as the basis of telephone or personal interviews. For example, United Parcel Service surveyed customers to find out how it could improve service. Surprisingly, clients wanted more interaction with drivers because they can offer practical advice on shipping. UPS thus added extra drivers, freeing up some time for drivers to get out of their trucks and spend time with customers.[21] However, surveys can be expensive and may vary widely in accuracy. In addition, because no firm can afford to survey everyone, marketers must be careful to contact representative groups of respondents. To address specific issues being researched, questions must be constructed carefully.

Focus Groups

In a **focus group**, 6 to 15 people are gathered in one place, where they are presented with an issue and asked to discuss it. The researcher takes notes but provides only a minimal amount of structure. At its best, this technique allows researchers to explore issues too

---

secondary data
Data readily available as a result of previous research

primary data
Data developed through new research

observation
Market research technique that involves simply watching and recording consumer behavior

survey
Market research technique using a questionnaire that is either mailed to individuals or used as the basis of interviews

focus group
Market research technique in which a group of people is gathered, presented with an issue, and asked to discuss it in depth

complex for questionnaires and can produce creative solutions. But because a focus group is small, its responses may not represent the feelings or opinions of the larger market. Thus focus groups are most often used as a first step to some other form of research.

Experimentation

Experimentation also tries to get answers to questions that surveys cannot address. As in scientific research, experimentation in market research tries to compare the responses of the same or similar people under different circumstances. For example, a firm trying to decide whether to include walnuts in a new candy bar probably would not learn much by asking people what they thought of the idea. But if it made up some bars with nuts and some without and then asked people to try both, the responses could be quite helpful. Unfortunately, however, experimentation is very expensive. Thus, in deciding whether to use it (or any other research method, for that matter) marketers must carefully weigh costs against possible benefits.

experimentation
Market research technique that attempts to compare the responses of the same or similar people under different circumstances

Understanding Consumer Behavior

Although marketing managers can tell us what qualities people want in a new VCR, they cannot tell us *why* people buy VCRs. What desire are they fulfilling? Is there a psychological or sociological explanation for why consumers purchase one product and not another? These questions and many others are addressed in the area of marketing known as **consumer behavior**: the study of the process by which customers decide to purchase and consume products.

consumer behavior
The various facets of the process by which customers decide to purchase and consume products

Influences on Consumer Behavior

According to the not-so-surprising title of one classic study, we are very much social animals.[22] To understand consumer behavior, then, marketers draw heavily on the fields of psychology and sociology. The result is a focus on four major influences on consumer behavior: psychological, personal, social, and cultural. By identifying the four influences that are most active, marketers try to explain consumer choices and predict future purchasing behavior:

- Psychological influences include a person's motivations, perceptions, ability to learn, and attitudes.

- Personal influences include lifestyle, personality, and economic status.

- Social influences include family, opinion leaders (people whose opinions are sought by others), and such reference groups as friends, co-workers, and professional associates.

- Cultural influences include culture (the way of living that distinguishes one large group from another), subculture (smaller groups, such as ethnic groups, with shared values), and social class (the cultural ranking of groups according to such criteria as background, occupation, and income).

All these factors can have a strong impact on the products that people purchase, often in complex ways. For example, many wealthy women wear real pearls for the prestige they represent. But Barbara Bush, the financially comfortable former First Lady, preferred to wear fake pearls. Personal influences thus outweighed social and cultural influences: The symbolism of real pearls did not match her self-image and social values.

On the other hand, the purchase of some products is influenced either very little or not at all by behavioral factors. For example, some consumers exhibit high brand loyalty; that is, they regularly purchase products because they are satisfied with their performance.

Such people (say, users of Quaker Oats) are generally less subject to typical influences and stick with preferred brands. Closer to home, however, the clothes you wear and the food you eat often reflect social and psychological influences on your consuming behavior.

The Consumer Buying Process

Students of consumer behavior have constructed various models to help marketers understand how consumers come to purchase products. Figure 11.3 presents one such model. At the core of this and similar models is an awareness of the psychosocial influences that lead to consumption. Ultimately, marketers use this information to develop marketing plans.

Problem/Need Recognition

The buying process begins when the consumer recognizes a problem or need. After strenuous exercise, for example, you may realize that you are thirsty and need refreshment. After the birth of twins, you may find your one-bedroom apartment too small for comfort.

Need recognition also occurs when you have a chance to change your purchasing habits. For example, when you obtain your first job after graduation, your new income may let you purchase items that were once too expensive for you. You may also discover a need for suits, apartment furnishings, and a car. American Express and Sears recognize this shift in typical needs when they market credit cards to college seniors.

Information Seeking

Once they have recognized a need, consumers often seek information. This search is not always extensive. If you are thirsty, for instance, you may simply ask someone to point you to a soft-drink machine. At other times, you may simply rely on your memory for information.

Before making major purchases, however, most people seek information from personal sources, marketing sources, public sources, and experience. For example, if you move to a new town, you will want to identify the best dentist, physician, hair stylist, butcher, or pizza maker in your area. To get this information, you may check with personal sources such as acquaintances, co-workers, and relatives. Before buying an exercise bike, you may go to the library or the Internet and read the relevant issue of *Consumer Re-*

Figure 11.3   The Consumer Buying Process

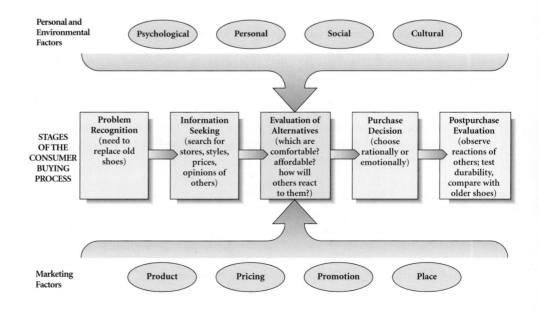

The Workplace Environment

After the Suit and Tie, Then What?

What makes people buy blue jeans? Levi Strauss & Co. clearly knows most of the reasons: comfort, style, fit, and price. But the venerable denim giant recently embarked on an unusual campaign: teaching office workers what to wear to work in the new "dress-down" corporate environment.

About 75 percent of U.S. businesses now allow workers to wear casual dress at least once a week, temporarily dispensing with the corporate uniform of skirts, suits, and ties. Employers anxious to satisfy workers but unwilling to sanction grunge began turning to Levi's for advice, and the clothier followed up with a passion.

Levi's has spent a mere $5 million so far and has kept its profile low. But through brochures, videos, consultations, seminars, an 800 number, and of course fashion shows, it's hoping to make Levi's brands, including the immensely popular Dockers label, the dress-down uniform of choice.

Among the 22,000 corporations it has advised in the last few years are Charles Schwab & Co., IBM, Nynex, and Aetna Life & Casualty.

Competitors such as Eddie Bauer and Gap Inc. have jumped in with their own dress-down promotions, including the Gap's recent sponsorship of a one-time-only dress-down Friday on the ultraconservative New York Stock Exchange floor. But Levi's early success showed that the firm had done its homework. Starting with a market research study in 1992 that documented the start of the dress-down trend, Levi's went on to build an extensive database of corporate workers and human resource managers. In 1996 the promotional effort went international, with a hip campaign consisting of ads and skits taking a light-hearted poke at traditional business wear.

"We did not create casual business wear," says Levi's consumer marketing director Daniel M. Chew. "What we did was identify a trend and see a business opportunity."

ports (a magazine that rates consumer goods). You may also question market sources such as sales clerks or rely on direct experience by test-riding several bikes before you buy.

By the same token, some sellers thus treat information as a value to be added to their products. For example, Glaxo Wellcome has prepared a Web site (www.zyban.com) dedicated to patient information about Zyban, the first nicotine-free pill for helping people quit smoking. One page at the site introduces nicotine replacement methods, discussing patches, gum, and nasal sprays, including information on the advantages and side effects of each method. The site provides a range of additional information such as the availability of patient support programs such as that of the American Lung Association. It also provides postings on upcoming events such as the GlaxoWellcome–sponsored live educational satellite broadcast, *Stop Smoking: Get Ready for Success.*[23]

Evaluation of Alternatives

If you are in the market for a set of skis, you probably have some idea of who makes skis and how they differ. You may have accumulated some of this knowledge during the information-seeking stage and combined it with what you knew before. By analyzing the product attributes that apply to a given product (color, price, prestige, quality, and service record), you will consider your choices and decide which product best meets your needs.

Purchase Decision

Ultimately, consumers must make purchase decisions. They may decide to defer a purchase or they may decide to buy now. Buy decisions are based on rational motives, emotional motives, or both. **Rational motives** involve the logical evaluation of product attributes: cost, quality, and usefulness. **Emotional motives** involve nonobjective factors and lead to nonrational decisions. Although not all nonrational decisions are sudden, many spur-of-the-moment decisions are emotionally driven. Emotional motives include socia-

rational motives
Reasons for purchasing a product that are based on a logical evaluation of product attributes

emotional motives
Reasons for purchasing a product that are based on nonobjective factors

Glaxo Wellcome Inc., a manufacturer of medicines and drugs, has a philosophy that includes giving the customer product information rather than the traditional sales pitch. In its print advertisements for Zyban, a prescription medicine for smoking cessation, the emphasis is on information for the patient regarding the product's purpose, its use, how it works, side effects, and warnings, along with access to additional educational messages on the product's Web site (www.zyban.com).

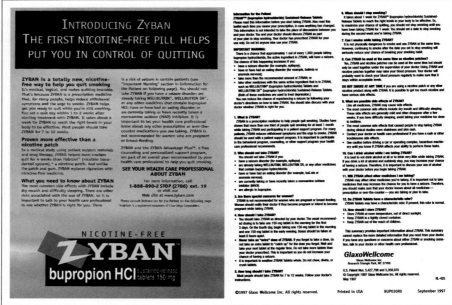

bility, imitation of others, and aesthetics. For example, you might buy the same brand of jeans as your friends to feel comfortable among that group, not because your friends happen to have the good sense to prefer durable, comfortable jeans.

Nonrational decisions can be either satisfying or, largely because they were not based on objective criteria, ill-considered. Gratifying a sudden urge for ice cream may not require much thought but may still produce a lot of enjoyment. On the other hand, we have all purchased items, taken them home, and then wondered, "Why in the world did I spend good money on this thing?"

Postpurchase Evaluations

Marketing does not stop with the sale of a product. It includes the process of consumption. What happens after the sale is thus quite important. Marketers want consumers to be happy after the consumption of products so that they are more likely to buy them again.

In fact, because consumers do not want to go through a complex decision process for every purchase, they often repurchase products they have used and liked.

Not all consumers are satisfied with their purchases, of course. Dissatisfied consumers may complain to sellers, criticize products publicly, or even file lawsuits. Needless to say, they are unlikely to purchase the same products again. Moreover, dissatisfied customers are much more likely to broadcast their experiences than are satisfied customers.

On the other hand, although they can have a negative impact, dissatisfied customers are potential sources of helpful information. At Hewlett-Packard, for example, every individual or corporate complaint is assigned to a specific employee. That person must check the H-P database to find out how common the problem is and what the company is doing about it. Then he or she is responsible for personally reporting back to the customer. One such complaint involved H-P's PerfView software, which is designed to monitor the speed of H-P networks. Customers pointed out that although PerfView did what it was supposed to do quite nicely, it did nothing else. The software was thus redesigned: It now tracks all the components of a network even if they are manufactured by different companies.[24]

Organizational Marketing and Buying Behavior

Buying behavior is observable daily in the consumer market, where marketing activities, including purchases, are visible to the public. Equally important, but far less visible, are organizational (or commercial) markets: 22 million organizations in the United States that buy goods and services to be used in creating and delivering consumer products. As we will see in the following sections, organizational marketers must deal with different kinds of organizational markets and with buying behaviors that are quite different from those found in consumer markets.

Organizational Markets

Organizational or commercial markets fall into three categories: industrial, reseller, and government/institutional markets. Taken together, these three markets do about $7 trillion annually—approximately three times the business done in the consumer market.

Industrial Market

The **industrial market** includes businesses that buy goods falling into one of two categories: goods to be converted into other products and goods that are used up during production. This market includes farmers, manufacturers, and some retailers. For example, Seth Thomas purchases electronics, metal components, and glass to make clocks for the consumer market. The company also buys office supplies, tools, and factory equipment items never seen by clock buyers to be used during production. Baskin-Robbins buys not only ingredients for ice cream but also paper bags and wrappers to package products for customers and freezer cabinets for storage.

The industrial market is huge, with some 21 million corporations, partnerships, and proprietorships. In iron and steel production alone, the U.S. market is $27 billion. In industrial electronics, annual sales total $30 billion for products with such industrial uses as testing, measuring, and manufacturing control devices.[25]

industrial market
Organizational market consisting of firms that buy goods that are either converted into products or used up during production

Reseller Market

Before products reach consumers, they pass through a **reseller market** consisting of intermediaries, including wholesalers and retailers, who buy the finished goods and resell them (wholesalers and retailers are discussed in detail in chapter 14). The Coast Distribution System, for example, is a leading distributor of parts and accessories for the pleasure boat market. It buys items such as lights, steering wheels, and propellers and resells them to marinas and boat repair shops. In the United States, 600,000 wholesalers have annual sales of $2.2 trillion.

reseller market
Organizational market consisting of intermediaries who buy and resell finished goods

Retailers, including department stores, drugstores, and supermarkets, buy clothing, appliances, foods, medicines, and other merchandise for resale to the consumer market. Some 3 million U.S. retailers purchase merchandise that, when resold to consumers, is valued at $2.3 trillion per year.[26] Retailers also buy such services as maintenance, housekeeping, and communications.

Government and Institutional Market

In addition to federal and state governments, there are more than 87,000 local governments (municipalities, counties, townships, and school districts) in the United States. State and local governments alone make annual purchases totaling $1.4 trillion for durable goods, nondurables, purchased services, and construction.[27] For example, EA Engineering Science & Technology is an environmental business with services ranging from hazardous waste testing to site cleanup management. Federal and state agencies have become EA's fastest-growing market, now accounting for 60 percent of its revenues. One of EA's best customers, the Defense Department, uses its consulting services in closing military bases, on which all hazardous wastes must be removed in order to meet environmental standards.[28]

institutional market
Organizational market consisting of such buyers of goods and services as hospitals, churches, museums, and charitable organizations

The **institutional market** consists of nongovernment organizations, such as hospitals, churches, museums, and charitable organizations, that also make up a substantial market for goods and services. Like organizations in other commercial markets, these institutions use supplies and equipment, as well as legal, accounting, and transportation services.

Organizational Buying Behavior

In many respects, industrial buying behavior bears little resemblance to consumer buying practices. For example, industrial product demand is stimulated by demand for consumer products and is less sensitive to price changes. Other differences include the buyers' purchasing skills, their decision-making activities, and buyer-seller relationships.

Differences in Demand

Recall our definition of *demand* in chapter 1: the willingness and ability of buyers to purchase a good or service. There are two major differences in demand between consumer and industrial products: derived demand and inelasticity of demand.

derived demand
Demand for industrial products that results from demand for consumer products

Derived Demand.   The term *derived demand* refers to the fact that demand for industrial products often results from demand for related consumer products (that is, industrial demand is often derived from consumer demand).

▶   Consider the chain of industrial demand that was ignited when Eastman Kodak Company realized how many consumers would buy the new digital cameras. To have the digital Kodaks on the market in 1996, renovations of manufacturing facilities were planned in 1994 and were then followed by construction. Such a project can require an array of services and materials such as structural steel, windows, bathroom fixtures, heating apparatus, and production equipment. In turn, these needs stimulate demand back up the supply chain. For example, in order to make the materials for the plant's construction, the steel supplier has to buy more scrap steel, carbon, and other raw materials from its suppliers. Once facilities were completed, there were new purchases of raw materials for production, including lenses, viewfinders, materials for the camera memory, photosensitive chips, liquid-crystal display, and the software that enables your photos to be downloaded into your computer's hard drive.

inelastic demand
Demand for industrial products that is not largely affected by price changes

Inelastic Demand.   **Inelastic demand** occurs when a price change for a product does not have much effect on demand. For instance, take the demand for cardboard used to package products such as file cabinets. Because cardboard packaging is such a small part of the manufacturer's overall cabinet cost, an increase in cardboard prices will not lessen the demand for cardboard. In turn, because cabinet buyers will see little price increase, demand for filing cabinets and for their accompanying cardboard packaging will remain at about the same level.

Differences in Buyers

Unlike most consumers, organizational buyers are professional, specialized, and expert (or at least well-informed):

- As professionals, organizational buyers are trained in arranging buyer-seller relationships and in methods for negotiating purchase terms. Once buyer-seller agreements have been reached, industrial buyers also arrange for formal contracts. Finally, they are often responsible for establishing buyer-seller transactions that comply with various laws, such as prohibitions against unfair collusion.

- As a rule, industrial buyers are company specialists in a line of items. As one of several buyers for a large bakery, for example, you may specialize in food ingredients such as flour, yeast, and butter. Another buyer may specialize in baking equipment (industrial ovens and mixers), and a third may purchase office equipment and supplies.

- Finally, industrial buyers are often experts about the products they are buying. On a regular basis, organizational buyers learn about competing products and alternative suppliers by attending trade shows, reading trade magazines, and conducting technical discussions with sellers' representatives.

Differences in Decision Making

Recall that we illustrated the five stages in the consumer buying process in Figure 11.3. As you can see in Figure 11.4, the organizational buyer's decision process differs in three important respects: developing product specifications, evaluating alternatives, and making postpurchase evaluations.

Developing Product Specifications. Following problem recognition, the first stage of the buying process, industrial buying takes an additional step, developing product specifications: A document is drawn up to describe the detailed product characteristics that are needed by the buyer and must be met by the supplier. These specifications are then used in the information-seeking stage, when buyers search for products and suppliers capable of meeting their specific needs.

Evaluating Alternatives. In evaluating alternatives, buyers carefully measure prospective suppliers against the product specifications developed earlier. Only suppliers that can meet those requirements are considered further. Then prospective vendors are evaluated according to other factors, such as price, reliability, and service reputation.

Making Postpurchase Evaluations. The final stage, postpurchase evaluation, is more systematic in organizational buying than in consumer buying. The buyer's organization examines the product and compares it, feature-by-feature, for conformance to product specifications. Buyers retain records on product and service quality received from sup-

Figure 11.4 The Industrial Buying Process

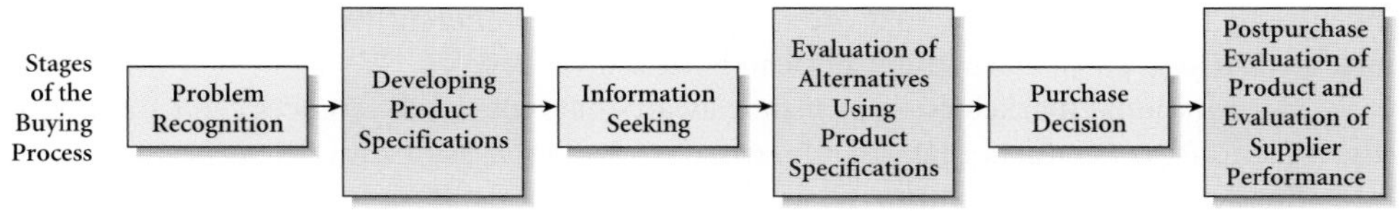

pliers as the basis for evaluating their performance. These performance ratings become important considerations for selecting future suppliers.

Differences in the Buyer-Seller Relationship

Consumer-seller relationships are often impersonal and fleeting one-time interactions. In contrast, industrial situations often involve frequent, enduring buyer-seller relationships. Accordingly, industrial sellers emphasize personal selling by trained representatives who can better understand the needs of each customer. Through extensive interaction with numerous buyers, sellers are better prepared to make suggestions for improving products and services that will benefit their customers.

The International Marketing Mix

Marketing products internationally means mounting a strategy to support global business operations. Obviously, this is no easy task. Foreign customers differ from domestic buyers in language, customs, business practices, and consumer behavior. When they decide to go global, marketers must thus reconsider each element of the marketing mix: product, pricing, promotion, and place.

International Products

Some products can be sold abroad with virtually no changes. Budweiser, Coca-Cola, and Marlboros are exactly the same in Peoria and Paris. In other cases, U.S. firms must create products with built-in flexibility, such as electric shavers that adapt to either 115- or 230-volt outlets.

As we noted earlier, however, sometimes only a redesigned or completely different product will meet the needs of foreign buyers. To sell the Macintosh in Japan, for example, Apple had to develop a Japanese-language operating system. Nevertheless, more companies are designing products for universal application. Whether designed for unique or universal markets, the branding and labeling of products are especially important for communicating global messages about them. For example, KFC (formerly Kentucky Fried Chicken) boxes and Pepsi-Cola cans display universal logos that are instantly recognizable in many nations.

International Pricing

When pricing for international markets, marketers must handle all the considerations of domestic pricing while also considering the higher costs of transporting and selling products abroad. Bass Pro Shops, for example, sells outdoor sports equipment to customers in Europe at higher prices that cover the added costs of delivery. In contrast, major products such as jet airplanes are priced the same worldwide because delivery costs are incidental; huge development and production costs are the major considerations regardless of customer location. Meanwhile, because of the higher costs of buildings, rent, equipment, and imported meat, a McDonald's Big Mac that sells for $2 in the United States costs over $10 in Japan.

International Promotion

Occasionally, a good advertising campaign here is a good advertising campaign just about everywhere else; that is, it can be transported to another country virtually intact.[29] Quite often, however, standard U.S. promotional devices do not succeed in other countries. In fact, many Europeans believe that your product must be inherently shoddy if you resort to any advertising, particularly the American hard-sell variety.

International marketers must also be aware that cultural differences can cause negative reactions to products that are advertised improperly. For example, some Europeans are offended by television commercials that show weapons or violence. Advertising practices are regulated accordingly. Consequently, Dutch commercials for toys do not feature the guns and combat scenes that are common on Saturday morning U.S. television.[30] Meanwhile, liquor and cigarette commercials that are banned from U.S. television are thriving in many Asian and European markets.

Symbolism is a sometimes surprising consideration. In France, for instance, yellow flowers suggest infidelity. In Mexico, they are signs of death, an association made in Brazil by the color purple. Clearly, product promotions must be carefully matched to the customs and cultural values of each country.

International Distribution

Finally, international distribution presents several problems. In some industries, delays in starting new distribution networks can be costly. Therefore, companies with existing distribution systems often enjoy an advantage over new businesses. Similarly, several companies have gained advantages in time-based competition by buying existing businesses. Procter & Gamble, for example, saved 3 years of startup time by buying Revlon's Max Factor and Beatrix cosmetics, both of which are well established in foreign markets. P&G can thus immediately use these companies' distribution and marketing networks for selling its own U.S. brands in the United Kingdom, Germany, and Japan.

Other U.S. companies contract with foreign firms or individuals to distribute and sell their products abroad. Foreign agents may perform personal selling and advertising, provide information about local markets, or serve as exporters' representatives. Of course, having to manage interactions with foreign personnel complicates a marketing manager's job. In addition, packaging practices in the United States must sometimes be adapted to withstand the rigors of transport to foreign ports and storage under conditions that differ radically from domestic conditions.

Given the need to adjust the marketing mix, success in international markets is hard won. Even experienced firms can err in marketing to other countries. International success requires flexibility and a willingness to adapt to the nuances of other cultures. Whether a firm markets in domestic or international markets, however, the basic principles of marketing still apply. It is only the implementation of those principles that changes.

Small Business and the Marketing Mix

As we noted in chapter 7, far more small businesses fail than succeed. Yet many of today's largest firms were yesterday's small businesses. McDonald's began with one restaurant, a concept, and one individual (Ray Kroc) who had foresight. Behind the success of many small firms lies a skillful application of the marketing concept and careful consideration of each element in the marketing mix.

Small Business Products

Some new products and firms are doomed at the start simply because few consumers want or need what they have to offer. Too often, enthusiastic entrepreneurs introduce products that they and their friends like but fail to estimate realistic market potential. Other small businesses offer new products before they have clear pictures of their target segments and how to reach them. They try to be everything to everyone, and they end up serving no one well.

In contrast, a thorough understanding of what customers want has paid off for many small firms. "Keep it simple" is a familiar key to success: Fulfill a specific need and do it efficiently. In 1996, for example, entrepreneur Marsha Serlin was named National Small Business Subcontractor of the Year by the U.S. Small Business Administration. Her recycling business, United Scrap Metal Inc., purchases scrap metal, paper, and plastic from other companies, then sorts, cleans, chops, bales, and resells it to customers such as U.S. Steel and Alcoa to be remade into other products. United Scrap's success, Serlin says, is due primarily to concentrating on what customers want; she learned the business and her customers' needs by asking questions: "My customer is the No. 1 person . . . I do everything as though it were for me. I put myself into the shoes of the customer, and I say, 'If I were him, what would I want from me?'" The result of this focused approach is United's annual revenues of $40 million and 120 employees.[31]

Small Business Pricing

Haphazard pricing that is often little more than guesswork can sink even a firm with a good product. Most often, small business pricing errors result from a failure to project operating expenses accurately. Owners of failing businesses have often been heard to say, "I didn't realize how much it costs to run the business!" and "If I price the product high enough to cover my expenses, no one will buy it!" But when small businesses set prices by carefully assessing costs, many earn very satisfactory profits—sometimes enough to expand or diversify.

Small Business Promotion

Many small businesses are also ignorant when it comes to the methods and costs of promotion. To save expenses, for example, they may avoid advertising and rely instead on personal selling. As a result, too many potential customers remain unaware of their products.

Successful small businesses plan for promotional expenses as part of startup costs. Some hold down costs by taking advantage of less expensive promotional methods. Local newspapers, for example, are sources of publicity when they publish articles about new or unique businesses. Other small businesses have succeeded by identifying themselves and their products with associated groups, organizations, and events.[32] Thus, a custom crafts gallery might join with a local art league and local artists to organize public showings of their combined products.

Small Business Distribution

Problems in arranging distribution can also make or break small businesses. Perhaps the most critical aspect of distribution is facility location, especially for new service businesses. The ability of many small businesses (retailers, veterinary clinics, and gourmet coffee shops) to attract and retain customers depends partly on the choice of location.

In distribution, as in other aspects of the marketing mix, smaller companies may have advantages over larger competitors, even in highly complex industries. They may be quicker in applying service technologies. Everex Systems Inc. of Fremont, California, sells personal computers to wholesalers and dealers through a system the company calls zero response time: Because the company is small and flexible, phone orders can be reviewed every 2 hours and factory assembly adjusted to match demand.

Summary of Learning Objectives

1 **Define *marketing*.** According to the American Marketing Association, marketing is the process of planning and executing the conception, pricing, promotion, and distribution of ideas, goods, and services to create exchanges that satisfy individual and organizational objectives.

2 **Describe the five forces that constitute the external marketing environment.** The external environment consists of the outside forces that influence marketing strategy and decision making. The political/legal environment includes laws and regulations, both domestic and foreign, that may define or constrain business activities. The social/cultural environment is the context within which people's values, beliefs, and ideas affect marketing decisions. The technological environment includes the technological developments that affect existing and new products. The economic environment consists of the conditions, such as inflation, recession, and interest rates, that influence both consumer and organizational spending patterns. Finally, the competitive environment is the environment in which marketers must persuade buyers to purchase their products rather than their competitors'.

3 **Explain market segmentation and show how it is used in target marketing.** Market segmentation is the process of dividing markets into categories of customers. Businesses have learned that marketing is more successful when it is aimed toward specific target markets: groups of consumers with similar wants and needs. Markets may be segmented by geographic, demographic, psychographic, or product use variables.

4 **Explain the purpose and value of market research.** Market research is the study of what buyers need and of the best ways to meet those needs. This process involves a study of the current situation, the selection of a research method, the collection of data, the analysis of data, and the preparation of a report that may include recommendations for action. The four most common research methods are observation, surveys, focus groups, and experimentation.

5 **Describe the key factors that influence the consumer buying process.** A number of personal and psychological considerations, along with various social and cultural influences, affect consumer behavior. When making buying decisions, consumers first determine or respond to a problem or need and then collect as much information as they think necessary before making a purchase. Postpurchase evaluations are also important to marketers because they influence future buying patterns.

6 **Discuss the three categories of organizational markets and explain how organizational buying behavior differs from consumer buying behavior.** The industrial market includes firms that buy goods falling into one of two categories: goods to be converted into other products and goods that are used up during production. Farmers and manufacturers are members of the industrial market. Members of the reseller market (mostly wholesalers) are intermediaries who buy and resell finished goods. Besides governments and agencies at all levels, the government and institutional market includes such nongovernment organizations as hospitals, museums, and charities.

There are four main differences between consumer and organizational buying behavior. First, the nature of demand is different in organizational markets; it is often derived (resulting from related consumer demand) or inelastic (largely unaffected by price changes). Second, organizational buyers are typically professionals, specialists, or experts. Third, organizational buyers develop product specifications, evaluate alternatives more thoroughly, and make more systematic postpurchase evaluations. Finally, they often develop enduring buyer-seller relationships.

Questions and Exercises

Questions for Review

1 What are the key similarities and differences between consumer buying behavior and organizational buying behavior?
2 Why and how is market segmentation used in target marketing?
3 What elements of the marketing mix may need to be adjusted to market a product internationally? Why?
4 How do the needs of organizations differ according to the different organizational markets of which they are members?

Questions for Analysis

5 Using examples of everyday products, explain why marketing plans must consider both the external marketing environment and the marketing mix.
6 Select an everyday product (books, CDs, skateboards, dog food, or shoes, for example). Show how different versions of your chosen product are aimed toward different market segments. Explain how the marketing mix differs for each segment.
7 Select a second everyday product and describe the consumer buying process that typically goes into its purchase.
8 If you were starting your own small business (say, marketing a consumer good that you already know something about), which of the forces in the external marketing

environment would you believe to have the greatest potential impact on your success?

Application Exercises

9 Interview the marketing manager of a local business. Identify the degree to which this person's job is oriented toward each element in the marketing mix.

10 Select a product made by a foreign company and sold in the United States. Compare it with a similar domestically made product in terms of product features, price, promotion, and distribution. Which of the two products do you believe is more successful with U.S. buyers? Why?

Building Your Business Skills

This exercise enhances the following SCANS workplace competencies: demonstrating basic skills, demonstrating thinking skills, exhibiting interpersonal skills, and working with information.

Goal To encourage students to analyze how various market segmentation variables affect business success.

Situation You and four partners are thinking of purchasing an automobile dealership that specializes in four-wheel-drive vehicles priced between $30,000 and $40,000. You are now in the process of deciding where that dealership should be. You are considering four locations: Miami, Florida; Westport, Connecticut; Dallas, Texas; and Spokane, Washington.

Method **Step 1:** Working with four classmates (your partnership group), do library research to learn how automakers market four-wheel-drive vehicles. Check for articles in *Wall Street Journal*, *Business Week*, *Fortune*, and other business publications.

Step 2: Continue your research. This time, focus on the specific marketing variables that define each prospective location. Check Census Bureau and Department of Labor data at your library and on the Internet and contact local Chambers of Commerce (by phone and via the Internet) to learn about each location's
- Geography
- Demography (especially age, income, gender, family status, and social class)
- Psychographic factors (lifestyles, interests, and attitudes)

Step 3: Come together with group members to analyze which location holds the greatest promise as a dealership site. Base your decision on your analysis of market segment variables and their effects on car sales.

Follow-Up Questions

1 Which location did you choose? Describe the market segmentation factors that influenced your decision?

2 Identify the two most important variables that you believe will have the greatest impact on the dealership's success. Why are these factors so important?

3 Which factors were least important in your decision? Why?

4 When automakers advertise four-wheel-drive vehicles, they often show them in precarious situations (on mountaintops, for example, or climbing the sides of buildings). Which market segments are these ads targeting? Describe these segments in terms of demographic and psychographic characteristics.

Business Case 11

Playing to Win at Toys Я Us

For a while it looked unstoppable. With its innovative no-frills store design, huge assortment, and moderate prices, Toys Я Us was on a roll in the 1980s. But its competitors caught up with it, and in the 1990s the big retailer was on the defensive.

Fighting discount stores that underpriced it, smarting from Federal Trade Commission charges of unfair pricing, and coming to grips with the realization that customers' tastes in shopping experiences have changed, Toys Я Us must enter a new era to survive. Earnings have fallen and its expansion overseas has stagnated. CEO Michael Goldstein has pushed a number of strategies to try to recoup the chain's luster. "We can't compete with prices at Wal-Mart and other discounters," he says, "So we're installing a wow factor."

Every aspect of the company's way of doing business has changed or is slated for change. Now a conglomerate of three distinct chains (Toys Я Us, Kids Я Us, and Babies Я Us), the firm announced plans to redesign all the toy stores to make the shopping experience more exciting. In the 13 stores refurbished so far, the sky-high shelving is down and the warehouse look is gone, color is everywhere, and a bright glass front has replaced the drab exteriors. The number of individual items stocked has been reduced 20 percent to make it easier to shop. All this redesign comes at a very high price, however, and the process of converting all 683 U.S. stores will be slow.

Megastores that combine all three elements of the chain in one location are planned as a way to compete with specialty stores and big department store chains. Covering 95,000 square feet, the new Kidsworld stores will open at the rate of two a year and will also house party areas, haircutting shops, and photo studios in an attempt to keep shoppers in the store longer. But one company board member worries that the stores are so big, "the country can only sustain so many."

Despite poor results so far, Toys Я Us is still adding stores overseas, with 40 new locations planned for 1997, most of them in Japan. Weakening economies in Europe and Asia may be partly responsible for the expansion's failure to hit the 30-percent-a-year growth goal, although Goldstein remains confident.

But Toys Я Us may benefit most from a powerful external force: a surging market for toys, helped along by a booming mini-industry in licensed toys related to popular movies such as *Star Wars*. After losing money when it ran out of stock on popular toys in the past, at least one redesigned Toys Я Us in New Jersey is ready with a giant *Star Wars* display.

Questions

1. How does Michael Goldstein's plan for redesigning the stores respond to customers' buying behavior?
2. Goldstein has chosen not to compete on price. What else can Toys Я Us offer consumers?
3. "There a point at which you get so much market share—in any industry—that there's nowhere to go but down," says investment portfolio manager Bernice Behar of John Hancock Funds. Comment on this assessment of Toys Я Us's prospects for the future.
4. The redesign of its stores and the construction of megastores will eat into the firm's capital budget for many years to come. Do you think this is a wise choice?
5. Should Toys Я Us continue to expand overseas? Why or why not?

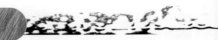

Connecting to the Web

The following Web sites will give you additional information and points of view about topics covered in this chapter. Many sites lead to other related Internet locations, so approach this list with the spirit of an explorer.

AMERICAN DEMOGRAPHICS/MARKETING TOOLS

http://www.demographics.com/home.htm

This site is your link to demographic data. Surfers gain access to summaries and articles from the archives of *American Demographics*, a publication targeted at marketers in search of consumer trends; *Marketing Tools*, a publication on information-based marketing; and *Forecast*, a newsletter of demographics and consumer economics. The site allows you to conduct keyword searches to target specific information.

AMERICAN MARKETING ASSOCIATION

http://www.ama.org/

This site introduces AMA publications (including *Marketing News* and the *Journal of Marketing*), conferences, and library and information services. It also includes on-line job listings in marketing. Many services cost money and are open only to AMA members.

BARNES & NOBLE

http://www.barnesandnoble.com

AMAZON.COM

http://www.amazon.com

With the achievement of its performance goal of expanding into on-line book retailing, Barnes & Noble is now going head to head with Amazon.com. To become more competitive, Barnes & Noble's Web storefront gives customers the opportunity to post and share book recommendations and reviews, just as they do on Amazon.com. Browse and compare the marketing approaches of these companies.

THE GALLUP ORGANIZATION

http://www.gallup.com

One of the world's premier market research companies is the Gallup Organization, which has conducted public opinion surveys since 1935. The Gallup Web site includes recent Gallup polls and special reports. It also introduces users to the marketing and management research available in the United States and abroad.

HARLEY-DAVIDSON

http://www.harley-davidson.com

HARLEY OWNERS GROUP

http://www.harley-davidson.com/experience/family/hog

Visit these Harley-Davidson sites for a look at relationship marketing on the Web. Events and festivals are announced and friendships among Harley owners are encouraged. Membership and special products are offered in the Harley Owners Group, which targets a specific consumer lifestyle.

HISPANIC MARKET CONNECTION: THE HISPANIC MARKET

http://www.hmc-research.com/market.html

Hispanic Market Connection is a marketing firm specializing in Hispanic-American consumers. The company's Web site explores the lifestyles, values, and culture of this growing market segment. Included is a Hispanic Market Report, which focuses on such vital marketing topics as cultural characteristics, media usage, and spending patterns. This is an important resource for students trying to learn more about how group identity influences consumer behavior.

LEVI STRAUSS & CO.

http://www.levistrauss.com

Visit the Web site of Levi Strauss and investigate how the company uses psychographic variables to market their casual business wear. Included is the Casual Businesswear Kit, a detailed guide for human resources managers for starting, maintaining, and updating a company's dress policy.

PURPLE MOON

http://www.purple-moon.com

Purple Moon's Web site promotes games such as *Rockett's New School* and *Secret Paths in the Forest.*

REEBOK

http://www.reebok.com/humnrights/index.html

The social and cultural environment moved Reebok to join with Amnesty International to sponsor the Human Rights Now! international concert tour and to create the Reebok Human Rights Award. Visit this site for an on-line look at Reebok's program.

SPALDING

http://www.spalding.com/womens.html

Marketing sporting goods to women is now big business. A case in point is Spalding's online marketing campaign, which includes a site dedicated exclusively to women's products.

U.S. DEPARTMENT OF COMMERCE GLOBAL EXPORT MARKET INFORMATION SYSTEM (GEMS) HOME PAGE

http://www.itaiep.doc.gov/

Managers who think there is a market for their products abroad will find help at this site, which was developed by the U.S. Department of Commerce. Included is the Central and Eastern Europe Business Information Center Online, which presents marketing opportunities for U.S. firms interested in doing business in the newly independent countries that were once part of the Soviet Union.

chapter 12

Developing and *pricing* products

When your new product is a blockbuster

These are tough times for Hollywood. Audiences are getting harder to please; top stars are pricey and volatile. Box-office hits are tougher to predict, and the make-or-break opportunity for success has narrowed to the crucial weekend when a new film opens. With the cost of filmmaking going through the roof, the stakes are higher than ever before. But the demand for films remains strong, and studios have no shortage.

There may be help on the financial front, with an innovative form of investment in which studios temporarily shift ownership of their movies to big outside investors. The investors pay for marketing and distribution but have no artistic control over the movies that are made. They share in any profits or losses, and after 5 years the studios buy back the films.

With the possibility of financial freedom in the offing, what does it really take to develop a new hit film? A good story, stars the public wants to see, and jazzy special effects may not be enough anymore. A new breed of directors is rising in the anything-goes atmosphere of Hollywood in the 1990s, and they bring an energy and intensity that seems to reflect the tastes of a generation raised on MTV and trendy TV commercials. Their style is variously described as overheated, overloud, overhyped, and overenergized, and if it lacks the subtlety and sophistication of an earlier generation, it does seem to sell well. The appeal of movies ranging from *Clueless* to *Men in Black*, though it may give up substance in favor of style, is widespread enough for their directors to be in as much demand as their stars. On the strength of such successes, the film industry expects markedly better times ahead.

Do such movies set new styles, or do they reflect the changing world in which they are made? It remains an open question. But one hot director, Baz Luhmann, has this answer: "There are, after all, only a

handful of stories, of plots, that don't change, but the way we communicate them does change. And that's our task, to find the language of the moment."

66 *There are, after all, only a handful of stories, of plots, that don't change, but the way we communicate them does change. And that's our task, to find the language of the moment.* 99

—Baz Luhmann, film director

Hollywood may represent an unusual industry, one known for making its own rules. But in fact its customer focus and sensitivity to costs are familiar to many business managers. Even its reliance on successful formulas in the form of copycat plots and sequels, is a mainstream product strategy.

By focusing on the learning objectives in this chapter, you will better understand such activities as product development and pricing. After reading this chapter, you should be able to

1 Identify a product and distinguish between consumer and industrial products.

2 Trace the stages of the product-life cycle.

3 Explain the importance of branding, packaging, and labeling.

4 Identify the various pricing objectives that govern pricing decisions and describe the price-setting tools used in making these decisions.

5 Discuss pricing strategies and tactics for both existing and new products.

In chapter 11 we introduced the four components of the marketing mix: product, price, promotion, and place (distribution). In this chapter we will look more closely at the first two of these components. Specifically, we will examine the complex nature of products. Managers must keep these complexities in mind when developing, naming, packaging, labeling, and pricing both new and existing products.

Let's begin by looking at the way in which one well-known company responded to competitive threats in its marketing environment.

▶ In 1997, Digital Equipment Corporation (DEC) Chairman Robert Palmer realized that his company had started to lose sight of the competitive landscape of the computer industry. Because the company was being outrun by competitor companies, DEC needed to make adjustments to recover from several quarters of disappointing earnings. The answer, DEC hopes, is its new pricing strategy on its line of Alpha servers and workstations. Prices are being aggressively reduced by up to 47 percent on midrange products such as the AlphaServer 4000 processor, with additional cuts of up to 27 percent of high-range products such as the AlphaServer 8400. For the price reductions to provide lasting pay-offs, however, DEC must cut some operating costs, add some new designs, and reconsider its methods of distribution.[1]

In making the decisions that it ultimately did, DEC faced a basic fact of business reality: It is virtually impossible to focus on one element of the marketing mix (pricing) without encountering one or more of the others (product design and distribution planning). In this chapter we will look more closely at the complex nature of perhaps the most important component in the marketing mix: the product. In particular, we will show why managers must keep in mind their wide variety when developing, naming, packaging, labeling, and pricing products.

What Is a Product?

In developing the marketing mix for any products, whether ideas, goods, or services, marketers must consider what consumers really buy when they purchase products. Only then can they plan their strategies effectively. We will begin this section where product strategy begins: with an understanding of product features and benefits. Next, we will describe the major classifications of products, both consumer and industrial. Finally, we will discuss the most important component in the offerings of any business: its product mix.

Features and Benefits

Customers do not buy products simply because they like the products themselves: They buy products because they like what the products can *do* for them, either physically or emotionally. To succeed, then, a product must include the right features and offer the right benefits. Product **features** are the qualities, tangible and intangible, that a company builds into its products, such as a 12-horsepower motor on a lawn mower. To be saleable, a product's features also must provide benefits: The mower must provide an attractive lawn.

Obviously, features and benefits play extremely important roles in the pricing of products. If you look carefully at the Price Waterhouse ad in Figure 12.1, you will realize that products are much more than just *visible* features and benefits. In buying a product, customers are also buying an image and a reputation. The marketers of the Price Waterhouse consulting services advertised here are well aware that brand name, labeling, and after-purchase satisfaction are indispensable facets of their product. The ad is designed to remind business customers that such features as getting results implemented, having practical ideas, and offering a global perspective go hand-in-hand with PW's commitment to integrity and trustworthiness.

feature
Tangible quality that a company builds into a product

Figure 12.1 Intangible Features and Benefits of Service Products

IF CONSULTANTS HAD TO EXECUTE EVERYTHING
THEY WROTE, PERHAPS THEY'D WRITE A LITTLE LESS.

Unfortunately, that's just the way most consultants work. They put everything on

paper, but hardly anything into practice. But at Price Waterhouse, we won't propose

an idea unless we can implement it. Whether we're helping a company build a global

supply chain or integrating its global operations, Price Waterhouse is committed to

taking ideas from conception to completion. To find out more about how we

work, call Price Waterhouse or visit our web site at http://www.pw.com

Price Waterhouse
Mind & Muscle™

Classifying Goods and Services

One way to classify a product is according to expected buyers. Buyers fall into two groups: buyers of consumer products and buyers of industrial products. As we saw in chapter 11, the consumer and industrial buying processes differ significantly. Not surprisingly, then, marketing products to consumers is vastly different from marketing them to other companies.

Classifying Consumer Products

Consumer products are commonly divided into three categories that reflect buyer behavior: convenience, shopping, and specialty products.

- **Convenience goods** (such as milk and newspapers) and **convenience services** (such as those offered by fast-food restaurants) are consumed rapidly and regularly. They are inexpensive and are purchased often and with little expenditure of time and effort.

- **Shopping goods** (such as stereos and tires) and **shopping services** (such as insurance) are more expensive and are purchased less often than convenience products.

convenience good/service
Inexpensive product purchased and consumed rapidly and regularly

shopping good/service
Moderately expensive, infrequently purchased product

Consumers often compare brands, sometimes in different stores. They may also evaluate alternatives in terms of style, performance, color, price, and other criteria.

specialty good/service
Expensive, rarely purchased product

■ **Specialty goods** (such as wedding gowns) and **specialty services** (such as catering for wedding receptions) are extremely important and expensive purchases. Consumers usually decide on precisely what they want and will accept no substitutes. They will often go from store to store, sometimes spending a great deal of money and time to get a specific product.

Classifying Industrial Products

Depending on how much they cost and how they will be used, industrial products can be divided into two categories: expense and capital items.

expense item
Industrial product purchased and consumed rapidly and regularly for daily operations

Expense Items. **Expense items** are any materials and services that are consumed within a year by firms producing other goods or supplying other services. The most obvious expense items are industrial goods used directly in the production process (for example, bulkloads of tea processed into tea bags).

In addition, support materials help to keep a business running without directly entering the production process. Oil, for instance, keeps the tea-bagging machines running but is not used in tea bags. Similarly, supplies (pencils, brooms, gloves, paint) are consumed quickly and regularly by every business. Finally, services such as window cleaning, equipment installation, and temporary office help are essential to daily operations. Because these items are used frequently, purchases are often automatic or require little decision making.

capital item
Expensive, long-lasting infrequently purchased industrial product such as a building

Capital Items. **Capital items** are permanent (that is, expensive and long-lasting) goods and services. All these items have expected lives of more than a year, and typically up to several years. Expensive buildings (offices, factories), fixed equipment (water towers, baking ovens), and accessory equipment (computers, airplanes) are capital goods. Capital services are those for which long-term commitments are made. These may include purchases for employee food services, building and equipment maintenance, or legal services. Because capital items are expensive and purchased infrequently, they often involve decisions by high-level managers.

The Product Mix

product mix
Group of products that a firm makes available for sale

The group of products that a company makes available for sale, whether consumer, industrial, or both, is its **product mix**. Black & Decker, for example, makes toasters, vacuum cleaners, electric drills, and a variety of other appliances and tools. 3M Corp. makes everything from Post-it notes to laser optics.

Many companies begin with a single product. Over time, however, they find that their initial products fail to suit all the consumers shopping for the product type. To meet market demand, therefore, they often introduce similar products designed to reach other consumers. ServiceMaster, for example, was among the first successful home services, offering mothproofing and carpet cleaning. Then they expanded into lawn care (TruGreen, ChemLawn), pest control (Terminix), cleaning (Merry Maids), and home warranty services (American Home Shield) for various residential services applications. A group of similar products intended for similar but not identical buyers who will use them in similar ways is a **product line**.

product line
Group of similar products intended for a similar group of buyers who will use them in similar ways

Companies may also extend their horizons and identify opportunities outside existing product lines. The result—multiple (or diversified) product lines—is evident at firms such as ServiceMaster. After years of serving residential customers, ServiceMaster has added product lines for business and industry called Commercial Services (landscaping and janitorial), Management Services (management of schools and institutions, including their physical facilities, financial and personnel resources, and management problems), and Healthcare Management Services (management of support services—plant operations, asset management, laundry/linen, clinical equipment maintenance—for long-term care facilities). Multiple product lines allow a company to grow more rapidly and can help to offset the consequences of slow sales in any one product line.

Developing New Products

To expand or diversify product lines—indeed, just to survive—firms must develop and successfully introduce streams of new products. Faced with competition and shifting consumer preferences, no firm can count on a single successful product to carry it forever. Even basic products that have been widely purchased for decades require nearly constant renewal. Consider the unassuming facial tissue. The white tissue in the low rectangular box has been joined (if not replaced) by tissues of many different colors and patterns. They arrive in boxes shaped and decorated for nearly every room in the house, and they are made to be placed or carried not only in the bathroom but in the purse, the briefcase, and the car.

In this section we will focus on the process by which companies develop the new goods and services that allow them to survive. We will also briefly discuss the special issues that arise when firms develop products for international markets.

The New Product
Development Process

▶ The demand for food and beverage ingredients will grow more than 6 percent per year, reaching $5 billion by the year 2000. Flavors and flavor enhancers will be the biggest part of that growth, especially artificial sweeteners. However, companies that develop and sell these products face a big problem: It costs between $30 and $50 million and can take as long as 8 to 10 years to get a new product through the approval process at the Food and Drug Administration. Testing, both for FDA approval and for marketing, can be the most time-consuming stage of development. For example, Hoechst Celanese Corp.'s acesulfame K sweetener has been through more than 90 safety studies and 1,000 technical studies to see how it performs in various kinds of beverages. Additional stages, after testing, include advertising and demonstration to food producers at the right time (when they are thinking of reformulating their products with new ingredients). A lot of time, patience, and money are required to cash in on the growth of ingredients for the food and beverage market.[2]

Like Hoechst Celanese Corp., many firms maintain research and development departments or divisions for exploring new product possibilities. Why do they devote so

"We're looking for the kind of bad taste that
will grab—but not appall."

many resources to thinking about products and exploring their possibilities, rejecting many seemingly good ideas along the way? How do they conduct these early explorations into new product possibilities?

We will address these questions in this section. We will see, for instance, that the high mortality rate for new ideas means that only a few new products eventually reach the market. Moreover, for many companies, speed to market with a product is often as important as care in developing it. Finally, product development is a long, complex, and expensive process. Companies do not dream up new products one day and ship them to retailers the next. In fact, new products usually involve carefully planned and sometimes risky commitments of time and resources.

Product Mortality Rates

It is estimated that it takes 50 new product ideas to generate one product that finally reaches the market. Even then, only a few of those survivors become *successful* products. Many seemingly great ideas have failed as products. Indeed, creating a successful new product has become more and more difficult, even for the most experienced marketers. For one thing, the number of new products hitting the market each year has increased dramatically. For example, 25,500 new household, grocery, and drugstore items were introduced in 1996. At any given time, however, the average supermarket carries a total of only 20,000 to 25,000 different items. There simply isn't enough room or customer demand in the marketplace, so about 9 out of 10 new products will fail.[3] The products with the best chances for success are the ones that are innovative and deliver unique benefits.

The Natural Environment

Where Green Products Yield Green Dollars

"The earth can't withstand a systematic increase of material things. If we grow by using more stuff, I'm afraid we'd better start looking for a new planet." With these words, Robert Shapiro, CEO of biotechnology firm Monsanto, states his case for pursuing environmentally friendly agricultural products to help feed the world. Scientists warn that unless things change, the expected doubling of Earth's population over the next 30 years will create a world of unimaginable scarcity and hardship. Shapiro believes that just to feed the planet we will need to get double the yield from every acre of land, and that doesn't begin to heal the already existing pockets of poverty and starvation.

Under his leadership Monsanto has begun intensive research in genetic engineering to come up with heartier pest- and disease-resistant seeds for such staples as cotton, potatoes, soybeans, and canola, and hormones to increase cows' milk production. Although some environmental groups worry that the long-term impact of creating biotechnology products is unknown, sales of the new products are strong.

> *"The earth can't withstand a systematic increase of material things. If we grow by using more stuff, I'm afraid we'd better start looking for a new planet."*
>
> —Robert Shapiro, CEO, Monsanto

That makes Shapiro happy too. He sees the interests of Earth, its population, and the company's shareholders as one. "I don't think it ultimately matters whether my soul is pure or I want to make a lot of money for shareholders; we come out at the same place: If Monsanto and other companies can get environmentally better products that people want to market faster at lower costs, we will kick butt in the marketplace."

Speed to Market

A product's chances for success are also better if it beats its competition to market. Consider the following scenario:

▶ A classic example of the advantage of getting a competitive head start is Miller Lite beer. Miller dominated the light beer market for years because it established itself with consumers before its competitors even got started. Miller was 1 year ahead of Schlitz Light, 2 years ahead of Anheuser-Busch Natural Light, and 3 years ahead of some 22 other brands. In 1994, after years of expensive advertising, Bud Light finally made up lost ground to take the lead in market share. Many additional years will pass, however, before Anheuser Busch recovers the higher profits that Miller Lite enjoyed during the decade of its market leadership.[4]

The principle reflected in this case is actually quite simple and applies to all industries: The more rapidly a product moves from the laboratory to the marketplace, the more likely it is to survive. By introducing new products ahead of competitors, companies quickly establish market leadership. They become entrenched in the market before being challenged by late-arriving competitors. How important is **speed to market**—that is, a firm's success in responding to customer demand or market changes? One study has estimated that any product that is only three months late to market (that is, 3 months behind the leader) sacrifices 12 percent of its lifetime profit potential. A product that is 6 months late will lose 33 percent.

speed to market
Strategy of introducing new products to respond quickly to customer or market changes

The Seven-Step Development Process

To increase their chances of developing a successful new product, many firms adopt some variation on a basic seven-step process. This process is not entirely the same for goods producers and service producers.

1 *Product ideas.* Product development begins with a search for ideas for new products. Product ideas can come from consumers, the sales force, research and development people, or engineering personnel.

2 *Screening.* The second stage is an attempt to eliminate all product ideas that do not mesh with the firm's abilities, expertise, or objectives. Representatives from marketing, engineering, and production must have input at this stage.

3 *Concept testing.* Once ideas have been screened, companies use market research to get consumers' input about product benefits and price.

4 *Business analysis.* After consumers have given their opinions, marketers must compare manufacturing costs and benefits to see whether the product meets minimum profitability goals.

5 *Prototype development.* Once the firm has determined the potential profitability of a product, engineering or research and development produce a preliminary version. Prototypes can be extremely expensive, often requiring extensive hand crafting, tooling, and development of components.

6 *Product testing and test marketing.* Using what it has learned from the prototype, the company goes into limited production. It then tests the product to see whether it meets performance requirements. If it does, it is made available for sale in limited areas. Because promotional campaigns and distribution channels must be established for test markets, this stage is quite costly.

7 *Commercialization.* If test-marketing results are positive, the company will begin full-scale production and marketing. Gradual commercialization, with the firm providing the product to more and more areas over time, prevents undue strain on initial production capabilities. On the other hand, delays in commercialization may give competitors a chance to bring out their own versions of the product.

You'll Never Get Lost Again

A new product is on its way to the consumer market that may soon be as indispensable as your spare tire, and it guarantees you'll never get lost on the road again.

The product, called on-board navigation, is a sophisticated method of pinpointing the car's location with input from both a global positioning satellite (GPS) and a dead reckoning system that monitors turns and direction. Digital maps of the continental United States are available on accompanying CDs that also offer a database of restaurants, gas stations, hotels, ATMs, and other common destinations around the country.

All you need to do is enter the desired destination, from a menu or from a personalized file in the system's address box, and start driving. The on-board navigator gives turn-by-turn directions, both on its screen and by voice output. If you miss a turn, the system automatically reprograms the chosen route to get you back where you belong.

General Motors and Ford will soon feature navigation systems in their new models, following BMW and Japanese and European car makers, who already offer them for about $2,800. Chrysler thinks it's too expensive, but a GPS supplier in California predicts the price will drop an average of 30 percent a year. Plans to combine navigation with other features such as a CD player, a no-hands cellular phone, or even a voice-activated personal computer should make the device more widely accepted.

Variations in the Process for Services

The development of services involves many of the same stages as goods development. Basically, steps 2, 3, 4, 6, and 7 are the same. There are, however, some important differences in steps 1 and 5:

definition of the service package
Identification of the features that characterize a service product

- *Service ideas.* The search for service ideas includes a task called **definition of the service package**: identification of the tangible and intangible features that characterize the service (see chapter 15) and service specifications.[5] For example, a firm that wants to offer year-end cleaning services to office buildings might commit itself to the following specifications: The building interior will be cleaned by midnight, January 5, including floor polishing of all aisles, carpets swept free of all dust and debris, and washbowls and lavatory equipment polished, with no interruption or interference to the customer.

service process design
Three aspects (process selection, worker requirements, and facilities requirements) of developing a service product

- *Service process design.* Instead of prototype development, services require a three-part **service process design**. Process selection identifies each step in the service, including the sequence and the timing. Worker requirements specify employee behaviors, skills, capabilities, and interactions with customers during the service encounter. Facility requirements designate all the equipment that supports delivery of the service.[6]

By using this process, Florida Power and Light (FPL), the third-largest investor-owned utility in the United States, has emerged as a stalwart in customer-focused services in its industry. FPL's Service Assurance Systems Group, which is responsible for improving the service quality of the company's phone operations, interviewed customers to find out what they expect when they call to conduct business. The results from interviews, focus groups, and surveys revealed that customers want to be treated politely while being kept on hold, wanted their business to be conducted in a timely manner, and wanted to be treated as a valued customer. As a result of this customer feedback, FPL revised the way they organize and retrieve information for incoming calls. They also revised processes used for different types of phone services at FPL customer service centers. The new processes specify each step in the service, including the sequence and the timing. Worker requirements are specified, including employee behaviors and types of interactions with customers during the service call. As customer satisfaction measures have improved, FPL has been able to provide the better service without increasing staff size, so costs have not increased.[7]

The Product Life Cycle

A product that reaches the market enters the **product life cycle** (**PLC**): a series of stages through which it passes during its profit-producing life. Depending on the product's ability to attract and keep customers over time, its PLC may be a matter of months, years, or decades. Strong products (Kellogg's Corn Flakes, Maxwell House coffee, H&R Block tax preparation) have had extremely long, productive lives.

product life cycle (PLC)
Series of stages in a product's profit-producing life

Stages in the Product Life Cycle

The life cycle for both goods and services is a natural process in which products are born, grow in stature, mature, and finally decline and die.[8] Figure 12.2 shows the four stages of the cycle, not yet complete, for VCRs. The product was introduced in the late 1970s and is widely used today. (Note that profits lag behind sales because of the extensive costs of developing new products.) If the market becomes saturated, sales will begin to decline. Sales will also fall if new products, such as double-sided digital video disk, send the VCR the way of the eight-track audio player.[9]

1 *Introduction.* The introduction stage begins when the product reaches the marketplace. During this stage, marketers focus on making potential consumers aware of the product and its benefits. Because of extensive promotional and development costs, profits are nonexistent.

2 *Growth.* If the new product attracts and satisfies enough consumers, sales begin to climb rapidly. During this stage, the product begins to show a profit. Other firms in the industry move rapidly to introduce their own versions.

3 *Maturity.* Sales growth begins to slow. Although the product earns its highest profit level early in this stage, increased competition eventually leads to price cutting and lower profits. Toward the end of the stage, sales start to fall.

4 *Decline.* During this final stage, sales and profits continue to fall. New products in the introduction stage take away sales. Companies remove or reduce promotional support (ads and salespeople) but may let the product linger to provide some profits.

Figure 12.2 The Product Life Cycle for VCRs

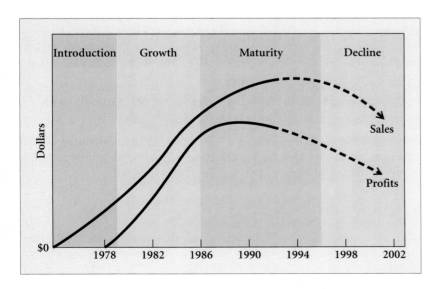

Table 12.1 Marketing Strategy Over the Life Cycle

	Introduction	Growth	Maturity	Decline
Marketing strategy emphasis	Market development	Increase market share	Defend market share	Maintain efficiency in exploiting product
Pricing strategy	High price, unique product/cover introduction costs	Lower price with passage of time	Price at or below competitors'	Set price to stay profitable or decrease to liquidate
Promotion strategy	Mount sales promotion for product awareness	Appeal to mass market; emphasize features, brand	Emphasize brand differences, benefits, loyalty	Reinforce loyal customers; reduce promotion expenditures
Place strategy	Distribute through selective outlets	Build intensive network of outlets	Enlarge distribution network	Be selective in distribution; trim away unprofitable outlets

Adjusting Marketing Strategy During the Life Cycle

As a product passes from stage to stage, marketing strategy changes, too. Each aspect of the marketing mix—product, price, promotion, place (distribution)—is reexamined for each stage of the life cycle. Changes in strategy for all four life-cycle stages are summarized in Table 12.1.

Extending Product Life: An Alternative to New Products

Not surprisingly, companies wish that they could maintain a product's position in the maturity stage for longer periods of time. Sales of television sets, for example, have been revitalized time and time again by introducing changes such as color, portability, miniaturization, and stereo capability. In fact, many companies have extended product life through a variety of creative means.[10] Foreign markets, for example, offer three approaches for longer life cycles:

product extension
Existing, unmodified product that is marketed globally

■ In **product extension**, an existing product is marketed globally, instead of just domestically. Coca-Cola and Levi's 501 jeans are prime examples of successful international product extensions.

product adaptation
Product modified to have greater appeal in foreign markets

■ With **product adaptation**, the basic product is modified to give it greater appeal in different countries. In Germany, for example, the McDonald's meal includes beer, and Ford puts the steering wheel on the right side for exports to Japan. Because it involves product changes, this approach is usually more costly than product extension.

reintroduction
Process of reviving for new markets products that are obsolete in older ones

■ **Reintroduction** means reviving for new markets products that are becoming obsolete in older ones. NCR, for example, has reintroduced manually operated cash registers in Latin America.

These examples show that the beginning of a sales downturn in the maturity stage is not necessarily the time to start abandoning a product; rather, it is often a time to realize that the old approach is starting to fade and to search for a new approach.

Identifying Products

As we noted earlier, developing a product's features is only part of a marketer's job. Marketers must also encourage consumers to identify products. Three important tools for accomplishing this task are branding, packaging, and labeling.

Branding Products

The name *Coca-Cola* is the best-known brand in the world. In fact, the name *Coca-Cola* is so valuable that its executives like to say that if all of the company's other assets were obliterated, they could walk over to the bank and borrow $100 billion for rebuilding, just on the strength of the brand name.[11] Brand names such as *Coca-Cola* are symbols for characterizing products and distinguishing them from one another. They were originally introduced to simplify the process when consumers are faced with a wealth of purchase decisions. **Branding**, then, is a process of using symbols to communicate the qualities of a particular product made by a particular producer. Brands are designed to signal uniform quality: Customers who try and like a product can return to it by remembering its name. Companies that spend the large amount of money needed to develop brands are looking for one thing from consumers: brand loyalty. That is, they want to attract customers who will keep coming back to the same brand.

An issue of growing importance in branding strategy is faced by firms that sell products internationally: They must also consider how product names will translate in various languages. In Spanish, for example, the name of Chevrolet's now-defunct Nova simply became *no va*: it does not go. Sales were particularly poor in South America. Similarly, Rolls-Royce was once going to name a new touring car: Silver Mist. Rolls changed the name to *Silver Shadow* when it discovered that *mist* is German for *manure*.[12] Naturally, foreign companies hoping to sell in the United States must be equally careful.

Types of Brand Names

Virtually every product has a brand name. Generally, the different types of brand names—national, licensed, and private brands—increase buyers' awareness of the nature and quality of products that must compete with any number of other products. When the consumer is satisfied with the quality of a recognizable product, marketers work to achieve brand loyalty among the largest possible segment of repeat buyers.

National Brands. Brand-name products that are produced by, widely distributed by, and carry the name of the manufacturer are called **national brands**. These brands (say, Scotch tape or Scope mouthwash) are often widely recognized by consumers because of national advertising campaigns. The costs of developing a positive image for a national brand are high. Some companies therefore use a national brand on several related products. Procter & Gamble, for instance, now markets Ivory shampoo, capitalizing on the widely recognized name of its bar soap and dishwashing liquid.

Most national brand names are valuable assets that signal product recognition and uniform quality. Not surprisingly, millions of dollars have been spent developing names such as Noxzema, Prudential, and Minute Maid. Millions more have been spent in getting consumers to attach meaning to these names. As a rule, therefore, they rarely change. In 1997, however, IBM Corp.'s new $10-million global PC ad campaign began emphasizing "solutions" rather than products. This shift in the positioning of the company's image reflects IBM's recognition that its true product is not the hardware but a package of services and computer technology to help IBM customers by offering customized solutions to their information technology problems. The "solution" may involve hardware, software, technical expertise, networking service, and financing for systems that help the customers to add value to their business operations.[13]

Licensed Brands. It has become increasingly common for nationally recognized companies (and even personalities) to sell the rights to place their names on products. These **licensed brands** are very big business today. Tie-ins with movies and other entertainment vehicles generate more than 20 percent of all licensed merchandise sales, such as products from the sixteenth James Bond film, *Goldeneye*. Some companies—Dixons Stores Group (United Kingdom) and Kodak—paid money up front to use the film's name in promotions that linked Bond to home-cinema equipment and professional photographers. Nintendo's U.K. distributor is launching a new *Goldeneye* game, and

branding
Process of using symbols to communicate the qualities of a product made by a particular producer

national brand
Brand-name product produced by, widely distributed by, and carrying the name of a manufacturer

licensed brand
Brand-name product for whose name the seller has purchased the right from an organization or individual

Each and every day, thousands of businesses build their sites on the Internet and wonder: When does the excitement begin? Where are the new customers, the improved relationships, the lower overhead? Surprise, surprise. You can't expect it to happen automatically.

It takes a solution. The good news is, a call to IBM can help put things in motion. **IBM Internet solutions** provide a unique combination of technology, professional services and know-how that can bring new value to just about every kind of business, making the most of existing investments. Here are some of our customers who are already reporting results:

Japan Airlines: uses Internet reservations to boost revenue by $4 million.

NHL: online store attracts more than a million hits per month.

Arena di Verona: expands opera audience using online ticketing.

Supervox: French wholesaler finds an $8 million opportunity in previously untapped market.

Find out how **the Internet can transform your business.** Visit us at www.ibm.com/internetsolutions or call us at 1 800 IBM-7080, ext. NC01, to enroll in our free seminar.

"the yippeee, we're on the Internet! now what?" solution

IBM.

Solutions for a small planet

IBM's new identity puts less emphasis on selling computers; it now focuses on helping businesses solve problems that will lead them to more profitable performance. The basic message is, "Why IBM? Because we will provide a high-value solution to your business problem." This "solutions" and "benefits" emphasis is highlighted in the ad with examples of boosting an airline's revenues with a new reservation system, using an online store for the National Hockey League to sell products to customer hockey fans, expanding an opera audience through online ticketing, and creating a new sales opportunity for a French wholesaler. Technology, professional services, and technical know-how are put together by IBM to solve any type of business problem relating to information technology. Getting a high-value result for the customer is important to IBM.

plans are under-way for a Bond restaurant chain and theme park attractions.[14] Shaq, Guns 'N' Roses, and Hard Rock Cafe will all make millions on licensed apparel sales this year. Free advertising from licensed T-shirts and other clothing is an added bonus.

> " *This year we'll net $10 million on licensing, and we should eventually be able to make $30 million to $35 million annually with very little commitment of capital.* "

— Michele Scannavini, manager of sales and marketing at Ferrari

For some companies, licensing has become as profitable than their main line of business. For example, Ferrari found that selling its name can be more profitable than selling its famous cars. Ferrari officials recognized that "Ferrari is as much style as substance . . . as much a legend as it is a car company." They reconceived the company name as a brand and decided to extend and exploit it. The famous stallion logo appears on luxury goods, sportswear, toys, and school supplies. In 1996 Ferrari earned just $2 million selling more than 3,000 cars; for 1997, says Michele Scannavini, manager of sales and marketing, "we'll net $10 million on licensing, and we should eventually be able to make $30 million to $35 million annually with very little commitment of capital."[15]

Private Brands. When a wholesaler or retailer develops a brand name and has the manufacturer place that name on the product, the resulting product name is a **private brand** (or **private label**). One of the best-known sellers of private brands is Sears, which carries such lines as Craftsman tools, Canyon River Blues denim clothing, and Kenmore appliances.

> Between 1989 and 1994, the share of private brand sales in supermarkets rose from 18.2 to 19.7 percent, and is projected to become 30 percent by 2002.[16] The increase has been steep enough for many marketers to resort to a tactic known as fighting brands: repricing national brands so that they represent a higher-quality but acceptably priced alternative to private brands. Miller Beer, for example, has repositioned its Miller High Life brand, and Procter & Gamble has cut prices on a host of products, including Joy detergent, Camay soap, and Luvs diapers. Like other companies, RJR Nabisco has decided to join the private brand parade as well as fight it by marketing its own private-brand cookies and crackers.[17]

▶ **THE WIDE WIDE WORLD OF PRIVATE LABELS.** The growth of consumer preference for private label products is even more evident in some foreign markets. Japan's Daiei supermarket chain, for example, launched its own Savings line of private label juices. Daiei's products include juice made from Brazilian oranges and are priced 40 percent below American national brands (such as Dole and Tropicana), and a pint of Daiei's premium ice cream sells for half the price of Lady Borden. (Ironically, Daiei buys its ice cream from the same supplier and packages it in cartons quite similar to Lady Borden's.)

> In the United Kingdom, private labels account for 36 percent of all grocery sales, compared with only 20 percent in the United States. The success stems partly from fewer national brand ads. In particular, because the British Broadcasting Corp. does not carry advertising, TV advertising, a key strategy for building brands and brand loyalty, is much less important than it is in the United States. The result is less brand loyalty among consumers. Industry structure is also a factor in the success of private labels offered by British retailers: Whereas Safeway and other major chains account for only one-fifth of U.S. grocery sales, Britain's five largest chains command nearly two-thirds of the grocery business.

> The story is much the same in North America. For example, Toronto-based Cott Corp. is putting pressure on big brands such as Coke and Pepsi. Under the Sam's American Choice label, Cott sells a billion cans of soft drinks each year at Wal-Mart. Meanwhile, Canada's Loblaw Co. Ltd. has created a line of upscale private brands called President's Choice (PC). Today, PC products, such as peanut butter and cookies, are found not only throughout Canada but in many U.S. grocery stores. The success of PC is one reason why the private label share of the Canadian soft drink market has reached 25 percent.[18]

Packaging Products

With a few exceptions (fresh fruits and vegetables, structural steel), products need some form of **packaging** in which to be sold. More important, a package also serves as an in-store advertisement that makes the product attractive, displays the brand name, and identifies features and benefits. It also reduces the risk of damage, breakage, or spoilage and increases the difficulty of stealing small products. Recent advances in product usage and the materials available for packaging have created additional roles for packaging. For example, a paper-based material that can be used as a cooking container has made Budget Gourmet dinners a low-cost entry in the dinner-entree market. No-drip-spout bottles have enhanced sales and brand loyalty for Clorox bleach.

private brand (or private label)
Brand-name product that a wholesaler or retailer has commissioned from a manufacturer

packaging
Physical container in which a product is sold, advertised, or protected

Packaging also produces about 50 million tons of waste each year—approximately one-third of all waste in the United States. It also consumes natural resources. Not surprisingly, it is a source of ongoing controversy. Business is responding to these concerns—especially the 46 members of a consortium in the United States. Some of their accomplishments:

▶ General Motors ordered suppliers to stop using Styrofoam dividers when shipping parts. Instead, they are to bolt down parts or use cardboard dividers. Landfill waste produced by every midsize GM car is down from 82 to 13 pounds.

▶ Sears nows sells nuts and bolts from open bins instead of separate blister packs. Plastic waste has been cut by 166,000 pounds per year.

▶ Digital Equipment Corp. spends $1 more per computer because it has redesigned one internal component to be more rugged. Packaging needs per unit dropped from $15.90 to $5.10.[19]

Labeling Products

label
Part of product packaging that identifies its name, manufacturer, and contents

Every product has a **label** on its package. Like packaging, labeling can help market the product. Information on package labels is often regulated by the federal government. For example, labels for foods, drugs, and health and beauty products come under the authority of the Food, Drug and Cosmetic Act of 1938, which empowers the Food and Drug Administration to check the accuracy of product ingredients as reported on labels. The Fair Packaging and Labeling Act of 1966 also requires labels to include the product name, the name and address of the manufacturer or distributor, and the net quantity of product contained in the package. In effect since January 1, 1995, the Child Safety Protection Act requires labels to identify toys that are choking hazards. It also stipulates criteria for clarity and placement (for instance, labels must be visible when packages are displayed on shelves).[20]

Determining Prices

pricing
Process of determining what a company will receive in exchange for its products

In product development, managers decide what products the company will offer to customers. In **pricing**, the second major component of the marketing mix, managers decide what the company will receive in exchange for its products. In this section we will first discuss the objectives that influence a firm's pricing decisions. Then we will describe the major tools companies use to meet those objectives.

Pricing to Meet Business Objectives

pricing objectives
Goals that producers hope to attain in pricing products for sale

Companies often price products to maximize profits. But sellers hope to attain other **pricing objectives**, or goals, in selling products. For example, some firms are more interested in dominating the market or securing high market share than in making the highest possible profits. Pricing decisions are also influenced by the need to survive in competitive marketplaces, by social and ethical concerns, and even by corporate image.

Profit-Maximizing Objectives
Pricing to maximize profits is tricky. If prices are set too low, the company will probably sell many units of its product but may miss the opportunity to make additional profit on each unit (and may even lose money on each exchange). Conversely, if prices are set too high, the company will make a large profit on each item but will sell fewer units. Again, the firm loses money. In addition, it may be left with excess inventory and may have to reduce or even close production operations. To avoid these problems, companies try to set prices to sell the number of units that will generate the highest possible total profits.

In calculating profits, managers weigh receipts against costs for materials and labor. However, they also consider the capital resources (plant and equipment) that the company must tie up to generate that level of profit. The costs of marketing (such as maintaining a large sales staff) can also be substantial. Concern over the efficient use of these resources has led many firms to set prices so as to achieve a targeted level of return on sales or capital investment.

Market Share Objectives

In the long run, of course, a business must make a profit to survive. Nevertheless, many companies initially set low prices for new products. They are willing to accept minimal profits, even losses, to get buyers to try products. In other words, they use pricing to establish **market share**: a company's percentage of the total market sales for a specific product type. Even with established products, market share may outweigh profits as a pricing objective. For a product such as Philadelphia brand cream cheese, dominating a market means that consumers are more likely to buy it because they are familiar with a well-known, highly visible product. Market domination means the continuous sales of more units and thus higher profits even at a lower unit price.

market share
As a percentage, total of market sales for a specific company or product

Other Pricing Objectives

In some instances, neither profit maximizing nor market share is the best objective. During difficult economic times, for instance, loss containment and survival may become a company's main objectives. Thus, in the mid-1980s John Deere priced agricultural equipment low enough to ensure the company's survival in a severely depressed farm economy.

A still different objective might be to provide a benefit to customers. To introduce its services to industrial clients, for example, International Graffiti Control offered a set-fee pricing system (typically charging $60 a month per building) to owners who needed graffiti removed from building walls. This method shifted the risk from the customer to IGC. It appeals to customers who never know from day to day how much new graffiti will appear but who do know that removal is covered by a fixed fee.[21]

Finally, social and ethical concerns may also affect pricing for some types of products. Consider the case of a large pharmaceutical company whose pricing strategies made global headlines:

▶ In 1987, drug maker Burroughs Wellcome received FDA approval to begin selling AZT, the first and at that time the only drug shown to be effective in combating AIDS. The demand for an AIDS treatment was growing, but a storm of protest erupted when Burroughs announced that a year's supply of AZT would cost $10,000. The public outcry was immediate and unrelenting. On editorial pages around the world, Burroughs found itself condemned as a price-gouging villain. Burroughs replied that it had to recapture the huge sums it had spent on developing AZT. However, these explanations failed to appease critics. After months of relentless pressure, Burroughs set a series of price reductions. A year's supply of AZT now runs about $2,300.[22]

Price-Setting Tools

Whatever a company's objectives, managers must measure the potential impact before deciding on final prices. Two basic tools are often used for this purpose: cost-oriented pricing and breakeven analysis. As a rule, these tools are combined to identify prices that will allow the company to reach its objectives.

Cost-Oriented Pricing

Cost-oriented pricing considers the firm's desire to make a profit and takes into account the need to cover production costs. A music store manager, for instance, would begin to price CDs by calculating the cost of making them available to shoppers. Included in this figure would be store rent, employee wages, utilities, product displays, insurance, and, of course, the cost of buying CDs from the manufacturer.

markup
Amount added to an item's cost in order to sell it at a profit

Let us assume that the cost from the manufacturer is $8.00 per CD. If the store sells CDs for this price, it will not make any profit. Nor will it make a profit if it sells CDs for $8.50 each or even $10.00 or $11.00. The manager must account for product and other costs and stipulate a figure for profit. Together, these figures constitute **markup**. In this case, a reasonable markup of $7.00 over costs would result in a $15.00 selling price.

Markup is usually stated as a percentage of selling price. Markup percentage is thus calculated as follows:

$$\text{Markup percentage} = \frac{\text{Markup}}{\text{Sales price}}$$

In the case of our CD retailer, the markup percentage is 46.7:

$$\text{Markup percentage} = \frac{\$7.00}{\$15.00} = 46.7\%$$

In other words, out of every dollar taken in, 46.7 cents will be gross profit for the store. From this profit, of course, the store must still pay rent, utilities, insurance, and all other costs.

Markup can also be expressed as a percentage of cost: The $7.00 markup is 87.5 percent of the $8.00 cost of a CD ($7.00/$8.00).

Breakeven Analysis: Cost-Volume-Profit Relationships

variable cost
Cost that changes with the quantity of a product produced or sold

fixed cost
Cost unaffected by the quantity of a product produced or sold

breakeven analysis
Assessment of the quantity of a product that must be sold before the seller makes a profit

breakeven point
Quantity of a product that must be sold before the seller covers variable and fixed costs and makes a profit

Using cost-oriented pricing, a firm will cover its **variable costs**: costs that change with the number of goods or services produced or sold. It will also make some money toward paying its **fixed costs**: costs that are unaffected by the number of goods or services produced or sold. But how many units must the company sell before all its fixed costs are covered and it begins to make a profit? To determine this figure, it needs a **breakeven analysis**.

To continue our music store example, suppose again that the variable cost for each CD (in this case, the cost of buying the CD from the producer) is $8.00. This means that the store's annual variable costs depend on how many CDs are sold: the number of CDs sold times $8.00 cost for each CD. Say that fixed costs for keeping the store open for 1 year are $100,000. These costs are unaffected by the number of CDs sold; costs for lighting, rent, insurance, and salaries are steady whether the store sells no CDs, 100 CDs, or 100,000 CDs. Therefore, how many CDs must be sold to cover both fixed and variable costs and to generate some profit? The answer to that question is the **breakeven point**, which is 14,286 CDs. We arrive at this number through the following equation:

$$\text{Breakeven point (in units)} = \frac{\text{Total fixed costs}}{\text{Price} - \text{Variable cost}}$$

$$= \frac{\$100,000}{\$15.00 - \$8.00} = 14,286 \text{ CDs}$$

Figure 12.3 shows the breakeven point graphically. If the store sells fewer than 14,286 CDs, it loses money for the year. If sales exceed 14,286 CDs, profits grow by $7.00 for each CD sold. If the store sells exactly 14,286 CDs, it will cover all its costs but will earn zero profit.

Zero profitability at the breakeven point can also be seen by using the profit equation:

Profit = Total revenue − (Total fixed cost + Total variable cost)

= (14,286 CDs × $15) − [$100,000 fixed cost

+ (14,286 CDs × $8.00 variable cost)]

$0 = $214,290 − [$100,000 + $114,288] (rounded to the nearest whole CD)

Figure 12.3 Breakeven Analysis

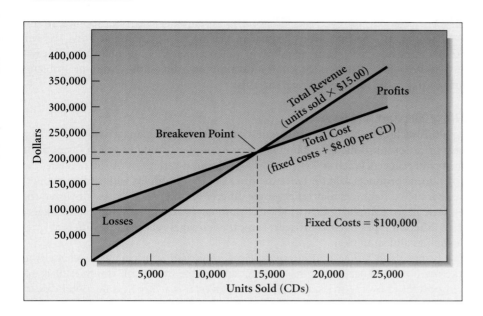

In reality, managers calculate breakeven points for each of several possible price levels. As the price per CD increases, the number of units that must be sold to reach the breakeven point decreases. As prices fall, the number of units that must be sold before reaching the breakeven point increases. Table 12.2 shows this relationship for a variety of prices. Prices below $8.00 are not considered: If the price does not exceed the item's variable cost, the breakeven point will never be reached.

The store owner would certainly like to hit the breakeven point as early as possible; after all, that is when profits will start rolling in. Why not charge $20.00 per CD, therefore, and break even earlier? The answer is that at $20.00 per CD, unit sales would drop. In setting a price, the manager must thus consider how much buyers will pay for a CD and what the store's local competitors charge.

Table 12.2 Comparative Breakeven Quantities

Price ($)	Number of CDs for Breakeven Quantity*
8.00	†
10.00	50,000
12.00	25,000
14.00	16,667
15.00	14,286
16.00	12,500
18.00	10,000
20.00	5,000

* Answer rounded to nearest whole CD.
† Doesn't exist at this price.

Pricing Strategies and Tactics

The pricing tools discussed in the previous section are valuable in helping managers set prices on specific goods. However, they do not help in setting pricing philosophies. In this section, we will discuss pricing strategy—that is, pricing as a planning activity. We will then describe some basic pricing tactics: ways in which managers implement a firm's pricing strategies. We will conclude this section by examining some of the common problems and solutions in pricing for international markets.

Pricing Strategies

Let's begin this section by addressing two questions. First: Can a manager really identify a single best price for a product? Probably not. For example, a study of prices for popular nonaspirin pain relievers (such as Tylenol and Advil) found variations of 100 percent.[23] In this market, some products sold for twice the price of other products with similar properties. Granted, such differences may reflect some differences in product costs. However, the issue is a little more complex. Such wide price differences reflect differing brand images that attract different types of customers. In turn, these images reflect vastly different pricing philosophies and strategies.

This brings us to our second question: How important is pricing as an element in the marketing mix? Because pricing has a direct and visible impact on revenues, it is extremely important to overall marketing plans. Moreover, it is a very flexible tool: It is certainly easier to change prices than to change products or distribution channels. In this section, we will focus on the ways in which pricing strategies for both new and existing products can result in widely differing prices for very similar products.

Pricing Existing Products

A firm has three options for pricing existing products:

- Pricing above prevailing market prices for similar products

- Pricing below market prices

- Pricing at or near market prices

Pricing above the market plays on the common assumption that higher price means higher quality. For example, Curtis Mathes, which manufactures televisions, VCRs, and stereos, promotes itself as the most expensive television set in the United States—but worth it. Companies such as Bloomingdale's, Godiva chocolates, and Rolls-Royce have also succeeded with this pricing philosophy.

In contrast, both Budget and Dollar car rental companies promote themselves as low-priced alternatives to Hertz and Avis. Similarly, ads for Suave hair-care products argue that Suave does what theirs does for a lot less. Pricing below prevailing market price can succeed if a firm can offer a product of acceptable quality while keeping costs below those of higher-priced competitors.

Finally, in some industries, a dominant firm called the **price leader** establishes product prices that other companies follow. This approach is called market pricing, and when it prevails, there are fewer price wars in an industry. Moreover, follower companies avoid the trouble of determining prices that consumers are willing to pay—the price leader has already done that. (Do not confuse this approach with price fixing, which occurs when producers illegally agree on prices among themselves.) Companies often resort to market pricing when products differ little in quality from one firm to another (for example, structural steel, gasoline, and many processed foods). These companies generally compete through promotion, personal selling, and service, not through price.

Pricing New Products

Companies introducing new products must often choose between two pricing policy options, selecting either very high prices or very low ones. The first option is called **price skimming**. The second is called **penetration pricing**.

price leader
Dominant firm that establishes product prices that other companies follow

price skimming
Setting an initial high price to cover new product costs and generate a profit

penetration pricing
Setting an initial low price to establish a new product in the market

Figure 12.4 Price Skimming on Cellular Phones, 1984–1996

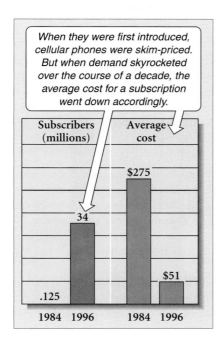

When they were first introduced, cellular phones were skim-priced. But when demand skyrocketed over the course of a decade, the average cost for a subscription went down accordingly.

Subscribers (millions)		Average cost	
.125	34	$275	$51
1984	1996	1984	1996

Price Skimming

Price skimming may allow a firm to earn a large profit on each item sold. The cash income is often needed to cover development and introduction costs. Skimming works only if marketers can convince consumers that a product is truly different from those already on the market. Moreover, the initial high profits will eventually attract competition. Microwave ovens, calculators, video games, and video cameras were all introduced at high skim prices. Naturally, prices fell as soon as new companies entered the market. As you can see from Figure 12.4, the same is true of cellular phones. As the number of subscribers has skyrocketed in the last decade, the original price has plummeted accordingly: The average monthly cost for a cellular subscription, skim-priced at $275 in 1984, had fallen to just over $50 twelve years later.[24]

Penetration Pricing

In contrast, penetration pricing seeks to generate consumer interest and stimulate trial purchase of new products. For example, new food products (convenience foods, cookies, and snacks) are often promoted at special low prices to stimulate early sales.

Penetration pricing provides for minimal (if any) profit. Thus, it can succeed only if sellers can raise prices as consumer acceptance grows. Of course, increases must be managed carefully to avoid alienating customers.

Pricing Tactics

Regardless of its pricing strategy, a company may adopt one or more pricing tactics, such as price lining or psychological pricing. Managers must also decide whether to use discounting tactics.

Price Lining

Companies selling multiple items in a product category often use **price lining**, offering all items in certain categories at a limited number of prices. A department store, for example, carries thousands of products. Obviously, setting separate prices for each brand and style of suit, glassware, or couch would take far too much time. With price lining, a store predetermines three or four price points at which a particular product will be sold. For men's

price lining
Setting a limited number of prices for certain categories of products

suits, the price points might be $175, $250, and $400: That is, all men's suits in the store will be priced at one of these three points. The store's buyers, therefore, must select suits that can be purchased and sold profitably at one of these three prices.

Psychological Pricing

psychological pricing
Pricing tactic that takes advantage of the fact that consumers do not always respond rationally to stated prices

Customers are not completely rational when making buying decisions, and **psychological pricing** takes advantage of this fact. For example, one type of psychological pricing, **odd-even pricing**, proposes that customers prefer prices that are not stated in even dollar amounts. That is, customers see prices of $1,000, $100, $50, and $10 as significantly higher than $999.95, $99.95, $49.95, and $9.95, respectively.

odd-even pricing
Psychological pricing tactic based on the premise that customers prefer prices not stated in even dollar amounts

Discounting

discount
Price reduction offered as an incentive to purchase

Of course, the price that is eventually set for a product is not always the price at which it is sold. Often, a seller must offer price reductions—**discounts**—to stimulate sales. At Filene's Basement, a Boston-based retail chain, this is the case more often than not. Filene's has built a profitable reputation by discounting designer clothing 20 to 60 percent below the prices charged by department stores. Analysts point out that this tactic accounts for Filene's success at times when larger upscale stores such as Macy's and Alexander's have suffered.

▶ **PRICE DICKERING: THE AUTO DEALER'S TRADITION.** In the mid-1980s, the Saturn division of General Motors implemented a revolutionary pricing method: Saturn would take the hassle out of the dealer-consumer relationship by selling vehicles for a fixed low price that would make negotiation unnecessary. Pricing experts believed that this no-haggle approach to auto pricing would appeal to consumers who hated to dicker.

Anyone who has ever visited a traditional new car dealership knows how it operates. Dealers slash prices by hundreds, and sometimes thousands, of dollars for aggressive customers who know how to shop around and haggle but hold fast to the manufacturer's suggested retail price—the sticker price—for customers with little negotiating skill. In contrast, fixed-price dealers average what they would have earned from aggressive customers and unsophisticated buyers. Then they charge every customer the same price. By maintaining this average price, fixed-price dealers are also able to maintain their profit margins.

Unfortunately, not all good ideas work in the marketplace, and many auto dealers now believe that the fixed-price approach has some serious practical flaws. For example, although thousands of consumers have embraced the fixed-price concept, many more continue to seek dealers who are willing to negotiate price. "A bunch of us thought people would be willing to pay an extra hundred bucks" for the convenience of fixed prices, admits John B. T. Campbell, who recently sold his fixed-price Ford and Mazda dealerships in Santa Ana, California. "We found that didn't prove to be the case." Instead, says Campbell, he attracted customers who browsed at his showroom but bought elsewhere because they regarded his prices as higher than those that they could negotiate elsewhere.

> **" A bunch of us thought people would be willing to pay an extra hundred bucks for the convenience of fixed prices. That didn't prove to be the case. "**
>
> —John B. T. Campbell, former owner of Ford and Mazda dealerships in Santa Ana, California

A recent survey conducted by the marketing-research firm of Dohring Co. found a sharp increase in the number of consumers who want to negotiate prices. According to

Dohring's report, "Automotive consumers need to feel that they get a good deal when they purchase a vehicle, and, for most, the only way is through negotiation." As a result, the number of haggle-free new car dealerships has plummeted in recent years: From a total of nearly 2,000 in 1994, the number had dropped to fewer than 1,200 to 1996. It seems that shoppers still want the option—and satisfaction—of negotiating final prices.[25]

International Pricing

▶ When Procter & Gamble reviewed the possibilities for marketing products in new overseas markets, it encountered an unsettling fact: Because it typically priced products to cover hefty R&D costs, profitably priced items were out of reach for too many foreign consumers. The solution was, in effect, to reverse the process: Now P&G conducts research to find out what foreign buyers can afford and then develops products that they can buy. The strategy is to penetrate markets with lower-priced items and encourage customers to trade up as they become acquainted with and can afford higher-quality P&G products.[26]

As P&G's experience shows, pricing products for sale in other countries is complicated because additional factors are involved. First, income and spending trends must be analyzed. In addition, the number of intermediaries varies from country to country, as does their effect on a product's cost. Exchange rates change daily (see chapter 3), shipping costs may occur, import tariffs must be considered (chapter 4), and different types of pricing agreements are permitted.

An alternative strategy calls for increasing foreign market share by pricing products below cost. As a result, a given product would be priced lower in a foreign market than in its domestic market. As we saw in chapter 4, this practice is called dumping, which is illegal. In recent years, for example, the U.S. International Trade Commission has agreed that motorcycles made by Honda and Kawasaki were being dumped on the U.S. market, as were computer memory chips. As a result, special U.S. tariffs were imposed on these products.

Finally, prices are sometimes determined not by individual companies, but rather by groups of sellers called cartels: associations of firms that produce similar products and cooperate to control their production and pricing. The best-known cartel is the Organization of Petroleum Exporting Countries (OPEC), which works to set petroleum production

Former Procter & Gamble CEO Edwin L. Artzt's push overseas went hand in hand with a revolution in P&G's pricing philosophy. In Brazil, for example, Pampers Uni is not quite the same quality diaper as the premium Pampers sold in the United States. It is priced so that Brazilians can afford it, and it is good enough to generate confidence in Pampers as a product— perhaps enough confidence to prompt consumers to "trade up" the next time around. The pricing strategy is designed to create global volume rather than to recover typically high R&D costs as quickly as possible.

quotas and prices among its members. Although price setting by means of such collusion is illegal in the United States, it is accepted in some nations.

Summary of Learning Objectives

1 **Identify a product and distinguish between consumer and industrial products.** Products are a firm's reason for being. Product features—the tangible and intangible qualities that a company builds into its products—offer benefits to buyers, whose purchases are the main source of most companies' profits. In developing products, firms must decide whether to produce consumer goods for direct sale to individual consumers or industrial goods for sale to other firms. Marketers must recognize that buyers will pay less for common, rapidly consumed convenience goods than for less frequently purchased shopping and specialty goods. In industrial markets, expense items are generally less expensive and more rapidly consumed than such capital items as buildings and equipment.

2 **Trace the stages of the product life cycle.** New products have a life cycle that begins with introduction and progresses through stage's of growth, maturity, and decline. Revenues rise through the early growth period and continue rising into maturity. Both sales and profits begin declining in late maturity and fall even lower during the decline stage.

3 **Explain the importance of branding, packaging, and labeling.** Each product is given an identity by its brand and the way it is packaged and labeled. The goal in developing brands symbols to distinguish products and signal their uniform quality is to increase brand loyalty (the preference that consumers have for a product with a particular brand name). National brands are products that are produced and widely distributed by the same manufacturer. Licensed brands are items for whose names sellers have bought the rights from organizations or individuals. Private brands (or private labels) are developed by wholesalers or retailers and commissioned from manufacturers.

Packaging provides an attractive container and advertises a product's features and benefits. It also reduces the risk of damage, spoilage, or theft. Labeling is the part of a product's packaging that usually identifies the producer's name, the manufacturer, and the contents. Labeling information is often heavily regulated.

4 **Identify the various pricing objectives that govern pricing decisions and describe the price-setting tools used in making these decisions.** A firm's pricing decisions reflect the pricing objectives set by its management. Although these objectives vary, they all reflect the goals that a seller hopes to reach in selling a product. They include profit maximizing (pricing to sell the number of units that will generate the highest possible total profits) and meeting market share goals (ensuring continuous sales by maintaining a strong percentage of the total sales for a specific product type). Other considerations include the need to survive in a competitive marketplace, social and ethical concerns, and even a firm's image.

Price-setting tools are chosen to meet a seller's pricing objectives. Cost-oriented pricing recognizes the need to cover the variable costs of producing a product (costs that change with the number of units produced or sold). In determining the price level at which profits will be generated, breakeven analysis also considers fixed costs (costs, such as facilities and salaries, that are unaffected by the number of items produced or sold).

5 **Discuss pricing strategies and tactics for both existing and new products.** Either a price-skimming strategy (pricing very high) or a penetration-pricing strategy (pricing very low) may be effective for new products. Depending on the other elements in the marketing mix, existing products may be priced at, above, or below prevailing prices for similar products. Guided by a firm's pricing strategies, managers set prices using

tactics such as price lining (offering items in certain categories at a set number of prices), psychological pricing (appealing to buyers' perceptions of relative prices), and discounting (reducing prices to stimulate sales).

Questions and Exercises

Questions for Review

1 What are the various classifications of consumer and industrial products? Give an example of a good and a service for each category other than those discussed in the text.

2 List the four stages in the product life cycle and discuss some of the ways in which a company can extend product life cycles.

3 Explain how brand names and packaging can be used to foster brand loyalty.

4 How do cost-oriented pricing and breakeven analysis help managers measure the potential impact of prices?

5 What is the overall goal of price skimming? Of penetration pricing?

Questions for Analysis

6 How would you expect the branding, packaging, and labeling of convenience, shopping, and specialty goods to differ? Why? Give examples to illustrate your answers.

7 Suppose that a small publisher selling to book distributors has fixed operating costs of $600,000 each year and variable costs of $3.00 per book. How many books must the firm sell to break even if the selling price is $6.00? If the company expects to sell 50,000 books next year and decides on a 40-percent markup, what will the selling price be?

8 Suppose your company produces industrial products for other firms. How would you go about determining the prices of your products? Describe the method you would use to arrive at a pricing decision.

Application Exercises

9 Interview the manager of a local manufacturing firm. Identify the company's different products according to their positions in the product life cycle.

10 Select a product with which you are familiar and analyze various possible pricing objectives for it. What information would you want to have if you were to adopt a profit-maximizing objective? A market share objective? An image objective?

Building Your Business Skills

This exercise enhances the following SCANS workplace competencies: demonstrating basic skills, demonstrating thinking skills, exhibiting interpersonal skills, and working with information.

Goal   To encourage students to evaluate how branding affects their personal purchasing decisions.

Method   **Step 1:** Working individually, walk around your room and bathroom at school or at home with pencil and paper in hand. List the brands of the various items you have purchased. For example, do you own a gallon of Tide laundry detergent or a store-bought equivalent? Is your toothpaste Crest or a private drug-store brand? Does your favorite sweater have a private Kmart label or is it a designer brand? Divide the items on the list into two columns: national brands and private brands.

Step 2: Come together with three or four classmates to compare your lists. Analyze the extent to which private brands have made inroads into your own purchases and the purchases of group members. Discuss the reasons for your specific brand choices.

Follow-Up Questions

1 Looking at your list of national brands, what motivated you to make these purchases? Were you influenced by brand reputation, advertising, quality, or a combination of several factors?

2 Looking at your list of private brands, what motivated you to make these purchases? Were you influenced mainly by price or were other factors involved?

3 Looking at a specific item—soap, for example—when one group member purchased a national brand and other group members purchased private brands, what factors were responsible for the different choices?

4 Based on this exercise, are you likely to continue your current buying habits, purchase more national brands, or purchase more store brands? Explain your answer.

In one of those lucky laboratory accidents, like the one that brought us 3M Post-It Notes, researchers at a biotechnology firm called Amgen, Inc., discovered a cheap and nonpolluting way to produce indigo, the dye that gives blue jeans their color. Because fabric dye wasn't an area the company planned to pursue, in 1989 Amgen sold the technology for the dyeing process to another firm called Genencor. Despite the dye's benefits, however, Genencor is having a tough time selling it to producers of indigo.

Produced by bacteria carrying a gene-spliced enzyme, the bio-dye costs a fraction of the price of existing dyes. The process relies on simple cornstarch to nourish the bacteria and produces no toxic byproducts. In contrast, conventional production of indigo, the world's most popular dye, yields poisonous cyanide and formaldehyde. In addition to being cheaper and cleaner to produce,

Genencor's dye is unlikely to cost a manufacturer the expense of complying with environmental regulations to clean up after itself.

The bio-dye recently received a boost from experts in the textile industry, who found it to be as good as the chemically produced version. And with consumers becoming ever more aware of environmental issues, particularly younger consumers who make up the prime market for blue jeans, the world would seem to be a friendly place for Genencor's remarkable product.

Yet the reaction to it has proven cool. Many indigo producers have been making a profit for years on their entrenched chemical processes and are less concerned about reducing their costs. Some are skeptical of the quality of the dye, and others are unwilling to pay for the research and development they feel it needs. The hunt for bio-tech versions of industrial

chemicals seems to have slackened for now. But Genencor's chief, W. Thomas Mitchell, is determined to make the new dye a success, and with strong market demand for denim and ever-more-stringent pollution laws behind him, it may only be a matter of time before he succeeds.

Questions

1 What might be some potential drawbacks of the new indigo dye?
2 Why do you think indigo producers are reluctant to adopt the new technology? Do you think their concerns are mostly financial, technical (related to quality control), or other? Does inertia play a role?
3 How might Mitchell reposition the dye in his search for a partner to produce and market it?
4 Do you think a direct appeal to consumers is likely to help matters? Why or why not?

Connecting to the Web

The following Web sites will give you additional information and points of view about topics covered in this chapter. Many sites lead to other related Internet locations, so approach this list with the spirit of an explorer.

3M

http://www.mmm.com/profile/innov/index.html

3M, a company known for encouraging innovation, has created more than 50,000 new products. Visit the 3M Innovation Network on the company Web site for a look at how 3M's corporate culture fosters creativity.

THE COCA-COLA COMPANY

http:www.cocacola.com/co/mission.html

Check out the mission statement on the Coca-Cola Company Web site for a profile of the company's worldwide business. You'll see the extent to which the Coca-Cola Company is following a strategy of international product extension. Also note the emphasis on the Coca-Cola brand name.

CURTIS MATHES

http://www.curtismathes.com

Curtis Mathes, which manufactures high-priced televisions, uses the Internet to introduce its state-of-the-art technology, called UniView. System features are explored, including Internet TV, e-mail, fax, phone, and caller ID. The Web site enhances the Curtis Mathes image as a manufacturer of expensive, high-quality electronic merchandise.

FERRARI NORTH AMERICA

http://www.ferrari.com/accessori/index.asp

Ferrari displays its licensed products on its Web site. Included is the Ferrari line of luggage, clothing and robes, and scale-model racing cars. Also examined is the licensing arrangement between Ferrari and Italian clothing designer Nino Cerruti.

FOOD AND DRUG ADMINISTRATION

http:www.fda.gov/

Visit this Web site for information on the premarket requirements imposed on manufacturers before bringing food additives, drugs, medical devices, and cosmetics to market. Meeting these requirements is part of the new product development process.

IBM CORPORATION

http://www.ibm.com

IBM's Web site reflects its global ad campaign, which emphasizes solutions over products.

OLDSMOBILE INTRIGUE

http://www.intriguecar.com/

OLDSMOBILE AURORA

http://www.auroracar.com/

Visit the Intrigue Web site to see how marketers are introducing this brand-new model (1998 was Intrigue's first model year.) Then move to the Aurora site for a look at the marketing strategy for a model introduced 3 years earlier.

SEARS, ROEBUCK AND CO.

http://www.sears.com/craftsman

Sears highlights its private brand of Craftsman tools.

U.S. PATENT AND TRADEMARK OFFICE

http://www.uspto.gov/

New product development often involves applying for patent protection. Patents promote innovation by ensuring that inventors will have the exclusive right to their products for a period of time specified by federal law. This site will introduce you to the patent application process.

WEDDINGS ONLINE: THE INTERNET'S WEDDING INFORMATION RESOURCE

http://weddings-online.com/wol.html

Consumers shopping for a wedding gown, caterer, florist, and music generally are looking for specialty goods with specific requirements. This site connects consumers to specific merchants who offer merchandise, often at discount prices. Web links allow users to visit various virtual storefronts.

chapter 13

Promoting products

Tiger, Tiger, burning bright

In 1997 Tiger Woods made history by being the youngest golfer and the only person of color ever to win the prestigious Masters Tournament, and overnight his name became the most sought-after product endorsement in sports. At 22 he is on his way to making a multi–million-dollar fortune from sponsorship contracts, even though in April 1997 he filed a tax return for the first time in his life.

Said Magic Johnson's agent of Woods, "He's a natural. . . . This kid is the real thing." Another sports agent declared, "Tiger has a chance to have an even broader appeal than Michael Jordan." With his youth, poise, good looks, and talent, Tiger could easily become a popular hero of the twenty-first century and become a role model for minority youth.

Still close to his family, Tiger worried that accepting too many deals would distract him from the game. His parents and his agency, International Management Group, agreed that limiting contracts to a few really big ones would increase, not dilute, Tiger's value as a spokesman for sports clothes and golf equipment. Nike, which signed its $40-million deal with Tiger just

before his historic win, hopes to see its growing golf business increase by 60 percent thanks to the use of his name. Both Nike and big equipment maker Titleist, which also has a deal with Tiger, hope his charisma and his Asian heritage will help them break into the huge Asian market for sports equipment in a big way. Beverage makers, automobile and credit card companies, and a major watchmaker all are interested in Tiger.

It's estimated that Tiger has already earned millions for the sport of golf through tournament revenue and by attracting younger people and nonwhites to the pricey game, traditionally played by older, wealthier whites. He may have ensured its future. His Masters appearance generated a record TV audience that is bound to have an impact on future television revenues from golf. And with the fifth largest endorsement contract in sports history, Tiger is also sure to influence the next generation of endorsement opportunities for other players.

In fact, Nike is betting that Tiger will become almost a brand unto himself, recognizable around the world. According to Nelson Farris, Nike's director of corporate education, Nike's CEO Philip Knight "saw that this kid represents the core stuff we always talk about around here. He has this unique character that transcends everything. Knight selected this kid to be a Nike guy because he saw that the pieces were there for greatness."

Will all the attention hurt Tiger's game? That seems to be the only thing he still controls. Either way, it's clear Tiger has opened the door to transforming the game of golf and the world of sports marketing.

❝ *This kid represents the core stuff we always talk about around here. He has this unique character that transcends everything. [CEO Philip] Knight selected this kid to be a Nike guy because he saw that the pieces were there for greatness.* **❞**

—Nelson Farris, Nike's director of corporate education

By focusing on the learning objectives of this chapter, you will become acquainted with the different approaches to promotional strategy and better understand when and why companies choose particular strategies and tools. After reading this chapter, you should be able to

1 Identify the important objectives of promotion and discuss the considerations entailed in selecting a promotional mix.

2 Discuss the most important advertising strategies and describe the key advertising media.

3 Outline the tasks involved in personal selling and list the steps in the personal selling process.

4 Describe the various types of sales promotions.

5 Describe the development of international promotional strategies.

6 Show how small businesses use promotional activities.

The Importance of Promotion

Let's begin by looking at the way in which two well-known companies responded to threats in their marketing environment:

▶ In 1996 McDonald's and Disney announced a decade-long cross-promotional agreement with an estimated value of $1 billion. A major benefit of the marketing partnership to Disney is the attraction of more direct and faster customer attention to its new movie and home video releases. McDonald's, meanwhile, stands to draw more restaurant customers who want popular tie-in toys from Disney movies. Other fast-food restaurants, notably Burger King, had recently profited from year-to-year tie-ins with Disney: BK, for example, had conducted highly successful promotional campaigns with Disney's *Lion King*, *Pocahontas*, and *Hunchback of Notre Dame* movies. But McDonald's arrangement with Disney is a strategic long-term decision that paves the way for the development of new and lasting promotional relationships between family restaurants and family entertainment. The potential marketing benefits for both companies is evident in plans calling for McDonald's to be the "presenting sponsor" of the Dinoland attraction at the 1998 opening of Disney's Animal Kingdom at Walt Disney World in Orlando.[1]

promotion
Aspect of the marketing mix concerned with the most effective techniques for selling a product

As we noted in Chapter 11, **promotion** is any technique designed to sell a product. It is part of the communication mix: the total message any company sends to consumers about its product. Promotional techniques, especially advertising, must communicate the uses, features, and benefits of products. Sales promotions also include various programs that add value beyond the benefits inherent in the product. For example, it is nice to get a high-quality product at a reasonable price but even better when the seller offers a rebate or a bonus pack with 20 percent more free. In promoting products, then, marketers have an array of tools at their disposal.

In this chapter we will look at the different objectives of and approaches to promotion. We will show when and why companies use particular strategies and tools and then describe the special promotional problems faced by both international and small businesses. First, however, we will explain the two general values to be gained from any promotional activity, regardless of the particular strategy or tools involved: communicating information and creating more satisfying exchanges.

Information and Exchange Values

In free-market systems, a business uses promotional methods to communicate information about itself and its products to consumers and industrial buyers. The purpose, of course, is to influence purchase decisions. From an information standpoint, promotions seek to accomplish four things with potential customers:

- Make them aware of products
- Make them knowledgeable about products
- Persuade them to like products
- Persuade them to purchase products

In terms of the exchange relationship, the firm hopes that marketing promotions will make its product more attractive. The buyer therefore gains more from the exchange (a more attractive product), as does the seller (more unit sales or higher prices). Additionally, as part of relationship marketing, promotions help to build lasting relationships with consumers. The Art Bell Show, for example, has worked to build a loyal following among its ever-growing late-night radio audience by providing a massive Internet Web site. Listeners can join the host by visiting Art's chat room, access information about guests, and see pictures of unusual show topics around the clock at www.artbell.com.

Successful promotions therefore provide communication about the product and create exchanges that satisfy both the customer's and the organization's objectives. However, because promotions are expensive, choosing the best promotional mix becomes critical. The promotional program, then, whether at the introduction stage (promoting for new product awareness) or maturity stage (promoting brand benefits and customer loyalty), can determine the success or failure of any business or product.

Promotional Objectives

Obviously, the ultimate objective of any promotion is to increase sales. In addition, marketers may use promotion to communicate information, position products, add value, and control sales volume.

Communicating Information

Promotion is effective in communicating information from one person or organization to another. Of course, consumers cannot buy products unless they have been informed about them. Information may thus advise customers that a product exists or educate them about its features. Soon after the New Year's holiday, for example, the Physicians' Weight Loss Centers' advertisement in *USA Today* not only announces the program's availability but educates the public on its health advantages over diets. Information may be communicated in writing (in newspapers and magazines), verbally (in person or over the telephone), or visually (on television, matchbook covers, or billboards). Today, in fact, the communication of information about a company's goods or services is so important that marketers try to place it everywhere consumers can be found: Experts estimate that the average consumer comes into contact with approximately 1,500 bits of promotional information each day.

Positioning Products

As we saw in chapter 11, **positioning** is the process of establishing an easily identifiable product image in the minds of consumers. Positioning a product is difficult because a company is trying to appeal to a specific segment of the market rather than to the market as a whole. First, therefore, it must identify which segments are likely to purchase its product and who its competitors are. Only then can it focus its strategy on differentiating its product from the competition's while still appealing to its target audience.

positioning
Process of establishing an identifiable product image in the minds of consumers

For the St. Louis Bread Company, for example, positioning has differentiated its restaurants from competitors throughout the Midwest. It offers a limited menu of light, healthful foods—for both eat-in and takeout—for morning, noon, and early evening service. The "light and healthy" theme of the menu—fresh, wholesome baked goods, soups, salads, sandwiches, and flavored coffees—is complemented by quiet surroundings, fresh flowers on the tables, light classical music, and cleanliness. Within any metropolitan area, its many sites are carefully chosen to ensure that a St. Louis Bread restaurant is not far away for upper-middle-class professionals to get a quick wholesome meal, reasonably priced, in a pleasant atmosphere.

Adding Value

Today's value-conscious customers gain benefits when the promotional mix is shifted so that it communicates value-added benefits in its products. Burger King, for instance, shifted its promotional mix by cutting back on advertising dollars and using those funds for customer discounts: Receiving the same food at a lower price is "value-added" for BK's customers. Similarly, in upstate New York, Lawless Container Corp., whose customers are other companies that buy cardboard boxes and packaging materials, has shifted its emphasis to certain unique services: special credit terms, storage, and delivery times that are valued by individual customers. Like BK's discounts, Lawless's new services add greater value for the dollar.

In addition to adding value, however, promotion is the main means of establishing a product's perceived value. It means creating communications and directing them to value-conscious customers. For example, customers must be given information about the value-adding characteristics—say, warranties, repair contracts, and after-purchase service—by which a product provides greater value than its competitors. For example, Lexus prides itself on adding value by providing superb treatment of customers. Sales representatives do not pry, solicit, or hover over buyers in the showroom. The first two scheduled maintenance jobs are free. Waiting customers can use offices, desks, or phones and can borrow cars or get rides. "We try to make it very hard for you to leave us," explains General Manager George Borst. "When you buy a Lexus, you don't buy a product. You buy a luxury package."[2]

> ## " We try to make it very hard for you to leave us. When you buy a Lexus, you don't buy a product. You buy a luxury package. "
>
> —George Borst, General Manager of Lexus

Controlling Sales Volume

Many companies, such as Hallmark Cards, experience seasonal sales patterns. By increasing promotional activities in slow periods, these firms can achieve more stable sales volume throughout the year. They can thus keep production and distribution systems running evenly. Promotions can even turn slow seasons into peak sales periods. For example, greeting-card companies and florists together have done much to create Grandparents' Day. The result has been increased consumer demand for cards and flowers in the middle of what was once a slow season for both industries.

Promotional Strategies

Once its larger marketing objectives are clear, a firm must develop a promotional strategy to achieve them. Two fundamentally different strategies are often used:

pull strategy
Promotional strategy designed to appeal directly to consumers who will demand a product from retailers

push strategy
Promotional strategy designed to encourage wholesalers or retailers to market products to consumers

■ A **pull strategy** is designed to appeal directly to consumers, who will demand the product from retailers. In turn, retailers will demand the product from wholesalers. When publishing a Stephen King novel, for example, Doubleday directs its promotions at horror story fans. If a bookstore does not stock the book, requests from readers will prompt it to order copies from Doubleday.

■ Using a **push strategy**, a firm aggressively markets its product to wholesalers and retailers, who then persuade consumers to buy it. Brunswick Corp., for instance, uses a push strategy to promote Bayliner boats, directing its promotions at dealers and persuading them to order more inventory. Dealers are then responsible for stimulating demand among boaters in their respective districts.

Many large firms use combination pull and push strategies. For example, General Foods uses advertising to create consumer demand (pull) for its cereals. At the same time, it pushes wholesalers and retailers to stock them.

The Promotional Mix

As we noted in chapter 12, there are four types of promotional tools: advertising, personal selling, sales promotions, and publicity and public relations. The best combination of these tools—that is, the best **promotional mix**—depends on many factors. The company's product, the characteristics of the target audience, and budget considerations are all important.

promotional mix
Combination of tools used to promote a product

The Product

Obviously, the nature of the product being promoted affects the promotional mix greatly. For example, advertising can reach a large number of widely dispersed consumers. Thus, it is the promotional tool used for products that are widely purchased, such as sunglasses, radios, snack foods, and thousands of others. Companies introducing new products also favor advertising because it reaches a large number of people very quickly and can repeat a message many times. Personal selling, on the other hand, is important when the product appeals to a very specific audience, such as an industrial company that needs highly specialized equipment. (We will discuss personal selling in more detail later in this chapter.)

The Target Audience: Promotion and the Buyer Decision Process

Another consideration in establishing the promotional mix is matching the promotional tool with the relevant stage in the buyer decision process. As we noted in chapter 11, this process can be broken down into five steps:

1   Buyers must first recognize the need to make a purchase. At this stage, marketers must make sure the buyer is aware that their products exist. Thus, advertising and publicity, which can reach a large number of people very quickly, are very important.

2   Buyers also want to learn more about available products. Advertising and personal selling are important in this stage because both can be used to educate the customer.

3   Buyers evaluate and compare competing products. Personal selling can be vital at this point: Sales representatives can demonstrate their product's quality and performance in direct relation to competitors' products.

4   Buyers decide on specific products and purchase them. Sales promotion is effective at this stage because it can give consumers an incentive to buy. Personal selling can also help by bringing products to convenient purchase locations.

5   Finally, buyers evaluate products after purchasing them. Advertising, or even personal selling, is sometimes used after the sale to remind consumers that they made a prudent purchase.

Figure 13.1 summarizes the effective promotional tools for each stage of the consumer buying process.

The Promotional Mix Budget

Choosing the promotional mix begins by determining the promotional budget—one of the marketing manager's most difficult decisions. The budget specifies how much of the firm's total resources will be spent on promotions. The combined costs of personal selling, advertising, sales promotion, and public relations must fall within the budgeted amount. Moreover, the elements of the mix must be balanced if they are to have the desired effects on attitudes and purchasing decisions.

Figure 13.1   The Consumer Buying Process and the Promotional Mix

Advertising Promotions

advertising
Promotional tool consisting of paid, nonpersonal communication used by an identified sponsor to inform an audience about a product

Advertising is paid, nonpersonal communication used by an identified sponsor to inform an audience about a product. In 1995, U.S. firms spent more than $160 billion on advertising, with $47 billion of this amount being spent by just 100 companies.[3]

In this section we will begin by describing some key elements in advertising strategy. Then we will describe each of the different types of advertising media, noting both advantages and limitations of each. We will also identify three main types of advertising according to product type and purpose. Next, we will describe the advertising campaign and the role of the advertising agency in designing it. Finally, we will touch on some key points in the regulation of advertising.

Advertising Strategies

The advertising strategies used for a product most often depend on which stage of the product life cycle (see chapter 12) the product is in. During the introduction stage, for example, informative advertising can help develop an awareness of the company and its product among buyers and help establish a demand for the product. Thus, when a new textbook is published, instructors receive direct-mail informative advertisements notifying them of the book's contents and availability.

As products become established and competition increases, advertising strategies must change. During a product's growth and maturity stages, for instance, marketers may choose one of three common approaches:

persuasive advertising
Advertising strategy that tries to influence consumers to buy one company's products instead of those of its rivals

comparative advertising
Advertising strategy that directly compares two or more products

reminder advertising
Advertising strategy that tries to keep a product's name in the consumer's mind

- **Persuasive advertising** seeks to influence consumers to buy the company's products rather than those of its rivals. This approach usually emphasizes the quality of the firm's goods or services. Major insurance companies, such as New York Life, are using persuasive advertising when they emphasize safety and security for policyholders.

- Another useful strategy during the maturity stage is **comparative advertising**, in which two or more products are compared directly. Broadly speaking, the goal is to steal sales from the competition.

- During the late part of the maturity stage and throughout the decline stage, **reminder advertising** can help to keep the product's name in the consumer's mind. Thus, Atari continues to advertise home video games even though market attention has shifted to newer competitors such as Nintendo, Sega, and Genesis.

Advertising Media

advertising media
Variety of communication devices for carrying a seller's message to potential customers

Bombarded with thousands of advertisements, consumers tend to ignore the bulk of the ads they see or hear. Marketers therefore must find out who their customers are, which media they attend to, what message will appeal to them, and how to get their attention. Marketers thus use several different **advertising media**—that is, specific communication devices for carrying a seller's message to potential customers. For example, IBM uses television ads to keep its name fresh in consumers' minds. It uses newspaper and magazine ads, however, to educate consumers on product features and trade publications to introduce new software. The following are the most common advertising media. Each medium has its own advantages and disadvantages.

Newspapers

Newspapers are the most widely used medium, accounting for about 25 percent of all advertising expenditures. Because each local market has at least one daily newspaper, newspapers provide excellent coverage. Each day, they reach more than 113 million U.S. adults.

The main advantage of newspaper advertising is flexible, rapid coverage: Ads can easily be changed from day to day. However, newspapers are generally thrown out after one day, are usually not printed in color, and have poor reproduction quality. Moreover, because their readership is so broad, newspapers do not usually allow advertisers to target audiences very well.

The Workplace Environment

"Shut Up and Buy It"

Fashions come and go, even in advertising. Canny marketers have always known they have to appeal to their audience with a combination of credibility and style, and it seems this has never been more true than now. The so-called Generation Xers, people born between 1965 and 1976, are coming into their own as big spenders, plunking down $125 billion a year for consumer goods, and marketers are honing their messages to this group to a finely crafted edge.

Slickness, hype, and the hard sell of materialism have been shown to turn off this savvy generation of consumers. To reach them, some big marketers such as Coca-Cola and Levi's are instead perfecting a style of advertising that can only be called "super slick." Typical tactics are to spoof the traditional hard sell, to appear to spurn the appeal of image and style, and even to have no apparent point at all. Memorable and even eccentric visuals are the norm, along with funky music and whimsical story lines. The product is often shown or named only at the very end of the message.

Coca-Cola, for instance, pretends to adopt the Gen-Xers' native skepticism by promoting Sprite with the line, "Image is nothing. Thirst is everything. Obey your thirst." Miller Genuine Draft Beer urges, "It's time to shut up and drink some beer." Other ads encourage the viewer to be aggressive, even selfish and impolite, about satisfying the desire to consume goods, drinks, and snack food.

> **" If you go out with the idea that you're not going to offend anybody, you probably won't make an impression. "**
>
> —Jamie Barrett,
> creative director of Wieden and Kennedy, Inc.

Some observers find the ads on the rude side and worry that what's being billed as humor is actually hostile. Says Robert Goldman, a professor of sociology at Lewis and Clark College in Portland, "The big issue is that [the new ads] seem to reflect a loss of civility. In this kind of world, jokes about personalism and materialism are funny."

But, says Jamie Barrett, creative director of Wieden and Kennedy, Inc., also of Portland, "if you go out with the idea that you're not going to offend anybody, you probably won't make an impression."

Television

Television accounts for about 22 percent of all advertising outlays. (See Figure 13.2). In addition to the major networks, cable television is fast becoming an important advertising medium. Cable network ad revenues have increased from $58 million in 1980 to $3.4 billion in 1995 and are projected to top $4 billion by 1997.[4]

Combining sight, sound, and motion, television appeals to a full complement of the viewer's senses. In addition, information on viewer demographics for a particular program allows advertisers to aim at target audiences. Finally, television reaches more people than any other medium. For example, recent Super Bowl games have consistently attracted over 40 million households and 115 million viewers. Unfortunately, the fact that there are so many commercials on TV often causes viewers to confuse products. For example, most people cannot recall whether a tire commercial advertised the goods of Firestone, Goodyear, or B. F. Goodrich. In addition, the brevity of TV ads makes television a poor medium in which to educate viewers about complex products. Finally, television is also the most expensive medium in which to advertise. Companies such as McDonald's, Pepsi, Frito-Lay, Anheuser-Busch, and Quaker State now pay about $1 million for 30-second commercials during the Super Bowl, with one 90-second Nike ad in 1995 becoming TV advertising's first $3-million spot. "If you're in the Super Bowl," reasoned one Nike executive, "you might as well give it your best shot."

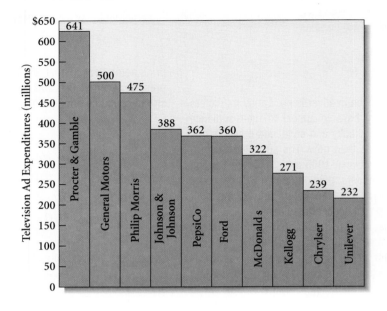

Figure 13.2   Top Ten Network TV Advertisers

> ❝ *If you're in the Super Bowl, you might as well give it your best shot.* ❞
>
> —Nike marketing executive on spending $3 million for a 90-second Super Bowl ad

direct mail
Advertising medium in which messages are mailed directly to consumers' homes or places of business

Direct Mail

Direct mail advertisements account for 18 percent of all advertising outlays. Direct mail involves fliers or other types of printed advertisements mailed directly to consumers' homes or places of business. It allows the company to select its audience and personalize its message. In addition, although many people discard junk mail, advertisers can predict in advance how many recipients will take a mailing seriously. These people have a stronger-than-average interest in the product advertised and are more likely than most to buy the promoted product. So although direct mail involves the largest advance costs of any advertising technique, it does appear to have the highest cost-effectiveness.

Radio

About 7 percent of all advertising outlays are for radio advertising. Over 180 million people in the United States listen to the radio each day, and radio ads are quite inexpensive. For example, a small business in a midwestern town of 100,000 people pays only about $20 for a 30-second local radio spot. (A television spot in the same area costs over $250.) In addition, stations are usually segmented into categories such as rock and roll, country and western, jazz, talk shows, news, and religious programming; thus their audiences are largely segmented. Unfortunately, radio ads, like television ads, are over quickly. Furthermore, they provide only audio presentations, and people tend to use the radio as background while doing other things.

Neither Rain, Nor Snow, Nor Electronic Filtering System . . .

What do your computer and your mailbox have in common? Junk mail. With the number of electronic mailboxes growing explosively (it is expected to reach over 150 million in the next year or so), the opportunities for enterprising electronic junk mailers seem limitless. After all, a single message costs well below a penny to send, and some firms charge ad rates of $30 to $70 per thousand viewers. One direct e-mail firm, Mercury Mail Inc., says it already sends over 1.1 million messages a day and, like many of its competitors, plans to add new features such as photos and multiply its business many times over. Sound and video aren't far behind.

From its earliest days, e-mail has been susceptible to the arrival of unsolicited advertising, popularly known as spam, but lately consumers have taken up arms. If you are receiving such mail, here are some recent developments from the battlefront.

- Thousands of people simply write to the offending firms asking them to stop sending ads and hope the problem will go away. A free program called Spam Hater (www.compulink.co.uk/) helps route form letters of protest back to advertisers' (often hidden) addresses.

- Some determined people use free software for removing their names from e-mail lists. Typical programs and help for this purpose are found at Web sites such as www.cancel-it.com, www.getlost.com, and www.junkbusters.com.

- AOL and CompuServe have gotten the U.S. District Court in Columbus, Ohio to uphold CompuServe's ban on unsolicited e-mail. AOL is looking into special filtering systems that would allow you to receive mail on only topics in which your previous Internet use indicates you have an interest.

- Netscape and Microsoft have pledged to pare down their users' mail with sorting systems and automatic purges, controlled by preset expiration dates the firms can apply to incoming ad messages.

- A renegade group of Internet users blocked or destroyed thousands of unsolicited ads and other messages sent by customers of an Internet service company called UUNet Technologies. UUNet's CEO John Sidgmore called the action "digital terrorism." The protesters set up a Web site at www.junkemail.org/scamspam to help other junk mail recipients determine whether mail they've received violates federal regulations and to inform the public about reporting the unwanted messages to the Federal Trade Commission.

- Some firms have hired human cyber-reps just to go through the company junk mail, filter out what's important, and forward it to the appropriate staff member.

If all else fails, you might be willing to just grin and bear it. A direct mail company in Louisville, KY, recently found that because of the extremely high rate of change in e-mail addresses, only 20 percent of its e-mail messages in a test mailing were actually delivered. In comparison, fewer than 1 percent of its snail-mail volume fails to reach its target.

Magazines

Magazine ads account for roughly 5 percent of all advertising. The huge variety of magazines provides a high level of ready market segmentation. Magazines also allow advertisers plenty of space for detailed product information. In addition, they allow for excellent reproduction of photographs and artwork. Finally, because magazines have long lives and tend to be passed from person to person, ads get constantly increased exposure. Ads must be submitted well in advance, however, and there is often no guarantee of where an ad will appear within a magazine.

Outdoor Advertising

Outdoor advertising—billboards, signs, and advertisements on buses, taxis, and subways—makes up about 1 percent of all advertising. These ads are inexpensive, face little competition for customers' attention, and are subject to high repeat exposure. Outdoor ad effectiveness was illustrated recently in a focused test of a Philip Morris brand, Altoids mints, which featured posters with images of an old-fashioned body builder and the simple headline: "Nice Altoids." Once the ads had been placed in neighborhoods of the target audience—affluent white-collar adults—sales skyrocketed more than 50 percent. Unfortunately, outdoor ads can present only very limited amounts of information, and sellers have little control over audiences.[5]

The Internet

The most recent advertising medium is the Internet, where such well-known names as Burlington Coat Factory, Miller Genuine Draft, MCI Communications, and Reebok have all placed ads. Although Internet advertising is still in its infancy and offers high potential, most marketers recognize that it also has limitations: In particular, consumers don't want to wade through electronic pages looking at details about hundreds of products. One expert offers the disappointing opinion that most of the commercial advertisements on the Internet may never be read by anyone. Even so, communication researchers are projecting that ad expenditures will rise from $301 million in 1996 to nearly $8 billion by 2002.[6]

Other Advertising Channels

A combination of many additional media, including catalogs, sidewalk handouts, Yellow Pages, skywriting, telephone calls, special events, and door-to-door communication, make up the remaining 22 percent of all U.S. advertising.

The Media Mix

media mix
Combination of advertising media chosen to carry message about a product

The combination of media that a company chooses to advertise its products is called its **media mix**. As Table 13.1 suggests, different industries use very different mixes, and most depend on a variety of different media, rather than using just one, for reaching their target audiences.

Types of Advertising

Regardless of the medium used, advertisements fall into one of these three categories:

brand advertising
Advertising promoting a specific brand

- **Brand advertising** promotes a specific brand, such as *People* magazine, Amtrak rail service, and Ricoh copiers. (A variation on brand advertising, product advertising promotes a general good or service, such as milk or dental services.)

advocacy advertising
Advertising promoting a cause, viewpoint, or candidate

- **Advocacy advertising** promotes a particular cause, viewpoint, or candidate. During the autumn of 1997, for example, several U.S. civic and business associations opposing the proposed United Nations global climate treaty ran ads where they might be seen by the public, the business community, and Congressional representatives. The ads stated that the treaty was unfair for the United States, provided a Web site for additional information, and concluded with the slogan "It's Not Global and It Won't Work."[7]

Table 13.1 Media Mix by Industry

Industry	Magazine	Newspaper	Outdoor	Television	Radio
Retail stores	4.2%	61.1%	1.9%	27.8%	5.0%
Industrial materials	29.3	7.8	0.3	52.8	9.8
Insurance and real estate	11.1	53.5	2.2	29.3	3.9
Food	14.9	0.7	0.3	80.5	3.6
Apparel	50.5	1.8	0.5	45.8	1.4

- **Institutional advertising** promotes a firm's long-term image. Hoechst, for example, runs a continuing series of ads to acquaint the public with its name, its industries, and its long-term vision: "Creating Value Through Technology." Their colorful ads cleverly capitalize on the firm's unusual name (pronounced "Herkst") and announces its leadership in diverse life sciences and other industries, such as crop protection, vaccines for animal health, drugs for allergies and cancer, and industrial gases and gas supply systems.

institutional advertising
Advertising promoting a firm's long-term image

Advertising to Specific Markets

Advertisements differ in their direction. In other words, the types of advertisements used by a company depend on its target market. In consumer markets, for instance, local stores usually concentrate retail advertising geographically to encourage local consumers to patronize the store. Larger retailers, such as Sears and J. C. Penney, use retail advertising to reach more geographically dispersed consumers on both the local and national levels.

Ads are also designed to reach a specific audience in terms of its demographics, such as gender, age, income level, or ethnicity. Naturally, advertising decisions about the tone of an ad, the type of medium (say, magazine versus television), and the specific vehicle (*People* versus *Cosmopolitan* magazine) are made with target groups in mind.

Target markets for advertising industrial products are often easier to identify than those for consumer goods. The existence of professional buyers, well-defined industrial groupings, and trade associations are, in effect, the demographics for defining the target audience. To reach the professional purchasing agents and managers at firms that buy raw materials or components, companies use industrial advertising. For example, American Standard, which makes toilets and other plumbing fixtures, advertises in *Hardware Retailer* to persuade large hardware stores to carry its products. Similarly, Chaparral Steel reaches its target audience of steel fabricators and distributors by advertising through trade shows, trade magazines, and direct mail. Finally, geographic location is simplified in industrial marketing because the professional target market has a limited number of buyers whose locations are well known within the industry.

Preparing the Campaign with an Advertising Agency

An **advertising campaign** is the arrangement of ads in selected media to reach target audiences. It includes several activities that, taken together, constitute a program for meeting a marketing objective, such as introducing a new product or changing a company's image in the public mind. A campaign typically includes six steps:

advertising campaign
Arrangement of ads in selected media to reach targeted audiences

- Identifying the target audience
- Establishing the advertising budget
- Defining the objectives of the advertising messages
- Creating the advertising messages
- Selecting the appropriate media
- Evaluating advertising effectiveness

Advertising agencies assist in the development of campaigns by providing specialized services. They are independent companies that provide some or all of their clients' advertising needs. The agency works together with the client company to determine the campaign's central message, create detailed message content, identify ad media, and negotiate media purchases.

advertising agency
Independent company that provides some or all of a client firm's advertising needs

The advantage that agencies offer is expertise in developing ad themes, message content, and artwork, as well as in coordinating ad production and advising on relevant legal matters. Today, even more specialized agencies have emerged to cater to clients with very specific goals in specific industries or market segments. For example, Medicus Consumer/D.M.B.&B., Kallir Phillips Ross, and Sudler & Hennessey are agencies experienced in the marketing of pharmaceuticals. Burrell Communications Group is the largest African-American advertising agency, and Conhill Advertising focuses on Hispanic consumers.[8]

As payment for its services, the agency usually receives a percentage, traditionally 15 percent of the media purchase cost. For example, if an agency purchases a $1-million television commitment for a client's campaign, it would receive $150,000 for its services.

▶ An example of an advertising agent's activities is the recent ad campaign for Starbucks, the upscale coffee vendor. The $8-million TV and radio campaign began in May 1997 and was developed by Goodby, Silverstein & Partners, a San Francisco agency. The campaign's objectives are to promote a cold drink—Frappuccino—and to define and build Starbucks' image as a friendly local purveyor of "coffee, tea, and sanity." Starbucks' previous ads were limited to outdoor efforts, newspaper ads, and occasional radio and TV to support its stores and beverages. But a change was needed for broader reach to keep up with Starbucks' growth; the current 1,200 stores in 25 states is expected to become 2,000 stores by 2000. Goodby has planned this new campaign as the first of a series of coordinated campaigns for the future. It includes three TV and three radio spots running for 8 weeks in 11 major North American markets. Each TV ad, using whimsical line drawings of animated characters, shows Starbucks' iced Frappuccino drink providing relief from the summer heat. The radio campaign features "Mr. Z," a man suffering in the heat, who finds relief with the iced drink. Frappuccino in particular was chosen for the campaign because Starbucks hopes the cold drink will increase sales during the normally slow summer period. The Goodby agency managed the entire campaign: the ad message and format, choice of media, number of spots, selection of markets, negotiation of the media purchases, and the timing for the ad appearances.[9]

Regulation of Advertising

Not surprisingly, advertising affects nearly every person in the United States. Because it can be used to deceive as well as inform buyers, it has long been the subject of some sort of regulation. The first regulatory activities came in 1914 with passage of the Federal Trade Commission Act. As we saw in chapter 4, this act created the Federal Trade Commission (FTC) to protect competition from unfair trade practices. In 1938 the Wheeler-Lea Act gave the FTC power to protect consumers against advertising that makes misleading claims or suggestions. In 1971 the FTC instituted a program requiring companies to furnish evidence that advertising claims are true.

To some degree, members of the advertising industry also regulate themselves. For example, advertising media, including television networks and local stations, magazines, and newspapers, often decline ads that they believe to be false or in poor taste. Thus, many newspapers will not allow classified ads offering or asking for the services of soldiers of fortune. The National Advertising Review Board (NARB) was established by a council of professional advertisers to investigate complaints against its members. If the NARB rules in favor of the complaining party, the advertiser must modify or withdraw its claim.

Overall, self-regulation has been successful. The NARB hears more than 400 cases a year, mostly initiated by businesses against competitors' claims. The cases heard by the NARB are handled quickly and at a lower cost than those processed by the FTC. However, if an advertiser rejects an NARB finding, the Board can do little except refer the matter to the FTC.

Personal Selling

personal selling
Promotional tool in which a salesperson communicates one-on-one with potential customers

In **personal selling**, a salesperson communicates one-to-one with potential customers to identify their needs and to line them up with the seller's products. The oldest form of selling, it provides the personal link between seller and buyer and adds to a firm's credibility because it allows buyers to interact with and ask questions of the seller. This professional intimacy is especially effective for relationship marketing: It places the seller closer to the buyer, it provides a clearer exposure of the customer's business, and the salesperson can then assist the buying company in creating value-adding services for the buyer's target customers.[10]

However, because it involves personal interaction, personal selling requires a certain level of trust between buyer and seller—a relationship that must often be established over time. Moreover, because presentations are generally made to only one or two individuals at a time, personal selling is the most expensive form of promotion per contact. Expenses may include salespeople's compensation and their overhead, usually travel, food, and lodging. Indeed, the average cost of a single industrial sales call has been estimated at approximately $300.[11]

Such high costs have prompted many companies to turn to telemarketing: using telephone solicitations to perform the personal selling process. Telemarketing can be used to handle any stage of the personal selling process or to set up appointments for outside salespeople. For example, it saves the cost of personal sales visits to industrial customers. Each industrial buyer requires an average of nearly four visits to complete a sale; some companies have thus realized savings in sales visits of $1,000 or more. Not surprisingly, such savings are stimulating the remarkable growth of telemarketing, which sold over $360 billion in goods and services in 1995, calling from some 60,000 call centers in the United States. The Direct Marketing Association estimates that telemarketing sales could grow to $600 billion, with as many as 5 million more people to be employed by the year 2000.[12]

Personal Selling Situations

Managers of both telemarketers and traditional salespeople must always consider the ways in which personal sales are affected by the differences between consumer and industrial products:

- **Retail selling** is selling a consumer product for the buyer's own personal or household use.

- **Industrial selling** is selling products to other businesses, either for the purpose of manufacturing other products or for resale.

> **retail selling**
> Personal selling situation in which products are sold for buyers' personal or household use

> **industrial selling**
> Personal selling situation in which products are sold to businesses, either for manufacturing other products or for resale

For example, Levi's sells jeans to the retail clothing operation The Gap (industrial selling). In turn, consumers purchase Levi's jeans at one of The Gap's stores (retail selling).

Each of these situations has distinct characteristics. In retail selling, for instance, the buyer usually comes to the seller. In contrast, the industrial salesperson almost always goes to the prospect's place of business. The industrial decision process also may take longer than a retail decision because more money, decision makers, and weighing of alternatives are involved. In addition, as we saw in chapter 11, industrial buyers are professional purchasing agents accustomed to dealing with salespeople. Consumers in retail stores, on the other hand, may actually be intimidated by salespeople.

Sales Force Management

Sales force management means setting goals at top levels of the organization, setting practical objectives for salespeople, organizing a sales force that can meet those objectives, and implementing and evaluating the success of the overall sales plan. Obviously, then, sales management is an important factor in meeting the marketing objectives of any large company.

IBM's U.S. industrial sales force, for example, is more than 30,000 strong. Traditionally, it has been organized geographically. In 1993, however, IBM announced that it would reorganize the staff to feature specialists who would be better able to help specific industries, buyers, and users on the features and applications of specific IBM products. The company's 12,000-person British sales force has already been organized into selling units concentrating on specific products from mainframes to minicomputers for specific industries. Similarly, by 1995 IBM had recast its U.S. sales staff to reflect a new company-wide strategy: It has become a supplier and consultant in information management systems for specific industries. Accordingly, the sales organization is arranged around 13 industry groups, such as banking and insurance.[13]

Personal Selling Tasks

One important aspect of sales force management is overseeing salespeople as they perform the three basic tasks generally associated with personal selling: order processing, creative selling, and missionary selling. Depending on the product and company, sales jobs usually require individuals to perform all three tasks to some degree.

Order Processing

order processing
Personal selling task in which salespeople receive orders and see to their handling and delivery

In **order processing**, a salesperson receives an order and sees to its handling and delivery. Route salespeople, who call on regular customers to check their supplies, are often order processors: With the customer's consent, they may determine the sizes of reorders, fill them directly from their trucks, and even stack the customer's shelves.

Creative Selling

creative selling
Personal selling task in which salespeople try to persuade buyers to purchase products by providing information about their benefits

When the benefits of a product are not entirely clear, **creative selling** can help to persuade buyers. Most industrial products involve creative selling, especially when a buyer is unfamiliar with a product or the features and uses of a specific brand. Personal selling is also crucial for high-priced consumer products, such as homes and cars, for which buyers comparison shop. Any new product can benefit from creative selling that works to differentiate it from competitors.

Missionary Selling

missionary selling
Personal selling tasks in which salespeople promote their firms and products rather than try to close sales

A company may also use **missionary selling** when its purpose is to promote itself and its products rather than simply to close a sale. For example, drug company representatives promote drugs to doctors who, in turn, prescribe them to patients. The sale, then, is actually made at the drugstore. In this case, the goal of missionary selling may be to promote the company's long-term image as much as any given product. Another form of missionary selling is the after-sale technical assistance that companies offer for complex products. For example, IBM uses after-sale missionary selling both to ensure that customers know how to use IBM equipment and to promote good will.

The Personal Selling Process

Although all three sales tasks are important to an organization that uses personal selling, perhaps the most complicated is creative selling. The creative salesperson is responsible for undertaking and following through on most of the steps in the personal selling process.[14]

prospecting
Step in the personal selling process in which salespeople identify potential customers

1 *Prospecting and qualifying.* In order to sell, a salesperson must first have a potential customer, or prospect. **Prospecting** is the process of identifying potential customers. Salespeople find prospects through past company records, customers, friends, relatives, company personnel, and business associates. Prospects must then be **qualified** to determine whether they have the authority to buy and the ability to pay.

qualifying
Step in the personal selling process in which salespeople determine whether prospects have the authority and ability to pay

2 *Approaching.* The first few minutes of a salesperson's contact with a qualified prospect make up the approach. Because it affects the salesperson's credibility, the success of later stages in the process depends on the prospect's first impression of the salesperson. For this reason, a salesperson must present a neat, professional appearance and greet prospects in a strong, confident manner.

3 *Presenting and demonstrating.* After the approach, the salesperson must present the promotional message to the prospect. A presentation is a full explanation of the product, its features, and its uses. Most important, it links the product's benefits to

the prospect's needs. A presentation may or may not include a demonstration of the product. However, because many people have trouble fully appreciating what they have been told verbally about a product's performance, experienced salespeople try to demonstrate products whenever possible.

4 *Handling objections.* No matter what the product, prospects will have some objections. At the very least, they will angle for a discount by objecting to price. Objections not only show the salesperson that the buyer is interested but also pinpoint the parts of the presentation with which the buyer has a problem. Obviously, the salesperson must then work to overcome these objections.

5 *Closing.* The most critical part of the selling process is the **closing**, in which the salesperson asks the prospective customer to buy the product. Successful salespeople recognize the signs that a customer is ready to buy. For example, prospects who start to figure out monthly payments for the product are clearly indicating a readiness to buy. The salesperson should then attempt to close the sale. Salespeople can either ask directly for the sale or imply a close indirectly. Questions such as "Could you take delivery Tuesday?" and "Why don't we start you off with an initial order of 10 cases?" are implied closes. Again, the experienced salesperson knows that indirect closes place the burden of rejecting the sale on the prospect, who may find it a little harder to say no.

closing
Step in the personal selling process in which salespeople ask prospective customers to buy products

6 *Following up.* Follow-up is a key activity, especially for relationship marketing. For lasting relationships with buyers, the sales process does not end with the close of the sale. Sellers want this sale to be so successful that the customer wants to buy from this seller again in the future. Therefore, sellers supply additional services that customers want: after-sale support that provides convenience and added value. Thus, they require sales follow-ups that include quick processing of the customer's orders, on-time delivery, and speedy repair service. Training the customer in the proper care and use of the purchase may also be part of the follow-up that stimulates repeated future sales.

Sales Promotions

Sales promotions are short-term promotional activities designed to stimulate consumer buying or cooperation from distributors, sales agents, or other members of the trade. They are important because they increase the likelihood that buyers will try products. They also enhance product recognition and can increase purchase size and amount. For example, soap is sometimes bound in packages of four with the promotion "Buy three and get one free."

    To be successful, sales promotions must be convenient and accessible when the decision to purchase occurs. For instance, if Harley-Davidson has a 1-week motorcycle promotion and you have no local dealer, the promotion is neither convenient nor accessible to you, and you will not buy. On the other hand, if Folgers offers a $1-off coupon that you can save for use later, the promotion is both convenient and accessible.

sales promotion
Short-term promotional activity designed to stimulate consumer buying or cooperation from distributors and sales agents

Types of Sales Promotions
The best-known forms of promotions are coupons, point-of-purchase displays, various purchasing incentives (especially free samples and premiums), trade shows, and contests and sweepstakes.

■ A certificate that entitles the bearer to a stated savings off a regular price is a **coupon**. Coupons may be used to encourage customers to try new products, to attract customers away from competitors, or to induce current customers to buy more of a product. They appear in newspapers and magazines, are included with other products, and are often sent through direct mail.

coupon
Sales promotion technique in which a certificate is issued entitling the buyer to a reduced price

■ To grab customers' attention as they walk through stores, some companies use **point-of-purchase (POP) displays**. Located at the ends of aisles or near checkout counters,

point-of-purchase (POP) display
Sales promotion technique in which product displays are located in certain areas to stimulate purchase

POP displays make it easier for customers to find products and easier for sellers to eliminate competitors from consideration.

premium
Sales promotion technique in which offers of free or reduced-price items are used to stimulate purchases

■ Free samples and premiums are purchasing incentives. Free samples allow customers to try products without risk. They may be given out at local retail outlets or sent by manufacturers to consumers by direct mail. **Premiums** are gifts, such as pens, pencils, calendars, and coffee mugs, that are given away to consumers in return for buying a specified product. Retailers and wholesalers also receive premiums for carrying some products.

trade show
Sales promotion technique in which various members of an industry gather to display, demonstrate, and sell products

■ Periodically, industries sponsor **trade shows** for members and customers. Trade shows allow companies to rent booths to display and demonstrate products to customers who have a special interest in them or who are ready to buy. Trade shows are inexpensive and, because the buyer comes to the seller already interested in a given type of product, are quite effective.

■ Customers, distributors, and sales representatives may all be persuaded to increase sales by means of contests. For example, consumers may be asked to enter their cats in the Purina Cat Chow calendar contest by submitting entry blanks from the backs of cat food packages.

Publicity and Public Relations

publicity
Promotional tool in which information about a company or product is transmitted by general mass media

Much to the delight of marketing managers with tight budgets, **publicity** is free. Moreover, because it is presented in a news format, consumers often see publicity as objective and highly believable. Thus, it is a very important part of the promotional mix. Unfortunately, however, marketers often have little control over publicity.

In 1994 Intel, the world's largest maker of computer chips, was presented with a crisis when a defect was discovered in its Pentium chip. When Thomas Nicely contacted Intel and asked for a replacement chip, his request was refused. Intel acknowledged that Pentium had a flaw but insisted that it would result in a computing error only once in 27,000 years. A frustrated Nicely expressed his dissatisfaction over the Internet. Word about the Pentium flaw—and Intel's response—spread quickly. After about 2 months of negative publicity in newspapers, on TV, and on the radio, Intel announced that it would provide an updated Pentium chip "for any owner who requests it, free of charge during the lifetime of their computer."[15]

public relations
Company-influenced publicity directed at building good will between an organization and potential customers

Public relations is company-influenced publicity that seeks to build good relations with the public and to deal with the effects of unfavorable events.[16] It attempts to establish good will with customers (and potential customers) by performing and publicizing a company's public service activities. McDonald's 1995 *Annual Report*, for example, proudly announces there were 168 Ronald McDonald houses in 12 countries serving more than 2,500 away-from-home families with seriously ill children every night. Southwest Airlines gained favor with the flying public when it announced in 1996 it would spend $20 million to replace the flight data recorders ("black boxes") on its fleet of 737s, and that it would do so ahead of mandated improvements already being considered by the Federal Aviation Administration. Southwest's plans were announced after two unexplained crashes of 737s operated by other airlines.[17]

International Promotional Strategies

As we saw in chapter 3, recent decades have witnessed a profound shift from home-country marketing to multicountry and now to global marketing. Nowhere is this rapidly growing global orientation more evident than in marketing promotions, especially advertising.

Growth of Worldwide Advertising

In the mid-twentieth century, companies began exporting to other countries when domestic sales stagnated. Advertising played a key role in these efforts because it was the best tool for creating product awareness in each country—that is, for stimulating sales by ex-

Table 13.2 Top 10 Global Advertising Spenders

World Rank	Advertiser	Headquarters	Primary Business	Worldwide Spending ($ million)	Non-U.S. Spending as % of Worldwide
1	Procter & Gamble	U.S.A.	Consumer products	2,713.3	34.4
2	Philip Morris	U.S.A.	Food	2,502.1	17.2
3	Unilever	Netherlands/England	Consumer products	1,744.2	65.4
4	General Motors	U.S.A.	Automotive	1,687.7	19.2
5	Nestlé	Switzerland	Food	1,143.0	46.8
6	McDonald's	U.S.A.	Restaurants	934.1	17.1
7	PepsiCo	U.S.A.	Food	913.8	14.0
8	Ford	U.S.A.	Automotive	870.7	30.9
9	Kellogg	U.S.A.	Food	823.7	25.7
10	Toyota	Japan	Automotive	739.8	43.6

plaining a product's benefits to new consumers. Today, worldwide advertising is a large part of many companies' promotional expenditures. The top 10 global spenders are listed in Table 13.2. The U.S. firms on the list spend an average of 24 percent of their ad budgets to reach non-U.S. audiences.

Emergence of the Global Perspective

Every company that markets its products in several countries faces a basic choice: use a decentralized approach with separate marketing management for each country or adopt a **global perspective** with a coordinated marketing program directed at one worldwide audience. The global perspective, therefore, is actually a company philosophy that directs marketing toward a worldwide rather than a local or regional market. American companies such as IBM, PepsiCo, and the accounting firm Arthur Andersen are in the forefront of global orientation in advertising. The movement is in the global direction, but "one world market" remains a concept more than a reality.

global perspective
Company's approach to directing its marketing toward worldwide rather than local or regional markets

Movement Toward Global Advertising

The truly global perspective means designing products for multinational appeal—that is, genuinely global products. A few brands, such as Coca-Cola, McDonald's, Mercedes, Rolex, and Xerox, enjoy global recognition in a variety of countries and cultures, and thus have become truly global brands. Not surprisingly, then, globalization is affecting many firms' promotional activities. In effect, they have already posed the question "Is it possible to develop global advertising?" Certainly one universal advertising program would be more efficient and cost-effective than developing different programs for each of many countries. For several reasons, however, global advertising is not feasible for many companies. Here, we will touch on four factors that make global advertising a challenging proposition: product variations, language differences, cultural receptiveness, and image differences.

Product Variations. First, even if a basic product has universal appeal, at least modest product variations, or slightly different products, are usually preferred in different cultures. In the magazine business, for example, Hearst Corporation has expanded to 33 editions of *Cosmopolitan* magazine, including one for Central America, English and Spanish editions for the United States, and local editions for Italy, Turkey, Russia, Hong Kong, and Japan. *Reader's Digest* has 48 editions in 19 languages. As noted by Jonathan Newhouse, chairman of publisher Condé Nast International, "The rest of the world has started to catch up to the West in economic development and in its thirst for information and advertised products. Increasingly, American publishers are adapting products to the regional tastes and styles of local audiences, relying on either joint venture partners or licensing their titles to local companies that control the content." Advertising must reflect these differences in order to communicate product variations, their features, and of course their advantages effectively to local consumers.[18]

> ❝ *The rest of the world has started to catch up to the West in economic development and in its thirst for information and advertised products.* ❞
>
> —Jonathan Newhouse, chairman of publisher Condé Nast International

Language Differences. Perhaps the most obvious barrier to the global ad is language. Compared with those in other languages, for example, ads in English require less print space and air time because English is an efficient language with greater precision of meaning than most. More importantly, translations from one language to another are often inexact and lead to confusion and misunderstanding. For these reasons, acquisitions and mergers of advertising agencies have resulted in the growth of worldwide agency networks that can coordinate an ad campaign's central theme and yet allow regional variations. This diversified language approach will be used in Campbell Soup Company's recent decision to establish its soup globally. In taking its core business international, Campbell's advertising agent will emphasize the soup's logoed containers, but the ad's message content will be adapted in the language of each region to best communicate Campbell's as a reliable, tasty soup.[19]

Cultural Receptiveness. Another variable is cultural receptiveness to alien ideas and products. For example, the threat of violence required police protection when Pizza Hut opened its first restaurant in India in the city of Bangalore in 1996. Political parties and farmers' groups opposed fast-food business because it might corrupt traditional eating habits. Similarly, there is considerable difference across nations regarding the acceptability of mass advertising for sensitive products or those that cause social discomfort (such as underwear, birth control products, personal hygiene products), not to mention those for which advertising may be legally restricted (pharmaceuticals, alcohol, cigarettes). Generally speaking, European countries have more liberal advertising environments than countries in North America, Asia, the Middle East, and Latin America.[20]

For worldwide advertising, magazines are the most popular medium for sensitive products because clear messages can be demographically targeted. Magazines such as *Cosmopolitan* and *Harper's Bazaar* are effective because they are published in a consistent format but with regional variations for the same target audience in many different countries.[21]

Image Differences. Each company's overall image can vary from nation to nation, regardless of any advertising appeals for universal recognition and acceptance. For example, a recent study comparing well-known global brands in the United States and the United Kingdom found that American Express, IBM, and Nestlé had higher-ranking images in the United States than in the United Kingdom. In contrast, Heinz, Coca-Cola, and Ford had higher-ranking images in the United Kingdom.[22]

Firms that are concerned about image and visibility use advertising to present desirable corporate images and to boost public awareness of their company and products. For example, Philips Electronics, the Dutch firm whose U.S. brands include Norelco and Magnavox, uses a worldwide campaign to make a more prominent connection between its product brands and its corporate name. Similarly, Chrysler Corporation has launched its first international corporate branding campaign for the Asia-Pacific region. Although its Jeep brand is globally recognized, Chrysler wants a stronger image for its other branded products, such as Neon, Voyager, Stratus, and Concorde. The $60-million campaign uses TV ads created especially for each market: one for Australia/New Zealand, others for China, Japan, South Korea, Thailand, and Taiwan. The international ad agency Bozell Worldwide used local offices abroad to handle the advertising and "to make sure that the ads were culturally correct in the way people were portrayed." Although the specifics differ for each country and product, all the ads contain one theme for positioning the Chrysler image with the following footage: "Once, traveling with the family was a bit confining. That was then, this is now."[23]

Universal Messages and Regional Advertising Skills

In recognizing national differences, many global marketers try to build on a universal advertising theme that nevertheless allows for variations. In doing so, they rely on help from different advertising agencies in various geographic regions. For example, KFC spends $80 million a year on non-U.S. advertising, including global branding campaigns. KFC has promoted a single message—its red and white three-letter logo—that is recognized around the world. At the same time, however, it still uses advertising variations that are developed by various ad agencies in different countries. KFC uses Ogilvy & Mather Worldwide (Europe, Canada, Mexico, Singapore, China, Ireland) as its international agency, John Singleton Advertising for its Australian and New Zealand activities, and Young & Rubicam in the United States, Latin America, Hong Kong, and Thailand.[24]

Promotional Practices in Small Business

From our discussion so far, you may think that only large companies can afford to promote their products. Although small businesses generally have fewer resources, cost-effective promotions can improve sales and allow small firms to compete with much larger firms.

Small Business Advertising

The type of advertising chosen by a small business depends on the market that the firm is trying to reach: local, national, or international.

Local Markets

Advertising in non–prime-time slots on local television or cable TV offers great impact at a cost that many small firms can afford. More often, however, small businesses with local markets use newspaper, radio, and, increasingly, direct mail. Although billboards are beyond the means of many small businesses, outdoor store signs can draw strong responses from passers-by.

The timing of advertising can be as critical for small businesses as the medium. For year-round advertising, the Yellow Pages are popular for advertising both industrial and consumer products in local markets. However, many small businesses, especially those selling to consumer markets, rely more on seasonal advertising. Retail stores, for instance, advertise for the holidays, and ads for lawn care and home maintenance services appear in the early spring.

National Markets

Many businesses have grown from small to large by using direct mail, particularly catalogs. Sears & Roebuck was once a small mail-order house, as was L.L. Bean. By purchasing mailing lists of other companies' customers, a small firm can reduce costs by targeting its mailings.

The ability to target an audience also makes specialized magazines attractive to small businesses. For example, Turnquist Lumber Co. of Foster, Rhode Island, advertises its specialty, the exporting of quality red oak, in *Southern Lumberman*, a trade magazine for the lumber industry. Similarly, Georgetown Galleries of Bethesda, Maryland, and Omaha Steaks of Omaha, Nebraska, reach for upscale nationwide audiences by advertising in *Smithsonian* magazine.

International Markets

Television, radio, and newspapers are seldom viable promotional options for small businesses to use in reaching international markets. For one thing, they are too expensive for many small firms. For example, the market research used by large companies to determine the best message and style for reaching the target audience is expensive. Additional costs are incurred in developing broadcast and newsprint advertisements with the necessary variations in language and cultural appeal. Instead, most small firms find direct mail and carefully targeted magazine advertising the most effective tools.

The Role of Personal Selling in Small Business

As with advertising, the personal selling strategies used by small businesses depend on their intended markets. Some small firms maintain sales forces to promote and sell their products, especially in local markets, where clients can be quickly visited. Others prefer not to do their own selling, but contract with sales agencies: companies that handle the products of several clients to act on their behalf. For national markets, however, the costs of operating a national sales force are high, so sales agencies and other methods such as telemarketing are used. By combining telemarketing with catalogs or other product literature, small businesses can sometimes compete against much larger companies on a national scale. For example, Syncsort Inc. combined a telemarketing staff with eight national sales representatives to become the number-one developer of computer software for sorting data into convenient formats. Number two is IBM.

Obviously, few small companies can afford to establish international offices. For most, even sending sales representatives overseas is expensive. An increasingly popular alternative for person-to-person selling is through alliances and joint ventures. For example, Megatrends Ltd., a research firm based in Telluride, Colorado, has established no fewer than 57 joint ventures in 42 countries. Personal selling is done by local representatives and, as a result, Megatrends has increased its global reach even though, in owner John Naisbitt's own words, "we are just four people".[25]

Small Business Promotions

Small companies use the same sales promotion incentives as larger companies. However, larger firms tend to use more coupons, POP displays, and sales contests. Because these tools are expensive and difficult to manage, smaller firms rely on premiums and special sales. For example, an automobile dealership might offer you a fishing reel at a bargain price if you just come on down and road-test a new four-wheel-drive vehicle. Gas stations use premiums when they offer free car washes with fill-ups. Special sale prices are commonly offered by service companies ranging from martial arts centers to remodelers and dry cleaners. One successful company, however, uses a variety of promotions to encourage lasting relationships with its customers. Zane's Cycles, a bicycle retailer in Branford, Connecticut, offers free coffee and soft drinks to waiting customers, even some who drop in on Saturday mornings, drink coffee, read the paper, and leave after 20 minutes. With revenues expected to pass $2 million in 1997, Zane's also offers the ultimate promotional incentive: Free lifetime service on each bike it sells.[26]

Summary of Learning Objectives

1 **Identify the important objectives of promotion and discuss the considerations entailed in selecting a promotional mix.** Although the ultimate goal of a promotion is to increase sales, other goals include communicating information, positioning a product, adding value, and controlling sales volume. In deciding on the appropriate promotional mix, marketers must consider the good or service being offered, charac-

teristics of the target audience and the buyer's decision process, and the promotional mix budget.

2 **Discuss the most important advertising strategies and describe the key advertising media.** Advertising strategies often depend on the product life cycle stage. In the introductory stage, informative advertising helps to build awareness. As a product passes through the growth and maturity stages, persuasive advertising, comparative advertising, and reminder advertising are often used. Advertising media include newspapers, television, direct mail, radio, magazines, and outdoor advertising, as well as other channels such as Yellow Pages, special events, and door-to-door selling. The combination of media that a company chooses is called its media mix.

3 **Outline the tasks involved in personal selling and list the steps in the personal selling process.** Personal selling tasks include order processing, creative selling (activities that help persuade buyers), and missionary selling (activities that promote firms and products rather than simply close sales). The personal selling process consists of six steps: prospecting and qualifying (identifying potential customers with the authority to buy), approaching (the first moments of contact), presenting and demonstrating (presenting the promotional message that explains the product), handling objections, closing (asking for the sale), and following up (processing the order and ensuring after-sale service).

4 **Describe the various types of sales promotions.** Coupons provide savings off the regular price of a product. Point-of-purchase (POP) displays are intended to grab attention and help customers find products in stores. Purchasing incentives include samples (which let customers try products without buying them) and premiums (rewards for buying products). At trade shows, sellers rent booths to display products to customers who already have an interest in buying. Contests are intended to increase sales by stimulating buyers' interest in products.

5 **Describe the development of international promotional strategies.** Many firms began exploring the possibilities of international sales when domestic sales flattened out in the mid-twentieth century. Because advertising is the best tool for stimulating product awareness on a country-by-country basis, it has played a key role in the growth of international marketing. Whereas some firms prefer a decentralized approach (separate marketing management for different countries), others have adopted a global perspective (coordinating marketing programs directed at one worldwide audience). Because the global perspective requires products designed for multinational markets, companies such as Coca-Cola, McDonald's, and many others have developed global brands. In promoting these products, global advertising must overcome such challenges as product variations, language differences, cultural receptiveness, and image differences.

6 **Show how small businesses use promotional activities.** Small business can advertise and engage in personal selling activities in local, national, and international markets. Because coupons and contests are more expensive and harder to manage, small business owners are likely to rely more heavily on premiums and special sales.

Questions and Exercises

Review Questions

1 What are the differences between push and pull strategies? Why would a firm choose one over the other?
2 Compare the advantages and disadvantages of different advertising media.
3 What are the advantages of personal selling over other promotional tools?
4 Which promotional tools have proven most useful in mounting global advertising campaigns? Why?
5 Is publicity more or less available to small firms than to larger firms? Why?

Questions for Analysis

6 Take a look at some of the advertising conducted by locally based businesses in your area. Choose two campaigns: one that you think effective and one that you think ineffective. What differences in the campaigns make one better than the other?

7 Select a good or a service that you have purchased recently. Try to retrace the relevant steps in the buyer decision process as you experienced it. Which steps were most important to you? Least important?

8 Find some examples of publicity about some business, either a local firm or a national firm. Did the publicity have, or is it likely to have, positive or negative consequences for the business involved? Why?

Application Exercises

9 Select a product that is sold nationally. Identify as many media used in its promotion as you can. Which medium is used most? On the whole, do you think the campaign is effective? Why or why not?

10 Interview the owner of a local small business. Identify the company's promotional objectives and strategies and the elements in its promotional mix. What (if any) changes would you suggest? Why?

Building Your Business Skills

This exercise enhances the following SCANS workplace competencies: demonstrating basic skills, demonstrating thinking skills, exhibiting interpersonal skills, and working with information.

Goal To encourage students to analyze the impact of color on newspaper advertising.

Situation You are the advertising manager of a newspaper with a daily circulation of 300,000. Although ad revenues have been steady for years, you see a way of boosting circulation, which would allow the paper to charge more for ads. Your solution is to print the paper in color. Your challenge is to convince the publisher that it is a financially sound decision.

Method **Step 1:** Come together with four or five classmates to research the switch to color in the *New York Times*. Find out why the *Times* added color and investigate the reaction of the public and advertisers.

Step 2: Draft a proposal to the publisher. Leaving budget and production factors to colleagues in accounting and production, list as many reasons as possible for shifting to color. Then defend each reason. Among the reasons to consider are the following:

- *The competitive environment:* Analyze the impact of newspapers that already print in color.
- *The expectations of the target market:* Do Generation Xers expect color?
- *The point-of-sale appeal:* Will a front-page color photo sell more papers?
- *The effect on advertisers:* Are they more likely to advertise because their ads have greater impact?

Follow-Up Questions

1 Why do you think the public wants colorful newspapers?

2 *USA Today* started this trend over a decade ago. Why do you think it took so long for other papers to make the switch?

3 What was your most convincing argument for shifting to color?

4 Can a newspaper continue to thrive without color when other papers are making the switch?

Business Case 13

Spike Lee Takes a Lease on Madison Avenue

An Oscar-winning film director (*Do the Right Thing, She's Gotta Have It*) who has already created a number of innovative ads (Nike's famous Air Jordan campaign), Spike Lee made his presence on Madison Avenue official with the recent formation of his own advertising agency. A joint venture between Lee and advertising giant DDB Needham Worldwide, the new agency, known as Spike DDB, got off to a fast start. Ad billings from the first roster of clients were expected to hit $35 million.

Lee wants to court clients who reach what he calls "the urban market." He sees this market as including young, trend-setting consumers with money to spend on sports and fashion. "It's all about telling a story," he told the *New York Times* about his agency's mission. "It's not specifically targeting African-Americans." Yet directors of some of the industry's biggest black-owned agencies disagree. Some feel Lee should have chosen a black agency as his business partner, and others feel the kind of mass marketing Spike DDB wants to do is dead. In apparent support of black agencies' reliance on more narrowly targeted campaigns is an advertising industry study showing that the lists of top 20 TV shows for white households and for black households intersect at only one point (*Monday Night Football*).

> **" I got tired of just being the hired gun. I wanted more creative input. I tell young people, especially African-Americans, that it's about ownership. "**

> —Spike Lee

Still, Spike DDB has already done work for the such mass market targeters as the Showtime channel and Anheuser-Busch, the maker of Budweiser beer.

Lee faces another challenge: keeping himself going. The energetic director has pledged his wholehearted effort to the advertising firm, yet he continues to work on a steady stream of new feature-length films and documentaries. In addition he directs commercials and music videos, acts in ads for other agencies, writes, and runs his own production company. He is not the only director at home in films and commercials, but he is so far the only one to set up his own agency: "I got tired of just being the hired gun. I wanted more creative input. I tell young people, especially African-Americans, that it's about ownership."

Questions

1 Do you think Spike Lee's continuing career as a successful filmmaker will help or hurt Spike DDB? Why?

2 How do you think Spike DDB should respond to criticism from black-owned ad agencies?

3 Do you think mass marketing is dead? Why or why not?

4 How should Spike DDB position itself for success in the advertising business?

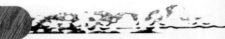

Connecting to the Web

The following Web sites will give you additional information and points of view about topics covered in this chapter. Many sites lead to other related Internet locations, so approach this list with the spirit of an explorer.

ADVERTISING AGE

http://www.adage.com

This interactive version of *Advertising Age*, the industry bible, allows you to search for specific articles and features.

CBBB: NATIONAL ADVERTISING REVIEW BOARD

http://www.bb.org/advertising/narb.html

The National Advertising Review Board was created by the Council of Better Business Bureaus to help ensure "truth and accuracy in national advertising." This site describes the NARB, its history and functions, as well as the industry's self-regulatory process.

CHAPARRAL STEEL

http://www.chaparralsteel.com/

Like its advertisements, Chaparral Steel's Web site is targeted at industrial users and distributors.

THE GAP

http://www.gap.com

Visit this Web site to see how The Gap uses the Internet for sales and promotion. Current advertising campaigns for such product lines as GapKids and Gap Jeans were found on a recent visit, as were outdoor advertising campaigns in Los Angeles, New York, and Tokyo.

HALLMARK CARDS

http://www.hallmark.com/

This site demonstrates some of the on-line promotional techniques used by Hallmark Cards in order to stabilize sales volume throughout the year.

LEXUS

http://www.lexuscar.com/

Visit the Lexus Web site for a glimpse of the high level of customer service that is a corporate value.

MGD TAPROOM

http://www.mgdtaproom.com/index.htm

With its "What's the point?" approach, this Miller Brewing Company Web site is designed to appeal to Generation Xers.

MOBIL CORPORATION: MOBILE NEWS AND VIEWS

http://www.mobil.com/this/news/indx.html

The Mobil Corporation takes editorial positions on issues critical to business and the general public and publishes these positions as paid advertisements in major newspapers throughout the country. Mobil's institutional advertising can be found on this Web site.

SPIKESITE

http://www.spikeddb.com/

This site introduces Spike Lee's joint advertising agency venture with DDB Needham Worldwide.

A TRIBUTE TO THE STARBUCKS FRAPPUCCINO

http://home.earthlink.net/~Ishinar/frappucino.html

This Web site is part of Starbucks' advertising campaign to promote Frappuccino to Generation Xers.

chapter 14

Distributing products

Welcome to the Cyberspace Mall!

Are you looking for a book? Some software? Milk, eggs, and hamburger rolls? How about rare stamps, a time-share, or airline tickets?

You can now get all these and more on the Internet. Up-to-the-minute technology, combined with tried and true sales techniques, are transforming the world's marketplace. Just about everything from computer hardware to perishables and collectibles is being offered on hundreds of Web sites in the new electronic mall, as close as your modem. With strategies from download-able catalogs with 3D images to auctions to electronic personal shoppers, sellers around the globe are zeroing in on the enormous number of people willing to browse and buy on the Net. There is even a close-out merchandiser in cyberspace, doing well enough to

branch out into franchise warehouses in South Africa and Australia.

The electronic marketplace is mostly populated by U.S. consumers; one estimate says that $4 out of $5 spent on-line are spent by Americans, and foreign firms are eager to sell to them. Cheaper labor costs abroad—and the unprecedented opportunity to compete only one click of a mouse away from the rest of the world—are helping international transactions increase as Internet shopping grows. Says Simon Croft, an English Web site designer who sells on the Net, "Many visitors do not seem to care, or do not stop to think about, where you are based on the planet."

Home-grown firms such as Elcom International, Inc., are confident too. Says CEO Robert J. Crowell of his firm's new venture into on-line grocery shopping, "We're going to change the way people shop." Food and drink sales on the Internet are still modest, perhaps understandably, but this market alone is pro-

A customer connects to www.amazon.com.

jected to zoom into the $300 million range in the next few years.

And, at least for now, on-line shoppers are largely avoiding the bane of mall shoppers everywhere: the state sales tax.

❝ We're going to change the way people shop. ❞

—Robert J. Crowell, CEO, Elcom International Inc.

Although on-line shopping has enormous potential, it is only one way of getting products to customers. As the fourth element in the marketing mix (place), distribution takes many forms. By focusing on the learning objectives of this chapter, you will better understand the importance of distribution in the marketing process. After reading this chapter, you should be able to

1 Identify the different channels of distribution and explain different distribution strategies.

2 Explain the differences between merchant wholesalers and agents/brokers.

3 Identify the different types of retail stores and explain the wheel of retailing.

4 Describe the major activities in the physical distribution process.

5 Compare the five basic forms of transportation and identify the types of firms that provide them.

The Distribution Mix

distribution mix
The combination of distribution channels by which a firm gets its products to end users

We have already seen that a company needs an appropriate product mix. But the success of any product also depends on its **distribution mix**: the combination of distribution channels that a firm selects to get a product to end users. In this section, we will consider some of the many factors that enter into the distribution mix. First, we will look at the role of the target audience and explain the need for intermediaries. We will then discuss the basic distribution strategies. Finally, we will consider some special issues in channel relationships—namely, conflict and leadership.

Intermediaries and Distribution Channels

intermediary
Individual or firm that helps to distribute a product

Once called middlemen, **intermediaries** are the individuals and firms who help to distribute a producer's goods. They are generally classified as wholesalers or retailers. **Wholesalers** sell products to other businesses, who resell them to final consumers. **Retailers** sell products directly to consumers. Some firms rely on independent intermediaries, and others employ their own distribution networks and sales forces. The decision normally hinges on three factors:

wholesaler
Intermediary who sells products to other businesses for resale to final consumers

■ The company's target markets

■ The nature of its products

retailer
Intermediary who sells products directly to consumers

■ The costs of maintaining distribution and sales networks

In this section we will examine these factors more closely by describing some of the distribution decisions that go into the marketing of consumer products.

Distribution of Consumer Products

distribution channel
Network of interdependent companies through which a product passes from producer to end user

A **distribution channel** is the path that a product follows from producer to end user. Figure 14.1 shows how the six primary distribution channels can be identified according to the kinds of channel members who participate in getting products to their ultimate destinations. As we move through this discussion, note first that all channels begin with a manufacturer and end with a consumer or an industrial user. Channels 1 through 4 are most often used for the distribution of consumer goods and services.

Figure 14.1 Channels of Distribution

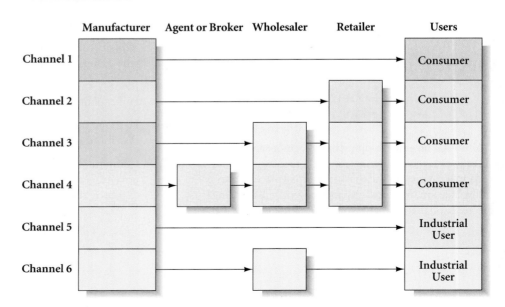

Channel 1: Direct Distribution of Consumer Products.   In a **direct channel**, the product travels from the producer to the consumer without intermediaries. Using their own sales forces, companies such as Avon, Fuller Brush, and Tupperware use this channel.

▶   Dell Computer Corp., for example, sells personal computers over the phone and customers receive their purchases by direct mail. Today, Dell Computer is a $3.4-billion-a-year business and the fourth-largest PC maker in the United States. By selling direct, Dell and rival Gateway 2000 have captured about 20 percent of the $45-billion PC market. Dell runs a bare-bones operation in Austin, Texas, where workers assemble off-the-shelf components into finished PCs as orders are received. As the first entrepreneur to sell computers by mail, Michael Dell feels confident that he knows his market better than anyone else. However, Dell's experience has also taught him that direct sales is more difficult than it looks: "It's not as easy as a couple of 1-800 lines and a bunch of picnic tables," he warns.[1]

> ❝ *It's not as easy as a couple of 1-800 lines and a bunch of picnic tables.* ❞
>
> —Computer entrepreneur Michael Dell

Channel 2: Retail Distribution of Consumer Products.   In Channel 2, manufacturers distribute products through retailers. Goodyear, for example, maintains its own system of retail outlets. Levi's has its own outlets but also produces jeans for other retailers such as The Gap. Liz Claiborne, on the other hand, relies on more than 9,300 retailers to sell its apparel worldwide. Claiborne uses its sales force to sell products to the retailers, who then sell them over the counter to consumers.

Channel 3: Wholesale Distribution of Consumer Products.   Until the mid-1960s, Channel 2 was the most widely used method of nondirect distribution. It requires a large amount of floor space, however, both for storing merchandise and for displaying it in retail stores. Faced with the rising cost of retail space, many retailers found that they could not afford both retail and storage space. Thus, wholesalers entered the distribution network to take over more and more of the storage service. An example of Channel 3 is combination convenience stores/gas stations. Approximately 90 percent of the space in these stores is used for merchandise displays; only about 10 percent is left for storage and office facilities. Merchandise in the store is stocked frequently by wholesalers.

At the same time, wholesale channels have always played a role in the distribution of some products. For example, many manufacturers distribute products only in large quantities. Thus, small businesses that cannot afford large-quantity purchases often rely on wholesalers to hold and supply inventories on short notice. For example, a family-owned grocery store that annually sells only 100 cases of canned spinach cannot afford a truckload order of 500 cases. Instead, it will order a few cases each month from a local wholesaler, who buys and stores large lots to resell in small quantities.

Channel 4: Distribution Through Sales Agents or Brokers.   Channel 4 uses **sales agents**, or **brokers**, who represent manufacturers and sell to wholesalers, retailers, or both. They receive commissions based on the price of goods they sell. Agents generally deal in the related product lines of a few producers, serving as their sales representatives on a long-term basis. For example, travel agents represent airlines, car rental companies, and hotels. In contrast, brokers are hired to assist in buying and selling temporarily, matching sellers and buyers as needed. This channel is often used in the food and clothing industries. The real estate industry also relies on brokers for matching buyers and sellers of property.

direct channel
Distribution channel in which a product travels from producer to consumer without intermediaries

sales agent/broker
Independent intermediary who usually represents many manufacturers and sells to wholesalers or retailers

Figure 14.2   A Typical Sequence of Markups

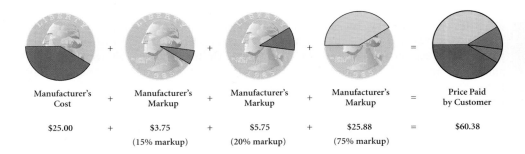

Manufacturer's Cost	+	Manufacturer's Markup	+	Manufacturer's Markup	+	Manufacturer's Markup	=	Price Paid by Customer
$25.00	+	$3.75	+	$5.75	+	$25.88	=	$60.38
		(15% markup)		(20% markup)		(75% markup)		

The Pros and Cons of Nondirect Distribution

Ultimately, each link in the distribution chain makes a profit by charging a markup or commission. Thus, nondirect distribution channels mean higher prices for end users: The more members in the channel—the more intermediaries—the higher the final price. Calculated as a percentage of cost, markups are applied each time a product is sold. Figure 14.2 highlights a typical series of markups as a product moves through the distribution channel. Markups may range from 10 to 40 percent for manufacturers, from 2 to 25 percent for wholesalers, and from 5 to 100 percent for retailers. Markup size depends on the particular industry and competitive conditions.

At the same time, however, intermediaries can save consumers both time and money. In doing so they provide added value for customers. Moreover, this value-adding activity continues and accumulates at each stage of the supply chain. In fact, intermediaries add value by making the right quantities of products available where and when you need them. For example, consider Figure 14.3, which illustrates the problem of making chili without benefit of a common intermediary—the supermarket. You would obviously spend a lot more time, money, and energy if you tried to gather all the ingredients yourself. Moreover, if we eliminated intermediaries, we would not eliminate either their functions or the costs entailed by what they do. Intermediaries exist because they perform necessary functions in cost-efficient ways.

Distribution of Industrial Products

industrial distribution
Network of channel members involved in the flow of manufactured goods to industrial customers

Industrial channels are important because every company is itself a customer that buys other companies products. The Kellogg Co., for example, buys grain to make breakfast cereals, and Humana, a nationwide chain of for-profit hospitals, buys medicines and other supplies to provide medical services. **Industrial distribution**, therefore, is the network of channel members involved in the flow of manufactured goods to industrial customers.

Figure 14.3   The Value-Adding Intermediary

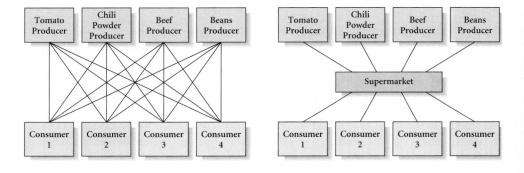

Unlike consumer products, industrial products are traditionally distributed through Channels 5 or 6 shown in Figure 14.1.

Channel 5: Direct Distribution of Industrial Products.

Most industrial goods are sold directly by the manufacturer to the industrial buyer. Lawless Container Corp., for instance, produces packaging containers that are sold directly to such customers as Fisher-Price (toys), Dirt Devil (vacuum cleaners), Peak anti-freeze, and Mr. Coffee (coffee makers). As contact points with their customers, manufacturers maintain **sales offices**. These offices provide all services for the company's customers and serve as headquarters for its salespeople.

Other products distributed through Channel 5 include steel, transistors, and conveyors. Intermediaries are often unnecessary because such goods are usually purchased in large quantities. In some cases, however, brokers or agents may enter the distribution chain between manufacturers and buyers.

sales office
Office maintained by a manufacturer as a contact point with its customers

Channel 6: Wholesale Distribution of Industrial Products.

Wholesalers function as intermediaries between manufacturers and end users in a very small percentage of industrial channels. Brokers and agents are even rarer. Channel 6 is most often used for accessory equipment (computer terminals, office equipment) and supplies (floppy disks, copier paper). Whereas manufacturers produce these items in large quantities, companies buy them in small quantities. For example, few companies order truckloads of paper clips. As with consumer goods, then, intermediaries help end users by representing manufacturers or by breaking down large quantities into smaller sales units.

In some areas, however, relationships are changing. In the office products industry, for instance, Channel 6 is being displaced by the emergence of a new channel that looks very much like Channel 3 for consumer products: Instead of buying office supplies from wholesalers (Channel 6), many users are shopping at office discount stores such as Staples, Office Depot, and Office Max. All three warehouse-like superstores target small and mid-size businesses, which generally buy supplies at retail stores, much as they target retail consumers. In these new discount stores for industrial users, customers stroll down the aisles behind shopping carts, selecting from 7,000 items at prices 20 to 75 percent lower than manufacturers' suggested prices.

Retailers such as Staples concentrate on dominant assortments of merchandise. Customers shopping for stationery or office equipment know beforehand that they will find what they are looking for. When such retailers maintain huge assortments in one product area, they complement wide selections with steep price discounts and are often called category killers. Other well-known category killers are Home Depot, Crown Books, Sports-Mart, and Toys Я Us. What they are killing is the habit of one-stop shopping at stores such as Wal-Mart and Kmart.

Choosing an appropriate distribution channel is sometimes much more difficult than it seems, especially with new products:

▶ An example is MicroFrige, a combination refrigerator-freezer and microwave oven for smaller housing units (apartments, dormatories, hotel rooms). CEO Bob Bennett chose 17 established large-appliance distributors, covering most of the United States, to carry his new product. After 5 months of near business failure, he realized that these distributors had no idea how to move his product. They had no contacts at colleges or army bases—organizations with large concentrations of dormatories. Bennett thus replaced his distributors by hiring four full-time sales representatives who focused on college and army-base housing directors. Today, 75 percent of the company's sales are made through direct sales to colleges and military bases. The changeover to direct distribution (Channel 5) saved MicroFrige from financial disaster.[2]

Distribution Strategies

Selecting an appropriate distribution network is vital. Distribution strategy determines not only the amount of market exposure that a product receives but also the cost of getting it.

Generally, distribution strategy depends on the product class and the degree of market exposure that is most effective in getting a product to the greatest number of customers. The goal is to make a product accessible in just enough locations to satisfy customers' needs. Whereas milk can be purchased in numerous retail outlets, there is only one Rolls-Royce distributor in any city, region, or even state. Different degrees of market exposure are available through strategies of intensive, exclusive, and selective distribution.

Intensive Distribution

intensive distribution
Strategy by which a product is distributed through as many channels as possible

Intensive distribution entails distributing a product through as many channels and channel members as possible (both wholesalers and retailers). It is normally used for low-cost consumer goods with widespread appeal, such as candy and magazines. Thus, M&M's candies enter the market through all suitable retail outlets—supermarkets, candy machines, drugstores, and so forth. Various retailers are supplied by many different wholesalers.

Exclusive Distribution

exclusive distribution
Strategy by which a manufacturer grants exclusive rights to distribute or sell a product to a limited number of wholesalers or retailers in a given geographic area

With **exclusive distribution**, a manufacturer grants the exclusive right to distribute or sell a product to a limited number of wholesalers or retailers, usually in a given geographic area. Such agreements are most common for high-cost prestige products. Rolex watches, for example, are sold only in selected jewelry stores. Jaguar automobiles are sold by a limited number of dealers serving large metropolitan areas, regions, or states.

Selective Distribution

selective distribution
Strategy by which a company uses only wholesalers and retailers who give special attention to specific products

Finally, **selective distribution** falls between intensive and exclusive distribution. Using this strategy, a producer selects only wholesalers and retailers who will give a product special attention in sales effort, display advantage, and so forth. Selective distribution policies are used most often for consumer products such as furniture and appliances. A company such as General Electric uses selective distribution for appliances because it can form good relationships with selected wholesalers who will emphasize GE rather than other brands. By dealing with a few devoted channel members, GE keeps distribution costs lower while giving its products good market coverage.

Channel Conflict and Channel Leadership

Manufacturers can choose to distribute through more than one channel or wholesaler. They can also choose to make new uses of existing channels. Similarly, most retailers (say, RiteAid drugstores) are free to strike agreements with as many producers (the makers of Tylenol, Advil, and Bayer) as capacity permits. In such cases, channel conflict may arise.

Conflicts are resolved when members' efforts are better coordinated. A key factor in coordinating the activities of independent organizations is channel leadership. Another strategy for improving coordination is the vertical marketing system.

Channel Conflict

Channel conflict occurs when members of the channel disagree over the roles they should play or the rewards they should receive. For example, John Deere would object if its dealers began distributing Russian and Japanese tractors. Similarly, when a manufacturer-owned factory outlet store discounts the company's apparel or housewares, it runs the risk of alienating the manufacturer's retail accounts. Channel conflict may also arise if one member has more power than the others or is viewed as receiving preferential treatment. Needless to say, such conflicts defeat the purpose of the system by disrupting the flow of goods to their destinations.

Consider the case of IBM, which sells both nondirectly, through wholesalers and retailers, and directly to major corporations. When IBM makes a direct sale, its dealers point out that they have lost a chance to earn money by making the sale themselves. If this pattern repeatedly frustrates one particular dealer, that dealer may take action (for example, by switching from IBM to Apple products).

Another example can be found in the pharmaceutical industry. The emergence of generic drugs in recent years has led to channel and ethical conflicts in the prescription drug market. Most drugstores carry both name brands and generic equivalents that sell for as little as one-third of the name-brand price. When considering generic substitution, customers seek the pharmacist's advice. Ethically, the pharmacist is placed in the position of balancing benefits for customers (lower prices) against benefits for the store (profitability). The conflict arises because the intermediary may undersell one producer's brand-name product by recommending another's generic.

Channel Leadership

Usually, one channel member is most powerful in determining the roles and rewards of other members. That member is the **channel captain**. Often, the channel captain is a manufacturer. For example, the jewelry made by New Orleans artisan Thomas Mann is so un-

channel conflict
Conflict arising when the members of a distribution channel disagree over the roles they should play or the rewards they should receive

channel captain
Channel member who is most powerful in determining the roles and rewards of other members

Although channel leaders are often large firms, sometimes they can be a sole proprietor. Jewelry artisan Thomas Mann of New Orleans, whose work is shown here, is an example. Mann's reputation for high-quality and popular designs has positioned him prominently in the art-jewelry industry. Mann selects the channel members for his unique hand-crafted products and sets the prices. In addition, his understanding of marketing and distribution channels has placed him in demand as a seminar leader at American Craft Council shows; Mann helps other artisans learn about running a successful business. Says Mann, "I think many very talented people have gotten disappointed with their lives as artists because they couldn't handle the business part."

usual and treasured that wholesalers and retailers wait years for the chance to distribute it. Mann selects channel members, sets prices, and determines product availability. In other industries, an influential wholesaler or a large retailer such as Wal-Mart or Sears may emerge as channel captain because of large sales volume.

Vertical Marketing Systems

To overcome problems posed by channel conflict and issues of channel leadership, the **vertical marketing system (VMS)** has emerged. In a VMS, separate businesses join to form a unified distribution channel, with one member coordinating the activities of the whole channel. There are three types of VMS arrangements:

vertical marketing system (VMS)
Unified distribution channel composed of separate businesses centrally controlled by a single member

- In a corporate VMS, all stages in the channel are under single ownership. The Limited, for example, owns both the production facilities that manufacture its apparel and the retail stores that sell it.

- In a contractual VMS, channel members sign contracts agreeing to specific duties and rewards. The Independent Grocers' Alliance (IGA), for example, consists of independent retail grocers joined with a wholesaler who contractually leads but does not own the VMS.

- In an administered VMS, channel members are less formally coordinated than in a corporate or contractual VMS. Instead, one or more of the members emerge as leaders and maintain control as a result of power and influence. Although the administered VMS is more fragile than the corporate and contractual forms, it is still more unified than channels relying on independent members.

Wholesaling

Now that you know something about distribution channels, we can consider the role played by intermediaries in more detail. Wholesalers provide a variety of services to customers who are buying products for resale or business use. For example, in addition to storing and providing an assortment of products, wholesalers offer delivery, credit, and product information. Of course, not all wholesalers perform all these functions. Services offered depend on the type of intermediary involved: merchant wholesalers or agents/brokers.

merchant wholesaler
Independent wholesaler who takes legal possession of goods produced by a variety of manufacturers and then resells them to other businesses

full-service merchant wholesaler
Merchant wholesaler who provides credit, marketing, and merchandising services in addition to traditional buying and selling services

limited-function merchant wholesaler
Merchant wholesaler who provides a limited range of services

drop shipper
Limited-function merchant wholesaler who receives customer orders, negotiates with producers, takes title to goods, and arranges for shipment to customers

rack jobber
Limited-function merchant wholesaler who sets up and maintains display racks in retail stores

Merchant Wholesalers

Most wholesalers are independent operations that sell various consumer or business goods produced by a variety of manufacturers. Merchant wholesalers, the largest single group of wholesalers, play dual roles, buying products from manufacturers and selling them to other businesses. Merchant wholesalers purchase and own the goods that they resell. Usually, they also provide storage and delivery. In the United States, the merchant wholesaling industry employs 5 million people with a total yearly payroll of $140 billion.

A full-service merchant wholesaler also provides credit, marketing, and merchandising services. Approximately 80 percent of all merchant wholesalers are **full-service merchant wholesalers**. **Limited-function merchant wholesalers** provide only a few services, sometimes merely storage. Their customers are normally small operations that pay cash and pick up their own goods. One such wholesaler, the **drop shipper**, does not even carry inventory or handle the product. Drop shippers receive orders from customers, negotiate with producers to supply goods, take title to them, and arrange for shipment to customers. The drop shipper bears the risks of the transaction until the customer takes title to the goods.

Other limited-function wholesalers, known as **rack jobbers**, market consumer goods (mostly nonfood items) directly to retail stores. Procter & Gamble, for example, uses rack jobbers to distribute products such as Pampers diapers. After marking prices, setting up display racks, and displaying diapers in one store, the rack jobber moves on to another outlet to check inventories and shelve products.

Agents and Brokers

Agents and brokers serve as sales forces for various manufacturers. They are independent representatives of many companies' products. They work on commissions, usually about 4 to 5 percent of net sales. Unlike merchant wholesalers, they do not take title to (that is, they do not own) the merchandise they sell. Rather, they serve as sales and merchandising arms of manufacturers who do not have their own sales forces.

The value of agents and brokers lies primarily in their knowledge of markets and their merchandising expertise. They also provide a wide range of services, including shelf and display merchandising and advertising layout. Finally, they maintain product salability by removing open, torn, or dirty packages, arranging products neatly, and generally keeping them attractively displayed. Many supermarket products are handled through brokers.

▶ A unique new brokerage service has emerged in the form of the on-line facilitator, Cendant Corporation International, for example, has launched NetMarket on the World Wide Web. As an on-line facilitator, NetMarket offers a database displaying more than 250,000 discount products and services and takes customer orders and payments. Orders are passed along to distributors and manufacturers, who ship products directly to buyers. Because the electronic intermediary has no need for expensive sales personnel, warehouses, inventories, or showrooms, an expected advantage for consumers is lower cost. "It's all leverage," explains one marketing researcher. "The brilliance is that they don't have to have a warehouse for just-in-time purchasing. It's the ideal middleman business."[3]

❝ *The brilliance is that they don't have to have a warehouse for just-in-time purchasing. It's the ideal middleman business.* ❞

—Marketing researcher Gary Arlen

Trends in Intermediary-Customer Relationships

Like so many relationships in today's business environment, intermediary-customer relationships are undergoing a variety of changes. Two emerging trends are the use of fewer intermediaries and more customer-supplier partnerships.

In some industries, intermediaries are losing sales because customers with access to new information sources are locating new channels for the products they want. Travel agents, for example, still sell about four-fifths of all U.S. airtravel tickets (a service for which they are paid by airlines). However, this service is now threatened with displacement by consumers who have such services as Prodigy and CompuServe, which give them direct computer access to airline reservation systems.[4]

A variety of other products are also becoming available without intermediaries. Readers can order books directly from the publisher by fax or toll-free telephone. Similarly, customers can place telephone orders for made-to-order Motorola pagers and for computers at IBM's PC Direct operation in North Carolina.[5]

Membership-based consumer sites allow members access to databases of hundreds of thousands of brand-name, discount-priced products. Web sites like this simulation display products, take orders, and collect payment. The advantage of shopping this way is the elimination of the showroom, warehouse, inventory, and sales personnel. The online retailer can offer close-to-cost prices because orders are sent directly to manufacturers that, in turn, ship products directly to consumers. The typical Web site features a huge array of consumer goods and such services as travel arrangements, dining selections, and used-auto sales.

Retailing

There are more than 2.5 million retail establishments in the United States. Most of them are small operations, often consisting of owners and part-time help. Indeed, over one-half of the nation's retailers account for less than 10 percent of all retail sales. Retailers also include huge operations such as Wal-Mart, the largest employer in the United States, and Sears. Although there are large retailers in many other countries—Kaufhof in Germany, Carrefour in France, and Daiei in Japan—more of the world's largest retailers are based in the United States than in any other country.

In this section we will begin by describing in some depth the different types of outlets, both store and nonstore, that dot the U.S. retailing landscape. We will also discuss how stores and chains evolve, in a concept called the wheel of retailing. Finally, we will discuss some of the key factors involved in a company's retailing strategy, notably location and type of outlet.

Types of Retail Outlets

U.S. retail operations vary as widely by type as they do by size. They can be classified in various ways: by pricing strategies, location, range of services, or range of product lines. Choosing the right types of retail outlets is a crucial aspect of every seller's distribution strategy. Consider the experience of the Sara Lee Corp., whose name usually conjures visions of cheesecake and chocolate brownies. The Sara Lee of the 1990s, however, has as much to do with pantyhose as it does pies. To achieve broad distribution on its pantyhose line, Sara Lee had to design product lines that appealed to a variety of retailers. To appeal to food retailers, Sara Lee developed two inexpensive hosiery lines: L'Eggs and Just My Size. In this section we describe U.S. retail stores by using two classifications: product line retailers and bargain retailers.

Product Line Retailers

Retailers that feature broad product lines include department stores, supermarkets, and hypermarkets; specialty stores are typified by narrow product lines.

Department Stores.   As the name implies, **department stores** are organized into specialized departments: shoes, furniture, women's petite sizes, and so on. Department stores are usually large and handle a wide range of goods. In addition, they usually offer a variety of services, such as generous return policies, credit plans, and delivery.

> **department store**
> Large product line retailer characterized by organization into specialized departments

In the past, department stores differentiated themselves by what they sold and the prices they charged. Today, however, consumers report that ambiance and service levels

It's Your Business

Sears: Todo Para La Mujer De Hoy ("For All the Women You Are")

If you think all Sears stores are alike, read on.

As one of the oldest Sears retail stores in the country, the outlet in Boyle Heights, a Hispanic neighborhood in downtown Los Angeles, had projected a middle-American image from its founding in 1927 until the mid-1990s. Promoting a classic Sears product line of everything from tractors to soccer shirts with "USA" in big letters on the front, the store was on a losing streak and destined for closing.

But Larry Vines, who became Sears' district general manager in 1994, thought he saw a way to save the store: "We wanted the customer to say, 'This store was built for me.'"

Vines set about changing the entire stock of the store to fit the needs of the Boyle Heights neighborhood. He replaced the tractors with workshop tools and the "USA" shirts with jerseys featuring Latin American teams. He stopped offering custom-made drapes and sold sewing machines in-

stead, brought in tortilla presses and juicers to replace bread makers and fancy appliances, and replaced men's and women's clothing with smaller sizes in brighter colors. Vines paid attention to details, too; his customers preferred solid-color underwear and conservative one-piece swimsuits. Signs in the store were carefully rewritten in Spanish, and Spanish-speaking salespeople were hired.

> " We wanted the customer to say, 'This store was built for me.' "
>
> —Larry Vines, Sears' district general manager

Now the store is one of the most profitable Sears in the area, even though its customers, recent Mexican and Central American immigrants, are generally poor. Sears has retained its buying power by coordinating district-level merchandising at corporate headquarters.

Sears is clearly riding the crest of a wave of new marketing efforts aimed at a growing market. Other chains such as J.C. Penney and Nordstrom are following suit.

differ more than merchandise and thus drive buyer preferences among stores. In New York, for example, Lord & Taylor is associated with tradition and security, Barney's is known as innovative, creative, and masculine, and Bergdorf Goodman is known for sophistication. Throughout the United States, high-end department stores offer attractive surroundings, sometimes with entertainment, that create the atmosphere that affluent shoppers seem to demand. Others offer rock-bottom pricing as their distinguishing feature. But those in between, without a distinct differentiating feature, are at risk of failure. As an example, the collapse of Montgomery Ward, one of the world's most famous department store chains, is due to the lack of a clear identity. Ward's shifted from low-priced mall stores to electronics, appliances, and home furnishings, and ended in malls without any specific identity. For success today, image is growing in importance; increasingly, the product is the store itself, including all of its intangibles.[6]

supermarket
Large product line retailer offering a variety of food and food-related items in specialized departments

Supermarkets.   The shift from the small corner grocery to supermarkets began in the second half of the 1930s. Like department stores, **supermarkets** are divided into departments of related products: food products, household products, and so forth. The emphasis is on low prices, self-service, and wide selection. The largest supermarkets are chain stores such as Safeway, Kroger, Lucky Stores, Winn-Dixie, A&P, and Albertson's.

hypermarket
Very large product line retailer carrying a wide variety of unrelated products

Hypermarkets.   A phenomenon begun in the late 1970s, **hypermarkets** are much larger than supermarkets (up to 200,000 square feet) and sell a much wider variety of products. They also practice **scrambled merchandising**: carrying any product, whether similar or dissimilar to the store's original product offering, that promises to sell. In Dallas, for example, Hypermart U.S.A. sells a wide range of food and grocery items, including specialty foods and fresh bakery goods. It also offers television sets, auto accessories, and dry-cleaning services.

scrambled merchandising
Retail practice of carrying any product that is expected to sell well regardless of a store's original product offering

specialty store
Small retail store carrying one product line or category of related products

Specialty Stores.   **Specialty stores** are small stores that carry one line of related products. They serve clearly defined market segments by offering full product lines in narrow product fields and often feature knowledgeable sales personnel. Sunglass Hut International, for example, has 1,600 outlets carrying a deep selection of sunglasses at competitive prices. In the United States, Canada, Europe, and Australia, its stores are located in malls, airports, and anywhere else that is convenient for quick, one-stop shopping. "People's time," contends CEO Jack B. Chadsey, "is so limited, they don't want to walk through a maze of categories. If they're looking for electronics, they're going to go to an electronics speciality store. Sunglasses are no different."[7]

> **❝** *People's time is so limited, they don't want to walk through a maze of categories.* **❞**
>
> —Jack B. Chadsey, CEO of Sunglass Hut International

Some specialty stores, such as Waldenbooks, are large nationwide chains of identical stores offering standardized product lines. Particularly in the apparel industry, the 1980s were the decade of the specialty store. Between 1980 and 1990, retailers such as The Gap, The Limited, and Ann Taylor spearheaded the growth spurt of a $100-billion industry in stylish upscale clothing.[8]

Bargain Retailers

bargain retailer
Retailer carrying a wide range of products at bargain prices

Bargain retailers carry wide ranges of products and come in many forms. Included in this category are discount houses, off-price stores, catalog showrooms, factory outlets, warehouse clubs, and convenience stores.

Discount Houses.   After World War II, some U.S. retailers began offering discounts to certain customers. These first **discount houses** sold large numbers of items such as televisions and other appliances by featuring substantial price reductions. As name-brand items became more plentiful in the early 1950s, discounters offered even better product assortments while still embracing a philosophy of cash-only sales conducted in low-rent facilities. As they became more firmly entrenched, they began moving to better locations, improving decor, and selling better-quality merchandise at higher prices. They also began offering a few department store services, such as credit plans and noncash sales.

discount house
Bargain retailer that generates large sales volume by offering goods at substantial price reductions

Off-Price Stores.   The 1980s witnessed the growth of the discount house variation commonly called the **off-price store**. Off-price stores buy the excess inventories of well-recognized high-quality manufacturers and sell them at prices up to 60 percent off regular department store prices. They are often prohibited from using manufacturers' names in their advertising because producers fear that a product's marketplace value and prestige will be compromised. One of the more successful off-price chains is Marshall's, which reduces prices on brand-name apparel for men, women, and children.

off-price store
Bargain retailer that buys excess inventories from high-quality manufacturers and sells them at discounted prices

Catalog Showrooms.   Another form of bargain store that has grown dramatically in recent years is the **catalog showroom**. These firms mail out catalogs with color pictures, product descriptions, and prices to attract customers into their showrooms. Once there, customers view display samples, place orders, and wait briefly while clerks retrieve orders from attached warehouses. Service Merchandise, Best Products, and LaBelle's are major catalog showroom retailers.

catalog showroom
Bargain retailer in which customers place orders for catalog items to be picked up at on-premises warehouses

Factory Outlets.   **Factory outlets** are manufacturer-owned stores that avoid wholesalers and retailers by selling merchandise directly from the factory to consumers. The first factory outlets featured apparel, linens, food, and furniture. Because they were usually located in warehouse-like facilities next to the factories, distribution costs were quite low. Lower costs were passed on to customers as lower prices.

factory outlet
Bargain retailer owned by the manufacturer whose products it sells

Warehouse Clubs.   The **warehouse club** (or **wholesale club**) offers large discounts on brand name clothing, groceries, appliances, automotive supplies, and other merchandise. Unlike customers at discount houses and factory outlets, club customers pay annual

warehouse club (or **wholesale club**)
Bargain retailer offering large discounts on brand-name merchandise to customers who have paid annual membership fees

membership fees. The first warehouse club, Price Club, opened in 1976. It merged with its rival Costco in 1993 to form the second-largest warehouse club in the nation (after Wal-Mart's Sam's Club).

Convenience Stores. Neighborhood food retailers such as 7-Eleven and Circle K stores are successful convenience store chains. As the name suggests, **convenience stores** offer ease of purchase: They stress easily accessible locations with parking, extended store hours (in many cases 24 hours), and speedy service. They differ from most bargain retailers in that they do not feature low prices. Like bargain retailers, however, they control prices by keeping in-store service levels to a minimum.

convenience store
Retail store offering easy accessibility, extended hours, and fast service

Nonstore Retailing

Of course, not all goods and services are sold in stores. In fact, some of the nation's largest retailers sell all or most of their products without stores. For example, certain types of consumer goods—soft drinks, candy, and cigarettes—lend themselves to distribution in vending machines. Even at $30 billion per year, however, vending machine sales still represent less than 5 percent of all U.S. retail sales.

Major Types of Nonstore Selling

In this section we will survey a few of the more important forms of nonstore retailing. In particular, we will examine **direct-response retailing**, in which firms make direct contact with customers both to inform them about products and to receive sales orders. This type of retailing includes mail marketing, video marketing, telemarketing, and electronic shopping. Another important form of nonstore retailing is direct selling.

direct-response retailing
Nonstore retailing by direct interaction with customers to inform them of products and to receive sales orders

Mail Marketing. Direct mail and mail-order marketing result in billions of sales dollars annually in both retail and industrial sales. In retailing, the world's largest mail-order business is run by Otto Versand, a privately held company based in Hamburg, Germany. Company founder Werner Versand began in mail order back in 1950 by pasting pictures of shoes in hand-bound catalogs. Today, with annual sales topping $13 billion, Otto Versand has used mail order to build itself into one of the world's biggest multinational retailers. In addition to mail-order companies in Hungary, Japan, Italy, France, Britain, and Germany, Otto Versand owns 90 percent of Spiegel and its Eddie Bauer subsidiary in the United States.[9]

Direct mail is effective because it targets audiences that have been identified from research lists as likely to be interested in specific products. The single mailings sent by insurance companies, magazine and book publishers, and clothing and furniture stores are expensive direct mail promotions. These various pamphlets, letters, brochures, and convenient order forms result in high-response sales rates. Charities rely on direct mail as a primary fundraising method. Although mail-order responses are increasing at both for-profit and nonprofit organizations, the industry faces difficulties from increasing postal rates and a backlash against the accumulation of unwanted catalogs in customers' mailboxes.

Mail Order (or Catalog Marketing). Firms that sell by **mail order** (or **catalog marketing**) typically send out splashy color catalogs describing a variety of merchandise. Currently, they garner sales of $45–$60 billion in the United States each year. L.L.Bean alone ships more than 10 million packages to mail-order customers annually. As a whole, the world of interactive commerce is an incredibly busy place: Each year, for example, AT&T's 800-line unit generates 13 billion calls, and competitors carry another 9 billion.[10]

Although mail-order firms have existed for a long time, computer technology and telephone charge transactions have made this a booming industry in recent years. Advances in communication technologies are permitting U.S. mail-order catalogers to expand by targeting overseas customers. Armed with 24-hour international toll-free phone

mail order (or **catalog marketing**)
Form of nonstore retailing in which customers place orders for catalog merchandise received through the mail

lines, overnight delivery, inexpensive fax machines, and credit-card offers, U.S.-based catalog marketing is now convenient and fast for consumers in Canada, Japan, Europe, and England. Japanese consumers can call a San Francisco outlet toll free around the clock, talk with a Japanese-speaking telemarketer, avoid import tariffs, and receive express mail delivery. Furthermore, they can buy U.S. mail-order merchandise at lower prices—sometimes one-third of the Japanese retailer's price—because Japan's many-layered distribution system escalates in-store costs.[11]

Video Marketing. More and more companies have begun using television to sell consumer commodities such as jewelry and kitchen accessories. Many cable systems now offer **video marketing** through home-shopping channels that display and demonstrate products and allow viewers to phone in orders. On one weekend in 1993, for instance, Ivana Trump's appearance on the Home Shopping Club netted $2 million in orders for her high-fashion apparel. Phone traffic was so brisk that the scheduled 2-day show had to be cut short because inventory had sold out.

video marketing
Nonstore retailing to consumers via standard and cable television

Meanwhile, QVC, another home-shopping network, has entered agreements with British Sky Broadcasting to reach into England, Ireland, and parts of Europe and with Mexico's Grupo Telvisa to send live broadcasts to Mexico, Spain, Portugal, and South America. Optimistic observers believe that home shopping is finally prepared to launch itself into the digital, interactive, multimedia retailing future. Microsoft's Bill Gates is among them: "I can ignore geographical limits to my shopping," explains Gates. "It changes the nature of competition, which becomes pure because you can no longer benefit from customer ignorance. If you believe in markets—and I love markets—this is a good thing. It makes all markets work more efficiently."[12]

Telemarketing. **Telemarketing** is the use of the telephone to sell directly to consumers. WATS (wide area telephone service) lines can be used to receive toll-free calls from consumers responding to television and radio ads. Using live or automated dialing, message delivery, and order taking, telemarketers can also use WATS lines to call consumers to promote products and services. Telemarketing is used not only for consumer goods but also for industrial goods and insurance and accounting services. Currently, telemarketing is experiencing exceptional growth in the United States, Canada, and Great Britain. With sales having topped $360 billion in 1995, the industry expects sales of up to $600 billion by the year 2000.[13]

telemarketing
Nonstore retailing in which the telephone is used to sell directly to consumers

Electronic Shopping. **Electronic shopping** is made possible by computer information systems that allow sellers to connect to consumers' computers with information about products. With over one million subscribers, Prodigy, which was formed as a joint venture of IBM and Sears, is among the largest home networks. As an Internet service company, it provides members with computer access showing available products, which range from airplane reservations to financial services to consumer goods. The viewer can examine detailed descriptions, compare brands, send for free information, or purchase by credit card from home. As an industry leader in Internet shopping transactions, Prodigy operates beyond the United States with networks in Africa, Asia, and Latin America.

electronic shopping
Nonstore retailing in which information about the seller's products and services is connected to consumers' computers, allowing consumers to receive the information and purchase the products in the home

Direct Selling. Possibly the oldest form of retailing, **direct selling** is still used by more than 600 U.S. companies that sell door-to-door or through home-selling parties. For example, some of us have attended Tupperware parties at friends' houses. Consider some current events at one of the world's best-known direct sellers:

direct selling
Form of nonstore retailing typified by door-to-door sales

▶ For more than a century, Avon Products Inc. has prospered by marketing cosmetics to American women through a direct sales organization. Today, even though most American consumers purchase cosmetics through such traditional retail channels as drugstores and department stores, Avon still rings up $4 billion in sales each year. In addition to its direct-selling effort in the United States, Avon is also moving quickly to take advantage of

Avon admits that since it entered the Chinese market in 1990, sales have grown slowly. Nevertheless, say company executives, it's a market with huge potential, and that's why Avon has a sales force of 25,000 there. Because Chinese consumers tend to be wary of door-to-door salespeople, Avon also maintains showrooms where interested buyers in large cities can sample products and consult with professional cosmeticians. The gamble on foreign markets is not hard to understand. Whereas Avon's U.S. sales are flat, sales in emerging markets, such as China, Argentina, Mexico, and Poland were up nearly 20 percent in a recent year.

growth opportunities in global markets. For example, even though low incomes limit expenditures on cosmetics and toiletries, sales in emerging countries such as Brazil and Mexico now total $1.3 billion a year. "Our distribution system," notes CEO James E. Preston, "is perfect for countries whose retail infrastructures are weak." In 1990, for example, Avon established a joint venture with Guangzhou Cosmetics Factory in the Chinese province of Old Canton. Avon thus became the first company officially permitted to sell door-to-door in China, and today, its Chinese sales force numbers 25,000. In 1993, sales reached $15 million. Avon has also moved into East Germany, Hungary, and Czechoslovakia.[14]

> ❝ *Our distribution system is perfect for countries whose retail infrastructures are weak.* ❞
>
> —Avon CEO James E. Preston

Office-to-office direct selling is also common in the wholesaling of such industrial goods as commercial copying equipment. Although direct selling is convenient and gives customers one-on-one attention, prices are usually driven up by labor costs (salespeople often receive commissions of 40 to 50 cents on every sales dollar). Even so, there are about 3.5 million direct salespeople in the United States, 80 percent of whom are women. Worldwide, 9 million direct salespeople now generate annual retail sales of $35 billion. In Japan alone, for instance, 1.2 million distributors have made Amway Corp. second only to Coca-Cola as the most profitable foreign retailer.

The Wheel of Retailing

wheel of retailing
Concept of retail evolution holding that low-service, low-price stores add services and raise prices until they lose price-sensitive customers and are replaced by new firms that enter the market to fill the need for low-price stores

As we saw earlier, many forms of retail outlets emerge, thrive, and then change into different formats. These changes reflect the evolution of retail stores described by a concept known as the **wheel of retailing**.

According to this theory, the wheel begins when new retailers emerge to offer lower prices than existing stores. These low-price stores keep prices down by providing fewer services, selling unknown brands, and locating in inexpensive facilities. As they become successful and upgrade their facilities they must cover increased costs by charging higher prices. As it continues to evolve, it tries to increase market share, offers expanded services, and offers name brand merchandise, all in upgraded stores. When the new store raises prices to cover increased costs, the wheel comes full circle. Meanwhile, as one company moves up in prices and offerings, new retailers appear to fill the gap in the lower-priced market.

Kmart is an example of the wheel of retailing in action. Initially, Kmart offered a variety of low-cost products in converted warehouses. Today, the firm has remodeled existing facilities and built entirely new ones. Kmart now offers a wide range of higher-quality merchandise in aesthetically pleasing surroundings. In response, however, a large number of bargain barns and other independent local retailers have filled the gap left by the original Kmart concept.

Physical Distribution

Physical distribution is the activities needed to move products efficiently from manufacturer to consumer. The goals of physical distribution are to make goods available when and where consumers want them, to keep costs low, and to provide services that keep customers satisfied. Thus physical distribution includes warehousing and transporting operations, as well as customer service operations such as order processing.

physical distribution
Activities needed to move a product efficiently from manufacturer to consumer

Warehousing Operations

Storing, or **warehousing**, is a major part of distribution management. In selecting a strategy, managers must keep in mind both the different characteristics and costs of warehousing operations.

warehousing
Physical distribution operation concerned with the storage of goods

Types of Warehouses

There are two basic types of warehouses: private and public. Facilities can be further divided according to their use as storage warehouses or distribution centers.

Public and Private Warehouses.   **Private warehouses** are owned and used by a single manufacturer, wholesaler, or retailer. Most are operated by large firms that deal in mass quantities and need storage on a regular basis. J.C. Penney, for example, eases the movement of products to retail stores by maintaining its own warehouses.

Public warehouses are independently owned and operated. Companies rent only the space they need. Public warehouses are popular with firms that need storage only during peak periods. They are also used by manufacturers needing multiple storage locations to get products to numerous markets.

private warehouse
Warehouse owned by and providing storage for a single company

public warehouse
Independently owned and operated warehouse that stores goods for many firms

Storage Warehouses and Distribution Centers.   **Storage warehouses** provide storage for extended periods of time. Producers of seasonal items, such as agricultural crops, use this type of warehouse. **Distribution centers** store products whose market demand is both constant and high. They are used by retail chains, wholesalers, and manufacturers that need to break down large quantities of merchandise into the smaller quantities that stores or customers demand.

Distribution centers are common in the grocery and food industry. Kellogg, for example, stores virtually no products at its plants. Instead, it ships cereals from factories directly to regional distribution centers. As wholesalers place orders for combinations of products, warehouses fill and ship them. Because warehouses are regional, wholesalers receive orders quickly.

storage warehouse
Warehouse providing storage for extended periods of time

distribution center
Warehouse providing short-term storage of goods for which demand is both constant and high

Warehousing Costs

Typical warehouse costs include such obvious expenses as storage space rental or mortgage payments (usually computed on a square-foot basis), insurance, and wages. They also include the costs of inventory control and materials handling.

inventory control
Warehouse operation that tracks inventory on hand and ensures that an adequate supply is in stock at all times

material handling
Warehouse operation involving the transportation, arrangement, and orderly retrieval of goods in inventory

Inventory Control.   **Inventory control** goes beyond keeping track of what is on hand at any time. It often involves the very tricky balancing act of ensuring that although an adequate supply of a product is in stock at all times, excessive supplies are avoided.

Material Handling.   Most warehouse personnel are involved in **material handling**: the transportation, arrangement, and orderly retrieval of inventoried goods. Holding down material-handling costs means developing a product storage strategy that takes into account product locations within the warehouse. Other considerations include packaging decisions, such as whether to store a product as individual units, in multiple packages, or in sealed containers.

One strategy for managing materials is unitization, which makes storage and handling more systematic by standardizing the weight and form of materials. For example, General Electric's Louisville, Kentucky, warehouse receives apartment-sized refrigerators from Europe in containers holding 56 refrigerators. Using the huge containers rather than individual boxes not only makes handling easier but also reduces theft and damage. It also optimizes shipping space and allows for easier restocking.

Transportation Operations

The highest cost faced by many companies is the cost of physically moving a product. Thus, cost is a major factor in choosing a transportation method. But firms must also consider several other factors: the nature of the product, the distance it must travel, the speed with which it must be received, and customer wants and needs.

Transportation Modes

Figure 14.4 compares the strengths of the major transportation modes: trucks, railroads, planes, water carriers, and pipelines. Not surprisingly, differences in cost are most directly related to delivery speed.

Trucks.   The advantages of trucks include flexibility, fast service, and dependability. Nearly all areas of the United States can be reached by truck. Because less breakage occurs than with railroad transport, trucked goods need less packing—a major cost savings. Trucks are a particularly good choice for short-distance distribution and for expensive products. They carry more freight than any other form of transport except rail carriers.

Railroads.   Railroads have been the backbone of the U.S. transportation system since the late 1800s. Until the 1960s, when trucking firms attracted many of their customers with lower rates, railroads were also fairly profitable. They are now used primarily to transport heavy, bulky items such as cars, steel, and coal. To regain market share, railroads have expanded services to include faster delivery times and piggyback service, in which truck trailers are placed on railcars. This service alone can save shippers up to one-half the cost of shipping by truck.

Planes.   Air is the fastest available mode of transportation. Other advantages include much lower costs in handling and packing and unpacking compared with other modes. Inventory carrying costs can also be reduced. Shipments of fresh fish, for example, can be picked up by restaurants each day, thus avoiding the risk of spoilage from packaging and storing. However, air freight is the most expensive form of transportation.

Water Carriers.   Of all transport modes, water is the least expensive. Modern networks of internal waterways, locks, rivers, and lakes allow water carriers to reach many areas in the United States and throughout the world. Unfortunately, water transport is also the slowest mode. Thus, boats and barges are used mostly for heavy, bulky materials and

Figure 14.4 Ranking Modes of Transportation

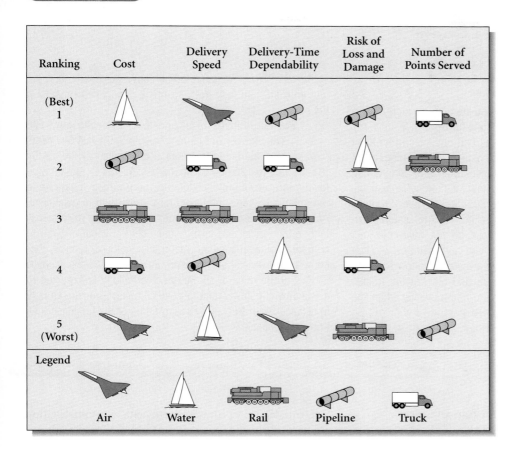

Ranking	Cost	Delivery Speed	Delivery-Time Dependability	Risk of Loss and Damage	Number of Points Served
(Best) 1	Water	Air	Pipeline	Pipeline	Truck
2	Pipeline	Truck	Truck	Water	Rail
3	Rail	Rail	Rail	Air	Air
4	Truck	Pipeline	Water	Truck	Water
5 (Worst)	Air	Water	Air	Rail	Pipeline

Legend

Air   Water   Rail   Pipeline   Truck

products (such as sand, gravel, oil, and grain), for which delivery speed is unimportant. Today, companies use water carriers because many ships are now specially constructed to hold large standardized containers.

Pipelines.   Like water transportation, pipelines are slow. Used to transport liquids and gases, pipelines are also inflexible. But pipelines do provide a constant flow of products and are unaffected by weather conditions. The Alaska Pipeline, for example, transports oil through Alaska on its route to the lower 48 states. Lack of adaptability to other products makes pipelines an unimportant transportation method for most industries.

Changes in Transportation Operations

For many years, U.S. transport companies specialized in one mode or another. Since deregulation in 1980, however, this pattern has changed. New developments in cost-efficiency and competitiveness include intermodal transportation, containerization, and information technology.

Intermodal Transportation.   **Intermodal transportation**—the combined use of different modes of transportation—has come into widespread use. For example, shipping by a combination of air and rail or truck is sometimes called birdyback transport. Large railroad companies, such as Burlington Northern and Union Pacific, are thus merging with trucking, air, and shipping lines. The goal is to offer simplified source-to-destination delivery by any necessary combination of methods.[15]

intermodal transportation
Combined use of several different modes of transportation

The Natural Environment

Faster Than a Speeding Bullet

What's faster than a speeding bullet and cleaner than a truck? Answer: the freight train of the future.

In a very real sense, the railroad business in its early days helped to build the United States. But in more recent times, it has seen its freight revenue erode from competition with trucks and ships. However, new technology is available that allows trains to run safely at 80 miles an hour, 25 miles an hour faster than currently. Satellite tracking systems can automatically control speed to head off potential collisions when trains are still miles apart, and automatic brakes can stop a train on a dime. Lightweight materials allow trains to carry heavier loads with less wear and tear on the tracks. Warnings are sent to the train yard automatically when the train needs maintenance, and new locomotives that run on alternating current are located throughout the train, not just at the ends. These trains are 50 percent more powerful, more fuel efficient, and less likely to break down than models in the past.

The rail industry is behind the new technology 100 percent. The number of freight cars sold in the last few years represents a tremendous increase over sales in the 1980s (from 5,000 to 120,000 cars) and is expected to remain high for the foreseeable future. Volume and productivity are up in rail shipping, even though the new equipment is expensive. As volume increases, however, rail shippers face the increasingly difficult task of making scheduling efficient enough to compete. Maintenance of the tracks, also expensive, becomes more crucial the more urgently the tracks are needed.

But the price of all the new technology is expected to come down, if slowly, and railroad shipping firms are already in alliances with truckers, sharing some of the business they hope to win back.

containerization
Transportation method in which goods are sealed in containers at shipping sources and opened when they reach final destinations

Containerization. To make intermodal transport more efficient, **containerization** uses standardized heavy-duty containers in which many items are sealed at points of shipment and opened only at final destinations. On the trip, containers may be loaded onto ships for ocean transit, transferred onto trucks, loaded onto railcars (piggyback service), and delivered to final destinations by other trucks. Sealed containers are then unloaded and returned for future use.

Information Technology. Up-to-the-minute information about the location and progress of in-transit shipments can be just as important as the method of transportation. American President Cos., a large U.S.-based steamship and train operator, uses a high-tech computer system to monitor and guide transportation shipments for customers throughout the world. For example, containers of toys bound for Toys Я Us are tracked from suppliers in Asia until they reach regional distribution centers in the United States. APC keeps Toys Я Us headquarters informed electronically on where every container is and what's in it; they know as much as 2 weeks in advance what product types, sizes, and colors are in each container and what their exact destinations are, and they are advised of potential delays. This enables the toy company to reorder missing products or divert cargo from one destination to another in order to keep store shelves adequately stocked.[16]

Companies Specializing in Transportation

The major modes of transport are available from four different types of companies:

common carrier
Transporting company, such as a truck line or railroad, that transports goods for any shipper

- **Common carriers** transport merchandise for any shippers: manufacturers, wholesalers, retailers, and even individuals. They maintain regular schedules and charge competitive prices. Truck lines and railroads are common carriers.

■ **Freight forwarders** are common carriers that lease bulk space from other carriers, such as railroads or airlines. They then resell parts of that space to smaller shippers. Once it has enough contracts to fill its leased bulk space, the freight forwarder picks up all merchandise to be shipped. It transports the goods to the bulk carrier, makes deliveries to specific destinations, and handles billing and inquiries.

■ **Contract carriers** transport products for any firm for a contracted price and time period. They are usually self-employed operators who own their vehicles. When they have delivered contracted shipments, they generally try to locate another shipment (often with a different manufacturer) for the return trip. Contract carriers often tailor services for customers with special needs. Dairy tankers, for example, are often contract carriers with specialized equipment and skills.

■ A few manufacturers and retailers are **private carriers** who maintain their own transport systems—usually fleets of trucks—to carry their own products. These are usually very large manufacturers and retail chains such as Kraft General Foods and Kroger.

freight forwarder
Transporting company that leases bulk space from other carriers to be resold to firms making smaller shipments

contract carrier
Independent transporting company that usually owns the vehicles in which it transports products

private carrier
Manufacturer or retailer that maintains its own transportation system

Customer Service Operations

Sometimes, buyers make direct contact with sellers only when placing orders. Thus, **order processing**—filling orders as they are received—affects the buyer's view of the seller's efficiency. In turn, the behavior of order-processing personnel is often critical to the seller's reputation.

Firms that satisfy customers and enjoy repeat business work to ensure fast, convenient, and polite service. For example, Bass Pro Shops (which sells fishing and other recreational gear) maintains a toll-free line staffed by courteous, knowledgeable representatives. These salespeople handle order-related queries ranging from methods of payment to dates and arrangements for shipping.

Similarly, many firms set standards for **order cycle times**: the total time elapsed between placement and receipt of order. Because customers obviously prefer faster and more predictable deliveries, rapid order cycle times can be a distinct competitive advantage. Many companies have found that the keys to improved order cycle time are computerized information and warehousing systems.

order processing
In customer service operations, the filling of orders as they are received

order cycle time
In customer service operations, total time elapsed between placement and receipt of orders

Distribution as a Marketing Strategy

Distribution is an increasingly important way of competing for sales. Instead of just offering advantages in product features and quality, price, and promotion, many firms have turned to distribution as a cornerstone of their business strategies. This approach means assessing and improving the entire stream of activities (wholesaling, warehousing, and transportation) involved in getting products to customers. Its importance is illustrated at Compaq Computer, which registered a loss of nearly $1 billion in sales for 1994 because products were unavailable when and where customers wanted them. To correct the problem, Compaq has placed distribution at the top of its list as the competitive strategy for the future. This commitment entails reworking the company's whole supply chain of distributors and transportation.

The Use of Hubs

One approach to streamlining is the use of **hubs**: central distribution outlets that control all or most of a firm's distribution activities. Two contrasting strategies have emerged from this approach: supply-side and prestaging hubs on one hand and distribution-side hubs on the other.

hub
Central distribution outlet that controls all or most of a firm's distribution activities

Supply-Side and Prestaging Hubs. Supply-side hubs make the most sense when large shipments of supplies flow regularly to a single industrial user, such as a large manufacturer. They are used by automobile factories, where thousands of incoming supplies can arrive by train, truck, and air. Incoming shipments can create a nightmare of traffic jams, loading-dock congestion, paperwork logjams, and huge storage space requirements.

To clear this congestion, some firms operate prestaging hubs. Saturn, for example, maintains such a facility—managed by Ryder System—located 2 miles from its factory. All incoming transportation schedules and supplies are managed by Ryder to satisfy one requirement: meeting Saturn's production schedules. The long-haul tractors at the hub are disconnected from trailers and sent on their return trips to any of 339 suppliers located in 39 states. Responding to Saturn's up-to-the-minute needs, hub headquarters arranges the transport of presorted and preinspected materials to the factory by loading them onto specially designed shuttle tractors.

The chief job of the hub, then, is to coordinate the customer's materials needs with supply chain transportation. If the hub is successful, the factory's inventories are virtually eliminated, storage space requirements are reduced, and long-haul trucks keep moving, instead of lining up at the customer's unloading dock. By outsourcing distribution activities to its hub, Saturn can focus on what it does best: manufacturing. Meanwhile, Ryder, the nation's largest logistics management firm, is paid for its speciality: handling transportation flows.[17]

Distribution-Side Hubs.   Whereas supply-side hubs are located near industrial customers, distribution-side hubs may be located much farther away, especially if customers are geographically dispersed.

▶   National Semiconductor, one of the world's largest chip makers, is an example. National's finished products, silicon microchips, are produced in plants throughout the world and shipped to customers such as IBM, Toshiba, Siemens, Ford, and Compaq at factory locations around the globe. On the journey from producer to customer, chips originally sat waiting at one location after another—on factory floors, at customs, in distributors' facilities, and in customers' warehouses. Typically, they traveled 20,000 different routes on as many as 12 airlines and spent time in 10 warehouses before reaching their customers. National has streamlined its delivery system by shutting down six warehouses around the world. Now it airfreights microchips worldwide from a single distribution center in Singapore. All of its activities—storage, sorting, shipping—are run by Federal Express. As a result, distribution costs have fallen, delivery times have been reduced by half, and sales have increased.[18]

Summary of Learning Objectives

1 **Identify the different channels of distribution and explain different distribution strategies.** In selecting a distribution mix, a firm may use all or any of six distribution channels. The first four are aimed at getting products to consumers, and the last two are aimed at getting products to industrial customers. Channel 1 involves direct sales to consumers. Channel 2 includes a retailer. Channel 3 involves both a retailer and a wholesaler, and Channel 4 includes an agent or broker who enters the system before the wholesaler and retailer. Channel 5 involves a direct sale to an industrial user. Channel 6, which is used infrequently, entails selling to industrial users through wholesalers. Distribution strategies include intensive, exclusive, and selective distribution, which differ in the number of products and channel members involved and the amount of service performed in the channel.

2 **Explain the differences between merchant wholesalers and agents/brokers.** Wholesalers act as distribution intermediaries. They may extend credit as well as store, repackage, and deliver products to other members of the channel. Full-service and limited-function merchant wholesalers differ in the number and types of distribution functions they offer. Unlike wholesalers, agents and brokers never take legal possession of products. Rather, they function as sales and merchandising arms of manufac-

turers that do not have their own sales forces. They may also provide such services as advertising and display merchandising.

3 Identify the different types of retail stores and explain the wheel of retailing. Retailers can be described according to two classifications: product line retailers and bargain retailers. Product line retailers include department stores, supermarkets, hypermarkets, and specialty stores. Bargain retailers include discount houses, off-price stores, catalog showrooms, factory outlets, warehouse clubs, and convenience stores. These retailers differ in terms of size, goods and services offered, and pricing. Some retailing also takes place without stores. Nonstore retailing may use direct mail catalogs, vending machines, video marketing, telemarketing, electronic shopping, and direct selling. According to the wheel of retailing concept, conventional retailers are periodically displaced by innovative, lower-priced competitors, who then become more conventional and are themselves displaced.

4 Describe the major activities in the physical distribution process. Physical distribution includes all the activities needed to move products from manufacturer to consumer, including customer service, warehousing, and transporting products. Warehouses may be public or private and may function either as long-term storage warehouses or as distribution centers. In addition to storage, insurance, and wage-related costs, the cost of warehousing goods also includes inventory control (maintaining adequate but not excessive supplies) and material handling (transporting, arranging, and retrieving supplies).

5 Compare the five basic forms of transportation and identify the types of firms that provide them. Trucks, railroads, planes, water carriers (boats and barges), and pipelines are the major transportation modes used in the distribution process. They differ in cost, availability, reliability, speed, and number of points served. Air is the fastest but most expensive mode; water carriers are the slowest but least expensive. Since transport companies were deregulated in 1980, they have become more cost-efficient and competitive by developing such innovations as intermodal transportation and containerization. Transportation in any form may be supplied by common carriers, freight forwarders, contract carriers, or private carriers.

Questions and Exercises

Questions for Review

1 From the manufacturer's point of view, what are the advantages and disadvantages of using intermediaries to distribute products? From the end user's point of view?

2 Identify the six channels of distribution. In what key ways do the four channels used for consumer products differ from the two channels used for industrial products?

3 Identify and explain the differences between the three distribution strategies.

4 Explain the different roles played by merchant wholesalers and agents/brokers.

5 Identify the five modes of transportation used in product distribution. What factors lead companies to choose one over the others to deliver products to end users?

Questions for Analysis

6 Give three examples (other than those in the chapter) of products that use intensive distribution. Do the same for products that use exclusive distribution and selective distribution. For which category was it easiest to find examples? Why?

7 Give examples of five products that typify the sort of products sold by video shopping networks. Explain why this form of nonstore retailing is effective for each of these different products.

8 If you could own a firm that transports products, would you prefer to operate an intermodal transportation business or one that specializes in a single mode of transportation (say, truck or air)? Explain your choice.

Application Exercises

9 Interview the manager of a local manufacturing firm. Identify the firm's distribution strategy and the channels of distribution that it uses. Where applicable, describe the types of wholesalers or retail stores used to distribute the firm's products.

10 Choose any consumer item at your local supermarket and trace the chain of physical distribution activities that brought it to the store shelf.

Building Your Business Skills

This exercise enhances the following SCANS workplace competencies: demonstrating basic skills, demonstrating thinking skills, exhibiting interpersonal skills, and working with information.

Goal   To encourage students to consider the value of on-line retailing as an element in a company's distribution system.

Situation   As the distribution manager of a privately owned clothing manufacturer, specializing in camping gear and outdoor clothing, you are convinced that your product line is perfect for on-line distribution. But the owner of the company is reluctant to expand distribution from a successful network of retail stores and a catalog operation. Your challenge is to convince the boss that retailing via the Internet can boost sales.

Method   **Step 1:**   Join together with four or five classmates to research the advantages and disadvantages of an on-line distribution system for your company. Among the factors to consider are

- The likelihood that target consumers are Internet shoppers. Camping gear is generally purchased by young, affluent consumers who are comfortable with the Web.
- The industry trend to on-line distribution. Are similar companies doing it? Have they been successful?
- The opportunity to expand inventory without increasing the cost of retail space or catalog production and mailing charges.
- The opportunity to have a store that never closes.
- The lack of trust many people have about doing business on the Web. Many consumers are reluctant to provide credit card data on the Web.
- The difficulty electronic shoppers have in finding a Web site when they do not know the store's name.
- The frustration and waiting time involved in Web searches.
- The certainty that the site will not reach consumers who do not use computers or who are uncomfortable with the Web.

Step 2:   Based on your findings, write a persuasive memo to the company's owner stating your position about expanding to an on-line distribution system. Include information that will counter expected objections.

Follow-Up Questions

1 What place does on-line distribution have in the distribution network of this company?

2 In your view, is on-line distribution the wave of the future? Is it likely to increase in importance as a distribution system for apparel companies? Why or why not?

Bookselling Goes Electronic, Twice

Inspired by a stint filling in as bookstore manager for his vacationing son, Walter Powell opened his own used bookstore in Portland, Oregon, in 1971. Today Powell's unique City of Books is the largest independent bookseller in the United States, if not the world. Covering 43,000 square feet of space with more than half a million new and used hardcover and paperback books, the store also features a comfortably low-key atmosphere and a homespun café. Kanth Godalpur, Powell's marketing manager, contrasts the firm with Borders, the giant book chain: "They don't sell 21 editions of *Catcher in the Rye*. We have old paperbacks that sell for $2, a signed first edition for $1,200, and everything in between."

Although Powell's established six satellite specialty stores in Portland during the 1980s, further expansion of the $30-million-a-year business seemed unlikely. Among the limiting factors was the logistical impossibility of duplicating the depth and breadth of its unique selection in another location.

The Internet offered the ideal solution, and Powell's brought the first part of its inventory (its computer booklist) on line in 1993. By 1996 the complete catalog of titles in 122 subject categories was listed on the City of Books website (www.powells.com), and sales have grown by 10 to 20 per-

cent a month ever since. Walter's son Michael, now in the business with him, estimates that in a few years a third of the store's business will come in via the Internet.

As unique as its successful formula may be, Powell's has to contend with at least one other major independent bookseller on the Internet, Amazon.com (its name and Web address are the same). Founded in 1994 by Jeff Bezos, Amazon has no retail outlet and warehouses only a few hundred of its top sellers. The rest of its orders (for new books only) are filled by distributors, and it offers more than 2.5 million titles.

Where Powell's competes against the big chains with the sheer variety it offers, Amazon's strategy was to get established on the Internet before Borders and Barnes & Noble could gain a foothold. Whereas Powell's has relied on word of mouth and basic customer service, Amazon spent heavily on promotion and of-

fers readers book reviews, related articles, and customized notices of new book arrivals.

Ultimately, however, they are in the same business. Yet Powell and

> ❝ *We have old paperbacks [of Catcher in the Rye] that sell for $2, a signed first edition for $1,200, and everything in between.* ❞
>
> —Kanth Godalpur, marketing manager, Powell's City of Books

Bezos both claim there's room for the two of them.

Questions:

1 Powell's focuses on used books whereas Amazon sells only new ones. Visit their Web sites and determine in what other ways they differ. Are they appealing to the same customers? Why or why not?

2 How well do you think Powell's can continue to compete against such large chains as Borders and Barnes & Noble? Does Amazon have an advantage here? If so, what is it?

3 Evaluate the two owners' statement that the firms can both succeed. Do you agree with Powell and Bezos? Why or why not?

Connecting to the Web

The following Web sites will give you additional information and points of view about topics covered in this chapter. Many sites lead to other related Internet locations, so approach this list with the spirit of an explorer.

THE AMWAY CORPORATION

http://www.amway.com

The site introduces Amway's system of direct sales, involving 2.5 million independent distributors worldwide, as well as the company's products, services, manufacturing, and distribution operations.

AVON: SHOPPING FOR COSMETICS AND BEAUTY ONLINE

http://www.avon.com/

Avon demonstrates its direct distribution of consumer products from producer to consumer without intermediaries. Avon reaches consumers through its corporate sales force and on-line shopping.

BLOOMINGDALE'S

http://www.bloomingdales.com

Bloomingdale's cultivates its high-priced image on the Web. Included in the retailer's site are a personal shopping service and special events for all Bloomingdale's stores.

KMART

http://www.kmart.com/

Kmart's Web site celebrates its image as a value discounter for the entire family.

QVC

http:www.qvc.com

Visit the Web site of QVC, one of the most successful video marketers, to find QVC, the company's interactive on-line shopping presence.

SAM'S CLUB

http://www.samsclub.com

The on-line site of Sam's Club, Wal-Mart's wholesale shopping club, features a virtual storefront where consumers can view a variety of merchandise, including electronics, automotive products, and appliances.

7-ELEVEN

http://www.7-eleven.com/

The Southland Corporation's 7-Eleven convenience store operation is highlighted on this Web site.

SHOPPING MALLS ONLINE: THE CYBERMALL.COM DIRECTORY

http://www.cybermall.com

Internet shopping made easy is what consumers will find here. The site screens premium, specialty, and regional cybermalls and selects those that offer the best home-shopping experience.

STAPLES

http://www.staples.com

Using the Staples Web site, small businesses have access to the deep discounts that were once available only to large corporations. The wholesale function is absent from this distribution channel.

SUNGLASS HUT INTERNATIONAL

http://www.sunglasshut.com

Sunglass Hut's specialty store presence is found on the Web. The site also leads to other specialty retailers in the chain, including Sunscription for prescription sunglasses and the Watch Station for watches.

Managing Operations and Information

Picture the ball dropping in New York City's Times Square on December 31, 1998, as millions celebrate the start of the last year of the twentieth century. Then picture thousands of weary technology and information managers who watch with a mixture of fear and dread. Are they Scrooges with little party spirit? It's possible. But it's more likely that they are preoccupied with the most serious—and universal—technology problem to hit business: getting the world's computers ready for the millennium, just 365 days away.

Facing these experts is a glitch that will wreak havoc on every aspect of business that operates via computer unless it is fixed in time. The problem goes by many names (the year 2000 bug, the millennium bomb, the Y2K problem) and will cost government, business, and individuals as much as $600 billion to repair (about a $1 to $2 for every line of computer code). The federal government alone will spend at least $4 billion, Chase Manhattan Bank $250 million, Prudential Insurance $110 million, and FedEx $75 million.

Why MM/DD/YY Is a Problem

The seeds of the millennium bomb were planted in the 1970s when the computer industry was still in its infancy and when a megabyte of computer memory cost $600,000, as compared to 10 cents today. To control costs, programmers limited dates to just six spaces: two for the month, two for the day, and two for the year (MM/DD/YY). This system works well for months and days, but with only two digits, rather than four, to represent the year, the computer can't handle the switch from the twentieth to the twenty-first century.

"The problem is that the computer doesn't interpret '00' as the year 2000 but rather 1900, and miscalculates all computations accordingly," explained Gary Fisher, a computer scientist with the Commerce Department's National Institute of Standards and Technology. This problem appears in mainframe computers and in the computer chips that control everything from ATMs to security systems.

How will this affect business? Examples of problems that have already surfaced tell a story of what lies ahead for companies that fail to find a workable solution:

- At a gourmet food store in Warren, Michigan, a customer tried to pay his bill with a credit card that expired in 2000. The simple act of swiping the card through the system caused the store's 10 computerized cash registers to lock shut for half a day.

- At Delta, American, and other airlines, problems associated with Y2K began in the mid-1990s, when maintenance cycles, pension programs, and even extended leaves of absence were being scheduled.

- When in 1997 a municipal sewage treatment plant tested Y2K changes, the fix failed and raw sewage spilled into a harbor, according to computer directions.

The year 2000 problem affects manufacturing as well as service companies that do long-term budget and production planning. At Reebok, the Massachusetts-based athletic shoe manufacturer, the year 2000 problem showed up when the company began its 18-month planning horizon on apparel and footwear. Banks, accounting firms, and other financial institutions may encounter automated computer backup routines that will overwrite new files with older, outdated information.

Defining the Problem

Most companies have gotten the message that if they ignore the problem, their computer systems may shut down or produce incorrect data that infects other systems. Sears, one of the country's retailing giants, has divided the problem into three parts.

Our first problem "is to bring the applications systems up to compliance level as well as the systems software that we have within our organization," explained chief information officer Joe Smialowski. "The second area is tougher to tackle: all those desktop applications we've all built . . . whether they be spreadsheets or database or word-processing applications. . . . In some cases, they are important to running the day-to-day business. We are focusing heavily on this area now.

"The third area concerns our suppliers, both merchandise suppliers and service providers," he said. "Hopefully, they're working toward compliance also. We have an active certification program that is under way that determines whether our suppliers are making the right level of progress on year 2000 compliance. Having a real year 2000 plan and being able to demonstrate it to our company is a condition of continuing to do business with Sears. If you [can't do it], your business is at risk with Sears."

Computer analysts in other industries see the problem in the same way. Debbie Freedman, vice president in American Airlines' Sabre system, is particularly concerned about desktop PCs. "Imagine the impact when the simple little PC package purchased by the local office to produce monthly sales statistics suddenly fails or provides wrong information." Worse yet, the information technology department has no centralized control over these PCs.

Fixing the Problem

In 1996, the International Air Transport Association established a Year 2000 Group (Y2KG) to coordinate efforts within the industry to solve the year 2000 problem on time. The group has defined seven steps to remedy the problem. These steps apply to other industries as well.

■ *Recognize the problem:* This requires that everyone in an organization as well as clients, vendors, and even government officials acknowledge the problem and its deadline.

■ *Inventory all software, hardware, and ancillary equipment run by computer chips:* In the case of the airline industry, that includes runway lights, which are operated with a computerized clock, security and access systems, and ticket machines.

■ *Study options and risks:* This involves establishing a budget and prioritizing so that critical computer functions are handled first.

■ *Plan the project:* Detailed plans and budgets are essential to meet the deadline, as is the development of controls to identify and correct problems that arise along the way.

■ *Make the changes:* This phase is time-consuming and requires a supply of trained computer programmers. According to Y2KG, the problems that are likely to arise at this stage include "missing or out-of-date documentation, lack of resources skilled in older technologies, and lack of knowledge of a system, especially the special 'fixes' that have been implemented over the years."

■ *Test the fixes:* Experts agree that this will represent more than half of the entire effort because it involves internal systems as well as interactions with vendors, clients, and other business partners.

■ *Post-2000 watch:* Thorough testing will not produce a fail-safe system. Companies must expect minor to serious problems in the early months of the new millennium.

The Gartner Group, a Stamford, Connecticut–based marketing research firm, estimates that half of all businesses will not make the fix in time, creating potential chaos for every computer connected to their systems. Some companies may fail because of the shortage of trained programmers. Aware of this labor shortage, Reebok, Safeway, and other companies are using programmers in India and other developing countries.

To put it mildly, chief information officers are not happy with the millennium bug. They view it as a hurdle they must jump to do business in the twenty-first century. "It's an opportunity," said Office Depot CIO Bill Seltzer, "only if our competitors fail to execute."

WEB LINKS

The following Web sites highlight the Y2K problem. The information in these sites will help you answer the questions that follow.

American Institute of Certified Public Accountants	http://www.aicpa.org/
Apple Products: Mac OS	http://www.apple.com/macos/info/2000.html
IBM Year 2000 Home Page	http://www.ibm.com.IBM/year2000/
ITAAs (Information Technology Association of America) Year 2000 Home Page	http://www.itaa.org/year2000.htm
The Millennium Bug	http://www.zebra..co.uk/workshop/year2000.htm
Survive 2000	http://www.sbhs.com/
Year 2000 Date Problem Support Centre	http://www.compinfo.co.uk/y2k.htm
The Year 2000 Information Center/Millennium	http://www.year2000.com/
Ymark2000	http://www.nstl.com/

CASE QUESTIONS

1 If a manufacturing company fails to fix its Y2K problem in time, how could the millennium bug affect operation processes? If a service company fails to fix its Y2K problem in time, how could the millennium bug affect operation processes?

2 How could the integrity and operation of a company's accounting system be affected by the Y2K problem? Why do you think the AICPA Web site pays so much attention to this issue?

3 Federal regulators are worried that some community banks and credit unions are not doing enough to handle their Y2K risk. As a chief financial officer, what steps would you take to safeguard the corporate accounting system if company assets were held by these institutions?

4 Some Y2K experts see the problem as an opportunity to upgrade a company's computer system. Considering what you learned in this case and on the Web links, do you consider this a feasible solution?

5 How are word processing programs, spreadsheets, and database management programs at risk from this problem? In what ways are users' concerns reflected on the IBM and Apple Web sites?

6 Consider this statement: Managing the Y2K problem is a quality control issue. Do you agree or disagree? Explain your answer.

chapter 15

Producing
services
and goods

Send in the clowns, and the dolls, and the toy trains

Along with seeing the Christmas tree–lighting ceremony in Rockefeller Center and Santa's workshop in Macy's on 34th Street, one of New York City's great holiday traditions is paying a visit to the enormous wonderland of toys at F.A.O. Schwarz's fabled flagship store on Fifth Avenue. In recent years, though, the store's fame made long waits at the door another December tradition. Stoic customers, and their not-so-stoic children, might wait up to an hour in lines that stretched to the next block; once inside, they faced intimidating crowds. Capacity was clearly not up to demand.

Now, however, the store has taken over a former bank branch next door. Thanks to a more than 50 percent increase in square footage, F.A.O. Schwarz will boast much shorter waits and an even broader assortment of toys, games, dolls, and other merchandise. It will now offer direct access to its mail selling floor from both Madison Avenue and Fifth Avenue, making it the only store in Manhattan to bridge the borough's two most upscale shopping streets. It also gains extra feet of frontage and window displays, as well as an additional floor, the former basement of the bank.

Most of the new space is already spoken for. For the first time in years there is room to display and sell model train sets. A miniature village 30 feet long is under construction for the purpose. There will also be a test track for remote-controlled toys that customers can play with, a giant model engine with moving parts, and a window full of moving stuffed animals.

It's estimated that as many as 60,000 people a day will visit the new F.A.O. Schwarz every December. The store's added retail capacity should make room for all those visitors, tourists and customers alike, to come in and find just what they're looking for.

Even success has its problems. Its undisputed popularity forced FAO Schwarz to do some creative capacity planning, one of the toughest challenges for any business, whether it produces goods or services or both. How do companies determine how much to provide, where to produce it, and what manufacturing methods (for goods) or delivery systems (for services) to use?

Solutions lie in the intricate set of strategies and operations called the production process. In this chapter we will examine how goods and services are produced and describe the key tools managers use to manage the production process.

After reading this chapter you should be able to

1 Explain the meaning of the term *production* or *operations* and describe the four kinds of utility it provides.

2 Describe and explain the three classifications of operations processes.

3 Identify the characteristics that distinguish service operations from goods production and explain the main differences in the service focus.

4 Describe the factors involved in operations planning.

5 Explain some of the activities involved in operations control, including materials management and the use of certain operation control tools.

Everywhere you go today, you encounter business activities that provide goods and services to their customers. You wake up in the morning, for example, to the sound of your favorite radio station. You stop at the corner newsstand for a newspaper on your way to the bus stop, where you catch the bus to work or school. Your instructors, the bus driver, the clerk at the 7-Eleven store, and the morning radio announcer are all examples of people who work in **service operations**: They provide you with tangible and intangible services, such as entertainment, transportation, education, and food preparation. The firms that make the tangible products you use so often—radios, newspapers, buses, textbooks—are engaged in **goods production**.

service operations
Produces tangible and intangible services, such as entertainment, transportation, and education

goods production
Produces tangible products, such as radios, newspapers, buses, and textbooks

A Short History of Production Operations

Before the Industrial Revolution began in England in the eighteenth century, the typical workplace was the small shop or the home. Leather and cloth were handmade, as were needles and other tools; clothing, harnesses, and other goods were made by craftspeople one at a time. In the late 1770s, however, a new institution emerged: Using machines, raw materials, industrial workers, and managers, the factory produced greater quantities of goods in an organized fashion. Throughout the nineteenth century, the factory remained the central institution for commerce. By then it was using water, and then electricity, as a power source. The factory also relied on smoke-laden heavy machinery that was cumbersome, powerful, and dangerous, and it was often used by children.

In the early 1900s Frederick W. Taylor began his scientific management studies and Henry Ford revolutionized industry with the Ford mass production system (see chapters 2 and 10). At least in theory, production had become the science of making products economically on a massive scale. Using specialization of labor for efficiency, the assembly line became the new tool for gaining economies of scale. Through the 1940s, the assembly line still depended heavily on human labor. By the 1960s, however, when mass production had reached its zenith, the factory culture had matured socially as well as commercially. As consumers continued to rely on access to the material goods from factories, attitudes toward production and production workers were changing. Children were no longer a part of the work force, and once "radical" ideas such as gender equality and ethnic diversity were soon to become accepted goals. People were also beginning to pay more attention to environmental concerns.

At the same time, countries continued to join the ranks of developed nations and to benefit from new and better manufacturing methods. As a result, global competition has reshaped production into a fast-paced, challenging business activity. Although the factory remains the centerpiece of manufacturing industries, it is virtually unrecognizable when compared to its counterpart of even a decade ago. The smoke, grease, and danger have been replaced in many companies by glistening high-tech machines, computers, and cleanrooms that are contaminant-free and carefully controlled for temperature.[1] Instead of continuous mass production, firms today face constant change. They must monitor consumer demands that are always in flux and develop ever-new technologies to respond to them. They must strive to design new products, get them into production, and deliver them to customers faster than their competitors.[2]

Although the term *production* has historically referred to companies engaged in goods production, the concept as we now use it means services as well as goods. An abundance of necessities and conveniences on which we rely, from fire protection and health care to mail delivery and fast food, are all produced by service operations. Yet many experts admit that it is still hard to describe the economic value of the service sector in quantitative terms.

This IBM plant in Charlotte, North Carolina, turns out products ranging from bar code readers to medical equipment and satellite communication devices. Serving each production team of about 12 workers are computers linked to the factory network. With computer screens displaying both up-to-the-minute lists of needed parts and detailed assembly instructions, teams can make 27 different IBM products simultaneously. This combination of computer networks, software, and highly trained human resources is called soft manufacturing. *It typifies a technique originating in American factories that have committed to using human judgment in jobs for which robots and other technologies are not well suited.*

One problem, according to marketing consultant Fred Reichheld, is the traditional view of the economy. "Most people," charges Reichheld, "still view the world through manufacturing goggles." In other words, management and accounting practices still focus on the financial value of equipment, inventory, and other tangible assets. In the service sector, says Reichheld, the profit and loss statement should reflect such valuable assets as employee brainpower and sensitivity to customer needs.

In this view, service sector managers should focus less on such manufacturing-centered goals as equipment and technology. Rather, they should stress the human element in their activities. Why? Because success or failure depends on contact with the customer during service delivery. The provider's employees—their human resources—who deal directly with their customers affect the customer's feelings about the service. As we will see throughout this chapter, one of the main differences between production and service operations is the customer's involvement in the latter.

Growth in the Service and Goods Sectors

Manufacturing industries today still account for about 25 percent of all private sector jobs in the United States—just as they have for the past four decades. Nevertheless, the economic significance of manufacturing activity is rising: For example, real income from manufacturing has been rising steadily, increasing by over 30 percent in the past 10 years. So effective are new manufacturing methods—and so committed are U.S. manufacturers to using them—that in 1994 the United States surpassed Germany and Japan in manufactured exports, returning to the number-one spot for the first time in a decade.[3] This re-

Figure 15.1 Employment in Goods and Service Sectors (millions of workers)

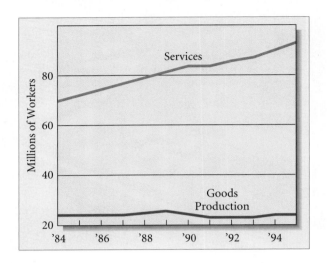

birth of industrial strength is reflected in the comment by CEO Jack Welch of General Electric: "The 1990s is the decade of manufacturing."

> **" The 1990s is the decade of manufacturing. "**
>
> —Jack Welch, CEO of General Electric

Naturally, both goods and service industries are important to the economy. However, as you can see from Figures 15.1 and 15.2, services have grown far more rapidly since 1984. For one thing, employment has risen significantly in the service sector while remaining stagnant in goods production (Figure 15.1). In fact, by 1995 employment in service industries accounted for almost 80 percent of the total U.S. work force: nearly 93 million

Figure 15.2 GDP from Goods and Services ($ billion)

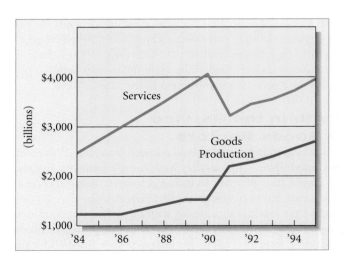

An old-line manufacturer for more than a century, Johnson Controls has discovered triple-digit growth in a service business that is actually an offshoot of its traditional manufacturing operations: It serves the heating, lighting, cleaning, and security operations of buildings such as this one in Malvern, Pennsylvania, which belongs to mutual fund giant Vanguard Group. "Much of our growth," says CEO James Keyes, "has come from the fact that we do more for our customers."

jobs. Much of this growth has been in finance, food and retailing, insurance and real estate, health care, and government. Employment projections indicate that services will remain the faster-growing employment source in the immediate future.[4] With this growth, the gap in average wages between the two sectors has closed to just $19 per week more for goods-producing workers. More importantly, however, the distribution of high-paying and low-paying jobs in each sector is now equal.

By 1995, the service sector also provided nearly 60 percent of national income, as opposed to just over 50 percent in 1947. As Figure 15.2 shows, the service sector's share of the U.S. gross domestic product—the value of all the goods and services produced by the economy, excluding foreign income—has climbed since 1984 until it is now nearly 50 percent greater than that of the goods-producing sector.

Remember that although companies are often classified as either goods producers or service providers, the distinction is often blurred. For one thing, all businesses are service operations to some extent. Consider Johnson Controls, a Milwaukee manufacturer of electronic controls for heating and cooling systems in schools, hospitals, and commercial buildings. Although Johnson has been making tangible products since 1883, it has prospered since 1989 in a brand-new but related, area: It manages the lighting, security, and cleaning operations of office buildings. "It's a market worth tens of billions of dollars in the U.S. alone," says vice president Terry Weaver.[5]

Creating Value Through Production

Measuring Utility

Not surprisingly, to understand the production processes of a firm we need to know how to measure the value of services and goods. Products provide businesses with economic results: profits, wages, and goods purchased from other companies. At the same time, they provide consumers with **utility**: the ability of a product to satisfy a human want.

utility
A product's ability to satisfy a human want

There are four basic kinds of production-based utility:

- When a company turns out ornaments in time for Christmas, it creates *time utility;* that is, it makes products available when consumers want them.

- When a department store opens its annual Trim-a-Tree department, it creates *place utility:* It makes products available where they are convenient for consumers.

- By making a product available for consumers to own and use, production creates ownership or *possession utility,* which customers enjoy when they buy boxes of ornaments and decorate their trees.

- Above all, production makes products available in the first place: By turning raw materials into finished goods, production creates *form utility,* as when an ornament maker combines glass, plastic, and other materials to create tree decorations.

Because the term *production* was historically associated just with manufacturing, writers have recently replaced it with *operations,* a term that reflects both service and goods production. **Operations** (or **production**) **management** is the systematic direction and control of the processes that transform resources into finished services and goods.[6] Thus, **operations** (or **production**) **managers** are ultimately responsible for creating utility for customers.

As Figure 15.3 shows, operations managers must draw up plans to transform resources into products. First, of course, they must bring together basic resources: knowledge, physical materials, equipment, and labor. Naturally, they must put those resources to effective use in the production facility. As demand for a product increases, managers must schedule and control work to produce the required amounts of products. Finally, they must also control costs, quality levels, inventory, and facilities and equipment.

Although some production managers work in factories, others work in large and small offices and retail stores ranging from giant discount outlets to specialty shops. Examples of inputs, transformations, and outputs for selected service operations are shown in Table 15.1.

Farmers are also operations managers. They create utility by transforming soil, seeds, fuel, and other inputs into soybeans, milk, and other outputs. As production managers, they may employ crews of workers to plant and harvest. Or they may opt for automated machinery or some combination of workers and machinery. Naturally, these decisions affect costs, the role of buildings and equipment in their operations, and the quality and quantity of goods that they produce.

operations (or **production**) **management**
Systematic direction and control of the processes that transform resources into finished products

operations (or **production**) **managers**
Managers responsible for production, inventory, and quality control

Figure 15.3 Resource Transformation Process

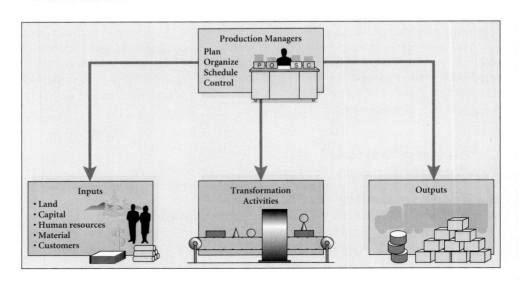

Table 15.1 Transformations in the Service Sector

Service Operation	Inputs	Transformations	Outputs
Airline	A resident of Boston, jet fuel, pilot and crew	Air travel	A vacationer in Florida
Home security	House, family with fear of theft, home security system, tools, installer	Installation of system	Safe house, peace of mind
Hospital	Sick and injured people, medical supplies, nurses, doctors, utilities	Medical care and treatment	Healthy people
Lawn service	Overgrown lawn, lawnmower, worker	Lawnmowing, yard work	Neat yard
Pizza shop	Hungry person, truck, pizza, delivery person, fuel	Delivery of pizza	Satisfied person
Theater	Expectant people, actors, costumes, seats, utilities	Theatrical production	Entertained people
TV repair shop	Inoperable television set, replacement parts, tools, skilled technician, utilities	Television repair	Operable television set
University	High school graduates, tuition, books, professors	Education	College graduates

Operations Processes

An **operations process** is a set of methods and technologies used in the production of a good or a service. We classify various types of production according to differences in their operations processes. In other words, we can describe goods according to the kind of transformation technology they require, or according to whether their operations process combines resources or breaks them into component parts. We can describe services according to the extent of customer contact required.

operations process
Set of methods used in the production of a good or service

Goods Manufacturing

All goods-manufacturing processes can be classified in two different ways: by the type of transformation technology that transforms raw materials into finished goods, and by the analytic or synthetic nature of the transformation process.

Classified by Transformation Technology. Manufacturers use the following types of transformation processes to turn raw materials into finished goods:

- In *chemical processes,* raw materials are chemically altered. Such techniques are common in the aluminum, steel, fertilizer, petroleum, and paint industries.

- *Fabrication processes* mechanically alter the basic shape or form of a product. Fabrication occurs in the metal-forming, woodworking, and textile industries.

- *Assembly processes* put together various components. These techniques are common in the electronics, appliance, and automotive industries.

- In *transport processes,* goods acquire place utility by being moved from one location to another. For example, bicycles are routinely moved by trucks from manufacturing plants to consumers through warehouses and discount stores.

- *Clerical processes* transform information. Combining data on employee absences and machine breakdowns into a productivity report is a clerical process. So is compiling inventory reports at a retail outlet.

The Natural Environment

How Clean Is Clean Enough?

Most companies define their productivity in terms of how cost-efficiently they can deliver goods and services. Soon, however, it may be equally important for them to demonstrate how effectively they can keep pollution out of the air at the same time.

In 1997 the Environmental Protection Agency (EPA) announced new standards that tightened existing guidelines for ozone and particulate air pollution. Particulates, microscopic particles released in fuel combustion, have never been regulated before but are believed to be responsible for many respiratory illnesses and deaths. Even though there are areas of the country where the air already meets the previous standards, U.S. epidemiologists estimate that 50,000 people a year still die from air pollution–related diseases such as asthma, stroke, bronchitis, and heart disease—more than are killed in car accidents over the same period.

Many industrial firms, their Congressional lobbyists, and even some scientists dispute claims that what the government calls "clean air" can still be bad for you. But one environmental economist who stands by his findings is a professor at Brigham Young University. After the 13-month closing in a labor dispute of a steel mill near Provo, Utah, C. Arden Pope collected admissions data from the three local hospitals and found a striking reduction in bronchitis, asthma, and pneumonia cases, particularly among children, while the plant was closed.

Although the matter is controversial, the weight of the evidence seems to be with Pope and other researchers. Protests from heavy industries such as oil, autos, utilities, and manufacturing say that expensive compliance with the new regulations will threaten the loss of thousands of jobs. But who will foot the bills for medical care, and how will we repair the damage to the environment? Like many tradeoffs, this one seems to lack an easy answer.

---

analytic process
Production process in which resources are broken down into components to create finished products

synthetic process
Production process in which resources are combined to create finished products

Classified by Analytic or Synthetic Nature.   An **analytic process** breaks down resources into components. Tyson, for example, reduces incoming whole chickens to the packaged parts we find at the meat counter. The reverse approach, a **synthetic process**, combines raw materials to produce a finished product. General Electric uses this approach in manufacturing refrigerators. It forms and shapes steel to produce the basic refrigerator, then it adds motors, lightbulbs, trays, and shelves. Finally, it packages the refrigerator in a shipping carton and delivers it to an appliance store.

Service Processes: Classified by Extent of Customer Contact

One way of classifying services is to ask whether a given service can be provided without the customer's being part of the production system. In answering this question, we classify services according to the extent of customer contact.

high-contact system
Level of customer contact in which the customer is part of the system during service delivery

High-Contact Processes.   Think for a moment about your local public transit system. The service provided is transportation, and when you purchase transportation, you must board a bus or train. For example, the Bay Area Rapid Transit System (BART) connects San Francisco with many of its outlying suburbs. Like all public transportation systems, BART is a **high-contact system**: To receive the service, the customer must be a part of the system. For this reason, BART managers must worry about the cleanliness of the trains and the appearance of the stations. This is usually not the case in low-contact systems: Large industrial concerns that ship coal in freight trains are generally not concerned with the appearance inside those trains.

Low-Contact Processes.   Now consider the check-processing operations at your bank. Workers sort the checks that have been cashed that day and dispatch them to the banks on which they were drawn. This operation is a **low-contact system**: Customers are not in contact with the bank while the service is performed. They receive the service— their funds are transferred to cover their checks—without ever setting foot in the check-processing center. Gas and electric utilities, auto repair shops, and lawn care services are also low-contact systems.

low-contact system
Level of customer contact in which the customer need not be a part of the system to receive the service

Differences Between Service and Manufacturing Operations

Focus on Performance

Not surprisingly, service and manufacturing operations share several important features. For example, both transform raw materials into finished products. In service production, however, the raw materials, or inputs, are not glass or steel. Rather, they are people who choose among sellers because they have either unsatisfied needs or possessions for which they need some form of care or alteration. In service operations, then, finished products or outputs are people with needs met and possessions serviced.

Therefore, there is at least one very obvious difference between service and manufacturing operations: Whereas goods are produced, services are performed. Thus, customer-oriented performance is a key factor in measuring the effectiveness of a service company.

■ For example, by studying the practices of service-oriented retailers such as L.L. Bean and Land's End, Baltimore Gas and Electric, which provides power to a million customers in Maryland, has designed a customer information system (CIS) to speed up its service calls. Now, with $50 million worth of computer hardware and software linked to mobile terminals, BG&E dispatches repair crews for same-day service. CIS even allows the company to call customers with a 30-minute lead time before arriving on maintenance calls.

■ Recent investment in computer technology now lets Banc One service representatives speed up the resolution of problems by calling up a customer's entire banking history. Banc One also makes representatives available via a 24-hour hotline. In addition, about 60 percent of Banc One's 1,400 branches in the Midwest and West are now open on Saturday; 20 percent are open on Sunday.[7]

In many ways, then, service operations are more complex than manufacturing operations. First, services are more intangible, customized, and unstorable than most products. Second, the customer is often present when the service is performed. Finally, quality considerations must be defined and managed differently in the service sector than in manufacturing operations.

Focus on Service Characteristics

Service companies' transactions always reflect the fact that service products are characterized by three key qualities: *intangibility, customization,* and *unstorability.*

Intangibility

Often, services cannot be touched, tasted, smelled, or seen. An important value, therefore, is the intangible experience of the customer in the form of pleasure, satisfaction, or a feeling of safety. For example, when you hire an attorney to resolve a problem, you purchase not only the intangible quality of legal expertise but also the equally intangible reassurance that sympathetic help is at hand. Although all services have some degree of intangibility, some provide tangible elements as well. For example, your attorney can draw up the living will that you want to keep in your safe deposit box.

Customization

When you visit a physician, you expect to be examined and your symptoms evaluated. Likewise, when you purchase insurance, get your pet groomed, or have your hair cut, you expect these services to be designed for your needs. Typically, therefore, services are customized.

Unstorability

Services such as trash collection, transportation, child care, and house cleaning cannot be produced ahead of time and then stored: If a service is not used when available, it is usually wasted.

Focus on the Customer-Service Link

Because they transform customers or their possessions, service operations often acknowledge the customer as part of the operations process. For example, to purchase a haircut you must usually go to the barbershop or beauty salon.

As part of the operations process, consumers of services have a unique ability to affect that process. In other words, as the customer, you expect the salon to be conveniently located, to be open for business at convenient times, to offer needed services at reasonable prices, and to extend prompt service. Accordingly, the manager arranges hours of operation, available services, and numbers of employees to meet your requirements and those of other customers.

It's Your Business

Better Service for You

If you've called customer service lately at Microsoft, Hewlett Packard, Canon, or Yamaha, their managers hope you've noticed a big improvement in the service you're getting. These giants are among the hundreds of companies, large and small, that have installed specially designed software to help them provide better customer service.

The new customer interaction programs are partially automated and can start by recognizing incoming calls and routing them to the right department. They also store and compile data to build a case file on each call. "We know exactly how we're doing," says Steven Thatcher, Yamaha's general manager for support at the company's Customer Satisfaction Group. "We can check recurring calls, see how long it takes us to get back to the customer, and track defects down to a single product and single serial number."

By capturing so much relevant data, the programs give user firms insights that can help them improve their products and support services. Flexibility, ease of integration with existing databases, and positive response from customers make up for the high price much of the new software commands. When combined with Web browsers and integrated telephone and computer services, the new programs will be powerful enough to let PC users get help directly from manufacturers' Web sites and databases and even open a voice line to speak with a company technician in real time.

> *When all the Internet hype finally settles, customer interaction and services will be the leading applications on the Net.*
>
> —John Longo, CEO of Vantive

According to John Longo, CEO of Vantive, one of the suppliers of customer interaction software, "When all the Internet hype finally settles, customer interaction and services will be the leading applications on the Net."

Focus on Quality Considerations

Finally, consumers use different criteria to judge services and goods. Service managers understand that quality of work and quality of service are not necessarily synonymous. For example, although your car may have been flawlessly repaired, you will feel dissatisfied with the service if it is not ready until a day later than promised.

Now that we've contrasted goods and services we can return to a more general consideration of production encompassing both goods and services. Like all good managers, we start with planning.

Operations Planning

Managers from many departments contribute to the firm's decisions about operations management. As Figure 15.4 shows, however, no matter how many decision makers are involved, the process can be described as a series of logical steps. The success of any firm depends on the final result of this logical sequence of decisions.

The overall business plan and forecasts developed by a company's top executives guide operations planning. The business plan outlines the firm's goals and objectives, including the specific goods and services that it will offer in the upcoming years. In this section we will survey the development of the main parts of operations planning. We will describe forecasting, and then we will discuss the planning five production elements: capacity, location, layout, quality, and methods planning.

Figure 15.4 Operations Planning and Control

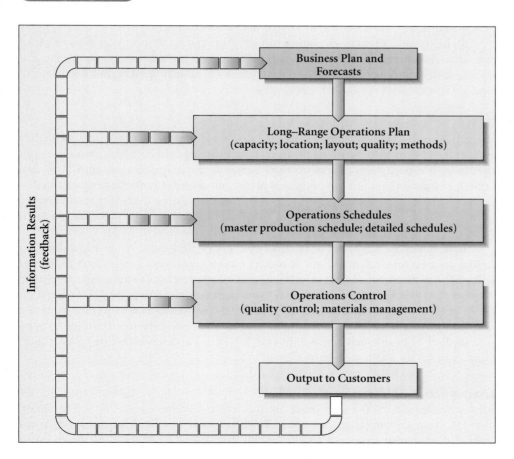

Forecasting

forecast
Facet of a long-range production plan that predicts future demand

In addition to the business plan, managers develop the firm's long-range production plan through **forecasts** of future demand for both new and existing products. The long-range plan covers a 2- to 5-year period. It specifically details the number of plants or service facilities, as well as the labor, equipment, and transportation and storage facilities, that will be needed to meet demand. It also specifies how resources will be obtained.

Forecasting uses both qualitative and quantitative methods. *Qualitative forecasts* may come from an expert or a group of experts who use their judgment and experience. *Quantitative forecasts* use statistical methods to project future demand from past demand patterns. For example, in developing a new line of mutual funds, T. Rowe Price might use quantitative methods to calculate demand for the next 3 years at 4 million new investor accounts per year. Its long-range production plan might translate this demand into a need to build a new office facility, acquire 100 computer workstations, and hire 200 new employees.

Capacity Planning

capacity
Amount of a product that a company can produce under normal working conditions

The amount of a product that a company can produce under normal working conditions is its **capacity**. The capacity of a goods or service firm depends on how many people it employs and the number and size of its facilities. Long-range planning must take into account both current and future capacity.

Capacity Planning for Producing Services

In low-contact processes, maintaining inventory lets managers set capacity at the level of *average demand*. For example, the J.C. Penney catalog sales warehouse may hire enough order fillers to handle 1,000 orders each day. When daily orders exceed this average demand, some orders are placed in inventory—set aside in a "to be done" file—to be processed on a day when fewer than 1,000 orders are received.

In high-contact processes, managers must plan capacity to meet *peak demand*. A supermarket, for instance, has far more cash registers than it needs on an average day. But on a Saturday morning or during the 3 days before Thanksgiving, all registers will be running full speed.

Capacity Planning for Producing Goods

Capacity planning for goods means ensuring that a manufacturing firm's capacity slightly exceeds the normal demand for its product. To see why this policy is best, consider the alternatives. If capacity is too small to meet demand, the company must turn away customers, a situation that not only cuts into profits but alienates both customers and salespeople. If capacity greatly exceeds demand, the firm is wasting money by maintaining a plant that is too large, by keeping excess machinery on-line, or by employing too many workers.

The stakes are high in the company's capacity decisions: While expanding fast enough to meet future demand and to protect market share from competitors, they must also weigh the increased costs of expanding. One reason that Intel Corp. enjoys more than 70-percent market share in the worldwide semiconductor business is the $11 billion it invested in capacity expansion between 1991 and 1995 (including $1.8 billion for its newest plant in Rio Rancho, New Mexico). Will demand for semiconductors continue to grow even further? With so much invested thus far, Intel must decide whether the risks of additional capacity are worth the potential gains.[8]

Location Planning

Because the location of a factory, office, or store affects its production costs and flexibility, sound location planning is crucial. Depending on the site of its facility, a company may be capable of producing a low-cost product or may find itself at an extreme cost disadvantage relative to its competitors.

Location Planning for Producing Services

In planning low-contact services, companies have some options: Services can be located near resource supplies, labor, or transportation outlets. For example, the typical Wal-Mart distribution center is located near the hundreds of Wal-Mart stores it supplies, not the companies that supply the distribution center. Distribution managers regard Wal-Mart stores as their customers: To better serve them, distribution centers are located so that truckloads of merchandise flow quickly to the stores.

On the other hand, high-contact services are more restricted: They must be near customers, who are a part of the system. Consider the following facts about the highest-volume sites of the United States' best-known fast-food companies:

- The McDonald's restaurant on Interstate 95 near the New York–Connecticut border serves more customers each day than any other restaurant in the chain. Open 24 hours, it sells 8,000 meals daily.

- The highest-volume KFC restaurant is on the U.S. Army base at Fort Campbell, Kentucky. Even though it serves as many as 2,000 customers each day, this outlet refuses to take its captive audience for granted. Promises vice president for operations Terry Rogers, "Employees who don't smile end up working in the kitchen."

- Located near the U.S. Marine Corps base in the Mojave Desert close to Twenty-Nine Palms, California, the biggest Domino's Pizza restaurant also thrives on military business. The restaurant's ovens can turn out 360 pies an hour.

The fundamental strategy establishes outlets where the customers are. As noted by Wayne Norbitz, president of Nathan's Famous Hotdogs: "You used to open a restaurant, advertise, and ask people to come to you. Today, the strategy is to find out where people already are and bring your product there.[9]

> **" *You used to open a restaurant, advertise, and ask people to come to you. Today, the strategy is to find out where people already are and bring your product there.* "**
>
> —Wayne Norbitz, president of Nathan's Famous Hotdogs

Location Planning for Producing Goods

Managers in goods-producing operations must consider many factors in location planning. Their location decisions are influenced by proximity to raw materials and markets, availability of labor, energy and transportation costs, local and state regulations and taxes, and community living conditions.

In 1993, for example, Mercedes-Benz selected Alabama as the location for its first North American assembly plant. Most important to Mercedes officials who were responsible for the decision was transportation costs. Part of their search, therefore, focused on locations with access to Atlantic or Gulf seaports. At the same time, however, midwestern sites in Nebraska and Iowa were considered because they were in the center of Mercedes's targeted market. Alabama finally won out because it not only afforded proximity to Mercedes distributors throughout the United States but also boasted favorable wage scales, positive worker attitudes, and a receptive local atmosphere. Along with its advantages, however, the new site has some drawbacks: This is Mercedes's first foreign plant, it is building its first sport utility vehicle, and its employees have never built a car. So, to ensure continuity of quality, hundreds of new Alabama employees were sent to work in the Mercedes plant in Germany for up to 6 months during 1996. And today some 70 German employees have moved to Alabama to provide training at the new plant.[10]

Some location decisions are now being simplified by the rise of industrial parks. Created by cities interested in attracting new industry, these planned sites come with the necessary zoning, land, shipping facilities, utilities, and waste disposal outlets already in place. Such sites offer flexibility, often allowing firms to open new facilities before competitors can get started in the same area. The ready-made site also provides faster construction startups because it entails no lead time in preparing the chosen site.

Layout Planning

Once a site has been selected, managers must decide on plant layout. Layout of machinery, equipment, and supplies determines whether a company can respond quickly and efficiently to customer requests for more and different products or finds itself unable to match competitors' production speed or convenience of service.

Layout Planning for Producing Goods

In facilities that produce goods, layout must be planned for three different types of space:

- *Productive facilities:* workstations and equipment for transforming raw materials, for example

- *Nonproductive facilities:* storage and maintenance areas

- *Support facilities:* offices, restrooms, parking lots, cafeterias, and so forth

In this section, we will focus on productive facilities. Alternatives include process, product, cellular, and fixed-position layouts.

process layout
Spatial arrangement of production activities that groups equipment and people according to function

Process Layouts. In a **process layout**, which is well suited to job shops that specialize in custom work, equipment and people are grouped together according to function. In a custom cake bakery, for instance, machines blend batter in an area devoted to mixing, baking occurs in the oven area, and cakes are decorated on tables in a finishing area before boxing. The various tasks are each performed in specialized locations. Machine, woodworking, and dry cleaning shops also feature process layouts.

product layout
Spatial arrangement of production activities designed to move resources through a smooth, fixed sequence of steps

Product Layouts. In a **product layout**, equipment and people are set up to produce one type of good in a fixed sequence of steps and are arranged according to its production requirements. Product layouts often use **assembly lines**, as in automobile, food-processing, and computer assembly plants.

Product layouts can be efficient and inexpensive because they simplify work tasks and use unskilled labor. However, they tend to be inflexible because they require a heavy investment in specialized equipment that is hard to rearrange for new applications. In addition, workers are subject to boredom, and when someone is absent or overworked, those farther down the line cannot help out.

assembly line
Product layout in which a product moves step by step through a plant on conveyor belts or other equipment until it is completed

Recently, many companies have experimented with variations on the product layout, to make standard production lines more flexible. Some firms have adopted **U-shaped production lines**: Because machines are close together, in slow periods one worker can complete all the tasks needed to make a product by easily moving from one location to another inside the U. In busier times, more workers can be added until there is one worker per machine. This flexibility enables the production line to be efficient during periods of both high and low demand for its products.[11]

U-shaped production line
Production layout in which machines and workers are placed in a narrow U shape rather than a straight line

cellular layout
Spatial arrangement of production facilities designed to move families of products through similar flow paths

Cellular Layouts. A newer workplace arrangement for some applications is often called the **cellular layout**. Cellular layouts are used when families of products can follow similar flow paths. A clothing manufacturer, for example, may establish a cell, or designated area, dedicated to making a family of pockets—say, pockets for shirts, coats, blouses, trousers, and slacks. Although each type of pocket is unique in shape, size, and style, all go through the same production steps. Within the cell, therefore, various types of equipment (for cutting, trimming, and sewing) are arranged close together in the appropriate sequence. All pockets pass stage by stage through the cell from beginning to end, in a nearly continuous flow.

Cellular layouts have several advantages. For example, because similar products require less machine adjustment, equipment setup time is reduced. Because flow distances are usually shorter, there is less material handling and transit time. Finally, inventories of goods in progress are lower and paperwork is simpler because material flows are more orderly.[12]

Fixed-Position Layouts. Sometimes, of course, the simplest layout is the most efficient. In a **fixed-position layout**, labor, materials, and equipment are brought to the work location. This layout is used in building ships, homes, skyscrapers, dams, and manufacturing facilities themselves.

fixed-position layout
Product layout that brings production activities (labor, materials, and equipment) to the location where the work is done

Layout Planning for Producing Services

Service firms use some of the same layouts as goods-producing firms. In a low-contact system, for instance, the facility should be arranged to enhance the production of the service. A mail-processing facility at UPS or Federal Express, therefore, looks very much like a product layout in a factory: Machines and people are arranged in the order in which they are used in the mass processing of mail. In contrast, Kinko's Copy Centers use process layouts for different custom jobs: Specific functions, such as photocopying, computing, binding, photography, and laminating, are performed in specialized areas of the store.

High-contact systems should be arranged to meet customer needs and expectations.[13] For example, Piccadilly Cafeterias focuses both layout and services on the groups that constitute its primary market: families and elderly people. As you can see in Figure 15.5, families enter to find an array of highchairs and rolling baby beds that make it convenient to wheel children through the line. Servers are willing to carry trays for elderly people and for those pushing strollers. Note, too, that customers must pass by the whole serving line before making selections. Not only does this layout help them make up their minds; it also tempts them to select more.

Quality Planning

In planning production systems and facilities, managers must keep in mind the firm's quality goals. Thus, any complete operations plan must ensure that products are produced to meet the firm's standards of quality. The American Society for Quality Control defines *quality* as "the totality of features and characteristics of a product or service that bear on its ability to satisfy stated or implied needs."[14]

In other words, operations processes must be geared to creating fitness for use, or offering features that customers want. Such features may include a product's reasonable

Figure 15.5 Layout of a Typical Piccadilly Cafeteria

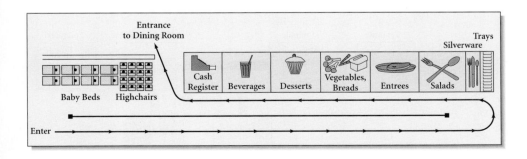

price and its consistent performance in delivering the benefit it promises. For example, Perrigo, the largest U.S. manufacturer of over-the-counter pharmaceuticals and personal-care products, treats quality planning as a central part of its competitive strategy. Quality is enhanced through the continuous improvement of manufacturing methods, the careful control of every step in production and packaging, and a quality improvement program that empowers employees to reduce waste and increase production capabilities.[15]

Methods Planning in Services

In designing operations systems, managers must clearly identify every production step and the specific methods for performing them. They can then work to reduce waste, inefficiency, and poor performance by examining procedures on a step-by-step basis—an approach sometimes called methods improvement.

Methods Improvement in Services

In a low-contact process, managers can use methods improvements to speed up services ranging from mowing lawns to filling prescriptions and drawing up legal documents. At First Chicago Bank, for example, the cash management unit collects accounts receivable for corporate clients; the sooner checks are collected and deposited, the sooner the client begins collecting interest. Delays, including the time required to check and adjust customer queries, are expensive, and speed and accuracy are of the essence. In First Chicago's methods planning, employees not only are trained to perform the specific requirements of their jobs but also are educated about the overall mission of the department, so they can make time- and money-saving judgments on their own.[16]

Service Flow Analysis

service flow analysis
Method for analyzing a service by showing the flow of processes that constitute it

By showing the flow of processes that make up a given service, **service flow analysis** helps managers decide whether all those processes are necessary. Moreover, because each process is a potential contributor to good or bad service, analysis also helps identify and isolate potential problems (known as *fail points*). For example, in Figure 15.6, the manager of a photofinishing shop has determined that the standard execution time for developing a roll of film is 48.5 minutes. She has also found that the "develop film" stage is the one most likely to delay service because it is the most complex. Thus, she has marked it as a potential fail point, as a reminder to give special attention to this stage of operations.

Designing to Control Employee Discretion in Services

Thus far, we have stressed the importance of the human factor in service activities—that is, the direct contact of server and customer. In some cases, however, the purpose of service design is to limit the range of activities of both employees and customers. By careful planning—and sometimes even by automating to control human discretion—managers can make services more customer-oriented because they can ensure product consistency.

Figure 15.6 Service Flow Analysis

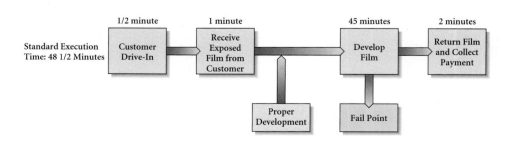

McDonald's, for example, has done an outstanding job of designing the fast-food business as a mass production system. By automating processes that would otherwise rely on judgment, McDonald's has been able to provide consistent service from a staff with little specialized training. At a central supply house, for instance, hamburger patties are automatically measured and packed. Specially designed scoops measure the same amount of french fries and other items into standard-sized containers. In addition, all drawers, shelves, and bins are designed to hold the ingredients for McDonald's standard product mixes only.

Sometimes, firms design ways to transfer discretion from employees to customers. For example, hospital patients connected to special equipment can administer their own pain-relieving drugs. This procedure offers more control to the patient and frees up nurses for other duties. (Of course, there are safeguards: Once a predetermined limit of drugs has been is used, the source shuts down.)

Design for Customer Contact in Services

In a high-contact service, the demands on system designs are somewhat different. Here, managers must develop procedures that clearly spell out the ways in which workers interact with customers. These procedures must cover such activities as exchanging information or money, delivering and receiving materials, and even making physical contact. The next time you visit your dentist's office, for instance, notice the way dental hygienists scrub up and wear disposable gloves. They also scrub after patient contact, even if they intend to work on equipment or do paperwork, and they rescrub before working on the next patient. The high-contact system in a dental office consists of very strict procedures designed to avoid contact that can transmit disease.

Methods Planning in Goods Production

Improvement of production for goods begins when a manager documents the current method. A detailed description, often using a diagram called the *process flow chart,* is usually helpful for organizing and recording all information. It identifies the sequence of production activities, movements of materials, and the work performed at each stage as the product flows through production. The flow can then be analyzed to identify wasteful activities, sources of delay in production flows, and other inefficiencies. The final step is implementing improvements.

▶ Mercury Marine, for example, used methods improvement to streamline the production of stern-drive units for power boats. Examination of the process flow from raw materials to assembly (the final production step) revealed numerous wastes and inefficiencies. Each product passed through 122 steps, traveled nearly 21,000 feet (almost 4 miles) in the factory, and was handled by 106 people. Analysis revealed that only 27 steps actually added value to the product (for example, drilling, painting). Work methods were revised to eliminate nonproductive activities. Mercury ultimately identified potential savings in labor, inventory, paperwork, and space requirements. Because production lead time was also reduced, customer orders were filled faster.

Operations Scheduling

Once plans identify needed resources and how they will be used to reach a firm's goals, managers must develop timetables for acquiring resources for production. This aspect of operations is called scheduling.

Scheduling Service Operations

Service scheduling may cover both work and workers. In a low-contact service, it can be based either on desired completion dates or on the time of order arrivals. For example, several cars may be scheduled for repairs at a local garage. If your car is not scheduled for work until 3:30, it may sit idle for several hours even if it was the first to be dropped off. In such businesses, reservation and appointment systems can help to smooth ups and downs in demand.

In high-contact situations, however, the precise scheduling of services may not be possible. If a hospital emergency room is overloaded, for example, patients cannot be asked to make appointments and come back later; the customer is part of the system and must be accommodated.

In scheduling workers, managers must also consider efficiency and costs. McDonald's, for example, guarantees workers that they will be scheduled for at least 4 hours at a time. To accomplish this goal without having workers idle, McDonald's uses overlapping shifts: The ending hours for some employees overlap the beginning hours for others to provide maximum coverage during peak periods.

A 24-hour-a-day service operation, such as a hospital, can be an even greater scheduling challenge. For example, nurses must be on duty around the clock, 7 days a week. However, few nurses want to work on weekends or during the wee hours of the morning. Similarly, although enough nurses must be scheduled to meet emergencies, most hospitals are on tight budgets and cannot afford to have too many on-duty nurses. Thus, incentives are often used to entice nurses to work at times they might not otherwise choose. For example, would you choose to work 12 hours a day, 7 days a week? Probably not. But what if you were entitled to have every other week off in exchange for working such a schedule? A number of hospitals use just such a plan to attract nurses.

Scheduling Goods Operations

master production schedule
Schedule showing which products will be produced, when production will take place, and what resources will be used

Scheduling of goods production occurs on different levels within the firm. First, a top-level or **master production schedule** shows which products will be produced, when production will occur, and what resources will be used during specified time periods.

▶ Consider the case of Logan Aluminum Inc. Logan produces coils of aluminum that its main customers, Atlantic Richfield and Alcan Aluminum, use to produce aluminum cans. Logan's master schedule extends out to 60 weeks and shows how many coils will be made each week. For various types of coils, the master schedule specifies how many of each will be produced. "We need this planning and scheduling system," says material manager Candy McKenzie, "to determine how much of what product we can produce each and every month."[17]

However, this information is not complete. For example, manufacturing personnel must also know the location of all coils on the plant floor and their various stages of production. Startup and stop times must be assigned, and employees must be given scheduled work assignments. Short-term detailed schedules fill in these blanks on a daily basis. These schedules use incoming customer orders and information about current machine conditions to update the sizes and variety of coils to make each day.

Operations Control

operations control
Process of monitoring production performance by comparing results with plans

follow-up
Production control activity for ensuring that production decisions are being implemented

Once long-range plans have been put into action and schedules have been drawn up, **operations control** requires production managers to monitor production performance by comparing results with detailed plans and schedules. If schedules or quality standards are not met, these managers must take corrective action. **Follow-up**—checking to ensure that production decisions are being implemented—is an essential and ongoing facet of operations control.

Operations control features materials management and production process control. Both these activities ensure that schedules are met and that production goals are fulfilled, both in quantity and in quality.

Materials Management

Both goods-producing and service companies use materials. For many manufacturing firms, material costs account for 50 to 75 percent of total product costs. For goods whose production uses little labor, such as petroleum refining, this percentage is even higher. Thus, companies have good reasons to emphasize materials management.

The process of **materials management** not only controls but also plans and organizes the flow of materials. Even before production starts, materials management focuses on product design by emphasizing materials **standardization**: the use of standard and uniform components rather than new or different components. Law firms, for example, maintain standardized forms and data files for estate wills, living wills, trust agreements, and various contracts that can be adjusted easily to meet your individual needs. And in manufacturing, Ford's engine plant in Romeo, Michigan, uses common parts for several different kinds of engines rather than unique parts for each. Once components were standardized, the total number of different parts was reduced by 25 percent. Standardization also simplifies paperwork, reduces storage requirements, and eliminates unnecessary material flows.

Once the product has been designed, materials managers purchase the necessary materials and monitor the production process through the distribution of finished goods. The five major areas of materials management are transportation, warehousing, purchasing, supplier selection and inventory control:

- *Transportation* includes the means of transporting resources to the company and finished goods to buyers.

- *Warehousing* is the storage of both incoming materials for production and finished goods for physical distribution to customers.

- *Purchasing* is the acquisition of all the raw materials and services that a company needs to produce its products; most large firms have purchasing departments to buy proper materials in the amounts needed.

- **Supplier selection** means finding and choosing suppliers of services and materials to buy from. It includes evaluating potential suppliers, negotiating terms of service, and maintaining positive buyer-seller relationships.

- **Inventory control** includes the receiving, storing, handling, and counting of all raw materials, partly finished goods, and finished goods. It ensures that enough materials inventories are available to meet production schedules.

Tools for Operations Process Control

A number of tools assist managers in controlling operations. Chief among these are worker training, just-in-time production systems, material requirements planning, and quality control.

Worker Training

Not surprisingly, customer satisfaction is closely linked to the employees who provide the service. As Bain & Co.'s Fred Reichheld puts it, "It's impossible to build a loyal book of customers without a loyal employee base."[18] Naturally, effective customer relationships do not come about by accident: Service workers can be trained and motivated in customer-oriented attitudes and behavior.

In service product design, it is important to remember that most services are delivered by people: That is, service system employees are both the producers of the product and the salespeople. Thus, human relations skills are vital in anyone who has contact with the public. Says Richard Bell-Irving, vice president for human resources at Marriott, "We used to hire people who were good at the keyboard, good at processing information. Now we want associates who can look you in the eye, carry on a conversation, and work well under stress."[19] Like Bell-Irving, more and more human resource experts now realize that

materials management
Planning, organizing, and controlling the flow of materials from design through distribution of finished goods

standardization
Use of standard and uniform components in the production process

supplier selection
Process of finding and selecting suppliers from whom to buy

inventory control
In materials management, receiving, storing, handling, and counting of all raw materials, partly finished goods, and finished goods

without employees trained in these skills, businesses such as airlines, employment agencies, and hotels can lose customers to better-prepared competitors.

> *We used to hire people who were . . . good at processing information. Now we want associates who can look you in the eye and carry on a conversation.*
>
> —Richard Bell-Irving, vice president for
> human resources at Marriott International

Managers realize how easily service employees with a poor attitude can reduce sales. Conversely, the right attitude is a powerful sales tool. "You never know," says Disney employee trainer Robert Sias, "when something seemingly insignificant out in the workplace is going to have an enormous impact on a guest."[20]

The Disney organization does an excellent job of remembering that no matter what their jobs, service employees are all links to the public. Of the 35,000 employees at Disney World Resort in Buena Vista, Florida, some 20,000 have direct contact with guests. For example, Disney World has a team of sweepers constantly at work picking up bits of trash as soon as they fall to the ground. When visitors have questions about directions or time, they often ask one of the sweepers. Because their responses affect visitors' overall impressions of Disney World, sweepers are trained to respond in appropriate ways. Their work is evaluated and rewarded based on strict performance appraisal standards. A pleased customer is more likely to return.

Just-in-Time Production Systems

just-in-time (JIT) production
Production method that brings together all materials and parts needed at each production stage at the precise moment they are required

To minimize manufacturing inventory costs, some managers use **just-in-time (JIT) production systems**. JIT brings together all the needed materials and parts at the precise moment they are required for each production stage, not before. All resources are continuously flowing, from their arrival as raw materials to subassembly, final completion, and shipment of finished products. JIT reduces to practically nothing the number of goods in process (that is, goods not yet finished) and saves money by replacing stop-and-go production with smooth movement. Once smooth movements become the norm, disruptions become more visible and thus get resolved more quickly. Finding and eliminating disruptions by continuous improvement of production is a major objective of JIT.[21]

By implementing JIT, Harley-Davidson reduced its inventories by over 40 percent, improved production work flows, and reduced its costs of warranty work, rework, and scrap by 60 percent. In addition, Harley motorcycles have retained their coveted quality reputation: The annual number of shipments more than doubled from 1988 to 1996. And, with the help of JIT, their Plan 2003 calls for another doubling of production for Harley's 100th anniversary in 2003.[22]

Material Requirements Planning

material requirements planning (MRP)
Production method in which a bill of materials is used to ensure that the right amounts of materials are delivered to the right place at the right time

bill of materials
Production control tool that specifies the necessary ingredients of a product, the order in which they should be combined, and how many of each are needed to make one batch

Like JIT, **material requirements planning (MRP)** also seeks to deliver the right amounts of materials at the right place and the right time for goods production. MRP uses a **bill of materials** that is basically a recipe for the finished product. It specifies the necessary ingredients (raw materials and components), the order in which they should be combined, and the quantity of each ingredient needed to make one batch of the product (say, 2,000 finished telephones). The recipe is fed into a computer that controls inventory and schedules each stage of production. The result is fewer early arrivals, less frequent stock shortages, and lower storage costs. MRP is most popular among companies whose products require complicated assembly and fabrication activities, such as automobile manufacturers, appliance makers, and furniture companies.

       Manufacturing resource planning (MRP II), is an advanced version of MRP that ties all parts of the organization into the company's production activities. For example, MRP inventory and production schedules are translated into cost requirements for the financial management department and into personnel requirements for the human resource department; information about available capacity for new orders goes to the marketing department.

Quality Control

Another operation control tool is **quality control**: the management of the production process so as to manufacture goods or supply services that meet specific quality standards. McDonald's, for example, has been a pioneer in quality control in the restaurant industry since the early 1950s. The company oversees everything from the farming of potatoes for French fries to the packing of meat for Big Macs. Quality assurance staffers even check standards for ketchup sweetness and French fry length. Our discussion of quality control is continued in chapter 16.

Special Production Control Problems in Service Operations

The unique characteristics of services—customization, unstorability, and the presence of customers within the production process—create special challenges. In this final section, we will consider some techniques for meeting these challenges.

Customization

The customized nature of services often makes scheduling difficult or impossible. This difficulty is one reason why you often have to wait at your doctor's office even though you have an appointment. Because the patients ahead of you also purchased customized services, the receptionist who schedules appointments can never know exactly when service will be completed.

       Because scheduling is harder in high-contact services, it can often be improved by reducing customer contact. Routine transactions, such as approval for small loans, for example, can be handled by telephone or mail; only exceptions need be handled on a face-to-face basis. Locating drop-off points away from main facilities also reduces the level of customer contact. Consider the success of automatic teller machines: Not only are they more convenient for customers, but they free bank tellers from processing routine deposits and withdrawals.

       Scheduling can also be improved by separating information gathering from provision of the service itself. For example, a well-run medical office will give you a medical history form to fill out while you wait. This system frees all office personnel, including the doctor, for other duties.

Unstorability

As we noted earlier, the unstorability of services creates a potential for waste. Many hotels therefore accept more reservations than they can accommodate on a given night: If some customers fail to keep reservations, the hotel's ability to provide rooms has not been wasted (although it does risk offending customers who must be turned away if everyone shows up). Likewise, airlines overbook flights because they can usually count on no-shows.

Customer Involvement

We have already seen that service production is complicated when customers are part of the process. However, some businesses have found a way to turn customer presence into an advantage: They actually get the customer more involved in the process. Consider the process of making a direct-dial long-distance telephone call. Back in 1970, over half of all long-distance calls were still being placed with the assistance of operators. Then in 1971,

manufacturing resource planning (MRP II)
Advanced version of MRP that ties together all parts of an organization into its production activities

quality control
Management of the production process designed to manufacture goods or supply services that meet specific quality standards

AT&T introduced special switching systems. It also introduced a major marketing program that explained the change, promised benefits to customers (reduced cost and faster connections), and requested customer cooperation. By the end of 1971, 75 percent of all long-distance calls were direct-dialed. Today, the figure is well over 90 percent. What AT&T had done was shift some productive effort to the customer.

Summary of Learning Objectives

1   **Explain the meaning of the term** *production* **or** *operations* **and describe the four kinds of utility it provides.** *Production* (or *operations*) refers to the processes and activities for transforming resources into finished services and goods for customers. The resources include knowledge, physical materials, equipment, and labor that are systematically combined in a production facility to create four kinds of utility for customers: time utility (makes products available when customers want them), place utility (available where they are convenient for customers), possession or ownership utility (customers benefit from possessing and using the product), and form utility (the creation of the product itself).

2   **Describe and explain the three classifications of operations processes.** Operations managers in manufacturing use one of two classifications to describe operations processes. Criteria include the type of technology used (chemical, fabrication, assembly, transport, or clerical) to transform raw materials into finished goods and whether products are submitted to analytic or synthetic processes (that is, whether the process breaks down resources into components or combines raw materials into finished products). Service operations are classified according to the extent of customer contact, as either high-contact systems (the customer is part of the system) or low-contact (customers are not in contact while the service is provided).

3   **Identify the characteristics that distinguish service operations from goods production and explain the main differences in the service focus.** Although the creation of both goods and services involves resources, transformations, and finished products, service operations differ from goods manufacturing in several important ways. In service production, the raw materials are not, say, glass or steel, but rather people who choose among sellers because they have unsatisfied needs or possessions in need of care or alteration. Therefore, whereas services are typically performed, goods are physically produced. In addition, services are largely intangible, more likely than physical goods to be customized to meet the purchaser's needs, and more unstorable than most products. Service businesses therefore focus explicitly on these characteristics of their products. Because services are intangible, for instance, providers work to ensure that customers receive value in the form of pleasure, satisfaction, or a feeling of safety. Often, they also focus on both the transformation process and the final product (say, making the loan interview a pleasant experience as well as providing the loan itself). Finally, service providers typically focus on the customer-service link, often acknowledging the customer as part of the operations process.

4   **Describe the factors involved in operations planning.** Operations planning involves the analysis of six key factors. Forecasts of future demand for both new and existing products provide information for developing production plans. In capacity planning, the firm analyzes how much of a product it must be able to produce. In high-contact services, managers must plan capacity to meet peak demand. Capacity planning for goods means ensuring that manufacturing capacity slightly exceeds the normal demand for its product. Location planning for goods and for low-contact services involves analyzing proposed facility sites in terms of proximity to raw materials and markets, availability of labor, and energy and transportation costs. Location planning for high-contact services, in contrast, involves locating the service near customers, who are part of the system. Layout planning involves designing a facility so that customer needs are supplied for high-contact services and so as to enhance production efficiency. Lay-

out alternatives include product, process, and cellular configurations. In quality planning, systems are developed to ensure that products meet a firm's quality standards. Finally, in methods planning, specific production steps and methods for performing them are identified. Service flow analysis and process flow charts are helpful for identifying all operations activities and eliminating wasteful steps from production.

5 **Explain some of the activities involved in operations control, including materials management and the use of certain operations control tools**. Operations control requires production managers to monitor production performance, by comparing results with detailed plans and schedules, and then to take corrective action as needed. Materials management is the planning, organizing, and controlling of the flow of materials. It focuses on the control of transportation (transporting resources to the manufacturer and products to customers), warehousing (storing both incoming raw materials and finished goods), purchasing (acquiring the raw materials and services that a manufacturer needs), supplier selection, and inventory control. To control operations processes, managers use various methods. For example, worker training programs can assist in quality control, the management of the operations process so as to ensure that services and goods meet specific quality standards. Just-in-time (JIT) production systems bring together all materials and parts needed at each production stage at the precise moment they are required. JIT reduces manufacturing inventory costs and reveals production problems that need improvement. Material requirements planning (MRP) is another method for ensuring that the right amounts of materials are delivered to the right place at the right time for manufacturing. It uses computer-controlled schedules for moving inventories through each stage of production.

Questions and Exercises

Review Questions

1 What are the four different kinds of production-based utility?
2 What are the major differences between goods production operations and service operations?
3 What are the major differences between high-contact and low-contact service systems?
4 What are the six major categories of operations planning?
5 How does a process layout differ from a product layout? How does a fixed-position layout differ from a U-shaped layout?
6 What factors must a manager consider when planning the layout of a service facility?

Questions for Analysis

7 What are the resources and finished products of the following services?
 • Real estate firm
 • Child care facility
 • Bank
 • City water and electric department
 • Hotel
8 Analyze the location of a local firm where you do business (perhaps a restaurant, a supermarket, or a manufacturing firm). What problems do you see and what recommendations would you make to management?
9 Why is high quality in the service sector so difficult to achieve?
10 Find good examples of a synthetic production process and an analytic process. Then classify each according to whether it is chemical, fabrication, assembly, transport, or clerical. Explain your analysis.
11 Develop a service flow analysis for some service that you use frequently, such as buying lunch at a cafeteria, having your hair cut, or riding a bus. Identify areas of potential quality or productivity failures in the process.

Application Exercises

12 Interview the owner of a local small manufacturing firm. Classify the firm's operations processes and then identify its major operations problems. Propose some solutions to these problems.

13 Interview the manager of a local service business, such as a laundry or dry-cleaning shop. Identify the major decisions that were involved in planning its service operations. Prepare a class report suggesting areas for improvement.

14 Select a high-contact industry. Write an advertisement to hire workers for this business. Draw up a plan for motivating the hired workers to produce high-quality services for the firm.

Building Your Business Skills

This exercise enhances the following SCANS workplace competencies: demonstrating basic skills, demonstrating thinking skills, exhibiting interpersonal skills, and working with information.

Goal   To encourage students to apply the concept of customization to an entrepreneurial idea.

Situation   Imagine that you are an entrepreneur with the desire to start your own service business. You are intrigued with the idea of creating some kind of customized one-on-one service that would appeal to baby boomers, who traditionally have been pampered, and working women, who have little time to get things done.

Method   **Step 1:**   Come together with three or four other students to brainstorm business ideas that would appeal to harried working people. Among the ideas to consider are
- A concierge service in office buildings that would handle such personal and business services as arranging children's birthday parties and booking guest speakers for business luncheons.
- A personal image consultation service aimed at helping clients improve their appearance, personal etiquette, and presentation style.
- A mobile pet care network in which veterinarians and personal groomers make house calls.

Step 2:   Choose an idea from these or others you might think of. Then write a memo explaining why you think your idea will succeed. Research may be necessary as you target
- A specific demographic group or groups. (Who are your customers and why would they buy your service?)
- The features that make your service attractive to this group.
- The social factors in your local community that would lead to success.

Follow-Up Questions

1 Why is the customization of and easy access to personal services so attractive as we approach the twenty-first century?

2 As services are personalized, do you think quality will become more or less important? Why?

3 Why does the trend to personalized, one-on-one service present unique opportunities for entrepreneurs?

4 In a personal one-on-one business, how important are the human relations skills of those delivering the service? Can you make an argument that they are more important than the service itself?

Business Case 15

Honda's "Global" Accord: A Customization Breakthrough

Even at the end of its 4-year sales cycle, the 1997 model Honda Accord was still among the best-selling cars in the United States, testimony to the brand's enormous and continuing popularity with baby boomers. Honda hopes to do even better with its newest Accord, which it will parlay into customized vehicles for several distinct global markets thanks to a revolutionary production change.

> **" Honda has come up with the best approach for going global. They can easily and inexpensively customize and design products for each market around the world. "**
>
> —Auto consultant Christopher Cedergren

The Japanese automaker plans to base seven new Accords on a single innovative platform or frame (the most expensive part of any new car design) that can readily be shrunk or expanded to accommodate car bodies of varying sizes. The cars will range from a mid-size American sedan to a sporty Japanese compact, a narrow European model, a minivan, a sport utility vehicle, and even two luxury cars due in 1998 and 1999. Honda's production breakthrough will allow it to differentiate each one of these cars from the others, inside and out.

By customizing the Accord, its maker hopes to increase market share worldwide, as it has already done in the United States. "Honda has come up with the best approach for going global," according to auto consultant Christopher Cedergren. "They can easily and inexpensively customize and design products for each market around the world." In the United States, Honda expects the customization to save about 20 percent of its production cost per vehicle, enabling it to keep the sticker price for the U.S. sedan at its current level (about $15,500) while increasing interior room and adding new features.

Other manufacturers have tried to capture a global market, but with a single car shipped around the world. Industry observers say Honda's advantage is in recognizing that U.S. drivers want different features than do Europeans—who don't want the same driving experience as Asians—and in coming up with a manufacturing solution to the problem of satisfying them all. Remarkably, the switchover to manufacturing the new model Accord was accomplished in 20 days (while the old model was still rolling off the production line) and required no layoffs or shutdowns.

With a much smaller research budget than its rival automakers ($2.1 billion compared to GM's $9 billion, for instance), Honda had a big incentive to innovate. Analysts think the bill for developing the new Accord may total $600 million, not bad compared with $2.6 billion for the Ford Taurus. So far, the gamble seems to be paying off.

Questions

1 How will Honda succeed in correctly customizing each of its new Accords? How can it ensure that it does not alienate trade-in customers who like the old model?

2 Toyota's Sienna minivan is based on the Camry chassis. Would you expect other competitors to try to adapt Honda's new production technology in their own bids for a global car? Why or why not?

3 What alternative strategies might competitors use instead of customization? What are their advantages and disadvantages?

4 U.S. automakers have been less successful at cutting costs than either Toyota or Honda. How can Honda promote its efficient cost management as a marketing strategy? Why might such a strategy also be dangerous?

Connecting to the Web

The following Web sites will give you additional information and points of view about topics covered in this chapter. Many sites lead to other related Internet locations, so approach this list with the spirit of an explorer.

AMERICAN DENTAL ASSOCIATION: TALKING INFECTION CONTROL

http://www.ada.org/

The high-contact service of dentistry involves stringent infection control procedures. These procedures are described for consumers in the American Dental Association's Web site, with the result that consumers expect dentists to meet ADA standards.

AMERICAN SOCIETY FOR QUALITY

http://www.asqc.org/

The American Society for Quality is dedicated to helping organizations improve customer satisfaction by identifying, communicating, and promoting high-quality goods and services. This Web site defines the ASQ's specific role in quality improvement.

AUSTRALIAN ORGANISATION FOR QUALITY

http://q2000.com/au/aoq/#obj

The Australian Organisation for Quality is the largest supplier of quality management training and education in Australia. This Web site introduces the quality issues faced by Australian corporations and government bodies.

BAY AREA RAPID TRANSIT DISTRICT

http://www.bart.org/

The San Francisco Bay Area Rapid Transit System (BART) is a high-contact service system. BART uses its Web site to help meet customers' varied needs through a menu of on-line services that includes trip planning assistance, information for senior riders and people with disabilities, and ticket information.

FAO SCHWARZ

http://www.faoschwarz.com/aboutfao/index.htm/

Visit this Web site for a look at FAO Schwarz's approach to service. Included are a personal shopping service, a catalog operation, and an on-line buying service.

JOHNSON CONTROLS: CONTROLS GROUP INTRODUCTION

http://www.johnsoncontrols.com/cg/html/intro_to_cg.htm

This Web page explains the comprehensive bundle of products and services offered by Johnson Controls, including the design, manufacture, installation, repair, operation, and maintenance of heating and cooling systems in nonresidential buildings as well as a host of on-site management and technical services.

KINKO'S COPY CENTERS

http://www.kinkos.com/main

This site describes the products and services offered by Kinko's Copy Centers. Using process layouts, managers place various functions in specialized store areas in order to better serve customers' needs.

MERCEDES-BENZ

http://www.mercedes-benz.com

Type the word *Alabama* into the search function of the Mercedes-Benz Web page to learn why the company built its first North American assembly plant in Tuscaloosa, Alabama.

U.S. ENVIRONMENTAL PROTECTION AGENCY

http://www.epa.gov

The Web site of the U.S. Environmental Protection Agency includes information on the latest air pollution standards.

VANTIVE

http://www.vantive.com/

Visit this site for a close look at Vantive's customer asset management software, which automates marketing, sales, customer support, quality tracking, field service, spare parts management, internal help desks, and Web interaction.

chapter 16

Managing for **quality** and **productivity**

Dell speeds its way to quality

Dell Computer Corp. has never done business in quite the same way that other computer makers have. One of the country's fastest-growing high-tech firms, Dell sells its computers directly to customers and is already making a big splash on the Internet, writing up $1 million worth of orders a day from its new Web site. It is now the number-one PC retailer on the Web and sales are still growing at an astounding 20 percent per month. In fact, Dell has led the way to a whole new world of selling: Direct buyers now account for a third of all new PC sales, double the number of just a few years ago.

What's the secret of Dell's success? Michael Dell, chairman and CEO, has stressed a few key production principles that drive productivity up and keep costs and inventories low. Perhaps the most important one is speed. Just-in-time manufacturing has al-

ways been a key tenet of the firm, and Dell has recently extended it to its suppliers. It now requires its supply chain to warehouse most computer components within 15 minutes of its factories in Texas, Ireland, and Malaysia, and it has dropped suppliers who can't comply. Dell doesn't even buy components until it's received an order for one of its computers, thus realizing big savings on parts whose prices can drop almost overnight. Despite the squeeze on suppliers, the firm can still book a custom order and ship the finished machine within 48 hours.

Dell also collects on sales faster than the competition, averaging 24 hours from order to cash. That's days sooner than rivals Gateway and Compaq.

"Speed is everything in this business," says CEO Dell. "We're setting the pace for the industry." With the firm's stock price continuing to climb, it seems that investors as well as customers must agree that Dell has figured out how to achieve an enviable mix of productivity and quality.

> ❝ *Speed is everything in this business. We're setting the pace for the industry.* ❞
>
> —Michael Dell,
> CEO of Dell Computer Corp.

It is no secret that productivity and quality are the watchwords in today's business competition. Companies are not only measuring productivity and insisting on improvements but also insisting that quality means bringing to market products that satisfy customers, improve sales, and boost profits.

By focusing on the learning objectives of this chapter, you will better understand the increasingly important concepts of productivity and quality.

After reading this chapter, you should be able to

1 Describe the connection between productivity and quality.

2 Explain the decline and recovery in U.S. productivity that has occurred in the last 25 or 30 years.

3 Explain total and partial measures of productivity and show how they are used to keep track of national, industrywide, and companywide productivity.

4 Identify the activities involved in total quality management and describe six tools that companies can use to achieve it.

5 List three trends in productivity and quality management and discuss three ways in which companies can compete by improving productivity and quality.

The Productivity-Quality Connection

Productivity is a measure of economic performance: It compares how much we produce with the resources we use to produce it. The formula is fairly simple: The more we can produce while using fewer resources, the more productivity grows and the more everyone—the economy, businesses, and workers—benefits.

However, productivity also refers to the quantity and quality of what we produce. When resources are used more efficiently, the quantity of output is certainly greater. But experience has shown marketers of goods and services that unless the resulting products are of satisfactory quality, consumers will reject them. Producing **quality**, then, means creating fitness for use, offering features that consumers want.

quality
A product's fitness for use; its success in offering features that consumers want

The importance of quality cannot be overstated. Poor quality, for example, has created some long-standing competitive problems for U.S. firms that have focused too narrowly on efficiency and quantity. In 1970, for instance, the United States enjoyed the highest levels of productivity in the industrialized world. Through the 1980s, however, productivity and quality grew faster in several other industrialized nations, and the United States lost ground to global competitors.

Recently, many U.S. firms have reversed this trend by focusing on the need for greater quantity and improved quality. United Parcel Service, for example, regularly surveys customers to identify and correct problems in its pickup and delivery services. Globe Metallurgical Inc. has become a leader in the metals industry by simultaneously increasing worker productivity and reducing customer complaints. As if to underscore the quality-productivity connection, the former American Productivity Center in Houston has been renamed the American Productivity and Quality Center. The center offers seminars, conferences, data exchanges, and other resources to assist companies in improving productivity and quality.

Responding to the Productivity Challenge

Productivity has both international and domestic ramifications. Obviously, when one country is more productive than another, it will accumulate more wealth. Similarly, a nation whose productivity fails to increase as rapidly as that of competitor nations will see its standard of living fall.

A Reality Check for International Business Survival

For decades, United States products dominated world markets because U.S. businesses were so successful in producing goods and distributing them in both domestic and foreign markets. The 1960s found U.S. manufacturers unchallenged as the world's industrial leaders. U.S. industry, it seemed, could make anything, and because U.S. products were the best, Americans could sell whatever they made, both at home and abroad. In the 1970s, however, U.S. productivity began a dramatic downslide that continued into the 1980s. Then, a remarkable turnaround in productivity occurred in the years leading up to 1994, when American businesses regained significant market shares in several large industries, including industrial machinery (Caterpillar), automobiles (Ford), and electronic equipment (IBM and Motorola). By 1997 U.S. companies remained the world's leading exporters in several major industries. Today, more and more Asian and European firms are once again concerned with catching U.S. businesses in a world of intense global competition.

How did this change in fortunes come about? For one thing, U.S. businesses that once focused on and complained about the foreign competition's advantage in lower labor rates began looking elsewhere for competitive advantage. For example, they studied ways to revitalize sagging sales. First, they concentrated on understanding the true meaning of productivity and devised means of measuring it. Soon learning that quality must be defined in terms of value to the customer, they redesigned their organizations and market-ing efforts so that the focus was more customer oriented. As quality improvement prac-tices were gradually implemented, more and more firms began to realize the payoffs from these efforts. These successes highlighted the interdependence of four key ingredients: cus-tomers, quality, productivity, and profits.

▶ *PRODUCTIVITY AMONG GLOBAL COMPETITORS.* A report by the consulting firm McKinsey & Co. reveals productivity in nine key industries and concludes that overall, U.S. manufacturers are more productive than their Japanese and German counterparts. Figure 16.1 shows productivity in those nine industries in terms of output per hour worked. In all cases, the index compares Japanese and German output to an American standard of 100 units. As you can see, there are wide variations, both from industry to in-dustry and nation to nation. In auto parts, for example, if the United States produces 100 units of output per hour, we trail Japan, which produces 124 units, but lead Germany, which produces 76 units, by an equally wide margin.

Figure 16.1 Competitive U.S. Productivity

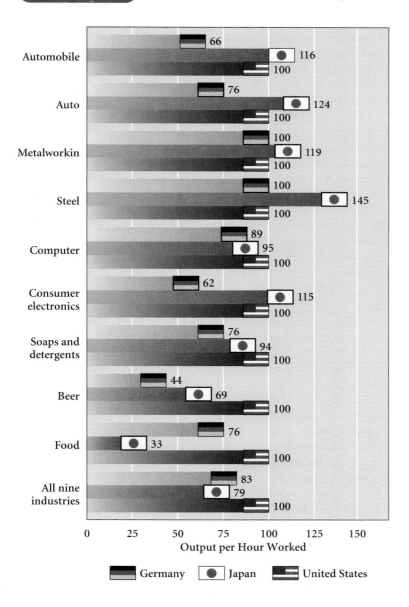

However, the study stresses that U.S. productivity is higher *overall*. Why? Consider the numbers in food production. In Japan, the food-production industry employs more workers than the automotive, computer, consumer electronics, and machine tool industries combined. It is also a fragmented, highly protected industry and, as you can see from Figure 16.1, an extremely inefficient one. Whereas a Japanese worker produces 33 units or $39 worth of food per hour, an American worker produces 100 units, or $119 worth. For all industries taken together, in the time that it takes a U.S. worker to produce $10 worth of goods, Japanese and German workers produce about $8 worth.[1] Thus at least according to one source, the road has been paved by U.S. manufacturers to more successful global competition.

Domestic Productivity

Nations must care about domestic productivity regardless of their global standing. A country that improves its ability to make something out of its existing resources can increase the wealth of all its inhabitants. Conversely, a decline in productivity shrinks a nation's total wealth. Therefore, an increase in one person's wealth comes only at the expense of others with whom he or she shares a social economic system. For example, additional wealth from higher productivity can be shared among workers (as higher wages), investors (as higher profits), and customers (as stable prices). When productivity drops, however, wages can be increased only by reducing profits (penalizing investors) or by increasing prices (penalizing customers).[2] It is understandable, then, that investors, suppliers, managers, and workers are all concerned about the productivity of specific industries, companies, departments, and even individuals. Accordingly, we next survey recent trends in U.S. productivity on various levels: national, industrywide, companywide, and departmental and individual.

National Productivity Trends

level of productivity
Dollar value of goods and services relative to the resources used to produce them

The United States remains the most productive nation in the world. In 1996, for instance, the value of goods and services produced by each U.S. worker was $63,900. This current **level of productivity** is higher than that of any other country. In second place, French and Belgian workers produced $61,000 per worker, followed by Italian workers at $59,100. Canadian workers produced $56,700.[3] As Figure 16.2 shows, the output per hour worked also rose steadily in the United States throughout most of the 1980s and 1990s.

Where, then, lies any cause for concern? Economists currently point to two disturbing trends in national productivity: slower growth rates and uneven growth in the manufacturing and service sectors.

Slower Growth Rates

growth rate of productivity
Annual increase in a nation's output over the previous year

Many observers are alarmed by an important trend that persisted throughout the 1980s: a slowdown in the **growth rate of productivity** (the annual increase in a nation's output over the previous year). In short, U.S. productivity was not increasing as fast as it had in the past: Business output grew only half as fast each year from 1979 to 1996 as it had each year from 1948 to 1973.

The growth of U.S. output was also slow in comparison with other nations. Figure 16.3 shows how fast productivity is growing in various countries. Largely because of modernized facilities and work methods, Japan and South Korea have experienced especially strong growth spurts. If current growth rates continue, per capita productivity in France, Belgium, and Italy will surpass that of the United States by the year 2000, and Japan and Austria will surpass the United States before 2005.[4]

Uneven Growth in the Manufacturing and Service Sectors

A close look at the manufacturing and service sectors reveals important productivity differences. Throughout most of the 1970s, productivity in the manufacturing sector trailed slightly behind that of the service sector. But U.S. service productivity averaged zero im-

Figure 16.2 U.S. Productivity, 1977–1996

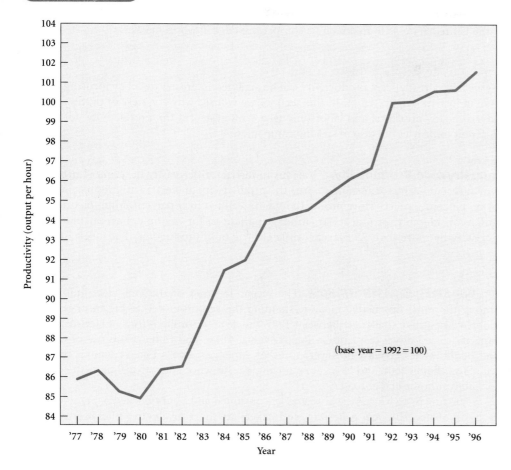

(base year = 1992 = 100)

provement in the years 1978–1990. By 1993 U.S. manufacturing productivity had grown to more than double the productivity of services. Between 1977 and 1994, the productivity of the federal government, a key service producer, grew 1 percent annually.[5]

Thus, manufacturing is primarily responsible for the recent increases in overall U.S. productivity. In 1996, for instance, the value of goods produced by each U.S. manufacturing worker was $114,000, compared with $44,000 for each service worker.[6] However, as

Figure 16.3 International Productivity Growth, 1986–1991

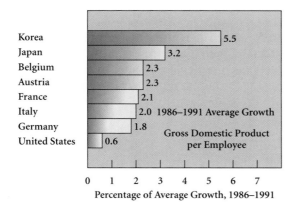

Korea	5.5
Japan	3.2
Belgium	2.3
Austria	2.3
France	2.1
Italy	2.0
Germany	1.8
United States	0.6

1986–1991 Average Growth

Gross Domestic Product per Employee

Percentage of Average Growth, 1986–1991

we saw in chapter 15, services are growing faster than goods production as a proportion of all U.S. business. For example, they now account for nearly 60 percent of national income. In the years ahead, therefore, productivity must increase more rapidly in the service sector if the United States is to maintain its competitive edge in world markets.

Productivity Within Industries and Firms

As we have already seen, productivity can be analyzed in greater detail by focusing on specific industries (Figure 16.1). In this section, we will see why a variety of parties, such as governments, investors, and labor unions, are interested in the productivity not only of different industries but also of specific companies.

Industrywide Productivity. Various industries differ vastly in terms of productivity. In recent years, for instance, while the productivity of electric utilities has increased by 35 percent, grocery store productivity has declined by 9 percent. Manufacturers also differ considerably: producers of laundry appliances, for example, have increased productivity by more than 25 percent while electric bulb productivity has fallen by nearly 15 percent.[7]

▶ **BIG STEEL RECASTS ITS ROLE.** The recent fortunes of the U.S. steel industry are among the most instructive in understanding the response of U.S. big business to the global competitive challenge. Between 1977 and 1987, 45 million tons of steel-producing capacity closed down in plants in Pennsylvania, Ohio, and Indiana because of cutbacks and bankruptcies. Today, however, some of American steel's biggest names, including U.S. Steel, Bethlehem, and LTV, are enjoying a resurgence after struggling with competitors both at home and abroad.

Judging by two key measures, energy consumed and hours worked per employee for each ton of steel shipped, American steelmakers are more productive than ever while offering improved quality. U.S. firms needed 10 labor hours to produce a ton of steel in 1972. Now they need only 5.3 labor hours to produce a ton, compared to 5.6 for Japanese and Canadian workers and 5.7 for most European workers.

One reason for the improvement is a new technology called continuous casting. Today, machines can turn molten metal into slabs that can be processed while still red hot; it is no longer necessary to cool the steel, strip off the molding, and then reheat it for processing. This new process has meant immense savings in both labor and energy. The heat needed to make a ton of steel is down from almost 35 million BTUs to less than 20 million BTUs. Because of cost savings in labor and energy, the price of producing a ton of steel in the United States dropped from $650 to under $520 between 1982 and 1996.

The steel industry's resurgence has been led by innovators such as Chaparral Steel and Nucor Corp. Beginning in the early 1980s, these firms achieved tremendous savings in energy costs by producing steel from scrap materials (shredded automobiles and appliances, for example) rather than ore. Today, Chaparral is the largest recycler of automobiles in the world (600,000 per year). Compared to traditional integrated plants that start the production process with raw materials taken from the ground, this new breed of plant, known as the mini-mill, pioneered a lower-cost (and cleaner) approach to steelmaking. Nucor's use of new technology resulted in an enviable growth record during the same years that most of the industry foundered: From a $22.3 million company in 1965, Nucor has grown to the fourth-largest U.S. steelmaker, with sales of nearly $3.6 billion in 1996.[8]

Naturally, the productivity of specific industries concerns different people for different reasons. For example, because highly productive industries can better afford raises than less productive industries, labor unions must consider productivity when negotiating contracts. Investors and suppliers consider industry productivity when making loans, buying securities, and planning production. Government bodies use productivity as a means of authorizing programs and projecting tax revenues.

The Workplace Environment

Outsourcing: The Cure or the Disease?

What's a good way for a company to save money? Outsourcing is the process of farming out work—from training and development to component manufacturing—to outside firms who promise to do the job for less than the company would spend to do the work inside.

What's a good way to risk getting locked into high-priced contracts, court production delays, and demoralize employees? If you said outsourcing, you're right.

Touted by consultants as the best new idea in productivity management, outsourcing offers the possibility of hiring specialists to do top-quality work at guaranteed prices and reducing internal staff, which can save firms big bucks in salaries, benefits, and bonus pay. The National Association of Purchasing Management reports that a 1997 study projects that the global outsourcing market will reach $121 billion by the year 2000, and the Outsourcing Institute in New York puts the figure at more than twice that. Although outsourcing seems to be more common in larger firms than in small businesses, *Inc.* magazine reports that more small and medium-size firms are looking at it as a means to grow. Unfortunately, outsourcing also seems to have some major drawbacks.

In some industries the price of outsourced work can drop, leaving the firm with a costly long-term contract at the old, higher, price. One retailer locked itself into a situation that could cost it an extra $36 million in information-processing costs; it has hired the accounting firm Deloitte & Touche to renegotiate the contract (for a fee).

Another danger lies in the aftermath of the layoffs that typically follow outsourcing deals. The lower-paid employees who are left on staff are often unenthusiastic about the prospect of working harder than before for less incentive, and sometimes they must also struggle with problems caused by outsourcing that fails to meet schedule, budget, or quality specifications.

Outsourcing that actually impedes the work of the firm is rare, but it can happen. General Electric Co. and Southern Pacific Rail Corp. have both suffered production delays caused by their outsource firms. "You rarely hear about the failures of these contracts, but there are many of them" according to John Wyatt, who heads the consulting firm James Martin & Co.

> **You rarely hear about the failures of these [outsourcing] contracts, but there are many of them.**
>
> —John Wyatt, president of James Martin & Co.

Smaller firms are more likely to use outsourcing, according to a Dun & Bradstreet report, and a California research firm reports that the most commonly outsourced business processes are payroll, accounting, and human resource administration. Despite the strategy's popularity, the moral of the story seems to be "look carefully before you leap."

Companywide Productivity.   High productivity gives a company a competitive edge because its costs are lower than those of other companies. A firm can thus choose to offer products at lower prices or to make a greater profit on each unit sold. Increased productivity also allows firms to pay higher wages without raising prices.

For all these reasons, the productivity of individual companies is important to investors, workers, and managers. For example, comparing the productivity of several companies in the same industry guides investors in buying and selling stocks. In addition, employee profit-sharing plans are often based on employers' annual productivity growth. Finally, managers use information about productivity trends to plan for new products, factories, and funds.

Departmental and Individual Productivity.   Within companies, managers are concerned with the productivity of various divisions, departments, workstations, and individuals. Improved productivity in any of these areas can improve a firm's overall productivity. However, an overemphasis on the performance of individuals and departments tends to discourage working together, as teams, for overall company improvement. For this reason, many companies are cautious about using departmental and individual productivity measures.

Measuring Productivity

To improve productivity, we must first be able to measure it. Otherwise, we cannot determine whether a given program has increased productivity. In this section we will describe several standard measures of productivity. Each measure is an equation, or ratio, and each compares goods and services produced with the resources required to produce them.

Total and Partial Measures of Productivity

total factor productivity ratio
Productivity measure that considers all types of input resources (labor, capital, materials, energy, and purchased business services)

Every productivity measure is a ratio of outputs to inputs. Outputs are goods and services produced. Inputs are the resources used to create outputs. In selecting a productivity measure, managers must first decide which inputs, or factors, are most important for their businesses. In other words, the choice of inputs determines the specific measure that a manager will use.

In some cases, all inputs are equally important. Managers thus use a **total factor productivity ratio**, which is calculated as follows:

$$\text{Total factor productivity} = \frac{\text{Outputs}}{\text{Labor} + \text{Capital} + \text{Materials} + \text{Energy inputs} + \text{Purchased business services}}$$

For example, if an insurance company sold $10 million in policies and used $2 million worth of resources, its total factor productivity would be 5.

partial productivity ratio
Productivity measure that considers only certain input resources

Sometimes a single input resource is so important for production that it deserves special attention and control. For some purposes, therefore, **partial productivity ratios** are used because they are designed to concentrate on just one factor.

materials productivity
Partial productivity ratio calculated by dividing total output by total material inputs

For example, **materials productivity**, although a partial productivity ratio, may be a fairly good measure of overall productivity in non–labor-intensive industries, where materials and equipment, not labor, constitute over 90 percent of operating costs. Material productivity is calculated thus:

$$\text{Materials productivity} = \frac{\text{Outputs}}{\text{Materials}}$$

"Productivity is up nine per cent since I made everyone a vice-president."

For instance, if a chemical plant uses 8 tons of chemicals to produce 2 tons of insecticide, its materials productivity is 0.25 (2/8).

Measures of Labor Productivity

When we examine productivity on a national or industrywide level, we see that a major input is labor. We can thus analyze productivity by calculating a ratio designed to determine **labor productivity**. Most countries use partial ratios of labor productivity to measure national productivity. In general, labor productivity is calculated as follows:

$$\text{Labor productivity} = \frac{\text{Outputs}}{\text{Labor}}$$

A country's labor productivity is usually calculated this way:

$$\text{Labor productivity of a country} = \frac{\text{Gross domestic product}}{\text{Total number of workers}}$$

In this equation, total number of workers represents the nation's total labor input. (This figure could also be total hours worked.) **Gross domestic product (GDP)** is the value of all goods and services produced in the economy, excluding foreign earnings and income. This figure represents the nation's total output. (Recall from chapter 1 that gross national product is the value of all goods and services produced by an economy, including foreign earnings and income.)

Labor productivity measures are popular because they are easy to calculate and compare. Thus, governments keep records on gross domestic product. For example, the U.S. Bureau of Labor Statistics and the U.S. Department of Commerce compile updated labor and GDP statistics each month. In showing output per hour worked, for example, Figures 16.1 and 16.2 reflect labor productivity in the private sector of U.S. business. Note that such figures are typically adjusted to erase the effects of inflation. The resulting data permit reliable year-to-year comparisons of national productivity—changes that, in turn, can be compared with the productivity of other countries. However, as labor-intensive industries become less important in many national economies, other measures, such as materials productivity, energy productivity, and even total factor productivity, are coming into wider use.

Measures of Company Productivity

Many companies have established productivity measures for individual divisions, plants, departments, and even jobs. Goals for productivity improvement are installed in the areas of greatest importance. They serve as guidelines for workplace changes and performance evaluations. For example, an automated, petroleum-fueled factory may place high priority on energy productivity. Its major goal, therefore, might be to raise the level of its sales per barrel of consumed fuel from $200 to $220. Employees would thus seek ways to conserve fuel while maintaining or increasing production and sales.

By contrast, retailers such as Circuit City have been successful in using sales per square foot of space and sales per employee as their main productivity measures. Similarly, a labor-intensive restaurant will use the dollar amount of food served per server. If it offers servers incentives to increase sales, they will encourage customers to order tempting (and highly profitable) specialties, drinks, and desserts.

A number of companies use a traditional measure of sales per employee: If the company can boost revenues without a corresponding increase in labor costs, it is more productive. Atlanta-based Equifax, a provider of credit and data services, is an example: Between 1991 and 1996, sales per employee rose an average of 10 percent annually. With sales of $128,000 per employee, they have become the world's largest provider of check authorizations for retailers. Although their business revenues have

labor productivity
Partial productivity ratio calculated by dividing total output by total labor inputs

gross domestic product (GDP)
The value of all goods and services produced by a nation's economy, excluding foreign earnings and income

multiplied through dozens of acquisitions, the number of employees has increased only modestly.[9]

Ford, Westinghouse, Control Data, and TRW Inc. are among a growing number of companies profiting from the development of major productivity programs. As part of their programs, these companies have established tailor-made productivity measures to reflect their own performances. Measures at TRW, a large diversified manufacturer, provide guidelines for evaluating the productivity of each of the company's inputs (labor, materials, capital, and energy). Using these measures, TRW can identify which resources are being overused and decide how to correct problems to gain higher productivity in each area.

Total Quality Management

It is not enough to measure productivity in terms of numbers of items produced; we must also take quality into account. For the past 50 years, the American Society for Quality (ASQ) has maintained standards for quality and provided services to assist U.S. industry's quality efforts.

Prominent people have promoted the need for quality. In the first years after World War II, for instance, U.S. business consultant W. Edwards Deming tried to persuade domestic firms that they needed to improve quality at least as much as quantity. Like many prophets, however, Deming was more honored abroad than in his homeland. His arguments appealed to the Japanese. Fortunately, many U.S. companies have also embraced Deming's message in the past decade.

Managing for Quality

total quality management (TMQ) (or quality assurance)
The sum of all activities involved in getting high-quality products into the marketplace

Total quality management (TQM) (sometimes called quality assurance) includes all of the activities necessary for getting high-quality goods and services into the marketplace. It must consider all parts of the business, including customers, suppliers, and employees (Figure 16.4). As noted by John Kay, director of Oxford University's School of Manage-

Figure 16.4   ADAC Laboratories Quality System

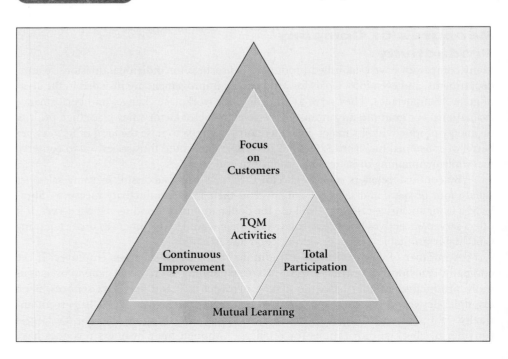

ment, "You can't run a successful company if you don't care about customers and employees, or if you are systematically unpleasant to suppliers."[10] To bring the interests of all these stakeholders together, TQM involves planning, organizing, directing, and controlling.

> **❝** *You can't run a successful company if you don't care about customers and employees, or if you are systematically unpleasant to suppliers.* **❞**
>
> —John Kay, director of Oxford University's School of Management

Planning for Quality

Planning for quality begins before products are designed or redesigned. To ensure that their needs are not overlooked, customers may be invited to participate in the planning process. In the predesign stage, managers must set goals for both performance quality and quality reliability. **Performance quality** refers to the performance features of a product. For example, Maytag gets premium prices for its appliances because they are perceived as offering more advanced features and a longer life than competing brands. Through its advertising, the firm has made sure that consumers recognize the Maytag repairman as the world's loneliest service professional.

Performance quality may or may not be related to a product's **quality reliability**— that is, the consistency of product quality from unit to unit. Toyotas, for example, enjoy high quality reliability; the firm has a reputation for producing very few lemons. In services, consistency is important. Custom Research, Inc., a marketing research firm that received the 1996 Malcolm Baldrige National Quality Award, was applauded for 99 percent on-time delivery of final research reports to its clients.[11] For both goods and services, consistency is achieved by controlling the quality of raw materials, encouraging conscientious work, and keeping equipment in good working order.

Some products offer both high quality reliability and high performance quality. Kellogg, for example, has a reputation for consistently producing cereals made of high-quality ingredients. As we saw in chapter 15, to achieve any form of high quality, managers must plan for production processes (equipment, methods, worker skills, and materials) that will result in high-quality products.

performance quality
The performance features offered by a product

quality reliability
Consistency of a product's quality from unit to unit

Organizing for Quality

Perhaps most important to the quality concept is the belief that producing high-quality goods and services requires an effort from all parts of the organization. Having a separate quality control department is no longer enough. Everyone from the chairperson of the board to the part-time clerk—purchasers, engineers, janitors, marketers, machinists, and other personnel—must work to ensure quality. In Germany's Messerschmitt-Boelkow-Blohm aerospace company, for example, all employees are responsible for inspecting their own work. The overall goal is to reduce eventual problems to a minimum by making the product right from the beginning. The same principle extends to teamwork practice at Heinz Co., where teams of workers are assigned to inspect virtually every activity in the company. Heinz has realized substantial cost savings by eliminating waste and rework.

Although everyone in a company contributes to product quality, responsibility for specific aspects of total quality management is often assigned to specific departments and jobs. In fact, many companies have quality assurance or quality control departments staffed by quality experts. These people may be called in to help solve quality-related problems in any of the firm's other departments. They keep other departments informed of the latest developments in equipment and methods for maintaining quality. In addition, they monitor all quality control activities to identify areas for improvement.

Directing for Quality

Too often, firms fail to take the initiative in making quality happen. Directing for quality means that managers must motivate employees throughout the company to achieve quality goals. Managers companywide must help employees see how they affect quality and how quality affects both their jobs and the company. Chrysler CEO Robert J. Eaton, for example, observed poor-fitting interior trim and engine noise when test-driving the prototype Cirrus sedan in March 1994. He immediately postponed production until corrections could be made and launched a major program to increase the overall quality of Chrysler cars. Eaton's willingness to take drastic action to ensure improvement was a visible display of a quality emphasis that had the added value of raising the quality consciousness of all Chrysler's employees.[12]

Like Eaton, leaders must continually find ways to foster a quality orientation by training employees, encouraging involvement, and tying compensation to work quality. Ideally, if managers succeed, employees will ultimately accept **quality ownership**: the idea that quality belongs to each person who creates it while performing a job.

Controlling for Quality

By monitoring its products and services, a company can detect mistakes and make corrections. First, however, managers must establish specific quality standards and measurements. For example, the control system for a bank's teller services might use the following procedure. Supervisors periodically observe the tellers' work and evaluate it according to a checklist. Specific aspects of each teller's work—appearance, courtesy, efficiency—are recorded. The results are reviewed with employees and either confirm proper performance or indicate changes needed to bring performance up to standards.

Tools for Total Quality Management

Many companies rely on proven tools to manage quality. Often, ideas for improving both the product and the production process come from competitive product analysis. For example, Toshiba might take apart a Xerox copier and test each component. Test results will then help managers decide which Toshiba product features are satisfactory, which features should be upgraded, and which operations processes need improvement.

In this section, we will survey six of the most commonly used tools for total quality management: value-added analysis, statistical process control, quality/cost studies, quality improvement teams, benchmarking, and getting closer to the customer.

Value-Added Analysis

One effective method of improving quality and productivity is **value-added analysis:** the evaluation of all work activities, material flows, and paperwork to determine the value that they add for customers. Value-added analysis often reveals wasteful or unnecessary activities that can be eliminated without harm to (and may even improve) customer service. When Hewlett-Packard, for example, simplified its contracts and reduced them from 20 pages to as few as 2 pages for all customers, computer sales rose by more than 18 percent.

Statistical Process Control

Although every company would like complete uniformity in its output, the goal is unattainable: Every business experiences unit-to-unit variations in products and services. Firms can better control product quality by understanding sources of variation. **Statistical process control (SPC)** refers to methods by which employees can gather data and analyze

---

quality ownership
Principle of total quality management that holds that quality belongs to each person who creates it while performing a job

value-added analysis
Process of evaluating all work activities, materials flows, and paperwork to determine the value they add for customers

statistical process control (SPC)
Methods for gathering data to analyze variations in production activities to see when adjustments are needed

Statistical process control (SPC) systems use sampling techniques: That is, they test a significant portion of a production lot instead of every single item. Even so, conventional methods for recording and evaluating the findings—check sheets and control charts, whether manual or computerized—are often used as well. Originally conceived as improvements of conventional inspection methods, SPC systems now permit testers to monitor operations while they are actually in progress. This employee at Farbex is checking the weight of plastic pellets to ensure they comply with quality requirements.

variations in production activities to determine when adjustments are needed. The Glidden Co., for example, uses SPC to control paint-making processes more effectively. Litton Precision Gear uses SPC to ensure the quality of transmission gears installed in military helicopters. At Farbex, a plastics manufacturer, SPC analysts spot-check numerous standards such as the weight of samples of plastic pellets at several different points in the production process. Forty percent of all North American pulp and paper mills use SPC to reduce waste and increase productivity during production.

Two of the most common SPC methods are process variation studies and control charts.

Process Variations

Variations in a firm's products arise from the inputs used in the production process. As employees, materials, work methods, and equipment change, so do production outputs (that is, the company's products). These variations are called **process variations.** Although some amount of process variation is inevitable, too much can result in poor quality and excessive operating costs.

Consider the box-filling operation for Honey Nuggets, a hypothetical cereal. Each automated machine fills two 14-ounce boxes per second. Even under proper conditions, slight variations in cereal weight from box to box are normal. However, company managers want to know how much variation is occurring. How much is acceptable?

Information about variation in a process can be obtained from a process capability study. At the Honey Nuggets factory, boxes are taken from the filling machines and weighed. The results are plotted, as in Figure 16.5, and compared for weight against upper and lower specification limits, which serve as acceptable quality limits. Boxes with over 14.2 ounces are considered wasteful giveaways of the company's product. Boxes with less than 13.8 ounces are also costly, not only because they will anger a lot of buyers but because they are unlawful.

Analyzing the results of the Honey Nuggets capability study, we see that the output from Machine A is acceptable; none of its boxes violates quality limits. Machine A, then, is

process variation
Variation in products arising from changes in production inputs

Figure 16.5 Process Variation Study at Honey Nuggets Cereal

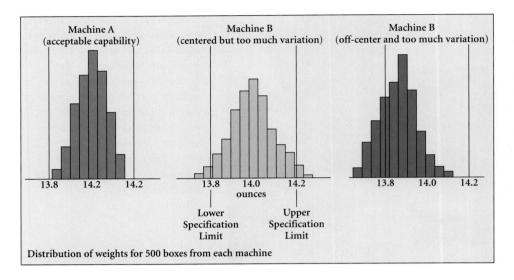

Distribution of weights for 500 boxes from each machine

fully capable of meeting company quality standards. Machines B and C, however, have problems. Neither machine reliably meets Honey Nuggets standards: They are not capable. Our process capability study reveals that unless Machines B and C are renovated, the company will continue to be plagued by substandard production quality.

Control Charts

Knowing that a process is capable of meeting quality standards is not enough. Managers must still monitor the production process to prevent it from going astray. To detect the beginning of departures from normal conditions, employees can check production periodically and plot the results on a control chart. Three or four times a day, for example, a machine operator at Honey Nuggets might weigh several boxes of cereal together to determine the average weight. That average is then plotted on the control chart.

Figure 16.6 shows the control chart for Machine A at the Honey Nuggets plant. As you can see, the first five points are randomly scattered around the center line, indicating

Figure 16.6 Process Control Chart at Honey Nuggets Cereal

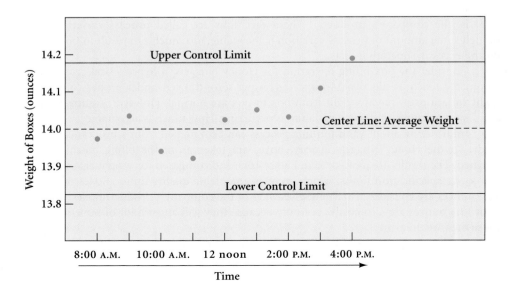

that the machine was operating well from 8 A.M. until noon. However, the points for samples 5 through 9 are all above the center line, indicating that something caused boxes to overfill. The last point falls outside the upper control limit, confirming that the process is out of control. At this point, the machine must be shut down so that an operator can investigate the cause of the problem, be it equipment, people, materials, or work methods. Control is completed when the problem is corrected and the process is restored to normal.

Quality/Cost Studies

Statistical process controls help keep operations up to existing capabilities. But in today's competitive environment, firms must consistently raise quality capabilities. However, any improvement in products or production processes means additional costs, whether for new facilities, equipment, training, or other changes. Managers thus face the challenge of identifying the improvements that offer the greatest promise. Quality/cost studies are useful because they not only identify a firm's current costs but also reveal areas with the largest cost-savings potential.

Quality costs are associated with making, finding, repairing, or preventing defective goods and services. All of these costs should be analyzed in a quality/cost study. For example, Honey Nuggets must determine its costs for **internal failures**. These are expenses including the costs of overfilling boxes and the costs of sorting out bad boxes incurred during production and before bad products leave the plant. Studies indicate that many U.S. manufacturers incur costs for internal failures up to 50 percent of total costs.

internal failures
Reducible costs incurred during production and before bad products leave a plant

Despite quality control procedures, however, some bad boxes may get out of the factory, reach the customer, and generate complaints from grocers and consumers. These **external failures** are discovered outside the factory. The costs of correcting them (refunds to customers, transportation costs to return bad boxes to the factory, possible lawsuits, and factory recalls) should also be tabulated in the quality/cost study.

external failures
Reducible costs incurred after defective products have left a plant

The percentage of costs in the different categories varies widely from company to company. Thus, every firm must conduct systematic quality/cost studies to identify the most costly and often the most vital areas of its operations. Not surprisingly, these areas should be targets for improvement. Too often, however, firms substitute hunches and guesswork for data and analysis.

Quality Improvement Teams

In their quest for quality, many U.S. businesses have adopted **quality improvement (QI) teams** (patterned after the Japanese concept of quality circles): groups of employees from various work areas who meet regularly to define, analyze, and solve common production problems. Their goal is to improve both their own work methods and the products they make.

quality improvement (QI) team
TQM tool in which groups of employees work together to improve quality

Many QI teams organize their own efforts, select leaders, and attack problems in their workplace. Frito-Lay Inc. has such a program at its plant in Lubbock, Texas. There, teams of 10 hourly workers oversee activities ranging from potato processing to machine maintenance. Their primary job is to cut costs while improving quality. The teams now assume such managerial responsibilities as rejecting products that fail to meet quality standards and sending home employees who are unneeded (for example, when machines break down). From a place in the bottom 20 of Frito-Lay's 48 plants, the Lubbock operation has jumped into the top six in terms of quality.[13]

One of the greatest benefits of QI teams, in addition to direct cost savings, is their effect on employees' attitudes. Instead of viewing themselves as passive production resources, employees develop a sense of self-worth and quality ownership. In short, the talents and job knowledge of team members, rather than being dormant, are put to use. Although QI teams can improve job satisfaction, they also involve risks. Not all employees want to participate. Moreover, management cannot always adopt group recommendations, no matter how much careful thought, hard work, and enthusiasm went into them. The challenge for management, then, is to make wise decisions about when and how to use quality improvement teams.

Since Frito-Lay introduced work teams at its Lubbock, Texas, plant, the number of managers has dropped by more than half. Most of their work, including crew scheduling and interviewing potential employees, is now done by team members. To help them improve quality, teams receive weekly reports on costs and service performance, and each team is advised of its success in relation to corresponding teams at 22 other factories. At the Lubbock plant, the hourly work force has grown by 20 percent since 1990, but costs have gone down and quality has risen significantly during the same period.

benchmarking
Process by which a company implements the best practices of other companies to improve its own products

Benchmarking

A powerful TQM tool that has been effective for some firms is called **benchmarking**: To improve its own products or its business procedures, one company finds and implements the best practices of others. Benchmarking begins with a critical review of competitors (or even companies in other lines of business) to determine which goods or services perform the best; these activities and products are called best practices. Why is one good or service better? Which specific features do customers like? Critical comparisons of the company's own products and procedures with selected benchmarks reveal specific areas where improvement is likely to result in greater competitiveness. L.L. Bean, for example, regularly attracts observers who want to see Bean's world-class methods for processing customer orders so efficiently.

Benchmarks are usually helpful in providing realistic targets for improvement. It is important to remember, however, that as the most innovative companies create better products and provide better services, the best benchmark targets keep changing. Nevertheless, many organizations continue to use benchmarking successfully. The U.S. Internal Revenue Service, for example, has identified American Express as a best-practice firm and benchmarked AmEx's billing procedures in an effort to improve its own. Similarly, when Motorola wanted to reduce the time between receipt and delivery of a customer's order for cellular phones, it studied Domino's Pizza's procedures for keeping 30-minute delivery cycles.

Getting Closer to the Customer

As one advocate of quality improvement puts it, "Customers are an economic asset. They're not on the balance sheet, but they should be."[14] One of the themes of this chapter has been that struggling companies have often lost sight of customers as the driving force for all business activity. Perhaps they waste resources designing products that customers do not want. Sometimes they ignore customer reactions to existing products or fail to keep up with changing consumer tastes. By contrast, the most successful businesses keep close to their customers and know what they want in the products they consume.

▶ For example, MBNA, a Wilmington, Delaware credit-card company, has learned that speed of service is vital for serving 4,300 groups with custom Visas and MasterCards, including such groups as the National Education Association and Ringling Brothers. These premium customers want good service and they want it now. MBNA was one of the first in the industry to make service representatives available 24 hours a day. Furthermore, MBNA continually monitors its own performance using 15 measures, many of them relating to speed of service. The phone must be picked up within two rings, incoming calls at the switchboard must be transferred within 21 seconds to the correct party, and customer address changes must be processed in 1 day. The companywide goal on the 15 standards is 98.5 percent. That means, for example, that responses to credit-line inquiries will be answered in half an hour 98.5 percent of the time and the phone will be answered within two rings 98.5 percent of the time. Results are posted daily on 60 scoreboards throughout the company. By placing the customer at the head of its organizational culture, MBNA is able to retain a remarkable 98 percent of its profitable customers and its common stock price has increased 600 percent in 5 years.[15]

> **" Customers are an economic asset. They're not on the balance sheet, but they should be. "**

—Claess Fornell, quality improvement advocate

Trends in Productivity and Quality Management

Intensified competition has stimulated some new considerations for quality management. Among these are the emergence of international quality standards and the radical redesign of business processes to improve products. A third approach emphasizes the need for quality improvement programs to show monetary benefits.

ISO 9000

Consider the following case in quality control diagnosis and correction:

▶ The Du Pont Company's Emigsville, Pennsylvania, plant had a problem: A molding press used to make plastic connectors for computers had a 30-percent defect rate. Efforts to solve the problem went nowhere until, as part of a plantwide quality program, press operators were asked to submit detailed written reports describing how they did their jobs. After comparing notes, operators realized that they were incorrectly measuring the temperature of the molding press; as a result, temperature adjustments were often wrong. With the mystery solved, the defect rate dropped to 8 percent.

The quality program that led to this solution is called ISO 9000 a certification program attesting to the fact that a factory, a laboratory, or an office has met the rigorous quality management requirements set by the International Organization for Standardization.

ISO 9000 (pronounced *ICE-o nine thousand*) originated in Europe as an attempt to standardize materials received from suppliers in such high-technology industries as electronics, chemicals, and aviation. Today, more than 90 countries have adopted ISO 9000 as a national standard. It is being adopted by U.S.-based multinationals such as General Electric, Eastman Kodak, Motorola, and Xerox. In turn, these companies are requiring certification from their own suppliers, including employment agencies. For example, 340 suppliers working with GE's plastics division were told to meet ISO 9000 standards if they wanted to continue doing business with the company.

ISO 9000 standards enable firms to demonstrate that they follow documented procedures for testing products, training workers, keeping records, and fixing product defects. To become certified, companies must document the procedures that workers follow during every stage of production. The purpose of ISO 9000, explains the International Division of the U.S. Chamber of Commerce, is to ensure that a manufacturer's product is exactly the same today as it was yesterday and as it will be tomorrow. The goal of standardization is to guarantee that goods will be produced at the same level of quality even if all the employees were replaced by a new set of workers.

Companies seeking ISO 9000 certification are audited by an elite group of quality system registrars. Not surprisingly, the certification process is time-consuming and costly: It can take up to 18 months for a manufacturing plant employing 300 workers and cost up to $200,000.

Why do companies put themselves through this ordeal? For one thing, an ISO 9000 certificate has become the passkey to doing business in Western Europe. Explains Richard Thompson, general manager of Caterpillar's engine division, whose Mossville, Illinois, plant was one of the first U.S. diesel engine factories to win certification: "Today, having ISO 9000 is a competitive advantage. Tomorrow, it will be the ante to the global poker game."[16]

Today, more and more U.S. companies are jumping on the ISO 9000 bandwagon. Currently, about 10,000 ISO 9000 certificates have been issued in the United States, compared to 53,000 in Great Britain. In total, some 128,000 certificates have been issued in 99 countries.[17]

> *Today, having ISO 9000 is a competitive advantage. Tomorrow, it will be the ante to the global poker game.*
>
> —Richard Thompson, general manager of Caterpillar's engine division

Reengineering

Consider another case in problem identification and solution:

▶ IBM Credit Corp., a financing subsidiary of IBM, was profitable but poorly run. Although the company existed to provide service to finance computers and software and furnish related services, employees often acted as if the customer did not matter. The entrenched approval process was the primary problem because every financing request involved five distinct steps to determine approval. Different specialists logged in requests, checked credit, determined the appropriate interest rates, and so on. Even though most customers needed an immediate answer, the process typically took 6 days to 2 weeks. The system was not customer friendly.

▶ Realizing that the very life of their business was at stake, two senior managers decided to troubleshoot the system. They began by walking a request through all five steps from start to finish. To their amazement, they found that the actual work took only 90 minutes. The rest of the time was spent shuffling forms from one department to another, and shuffled forms wound up sitting on unattended desks.

▶ To solve the problem, IBM Credit decided that one person could handle the entire job of approving a single credit request. The company thus replaced its team of specialists with generalists, each of whom handled all five steps. The result was a routine 4-hour turnaround and a hundredfold increase in the number of requests handled.

These astounding results are the direct result of a difficult and often painful process known as **reengineering**, a process that focuses on both productivity and quality and entails rethinking each step of operations by starting over from scratch. Reengineering can be defined as the fundamental rethinking and radical redesign of business processes to achieve dramatic improvements in measures of performance such as cost, quality, service, and speed.[18]

reengineering
Quality improvement process that entails rethinking an organization's approach to productivity and quality

The bottom line in every reengineering process is redesigning systems to better serve the needs of customers and to adopt a customer-first value system throughout the company. This redesign is dominated by a desire to improve operations so that goods and services are produced at the lowest possible cost and at the highest value for the customer.

Return on Quality

The motto of another approach to quality management is expressed in the words of one of its leading proponents: "If we're not going to make money off of it, we're not going to do it." This approach is by no means a rejection of TQM and such developments as quality standards and reengineering. Rather, it reflects a determination to ensure that sophisticated and expensive quality improvement programs pay off.

▶ AT&T knows very well that when customers perceive improved quality, the bottom line benefits. Today, however, AT&T has more stringent criteria for going ahead with quality initiatives: All programs must yield not only a 30-percent drop in defects but a 10-percent return on investment.

Thus, when the company realized that it had to reduce service outages in its 800-number business—customers' biggest complaint—it considered its options differently. One solution was a complete modernization program. It would certainly have solved the problem, but it would have cost more than $1 billion. How many new customers would this solution have gained? Quite a few, perhaps, but certainly not enough to generate a 10-percent return on investment. Instead, AT&T invested $300 million in equipment to back up its existing system. Explains AT&T corporate quality officer Phillip M. Scanlon: "It isn't the old 'Give me money and I'll fix it' stuff. We're taking the cost out of making our system better."

The approach adopted by AT&T is often called return on quality (ROQ). Like most approaches to quality improvement, ROQ has a customer focus. ROQ advocates argue that there is a difference—one that is clearly at work, they say, in the case of AT&T's decision in dealing with its 800-number system. They contend that too many quality improvement programs are designed to attract new customers by impressing them with dazzling numerical displays of accomplishments in quality procedures and products. ROQ asserts that it is cheaper to increase market share by selling more products to the customers that a company already has. AT&T's decision was made not to lure new customers, but rather to improve service to and increase business among existing customers.[19]

Productivity and Quality as Competitive Tools

A company's ability to compete by improving productivity and quality depends on participation by all parts of the firm. And total firm involvement stems from having company-wide strategies that we consider in this section: the company's willingness to invest in innovation, its long-run perspective on its goals, its concern for the quality of work life, and the streamlining of its service operations.

Investing in Innovation and Technology

Many U.S. firms that have continued to invest in innovative technology have enjoyed rising productivity and rising incomes. For example, computer software products made by Deneb Robotics simulate many aspects of manufacturing: machine tools cutting metal, workers carrying heavy loads, flows of materials, and all the factory's operations. Deneb's software is used by more than 1,000 companies. The user observes digitized images of people and machines on a computer screen to examine their motions as they walk, lift, and turn in the simulated work environment. The software brings to life any proposed

AlliedSignal's microturbine will help increase energy productivity by enabling small firms to make their own power at lower cost than from utility companies. Simple in design, this generator's turbine has only one moving part, is almost noiseless, and burns natural gas with virtually no pollution.

factory activity so it can be observed in the design phase, before the real system is built. The software prevents problems before they arise by revealing occupational risks and equipment problems that would otherwise result in expensive damage and wasteful activities. Then, the design can be improved quickly before making any real changes in the factory. For example, General Motors uses Deneb software to maximize the efficiency of work teams making automobile doors. McDonnell Douglas Aerospace uses it to find new ways to make parts for the F-15 fighter in less time and at lower cost. The savings of labor, materials, energy, and equipment from the Deneb simulation technology boosts productivity and improves quality.[20]

Similarly, innovative product technologies are creating changes in electricity distribution services. For example, in most big cities the major cost of delivering electricity, one-third to one-half of your bill, is in the distribution lines that bring the electricity to your house. The cost of delivering by underground wires is eight times higher than sending it on wires and poles above ground. One way to avoid expensive distribution charges is with a microturbine: a refrigerator-size generator that businesses can install to make their own electricity. A generator offered by AlliedSignal, the jet engine and auto parts company, can provide enough electricity for a small business and pay for itself ($15,000) in 2 years. These lower energy costs result in higher energy productivity for office buildings, apartments, restaurants, and other businesses that adopt the new electricity-generating technology.[21]

Adopting a Long-Run Perspective

continuous improvement
An ongoing commitment to improving products and processes in the pursuit of ever-increasing customer satisfaction

Many quality-oriented firms are committed to long-term efforts at **continuous improvement**: the ongoing commitment to improving products and processes, step by step, in pursuit of ever-increasing customer satisfaction. Motorola is a good example of a company that emphasizes continuous, long-run improvement. Its Six Sigma program called for the unheard-of target of having only three defects per million parts; for all practical purposes this would be zero defects. In 1981, to get started, the firm adopted a 5-year goal of a 90 percent reduction of errors. In 1986, it extended that goal to a 99 percent reduction of errors by 1992. During just 5 years the defect rate dropped from 6,000 defects per million to just 40 by 1992. When, by 1996, Six Sigma quality had been achieved, Motorola began planning for errors per billion rather than just errors per million quality levels. As of 1997, their goals call for a 90 percent reduction of errors every 2 years, to result in an unimaginable 1 defect per billion parts.[22]

Emphasizing Quality of Work Life

The products and services of businesses represent such a large part of total national output that the well-being and participation of their workers is central to improving national productivity. How can firms make their employees' jobs more challenging and interesting? Many companies are enhancing workers' physical and mental health through recreational facilities, counseling services, and other programs. In addition, more and more firms have started programs to empower and train employees.

Employee Empowerment

Many firms are replacing the environments of yesterday, based on management-directed mass production, with worker-oriented environments that foster loyalty, teamwork, and commitment. Trident Precision Manufacturing, winner of the 1996 Malcolm Baldrige National Quality Award, has a program for full employee involvement. Over 95 percent of employee recommendations for process improvements have been accepted since 1991. As a result, employee turnover has fallen from 41 percent to less than 5 percent and sales per employee more than doubled.[23] Firms using this approach have found success in the concept of **employee empowerment:** the principle that all employees are valuable contributors to a business and should be entrusted with certain decisions regarding their work. The Hampton Inns motel chain, for example, initiated a program of refunds to customers who were dissatisfied with their stays for any reason. Managers were pleased, and the refund policy created far more additional business than it cost. A surprise bonus was the increased morale when employees—everyone from front-desk personnel to maids—were empowered to grant refunds. With greater participation and job satisfaction, employee turnover was reduced to less than one-half its previous level.[24] Such confidence in employee involvement contrasts sharply with the traditional belief that managers are the primary source of decision making and problem solving.

employee empowerment
Concept that all employees are valuable contributors to a firm's business and should be entrusted with decisions regarding their work

The prestigious Malcolm Baldrige National Quality Award is given annually by the National Bureau of Standards and Technology, part of the U.S. Department of Commerce. It recognizes outstanding achievement in these areas, in descending order of importance: customer satisfaction, quality results, quality assurance of products and services, human resource utilization, strategic quality planning, information and analysis, and leadership. Customer satisfaction counts almost twice as much as the next most important standard in determining a candidate firm's quality performance.

Employee Training

For employee involvement to be effective, it must be implemented with preparation and intelligence. Training is one of the proven methods for avoiding judgments and actions that can lead to impaired performance. In a recent survey, for example, insufficient training is the most common barrier reported by work teams. The study reconfirms the belief that training is a key to implementing a successful quality management program. At Heath Tecna Aerospace Co., for instance, team members are taught how to work in groups, as well as trained in job skills, work flow planning, and basic knowledge about the company's markets and operations. With increased training and experience, the rate of material waste has diminished and product quality has increased.[25]

Improving the Service Sector

As important as employee attitude is to goods production, it is even more crucial to service production, where employees often are the service. Although the U.S. service sector has grown rapidly (far more rapidly than the service sectors of other nations), this growth has often been accompanied by high levels of inefficiency. For one thing, many newly created service jobs have not been streamlined. In addition, whereas some companies, such as UPS and Federal Express, operate effectively, many others are so inefficient that they drag down overall U.S. productivity. As new companies enter these markets, increased competition is giving service providers a better understanding of how to operate more productively by emphasizing service quality.

It's Your Business

The Skies Are Getting Friendlier Again

It's usually pretty easy to define quality in a service business: It's whatever makes customers happy and satisfied. Airlines are learning that simple lesson all over again as they refocus their attention on their passengers.

Rising complaints about canceled flights, late arrivals, reduced amenities such as movies and food, and slip-ups in baggage handling have prompted many carriers to reexamine the prominence they've been giving to cost cutting, and to look again at customer satisfaction as a measure of quality. Among the newly refocused airlines are Delta, Continental, and American, whose CEO Robert Crandall admits that cost cutting has "diverted our attention from the nuts and bolts of our business. Our customers have noticed." Delta's chief blames cost-cutting, too: "In some cases we did cut too deeply," says Ronald Allen.

Continental has made some of the biggest strides, zooming up from nearly last place in Department of Trans-

portation rankings to post top grades in on-time arrivals, baggage handling, and customer satisfaction. CEO Gordon Bethune has been pitching quality for several years and claims to be winning market share from rival carriers.

> **"** [Cost-cutting has] diverted our attention from the nuts and bolts of our business. Our customers have noticed. **"**
>
> —Robert Crandall, CEO of American Airlines

Customers do seem to respond to upgrades in safety, comfort, and reliability. That's why Northwest is cleaning airplane bathrooms more often, America West is improving food, entertainment, and in-flight phone services as well as speeding mechanical repairs, and Delta plans to restore some meals and rehire hundreds of ground personnel to smooth baggage handling and service at the gate.

If a flight is in your future, you can probably expect to enjoy it a little more.

In trying to offer more satisfactory services, many companies have discovered five criteria that customers use to judge service quality:[26]

■ *Reliability.* Perform the service as promised, both accurately and on time.

■ *Responsiveness.* Be willing to help customers promptly.

■ *Assurance.* Maintain knowledgeable and courteous employees who will earn the trust and confidence of customers.

■ *Empathy.* Provide caring, individualized attention.

■ *Tangibles.* Maintain a pleasing appearance among personnel and in materials and facilities.

Among the 1,600 customers surveyed in one recent study, reliability was mentioned most often as the essence of good service. In the performance of many services, however, these criteria are difficult to separate. Consider two seemingly different service products: window designs from Andersen Windows and swimsuit designs offered by Software Sportswear. What they share in common is designs that are created by customers using interactive computers at the retailer's showroom. Using this tool, the window salesperson helps customers choose the features and shapes that please them. After the computer checks the window design for structural soundness, it gives a price quote. Then the computer transmits the order to the factory for production. Software Sportswear makes custom swimsuits with the aid of a computerized video camera. With the customer's profile displayed on a computer screen, a variety of styles are superimposed on the monitor. The digital display shows the customer's image clothed in each of hundreds of individually tailored designs. The patterns can then be stored for future use with new designs for each customer. These services certainly provide empathy (individualized attention and care). Moreover, by using the customer's recipe for a custom product, both companies are prepared to provide both reliability and responsiveness in future transactions with each customer.[27]

Summary of Learning Objectives

1 **Describe the connection between productivity and quality.** Productivity is a measure of economic performance: It compares how much is produced with the resources used to produce it. Quality is a product's fitness for use. However, an emphasis solely on productivity or solely on quality is not enough. Profitable competition in today's business world demands high levels of both productivity and quality.

2 **Explain the decline and recovery in U.S. productivity that has occurred over the last 25 or 30 years.** Although the United States is the most productive country in the world, by the early 1970s other nations had begun catching up with U.S. productivity. In particular, the U.S. growth rate of productivity slowed from about 1979 to 1991. Moreover, even though U.S. manufacturing productivity is increasing, the service sector is bringing down overall productivity growth. Because services now account for 60 percent of national income, productivity in this area must improve. Finally, certain industries and companies remain less productive than others. If such trends continue, several other countries will surpass the United States in productivity by 2005.

On the other hand, in the years just before 1994, U.S. firms regained significant market share in such industries as industrial machinery, automobiles, and electronics. Abandoning a long-standing focus on lower wage rates in other countries, U.S. companies focused instead on revitalizing productivity by becoming more customer-oriented. In addition, quality improvement practices were widely implemented.

Recovery has resulted from a recognition of the connection among customers, quality, productivity, and profits.

3 **Explain total and partial measures of productivity and how they are used to keep track of national, industrywide, and companywide productivity.** Productivity measures are ratios of outputs (goods and services produced) and inputs (the resources needed to produce outputs). Total factor productivity includes all types of input resources: materials, labor, capital, energy, and purchased business services. In contrast, partial productivity measures focus on certain key input factors while ignoring others. Thus, materials productivity focuses on the productivity of materials and is especially important in non–labor-intensive industries. Labor productivity, the most common national productivity measure, focuses on labor as an input. The United States also measures capital productivity, which focuses on money and investment as input factors.

4 **Identify the activities involved in total quality management and describe six tools that companies can use to achieve it.** Total quality management (TQM) is the planning, organizing, directing, and controlling of all the activities needed to get high-quality goods and services into the marketplace. Managers must set goals for and implement the processes needed to achieve high quality and reliability levels. Value-added analysis evaluates all work activities, materials flows, and paperwork to determine what value they add for customers. Statistical process control methods, such as process variation studies and control charts, can help keep quality consistently high. Quality/cost studies, which identify potential savings, can help firms improve quality. Quality improvement teams also can improve operations by more fully involving employees in decision making. Benchmarking—studying the best practices of other companies and using the knowledge to improve a company's own goods and services—has become an increasingly common TQM tool. Finally, getting closer to the customer provides a better understanding of what customers want so that firms can satisfy them more effectively.

5 **List three trends in productivity and quality management and discuss three ways in which companies can compete by improving productivity and quality.** Recent trends include ISO 9000, a certification program (originating in Europe) attesting that an organization has met certain international quality management standards. Reengineering involves some fundamental redesign of business operations in the interest of improvements in quality, cost, and service. Advocates of return on quality (ROQ) argue that successful quality improvement programs should show quantifiable financial payoffs.

Productivity and quality can be competitive tools only if firms attend to all aspects of their operations. To increase quality and productivity, businesses must invest in innovation and technology. They must also adopt a long-run perspective for continuous improvement. In addition, they should realize that placing greater emphasis on the quality of work life can also help firms compete. Satisfied, motivated employees are especially important in increasing productivity in the fast-growing service sector.

Questions and Exercises

Questions for Review

1 What is the relationship between productivity and quality?
2 Why do labor unions care about the productivity of an industry?
3 How do total factor productivity ratios differ from partial factor ratios?
4 What activities are involved in total quality management?

5 In what key way does the emphasis on return on quality differ from that of reengineering?

Questions for Analysis

6 How would you suggest that benchmarking be used to increase productivity in the service sector?

7 Why is employee empowerment essential to successful quality improvement teams?

8 Why is high productivity in the service sector so difficult to achieve?

Application Exercises

9 Using a local company as an example, show how you would conduct a quality/cost study. Identify the cost categories and give some examples of the costs in each category. Which categories do you expect to have the highest and lowest costs? Why?

10 Select a company of interest to you and consider the suggestions for competing that are detailed in this chapter. Which of these suggestions apply to this company? What additional suggestions would you make to help this company improve its overall quality and productivity?

Building Your Business Skills

This exercise enhances the following SCANS workplace competencies: demonstrating basic skills, demonstrating thinking skills, exhibiting interpersonal skills, and working with information.

Goal To encourage students to understand how benchmarking can help improve quality and productivity.

Situation As the director of maintenance for a regional airline, you are disturbed to learn that the cost to maintain your 100-plane fleet is skyrocketing. A major factor in this cost escalation is repair time: When maintenance or repairs are required, work often proceeds slowly, with the result that additional aircraft are required to meet the schedule. You decide to do a benchmarking study to learn how other companies have managed similar problems. Your goal is to apply the best practices to your own maintenance and repair operation.

Method **Step 1:** Working with three or four other students, choose your benchmarking target from among the following choices:

• The maintenance and repair operation of a competing airline
• The pit crew operation of an Indianapolis 500 race car team
• The maintenance and repair operation of a nationwide trucking company

Write a memo explaining the reasons for your choice.

Step 2: Write up a list of benchmarking questions that will help you learn the best practices of your targeted company. Your goal is to ask questions that will help you improve your own operation. These questions will be asked during on-site visits.

Step 3: As part of a benchmarking project, you will be dealing with your counterparts in other companies. You have a responsibility to prepare for these encounters and to understand that what you learn during benchmarking is privileged information. Based on this, describe what steps you would take before your first on-site visit and how you would define your benchmarking code of ethics.

Follow-Up Questions

1 Why is benchmarking an important method for improving quality?

2 Why did you make your benchmarking choice? Explain why the company you selected holds more promise than other companies in helping you solve your internal maintenance problems.

3 What kind of information would help you improve the efficiency of your operations? Are you interested in management information, technical information, or both?

4 In an age of heightened competition, why do you think companies are willing to benchmark with each other?

Business Case 16
Samsung Takes to the Road

Already a powerhouse in finance, machinery, chemicals, and especially electronics, Samsung, the huge South Korean manufacturer, is planning on getting into the auto business. Although there is a worldwide glut of new cars, Samsung's chairman Lee Kun Hee is determined to produce a car good enough to vault the firm into the world's top 10 automakers in the next dozen years. With production plans to build 1.5 million cars a year, Samsung must succeed at the expense of its entrenched competitors. As one analyst put it, "There's no logical opening in the marketplace where Samsung can step in and fill a vacuum. Its sales will have to come out of someone else's hide."

Despite its advantage in electronics, which accounts for more and more of the inner workings of today's new cars, Samsung faces a difficult road test. It has never manufactured a car before, and the global market's perception of the quality of Korean autos tends to be low. Its Korean competitors have apparently convinced their parts suppliers not to sell to their new rival, so Samsung is getting parts from a number of manufacturers as new to the car industry as itself.

The new venture is also costly: The bill has run to $3.5 billion so far,

almost a third more than planned. And Jeong Ju Wha, the firm's head of production, will conduct nearly a year's worth of expensive trial production runs before releasing the first model for sale. "It's the only way we can win," he says.

But Samsung has one or two other forces working in its favor. First, it has very deep pockets for new ventures, having already succeeded in another supposedly saturated industry, semiconductors. Second, it adheres to the Korean tradition of preserving jobs and creating new industries to provide them. So committed is the firm to this philosophy of work that its 160,000 workers have been promised no one will be laid off.

Its expertise in electronics will undoubtedly also weigh in Samsung's favor as features such as satellite navigation systems become more common in cars. And finally, Samsung has the unusual benefit of assistance from Nissan, the Japanese auto manufacturer, which is providing production expertise, design input, worker training, and even an aluminum engine plant. Samsung will pay Nissan a fee for its help and turn over 2 percent of the factory price of each car sold, which Nissan hopes will bring it up to $1 billion in revenues.

Samsung still faces a big marketing challenge: It has to distinguish its new product in a seriously crowded market, and then it has to convince drivers around the world to buy it.

Questions

1 How do you think Samsung can achieve quality in its new venture?

2 How can Samsung measure the quality of its products? What would a comparison with U.S. products tell the firm? How should Samsung make such a comparison?

3 What productivity measures can Samsung rely on?

4 How can Samsung identify problems in quality and productivity when they arise? What solutions do you suggest?

5 What is the upside of Samsung's extensive quality testing? How might the firm promote that to its advantage?

6 One of the marketing strategies under consideration at Samsung is the purchase of one of its rival car makers, the Korean firm Kia Motors, which recently sold 770,000 cars in 1 year with earnings of $8.2 million. How would such a purchase affect Samsung's quality control procedures? What impact might it have on productivity?

Connecting to the Web

The following Web sites will give you additional information and points of view about topics covered in this chapter. Many sites lead to other related Internet locations, so approach this list with the spirit of an explorer.

AMERICAN CUSTOMER SATISFACTION INDEX (ACSI)

http://acsi.asq.org/

Run by the American Society for Quality and the University of Michigan Business School, this Web site presents the nationally known American Customer Satisfaction Index: an economic indicator that measures customer satisfaction with goods and services available in the United States.

AMERICAN PRODUCTIVITY & QUALITY CENTER

http://www.apqc.org/

The American Productivity & Quality Center has vast resources to improve the quality and productivity of business organizations. Visit this site for information on benchmarking, knowledge management, measurement, customer satisfaction, and productivity and quality.

THE BENCHMARKING EXCHANGE

http://www.benchnet.com/

The Benchmarking Exchange provides a comprehensive forum for all phases of benchmarking. Although this site is designed for benchmarking practitioners, a visit will introduce you to available services and resources.

BLS NEWS RELEASES

http://stats.bls.gov/newsrels.htm

On a recent visit to this U.S. Bureau of Labor Statistics site, we found news releases comparing U.S. productivity to the productivity of other countries, productivity comparisons by industry, and regional productivity information for Boston, New York, Philadelphia, Atlanta, Chicago, Dallas, Kansas City, and San Francisco.

CENTER FOR QUALITY AND PRODUCTIVITY IMPROVEMENT

http://www.engr.wisc.edu/centers/cqpi/

Located at the University of Wisconsin–Madison, the Center for Quality and Productivity Improvement conducts quality improvement research and shares its findings among interested parties in industry, government, and academia. Contact this Web site to learn more about the reports, courses, and other resources available through this organization.

CURIOUS CAT MANAGEMENT IMPROVEMENT LIBRARY

http://curiouscat.com/guides/library.htm

Visit this site for a collection of Web-based documents related to management improvement.

ISO-9000

http://www.asq.org.standcert/iso.html

This American National Standards Institute (ANSI) site answers the most frequently asked questions about ISO-9000.

NIST QUALITY PROGRAM

http://www.quality.nist.gov/

This site, run by the National Institute of Standards and Technology, is the home of the Malcolm Baldrige National Quality Award.

ONLINE QUALITY RESOURCES

http://deming.eng.clemson.edu/onlineq.html

Run out of Clemson University, this site has links to on-line resources on quality and productivity.

QUALITY TEXAS AND TEXAS QUALITY AWARD

http://www.texas-quality.org/index.html

Quality Texas helps Texas-based organizations improve product and service quality, customer satisfaction, and performance excellence and recognizes superior achievement through the annual Texas Quality Award. Visit this site for a look at what this organization does and for a close-up look at award-winning companies.

chapter 17

Managing information systems and communication technology

Area codes go global with the internet

The keyword in the new world of business is *communication,* and its essence is perfectly captured by the Internet. Nothing seems to have made as big an impact on the way we exchange information since the invention of movable type.

Among its other wonders, the Internet, which began as a Pentagon research project to transmit vital data in the event of war, can let users with the proper software make their own phone calls without the aid—or the fees—of a phone company. Because phone companies price calls according to duration and distance, and Internet providers charge flat rates for access to the same communication lines, phone calling via the Internet is clearly a better deal for long-distance calling. Although the sound quality still needs improvement and both parties must be logged on at the same time, Internet calls can cost just pennies per minute to anywhere in the world, and there's no limit on the length of the call. Faxes, which make up about 50 percent of transatlantic

connections, are another application where cost savings promise to be enormous.

Firms that are savvy about using the Net are already taking full advantage of the new software packages that make bypassing phone companies possible. Among the providers are firms such as Vocaltec, Voxware, Quarterdeck, and NetSpeak, and a worldwide organization of over 300 volunteers called the Free World Dial-Up Project (www.pulver.com/fwd) is working to patch Internet calls into local phone networks using their own computers. Vocaltec itself is already saving $10,000 a month on calls between its offices in Israel and New Jersey using its own software to dial over the Net. Eli Noam, an economics professor at Columbia University, predicts that in the long term Internet calling will profoundly change the telephone business, and most technology experts agree that although it isn't perfect yet, the new service will grow to compete strongly with traditional phone service.

It's easy to see why. With features such as telephone-linked Web sites and the equivalent of conference calls hooked up to standard word-processing programs, Internet calling can offer a wide range of

services designed for corporate users looking for speed, convenience, and cost savings. Even on-line shoppers and kids playing games will find applications just for them.

Don't expect phone companies to take the threat lying down, however. Increasing competition in the deregulated telephone industry should force conventional long-distance rates down, and ballooning traffic on the Internet may drive access providers to raise their rates. For now, though, the window of opportunity is open for business.

In today's business environment, the need to communicate and manage information efficiently and quickly is crucial. Information can take many forms: information about customers' locations and order patterns, information about supplies and finished goods on hand, information about workers' pay and productivity, information about products and development, and information about competitors. We communicate it by telephone, voice mail, e-mail, and fax, and we store it on floppy disk, hard drive, magnetic tape, and CD-ROM.

By focusing on the learning objectives of this chapter, you will better understand why the options are so many and so accessible. You will also appreciate the role of the computer at the forefront of contemporary information management. After reading this chapter, you should be able to

1 Show why businesses must manage information and show how computers have revolutionized information management.

2 Identify and briefly describe the main elements of a computer system.

3 Identify the role played by databases and describe four important types of business applications programs.

4 Classify computer systems by size and structure.

5 List some trends in the application of computer technology to business information management.

6 Identify how the Internet and the World Wide Web are affecting information management.

Information Management: An Overview

In this section we will explore the ways in which companies manage information with computers and related information technologies. First, however, in order to understand information management, you must understand what information is and what it is not. Only then can you appreciate what computers do and how they do it.

Businesspeople are bombarded with facts and figures. Modern communications permit businesses to receive up-to-the-minute information from remote plants, branches, and sales offices. To find the information that they need to make critical decisions, managers must often sift through a virtual avalanche of reports, memos, magazines, and phone calls. How can businesses get useful information to the right people at the right time?

information managers
Managers responsible for designing and implementing systems to gather, organize, and distribute information

Most businesses regard their information as a private resource—an asset that they plan, develop, and protect. It is not surprising, then, that companies have **information managers**, just as they have production, marketing, and finance managers. Information management is an internal operation that determines business performance and outcomes. For example, the performance of Chaparral Steel—customer service, delivery times, sales, profits, and customer loyalty—has been boosted by an information system that gives customers fast access to lists of the steel products that are currently available in Chaparral's inventories. The technology that allows customers to shop electronically through its storage yards gives Chaparral greater agility, and because it can respond more rapidly than its competitors, it gets more sales.

Data Versus Information

Although businesspeople often complain that they get too much information, what they usually mean is that they get too many data. **Data** are raw facts and figures. **Information** is the useful interpretation of data.

data
Raw facts and figures

information
The meaningful, useful interpretation of data

For example, consider the following data:

- Last year, 1.4 billion tubes of toothpaste were sold in the United States.

- The U.S. birth rate is rising.

- Two years ago, 1.2 billion tubes of toothpaste were sold.

- Advertising for toothpaste increased 6 percent last year.

- A major dentists' group recently came out in favor of using dental floss daily.

If all these data were put together in a meaningful way, they might produce information about what sells toothpaste and, in particular, whether toothpaste manufacturers should construct new plants to meet increasing demand. The challenge for businesses, then, is to turn a flood of data into manageable information.

Management Information Systems

management information system (MIS)
System for transforming raw data into information that can be used in decision making

One response to this challenge has been the growth of **management information systems (MIS)**: systems for transmitting and transforming data into information that can be used in decision making. Those charged with running a company's MIS must first determine what information will be needed. Then they must gather the data and provide ways to convert data into desired information. They must also control the flow of information so that it goes only to people who need it.

Information supplied to employees and managers varies according to such factors as the functional areas in which they work (say, accounting or marketing) and the levels of management they occupy. The quality of the information transmitted to all levels depends increasingly on an organization's technological resources and on the people who manage it. In this section we will discuss the evolution of the technology that processes information and then describe the information requirements at various managerial levels in today's organization.

The Computer Revolution

Today, managing information means managing computers as information tools. Although individual computers are marvelous information processors, the networking of computers offers far greater advantages. Changes in computer technology—powerful new equipment, the formation of networks within firms, and worldwide networking through the Internet—have revolutionized the way businesses manage information. As recently as 20 years ago, for instance, automated banking machines were virtually unheard of. Now national banking networks such as Plus and Cirrus routinely let a New York City bank customer who has run out of cash in Las Vegas withdraw money from a machine in the Caesar's Palace lobby. That same Caesar's Palace guest, in the privacy of his or her room, can connect a personal laptop computer into the Internet, access American Airlines' SABRE system to change airline reservations, then connect to a PC at home or on their business network to discuss recent developments in New York. Computers offer businesses and individuals a wide range of capabilities: You can chat, shop, get the latest news, and share information on just about any subject.

Not surprisingly, the emergence of information technology has made possible the development of numerous new businesses, many of them in the fields of information and communication products:

▶ Brøderbund (www.broderbund.com), based in Novato, California, makes best-selling software such as The Print Shop® Signature Greetings™, a program for creating personalized greeting cards and envelopes. Its Living Books Library series consists of CD-ROM software that not only reads stories to children but allows them to call up moving characters and props.

▶ Auto-By-Tel (ABT) sells cars over the Internet using a network of 2,000 dealers throughout the U.S. Located in Orange County, California, ABT receives purchase requests from customers via computer, then routes them to the nearest accredited dealer. Within 24–48 hours the dealer contacts the customer with a low, firm price. With 75 percent lower transaction costs than the traditional walk-in sale, ABT receives more than 60,000 customer requests every month.[1]

▶ In Redwood City, California, The Espresso Lane, a coffee drive-through, found a way to speed up service for busy customers hurrying to work. Their computer-based system starts with a plastic card with the customer's favorite orders bar-coded on the card's surface. An infrared scanner reads the order, a computer processes the order onto the customer's screen and onto a printer in the kitchen. The system has reduced rush-hour turnaround time to just 3 minutes and boosted sales by 10 percent.[2]

The Digital Age. As we will see throughout this chapter, the advent of the digital age is an important event in the annals of high-tech business. The "digital age has arrived," declares Joseph P. Clayton, executive vice president of Thomson Consumer Electronics. "Consumers are becoming more comfortable with sophisticated electronic devices." His point is borne out by the sales figures highlighted in Figure 17.1. In 1996, U.S. consumers bought 23.5 million TV sets and 9.2 million personal computers. The value in total sales, however, was much closer: For the first time Americans spent more on PCs ($11 billion) than on TV sets ($8.6 billion).[3]

Figure 17.1 Sales of Personal Computers and Televisions, 1990–1996

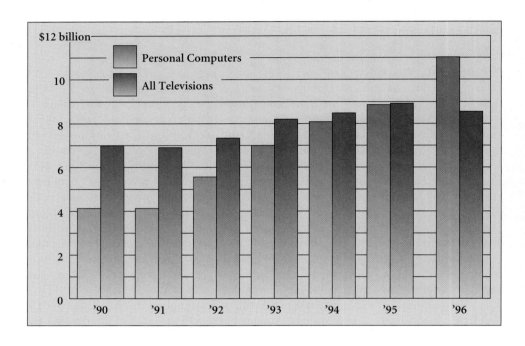

> **The digital age has arrived. Consumers are becoming more comfortable with sophisticated electronic devices.**
>
> —Joseph P. Clayton, executive vice president of Thompson Consumer Electronic

The Key Features of the Computer. Why are computers having such an impact on business? Although it is really nothing more than a machine, the computer boasts four features that make it especially useful:

- *Speed of processing.* The computer is fast: Manual calculations requiring several lifetimes can be performed in less than one second by computers.

- *Accuracy of processing.* Computers have built-in error-checking ability that allows them to perform error-free calculations.

- *Ability to store programs.* One of the most important breakthroughs of the computer revolution is the stored-program concept: Computers store and handle not only the data that need processing, but also the instructions (programs) needed to process the data.

- *Ability to make comparisons.* Although computers cannot think, they can make comparisons. Based on the results of those comparisons, they can take different courses of action—that is, they can execute a huge variety of programmed instructions.

Remember that, for all its virtues, the computer is far from perfect. Unfortunately, the computer will process incorrect data just as readily as it processes correct data. The accuracy of what you receive from the computer depends on the accuracy of what you put in. People in the computer field have coined a term for this phenomenon: GIGO (garbage in, garbage out). In other words, if the computer is given the wrong data to process, it is likely to give you back information that you cannot use.

Elements of the Computer System

The computer is a powerful electronic machine. However, it is only one part of the complete **computer system** designed to turn data into information. As shown in Figure 17.2, every system has five parts:

computer system
Electronic system designed to turn data into information

- Hardware
- Software
- People
- Control
- Data

Figure 17.2 The Five Parts of a Computer System

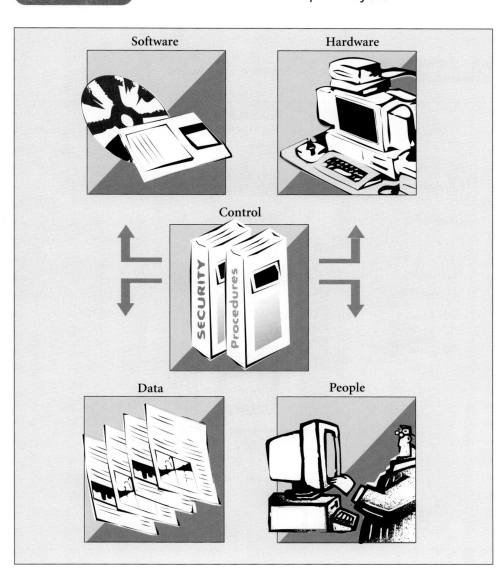

In this section we will describe each of the first four components in detail. We will reserve our discussion of data and its organization and processing for the next section. Remember that all five of these components must be present and properly coordinated for a computer system to function effectively.

Hardware

hardware
Physical components of a computer system

Figure 17.3 shows the various systems and components that make up the **hardware**: the physical components of a computer system. The functioning of a computer's hardware is not as complicated as it looks. To get a bird's-eye view of how the system works, suppose that you are a very simple piece of data (say, the number 3).

Inputting

input device
Part of the computer system that enters data into it

central processing unit (CPU)
Part of the computer system where data processing takes place

To get into the computer, data must be entered by an **input device**. Optical scanners, voice pickups, CD-ROM drives, and mice are all input devices, but let's assume that you are entered by a friend using the most common input device, a keyboard. When your friend presses the number 3 on the keyboard, an electronic signal is sent to the computer's **central processing unit (CPU)**, where the actual processing of data takes place.

Figure 17.3   Computer System Hardware

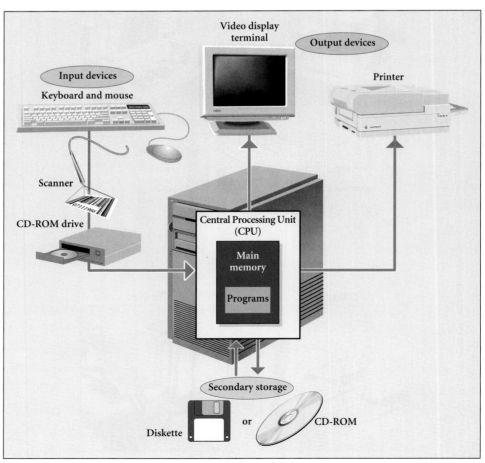

Digital Data

Actually, the CPU does not receive a signal that is *3*. Rather, it receives a special code that stands for *3*. This code consists of eight digits called bits. Each bit is binary, meaning it is either the digit *0* or the digit *1*. To understand how bits work, remember that the earliest computers had mechanical switches, much like the on/off light switches in your home. Although modern computers have no mechanical switches, the principle remains the same: The electronic signals tell the computer to set a particular switch in one of two positions: on or off. In a computer, these two positions represent the flow or lack of flow of electricity.

Obviously, however, we need different input signals for all the input characters that go into the computer (the letters, digits, and other symbols on the keyboard). A single switch (bit), therefore, is not enough. Taken together, a series of eight bits, called a byte, can represent any character on the keyboard. As the number *3*, for example, you would be sent to the computer as a command to turn bits 1, 2, 3, 4, 7, and 8 on and bits 5 and 6 off. The binary code for *3* thus works out as 11110011. Every symbol on the keyboard has its own binary code.

Main Memory

You are now inside the CPU in a form that the computer can handle. Now what happens? As a piece of data, you must go first to **main memory** the part of the computer's CPU that stores those programs that it needs in order to operate.

Programs

At this point, the CPU searches through its memory for instructions—**programs**—on what to do with you. Using the appropriate instructions, it then performs the calculations (addition, subtraction, multiplication, and division) and comparisons as directed by the program. Then, the CPU sends the results into one or more **output devices**: a video display terminal (VDT) or a printer.

Secondary Storage

If someone turned off the computer at this point, it would forget both the data (you) and information that resulted. Why? The computer's active memory is a short-term form of memory that lasts only as long as the computer stays on. It is called **random access memory (RAM)** because any part of it can be called upon for processing at any time.

Disks and CD-ROM. For long-term memory, however, we need **secondary storage**: that is, any medium for storing data or information outside the computer's CPU. Magnetic tape, hard disks, diskettes, and CD-ROM can all be used for secondary storage. Digital data that are stored can later be retrieved (that is, read) from storage by the user. **Hard disks** are rigid metal disks permanently enclosed in the computer. **Diskettes** are portable and can be easily inserted and removed.

CD-ROMs (for compact disk **read-only memory**) look just like music CDs and can hold as much data as 400 regular diskettes. They are convenient for storing sound and video images but do not allow users to write new data onto them. A CD recorder is required for adding new data. The recorder uses special software to laser-cut grooves into the CD. Popular CD-ROMs include large-volume materials such as encyclopedias. Brøderbund Software, for example, offers Encyclopaedia Britannica CD 98, which includes the entire text of the 32 volumes, 72,000 articles, 8,000 photos and illustrations, sound clips, animation and video, Webster's Collegiate® Dictionary, and 15,000 related Internet links.[4] CD-ROMS are especially useful for storing multimedia technical presentations that use overhead projections, videos, voice, and sound.

Now that you have an inside view of computer hardware operations, let's look at things from the outside. Suppose you have a part-time job in the registrar's office at

---

main memory
Part of the computer CPU that houses the memory of programs it needs to operate

program
Set of instructions used by a computer to perform specified activities

output device
Part of a computer system that presents results, either visually or in printed form

random access memory (RAM)
Short-term memory that is active while the computer is performing its functions

secondary storage
Any medium (such as disks) for storing data or information outside the computer's CPU

hard disk
Secondary storage device permanently installed in a computer

diskette
Portable, easily removed secondary storage device

CD-ROM
Secondary storage device that can store sound and video data but accepts no new written data

read-only memory (ROM)
Secondary storage device that can hold instructions to be read by the computer but accepts no written instructions

your school. Let's say that a student requests information about an introductory accounting class. You insert a diskette and type the request on your keyboard—your link to the CPU. Although the keyboard does no processing itself, it lets you issue commands to the CPU.

Next, the CPU takes over. It issues an electronic command that finds data about accounting classes in secondary storage and copies it into the main memory. A program in the CPU tells the computer how to search through the lists for the introductory course requested by the student. Finally, the CPU transfers the results to your video display. In a matter of seconds, you can tell the student that the class meets at 8:30 A.M. every day and that three seats are still open.

Software

Although hardware is a vital component of a computer system, it is useless without the other components. As we have just seen, hardware needs programs—**software**—to function. There are basically two types of software programs: system and application.

System Programs

System programs tell the computer what resources to use and how to use them. For example, an operating system program tells the computer how and when to transfer data from secondary to primary storage and to return information to the user. You have probably heard of DOS, the disk operating system used by the IBM PC, its clones, and almost all other personal computers. It is called DOS because a disk is used to store the operating system software.

Another type of system program, the **language program**, allows computer users to write specialized instructions for their computers. For example, FORTRAN (for *formula translator*) is used in engineering and the sciences because it is designed for the rapid calculation of large numbers. Visual Basic and Visual C are popular general-purpose languages for specialists who like to write their own programs. Many educators prefer PASCAL because it teaches good programming habits and makes both reviewing and debugging fairly simple.

Application Programs

Most computer users do not write programs but use **application programs**: software written by others. Each different type of application (such as financial analysis, word processing, or Web browsing) uses a program that meets that need. Thus, a computer system usually has many application programs available, such as Lotus 1-2-3, Quicken, and WordPerfect. We will consider the types of application programs most often used in business later in this chapter.

Graphic User Interface

One of the most helpful software developments is the **graphic user interface (GUI)**: the user-friendly visual display that helps users select from among the many possible applications on the computer. Typically, the screen displays numerous **icons** (small images) representing such choices as word processing, graphics, DOS, fax, printing, CD, or games. The user tells the computer what to do by moving a pointing device (usually an arrow) around the screen to activate the desired icon. Printed text presents simple instructions for using activated features. Today, Microsoft Windows is the most popular GUI because it simplifies computer use while actually making it fun.

People

We think and speak of computer systems as if they were only hardware and software. In large part, however, a computer system is a function of the people who construct and use it. The people in a computer system can be divided into three categories: programming personnel, operations personnel, and end users.

software
Programs that instruct a computer in what to do

system program
Software that tells the computer what resources to use and how to use them

language program
System program (such as FORTRAN) that allows users to give computers their own instructions

application program
Software (such as Lotus 1-2-3) that processes data according to a user's special needs

graphic user interface (GUI)
Software that provides a visual display to help users select applications

icon
Small image in a GUI that enables users to select applications or functions

Programming Personnel

Programming personnel include both systems analysts and application or systems programmers:

- Systems analysts deal with the entire computer system. They work with users to learn their requirements and then design systems to meet them. Generally, they decide on the type and size of computer and on how to set up linkages among computers to form a network of users.

- Using various language programs, programmers write the instructions that tell computers what to do. Application programmers, for example, write instructions to address particular problems. Systems programmers ensure that a system can handle the requests made by various application programs.

Operations Personnel

People who run the computer equipment are called operations personnel: They make sure that the right programs are run in the correct sequence and monitor equipment to ensure that it is operating properly. Many organizations also have data-entry personnel who key data into the system for processing.

End Users

Finally, end users of the system obtain information from it. Systems analysts realize that effective systems can be created only if intended users play a part in designing them, and users at different levels in the firm have different informational needs. For example, low-

The Workplace Environment

"Your CEO Wears Combat Boots!"

How far do you think a business executive should go to learn about information technology? How about all the way to the U.S. Army?

That's precisely where executives from Oracle, Corning, IBM, Eastman Kodak, GTE, and other firms have come, for a kind of MIS bootcamp that runs for 14 weeks. The Army's Information Resources Management College, part of its National Defense University (NDU) in Washington, D.C., offers an intensive course in information technology that draws 100 students a year from private companies as well as government departments at home and abroad. Executives can rub shoulders with participants from the Environmental Protection Agency, the FBI, or the Philippine Navy. Course titles range from "Virtual Reality for Managers" to "Innovative Thinking for the Information Age," and the methodology includes everything from corporate field trips to simulated interplanetary combat. Teamwork, brainstorming, and group problem-solving are paramount.

Students are equipped on arrival with networked laptop computers and a mountain of software such as Lotus Notes, Powerpoint, and other groupware and database programs. All the courseware is already stored in a database, ready to be taken back home to the graduates' own organizations and shared with others.

> " You fight the way you organize for business. "
>
> —Robert Neilson, a professor at National Defense University

The core of the curriculum focuses on competition as combat—and vice versa—in the context of how digital technologies will change war, business, and society. "You fight the way you organize for business," says Robert Neilson, a professor at NDU. Indeed, it seems that NDU gives new meaning to the idea that for today's executives, "it's a war out there."

Figure 17.4 Information Needs at Different Management Levels

level (first-line) managers need information to oversee the day-to-day operations of the business. Meanwhile, middle managers need summaries and analyses to help them set intermediate and long-range goals. Finally, top management needs analyses of broader trends in the economy and the overall business environment in order to conduct long-range and corporate planning.

Consider the information needs of various managers for a flooring manufacturer. Sales managers (first-line managers) supervise salespeople, assign territories to the sales force, and handle customer service and delivery problems. They need current and accurate information on the sales and delivery of flooring products: lists of incoming customer orders and daily delivery schedules to customers in their territories. Regional managers (middle managers) set sales quotas for each sales manager, prepare budgets, and plan staffing needs for the next year. To do so, they need total monthly sales by product and region. Finally, top management needs sales data summarized by product, customer type, and geographic region, along with comparisons to previous years and competitors' sales. Just as important as internal operations information is external environmental information (say, consumer behavior patterns, the competition's success record, and related economic forecasts).

Figure 17.4 illustrates the different kinds of information needed at the different levels of management. As you can see, information is increasingly condensed and summarized as it moves up through the management hierarchy.

Control

Control ensures that the system is operating according to specific procedures and within specific guidelines. These procedures include guidelines for operating the system, the responsibilities of the personnel involved with it, and plans for dealing with system failure. For example, a key aspect of information management is controlling two groups of people: those who have access to input or change the system's data and those who receive output from it. Thus, for example, most firms limit access to salary information.

Problems of Privacy, Piracy, and Security

"Breaking and entering" no longer refers merely to physical intrusions into one's home or business. Today, it applies to computer system intrusions as well. In this section we will describe the three most common forms of computer intrusion: privacy invasion, viruses, and piracy. We will also discuss some of the methods that companies use to provide security for their information systems.

Privacy Invasion.   In the computer world, privacy invasion occurs in two forms. First, intruders (hackers) gain unauthorized access, either to steal information, money, or property or to tamper with data. We have all read about computer enthusiasts who have gained access to school systems to change grades. In 1994, a 16-year-old British hacker made 150 intrusions into the Air Force's top command-and-control facility. He then used those entries to get access to computers of several defense contractors and the South Korean Atomic Research Institute. In a 1997 survey, 40 percent of the companies surveyed reported recent break-ins. FBI Director Louis Freeh reports that 23 countries are engaged in economic spying against American business, including at least seven nations that are training intelligence agents to hack U.S. computers for commercial data. Help for the professional hacker is openly available: Programs called Crack (for decoding stolen passwords) and Rootkit (a program for scanning phone numbers in search of those connected to modems) are even available on the Internet for free![5]

Viruses.   A second form of intrusion involves passing a computer virus into the system. Viruses are harmful programs created and spread by vandals seeking to destroy or disrupt computer operations. In effect, the virus is an unwanted disease that spreads from computer to computer, damaging data, programs, and even hardware.

   Whereas some viruses erase databases or programs immediately, others spread slowly like a cancer. Some may even lie dormant for weeks before suddenly activating. Viruses can be transmitted electronically from one system to another and can be distributed by virus-infected disks. Programs such as Norton AntiVirus Netware screen for viruses on diskettes, the computer network, or the Internet and prevent them from entering the user's system.

Piracy.   Computer piracy is the unauthorized copying of software. Although general-purpose software, such as WordPerfect or Lotus 1-2-3, is protected by the Copyright Law of 1974, some users ignore the law, illegally copying programs for friends and family, who can thus avoid buying additional copies for personal use.

   Another form of piracy involves proprietary software for special applications. For example, one company's computer staff may develop its own program for computer-aided design. Piracy occurs when it is stolen from the developer company and illegally sold to other firms. A third form of piracy occurs when a buyer distributes unauthorized copies of software throughout the company. Most software suppliers offer site license agreements that authorize companywide use of software in return for fees.

Security.   Security measures for protection against intrusion and piracy are a constant challenge for many firms.[6] To prevent unlawful modification of software, code words allowing access to it can be changed periodically. The activities of users can also be monitored, and some procedures require second-person confirmation before any one person can make changes in software programs. To gain entry into any system, computer users have protected passwords that guard against unauthorized access.

   To protect against intrusions by unauthorized outsiders, companies use security devices, called electronic **firewalls**, in their computer systems. Firewalls are software programs that allow employees access to both the Internet and the company's internal computer network while barring entry by outsiders.

   Protection for data files and databases is not foolproof and typically involves making backup copies to be stored outside the computer system, usually in a safe. Thus, if system files are damaged, they can be replaced by backup. Another security problem is the interception of data communication during transit from one location to another. To prevent interception, encryption software scrambles the transmission signals so that only personnel with the deciphering codes can read them.

firewall
Software program that prevents outsiders from accessing a company's network

Finally, the most important security factor is the people in the system. At most firms, personnel are trained in the responsibilities of computer use and warned of the penalties for violating system security. For example, each time the computer boots up, a notice displays the warning that software and data are protected and spells out penalties for unauthorized use.[7]

Databases and Applications Programs

As we noted earlier, all computer processing is the processing of data. This processing is carried out by programs: instructions that tell the computer to perform specified functions. In this section we will begin by briefly describing the nature of computer data and databases. We then discuss a few of the specialized applications programs designed for business use.

Data and Databases

database
Centralized, organized collection of related data

Computers convert data into information by organizing it in some meaningful manner. Within a computer system, chunks of data numbers, words, and sentences are stored in a series of related collections called fields, records, and files. Taken together, all these data files constitute a **database**: a centralized, organized collection of related data.

It's Your Business

How Much Is Information Worth?

Define the word *free*. If your definition included the idea of getting something for nothing, you may be surprised to discover that some state agencies don't agree with you.

In the last several years a number of state governments have begun charging fees for information stored in government records to which the public is guaranteed access. Driving records, tax assessments, liquor license records, and many other kinds of data are beginning to look like found money to the states that compile and store them.

Just in case you thought their fees might be nominal processing costs, consider the price tag on a recent request for computerized driver's license data that the Belleville, Illinois *News-Democrat* needed for a story on voter fraud. The Illinois Secretary of State was glad to oblige—for $37.5 million. In hard copy form, the information had always been free. When Rhode Island wanted $9.7 million for computerized traffic ticket data requested by the Providence *Journal-Bulletin*, the paper sued (the case is still pending).

Those in the newspaper industry trace the onset of fees to the early 1990s, when marketing firms discovered

the value of the personal and demographic data available from state and local governments and were willing to pay for it. Illinois already makes about $10 million a year selling its data. Reporters and editors argue that the fees states now collect are detrimental to their work, which benefits the wider public. Rather than paying for partial data, as some marketers can do, they often need to study an entire city- or statewide database to unearth broader trends. In the new seller's market, those data can be prohibitively expensive.

Is the public worried? Perhaps it should be. Only the intervention of a state legislator allowed the Houston *Chronicle* to access computerized motorist arrest records without paying the proposed $75-million price tag, which would have killed what proved to be an award-winning story showing that minorities in certain communities were twice as likely to get traffic tickets as whites. An editor at the Providence *Journal-Bulletin*, awaiting the outcome of its suit for motor vehicle records, recalled a story he wrote in the 1980s using three separate statewide databases to identify school bus drivers with multiple traffic violations and even drug convictions. In response, Rhode Island tightened the rules on school bus operators, and deaths of children in school bus accidents stopped. Total cost of the story: $500.

As for the Belleville *News-Democrat*'s story on voter fraud, it was never written.

Processing

Once data are entered into the database, they can be manipulated, sorted, combined, or compared. In **batch processing**, data are collected over some time period and then processed as groups or batches. Payrolls, for example, are usually run in batches: Because most employees get paid on either a weekly or a biweekly basis, the data (the hours worked) are accumulated over the pay periods and processed at one time.

Batch processing was once the only type of computer processing. Although it is still widely used, companies today have such choices as **real-time processing**, in which data are entered and processed immediately. This system is always used when the results of each entry affect subsequent entries. For example, if you book seat F6 on Continental Flight 253 on December 23, the computer must thereafter keep other passengers from booking the same seat.

batch processing
Method of collecting data over a period of time and then processing them as a group or batch

real-time processing
Method of entering data and processing them immediately

Application Programs

Programs are available for a huge variety of business-related tasks. Some of these programs address such common needs as accounting, payroll, and inventory control. Others have been developed for an endless variety of specialized needs. Most business applications programs fall into one of four categories: word processing, spreadsheets, database management, and graphics.

Word Processing

Popular **word-processing programs** such as Microsoft Word and WordPerfect allow computer users to store, edit, display, and print documents. Sentences or paragraphs can be added or deleted without retyping or restructuring an entire document, and mistakes are easily corrected. At *USA Today*, for example, hundreds of reporters and editors use word processing to write, edit, and store articles on computer terminals that are linked to a central system. Within minutes after stories are completed, the system sends typeset text via satellite to printing sites throughout the United States, where the paper is printed and distributed to newsstands each day.

word-processing program
Applications program that allows computers to store, edit, and print letters and numbers for documents created by users

Spreadsheets

Electronic spreadsheets spread data across and down the page in rows and columns. Users enter data, including formulas, at row and column intersections, and the computer automatically performs the necessary calculations. Payroll records, sales projections, and a host of other financial reports can be prepared in this manner.

Spreadsheets are useful planning tools because they allow managers to see how making a change in one item will affect related items. For example, a manager can insert various operating cost percentages, tax rates, or sales revenues into the spreadsheet. The computer will automatically recalculate all the other figures and determine net profit. Three popular spreadsheet packages are Lotus 1-2-3, Quattro Pro, and Microsoft Excel.

electronic spreadsheet
Applications program with a row-and-column format that allows users to store, manipulate, and compare numeric data

Database Management

Database management programs, such as dBase and R-Base, can keep track of all of a firm's relevant data. They can then sort and search through data and integrate a single piece of data into several different files. Figure 17.5 illustrates how a database management program might be used at a company called Artists' Frame Service. In this case, the program is integrating the file for customer orders with the company's inventory file. When sales to Jones and Smith are entered into the Customer Orders File, the database system automatically adjusts the Frame Inventory File; the quantities of materials B5 and A3 are reduced because those materials were used in making the frames for Jones and Smith.

database management program
Applications program for creating, storing, searching, and manipulating an organized collection of data

Graphics

Computer graphics programs convert numeric and character data into pictorial information such as charts, graphs, and cartoon characters. These programs make computerized information easier to use and understand in two ways. First, graphs and charts summarize

computer graphics program
Applications program that converts numeric and character data into pictorial information such as graphs and charts

Figure 17.5 Artists' Frame Service Database Management Program

Customer Orders File				Frame Inventory File		
Job Order Number	Customer Name	Quantity Ordered (inches)	Frame Material Number	Frame Material Number	Description	Quantity on Hand
12345	JONES, JOHN	42	B5	A3	ITALIAN OLIVE	500
25974	SMITH, MARY	89	A3	B2	PLASTIC BLACK	010
				B5	PLASTIC GREEN	272

data and allow managers to detect problems, opportunities, and relationships more easily. Second, graphics are valuable in creating clearer and more persuasive reports and presentations.

Presentation graphics software, such as Microsoft PowerPoint, uses slides, video, and sound splices for professional presentations. The ability to vary color and size, and to use pictures and charts with three-dimensional effects, shadows, and shading along with animation and sound is more visually interesting than static presentations.

presentation graphics software
Applications that enable users to create visual presentations that can include animation and sound

This fashion designer is using a graphic tablet to design a dress on her computer. The initial design can easily be changed electronically to try new features and styles. The final design is stored for future use. Graphics programs and applications can now create everything from a simple slide presentation to award-winning special effects for film and television.

Computer graphics capabilities extend beyond mere data presentation. They also include standalone programs for artists and special effects designers. Everything from simple drawings to fine art, television commercials, and motion picture special effects are now created by computer graphics software. The realism of the dinosaurs in *Jurassic Park* and the physical appearance of the legless Vietnam veteran in *Forrest Gump* are special effects created with computer graphics.

Some of the latest software for **desktop publishing** combines word-processing and graphics capability to produce typeset-quality text with stimulating visual effects from personal computers. Quark XPress, for example, is able to manipulate text, graphics, and full-color photographs. Desktop publishing eliminates costly printing services for reports and proposals, and Quark is also used by ad agencies such as J. Walter Thompson, where computer-generated designs offer greater control over color and format.

desktop publishing
Process of combining word-processing and graphics capability to produce virtually typeset-quality text from personal computers

Types of Computer Systems

Although all computer systems share basic common elements, they vary dramatically in size, capacity, and cost. In the following section we will stress differences. Remember, however, that all computers have essentially the same capabilities: They process, store, and input and output data.

Categorizing Systems by Size

Grouping computer systems by cost, capacity, and capability results in four basic categories: microcomputers, minicomputers, mainframes, and supercomputers. Computers in each category differ in the ways in which data enter and are represented by the system. They are supported by different software programs, and as we will see in the following sections, the biggest differences lie in the uses to which they are put.

Microcomputers

Most of the computers that you see sitting on desks are **microcomputers** (also called personal computers). The convenience and power of microcomputers such as the IBM PC and Apple Macintosh have shifted the balance of computing power to smaller systems. Smaller, portable PCs include laptops, notebooks, and palmtops. Light in weight, ranging from a few ounces (palmtops) to 15 pounds (laptops), portables have external power sources (such as rechargeable batteries) and many, but not all, of the features of desktops. Notebooks and palmtops have more limited keyboards and smaller memories, and palmtops have very small monitors. Their advantages—they are lightweight, transportable, and storable (some are small enough for your pocket)—make them attractive timesavers for commuters and travelers.

microcomputer (or **personal computer**)
Smallest, slowest, least expensive form of computer

Because PCs are so convenient, they are the fastest-growing segment of computer sales. Indeed, the percentage of U.S. households with PCs has risen from under 25 percent in 1989 to more than 40 percent in 1996.[8] Equally interesting, in terms of percentage share, shipments of PCs to home users have been rising steadily since 1993 and will soon pass shipments to business users. By the year 2000, the home will be the biggest PC segment in the United States. Moreover, says Ronald Chwang, president of Acer America Corp., "we used to think the home computer was the low-end computer. Now it's driving the technology." Much of that technology is for younger users: interactive story programs, high-tech games featuring visuals, music, and sound effects, and access to the Internet.[9]

❝ *We used to think the home computer was the low-end computer. Now it's driving the technology.* ❞

—Ronald Chwang, president of Acer America Corp.

minicomputer
Computer whose capacity, speed, and cost fall between those of microcomputers and mainframes

mainframe
Computer whose capacity and speed enable it to serve many users simultaneously

supercomputer
Largest, fastest, most expensive form of computer

system architecture
Location of a computer system's elements (data-entry and data-processing operations, database, data output, and computer staff)

centralized system
Form of computer system architecture in which all processing is done in one location through a centralized computer, database, and staff

decentralized system
Form of computer system architecture in which processing is done in many locations by means of separate computers, databases, and personnel

computer network
Group of interconnected computer systems able to exchange information with one another from different locations

wide area network
Network of computers and workstations located far from one another and linked by telephone wires or by satellite

local area network (LAN)
Network of computers and workstations, usually within a company, that are linked together by cable

Minicomputers

Larger, faster, and more sophisticated than microcomputers, **minicomputers** can process millions of instructions per second (mips). They can also support multiple users in a network and provide much more storage than micros.

Mainframes

Still bigger and faster are **mainframes**. Costing $1 million or more, they can store and access billions of characters and process hundreds of millions of instructions per second. Mainframes are most often found in banks and other commercial organizations where large volumes of data must be processed.[10]

Supercomputers

The largest, fastest, and most expensive of all computers, **supercomputers** are used mainly in scientific applications in which huge numbers of complex calculations must be performed very quickly. Intel Corp.'s supercomputer, a $46-million machine installed at Sandia National Laboratories, passed the speed of 1 teraflop (one trillion calculations per second) in 1996. The U.S. Energy Department's other laboratories are scheduled to receive even faster supers: a 3-teraflop system by 1998 and, if the program gets an additional extension, a 500-teraflop system by 2005. This giant, compared to today's best personal computers, would be like traveling to the moon and back while the PC travels just two long city blocks.[11]

System Architectures

Whereas differences in computer capacity and ability are shrinking, system architecture has remained a fairly constant feature. **System architecture** refers to the location of the various parts of the system: its data-entry and data-processing operations, database, data output, and computer staff. System architecture is classified according to the organization of a system's parts.

Centralized Systems

In a **centralized system**, most of the processing is done in one location. For example, all of a bank's branch teller machines need the same information. Thus, they are all linked to the main office mainframe, which houses all customer information files in a central database. Centralized systems do have drawbacks: For example, when the central computer fails or communication lines to it go down, all the branches also go down.

Decentralized Systems

In a **decentralized system**, each location determines the needs of its own system (physical components, programs, databases, personnel). Locations are independent of centralized mainframes, and there are no communication links between locations. Problems occur if different locations independently adopt incompatible components or programs. It may then become difficult or impossible for systems at separate locations to share important data.

Computer Networks

Networking allows otherwise decentralized computers to exchange data quickly and easily. A **computer network** is a group of interconnected computers at several different locations that can exchange information. Networks may link computers statewide or even nationwide through telephone wires or satellites, as in **wide area networks**. Wal-Mart Stores, for example, depends heavily on its private satellite network that links more than 2,000 retail stores to its Bentonville, Arkansas, headquarters.

Internal networks may link all of a firm's computers through cables, as in **local area networks (LANs)**. The computers in internal networks share processing duties, software, storage areas, and data. On cable TV's *Home Shopping Network*, for example, hundreds of operators seated at monitors in a large room are united by a LAN for entering call-in orders from customers. This arrangement allows the use of a single computer system with one database and software system.

Combination systems using local and wide area networks are also possible. For example, separate plants or offices might handle orders locally while electronically transmitting sales summaries to a corporate office. Computer networks thus give companies the advantages of both centralized and decentralized processing. Using a personal computer with a **modem**—a computer-to-computer link over telephone wires—users can conduct searches in a remote database and exchange messages.

The materials used for making local and wide area networks are changing rapidly. **Fiber optic cable** is made from hairlike, ultra-thin glass fibers that carry data faster, are lighter, and are less expensive than the older copper wire cables. The copper wire cables carry data as electrical signals, whereas fiber optic cable carries data as laser-generated light beams.[12] Wire cables throughout the world are being replaced daily with fiber optic cable, but the change will require many years of effort. Tele Danmark, Denmark's leading telecom company, is prominent in the transition. In 1996 it installed the BALTICA submarine cable, 400 kilometers long, between Poland, Denmark, and Sweden, and a 700-kilometer cable underwater in Brazil. Its cable ships are routinely engaged in cable maintenance in the North Sea.[13]

Client Server Systems. An advantage of networks is the sharing, rather than costly and unnecessary duplication, of resources. Any component that can be shared by network users is called a **server**. The powerful minicomputer at the network hub, for example, may be the server for the surrounding **client PCs** in the network.

More specifically, it may act as a file server, a print server, and a fax server. As a file server, the mini has a large-capacity disk for storing the programs and data shared by all the PCs in the network. It contains customer files plus the database, word-processing, graphics, and spreadsheet programs that may be used by clients. As a print server, the mini controls the printer, stores printing requests from client PCs, and routes jobs to the printer as it becomes available. And as the fax server, the mini receives, sends, and otherwise controls the system's fax activities. Only one disk drive, one printer, and one fax, therefore, are needed for the entire system of users.

By linking and sharing computing resources, server-client LANs are fast replacing standalone minis and mainframes. At Motorola, for instance, networking rings in three LANs now route data requests from 1,000 workstation clients through 30 minicomputer servers. Since the system was installed, cost of the company's MIS has dropped from 3.7 percent to 1.2 percent of sales.[14]

Miniaturization

The year 1971 witnessed the first commercial introduction of the **microprocessor chip**. This chip, the size of a small paper clip, contains the computer's central processing unit. Before 1971, computers had specialized chips for logic, programming, and so forth. Intel Corp.'s development of the microprocessor made it possible to put all the computer's functions on a single chip. Today, many cars, watches, and televisions also use microprocessors.

Continued miniaturization has made it possible to put even more circuits on a single chip. The result is known as large-scale integration (LSI) and very-large-scale integration (VLSI). Today's super chips have room for millions of miniature transistors on a space no thicker than a human hair. They permit software and printers to react more quickly with each other and with the computer. Coupled with improvements in software, the latest computers are faster and easier for nonprogrammers to use.

Although no one is sure what the next generation of computing will be like, the continuing miniaturizing of transistor circuits is creating almost daily new possibilities in both speed and storage capacity. A microprocessor's speed determines how fast it can process software instructions. Smaller circuit sizes mean that more transistors can be

modem
Device that provides a computer-to-computer link over telephone wires

fiber optic cable
Hairlike glass fiber cables that carry data in the form of light pulses

server
Any user-shared component (such as a minicomputer) at the center of a local area network

client PC
Any computer attached to a network server

microprocessor chip
Single silicon chip containing a computer's central processing unit

placed on a single silicon chip. They can also be placed closer together, and reduced distance means faster processing. More circuits per chip means much larger memory capacity. Recent capacities were measured in megabits (millions of bits), but chip technology has reached the gigabit (billion-bit) range. The 586-class chip common in today's PCs has millions of transistors, making it more powerful than the mainframes of 10 years ago. It is just one product of a computing power explosion that has been growing by a factor of four every 3 years since 1979. In other words, the performance of this year's PC is about four times that of the PC of just 3 years ago. And today's PC is priced lower.[15]

The Marriage of Information and Communication Technology

Although computing is constantly evolving, some of its foundational elements are here: artificial intelligence, expert systems, office information technologies, executive information systems, operations information systems, data communication networks, and multimedia communication systems. The most powerful vehicle for using these elements to their full potential is the marriage of computers to communication technologies. Thanks to lower-cost, higher-capacity networks, the joining of computers, communication, and the mass media is already in its first stages.

This marriage promises to change the future of business—indeed, of society itself. "Personal computing," observes Microsoft's Bill Gates, "was qualitatively a very, very different thing than the computing that came before. The advances in communication likewise will create new ways of using communication for learning, education, and commerce that go far beyond anything done to date." Both independently and through joint ventures, companies such as Microsoft, AT&T, Hewlett-Packard, Oracle Corp., and Telecommunications Inc. are pursuing such products as personal digital assistants, digital TVs, digital photography, and devices for tapping into high-bandwidth networks, multimedia information, and online services.[16] In this section we briefly discuss the progress of some of these projects.

> **66** *Personal computing was qualitatively a very, very different thing than the computing that came before. The advances in communication likewise will create new ways of using communication for learning, education, and commerce that go far beyond anything done to date.* **99**
>
> —Bill Gates, CEO, Microsoft Corp.

Artificial Intelligence

artificial intelligence (AI)
Construction and programming of computers to imitate human thought processes

Artificial intelligence (AI) can be defined as the construction and programming of computers to imitate human thought processes. In developing components and programs for AI, computer scientists are trying to design computers capable of reasoning so that computers, instead of people, can perform useful activities.

Robotics is one category of AI. With their "reasoning" capabilities, robots can "learn" repetitive tasks such as painting, assembling components, and inserting screws. Furthermore, they avoid repeating mistakes by "remembering" the causes of past mistakes and, when those causes reappear, adjusting or stopping until adjustments are made.

Using the latest techniques in knowledge engineering and computer technology, this GE Capital Services team was able to put together in one program all the loan and collateral requirements, cash flow analyses, market reports, risk factors, and other criteria that go into a complex real estate investment decision. Thanks to this expert system, which can be accessed with a laptop, GE field staff will now be able to quote, underwrite, and review a real estate deal more quickly and effectively, helping to reduce overall cycle time by two-thirds.

Computer scientists are also designing AI systems that possess sensory capabilities (vision with lasers, as well as hearing and feeling). In addition, as machines become more sophisticated in processing natural languages, humans will be able to give instructions and ask questions just by speaking to the computer.

Expert Systems

A special form of artificial intelligence programs, the **expert system**, tries to imitate the behavior of human experts in a particular field. Expert systems incorporate the rules that an expert applies to specific types of problems. In effect, they supply everyday users with "instant expertise."[17] General Electric's Socrates Quick Quote™ is an example. As shown in the photo above, it places a package of technical knowledge about real estate transactions at the fingertips of real estate dealers on GE's private computer network.[18]

expert system
Form of artificial intelligence that attempts to imitate the behavior of human experts in a particular field

Office Information Technologies

Office information technologies (OIT) are the computer-based devices and applications whose function is to enhance the performance and productivity of general office activities. In this section we will survey three of the most solidly entrenched innovations in today's automated office: fax machines, voice mail, and e-mail.

Fax Machines

Fax machines (short for *facsimile-transceiver machines*) can transmit text documents, drawings, and photograph images over telephone lines in a matter of seconds, thus permitting written communication over long distances. Fax machines are popular with both large and small firms because of speed and low cost.

fax machine
Machine that can transmit copies of documents (text and graphics) over telephone lines

Voice Mail

Voice mail is a computer-based system for receiving and delivering incoming telephone calls. Incoming calls are never missed because a voice responds to the caller, invites a message, and stores it. A company with voice mail has each employee's phone networked for receiving, storing, and forwarding calls.

voice mail
Computer-based system for receiving and delivering incoming telephone calls

Voice mail software links the communication device (telephone) with a computer. The input from the telephone is sent to the computer, which uses software to digitize the voice data and stores it on a disk. The employee can then call the voice-mail center to retrieve from storage a recording of waiting calls and voice messages. By combining technologies, voice mail can receive and store an incoming fax message until the recipient requests that the fax be printed.

E-Mail

electronic mail (e-mail)
Computer system that electronically transmits letters, reports, and other information between computers

An **electronic mail** (or **e-mail**) system electronically transmits letters, reports, and other information between computers, whether in the same building or in another country. It is also used for voice transmission and for sending graphics and videos from one computer to another. E-mail thus substitutes for the flood of paper and telephone calls that threatens to engulf many offices.

Executive Information Systems

executive information system (EIS)
Easy-access information cluster specially designed for upper-level managers

Executive information systems (EIS) are quick-reference, easy-access information clusters specially designed for instant access by upper-level managers. Business planning, strategy sessions, and competitive evaluations depend on convenient information retrieval by senior-level managers, who do not typically possess technical computer skills. An EIS is easily accessible with simple keyboard strokes or even voice commands.

Operations Information Systems

operations information system
Computer system used to manage production and manufacturing operations

Computer technology is having a major impact on production and manufacturing through the use of **operations information systems** which includes computer-aided design (CAD), computer-aided manufacturing (CAM), and computer operation control. CAD assists in designing products by simulating the real product and displaying it in three-dimensional graphics. Immersion's MicroScribe-3D software (www.immerse.com), for example, uses a penlike tool to scan the surface of any three-dimensional object, such as a football helmet, and electronically transforms it into a 3D graphic. The helmet designer can then try different shapes and surfaces for the helmet in the computer and observe the new designs on the video monitor.[19] For many design applications, CAD creates faster designs at lower cost than manual modeling methods. CAM is a similar tool, but it is used for designing the manufacturing equipment, facilities, and plant layouts for better product flows and productivity.

Computer operations control is any system for managing the day-to-day production activities for either goods or service production. Hospitals use computer-based scheduling for preparing patients' meals, just as manufacturers do for making autos,

"Dennis, I would like to talk to you for a minute—off line."

A designer using a light pen works on the computer-aided design of new shoes for Clarke's, the shoe manufacturer. After electronically testing for strength, appearance, and durability, the designer can make improvements to reach the final design. The electronic files of the design are then transferred to manufacturing, where computer-controlled production cuts the materials and assembles them into new shoes.

clocks, and paper products. GE, for example, has developed an operations control system for improving railway service, as shown in the photo below.[20]

Data Communication Networks

Gaining popularity on both home and business computers are public and private **data communication networks**: global networks that carry streams of digital data (electronic messages, documents, and other forms of video and sound) back and forth quickly and economically on telecommunication systems. The most prominent networks, the Internet and the World Wide Web, have emerged as powerful communication technologies.[21]

data communication network
Global network (such as the Internet) that permits users to send electronic messages and information quickly and economically

The new Railway Control and Management System, developed by GE–Harris Railway Electronics and demonstrated here by one of the firm's scientists, can coordinate the movement of all trains and work crews across an entire railroad network, allowing railroads to make the best use of existing lines and to avoid expensive investments in new rail infrastructure. The improved flow of train traffic will allow for better on-time performance as well. This is a prime example of how computers can assist in operations information systems.

The Internet

Internet
Global data communication network serving millions of computers with information on a wide array of topics and providing communication flows among certain private networks

The **Internet** (or the Net, for short) is the largest public network, serving millions of computers with information on business, science, and government and providing communication flows among certain private networks, including CompuServe and MCI Mail. Originally commissioned by the Pentagon as a communication tool for use during war, the Internet allows personal computers in virtually any location to be linked together by means of large computers known as network servers. The Net has gained in popularity because it makes available an immense wealth of academic, technical, and business information. Another major attraction is its capacity to transmit e-mail. For thousands of businesses, therefore, the Net is joining—and even replacing—the telephone, the fax machine, and express mail as a standard means of communication.

In 1994 the number of Net users doubled, to 15 million, with links to 138 countries. In 1995, more than 25 million people and 22,000 businesses had access to the Net.[22] Its use continues to grow because it offers new opportunities for computing enhancements. Consider Java by Sun Microsystems Inc. Java is a software language that can be used by software developers on any type of PC. By instantaneously connecting software writers with software users on the Internet, it provides an entirely new, convenient way of creating, selling, delivering, and using software. Software writers like it because they can create a new tool then send it on the Net to users. When the program arrives it automatically loads itself and runs on the requestor's PC. Thus, the user avoids having to install a big program. Suppose you want to create a Web site and you are not a programmer. Just use Java to call up "Webra" and you'll get assistance. If you want to create animation for your Web site, use Java to call up "Dimension X" and you get programs to create animation with just a few mouse clicks. Each time the program is needed you call up Java and it comes across the Net, then leaves when you're finished. As with the Java example, these applets (short applications or mini-programs) can be retrieved from many suppliers' Web sites, they perform a specific function, then disappear after the user is finished. One danger is that when you import these just-in-time programs they may carry viruses that infect users' systems, so security is a problem.[23]

The Net's power to change the way business is conducted has already been amply demonstrated. Digital Equipment Corp., for instance, is a heavy Internet user: With more than 31,000 computers connected to the network, DEC's monthly e-mail volume has jumped to an average of 700,000 messages. DEC has also linked its new Alpha AXP high-speed business computer to the Internet so that potential buyers and software developers can spend time using and evaluating it. Gail Grant, Internet administrator at DEC, reports that in just a few months, 2,500 computer users in 27 countries have taken advantage of the opportunity to explore the Alpha AXP.

The Net has also benefitted small companies, especially as a means of expanding market research and improving customer service.[24] In Ann Arbor, Michigan, Grant's Flowers and Greenhouses has used the Net to establish an international presence. Owner Larry Grant reports that the Net now generates nearly as many orders as FTD. "We're getting orders from all over the country," he reports. "We even got an order from someone in Japan." "Basically," confirms Jon R. Zeef, the Internet service provider who put Grant's Flowers on the Net for a $28 monthly fee, "your small-town store can suddenly have an international presence in a cost-effective manner."[25]

World Wide Web

World Wide Web
Subsystem of computers providing access to the Internet and offering multimedia and linking capabilities

Thanks to a subsystem of 7,000 computers known as the **World Wide Web** (WWW, or simply the Web), the Internet is easier to use than ever before. It has made the Internet usable to a general audience, rather than just to technical users. The Federal Express Web site, for example, gives customers access to the FedEx package-tracking database. Each day up to 12,000 customers look through the FedEx Web pages and find out the status of their packages without any help from FedEx employees. This customer self-help saves FedEx up to $2 million each year.

The computers linked by the Web are known as Web servers. They are owned by corporations, colleges, government agencies, and other large organizations. There are now well over 200,000 such sites serving up tens of millions of pages of publicly accessible information.[26] The user can connect with the Web by means of **browser** software (such as Netscape, Netcruiser, WebExplorer, and Mosaic). Browsers support the graphics and linking capabilities needed to navigate the Web. The user must simply point and click, and experts predict that as more people become familiar with browsers, the number of Net users will grow by 10 to 15 percent a month. Netscape Navigator currently enjoys an 80-percent market share, although it is being challenged by new entries, including its own Netscape Communicator and Microsoft Corp.'s Explorer.

Among the most successful enterprises to take advantage of the Web are those that operate search engines. Companies such as InfoSeek, Lycos, and Yahoo maintain free-to-use public directories of the Web's ever-increasing content. These indexes constantly scan the Web to stay up to date. A search engine may respond to approximately 10 million inquiries per day. It is thus no surprise that search engines are packed with paid ads placed by companies such as Honda and AT&T.

Intranets

The success of the Internet has led some companies to extend the Net's technology internally, for browsing internal Web sites containing information throughout the firm. These private networks, or **intranets**, are accessible only to employees via entry through electronic firewalls. At Compaq Computer Corp., the intranet allows employees to shuffle their retirement savings among various investment funds. Ford Motor Co.'s intranet, with links to design centers in Asia, Europe, and the United States, helped engineers design the 1996 Taurus. A major advantage of these intranets is their use of a more standardized electronic system for information storage and access. The revolutionary new information links were previously impossible among departments and offices separated by distance or by incompatible software, computers, and databases. The new technology uses a more standardized system based on the same structure used in the Internet.[27]

Multimedia Communication Systems

Today's information systems include not only computers but also **multimedia communication systems**: connected networks of communication appliances such as faxes, televisions, sound equipment, cell phones, printing machines, and photocopiers that may also be linked with such mass media as TV and radio broadcast programming, news and other print publications, and library collections. Not surprisingly, the integration of these elements is already changing the ways we live our lives and manage our businesses. A good example is T. Rowe Price's TeleAccess, a customer service in which investors make their own financial transactions by interacting with a computer on the phone, or use their home computers to track their investments and electronically change their portfolios.

Multimedia Technology

Multimedia communication technology is profoundly expanding the applications of PCs. Today's programs incorporate sound, animation, and photography as well as ordinary graphics and text. Communication power has multiplied through on-line information services such as Prodigy and CompuServe that provide instant access to financial and news data. Electronic discussion groups and business meetings display interactive dialogue on screens for the benefit of conference callers in widespread locations. America Online, for example, has some 14,000 chat rooms that allow PC users to exchange electronic messages in real time.[28] Today's PCs have built-in TV circuits so that you can tune in your favorite TV show on the computer monitor, watch movies from CD-ROMs, and listen to your favorite music.

Communication Channels. Communication channels are the media that make all these transmissions possible. These include coaxial and fiberoptic cable and infrared, microwave, and satellite transmission. In particular, the use of satellite channels is increasing to meet the growing demand for wireless transmission. GE's Technical Response Center, shown in the photo on page 468 illustrates the value of satellites for improving aircraft

browser
Software supporting the graphics and linking capabilities necessary to navigate the World Wide Web

intranet
Private network of internal Web sites and other sources of information available to a company's employees

multimedia communication system
Connected network of communication appliances (such as faxes or TVs) that may be linked to forms of mass media (such as print publications or TV programming)

Demonstrating how computers have changed communications, these engineers at GE's corporate research and development center can monitor engines in flight from the ground via satellite. The new system can diagnose potential engine problems, plan for maintenance or overhaul, and resolve problems more quickly than ever. In addition to improving safety and reliability, real-time remote monitoring and diagnostics can lower operating costs for airlines by reducing delays and cancellations.

engine maintenance and safety.[29] With wireless systems instead of fiber cables underground, laser beams or radio waves will transmit signals from satellite to satellite. Using satellite networks under development by McCaw, Hughes, Motorola, AT&T, and Loral, the Net becomes accessible in remote areas where underground cable isn't feasible; all the world is within instant reach on the Internet.[30] Most of us use communication channels when we use some type of telephone system. Even today, however, the bulk of telephone transmissions are data, not conversations. Fax data account for 90 percent of all telephone signals between the United States and Japan.

The need for more capacity in communication channels is the biggest factor in the push toward more sophisticated wireless technology. In conjunction with electronics and communication giants such as IBM, Motorola, BellSouth, and McCaw Cellular Communications, specialty firms such as Ardis, Ram Mobile Data, Metricom, and Orbcomm are developing wireless devices that use credit-card–size modems to transmit data over radio signals traveling from tiny PCs to a series of strategically placed receivers. Experts expect such devices to find a ready market among businesspeople who cannot afford to be out of touch.

Smart Software.   Software for many multimedia components actually permits them to perform some activities automatically. Smart modems perform such functions as dialing, answering the phone, and transmitting. Smart TVs remember your program preferences, remind you of upcoming programs, and even make suggestions for your viewing pleasure. Similar software is available for watches, ovens, automobiles, airplanes, and air conditioners. Software is also available for integrating the activities of multimedia hardware. Microsoft at Work, for example, can be installed in office equipment hardware (phones, fax machines, copiers) so that they can all be controlled by PCs.[31]

Information Technology and the Paperless Workplace

A realistic possibility stemming from modern information technology is the emergence of the paperless workplace, without paperwork and, more importantly, the delays that come with it. At Chaparral Steel, for example, there are no file cabinets in the accounting department, and information is stored as images on laser disks. When a packing slip arrives from an outside vendor it is scanned, indexed, and filed electronically. To call up the data, accounting managers can access the index from desktop PCs. In the same way, all documents generated from within the company are electronically transmitted from the mainframe to the scanning unit. "Our goal," says Jack Loteryman, Chaparral's Manager of Information Systems, "is to have information flowing among departments so customer orders are processed faster. A sales order would flow at once to quality control, manufacturing, and engineering and would be immediately added to the general ledger."

Although the accounting department is leading the way in eliminating paperwork, the rest of the company is rapidly working in the same direction. "Who needs paper anyway?" asks Loteryman. "And, besides, every company wants to be 'green.'"

" Who needs paper anyway?"

—Jack Loteryman, manager of information systems, Chaparral Steel

Summary of Learning Objectives
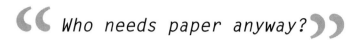

1 **Show why businesses must manage information and show how computers have revolutionized information management.** Because businesses are faced with an overwhelming amount of data and information about customers, competitors, and their own operations, the ability to manage this information can mean the difference between success and failure. Because of their speed, accuracy, storage capabilities, and ability to make comparisons, computers have emerged as a powerful tool for information management.

2 **Identify and briefly describe the main elements of a computer system.** Hardware is a computer's physical components. It consists of an input device (such as a keyboard), a central processing unit (CPU), disk drives, a main memory (hard disk), diskettes for data storage, and output devices (such as video monitors and printers). Software includes the computer's operating system and applications such as spreadsheets, graphics programs, and programs for word processing and desktop publishing.

People are also part of the computer system. Systems analysts, for example, design systems, and programmers write instructions. Operations personnel run the computers, and users log onto computers to obtain and manipulate the data needed to perform their jobs. Control is important to ensure not only that the system operates correctly but also that data and information are transmitted through secure channels to people who really need them.

3 **Identify the role played by databases and describe four important types of business applications programs.** Through sequences of instructions called programs, computers are able to process data and perform specific functions. Once data (raw facts and figures) are centralized and organized into meaningful databases, they can be manipulated, sorted, combined, or compared according to program instructions.

Four major types of applications programs for businesses are word processing (which allows computers to act like sophisticated typewriters), electronic spreadsheets (which enter data in rows and columns and perform calculations), database management (which organizes and retrieves a company's relevant data), and graphics (which convert numeric and character data into pictorial information).

4 **Classify computer systems by size and structure.** Computers can be classified according to cost, capacity, and capability. The smallest, slowest, and least expensive computers are microcomputers. The largest, fastest, and most expensive are supercomputers. Minicomputers and mainframes fall in between, but these distinctions are beginning to blur. In contrast, computer systems differ sharply in architecture. In centralized systems, most processing is done from one location, using a centralized database. In decentralized systems, each location handles its own processing from its own database. Computer networks allow branch computers to communicate, offering some of the advantages of both centralized and decentralized systems.

5 **List some trends in the application of computer technology to business information management.** The next generation of computing promises exciting developments in information management. Recent advances include artificial intelligence (programming computers to imitate human thought processes), expert systems

(which try to imitate the behavior of experts in a given field), office information technologies (which includes fax machines, voice mail, and e-mail for streamlining communication), executive information systems (which provide upper-level managers with easy access to information), and operations information systems (which increase operations productivity). All of these technologies assist businesspeople in making decisions and solving problems.

Multimedia communication systems link connected networks of communication appliances (such as faxes and cell phones) with such mass media as print publications and TV programming. New technology for multimedia has made on-line information services available, along with electronic discussion groups and interactive on-screen dialogue. Data communication networks such as the Internet and the World Wide Web permit users to send electronic messages and video and audio information quickly and economically.

6 **Identify how the Internet and the World Wide Web are affecting information management.** These global networks carry information from documents, video, and sound back and forth quickly and economically on telecommunication systems. They give millions of people and companies access to remote technical and commercial information for improving business operations. Instant communication through e-mail provides up-to-the-minute status reports. Business transactions, from beginning dialogue through product exposure to closing the sale, can be conducted nearly instantaneously through remote video and sound interaction. Users can access Web sites to discover various companies' product offerings, make purchases, and network with remote groups in electronic chat rooms. For software developers and users, the Internet provides a new channel for distributing, retrieving, and temporarily using myriad new applications programs (applets) quickly, thus avoiding the cost of buying and permanently installing them on the user's computer.

Questions and Exercises

Questions for Review

1 Why does a business need to manage information as a resource?
2 Describe the components of a computer system. Explain how each of the parts is related to the others.
3 Rank microcomputers, minicomputers, mainframes, and supercomputers according to cost, processing speed, and capacity.
4 Why has miniaturization been so crucial to the latest developments in computer and communication technology?
5 How can an e-mail system increase office productivity and efficiency?

Questions for Analysis

6 Give two examples (other than those in this chapter) for each of the four major types of applications programs used in businesses.
7 Describe the types of work or activities for which a local department store might choose to use batch processing. Do the same for real-time processing.
8 Describe three or four activities in which you regularly engage that might be made easier by multimedia technology.
9 Analyze the ways in which businesses will be affected by the change to wireless from wire and cable communication technologies.

Application Exercises

10 Describe the computer system at your college or university. Identify its components, capacity and speed, and architecture.

11 Visit a small business in your community to investigate the ways that it is using computers and communication technology and the ways it plans to use them in the future. Prepare a report for presentation in class.

Building Your Business Skills

This exercise enhances the following SCANS workplace competencies: demonstrating basic skills, demonstrating thinking skills, exhibiting interpersonal skills, working with information, applying system knowledge, and using technology.

Goal To encourage students to understand the difference between World Wide Web directories and search engines and to compare the usefulness of each tool in a research project.

Background The World Wide Web is jam-packed with information. The challenge is to access sites that have the information you need. Among the most useful mechanisms for navigating the Web are search engines and directories. Whereas search engines index every word at a Web site, directories catalog information into subject categories, subcategories, and subsubcategories. Search engines pull up the largest number of sites, but are more difficult to use because of the sheer volume of material.

Yahoo! (http://www.yahoo.com) and the Britannica Information Guide (http://www.ebig.com) are directories, whereas altavista (http://altavista.digital.com), excite (http://www.excite.com), hotbot (http://www.hotbot.com), infoseek (http://www.infoseek.com), and lycos (http://www.lycos.com) are search engines.

Method **Step 1:** Divide into groups of four or five people. Then choose a business-related research topic that interests every group member. It could be a company such as Coca-Cola or CBS, a business leader such as Microsoft CEO Bill Gates or Federal Reserve Chairman Allan Greenspan, or a current issue such as business ethics, Internet marketing, or product liability. Working with group members, narrow your topic so it is manageable. For example, you might choose to investigate product liability cases related to automobile air bags or the changes in corporate leadership at Coca-Cola after the death in 1997 of chairperson and CEO Roberto C. Goizueta.

Step 2: Go to the directories and search engines listed in this exercise. Start by reading through each site's help section for search advice. Focus on advanced search commands that will help narrow results. For example, you will learn that using quotation marks around a phrase means that the directory or search engine will look for the phrase instead of the separate words that make up the phrase.

Step 3: Type your topic into the directories and search engines listed in this exercise. Working with group members, analyze each response list to determine where you got the most useful results.

Follow-Up Questions

1 Which site gave you the most useful information?
2 What differences did you notice between the broad categories of directories and search engines?
3 What differences did you notice between specific directories and among specific search engines?
4 What mechanisms did you discover to help you conduct successful future searches?
5 What directory or search engine would you go to first with your next research question? Why?
6 How has the World Wide Web changed the nature of business research?

Is Your Computer a Television?
Or Is Your TV a Computer?

Picture yourself watching the World Series on TV and using a wireless keyboard to open a window on the television screen. Now you can download the pitcher's career stats from the team's home page on the Internet without even missing an out.

There is little doubt in most observers' minds that some day soon the functions of the family television and the home office computer will be joined in a single machine. Whether that machine will be a computer that picks up TV feeds from the Internet, or a TV with computer and Internet capabilities, is a question that threatens to shake up both the computer and television manufacturing industries, with broadcasters caught in the middle.

In an escalating series of news conferences, product unveilings, and sweeping statements about the future as they see it, executives of consumer electronics firms and computer makers have been squaring off for several years. Neither has had much success breaking into the other's market yet, but neither is giving up any time soon. Gateway 2000 Inc., which makes PCs, also sells a big-screen computer television under the brand name Destination. Several electronics firms have marketed Web TV devices that allow users to access the Internet on conventional TVs. Sales of both products have been disappointing.

By most estimates, 99 percent of U.S. households own one or more TVs, and about 40 percent own a personal computer. Both industries are assuming that with the arrival of digital or high-definition television technology, people will have to begin replacing their TVs before the scheduled end of conventional broadcasting in 2006. With the prospect of $150 billion in revenues just from sales of the new sets, the stakes are high for what may be the biggest market shakeout of the computer age.

PC makers want to produce their television pictures in a format incompatible with the one that broadcasters use, which uses 525 lines per screen but gets higher resolution than normal with extra channel capacity. TV manufacturers, anticipating the announced plans of major broadcasters who lobbied hard for—and secured—the right to broadcast HDTV, expect to produce high-definition TVs or PC/TVs that accept 1,080 lines per screen. The Federal Communication Commission (FCC) has urged an agreement over technology and doesn't want to arbitrate the coming clash.

The computer industry is counting on the decline of television viewing and the rise of the Internet to change the way people use their TVs.

It's already clear that most browsing on the Net is occurring during television's traditional prime time hours. And "we think it is much easier to have a PC do television than to add personal computing capabilities to TVs," says Intel executive Rob Siegal. "The PC has just got to migrate from the home office to the family room." In fact, within the next year, every new PC sold in the United States will include a digital TV receiver as standard equipment, and computer industry executives expect to sell 40 million PCs with digital TV decoders by the year 2002.

Consumer electronics firms, even while they explore the interactive potential, defend the simplicity and single function of their traditional product, the television set. "I think people will buy these (digital) TVs for entertainment—a great high-definition picture on a big screen," says Richard Kraft, president of Matsushita Electric's U.S. subsidiary, which makes the Panasonic and Quasar brands. Sony's president, Carl Yankowski, says, "One of the reasons we are ubiquitous in American homes is that TVs are simple and easy to use." But in the meantime, broadcasters have slowed their drive toward

> ❝ *All of a sudden we got this thing approved, and nobody has a clue what they are going to do.* ❞
>
> —Michael Jordan, chairperson of Westinghouse Electric Corp.

HDTV, risking Congressional ire if they miss federal deadlines for broadcasting. Says Michael Jordan, chairperson of Westinghouse Electric Corp. which owns CBS, "All of a sudden we got this thing approved, and nobody has a clue what they are going to do."

Those in the computer camp counter that with the new digital technology, the "PC theater," a computer that combines traditional TV programming with computer functions, will be transparently easy to use. But is it what the customer ordered? Jim Meyer, vice president of Thomson Consumer Electronics, which makes the RCA and Proscan brands, doesn't think so. "I'm not 100 percent convinced that interactivity is going to be the service that drives this product," he says. "Interactivity may sell in Silicon Valley. But will it sell in Gary (Indiana)? I don't know."

Questions

1 The combination of broadcast and computing functions in a single machine is known in the communication industry as convergence. Do you think convergence is an idea whose time has come? Why or why not?

2 Do you think consumers place greater value on simplicity of use or functionality? Which do you prefer?

3 Television networks are concentrating on perfecting digital high-definition programming and getting it on the air by 1999, as mandated by the FCC. For now they are not planning any of the kind of interactive programming that computer makers want to offer with their PC/TVs. How might a change in the networks' plans affect the computer and consumer electronics industries? How do you think the networks should use whatever power they have to influence the outcome?

4 Do you foresee any way in which computer and television makers can successfully divide the consumer computing and entertainment markets between them? What would this mean for the consumer?

5 Why might the FCC be unwilling to mandate a solution to the problem of incompatible technologies? Do you agree with the FCC's decision to force the market to choose?

Connecting to the Web

The following Web sites will give you additional information and points of view about topics covered in this chapter. Many sites lead to other related Internet locations, so approach this list with the spirit of an explorer.

BRØDERBUND SOFTWARE

http://www.broderbund.com

This site introduces Brøderbund's computer software and CD-ROMs, including Encyclopaedia Britannica's CD-ROM Multimedia Edition and the Print Shop graphics program.

FEDEX STANDARD TRACKING

http://www.fedex.com/track_it.html

Visit the FedEx Web site to see how easy it is to track a FedEx package any time, anywhere in the world.

JAVA COMPUTING

http://www.sun.com/javastation/index.html

The software language developed by Sun Microsystem's Java unit offers a range of Internet strategies that facilitate communication.

MICROSOFT CORPORATION HOME PAGE

http://www.microsoft.com/microsoft.htm

Visit the Microsoft home page to learn about the Microsoft products and services that have defined and revolutionized the information age.

NATIONAL DEFENSE UNIVERSITY: INFORMATION RESOURCES MANAGEMENT COLLEGE

http://www.ndu.edu

Click on the Informational Resources Management College to learn what the 14-week graduate-level program run by the U.S. Army offers senior executives. The site describes program goals.

PERSPECTIVES OF THE SMITHSONIAN: SMITHSONIAN COMPUTER HISTORY

http://www.si.edu/resource/tours/comp_hist/computer.htm

Take an on-line tour of the Smithsonian's division of computers to learn about computer history, to locate computer links around the world, to study the accomplishments of award-winning computer scientists, and more.

QUARKXPRESS

http://www.quark.com/qxp001.htm

This site introduces the features of the integrated publishing package QuarkXPress, which lets users combine text, pictures, typography, writing, editing, and printing.

WELCOME TO McAFEE

http://www.mcafee.com/main.asp

McAfee, a world leader in network scanning and security services, offers powerful antivirus programs and security services that prevent thieves and hackers from stealing data from computer networks.

WELCOME TO NETSCAPE

http://www.netscape.com/

This site introduces the Netscape browser and other Internet communication software.

YAHOO!

http://www.yahoo.com/

The Yahoo! directory categorizes and accesses data on the World Wide Web according to specific user requests. Visit the site, plug in a request, and see what sites Yahoo! brings up.

chapter 18

Understanding
principles of
accounting

Too shady even for an audit?

Things are changing in the usually stable world of accounting. Mergers, acquisitions, competition, advertising campaigns, and new services are some of the trends. Another change is less positive: Since the early 1990s accounting firms have paid an unprecedented $1 billion to settle civil lawsuits that have been brought against them. The charges revolved around financial frauds and scandals that went undetected by accountants' audits. Investors who lost out in the disasters that followed wanted to blame somebody, and the accounting profession woke up fast.

New standards have just been enacted by the Auditing Standards Board of the accounting profession's governing body, the American Institute of Certified Public Accountants (AICPA). Unlike past standards—which Dan Guy, an AICPA vice president, admits "obviously didn't do the job"—the new rules require auditors to look actively for a checklist of specific risk factors in a firm. For example, are earnings growing while cash flow isn't? Is management too aggressively pursuing revenue targets? Are those targets unrealistic? "Instead of a nebulous and unspecified means of testing for fraud, now you've got a checklist," says accounting professor William Coyle at Babson College, Massachusetts. "This is a significant change."

The intent is to focus auditors' efforts and to give them the means to document their assessment of the audited firm. What still worries some critics, however, is the potential for abuse to occur because of the commercial relationship between auditors and their clients. Accounting firms may want to sell other, more profitable services to the clients they audit, such as tax preparation and financial consulting. The possibility of booking future business, say skeptics, will tempt auditors to overlook potential fraud at a client firm.

One cure would be for accounting firms to restructure their pricing so that audits alone could bring in enough profit to make objectivity pay for itself. Whether that happens, and whether the temptation to collude with shady clients is really that great, time and the new standards will tell. If nothing else, the stricter rules should encourage accountants to look more critically at future clients. After all, would you really want to work with a firm that showed every risk indicator of fraud?

  ❝ *Instead of a nebulous and unspecified means of testing for fraud, now you've got a checklist. This is a significant change.* **❞**

—William Coyle, accounting professor at Babson College, MA

Of all the business disciplines, probably none has the universal reach of accounting, which is found in nearly every community in the world. In most businesses, accountants play a role in virtually all activities. By focusing on the learning objectives of this chapter, you will become acquainted with accountants: who they are, what they do, what concepts and rules they apply, and how these rules are formulated. You will also understand more about the most important part of accounting: the basic financial reports of economic activity that are the primary reason for accounting. After reading this chapter, you should be able to

1 Explain the role of accountants and distinguish between the kinds of work done by public and private accountants.

2 Explain how the following three concepts are used in recordkeeping: the accounting equation, double-entry accounting, and T-accounts for debits and credits.

3 Describe the three basic financial statements and show how they reflect the activity and financial condition of a business.

4 Discuss the importance of budgets in internal planning and control.

5 Explain how computing key financial ratios can help in analyzing the financial strengths of a business.

6 Explain some of the special issues facing accountants at firms that do international business.

What Is Accounting and Who Uses Accounting Information?

accounting
Comprehensive system for collecting, analyzing, and communicating financial information

Accounting is a comprehensive system for collecting, analyzing, and communicating financial information. It is a system for measuring business performance and translating those measures into information for management decisions. Accounting also uses performance measures to prepare performance reports for owners, the public, and regulatory agencies. To meet these objectives, accountants keep records of such transactions as taxes paid, income received, and expenses incurred. They also analyze the effects of these transactions on particular business activities. By sorting, analyzing, and recording thousands of transactions, accountants can determine how well a business is being managed and how financially strong it is.

bookkeeping
The recording of accounting transactions

Bookkeeping, which is sometimes confused with accounting, is just one phase of accounting: the recording of accounting transactions. Clearly, accounting is much more comprehensive than bookkeeping because accounting involves more than just the recording of information.

accounting system
Organized means by which financial information is identified, measured, recorded, and retained for use in accounting statements and management reports

Because businesses engage in many thousands of transactions, ensuring consistent, dependable financial information is mandatory. This is the job of the **accounting system**: an organized procedure for identifying, measuring, recording, and retaining financial information so that it can be used in accounting statements and management reports. The system includes all the people, reports, computers, procedures, and resources for compiling financial transactions.[1]

Users of Accounting Information

On November 18, 1997, Noranda Inc., Canada's biggest natural resource company, announced plans to refocus on the mining and metals side of its activities by selling its forest products and oil and natural gas interests. In preparation for the announcement, corporate officers relied on accounting to provide information for everyone who might be interested in the firm's activities. Its 49-percent ownership of Norcen Energy Resources Ltd. will be sold. Its oil and gas subsidiary, Canadian Hunter Exploration Ltd., will be distributed as a dividend to Noranda shareholders, as will its interest in Noranda Forest Inc., a forest products company. A statement issued to shareholders and the public will show clearly how much each of the three segments contributed to Noranda's overall sales, expenses, and earnings. Current and potential stockholders will also be told how the new stock shares will be distributed.[2]

Noranda accountants must tabulate financial projections for the separation because stakeholders have important questions about the soon-to-be three companies: Do the business prospects indicate that as separate companies they are good credit risks? As investments, will they pay sufficient financial returns to owners? Have adequate arrangements been made for employee retirement funds and benefits? Do their business prospects look healthy enough to support current employment levels? Upon receiving accounting answers to questions such as these, different information users (owners, employees, regulatory agencies, lenders, and the public) are better prepared to make decisions for themselves and for their organizations.

As the Noranda example illustrates, there are numerous users of accounting information:

- *Business managers* use accounting information to set goals, develop plans, set budgets, and evaluate future prospects.

- *Employees and unions* use accounting information to get paid and to plan for and receive such benefits as health care, insurance, vacation time, and retirement pay.

- *Investors and creditors* use accounting information to estimate returns to stockholders, determine a company's growth prospects, and determine whether it is a good credit risk before investing or lending.

■ *Tax authorities* use accounting information to plan for tax inflows, determine the tax liabilities of individuals and businesses, and ensure that correct amounts are paid on time.

■ *Government regulatory agencies* rely on accounting information to fulfill their duties. The Toronto Stock Exchange in Canada and the Securities and Exchange Commission in the United States, for example, require firms to file financial disclosures so that potential investors have valid information about a company's financial status.

Who Are Accountants and What Do They Do?

At the head of the accounting system is the **controller**, who manages all the firm's accounting activities. As chief accounting officer, the controller ensures that the accounting system provides the reports and statements needed for planning, controlling, and decision-making activities. This broad range of activities requires different types of accounting specialists. In this section we will begin by distinguishing between the two main fields of accounting: financial and managerial. Then we will discuss the different functions and activities of certified public accountants and private accountants.

controller
Person who manages all of a firm's accounting activities (chief accounting officer)

Financial Versus Managerial Accounting

In any company, two fields of accounting (financial and managerial) can be distinguished by the different users they serve. As we have just seen, it is both convenient and accurate to classify users of accounting information as users outside the company and users inside the company. This same distinction allows us to categorize accounting systems as either financial or managerial.

Financial Accounting

A firm's **financial accounting system** is concerned with external users of information: consumer groups, unions, stockholders, and government agencies. It prepares and publishes income statements and balance sheets at regular intervals, as well as other financial reports that are published for shareholders and the general public. All of these documents focus on the activities of the company as a whole, rather than on individual departments or divisions.

financial accounting system
Field of accounting concerned with external users of a company's financial information

In reporting data, financial accountants must conform to standard reporting formats and procedures imposed by both the accounting profession and government agencies. This requirement helps ensure that users can clearly compare information, whether from many different companies or from the same company at different times. The information in such reports is mostly historical; that is, it summarizes financial transactions that have occurred during past accounting periods.

Managerial Accounting

In contrast, **managerial** (or **management**) **accounting** serves internal users. Managers at all levels need information to make decisions for their departments, to monitor current projects, and to plan for future activities. Other employees also need accounting information. Engineers, for instance, want to know the costs for materials and production so that they can make product or operations improvements. To set performance goals, salespeople need data on past sales by geographic region. Purchasing agents use information on materials costs to negotiate terms with suppliers.

managerial (or management) accounting system
Field of accounting that serves internal users of a company's financial information

Reports to these users serve the company's individual units, whether departments, projects, plants, or divisions. Internal reports may be designed in any form that will assist internal users in planning, decision-making, and controlling. Furthermore, as projections and forecasts of both financial data and business activities, internal reports are an extremely important part of the management accounting system: They are forward-looking rather than historical in nature.

Certified Public Accountants

certified public accountant (CPA)
Accountant licensed by the state and offering services to the public

Certified public accountants (CPAs) offer accounting services to the public. CPAs are licensed at the state level after passing a 3-day written exam prepared by the American Institute of Certified Public Accountants (AICPA), which is the national professional organization of CPAs. The AICPA also provides technical support to members and discipline in matters of professional ethics.[3]

Professional Practice and the Big 4

Whereas some CPAs work as individual practitioners, many join with one or more other CPAs in partnerships or professional corporations. More than 40,000 CPA firms practice in the United States. However, nearly one-half of accounting's total revenues in the United States are received by the so-called Big 6 (soon to be the Big 4) accounting firms: Arthur Andersen & Company, Coopers & Lybrand, Deloitte and Touche, Ernst & Young, KPMG Peat Marwick, and Price Waterhouse & Co.[4] The merger of Coopers & Lybrand with price Waterhouse is planned for December 1997. Then, in 1998 Ernst & Young is expected to merge with KPMG, leaving just four "Big" firms. In addition to their prominence in the United States, international growth into worldwide accounting operations is a major expansion area for Big 4 firms.

CPA Services

Virtually all CPA firms, whether consisting of 10,000 employees in 100 nationwide offices or just one person in a small private facility, provide auditing, tax, and management services. Larger firms earn 60 to 70 percent of their revenue from auditing services. Smaller firms typically earn most of their income from tax and management services.

audit
Systematic examination of a company's accounting system to determine whether its financial reports fairly represent its operations

Auditing.   An **audit** examines a company's accounting system to determine whether its financial reports fairly present its operations. Companies must normally provide audit reports when applying for loans or selling stock. In 1996, for example, auditors from the accounting firm Deloitte and Touche disclosed that Baby Superstore Inc., a competitor of Toys Я Us, may have overstated cash reserves in its 1996 financial statements. An imme-

As a retailer of both toys and childcare products, Toys 'Я' Us experiences a wide range of turnover rates. For example, seasonal toys turn over less than three times per year. On the other hand, baby formula and diapers turn over more than 12 times annually. The average for an entire store is about three times per year. The highest and lowest points? October 31 and January 31, respectively. The benefits of high turnover include fewer markdowns and less depreciation, lower inventory expenses (such as storage and insurance costs), and a higher rate of return on inventory investment.

diate result of the disclosure was a 29-percent plunge in the share price of Baby Superstore stock. Company officials hastened to report that the overstatement was a result of its accounting procedures, not of any illegal or improper management conduct.[5]

The auditor must also ensure that the client's accounting system follows **generally accepted accounting principles (GAAP)**: rules and procedures governing the content and form of financial reports. GAAPs are formulated by the Financial Accounting Standards Board (FASB) of the AICPA.[6] By using GAAP, the audit should determine whether a firm has controls to prevent errors and fraud. Ultimately, the auditor will certify whether the client's financial reports comply with GAAP.

generally accepted accounting principles (GAAP)
Accepted rules and procedures governing the content and form of financial reports

Tax Services.   Tax laws are immensely complex. Tax services thus include assistance not only with tax return preparation but also with tax planning. A CPA's advice, for example, can help a business structure (or restructure) operations and investments and perhaps save millions of dollars in taxes. In order to best serve their clients, accountants must stay abreast of changes in tax laws. This is no simple matter: Legislators made more than 70 pages of technical corrections to the 1986 Tax Reform Act before it even became law.

Management Advisory Services.   When hired as consultants, accounting firms provide **management advisory services** ranging from personal financial planning to planning corporate mergers. Other services include plant layout and design, production scheduling, computer feasibility studies, and accounting system design. Some CPA firms even assist in executive recruitment. On staff at the largest firms are engineers, architects, mathematicians, and psychologists.

management advisory services
Specialized accounting services to help managers resolve a variety of business problems

The Workplace Environment

Closing the Gender Cap in Accounting

If you thought the accounting profession was male-dominated, think again. According to a recent study by researchers at Bentley College, Massachusetts, women now account for an impressive 55 percent of bachelor's degrees in accounting, up from less than 10 percent in 1970. Women also make up 77 percent of graduates with associate's degrees in the subject. In fact, slightly more than half of all U.S. accountants are female, double the percentage in the legal and medical professions.

That's the good news. The Bentley College researchers concluded that women may have gone as far in accounting as they can, for now. Men are getting interested in the profession again, and many new hires at accounting firms are men, some in related fields that don't require degrees in accounting. And once hired, some female accountants may be rejecting the long hours and rigid schedules required to make partner in the firm. At the moment only about 13 percent of accounting partners are female. A sizable number of

women in accounting are paraprofessionals with lesser degrees and correspondingly lower pay.

These statistics raise the question of whether accounting will respond to its new-found diversity with family-friendly benefits to attract and keep female employees, or whether it will solidify into a two-tiered profession with higher-paid jobs for men at the top and lower-paying jobs for women at the bottom.

There is some encouraging news. The accounting firm of Ernst & Young has undertaken an unusually thorough effort to retain its female professionals by changing the way the firm is managed. "It's like this revelation," says Mary Stern, a tax manager at the firm. Planned to last a year and intended to combat reported bias toward men, the campaign will take ambitious steps to reduce the job stress felt by both men and women but particularly by women, who tend to have a working spouse and correspondingly greater personal and family needs. Flexible schedules, a ban on weekend e-mail, and a broader range of acceptable client-entertainment activities that includes family-friendly picnics and ballgames are some of the innovations the firm will make.

Can the profession be changed in time? Stay tuned.

Noncertified Public Accountants

Many accountants choose not to take the CPA exam; others work in the field while preparing to take it or while fulfilling requirements for state certification. Many small businesses, individuals, and even larger firms rely on these noncertified public accountants for income tax preparation, payroll accounting, and financial planning services.

Private Accountants

private accountant
Salaried accountant hired by a business to carry out its day-to-day financial activities

To ensure integrity in reporting, CPAs are always independent of the firms they audit. As employees of accounting firms, they provide services for many clients. However, many businesses also hire their own salaried employees—**private accountants**—to carry out day-to-day activities.

Private accountants perform a variety of jobs. An internal auditor at Phillips Petroleum, for example, might fly to the North Sea to confirm the accuracy of oil flow meters on offshore drilling platforms. Meanwhile, a supervisor responsible for $2 billion in monthly accounts payable to vendors and employees may travel no farther than the executive suite. Large businesses employ specialized accountants in such areas as budgets, financial planning, internal auditing, payroll, and taxation. In small businesses, a single person may handle all accounting tasks.

certified management accountant (CMA)
Certified accountant specializing in management accounting

As we have already seen, most private accountants are management accountants who provide services to support company managers in a variety of activities (marketing, production, engineering, and so forth). Management accountants who become **certified management accountants (CMAs)** are recognized as professional specialists. Certification is granted by the Institute of Management Accounting.[7]

Tools of the Accounting Trade

All accountants rely on recordkeeping to enter and track business transactions. Underlying all recordkeeping procedures are the three key concepts of accounting: the accounting equation, double-entry accounting, and T-accounts for debits and credits.

Record Keeping with Journals and Ledgers

As Figure 18.1 shows, recordkeeping begins with initial records of a firm's financial transactions. These transactions include sales orders, invoices for incoming materials, employee time cards, and customer installment payments. Large companies receive and

Figure 18.1   Accounting and Recordkeeping

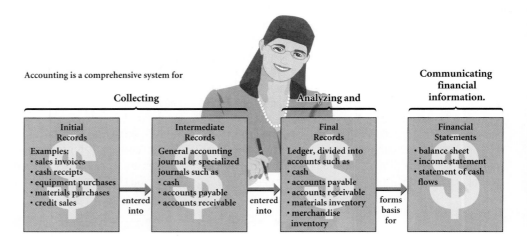

Accounting is a comprehensive system for			Communicating financial information.
Collecting		Analyzing and	
Initial Records	**Intermediate Records**	**Final Records**	**Financial Statements**
Examples: • sales invoices • cash receipts • equipment purchases • materials purchases • credit sales	General accounting journal or specialized journals such as • cash • accounts payable • accounts receivable	Ledger, divided into accounts such as • cash • accounts payable • accounts receivable • materials inventory • merchandise inventory	• balance sheet • income statement • statement of cash flows
	entered into	entered into	forms basis for

process tens of thousands of these documents every day. For example, before switching to credit cards with magnetic strips, Amoco Oil Co. received 650,000 sales receipts daily. Each receipt represented a transaction. Of course, few companies today are deluged with such waves of paper, but even in the age of digitized information flows, managers can track and control a company's progress only if its transactions are analyzed and classified in an orderly fashion.

Journals and Ledgers

As initial records are received, they are sorted and entered into a **journal**: a chronological record of financial transactions, including a brief description of each. They are now intermediate records. Most companies keep specialized journals for different transactions, such as cash receipts, sales, and purchases.

Journal transactions are summarized, usually on a monthly basis, in a final record called the **ledger**. In the term *auditing the books*, the book is the ledger. Like specialized journals, the ledger is divided into accounts, such as cash, inventories, and receivables. The cash account, for example, is a detailed record of all the firm's changes in cash. Other accounts record changes in each type of asset and liability. Ledgers also feature an important column labeled *Balance*, which shows the current total dollar amount in each account. If a balance in a given account is unexpectedly high or low, tracking backward to the corresponding journal entry should reveal the cause of the unexpected figure.

Financial Reports and the Fiscal Year

At the end of the year, all the accounts in the ledger are totaled, and the firm's financial status is assessed. This summation is the basis for annual financial reports. With the preparation of reports, the old accounting cycle ends and a new cycle begins. The timing of the annual accounting cycle is called the **fiscal year**: the 12-month period used for financial reporting purposes. Although most companies adopt the calendar year, many companies use 12-month periods that reflect the seasonal nature of their industries. For example, to close its fiscal year at the completion of harvesting, a fruit orchard may select the period from September 1, 1998, to August 31, 1999.

journal
Chronological record of a firm's financial transactions, including a brief description of each

ledger
Record, divided into accounts and usually compiled on a monthly basis, containing summaries of all journal transactions

fiscal year
Twelve-month period designated for annual financial reporting purposes

Figure 18.2

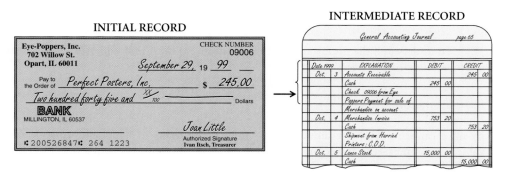

Entering a check in the general journal. The transaction begins when Perfect Posters receives a check from Eye-Poppers. Along with a brief explanation, the amount of the check is entered on the *debit* side of the Perfect Posters general accounting journal. Note that the amount, $245, has also been entered on Oct. 3 as an *accounts receivable*. The accountant has noted both a *decrease* in the company's assets (money owed Perfect Posters by Eye-Poppers) and an *increase* (money paid to Perfect Posters by Eye-Poppers). As we will see, these entries will be balanced in the firm's general ledger (Figure 18.3).

Figure 18.3

| General Ledger | | | | Page 19 |
Accounts Receivable Account				
Date 1999		Debit	Credit	Balance
Sept.	30			4546 61
Sept.	30 No Blond Looks		324 46	4222 15
Oct.	3 Eye Poppers		245 00	3977 15
Oct.	6 Walls R Us	5131 32		9108 47
Oct.	10 Cover All		123 45	8985 02

| General Ledger | | | | |
Cash Account				
Date 1999		Debit	Credit	Balance
Oct.	3			98,563 43
Oct.	3 Eye Poppers	245 00		98,808 43
Oct.	4 Harried Printers		753 20	98,055 23
Oct.	5 Lance		15,000 00	83,055 23
Oct.	5 Walls R Us		5,131 20	77,924 03

Entering a check in the general ledger. Perfect Poster's accountant now transfers the entry from the general journal to the general ledger. The ledger is divided into two accounts: *accounts receivable* and cash. Note that a new column, *balance,* also appears; total dollar amounts for each type of account are entered here. As we will see, the accountant has used the *double-entry accounting system:* The $245 check from Eye-Poppers decreases Perfect Posters' accounts receivable account (it is no longer owed the money) *and* increases its cash account. On the company's balance sheet (Figure 18.5), both balances will appear as *current assets.*

As an example of the recordkeeping process, consider Figures 18.2 and 18.3, which illustrate a portion of the process for Perfect Posters, Inc., a hypothetical wholesaler. In Figure 18.2, a check from Eye-Poppers (an initial record) is entered in Perfect Posters' general accounting journal (an intermediate record).

In Figure 18.3, this entry eventually turns up in Perfect Posters' general ledger, where it becomes a final record showing a cash account balance of $98,808.43. In the next section we will see how this entry is ultimately reflected in the financial reports that Perfect Posters submits to its stockholders and its bank.

The Accounting Equation

At various points in the year, accountants use the following equation to balance the data in journals and ledgers:

$$\text{Assets} = \text{Liabilities} + \text{Owners' equity}$$

To understand the importance of this equation, we must first understand the terms *assets*, *liabilities*, and *owners' equity*.

asset
Any economic resource expected to benefit a firm or an individual who owns it

liability
Debt owed by a firm to an outside organization or individual

owners' equity
Amount of money that owners would receive if they sold all of a firm's assets and paid all of its liabilities

Assets and Liabilities

Charm and intelligence are often said to be assets, and a nonswimmer is no doubt a liability on a canoeing trip. Accountants apply these same terms to items with quantifiable value. Thus, an **asset** is any economic resource that is expected to benefit a firm or an individual who owns it. Assets include land, buildings, equipment, inventory, and payments due the company (accounts receivable). A **liability** is a debt that the firm owes to an outside organization or individual.

Owners' Equity

You may also have heard someone speak of the equity that he or she has in a home—that is, the amount of money that could be made by selling the house and paying off the mortgage. Similarly, **owner's equity** is the amount of money that owners would receive if they sold all of a company's assets and paid all of its liabilities. We can rewrite the accounting equation to show this definition:

$$\text{Assets} - \text{Liabilities} = \text{Owners' equity}$$

If a company's assets exceed its liabilities, owners' equity is positive: If the company goes out of business, the owners will receive some cash (a gain) after selling assets and paying off liabilities. If liabilities outweigh assets, however, owners' equity is negative: There are insufficient assets to pay off all debts. If the company goes out of business, the owners will get no cash and some creditors will not be paid. Owners' equity is a meaningful number to both investors and lenders. For example, before lending money to owners, lenders want to know the amount of owners' equity existing in a business.

Owners' equity consists of two sources of capital:

- The amount that the owners originally invested

- Profits earned by and reinvested in the company

When a company operates profitably, its assets increase faster than its liabilities. Owners' equity, therefore, will increase if profits are retained in the business instead of paid out as dividends to stockholders. Owners' equity can also increase if owners invest more of their own money to increase assets. However, owners' equity can shrink if the company operates at a loss or if the owners withdraw assets.

Double-Entry Accounting

If your business purchases inventory with cash, you decrease your cash and increase your inventory. Similarly, if you purchase supplies on credit, you increase your supplies and increase your accounts payable. If you invest more money in your business, you increase the company's cash and increase your owners' equity. In other words, every transaction affects two accounts. Accountants thus use a **double-entry accounting system** to record the dual effects of financial transactions.

Recording dual effects ensures that the accounting equation always balances. As the term implies, the double-entry system requires at least two bookkeeping entries for each transaction. This practice keeps the accounting equation in balance.

Debits and Credits: The T-Account

Another accounting tool uses debits and credits as a universal method for keeping accounting records. To understand debits and credits, we first need to understand the **T-account**. The format for recording transactions takes the shape of a *T* whose vertical line divides the account into two sides. As pictured below, for example, Perfect Posters' general accounting journal has the following T format:

double-entry accounting system
Bookkeeping system that balances the accounting equation by recording the dual effects of every financial transaction

T-account
Bookkeeping format for recording transactions that takes the shape of a *T* whose vertical line divides the account into debits (left side) and credits (right side)

Cash

Left side	Right side
Debit	Credit

In bookkeeping, *debit* and *credit* refer to the side on which account information is to be entered. The left column of any T-account is called the debit side, and the right column is the credit side:

$$\text{debit} = \text{left side}$$
$$\text{credit} = \text{right side}$$

When an asset increases, it is entered as a debit. When it decreases, it is entered as a credit. Thus, when Perfect Posters received payment from Eye-Poppers, it received more

debit
Bookkeeping entry in a T-account that records increases in assets

credit
Bookkeeping entry in a T-account that records decreases in assets

Figure 18.4 The T-Account and the Accounting Equation

Accounting Equation	Assets		=	Liabilities		–	Owners' Equity	
Rules of the T-Account	Debit for Increase	Credit for Decrease		Debit for Decrease	Credit for Increase		Debit for Decrease	Credit for Increase

cash—an asset. It thus debited the general accounting journal (Figure 18.2) by placing $245 on the left side of that T-account.

Figure 18.4 shows how the rules of the T-account are consistent with the terms of the accounting equation. Debits and credits provide a system of checks and balances. Every debit entry in a journal must have an offsetting credit entry elsewhere. If not, the books will not balance because some error (or deliberate deception) has been introduced in the recordkeeping. To ensure accurate financial records, accountants must find and correct such errors.

T-accounts and the double-entry system, therefore, provide an important method of accounting control. At the end of the accounting cycle, debits and credits must balance; total debits must equal total credits in the account balances recorded in the general ledger. An imbalance indicates improper accounting that must be corrected. Balancing the books, then, is a control procedure to ensure that proper accounting has been used.

Financial Statements

As we noted earlier, the primary purposes of accounting are to summarize the results of a firm's transactions and to issue reports to help managers make informed decisions. Among the most important reports are **financial statements**, which fall into three broad categories: balance sheets, income statements, and statements of cash flows. In this section, we also explain the function of the budget as an internal financial statement.

Balance Sheets
Balance sheets supply detailed information about the accounting equation factors: assets, liabilities, and owners' equity. Because they also show a firm's financial condition at one point in time, balance sheets are sometimes called statements of financial position. Figure 18.5 shows the balance sheet for Perfect Posters.

Assets
As we have seen, an asset is any economic resource that a company owns and from which it can expect to derive some future benefit. From an accounting standpoint, most companies have three types of assets: current, fixed, and intangible.

Current Assets. **Current assets** include cash and assets that can be converted into cash within the following year. They are normally listed in order of **liquidity**: the ease with which they can be converted into cash. Business debts, for example, can usually be satisfied only through payments of cash. A company that needs but cannot generate cash—in other words, a company that is not liquid—may thus be forced to sell assets at sacrifice prices or even go out of business.

By definition, cash is completely liquid. Marketable securities purchased as short-term investments are slightly less liquid but can be sold quickly if necessary. Marketable securities include stocks or bonds of other companies, government securities, and money market certificates. There are three other important nonliquid assets held by many companies: accounts receivable, merchandise inventory, and prepaid expenses.

---

financial statement
Any of several types of reports summarizing a company's financial status to aid in managerial decision making

balance sheet
Financial statement detailing a firm's assets, liabilities, and owners' equity

current asset
Asset that can or will be converted into cash within the following year

liquidity
Ease with which an asset can be converted into cash

Figure 18.5

□□□□□□□□□□□□ **Perfect Posters**, INC.			
555 RIVERVIEW, CHICAGO, IL 60606			

Perfect Posters, Inc.
Balance Sheet
As of December 31, 1999

Assets

Current Assets:
Cash		$7,050	
Marketable securities		2,300	
Accounts receivable	$26,210		
Less: Allowance for doubtful accounts	(650)	25,560	
Merchandise inventory		21,250	
Prepaid expenses		1,050	
Total current assets			$ 57,210

Fixed assets:
Land		18,000	
Building	65,000		
Less: Accumulated depreciation . .	(22,500)	42,500	
Equipment	72,195		
Less: Accumulated depreciation . .	(24,815)	47,380	
Total fixed assets			107,880

Intangible assets:
Patents	7,100		
Trademarks	900		
Total intangible assets		8,000	

| Total assets . . . . | | | $173,090 |

Liabilities and Owners' Equity

Current liabilities:
Accounts payable	$16,315	
Wages payable	3,700	
Taxes payable	1,920	
Total current liabilities		$ 21,935

Long-term liabilities:
Notes payable, 8% due 2001	10,000	
Bonds payable, 9% due 2003	30,000	
Total long-term liabilities	40,000	

| Total liabilities . . . . | | $ 61,935 |

Owners' Equity:
Common stock, $5 par	40,000	
Additional paid-in capital	15,000	
Retained earnings	56,155	
Total owners' equity		111,155

| Total liabilities and owners' equity . . . . | | $173,090 |

Perfect Posters' balance sheet as of December 31, 1999. Perfect Posters' balance sheet shows clearly that the firm's total assets equal its total liabilities and owners' equality.

Accounts receivable are amounts due from customers who have purchased goods on credit. Most businesses expect to receive payment within 30 days of a sale. In our hypothetical example, the entry labeled *Less: Allowance for doubtful accounts* in Figure 18.5 indicates $650 in receivables that Perfect Posters does not expect to collect. Total accounts receivable assets are decreased accordingly.

Although doubtful accounts is a small item for Perfect Posters, it is a serious problem in some industries, such as health care. For example, the Bayfront Medical Center in St. Petersburg, Florida, chronically suffers uncollectible accounts amounting to over 20 percent of total revenues. Accordingly, Bayfront's assets are considerably lower than they would be if the hospital had succeeded in adopting stricter payment requirements.

Following accounts receivable on the Perfect Posters balance sheet is **merchandise inventory**: the cost of merchandise that has been acquired for sale to customers and is still on hand. Accounting for the value of inventories on the balance sheet is difficult because inventories are flowing in and out throughout the year. Therefore, assumptions must be made about which ones were sold and which ones remain in storage.

The **LIFO (last-in-first-out) method** assumes that inventories received last (most recently) are sold first, thus leaving older inventories on hand for future use. In contrast, the **FIFO (first-in-first-out) method** assumes that older inventories (first in) are sold first and newer inventories are held for later use. The method used in calculating inventory (LIFO or FIFO) must be disclosed in a firm's financial statements. It must also be used consistently year after year.

Prepaid expenses include supplies on hand and rent paid for the period to come. They are assets because they have been paid for and are available to the company. In all, Perfect Posters' current assets as of December 31, 1999, totaled $57,210.

account receivable
Amount due from a customer who has purchased goods on credit

merchandise inventory
Cost of merchandise that has been acquired for sale to customers and is still on hand

LIFO (last-in-first-out) method
Method of valuing inventories that assumes that those received most recently (last in) are sold first

FIFO (first-in-first-out) method
Method of valuing inventories that assumes that older inventories (first in) are sold first

prepaid expense
Expense, such as prepaid rent, that is paid before the upcoming period in which it is due

fixed asset
Asset with long-term use or value, such as land, buildings, and equipment

depreciation
Process of distributing the cost of an asset over its life

intangible asset
Nonphysical asset, such as a patent or trademark, that has economic value in the form of expected benefit

goodwill
Amount paid for an existing business above the value of its other assets

Fixed Assets. The next major classification on the balance sheet is usually **fixed assets**. Items in this category have long-term use or value (for example, land, buildings, and equipment). As buildings and equipment wear out or become obsolete, their value decreases. To reflect decreasing value, accountants use depreciation to spread the cost of an asset over the years of its useful life. **Depreciation** means calculating an asset's useful life in years, dividing its worth by that many years, and subtracting the resulting amount each year. Each year, therefore, the asset's remaining value decreases on the books. In Figure 18.5, Perfect Posters shows fixed assets of $107,880 after depreciation.

Intangible Assets. Although their worth is hard to set, **intangible assets** have monetary value. Intangible assets usually include the cost of obtaining rights or privileges such as patents, trademarks, copyrights, and franchise fees. **Goodwill** is the amount paid for an existing business beyond the value of its other assets.

A purchased firm, for example, may have a particularly good reputation or location. In fact, a company's goodwill may be worth more than its tangible assets. For example, when Ford purchased Jaguar for $2.5 billion, $2 billion was recorded as goodwill. Similarly, when General Motors paid $5 billion for Hughes Aircraft, only $1 billion could be associated with assets on Hughes's balance sheet; the remaining $4 billion was paid for goodwill.

Perfect Posters has no goodwill assets. However, it does own trademarks and patents for specialized storage equipment. These are intangible assets worth $8,000. Larger companies, of course, have intangible assets that are worth much more.

Liabilities

current liability
Debt that must be paid within the year

accounts payable
Current liabilities consisting of bills owed to suppliers, plus wages and taxes due within the upcoming year

long-term liability
Debt that is not due for more than 1 year

Like assets, liabilities are often separated into different categories. **Current liabilities** are debts that must be paid within 1 year. These include **accounts payable**: unpaid bills to suppliers for materials as well as wages and taxes that must be paid in the coming year. Perfect Posters has current liabilities of $21,935.

Long-term liabilities are debts that are not due for at least a year. These normally represent borrowed funds on which the company must pay interest. Perfect Posters' long-term liabilities are $40,000.

Owners' Equity

paid-in capital
Additional money, above proceeds from stock sale, paid directly to a firm by its owners

retained earnings
Earnings retained by a firm for its use rather than paid as dividends

income statement (or **profit-and-loss statement**)
Financial statement listing a firm's annual revenues and expenses so that a bottom line shows annual profit or loss

The final section of the balance sheet in Figure 18.5 shows owners' equity broken down into common stock, paid-in capital, and retained earnings. When Perfect Posters was formed, the declared legal value of its common stock was $5 per share. By law, this $40,000 ($5 × 8,000 shares) cannot be distributed as dividends. **Paid-in capital** is additional money invested in the firm by its owners. Perfect Posters has $15,000 in paid-in capital.

Retained earnings are net profits minus dividend payments to stockholders. Retained earnings accumulate when profits, which could have been distributed to stockholders, are kept instead for use by the company. At the close of 1999, Perfect Posters had retained earnings of $56,155.

Income Statements

The **income statement** is sometimes called a profit-and-loss statement because its description of revenues and expenses results in a figure showing the firm's annual profit or loss. In other words,

$$\text{Revenues} - \text{Expenses} = \text{Profit (or loss)}$$

Popularly known as the bottom line, profit or loss is probably the most important figure in any business enterprise. Figure 18.6 shows the 1999 income statement for Perfect Posters, whose bottom line that year was $12,585. Like the balance sheet, the income statement is divided into three major categories: revenues, cost of goods sold, and operating expenses.

Figure 18.6

```
□□□□□□□□□□□ Perfect Posters, INC.
              555 RIVERVIEW, CHICAGO, IL 60606
```

Perfect Posters, Inc.
Income Statement
Year Ended December 31, 1999

Revenues (gross sales)			$256,425
Cost of goods sold:			
Merchandise inventory, January 1, 1999.	$22,380		
Merchandise purchases during year	103,635		
Goods available for sale		$126,015	
Less: Merchandise inventory			
December 31, 1999		21,250	
Cost of goods sold			104,765
Gross profit			151,660
Operating expenses:			
Selling and repackaging expenses:			
Salaries and wages			
Advertising	49,750		
Depreciation—warehouse and repackaging	6,380		
equipment			
Total selling and repackaging expenses	3,350		
Administrative expenses:		59,480	
Salaries and wages			
Supplies	55,100		
Utilities	4,150		
Depreciation—office equipment	3,800		
Interest expense	3,420		
Miscellaneous expenses	2,900		
Total administrative expenses	1,835	71,205	
Total operating expenses			130,685
Operating income (income before taxes) . . .			20,975
Income taxes			8,390
Net income			$12,585

Perfect Posters' income statement for year ended December 31, 1999. The final entry on the income statement, the bottom line, reports the firm's profit or loss.

Revenues

When a law firm receives $250 for preparing a will or when a supermarket collects $65 from a customer buying groceries, both are receiving **revenues**: the funds that flow into a business from the sale of goods or services. In 1999, Perfect Posters reported revenues of $256,425 from the sale of art prints and other posters.

Cost of Goods Sold

In Perfect Posters' income statement, the category labeled *Cost of goods sold* shows the costs of obtaining materials to make the products sold during the year. Perfect Posters began 1999 with posters valued at $22,380. Over the year, it spent another $103,635 to purchase posters. During 1999, then, the company had $126,015 worth of merchandise available to sell. By the end of the year, it had sold all but $21,250 of those posters, which remained as merchandise inventory. The cost of obtaining the goods sold by the firm was thus $104,765.

Gross Profit (or Gross Margin)

You subtract cost of goods sold from revenues to calculate **gross profit** (or **gross margin**). Perfect Posters' gross profit in 1999 was $151,660 ($256,425 − $104,765). Expressed as a percentage of sales, gross profit is 59.1 percent ($151,660/$256,425).

Gross profit percentages vary widely across industries. In retailing, for instance, Safeway's gross profit percentage is 27 percent; in food processing, General Mills's is 48

revenues
Funds that flow into a business from the sale of goods or services

cost of goods sold
Total cost of obtaining materials for making the products sold by a firm during the year

gross profit (or **gross margin**)
Revenues obtained from goods sold minus cost of goods sold

percent; and in the software industry, Microsoft's gross margin is 80 percent. For companies with low gross margins, product costs are a big expense. If a company has a high gross margin, it probably has low cost of goods sold but high selling and administrative expenses.

Operating Expenses

operating expenses
Costs, other than the cost of goods sold, incurred in producing a good or service

In addition to costs directly related to acquiring goods, every company has general expenses ranging from erasers to the president's salary. Like cost of goods sold, **operating expenses** are resources that must flow out of a company for it to earn revenues. As you can see from Figure 18.6, Perfect Posters had 1999 operating expenses of $130,685. This figure consists of $59,480 in selling and repackaging expenses and $71,205 in administrative expenses.

Selling expenses result from activities related to selling the firm's goods or services. These may include salaries for the sales force, delivery costs, and advertising expenses. General and administrative expenses, such as management salaries, insurance expenses, and maintenance costs, are expenses related to the general management of the company.

operating income
Gross profit minus operating expenses

net income (or net profit or net earnings)
Gross profit minus operating expenses and income taxes

Operating and Net Income

Sometimes managers must determine **operating income**, which compares the gross profit from business operations against operating expenses. This calculation for Perfect Posters ($151,660 − $130,685) reveals an operating income, or income before taxes, of $20,975. Subtracting income taxes from operating income ($20,975 − $8,390) reveals **net income** (also called **net profit** or **net earnings**). In 1999, Perfect Posters's net income was $12,585.

Statements of Cash Flows

statement of cash flows
Financial statement describing a firm's yearly cash receipts and cash payments

Some companies prepare only balance sheets and income statements. However, the Securities and Exchange Commission also requires all firms whose stock is publicly traded to issue a third report: a **statement of cash flows**. This statement describes a company's yearly cash receipts and cash payments. It shows the effects on cash of three business activities:

- *Cash flows from operations.* This part of the statement is concerned with the firm's main operating activities: the cash transactions involved in buying and selling goods and services. It reveals how much of the year's profits result from the firm's main line of business (for example, Jaguar's sales of automobiles) rather than from secondary activities (for example, licensing fees a clothing firm paid to Jaguar for using the Jaguar logo on shirts).

- *Cash flows from investing.* This section reports net cash used in or provided by investing. It includes cash receipts and payments from buying and selling stocks, bonds, property, equipment, and other productive assets.

- *Cash flows from financing.* The final section reports net cash from all financing activities. It includes cash inflows from borrowing or issuing stock as well as outflows for payment of dividends and repayment of borrowed money.

The overall change in cash from these three sources provides information to lenders and investors. When creditors and stockholders know how firms obtained and used their funds during the course of a year, it is easier for them to interpret the year-to-year changes in the firm's balance sheet and income statement.

The Budget: An Internal Financial Statement

budget
Detailed statement of estimated receipts and expenditures for a period of time in the future

In addition to financial statements, managers need other types of accounting information to aid in internal planning, controlling, and decision making. Probably the most crucial internal financial statement is the budget. A **budget** is a detailed statement of estimated receipts and expenditures for a period of time in the future. Although that period is usually 1 year, some companies also prepare budgets for 3- or 5-year periods, especially when considering major capital expenditures.

Budgets are also useful for keeping track of weekly or monthly performance. Procter & Gamble, for example, evaluates all of its business units monthly by comparing actual financial results with monthly budgeted amounts. Discrepancies in actual versus budget totals signal potential problems and initiate action to get financial performance back on track.

Pssst! Want a New Credit Card?

Do you *need* another credit card? Credit card spending, without the discipline of a budget, can spell financial disaster. And plenty of banks are anxious to offer you cards, as consumers ride the highest tide of easy credit in memory.

Just think about the numbers. Consumer debt has almost doubled since 1995 and is at record levels of over 20 percent of disposable income. A quarter of all families earning less than $10,000 a year now spend with credit cards, and in households earning under $50,000 monthly credit card payments have jumped to almost 18 percent of total income. Late payments and defaults are at record highs, interest rates and fees are on the rise, with annual averages at around $1,000 per card holder, and in 1996 the number of personal bankruptcy filings rose past 1.1 million with no end in sight.

Aggressive promotion, particularly on college campuses, and unsolicited mailings of over 2 billion credit card offers a year are partly responsible for the gigantic rise in consumer spending. "People today feel they deserve the good life, and if someone's dumb enough to send them a credit card, they're going to use it to pay for a style they can't afford," says A. Gary Shilling, a financial consultant. And therein lies the rub. The ugly downside of the rush to credit card spending is a massive pileup of debt that consumers will struggle with for years to come. And some will just go under.

LaToya Dailey, a student at University of Alabama (Tuscaloosa), racked up more than $8,000 in debt by her sophomore year. Richard Matson, who attends Columbia College in Chicago, is making monthly payments of $900 on credit card debts that bit too deeply into the money his par-

ents had saved for his tuition. To complete his degree, he'll be taking out a loan. And Carol Stedman, who earns $36,000 as assistant manager in a San Francisco supermarket, charged $25,000 worth of vacations, clothes, and restaurant meals. When the interest on her debt surpassed her monthly credit card bill, it was like "a diet where you lose 20 pounds and gain back 30," she says.

> ❝ *People today feel they deserve the good life, and if someone's dumb enough to send them a credit card, they're going to use it to pay for a style they can't afford.* ❞
>
> —Financial consultant A. Gary Shilling

Credit card companies are themselves caught in a trap. To cover losses from bad debt they must continually seek out new customers whose spending makes up the difference. Some bankers are confident that consumers are in control of their finances and thus continue to push credit on the sometimes unworthy, but consumer advocates are nervous. "Given widespread job insecurity," says consultant Shilling, "people ought to be putting something aside for a rainy day."

Here's some other good advice: Make a personal budget of required monthly expenses and average monthly income, so you'll know what you can afford. Pay for smaller purchases with cash. Always read the fine print on credit card agreements, and don't fall for promotions and giveaways. Make it a point to pay on time. And, if all else fails, before you buy ask yourself, "Do I really need this item?" The answer might surprise you.

Figure 18.7 The Sales Budget

Perfect Posters, INC.
555 RIVERVIEW, CHICAGO, IL 60606

Perfect Posters, Inc.
Sales Budget
First Quarter, 2000

	January	February	March	Quarter
Budgeted sales (units)	7,500	6,000	6,500	20,000
Budgeted selling price per unit	$3.50	$3.50	$3.50	$3.50
Budgeted sales revenue	$ 26,250	$ 21,000	$ 22,750	$ 70,000
Expected cash receipts:				
From December sales	$26,210[a]			$26,210
From January sales	17,500[b]	$8,750		26,250
From February sales		14,000	$7,000	21,000
From March sales			15,200	15,200
Total cash receipts:	$ 43,710	$ 22,750	$ 22,200	$ 88,660

[a]This cash from December sales represents a collection of the accounts receivable appearing on the December 31, 1999, balance sheet.
[b]The company estimates that two-thirds of each month's sales revenues will result in cash receipts during the same month. The remaining one-third is collected during the following month.

Although the accounting staff coordinates the budget process, it requires input from many people in the company regarding proposed activities, needed resources, and input sources.[8] Figure 18.7, for example, is a sample sales budget. In preparing such a budget, the accounting department must obtain from the sales group both its projections for units to be sold and expected expenses for each quarter of the coming year. Accountants then draw up the final budget, and throughout the year, the accounting department compares the budget to actual expenditures and revenues in the sales group.

Analyzing Financial Statements

Financial statements present a great deal of information. But what does it all mean? How, for example, can statements help investors decide what stock to buy or help managers decide whether to extend credit? Statements provide data. These data can in turn be applied to various ratios (comparative numbers). These ratios can then be used to analyze the financial health of one or more companies. They can also be used to check a firm's progress by comparing current and past statements.

solvency ratio
Financial ratio, either short- or long-term, for estimating the risk in investing in a firm

profitability ratio
Financial ratio for measuring a firm's potential earnings

activity ratio
Financial ratio for evaluating management's use of a firm's assets

Ratios are normally grouped into three major classifications:

- **Solvency ratios**, both short- and long-term, estimate risk.
- **Profitability ratios** measure potential earnings.
- **Activity ratios** reflect management's use of assets.

Depending on the decisions to be made, a user may apply none, some, or all the ratios in a particular classification.

Short-Term Solvency Ratios

In the short run, a company's survival depends on its ability to pay its immediate debts. Such payments require cash. Short-term solvency ratios measure a company's relative liquidity and thus its ability to pay immediate debts. The higher a firm's **liquidity ratios**, then, the lower the risk involved for investors. The two most commonly used liquidity ratios are the current and quick (or acid test) ratios.

liquidity ratio
Solvency ratio measuring a firm's ability to pay its immediate debts

Current Ratio

The **current ratio** has been called the banker's ratio because it concerns a firm's creditworthiness. The current ratio measures a company's ability to meet current obligations out of current assets. It thus reflects a firm's ability to generate cash to meet obligations through the normal, orderly process of selling inventories and collecting accounts receivable. It is calculated by dividing current assets by current liabilities.

As a rule, a current ratio is satisfactory if it is 2:1 or higher—that is, if current assets more than double current liabilities. A smaller ratio may indicate that a company will have difficulty paying its bills. Note, however, that a larger ratio may imply that assets are not being used productively and should be invested elsewhere.

How does Perfect Posters measure up? Look again at the balance sheet in Figure 18.5. Judging from its current assets and current liabilities at the end of 1999, we see that

current ratio
Solvency ratio that determines a firm's credit worthiness by measuring its ability to pay current liabilities

$$\frac{\text{Current assets}}{\text{Current liabilities}} = \frac{\$57,210}{\$21,935} = 2.61$$

How does Perfect Posters' ratio compare with those of other companies? Not bad: It is higher than those of Johnson & Johnson (1.83), Boeing (1.41), and Northeast Utilities (0.95). Although Perfect Posters may be holding too much uninvested cash, it looks like a good credit risk.

Working Capital. A related measure is **working capital**: the difference between the firm's current assets and its current liabilities. Working capital indicates the firm's ability to pay off short-term debts (liabilities) that it owes to outsiders. At the end of 1999, Perfect Posters' working capital was $35,275 (that is, $57,210 − $21,935). Because current liabilities must be paid off within 1 year, current assets are more than enough to meet current obligations.

working capital
Difference between a firm's current assets and current liabilities

Quick (Acid Test) Ratio

The current ratio represents a company's ability to meet expected demands for cash. In contrast, the **quick**, or **acid-test**, **ratio**, which divides quick assets by current liabilities, measures a firm's ability to meet emergency demands for cash. **Quick assets** include cash and assets just one step removed from cash: marketable securities and accounts receivable. Inventory is excluded from this measure because it can be liquidated quickly only at sacrifice prices. Thus, the quick ratio is a more stringent test of liquidity than is the current ratio. As a rule, a quick ratio of 1.0 or more is satisfactory, although it varies from industry to industry. Whirlpool Corp., for example, has a quick ratio of 0.92. WalMart, meanwhile, with a very low ratio of only 0.8, is still regarded by many as a safe bet for meeting emergency demands for short-term obligations.

If we consider Perfect Posters' position at the end of 1999 (again using data from Figure 18.5), we see that

quick (or **acid-test**) **ratio**
Solvency ratio for determining a firm's ability to meet emergency demands for cash

quick asset
Cash plus assets one step removed from cash (marketable securities and accounts receivable)

$$\frac{\text{Quick assets}}{\text{Current liabilities}} = \frac{\$7,050 + 2,300 + 26,210 - 650}{\$21,935} = 1.59$$

In an emergency, the firm apparently can pay off all current obligations without having to liquidate inventory.

Long-Term Solvency Ratios

To survive in the long run, a company must be able to meet both its short-term (current) debts and its long-term liabilities. These latter debts usually involve interest payments. A firm that cannot meet them is in danger of collapse or takeover—a risk that makes creditors and investors quite cautious. The 1998 Asian financial crisis was fueled by a loss of confidence by investors in large firms in Japan and Korea that could not meet their long-term cash obligations.

Debt-to-Owners' Equity Ratio

debt ratio
Solvency ratio measuring a firm's ability to meet its long-term debts

debt-to-owners' equity ratio (or **debt-to-equity ratio**)
Solvency ratio describing the extent to which a firm is financed through borrowing

debt
A firm's total liabilities

To measure the risk that a company may encounter this problem, we use the long-term solvency ratios called **debt ratios**. The most commonly used debt ratio is the **debt-to-owners' equity ratio** (or **debt-to-equity ratio**), which describes the extent to which a firm is financed through borrowed money. It is calculated by dividing **debt** (total liabilities) by owners' equity.

This ratio is commonly used to compare a given company's status with industry averages. For example, companies with debt-to-equity ratios above 1 are probably relying too much on debt. Such firms may find themselves owing so much debt that they lack the income needed to meet interest payments or to repay borrowed money.

For example, after George Fisher became CEO of Kodak in 1993, he immediately zeroed in on the company's debt burden. Kodak's previous regime had made a number of acquisitions, including the 1988 purchase of Sterling Drug, a large pharmaceutical distributor. As a result, debt had ballooned to over $9 billion and stood at $7.5 billion when Fisher arrived. Moreover, income from core photography and imaging products was being used to pay interest on the debt rather than fund innovation. "We were going to milk the imaging business to death," said Fisher, who moved swiftly to strengthen Kodak's balance sheet. First and foremost, he sold Sterling and other assets (namely the firm's health and household products divisions) not directly related to photography and imaging. With the proceeds from these sales ($7.9 billion), Fisher was able to reduce the company's debt. Figure 18.8 shows the results of his efforts. The reductions of long-term debt caused the downward trend in Kodak's debt-to-equity ratio. With less debt and, hence, lower interest payments, most of the firm's cash flow was freed up to pursue profitable, more tightly focused activities. In the case of Perfect Posters, we can see from the balance sheet in Figure 18.5 that the debt-to-equity ratio works out as follows:

$$\frac{\text{Debt}}{\text{Owner's equity}} = \frac{\$61,935}{\$111,155} = 0.56$$

Figure 18.8 Kodak's Trends in Long-Term Debt and Debt-to-Equity Ratio

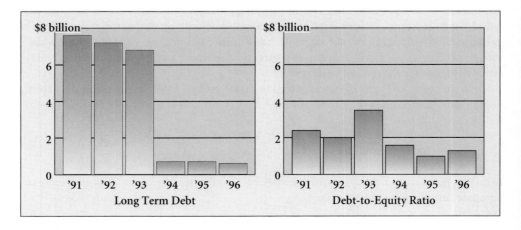

"I realize, gentlemen, that thirty million dollars is a lot of money to spend. However, it's not real money and, of course, it's not our money either."

Because the ratio is well below 1, all creditors would be protected if the firm developed difficulties severe enough to force liquidation. In other words, owners' equity is more than sufficient to meet all debts.

Leverage. Note that a fairly high debt-to-equity ratio may sometimes be not only acceptable but desirable. Borrowing funds provides **leverage**: the ability to make otherwise unaffordable purchases. In leveraged buyouts (LBOs), firms have willingly taken on sometimes huge debt in order to buy out other companies. When the purchased company allows the buying company to earn profits above the cost of the borrowed funds, leveraging makes sound financial sense, even if it raises the buyer's debt-to-equity ratio. Unfortunately, many buyouts have fallen into financial trouble when actual profits dropped short of anticipated levels or when rising rates increased interest payments on the debt acquired by the buyer.

leverage
Ability to finance an investment through borrowed funds

Profitability Ratios

Although it is important to know that a company is solvent in both the long and the short term, safety or risk alone is not an adequate basis for investment decisions. Investors also want some measure of the returns they can expect. Return on sales, return on investment, and earnings per share are three commonly used profitability ratios.

Return on Sales

Also called the **net profit margin**, **return on sales** is calculated by dividing net income by sales. This ratio indicates the percentage of income that is profit to the company. There is no single right net profit margin. The figure for any one company must be compared with figures for other firms in the industry to determine how well a business is doing. Typical return on sales ratios are 1 percent for meat-packing plants, 3 percent for wholesalers such as Perfect Posters, and 6 percent for machinery manufacturers.

Using data from Figure 18–6, we see that return on sales for Perfect Posters in 1999 was

net profit margin (or **return on sales**)
Profitability ratio indicating the percentage of its income that is a firm's profit

$$\frac{\text{Net income}}{\text{Sales}} = \frac{\$12,585}{\$256,425} = 0.049 = 4.9\%$$

In other words, the business realized a 4.9-cent profit on each dollar of sales—well above the 3-percent standard for its industry.

return on investment (or **return on equity**)
Profitability ratio measuring income earned for each dollar invested

Owners are interested in the net income earned by a business for each dollar invested. **Return on investment** (sometimes called **return on equity**) measures this performance by dividing net income (recorded in the income statement, Figure 18.6) by total owners' equity (recorded in the balance sheet, Figure 18.5). For Perfect Posters, the return-on-investment ratio in 1999 can be calculated as follows:

$$\frac{\text{Net income}}{\text{Total owners' equity}} = \frac{\$12,585}{\$111,155} = 11.3\%$$

Is this figure good or bad? There is no set answer. If Perfect Posters' ratio for 1999 is higher than in previous years, owners and investors should be encouraged. But if 11.3 percent is lower than the ratios of other companies in the same industry, they should be concerned.

Defined as net income divided by the number of shares of common stock outstanding, **earnings per share** determines the size of the dividend that a company can pay its shareholders. Investors use this ratio to decide whether to buy or sell a company's stock. As the ratio gets higher, the stock value increases, because investors know that the firm can better afford to pay dividends. Naturally, stock will lose market value if the latest financial statements report a decline in earnings per share.

For Perfect Posters, we can use the net income total from the income statement in Figure 18.6 to calculate earnings per share as follows:

earnings per share
Profitability ratio measuring the size of the dividend that a firm can pay shareholders

$$\frac{\text{Net income}}{\text{Number of common shares outstanding}} = \frac{\$12,585}{8,000} = \$1.57 \text{ per share}$$

As a baseline for comparison, Wal-Mart's recent earnings per share was $1.19.

Activity Ratios
The efficiency with which a firm uses resources is linked to profitability. As a potential investor, then, you want to know which company gets more mileage from its resources. Activity ratios measure this efficiency. For example, say that two firms use the same amount of resources or assets. If Firm A generates greater profits or sales, it is more efficient and thus has a better activity ratio.

By the same token, if a firm needs more resources to make products comparable to its competitors', it has a worse activity ratio. In June 1994, for instance, the consulting firm of Harbour & Associates Inc. released a study showing that in order to match Ford's efficiency, General Motors would have to cut 20,000 workers. According to the report, production inefficiency at its plants costs GM $2.2 billion annually in excess labor costs. On the upside, however, GM is making substantial progress. A similar report issued 2 years earlier had concluded that GM needed to cut 70,000 workers because excess labor costs were $4 billion.[9]

inventory turnover ratio
Activity ratio measuring the average number of times that inventory is sold and restocked during the year

Certain specific measures can be used to explain how one firm earns greater profits than another. One of the most important is the **inventory turnover ratio**, which measures the average number of times that inventory is sold and restocked during the year—that is, how quickly it is produced and sold. First, you need to know your average inventory: the typical amount of inventory on hand during the year. You can calculate average inventory by adding end-of-year inventory to beginning-of-year inventory and dividing by 2. You can now find your inventory turnover ratio, which is expressed as the cost of goods sold divided by average inventory:

$$\frac{\text{Cost of goods sold}}{\text{Average inventory}} = \frac{\text{Cost of goods sold}}{(\text{Beginning inventory} + \text{Ending inventory})/2}$$

A high inventory turnover ratio means efficient operations: Because a smaller amount of investment is tied up in inventory, the company's funds can be put to work elsewhere to earn greater returns. However, inventory turnover must be compared with both prior years and industry averages. An inventory turnover rate of 5, for example, might be excellent for an auto supply store, but it would be disastrous for a supermarket, where a rate of about 15 is common. Rates can also vary within a company that markets a variety of products.[10]

To calculate Perfect Posters' inventory turnover ratio for 1999, we take the merchandise inventory figures for the income statement in Figure 18.6. The ratio can be expressed as follows:

$$\frac{\$104,765}{(\$22,380 + \$21,250)/2} = 4.8$$

In other words, new merchandise replaces old merchandise every 76 days (365 days/4.8). The 4.8 ratio is below the average of 7 for comparable wholesaling operations, indicating that the business is slightly inefficient.

As an example of its importance, improved inventory management contributed to the resurgence of Adidas in the United States. After once leading the U.S. market, Adidas America's market share fell to the low single digits while Nike and Reebok's combined share climbed to 50 percent. When a new management team was brought aboard in 1989, they immediately recognized the need to revamp information and reporting systems. For example, when the CFO asked for figures on normal inventory turnover rates, no one could tell him. When he finally found out, the news was not good: Whereas Nike and Reebok turned U.S. inventories five times per year, Adidas America did so only twice. After setting up a new reporting system that generated inventory data, Adidas was able to make substantial improvements in the turnover ratio. The same system also allowed them to pinpoint critical marketing information, such as product lines with high gross margins. For example, they discovered that although basketball shoes are high-volume sellers, soccer and tennis shoes are much more profitable. Such enlightenment led to a marketing push of profitable products and a $30-million increase in gross profit.[11]

International Accounting

More and more U.S. companies are buying and selling goods and services in other countries. Coca-Cola and Boeing, for example, receive large portions of their operating revenues from sales in many countries around the globe.[12] Conversely, firms such as Toastmaster Inc. buy components for electric appliances from suppliers in Asia. Retailers such as Sears and Kmart buy merchandise from other countries for merchandising in the United States. In addition, more and more companies own subsidiaries in other countries. Obviously, accounting for foreign transactions involves some special procedures. One of the most basic is translating the values of the currencies of different countries.

Foreign Currency Exchange

A unique consideration in international accounting is the value of currencies and their exchange rates. As we saw in chapter 3, the value of any country's currency is subject to occasional change. Political and economic conditions, for instance, affect the stability of a nation's currency and its value relative to the currencies of other countries. Whereas the Swiss franc, for example, has a long history of stability, the Brazilian real has a history of instability.

As it is traded each day around the world, any currency's value is determined by market forces: what buyers are willing to pay for it. The resulting values are called **foreign currency** exchange rates. How volatile are such rates? Table 18.1 shows the changes in exchange rates for some foreign currencies during a 1-year period. When a nation's currency becomes unstable, as when the Mexican peso began a disastrous plunge in December 1994, it is re-

foreign currency exchange rate
Value of a nation's currency as determined by market forces

Table 18.1   Foreign Currency Exchange Rates

Country	Monetary Unit	Dollar Value December 23, 1996	Dollar Value December 23, 1997	% Change in Value
Canada	dollar	0.7318	0.6956	−4.9
France	franc	0.1906	0.1684	−11.3
Japan	yen	0.0088	0.0077	−12.5
Switzerland	franc	0.7479	0.6974	−6.8

garded as a weak currency. On the other hand, the Swiss franc is said to be a strong currency because its value historically rises or holds steady in comparison to the U.S. dollar. As exchange rate changes occur, they must be considered by accountants when recording a firm's international transactions. They will have an impact, perhaps profound, on the amount that a firm pays for foreign purchases and the amount it gains from sales to foreign buyers.

International Purchases

On the most basic level, accounting for international transactions involves two steps: translating from one currency to another and reflecting gains or losses due to exchange rate changes. Let's explain these two steps by developing an extended illustration. Suppose, for example, that on March 7, Village Wine and Cheese Shops import Bordeaux wine from Pierre Bourgeois in France. The price is 32,000 francs, and the exchange rate on March 7 is $0.18 per French franc.

Translating Currencies

As a standard practice, Village's accounting system is maintained consistently in one currency (U.S. dollars). Accordingly, the first step for its accountant is to translate the price of the transaction into dollars:

$$\text{Price in French francs} = 32{,}000 \text{ Fr}$$
$$\text{Price in U.S. dollars} = (32{,}000 \text{ Fr}) (\$0.18) = \$5{,}760$$

The accounting system whereby multinational firms report cross-border transactions among subsidiaries is called transfer pricing. *The Internal Revenue Service and its counterparts in several other countries suspect that many companies use this procedure to underreport profits and thus minimize taxes. At year-end 1996, for example, a $269-million tax assessment was still pending against Coca-Cola Co. by the Japanese tax authorities. Japan's National Tax Administration Agency levied the bill, claiming back taxes for the years since 1990. Coke's managers in Japan, charges the NTAA, cut into their profits by overreporting royalty payments made to their American parent. Back in the United States, meanwhile, the IRS has handed hefty penalties to such Japanese firms as Nissan, Hitachi, and Yamaha for similar violations. Says one Japanese lawyer: "There's clearly a war going on."*

Next, the transaction must be recorded in Village's books. Which accounts will be affected? It depends on whether the sale involves a cash payment or credit.

Cash Payment Although cash transactions are unusual in international trade, they do occur occasionally. If the transaction is settled immediately—that is, if Village pays Bourgeois on March 7—Village's accounting records will appear as follows:

		Debit	Credit
March 7	Inventory . . .	5,760	
	Cash		5,760

Purchase on Credit Suppose, however, that Village purchases on credit and that Bourgeois requires payment within 30 days. Village's accounting records will then appear as follows:

		Debit	Credit
March 7	Inventory	5,760	
	Accounts payable . . .		5,760

Then, on April 1, when Village pays Bourgeois, the payment entry will appear this way:

		Debit	Credit
April 1	Accounts payable . . .	5,760	
	Cash		5,760

Purchase on Credit with Shifting Exchange Rates. Thus far, our bookkeeping has been straightforward because Village's accountants have assumed a constant exchange rate of $0.18 per franc. The preceding entries are correct if the exchange rate for francs on April 1 is the same as it was on March 7 ($0.18 per franc). However, because exchange rates rise and fall daily, some change will no doubt occur during the month in question.

Let's say, for example, that on April 1 the value of the French franc has fallen below $0.18. Village Cheese therefore will enjoy a foreign currency transaction gain: It can pay its debt with fewer dollars. Suppose that the franc has fallen to $0.17 by the time Village pays Bourgeois on April 1. The payment entry therefore will appear as follows:

		Debit	Credit
April 1	Accounts payable	5,760	
	Cash (32,000 × $0.17)		5,440
	Foreign currency transaction gain . . .		320

In other words, when the value of the franc decreased, Village needed only $5,440 to pay the original account payable of $5,760. Of course, had the franc increased to a value above $0.18, Village would have paid more than the original $5,760. It would have suffered a foreign currency transaction loss.

International Sales on Credit

Sales made on credit to customers in other countries can also be recorded to reflect both translations from foreign currency and changes in currency exchange rates. Suppose, for instance, that on June 1, Motorola sells some cellular phones on credit to the Japanese distributor Hirotsu. The total price of the phones is 50 million yen, and the exchange rate is $0.01 per yen. Motorola's transaction is thus recorded as follows:

		Debit	Credit
April 1	Accounts receivable		
	(50,000,000 × $0.01) . . .	500,000	
	Sales revenue		500,000

Let's suppose that when Hirotsu pays Motorola (say, on June 30), the exchange rate has fallen to $0.0095 per yen. Motorola, therefore, will receive fewer dollars than were recorded in its June 1 accounts receivable entry. It will suffer the foreign currency transaction loss shown in the following entry:

		Debit	*Credit*
June 30	Cash (50,000,000 × $0.0095)	475,000	
	Foreign currency transaction loss . . .	25,000	
	Accounts receivable		500,000

At the end of an accounting period, all exchange rate gains and losses are combined to reveal a net gain or loss. This figure can then be shown on the income statement as other revenue and expense. In other words, it need not be combined with conventional revenues and expenses from normal operations.

Accounting for International Subsidiaries

After the fall of the Mexican peso in 1994, many parent companies with Mexican subsidiaries needed to know how their balance sheets would be affected. Here is one example. In 1991, Austin Design Specialties, a U.S. interior-decorating and construction firm, purchased Puebla Artifacts, a Mexican art firm. Puebla's balance sheet is expressed in pesos. In 1997, Austin wants to consolidate Puebla's balance sheet into its own in order to reflect the parent company's overall status. Doing so involves a translation adjustment reflecting changes in the value of the peso.

To do the job of Austin's accountants, let's begin with the numbers in Table 18.2. This table focuses on selected entries from Puebla's balance sheet (assets, liabilities, and owners' equity). Also note that when Austin bought Puebla, the peso was worth $0.35. Thus, the dollar translation for common stock reflects that exchange rate:

500,000 pesos @ $0.35 each = $175,000

During the years 1990–1997, when income was being retained by Puebla, the average value of the peso was $0.21. This is the rate at which retained earnings have been translated. Similarly, to express the value of assets and liabilities in dollars, we must translate them using the current exchange rate, which is now substantially lower than it was in the past.

Observing the translations into dollars, you can see why a translation adjustment is needed. The accounting equation is out of balance: Assets no longer equal liabilities plus

Table 18.2   Translating Pesos into Dollars

Selected Entries from Puebla Artifacts Balance Sheet	Pesos	Exchange Rate	Dollars
Assets	4,000,000	$0.12	$480,000
Liabilities	2,500,000	0.12	300,000
Owners' equity:			
Common stock	500,000	0.35	175,000
Retained earnings	1,000,000	0.21	210,000
Translation adjustment	—		(205,000)
	4,000,000		480,000

owners' equity. Why the imbalance? The problem is the change in exchange rates. The translation adjustment is needed because the subsidiary's assets must equal liabilities plus owners' equity when expressed in dollars. That adjustment is the balancing amount by which owners' equity must be changed (increased).

The compensating adjustment in this case is negative ($205,000). Resulting owners' equity is $180,000:

$$\$175,000 + 210,000 - 205,000 = \$180,000$$

When Austin now compiles its consolidated balance sheet, the items expressed in dollars from Table 18.2 will be reported along with the corresponding items for the parent company itself. Translation adjustment will appear as a new, additional item under the owners' equity section of the firm's financial report.

Summary of Learning Objectives

1 **Explain the role of accountants and distinguish between the kinds of work done by public and private accountants.** By collecting, analyzing, and communicating financial information, accountants provide business managers and investors with an accurate picture of the firm's financial health. Certified public accountants (CPAs) are licensed professionals who provide auditing, tax, and management advisory services for other firms and individuals. Public accountants who have not yet been certified perform similar tasks. Private accountants provide diverse specialized services for the specific firms that employ them.

2 **Explain how the following three concepts are used in recordkeeping: the accounting equation, double-entry accounting, and T-accounts for debits and credits.** The accounting equation (assets = liabilities + owners' equity) is used to balance the data in both journals and ledgers. Double-entry accounting acknowledges the dual effects of financial transactions and ensures that the accounting equation always balances. Using the T-account, accountants record financial transactions in the shape of a T, with the vertical line dividing the account into debit and credit columns. These tools enable accountants not only to enter but to track transactions.

3 **Describe the three basic financial statements and show how they reflect the activity and financial condition of a business.** The balance sheet summarizes a company's assets, liabilities, and owners' equity at a given point in time. The income statement details revenues and expenses for a given period of time and identifies any profit or loss. The statement of cash flows reports cash receipts and payments from operating, investing, and financing activities.

4 **Discuss the importance of budgets in internal planning and control.** To ensure the overall efficient use of resources, accountants and other managers develop budgets. A budget shows where funds will be obtained (the sources) and where they will be spent (the uses.) Throughout the year, the budget is monitored to ensure that costs are not exceeding revenues.

5 **Explain how computing key financial ratios can help in analyzing the financial strengths of a business.** Drawing on data from financial statements, ratios can help creditors, investors, and managers assess a firm's finances. The liquidity, current, quick (or acid test), and debt-to-equity ratios all measure solvency (a firm's ability to pay its debt) in both the short and the long run. Return on sales, return on investment, and earnings per share are all ratios that measure profitability. Inventory turnover ratios show how efficiently a firm is using its funds.

6 **Explain some of the special issues facing accountants at firms that do international business.** Accounting for foreign transactions involves some special procedures. First, accountants must consider the fact that the exchange rates of national currencies

change. Accordingly, the value of a foreign currency at any given time, its foreign currency exchange rate, is what buyers are willing to pay for it.

Exchange rates affect the amount of money that a firm pays for foreign purchases and the amount that it gains from foreign sales. U.S. accountants, therefore, must always translate foreign currencies into the value of the dollar. Then, in recording a firm's transactions, they must make adjustments to reflect shifting exchange rates over time. Shifting rates may result in either foreign currency transaction gains (a debt, for example, may be paid with fewer dollars) or foreign currency transaction losses.

Questions and Exercises

Questions for Review

1 Identify the three types of services performed by CPAs.
2 How does the double-entry system reduce the chances of mistakes or fraud in accounting?
3 What are the three basic financial statements and what major information items does each contain?
4 Identify the three major classifications of financial statement ratios and give an example of one ratio in each category.
5 Explain how financial ratios allow managers to monitor their own efficiency and effectiveness.

Questions for Analysis

6 Suppose that Inflatables Inc., makers of air mattresses for swimming pools, has the following transactions one week:
  • Sale of three deluxe mattresses to Al Wett (paid cash $75) on 7/16
  • Received check on 7/13 from Ima Flote in payment for mattresses bought on credit ($90) on 7/13
  • Received new shipment of 200 mattresses from Airheads Mfg. (total cost, $2,000) on 7/17
  • Construct a journal for Inflatables Inc.
7 If you were planning to invest in a company, which of the three types of financial statements would you most want to see? Why?
8 Dasar Co. reports the following data in its September 30, 1998, financial statements:
  • Gross sales $225,000
  • Current assets   40,000
  • Long-term assets   100,000
  • Current liabilities   16,000
  • Long-term liabilities   44,000
  • Owners' equity   80,000
  • Net income   7,200
Compute the following ratios: current ratio, debt-to-equity ratio, return on sales, and return on owners' equity.

Application Exercises

9 Interview an accountant at a local manufacturing firm. Trace the process by which budgets are developed in that company. How does the firm use budgets? How does budgeting help managers plan business activities? How does budgeting help them control business activities? Give examples.
10 Interview the manager of a local retail or wholesale business about taking inventory. What is the firm's primary purpose in taking inventory? How often is it done?

Building Your Business Skills

This exercise enhances the following SCANS workplace competencies: demonstrating basic skills, demonstrating thinking skills, exhibiting interpersonal skills, working with information, and applying system knowledge.

Goal   To encourage students to think about the advantages and disadvantages of using an electronic system for handling accounts receivable and accounts payable.

Method   **Step 1:**   Study Figure 18.A. The outside circle depicts the seven steps involved in the issuing of paper bills to customers, the payment of these bills by customers, and the handling by banks of debits and credits for the two accounts. The inside circle shows the same bill issuance and payment process handled electronically.

Step 2:   As the chief financial officer of a midwestern utility company, you are analyzing the feasibility of switching from a paper to an electronic system of billing and bill payment. You decide to discuss the ramifications of the choice with three business associates (choose three classmates to take on these roles). Your discussion requires that you research electronic payment systems now being developed. Specifically, using on-line and library research, you must find out as much as you can about the electronic bill-paying systems being developed by Visa International, Intuit, IBM, and the Checkfree Corporation. After you have researched this information, brainstorm the advantages and disadvantages of using an electronic bill-paying system in your company.

Follow-Up Questions

1 What cost savings are inherent in the electronic system for both your company and its customers? In your answer, consider such costs as handling, postage, and paper.

2 What consequences would your decision to adopt an electronic system have on others with whom you do business, including manufacturers of check-sorting equipment, the U.S. Postal Service, and banks?

3 Switching to an electronic bill-paying system would require a large capital expenditure for new computers and computer software. How could analyzing the company's income statement help you justify this expenditure?

4 How are consumers likely to respond to paying bills electronically? Are you likely to get a different response from individuals than you get from business customers?

Figure 18.A Managing Operations and Information

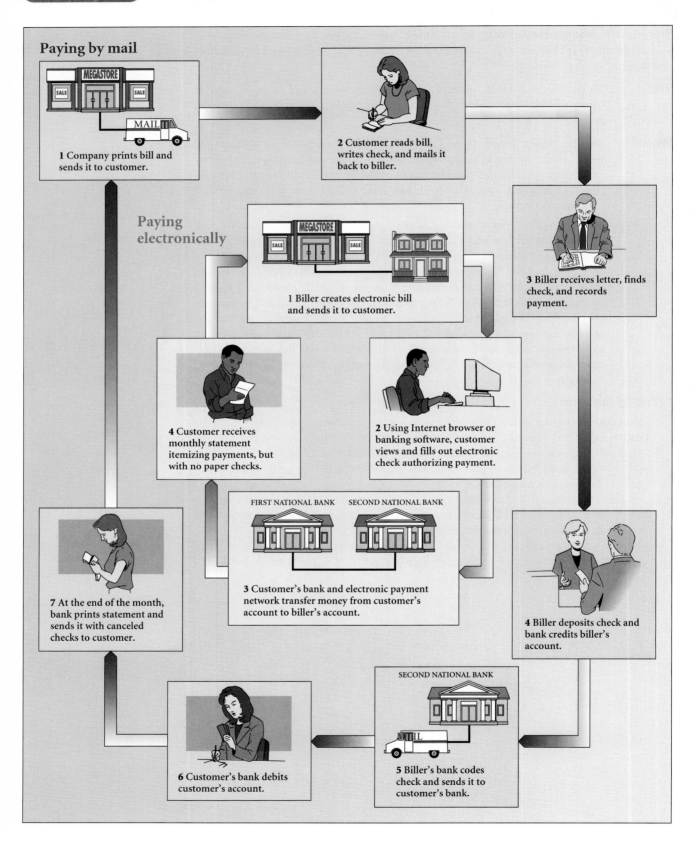

Paying by mail

1 Company prints bill and sends it to customer.

2 Customer reads bill, writes check, and mails it back to biller.

3 Biller receives letter, finds check, and records payment.

Paying electronically

1 Biller creates electronic bill and sends it to customer.

2 Using Internet browser or banking software, customer views and fills out electronic check authorizing payment.

4 Customer receives monthly statement itemizing payments, but with no paper checks.

FIRST NATIONAL BANK   SECOND NATIONAL BANK

3 Customer's bank and electronic payment network transfer money from customer's account to biller's account.

4 Biller deposits check and bank credits biller's account.

7 At the end of the month, bank prints statement and sends it with canceled checks to customer.

SECOND NATIONAL BANK

6 Customer's bank debits customer's account.

5 Biller's bank codes check and sends it to customer's bank.

The Food Was All Right, but What About the Books?

Boston Chicken seemed to come out of nowhere to take the fast-food market by storm in the 1990s. Its healthful menu of take-home dinners featuring chicken, turkey, meatloaf, and vegetables pleased the palates of harried consumers who were grateful to eat well without having to cook. Reported earnings soon soared, and CEO Scott Beck hoped to open 3,600 restaurants by 2003. Although its stock price rose, the restaurant chain's accounting procedures raised a whiff of controversy that put some restaurant industry watchers on the alert.

Investors remained optimistic, however, for as far as they could tell earnings had risen from $1.6 million in 1993 to $34 million in 1995. But accurate information about the company's finances was hard to get (unless you delved into the data it filed with the SEC). Because the firm is organized into more than a dozen standalone regional franchise groups, called financial area developers (FADs), Boston Chicken was able to avoid recording millions of dollars in operating losses in its corporate accounts. Instead, these losses were written against the FADs, until they more than canceled out the parent company's reported earnings.

Another feature of the chain's accounting that worried analysts was its practice of recording operating expenses such as food and labor costs as overhead for development, which artificially reduced operating expenses at the store level and inflated cash flow earnings. Furthermore, the company provided operating results only for what it called mature stores, about 72 percent of the total. All

other retailers and restaurant chains provide same-store figures for every location open a year or more.

The firm's unusual accounting methods were no secret, but Wall Street investment firms ignored them—and their consequences—and kept promoting the company's stock through 1996. Beck insisted the chain was profitable, and that it was rapid expansion, not losses, that necessitated a steady stream of loan money flowing into its 1,159 franchisees.

However most of Boston Chicken's revenue came not from sales of its homestyle chicken dinners but from royalties and interest being paid back on the big loans the company made to its franchisees. And the franchisees were losing money; by mid-1997 they had lost $356 million over a 3-year period, a figure Boston Chicken never reported in its corporate books. The firm claimed such reporting was not required, but one analyst concluded that Boston Chicken's unusual financial structure was "designed to decouple reported earnings from economic reality."

Meanwhile, the firm was able to raise nearly $300 million by issuing bonds, thanks in part to the backing of the same Wall Street firms that had rated its stock so highly and kept the price inflated. Then the bottom fell out of Boston Chicken's stock price in early 1997. Shares dropped 50 percent as the company's executives admitted sales were falling short. By spring top management had been realigned, expansion plans were on hold, and 115 employees had been laid off. A lot of shareholders were angry.

Questions

1 Boston Chicken's accounting procedures were not illegal, but they do appear to have misled at least some investors. Do you think the procedures were unethical? Why or why not? What, if anything, would you change about the firm's accounting practices?

2 The firm's chief financial officer, Mark Stephens, was quoted as saying that although sales were down, the company's problems had "nothing to do with accounting." Do you agree? Why or why not?

3 Boston Chicken's Wall Street backers made money from handling the restaurant chain's bond issue and that of its subsidiary, Einstein/Noah Bagel Corp., as well as its many loans, so Boston Chicken's profitability was critical to them. Did they have a responsibility to look more closely at the firm's actual finances and disclose what they found? Or should the individual shareholders have been more cautious?

4 Most recently, the chain has tried to refocus its marketing efforts with an expensive new ad campaign and has slowed its expansion in order to increase sales at existing stores. Do you think these attempts to make the firm profitable will restore investors' confidence in Boston Chicken's performance? Why or why not?

5 One writer for *Fortune* magazine called the story of Boston Chicken's rise and fall one of "ignorance, shortsightedness, self-interest, and . . . greed." Do you agree with this assessment? Why or why not?

Connecting to the Web

The following Web sites will give you additional information and points of view about topics covered in this chapter. Many sites lead to other related Internet locations, so approach this list with the spirit of an explorer.

ACCOUNTANTS FOR THE PUBLIC INTEREST

http://www.accountingnet.com/asso/api/index.html

Accountants for the Public Interest is a national organization that encourages accountants to volunteer their time and expertise to nonprofits, small businesses, and individuals who cannot afford professional accounting services. Visit this site to learn about becoming an API volunteer.

ACCOUNTING BOARD OF OHIO

http://www.state.oh.us/acc/

If you're thinking of becoming an accountant in Ohio or are one, visit this site for board functions, including complaint procedures, disciplinary action, administering CPA exams, ethics standards, and continuing education.

THE ACCOUNTING HALL OF FAME

http://www.cob.ohio-state.edu.dept/acctmis/hot/hall.html

Developed by the Fisher College of Business at Ohio State University, the Accountants Hall of Fame honors accountants who have made significant contributions to the advancement of accounting. Visit this site to learn about the 60 accountants who are members of this honored group.

AMERICAN INSTITUTE OF CERTIFIED PUBLIC ACCOUNTANTS (AICPA)

http://www.aicpa.org/

The American Institute of Certified Public Accountants is the most influential and important national association for CPAs. Its mission is to provide members with resources, information, and leadership so they can perform at the highest professional levels. The AICPA is involved in certification and licensing, recruitment and education, the establishment of professional performance standards, member communication, and member advocacy before government and regulatory bodies.

AMERICAN SOCIETY OF WOMEN ACCOUNTANTS

http://www.aswa.org/

The mission of the American Society of Women Accountants is to create opportunities for women in the accounting field and to help women achieve their personal, professional, and economic potential. Visit this site for the benefits of membership.

ARTHUR ANDERSEN

http://www.arthurandersen.com/homepage.htm

Visit this Web page to learn about the accounting and consulting services offered by Arthur Andersen to help client firms improve performance in management, business processes, operations, information technology, and finance. You'll also learn about career opportunities with leading business consultants.

DELOITTE TOUCHE TOHMATSU INTERNATIONAL

http://www.deloitte.com

Visit this site to learn about the national practices of Deloitte Touche Tohmatsu International and, specifically, about the company's accounting, tax, and consulting services in Africa, Asia-Pacific, Europe, North America, and South America.

FINANCIAL ACCOUNTING STANDARDS BOARD (FASB)

http://www.rutgers.edu/Accounting/raw/fasb/home.htm

The Financial Accounting Standards Board determines the accounting rules by which U.S. companies must operate as they prepare financial reports. FASB standards are officially recognized by the Securities and Exchange Commission and the American Institute of Certified Public Accountants. Visit this site for information on specific organizational functions.

INTERNAL AUDITING WORLD WIDE WEB (IAWWW)

http://www.bitwise/net/iawww/

This organization shares information and knowledge pertaining to the internal auditing profession across associations, industries, and countries.

WORLD LECTURE HALL: ACCOUNTING

http://www.utexas.edu/world/lecture/acc/

This Web site contains links to faculty worldwide and includes lectures, syllabi, and other accounting-related information.

part six

Understanding **financial** issues

It's 10 A.M. on Saturday morning—a good time to have some coffee, if only you had the sugar and cream that make it taste so good. Your refrigerator is empty, you're yearning for caffeine, and the supermarket beckons. And so does the market's in-store banking center, where you plan to spend a few extra minutes depositing your paycheck and applying for a home equity loan.

Welcome to the new world of banking, where full-service supermarket branches are located right down the aisle from Kellogg's cereals and where branch managers are learning to sell as hard as Coke and Pepsi. There are now more than 5,000 in-store banks across the country, and the number is climbing every year. "It's a concept whose time has come," said John W. Garnett, president of International Banking Technologies, an Atlanta-based consulting firm.

"There's tremendous potential for new business and the bank does not have to spend one nickel to advertise to bring the people in."

Barely a blip on bankers' radar screen just a few years ago, supermarket banking is now the location of choice for many of the country's largest banks, including Wells Fargo, Bank of America, Barnett Banks, NationsBank, and First Union. San Francisco–based Wells Fargo already has more than 700 supermarket sites and is so confident of its location strategy that it is selling its branch real estate.

Supermarket branches have helped level the playing field for community banks, which lack the resources to go head to head with larger competitors in the normal branch system. For a mere $100,000, instead of $1 million or more for a standalone branch, a small bank can set up shop in a supermarket and compete with the big guys.

Put Branches in Supermarkets and Customers Will Come

Supermarket branches make sense because they give customers what they want: the ability to bank while shopping. As they become more popular, they are forcing bankers to redefine the branch concept. In a 300-square-foot space in the corner of a supermarket, the focus is no longer on operations, but on customer service. "The real issue is, 'Is the customer changing?" explained Don Horner, vice chairperson of First Hawaiian Bank. "And, if so, how can we better serve him and what facility can we use to do it?"

Research has shown that customers want convenience in the form of one-stop banking and that they are willing to use technology to expedite service. At Barnett Bank in Jacksonville, Florida, self-service delivery channels, including ATMs and voice mail systems, account for half of all transactions. Some banks use video technology to augment in-store staff. At the Bank of Oklahoma in Tulsa, a two-way video unit is connected to the bank's call center, via a high-speed (ISDN) telephone hook-up. Customers who want to open an account or apply for a loan dial into the system. The machine can even print temporary checks and ATM cards.

Thanks to this technology, banks are providing full service with fewer employees. Wells Fargo runs its in-store branches with just six employees, half the number in a typical stand-alone branch. But customers don't seem to mind because they can make transactions, set up new accounts, arrange for home and auto loans, and buy insurance and investments without leaving the market.

What Happened to All Those Stuffy Bankers?

If Christopher H. Stephenson is typical, bankers aren't what they used to be. At age 25, Stephenson is a supermarket branch manager for National Commerce Bancorp in suburban Memphis. In a typical month, he and his staff must sell 26 new checking accounts, 26 new money market accounts, as well as other banking products. If the business doesn't come to the window, Stephenson walks the aisles to find it in the market.

This go-out-and-find-the-customer attitude is echoed at the in-store operation of National City Bank in Dublin, Ohio. Since the branch opened in the Big Bear supermarket in 1996, monthly sales, including those produced by telemarketing, have averaged 250 products. A top seller is the home equity loan, which, in just 8 months, has brought in more than $1.2 million.

The greatest challenge this new breed of bankers face is to entice new customers to give them a try. Although supermarket shoppers average 2.5 visits a week, 80 percent have never used an in-store bank. Experience has shown that traditional bank sales strategies don't work in the supermarket setting.

What does work? The same dynamic sales techniques used by food marketers. Francie Henry, vice president and regional manager of Cincinnati-based Fifth Third Bancorp, has learned that banks, like food stores, must capture consumer interest before they can make sales. "We have a product-of-the-month promotion and we always decorate to match the theme," said Henry. "The goal is to keep the message fresh and to keep moving around." She means that literally. Bank employees discuss loans in the bakery aisle, open money market accounts in the meat department, and arrange for certificates of deposit next to containers of Clorox Bleach.

Will Supermarket Branches Be Tomorrow's One-Stop Banking and Investment Center?

As the popularity of in-store branches grows, their product lines are also growing from federally insured vehicles, such as bank money market accounts, to uninsured vehicles, including mutual funds. Large banks, which see themselves as financial supermarkets, are expanding their product lines in both branch and in-store settings.

This worries the National Association of Securities Dealers (NASD), which cites the potential for consumer confusion in the small space of a supermarket bank. NASD spokesman Michael Robinson, explains: "If you walk into a [regular] bank, it's pretty easy to understand that in one section they sell treasury bonds that are federally insured, while in other areas they sell mutual funds. In a supermarket branch, it's much more difficult to make that distinction."

Sandra Deem, a spokesperson for Connecticut-based First Union Corp., considers this distinction unnecessary because most First Union customers use in-store branches for check-cashing and other simple transactions. "People don't often come in to talk about a mutual fund," said Deem. "The people who are coming in to shop for groceries often don't generate the type of business we are looking for."

Despite First Union's skepticism, industry analysts expect approximately 7,500 in-store branches by the year 2000. Will banking and banking relationships ever be the same?

WEB LINKS

The following Web sites will help you examine the issues that surround in-store banking and answer the questions that follow.

American Banker Online	http://www.americanbanker.com/
Barnett Bank	http://www.barnett.com
NationsBank	http://www.nationsbank.com/
New York Stock Exchange	http://www.nyse.com/
Wells Fargo	http://wellsfargo.com/home/
U.S. Securities and Exchange Commission	http://sec.gov/

CASE QUESTIONS

1   In an environment where millions of Americans are taking money out of banks to invest in the stock market (via mutual funds and individual stocks), can you make an argument that supermarket banking is critical to the survival of the banking industry? Explain your answer. (Consult the New York Stock Exchange Web site for investor information.)

2   Do you think that the same consumers who use on-line banking services are likely to use supermarket banking services? Why or why not? (See bank Web sites for information about on-line banking.)

3   Do you agree or disagree with the concerns of the National Association of Securities Dealers about consumer confusion between insured and uninsured investments in the small space of a supermarket bank? What role do you think the U.S. Securities and Exchange Commission should play in addressing these concerns? (See the SEC Web site for information on the agency's regulatory activities.)

4   What effect do you think the Interstate Banking Efficiency Act of 1994 has had on the spread of in-store banks?

5   Do you agree that in-store banking puts small banks on an equal footing with larger institutions?

6   As banks achieve greater efficiencies and lower costs by closing stand-alone branches in favor of in-store branches, how do you think bank stock prices will change? How important do you think these efficiencies are in maintaining a high stock price?

7   Should banks target specific in-store branches for small business owners? What kinds of financial products should they sell?

8   What risks does Wells Fargo face in closing traditional branches in favor of supermarket branches?

chapter 19

Understanding **money** and banking

Who needs cash anyway?

Do your pockets wear out because of all the loose change you carry? That's the complaint of Jay Strom, a Canadian corn farmer who has wholeheartedly embraced an experimental form of money being promoted by the British financial service company Mondex International. "I like the idea," says Strom. "No cash."

Called an electronic cash card or smartcard, the new cashless money has already been market tested globally with moderate success. It has recently appeared in New York City under the watchful eyes of participating financial institutions Citibank, Chase Manhattan, Visa, and MasterCard. It consists of a plastic card with embedded computer chip that can be programmed to record and pay for up to $1,000 worth of purchases at any participating store, or even in parking meters equipped to accept it.

For now Mondex is giving away free the equipment retailers need to accept the card from customers. Cardholders pay 75 cents to $1 for downloading cash electronically or over the phone, but there are no transactions fees to either party. The card's carrying case keeps track of the user's balance, but the chip carries no ID. However, it can be locked with a number code, similar to a PIN.

The experiment may do well in Canada if Jay Strom is an indication. It got off to a slow start in New York, however, where an entire neighborhood on the West Side was given unsolicited cards in the mail. Most of the card-reading equipment was delayed in reaching the stores in the program, and some of it did not function properly. Inertia played a role, too. "Some people still consider cash to be sacred," said David Breault, Mondex's project manager.

And one cashless reporter for the *Wall Street Journal*, foiled in his attempt to use the card for coffee at Starbucks on the first day of the program, had to

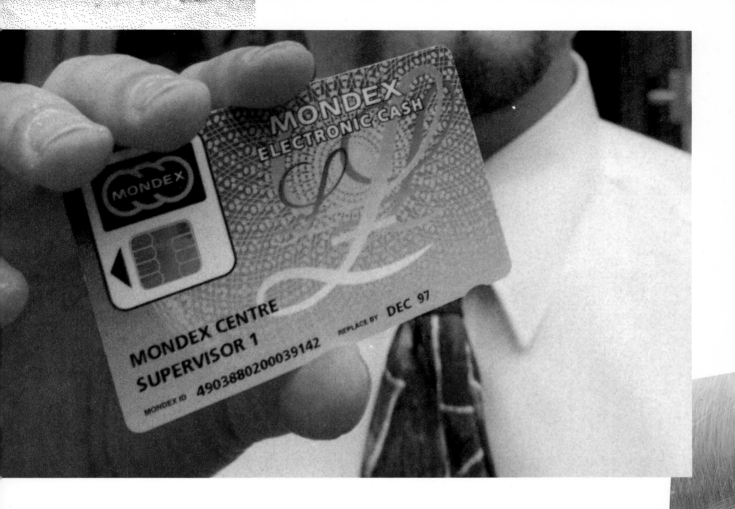

make do with a complimentary cup when the manager took pity on him.

“ *Some people still consider cash to be sacred.* ”

—David Breault,
Mondex's project manager

Meeting the money needs of an entire economy obviously requires a complex system. The U.S. system thus consists of financial institutions, especially banks, that are subject to government regulation. As the needs of the system change, so does the structure of the financial industry that has grown up to serve it. The Mondex electronic cash card is one example of how financial institutions respond to the changing financial environment. By focusing on the learning objectives of this chapter, you will better understand that environment and the different kinds of institutions that conduct business in it. After reading this chapter, you should be able to

1. Define money and identify the different forms it takes in the nation's money supply.

2. Describe the different kinds of financial institutions that make up the U.S. financial system and explain the services they offer.

3. Explain how banks create money and describe the means by which they are regulated.

4. Discuss the functions of the Federal Reserve System and describe the tools it uses to control the money supply.

5. Identify five important ways in which the financial industry is changing.

6. Understand some of the key activities in international banking and finance.

What Is Money?

When someone asks you how much money you have, do you count the dollar bills and coins in your pockets? Do you include your checking and savings accounts? What about stocks and bonds? Do you count your car? Taken together, the value of all these things is your personal wealth. Not all of it, however, is money. In this section, we consider more precisely what money is and does.

The Characteristics of Money

money
Any object that is portable, divisible, durable, and stable and serves as a medium of exchange, a store of value, and a unit of account

Modern money often takes the form of stamped metal or printed paper: U.S. dollars, British pounds, French francs, Japanese yen issued by governments. Theoretically, however, just about any object can serve as **money** if it is portable, divisible, durable, and stable. To appreciate these qualities, imagine using something that lacks them—say, a 70-pound salmon:

- *Portability.* Try lugging 70 pounds of fish from shop to shop. In contrast, modern currency is lightweight and easy to handle.

- *Divisibility.* Suppose you want to buy a hat, a book, and some milk from three different stores. How would you divide your fish-money? Is a pound of its head worth as much as, say, two gills? Modern currency is easily divisible into smaller parts, each with a fixed value. A dollar, for example, can be exchanged for four quarters. More importantly, units of money can be easily matched with the value of all goods.

- *Durability.* Whether or not you spend it, your salmon will lose value every day (in fact, it will eventually be too smelly to be worth anything). Modern currency neither dies nor spoils, and if it wears out, it can be replaced. It is also hard to counterfeit it— certainly harder than catching more salmon.

- *Stability.* If salmon were in short supply, you might be able to make quite a deal for yourself. But in the middle of a salmon run, the market would be flooded with fish. Sellers of goods would soon have enough fish and would refuse to produce anything for which they could get only salmon. Goods would become scarcer, but the salmon would continue (or cease) running regardless of the plenitude or scarcity of buyable goods. The value of our paper money also fluctuates, but it is considerably more stable than salmon. Its value is certainly related to what we can buy with it.

The Functions of Money

Imagine a successful fisherman who needs a new sail for his boat. In a barter economy (one in which goods are exchanged directly for one another) he would have to find someone who not only needs fish but who is also willing to exchange a sail for it. If no sailmaker

"Over there is the first dollar we ever made; next to that is the second dollar we ever made; next to that is the third dollar..."

wants fish, the fisherman must find someone else—say, a shoemaker who wants fish. Then the fisherman must hope that the sailmaker will trade for his new shoes. Clearly, barter is quite inefficient in comparison to money. In a money economy, the fisherman would sell his catch, receive money, and exchange the money for such goods as a new sail.

Money serves three functions:

■ *Medium of exchange.* Like the fisherman trading money for a new sail, we use money as a way of buying and selling things. Without money, we would be bogged down in a system of barter.

■ *Store of value.* Pity the fisherman who catches a fish on Monday and wants to buy a few bars of candy on, say, the following Saturday, by which time the fish would have spoiled and lost its value. In the form of currency, however, money can be used for future purchases and so stores value.

■ *Unit of account.* Money lets us measure the relative values of goods and services. It acts as a unit of account because all products can be valued and accounted for in terms of money. For example, the concepts of $1,000 worth of clothes or $500 in labor costs have universal meaning because everyone deals with money every day.

The Spendable Money Supply: M-1

For money to serve its basic functions, both buyers and sellers must agree on its value. That value depends in part on its supply, or how much money is in circulation. When the money supply is high, the value of money drops. When it is low, that value increases.

Unfortunately, it is not easy to measure the supply of money. One of the most commonly used measures, known widely as **M-1**, counts only the most liquid—that is, spendable forms of money (currency, demand deposits, and other checkable deposits). These are all non–interest or low-interest-bearing forms of money. In July 1997, M-1 in the United States was measured at just over $1 trillion.[1]

M-1
Measure of the money supply that includes only the most liquid (spendable) forms of money

Currency

Currency is the paper money and metal coins issued by the government. It is widely used for small exchanges. As the U.S. dollar bill states, currency is legal tender for all debts, public and private—that is, the law requires creditors to accept it in payment of debts. The average adult in the United States carries about $45 in currency. In July 1997, currency in circulation in the United States amounted to $410 billion, or about 39 percent of M-1. Traveler's checks, bank cashier's checks, and money orders, which are all accepted as currency, accounted for another $8 billion.

currency
Government-issued paper money and metal coins

Demand Deposits

A **check** is essentially an order instructing a bank to pay a given sum to a payee. Checks permit buyers to make large purchases without having to carry large amounts of cash. Although not all sellers accept them as payment, many do. Checks are usually acceptable in place of cash because they are valuable only to specified payees and can be exchanged for cash. Checking accounts, which are known as **demand deposits**, are counted in M-1 because funds may be withdrawn at any time on demand. Eighty-four percent of all U.S. households have checking accounts, and in July 1997, demand deposits account for $396 billion, or about 37 percent of M-1.

check
Demand-deposit order instructing a bank to pay a given sum to a specified payee

demand deposit
Bank account funds that may be withdrawn at any time

Other Checkable Deposits

Other checkable deposits—that is, deposits on which checks can be written—include automated teller machine (ATM) account balances and NOW accounts. NOW (negotiable order of withdrawal) accounts are interest-bearing accounts that can be held only in savings banks and savings and loan associations by individuals and nonprofit organizations. Checkable deposits exceeded $247 billion in July 1997, or 23 percent of M-1.

M-1 Plus the Convertible Money Supply: M-2

M-2
Measure of the money supply that includes all the components of M-1 plus the forms of money that can be easily converted into spendable form

M-2 includes everything in M-1 plus items that cannot be spent directly but are easily converted to spendable forms. The major components of M-2 are M-1, time deposits, money market mutual funds, and savings deposits. Totaling $3.9 trillion in July 1997, M-2 accounts for nearly all the nation's money supply. It thus measures the store of monetary value that is available for financial transactions. As this overall level of money increases, more is available for consumer purchases and business investment. When the supply is tightened, less money is available, and financial transactions, spending, and business activity thus slow down.

Time Deposits

time deposit
Bank funds that cannot be withdrawn without notice or transferred by check

Unlike demand deposits, **time deposits** require prior notice of withdrawal and cannot be transferred by check. On the other hand, however, time deposits pay higher interest rates. Thus, the supply of money in time deposits such as certificates of deposit (CDs) and savings certificates grew rapidly in the 1970s and 1980s after government ceilings on interest rates were removed. Depositors can now invest for both short and long periods of time. Time deposits in M-2 include only accounts of less than $100,000 that can be redeemed on demand with small penalties. Large time deposits, usually those made by businesses, cannot be redeemed early and are not included in M-2. In July 1997, U.S. time deposits amounted to nearly $961 billion—more than 24 percent of M-2.

Money Market Mutual Funds

money market mutual fund
Fund of short-term, low-risk financial securities purchased with the assets of investor-owners pooled by a nonbank institution

Money market mutual funds are operated by investment companies that bring together pools of assets from many investors. The fund buys a collection of short-term, low-risk financial securities. Ownership of and profits (or losses) from the sale of these securities are shared among the fund's investors.

Money market funds attracted many investors in the 1980s because they paid high rates and often allowed investors to write checks against their shares. Why do mutual funds pay higher returns than most individuals can get on their own? There are two reasons:

■ Funds can buy into higher-paying securities that require larger investments than most individuals can afford.

■ They are managed by professionals who monitor changing investment opportunities.

Shortly after being introduced in 1974, money market mutual funds attracted $1.7 billion. By July 1997, they totaled $579 billion—15 percent of M-2.

Savings Deposits

In the wake of new, more attractive investments, traditional savings deposits, such as passbook savings accounts, have declined in popularity. Savings deposits represented 40 percent of M-2 in 1971 but only 34 percent by 1997.

Figure 19.1 shows how the two measures of money (M-1 and M-2) have grown since 1959. For many years, M-1 was the traditional measure of liquid money. Because it was closely related to gross domestic product, it served as a reliable predictor of the nation's economic health. This situation changed in the early 1980s, however, with the introduction of new types of investments and easier transfer of money among investment funds to gain higher interest returns. As a result, M-2 today is a more reliable measure than M-1 and is often used by economists for economic planning.

▶ *A PERCENTAGE SAVED.* For the past several years, Americans have been saving less money than they used to. For nearly three decades after World War II, for example, annual savings amounted to 9 percent of national income. If you look at Figure 19.2, however, you can see that by the early 1980s, that number dropped to below 5 percent. By 1997, it had dipped to 3 percent of national income. On a national scale, the consequences have been

Figure 19.1 Money Supply Growth

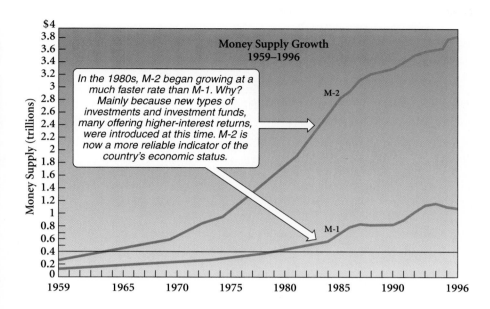

significant: Business has had less to invest, and the United States has been forced to borrow money from abroad, more than $1 trillion over the past 10 years, to finance the trade and budget deficits. The finger of blame is often pointed at baby boomers, people born between 1946 and 1964. Boomers have typically been accused of leading free-spending, self-indulgent lifestyles characterized by too much buying and too little saving. For some time, experts have warned boomers that they will not be financially secure at retirement.

However, new evidence suggests that boomers have gotten a bad rap. According to recent studies, it is actually people 55 years of age and older who are spending at a faster rate. Data show that Americans who are nearing retirement or who are already retired are saving less and consuming more than in previous generations. One reason is the nation's health care and retirement system. Overall, the percentage of household income spent on medical needs has jumped from 6 percent in the 1960s to 15 percent today. Obviously, much of that increase comes from the elderly. But there is another side to the coin: Our medical care and retirement system is also a safety net for many of our elderly. "For many people," concludes one economist, "we've basically eliminated the need to save, because you can have a comfortable retirement without saving." Thus a study by the Federal Reserve Bank of Cleveland shows that an 80-year-old spends $1.16 for every $1.00 that a 30-year-old spends.

> **❝ For many people, we've eliminated the need to save, because you can have a comfortable retirement without saving. ❞**
>
> —John Sabelhaus, economist at the Urban Institute

Of course, boomers must still save something for retirement. And they are. But are they saving enough? Studies show that boomers save 9.5 percent of their incomes, close to their parents' rate of 9.6 percent. To some, that figure refutes the doom-and-gloom scenarios depicting the decline and fall of the baby-boomer standard of living. Those who say it is going to be awful, explains demographer Charles Longino, don't understand that boomers have multiple sources of income and multiple retirement packages for husbands and wives.

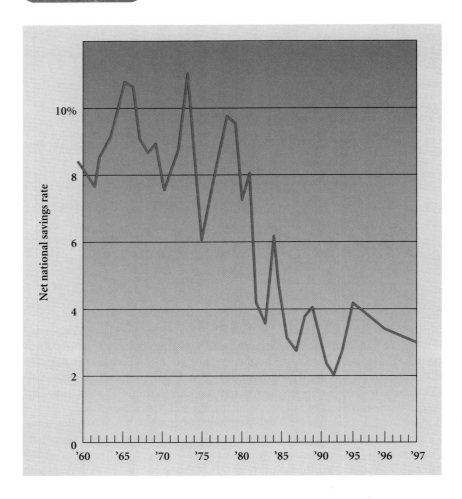

Figure 19.2 The U.S. National Savings Rate, 1960–1997

Of course, not everyone shares Longino's optimism. Merrill Lynch, for instance, has compiled a Baby Boom Retirement Index. According to this study, if they want to maintain their current standard of living in retirement, boomer households are saving just one-third of what they should be saving in order to retire at age 65. "We think there's a very large problem, " says one Merrill Lynch analyst, "and it's going to be worse."[2]

Credit Cards

Citicorp is the nation's largest credit card issuer, with over 38 million accounts among the 124 million U.S. card holders who carry more than 1 billion cards.[3] Spending with general-purpose credit cards reached $731 billion in 1994 and is projected to reach $1.4 trillion—almost half of all transactions—by the year 2000.[4] Indeed, the use of credit cards has become so widespread that many people call them plastic money.

Credit cards are big business for two reasons. First, they are quite convenient. Second, they are extremely profitable for issuing companies. Profits derive from two sources:

- Some cards charge annual fees to holders. All charge interest on unpaid balances. Depending on the issuer and on certain state regulations, cardholders pay interest rates ranging from 11 to 20 percent.

- Merchants who accept credit cards pay fees to card issuers. Depending on the merchant's agreement with the issuer, 2 to 5 percent of total credit sale dollars goes to card issuers.

Credit card loans have also been increasing at the rate of 20 percent per year since 1994. In 1995, for example, CitiCorp issued $44.8 billion in credit card loans. Discover Card issued $27.8 billion in loans. By 1996 credit card debt issued by banks and by nonbank companies had reached 11 percent of commercial bank loan portfolios. Why are banks and other card issuers so willing to grant this kind of credit? Returns are up to three times higher than those from other forms of banking.[5]

Of course, credit cards are not a strictly U.S. phenomenon. Annually, more than 28 million cards are used in the United Kingdom and 25 million in Canada. Likewise, the accompanying problems are international in scope. The number of cards issued in Japan, for instance, doubled (to 166 million) from 1985 to 1990 and so did the number of delinquencies. Many younger Japanese, it seems, have incurred large debts by using credit cards to purchase high-ticket items such as travel packages and automobiles. In South Korea, because heavy spending by young people is contributing to higher inflation, the Finance Ministry has actually curbed the issuance of credit cards: No more cards can be issued to college students, to people younger than 20, or to workers who have held jobs for less than 1 year.[6]

The U.S. Financial System

Many forms of money, especially demand deposits and time deposits, depend on the existence of financial institutions to provide a broad spectrum of services to both individuals and businesses. Just how important are reliable financial institutions to businesses and individuals? Try asking financial consumers in a country where commercial banking can be an adventure.

▶ In Russia, there is almost no banking regulation and no way to distinguish qualified from unscrupulous bankers in thousands of different financial institutions, large and small. The Moscow City Bank has no deposit insurance, no customer service desk, no loan officers, and no cash machine. Businesses need stable financial institutions to underwrite modernization and expansion, and individuals need them to handle currency. Imagine the disappointment of Vladimir Shcherbakov, who needed to withdraw $500 from his account to buy a car but was turned away by a sign announcing that no withdrawals would be allowed for 10 days. "I'm resigned to losing my money," sighed Shcherbakov. "But if I do get it back, I'll change my rubles into dollars and hold onto it myself."[7]

❝ *I'm resigned to losing my money. But if I do get it back, I'll change my rubles into dollars and hold onto it myself.* ❞

—Russian bank customer lamenting the instability the country's financial system

In the sections that follow, we describe the major types of financial institutions, explain how they work when they work as they are supposed to, and survey some of the special services that they offer. We also explain their role as creators of money and discuss the regulation of the U.S. banking system.

Financial Institutions

The main function of financial institutions is to ease the flow of money from sectors with surpluses to those with deficits. They do this by issuing claims against themselves and using the proceeds to buy the assets of and thus invest in other organizations. A bank, for instance, can issue financial claims against itself by making available funds for checking and savings accounts. In turn, its assets will be mostly loans invested in individuals and

It's Your Business

On-Line Banking: An Idea Whose Time Has Come?

Do you write a lot of checks? Do you have two or more accounts at your bank, and do you often transfer money between them? Do you keep track of inflows and outflows in your accounts? If you answered yes to all these, you might be one of the growing number of people doing their banking on-line. The number of banks offering electronic banking could soon reach 600 and is expected to keep climbing fast. The wide range of services they offer and the convenience of banking at home are attracting millions of customers, and improved encryption techniques promise greater security than ever before. Most banks will cover any monetary losses you suffer in the unlikely event of an electronic break-in (although the loss of privacy would be yours to bear).

On the plus side, here's what you can expect in the way of services. With on-line banking you should be able to track balances, list recent transactions, transfer funds, see checking and savings statements, and pay bills (as long as the merchant or institution is set up to receive electronic payment; for the 60 percent that are not, the bank turns your electronic payment command into a paper check it then sends through the mail).

There are a few drawbacks. Electronically paid bills leave no paper trail, so if errors or delays occur it can be difficult to resolve problems. It is rare for funds to go astray in cyberspace, but it can happen, and some banks will make good only if they are sure the error is theirs and not yours. Most banks require a minimum balance for customers paying bills by computer, and many charge up to $10 a month for this service. That could be more than the cost of postage and paper checks if you don't have many bills to pay, but it does represent a big drop in price from just a couple of years ago.

You can make your on-line banking more secure by taking a few simple and familiar precautions. Never give your password or PIN number to anyone. If you write them down, don't also write what they're for, and put them in a secure place. Keep your software up to date; if you use a browser (as opposed to your bank's own software), download updates whenever they become available. Finally, keep a close watch on all your accounts to spot any suspicious activity.

If the benefits sound appealing to you, you'll be glad to know that you can soon get a new peripheral that lets you download cash yourself from your checking account onto a chip card like the one mentioned at the beginning of the chapter. It's called the Personal ATM.

---

businesses and perhaps government securities. In this section we discuss each of the major types of financial institutions: commercial banks, savings and loan associations, mutual savings banks, credit unions, and various organizations known as nondeposit institutions.

Commercial Banks

commercial bank
Federal- or state-chartered financial institution accepting deposits that it uses to make loans and earn profits

The United States today boasts more than 10,000 **commercial banks**: companies that accept deposits that they use to make loans and earn profits. Commercial banks range from the very largest institutions in New York, such as Citibank and Chase Manhattan, to extremely small banks dotting the rural landscape. Bank liabilities include checking accounts and savings accounts. Assets consist of a wide variety of loans to individuals, businesses, and governments.

state bank
Commercial bank chartered by an individual state

national bank
Commercial bank chartered by the federal government

All commercial banks must be chartered. Until 1863 all banks were chartered by individual states. Today, nearly 70 percent of all commercial banks remain **state banks**. Most of the largest U.S. banks, however, are **national banks**, chartered by the federal government. The nine largest U.S. commercial banks are all nationally chartered. In 1996 these nine institutions had combined profits of $18.1 billion. Taken together, all state and national banks hold $4.4 trillion in domestic assets and $2.5 trillion in loans.[8]

Diversification and Mergers. Many observers today believe that traditional banking has become a mature industry—one whose basic operations have expanded as broadly as they can. For instance, 1993 marked the first year in which the money invested in mutual

Figure 19.3   Market Share in the Financial Industry, 1980–1995

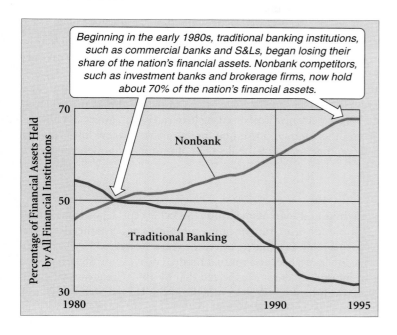

Beginning in the early 1980s, traditional banking institutions, such as commercial banks and S&Ls, began losing their share of the nation's financial assets. Nonbank competitors, such as investment banks and brokerage firms, now hold about 70% of the nation's financial assets.

funds (almost $2 trillion) equaled the amount deposited in U.S. banks. Thus, financial industry competitors in areas such as mutual funds are growing, sometimes rapidly.

As consumers continue to look for alternatives to traditional banking services, commercial banks and savings and loan associations find themselves with a dwindling share of market. As you can see from Figure 19.3, nonbank competitors have increased their share of market to nearly 70 percent. Investment bank Merrill Lynch, for example, has originated billions of dollars in commercial loans, formerly the province of commercial banks. Savers are putting their savings into the money market funds, stocks, and bonds offered by companies such as Charles Schwab instead of into the traditional savings accounts offered by banks. Many observers contend that in order to compete, banks must diversify their offerings. The only way that banks can compete, says banking analyst Thomas Brown, "is to transform themselves into successful retailers of financial services, which involves dramatic, not incremental change."[9]

❝ *The only way that banks can compete is to transform themselves into successful retailers of financial services.* ❞

—Banking analyst Thomas Brown

A related option seems to be to get bigger. In efforts to regain competitiveness, banks have been merging at a record-setting pace in the 1990s. In 1995 there were more than 400 mergers worth $60 billion—more than double the old record set in 1991.[10] BancOne, for example, which operates 62 separately chartered banks in 12 states, made 31 acquisitions between 1990 and 1994. One single merger in 1996 involved institutions with combined assets of $3 billion. Chase Manhattan Corp. became the largest U.S. bank when it merged with Chemical Banking Corp. The new company offers a wide range of services for both consumers and businesses, including private banking, credit card services, mortgages, and loans. Mergers are the trend in U.S. banking, and fewer but larger banks are offering a wide range of financial products. The strategy streamlines operations to reduce costs and focuses on providing products that will win back customers.[11]

Commercial Interest Rates. Every bank receives a major portion of its income from interest paid on loans by borrowers. As long as terms and conditions are clearly revealed to borrowers, banks are allowed to set their own interest rates. Traditionally, the lowest rates were made available to the bank's most creditworthy commercial customers. That rate is called the **prime rate**. Most commercial loans are set at markups over prime. However, the prime rate is no longer a strong force in setting loan rates. Borrowers can now get funds less expensively from other sources, including foreign banks that set lower interest rates. To remain competitive, therefore, U.S. banks now offer some commercial loans at rates below prime.

Savings and Loan Associations

Like commercial banks, **savings and loan associations (S&Ls)** accept deposits and make loans. In the past, they lent money primarily for home mortgages because they were created specifically to provide financing for homes. In recent years, however, they have ventured into consumer loans, life insurance, and mutual funds. Today, some S&Ls have less than half of their assets in mortgages and it is expected that by 1999 Congress will eliminate the legal difference between banks and S&Ls.[12] S&Ls in the United States now hold nearly $1 trillion in assets and deposits of $742 billion.[13]

Mutual Savings Banks

In **mutual savings banks**, all depositors are considered owners of the bank. All profits, therefore, are divided proportionately among depositors, who receive dividends. Like S&Ls, mutual savings banks attract most of their funds in the form of savings deposits, and funds are then lent out in the form of mortgages. Although 90 percent of all mutual savings bank deposits are held in five northeastern states, these institutions nationwide held assets totaling some $1 trillion in 1994.[14]

Credit Unions

Credit unions accept deposits only from members who meet specific qualifications—usually working for a particular employer. Most universities run credit unions, as do the U.S. Navy and the Pentagon. Credit unions make loans for automobiles and home mortgages as well as other types of personal loans. More than 12,000 credit unions now operate in the United States, nearly double the number operating in 1945. They hold $270 billion in savings and checking accounts for more than 72 million members.[15]

Nondeposit Institutions

In addition to banks, a variety of other organizations take in money, provide interest or other services, and make loans. We will describe four of the most important: pension funds, insurance companies, finance companies, and securities dealers.

Pension Funds. A **pension fund** is essentially a pool of funds managed to provide retirement income for its members. Public pension funds include Social Security and $1 trillion in retirement programs for state and local government employees. Private pension funds, operated by employers, unions, and other private groups, cover about 80 million people and have total assets of $5.4 trillion.[16] The Teachers Insurance and Annuity Association (TIAA) operates the largest private fund in the United States, with assets totaling $168 billion in 1997.

Insurance Companies. **Insurance companies** collect large pools of funds from the premiums charged for coverage. Funds are invested in stocks, real estate, and other assets. Earnings pay for insured losses, such as death benefits, automobile damage, and health

prime rate
Interest rate available to a bank's most creditworthy customers

savings and loan association (S&L)
Financial institution accepting deposits and making loans primarily for home mortgages

mutual savings bank
Financial institution whose depositors are owners sharing in its profits

credit union
Financial institution that accepts deposits from, and makes loans to, only its members, usually employees of a particular organization

pension fund
Nondeposit pool of funds managed to provide retirement income for its members

insurance company
Nondeposit institution that invests funds collected as premiums charged for insurance coverage

care expenses (see Appendix I). At the end of 1994, insurance companies had total assets of over $2.5 trillion.[17]

Finance Companies. **Finance companies** specialize in making loans to businesses and individuals. Commercial finance companies lend to businesses needing capital or long-term funds. For instance, they may lend to a manufacturer who needs new assembly line equipment. Consumer finance companies devote most of their resources to small noncommercial loans to individuals. Consumer finance companies take greater risks and generally charge higher interest rates than banks. Most loans pay for such items as cars, appliances, medical bills, and vacations. By the end of 1996, U.S. finance companies had issued credit totaling $762 billion.[18]

finance company
Nondeposit institution that specializes in making loans to businesses and consumers

Securities Dealers. **Securities investment dealers (brokers)**, such as Merrill Lynch and A.G. Edwards & Sons, buy and sell stocks and bonds on the New York and other stock exchanges for client investors. They also invest in securities—that is, they buy stocks and bonds for their own accounts in hopes of reselling them later at a profit. These companies hold large sums of money for transfer between buyers and sellers. Investment bankers match buyers and sellers of newly issued securities and receive commissions for the service. They are thus financial intermediaries. At the end of 1994, U.S. investment dealers

securities investment dealer (broker)
Nondeposit institution that buys and sells stocks and bonds both for investors and for its own accounts

The Workplace Environment

His Bank Pushed Him "Into the Pool"

When Wayne Reece, CEO of Clarklift/FIT, a Florida forklift dealer, and his CFO, Ken Daley, went to Citicorp to look for badly needed capital for their business, they probably thought money was all they would get. Instead, in a relationship that is becoming more and more typical between commercial banks and small business owners, Citicorp's Global Equipment Finance Division lent the money on the condition that Reece prove his firm's computer systems could provide the level of information tracking and financial analysis the bank required. "It's simple," said Citicorp VP David Hilton. "If clients don't have the proper systems to automatically generate the sorts of financial reports we need on a monthly basis, this sort of loan would overwhelm them."

Computerized accounting had not been a big feature of Clarklift's operations, but in response to the bank's request Daley plunged into the firm's underused software programs and learned how to pull out the reports and data Citicorp required. He and Reece also discovered that the rapidly growing firm had picked up some bad business habits such as stocking unused parts that were costing it money. That problem solved, they moved on to a spreadsheet program that laid out forklift rental data, sales data, a brand new corporate database, and automatic posting of

sales quotes to Reece's file and the database. Says Reece, "I just read the (software) manual until the cover fell off." Improved accounts receivable management and targeted marketing campaigns also spring from the firm's new focus on technology.

> ❝ If clients don't have the proper systems to automatically generate the sorts of financial reports we need on a monthly basis, this sort of loan would overwhelm them. ❞
>
> —Citicorp vice president David Hilton

Citicorp recently gave Reece and Daley its Distinguished Dealer Award, and Reece and Daley credit the bank's information requirements with helping the firm use technology to the fullest, contributing to a 33-percent increase in Clarklift's return on assets. This "push into the pool," which was how Reece described the experience of working with the bank, taught the company how to swim.

and investment bankers held $443 billion in assets.[19] (We will discuss the activities of brokers and investment bankers more fully in chapter 20.)

Special Financial Services

The finance business today is a highly competitive industry. No longer is it enough for commercial banks to accept deposits and make loans. For example, most now offer bank-issued credit cards and safe deposit boxes. In addition, many offer pension, trust, international, and brokerage services and financial advice. Most offer automated teller machines and electronic money transfer.

Pension Services

individual retirement account (IRA)
Tax-deferred pension fund with which wage earners supplement other retirement funds

Most banks help customers establish savings plans for retirement. **Individual retirement accounts (IRAs)** are pension funds that wage earners and their spouses can set up to supplement other retirement funds. All wage earners can invest up to $2,000 annually of earned income in an IRA. IRAs offer a significant tax benefit: Under some circumstances, taxes on principal and earnings are deferred until funds are withdrawn upon retirement. Under the 1997 tax changes, some IRAs are entirely tax-free. Banks serve as financial intermediaries by receiving funds and investing them in IRAs as directed by customers. They also provide customers with information on investment vehicles available for IRAs (deposit accounts, mutual funds, stocks, and so forth).

Keogh plan
Tax-deferred pension plan for the self-employed

Banks also assist customers in establishing **Keogh plans**. Though similar to IRAs, Keogh plans can be opened only by self-employed people, such as doctors, small business owners, and consultants. Taxes on Keogh plans are always deferred until earners withdraw the funds. If a depositor needs to withdraw funds from a Keogh or an IRA before age 59½, however, the Internal Revenue Service will impose a penalty of 10 percent on the withdrawn amount.

Trust Services

trust services
Bank management of an individual's investments, payments, or estate

Many commercial banks offer **trust services**: the management of funds left in the bank's trust. In return for a fee, the trust department will perform such tasks as making your monthly bill payments and managing your investment portfolio. Trust departments also manage the estates of deceased people.

International Services

The three main international services offered by banks are currency exchange, letters of credit, and banker's acceptances. Suppose that a U.S. company wants to buy a product from a French supplier. For a fee, it can use one or more of three services offered by its bank:

■ It can exchange U.S. dollars for French francs at a U.S. bank and then pay the French supplier in francs.

letter of credit
Bank promise, issued for a buyer, to pay a designated firm a certain amount of money if specified conditions are met

■ It can pay its bank to issue a **letter of credit**: a promise by the bank to pay the French firm a certain amount if specified conditions are met.

■ It can pay its bank to draw up a **banker's acceptance**, which promises that the bank will pay some specified amount at a future date.

banker's acceptance
Bank promise, issued for a buyer, to pay a designated firm a specified amount at a future date

A banker's acceptance requires payment by a particular date. Letters of credit are payable only after certain conditions are met. For example, the French supplier may not be paid until shipping documents prove that the merchandise has been shipped from France.

Financial Advice and Brokerage Services

Many banks, both large and small, help their customers manage their money. Depending on the customer's situation, the bank may recommend different investment opportunities. The recommended mix might include CDs, mutual funds, stocks, and bonds. Many

Citibank has realized a big payoff from its 20-year commitment to consumer banking technology—that is, to the world's most advanced ATM technology. In one recent year, for example, the consumer banking division earned more than all the bank's other divisions combined. That's why Citibank now has consumer banking outlets in 41 countries, where it strives to make its once specialized products universal. At this ATM machine in Budapest, Hungary, for example, Americans can access their U.S. accounts in English. Then, says Victor Meneszes, head of Citibank's U.S./Europe consumer banking operations, "they can withdraw cash and go across the street to McDonald's. They feel completely at home."

banks also serve as securities intermediaries, using their own stockbrokers to buy and sell securities and their own facilities to hold them.

Automated Teller Machines

Automated teller machines (ATMs) are electronic machines that allow customers to withdraw money and to make deposits 24 hours a day, 7 days a week. They also allow transfers of funds between accounts and provide information on account status. Some 165,000 machines are now located at bank buildings, grocery stores, airports, shopping malls, and other locations in the United States. Some banks offer cards that can be used in affiliated worldwide systems. U.S. bank customers conduct 11 billion ATM transactions a year, withdrawing an average of $50 per transaction.[20]

> **automated teller machine (ATM)**
> Electronic machine that allows customers to conduct account-related activities 24 hours a day, 7 days a week

Increasingly, ATMs are becoming global fixtures. In fact, among the world's 545,000 ATMs, 80 percent are located outside the United States. The world total is expected to reach nearly 950,000 machines by the year 2000. Many U.S. banks offer international ATM services. In China, for example, CitiCorp has installed Shanghai's first 24-hour ATM and is the first foreign bank to receive approval from the People's Bank of China to issue local currency through ATMs. Elsewhere, Citibank machines feature touch screens that take instructions in 10 languages.[21]

Electronic Funds Transfer

ATMs are the most popular form of **electronic funds transfer (EFT)**. EFT systems transfer many kinds of financial information via electrical impulses over wire, cable, or microwave. In addition to ATMs, EFT systems include automatic payroll deposit, bill payment, and automatic funds transfer. Such systems can help you close an important business deal by transferring money from San Francisco to Miami within a few hours.

> **electronic funds transfer (EFT)**
> Communication of fund-transfer information over wire, cable, or microwave

Banks as Creators of Money

In the course of their activities, financial institutions provide a special service to the economy: they create money. This is not to say that they mint bills and coins. Rather, by taking in deposits and making loans, they expand the money supply.

As Figure 19.4 shows, the money supply expands because banks are allowed to lend out most (although not all) of the money that they take in from deposits. Suppose that you deposit $100 in your bank. If banks are allowed to lend out 90 percent of all their deposits, then your bank will hold $10 in reserve and lend $90 of your money to borrowers. (Of course, you still have $100 on deposit.) Meanwhile, borrowers or the people they pay will deposit the $90 loan in their own banks. Together, the borrowers' banks will then

Figure 19.4 How Banks Create Money

Deposit	Money Held in Reserve by Bank	Money to Lend	Total Supply
$100.00	$10.00	$90.00	$190.00
90.00	9.00	81.00	271.00
81.00	8.10	72.90	343.90
72.90	7.29	65.61	409.51
65.61	6.56	59.05	468.56

have $81 (90 percent of $90) available for new loans. Banks, therefore, have turned your original $100 into $271 ($100 + $90 + $81). The chain continues, with borrowings from one bank becoming deposits in the next.

Regulation of Commercial Banking

Because commercial banks are critical to the creation of money, the government regulates them to ensure a sound and competitive financial system. Later in this chapter we will see how the Federal Reserve System regulates many aspects of U.S. banking. Other federal and state agencies including the Comptroller of the Currency and the Federal Deposit Insurance Corporation also regulate banks to ensure that the failure of some banks due to competition will not cause the public to lose faith in the banking system itself.

Comptroller of the Currency

Every national bank is subject to regulation by the Comptroller of the Currency, an office established in 1863 as an agency within the Treasury Department. At least once a year, examiners study each bank's financial statements, business records, and management competence. For example, an examiner may choose a loan at random and study its payment history to determine whether the bank accurately reported that loan's status in statements made to the Comptroller's office.

If audits reveal unsatisfactory practices, the bank must correct the problems. The Comptroller of the Currency can act to ensure a bank's soundness, safety, and security in many ways. For example, it can require changes in credit policies. It can shut down a bank and even require one bank to merge with another.

Federal Deposit Insurance Corporation

Federal Deposit Insurance Corporation (FDIC)
Federal agency that guarantees the safety of all deposits up to $100,000 in the financial institutions that it insures

The **Federal Deposit Insurance Corporation (FDIC)** insures deposits in member banks. More than 99 percent of the nation's commercial banks pay fees for membership in the FDIC. In return, the FDIC guarantees, through its Bank Insurance Fund (BIF), the safety of all deposits up to the current maximum of $100,000. If a bank collapses, the FDIC promises to pay its depositors through the BIF for losses up to $100,000 per person. (A handful of the nation's 10,000 commercial banks are state-insured rather than covered by the BIF.)

To insure against multiple bank failures, the FDIC maintains the right to examine the activities and accounts of all member banks. Such regulation was effective from 1941 through 1980, when fewer than 10 banks failed per year. At the beginning of the 1980s, however, banks were deregulated, and between 1981 and 1990, losses from nearly 1,100 bank failures depleted the FDIC's reserve fund. In recent years, the FDIC has thus raised the premiums charged to member banks to keep up with losses incurred by failed banks.

The Federal Reserve System

Perched atop the U.S. financial system and regulating many aspects of its operation is the Federal Reserve System. Established by Congress in 1913, the **Federal Reserve System**, popularly called **the Fed**, is the nation's central bank. In this section we describe the structure of the Fed, its functions, and the tools that it uses to control the nation's money supply.

The Fed's Structure

The Federal Reserve System consists of a Board of Governors, a group of Reserve Banks, and member banks. As originally established by the Federal Reserve Act of 1913, the system consisted of 12 autonomous banks and a seven-member committee whose powers were limited to coordinating their activities. By the 1930s, however, both the structure and function of the Fed had changed dramatically.

The Board of Governors

The Fed's Board of Governors consists of seven members appointed by the president for overlapping terms of 14 years. The chair of the board serves on major economic advisory committees and works actively with the administration to formulate economic policy. The board plays a large role in controlling the money supply. It alone determines the reserve requirements, within statutory limits, for depository institutions. It also works with other members of the Federal Reserve System to set discount rates and handle the Fed's sale and purchase of government securities.

Reserve Banks

Figure 19.5 shows the 12 administrative areas and 12 banks in the Federal Reserve System. Each Federal Reserve Bank holds reserve deposits from and sets the discount rate for commercial banks in its region. Reserve Banks also play a major role in the nation's check-clearing process.

Federal Reserve System (the Fed)
The central bank of the United States, which acts as the government's bank, serves member commercial banks, and controls the nation's money supply

Figure 19.5   The Federal Reserve System

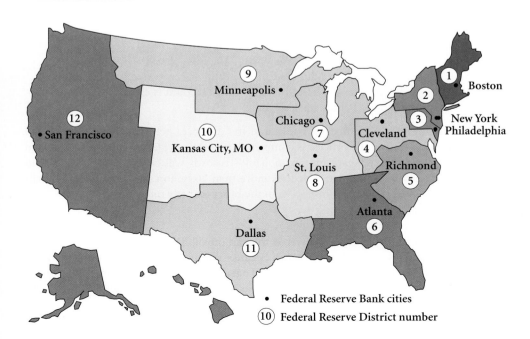

• Federal Reserve Bank cities
⑩ Federal Reserve District number

Member Banks

As we noted earlier, all nationally chartered commercial banks are members of the Federal Reserve System, as are some state-chartered banks. The accounts of all member bank depositors are automatically covered by the FDIC/BIF. Although many state-chartered banks do not belong to the Federal Reserve System, most pay deposit insurance premiums and are covered by the FDIC.

The Functions of the Fed

In addition to chartering national banks, the Fed serves as the federal government's bank and the bankers' bank, regulating a number of banking activities. Most importantly, however, it controls the money supply. In this section we describe these functions in some detail.

The Government's Bank

Two of the Fed's activities are producing the nation's paper currency and lending money to the government. The Fed decides how many bills to produce and how many to destroy. To lend funds to the government, the Fed buys bonds issued by the Treasury Department. The borrowed money is then used to help finance the national deficit.

The Bankers Bank

Individual banks that need money can borrow from the Federal Reserve and pay interest on the loans. In addition, the Fed provides storage for commercial banks, which are required to keep funds on reserve at a Federal Reserve Bank.

Check Clearing. The Fed also clears checks for commercial banks. To understand the check-clearing process, imagine that you are a photographer living in New Orleans. To participate in a workshop in Detroit, you must send a check for $50 to the Detroit studio. Figure 19.6 traces your check through the clearing process:

1 You send your check to the Detroit studio, which deposits it in its Detroit bank.

2 This bank deposits the check in its own account at the Federal Reserve Bank of Chicago.

3 The check is sent from Chicago to the Atlanta Federal Reserve Bank for collection because you, the check writer, are in the Atlanta district.

4 Your New Orleans bank receives the check from Atlanta and deducts the $50 from your personal account.

5 Your bank then has $50 deducted from its deposit account at the Atlanta Federal Reserve Bank.

6 The $50 is shifted from Atlanta to the Chicago Federal Reserve Bank. The studio's Detroit bank gets credited, whereupon the studio's account is credited $50. Your bank mails the canceled check back to you.

Depending on the number of banks and the distances between them, a check will clear in 2 to 6 days. Until the process is completed, the studio's Detroit bank cannot spend the $50 deposited there. Meanwhile, your bank's records will continue to show $50 in your account. Each year, the Fed processes more than 20 billion checks totaling $12 trillion. The term *float* refers to all the checks in the process at any one time.

float
Total amount of checks written but not yet cleared through the Federal Reserve

Overseeing the Banking Community

The Federal Reserve System is empowered to examine all banks in its system. In reality, however, it examines only the state banks because national banks are examined by the Comptroller of the Currency and the FDIC. Together, these auditing efforts ensure the safety and stability of the state and national banks that are members of the Federal Reserve System.

Figure 19.6 Clearing a Check

Controlling the Money Supply

Finally, the Federal Reserve System is responsible for the conduct of U.S. **monetary policy**: the management of the nation's economic growth by managing money supply and interest rates. By controlling these two factors, the Fed influences the ability and willingness of banks throughout the country to lend money.

Inflation Management.   As we defined it in chapter 1, inflation is a period of widespread price increases throughout an economic system. It occurs if the money supply grows two large: Demand for goods and services increases, and the prices rise. (In contrast, too little money means that an economy lacks the funds to maintain high levels of employment.) Because commercial banks are the main creators of money, much of the Fed's management of the money supply takes the form of regulating the supply of money through commercial banks.

▶   Consider the following illustration from 1995. In July the Fed announced a decrease in the Federal funds rate (also called the discount rate), the interest rate charged on overnight loans made among banks, from 6 percent to 5.75 percent. Inflationary trends had been easing since early 1994, and the step was intended to keep the economy from slowing down too much. Thus, the Fed's action completed a classic cycle of rate changes that it had begun in 1990, when the Fed had decreased interest rates to stimulate the re-

monetary policy
Policies by which the Federal Reserve manages the nation's money supply and interest rates

cessionary economy. The Fed steadily cut rates until September 1992, when it became apparent that its actions were having the desired effect: Consumer and business borrowing were increasing and business activity showed signs of increasing during 1993. At that point, therefore, the Fed stopped decreasing the rate. Again, the decision was effective: Although the rate was unchanged throughout 1993, business activity continued to grow.

By 1994, however, the Fed perceived indications that the economy might be growing too fast. Thus, it began gently increasing the interest rate to head off inflation. The first graph in Figure 19.7 shows that, in order to keep inflation under control, the central bank raised the

Figure 19.7   The Fed and the Federal Funds Rate, 1992–1995

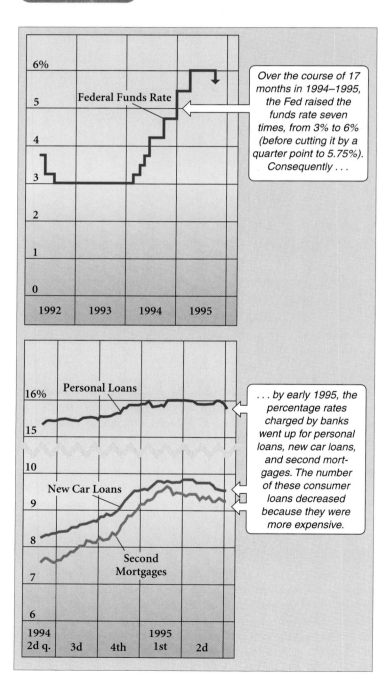

funds rate seven times during the next 17 months. The second graph in Figure 19.7 shows that by early 1995 it was evident that the higher rates were having the desired effect. Because of higher interest rates, for example, consumer loans became more expensive; as consumers borrowed (and spent) less, overall economic activity slowed down. Inflationary pressures were under control. Finally, by mid-1995, there were indications of that another economic slowdown might be under way. Therefore, the Fed cut the rate for the first time since 1992.[22]

The Fed's Tools

According to the Fed's original charter, its primary duties were to supervise banking and to manage both the currency and commercial paper. Gradually, however, the duties of the Fed evolved along with a predominant philosophy of monetary policy. That policy includes an emphasis on the broad economic goals that we discussed in chapter 1: stability, full employment, and growth. The Fed's role in controlling the nation's money supply results from its role in setting policies to help reach these goals. To control the money supply, the Fed uses four primary tools: reserve requirements, discount rate controls, open-market operations, and selective credit controls.

Reserve Requirements

The **reserve requirement** is the percentage of its deposits that a bank must hold, in cash or on deposit, with a Federal Reserve Bank. High requirements mean that banks have less money to lend. Thus, a high reserve requirement reduces the money supply. Conversely, low requirements permit the supply to expand. Because the Fed sets requirements for all depository institutions, it can adjust them to make changes in the overall supply of money to the economy.

> **reserve requirement**
> Percentage of its deposits that a bank must hold in cash or on deposit with the Federal Reserve

Reserve requirements are based on the Fed's assessment of the economic climate in each bank's region. Large cities, for example, are generally regarded as more active because large deposits change hands daily. Meanwhile, deposit activities in so-called country climates are generally more stable because there is less risk of a bank running short of funds from surprisingly heavy activity. As a result, reserve requirements may range from 6 percent in more stable regions to 12 percent in more active regions.

The reserve rate largely determines the lending ability of the financial system. Moreover, rate changes tend to have sudden and dramatic impact on the entire economy. For the sake of economic stability, then, the Fed rarely uses this tool to adjust the money supply.

Discount Rate Controls

As the bankers' bank, the Fed lends money to banks. The interest rate on these loans is known as the **discount rate**. If the Fed wants to reduce the money supply, it increases the discount rate, making it more expensive for banks to borrow money and less attractive for them to lend it. Conversely, low rates encourage borrowing and lending and expand the money supply.

> **discount rate**
> Interest rate at which member banks can borrow money from the Federal Reserve

Open-Market Operations

The third instrument for monetary control is probably the Fed's most important tool. **Open-market operations** are the Fed's sale and purchase of securities (usually U.S. Treasury notes and bonds) in the open market. Open-market operations are particularly effective because they act quickly and predictably on the money supply. How so? The Fed buys securities from dealers. Because the dealer's bank account is credited for the transaction, its bank has more money to lend and so expands the money supply. The opposite happens when the Fed sells securities.

> **open-market operations**
> The Federal Reserve's sales and purchases of securities in the open market

Selective Credit Controls

Finally, the Federal Reserve can exert considerable influence on business activity by exercising **selective credit controls**. The Fed may set special requirements for consumer stock purchases and credit rules for other consumer purchases.

> **selective credit controls**
> Federal Reserve authority to set both margin requirements for consumer stock purchases and credit rules for other consumer purchases

As we will see in chapter 20, investors can set up credit accounts with stockbrokers to buy stocks and bonds. A margin requirement set by the Fed stipulates the amount of credit that the broker can extend to the customer. For example, a 60-percent margin rate means that approved customers can purchase stocks having $100,000 market value with $60,000 in cash (60 percent of $100,000) and $40,000 in loans from the dealer. If the Fed wants to increase securities transactions, it can lower the margin requirement. Customers can then borrow greater percentages of their purchase costs from dealers, thus increasing their purchasing power and the amount of securities they can buy.

Within stipulated limits, the Fed is also permitted to specify the conditions of certain credit purchases. This authority extends to such conditions as allowable downpayment percentages for appliance purchases and repayment periods on automobile loans. The Fed has chosen not to use these powers much in recent years.

The Changing Money and Banking System

The U.S. money and banking systems have changed, sometimes dramatically, in recent years and continue to change today. Deregulation and interstate banking, for example, have increased competition not just among banks but between banks and other financial institutions. Electronic technologies affect not only how you obtain money but also how much interest you pay for it.

Deregulation

The Depository Institutions Deregulation and Monetary Control Act (DIDMCA) of 1980 brought many changes to the banking industry. Before its passage, there were clear distinctions between the types of services offered by different institutions. For example, although all institutions could offer savings accounts, only commercial banks could offer checking accounts, and S&Ls and mutual savings banks generally could not make consumer loans. The DIDMCA and subsequent laws sought to promote competition by eliminating many such restrictions.

A crucial aspect of this act was the deregulation of interest rates. Before 1980, checking accounts could not earn interest, and S&L savings accounts paid very low rates. However, the DIDMCA introduced free competition by granting institutions largely free rein in setting rates.

Under deregulation, many banks were unable to survive in the new competitive environment. In the 1980s, more than 1,000 banks—more than 7 percent of the total—failed, as did 835 savings and loans.[23] However, many economists regard some bank closings as a beneficial weeding out of inefficient competitors.

Interstate Banking

Since 1927, the Pepper-McFadden Act has forbidden interstate banking. During the early 1990s, however, banking institutions became increasingly creative in expanding their activities across state boundaries. For example, Citicorp, the holding company for Citibank, has purchased chains of S&Ls in both California and Florida. In important respects, this strategy gave Citicorp a network of depository institutions in many states—in other words, a first step in interstate banking.

Interstate Banking Efficiency Act of 1994

The Interstate Banking Efficiency Act was passed into law in September 1994, thus allowing banks to enter (gradually) into interstate banking. It also mandates regulation by government agencies to ensure proper operation and competition. The key provisions in this act are as follows:

■ Limited nationwide banking was permitted, beginning in 1995. Bank holding companies can acquire subsidiaries in any state.

- The ultimate size of any company is limited. No one company can control more than 10 percent of nationwide insured deposits. No bank can control more than 30 percent of a state's deposits (each state is empowered to set its own limit).

- Beginning in 1995, banks can provide limited transactions for affiliated banks in other states. They can thus accept deposits, close loans, and accept loan payments on behalf of other affiliated banks. However, they cannot originate loans or open deposit accounts for affiliates.)

- Beginning in June 1997, banks can convert affiliates into full-fledged interstate branches.

- Regulation of the new system involves a commission, established by the Secretary of the Treasury, to study its strengths and weaknesses in meeting customer needs. The Federal Reserve, Government Accounting Office (GAO), and FDIC have new duties for evaluating, monitoring, and reporting on interstate banking activities.[24]

Interstate banking offers certain efficiencies. For example, it allows banks to consolidate services and eliminate duplicated activities. Opponents remain concerned that some banks will gain undue spheres of influence, dominate other banks, and hinder competition. Critics also point to the risk of financial loss from the collapse of large banks with huge resources.

The new law addresses these concerns through regulation by both federal and state agencies to ensure antitrust compliance. The Federal Reserve, for example, uses an index to test how a given merger would upset the competitive balance in bank deposits. It also tests for effects on lending to prevent any unfair advantage that would hinder competition.[25]

The Impact of Electronic Technologies

Like so many other businesses, banks are increasingly investing in technology as a way to improve efficiency and customer service levels. Many banks offer ATMs and EFT systems. Some offer TV banking, in which customers use television sets and terminals or home computers to make transactions. The age of electronic money has arrived. Each business day more than $2 trillion exists in and among banks and other financial institutions in purely electronic form. Digital money is replacing cash in stores, taxicabs, subway systems, and vending machines. Each year the Fed transfers electronically more than $200 trillion in transactions.

Debit Cards

One of the fast-growing electronic offerings from the financial industry is the debit card. More than 1.3 million debit cards are being issued each month and banking experts expect that two-thirds of U.S. households will have one by the year 2000.[26] Unlike credit cards, **debit cards** allow only the transfer of money between accounts. They do not increase the funds at an individual's disposal. However, they can be used to make retail purchases.

For example, in stores with **point-of-sale (POS) terminals**, customers insert cards that transmit to terminals information relevant to their purchases. The terminal relays the information directly to the bank's computer system. The bank automatically transfers funds from the customer's account to the store's account.

Smartcards

The smartcard is the size of a credit card with an integrated circuit chip embedded in the plastic. The computer chip stores information and can be programmed with electronic money. Also known as electronic purses or stored-value cards, smartcards have actually existed for nearly a decade. Shoppers in Europe and Asia are the most avid users, holding the majority of the 33 million cards in circulation at the beginning of 1995.[27]

debit card
Plastic card that allows an individual to transfer money between accounts

point-of-sale (POS) terminal
Electronic device that allows customers to pay for retail purchases with debit cards

Commuters in metropolitan New York are getting accustomed to paying bridge and tunnel tolls with the E-Z Pass, a debit device that the driver attaches to the front windshield. A scanner electronically records trips through participating bridge and tunnel toll booths and debits an account established with the customer's credit card. Currently offered by the Metropolitan Transit Authority and the Port Authority of New York and New Jersey, the E-Z Pass will soon be offered by other transportation authorities in New Jersey, Pennsylvania, Delaware, and Maryland.

Why are smartcards increasing in popularity today? For one thing, the cost of producing them has fallen dramatically, from as much as $10 to as little as $1. Convenience is equally important, notes Donald J. Gleason, president of Electronic Payment Services' Smart Card Enterprise division. "What consumers want," Gleason contends, "is convenience, and if you look at cash, it's really quite inconvenient."[28]

> **What consumers want is convenience, and if you look at cash, it's really quite inconvenient.**
>
> —Donald J. Gleason, president of Smart Card Enterprise

Smartcards can be loaded with money at ATM machines or, with special telephone hookups, even at home. After using your card to purchase an item, you can then check an electronic display to see how much money your card has left. Analysts predict that in the near future, smartcards will function as much more than electronic purses. For example, travel industry experts predict that people will soon book travel plans at home on personal computers and then transfer their reservations onto their smartcards. The cards will then serve as airline tickets and boarding passes. As an added benefit, they will allow travelers to avoid waiting in lines at car rental agencies and hotel front desks.

E-Cash

A new world of electronic money has begun to emerge with the rapid growth of the Internet. Electronic money, known as e-cash, is money that moves back and forth between consumers and businesses via digital electronic transmissions. E-cash moves outside the established network of banks, checks, and paper currency overseen by the Federal Reserve. Companies as varied as new startup Mondex and giant Citicorp are developing their own forms of electronic money that allows consumers and businesses to spend money more conveniently, quickly, and cheaply than they can through the banking system. In fact, some observers predict that by 2005, as much as 20 percent of all household expenditures will take place on the Internet. "Banking," comments one investment banker, "is essential to the modern economy, but banks are not."

" Banking is essential to the modern economy, but banks are not. "

—J. Richard Fredericks, senior managing director at Montgomery Securities

How does e-cash work? Traditional currency is used to buy electronic funds, which are downloaded over phone lines into your PC or a portable electronic wallet that can store and transmit e-cash. E-cash is purchased from any company that issues (sells) it, including companies such as Mondex, Citicorp, and banks. When shopping on-line—say, to purchase jewelry—a shopper sends digital money to the merchant instead of using traditional cash, checks, or credit cards. Businesses can purchase supplies and services electronically from any merchant that accepts e-cash. E-cash flows from the buyer's into the seller's e-cash funds, which are instantaneously updated and stored on a microchip. Or, funds can be transferred between cards, from person to person. One system, operated by CyberCash, tallies all e-cash transactions in the customer's account and, at the end of the day, converts the e-cash balance back into dollars in your conventional banking account.

Although e-cash transactions are cheaper than handling checks and the paper records involved with conventional money, there are some potential problems. Hackers may break into e-cash systems and drain them instantaneously. Moreover, if the issuer's computer system crashes, it is conceivable that money banked in memory may be lost forever. Finally, regulation and control of e-cash systems remain largely nonexistent; there is virtually none of the protection that covers government-controlled money systems.[29]

International Banking and Finance

Along with international banking networks, electronic technologies now permit nearly instantaneous financial transactions around the globe. The economic importance of international finance is evident from both the presence of foreign banks in the U.S. market and the sizes of certain banks around the world. In addition, each nation tries to influence its currency exchange rates for economic advantage in international trade. The subsequent country-to-country transactions result in an international payment process that moves money among buyers and sellers on different continents.

International Banking at U.S. Banks

The United States is heavily involved in international transactions that often entail exchanges between U.S. banks and other banks around the world. In 1996 these transactions amounted to some $2 trillion. Such sums have obviously attracted foreign banks to the U.S. market, where many now maintain a significant presence. In their U.S. branches and agencies, these banks hold $907 billion in assets and $367 billion in loans, mostly in New York, California, and Illinois. Meanwhile, foreign branches of U.S. banks, most notably in the United Kingdom, the Bahamas, and the Cayman Islands, hold $700 billion in assets.[30]

Interestingly, the largest banks in the world are not U.S. banks. In fact, the largest American institution, Chase Manhattan Corp., ranks only eighteenth worldwide, with assets equal to about one-half of the world's largest bank: Japan's Bank of Tokyo-Mistsubishi, which holds $700 billion in assets.[31]

Exchange Rates and International Trade

As we saw in chapter 18, every country's currency exchange rate affects its ability to buy and sell on the global market. The value of a given currency (say, the Canadian dollar) reflects the overall supply and demand for Canadian dollars both at home and abroad. This value changes with economic conditions. Worldwide, therefore, firms will watch those trends. For example, what is the current exchange rate between their own currencies and that of Canada? Decisions about whether to do business in Canada will be affected by more or less favorable exchange rates. How do firms determine when rates are favorable?

The Law of One Price

When a country's currency becomes overvalued, its exchange rate is higher than warranted by its economic conditions. Its high costs make it less competitive: Because its products are too expensive to make and buy, fewer are purchased by other countries. The likely result is a trade deficit (see chapter 3). In contrast, an undervalued currency means low costs and low prices: It attracts purchases by other countries, usually leading to a trade surplus.

law of one price
Principle holding that identical products should sell for the same price in all countries

How do we know whether a currency is overvalued or undervalued? One method involves a simple concept called the **law of one price**: the principle that identical products should sell for the same price in all countries. In other words, if the different prices of a Rolex watch in different countries were converted into a common currency, the common-denominator price should be the same everywhere.

But what if prices are not equal? In theory, the pursuit of profits should equalize them: Sellers in high-priced countries will have to reduce prices if they are to compete successfully and make profits. As prices adjust, so should the exchange rates between different currencies until the Rolex can be purchased for the same price everywhere.

Big MacCurrencies. A simple example that illustrates over- and undervalued currencies is the Big MacCurrencies, an index published annually in the British magazine *The Economist*. The identical product here is always McDonald's Big Mac, which is made locally in 68 countries. The first two columns in Table 19.1 list several countries and Big

Table 19.1   The Big Mac Currency Index

Country	Big Mac Prices in Local Currency	Big Mac Prices in Equivalent U.S. Dollars	Local Currency Overvaluation (+) or Undervaluation (−)
United States	**$2.42**	**$2.42**	
Switzerland	5.90 francs	4.02	+66%
Denmark	25.75 krone	3.95	+63
Belgium	109 francs	3.09	+28
Chile	1,200 pesos	2.88	+19
S. Korea	2,300 won	2.57	+6
Argentina	2.50 pesos	2.50	+3
Taiwan	$68 Taiwanese	2.47	+2
Japan	294 yen	2.34	−3
Canada	$2.88 Canadian	2.06	−14
Australia	$2.50 Australian	1.94	−20
Poland	4.30 zloty	1.39	−43
China	9.70 yuan	1.16	−52

Mac prices in terms of local currencies. Each country's price is then converted into dollars (based on recent exchange rates). As you can see, the Swiss price (SFr5.90) is most expensive, and the Chinese is the cheapest.

According to the Big Mac index, then, the Swiss franc is the most overvalued currency (against the dollar), and the Chinese yuan is the most undervalued. In theory, this means that you could buy Big Macs in China (using yuan) and resell them in Switzerland (for Swiss francs) at a handsome profit. In China, therefore, the demand for burgers would increase, driving the price up toward the higher prices in the other countries. In other words, the law of one price would set in. The index also indicates that the exchange rates of Taiwan, Argentina, and Japan are barely overvalued or undervalued against the dollar. Governments and businesses use far more sophisticated methods to measure the purchasing power of different currencies in making much more complex transactions.

Government Influences on Exchange Rates

What happens in reality when a currency becomes overvalued or undervalued? A nation's economic authorities may take action to correct its balance-of-payments conditions. Typically, they will devalue or revalue the nation's currency. The purpose of devaluing is to cause a decrease in the home country's exchange value. It will then be less expensive for other countries to buy the home country's products. As more of its products are purchased, the home country's payment deficit goes down. The purpose of revaluation, of course, is the reverse: to increase the exchange value and reduce the home country's payment surplus.

As an example, at the beginning of December 1994, the exchange rate was 3.5 Mexican pesos per U.S. dollar. Three weeks later, Mexican officials announced a devaluation, and the rate quickly changed to 4.65 pesos per dollar. By December 1997, the rate had gone to 8.16 on the world market. Mexican officials expect the more favorable exchange rate to encourage other countries to buy more Mexican products, thereby reducing Mexico's payments deficit.

The International Payment Process

Now we know why a nation tries to control its balance of payments and what it can do about an unfavorable balance. When transactions are made among buyers and sellers in different countries, exactly how are payments made? Payments are simplified through the services provided by their banks. For example, payments from buyers flow through a local bank that converts them from the local currency into the foreign currency of the seller. The local bank receives and converts incoming money from the banks of foreign buyers. The payment process is shown in Figure 19.8.[32]

1 A U.S. olive importer withdraws $1,000 from its checking account in order to buy olives from a Greek exporter. The local U.S. bank converts those dollars into Greek drachmas at the current exchange rate (230 drachmas per dollar).

2 The U.S. bank sends the check for 230,000 drachmas (230 × 1,000) to the exporter in Greece.

3 and 4 The exporter sends olives to its U.S. customer and deposits the check in its local Greek bank. The exporter now has drachmas that can be spent in Greece, and the importer has olives to sell in the United States.

At the same time, a separate transaction is being made between a U.S. machine exporter and a Greek olive oil producer. This time, importer/exporter roles are reversed between the two countries: The Greek firm needs to import a $1,000 olive oil press from the United States.

5 and 6 Drachmas (230,000) withdrawn from a local Greek bank account are converted into $1,000 U.S. dollars and sent via check to the U.S. exporter.

7 and 8 The olive oil press is sent to the Greek importer, and the importer's check is deposited in the U.S. exporter's local bank account.

Figure 19.8 The International Payment Process

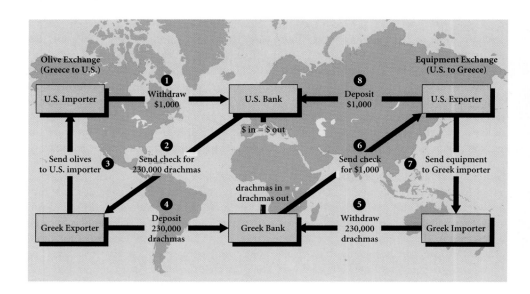

In this example, trade between the two countries is in balance: Money inflows and outflows are equal for both countries. When such a balance occurs, money does not actually have to flow between the two countries. Within each bank, the dollars spent by local importers offset the dollars received by local exporters. In effect, therefore, the dollars have simply flowed from U.S. importers to U.S. exporters. Likewise, the drachmas have moved from Greek exporters to Greek importers.

International Bank Structure

There is no worldwide banking system that is comparable, in terms of policy-making and regulatory power, to the system of any industrialized nation. Rather, worldwide banking stability relies on a loose structure of agreements among individual countries or groups of countries.

The World Bank and the IMF

Two United Nations agencies, the World Bank and the International Monetary Fund, help to finance international trade. Unlike true banks, the **World Bank** (technically the International Bank for Reconstruction and Development) provides only a very limited scope of services. For instance, it funds national improvements by making loans to build roads, schools, power plants, and hospitals. The resulting improvements eventually enable borrowing countries to increase productive capacity and international trade.

The **International Monetary Fund (IMF)** is a group of some 150 nations that have combined resources for the following purposes:

■ To promote the stability of exchange rates

■ To provide temporary, short-term loans to member countries

■ To encourage members to cooperate on international monetary issues

■ To encourage development of a system for international payments

The IMF makes loans to nations suffering from temporary negative trade balances. By making it possible for these countries to continue buying products from other countries, the IMF facilitates international trade. However, some nations have declined IMF funds rather than accept the economic changes that the IMF demands. For example, some

World Bank
United Nations agency that provides a limited scope of financial services, such as funding national improvements in undeveloped countries

International Monetary Fund (IMF)
United Nations agency consisting of about 150 nations that have combined resources to promote stable exchange rates, provide temporary short-term loans, and serve other purposes

developing countries reject the IMF's requirement that they cut back social programs and spending in order to bring inflation under control.

Summary of Learning Objectives

1 **Define money and identify the different forms it takes in the nation's money supply.** Any item that is portable, divisible, durable, and stable satisfies the four basic characteristics of money. Money also serves three functions: It is a medium of exchange, a store of value, and a unit of account. The nation's money supply is often determined by two measures. M-1 includes liquid (or spendable) forms of money: currency (bills and coins), demand deposits, and other checkable deposits (such as ATM account balances and NOW accounts). M-2 includes M-1 plus items that cannot be directly spent but can be converted easily to spendable forms: time deposits, money market funds, and savings deposits. Credit must also be considered as a factor in the money supply.

2 **Describe the different kinds of financial institutions that make up the U.S. financial system and explain the services they offer.** The U.S. financial system includes federal- and state-chartered commercial banks, savings and loan associations, mutual savings banks, credit unions, and nondeposit institutions such as pension funds and insurance companies. These institutions offer a variety of services, including pension, trust, and international services, financial advice and brokerage services, and electronic funds transfer (EFT), including automated teller machines.

3 **Explain how banks create money and describe the means by which they are regulated.** By taking in deposits and making loans, banks create money or, more accurately, expand the money supply. The overall supply of money is governed by several federal agencies. The Comptroller of the Currency and the Federal Deposit Insurance Corporation (FDIC) are the primary agencies responsible for ensuring a sound, competitive financial system.

4 **Discuss the functions of the Federal Reserve System and describe the tools it uses to control the money supply.** The Federal Reserve System (or the Fed) is the nation's central bank. As the government's bank, the Fed produces currency and lends money to the government. As the bankers' bank, it lends money (at interest) to member banks, stores required reserve funds for banks, and clears checks for them. The Fed is empowered to audit member banks and sets U.S. monetary policy by controlling the country's money supply. To control the money supply, the Fed specifies reserve requirements (the percentage of its deposits that a bank must hold with the Fed). It sets the discount rate at which it lends money to banks and conducts open-market operations to buy and sell securities. It also exerts influence through selective credit controls (such as margin requirements governing the credit granted to buyers by securities brokers).

5 **Identify five important ways in which the financial industry is changing.** Many changes have affected the financial system in recent years. Deregulation, especially of interest rates, and the rise of interstate banking have increased competition. Electronic technologies offer a variety of new financial conveniences to customers. Debit cards are plastic cards that permit users to transfer money between bank accounts. Smartcards are credit card-sized computers that can be loaded with electronic money at ATMs or over special telephone hookups. E-cash is money that can be moved among consumers and businesses via digital electronic transmissions. Another change is the increase in foreign banks now maintaining a significant presence in the United States to aid international trade.

6 **Understand some of the key activities in international banking and finance.** Electronic technologies now permit speedy global financial transactions to support the growing importance of international finance. Country-to-country transactions are

conducted according to an international payment process that moves money among buyers and sellers in different nations. Each nation tries to influence its currency exchange rates to gain advantage in international trade. For example, if its currency is overvalued, a higher exchange rate usually results in a trade deficit. Conversely, undervalued currencies can attract buyers and create trade surpluses. Governments may act to influence exchange rates by devaluing or revaluing their national currencies (that is, by decreasing or increasing them). Devalued currencies make it less expensive for other countries to buy the home country's products.

Questions and Exercises

Questions for Review

1 What are the components of M-1? Of M-2?
2 Explain the roles of commercial banks, savings and loan associations, and nondeposit institutions in the U.S. financial system.
3 Explain the types of pension services that commercial banks provide for their customers.
4 Describe the structure of the Federal Reserve System.
5 Show how the Fed uses the discount rate to manage inflation in the U.S. economy.

Questions for Analysis

6 Do you think credit cards should be counted in the money supply? Why or why not? Support your argument by using the definition of money.
7 Should commercial banks be regulated, or should market forces be allowed to determine the money supply? Why?
8 Identify a purchase made by you or a family member in which payment was made by check. Draw a diagram to trace the steps in the clearing process followed by that check.

Application Exercises

9 Start with a $1,000 deposit and assume a reserve requirement of 15 percent. Now trace the amount of money created by the banking system after five lending cycles.
10 Interview the manager of a local commercial bank. Identify several ways in which the Fed either helps the bank or restricts its operations.

Building Your Business Skills

This exercise enhances the following SCANS workplace competencies: demonstrating basic skills, demonstrating thinking skills, exhibiting interpersonal skills, working with information, and applying system knowledge.

Goal   To encourage students to understand the economic factors considered by the Federal Reserve Board to determine current interest rates.

Background One of the Federal Reserve's most important tools in setting monetary policy is the adjustment of the interest rates it charges member banks to borrow money. To determine interest rate policy, the Fed analyzes current economic conditions from its 12 districts. Its findings are published eight times a year in a report commonly known as the *Beige Book*.

Method   **Step 1:** Working with three other students, access the Federal Reserve's Web site at http://www.bog.frb.fed.us/. Look for the heading "Federal

Open Market Committee," then click on the subheading *"Beige Book."* When you reach that page, click on the "Summary" of the "Current Report."

Step 2: Working with group members, study each of the major summary sections:
- Consumer spending
- Manufacturing
- Construction and real estate
- Banking and finance
- Nonfinancial services
- Labor market, wages, and pricing
- Agriculture and natural resources

Then, working with team members, discuss how you think key information contained in the summary might affect the Fed's decision to raise, lower, or maintain interest rates.

Step 3: At your library find back issues of *Barron's,* the highly respected weekly financial publication. Look for the issue published right after the current *Beige Book,* and search for articles analyzing the report. Discuss with group members what the articles say about current economic conditions and interest rates.

Step 4: Based on your research and analysis, what factors do you think the Fed will take into account to control inflation? Working with group members, explain your answer in writing.

Step 5: Working with group members, research what the Federal Reserve chairman says next about interest rates. Do his reasons for raising, lowering, or maintaining rates agree with your group's analysis?

Follow-Up Questions

1 What are the most important factors in the Fed's interest rate decision?
2 Based on your research and analysis, why do you think economists have such varying opinions? (There is a common joke about economists that goes like this: When there are four economists in a room analyzing current economic conditions, there are at least eight different opinions.)

Under the Federal Credit Union Act, credit unions come under a Federal regulation that limits their membership to "groups having a common bond of occupation or association," or belonging to a particular community. In their early days, credit unions were limited to members of a single firm or occupation. But as it is now interpreted, that wording can mean unrelated groups, each defined by its own common bond.

The result of the new interpretation, which was issued by the National Credit Union Administration in 1982, was to greatly increase the number of credit unions and their members. There are now 7,000 federally chartered credit unions, and about half those, including many of the largest ones, encompass multiple groups of members.

Credit unions have expanded their services and now compete directly with banks in many areas. They provide home mortgages, car loans, checking accounts, and of course savings (or "share") accounts. As non-profit, tax exempt cooperatives staffed mostly by volunteers, credit unions can offer more financial products and services at lower costs than banks, with which they have recently begun to compete in earnest.

It should come as no surprise, then, that banks are anxious to abridge some of the credit unions' new growth. The American Bankers Association has challenged the 1982 interpretation in a suit now before the Supreme Court. The government supports the broader interpretation of the rule and is relying on the ambiguity of the original wording (written in 1934) to support its case that *group* can mean multiple "groups." It also asserts that the purpose of the regulation was not to protect banks from competition.

The bankers, on the other hand, want to apply the stricter interpretation, which would reduce the scope of many established credit unions. (It is not clear yet what would happen to current member groups if the banks were to prevail.)

In any case a bill already before Congress would make the 1982 regulation into law. If they lose in court, the credit unions will certainly push for its passage.

Questions

1 Do you think the banks have the right to challenge the 1982 regulation, which does not directly address them? Or do you feel their interest in the outcome gives them a stake in the ruling?

2 Is competition between banks and credit unions good for the consumer? Why or why not?

3 Other than the fight over the 1982 rule, what might banks do to step up their competition with credit unions?

4 What would you expect credit unions to do in response?

Connecting to the Web

The following Web sites will give you additional information and points of view about topics covered in this chapter. Many sites lead to other related Internet locations, so approach this list with the spirit of an explorer.

THE AMERICAN BANKER

http://www.americanbanker.com/

The American Banker, the daily newspaper of the banking industry, is available on-line. Visit on the site to learn about the industry's current issues.

BOARD OF GOVERNORS OF THE FEDERAL RESERVE SYSTEM

http://www.bog.frb.fed.us/

This site explores the purposes and functions of the Federal Reserve System in ensuring a safe, flexible, stable monetary and financial system.

CITIBANK

http://www.citicorp.com/

Citibank's Web site highlights the diversity of today's commercial banks. The Web site allows you to visit Citibank's PC banking, credit card, investment center as well as traditional banking services.

INTERNATIONAL MONETARY FUND

http://www.imf.org/

Chartered in 1945, the International Monetary Fund currently has 182 member countries. Among its functions are the promotion of international monetary cooperation and foreign trade and the distribution of general resources to member countries that are experiencing balance of payments difficulties. Visit this site to explore IMF functions and recent activities.

MONDEX INTERNATIONAL

http://www.mondex.com

Visit this site to learn how Mondex uses smartcard technology to offer an alternative to traditional cash.

THE OSU VIRTUAL FINANCE LIBRARY

http://www.cob.ohio-state.edu/dept/fin/overview.htm

Developed and maintained by Ohio State's Department of Finance, this Web site explores various financial institutions including banks, investment banks, insurers, exchanges, and world markets. The site is open to all, including students, researchers, investors, and executives. Visit this site to learn about the top five minority and women-owned financial institutions.

THE SMART CARD FORUM

http:www.smartcardforum.org/

The Smart Card Forum is an advocacy group that tries to increase the acceptance and application of smartcard technology by bringing together leading users and technologists in government and the private sector.

SMITH BARNEY

http://www.smithbarney.com/

Solomon Smith Barney allows investors to monitor their portfolios, do financial planning, and analyze financial products and services on-line.

chapter 20

Understanding **securities** and **investments**

Investing in a team of your own

In 1988 it cost about $25,000 to own a team in the East Coast Hockey League. Today the team is worth about $1.5 million.

Although it sounds like a good investment, that rate of appreciation in value is rare in pro sports. But most teams do appreciate over time even if they aren't profitable, and the opportunity to own or at least invest in a team has its own appeal. Pro sports, particularly women's sports, are growing, fueled in part by the expansion of TV broadcasts of sports events. Arena football, women's basketball, indoor soccer, team bicycling, and roller hockey are some of the expanding sports leagues in the United States today, and investing in them wisely requires the same careful scrutiny of hidden costs and future earning power that you'd expect to use for more traditional investments such as stocks and bonds.

In addition to the purchase price, which can range from $50,000 for a team in the Professional Bicycle League to $1 million for a franchise in the Continen-

tal Basketball Association, you should expect to pay another 150 to 200 percent of the price every year in operating costs. And, says Jason Klein, owner of the Buffalo Wings roller hockey team, "it takes a lot more marketing muscle and resources than you anticipated."

Then there are the owners' responsibilities to negotiate contracts, leases on arenas or stadiums, and media rights. And there's always the risk of failure, which struck the owners of the Huntington Club, a West Virginia baseball team in the minor leagues. When the owners' partners, the Chicago Cubs, let their contract to co-manage the team lapse, the team disbanded and the investors lost their money. But owning a sports team still holds allure. Says Mike Veeck, who owns five minor league baseball teams, "It's possible to make money, and it's also possible to lose a lot very quickly. . . . [But] at the end of the day, no matter how rotten the day is, my office is a ball field."

And there soon may be a safer way to own a piece of your favorite team. The Florida Panthers, an ice hockey team, is selling stock in itself for only $10 a share.

> ❝ *It's possible to make money, and it's also possible to lose a lot very quickly.... [But] at the end of the day, no matter how rotten the day is, my office is a ball field.* ❞
>
> —Mike Veeck, owner of five minor league baseball teams

As you will see in this chapter, business success is increasingly determined by investors' evaluations of the stocks and bonds that firms issue to raise needed capital. The East Coast Hockey League, for example, was able to expand and prosper, so the teams became financially attractive to investors. New professional teams sometimes raise investment capital with low-cost initial offerings of common stock. However, the sports industry also demonstrates how investor expectations of high growth can subject them and the companies in which they invest to financial risks in an extremely competitive business environment. By focusing on the learning objectives of this chapter, you will better understand the importance of the marketplaces in which securities are traded and the nature of such investment vehicles as stocks and bonds, mutual funds, and commodities. After reading this chapter, you should be able to

1 Explain the difference between primary and secondary securities markets.

2 Discuss the value to shareholders of common and preferred stock and describe the secondary market for each type of security.

3 Distinguish among various types of bonds in terms of their issuers, safety, and retirement.

4 Describe the investment opportunities offered by mutual funds and commodities.

5 Explain the process by which securities are bought and sold.

6 Explain how securities markets are regulated.

Securities Markets

securities
Stocks and bonds representing secured, or asset-based, claims by investors against issuers

Stocks and bonds are known as **securities** because they represent secured, or asset-based, claims on the part of investors. In other words, holders of stocks and bonds have a stake in the business that issued them. As we saw in chapter 2, stockholders have claims on some of a corporation's assets (and a say in how the company is run) because each share of stock represents part ownership.

In contrast, bonds represent strictly financial claims for money owed to holders by a company. Companies sell bonds to raise long-term funds. The markets in which stocks and bonds are sold are called securities markets.

Primary and Secondary Securities Markets

primary securities market
Market in which new stocks and bonds are traded

In **primary securities markets**, new stocks and bonds are bought and sold by firms and governments. Sometimes, new securities are sold to single buyers or small groups of buyers. These so-called private placements are desirable because they allow issuers to keep their plans confidential.

In 1995, $122 billion in new private placements were purchased in the United States by large pension funds and other institutions that privately negotiated prices with sellers.[1] Because private placements cannot be resold in the open market, buyers generally demand higher returns from the issuers.

Investment Banking

investment banker
Financial institution engaged in purchasing and reselling new securities

Most new stocks and some bonds are sold on the wider public market. To bring a new security to market, the issuing firm must get approval from the Securities and Exchange Commission, the government agency that regulates securities markets. It also needs the services of an **investment banker**: a financial specialist in purchasing and reselling new securities. Such bankers as Merrill Lynch and Morgan Stanley provide three important services:

- They advise companies on timing and financial terms for new issues.

- By underwriting (that is, buying new securities), they bear some of the risks of issuing them.

- They create the distribution networks for moving new securities through groups of other banks and brokers into the hands of individual investors.

secondary securities market
Market in which existing stocks and bonds are traded

In 1996, U.S. investment bankers brought to the market $116 billion in new corporate stocks and $386 billion in new corporate bonds.[2] However, new securities represent only a very small portion of traded securities. Existing stocks and bonds are sold in the **secondary securities market**, which is handled by such familiar bodies as the New York Stock Exchange. We consider the activities of these markets later in this chapter.

Stocks

Each year, financial managers, along with millions of individual investors, buy and sell the stocks of thousands of companies. This widespread ownership has become possible because of the availability of different types of stocks and because markets have been established for conveniently buying and selling them. In this section, we focus on the value of common and preferred stock as securities. We also describe the stock exchanges where they are bought and sold.

Common Stock

Individuals and other companies purchase a firm's common stock in the hope that it will increase in value, provide dividend income, or both. But how is the value of a common stock determined? Stock values are expressed in three different ways: as par, market, and book value.

An Unusual Investment in the Future

What do investment bankers do in their spare time? Recently about 100 managers from Goldman, Sachs, the Wall Street investment firm, spent a day at New York's P.S. 98 teaching low-income students about business and economics.

A combined effort of Goldman, Sachs and Junior Achievement of New York, the 1-day program was designed to compensate for the fact that few volunteers have been signing up to run the traditional Junior Achievement program, which is designed to last a whole semester. Instead, over the course of a month, about 2,000 Goldman, Sachs employees visited 28 New York City schools to talk about who producers and consumers are, how municipal government works, what overhead consists of, and how profit margins are calculated. Says the principal of P.S. 98, Lisandro Garcia-Marchi, "This shows the kids that they are important. It gives them a taste of what the business world is about and a sense that they can join it."

The Junior Achievement organization is pleased too. "Even a one-day visit shows the kids that not all successful white guys grew up rich, that women can get high-level jobs, that poor kids can have opportunities too," says the organization's executive vice president Peter Mertens. And the volunteers found that the learning experience worked both ways. It was members of the first group, who traveled to a school in the Bronx, who took the initiative in signing up colleagues for the other trips. And it appeared that the relationship would not end with the program: One volunteer sent a set of encyclopedias, and another took an entire class to see a Broadway show.

> *Even a one-day visit shows the kids that not all successful white guys grew up rich, that women can get high-level jobs, that poor kids can have opportunities too.*
>
> —Junior Achievement executive vice president Peter Mertens

Par Value

Par value is the face value of a share of stock at the time it is originally issued. It is set by the issuing company's board of directors. In order to receive their corporate charters, all companies must declare par values for their stocks. Each company must preserve the par value money in its retained earnings, and it cannot be distributed as dividends. However, because this procedural protection is largely a formality, par value usually bears no relationship to a stock's true value. In 1997, for example, Rayovac, a company that manufactures batteries, issued stock with a par value of only $0.01 per share. The firm proceeded to sell the stock to the public for $14 a share.[3] The choice of $14 reflects the price that Rayovac management believed investors would be willing to pay based on Rayovac's assets and earnings potential.

par value
Face value of a share of stock, set by the issuing company's board of directors

Market Value

A stock's real value, then, is its **market value**: the current price of a share in the stock market. Rayovac shares, for example, sold for up to $19.62 a share in 1997, indicating that investors value the stock at more than the original $14. Market value, therefore, reflects buyers' willingness to invest in a company. It depends on a firm's history of dividend payments, its earnings potential, and investors' expectations of **capital gains**—that is, profits to be made from selling the stock for more than it cost. Investors are concerned primarily with market value.

market value
Current price of a share of stock in the stock market

capital gain
Profit earned by selling a share of stock for more than its cost

▶ *AT&T TAKES A BUMPY MARKET RIDE.* To get an idea of how perceptions about future performance can affect market value, consider the prices of AT&T, the nation's

Figure 20.1 AT&T Stock Price, September 1995–
September 1996

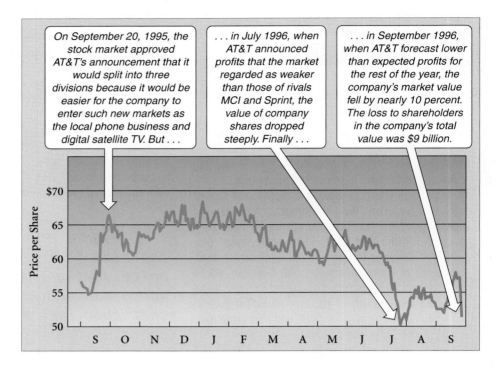

On September 20, 1995, the stock market approved AT&T's announcement that it would split into three divisions because it would be easier for the company to enter such new markets as the local phone business and digital satellite TV. But . . .

. . . in July 1996, when AT&T announced profits that the market regarded as weaker than those of rivals MCI and Sprint, the value of company shares dropped steeply. Finally . . .

. . . in September 1996, when AT&T forecast lower than expected profits for the rest of the year, the company's market value fell by nearly 10 percent. The loss to shareholders in the company's total value was $9 billion.

most widely held stock. On September 20, 1995, the stock gained 6⅛ points ($6.12) in one day with the announcement that AT&T would split into three companies. As you can see in Figure 20.1, this increase was followed by less dramatic ups and downs through June 1996. During this period, the company faced certain financial struggles with new business activities, such as wireless service, local service, and Internet access. In July, AT&T reported quarterly profits higher than those in the same quarter the previous year. However, industry analysts interpreted the numbers as weak and not up to the stronger earnings of competitors MCI Communications and Sprint Corp. As a result, AT&T's market price declined sharply. Then, on September 24, 1996, AT&T's market value fell nearly 10 percent ($9 billion in total value). The stock price plunged 5⅝ a share ($5.63) when the company announced that earnings for the rest of 1996 would be less than previously expected. The stock price dropped because shareholders bid down the market price to reflect AT&T's lower future earnings power. Most analysts blamed AT&T's inability to keep pace with its competition. AT&T, suspects one investment banker, "was a bureaucratic, regulated beast asked to become a hard-charging competitor in a communications and information environment that's been totally unstable."[4]

> ❝ *AT&T was a bureaucratic, regulated beast asked to become a hard-charging competitor in an environment that's been totally unstable.* ❞

—Wall Street analyst on the 1996
drop in AT&T market value

Book Value

Recall from chapter 18 our definition of stockholders' equity: the sum of a company's common stock par value, retained earnings, and additional paid-in capital. The **book value** of common stock represents stockholders' equity divided by the number of shares. At the end of fiscal year 1996, for example, Rayovac had stockholders' equity of $61.6 million. There were 27.4 million shares outstanding.[5] Therefore, the book value of Rayovac stock was $2.25 per share ($61.6/27.4).

Book value is used as a comparison indicator because, for successful companies, the market value is usually greater than its book value. Thus, when market price falls to near book value, some investors buy the stock on the principle that it is underpriced and will increase in the future.

Investment Traits of Common Stock

Common stocks are among the riskiest of all securities. Uncertainties about the stock market itself, for instance, can quickly change a given stock's value. Furthermore, when companies have unprofitable years, they often cannot pay dividends. Therefore, shareholder income—and perhaps share price—drops.

Even companies with solid reputations sometimes have downturns. IBM is an example. IBM has paid cash dividends continuously to shareholders every year since 1916. Figure 20.2 traces the share price of IBM stock between December 1960 and November 1996. As you can see, price per share rose steadily from the 1970s to 1987 but began falling until 1993, when IBM showed a financial loss. Along with lower earnings per share during 1990–1993, IBM paid smaller dividends to shareholders each year. During this period, IBM's stock price fell steadily, from a 1990 high of $123 per share to a 1993 low of $41. By 1995, however, profits had again increased, and IBM's stock price rose in 1996 to a high of $135. In 1996, things got even better, as IBM enjoyed a significant increase in its core business (selling computers and information technology to major corporations). In November 1996, IBM stock hit a 9-year high of $158.50. "I wish I had kept more," sighs one mutual fund manager who sold at $90. "It's a changed company."[6]

book value
Value of a common stock expressed as total shareholders' equity divided by the number of shares of stock

Figure 20.2 IBM Stock Price, December 1960–November 1996

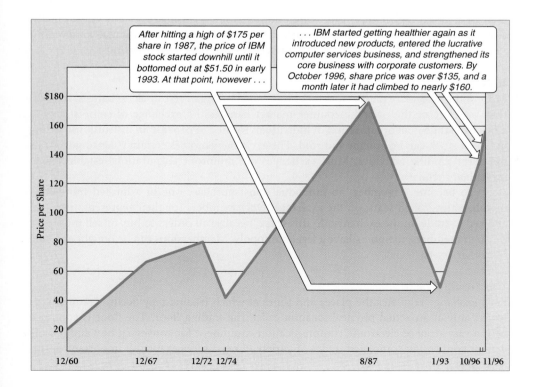

❝ *I wish I had kept more.* ❞

—Mutual fund manager James Cramer, who sold IBM stock at $90, when it reached $158.50

blue chip stock
Common stock issued by a well-established company with a sound financial history and a stable pattern of dividend payouts

However, common stocks offer high growth potential. Naturally, the prospects for growth in various industries change from time to time, but the **blue chip stocks** of well-established, financially sound firms such as Ralston Purina, Exxon, and many others have historically provided investors steady income through consistent dividend payouts.

Preferred Stock

Preferred stock is usually issued with a stated par value, and dividends are typically expressed as a percentage of par value. For example, if a preferred stock with a $100 par value pays a 6-percent dividend, holders will receive an annual dividend of $6 per share.

Some preferred stock is callable: The issuing firm can call in shares by requiring preferred stockholders to surrender them in exchange for cash payments. The amount of this payment, the call price, is specified in the purchase agreement between the firm and its preferred stockholders.

Investment Traits of Preferred Stock

cumulative preferred stock
Preferred stock on which dividends not paid in the past must be paid to stockholders before dividends can be paid to common stockholders

Because preferred stock has first rights to dividends, income is less risky than income from the same firm's common stock. Moreover, most preferred stock is **cumulative preferred stock**, which means that any missed dividend payments must be paid as soon as the firm is able to do so. In addition, the firm cannot pay any dividends to common stockholders until it has made up all late payments to preferred stockholders. Let's take the example of a firm with preferred stock having a $100 par value and paying a 6-percent dividend. If the firm fails to pay that dividend for 2 years, it must make up arrears of $12 per share to preferred stockholders before it can pay dividends to common stockholders.

Of course, there are disadvantages to cumulative preferred stock. For example, income is less certain than income from the same company's corporate bonds. In addition, whereas a company's preferred dividend is a fixed amount, its common dividend can be increased, giving higher returns to common shareholders during profitable years. Finally, although market prices of preferred stock can fluctuate, its growth potential is more limited than that of common stock because preferred stock pays fixed dividends.

Stock Exchanges

stock exchange
Organization formed to provide an institutional setting in which stock can be traded

Most of the secondary market for stocks is handled by organized stock exchanges. In addition, a dealer or the over-the-counter market handles the exchange of some stocks. A **stock exchange** is an organization of individuals formed to provide an institutional setting in which stock can be bought and sold. The exchange enforces certain rules to govern its members' trading activities. Most exchanges are nonprofit corporations established to serve their members.

To become a member, an individual must purchase one of a limited number of memberships, called seats, on the exchange. Only members (or their representatives) are allowed to trade on the exchange. In this sense, because all orders to buy or sell must flow through members, members have a legal monopoly. Memberships can be bought and sold like other assets.

The Trading Floor

Each exchange regulates the places and times at which trading may occur. Trading is allowed only at an actual physical location called the trading floor. The floor is equipped with a vast array of electronic communication equipment for conveying buy and sell orders or confirming completed trades. A variety of news services furnish important up-to-the-minute information about world events as well as business developments. Any change in these factors may be swiftly reflected in share prices.

Brokers

Some of the people on the trading floor are employed by the exchange. Others are trading stocks for themselves. Many are **brokers** who receive and execute buy and sell orders from nonexchange members. Although they match buyers with sellers, brokers do not own the securities. They earn commissions from the individuals and organizations for whom they place orders. Like many products, brokerage assistance can be purchased at either discount prices or at full-service prices.

broker
Individual or organization who receives and executes buy and sell orders on behalf of other people in return for commissions

▶ **WALL STREET'S BEST MOUSETRAP.** Charles Schwab & Co., the largest discount brokerage firm in the United States, offers well-informed individual investors a fast, low-cost way to participate in the market. Schwab's customers know what they want to buy or sell and they usually make trades simply by using personal computers or Schwab's automated telephone order system, without talking with a broker. Why are discount brokerage services less expensive? For one thing, their sales personnel receive fees, not commissions. Unlike many full-service brokers, they offer no investment advice and hold no person-to-person sales conversations.

The discount approach has filled a previously neglected niche among investors: At Schwab alone, active accounts rose from about 1 million in 1988 to about 3 million in 1994. By 1997 Schwab had captured 51 percent of the discount brokerage market.[7] Why are investors coming to Schwab? The reason, according to Tom D. Seip, Schwab's vice president for branch services, is fairly simple. "Many people come to us—it sounds sad, but it's true—after they have been shafted somewhere else." Today, Schwab's competition includes other discount brokers such as Fidelity Brokerage Services and National Discount, which have already undercut some of Schwab's fees. On-line trading, offered by Schwab and specialty firms such as E*TRADE®, allows investors to manage their own portfolios while paying low commissions for trading stocks on the Web.[8]

There is an important market for full-service brokerages to advise new, uninformed investors and for experienced investors who don't have time to keep track of the latest stock market developments. When you deal with busy people who want to invest successfully, says Joseph Grano of PaineWebber, "you can't do it through a telephone-response system. In a world that's growing more and more complicated, the advice and counsel of a broker will be more important, not less important."[9]

> **❝ Many people come to us after they have been shafted somewhere else. ❞**
>
> —Tom D. Seip, vice president for branch services at Charles Schwab & Co.

The Major Exchanges and the OTC Market

There are two major stock exchanges in the United States: the New York and American Stock Exchanges. The New York Stock Exchange, although still the largest, has recently begun to face stiff competition from both smaller regional U.S. exchanges and larger foreign exchanges, especially in London.

Perhaps the most important difference between the exchanges and the over-the-counter market is the number and activity of dealers. On the exchanges, one dealer, called a specialist, is appointed to control trading for each stock. The specialist buys and sells that stock for his or her own inventory and acts as exclusive auctioneer for it. The OTC, on the other hand, permits multiple dealers for each stock.

The New York Stock Exchange.

For many people, "the stock market" means the New York Stock Exchange (NYSE). Also known as "The Big Board," NYSE was founded in 1792 and is located at the corner of Wall and Broad Streets in New York City. The largest of all U.S. exchanges is the model for exchanges worldwide. With an average of 527 million shares changing hands each day, about 45 percent of all shares traded on U.S. exchanges are traded here. The value of trading each day averages $23 billion.

Only firms meeting certain minimum requirements—earning power, total value of outstanding stock, and number of shareholders—are eligible for listing on the NYSE. Nearly 2,700 listings are traded on the NYSE, with total market values of $11 trillion. At mid-1997, General Electric's common shares had the highest market value: $169 billion. NYSE trading volume in 1997 was over 133 billion shares.[10]

The American Stock Exchange.

The second-largest U.S. exchange, the American Stock Exchange (AMEX), is also located in New York. It accounts for 3 percent of all shares traded on U.S. exchanges. Like the NYSE, the AMEX has minimum requirements for listings. However, they are less stringent. The minimum number of publicly held shares, for example, is 500,000, versus 1.1 million for the NYSE. The AMEX currently lists about 1,000 stocks of companies around the world. Indeed, in 1996 foreign stocks made up 10 percent of the total market value traded on the AMEX. As firms grow, they often transfer their listings from the AMEX to the NYSE. Well-known companies, with stocks listed on the AMEX include Turner Broadcasting, TWA, and The New York Times Co.

Regional Stock Exchanges.

Established long before the advent of modern communications, the seven regional stock exchanges were organized to serve investors in places other than New York. The largest regional exchanges are the Midwest Stock Exchange in Chicago and the Pacific Stock Exchange in Los Angeles and San Francisco. Other exchanges are located in Philadelphia, Boston, Cincinnati, and Spokane. Many corporations list their stocks both regionally and on either the NYSE or the AMEX.

Foreign Stock Exchanges.

As recently as 1980, the U.S. market accounted for over half the value of the world market in traded stocks. Indeed, as late as 1975, the equity of IBM alone was greater than the national market equities of all but four countries. Market activities, however, have shifted as the value of shares listed on foreign exchanges continues to grow. The annual dollar value of trades on exchanges in London, Tokyo, and other cities is in the trillions. In fact, the London exchange exceeds even the NYSE in number of stocks listed; in market value, transactions on U.S. exchanges are now second to those on Japanese exchanges. New exchanges are also beginning to flourish in cities from Shanghai to Warsaw.

over-the-counter (OTC) market Organization of securities dealers formed to trade stock outside the formal institutional setting of the organized stock exchanges

Over-the-Counter Market, NASDAQ and NASD.

The **over-the-counter (OTC) market** is so called because its original traders were somewhat like retailers. They kept supplies of shares on hand and sold them over the office counter to interested buyers as opportunities arose. Even today, the OTC market has no trading floor. Instead, it consists of many people in different locations who hold an inventory of securities that are not listed on NASDAQ or any of the national U.S. securities exchanges. Unlike brokers, the OTC consists of independent dealers who own the securities they buy and sell, at their own risk.

Separate from the OTC market is the National Association of Securities Dealers (NASD), which has nearly 5,500 member firms. NASD includes dealers (not brokers) who have joined together to coordinate investment activities. They must pass qualification exams and meet certain standards for financial soundness. The privilege of trading in the market is granted by federal regulators and by NASD. NASD's electronic communication system includes the **National Association of Securities Dealers Automated Quotation (NASDAQ) system**, which operates the NASDAQ Stock Market. Currently, the NASD is working with officials in an increasing number of countries, especially in Asia and Latin America, who want to replace the trading floors of traditional exchanges with electronic networks like NASDAQ.[11]

National Association of Securities Dealers Automated Quotation (NASDAQ) system Organization of over-the-counter dealers who own, buy, and sell their own securities over an electronic network

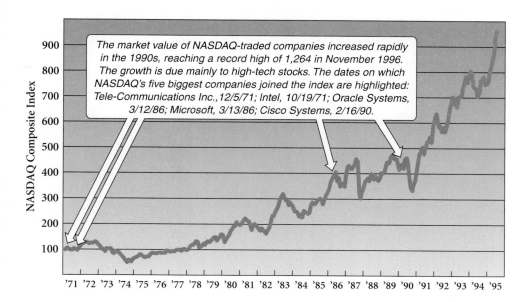

Figure 20.3 NASDAQ Composite Index, 1971–1995

The market value of NASDAQ-traded companies increased rapidly in the 1990s, reaching a record high of 1,264 in November 1996. The growth is due mainly to high-tech stocks. The dates on which NASDAQ's five biggest companies joined the index are highlighted: Tele-Communications Inc.,12/5/71; Intel, 10/19/71; Oracle Systems, 3/12/86; Microsoft, 3/13/86; Cisco Systems, 2/16/90.

Some 5,500 companies' stocks are traded by NASDAQ. Newer firms are often listed here when their stocks first become available in the secondary market. Many of these later become well known, including companies such as MCI Communications, Apple Computer, and Yellow Freight, along with many high-technology stocks in such industries as biotechnology, medical advancements, and electronics. Figure 20.3 shows rapid increases in market value of NASDAQ stocks during the 1990s, as reflected in the NASDAQ Composite Index. The index reached a record high of 1,953 in September 1997. In October 1997, NASDAQ became the first U.S. stock market to trade more than 1 billion shares in 1 day. Although the number of shares traded surpasses the New York Stock Exchange volume, the market value of NASDAQ stocks is only about one-fifth of those on the NYSE. Figure 20.4 shows the number of shares traded on the various exchanges and the NASDAQ system.

Bonds

A **bond** is an IOU: a promise by the issuer to pay the buyer a certain amount of money by a specified date, usually with interest paid at regular intervals. The U.S. bond market is supplied by three major sources: the U.S. government, municipalities, and corporations. Bonds differ in terms of maturity dates, tax status, and level of risk and potential yield.

To aid bond investors in making purchase decisions, several services rate the quality of bonds. Table 20.1 shows the systems of two well-known services: Moody's and Standard & Poor's. Ratings measure default risk—that is, the chance that one or more promised payments will be deferred or missed altogether. The highest grades are AAA and Aaa, the lowest C and D. Low-grade bonds are usually called junk bonds.

U.S. Government Bonds

The U.S. government is the world's largest debtor. New federal borrowing from the public exceeded $145 billion in 1996, when the total U.S. debt reached $5.4 trillion.[12] To finance its debt, the federal government issues a variety of government bonds. The U.S. Treasury issues Treasury bills (T-bills), Treasury notes, and Treasury bonds (including U.S. savings bonds). Many government agencies (for example, the Federal Housing Administration) also issue bonds.

Government bonds are among the safest investments available. Securities with longer maturities are somewhat riskier than short-term issues because their longer lives expose them to more political, social, and economic changes. However, all federal bonds

bond
Security through which an issuer promises to pay the buyer a certain amount of money by a specified date

government bond
Bond issued by the federal government

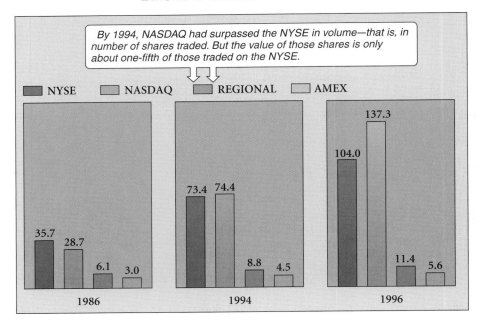

Figure 20.4 Trading Levels on U.S. Stock Exchanges, Billions of Shares

By 1994, NASDAQ had surpassed the NYSE in volume—that is, in number of shares traded. But the value of those shares is only about one-fifth of those traded on the NYSE.

are backed by the U.S. government. Government securities are sold in large blocks to institutional investors who buy them to ensure desired levels of safety in their portfolios. As their needs change, they may buy or sell government securities to other investors.

Municipal Bonds

municipal bond
Bond issued by a state or local government

State and local governments issue **municipal bonds** to finance school and transportation systems and a variety of other projects. In 1996, more than 7,000 new municipal bonds were issued at a value of more than $171 billion.[13]

Some bonds, called obligation bonds, are backed by the issuer's taxing power. In 1994, for example, the Albany School District in Minnesota issued $15 million in obligation bonds to fund two new elementary schools and a junior high school. The issuer intends to retire the bonds from future tax revenues. In contrast, revenue bonds are backed only by the revenue generated by a specific project. Thus, Dade County Airport issued $142 million in revenue bonds in 1994 to expand aviation facilities. Operating revenues from building rentals and aviation fees will eventually pay both principal and interest.[14]

The most attractive feature of municipal bonds is the fact that investors do not pay taxes on interest received. Commercial banks invest in bonds nearing maturity because they are safe, liquid investments. Pension funds, insurance companies, and even private citizens also make longer-term investments in municipals.

▶ *INVESTMENT TURNS SOUR FOR TYRONE, PENNSYLVANIA.* This is not to say that municipal bonds cushion portfolios like security blankets. Consider the following case, which

Table 20.1 Bond Rating Systems

	High Grades	**Medium Grades (Investment Grades)**	**Speculative**	**Poor Grades**
Moody's	Aaa, Aa	A, Baa	Ba, B	Caa to C
Standard & Poor's	AAA, AA	A, BBB	BB, B	CCC to D

has several school districts in Pennsylvania concerned about their financial future. Like many school districts, the small town of Tyrone issued bonds—$21 million—to finance the construction of a new school complex. School administrators needed to invest the district's money until the new construction was to begin, so they handed the funds over to Devon Capital Management, which handled investments for 64 school districts and other agencies located in six states. Now the school districts stand to lose millions because Devon, located in Tyrone, was shut down in 1997 when the Securities and Exchange Commission charged John Black, Devon's owner and long-time Tyrone citizen, with fraud. The SEC claims that Black used the funds to buy and sell high-risk bonds and then hid the losses while he got more money from new clients. By the time of the shutdown, Devon had lost $70 million of the schools' funds, and Tyrone's school district was the biggest investor. Instead of making extra money, Tyrone stands to lose millions from Black's volatile investments. School superintendent William Miller commented, "He was respected as a financial wizard, and he lives right here."

" He was respected as a financial wizard, and he lives right here. "

—William Miller, Tyrone School superintendent

The Tyrone incident is similar to the lesson from Orange County, California, just a few years earlier. Like that of many county treasurers, Robert Citron's job was to invest tax revenues and money raised through municipal bond offerings. Investment proceeds were used for such expenses as education, construction projects, and public employee salaries. As the treasurer of Orange County, Citron had amassed an impressive track record: In the 10-year period between 1984 and 1994, income from Orange County's investment portfolio nearly quadrupled, to $666 million.

How did Citron achieve such phenomenal results? He was particularly fond of an investment called a reverse repurchase, an arrangement whereby the county sold short-term securities with the promise to buy them back for a higher price. Meanwhile, Citron invested the proceeds from the sales in longer-term securities at higher rates of interest. It is basically a sound idea: The difference between the higher returns and the contracted buyback price allowed Citron to repurchase the county's securities and still have money left over.

The strategy was hugely successful as long as interest rates fell. This they did in the late 1980s and early 1990s. Meanwhile, Citron also borrowed money from Wall Street brokers (in particular, Merrill Lynch). In other words, he purchased securities by borrowing money from brokers, who, in turn, got the money from banks. The collateral for these loans consisted of the purchased securities, whose values, of course, were subject to change. Using the county's $7.4 billion as collateral, Citron built a portfolio valued at $20 billion. For many years, he was a local hero because his dealings helped finance Orange County's growing needs without substantially raising taxes.

Eventually, however, the inherent risks in Citron's strategy became apparent. Early in 1994, interest rates began to rise. When that happens, the share prices of the underlying assets shrink. Orange County's lenders began to demand more collateral to back up the portfolio assets that the county had purchased with borrowed money. Meeting those demands drained hundreds of millions from the county treasury. On December 1, county representatives announced that the value of Orange County's portfolio had dropped $1.5 billion. A few days later, unable to make a scheduled debt payment, Orange County declared bankruptcy in federal court.

Who stands to lose from the Orange County debacle? For one thing, investors holding $500 million in tax-exempt Orange County bonds may have trouble getting their money back because the county may not have the money to redeem them. It was no surprise, then, that the bond market was shaken by fears that other municipalities might be in the same situation as Orange County. Jittery investors needed reassurance that municipal bonds were still safe investments.[15]

Corporate Bonds

Although the U.S. government and municipalities are heavy borrowers, corporate long-term borrowing is even greater. **Corporate bonds** issued by U.S. companies are a large source of financing, involving more money than government and municipal bonds combined. U.S. companies raised nearly $600 billion from new bond issues in 1995. Bonds have traditionally been issued with maturities ranging from 20 to 30 years. In the 1980s, 10-year maturities came into wider use.

Like municipal bonds, longer-term corporate bonds are somewhat riskier than shorter-term bonds. To help investors evaluate risk, Standard & Poor's and Moody's rate both new and proposed issues on a weekly basis. Remember, however, that negative ratings do not necessarily keep issues from being successful. Rather, they raise the interest rates that issuers must offer. Corporate bonds may be categorized in terms of the method of interest payment or in terms of whether they are secured or unsecured.

Interest Payment: Registered and Bearer Bonds

Registered bonds register the names of holders with the company, which simply mails out checks. Certificates are of value only to registered holders. **Bearer (or coupon) bonds** require bondholders to clip coupons from certificates and send them to the issuer in order to receive payment. Coupons can be redeemed by anyone, regardless of ownership.

Secured Bonds

With **secured bonds**, issuers can reduce the risk to holders by pledging assets in case of default. Bonds can be backed by first mortgages, other mortgages, or other specific assets. In 1994, for example, Union Pacific Railroad Co. issued $76 million in bonds to finance the purchase and renovation of equipment. Rated Aaa (prime) by Moody's and maturing in 2012, the bonds are secured by the newly purchased and rehabilitated equipment: 80 diesel locomotives, 1,300 hopper cars, and 450 auto rack cars.[16]

Debentures

Unsecured bonds are called **debentures**. No specific property is pledged as security. Rather, holders generally have claims against property not otherwise pledged in the company's other bonds. Thus, debentures are said to have inferior claims on a corporation's assets. Financially strong firms often use debentures. An example is Boeing's $175-million debenture issued in 1993, with maturity on April 15, 2043.[17] Similar issues by weaker companies often receive low ratings and may have trouble attracting investors.

The Retirement of Bonds

Maturity dates on bonds of all kinds may be very long. Of course, all bonds must be paid off, or retired, at some point. With regard to maturity dates, there are three types of bonds: callable, serial, and convertible.

Callable Bonds

The issuer of **callable bonds** may call them in and pay them off at a price stipulated in the indenture, or contract. Usually, the issuer cannot call the bond for a certain period of time after issue. For example, most Treasury bonds cannot be called within the first 5 years.

Issuers usually call in existing bonds when prevailing interest rates are lower than the rate being paid on the bond. The issuer must still pay a call price in order to call in the bond. The call price usually gives a premium to the bondholder. The premium is merely the difference between the face value and call price. For example, a bond offered by the Wisconsin Power Co. bears a $100 face value and can be called by the firm for $108.67 any time during the first year after issue. The call price and the premium decrease annually as bonds approach maturity.

corporate bond
Bond issued by a business as a source of long-term funding

registered bond
Bond bearing the name of the holder and registered with the issuing company

bearer (or coupon) bond
Bond requiring the holder to clip and submit a coupon in order to receive an interest payment

secured bond
Bond backed by pledges of assets to the bondholders

debenture
Unsecured bond for which no specific property is pledged as security

callable bond
Bond that may be called in and paid for by the issuer before its maturity date

Sinking Funds. Callable bonds are often retired by the use of **sinking fund provisions**. The issuing company is required annually to put a certain amount of money into a special bank account. At the end of a certain number of years, the money (including interest) will be sufficient to redeem the bonds. Failure to meet the sinking fund provision places the issue in default. Obviously, such bonds are generally regarded as safer investments than many other bonds.

Serial and Convertible Bonds

Some corporations issue serial or convertible bonds. With a **serial bond**, the firm retires portions of the bond issue in a series of different preset dates. For example, a company with a $100-million issue maturing in 20 years may retire $5 million each year. Serial bonds are most popular among local and state governments.

Only corporations, however, can issue **convertible bonds**. These bonds can be converted into the common stock of the issuing company. At the option of the holder, payment is made in stock instead of in cash. When holders are given such flexibility and the potential benefits of converting bonds into stock, firms can offer lower interest rates when the bonds are issued. However, because holders cannot be forced to accept stock instead of cash, conversion works only when the bond buyer also regards the issuing corporation as a good investment.

Secondary Markets for Bonds

Nearly all secondary trading in bonds occurs in the over-the-counter market rather than on organized exchanges. Thus, precise statistics about annual trading volumes are not recorded. As with stocks, however, market values and prices change daily. The direction of bond prices moves opposite to interest rate changes. As interest rates move up, bond prices tend to go down. The prices of riskier bonds fluctuate more widely than those of higher-grade bonds.

Other Investments

Stocks and bonds are not the only marketable securities available to businesses. Financial managers are also concerned with financial opportunities in mutual funds and commodities.

Mutual Funds

Companies called **mutual funds** pool investments from individuals and organizations to purchase a portfolio of stocks, bonds, and other securities. Investors are thus part owners of the portfolio. For example, if you invest $1,000 in a mutual fund with a portfolio worth $100,000, you own 1 percent of that portfolio. Investors in **no-load funds** are not charged sales commissions when they buy into or sell out of funds. Investors in **load funds** generally pay commissions of 2 to 8 percent.

Reasons for Investing

The total assets invested in U.S. mutual funds has grown significantly every year since 1991, to a total of nearly 9,000 different funds.[18] Why do investors find them so attractive? Remember first of all that mutual funds vary in their investment goals. Naturally, different funds are designed to appeal to the different motives and goals of investors. Funds stressing safety often include money market mutual funds and other safe issues offering immediate income. Investors seeking higher current income must generally sacrifice some safety. Typically, these people look to long-term municipal bond, corporate bond, and income mutual funds that invest in common stocks with good dividend-paying records.

Mutual funds that stress growth include balanced mutual funds: portfolios of bonds and preferred and common stocks, especially the common stocks of established firms. Aggressive growth funds seek maximum capital appreciation. They sacrifice current income and safety and invest in stocks of new (and even troubled) companies and other high-risk

---

sinking fund provision
Method for retiring bonds whereby the issuer puts enough money into a bank account to redeem the bonds at maturity

serial bond
Bond retired when the issuer redeems portions of the issue at different preset dates

convertible bond
Bond that can be retired by converting it to common stock

mutual fund
Company that pools investments from individuals and organizations to purchase a portfolio of stocks, bonds, and short-term securities

no-load fund
Mutual fund in which investors pay no sales commissions when they buy in or sell out

load fund
Mutual fund in which investors are charged sales commissions when they buy in or sell out

The Natural Environment

How Do You Put Your Money Where Your Mouth Is?

Common advice for investors is to look for the highest return compatible with the acceptable level of risk. But a growing number of people are instead seeking out unusual mutual funds that focus on firms whose activities are in line with investors' ethical or religious beliefs.

The Revered M. Paige Brown, for instance, put his retirement savings into the Timothy Plan, a mutual that screens out firms, such as General Mills, whose activities are at odds with Christian fundamentalist beliefs. (General Mills contributed money to Planned Parenthood, which supports the right to abortion.) The Timothy Plan returned around 15 percent in early 1997, well below the S&P 500 rate of 23 percent for the same period.

But for those who believe that not only abortion but also homosexuality and violent or sexually explicit movies and TV programs are morally wrong, the 4-year-old Timothy Plan provides a way to invest without experiencing a crisis of conscience. It can even filter out firms that offer medical benefits to gay employees' partners.

Ethical or socially responsible investing, as it is known, has traditionally focused on liberal ideals. Domini Social Equity, Calvert Social Equity, and Dreyfus Third Century, for instance, don't include firms that discriminate against homosexuals, promote tobacco and alcohol use, or create pollution. Others shun weapons makers and nuclear power plants and seek out firms that contribute to local communities or protect the environment.

One newer fund, the Meyers Pride Value Fund, did nearly as well as the S&P 500 in 1997. As a group, though, socially responsible funds, both liberal and conservative, have performed less well than more broadly based investment vehicles.

But John Clark, cofounder of Guardian Investments brokerage in Front Royal, Virginia, whose clients are opposed to abortion, says "I'm unwilling to admit you will underperform because you invest in your beliefs." And fund managers do apply standard financial criteria. Some choose undervalued companies with bright prospects or small-cap companies with excess cash flow, low price-earnings ratios, and high insider stock ownership. The Social Investment Forum in Washington, DC, estimates that about $635 billion is currently invested in stocks, funds, or other investments attuned to investors' religious and ethical beliefs.

securities. Figure 20.5 shows how total assets in mutual funds are divided among different types of investments.[19] As you can see, the distribution of assets has shifted since the early 1980s in order to meet changing investor goals and attitudes toward financial risk.

In 1995 the nation's mutual funds had assets of nearly $3 trillion in 132 million shareholder accounts. The 40 million individual shareholders include many small investors representing 31 percent of U.S. households holding mutual find assets totaling $1.5 trillion. Institutional investors are also more heavily involved in mutual funds, especially in safer money market and short-term municipal bond funds. In 1960, for instance, institutional investors accounted for only $1.2 billion of the money in mutual funds. By 1995 that figure had risen above $1 trillion, more than one-third of all mutual fund assets.[20]

Commodities

futures contract
Agreement to purchase specified amounts of a commodity at a given price on a set date

commodities market
Market in which futures contracts are traded

Individuals and businesses can buy and sell commodities as investments. **Futures contracts**—agreements to purchase specified amounts of commodities at given prices on set dates—can be bought and sold in the **commodities market**. These contracts are available not only for stocks but also for commodities ranging from coffee beans and hogs to propane and platinum. Because selling prices reflect traders' estimates of future events and values, futures prices are quite volatile and trading is risky.

To clarify the workings of the commodities market, let's look at an example. On March 14, 1997, the price of gold on the open market was $352 per ounce. Futures contracts for October 1997 gold were selling for $376 per ounce. This price reflected investors'

Figure 20.5   Types of Mutual Fund Investments

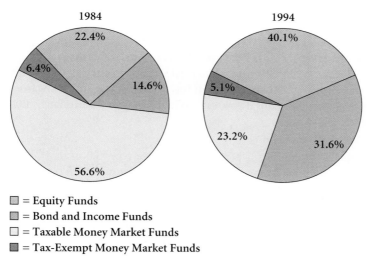

Types of Mutual Fund Investments

1984

1994

☐ = Equity Funds
▨ = Bond and Income Funds
☐ = Taxable Money Market Funds
▨ = Tax-Exempt Money Market Funds

judgment that gold prices would be higher the following October. Now suppose that you purchased a 100-ounce gold futures contract in March for $37,600 ($376 × 100). If in May 1997 the October gold futures sold for $401, you could sell your contract for $40,100. Your profit after the 2 months would be $2,500.

Margins

Usually, buyers of futures contracts need not put up the full purchase amount. Rather, the buyer posts a smaller amount—the **margin**—that may be as small as $3,000 for contracts up to $100,000. Let's look again at our gold futures example. As we saw, if you had posted a $3,000 margin for your October gold contract, you would have earned a $2,500 profit on that investment of $3,000 in only 2 months.

   However, you also took a big risk involving two big *ifs*: If you had held onto your contract until October, and if gold had dropped, say to $327 (as it really did by October 1997), you would have lost $4,900. If you had posted a $3,000 margin to buy the contract, you would have lost all of that margin and owed an additional $1,900. In fact, between 75 and 90 percent of all small time investors lose money in the futures market. For one thing, the action is fast and furious, with small investors trying to keep up with professionals ensconced in seats on the major exchanges. Although the profit potential is exciting, experts recommend that most novices retreat to safer stock markets. Of course, as one veteran financial planner puts it, commodities are tempting. "After trading commodities," he reports, "trading stocks is like watching the grass grow."[21]

margin
Percentage of the total sales price that a buyer must put up to place an order for stock or futures contracts

> ❝ *After trading commodities, trading stocks is like watching the grass grow.* ❞
>
> —Rick Powers, professional financial planner

   Most commodities investors have no intention of ever taking possession of the commodities in question. They merely buy and sell the futures contracts. Some companies buy futures to protect the prices of commodities important to their businesses. Hormel Meats, for example, trades in hog futures to protect the prices of pork and pork products.

Buying and Selling Securities

The process of buying and selling securities is complex. First, you need to find out about possible investments and match them to your investment objectives. Then you must select a broker and open an account. Only then can you place orders and make different types of transactions.

Financial Information Services

Have you ever looked at the financial section of your daily newspaper and wondered what all those tables and numbers mean? It is a good idea to know how to read stock, bond, and mutual fund quotations if you want to invest in issues. Fortunately, this skill is easily mastered.

Stock Quotations

Daily transactions for NYSE securities are reported in most city newspapers. Figure 20.6 shows part of a listing from the *Wall Street Journal*, with columns numbered 1 through 12. Let's analyze the listing for The Gap Inc.

- The first two columns ("High" and "Low") show the highest and lowest prices paid for one share of The Gap stock during the past year. Note that stock prices throughout are expressed in dollars per share, with the smallest fraction of a dollar being $\frac{1}{16}$ or 6¼ cents. In the past year, then, The Gap's stock ranged in value from $36.50 to $20.50 per share. This range reveals a fairly volatile stock price.

- The third column ("Stock") is the abbreviated company name. (Sometimes the notation "pf" appears after the company's name to show that the stock is preferred, not common. The listing reveals that GeminiII offers both a preferred stock and a common stock.)

- The NYSE symbol for the stock is listed in column 4 ("Sym").

- The fifth column ("Div") indicates that The Gap pays an annual cash dividend of $.30 per share. This can be compared to payouts by other companies.

- Column 6 ("Yld %") is the dividend yield, expressed as a percentage of the stock's current price (shown in column 11). The Gap's dividend yield is 1.0 percent (.30 ÷ 30.125, rounded). Potential buyers can compare this yield to returns that they might get from other investments.

price-earnings ratio
Current price of a stock divided by the firm's current annual earnings per share

- Column 7 ("PE") shows the **price-earnings ratio**: the current price of the stock divided by the firm's current annual earnings per share. On this day, The Gap's PE is 21, meaning that investors are willing to pay $21 for each dollar of reported profits to own The Gap stock. This figure can be compared to PE ratios of other stocks when deciding which would be the better investment.

- The last five columns detail the day's trading. Column 8 ("Vol 100s") shows the number of shares (in hundreds) that were traded (in this case 11,822). Some investors interpret increases in trading volume as an indicator of forthcoming price changes in a stock.

- Column 9 ("High") shows the highest price paid that day ($30.625). Column 10 ("Low") shows the lowest price paid that day ($30).

- Column 11 ("Close") shows that The Gap's last sale of the day was for $30.125.

- The final column ("Net Chg") shows the difference between the previous day's close and the close on the day being reported. The closing price of The Gap stock is ¼ higher than it was on the previous business day. Day-to-day changes are indicators of recent price stability or volatility.

Finally, look back at the far-left column, which has no heading. This column reports unusual conditions of importance to investors. Note the *s* to the left of the "52-Week

Figure 20.6 Reading a Stock Quotation

	52 Weeks High	52 Weeks Low	Stock	Sym	Div	Yld %	PE	Vol 100s	High	Low	Close	Net Chg
	(1)	(2)	(3)	(4)	(5)	(6)	(7)	(8)	(9)	(10)	(11)	(12)
s	$36\frac{1}{2}$	$20\frac{1}{2}$	Gap Inc	GPS	.30	1.0	21	11822	$30\frac{5}{8}$	30	$30\frac{1}{8}$	$+\frac{1}{4}$
▲	$28\frac{1}{4}$	$18\frac{3}{4}$	GaylrdEntn	GET	.36b	1.8	15	1352	$19\frac{7}{8}$	$19\frac{5}{8}$	$19\frac{3}{4}$	$-\frac{1}{8}$
	$27\frac{1}{4}$	$23\frac{3}{8}$	Geminill	GMI	.11e	.4	...	139	$27\frac{3}{4}$	$27\frac{3}{8}$	$27\frac{3}{4}$	$+\frac{1}{4}$
	$10\frac{3}{4}$	$9\frac{1}{2}$	Geminill pf		1.40	14.5	...	88	$9\frac{3}{4}$	$9\frac{5}{8}$	$9\frac{5}{8}$	$+\frac{1}{8}$
	17	$10\frac{1}{4}$	GenCorp	GY	.60	3.7	22	3287	$16\frac{3}{8}$	$15\frac{3}{4}$	$16\frac{3}{8}$	$+\frac{1}{2}$
	$55\frac{3}{8}$	$50\frac{3}{8}$	Genentech	GNE		...	49	460	$53\frac{7}{8}$	$53\frac{5}{8}$	$53\frac{7}{8}$	$+\frac{1}{4}$
	$23\frac{1}{2}$	$19\frac{1}{8}$	GenAmInv	GAM	.32e	1.4	...	201	$23\frac{1}{2}$	$23\frac{1}{4}$	$23\frac{1}{2}$	$+\frac{3}{8}$
n	21	$16\frac{5}{8}$	GenlChemGp	GCG	.08e	.4	...	555	19	$18\frac{3}{8}$	$18\frac{1}{2}$	$-\frac{1}{4}$
	$21\frac{7}{8}$	$9\frac{1}{8}$	GenData	GDC		...	dd	662	$10\frac{3}{4}$	$10\frac{1}{4}$	$10\frac{1}{2}$	$+\frac{1}{8}$
	72	$56\frac{3}{8}$	GenDynam	GD	1.64	2.4	15	2315	$67\frac{3}{4}$	$66\frac{3}{4}$	$67\frac{1}{4}$	$+\frac{1}{4}$
▲	$99\frac{3}{8}$	$63\frac{3}{8}$	GenElec	GE	1.84	1.8	24	27767	$101\frac{5}{8}$	$98\frac{5}{8}$	$101\frac{5}{8}$	$+2\frac{7}{8}$

High" column for The Gap. This symbol indicates either a stock split (a division of stock that gives stockholders a greater number of shares but does not change each individuals' proportionate share of ownership) or an extra stock dividend paid during the past 52 weeks. The *n* accompanying the General Chemical Group indicates that this stock was newly issued during the past 52 weeks. The dagger symbol (▲) indicates new 52-week highs in the prices of Gaylord and General Electric stocks.

Bond Quotations

Daily quotations on corporate bonds from the NYSE are also widely published. As you can see in Figure 20.7, bond quotations contain essentially the same type of information as stock quotations. One difference, however, is that the year in which it is going to mature is listed beside each bond. Again, let's focus on the first bond listed, Best Buy.

Figure 20.7 Reading a Bond Quotation

Bonds		Cur Yld	Vol	Close	Net Chg
(1)		(2)	(3)	(4)	(5)
BstBuy	$8\frac{5}{8}00$	8.6	153	$100\frac{7}{8}$	$+\frac{3}{8}$
BethSt	$8\frac{3}{8}01$	8.1	23	103	$+1\frac{1}{8}$
BethSt	8.45 s05	8.3	25	$101\frac{1}{4}$	$+\frac{3}{4}$
Bluegrn	$8\frac{1}{4}12$	CV	10	93	...
Bordn	$8\frac{3}{8}16$	8.3	38	$100\frac{3}{4}$	$-\frac{1}{8}$
BorgWS	$9\frac{1}{8}03$	8.9	70	$102\frac{1}{8}$	$-1\frac{3}{8}$
BoydGm	$9\frac{1}{4}03$	8.9	160	$104\frac{3}{8}$	$-\frac{3}{8}$
ChaseM	$7\frac{1}{2}03$	7.2	5	$103\frac{5}{8}$	$-\frac{5}{8}$
ChaseM	8 s04	7.8	30	$102\frac{7}{8}$	...
ChaseM	$7\frac{7}{8}04$	7.8	25	$101\frac{1}{2}$	$-\frac{1}{4}$

- Column 1 ("Bonds") is the bond identifier: the abbreviation for both the company and a specific bond issue. Here, we see that the Best Buy bond bears an annual interest payment of 8⅝ percent of the bond's face value. The digits *00* mean that the bond matures in the year 2000. (The *s* that sometimes appears between the rate and maturity year is meaningless; it simply keeps numbers from running together.)

- Column 2 shows the current yield: the annual dollar coupon amount divided by the current market price. Holders can turn in bonds each year. For every $100 worth of bonds they own, they will receive $8⅝ ($8.625) in cash. If we jump ahead momentarily to column 4 ("Close"), we see that the same bond (and remaining coupons) can now be purchased for $100 ⅞. This means that the bond currently yields an annual return of 8.55 percent (8⅝ divided by 100⅞). (The designation *CV* in column 2 means that the bond is convertible.)

- Columns 3, 4, and 5 refer to the current day's activities. Under "Vol", for example, we see that 153 Best Buy bonds were traded.

   "Close" is the particular bond's closing price. Note that this price, 100⅞, is expressed as a percentage of the bond's par value. Let's say that Best Buy had set a par value of $1,000. Today's closing price means that the actual price to a buyer would be 100.825 percent of par value: that is, $1,008.25 instead of $1,000.

   "Net Chg" refers to the difference between today's closing price and yesterday's. This bond is currently up ⅜ of a dollar, or $0.375.

OTC Quotations

Most OTC stock quotations are reported in the same format as exchange-listed stock quotations. However, some OTC trades are reported in terms of bid and asked quotations. For example, a quotation might show 7¼ as the bid price and 7¾ as the asked price. The **bid price** is the amount that the OTC dealer pays to obtain each share. The **asked price** is the amount the dealer charges clients to buy a share. The difference between bid and asked prices, in this case, ½, is the dealer's gain for making the transaction.

Mutual Funds Quotations

Selling prices for mutual funds are reported daily in most city newspapers. Additional investor information is also available in the financial press. Figure 20.8 shows how to read a typical weekly mutual funds quotation.

- Column 1 is the net asset value (NAV), or the value of a single share as calculated by the fund.

- Column 2 shows the net asset value change, the gain or loss based on the previous day's NAV.

- Column 3 lists the fund family at the top and the individual fund names beneath the family name.

- Column 4 reports each fund's objective. The "IB" code stands for an intermediate-term bond fund; "GR" indicates a growth stock fund. This allows readers to compare the performance of funds with similar objectives.

- The next five columns report each fund's recent and long-term performance, and rank the funds within each investment objective. These numbers reflect the percentage change in NAV plus accumulated income for each period, assuming that all distributions are reinvested in the fund. These five columns show the return of the fund for the year to date, the last 4 weeks, 12 months, 3 years, and 5 years. The numbers for periods exceeding one year show an average annual return for the period, and are followed by letters indicating the fund's performance relative to other funds with the same objective. "A" means the fund was among the top 20 percent of funds in that category, "B" indicates the second 20 percent, and so on.

bid price
Price that an OTC broker pays for a share of stock

asked price
Price that an OTC broker charges for a share of stock

Figure 20.8 Reading Mutual Fund Quotations

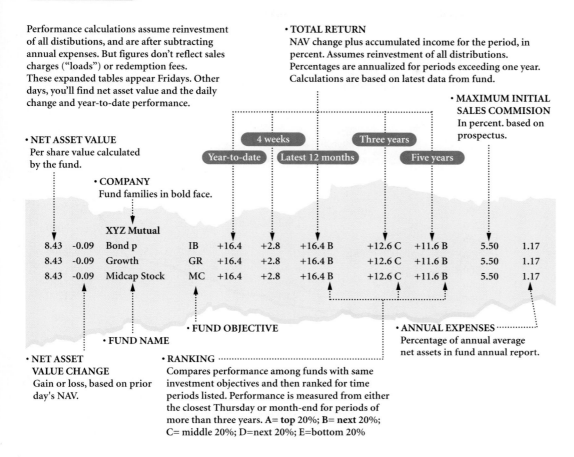

Performance calculations assume reinvestment of all distibutions, and are after subtracting annual expenses. But figures don't reflect sales charges ("loads") or redemption fees. These expanded tables appear Fridays. Other days, you'll find net asset value and the daily change and year-to-date performance.

• **TOTAL RETURN**
NAV change plus accumulated income for the period, in percent. Assumes reinvestment of all distributions. Percentages are annualized for periods exceeding one year. Calculations are based on latest data from fund.

• **MAXIMUM INITIAL SALES COMMISION**
In percent. based on prospectus.

• **NET ASSET VALUE**
Per share value calculated by the fund.

• **COMPANY**
Fund families in bold face.

			4 weeks			Three years				
		Year-to-date		Latest 12 months			Five years			
		XYZ Mutual								
8.43	-0.09	Bond p	IB	+16.4	+2.8	+16.4 B	+12.6 C	+11.6 B	5.50	1.17
8.43	-0.09	Growth	GR	+16.4	+2.8	+16.4 B	+12.6 C	+11.6 B	5.50	1.17
8.43	-0.09	Midcap Stock	MC	+16.4	+2.8	+16.4 B	+12.6 C	+11.6 B	5.50	1.17

• **FUND OBJECTIVE**

• **ANNUAL EXPENSES**
Percentage of annual average net assets in fund annual report.

• **FUND NAME**

• **NET ASSET VALUE CHANGE**
Gain or loss, based on prior day's NAV.

• **RANKING**
Compares performance among funds with same investment objectives and then ranked for time periods listed. Performance is measured from either the closest Thursday or month-end for periods of more than three years. A= **top** 20%; B= **next** 20%; C= middle 20%; D=next 20%; E=bottom 20%

■ The next column reports the maximum initial sales commission, expressed in percent, which the investor would have to pay to purchase shares in the fund

■ The last column shows the fund's average annual expenses, as a percentage of the fund's assets, paid annually by investors in the fund.

Market Indexes

Although they do not indicate the status of particular securities, **market indexes** provide useful summaries of trends, both in specific industries and in the stock market as a whole. Market indexes, for example, reveal bull and bear market trends. **Bull markets** are periods of upward-moving stock prices. Periods of falling stock prices are called **bear markets**.

As Figure 20.9 shows, for example, the years 1981 to 1998 boasted a strong bull market, the longest in history. Inflation was under control as business flourished in a healthy economy. The period 1972–1974, on the other hand, was characterized by a bear market. The Mideast oil embargo caused a business slowdown, and inflation was beginning to dampen economic growth. As you can see, the data that characterize such periods are drawn from two leading market indexes: the Dow Jones and Standard & Poor's.

The Dow and S&P. The **Dow Jones Industrial Average** is the most widely cited U.S. index. The Dow is the sum of market prices for 30 of the largest industrial firms listed on the NYSE. By tradition, it is an indicator of blue-chip stock price movements.

In February 1995, the Dow topped 4,000 for the first time ever. In November 1996, it broke the 6,400 barrier for the first time, and for 1997 the Dow ended above 7,900. For the first time ever, the Dow gained more than 20 percent a year for 3 consecutive years,

market index
Summary of price trends in a specific industry or the stock market as a whole

bull market
Period of upward-moving stock prices

bear market
Period of falling stock prices

Dow Jones Industrial Average
Market index based on the prices for 30 of the largest industrial firms listed on the NYSE

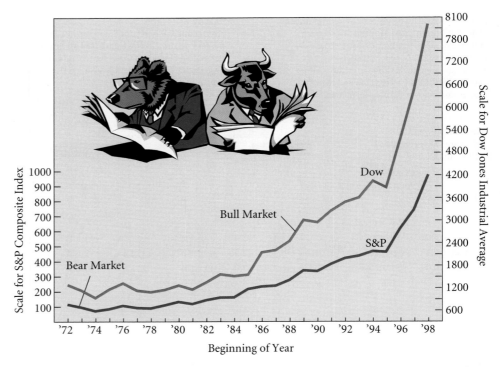

Figure 20.9 Bull and Bear Markets, 1972–1998

from 1995 to 1997. Why such optimism on the part of investors? What does the Dow's performance say about attitudes toward the economy? Though unable to pinpoint one single reason for the Dow's performance, experts cited at least three factors in the surge:

- Continued growth in corporate profits

- Continued acquisition and merger activity among corporations

- Indications from the Federal Reserve that inflation was under control and that interest rates would remain at present levels

As you can see in Figure 20.10, the Dow's movement has generally been opposite the trend for interest rates on long-term bonds. Why is this so? As bond rates decrease, investors tend to become more interested in stocks as vehicles for higher financial returns. Furthermore, because lower interest rates mean cheaper borrowing for businesses, business expenses are reduced and businesses become more profitable. Thus, investor hopes for even greater profits continue. How high will the Dow reach before it begins to fall? No one knows. Says Jack Bogle, chairperson of the Vanguard Group, "Hope can turn to fear

Figure 20.10   The Dow and Interest Rates, 1983–1996

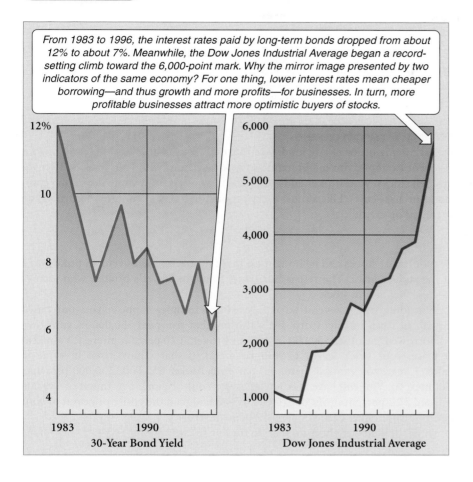

From 1983 to 1996, the interest rates paid by long-term bonds dropped from about 12% to about 7%. Meanwhile, the Dow Jones Industrial Average began a record-setting climb toward the 6,000-point mark. Why the mirror image presented by two indicators of the same economy? For one thing, lower interest rates mean cheaper borrowing—and thus growth and more profits—for businesses. In turn, more profitable businesses attract more optimistic buyers of stocks.

30-Year Bond Yield

Dow Jones Industrial Average

and greed pretty quickly. I think there's too much confidence in the market at these [1996] levels."[22]

Because it considers very few firms, the Dow is a limited gauge of the overall stock market. **Standard & Poor's Composite Index** is a broader report. The S&P 500 consists of 500 stocks, including 400 industrial firms, 40 utilities, 40 financial institutions, and 20 transportation companies. Interestingly, on the same day that the Dow topped 6,400, the S&P Index also jumped to a new record.

Placing Orders

After doing your own research and getting recommendations from your broker, you can choose to place several different types of orders:

■ A **market order** requests a broker to buy or sell a certain security at the prevailing market price at the time of the order. For example, look again at Figure 20.6: On that day, your broker would have sold your Gap Inc. stock for between 30.00 and 30.625 per share.

Note, however, that when you gave your order to sell, you did not know exactly what the market price would be. This situation can be avoided with limit and stop orders, which allow for buying and selling only if certain price conditions are met.

■ A **limit order** authorizes the purchase of a stock only if its price is less than or equal to a specified limit. For example, an order to buy at $30 per share means that the bro-

Standard & Poor's Composite Index
Market index based on the performance of 400 industrial firms, 40 utilities, 40 financial institutions, and 20 transportation companies

market order
Order to buy or sell a security at the market price prevailing at the time the order is placed

limit order
Order authorizing the purchase of a stock only if its price is equal to or less than a specified amount

stop order
Order authorizing the sale of a stock if its price falls to or below a specified level

round lot
Purchase or sale of stock in units of 100 shares

odd lot
Purchase or sale of stock in fractions of round lots

ker is to buy if and only if the stock becomes available for a price of $30 or less. A **stop order** instructs the broker to sell if a stock price falls to a certain level. For example, an order of $25 on a particular stock means that the broker is to sell that stock if and only if its price falls to $25 or below.

■ Orders also differ by size. An order for a **round lot** requests 100 shares of a particular stock or some multiple thereof. Fractions of round lots are called **odd lots**. Because an intermediary—an odd-lot broker—is often involved, odd-lot trading is usually more expensive than round-lot trading.

Financing Purchases

When you place a buy order of any kind, you must tell your broker how you will pay for the purchase. For example, you might maintain a cash account with your broker. Then, as you buy and sell stocks, your broker adds proceeds to your account while deducting commissions and purchase costs. Like almost every product in today's economy, securities can also be purchased on credit.

Margin Trading

Like futures contracts, stocks can be bought on margin; that is, the buyer can put down a portion of the stock's price. The rest is borrowed from the buyer's broker, who secures special-rate bank loans with stock.

Margin trading offers several advantages. For example, suppose you purchased $100,000 worth of stock in Intel Corp. Let's also say that you paid $50,000 of your own money and borrowed the other $50,000 from your broker at 10 percent interest. Valued at its market price, your stock serves as your collateral. If shares have risen in value to $115,000 after 1 year, you can sell them and pay your broker $55,000 ($50,000 principal plus $5,000 interest). You will have $60,000 left over. Your original investment of $50,000 will have earned a 20-percent profit of $10,000. If you had paid the entire price out of your own pocket, you would have earned only a 15-percent return.

Meanwhile, brokers benefit from margin trading in two ways:

■ Because it encourages more people to buy more stock, brokers earn more commissions.

■ Because they charge buyers higher interest rates than they pay banks, brokers earn profits on their loans.

Although investors often recognize possible profits to be made in margin trading, they sometimes fail to consider that losses can be amplified:

▶ Suppose, for example, that you decided on June 26, 1996, to buy 1,000 shares of Acme Electric, a producer of power conversion equipment, for $36 per share. You put up $18,000 of your own money and borrow $18,000 from your broker. As the stock rises, you reason, the loan will enable you to profit from twice as many shares. Now let's say that, shortly thereafter you purchase your stock Acme's market price begins to fall. You decide to hold on until it recovers. By June 26, 1997, when the price has fallen to $8.50 a share, you give up hope and sell.

Now let's see how margin trading has amplified your losses. If you had invested your own $18,000, instead of borrowing it, you would recover $8,500 of your $36,000 investment (excluding commissions). Your loss, therefore, would be 76 percent ($27,500 loss/$36,000 invested). By trading on margin, however, even though you still recover $8,500 of your $18,000 investment, you must repay the $18,000 that you borrowed, plus $1,800 in loan interest (at a 10-percent annual rate). In this case, your losses total $29,300 ($37,800 in outlays less $8,500 recovered). The percentage loss is 163 percent of your investment ($29,300 loss/$18,000 investment), much greater than the 76-percent loss you would have suffered without margin trading.[23]

Short Sales

In addition to lending money, brokerages also lend securities. A **short sale** begins when you borrow a security from your broker and sell it (one of the few times that it is legal to sell something that you do not own). At a given point in the future, you must restore an equal number of shares of that issue to the brokerage, along with a fee. Let's go back to our Gap Inc. example. Suppose that in January, you believe the price of Gap stock will soon fall. You therefore order your broker to "sell short" 100 shares at the market price of $30.125 per share. Your broker will make the sale and credit $3,012.50 to your account. If The Gap's price falls to $25 per share in July, you can buy 100 shares for $2,500 and use them to repay your broker. You will have made a $512.50 profit (before commissions). Of course, your risk is that The Gap's price may not fall: If it holds steady or rises, you will take a loss.

short sale
Stock sale in which investors borrow securities from their brokers to be sold and then replaced at a specified date

Securities Market Regulation

▶ The U.S. stock market was definitely bearish in October 1987. That month witnessed the greatest 1-month plunge in the market's history. When the fall began, stockholders throughout the nation issued sell orders. The result of massive selling was an even greater plunge. Nevertheless, many sellers tried to salvage at least something from their investments by continuing to sell their stocks at lower and lower prices. At month's end, stocks had lost 23 percent of their pre-October value. Losses totaled $0.5 trillion.

One oft-cited cause of the 1987 panic is **program trading**: the purchase or sale of a group of stocks valued at $1 million or more, often triggered by computerized trading programs that can be launched without human supervision or control. It works this way: As market values change during the course of a day, computer programs are busy recalculating the future values of stocks. Once a calculated value reaches a critical point, the program automatically signals a buy or sell order. Because electronic trading could cause the market to spiral out of control, the NYSE has set up circuit breakers that suspend trading

program trading
Large purchase or sale of a group of stocks, often triggered by computerized trading programs that can be launched without human supervision or control

New York Stock Exchange traders celebrate at the closing bell on December 31, 1997. The Dow Jones Industrial Average had just finished the year up 22.6 percent, marking the first time in the 101-year history of the Dow that the index had risen more than 20 percent in each of three consecutive years. The Dow continued its rise from 1981 to mid-1998, representing the strongest bull run in stock market history.

for a preset length of time (usually an hour). The interruption provides a cooling-off period that slows down trading activity and allows computer programs to be revised or shut down.

The Securities and Exchange Commission

To protect the investing public and to maintain smoothly functioning markets, the **Securities and Exchange Commission (SEC)** oversees many phases in the process through which securities are issued. The SEC regulates the public offering of new securities by requiring that all companies file prospectuses before proposed offerings commence. To protect investors from fraudulent issues, a **prospectus** contains pertinent information about both the offered security and the issuing company. False statements are subject to criminal penalties.

Unfortunately, to ensure full disclosure, the typical prospectus is highly technical and not easily understood by most investors. To overcome this difficulty and to make the document more user-friendly, the SEC is encouraging experimentation with a "profile prospectus." This new abbreviated document is being tested by mutual fund companies. It contains summarized information about the fund's goals, risks, investment strategy, and past performance so investors can compare it with other funds. It also fits on one piece of paper instead of requiring an entire booklet. At the very least, says A. Michael Lipper of Lipper Analytical Securities Corp., "This prospectus could save trees and lower costs to investors, and that's positive."[24]

> ❝ *This prospectus could save trees and lower costs to investors, and that's positive.* ❞
>
> —Investment analyst A. Michael Lipper, on the one-page, user-friendly securities prospectus

The SEC also enforces laws against **insider trading**: the use of special knowledge about a firm for profit or gain. In May 1996, for example, the U.S. prosecutor in Boston indicted a dentist on charges of gaining $140,000 in illegal profits by buying and selling shares of Purolator Products Co. The dentist allegedly had access to some advance, nonpublic information (a tip). Another company was preparing to purchase Purolator and, once the news became public, the price of Purolator shares would probably increase. The dentist is accused of benefiting unfairly by buying shares before public announcement of the intended buyout of Purolator.

Along with the SEC's enforcement efforts, the stock exchanges cooperate in detecting and stopping insider action. In 1995, for example, NASD referred 113 cases to the SEC for possible insider trading. The New York Stock Exchange and the American Stock Exchange have spent millions on self-regulation. They use sophisticated surveillance methods that electronically monitor transactions to detect unusual trading patterns. In May 1996, for example, the Pacific Stock Exchange asked the SEC to investigate the trading patterns of several investors believed to have ties to toymaker Hasbro Inc. The investigation began when the exchange observed a sudden rise in their trading of Hasbro stock just before Mattel Inc. announced its bid to purchase Hasbro. To stem the increase in illegal insider trading, the SEC is also using tougher enforcement, including criminal prosecution against offenders.[25]

State governments also regulate the sale of securities. For example, commenting that some promoters would sell stock "to the blue sky itself," one legislator's speech led to the phrase **blue-sky laws** and the passage of statutes requiring securities to be registered with

---

Securities and Exchange Commission (SEC)
Federal agency that administers U.S. securities laws to protect the investing public and maintain smoothly functioning markets

prospectus
Registration statement filed with the SEC before the issuance of a new security

insider trading
Illegal practice of using special knowledge about a firm for profit or gain

blue-sky laws
Laws requiring securities dealers to be licensed and registered with the states in which they do business

state officials. In addition, securities dealers must be registered and licensed by the states in which they do business. Finally, states may prosecute the sale of fraudulent securities.

Summary of Learning Objectives

1 **Explain the difference between primary and secondary securities markets.** Primary securities markets involve the buying and selling of new securities, either in public offerings or through private placements (sales to single buyers or small groups of buyers). Investment bankers specialize in selling securities in primary markets. Secondary markets involve the trading of existing stocks and bonds through such familiar bodies as the New York and American Stock Exchanges.

2 **Discuss the value to shareholders of common and preferred stock and describe the secondary market for each type of security.** Common stock affords investors the prospect of capital gains and dividend income. Common stock values are expressed in three ways: as par value (the face value of a share when it is issued), market value (the current market price of a share), and book value (the value of shareholders' equity divided by the number of shares). Market value is most important to investors. Preferred stock is less risky; for example, cumulative preferred stock entitles holders to missed dividends when the company is financially capable of paying. It also offers the prospect of steadier income. Shareholders of preferred stock must be paid dividends before shareholders of common stock.

   Both common and preferred stock are traded on stock exchanges (institutions formed to conduct the trading of existing securities) and in over-the-counter (OTC) markets (trades of securities outside stock exchange settings). Members who hold seats on exchanges act as brokers (agents who execute buy and sell orders for nonmembers). Exchanges include the New York, American, NASDAQ Stock Exchange, and regional and foreign exchanges. In the NASDAQ market, licensed dealers serve functions similar to those of brokers on other stock exchanges.

3 **Distinguish among various types of bonds in terms of their issuers, safety, and retirement.** U.S. government bonds are quite safe because they are backed by government institutions and agencies such as the Treasury Department and the Federal Housing Administration. Municipal bonds, which are offered by state and local governments to finance a variety of projects, are also usually safe, and the interest is often tax-exempt. Corporate bonds are issued by businesses to gain long-term funding. They may be secured (backed by pledges of the issuer's assets) or unsecured and offer varying degrees of safety. The safety of bonds issued by various borrowers is rated by such services as Moody's and Standard & Poor's. Only government and corporate bonds are callable (that is, can be paid off by the issuer before their maturity dates). Serial bonds are retired as portions are redeemed at preset dates; convertible bonds are retired by conversion into the issuer's common stock.

4 **Describe the investment opportunities offered by mutual funds and commodities.** Like stocks and bonds, mutual funds companies that pool investments to purchase portfolios of financial instruments offer investors different levels of risk and growth potential. Load funds require investors to pay commissions of 2 to 8 percent; no-load funds do not charge commissions when investors buy in or out. Futures contracts—agreements to buy specified amounts of commodities at given prices on preset dates—are traded in the commodities market. Commodities traders often buy on margins (percentages of total sales prices that must be put up to order futures contracts).

5 **Explain the process by which securities are bought and sold.** Investors generally begin with some homework to study such financial information services as newspaper stock, bond, and OTC quotations. Market indexes such as the Dow Jones Industrial Average and Standard & Poor's Composite Index provide useful summaries of trends, both in specific industries and in the market as a whole. Investors can then place dif-

ferent types of orders. Market orders are orders to buy or sell at current prices. Because investors do not know exactly what prices will be when market orders are executed, they may issue limit or stop orders that are to be executed only if prices rise to or fall below specified levels. Round and odd lots are purchases ordered, respectively, in multiples or fractions of 100 shares. Securities can be bought on margin or as part of short sales (sales in which investors sell securities that are borrowed from brokers and returned at a later date).

6 **Explain how securities markets are regulated.** To protect investors, the Securities and Exchange Commission (SEC) regulates the public offering of new securities and enforces laws against such practices as insider trading (using special knowledge about a firm for profit or gain). To guard against fraudulent stock issues, the SEC lays down guidelines for prospectuses (statements of information about stocks and their issuers). Many state governments also prosecute the sale of fraudulent securities and enforce blue-sky laws and statutes that require dealers to be licensed and registered where they conduct business.

Questions and Exercises

Questions for Review

1 What are the purposes of the primary and secondary markets for securities?
2 Which of the three measures of common stock value is most important? Why?
3 How do government, municipal, and corporate bonds differ from one another?
4 How might an investor lose money in a commodities trade?
5 How does the Securities and Exchange Commission regulate securities markets?

Questions for Analysis

6 What are your personal financial goals at this time? What types of stocks, bonds, or mutual funds would be best for meeting those goals? Why?
7 Which type of mutual fund would be most appropriate for your investment purposes at this time? Why?
8 Using a newspaper, select an example of a recent day's transactions for each of the following: a stock on the NYSE, a stock on the AMEX, a stock on the NASDAQ exchange, a bond on the NYSE, and a mutual fund quotation. Explain the meaning of each element in the listing.

Application Exercises

9 Interview the financial manager of a local business or your school. What are the investment goals of this person's organization? What securities does it use? What advantages and disadvantages do you see in its portfolio?
10 Either in person or through a toll-free number, contact a broker and request information about setting up a personal account for trading securities. Prepare a report on the broker's policies regarding buy/sell orders, credit terms, cash account requirements, services available to investors, and commissions and fee schedules.

Building Your Business Skills

This exercise enhances the following SCANS workplace competencies: demonstrating basic skills, demonstrating thinking skills, exhibiting interpersonal skills, working with information, and applying system knowledge.

Goal   To encourage students to understand the forces that affect fluctuations in stock price.

Background   Investing in stocks requires an understanding of the various factors that affect stock price. These factors may be intrinsic to the company itself or part of the external environment.

- *Internal factors* relate to the company itself, such as an announcement of poor or favorable earnings, earnings that are more or less than expected, major layoffs, labor problems, management issues, and mergers.

- *External factors* relate to world or national events, such as a threatened war in the Persian Gulf, the Asian currency crisis, weather conditions that affect sales, the Federal Reserve Board's adjustment of interest rates, and employment figures that were higher or lower than expected.

By analyzing these factors, you'll often learn a lot about why a stock did well or why it did poorly. Being aware of these influences will help you anticipate future stock movements.

Method   **Step 1:**   Working alone, choose a common stock that has experienced considerable price fluctuations in the past few years. Here are several examples, but there are many others: IBM, Chase Manhattan Bank, AT&T, Southern New England Telephone, Oxford Health Care, Apple Computer. Find the symbol for the stock (for example, Chase Manhattan Bank is CMB) and the exchange on which it is traded (CMB is traded on the New York Stock Exchange).

Step 2:   At your library, find the *Daily Stock Price Record*, a publication that provides a historical picture of daily stock closings. There are separate copies for the New York Stock Exchange, the American Stock Exchange, and the over-the-counter markets. Find your stock and study its trading pattern.

Step 3:   Find 4 or 5 days over a period of several months or even a year where there have been major price fluctuations in the stock. (A two- or three-point price change from one day to the next is considered major.) Then research what happened on that day that might have contributed to the fluctuation. The best place to begin is with the *Wall Street Journal* or on the business pages of a national newspaper, such as the *New York Times* or the *Washington Post*.

Step 4:   Write a short analysis that links changes in stock price to internal and external factors. As you analyze the data, be aware that sometimes it is difficult to know why a stock price fluctuates.

Step 5:   Get together with three other students who studied different stocks. As a group, discuss your findings, looking for fluctuation patterns.

Follow-Up Questions

1 Do you see any similarities in the movement of the various stocks during the same period? For example, did the stocks move up or down at about the same time? If so, do you think the stocks were affected by the same factors? Explain your thinking.

2 Based on your analysis, did internal or external factors have the greatest impact on stock price? Which factors had the most long-lasting effect? Which factors had the shortest effect?

3 Why do you think it is so hard to predict changes in stock price on a day-to-day basis?

Investment clubs are formed by groups of investors who want to pool their funds and their knowledge in order to invest in their own financial security by buying and selling stocks, bonds, and mutual funds. They appeal to all kinds of individual investors, and some are even operated by forward-thinking parents acting as custodians for their children. By pooling their funds, club members are able to diversify their investments more than they could do as individual risk-takers in the stock and bond markets. They can also take advantage of their fellow members' willingness to share the effort of researching information, reading annual reports and news stories, tracking various industries and firms, and making informed decisions.

a way to improve their own financial security but also as a means to involve their children in the economic mainstream.

"Many brokerage firms haven't made it a priority to market to the black community," according to Larry Folmar of the financial planning firm Folmar Financial, Inc., in Michigan. His firm advises investment clubs geared toward young black professionals. Many investment club members would like to redress that oversight, as does Curtis White, a retired insurance agent from Detroit who tells young blacks, "There is room in the market for everybody's money." About the young people he tries to reach, White says, "The kids starting clubs now have a chance to really change some things."

industries she formed the club to invest in local, private, minority businesses in her Los Angeles area. Now with 200 active members, the club has about $150,000 in assets and has hired a trader to monitor foreign currencies and commodities for its members. Pierce sees another purpose in the club: to open up avenues for blacks "who say they don't have any money to invest. We show them they do." She means it literally and has been known to work out household budgets for new club members to help them find a way to put cash aside for investment every month.

Curtis White would approve. "You don't have to be rich and you may not get rich. The goal is to build something to show for your life," he says.

> **❝** *You don't have to be rich and you may not get rich. The goal is to build something to show for your life.* **❞**
>
> —Curtis White, retired insurance agent

The National Association of Investment Clubs reports that the number of investment clubs is growing, and that black Americans in particular are forming and joining all-black clubs that share the same investment philosophies. Many blacks are enjoying rising incomes and are seeing investment not only as

One investment club founder saw the need for social change as a prime motivation for forming the club. Annie Pierce started Community Financial Investment Groups after neighborhood reaction to the verdict in the Rodney King case in 1992 left local businesses literally in flames. With friends in business and media

Questions

1 Is there an investment club for students at your school? Investigate it, if so, and determine how well the club's assets have performed in the last 5 years. How does the rate of return compare with the S&P 500 over the same period? What particular kinds of investments does the club make, and has its investment strategy changed since its formation? If it has, how and why?

2 If there is no investment club on your campus, what would it take to form one? What common ground might the members share if such a club were started?

What do you think would be an appropriate investment strategy for the group based on its demographics: Would it be risk-averse? Risk-seeking?

3 What sort of investments would your club undertake, if you formed one? Would it prefer high-tech stocks, for example, or communication industries, or environmentally conscious firms? How would club members determine where to put the assets of the club?

4 How would you divide the research work needed to keep the club performing well in the market you chose? In assigning tasks, consider what use you would make of the Internet and on-line investment services such as Pointcast (www.pointcast.com), Thomson Investors Network (www.thomsoninvest.net), and Closing Bell (www. merc.com). Research these sites enough to discover how their services differ and how you might customize their offerings for your club.

Connecting to the Web

The following Web sites will give you additional information and points of view about topics covered in this chapter. Many sites lead to other related Internet locations, so approach this list with the spirit of an explorer.

AMERICAN STOCK EXCHANGE

http://www.amex.com/

Visit this site for market information on AMEX-listed companies, options, and other financial instruments.

BLOOMBERG ONLINE

http://www.bloomberg.com/welcome.html

Bloomberg Online is an important commercial source of international financial news, including financial research and market commentary. You'll find real-time and historical data relating to the financial markets.

CHICAGO BOARD OF TRADE

http://www.cbot.com/

Visit the Web site of the world's leading futures and commodities exchange. Although much of the site is designed for traders, a special section called Academic Hall has courses for students and educators who want to learn about the commodities markets.

DREYFUS CORPORATION

http://www.dreyfus.com/funds/

Click on this site for a list and description of the Dreyfus family of mutual funds. Funds are designed for different investment purposes, and this site helps investors choose the fund that is right for them based on personal financial goals. The site also includes current economic and market information.

HOOVER'S ONLINE

http://www.hoovers.com

Billing itself as the "ultimate source for company information," Hoover's provides all the information you'll need about a company's financial history. Included are company profiles and access to the financial backgrounds of public and private companies.

INVESTORGUIDE: THE LEADING GUIDE TO INVESTING ON THE WEB

http://www.investorguide.com/

Visit this free comprehensive resource for investing and personal finance for information on stocks, electronic commerce, brokers, bonds, mutual funds, investment clubs, international investing, and more. The site has links to over 7,000 other investment sites.

NATIONAL ASSOCIATION OF SECURITIES DEALERS

http://www.nasd.com/

This Web site introduces the National Association of Securities Dealers, the largest securities industry self-regulatory organization in the United States. NASD sets the rules and regulations for investment activities conducted by more than 5,400 securities firms, with more than 58,000 branch offices. The NASD Web site also includes investor services such as investor training.

NEW YORK STOCK EXCHANGE

http://www.nyse.com/

Take a virtual tour of the New York Stock Exchange, the world's largest equities market in which securities are traded through a competitive agency auction system. Learn the role of the "Big Board" in raising capital for new companies through initial public offerings (IPOs).

SOCIAL INVESTMENT FORUM

http://www.socialinvest.org/

This site introduces the Social Investment Forum, a national nonprofit membership organization promoting the concept and growth of socially responsible investing. The areas of activity of the Social Investment Forum are networking and continuing education, research, direct member services and information, industry growth and client services, and industry advocacy.

U.S. SECURITIES AND EXCHANGE COMMISSION (SEC)

http://www.sec.gov/

Visit this Web site to learn how the SEC regulates the securities industry and protects investors from fraudulent schemes, in part by requiring full disclosure of investment information.

chapter 21

Understanding **financial** and risk management

Financing a recipe into an empire

Most people have heard the legend of Apple Computer's founding by two young men who put together a prototype computer in a California garage. The story is unusual but not unique: Two young men in Nantucket, Massachusetts, have begun a booming juice drink company with little more than an original recipe once concocted for a cooking contest and a collection of recycled wine bottles to sell it in.

Now bringing in $60 million a year and rapidly growing in a market dominated by giants such as Coca-Cola and Tropicana, the firm, Nantucket Allserve Inc., was started by Tom First and Tom Scott, who recall their beginning as "a combination of passion and naivete." In their early days in business the two Toms did indeed stumble into success heavily mixed with near-disaster. Some of their drink flavors were bizarre, their salesmanship was as inept as their

skill at distribution, and their employees stole more than $100,000 in merchandise from their new Boston warehouse without being detected. "We were just clueless," says Tom First. Even their radio ads were homemade.

But Michael Egan, a business executive who had made millions on the sale of his Alamo car rental company, saw the potential in their "new age" product and breezy attitude. So in 1993 he gave them $500,000 for a half share in their company. "These guys were just personally attractive, very hard working, dedicated, visionary, and so on," he says. "Really, when you invest in a business, especially a start-up business, you invest in the people."

Egan's investment has proven to be a smart risk. With a new outsourced distribution system, 100 employees, and 33 "nectar" flavors, Nantucket Allserve is enjoying 200-percent increases in revenue and plans to expand its fledgling juice bars across the United States. From a few bottles sold off the back of a boat in Nantucket harbor to an empire that sells its products as far away as Latin America

and Europe, the two Toms have made the most of their opportunities.

> ❝ *Really, when you invest in a business, especially a start-up business, you invest in the people.* ❞
>
> —Michael Egan,
> investor in Nantucket Allserve

Tom First and Tom Scott's experience reflects one of the most basic lessons in business: The difference between a firm's life and death can hinge on the handling of its finances. This fundamental truth applies equally to established firms and startups. Nantucket Allserve needed startup capital, revenue from sales, and internal financial controls. In this chapter we will examine the role of financial managers and show why businesses need financial management. By focusing on this chapter's learning objectives, you will see how risks arise when companies deploy their funds and how management works to protect firms from unnecessary financial loss. After reading this chapter, you should be able to

1 Describe the responsibilities of a financial manager.

2 Identify four sources of short-term financing for businesses.

3 Distinguish among the various sources of long-term financing and explain the risks entailed by each type.

4 Identify the most important financial management issues facing small businesses.

5 Explain how risk affects business operations and identify the five steps in the risk management process.

The Role of the Financial Manager

finance (or corporate finance)
Activities concerned with determining a firm's long-term investments, obtaining the funds to pay for them, conducting the firm's everyday financial activities, and managing the firm's risks

The business activity known as **finance** (or **corporate finance**) typically entails four responsibilities:

- Determining a firm's long-term investments
- Obtaining funds to pay for those investments
- Conducting the firm's everyday financial activities
- Helping to manage the risks that the firm takes

As we saw in chapter 12, marketing managers plan and control the development and marketing of products. In chapter 15, we saw that production managers plan and control the output of goods and services. Similarly, **financial managers** plan and control the acquisition and dispersal of a firm's financial resources. In this section we will see in some detail how those activities are channeled into specific plans for protecting and enhancing a firm's financial well-being.

financial manager
Manager responsible for planning and controlling the acquisition and dispersal of a firm's financial resources

Responsibilities of the Financial Manager

Financial managers collect funds, pay debts, establish trade credit, obtain loans, control cash balances, and plan for future financial needs. But a financial manager's overall objective is to increase a firm's value and thus stockholders 'wealth. Whereas accountants create data to reflect a firm's financial status, financial managers make decisions for improving that status. Financial managers, then, must ensure that a company's earnings exceed its costs—in other words, that it earns a profit. In sole proprietorships and partnerships, profits translate directly into increases in owners' wealth. In corporations, profits translate into an increase in the value of common stock.

The various responsibilities of the financial manager in increasing a firm's wealth fall into three general categories: cash flow management, financial control, and financial planning.

Cash Flow Management

cash flow management
Management of cash inflows and outflows to ensure adequate funds for purchases and the productive use of excess funds

To increase a firm's value, financial managers must ensure that it always has enough funds on hand to purchase the materials and human resources that it needs to produce goods and services. At the same time, of course, there may be funds that are not needed immediately. These must be invested to earn more money for the firm. This activity, **cash flow management**, requires careful planning. If excess cash balances are allowed to sit idle instead of being invested, a firm loses the cash returns that it could have earned.

How important to a business is the management of its idle cash? A study by Merrill Lynch has revealed that companies averaging $2 million in annual sales typically hold $40,000 in non–interest-bearing accounts. Larger companies hold even larger sums: For example, Coca-Cola's balance sheet showed $1.4 billion in cash on hand in December 1996.[1] More and more companies are learning that these idle funds can become working funds. By locating idle cash and putting it to work, they can avoid borrowing from outside sources. The savings on interest payments can be substantial.[2]

Although accurate information about current cash status is necessary, it does not, by itself, ensure good cash management. Managers must also plan cash flows ahead of time. For one thing, accurate projections of excess cash allow firms to take advantage of high-yield investment opportunities. In 1996, for example, Gucci, designers of luxury accessories, earned $14 million in interest income during the year by investing otherwise idle incoming cash that was not needed immediately to meet other obligations.[3]

Financial Control

Because things rarely go exactly as planned, financial managers must make adjustments for actual financial changes that occur each day. **Financial control** is the process of checking actual performance against plans to ensure that desired financial results occur. For example, planned revenues based on forecasts usually turn out to be higher or lower than actual revenues because sales are largely unpredictable. Control involves monitoring revenue inflows and making appropriate financial adjustments. Excessively high revenues, for instance, may be deposited in short-term interest-bearing accounts. Or they may be used to pay off short-term debt. In contrast, lower-than-expected revenues may necessitate short-term borrowing to meet current debt obligations.

Budgets (as we saw in chapter 18) are often the backbone of financial control. The budget provides the measuring stick against which performance is evaluated. The cash flows, debts, and assets not only of the whole company but also of each department are compared at regular intervals against budgeted amounts. Discrepancies indicate the need for financial adjustments so that resources are used to the best advantage.

financial control
Management process of checking actual performance against plans to ensure that desired financial results occur

Financial Planning

The cornerstone of effective financial management is the development of a financial plan. A **financial plan** describes a firm's strategies for reaching some financial position. In constructing the plan, a financial manager must ask several questions:

- What amount of funds does the company need to meet immediate needs?

- When will it need more funds?

- Where can it get the funds to meet its short- and long-term needs?

To answer these questions, a financial manager must develop a clear picture of why a firm needs funds. Managers must also assess the costs and benefits of potential funding sources. In the sections that follow we will examine the main reasons for which companies generate funds and describe the main sources of business funding for the short term and the long term.

financial plan
A firm's strategies for reaching a desired financial position

Why Do Businesses Need Funds?

Every company must spend money to survive. According to the simplest formula, funds that are spent on materials, wages, and buildings eventually lead to the creation of products, revenues, and profits. In planning for funding requirements, financial managers must distinguish between two different kinds of expenditures: short-term (operating) and long-term (capital) expenditures.

Short-Term (Operating) Expenditures

Short-term expenditures are incurred regularly in a firm's everyday business activities. Managing these outlays requires special attention to accounts payable, accounts receivable, and inventories. There are also innovative measures that many firms are taking to raise profits and improve efficiency by managing the funds known as working capital.

Accounts Payable

In chapter 18, we defined accounts payable as unpaid bills owed to suppliers plus wages and taxes due in the upcoming year. For most companies, this is the largest single category of short-term debt. To plan for funding flows, financial planners want to know in advance the amounts of new accounts payable as well as when they must be paid. For information about such obligations and needs (say, the quantity of supplies required by a certain department in an upcoming period), financial managers must rely on other managers. For example, financial plans at *People* magazine rely on information from production about the amount of ink and paper needed to print the magazine, and when these supplies are needed. Usually, it is in a buying firm's best interest to withhold payment as long as it can. The longer it withholds payment, the longer it will have that cash available for investments or other uses.

Accounts Receivable

As we also saw in chapter 18, accounts receivable consist of funds due from customers who have bought on credit. A sound financial plan requires accurate projections of both how much and when buyers will make payments on these accounts. For example, managers at Kraft Foods must know how many dollars' worth of cheddar cheese Kroger's supermarkets will order each month. They must also know Kroger's payment schedule. Because they represent an investment in products for which a firm has not yet received payment, accounts receivable temporarily tie up its funds. Clearly, the seller wants to receive payment and put the funds to use as quickly as possible.

credit policy
Rules governing a firm's extension of credit to customers

Credit Policies.   Predicting payment schedules is a function of **credit policy**: the rules governing a firm's extension of credit to customers. This policy sets standards as to which buyers are eligible for what type of credit. Typically, credit is extended to customers who have the ability to pay and who honor their obligations. Credit is denied to firms with poor payment histories. Information about such histories is available from many sources, including the Credit Interchange developed by the National Association of Credit Management.

Credit policy also sets payment terms. For example, credit terms of 2/10, net 30 mean that the selling company offers a 2-percent discount if the customer pays within 10 days. The customer has 30 days to pay the regular price. Under these terms, the buyer would have to pay only $980 on a $1,000 invoice on days 1 to 10, but all $1,000 on days 11 to 30. The higher the discount, the more incentive buyers have to pay early. Sellers can thus adjust credit terms to influence when customers pay their bills.

Inventories

Between the time a firm buys raw materials and the time it sells finished products, it ties up funds in **inventory**: materials and goods that it will sell within the year. There are three basic types of inventories:

inventory
Materials and goods that are held by a company but will be sold within the year

- The supplies that a firm purchases for use in production are its raw materials inventory. For example, raw materials inventory at Lee Apparel Co. includes huge rolls of denim.

- Work-in-process inventory consists of goods that have moved partway through the production process. Thus, jeans that have been cut out but not yet sewn are work-in-process inventory at Lee.

- Finished-goods inventory consists of items ready for sale. Completed blue jeans ready for shipment to dealers are part of Lee's finished-goods inventory.

Failure to manage inventory can have grave financial consequences. Too little inventory of any kind can cost a firm sales. Too much inventory means tied-up funds that cannot be used elsewhere. In extreme cases, a company may have to sell excess inventory at low profits simply to raise cash.

Working Capital

working capital
The difference between a firm's current assets and current liabilities; its liquid current assets on hand

Working capital consists of a firm's current assets on hand minus its liabilities. In other words, it is liquid assets out of which current debts can be paid. Most working capital assets are in the form of the following:

- Inventories (that is, raw materials, work-in-process, and finished goods on hand)

- Accounts receivable (minus accounts payable)

The Workplace Environment

Lasers to Keep Publisher's Inventory Under Control

Holtzbrinck, the German media giant that owns several big U.S. publishers, is betting that digital instructions and laser-wand technology can cure the stubborn inefficiency of the distribution end of the book business. The owner of Farrar, Straus & Giroux, Henry Holt, and St. Martin's Press unveiled a new inventory management system in a $30-million warehouse it built in Gordonsville, Virginia, and it has high hopes for dramatic cost savings from its state-of-the-art inventory equipment.

Small digital wands that can be waved over the inventory will transmit picking instructions to warehouse workers, who will use blinking lights on the shelves to note which books and how many of each are needed to fill each order. The packed boxes will travel on forklifts that ride along a narrow magnetic strip etched in the warehouse floor. Workers can still check orders by hand as a backup to the new system.

Some of Holtzbrinck's rival publishers credit the firm's innovation while steering well clear of adopting such experimental methods themselves. Jo Kiener, COO at HarperCollins, notes that debugging such a system can take months and could rule out Holtzbrinck's getting any competitive advantage from the new warehouse. But Holtzbrinck executives are confident they'll see 35 percent cost reductions among the five publishers the firm owns in the United States, a total of almost $6 million a year. And that could be a significant advantage in an industry increasingly suffering from flat margins and merchandise returns averaging 45 percent.

How much money is tied up in working capital? Fortune 500 companies typically devote 20 cents of every sales dollar to working capital. Although inventories and accounts receivable are necessary for creating sales and revenues, beyond some point they can grow too large and become wasteful.

What are the benefits of reducing excessive working capital? There are two very important pluses:

- Every dollar that is not tied up in working capital becomes a dollar of more useful cash flow.

- Reduction of working capital raises earnings permanently.

The second advantage results from the fact that money costs money (in interest payments and the like). Reducing working capital, therefore, means saving money.

Long-Term (Capital) Expenditures

In addition to funds for operating expenditures, companies need funds to cover long-term expenditures on fixed assets. As we saw in chapter 18, fixed assets are items with long-term use or value, such as land, buildings, and machinery.

Long-term expenditures are usually more carefully planned than short-term outlays because they pose special problems. They differ from short-term outlays in the following ways, all of which influence the ways that long-term outlays are funded:

- Unlike inventories and other short-term assets, they are not normally sold or converted into cash.

- Their acquisition requires a very large investment.

- They represent a binding commitment of company funds that continues long into the future.

Sources of Short-Term Funds

Firms can call on many sources for the funds they need to finance day-to-day operations and to implement short-term plans. These sources include trade credit, secured and unsecured loans, and factoring accounts receivable.

Trade Credit

trade credit
Granting of credit by one firm to another

Accounts payable are not merely expenditures. They also constitute a source of funds for the buying company. Until it pays its bill, the buyer has the use of both the purchased product and the price of the product. This situation results when the seller grants **trade credit**, which is effectively a short-term loan from one firm to another. Trade credit can take several forms:

open-book credit
Form of trade credit in which sellers ship merchandise on faith that payment will be forthcoming

- The most common form, **open-book credit**, is essentially a good-faith agreement. Buyers receive merchandise along with invoices stating credit terms. Sellers ship products on faith that payment will be forthcoming.

promissory note
Form of trade credit in which buyers sign promise-to-pay agreements before merchandise is shipped

- When sellers want more reassurance, they may insist that buyers sign legally binding **promissory notes** before merchandise is shipped. The agreement states when and how much money will be paid to the seller.

trade draft
Form of trade credit in which buyers must sign statements of payment terms attached to merchandise by sellers

- The **trade draft** is attached to the merchandise shipment by the seller and states the promised date and amount of payment due. To take possession of the merchandise, the buyer must sign the draft. Once signed by the buyer, the document becomes a **trade acceptance**. Trade drafts and trade acceptances are useful forms of credit in international transactions.

trade acceptance
Trade draft that has been signed by the buyer

Secured Short-Term Loans

collateral
Legal asset pledged by borrowers that may be seized by lenders in case of nonpayment

For most firms, bank loans are a very important source of short-term funding. Such loans almost always involve promissory notes in which the borrower promises to repay the loan plus interest. In secured loans, banks also require **collateral**: a legal interest in certain assets that can be seized if payments are not made as promised.

secured loan
Loan for which the borrower must provide collateral

Secured loans allow borrowers to get funds when they might not qualify for unsecured credit. Moreover, they generally carry lower interest rates than unsecured loans. Collateral may be in the form of inventories or accounts receivable, and most businesses have other types of assets that can be pledged. For instance, some own marketable securities, such as stocks or bonds of other companies. Many more own fixed assets, such as land, buildings, or equipment. However, fixed assets are generally used to secure long-term rather than short-term loans. Most short-term business borrowing is secured by inventories and accounts receivable.

Inventory Loans

When a loan is made with inventory as a collateral asset, the lender lends the borrower some portion of the stated value of the inventory. Obviously, inventory is more attractive as collateral when it provides the lender with real security for the loan amount. For example, if the inventory can be readily converted into cash, it is more valuable as collateral. Other inventory (say, boxes full of expensive, partially completed lenses for eyeglasses) is of little value on the open market. Meanwhile, a thousand crates of boxed, safely stored canned tomatoes might well be convertible into cash.

Accounts Receivable

pledging accounts receivable
Using accounts receivable as loan collateral

When accounts receivable are used as collateral, the process is called **pledging accounts receivable**. In the event of nonpayment, the lender may seize the receivables. If these assets are not enough to cover the loan, the borrower must make up the difference. Loans on receivables are granted only when lenders are confident that they can recover funds from the borrower's debtors. Receivables are especially important to service companies such as accounting firms and law offices because they do not maintain inventories of physical products; accounts receivable are their main source of collateral.

Typically, lenders who will accept accounts receivable as collateral are financial institutions with credit departments capable of evaluating the quality of the receivables.

Unsecured Short-Term Loans

With an **unsecured loan**, the borrower does not have to put up collateral. In many cases, however, the bank requires the borrower to maintain a compensating balance: The borrower must keep a portion of the loan amount on deposit with the bank in a non–interest-bearing account.

The terms of the loan amount, duration, interest rate, and payment schedule are negotiated between the bank and the borrower. To receive an unsecured loan, then, a firm must ordinarily have a good banking relationship with the lender. Once an agreement is made, a promissory note will be executed and the funds transferred to the borrower. Although some unsecured loans are one-time-only arrangements, many take the form of lines of credit, revolving credit agreements, or commercial paper.

unsecured loan
Loan for which collateral is not required

Line of Credit

A **line of credit** is a standing agreement between a bank and a business in which the bank promises to lend the firm a maximum amount of funds on request. Suppose, for example, that First National Bank gives Sunshine Tanning Inc. a $100,000 line of credit for the coming year. Under this arrangement, Sunshine's borrowings can total up to $100,000 at any time, and Sunshine benefits by knowing in advance that the bank regards it as creditworthy and will lend funds on short notice.

line of credit
Standing arrangement in which a lender agrees to make available a specified amount of funds upon the borrower's request

Revolving Credit Agreement

Revolving credit agreements are similar to consumer bank cards. A lender agrees to make some amount of funds available on a continuing basis. The lending institution guarantees that these funds will be available when sought by the borrower. In return for this guarantee, the bank charges the borrower a commitment fee for holding the line of credit open. This fee is payable even if the customer does not borrow any funds. It is often expressed as a percentage of the loan amount (usually .5 to 1 percent of the committed amount).

For example, say that First National agrees to lend Sunshine Tanning up to $100,000 under a revolving credit agreement. If Sunshine borrows $80,000, it still has access to $20,000. If it pays off $50,000 and reduces its debt to $30,000, it then has $70,000 available. Sunshine pays interest on the borrowed funds, plus a fee on the unused funds in its line of credit.

revolving credit agreement
Arrangement in which a lender agrees to make funds available on a continuing basis

Commercial Paper

Some firms can raise short-term funds by issuing **commercial paper**: short-term securities, or notes, containing the borrower's promise to pay. Because it is backed solely by the issuing firm's promise to pay, commercial paper is an option for only the largest and most creditworthy firms.

How does commercial paper work? Corporations issue commercial paper with a certain face value. Buying companies pay less than that value. At the end of a specified period (usually 30 to 90 days, but legally up to 270 days), the issuing company buys back the paper at face value. The difference between the price paid and the face value is the buyer's profit. For the issuing company, the cost is usually lower than prevailing interest rates on short-term loans.

For example, if Consolidated Edison needs to borrow $10 million for 90 days, it might issue commercial paper with a face value of $10.2 million. Who will buy the paper? Among other investors, insurance companies with $10 million in available cash may buy it. After 90 days, Consolidated Edison will pay a total of $10.2 million to the insurance companies who invested.

commercial paper
Short-term securities, or notes, containing a borrower's promise to pay

Factoring Accounts Receivable

factoring
Practice of raising funds by selling a firm's accounts receivable to another company

A firm can raise funds rapidly by **factoring**: selling the firm's accounts receivable. In this process, the purchaser of the receivables, usually a financial institution, is known as the factor. The factor pays some percentage of the full amount of receivables due to the selling firm. The seller gets this money immediately.

For example, a factor might buy $40,000 worth of receivables for 60 percent of that sum ($24,000). The factor profits to the extent that the money it eventually collects exceeds the amount it paid. This profit depends on the quality of the receivables, the cost of collecting them, and interest rates.

Sources of Long-Term Funds

Firms need long-term funding to finance expenditures on fixed assets: the buildings and equipment necessary for conducting their business. They may seek long-term funds through debt financing (that is, from outside the firm) or equity financing (by drawing on internal sources). In this section we discuss both options at length and, more briefly, a middle ground called hybrid financing. We also analyze some of the options that enter into decisions about long-term financing, as well as the role of the risk–return relationship in attracting investors to a firm.

Debt Financing

debt financing
Long-term borrowing from sources outside a company

Long-term borrowing from sources outside the company—**debt financing**—is a major component of most firms' long-term financial planning. Long-term debts are obligations that are payable more than 1 year after they were originally issued. The two primary sources of such funding are long-term loans and the sale of corporate bonds.

Long-Term Loans

Most corporations get long-term loans from commercial banks, usually those with which they have long-standing relationships. Credit companies (such as Household Finance Corp.), insurance companies, and pension funds also grant long-term business loans.

Long-term loans are attractive to borrowers for several reasons:

- Because the number of parties involved is limited, loans can often be arranged very quickly.

- The firm need not make public disclosure of its business plans or the purpose for which it is acquiring the loan. (In contrast, a public offering of corporate bonds requires such disclosure.)

- The duration of the loan can easily be matched to the borrower's needs.

- If the firm's needs change, loans usually contain clauses making it possible to change terms.

Long-term loans also have some disadvantages. For instance, borrowers may have trouble finding lenders to supply large sums. Long-term borrowers may also face restrictions as conditions of the loan. For example, they may have to pledge long-term assets as collateral or agree to take on no more debt until the loan is paid.

Interest Rates. Interest rates are negotiated between borrower and lender. Although some bank loans have fixed rates, others have floating rates tied to the prime rate that the bank charges its most creditworthy customers (see chapter 19). A loan at 1 percent above prime, then, is payable at 1 percentage point higher than the prime rate. This rate may fluctuate, or float, because the prime rate itself goes up and down as market conditions change.

Corporate Bonds

As we saw in chapter 20, a corporate bond is a contract a promise by the issuer to pay the holder a certain amount of money on a specified date. However, bond issuers do not retire their debt quickly. In many cases, bonds may not be redeemable for 30 years. Also, most bonds pay bondholders a stipulated sum of annual or semiannual interest. If the company fails to make a bond payment, it is said to be in default.

Bonds are the major source of long-term debt financing for most corporations. They are attractive when firms need large amounts for long periods of time. The issuing company also gains access to large numbers of lenders through nationwide bond markets and stock exchanges. On the other hand, bonds entail high administrative and selling costs. They may also require stiff interest payments, especially if the issuing company has a poor credit rating.

Bond Indentures. The terms of a bond, including the amount to be paid, the interest rate, and the maturity date (the date when the principal is to be paid) differ from company to company and issue to issue. They are spelled out in the bond contract, or **bond indenture**. The indenture also identifies which of the firm's assets, if any, are pledged as collateral for the bonds.

PPG Industries, a leading manufacturer of fiberglass, industrial chemicals, and medical supplies, has a $150-million debt issue that matures on May 1, 2021. Until the maturity date, the bondholders, including those who purchased the initial offering in 1991, will be paid 9.12 percent interest each year. In addition, they will receive a total of $150 million, the principal amount owed by PPG, when the bonds mature and are retired. The bond indenture contained no specific pledge of particular assets for security.[4]

bond indenture
Statement of the terms of a corporate bond

Equity Financing

Although debt financing often has strong appeal, looking inside the company for long-term funding is sometimes preferable. In small companies, for example, founders may increase personal investments in their own firms. In most cases, **equity financing** means issuing common stock or retaining the firm's earnings. Both options involve putting the owners' capital to work.

equity financing
Use of common stock or retained earnings to raise long-term funding

Common Stock

Investors who purchase common stock seek profits in two forms: dividends and appreciation. Overall, shareholders hope for an increase in the market value of their stock (appreciation) because they expect the firm to profit and grow. By issuing shares of stock, the company gets the funds it needs for buying land, buildings, and equipment.

Suppose, for example, that Sunshine Tanning's founders invested $10,000 by buying the original 500 shares of common stock (at $20 per share) in 1990. The company used

"First we develop the concept for our web site. Next we hire someone to design and execute it. Then we find investors to form the company."

Table 21.1 Stockholders' Equity for Sunshine Tanning

Common stockholders' equity, 1990	
Initial common stock (500 shares issued @ $20 per share, 1990)	$10,000
Total stockholders' equity	$10,000
Common stockholders' equity, 1998	
Initial common stock (500 shares issues @ $20 per share, 1990)	$10,000
Additional paid-in capital (500 shares issued @ $100 per share, 1998)	50,000
Total stockholders' equity	$60,000

these funds to buy equipment, and it succeeded financially. By 1998, it needed funds for expansion. A pattern of profitable operations and regularly paid dividends now allows Sunshine to raise $50,000 by selling 500 new shares of stock at $100 per share. This $50,000 would constitute paid-in capital: additional money, above the par value of its original stock sale, paid directly to a firm by its owners (see chapter 18). As Table 21.1 shows, this additional paid-in capital would increase total stockholders' equity to $60,000.

initial public offering (IPO)
First public offering of common stock by a company

The first public offering of its common stock by a company is called an **initial public offering (IPO)**. In 1996, for example, the IPO for Pixar Animation Studios in California made a spectacular debut when its stock price rose from $22 to $39 in its first day on the market.[5]

Finally, we should note that the use of equity financing by means of common stock can be expensive because paying dividends is more expensive than paying bond interest. Why? Because interest paid to bondholders is a business expense and, therefore, a tax deduction for the firm. Stock dividends are not tax-deductible.

Retained Earnings

Again, recall our discussion in chapter 18, where we defined retained earnings as profits retained for the firm's use rather than paid out in dividends. If a company uses retained earnings as capital, it will not have to borrow money and pay interest.

If a firm has a history of reaping profits by reinvesting retained earnings, it may be very attractive to some investors. However, retained earnings mean smaller dividends for shareholders. In this sense, then, the practice may decrease the demand for and thus the price of the company's stock.

For example, if Sunshine Tanning had net earnings of $50,000 in 1998, it could pay a $50-per-share dividend on its 1,000 shares of common stock. Let's say, however, that Sunshine plans to remodel at a cost of $30,000, intending to retain $30,000 in earnings to finance the project. Only $20,000 ($20 per share) will be available for shareholders.

Financial Burden on the Firm

As we have already noted, a firm cannot deduct paid-out dividends as business expenses, but it can deduct the interest that it pays on bonds. If equity funding can be so expensive, why do firms not rely entirely on debt financing? Loans and bonds carry fixed interest rates and represent fixed promises to pay, regardless of changes in economic conditions. If a firm defaults on its obligations, it may lose assets and may even go bankrupt. Indeed, following the deregulation of the savings and loan industry, widespread defaulting on loans made in the 1980s brought about the U.S. savings and loan catastrophe. S&Ls had granted loans to farmers, foreign businesses, and U.S. businesses that were unable to repay debts during the economic downturn.

Similarly, in the 1997 Asian financial crisis, Korean banks suffered when borrowers (large companies) could not repay outstanding debt. Companies went bankrupt, frightened

Thomas Balino (left), *head of the three-person International Monetary Fund (IMF) advance guard, talks with South Korean Choi Yon-Chong, Vice President of the Bank of Korea. Balino and his team came to Korea to work out the terms of a multibillion-dollar loan intended to bail out South Korea from its financial crisis. The crisis was fueled by firms that could not repay borrowed money, thus defaulting on the terms of their loans.*

foreign investors pulled their money out of the country, and borrowing costs soared as global lenders demanded higher returns for the increased risks of loaning funds to Korean firms. As more and more borrowers teetered on the verge of default, the Korean economy weakened. For example, Hyundai Motor Co. was forced to halt car production because of lack of parts from Mando Machinery, which had to file for court protection from creditors. With so much investor pessimism, how could firms raise badly needed funds to pay their debts? Several remedies were considered for regaining investor confidence. First, the Korean government could issue bonds with guaranteed payment to lenders. Another proposal was to consolidate all of Korea's private bank debt and convert it into government-backed bonds. Still another alternative would convert existing short-term debt into debt with longer-term maturities. Doing so would avoid the pressure of coming up with cash now and, instead, would allow payment of the debt at some time in the future. This option would buy time for creditors to weigh the risks of loans and for borrowers to figure out ways to meet their debt obligations. As of early 1998 the debate on what to do remained unresolved.[6]

Because of the risk of default, debt financing appeals most strongly to companies in industries that have predictable profits and cash flow patterns. For example, demand for electric power is quite steady from year to year and predictable from month to month. Thus, electric utility companies enjoy steady streams of income and can carry substantial amounts of debt. Detroit Edison Co., a major privately owned utility, is a representative example. About 63 percent of its long-term funding is in the form of debt. Equity from common stock provides only 32 percent. The remaining 5 percent of Edison's long-term capital is equity from preferred stock, a topic discussed in the next section.

Hybrid Financing: Preferred Stock

A middle ground between debt financing and equity financing is the use of preferred stock (see chapter 20). Preferred stock is a hybrid because it has some of the features of both corporate bonds and common stocks. As with bonds, for instance, payments on preferred stock are fixed amounts such as $6 per share per year. Unlike bonds, however, preferred stock never matures; like common stock, it can be held indefinitely. In addition, preferred stocks have first rights (over common stock) to dividends.

A major advantage to the issuer is the flexibility of preferred stock. Because preferred stockholders have no voting rights, the stock secures funds for the firm without jeopardizing corporate control of its management. Furthermore, corporations are not obligated to repay the principal and can withhold payment of dividends in lean times.

Choosing Between Debt and Equity Financing

Needless to say, an aspect of financial planning is striking a balance between debt and equity financing. A firm relies on a mix of debt and equity to raise the cash needed for capital outlays, and that mix is called its **capital structure**. Financial plans thus contain targets for capital structure; an example would be 40 percent debt and 60 percent equity. But choosing a target is not easy. A wide range of mixes is possible, and strategies range from conservative to risky.

The most conservative strategy is all-equity financing and no debt: A company has no formal obligations to make financial payouts. As we have seen, however, equity is an expensive source of capital. The riskiest strategy is all-debt financing. Although less expensive than equity funding, indebtedness increases the risk that a firm will be unable to meet its obligations (and even go bankrupt). Somewhere between the two extremes, financial planners try to find mixes that will increase stockholders' wealth with a reasonable exposure to risk.

Indexes of Financial Risk

To help understand and measure the amount of financial risk they face, financial managers often rely on published indexes for various investments. *Financial World*, for example, publishes independent appraisals of mutual funds (see chapter 20), using risk-reward ratings of A (very good) to E (poor) to indicate each fund's riskiness in comparison to its anticipated financial returns. An A-rated fund is judged to offer very good returns relative to the amount of risk involved. An E-rated fund carries the greatest risk with smaller returns. Similarly, Standard & Poor's publishes various indexes for numerous funds and for stocks that are available for purchase by financial managers.[7]

By using such indexes, financial managers can determine how a particular investment compares to other opportunities in terms of its stability. A bond, for example, is considered investment grade if it qualifies for one of the top four ratings by either S&P or Moody's. Bonds below investment grade are called junk bonds because they have unusually high default rates. Nonetheless, junk bonds appeal to many investors because they promise uncommonly high yields.

The Risk-Return Relationship

While developing plans for raising capital, financial managers must be aware of the different motivations of individual investors. Why, for example, do some individuals and firms invest in stocks whereas others invest only in bonds? Investor motivations determine who is willing to buy various securities. Investors give money to firms and, in return, anticipate receiving future cash flows. Thus, everyone who invests money is expressing a personal preference for safety or risk.

Although some cash flows are more certain than others, investors generally expect to receive higher payments for higher uncertainty. They do not generally expect large returns for secure investments such as government-insured bonds. Each type of investment, then, has a **risk–return relationship**, reflecting the principle that whereas safer investments tend to offer lower returns, riskier investments tend to offer higher returns. Figure 21.1 shows the general risk–return relationship for various financial instruments. High-grade corporate bonds, for example, rate low in terms of risk on future returns but also low on size of expected returns. The reverse is true of junk bonds.

Risk-return differences are recognized by financial planners, who try to gain access to the greatest funding at the lowest possible cost. By gauging investors' perceptions of its riskiness, a firm's managers can estimate how much they must pay to attract funds. Over time, a company can reposition itself on the risk continuum by improving its record on dividends, interest payments, and debt repayment.

capital structure
Mix of a firm's debt and equity financing

risk–return relationship
Principle that safer investments tend to offer lower returns and riskier investments tend to offer higher returns

Figure 21.1 The Risk–Return Relationship

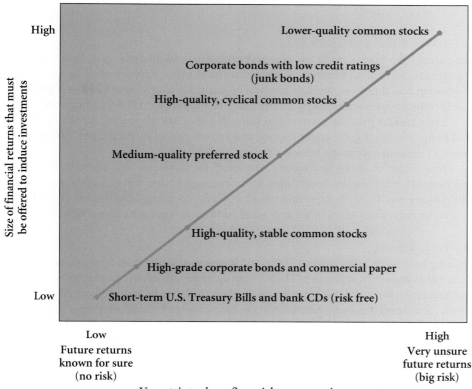

Size of financial returns that must be offered to induce investments

High

Low

Uncertainty about financial returns on investments

Low
Future returns
known for sure
(no risk)

High
Very unsure
future returns
(big risk)

Lower-quality common stocks

Corporate bonds with low credit ratings
(junk bonds)

High-quality, cyclical common stocks

Medium-quality preferred stock

High-quality, stable common stocks

High-grade corporate bonds and commercial paper

Short-term U.S. Treasury Bills and bank CDs (risk free)

Financial Management for Small Business

A recent study cites 10 common reasons why businesses fail.[8] As you can see, the first seven of these causes of failure are financial management lapses:

■ The business is undercapitalized.

■ Cash flow problems accumulate due to overextension of credit or poor collection.

■ Tax obligations have accumulated.

■ The company fails to collect payments.

■ They have lost the support of their financial backers.

■ Managers fail to consider the financial consequences of their activities.

■ They sign long-term property leases that turn out to be too burdensome.

■ Market conditions are unfavorable.

■ The entrepreneur knows little about the business and is unprepared for its challenges.

■ The entrepreneur fails to effectively manage the various stages of company growth.

Among these sources, undercapitalization may be the strongest. New business success and failure are often closely related to adequate or inadequate funding. For example, one study of nearly 3,000 new companies revealed a survival rate of 84 percent for new businesses with initial investments of at least $60,000 (expressed in 1998 dollars). Those with less funding have a much lower survival rate.[9] Why are so many startups underfunded? For one thing, entrepreneurs often underestimate the value of establishing bank credit as a source of funds and use trade credit ineffectively. In addition, they often fail to consider venture capital as a source of funding, and they are notorious for not planning cash flow needs properly.

Establishing Bank and Trade Credit

Some banks have liberal credit policies and offer financial analysis, cash flow planning, and suggestions based on experiences with other local firms. Some provide loans to small businesses in bad times and work to keep them going. Of course, some do not. Obtaining credit therefore begins with finding a bank that will support a small firm's financial needs.

Credit seekers must be prepared to show that they are worthy of the bank's help. A sound financial plan, a good credit history, and proven capability on the part of the entrepreneur all demonstrate that a business can succeed.

Once a line of credit is obtained, the small business can seek more liberal credit terms from other businesses. Sometimes, for instance, suppliers will give customers longer credit periods say, 45 or 60 days rather than 30 days. Receiving liberal trade credit terms lets firms increase short-term funds and avoid additional borrowing from banks.

Long-Term Funding

Obtaining long-term loans is more difficult for new businesses than for established companies. With unproven repayment ability, startup firms can expect to pay higher interest rates than older firms. If a new enterprise displays evidence of sound financial planning, however, the Small Business Administration (see chapter 7) may support a guaranteed loan.

How to Write a Business Plan

If you have never explained your business on paper, here's help to get started. The following four steps are taken from the business plan for entrepreneur David Cupp's Hilliard, Ohio, firm, Photos Online, and from information provided by Bank One, Columbus, and others.

1 Write a statement of purpose. If you can't explain your venture in 25 words or less, it's probably not a good idea. Following your explanation, tell how your business will work, who will own it, and why it will succeed.

2 Describe the business in detail. Tell what products or services you'll provide and to whom. Discuss the market for your business and the competition. Then explain how your company will be managed and by whom. List their credentials. Tell where your company will be located and why. Also, tell how you'll apply the loan, and list its expected benefits.

3 Supply financial data. You'll need 3 years of projected financial statements. They include income, loss, and cash-flow projections—by month for the first year, and by quarter for the next two.

If you must buy equipment, list the items, their costs, and what you'll use for collateral. Resist using your house and other personal property. Instead, list savings, bank accounts, and vehicles. Include notes of explanation whenever figures seem contradictory or otherwise questionable.

If you're asking for $50,000 or more, provide quick and current ratios comparing assets to liabilities, with and without inventory.

4 Attach supporting documents. Examples include résumés of principals; references from creditors, potential clients, and suppliers; the names of your accountant and attorney; evidence of hazard insurance; a lease agreement, if any; and articles of incorporation, if appropriate.

Then take your plan to a banker. If he or she says no, try another one. A sound plan will eventually find a lender. If you still need convincing, just ask David Cupp.

The Business Plan as a Tool for Credit. Startup firms without proven financial success usually must present a business plan to demonstrate that the firm is a good credit risk. The **business plan** is a document that tells potential lenders why the money is needed, the amount, how the money will be used to improve the company, and when it will be paid back. Photographer David Cupp, for example, needed $50,000 funding for his new firm, Photos Online, Inc., in Columbus, Ohio, which displays and sells photos over the Internet. His business plan had to be rewritten many times until it became understandable, in financial terms, to potential lenders. The plan eventually reached 35 pages and contained information on the competition as well as cash flow projections. After four failed attempts, the fifth bank approved a $26,000 term loan and granted a $24,000 line of credit, to be used for computers, software, and living expenses to get the business started.[10] Cupp's four-step approach to the business plan is summarized in the "It's Your Business" box.

business plan
Document that tells potential lenders why money is needed, how it will be used, and when it will be repaid

Venture Capital

Many newer businesses, especially those undergoing rapid growth, cannot get the funds they need through borrowing alone. They may therefore turn to **venture capital**: outside equity funding provided in return for part ownership. Venture capital firms actively seek chances to invest in new firms with rapid growth potential. Because failure rates of new startups are high, investors typically demand high returns, which are now often 20 to 30 percent.

venture capital
Outside equity financing provided in return for part ownership of the borrowing firm

Planning for Cash Flow
Requirements

Although all businesses should plan for their cash flows, this planning is especially important for small businesses. Success or failure may hinge on anticipating times when cash will be short or excess cash can be expected.

Figure 21.2 shows anticipated cash inflows, cash outflows, and net cash position (inflows minus outflows), month by month, for Slippery Fish Bait Supply, a highly seasonal business. As you can see, bait stores buy heavily from Slippery during the spring and summer. Revenues outpace expenses, leaving surplus funds that can be invested. During the fall and winter, however, expenses exceed revenues. Slippery must borrow funds to keep going until revenues pick up again in the spring. Comparing predicted cash inflows from sales with outflows for expenses shows the firm's expected monthly cash flow position.

Such information can be invaluable. By anticipating shortfalls, the firm's manager can seek funds in advance and minimize their cost. By anticipating excess cash,

Figure 21.2 Projected Cash Flow for Slippery Fish Bait Supply Co.

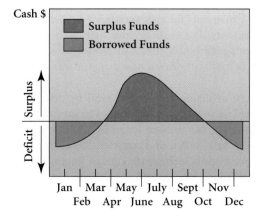

the manager can develop plans to put the funds to work in short-term, interest-earning investments.

Risk Management

Financial risks are not the only risks faced every day by companies (and individuals). In this section, we describe various other types of risks that businesses face and analyze some of the ways in which they typically manage them.

Coping with Risk

risk
Uncertainty about future events

speculative risk
Risk involving the possibility of gain or loss

pure risk
Risk involving only the possibility of loss or no loss

risk management
Process of conserving the firm's earning power and assets by reducing the threat of losses due to uncontrollable events

Businesses constantly face two basic types of **risk** (uncertainty about future events). **Speculative risks**, such as financial investments, involve the possibility of gain or loss. **Pure risks** involve only the possibility of loss or no loss. Designing and distributing a new product, for example, is a speculative risk. The product may fail or it may succeed and earn high profits. In contrast, the chance of a warehouse fire is a pure risk.

For a company to survive and prosper, it must manage both types of risk in a cost-effective manner. We can thus define the process of **risk management** as conserving the firm's earning power and assets by reducing the threat of losses due to uncontrollable events."[11] Every company must be alert for risks to the firm and their impact on profits. The risk management process usually entails the following five steps.

Step 1: Identify Risks and Potential Losses
Managers analyze a firm's risks to identify potential losses. For example, a firm with a fleet of delivery trucks can expect that one of them will eventually be involved in an accident. The accident may cause bodily injury to the driver or others, may cause physical damage to the truck or other vehicles, or both.

Step 2: Measure the Frequency and Severity of Losses and Their Impact
To measure the frequency and severity of losses, managers must consider both past history and current activities. How often can the firm expect the loss to occur? What is the likely size of the loss in dollars? For example, our firm with the fleet of delivery trucks may have had two accidents per year in the past. If it adds trucks, however, it may reasonably expect the frequency of accidents to increase.

Step 3: Evaluate Alternatives and Choose the Techniques That Will Best Handle the Losses
Having identified and measured potential losses, managers are in a better position to decide how to handle them. With this third step, they generally have four choices: risk avoidance, control, retention, or transfer.

risk avoidance
Practice of avoiding risk by declining or ceasing to participate in an activity

Risk Avoidance. A firm opts for **risk avoidance** by declining to enter or by ceasing to participate in a risky activity. For example, our firm with the delivery trucks could avoid any risk of physical damage or bodily injury by closing down its delivery service. Similarly, a pharmaceutical maker may withdraw a new drug for fear of liability suits.

risk control
Practice of minimizing the frequency or severity of losses from risky activities

Risk Control. When avoidance is not practical or desirable, firms can practice **risk control** (say, the use of loss prevention techniques to minimize the frequency of losses). A delivery service, for instance, can prevent losses by training its drivers in defensive driving techniques, mapping out safe routes, and conscientiously maintaining its trucks.

Although loss prevention techniques cannot guarantee that losses will not occur, they try to minimize their severity. Seatbelts or airbags, for example, can reduce injuries to truck drivers when accidents do happen. Similarly, most firms use fire extinguishers, fire alarms, or burglar alarms to reduce loss.

All risk control techniques involve costs. The risk manager's job, therefore, is to find techniques whose benefits exceed their costs. For example, a new sprinkler system may cost $100,000. But if it reduces losses by $150,000, it is money well spent.

Risk Retention.   When losses cannot be avoided or controlled, firms must cope with the consequences. When such losses are manageable and predictable, firms may decide to cover them out of company funds. The company is thus said to assume or retain the financial consequences of the loss; hence, the practice known as **risk retention**. For example, our firm with the fleet of trucks may find that vehicles suffer vandalism totaling $100 to $500 per year. Depending on its coverage, the company may find it cheaper to pay for repairs out of pocket rather than to submit claims to its insurance company.

risk retention
Practice of covering a firm's losses with its own funds

Risk Transfer.   When the potential for large risks cannot be avoided or controlled, managers often opt for **risk transfer**. They transfer the risk to another firm (namely, an insurance company). In transferring risk to an insurance company, a firm pays a sum called a **premium**. In return, the insurance company issues an insurance policy: a formal agreement to pay the policyholder a specified amount in the event of certain losses. In some cases, the insured party must also pay a deductible: an agreed-upon amount of the loss that the insured must absorb before reimbursement. Thus, our hypothetical company may buy insurance to protect itself against theft, physical damage to trucks, and bodily injury to drivers and others involved in an accident. (We discuss insurance more fully in Appendix 2 of this book.)

risk transfer
Practice of transferring a firm's risk to another firm

premium
Fee paid by a policyholder for insurance coverage

Step 4: Implement the Risk Management Program
The means of implementing risk management decisions depends on both the technique chosen and the activity being managed. For example, risk avoidance for certain activities can be implemented by purchasing those activities from outside providers (outsourcing)—say, hiring delivery services instead of operating delivery vehicles. Risk control might be implemented by training employees and designing new work methods and equipment for on-the-job safety. For situations in which risk retention is preferred, reserve funds can be set aside out of revenues. When risk transfer is needed, implementation means selecting an insurance company and buying the right policies.

Step 5: Monitor Results
Because risk management is an ongoing activity, follow-up is always essential. New types of risks emerge with changes in customers, facilities, employees, and products. Insurance regulations change, and new types of insurance become available. Consequently, managers must continually monitor a company's risks, reevaluate the methods used for handling them, and revise them as necessary.

The Contemporary Risk Management Program
Virtually all business decisions involve risks having financial consequences. As a result, the company's chief financial officer, along with managers in other areas, has a major voice in applying the risk management process. In some industries, most notably insurance, the companies' main line of business revolves around risk taking and risk management for themselves and their clients.

Today, many firms are taking a new approach to risk management.[12] The key to that approach is developing a program that is both comprehensive and companywide. In the past, risk management was often conducted by different departments or by narrowly focused financial officers. Now, however, more and more firms have not only created high-level risk-management positions, but also are stressing the need for middle managers to practice risk management on a daily basis. Advises one global risk management expert: "The breadth of products offered, the complexity of those products, and the global nature of markets, all make top-down, centralized risk management a necessity."

❝ *The breadth of products offered, the complexity of those products, and the global nature of markets, all make top-down, centralized risk management a necessity.* **❞**

—Thomas B. Whelan, risk-management consultant at Morgan Stanley & Co.

Summary of Learning Objectives

1 **Describe the responsibilities of a financial manager.** The job of the financial manager is to increase the firm's value by planning and controlling the acquisition and dispersal of its financial assets. This task involves three key responsibilities: cash flow management (making sure the firm has enough available money to purchase the materials it needs to produce goods and services), financial control (checking actual performance against plans to ensure that desired financial results occur), and financial planning (devising strategies for reaching future financial goals).

2 **Identify four sources of short-term financing for businesses.** To finance short-term expenditures, firms rely on trade credit (credit extended by suppliers) and loans. Secured loans require collateral (legal interest in assets that may include inventories or accounts receivable). Unsecured loans may be in the form of lines of credit or revolving credit agreements. Smaller firms may choose to factor accounts receivable (that is, sell them to financial institutions).

3 **Distinguish among the various sources of long-term financing and explain the risks entailed by each type.** Long-term sources of funds include debt financing, equity financing, and the use of preferred stock. Debt financing uses long-term loans and corporate bonds (promises to pay holders specified amounts by certain dates), both of which obligate the firm to pay regular interest. Equity financing involves the use of owners' capital, either from the sale of common stock or from retained earnings. Preferred stock is a hybrid source of funding that has some of the features of both common stock and corporate bonds. Financial planners must choose the proper mix of long-term funding. All-equity financing is the most conservative, least risky, and most expensive strategy. All-debt financing is the most speculative option.

4 **Identify the most important financial management issues facing small businesses.** Small business owners must establish lines of credit with banks and suppliers. For long-term funds, they can turn to the Small Business Administration. Venture capital firms may provide equity funding in exchange for shares of ownership. Finally, small business owners must take great care when planning cash flow requirements. Development of a sound business plan provides evidence that the borrower is creditworthy.

5 **Explain how risk affects business operations and identify the five steps in the risk management process.** Businesses operate in an environment pervaded by risk. Speculative risks involve the prospect of gain or loss. Pure risks involve only the prospect of loss or no loss. Firms manage their risks by following some form of a five-step process: identifying risks, measuring possible losses, evaluating alternative techniques,

implementing chosen techniques, and monitoring programs on an ongoing basis. Four general methods for dealing with risk are risk avoidance, control, retention, and transfer.

Questions and Exercises

Questions for Review

1 What are four short-term sources of funds for financing day-to-day business operations? Identify the advantages and disadvantages of each.
2 In what ways do the two sources of debt financing differ from each other? How do they differ from the two sources of equity financing?
3 Describe the relationship between investment risk and return. In what ways might the risk–return relationship affect a company's financial planning?
4 What are the main sources of credit for small businesses?
5 Describe the risk management process. What are the major roles of a company's risk manager?

Questions for Analysis

6 How would you decide on the best mix of debt, equity, and preferred stock for a company?
7 Why is liability insurance important to business firms?
8 As a risk manager of a large firm, what risks do you think your firm faces? For a small firm? What accounts for the most important differences?

Application Exercises

9 Interview the owner of a small local business. Identify the types of short-term and long-term funding that this firm typically uses. Why has the company made the financial management decisions that it has?
10 Interview the owner of a small local business. Ask this person to describe the risk management process that he or she follows. What role, for example, is played by risk transfer? Why has the company made the risk management decisions that it has?

Building Your Business Skills

This exercise enhances the following SCANS workplace competencies: demonstrating basic skills, demonstrating thinking skills, exhibiting interpersonal skills, working with information, and applying system knowledge.

Goal   To encourage students to better understand the major financial and risk management issues that face large companies.

Background In 1997–1998, all of the following companies reported financial problems relating to risk management:
- Oxford Health Care
- Eastman Kodak
- Apple Computer
- United Parcel Service
- Citibank

Method   **Step 1:** Working alone, research one of the companies listed here to learn more about the financial risks that were reported in the news.

Step 2: Write a short explanation of the financial and management issues that were faced by the firm that you researched.

Step 3: Join in teams with students who researched other companies and compare your findings.

Follow-Up Questions

1 Were there common themes in the "big stories" in financial management?
2 What have the various companies done to minimize future risks and losses?

Business Case 21

Business Plastic

Where do most small firms get their financing? An increasing number of them are relying on a particularly risky source: the low-rate introductory offers made by credit card companies.

One-third of the respondents to a recent survey by accounting firm Arthur Andersen and the National Small Business United (NBSU) organization said they use credit cards as one of their sources of financing—a big increase over the 17 percent who did so in 1993. Firms with 19 or fewer workers rely less on commercial bank loans; their numbers are down to about 38 percent from 49 percent. "Credit cards present one method of obtaining financing very quickly without the need for a business plan or inspections that banks or venture capitalists need," says Todd McCracken, president of NBSU.

Some small business owners take advantage of the convenience credit cards offer, and the five-figure credit lines can provide a big boost for many firms. The amount of time required to secure cheaper credit is what holds back Brian Williford, who owns a Web-site design firm in

Washington. "The last thing I have right now is time," he says.

In the last few years credit card companies have become even more aggressive in marketing corporate credit cards to businesses of all sizes. American Express, Visa USA, and MasterCard International all are planning to make their offers even more attractive to small businesses in particular. They are introducing revolving balance cards, more discounts from hotels and airlines, and even special small business debit cards. Although it takes effort to juggle balances looking for the best rate, especially when they are using several credit card accounts, some small business owners may opt for the promise of ready cash.

Questions

1. What are some of the advantages small business owners see in using credit card financing for their firms? The disadvantages?
2. What alternative sources of financing might they be overlooking or underusing? What are the advantages and disadvantages of these?
3. Credit card financing is more impersonal than having a lending or credit relationship with a bank. What are some of the consequences for a small business, particularly a new one, of bypassing a relationship with a bank?

> **Credit cards present one method of obtaining financing very quickly without the need for a business plan or inspections that banks or venture capitalists need.**
>
> —Todd McCracken, president of NBSU

Connecting to the Web

The following Web sites will give you additional information and points of view about topics covered in this chapter. Many sites lead to other related Internet locations, so approach this list with the spirit of an explorer.

BANK ONE: SMALL BUSINESS SOLUTIONS

http://www.bancone.com/busbank/

This Web site offers small business owners information on loans, cash flow management, capitalization needs, technology and finance, and more. It also includes a financial worksheet that answers such critical questions as "How big a loan can I afford?"

MOODY'S INVESTORS SERVICE

http://www.moodys.com

Visit this site to learn about Moody's bond ratings for corporations.

NET EARNINGS: AMERICA'S SMALL BUSINESS FINANCIAL CENTER

http://www.netearnings.com/

Net Earnings helps small businesses use the Internet to obtain financial and management services. Visit this site for information on loans, customer credit checks, and other financial services.

NEW YORK STOCK EXCHANGE: GLOBAL INVESTING

http://www.nyse.com/public/intview/4c/4cix.htm

The New York Stock Exchange plays a critical role in raising capital for non-U.S. companies, including the more than 300 foreign firms now on the exchange. Visit the site for information on this global financial topic.

NEW YORK STOCK EXCHANGE: HOW TO GET LISTED

http://www.nyse.com/public/listed/3b/3bix.htm

To list a company on the New York Stock Exchange, the company must meet stringent requirements that are described on this Web page.

ONLINE WOMEN'S BUSINESS CENTER: FINANCE CENTER

http://www.onlinewbc.org/docs/finance/index.html

This site provides an excellent primer on financial management for small business. Included is extensive coverage of borrowing and lending, banking, capital alternatives (sources of money), and financing your growing business. Although the site is intended for women, it has important information for everyone involved in small business financing.

SECURITIES AND EXCHANGE COMMISSION: SMALL BUSINESS Q & A

http://www.sec.gov/smbus/qasbsec.htm

The Securities and Exchange Commission has rules for small businesses that want to go public. Visit this site for information on registering a public offering.

SMALL BUSINESS ADMINISTRATION: BUSINESS PLAN OUTLINE

http://www.sbaonline.sba.gov/starting/businessplan.html

The Small Business Administration provides a detailed outline of a business plan. A must for every aspiring businessperson.

SMALL BUSINESS ASSOCIATION: FINANCING YOUR BUSINESS

http://www.sbaonline.sba.gov/financing/

The site explores the SBA's loan program and its role in working with intermediaries, banks, and other lenders to provide loans and venture capital financing to small businesses unable to secure financing through normal lending channels.

U.S. BUSINESS ADVISOR

http://www.business.gov/

Visit this site for information all businesses need to know on such government-related financial issues as taxes and Social Security.

Understanding the Legal Context of Business

In this appendix, we will describe the basic tenets of U.S. law and show how these principles work through the court system. We will also survey a few major areas of business-related law. By focusing on the learning objectives of this appendix, you will see that laws may create opportunities for business activity just as readily as they set limits on them.

The U.S. Legal and Judicial Systems

If people could ignore contracts or drive down city streets at any speed, it would be unsafe to do business on Main Street—or even to set foot in public. Without law, people would be free to act "at will," and life and property would constantly be at risk. **Laws*** are the codified rules of behavior enforced by a society. In the United States, laws fall into three broad categories according to their origins: *common*, *statutory*, and *regulatory*.[1] After discussing each of these types of laws, we will briefly describe the three-tier system of courts through which the judicial system administers the law in the United States.

Types of Law

Law in the United States originates primarily with English common law.[2] Its sources include the U.S. Constitution, state constitutions, federal and state statues, municipal ordinances, administrative agency rules and regulations, executive orders, and court decisions.

Common Law Court decisions follow *precedents*, or the decisions of earlier cases.[3] Following precedent lends stability to the law by basing judicial decisions on cases anchored in similar facts. This principle is the keystone of **common law**: the body of decisions handed down by courts ruling on individual cases. Although some facets of common law predate the American Revolution (and even hearken back to medieval Europe), common law continues to evolve in the courts today.

Statutory Law Laws created by constitutions or by federal, state, or local legislative acts constitute **statutory law**. For example, Article I of the U.S. Constitution is a statutory law that empowers Congress to pass laws on corporate taxation, the zoning authority of municipalities, and the rights and privileges of business operating in the United States.

State legislatures and city councils also pass statutory laws. Some state laws, for example, prohibit the production or sale of detergents containing phosphates, which are believed to be pollutants. Nearly every town has ordinances specifying sites for certain types of industries or designating areas where cars cannot be parked during certain hours.

Regulatory Law Statutory and common law have long histories. Relatively new, is **regulatory** (or **administrative**) **law**: law made by the authority of administrative agencies. By and large, the expansion of U.S. regulatory law has paralleled the nation's economic and technological development. Lacking the technical expertise to develop specialized legislation for specialized business activities, Congress established the first administrative agencies to create and administer the needed laws in the late 1800s. Before the early 1960s, most agencies concerned themselves with the *economic* regulation of specific areas of business—say, transportation or securities. Since then many agencies have been established to pursue narrower *social* objectives. They focus on issues that cut across different sectors of the economy—clean air, for example, or product testing.[4]

Today a host of agencies, including the Equal Employment Opportunity Commission (EEOC), the Environmental Protection Agency (EPA), the Food and Drug Administration (FDA), the Federal Trade Commission (FTC), and the Occupational Safety and Health Administration (OSHA) regulate U.S. business practices. Figure A.1 shows the growth in the number of federal agencies from 1900 to 1979, when the dramatic growth spurt of new agencies, begun in the 1960s, peaked.

*Key terms appearing in this appendix are defined in the glossary at the end of the book.

Figure A.1 The Growth of Federal Regulatory Agencies

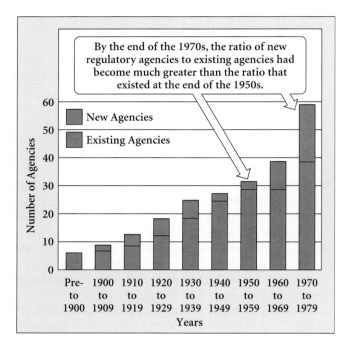

In this section, we look briefly at the nature of regulatory agencies and describe some of the key legislation that makes up administrative law in this country. We also discuss an area of increasing importance in the relationship between government and business; *regulation*—or, more accurately, *deregulation*.

Agencies and Legislation. Although Congress retains control over the scope of agency action, once passed regulations have the force of statutory law. Government regulatory agencies act as a secondary judicial system, determining whether or not regulations have been violated and imposing penalties. A firm that violates OSHA rules, for example may receive a citation, a hearing, and perhaps a heavy fine. Much agency activity consists of setting standards for safety or quality and monitoring the compliance of businesses. The FDA, for example, is responsible for ensuring that food, medicines, and even cosmetics are safe and effective.

Regulatory laws have been on the books for nearly a century. As early as 1906, for example, the Pure Food and Drug Act mandated minimum levels of cleanliness and sanitation for food and drug companies. More recently, the Children's Television Act of 1990 requires that broadcasters meet the educational and informational needs of younger viewers and limit the amount of advertising broadcast during children's programs. In 1996, a sweeping new law to increase competition in the communications industry required television makers to install a "V-chip," which allows parents to block undesirable programming.

And Congress continues to debate the possibility of regulating the Internet.

Congress has created many new agencies in response to pressure to address social issues. In some cases, agencies were established in response to public concern about corporate behavior. The activities of these agencies have sometimes forced U.S. firms to consider the public interest almost as routinely as they consider their own financial performance.[5]

The Move Toward Deregulation. Although government regulation has benefited U.S. business in many ways, it is not without its drawbacks. Businesspeople complain—with some justification—that government regulations require too much paperwork. In order to comply with just one OSHA regulation for one year, Goodyear once generated 345,000 pages of computer reports weighing 3,200 pounds. It now costs Goodyear $35.5 million each year to comply with the regulations of six government agencies, and it takes 36 employee-years annually (the equivalent of one employee working full-time or 36 years) to fill out the required reports.

Not surprisingly, many people in both business and government support broader **deregulation**: the elimination of rules that restrict business activity. Advocates of both regulation and deregulation claim that each acts to control business expansion and prices, increase government efficiency, and right wrongs that the marketplace cannot or does not handle itself. Regulations such as those enforced by the EEOC, for example, are supposed to control undesirable business practices in the interest of social equity. In contrast, the court-ordered breakup of AT&T was prompted by a perceived need for greater market efficiency. For these and other reasons, the federal government began deregulating certain industries in the 1970s.

It is important to note that the United States is the only industrialized nation that has deregulated key industries—financial services, transportation, telecommunications, and host of others. Most recently, for instance, a 1996 law allowed the seven "Baby Bells"—regional phone companies created when AT&T was broken up—to compete for long-distance business. It also allowed cable television and telephone companies to enter each other's markets by offering any combination of video, telephone, and high-speed data communications services.[6] Many analysts contend that such deregulation is now and will become an even greater advantage in an era of global competition. Deregulation, they argue, is a primary incentive to innovation.

According to this view, deregulated industries are forced to innovate in order to survive in fiercely competitive industries. Those firms that are already conditioned to compete by being more creative will outperform firms that have been protected by regulatory climates in their home countries. "What's important," says one economist, "is that competition energizes new ways of doing things." The U.S. telecommunications industry, proponents of this view say, is twice as productive as its European counterparts because it is the only such industry forced to come out from under a protective regulatory umbrella.[7]

The U.S. Judicial System

Laws are of little use unless they are enforced. Much of the responsibility for law enforcement falls to the courts. Although few people would claim that the courts are capable of resolving every dispute, there often seem to be more than enough lawyers to handle them all: Indeed, there are 140 lawyers for every 100,000 people in the United States. Litigation is a significant part of contemporary life, and we have given our courts a voice in a wide range of issues, some touching profoundly personal concerns, some ruling on matters of public policy that affect all our lives. In this section, we look at the operations of the U.S. judicial system.

The Court System As Figure A.2 shows, there are three levels in the U.S. judicial system—*federal*, *state*, and *local*. These levels reflect the *federalist* structure of a system in which a central government shares power with state or local governments. Federal courts were created by the U.S. Constitution. They hear cases on questions of constitutional law, disputes relating to maritime laws, and violations of federal statutes. They also rule on regulatory actions and on such issues as bankruptcy, postal law, and copyright or patent violation. Both the federal and most state systems embody a three-tiered system of *trial*, *appellate*, and *supreme courts*.

Trial Courts. At the lowest level of the federal court system are the **trial courts**, general courts that hear cases not specifically assigned to another court. A case involving contract violation would go before a trial court. Every state has at least one federal trial court, called a *district court*.

Trial courts also include special courts and administrative agencies. *Special courts* hear specific types of cases, such

as cases involving tax evasion, fraud, international disputes, or claims against the U.S. government. Within their areas of jurisdiction, administrative agencies also make judgments much like those of courts.

Courts in each state system deal with the same issues as their federal counterparts. However, they may rule only in areas governed by state law. For example, a case involving state income tax laws would be heard by a state special court. Local courts in each state system also hear cases on municipal ordinances, local traffic violations, and similar issues.

Appellate Courts. A losing party may disagree with a trial court ruling. If that party can show grounds for review, the case may go before a federal or state **appellate court**. These courts consider questions of law, such as possible errors of legal interpretation made by lower courts. They do not examine questions of fact. There are now 13 federal courts of appeal, each with 3 to 15 judges. Cases are normally heard by three-judge panels.

Supreme Courts. Cases still not resolved at the appellate level can be appealed to the appropriate state supreme courts or to the U.S. Supreme Court. If it believes that an appeal is warranted or that the outcome will set an important precedent, the U.S. Supreme Court also hears cases appealed from state supreme courts. Each year, the U.S. Supreme Court receives about 5,000 appeals but typically agrees to hear fewer than 200.

Business Law

Most legal issues confronted by businesses fall into one of six basic areas: *contract*, *tort*, *property*, *agency*, *commercial*, or *bankruptcy law*. These areas cover a wide range of business activity.

Figure A.1 The U.S. Judicial System

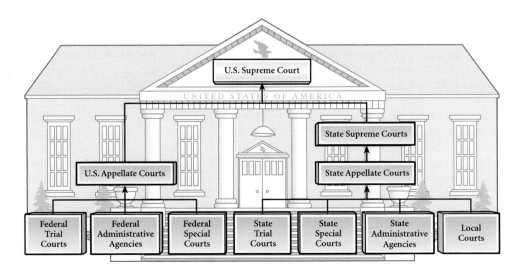

Contract Law

A **contract** is any agreement between two or more parties that is enforceable in court. As such, it must meet six conditions. If all these conditions are met, one party can seek legal recourse from another if the other party breaches (that is, violates) the terms of the agreement.[8]

1 *Agreement.* Agreement is the serious, definite, and communicated offer and acceptance of the same terms. Let us say that an auto parts supplier offers in writing to sell rebuilt engines to a repair shop for $500 each. If the repair shop accepts the offer, the two parties have reached an agreement.

2 *Consent.* A contract is not enforceable if any of the parties has been affected by an honest mistake, fraud, or pressure. For example, a restaurant manager orders a painted sign, but the sign company delivers a neon sign instead.

3 *Capacity.* To give real consent, both parties must demonstrate legal **capacity** (competence). A person under legal age (usually 18 or 21) cannot enter into a binding contract.

4 *Consideration.* An agreement is binding only if it exchanges **considerations**, that is, items of value. If your brother offers to paint your room for free, you cannot sue him if he changes his mind. Note that "items of value" do not necessarily entail money. For example, a tax accountant might agree to prepare a homebuilder's tax return in exchange for a new patio. Both services are items of value. Contracts need not be "rational," nor must they provide the "best" possible bargain for both sides. They need only include "legally sufficient" consideration. The terms are met if both parties receive what the contract details.

5 *Legality.* A contract must be for a lawful purpose and must comply with federal, state, and local laws and regulations. For example, an agreement between two competitors to engage in price fixing—that is, to set a mutually acceptable price—is not legal.

6 *Proper form.* A contract may be written, oral, or implied from conduct. It must be written, however, if it involves the sale of land or goods worth more than $500. It must be written if the agreement requires more than a year to fulfill—say, a contract for employment as an engineer on a 14-month construction project. All changes to written contracts must also be in writing.

Look Before You Compete

How much does it mean to you to feel wanted on the job?

A specialized type of contract that is rapidly becoming more common in business is the employment contract. While it can promise a high-level or professional employee a certain degree of protection against dismissal, it is often written primarily to benefit the employer, particularly if it contains a noncompete clause.

Noncompete clauses are an attempt by firms to keep their most valued people on staff as long as possible by making it less attractive for them to leave. They bind the departing employee to a promise not to work for a competitor for a certain period of time or within a specified geographic distance, or both. Says Michael C. Lasky, a New York lawyer who specializes in such issues, "If you are legally constrained from servicing [your accustomed] business for a year, it certainly is going to impact how attractive you are to your next employer." Recently more companies have begun enforcing legal penalties against defectors who defy such clauses, and sometimes they win.

Here is some advice from Lasky and another employment lawyer, Alan Sklover, to take the sting out of being wanted. Before you sign on with a firm that demands a noncompete clause, negotiate for more favorable terms. Ask for a reduced time period for the agreement, or for a smaller geographic territory to be placed off-limits. Try to make the contract specify the jobs and locations to which it doesn't apply, including related industries where you think you can comfortably work out the duration of the clause if and when you leave. Remember that the best time to negotiate is before you're hired, when the employer is still putting its best foot forward to get you on board.

If you decide to leave the firm, shift into self-defense mode. Says Lasky, "Take nothing with you other than the picture of the wife, kids, and dog. Don't take the Rolodex or files. Don't come into the office at hours when no one else is there. Even if it's innocent, it will be seen as an attempt to steal business." Finish or responsibly delegate all your projects and obligations; tie up all loose ends. As for filling in the time until you can compete with your old employer, you might be able to work in a related field if you managed your contract negotiations well. Failing that, you can look for a possible breach of contract on your employer's part to void the pact, or you might consider moving out of state to a new job in a state where noncompete clauses aren't honored.

Breach of Contract What can one party do if the other fails to live up to the terms of a valid contract? Contract law offers a variety of remedies designed to protect the reasonable expectations of the parties and, in some cases, to compensate them for actions taken to enforce the agreement.

As the injured party to a breached contract, any of the following actions might occur:

- You might cancel the contract and refuse to live up to your part of the bargain. For example, you might simply cancel a contract for carpet shampooing if the company fails to show up.

- You might sue for damages up to the amount that you lost as a result of the breach. Thus, you might sue the original caterer if you must hire a more expensive caterer for your wedding reception because the original company canceled at the last minute.

- If money cannot repay the damage you suffered, you might demand specific performance—that is, require the other party to fulfill the original contract. For example, you might demand that a dealer in classic cars sell you the antique Stutz Bearcat he agreed to sell you and not a classic Jaguar instead.

Tort Law

Tort law applies to most business relationships *not governed by contracts*. A **tort** is a *civil*—that is, noncriminal—injury to people, property, or reputation for which compensation must be paid. For example, if a person violates zoning laws by opening a convenience store in a residential area, he or she cannot be sent to jail as if the act were a criminal violation. But a variety of other legal measures can be pursued, such as fines or seizure of property. Trespass, fraud, defamation, invasion of privacy, and even assault can be torts, as can interference with contractual relations and wrongful use of trade secrets. In this section, we explain three classifications of torts: *intentional*, *negligence*, and *product liability*.

Intentional Torts **Intentional torts** result from the deliberate actions of another person or organization—for instance, a manufacturer knowingly fails to install a relatively inexpensive safety device on a product. Similarly, refusing to rectify a product design flaw—as in the case of the space shuttle *Challenger* disaster—can render a firm liable for an intentional tort. The actions of employees on the job may also constitute intentional torts—say, an overzealous security guard who wrongly accuses a customer of shoplifting. To remedy torts, courts will usually impose **compensatory damages**: payments intended to redress an injury actually suffered. They may also impose **punitive damages**: fines that exceed actual losses suffered by plaintiffs and that are intended to punish defendants.

In 1992, for example, a jury awarded $300,000 in compensatory damages plus $4 million in punitive damages to a couple who alleged that a two-way mirror in their penthouse suite had allowed strangers to spy on them at a local hotel. The compensatory damages were awarded because the jury agreed that the couple's privacy had been invaded. The large punitive award cited the plaintiffs's emotional distress in the aftermath of the incident. (The case was later settled for $1 million in total damages.)[9]

Negligence Torts Ninety percent of tort suits involve charges of **negligence**, conduct falling below legal standards for protecting others against unreasonable risk. If a company installs a pollution-control system that fails to protect a community's water supply, it may later be sued by an individual who gets sick from drinking the water.

Negligence torts may also result from employee actions. For example, if the captain of a supertanker runs aground and spills 11 million gallons of crude oil into coastal fishing waters, the oil company may be liable for potentially astronomical damages. Thus in September 1994, a jury in Alaska ordered Exxon Corp. to pay $5 billion in punitive damages to 34,000 fishermen and other plaintiffs as a consequence of the *Exxon Valdez* disaster of 1989. (Plaintiffs had asked for $15 billion.) A month earlier, the jury had awarded plaintiffs $287 million in compensatory damages. In 1993, the firm responsible for pipeline operations at the Valdez, Alaska, terminal (which is partially owned by Exxon) agreed to pay plaintiffs in the same case $98 million in damages. In a separate case, Exxon paid $20 million in damages to villages whose food supply had been destroyed. A separate state jury will consider another $120 million in claims by Alaskan corporations and municipalities. Even before any of these awards was handed down, Exxon had spent $2.1 billion on the cleanup effort and paid $1.3 billion in civil and criminal penalties.[10]

Product Liability Torts In cases of **product liability**, a company may be held responsible for injuries caused by its products. Product liability is an issue in each of the following situations:

- In a raft of recent lawsuits, plaintiffs have charged that certain three-wheel all-terrain vehicles are unsafe; they contend that they are unstable and too easily overturned. They argue that manufacturers are liable for injuries suffered by drivers operating those vehicles.

- In 1997, suits were filed against Mattel. During the preceding Christmas season, the toymaker had sold thousands of Cabbage Patch dolls with a brand-new feature: the dolls could "chew" play food. Unfortunately, they were also prone to gnaw on the hair of young children.

According to a special government panel on product liability, about 33 million people are injured and 28,000 killed by consumer products each year. Even so, U.S. courts seem to be taking a harder look at many product liability claims, especially when they are based on "soft" science:

- An appeals court overturned a $1 million award to a psychic who claimed that a CAT scan destroyed her special abilities.

- A federal judge barred as "unreliable" medical testimony linking carpal tunnel syndrome to a computer keyboard made by Unisys.

- Another federal judge dismissed a case claiming that cellular phone use caused a woman's brain tumor.[11]

Strict Product Liability. Since the early 1960s, businesses have faced a number of legal actions based on the relatively new principle of **strict product liability**: the principle that liability can result not from a producer's negligence but from a defect in the product itself. An injured party need show only that

1 The product was defective.

2 The defect was the cause of injury.

3 The defect caused the product to be unreasonably dangerous.

Many recent cases in strict product liability have focused on injuries or illnesses attributable to toxic wastes or other hazardous substances that were legally disposed of. Because plaintiffs need not demonstrate negligence or fault, these suits frequently succeed. Not surprisingly, the number of such suits promises to increase.[12]

Property Law

As the name implies, *property law* concerns property rights. But what exactly is "property"? Is it the land under a house? The house itself? A car in the driveway? A dress in the closet? The answer in each case is yes: in the legal sense, **property** is anything of value to which a person or business has sole right of ownership. Indeed, property is technically those *rights*.

Within this broad general definition, we can divide property into four categories. In this section, we define these categories and then examine more fully the legal protection of a certain kind of property—intellectual property.

- **Tangible real property** is land and anything attached to it. A house and a factory are both tangible real property, as are built-in appliances or the machines inside the buildings.

- **Tangible personal property** is any movable item that can be owned, bought, sold, or leased. Examples are automobiles, clothing, stereos, and cameras.

- **Intangible personal property** cannot be seen but exists by virtue of written documentation. Examples are insurance policies, bank accounts, stocks and bonds, and trade secrets.

- **Intellectual property** is created through a person's creative activities. Books, articles, songs, paintings, screenplays, and computer software are all intellectual property.

Protection of Intellectual Rights The U.S. Constitution grants protection to intellectual property by means of copyrights, trademarks, and patents. Copyrights and patents apply to the tangible expressions of an idea—not to the ideas themselves. Thus, you could not copyright the idea of cloning dinosaurs from fossil DNA. Michael Crichton, could copyright his novel *Jurassic Park*, which is a tangible result of that idea, and sell the film rights to producer-director Steven Spielberg. Both creators are entitled to the profits, if any, that may be generated by their tangible creative expressions.

Copyrights. Copyrights give exclusive ownership rights to the creators of books, articles, designs, illustrations, photos, films, and music. Computer programs and even semiconductor chips are also protected. Copyrights extend to creators for their entire lives and to their estates for 50 years thereafter. All terms are automatically copyrighted from the moment of creation.

Trademarks. Because the development of products is expensive, companies must prevent other firms from using their brand names. Often they must act to keep competitors from seducing consumers with similar or substitute products. A producer can apply to the U.S. government for a **trademark**—the exclusive legal right to use a brand name.[13]

Trademarks are granted for 20 years and may be renewed indefinitely if a firm continues to protect its brand name. If a firm allows the brand name to lapse into *common usage*, it may lose protection. Common usage takes effect when a company fails to use the ® symbol to indicate that its brand name is a registered trademark. It also takes effect if a company seeks no action against those who fail to acknowledge its trademark. Recently, for example, the popular brand-name sailboard Windsurfer lost its trademark. Like *trampoline*, *yo-yo*, and *thermos*, *windsurfer* has become the common term for the product and can now be used by any sailboard company. In contrast, Formica Corp. successfully spent the better part of a decade in court to protect the name *Formica* as a trademark. The Federal Trade Commission had contended that the word had entered the language as a generic name for any similar laminate material.

Patents. Patents provide legal monopolies for the use and licensing of manufactured items, manufacturing processes, substances, and designs for objects. A patentable invention must be *novel, useful,* and *nonobvious.* Since June 1995, U.S. patent law has been in harmony with that of most developed nations. For example, patents are now valid for 20 years rather than 17 years. In addition, the term now runs from the date on which the application was *filed,* not the date on which the patent itself was *issued.*[14]

Although the U.S. Patent Office issues about 1,200 patents a week, requirements are stringent, and U.S. patents actually tend to be issued at a slow pace. While Japan and most European countries have installed systems to speed up patent filing and research, the U.S. system can extend the process to years. Other observers argue that American firms trail their foreign counterparts in patents because of the sluggishness with which U.S. companies move products through their own research and development programs.

About 50 percent of all U.S. patents granted each year are awarded to foreign companies. However, the percentage of patents awarded to U.S. companies is increasing as U.S. companies become more aggressive. In 1992, for example, Digital Equipment Corp. won 223 U.S. patents, up from a mere 20 in 1985. Intel Corp. increased the number of its filings from 100 in 1990 to 400 in 1993.[15]

Restrictions on Property Rights

Property rights are not always absolute. For example, rights may be compromised under any of the following circumstances:

- Owners of shorefront property may be required to permit anglers, clam diggers, and other interested parties to walk near the water.

- Utility companies typically have rights called easements, such as the right to run wire over private property or to lay cable or pipe under it.

- Under the principle of **eminent domain**, the government may, upon paying owners fair prices, claim private land to expand roads or erect public buildings.

Agency Law

The transfer of property—whether the deeding of real estate or the transfer of automobile title—often involves agents. An **agent** is a person who acts for, and in the name of, another party, called the **principal**. The most visible agents are those in real estate, sports, and entertainment. Many businesses, however, use agents to secure insurance coverage and handle investments. Every partner in a partnership and every officer and director in a corporation is an agent of that business. Courts have also ruled that both a firm's employees and its outside contractors may be regarded as its agents.

Authority of Agents

Agents have the authority to bind principals to agreements. They receive that authority, however, from the principals themselves; they cannot create their own authority. An agent's authority to bind a principal can be express, implied, or apparent. The following illustration involves all three forms of agent authority:

> Ellen is a salesperson in Honest Sam's Used Car Lot. Her written employment contract gives her **express authority** to sell cars, to provide information to prospective buyers, and to approve trade-ins up to $2,000. Derived from the custom of used-car dealers, she also has **implied authority** to give reasonable discounts on prices and to make reasonable adjustments to written warranties. Furthermore, Ellen may—in the presence of Honest Sam—promise a customer that she will match the price offered by another local dealer. If Honest Sam assents—perhaps merely nods and smiles—Ellen may be construed to have the **apparent authority** to make this deal.

Responsibilities of Principals

Principals have several responsibilities to their agents. They owe agents reasonable compensation, must reimburse them for related business expenses, and should inform them of risks associated with their business activities. Principals are liable for actions performed by agents *within the scope of their employment.* Thus, if agents make untrue claims about products or services, the principal is liable for making amends. Employers are similarly responsible for the actions of employees. In fact, firms are often liable in tort suits because the courts treat employees as agents.

Businesses are increasingly being held accountable for *criminal* acts by employees. Court findings, for example, have argued that firms are expected to be aware of workers' propensities for violence, to check on their employees' pasts, and to train and supervise employees properly. Suppose, for instance, that a delivery service hires a driver with a history of driving while intoxicated. If the driver has an accident with a company vehicle while under the influence of alcohol, the company may be liable for criminal actions.

Commercial Law

Managers must be well acquainted with the most general laws affecting commerce. Specifically, they need to be familiar with the provisions of the *Uniform Commercial Code,* which sets down rules regarding *warranties.*

The Uniform Commercial Code

For many years, companies doing business in more than one state faced a special problem: laws governing commerce varied, sometimes widely, from state to state. In 1952, however, the National Conference of Commissioners on Uniform State Laws and the American Law Institute drew up the **Uniform Commercial Code (UCC)**. Subsequently accepted by every state except Louisiana, the UCC describes the rights of buyers and sellers in transactions.

For example, buyers who believe that they have been wronged in agreements with sellers have several options. They can cancel contracts, refuse deliveries, and demand the return of any deposits. In some cases, they can buy the same products elsewhere and sue the original contractors to recover any losses incurred. Sellers, too, have several options. They can cancel contracts, withhold deliveries, and sell goods to other buyers. If goods have already been delivered, sellers can repossess them or sue the buyers for purchase prices.

Warranties. A **warranty** is a seller's promise to stand by its products or services if a problem occurs after the sale. Warranties may be express or *implied*. The terms of an **express warranty** are specifically stated by the seller. For example, many stereo systems are expressly warranted for 90 days. If they malfunction within that period, they can be returned for full refunds.

An **implied warranty** is dictated by law. Implied warranties embody the principle that a product should (1) fulfill the promises made by advertisements and (2) serve the purpose for which it was manufactured and sold. If you buy an advertised frost-free refrigerator, the seller implies that the refrigerator will keep your food cold and that you will not have to defrost it. It is important to note, however, that warranties, unlike most contracts, are easily limited, waived, or disclaimed. Consequently, they are the source of more and more tort action, as dissatisfied customers seek redress from producers.

Bankruptcy Law

At one time, individuals who could not pay their debts were jailed. Today, however, both organizations and individuals can seek relief by filing for **bankruptcy**—the court-granted permission not to pay some or all debts.

Hundreds of thousands of individuals and tens of thousands of businesses file for bankruptcy each year, and their numbers continue to increase. Filings have doubled since 1985, peaking in 1996 at 1.1 million (a 25-percent increase over 1995).[16] Why do individuals and businesses file for bankruptcy? Cash-flow problems and drops in farm prices caused many farmers, banks, and small businesses to go bankrupt. In recent years, large enterprises such as Continental Airlines and R. H. Macy have sought the protection of bankruptcy laws as part of strategies to streamline operations, cut costs, and regain profitability.

Three main factors account for the increase in bankruptcy filings:

1 The increased availability of credit

2 The "fresh-start" provisions in current bankruptcy laws

3 The growing acceptance of bankruptcy as a financial tactic

In some cases, creditors force an individual or firm into **involuntary bankruptcy** and press the courts to award them payment of at least part of what they are owed. Far more often, however, a person or business chooses to file for court protection against creditors. In general, individuals and firms whose debts exceed total assets by at least $1,000 may file for **voluntary bankruptcy**.

Business Bankruptcy A business bankruptcy may be resolved by one of three plans:

- Under a *liquidation plan*, the business ceases to exist. Its assets are sold and the proceeds used to pay creditors.

- Under a *repayment plan*, the bankrupt company simply works out a new payment schedule to meet its obligations. The time frame is usually extended, and payments are collected and distributed by a court-appointed trustee.

- *Reorganization* is the most complex form of business bankruptcy. The company must explain the sources of its financial difficulties and propose a new plan for remaining in business. Reorganization may include a new slate of managers and a new financial strategy. A judge may also reduce the firm's debts to ensure its survival. Although creditors naturally dislike debt reduction, they may agree to the proposal, since 50 percent of one's due is better than nothing at all.

New legislation passed in 1994 has made some major revisions in bankruptcy laws. For example, it is now easier for individuals with up to $1 million in debt to make payments under installment plans instead of liquidating assets immediately. In contrast, the new law restricts how long a company can protect itself in bankruptcy while continuing to do business. Critics have charged, for instance, that many firms have succeeded in operating for many months under bankruptcy protection. During that time, they were able to cut costs and prices, not only competing with an unfair advantage but dragging down overall industry profits. The new laws place time limits on various steps in the filing process. The intended effect is to speed up the process and prevent assets from being lost to legal fees.

The International Framework of Business Law

Laws can vary dramatically from country to country, and many businesses today have international markets, suppliers, and competitors. It follows that managers need a basic understanding of the international framework of business law that affects the ways in which they can do business.

National laws are created and enforced by countries. The creation and enforcement of international law is more complicated. For example, if a company shipping merchandise between the United States and Mexico breaks an environmental protection law, to whom is that company accountable? The answer depends on several factors.

Which country enacted the law in question? Where did the violation occur? In which country is the alleged violator incorporated?

Issues such as pollution across border are matters of **international law**: the very general set of cooperative agreements and guidelines established by countries to govern the actions of individuals, businesses, and nations themselves. In this section, we examine the various sources of international law. We then discuss some of the important ways in which international trade is regulated and place some key U.S. trade laws in the international context in which they are designed to work.

Sources of International Law

International law has several sources. One source is custom and tradition. Among countries that have been trading with each other for centuries, many customs and traditions governing exchanges have gradually evolved into practice. Although some trading practices still follow ancient unwritten agreements, there has been a clear trend in more recent times to approach international trade within more formal legal framework. Key features of that framework include a variety of formal trade agreements.

Trade Agreements In addition to subscribing to international rules, virtually every nation has formal trade treaties with other nations. A *bilateral agreement* is one involving two countries; a *multilateral agreement* involves several nations.

General Agreement on Tariffs and Trade. The **General Agreement on Tariffs and Trade (GATT)** was first signed shortly after the end of World War II. Its purpose is to reduce or eliminate trade barriers, such as tariffs and quotas. It does so by encouraging nations to protect domestic industries within internationally agreed-upon limits and to engage in multilateral negotiations.

In December 1994, the U.S. Congress ratified a revision of GATT that had been worked out by 124 nations over a 12-year period. Still, many issues remain unresolved—for example, the opening of foreign markets to most financial services. Governments may still provide subsidies to manufacturers of civil aircraft, and no agreement was reached on limiting the distribution of American cultural exports—movies, music, and the like—in Europe With those agreements that have been reached, however, one international economic group predicts that world commerce will have increased by $270 billion by 2002.[17]

North American Free Trade Agreement. The **North American Free Trade Agreement (NAFTA)** was negotiated to remove tariffs and other trade barriers among the United States, Canada, and Mexico. NAFTA also included agreements to monitor environmental and labor abuses. It took effect on January 1, 1994, and immediately eliminated some

tariffs; others will disappear after 5-, 10-, or 15-year intervals.

In the first year after its passage, observers agreed that, by and large, NAFTA achieved what it was supposed to: a much more active North American market. The following were among the results after one year:[18]

- Direct foreign investment increased. U.S. and Canadian firms, for example, accounted for 55 percent of all foreign investment in Mexico, investing $2.4 billion. Companies from other nations—for instance, Toyota Motor Corp.—also made new investments, such as expanding production facilities, to take advantage of the freer movement of goods in the new market.

- U.S. exports to Mexico increased by about 20 percent. Procter & Gamble, for example, enjoyed an increase of nearly 75 percent, and the giant agribusiness firm of Archer Daniels Midland reported a tripling of its exports to Mexico. Mexico passed Japan as the second-largest buyer of U.S. goods, and trade with Canada rose 10 percent (twice the gain in Europe and Asia).

- U.S. imports from Mexico and Canada rose even faster than rates in the opposite direction, setting records of $48 billion and $120 billion, respectively. In particular, electronics, computers, and communications products came into the United States twice as fast as they went out. "We pointed out," says one NAFTA opponent, "that there was a fairly sophisticated manufacturing base in Mexico that pays peanuts, and the numbers bear that out."

- NAFTA created fewer jobs than proponents had hoped. Although the U.S. economy added 1.7 million new jobs in 1994, the Labor Department estimates that only 100,000 jobs were NAFTA-related. At the same time, however, the flood of U.S. jobs to Mexico predicted by Ross Perot and other NAFTA critics, especially by labor union officials, did not occur. In fact, the president of Ford Motor Co.'s Mexico operations has boasted that his activities "have created jobs here and in the U.S." His reasoning: Ford's exports of Mexican-made vehicles to the United States are up 30 percent, and 80 percent of all components in those cars are made in the United States. Ford also reports that its exports of American-made cars to Mexico rose from 1,200 to 30,000 in NAFTA's first year.

European Union. Originally called the Common Market, the **European Union (EU)** includes the principal Western European nations. These countries have eliminated most quotas and have set uniform tariff levels on products imported and exported within their group. In 1992, virtually all internal trade barriers were eliminated, making the European Union the largest free marketplace in the world.

Understanding
Insurance

To deal with some risks, both businesses and individuals may choose to purchase one or more of the products offered by insurance companies. Buyers find insurance appealing for a very basic reason: In return for a relatively small sum of money, they are protected against certain losses, some of them potentially devastating. In a sense, then, buying insurance is a function of risk management. With insurance, individuals and businesses share risks by contributing to a fund out of which those who suffer losses are paid. But why are insurance companies willing to accept these risks for other companies?

The Business of Insuring

Insurance companies make profits by taking in more money in **premiums*** than they pay out to cover policyholders' losses. Quite simply, although many policyholders are paying for protection against the same type of loss, by no means all of them will suffer such a loss.

The Statistical Basis of Insurance

Consider a town with 5,000 insured houses. Based on past history, insurers know that each year, 50 of these houses will be involved in fires. Damages will average $40,000 per house. Insurers, therefore, can expect to pay $2,000,000 ($40,000 × 50) to cover their policyholders. By charging each household $500 annually for fire insurance, the company effectively spreads out the risk. It also earns a gross profit of $500,000 ($2,500,000 in premiums versus $2,000,000 in damages). This profit, then, is the insurer's gain for providing its service—namely, spreading risk.

To earn a profit, then, insurers must know the likelihood of a particular loss. The more they know, the better their predictions will be. Rates, of course, are set accordingly. Insurers also benefit from a statistical principle called the **law of large numbers**: As the number of people seeking insurance rises, so does the chance that the actual loss *rate* will be the same as the statistically calculated rate.

Insurance Ratings Systems As an aid in pricing policies, insurers use a classification system that rates possible losses based on certain characteristics. For example, the probability of loss from an automobile accident varies with the number of miles driven per year. Variation also occurs according to whether the driving is done in rural or urban areas or done by experienced or inexperienced drivers.

Thus an experienced driver traveling fewer than 3,000 miles per year on uncongested roads will probably have fewer accidents than a 16-year-old who drives the freeways of Los Angeles every day. Therefore, drivers with lower probabilities of accidents—as determined by such classification characteristics as experience and average miles driven—should pay relatively lower premiums.

Indemnification The ultimate purpose of insurance is to *indemnify* policyholders: That is, policyholders should be restored to their financial positions prior to their losses. No policyholder, however, should *gain* financially from insurance. To remain financially viable, an insurance company must follow two very basic rules: never pay for losses not covered by the policy and never pay too much for each loss.

Insurable versus Uninsurable Risks

Like every business, insurance companies must avoid certain risks. Insurers thus divide potential sources of loss into *insurable* and *uninsurable risks*. Obviously, they issue policies only for insurable risks. Although there are some exceptions, an insurable risk must meet the four criteria described in the following sections.

Predictability The insurer must be able to use statistical tools to forecast the likelihood of a loss. For example, an auto insurer needs information about the number of car accidents in the past year to estimate the expected number of accidents for the following year. With this knowledge, the insurer can translate expected numbers and types of accidents into expected dollar losses. The same forecast, of

---

*Key terms appearing in this appendix are defined in the glossary at the end of the book.

course, also helps insurers determine premiums charged to policyholders.

Because accurate forecasts of business conditions are difficult (if not impossible), business downturns are uninsurable risks. Thus you cannot insure your company against future losses due to recessions or changes in consumer tastes.

Casualty A loss must result from an accident, not from an intentional act by the policyholder. Insurers do not have to cover damages if a policyholder deliberately sets fire to corporate headquarters. To avoid paying in cases of fraud, insurers may refuse to cover losses when they cannot determine whether policyholders' actions contributed to them.

Note, however, that even good intentions can cause uninsurability if outcomes are within a company's control. For example, a food-processing company that installs new technology for making bologna faces two uninsurable risks:

1 The new equipment may yield substandard bologna.

2 The new equipment may be inefficient and too costly to operate.

Such risks are uninsurable because they are within the control of the food-processing company: With careful engineering and skillful production, the equipment can and should make the desired products efficiently.

Unconnectedness Potential losses must be random and must occur independently of other losses. No insurer can afford to write insurance when a large percentage of those who are exposed to a particular kind of loss are likely to suffer such a loss. One insurance company, for instance, would not want all the hurricane coverage in Miami or all the earthquake coverage in Los Angeles. By carefully choosing the risks that it will insure, an insurance company can reduce its chances of a large loss or even insolvency.

Verifiability Finally, insured losses must be verifiable as to cause, time, place, and amount. Did an employee develop emphysema because of a chemical to which she was exposed or because she smoked 40 cigarettes a day for 30 years? Did the policyholder pay the renewal premium before the fire destroyed his factory? Were the goods stolen from company offices or from the president's home? What was the insurable value of the destroyed inventory? When all these points have been verified, payment by the insurer goes more smoothly.

Types of Insurance Companies

Insurance companies are organized in two ways: either as *public* or *private insurers*. The first type is sometimes called *governmental* insurance. Its market share in the important areas of property and liability insurance is small. The prevailing philosophy is that government will insure only in areas where the private sector fails to do so. Typically, these have been areas in which the magnitude of the risk is regarded as potentially catastrophic.

Public Insurers Most business insurance is written by private insurance companies. But some of it— and a great deal of individual insurance—is provided by public insurance companies that are, in fact, government agencies. For example, the Federal Deposit Insurance Corp. (FDIC) insures savers against loss in case an insured bank fails (see chapter 19). Other forms of public insurance include unemployment insurance, workers' compensation, social security, and Medicare. The National Flood Insurance Association provides property protection in flood-prone areas that private companies consider too risky to cover.

Private Insurers Private insurers may be stockholder-owned or mutually owned. **Stock insurance companies** are like any other corporation: They sell their stock to the public, which hopes to earn a profit on the investment. Stockholders can be—but do not have to be—policyholders. American International Group Inc. is the largest stock insurance company in the United States (you can visit American International on the Internet at www.aig.com).

Mutual insurance companies are owned by their policyholders, for whom they seek to provide insurance at lower costs. As *cooperative* operations, they divide profits among policyholders, either by issuing dividends or by reducing premiums. In other words, the company's profits are generated for the direct benefit of policyholders rather than for outside stockholders. Some of the biggest names in insurance are mutual companies, such as Prudential, New York Life, State Farm, and Northwestern Mutual.

Underwriting and Marketing Insurance Two of the most important activities of private insurers are the underwriting and marketing of insurance offerings. **Underwriting** involves two basic tasks:

1 Determining which applications for insurance to accept and which ones to reject

2 Deciding what rates the insurer will charge

These decisions are made by *underwriters*—experts who gather information and tabulate data, assess loss probabilities, and decide which applications to accept. The purpose of all these functions, of course, is to maximize the insurer's profits.

Agents and brokers are the people who market insurance. An **insurance agent** represents and is paid a commission by an insurance company. The agent, then, represents the insurance seller. An **insurance broker**, on the other hand, is a free-lance agent who represents insurance buyers rather than sellers. Brokers work for clients by seeking the best coverage for them. They are then paid commissions by the insurers whom they recommend to their clients. Some brokers also offer risk-management advice.

The Insurance Product

Insurance companies are often distinguished by the types of insurance coverage they offer. While some insurers offer only one area of coverage—life insurance, for example—others offer a broad range. In this section, we describe the four major categories of business insurance: *liability*, *property*, *life*, and *health*. As we will see, each of these broad categories includes a wide variety of coverage plans and options.

Liability Insurance

As we saw in Appendix 1, *liability* means responsibility for damages in case of accidental or deliberate harm to individuals or property. Who, for example, might be financially responsible—liable—for the medical expenses, lost wages, and pain and suffering incurred by an individual temporarily or permanently disabled because of another's actions? **Liability insurance** covers losses resulting from damage to people or property when the insured party is judged liable.[1]

To meet this growing need, insurance companies offer a wide variety of liability insurance policies. All policies, however, offer two basic types of coverage:

1 The insurer promises to defend the policyholder in a court of law.

2 The insurer promises to pay damages assessed against the policyholder if the policyholder is held to be legally liable.

General Liability   General liability policies protect business policyholders in cases involving four types of problems:

- **Personal liability** coverage would protect a firm if one of its truck drivers runs over a customer's foot.

- **Professional liability** coverage would protect a surgeon who leaves a pair of scissors inside a patient.

- **Product liability** coverage would protect the maker of a new hair conditioner that causes users' hair to fall out.

- **Premises liability** coverage would protect a firm if a customer slips on a wet floor and suffers a severe concussion.

Selected Types of Liability Coverage   Businesses often choose to purchase comprehensive general liability policies, which provide coverage for all these problems and more. In

As You Drive, So Shall You Pay

If you drive a sport utility vehicle or pickup truck, then you might want to keep an eye on your liability insurance. Current research shows that in road accidents these heavier vehicles inflict greater than usual damage to other vehicles and their human occupants, and insurance firms, who have been paying out larger claims as a result, have taken notice. In an attempt to force auto makers to make these vehicles safer, and to more fairly distribute the cost of insuring them, insurers are funding additional research and far-reaching experiments and crash tests—and raising their rates.

   Sport utility vehicles not only greatly outweigh the typical sedan, often by two to three thousand pounds; they also have sturdy frames and ride higher off the ground, tending to nullify the protective features built into smaller cars. "It's pretty obvious the size and weight of these vehicles and the way they're built is

contributing to the loss experience," said Jonathan Adkisson, an actuary at Farmers Insurance Group. "So it seems appropriate to charge the drivers of those vehicles higher premiums."

   Some larger U.S. insurers, such as Farmers and the Progressive Corporation, have already changed their rate structure, while several others, including Allstate, Nationwide, and Geico, plan to do so after further research is completed in 1998.

   Before the changes in rates, all drivers were essentially subsidizing the higher property damage costs incurred by drivers of utility vehicles and pickups. The Highway Loss Data Institute has estimated that cost at around 25% above normal on average for vans, pickups, and sport utility vehicles, although for the latter the difference can exceed 60%. Ironically, the subsidized vehicles are more expensive and are often purchased by more affluent drivers.

   After the dust settles, drivers of the larger vehicles could face increases of $50 to $700 a year in liability insurance premiums, while car drivers might see savings of perhaps $25 to $350. Whether the higher rates (and the potential for further costs levied on their high pollution emissions) will affect the sale of vans and sport utility vehicles remains to be seen.

this section, we focus on three types of such coverage: *umbrella policies*, *automobile policies*, and *workers' compensation*.

Umbrella Policies Because the dollar value of a liability loss can be huge, many insurers will write coverage only up to a certain limit. Moreover, many liability contracts exclude certain types of losses. To cover financial consequences that exceed the coverage of standard policies, some businesses buy **umbrella insurance**: insurance intended to cover losses in addition to or excluded by an underlying policy.

For example, suppose that a business has an automobile policy with a limit of $500,000 for bodily injury and property damage, a premises liability policy with a limit of $500,000, and a product liability policy with a limit of 750,000. An additional policy—the umbrella—might extend the coverage in any of the three insured areas not covered by the existing policies.

Automobile Policies A firm that owns and maintains automobiles for business use needs a *business automobile policy*. This policy will protect it against liability for bodily injury and property damage inflicted by its vehicles. Typically, such policies provide the following types of coverage:

- *Bodily injury and property damage.* Coverage that pays the firm if it is held legally liable for bodily injury or property damage.

- *Medical.* Coverage that pays for medical expenses incurred by persons in an insured vehicle.

- *Uninsured motorists.* Coverage that pays bodily injury expenses when injury to an insured driver is caused by an uninsured motorist, a hit-and-run driver, or a driver whose employer is insolvent.

An important type of automobile insurance now mandated in several states is **no-fault auto insurance**. Under no-fault plans, the parties injured in an accident are compensated by their own insurers for bodily injuries and property damage—regardless of which party is at fault. (Under traditional plans, an accident victim must seek compensation from the other driver's insurer.) No-fault simplifies the settlement of damage claims and prevents many cases from going to court.

Workers' Compensation A business is liable for any injury to an employee when the injury arises from activities related to occupation. When workers are permanently or temporarily disabled by job-related accidents or disease, employers are required by law to provide **workers' compensation coverage** for medical expenses, loss of wages, and rehabilitation services. U.S. employers now pay out approximately $60 billion in workers' compensation premiums each year, much of it to public insurers.[2] Since 1991, 34 states have passed revised workers' compensation laws: Eligibility requirements are tougher for disability benefits, pos-

sible fraud is examined more closely, and claimants' recourse to the courts has been restricted.[3]

Property Insurance

Firms purchase **property insurance** to cover injuries to themselves resulting from physical damage to or loss of real estate or personal property. Property losses may result from fire, lightning, wind, hail, explosion, theft, vandalism, or other destructive forces. Losses from fire alone in the United States come to about $12 billion per year.[4] In this section, we describe five of the most important types of property insurance: *fire* (including *allied lines*), *marine*, *title*, *business interruption*, and *credit insurance*. We also describe *multiline policies* and discuss the option known as *coinsurance*.

Fire and Allied Lines One of the policies most often purchased by businesses is the 1943 **Standard Fire Policy (SFP)**. The SFP covers specified property against damage or loss from fire, lightning, or theft. Coverage can be extended to cover other perils such as windstorm, hail, riot, smoke, explosion, and vandalism. Additional coverage is available in separate policies called **allied lines**: policies that insure the firm's property against catastrophes ranging from sprinkler leakage to floods and nuclear accidents.

With fire insurance, as with any other type of property insurance, the insured must know exactly what type of coverage he or she has *prior to incurring a loss*. Coverage comes in two basic types:

- When fire destroys the sofa in a dentist's office, **replacement value coverage** will provide the insured with sufficient funds to buy a new sofa.

- **Depreciated value coverage** deducts a certain amount for the prior use of the property before it was damaged. For example, suppose that our dentist's sofa had been purchased with a total expected life of five years and had been in the office for two years before the fire. In this case, depreciated value coverage would pay for only three-fifths of the cost of the sofa (the unused life of the property).

Marine Insurance Marine insurance includes two distinct types of insurance: ocean and inland marine. *Ocean marine insurance* covers the liability and loss of or damage to ships and their cargo. Meanwhile, although *inland marine insurance* sounds like a conflict in terms, it is truly an extension of the ocean marine form: It covers transportation (whether by truck, rail, or plane) and transported property. There are four main categories:

- *Property in transit.* Coverage protects property while it is being transported.

- *Bailee liability.* Coverage reimburses customers for losses that occur when their property is in the custody of another party.

- *Instrumentalities of transportation.* Coverage protects against losses from natural or accidental destruction.

- *Mobile property.* Coverage protects against losses from damages to pleasure boats and commercial vessels.

Title Insurance When land and buildings are purchased it is customary to research the *title*—that is, ownership—in order to determine whether it is free of encumbrances. The easiest way to ensure that the seller has clear legal right to sell a property is to purchase **title insurance**. A title insurance company will search a variety of sources and guarantee not only that the seller is the proper owner but also that there are no unknown debts or liens against the property.

For instance, if the seller once owned the property with a former spouse, a title search would verify whether he or she has the legal right to sell it. But what if the title insurance company erroneously indicates that the title is clear? What if the policyholder subsequently suffers a loss because of the error? In such cases, the title insurance company must reimburse the insured to the amount specified in the policy.

Business Interruption Insurance In some cases, loss to property is minimal in comparison to loss of income. A manufacturer, for example, may have to close down for an extended time while repairs to fire damage are being completed. During that time, of course, the company is not generating income. Even so, however, certain expenses—such as taxes, insurance premiums, and salaries for key personnel—may continue. To cover such losses, a firm may buy **business interruption insurance**.[5]

One form, **contingent business interruption insurance**, provides coverage if a business is interrupted because it is dependent on another business that suffers damage. For example, Mead Paper Corp. would have to shut down if its paper supplier burned down. Mead's contingent business interruption insurance would cover both its loss of profits and its fixed costs until it could find another supplier.

Credit Insurance In addition to protecting its physical assets, a firm may buy **credit insurance** to protect its financial assets. For example, if one or more customers cannot or do not pay their debts, the firm loses the value of the goods or services that it had provided to them on credit. Even firms that manage their credit policies well sometimes experience such losses. For instance, even a well-managed customer with a fine credit record may suffer property losses—and income disruption—from such natural disasters as tornadoes, flood, or fire. Credit insurance protects creditors from many kinds of accounts-receivable losses.

Multiline Policies Because companies have many risks, they may need many kinds of insurance. Rather than pur-

chasing separate policies, however, firms may choose to buy a **multiline policy**: one that combines coverage for property and liability losses.

One such policy is the Special Multiperil Policy (SMP) for owners of large businesses. SMPs usually include four broad areas of coverage:

- Property coverage for buildings and their contents

- Liability coverage

- Crime coverage

- Coverage against malfunctions of electrical and mechanical equipment

Another multiline plan, the Businessowners Policy (BOP), is designed for small- to medium-size retail stores, office buildings, apartment buildings, and similar firms. BOPs include coverage for fires to buildings and contents, loss of income, business interruption, and general liability.

Coinsurance Because a *total* loss of property is not highly probable, owners have traditionally purchased less than the total value in coverage. This approach means that the owner receives coverage against losses on all parts of the insured property. The insurer, however, receives a premium that reflects only a fraction of the property's value.

To counter this problem, many policies include **coinsurance** provisions: Policyholders must insure a certain minimum percentage of the property's total value. If the policyholder carries the stipulated coverage, the insurer will cover the entire value of a loss (up to a maximum amount). If the policyholder fails to insure to the required percentage, the insurer will pay less than the entire value of the loss. The smaller amount is determined by the following formula:

$$\frac{amount\ of\ insurance\ owned}{amount\ of\ insurance\ required} \times amount\ of\ property\ loss$$

$$= insurance\ company's\ payment$$

Let's say, for example, that a building has a replacement value of $80,000. The owner's insurance policy has an 80-percent coinsurance requirement. The owner, therefore, is required to carry $64,000 in coverage ($80,000 × .80). If the owner carries $64,000 worth of insurance then a $25,00 loss will be paid in full, as will any other loss up to $64,000. Let's say, however, that the owner carries only $50,000 in coverage. In this case, the insurer will pay only $19,531.25 of the $25,000 loss. Why? The figure is determined by the following calculation:

$$\frac{\$50,000}{\$64,000} \times \$25,000 = \$19,531.25$$

The policyholder then bears the remainder of the loss ($25,000.00 − $19,531.25 = $5,468.75)—in effect, a penalty for underinsuring the property.

Life Insurance

Insurance can also protect a company's human assets. As part of their benefits packages, many businesses purchase **life insurance** for employees. Life insurance companies accept premiums in return for the promise to pay beneficiaries after the death of insured parties. A portion of the premium is used to cover the insurer's own expenses. The remainder is invested in various types of financial instruments such as corporate bonds and stocks. The concept has created some very profitable businesses. In 1996, for example, life insurance companies paid benefits of $35 billion on premiums of $354 billion.[6]

Whole Life Insurance With a **whole life insurance** policy, a business or individual pays a sum that is sufficient to keep the policy in force for the whole of the person's life. This sum can be paid on a yearly basis for life or for a stated period of years (such as 20 years). For example, a woman may pay $115 each year for the rest of her life and be assured that her beneficiary, her husband, will receive the stated face value of the policy upon her death. Alternatively, she could pay $198 each year for 20 years and receive the same benefit. In both cases, the policy is said to be *paid-up*.

Cash Value Whole life policies have an internal buildup called a *cash value*. This value can never be forfeited even if the policyholder chooses to quit paying the premium. In some cases, the policyholder can borrow against this value. Sometimes, a policyholder can surrender (discontinue) the insurance policy and receive its cash value from the insurer. Cash value makes whole life policies very attractive to some insurance purchasers.

Term Life Insurance As its name suggests, **term insurance** provides coverage for a term (a temporary time period) stated in the policy. The term can be for 1, 5, 10, or 20 years. Term insurance has no cash value and is less expensive than any of the other forms of insurance discussed in this section. A term insurance policyholder purchases a larger after-death benefit for his or her beneficiaries than does a whole life policyholder who pays the same premium. For this reason, an individual who has a very limited insurance budget but a significant need for life insurance should consider term insurance. Term insurance is the form of life insurance typically supplied by companies to their employees.

Endowments An **endowment** pays the face value of the policy after a fixed period of time whether the policyholder is dead or alive. The purpose of an endowment is to allow accumulation of a fund. For example, a father might buy a $20,000 ten-year endowment in order to accumulate $20,000 within a ten-year period for his daughter's college education. If he dies before the ten years are up, the insurer will pay his beneficiary (his daughter). However, if the father lives to the tenth year, the company turns the accumulated $20,000 over to him.

Universal Life Insurance For many years, the three policies described above provided the life insurance industry with very good profits. Whole life was the backbone of the industry. However, as interest rates increased in the 1960s and 1970s, many policyholders became unhappy with the low return rates earned by whole life and endowment policies. They began surrendering policies and investing funds in higher-yielding instruments, such as money market funds. Life insurance companies responded by developing a new product. **Universal life policies** combine the protection of term life insurance with the higher yields of money market funds and similar investments.

Policyholders enjoy some flexibility in designing policies to meet their changing needs. For example, they can choose the mix of death benefit and accumulated cash value, and they can change that mix as their needs change. Although initial premiums tend to be high, payments are flexible and interest earned on the policy's savings component is competitive with other money market instruments.

Variable Life Insurance Another form of life insurance is a modified form of whole life insurance. **Variable life insurance (VLI)** allows flexibility regarding the minimum face value of the policy, the types of investments supporting it, and even the amount and timing of the premiums. VLI policies emerged in the inflationary 1970s to offset some of the loss in the dollar's purchasing power.

How does VLI work? Instead of buying a whole life policy with a fixed face value of $100,000, a policyholder may choose a variable life policy with a $100,000 *minimum* face value. The actual face value can exceed the minimum, depending on the market performance of the VLI investment portfolio. VLI policyholders can stipulate the portfolio mix, choosing among a variety of investment instruments such as common stocks, short-term bonds, and high-yield money market securities. The increase in the policy's face value depends on the success of the underlying investments. VLIs are a growing segment of the insurance market because they offer more flexibility than traditional policies.

Group Life Insurance Most companies buy **group life insurance**, which is underwritten for groups as a whole rather than for each individual member. The insurer's assessment of potential losses and its pricing of premiums are based on the characteristics of the whole group. Johnson & Johnson's benefit plan, for example, includes group life coverage with a standard program of protection and benefits—a master policy purchased by J&J—that applies equally to all employees.

Health Insurance

Health insurance covers losses resulting from medical and hospital expenses as well as income lost from injury or disease. It is, of course, no secret that the cost of health insurance has skyrocketed in recent years. Today, for example, companies pay about $4,000 per employee on health insurance premiums to both *commercial insurers* like Prudential, Metropolitan, and Nationwide and *special providers* like Blue Cross/Blue Shield, and to health maintenance organizations and preferred provider organizations.[7]

National health expenditures, including government programs like Medicare and Medicaid, reached $1 trillion in 1996. This average annual expenditure of $4,000 for every person in the nation is expected to increase to $5,500 by the year 2002.[8] These figures reflect both the high demand for health-care services and escalating costs.

Disability Income Insurance **Disability income insurance** provides continuous income when disability keeps the insured from gainful employment. Many health insurance policies cover "short-term" disabilities, sometimes up to two years. Coverage for permanent disability furnishes some stated amount of weekly income—usually 50 to 70 percent of the insured's weekly wages—with payments beginning after a six-month waiting period. Group policies account for over 70 percent of all disability coverage in the United States.

Commercial Health Insurers Commercial insurers provide a variety of policies to cover expenses incurred because of sickness or injury. Many types of coverage are available:

- *Hospital expenses.* Coverage pays for medical expenses incurred while in the hospital. Such expenses include room and board charges, laboratory charges, X-ray fees, and costs of prescription medication.

- *Surgical expenses.* Coverage pays for physician fees for surgery performed in the hospital or elsewhere.

- *Physicians' expenses.* Coverage pays for nonsurgical care provided by a physician in the hospital, at home, or in the doctor's office.

- *Dental and vision.* Coverage pays a fixed percentage of expenses for certain dental services and doctor-prescribed eyeglasses and contact lenses.

- *Disability income.* Coverage pays a certain percentage of income to a policyholder who is unable to work as a result of a nonoccupational sickness or injury.

- *Comprehensive medical.* Coverage provides a variety of coverages like those listed above. This form of coverage is usually characterized by a deductible and a percentage-participation provision that requires some contribution by the policyholder.

Special Health-Care Providers Instead of reimbursement for a health professional's services, Blue Cross/Blue Shield, which is made up of nonprofit health-care membership groups, provides specific service benefits to its subscribers. Many other commercial insurers do the same. What is the advantage to the subscriber or policyholder? No matter what the service actually costs, the special health-care provider will cover the cost. In contrast, when policies provide reimbursement for services received, the policyholder may pay for a portion of the expense if the policy limit is exceeded. Other important options include HMOs and PPOs.

HMOs A **health maintenance organization (HMO)** is an organized health-care system providing comprehensive medical care to its members for a fixed, prepaid fee. In an HMO, all members agree that, except in emergencies, they will receive their health care through the organization.

HMOs emphasize prevention of illness. For example, one typical HMO benefit—paid office visits—encourages timely physical exams. Financial incentives are also given for ongoing exercise, smoking-cessation, and weight-loss programs.

PPOs A **preferred provider organization (PPO)** is an arrangement whereby selected hospitals and doctors agree to provide services at reduced rates and to accept thorough review of their recommendations for medical services. The objective of the PPO is to help control health-care costs by encouraging the use of cost-effective, efficient providers' health-care services.

Government Programs Many Americans rely on government programs to cover all or most of their health-care costs. In this section, we cover the two most important and best-known of these programs: Medicare and Medicaid.

Medicare Medicare, a government-sponsored program that funds medical services for the elderly, was created in 1965 as an amendment to the Social Security Act. Between 1968 and 1995, enrollment in the Medicare program increased from 20 million to almost 38 million people. Medicare recipients received $131 billion in services in 1995.

The Medicare program consists of Hospital Insurance (Part A) and Supplementary Medical Insurance (Part B). Part A, which is provided to all persons 65 years and older, covers inpatient hospital services, skilled nursing-facility services, home health-care services, and hospice care. It is funded by Social Security deductions.

Part B is a voluntary program that is supported by premiums paid by Medicare-eligible individuals. It covers physicians' fees and other related medical services. As health-care costs increase and Medicare recipients are responsible for higher deductibles and copayments, more commercial insurers and Blue Cross/Blue Shield organizations are offering Medicare supplement policies. These policies cover costs not paid for by Medicare.

Medicaid Like Medicare, the Medicaid program began in 1965 as an amendment to the Social Security Act. Medicaid makes health-care services available to low-income individuals and families. The program is administered by each state based on guidelines provided by the federal government. It is financed by both state and federal funds. In 1995, the Medicaid program paid $120 billion to 35 million recipients.[10]

Life and Health Insurance for Small Business Businesses spend a great deal of money to include life and health insurance in their employee benefit programs. Although some large firms have been able to absorb rising costs or pass them on to consumers, smaller firms are often unable to do either. Indeed, many small and midsized firms are beginning to question whether they can afford the basic benefit programs that workers have come to expect.

In recent years, small businesses have experimented with two new solutions to the problem of rising costs: *employee leasing* and *health-care coalitions*.

Employee Leasing Employee leasing means that instead of hiring their own employees, many small businesses "lease" them from firms that provide personnel services. The personnel firm also screens applicants, prepares payrolls, pays payroll taxes and workers' compensation premiums, and maintains personnel records. The employer, then, is not locked into obligations to a permanent work force and so avoids the costs of administering benefits plans.

Health-Care Coalitions In **health-care coalitions**, small firms join together not only to lower premiums but to practice preventive health care. By 1994, some 10,000 small businesses in California and Florida alone were among the growing number that are forming these new alliances.[11] Coalition members share ideas on preventing employee illness and information about the latest developments in health care. By working as groups, they get better insurance and prescription prices and negotiate doctor and hospital costs more effectively than if each member negotiated alone.

Special Forms of Business Insurance

Many forms of insurance are attractive to both businesses and individuals. For example, homeowners are as concerned about insuring property from fire and theft as are businesses. Businesses, however, have some special insurable concerns. In this section, we will discuss two forms of insurance that apply to the departure or death of key employees or owners.

Key Person Insurance Many businesses choose to protect themselves against loss of the talents and skills of key employees. For example, if a salesperson who rings up $2.5 million annually dies or takes a new job, the firm will suffer loss. It will also incur recruitment costs to find a replacement and training expenses once a replacement is hired. **Key person insurance** is designed to offset both lost income and additional expenses.

Business Continuation Agreements Who takes control of a business when a partner or associate dies? Surviving partners are often faced with the possibility of having to accept an inexperienced heir as a management partner. This contingency can be handled in **business continuation agreements**, whereby owners make plans to buy the ownership interest of a deceased associate from his or her heirs. The value of the ownership interest is determined when the agreement is made. Special policies can also provide survivors with the funds needed to make the purchase.

Self-Insurance

Some large organizations choose to build up their own pools of funds as a reserve to cover losses that would otherwise be covered by commercial insurance. This type of coverage is called **self-insurance**.

The primary motive for self-insurance is to avoid the high cost of buying coverage from commercial insurers. For example, part of a firm's paid premiums go to cover the insurer's administrative, advertising, and sales costs. Obviously, self-insurance avoids these costs. Suppose, for instance, that an athletic club pays $100,000 in premiums annually but experiences average losses of only $20,000. Let's say, however, that the club decides instead to set up its own reserve fund of $50,000 annually. If it also establishes efficient procedures for handling damages and other losses, it might achieve comparable coverage through self-insurance *and* save $50,000 in annual premiums.

As a practical matter, self-insurance is not a reasonable alternative for smaller or new companies (even large ones) that have not yet built up sizable reserves. For example, what will happen if our athletic club suffers a $1 million fire loss when its reserve fund has grown to only $100,000? It may be forced to close. Had its previous commercial coverage been in effect, however, the entire loss might have been covered. Then it could have resumed operations after the club was renovated.

Integrative
Video Case 1
SHOWTIME.

It's Showtime

This is the first of six cases that explore a variety of management-related issues at Showtime Networks Inc., a premium television network company. This installment is designed to be a general introduction. You may want to refer to it when you are studying the other integrative video cases.

The Company

Showtime Networks Inc. (SNI) is a wholly owned subsidiary of Viacom Inc., a giant media conglomerate, and operates the premium television networks Showtime, The Movie Channel (TMC), Flix, Showtime *en Español* (a separate audio feed of Showtime for its Spanish-speaking audience), and Showtime Extreme, an action-oriented channel that SNI plans to launch in the spring of 1998. It also operates and manages the premium television network Sundance Channel, a joint venture with Robert Redford and PolyGram Filmed Entertainment. Finally, the company also has a distinct pay-per-view distribution service that creates, markets, and distributes sports and entertainment events.

SNI's parent, Viacom, also owns Simon & Schuster, Paramount Pictures, Blockbuster Video, MTV, Nickelodeon, and VH1. SNI has exclusive movie distribution contracts with Paramount and other top movie studios such as Metro-Goldwyn-Mayer (MGM) and PolyGram.

Showtime, SNI's leading brand, is an award-winning and critically acclaimed network, having won Oscar, Emmy, and Cable ACE awards for its original programs. Together, SHO and TMC account for almost 99 percent of SNI's premium-service revenues. SNI's major competitor is Home Box Office Inc. (HBO), the category leader. HBO, which also includes Cinemax, has approximately 40 million subscribers to SNI's approximately 18 million (for Showtime and The Movie Channel).

The Industry

Above the basic level of cable or satellite service is **premium**, a cable- or satellite-delivered service that generally features uncut, commercial-free programming to consumers for which cable or satellite distributors typically charge a monthly incremental fee. The largest outlet for premium television networks is the cable industry, which has about 65 million subscribers for basic services in the United States. Cable operators sell one or more premium services as an additional purchase over and above the basic level of service. Premium services are also delivered via other technologies such as wireless cable, backyard dishes, and the newer Direct Broadcast Satellite

(DBS) business, which utilizes smaller backyard satellite dishes.

All SNI's business operations, including programming, sales, and marketing, face competitive pressures. One of the most significant factors facing SNI is that it is not affiliated with any cable operator, while HBO and Encore Media Group, a new entrant in the premium service category, are affiliated with the two largest cable operators, Time Warner and TCI, respectively.

It was thus against a complex and constantly changing backdrop that Matt Blank, new chairman of SNI, developed fresh and aggressive goals for the firm. To accomplish these he reorganized the company and made major strategic shifts. The reorganization included the executive ranks, since Matt knew he needed a group of talented and aggressive executives on his top management team.

The Top Management Team

Matt Blank became chairman of SNI in February 1995. A television industry veteran who has made an indelible mark on the cable industry, Matt joined SNI in 1988 after holding several senior executive positions at HBO. He has served as executive vice president of marketing at Showtime, and later as president and chief operating officer as well as president and chief executive officer. As chairman of SNI Matt began to carry out a new vision for the firm.

Gwen Marcus was promoted to executive vice president, general counsel and administration, in January 1996. In her new position she added responsibility for the human resources and administration departments to her existing position of general counsel. After beginning her legal career as an entertainment lawyer at a major New York law firm, Gwen joined SNI in 1984 as assistant counsel and has moved up the ranks since then to her present position.

Jerry Cooper, executive vice president, finance and operations, is responsible for the company's financial activities, information services, operations, and corporate development. He was formerly chief financial officer for Young Broadcasting, and before that he spent 16 years at Viacom where, among other positions, he served as senior vice president and general manager of Lifetime.

Len Fogge was hired in April 1996 as executive vice president, creative/marketing services. He had been president of Franklin Spier Inc., the leading advertising agency for publishing, and earlier, as president of Grey Entertainment, he helped build that company into the largest entertainment advertising agency in the United States.

Mark Greenberg was promoted to executive vice president, corporate marketing and communications in January 1996, from his position as senior vice president of marketing. His responsibilities include overseeing the company's marketing strategy and planning activities, its marketing campaigns and promotions, the corporate communications department, the new sports and event programming group, and all market research. The sports and event programming group is a major operating group responsible for putting on premier boxing events such as the two historic Holyfield vs. Tyson matches and major concerts such as the Spice Girls and, in years past, the Rolling Stones and the Grateful Dead. In June 1996 Mark assumed additional responsibilities for leading SNI's efforts to evaluate its strategic priorities and identify its competitive advantages. Before joining the firm in 1989 he held several sales and marketing positions at HBO.

Jerry Offsay, president of programming for SNI, is responsible for all the programming functions of the company. Because he deals with movie studios and generates a massive amount of original programming, his offices are in California to give him ready access to the film industry. Jerry was previously executive vice president of ABC Productions and has been an executive producer

of several films. He started his career as an entertainment attorney.

As executive vice president, sales and affiliate marketing, Showtime Networks sales and marketing, Jeff Wade is responsible for sales activities and affiliate marketing efforts throughout the company. Before coming to SNI as South Central regional director in 1981, he was executive vice president for affiliate relations at QVC. He serves on the board of the Sundance Channel.

We will learn more about other key managers in the cases that follow.

Questions

1 How would you characterize SNI's industry environment? What types of management skills would you expect to be most useful in that environment?

2 Given the information in the case, how would you evaluate SNI's management strength?

3 What do you think are the implications of the fact that some of SNI's managers are former employees of HBO? What do you think in general of having former competitors in management positions within a firm? What are likely to be the strengths and weaknesses they bring to their new employer?

Shaping the Corporate Culture at Showtime

This is the second of six cases that explore a variety of management-related issues at Showtime Networks Inc., a premium television network company. The first installment is a general introduction. You may want to refer to it when you are studying the case that follows.

One of the most powerful but most intangible qualities of any firm is the company's unique identity, called its corporate culture. Culture is embodied in the shared experiences, stories, beliefs, and norms that characterize the organization. Like any firm, Showtime has built its culture from elements of its management style and organizational structure.

Len Fogge, executive vice president, creative/marketing services, credits CEO Matt Blank with trying to reinvent SNI's culture, which emphasizes creativity, risk-taking, and the value of the individual. "There's a real change going on here," he said. "It's in the air; it's very palpable."

Focus on People as a Shared Belief

Its focus on valuing people is most evident in SNI's culture when it comes to human resources. Diversity is a goal the firm actively seeks. At every stage, from selection to train-ing to benefits planning (where SNI's innovative work and family policies have created a model for the industry), SNI lives up to its collective belief that people are its greatest resource. Managers look for and nurture what Matt Blank hopes to call "the next generation of leaders in our industry."

Mark Greenberg, executive vice president of corporate marketing and communications, readily articulates the culture's emphasis on people. He defines SNI's culture in terms of the firm's primary assets. "The assets leave every night in the elevator, and they come back every morning in the elevator. Our assets are the people who work here. We really value both the diversity and the individuality of our people."

Communication as a Shared Experience

Another way in which the culture becomes visible at SNI is at the "town meeting." About twice a year the 500 or so New York employees gather in an auditorium across the street from their offices; the regional offices have participated by means of videoconferencing. In line with CEO Matt Blank's emphasis on commu-nication, Matt and sometimes others in his top management team make presentations designed to inform and motivate everyone as a group. It's important, said Matt, for every-one to feel that what they are doing at Showtime is special, and although the logistics of town meetings are difficult, he feels the effort is well worthwhile.

When a dynamic new commercial for Showtime was aired for employ-ees at a recent town meeting, he said, "the group stood up and cheered. That motivated everybody in the company, not just the people in pro-gramming or advertising." Shared communication thus creates another element of the corporate culture.

Creativity as a Shared Norm

SNI's culture is exemplified by an ample allowance for creativity and a high tolerance for risk. Many man-agers make a conscious effort to in-still a creative spirit, to encourage employees to take risks, and to be supportive of their efforts as the company strives for what Matt has described as a new and "creative self-image." "I don't think *passion* is a word that you would have used around here several years ago," he said. "We use it today."

Ray Gutierrez, senior vice presi-dent, human resources and adminis-tration, explains, "To stay in the forefront of business we have to be creative everywhere."

Leadership as a Shared Norm

The firm is generally organized along functional lines; the one major exception is a separate entity that manages Sundance Channel, which is a joint venture with several partners. A stronger influence on the prevailing culture than the organizational chart, however, is Matt Blank's desire to have top management develop a collaborative approach to their work.

A close-knit group of just six or seven people, many of whom were hired by Matt Blank, SNI's senior executives are encouraged to work very closely together, sharing information freely and sharing responsibility in an informal matrix that exists apart from any formal organizational structure. This planned flexibility and cooperation is a key aspect of their leadership, and a strong influence on the company's dynamic culture.

The Competitive Environment as a Shared Story

The technology of the entertainment business is changing almost as fast as anyone can keep up with it, along with audience demographics and the prospects for government regulation. Competition is and will continue to be fierce; the cable industry has consolidated in the last few years, and future growth in cable is expected to be slow. As a "scrappy underdog," however, SNI can still grow within the premium category, while HBO, its biggest competitor, must actually grow the category.

SNI's culture has been described as spirited, even aggressive. Clearly its people feel they are up to the challenge they face and even welcome it. "This is a business that changes so dramatically and so quickly," said Matt. Yet this very aspect of the industry is what draws many SNI employees. Not being certain what the environment will look like even two years ahead adds a challenge to the job that SNI's culture encourages people to attack with energy.

Questions

1 Matt Blank has said of SNI that "the concept of prevailing is very important to us." How do you think that concept is reflected in SNI's corporate culture?

2 Suggest some day-to-day ways in which SNI's managers can keep alive the spirit of teamwork and camaraderie achieved at the town meetings.

3 What influence might the firm's functional organization have on its culture, and how do think SNI's informal top-management "matrix" modifies those effects?

Integrative Video Case 3 SHOWTIME®

Leading a Motivated Workforce

This is the third case that explores a variety of management-related issues at Showtime Network Inc., a premium television network company. The first installment is a general introduction. You may want to refer to it when you are studying the case that follows.

One of the biggest challenges of leadership, at SNI as anywhere, is attracting, retaining, and motivating a committed workforce. As demographic changes that began in the 1980s continue into the next century, managers at all levels find they must address not only the traditional motivation issues of advancement and compensation, but also new "work and family" issues that arise where employees' personal lives and their work lives intersect. Such intersections are becoming increasingly common as diversities of age, race, gender, and lifestyle become more widespread and even sought after in the workplace.

Even recruitment has changed; for example, visitors to Showtime's website (www.showtimeonline.com) find an opportunity there to explore job opportunities.

A company that is more attractive to work for will attract and keep better-qualified employees, as SNI knows. Here is a look at how SNI uses the newest tools of motivation.

Embracing Diversity

More and more executives today realize that having a diverse workforce is not only the right thing to do; it is also a tremendous competitive advantage. Diversity of opinion, best obtained in a diverse workforce, is also a strong defense against group think.

Nat Fuchs, SNI's vice president of human resource development, sought to define exactly what diversity meant to the firm. SNI put together a committee of employees who were "impassioned" about diversity and who were influential leaders in their respective areas within the firm. Together they looked first at visible diversity, a concept they later expanded to include differences in both visible and invisible factors such as race, age, gender, sexual orientation, physical challenge, and composition of family. Their goal was to encourage all departments to seek diversity, in staffing and even in programming.

Gwen Marcus, executive vice president, general counsel and administration, recalls that at first diversity in staffing raised red flags among people who thought it meant nothing more than "hiring people of color." Over time, however, that misperception was erased as people realized that SNI's commitment to diversity is not intended to promote preferential hiring on the basis of factors such as race, but rather that it

addresses broader issues such as offering employee benefits programs such as telecommuting, flexible work schedules, and similar work and family initiatives to accommodate the needs of a workforce with diverse backgrounds and lifestyles.

"We were the first in the industry to offer same-sex life partner insurance programs," said Nat. SNI was eventually recognized for its commitment to diverse life styles when it received the GLAAD (Gay Lesbian Alliance Against Defamation) Fairness Award in 1997.

The company also took a pioneering stand in favor of alternative work arrangements, which were designed to ease the difficulties faced not only by working parents but also by those caring for elderly parents or pursuing personal commitments outside SNI. As an example, said Gwen, "one of my most talented staff members is our paralegal by day and a novelist by night. He came to a point where he needed either to work a compressed work week or to quit SNI entirely. To retain the talents of a person like this, we accepted the change in hours, and it works great." Nat comments, "Nowadays, we don't even ask why you want it."

The alternative work arrangements SNI now offers weren't incorporated so easily at first. Some skepticism accompanied the initial three-month trial, but SNI imposed some conditions to increase the chances of success. Arrangements such as job sharing, flextime, staggered work hours, compressed work weeks, and telecommuting were offered only where they were consistent with the workload and work flow of the affected employees and departments. Success eventually followed, and one way in which SNI was recognized for its achievements in accommodating diversity in life style is being nominated for the Women in Cable Award for Work Environment. Another telling commendation is the high proportion of new hires who are referred by current employees.

The concept of diversity continues to expand at SNI, according to Ray Gutierrez, senior vice president of human resources and administration: "We keep expanding diversity as it plays into our business needs, continuing to define it. We have 700 full-time regular employees, plus consultants, freelancers, and temps; therefore, we work around their needs. We guide managers to help employees deal with diversity with in-house workshops and training programs, sometimes facilitated with outside consultants."

The rewards have been tangible. Nat Fuchs explains, "Our general business successes were identified with our diversity process, and so we became a model for the industry. Showtime is now seen as a leader; it has a genuine commitment and a business philosophy that encourages diversity in all aspects of its business, not a set of bureaucratic formulas or programs sitting on a shelf."

Rewarding Achievement

With the right people in place, SNI seeks to retain employees not only by addressing their varying needs but also by recognizing and rewarding their skills and achievement.

As in any company, promotions are motivating, and SNI has sought to make them highly prized. The practice of promoting people in order to enhance their credibility with outsiders is discouraged; promotions are earned. That said, about 90 percent of jobs at SNI are filled from within.

Performance measurement is critical since the firm is performance driven, and SNI has streamlined its appraisal process from six different systems to one. "We do upward feedback, which was initiated by employees, not management, and in some areas 360° feedback," said Ray. "We also do climate surveys asking how our employees want to be managed." Merit reviews are conducted once a year.

Awards and bonuses are many and varied, and they are not confined to the executive levels. Spot bonuses are awarded for exceptional achievements; field sales people are given incentive awards, and long-term incentives are awarded according to the overall performance of Showtime or of its parent company, Viacom. Individual employees are recognized in various ways, including the Chairman's Award, which is given by the chairman of Viacom, and the Unsung Hero Award. Both awards are designated for nonmanagerial employees who are compensated below

a specified salary cap, in recognition of the fact that critical support people provide invaluable service to the firm. Awards are also given for long-term tenure and in team-based merit reviews SNI's work teams determine the level (although not the amount) of raises given to team members. At every level SNI tries to offer employees the opportunity to be recognized and rewarded.

Questions

1 How would you describe SNI's definition of diversity to a new employee of the firm? What other kinds of "invisible" diversity do you think might be identified, and how could a firm ensure that they were considered appropriately, that is, in light of its business needs?

2 If some employees do not qualify for "work and family" benefits, do you think there would be a negative backlash to such innovations, and how would you handle them to ensure fairness to all?

3 What might a firm like SNI do to prepare its employees for promotions that depend on having business and management skills?

4 How do SNI's focus on diversity of all kinds and its efforts to reward performance at all levels of the firm reinforce each other as motivational tools for management?

**Integrative
Video Case 4
SHOWTIME®**

Reorganizing Marketing Communication and Advertising

This is the fourth case that explores a variety of management-related issues at Showtime Networks Inc., a premium television network company. The first installment is a general introduction. You may want to refer to it when you are studying the case that follows.

As part of his general reorganization of Showtime Networks Inc. (SNI), chairman and CEO Matt Blank sought to foster more creativity within the firm by reorganizing the advertising and creative services departments. Among the steps he took to accomplish this was to hire Len Fogge as the company's executive vice president of creative/marketing services, and to consolidate advertising and on-air promotions under Len's direction.

After auditing the departments reporting to him, Len concluded that SNI had a strong product offering, distinct from other channels, but that it lacked a comparably strong branding function. Consumer and trade advertising and promotional materials were not issued from a central office, various people had input into what was being said, and, while the resulting marketing messages were factually correct, they represented a kind of consensus decision making that did not accurately represent what SNI's distinct strengths were or what the Showtime brand was all about.

Len identified three key messages that he wanted SNI's marketing to convey:

- SNI provides programs different from anything shown on network TV.

- SNI makes films that move people because they are about something important.

- SNI makes "thrill-ride" viewing with programs like *Showtime Championship Boxing* and original series inspired by hit movies such as *Stargate* and *Total Recall.*

Len's goal was to make sure people understood "they get an experience from Showtime they can't get anywhere else."

Conducting the Agency Review

A common occurrence in the advertising business is the agency review, in which the client firm (in this case, SNI) reviews the qualifications of several advertising agencies that are invited to bid for the opportunity to work with the firm (or, in advertising jargon, to "pitch the account"). The firm's current ad agency may or may not be invited to participate.

Len's newly consolidated department soon conducted an agency review that included quite a few major national and international advertising agencies—and one candidate

that asked to pitch the account, the in-house group that had been responsible for SNI on-air and print promotions in the past. Prepared to be impressed, Len was nevertheless "blown away" by what he characterized as this group's "total communication of the product, a demonstrable understanding of the issues, and a brand concept that reflected Showtime." The in-house team, which came to be formalized as an in-house agency known as the Red Group, easily won the account.

The Red Group brainstormed around its winning concept that there are "no limits" to what Showtime can offer viewers who seek challenge, escape, and entertainment. The resulting campaign stressed as its theme the "no-limits viewing experience," in which the viewer would find no emotional or experiential limits to Showtime's dynamic programming.

Managing On-Air Time

In the past Showtime had filled the time between shows, known as interstitial time, with miscellaneous promotions for its upcoming programs. In keeping with his strategy to unify SNI's branding messages, however, Len added to the Red Group a media group to analyze the content of these interstitial spots. This group's responsibility was to integrate promotional communication with the adjacent programming, so that viewers of particular programs would see between-show spots for other shows that might appeal to the same audience.

"Our interstitial time is worth $100 million," said Len. "In the past, we would schedule but not plan it. Now we analyze and plan it, tying together promos with programs."

Managing Creative People

When creative people are rewarded for their work by being given promotions into administrative work, their creativity sometimes suffers as a result. And when pure administrators can make or veto creative decisions, the results are sometimes less than optimal. Len changed the practice at SNI by giving administrative duties to administrators in his group and allowing the "creatives" to concentrate on what they did best. An added advantage of the change is that while managers, directors, vice presidents, and other strategic people have input to creative decisions, the final results now rest with the writers, producers, and art directors whose work is on the line.

To offer creatives a place to gather in a relaxed and playful atmosphere, Len also designed "the Quad," a large open office area flanked by windows and filled with comfortable furniture and golf and basketball paraphernalia. Here members of the Red Group collect to talk, play, or just look out the windows and think. Away from their offices, they can refresh their creativity or get new perspective on a problem, alone or with colleagues. The Quad is a good example of the way in which Len views his role as a "facilitator" whose job is to allow people the freedom to do what they enjoy and do best.

Encouraging Risk Taking

A final step in Len's effort to integrate a consistent message for SNI was to create an environment in which creative people could thrive on the challenge of risk taking. "They must push the envelope," he said. "I encourage risk and I have only two responses, which are both visceral—'This is great,' or 'This is terrible.' Whichever it is, I tell people, 'You risked something; you took a step. It's not mediocre, which is the most important thing.' And they always come back with better stuff."

Questions

1 What are some of the less obvious advantages for management of the newly centralized creative/marketing services operation at SNI? Can you think of any potential disadvantages?

2 How do you think the introduction of a consistent marketing message will affect SNI's effort to strengthen Showtime's brand recognition in the cable market? List some specific results you might expect.

3 What criteria do you think were applied to the selection process that followed the agency review? List some qualities about the in-house group that might have led to its selection. How can the group continue to exploit its unique position for Showtime's benefit?

Integrative
Video Case 5
SHOWTIME®

Reengineering the Finance Department

This is the fifth case that explores a variety of management-related issues at Showtime Network Inc., a premium television network company. The first installment is a general introduction. You may want to refer to it when you are studying the case that follows.

The Problem

The contracts that cover the distribution of SNI's program services to local cable systems are unique and complex. One of the disadvantages of their complexity was an inefficient billing process, which relied on cable operators to interpret the terms of their contracts themselves and determine what they thought they owed SNI. SNI, in turn, based its bills on these estimates, which often under-reported the amount of money to SNI. Since the audit department could audit only about 30 percent of its 10,000 member cable systems a year, some operators owed SNI large sums of money by the time billing errors were discovered and corrected.

Confronting cable operators with corrected bills was, of course, a painful control procedure that sometimes resulted in angry customers, difficult situations for SNI salespeople, who were simultaneously trying to sell these same cus-

tomers new services, and uncollectable fees that sometimes cost SNI millions of dollars in revenue a year.

The Solution

When Jerry Cooper, executive vice president of finance and operations, decided to reengineer the finance department, his goal was to devise a way for SNI to get paid correctly and on time, without audits, by putting the controls at the front end of the billing procedure. True to the spirit of the reengineering process, Jerry began with "a blank sheet of paper." In essence, he turned the organization on its side, eliminating the traditional accounting areas of accounts receivable, accounts payable, billing, travel and entertainment (T&E), and so on and replacing them with cross-functional, self-directed teams he called "rings." Each ring was designed to serve a particular area of SNI, beginning with sales.

The sales department was put first because it was the biggest and most complex area served by the finance department, and because the field sales reps worked directly with SNI's customers to administer the problematic contracts. As Jerry Scro, senior vice president and CFO, recalled, "There was a compelling business reason to begin on the sales side."

When the reengineering had been completed, each ring consisted of a

small group of finance people, who came to be called financial business analysts (FBAs), and a team leader. These employees worked exclusively with the sales department *and* the customer to build a payment template with the terms and conditions of the contract. Rather than having to depend on estimates for revenue collection, SNI was now able to have the customer input the number of subscribers in the template, and the template then supplied the amount due. Billing became objective and automatic, customers were saved a great deal of work, and SNI began to realize the appropriate amounts of revenue from sales. In time the rings were actually moved out of headquarters and relocated to the regional offices, to be closer to the customers and field reps with whom they worked.

The change in structure was so successful that it was eventually expanded to the rest of the finance department and even to other departments, where informal rings work with their own particular in-house customers in creative and design services, marketing, law and human resources. But however successful, change is never easy. Jerry Cooper estimates that it took six to nine months just to begin the reengineering process and two years to complete it, and before it was over the dedication and resolve of those committed to improving SNI's revenue controls had been repeatedly tested. "Radical change creates conflict and dissension," notes Jerry. "It was necessary to find people in the organization who understood that changes were coming in job descriptions, information systems, compensation and incentives, and the corporate culture."

The Process

The first concrete step was to look carefully at the existing finance group, which had 60 or 70 employees. Many had individual ways of doing things that made the prospect of working in teams challenging. To ensure that they could work together well, and to reinforce the new mandate that rings would select, hire, and succeed or fail as teams, management allowed the rings to choose their own members, with the understanding that new competencies and capabilities would be required of all. Everyone was given an opportunity to retrain in an internal facility, set up to cover not only basic accounting procedures but also analysis and planning skills.

Said Jerry Cooper, "A different culture was created that led to team initiatives, conflict resolution training, 360° feedback, and so on. We let go of simple clerical functions and kept raising the bar." Although some employees left the firm in this early phase of the reengineering, SNI was confident that those who remained would become new leaders in the organization.

Among the many changes that took place in finance department job descriptions were the addition of revenue-generating responsibility and the opportunity and responsibility for finance people to deal well with customers. Finance people had never dealt with customers before and had never been considered part of a revenue-generating unit. Team members in the rings also had to learn to understand the sales function, and sales people learned how to use their rings as partners and resources in serving the customers' needs.

"This is the right way to work," said Jerry Cooper. "People are happier; they have greater job satisfaction and the ability to enhance their own careers. We put a customer focus in everything we do now, and morale is great." And, no small point, revenues are up.

Questions

1 Compare the effectiveness of SNI's past and present billing processes in terms of control. Use your conclusions to explain why SNI would view its billing function as a revenue-generating business process.

2 Assess the probable effect of the reengineering on productivity in the finance department. What good or service do the rings provide to the firm?

3 List some of the changes you think SNI needed to make in its financial information systems in the course of the reengineering described in this case.

Controlling the Uncontrollable—Risk Management at Showtime

This is the last of six cases that explore a variety of management-related issues at Showtime Networks Inc., a premium television network company. The first installment is a general introduction. You may want to refer to it when you are studying the case that follows.

Showtime Event Television (SET) Pay Per View is an industry leader in pay-per-view sports and event distribution. This division of SNI has produced and distributed eight of the top ten pay-per-view events of all time.

While live events such as rock concerts and boxing matches bring excitement to any programming lineup, they also carry certain risks. Performers can become ill, unforeseen news or cultural events can lure audiences away, and even technological problems with satellite transmission can mar a planned telecast. SET has faced the risks inherent in every stage of developing and producing such high-profile events, an its managers have developed a complex array of risk-management strategies that can be classified as risk control and risk transfer.

As a case in point, consider the scheduled boxing match between Mike Tyson and Bruce Seldon, which was to be held in July 1996 and broadcast live by SET. SET had purchased insurance on the participants in the event that one of them might be unable to perform due to illness, so the risk of nonperformance was effectively transferred to the insurance firm. And, although most of the promotional plans for the fight were laid months in advance, the major marketing expenditures would take place in the two weeks before the fight, when the decision to buy the event is typically made. Thus the risk of spending money on an event that might not occur as scheduled was controlled until the last possible moment.

As luck would have it, however, Tyson did fall ill with bronchitis at the last minute and was ordered by his doctors not to fight for several weeks. SET acted quickly to cancel its promotion and broadcast plans and shift everything to a later date. Still, some promotional materials had to be redone due to the change in dates, and so some unavoidable risk retention occurred for SET. A larger problem arose with the insurance company. Its management claimed that SET had not provided the firm with a medical report on Tyson and refused to pay SET's insurance claim. With its major means of risk transfer threatened, SET sought legal recourse and eventually recovered a substantial initial judgment against the insurance firm. Tyson recovered, the fight was rescheduled, and SET's risks were minimized as planned.

Other risks associated with live broadcasts are varied. In selecting a setting, or venue, for an event, SET considers such factors as the availability of back-up dates at the hall or arena and other events occurring in that city at the time. If there is too much competition for a live audience at a particular place, the venue might need to be changed.

Time is another risk factor. In addition to such obvious decisions as choosing the right day of the week, SET considers the occurrence of local and national holidays and cultural events, which influence audience size both at home and abroad. For instance, according to Jay Larkin, senior vice president, sports and event programming, Latin American holidays are particularly good days to stage boxing matches featuring Latin American fighters, since many people are celebrating their heritage and welcome a chance to cheer a local hero. (Interestingly, a different strategy governs the choice of dates for telecasting other events in pay-per-view. Since many people are not at home on holidays, the television audience is typically down at such times, so these dates are avoided.)

Another aspect of time risk is the occurrence of other headline-grabbing events. While the transfer of

Hong Kong from British to Chinese control in June 1997 probably did not take away much of the audience for SET's Mike Tyson–Evander Holyfield rematch, its significance in the history and economic life of South East Asia meant that news organizations all over the world had already booked huge blocks of satellite transmission time to cover it. SET put its Asian satellite connections together in time for the fight, but it was a more difficult task than it would have been at almost any other time.

The logistics of satellite transmission bring their own technological problems. There is always a chance that uplinks and downlinks to television satellites can fail, or that the mechanisms for scrambling the signal can go down. SET manages such risks in two ways, control and transfer. It controls risks by implementing extensive backup systems for all its satellite links, what Jay Larkin calls "built-in redundancy." These precautions serve the firm well. However, SET also buys signal insurance, whose price is negotiated with the insurer based on SET's expected revenues from the covered event.

As a service to its cable system customers, SET offers pass-along signal insurance, but some cable systems are unwilling to take on the cost of insuring a structure that seldom fails. But there are no guarantees in live television. If the cable system goes down for any reason and local customers don't get the show they paid for, it is the cable operator, not SET, who must shoulder the problem.

Questions

1 SET has chosen to rely most heavily on risk control and risk transfer. Why do you think risk retention forms so small a part of its risk management strategy?

2 Can you think of any area in which SET appears to practice risk avoidance? Why?

3 SET is protected against financial loss that might occur from the postponement or cancellation of its scheduled events. Do you think it incurs any nonfinancial losses from such disruptions to its programming plans, and how does the firm protect itself?

absolute advantage A nation's ability to produce something more cheaply than any other country can [59]

accountability Liability of subordinates for accomplishing tasks assigned by managers [139]

accounting Comprehensive system for collecting, analyzing, and communicating financial information [478]

accounting system Organized means by which financial information is identified, measured, recorded, and retained for use in accounting statements and management reports [478]

accounts payable Current liabilities consisting of bills owed to suppliers, plus wages and taxes due within the upcoming year [488]

accounts receivable Amount due from a customer who has purchased goods on credit [487]

acquisition The purchase of one company by another [47]

Active Corps of Executives (ACE) SBA program in which currently employed executives work with small businesses on a volunteer basis [170]

activity ratio Financial ratio for evaluating management's use of a firm's assets [492]

advertising Promotional tool consisting of paid, nonpersonal communication used by an identified sponsor to inform an audience about a product [334]

advertising agency Independent company that provides some or all of a client firm's advertising needs [339]

advertising campaign Arrangement of ads in selected media to reach targeted audiences [339]

advertising media Variety of communication devices for carrying a seller's message to potential customers [334]

advocacy advertising Advertising promoting a cause, viewpoint, or candidate [338]

affirmative action program Legally mandated program for recruiting qualified employees belonging to racial, gender, or ethnic groups who are underrepresented in an organization [197]

agency shop Workplace in which workers must pay union dues even if they do not join [251]

American Federation of Labor (AFL) Group of craft unions formed in 1866 to stress collective bargaining, economic action, and a pragmatic approach to union-management relations [242]

analytic process Production process in which resources are broken down into components to create finished products [394]

applications program Software (such as Lotus 1-2-3) that processes data according to a user's special needs [432]

articles of incorporation Document detailing the corporate governance of a company, including its name and address, its purpose, and the amount of stock it intends to issue [45]

artificial intelligence (AI) Construction and programming of computers to imitate human thought processes [462]

asked price Price that an OTC broker charges for a share of stock [562]

assembly line Product layout in which a product moves step by step through a plant on conveyor belts or other equipment until it is completed [400]

asset Any economic resource expected to benefit a firm or an individual who owns it [484]

audit Systematic examination of a company's accounting system to determine whether its financial reports fairly represent its operations [480]

authority Power to make the decisions necessary to complete a task [139]

autocratic style Managerial style in which managers generally issue orders and expect them to be obeyed without question [229]

automated teller machine (ATM) Electronic machine that allows customers to conduct account-related activities 24 hours a day, 7 days a week [525]

balance of payments Flow of all money into and out of a country [60]

balance of trade Total economic value of all products that a country imports minus the total economic value of all products that it exports [60]

balance sheet Financial statement detailing a firm's assets, liabilities, and owner's equity [486]

banker's acceptance Bank promise, issued for a buyer, to pay a designated firm a specified amount at a future date [524]

bargain retailer Retailer carrying a wide range of products at bargain prices [366]

bargaining unit Designated group of employees who will be represented by a union [252]

batch processing Method of collecting data over a period of time and then processing them as a group or batch [457]

bear market Period of falling stock prices [563]

bearer (or coupon) bond Bond requiring the holder to clip and submit a coupon in order to receive an interest payment [556]

benchmarking Process by which a company implements the best practices of other companies to improve its own products [430]

benefits Compensation other than wages and salaries [193]

bid price Price that an OTC broker pays for a share of stock [562]

bill of materials Production control tool that specifies the necessary ingredients of a product, the order in which they should be combined, and how many of each are needed to make one batch [406]

blue chip stock Common stock issued by a well-established company with a sound financial history and a stable pattern of dividend payouts [550]

blue-sky laws Laws requiring securities dealers to be licensed and registered with the states in which they do business [568]

board of directors Governing body of a corporation, which reports to its shareholders and delegates power to run its day-to-day operations [46]

bond Security through which an issuer promises to pay the buyer a certain amount of money by a specified date [554]

bond indenture Statement of the terms of a corporate bond [585]

bonus Individual performance incentive in the form of a special payment above the employee's salary [193]

book value Value of a common stock expressed as total shareholders' equity divided by the number of shares of stock [549]

bookkeeping The recording of accounting transactions [478]

boycott Labor action in which workers refuse to buy the products of a targeted employer [257]

branch office Foreign office set up by an international or multinational firm [68]

brand advertising Advertising promoting a specific brand [273, 338]

brand competition Competitive marketing that appeals to consumer perceptions of similar products [273]

branding Process of using symbols to communicate the qualities of a product made by a particular producer [311]

breakeven analysis Assessment of the quantity of a product that must be sold before the seller makes a profit [316]

breakeven point Quantity of a product that must be sold before the seller covers variable and fixed costs and makes a profit [316]

broker Individual or organization who receives and executes buy and sell orders on behalf of other people in return for commissions [551]

browser Software supporting the graphics and linking capabilities necessary to navigate the World Wide Web [467]

budget Detailed statement of estimated receipts and expenditures for a period of time in the future [490]

budget deficit Situation in which a government body spends more money in 1 year than it takes in [24]

bull market Period of upward-moving stock prices [563]

business An organization that provides goods or services in order to earn profits [6]

business agent (or **business representative**) Full-time official who acts as liaison between members of a large union and their supervisors [249]

business ethics Beliefs about acceptable and unacceptable business practices [82]

business plan Document that tells potential lenders why money is needed, how it will be used, and when it will be repaid [591]

business practice laws Laws or regulations that legalize in one country practices that are illegal in another [74]

bylaws Document detailing corporate rules and regulations, including election and responsibilities of directors and procedures for issuing new stock [45]

cafeteria benefit plan Benefit plan that sets limits on benefits per employee, each of whom may choose from a variety of alternative benefits [194]

callable bond Bond that may be called in and paid for by the issuer before its maturity date [556]

capacity Amount of a product that a company can produce under normal working conditions [398]

capital The funds needed to create and operate a business enterprise [7]

capital gain Profit earned by selling a share of stock for more than its cost [547]

capital item Expensive, durable, infrequently purchased industrial product such as a building [304]

capital structure Mix of a firm's debt and equity financing [588]

capitalism Market economy that provides for private ownership of production and encourages entrepreneurship by offering profits as an incentive [8]

cartel Association of producers whose purpose is to control supply and prices [74]

cash flow management Management of cash inflows and outflows to ensure adequate funds for purchases and the productive use of excess funds [578]

catalog showroom Bargain retailer in which customers place orders for catalog items to be picked up at on-premises warehouses [367]

CD-ROM Secondary storage device that can store sound and video data but accepts no new written data [451]

cellular layout Spatial arrangement of production facilities designed to move families of products through similar flow paths [400]

central processing unit (CPU) Part of the computer system where data processing takes place [450]

centralized organization Organization in which most decision-making authority is held by upper-level management [139]

centralized system Form of computer system architecture in which all processing is done in one location through a centralized computer, database, and staff [460]

certified management accountant (CMA) Certified accountant specializing in management accounting [482]

certified public accountant (CPA) Accountant licensed by the state and offering services to the public [480]

chain of command Reporting relationships within a company [134]

channel captain Channel member who is most powerful in determining the roles and rewards of other members [361]

channel conflict Conflict arising when the members of a distribution channel disagree over the roles they should play or the rewards they should receive [361]

check Demand-deposit order instructing a bank to pay a given sum to a specified payee [515]

check kiting Illegal practice of writing checks against money that has not yet been credited at the bank on which checks are drawn [94]

chief executive officer (CEO) Top manager hired by the board of directors to run a corporation [46]

classical theory of motivation Theory holding that workers are motivated solely by money [214]

client PC Any computer attached to a network server [461]

closed promotion system System by which managers, often informally, decide which workers are considered for promotions [187]

closed shop Workplace in which an employer may hire only workers already belonging to a union [251]

closing Step in the personal selling process in which salespeople ask prospective customers to buy products [343]

collateral Legal asset pledged by borrowers that may be seized by lenders in case of nonpayment [582]

collective bargaining Process by which labor and management negotiate conditions of employment for union-represented workers [240]

collusion Illegal agreement between two or more companies to commit a wrongful act [92]

commercial bank Federal- or state-chartered financial institution accepting deposits that it uses to make loans and earn profits [520]

commercial paper Short-term securities, or notes, containing a borrower's promise to pay [583]

committee and team authority Authority granted to committees or work teams involved in a firm's daily operations [142]

commodities market Market in which futures contracts are traded [558]

common carrier Transporting company, such as a truck line or railroad, that transports goods for any shipper [374]

common stock Stock that guarantees corporate voting rights but has last claims over assets [45]

comparable worth Principle that women should receive the same pay for traditionally "female" jobs of the same worth to a company as traditionally "male" jobs [198]

comparative advantage A nation's ability to produce some products more cheaply or better than others [60]

comparative advertising Advertising strategy that directly compares two or more products [334]

compensation system Total package offered by a company to employees in return for their labor [191]

competition Vying among businesses for the same resources or customers [15]

compulsory arbitration Method of resolving a labor dispute in which both parties are legally required to accept the judgment of a neutral party [258]

computer graphics program Applications program that converts numeric and character data into pictorial information such as graphs and charts [457]

computer network Group of interconnected computer systems able to exchange information with one another from different locations [460]

computer system Electronic system designed to turn data into information [449]

conceptual skills Abilities to think in the abstract, diagnose and analyze different situations, and see beyond the present situation [121]

Congress of Industrial Organizations (CIO) Group of industrial unions formed in 1938 that rapidly organized the auto, steel, mining, meatpacking, paper, textile, and electrical industries [243]

consumer behavior The various facets of the process by which customers decide to purchase and consume products [285]

consumer goods Products purchased by consumers for personal use [270]

consumerism Form of social activism dedicated to protecting the rights of consumers in their dealings with businesses [92]

containerization Transportation method in which goods are sealed in containers at shipping sources and opened when they reach final destinations [374]

contingency approach Approach to managerial style holding that the appropriate behavior in any situation is contingent on the unique elements of that situation [231]

contingency planning Identifying aspects of a business or its environment that might entail changes in strategy [115]

contingent worker Employee hired to supplement an organization's permanent work force [203]

continuous improvement An ongoing commitment to improving products and processes in the pursuit of ever-increasing customer satisfaction [434]

contract carrier Independent transporting company that usually owns the vehicles in which it transports products [375]

controller Person who manages all of a firm's accounting activities (chief accounting officer) [479]

controlling Management process of monitoring an organization's performance to ensure that it is meeting its goals [118]

convenience good/service Inexpensive product purchased and consumed rapidly and regularly [303]

convenience store Retail store offering easy accessibility, extended hours, and fast service [368]

convertible bond Bond that can be retired by converting it to common stock [557]

cooperative Form of organization in which a group of sole proprietorships or partnerships agrees to work together for common benefits [44]

corporate bond Bond issued by a business as a source of long-term funding [556]

corporate culture The shared experiences, stories, beliefs, and norms that characterize an organization [123]

corporate governance Roles of shareholders, directors, and other managers in corporate decision making [45]

corporation Business that is legally considered an entity separate from its owners and is liable for its own debts; owners' liability extends to the limits of their investments [42]

cost of goods sold Total cost of obtaining materials for making the products sold by a firm during the year [489]

cost-of-living adjustment (COLA) Labor contract clause tying future raises to changes in consumer purchasing power [254]

coupon Sales promotion technique in which a certificate is issued entitling the buyer to a reduced price [343]

craft union Union representing workers whose common interest is a specific job [240]

creative selling Personal selling task in which salespeople try to persuade buyers to purchase products by providing information about their benefits [342]

credit Bookkeeping entry in a T-account that records decreases in assets [485]

credit policy Rules governing a firm's extension of credit to customers [485, 580]

credit union Financial institution that accepts deposits from, and makes loans to, only its members, usually employees of a particular organization [522]

crisis management An organization's methods for dealing with emergencies [116]

cumulative preferred stock Preferred stock on which dividends not paid in the past must be paid to stockholders before dividends can be paid to common stockholders [550]

currency Government-issued paper money and metal coins [515]

current asset Asset that can or will be converted into cash within the following year [486]

current liability Debt that must be paid within the year [488]

current ratio Solvency ratio that determines a firm's creditworthiness by measuring its ability to pay current liabilities [493]

customer departmentalization Departmentalization according to types of customers likely to buy a given product [137]

data Raw facts and figures [446]

data communication network Global network (such as the Internet) that permits users to send electronic messages and information quickly and economically [465]

database Centralized, organized collection of related data [456]

database management program Application program for creating, storing, searching, and manipulating an organized collection of data [457]

debenture Unsecured bond for which no specific property is pledged as security [556]

debit Bookkeeping entry in a T-account that records increases in assets [485]

debit card Plastic card that allows an individual to transfer money between accounts [533]

debt A firm's total liabilities [494]

debt financing Long-term borrowing from sources outside a company [584]

debt ratio Solvency ratio measuring a firm's ability to meet its long-term debts [494]

debt-to-owners' equity ratio (or **debt-to-equity ratio**) Solvency ratio describing the extent to which a firm is financed through borrowing [494]

decentralized organization Organization in which a great deal of decision-making authority is delegated to levels of management at points below the top [139]

decentralized system Form of computer system architecture in which processing is done in many locations by means of separate computers, databases, and personnel [460]

decision-making skills Skills in defining problems and selecting the best courses of action [121]

definition of the service package Identification of the features that characterize a service product [308]

delegation Assignment of a task, responsibility, or authority by a manager to a subordinate [139]

demand and supply schedule Assessment of the relationships between different levels of demand and supply at different price levels [12]

demand The willingness and ability of buyers to purchase a good or service [12]

demand curve Graph showing how many units of a product will be demanded (bought) at different prices [12]

demand deposit Bank account funds that may be withdrawn at any time [515]

democratic style Managerial style in which managers generally ask for input from subordinates but retain final decision-making power [229]

demographic variables Characteristics of populations that may be considered in developing a segmentation strategy [279]

demotion Action, such as removal to a lower position, taken by management in response to an employee's poor performance [190]

department store Large product line retailer characterized by organization into specialized departments [365]

departmentalization Process of grouping jobs into logical units [136]

depreciation Process of distributing the cost of an asset over its life [488]

depression Particularly severe and long-lasting recession [19]

derived demand Demand for industrial products that results from demand for consumer products [290]

desktop publishing Process of combining word-processing and graphics capability to produce virtually typeset-quality text from personal computers [459]

direct channel Distribution channel in which a product travels from producer to consumer without intermediaries [357]

direct investment Arrangement in which a firm buys or establishes tangible assets in another country [69]

direct mail Advertising medium in which messages are mailed directly to consumers' homes or places of business [336]

direct selling Form of nonstore retailing typified by door-to-door sales [369]

direct-response retailing Nonstore retailing by direct interaction with customers to inform them of products and to receive sales orders [368]

directing Management process of guiding and motivating employees to meet an organization's objectives [118]

disciplinary action Action taken by management in response to employee behavior that is considered dangerous or disruptive [190]

discount Price reduction offered as an incentive to purchase [320]

discount house Bargain retailer that generates large sales volume by offering goods at substantial price reductions [367]

discount rate Interest rate at which member banks can borrow money from the Federal Reserve [531]

diskette Portable, easily removed secondary storage device [451]

distribution Part of the marketing mix concerned with getting products from producers to consumers [277]

distribution center Warehouse providing short-term storage of goods for which demand is both constant and high [371]

distribution channel Network of interdependent companies through which a product passes from producer to end user [356]

distribution mix The combination of distribution channels by which a firm gets its products to end users [356]

diversity training Programs designed to improve employees' understanding of differences in co-workers' attitudes and behaviors [202]

divestiture The selling of one or more business units by a corporation [48]

division Department that resembles a separate business in producing and marketing its own products [144]

divisional organization Organizational structure in which corporate divisions operate as autonomous businesses under the larger corporate umbrella [144]

double taxation Situation in which taxes may be payable both by a corporation on its profits and by shareholders on dividend incomes [44]

double-entry accounting system Bookkeeping system that balances the accounting equation by recording the dual effects of every financial transaction [485]

Dow Jones Industrial Average Market index based on the prices for 30 of the largest industrial firms listed on the NYSE [563]

downsizing Process of consolidating internal operations to make a firm more flexible and productive [191]

drop shipper Limited-function merchant wholesaler who receives customer orders, negotiates with producers, takes title to goods, and arranges for shipment to customers [362]

dumping Practice of selling a product abroad for less than the comparable price charged at home [74]

earnings per share Profitability ratio measuring the size of the dividend that a firm can pay shareholders [496]

economic strike Strike usually triggered by stalemate over one or more mandatory bargaining items [256]

economic system A nation's system for allocating its resources among its citizens [6]

electronic funds transfer (EFT) Communication of fund-transfer information over wire, cable, or microwave [525]

electronic mail (e-mail) Computer system that electronically transmits letters, reports, and other information between computers [464]

electronic shopping Nonstore retailing in which information about the seller's products and services is connected to consumers' computers, allowing consumers to receive the information and purchase the products in the home [369]

electronic spreadsheet Application program with a row-and-column format that allows users to store, manipulate, and compare numeric data [457]

embargo Government order banning exportation or importation of a particular product or all the products from a particular country [72]

emotional motives Reasons for purchasing a product that are based on nonobjective factors [287]

employee empowerment Concept that all employees are valuable contributors to a firm's business and should be entrusted with decisions regarding their work [435]

Employee Retirement Income Security Act (ERISA) Federal law regulating private pension plans [194]

employee stock ownership plan (ESOP) Arrangement in which a corporation holds its own stock in trust for its employees, who gradually receive ownership of the stock and control its voting rights [49]

employment at will Principle, increasingly modified by legislation and judicial decision, that organizations should be able to retain or dismiss employees at their discretion [199]

entrepreneur Businessperson who accepts both the risks and the opportunities involved in creating and operating a new business venture [7, 162]

environmental analysis Process of scanning the business environment for threats and opportunities [114]

Environmental Protection Agency (EPA) Federal agency established to protect and encourage the conservation of natural resources [90]

equal employment opportunity Legally mandated nondiscrimination in employment on the basis of race, creed, sex, or national origin [195]

equity financing Use of common stock or retained earnings to raise long-term funding [585]

equity theory Theory of motivation holding that people evaluate their treatment by employers relative to the treatment of others [218]

ethical behavior Behavior conforming to generally accepted social norms concerning beneficial and harmful actions [82]

ethics Beliefs about what is right and wrong or good and bad in actions that affect others [82]

exchange rate Rate at which the currency of one nation can be exchanged for that of another [61]

exclusive distribution Strategy by which a manufacturer grants exclusive rights to distribute or sell a product to a limited number of wholesalers or retailers in a given geographic area [360]

executive information system (EIS) Easy-access information cluster specially designed for upper-level managers [464]

expectancy theory Theory of motivation holding that people are motivated to work toward rewards that they want and that they believe they have a reasonable chance of obtaining [218]

expense item Industrial product purchased and consumed rap-idly and regularly [304]

experimentation Market research technique that attempts to compare the responses of the same or similar people under different circumstances [285]

expert system Form of artificial intelligence that attempts to imitate the behavior of human experts in a particular field [463]

export Product made or grown domestically but shipped and sold abroad [56]

exporter Firm that distributes and sells products to one or more foreign countries [66]

external environment Outside factors that influence marketing programs by posing opportunities or threats [270]

external failures Reducible costs incurred after defective products have left a plant [429]

factoring Practice of raising funds by selling a firm's accounts receivable to another company [584]

factors of production Resources used in the production of goods and services (natural resources, labor, capital, and entrepreneurs) [7]

factory outlet Bargain retailer owned by the manufacturer whose products it sells [367]

Fair Labor Standards Act Federal law (1938) setting minimum wage and maximum number of hours in the work week [250]

fax machine Machine that can transmit copies of documents (text and graphics) over telephone lines [463]

feature Tangible quality that a company builds into a product [302]

Federal Deposit Insurance Corporation (FDIC) Federal agency that guarantees the safety of all deposits up to $100,000 in the financial institutions that it insures [526]

Federal Reserve System (the Fed) The central bank of the United States, which acts as the government's bank, serves member commercial banks, and controls the nation's money supply [527]

fiber optic cable Hairlike glass fiber cables that carry data in the form of light pulses [461]

FIFO (first-in-first-out) method Method of valuing inventories that assumes that older inventories (first in) are sold first [487]

finance (or corporate finance) Activities concerned with determining a firm's long-term investments, obtaining the funds to pay for them, and conducting the firm's everyday financial activities [578]

finance company Nondeposit institution that specializes in making loans to businesses and consumers [523]

financial accounting system Field of accounting concerned with external users of a company's financial information [479]

financial control Management process of checking actual performance against plans to ensure that desired financial results occur [579]

financial manager Manager responsible for planning and controlling the acquisition and dispersal of a firm's financial resources [568]

financial plan A firm's strategies for reaching a desired financial position [579]

financial statement Any of several types of reports summarizing a company's financial status to aid in managerial decision making [486]

firewall Software program that prevents outsiders to access a company's network [455]

first-line managers Managers responsible for supervising the work of employees [119]

fiscal policies Government economic policies centered on how the government collects and spends its revenues [25]

fiscal year Twelve-month period designated for annual financial reporting purposes [483]

fixed asset Asset with long-term use or value, such as land, buildings, and equipment [488]

fixed cost Cost unaffected by the quantity of a product produced or sold [316]

fixed-position layout Product layout that brings production activities (labor, materials, and equipment) to the location where the work is done [401]

flextime programs Method of increasing job satisfaction by allowing workers to adjust work schedules on a daily or weekly basis [225]

float Total amount of checks written but not yet cleared through the Federal Reserve [528]

focus group Market research technique in which a group of people is gathered, presented with an issue, and asked to discuss it in depth [284]

follow-up Production control activity for ensuring that production decisions are being implemented [404]

forecast Facet of a production plan that predicts future demand [398]

foreign currency exchange rate Value of a nation's currency as determined by market forces [497]

franchise Arrangement in which a buyer (franchisee) purchases the right to sell the good or service of the seller (franchiser) [171]

free-rein style Managerial style in which managers typically serve as advisers to subordinates, who are allowed to make decisions [229]

freight forwarder Transporting company that leases bulk space from other carriers to be resold to firms making smaller shipments [375]

full-service merchant wholesaler Merchant wholesaler who provides credit, marketing, and merchandising services in addition to traditional buying and selling services [362]

functional departmentalization Departmentalization according to groups' functions or activities [137]

functional organization Form of business organization in which authority is determined by the relationships between group functions and activities [144]

futures contract Agreement to purchase specified amounts of a commodity at a given price on a set date [558]

gain-sharing plan Incentive program for distributing bonuses to employees whose performances improve productivity [193]

general partner Partner who actively manages a firm and who has unlimited liability for its debts [40]

general partnership Business with two or more owners, who share in both the operation of the firm and financial responsibility for its debts [38]

generally accepted accounting principles (GAAP) Accepted rules and procedures governing the content and form of financial reports [481]

geographic departmentalization Departmentalization according to areas served by a business [137]

geographic variables Geographic units that may be considered in developing a segmentation strategy [279]

giveback clause Labor contract clause by which a union agrees to give up wage increases won in earlier contracts [254]

global perspective Company's approach to directing its marketing toward worldwide rather than local or regional markets [345]

globalization Process by which the world economy is becoming a single interdependent system [56]

goal Objective that a business plans to achieve [111]

goodwill Amount paid for an existing business above the value of its other assets [488]

government bond Bond issued by the federal government [554]

graphic user interface (GUI) Software that provides a visual display to help users select applications [452]

gross domestic product (GDP) Total value of all the goods and services consumed by one nation in a 1-year period [22, 423]

gross national product (GNP) Total value of all the goods and services produced by an economic system in a 1-year period [22]

gross profit (or **gross margin**) Revenues from goods sold minus cost of goods sold [489]

growth Increase in the amount of goods and services produced by a nation's resources [21]

growth rate of productivity Annual increase in a nation's output over the previous year [418]

guaranteed loans program Program in which the SBA guarantees to repay 75 to 85 percent of small business commercial loans up to $750,000 [169]

hard disk Secondary storage device permanently installed in a computer [451]

hardware Physical components of a computer system[450]

Hawthorne effect Tendency for productivity to increase when workers believe they are receiving special attention from management [215]

hierarchy of human needs model Theory of motivation describing five levels of human needs and arguing that basic needs must be fulfilled before people work to satisfy higher-level needs [216]

high-contact system Level of customer contact in which the customer receives the service by participating as part of the system [394]

hub Central distribution outlet that controls all or most of a firm's distribution activities [375]

human relations Interactions between employers and employees and their attitudes toward one another [212]

human relations skills Skills in understanding and getting along with other people [121]

human resource management Development and administration of programs to enhance the quality and performance of a company's work force [184]

human resource managers Managers responsible for hiring, training, evaluating, and compensating employees [184]

hypermarket Very large product line retailer carrying a wide variety of unrelated products [366]

icon Small image in a GUI that enables users to select applications or functions [452]

immediate participation loans program Program in which small businesses are lent funds put up jointly by banks and the SBA [169]

import Product made or grown abroad but sold domestically [56]

importer Firm that buys products in foreign markets and then imports them for resale in its home country [66]

incentive program Special compensation program designed to motivate high performance [192]

income statement (or **profit-and-loss statement**) Financial statement listing a firm's annual revenues and expenses so that a bottom line shows annual profit or loss [488]

independent agent Foreign individual or organization who agrees to represent an exporter's interests [67]

individual retirement account (IRA) Tax-deferred pension fund with which wage earners supplement other retirement funds [524]

industrial distribution Network of channel members involved in the flow of manufactured goods to industrial customers [358]

industrial goods Products purchased by companies to produce other products [270]

industrial market Organizational market consisting of firms that buy goods that are either converted into products or used up during production [289]

industrial selling Personal selling situation in which products are sold to businesses, either for manufacturing other products or for resale [341]

industrial unionism Organizing of workers by industry rather than skill or occupation [243]

inelastic demand Demand for industrial products that is not largely affected by price changes [290]

inflation Period of widespread price increases throughout an economic system [17]

informal organization Network, unrelated to the firm's formal authority structure, of everyday social interactions among company employees [147]

information The meaningful, useful interpretation of data [446]

information managers Managers responsible for designing and implementing systems to gather, organize, and distribute information [446]

initial public offering (IPO) First public offering of common stock by a company [586]

input device Part of the computer system that enters data into it [450]

insider trading Use of confidential information to gain from the purchase or sale of stocks [95, 568]

institutional advertising Advertising promoting a firm's long-term image [339]

institutional investors Large investors, such as mutual funds and pension funds, that purchase large blocks of corporate stock [49]

institutional market Organizational market consisting of such buyers of goods and services as hospitals, churches, museums, and charitable organizations [290]

insurance company Nondeposit institution that invests funds collected as premiums charged for insurance coverage [522]

intangible asset Nonphysical asset, such as a patent or trademark, that has economic value in the form of expected benefit [488]

intensive distribution Strategy by which a product is distributed through as many channels as possible [360]

intermediary Individual or firm that helps to distribute a product [356]

intermediate goals Goals set for a period of 1 to 5 years into the future [113]

intermodal transportation Combined use of several different modes of transportation [373]

international competition Competitive marketing of domestic against foreign products [273]

international firm Firm that conducts a significant portion of its business in foreign countries [66]

International Monetary Fund (IMF) United Nations agency consisting of about 150 nations that have combined resources to promote stable exchange rates, provide temporary short-term loans, and serve other purposes [538]

international organizational structures Approaches to organizational structure developed in response to the need to manufacture, purchase, and sell in global markets [146]

Internet Global data communication network serving thousands of computers with information on a wide array of topics and providing communication flows among certain private networks [466]

intranet Private network of internal Web sites and other sources of information available to a company's employees [467]

intrapreneuring Process of creating and maintaining the innovation and flexibility of a small business environment within the confines of a large organization [148]

inventory Materials and goods that are held by a company for future sale or use [580]

inventory control Warehouse operation that tracks inventory on hand and ensures that an adequate supply is in stock at all times [372, 405]

inventory turnover ratio Activity ratio measuring the average number of times that inventory is sold and restocked during the year [496]

investment banker Financial institution engaged in purchasing and reselling new securities [546]

job analysis Evaluation of the duties and qualities required by a job [184]

job description Outline of the objectives, tasks, and responsibilities of a job [184]

job enrichment Method of increasing job satisfaction by adding one or more motivating factors to job activities [222]

job redesign Method of increasing job satisfaction by creating a more satisfactory fit between workers and their jobs [222]

job relatedness Principle that all employment decisions should be based on the requirements of the jobs in question [184]

job satisfaction Degree of enjoyment that people derive from their jobs [212]

job specialization The process of identifying the specific jobs that need to be done and designating the people who will perform them [135]

job specification Description of the skills, education, and experience required by a job [184]

joint venture (or **strategic alliance**) Collaboration between two or more organizations on an enterprise [49]

journal Chronological record of a firm's financial transactions, including a brief description of each [483]

just-in-time (JIT) production Production method that brings together all materials and parts needed at each production stage at the precise moment they are required [406]

Keogh plan Tax-deferred pension plan for the self-employed [524]

label Part of product packaging that identifies its name, manufacturer, and contents [314]

labor (or **human resources**) The physical and mental capabilities of people as they contribute to economic production [7]

labor productivity Partial productivity ratio calculated by dividing total output by total labor inputs [423]

Labor-Management Relations Act (Taft-Hartley Act) Federal law (1947) defining certain union practices as unfair and illegal [251]

Labor-Management Reporting and Disclosure Act (Landrum-Griffin Act) Federal law (1959) imposing regulations on internal union procedures, including elections of national leaders and filing of financial disclosure statements [251]

language program System program (such as FORTRAN) that allows users to give computers their own instructions [452]

law of demand Principle that buyers will purchase (demand) more of a product as its price drops and less as its price increases [12]

law of one price Principle holding that identical products should sell for the same price in all countries [536]

law of supply Principle that producers will offer (supply) more of a product for sale as its price rises and less as its price drops [12]

leadership Process of motivating others to work to meet specific objectives [228]

ledger Record, divided into accounts and usually compiled on a monthly basis, containing summaries of all journal transactions [483]

letter of credit Bank promise, issued for a buyer, to pay a designated firm a certain amount of money if specified conditions are met [524]

level of productivity Dollar value of goods and services relative to the resources used to produce them [419]

leverage Ability to finance an investment through borrowed funds [495]

liability Debt owed by a firm to an outside organization or individual [484]

licensed brand Brand-name product for whose name the seller has purchased the right from an organization or individual [311]

licensing arrangement Arrangement in which firms choose foreign individuals or organizations to manufacture or market their products in another country [68]

LIFO (last-in-first-out) method Method of valuing inventories that assumes that those received most recently (last in) are sold first [487]

limit order Order authorizing the purchase of a stock only if its price is equal to or less than a specified amount [565]

limited liability Legal principle holding investors liable for a firm's debts only to the limits of their personal investments in it [43]

limited partner Partner who does not share in a firm's management and is liable for its debts only to the limit of his or her investment [40]

limited partnership Type of partnership consisting of limited partners and an active or managing partner [40]

limited-function merchant wholesaler Merchant wholesaler who provides a limited range of services [362]

line authority Organizational structure in which authority flows in a direct chain of command from the top of the company to the bottom [141]

line department Department directly linked to the production and sales of a specific product [141]

line of credit Standing arrangement in which a lender agrees to make available a specified amount of funds upon the borrower's request [583]

liquidity Ease with which an asset can be converted into cash [486]

liquidity ratio Solvency ratio measuring a firm's ability to pay its immediate debts [493]

load fund Mutual fund in which investors are charged sales commissions when they buy in or sell out [557]

local area network (LAN) Network of computers and workstations, usually within a company, that are linked together by cable [460]

local content law Law requiring that products sold in a particular country be at least partly made there [74]

local development companies (LDCs) program Program in which the SBA works with local for-profit or nonprofit organizations seeking to boost a community's economy [169]

local union (local) Union organized at the level of a single company, plant, or small geographic region [249]

lockout Management tactic whereby workers are denied access to the employer's workplace [257]

long-term goals Goals set for extended periods of time, typically 5 years or more into the future [113]

long-term liability Debt that is not due for more than 1 year [488]

low-contact system Level of customer contact in which the customer need not be a part of the system to receive the service [395]

M-1 Measure of the money supply that includes only the most liquid (spendable) forms of money [515]

M-2 Measure of the money supply that includes all the components of M-1 plus the forms of money that can be easily converted into spendable form [516]

mail order (or **catalog marketing**) Form of nonstore retailing in which customers place orders for catalog merchandise received through the mail [368]

main memory Part of the computer CPU that houses the memory of programs it needs to operate [451]

mainframe Computer whose capacity and speed enable it to serve many users simultaneously [460]

management Process of planning, organizing, directing, and controlling an organization's resources in order to achieve its goals [116]

management advisory services Specialized accounting services to help managers resolve a variety of business problems [481]

management consultant Independent outside specialist hired to help managers solve business problems [169]

management development program Program designed to enhance the conceptual, analytical, and problem-solving skills of management personnel [189]

management information system (MIS) System for transforming raw data into information that can be used in decision making [446]

management of objectives (MBO) Set of procedures involving both managers and subordinates in setting goals and evaluating progress [220]

managerial (or **management**) **accounting system** Field of accounting that serves internal users of a company's financial information [479]

managerial style Pattern of behavior that a manager exhibits in dealing with subordinates [229]

manufacturing resource planning (MRP II) Advanced version of MRP that ties together all parts of an organization into its production activities [407]

margin Percentage of the total sales price that a buyer must put up to place an order for stock or futures contracts [559]

market Mechanism for exchange between buyers and sellers of a particular good or service [8]

market economy Economy in which individuals control production and allocation decisions through supply and demand [8]

market index Summary of price trends in a specific industry or the stock market as a whole [563]

market order Order to buy or sell a security at the market price prevailing at the time the order is placed [565]

market price (or **equilibrium price**) Profit-maximizing price at which the quantity of goods demanded and the quantity of goods supplied are equal [14]

market research The study of consumer needs and wants and the ways in which sellers can best meet them [283]

market segmentation Process of dividing a market into categories of customer types [278]

market share As a percentage, sales for a specific company's product as compared to the total market for that product [315]

market value Current price of a share of stock in the stock market [547]

marketing The process of planning and executing the conception, pricing, promotion, and distribution of ideas, goods, and services to create exchanges that satisfy individual and organizational objectives [270]

marketing concept Philosophy that in order to be profitable, a business must focus on identifying and satisfying consumer wants [36]

marketing manager Manager who plans and implements the marketing activities that result in the transfer of products from producer to consumer [273]

marketing mix The combination of product, pricing, promotion, and distribution strategies used to market products [274]

marketing plan Detailed and focused strategy for gearing marketing efforts to meet consumer needs and wants [273]

markup Amount added to an item's cost in order to sell it at a profit [316]

master limited partnership Form of organization that sells shares to investors who receive profits and pay taxes on individual income from profits[41]

master production schedule Schedule showing which products will be produced, when production will take place, and what resources will be used [404]

material requirement planning (MRP) Production method in which a bill of materials is used to ensure that the right amounts of materials are delivered to the right place at the right time [406]

materials productivity Partial productivity ratio calculated by dividing total output by total material inputs [422]

materials handling Warehouse operation involving the transportation, arrangement, and orderly retrieval of goods in inventory [372]

materials management Planning, organizing, and controlling the flow of materials from design through distribution of finished goods [405]

matrix structure Organizational structure in which teams are formed and team members report to two or more managers [145]

media mix Combination of advertising media chosen to carry message about a product [338]

mediation Method of resolving a labor dispute in which a third party suggests, but does not impose, a settlement [257]

mentor Experienced manager who sponsors and teaches younger, less experienced managers [189]

merchandise inventory Cost of merchandise that has been acquired for sale to customers and is still on hand [487]

merchant wholesaler Independent wholesaler who takes legal possession of goods produced by a variety of manufacturers and then resells them to other businesses [362]

merger The union of two corporations to form a new corporation [47]

merit salary system Incentive program linking compensation to performance in nonsales jobs [193]

microcomputer (or **personal computer**) Smallest, slowest, least expensive form of computer [459]

microprocessor chip Single silicon chip containing a computer's central processing unit [461]

middle managers Managers responsible for implementing the strategies, policies, and decisions made by top managers [119]

minicomputer Computer whose capacity, speed, and cost fall between those of microcomputers and mainframes [460]

minority enterprise small business investment company (MESBIC) Federally sponsored company that specializes in financing minority-owned and -operated businesses [168]

mission statement Organization's statement of how it will achieve its purpose in the environment in which it conducts its business [113]

missionary selling Personal selling tasks in which salespeople promote their firms and products rather than try to close sales [342]

mixed market economy Economic system featuring characteristics of both planned and market economies [9]

modem Device that provides a computer-to-computer link over telephone wires [461]

monetary policies Government economic policies that focus on controlling the size of a nation's money supply [25]

monetary policy Policies by which the Federal Reserve manages the nation's money supply and interest rates [529]

money Any object that is portable, divisible, durable, and stable and serves as a medium of exchange, a store of value, and a unit of account [514]

money market mutual fund Fund of short-term, low-risk financial securities purchased with the assets of investor-owners pooled by a nonbank institution [516]

monopolistic competition Market or industry characterized by a large number of buyers and a large number of sellers trying to differentiate products from those of competitors [16]

monopoly Market or industry in which there is only one producer, which can therefore set the prices of its products [17]

morale Overall attitude employees have toward their workplace [212]

motivation The set of forces that cause people to behave in certain ways [214]

multimedia communication system Connected network of communication appliances (such as faxes or TVs) that may be linked to forms of mass media (such as print publications or TV programming) [467]

multinational firm Firm that designs, produces, and markets products in many nations [67]

municipal bond Bond issued by a state or local government [554]

mutual fund Company that pools investments from individuals and organizations to purchase a portfolio of stocks, bonds, and short-term securities [557]

mutual savings bank Financial institution whose depositors are owners sharing in its profits [522]

National Association of Securities Dealers Automated Quotation (NASDAQ) system Organization of over-the-counter dealers who own, buy, and sell their own securities over an electronic network [552]

national bank Commercial bank chartered by the federal government [520]

national brand Brand-name product produced by, widely distributed by, and carrying the name of a manufacturer [311]

national debt Total amount that a nation owes its creditors [24]

National Labor Relations Act (Wagner Act) Federal law (1935) protecting the rights of workers to form unions, bargain collectively, and engage in strikes to achieve their goals [250]

National Labor Relations Board (NLRB) Federal agency established by the National Labor Relations Act to enforce its provisions [250]

natural monopoly Industry in which one company can most efficiently supply all needed goods or services [17]

natural resources Materials supplied by nature (such as land, water, mineral deposits, and trees) [7]

net income (or **net profit** or **net earnings**) Gross profit minus operating expenses and income taxes [490]

net profit margin (or **return on sales**) Profitability ratio indicating the percentage of its income that is a firm's profit [495]

networking Interactions among businesspeople for the purpose of discussing mutual problems and opportunities and perhaps pooling resources [170]

no-load fund Mutual fund in which investors pay no sales commissions when they buy in or sell out [557]

Norris-LaGuardia Act Federal law (1932) limiting the ability of courts to issue injunctions prohibiting certain union activities [250]

observation Market research technique that involves simply watching and recording consumer behavior [284]

Occupational Safety and Health Administration (OSHA) Federal agency that sets and enforces guidelines for protecting workers from unsafe conditions and potential health hazards in the workplace [199]

odd lot Purchase or sale of stock in fractions of round lots [566]

odd-even pricing Psychological pricing tactic based on the premise that customers prefer prices not stated in even dollar amounts [320]

off-price store Bargain retailer that buys excess inventories from high-quality manufacturers and sells them at discounted prices [367]

oligopoly Market or industry characterized by a handful of (generally very large) sellers with the power to influence the prices of their products [16]

on-the-job training Training, sometimes informal, conducted while an employee is at work [188]

open promotion system System by which employees apply, test, and interview for available jobs whose requirements are posted [187]

open-book credit Form of trade credit in which sellers ship merchandise on faith that payment will be forthcoming [582]

open-market operations The Federal Reserve's sales and purchases of securities in the open market [531]

operating expenses Costs, other than the cost of goods sold, incurred in producing a good or service [490]

operating income Gross profit minus operating expenses [490]

operational plans Plans setting short-term targets for daily, weekly, or monthly performance [115]

operations control Process of monitoring production performance by comparing results with plans [404]

operations information system Computer system used to manage production and manufacturing operations [464]

operations (or **production**) **management** Systematic direction and control of the processes that transform resources into finished products [392]

operations (or **production**) **managers** Managers responsible for production, inventory, and quality control [392]

operations process Set of methods used in the production of a good or service [393]

order cycle time In customer service operations, total time elapsed between placement and receipt of orders [375]

order processing Personal selling task in which salespeople receive orders and see to their handling and delivery [342, 375]

organization chart Diagram depicting a company's structure and showing employees where they fit into its operations [134]

organizational analysis Process of analyzing a firm's strengths and weaknesses [114]

organizational structure Specification of the jobs to be done within an organization and the ways in which they relate to one another [134]

organizing Management process of determining how best to arrange an organization's resources and activities into a coherent structure [116]

output device Part of a computer system that presents results, either visually or in printed form [451]

over-the-counter (OTC) market Organization of securities dealers formed to trade stock outside the formal institutional setting of the organized stock exchanges [552]

owners' equity Amount of money that owners would receive if they sold all of a firm's assets and paid all of its liabilities [484]

packaging Physical container in which a product is sold, advertised, or protected [313]

paid-in capital Additional money, above proceeds from stock sale, paid directly to a firm by its owners [488]

par value Face value of a share of stock, set by the issuing company's board of directors [547]

partial productivity ratio Productivity measure that considers only certain input sources [422]

participative management and empowerment Method of increasing job satisfaction by giving employees a voice in the management of their jobs and the company [221]

pay for performance (or **variable pay**) Individual incentive that rewards a manager for especially productive output [193]

pay-for-knowledge plan Incentive program to encourage employees to learn new skills or become proficient at different jobs [193]

penetration pricing Setting an initial low price to establish a new product in the market [318]

pension fund Nondeposit pool of funds managed to provide retirement income for its members [522]

performance appraisal Evaluation, often in writing, of an employee's job performance [189]

performance quality The performance features offered by a product [425]

personal selling Promotional tool in which a salesperson communicates one-on-one with potential customers [340]

erson-job matching Process of matching the right person to the right job [184]

persuasive advertising Advertising strategy that tries to influence consumers to buy one company's products instead of those of its rivals [334]

physical distribution Activities needed to move a product efficiently from manufacturer to consumer [371]

picketing Labor action in which workers publicize their grievances at the entrance to an employer's facility [257]

planned economy Economy that relies on a centralized government to control all or most factors of production and to make all or most production and allocation decisions [7]

planning Management process of determining what an organization needs to do and how best to get it done [116]

pledging accounts receivable Using accounts receivable as loan collateral [582]

point-of-purchase (POP) display Sales promotion technique in which product displays are located in certain areas to stimulate purchase [343]

point-of-sale (POS) terminal Electronic device that allows customers to pay for retail purchases with debit cards [533]

positioning Process of establishing an identifiable product image in the minds of consumers [331]

preferred stock Stock that guarantees its holders fixed dividends and priority claims over assets but no corporate voting rights [45]

premium Sales promotion technique in which offers of free or reduced-price items are used to stimulate purchases [344, 593]

prepaid expense Expense, such as prepaid rent, that is paid before the upcoming period in which it is due [487]

presentation graphics software Application that enables users to create visual presentation that can include animation and sound [458]

price leader Dominant firm that establishes product prices that other companies follow [318]

price lining Setting a limited number of prices for certain categories of products [319]

price skimming Setting an initial high price to cover new product costs and generate a profit [318]

price-earnings ratio Current price of a stock divided by the firm's current annual earnings per share [560]

pricing Process of determining what a company will receive in exchange for its products [314]

pricing objectives Goals that producers hope to attain in pricing products for sale [314]

primary data Data developed through new research [284]

primary securities market Market in which new stocks and bonds are traded [546]

prime rate Interest rate available to a bank's most creditworthy customers [522]

private accountant Salaried accountant hired by a business to carry out its day-to-day financial activities [482]

private brand (or **private label**) Brand-name product that a wholesaler or retailer has commissioned from a manufacturer [313]

private carrier Manufacturer or retailer that maintains its own transportation system [375]

private corporation Corporation whose stock is held by only a few people and is not available for sale to the general public [43]

private enterprise Economic system that allows individuals to pursue their own interests without undue government restriction [14]

private property The right to buy, own, use, and sell almost any form of property [14]

private warehouse Warehouse owned by and providing storage for a single company [371]

privatization Process of converting government enterprises into privately owned companies [9]

process departmentalization Departmentalization according to production process used to create a good or service [137]

process layout Spatial arrangement of production activities that groups equipment and people according to function [400]

product Good, service, or idea that is marketed to fill consumer needs and wants [274]

product adaptation Product modified to have greater appeal in foreign markets [310]

product departmentalization Departmentalization according to specific products being created [137]

product differentiation Creation of a product or product image that differs enough from existing products to attract consumers [275]

product extension Existing, unmodified product that is marketed globally [310]

product layout Spatial arrangement of production activities designed to move resources through a smooth, fixed sequence of steps [400]

product life cycle (PLC) Series of stages in a product's profit-producing life [309]

product line Group of similar products intended for a similar group of buyers who will use them in similar ways [304]

product mix Group of products that a firm makes available for sale [304]

product use variables Consumer characteristics based on the ways in which a product is used, the brand loyalty it enjoys, and the reasons for which it is purchased [283]

production era Period during the early twentieth century in which U.S. business focused almost primarily on improving productivity and manufacturing efficiency [36]

productivity Measure of economic growth that compares how much a system produces with the resources needed to produce it [22]

profit center Separate company unit responsible for its own costs and profits [136]

profit-sharing plan Incentive program for giving employees company profits above a certain level [193]

profitability ratio Financial ratio for measuring a firm's potential earnings [492]

profits The difference between a business's revenues and its expenses [6]

program Set of instructions used by a computer to perform specified activities [451]

program trading Large purchase or sale of a group of stocks, often triggered by computerized trading programs that can be launched without human supervision or control [567]

promissory note Form of trade credit in which buyers sign promise-to-pay agreements before merchandise is shipped [582]

promotion Aspect of the marketing mix concerned with the most effective techniques for selling a product [330]

promotional mix Combination of tools used to promote a product [332]

prospecting Step in the personal selling process in which salespeople identify potential customers [342]

prospectus Registration statement filed with the SEC before the issuance of a new security [568]

protectionism Practice of protecting domestic business at the expense of free-market competition [73]

proxy Authorization granted by a shareholder for someone else to vote his or her shares [46]

psychographic variables Consumer characteristics, such as lifestyles, opinions, interests, and attitudes, that may be considered in developing a segmentation strategy [282]

psychological pricing Pricing tactic that takes advantage of the fact that consumers do not always respond rationally to stated prices [320]

public corporation Corporation whose stock is widely held and available for sale to the general public [43]

public relations Company-influenced publicity directed at building good will between an organization and potential customers [344]

public warehouse Independently owned and operated warehouse that stores goods for many firms [371]

publicity Promotional tool in which information about a company or product is transmitted by general mass media [344]

pull strategy Promotional strategy designed to appeal directly to customers who will demand a product from retailers [332]

pure competition Market or industry characterized by a very large number of small firms producing an identical product [16]

pure risk Risk involving only the possibility of loss or no loss [592]

push strategy Promotional strategy designed to encourage wholesalers or retailers to market products to consumers [332]

qualifying Step in the personal selling process in which salespeople determine whether prospects have the authority and ability to pay [342]

quality A product's fitness for use; its success in offering features that consumers want [416]

quality control Management of the production process designed to manufacture goods or supply services that meet specific quality standards [407]

quality improvement (QI) team TQM tool in which groups of employees work together to improve quality [429]

quality ownership Principle of total quality management that holds that

quality belongs to each person who creates it while performing a job [426]

quality reliability Consistency of a product's quality from unit to unit [425]

quick (or **acid-test**) **ratio** Solvency ratio for determining a firm's ability to meet emergency demands for cash [493]

quick asset Cash plus assets one step removed from cash (marketable securities and accounts receivable) [493]

quota Restriction on the number of products of a certain type that can be imported into a country [72]

rack jobber Limited-function merchant wholesaler who sets up and maintains display racks in retail stores [362]

random access memory (RAM) Short-term memory that is active while the computer is performing its functions [451]

rational motives Reasons for purchasing a product that are based on a logical evaluation of product attributes [287]

read-only memory (ROM) Secondary storage device that can hold instructions to be read by the computer but accepts no written instructions [451]

real gross national product Gross national product adjusted for inflation and changes in the value of a country's currency [22]

real-time processing Method of entering data and processing them immediately [457]

recession Period characterized by decreases in employment, income, and production [19]

reengineering Quality improvement process that entails rethinking an organization's approach to productivity and quality [432]

registered bond Bond bearing the name of the holder and registered with the issuing company [556]

reinforcement Theory that behavior can be encouraged or discouraged by means of rewards or punishments, respectively [219]

reintroduction Process of reviving for new markets products that are obsolete in older ones [310]

relationship marketing Strategy that emphasizes lasting relationships with customers and supplies [270]

reminder advertising Advertising strategy that tries to keep a product's name in the consumer's mind [334]

reseller market Organizational market consisting of intermediaries who buy and resell finished goods [289]

reserve requirement Percentage of its deposits that a bank must hold in cash or on deposit with the Federal Reserve [531]

responsibility Duty to perform an assigned task [138]

retail selling Personal selling situation in which products are sold for buyers' personal or household use [341]

retailer Intermediary who sells products directly to consumers [356]

retained earnings Earnings retained by a firm for its use rather than paid as dividends [488]

return on investment (or **return on equity**) Profitability ratio measuring income earned for each dollar invested [496]

revenues Funds that flow into a business from the sale of goods or services [489]

reverse discrimination Practice of discriminating against well-represented groups by overhiring members of underrepresented groups [197]

revolving credit agreement Arrangement in which a lender agrees to make funds available on a continuing basis [583]

right-to-work laws Statutes making it illegal to require union membership as a condition of employment [251]

risk avoidance Practice of avoiding risk by declining or ceasing to participate in an activity [592]

risk control Practice of minimizing the frequency or severity of losses from risky activities [592]

risk management Process of conserving the firm's earning power and assets by

reducing the threat of losses due to uncontrollable events [592]

risk retention Practice of covering a firm's losses with its own funds [593]

risk transfer Practice of transferring a firm's risk to another firm [593]

risk–return relationship Principle that safer investments tend to offer lower returns and riskier investments tend to offer higher returns [588]

risk Uncertainty about future events [592]

round lot Purchase or sale of stock in units of 100 shares [566]

royalty Payment made to a license granter from a licensee in return for the rights to market the licenser's product [68]

salary Compensation in the form of money paid for discharging the responsibilities of a job [191]

sales agent/broker Independent intermediary who usually represents many manufacturers and sells to wholesalers or retailers [357]

sales office Office maintained by a manufacturer as a contact point with its customers [359]

sales promotion Short-term promotional activity designed to stimulate consumer buying or cooperation from distributors and sales agents [343]

savings and loan association (S&L) Financial institution accepting deposits and making loans primarily for home mortgages [522]

scientific management Theory of management that uses scientific analysis of individual jobs to increase productivity and efficiency [214]

scrambled merchandising Retail practice of carrying any product that is expected to sell well regardless of a store's original product offering [366]

secondary data Data readily available as a result of previous research [284]

secondary securities market Market in which existing stocks and bonds are traded [546]

secondary storage Any medium (such as disks) for storing data or information outside the computer's CPU [451]

secured bond Bond backed by pledges of assets to the bondholders [556]

secured loan Loan for which the borrower must provide collateral [582]

securities Stocks and bonds representing secured, or asset-based, claims by investors against issuers [546]

Securities and Exchange Commission (SEC) Federal agency that administers U.S. securities laws to protect the investing public and maintain smoothly functioning markets [568]

securities investment dealer (broker) Nondeposit institution that buys and sells stocks and bonds both for investors and for its own accounts [523]

selective credit controls Federal Reserve authority to set both margin requirements for consumer stock purchases and credit rules for other consumer purchases [531]

selective distribution Strategy by which a company uses only wholesalers and retailers who give special attention to specific products [360]

separation (or **termination**) Dismissal of an employee, usually for unacceptably poor performance [190]

serial bond Bond retired when the issuer redeems portions of the issue at different preset dates [557]

server Any user-shared component (such as a minicomputer) at the center of a local area network [461]

Service Corps of Retired Executives (SCORE) SBA program in which retired executives work with small businesses on a volunteer basis [170]

service flow analysis Method for analyzing a service by showing the flow of processes that constitute it [402]

service process design Three aspects (process selection, worker requirements, and facilities requirements) of developing a service product [308]

services Intangible products, such as time, expertise, or some activity, that can be purchased [270]

shop steward Union employee who acts as liaison between union members and supervisors [249]

shopping good/service Moderately expensive, infrequently purchased product [303]

short sale Stock sale in which investors borrow securities from their brokers to be sold and then replaced at a specified date [567]

short-term goals Goals set for the very near future, typically less than 1 year [113]

shortage Situation in which quantity demanded exceeds quantity supplied [14]

sinking fund provision Method for retiring bonds whereby the issuer puts enough money into a bank account to redeem the bonds at maturity [557]

slowdown Labor action in which workers perform jobs at a slower than normal pace [257]

small business Independently owned and managed business that does not dominate its market [156]

Small Business Administration (SBA) Federal agency charged with assisting small businesses [156]

Small Business Development Center (SBDC) SBA program designed to consolidate information from various disciplines and to make it available to small businesses [170]

Small Business Institute (SBI) SBA program in which college and university students and instructors work with small businesspeople to help solve specific problems [170]

Small Business Investment Company (SBIC) Federally licensed company that borrows money from the SBA to invest in or make loans to small businesses [168]

social audit Systematic analysis of a firm's success in using funds earmarked for meeting its social responsibility goals [98]

social obligation approach Approach to social responsibility by which a company meets only minimum legal requirements in its commitments to groups and individuals in its social environment [96]

social reaction approach Approach to social responsibility by which a company, if specifically asked to do so, exceeds legal minimums in its commitments to groups and individuals in its social environment [96]

social response approach Approach to social responsibility by which a company actively seeks opportunities to contribute to the well-being of groups and individuals in its social environment [96]

social responsibility The attempt of a business to balance its commitments to groups and individuals in its environment, including customers, other businesses, employees, and investors [85]

socialism Planned economic system in which the government owns and operates only selected major sources of production [10]

software Programs that instruct a computer in what to do [452]

sole proprietorship Business owned and usually operated by one person, who is responsible for all of its debts [37]

solvency ratio Financial ratio, both short- and long-term, for estimating the risk in investing in a firm [492]

span of control Number of people supervised by one manager [139]

specialty good/service Expensive, rarely purchased product [304]

specialty store Retail store carrying one product line or category of related products [366]

speculative risk Risk involving the possibility of gain or loss [592]

speed to market Strategy of introducing new products to respond quickly to customer or market changes [307]

spin-off Taking one or more business units from an existing corporation and setting it up as a new, independent corporation [48]

stability Condition in which the balance between the money available in an economy and the goods produced in it remains about the same [17]

staff authority Authority based on expertise that usually involves advising line managers [141]

staff members Advisers and counselors who aid line departments in making decisions but do not have the authority to make final decisions [141]

Standard & Poor's Composite Index Market index based on the performance of 400 industrial firms, 40 utilities, 40 financial institutions, and 20 transportation companies [565]

standardization Use of standard and uniform components in the production process [405]

state bank Commercial bank chartered by an individual state [520]

statement of cash flows Financial statement describing a firm's yearly cash receipts and cash payments [490]

stock A share of ownership in a corporation [45]

stock exchange Organization formed to provide an institutional setting in which stock can be traded [550]

stockholder (or **shareholder**) An owner of shares of stock in a corporation [45]

stop order Order authorizing the sale of a stock if its price falls to or below a specified level [566]

storage warehouse Warehouse providing storage for extended periods of time [371]

strategic alliance (or **joint venture**) Arrangement in which a company finds a foreign partner to contribute approximately equal amounts of resources and capital to a new business in the partner's country [68]

strategic goals Long-term goals derived directly from a firm's mission statement [113]

strategic plans Plans reflecting decisions about resource allocations, company priorities, and steps needed to meet strategic goals [115]

strategy formulation Creation of a broad program for defining and meeting an organization's goals [113]

strike Labor action in which employees temporarily walk off the job and refuse to work [256]

strikebreaker Worker hired as permanent or temporary replacement for a striking employee [257]

subsidy Government payment to help a domestic business compete with foreign firms [73]

substitute product Product that is different from those of competitors but can fulfill the same need [273]

supercomputer Largest, fastest, most expensive form of computer [460]

supermarket Large product line retailer offering a variety of food and food-related items in specialized departments [366]

supplier selection Process of finding and selecting suppliers from whom to buy [405]

supply The willingness and ability of producers to offer a good or service for sale [12]

supply curve Graph showing how many units of a product will be supplied (offered for sale) at different prices [12]

surplus Situation in which quantity supplied exceeds quantity demanded [14]

survey Market research technique using a questionnaire that is either mailed to individuals or used as the basis of interviews [284]

sympathy strike (or **secondary strike**) Strike in which one union strikes to support action initiated by another [256]

synthetic process Production process in which resources are combined to create finished products [394]

system architecture Location of a computer system's elements (data-entry and data-processing operations, database, data output, and computer staff) [460]

system program Software that tells the computer what resources to use and how to use them [452]

T-account Bookkeeping format for recording transactions that takes the shape of a *T* whose vertical line divides the account into debits (left side) and credits (right side) [485]

tactical plans Generally short-range plans concerned with implementing specific aspects of a company's strategic plans [115]

target market Group of people who have similar wants and needs and who can be expected to show interest in the same products [278]

tariff Tax levied on imported products [72]

technical skills Skills needed to perform specialized tasks [121]

telecommuting Form of flextime that allows people to perform some or all of a job away from standard office settings [226]

telemarketing Nonstore retailing in which the telephone is used to sell directly to consumers [369]

Theory X Theory of motivation holding that people are naturally irresponsible and uncooperative [216]

Theory Y Theory of motivation holding that people are naturally responsible and growth-oriented, self-motivated, and interested in being productive [216]

time deposit Bank funds that cannot be withdrawn without notice or transferred by check [516]

time management skills Skills associated with the productive use of time [122]

time-and-motion studies Scientific management studies using industrial engineering techniques to analyze each facet of a job in order to determine how to perform it most efficiently [214]

top managers Managers responsible to the board of directors and stockholders for a firm's overall performance and effectiveness [119]

total factor productivity ratio Productivity measure that considers all types of input resources (labor, capital, materials, energy, and purchased business services) [422]

total quality management (TMQ) (or **quality assurance**) The sum of all activities involved in getting high-quality products into the marketplace [424]

trade acceptance Trade draft that has been signed by the buyer [582]

trade credit Granting of credit by one firm to another [582]

trade deficit Situation in which a country's imports exceed its exports, creating a negative balance of trade [60]

trade draft Form of trade credit in which buyers must sign statements of payment terms attached to merchandise by sellers [582]

trade show Sales promotion technique in which various members of an industry gather to display, demonstrate, and sell products [344]

trade surplus Situation in which a country's exports exceed its imports, creating a positive balance of trade [60]

trust services Bank management of an individual's investments, payments, or estate [524]

two-factor theory Theory of motivation holding that job satisfaction depends on two types of factors: hygiene and motivating [217]

U-shaped production line Production layout in which machines and workers are placed in a narrow U shape rather than a straight line [400]

unemployment Level of joblessness among people actively seeking work [20]

unethical behavior Behavior that violates generally accepted social norms concerning beneficial and harmful actions [82]

union shop Workplace in which workers must join a union within a specified period after being hired [251]

unlimited liability Legal principle holding owners responsible for paying off all the debts of a business [38]

unsecured loan Loan for which collateral is not required [583]

utility A product's ability to satisfy a human want [391]

variable cost Cost that changes with the quantity of a product produced or sold [316]

venture capital Outside equity financing provided in return for part ownership of the borrowing firm [591]

venture capital firm Group of small investors that invests money in companies with rapid growth potential [168]

vertical marketing system (VMS) Unified distribution channel composed of separate businesses centrally controlled by a single member [362]

vestibule training Off-the-job training conducted in a simulated environment [188]

video marketing Nonstore retailing to consumers via standard and cable television [369]

voice mail Computer-based system for receiving and delivering incoming telephone calls [463]

voluntary arbitration Method of resolving a labor dispute in which both parties agree to submit to the judgment of a neutral party [258]

wage reopener clause Clause allowing wage rates to be renegotiated during the life of a labor contract [254]

wages Compensation in the form of money paid for time worked [191]

warehouse club (or **wholesale club**) Bargain retailer offering large discounts on brand-name merchandise to customers who have paid annual membership fees [367]

warehousing Physical distribution operation concerned with the storage of goods [371]

wheel of retailing Concept of retail evolution holding that low-service, low-price stores add services and raise prices until they lose price-sensitive customers and are replaced by new firms that enter the market to fill the need for low-price stores [370]

whistle-blower Employee who detects and tries to put an end to a company's unethical, illegal, or socially irresponsible actions by publicizing them [94]

wholesaler Intermediary who sells products to other businesses for resale to final consumers [356]

wide area network Network of computers and workstations located far from one another and linked by telephone wires or by satellite [460]

wildcat strike Strike that is unauthorized by the strikers' union [256]

word-processing program Application program that allows computers to store, edit, and print letters and numbers for documents created by users [457]

work sharing (or **job sharing**) Method of increasing job satisfaction by allowing two or more people to share a single full-time job [224]

work-force diversity Range of workers' attitudes, values, and behaviors that differ by gender, race, and ethnicity [200]

worker's compensation insurance Legally required insurance for compensating workers injured on the job [193]

working capital Difference between a firm's current assets and current liabilities [493, 580]

World Bank United Nations agency that provides a limited scope of financial services, such as funding national improvements in undeveloped countries [538]

World Wide Web Subsystem of computers providing access to the Internet and offering multimedia and linking capabilities [466]

yellow-dog contract Illegal contract clause requiring workers to begin and continue employment without union affiliation [250]

Reference Notes

Chapter 1

[1]John Huey, "Waking Up to the New Economy," *Fortune*, June 27, 1994, pp. 36–46.

[2]Karl E. Case and Ray C. Fair, *Principles of Economics*, 3d ed. (Englewood Cliffs, NJ: Prentice Hall, 1994), p. 77

[3]Page Smith, *The Rise of Industrial America* (New York: Viking Penguin, 1990).

[4]Barnaby J. Feder, "Crop Subsidies: Help and Headaches," *New York Times*, July 5, 1994, pp. D1, D2.

[5]Nathaniel C. Nash, "Privatizing in Hungary: A Door Reopens," *New York Times*, October 17, 1995, pp. D1, D6; Jane Perlez, "Post-Marxist Hungarian Bus Maker Takes to Capitalist Road," *New York Times*, August 10, 1995, p. D3.

[6]Case and Fair, *Principles of Economics*, p. 102.

[7]Nicholas C. Siropolis, *Small Business Management*, 7th ed. (Boston: Houghton Mifflin, 1999).

[8]John Rossant et al., "OPEC's Joyride Was Great While It Lasted," *Business Week*, June 3, 1996, p. 52.

[9]Christoper Farrell and Michael Mandel, "Why Are We So Afraid of Growth?" *Business Week*, May 16, 1994, pp. 62–65.

[10]U.S Bureau of the Census, *Statistical Abstract of the United States 1996*, 116th ed. (Washington, DC: U.S. Government Printing Office, 1997)

[11]Case and Fair, *Principles of Economics*, pp. 61–63, 570–571.

[12]"Economy Surging at 3.6%" Associated Press news release, August 29, 1997.

[13]W. Bruce Chew, "No-Nonsense Guide to Measuring Productivity," *Harvard Business Review*, January–February 1988, pp. 110–118.

[14]Thomas May, Jr., "Gearing Up for Steady Growth," *Fortune*, July 29, 1991, pp. 83–102.

Chapter 2

[1]Kevin Keasey, Steve Thompson, and Mike Wright, *Corporate Governance* (Oxford, UK: Oxford University Press, 1997)

[2]Roger E. Meiners et al., *The Legal Environment of Business*, 5th ed. (Minneapolis: West, 1994), pp. 407–408.

[3]U.S. Department of Commerce, *Statistical Abstract of the United States* (Washington, DC: Bureau of the Census, 1990), p. 521.

[4]George W. Spiro, *The Legal Environment of Business: Principles and Cases* (Englewood Cliffs, NJ: Prentice Hall, 1993), pp. 237–238.

[5]*Statistical Abstract of the United States*, p. 521.

[6]Linda Himelstein et al., "Boardrooms: The Ties That Bind?" *Business Week*, May 2, 1994, pp. 112–114; Thomas McCarroll, "Board Games," *Time*, February 8, 1993, p. 55.

Chapter 3

[1]Alan Farnham, "Global—or Just Globaloney?" *Fortune*, June 27, 1994, pp. 97–98, 100.

[2]For an overview, see Ricky W. Griffin and Michael Pustay, *International Business: A Managerial Perspective*, 2d ed. (Reading, MA: Addison-Wesley, 1999).

[3]Bill Saporito, "Where the Global Action Is," *Fortune*, Autumn–Winter 1993, pp. 62–65.

[4]Neal Templin, "Mexican Industrial Belt Is Beginning to Form as Car Makers Expand," *Wall Street Journal*, June 29, 1994, pp. A1, A10; Allen R. Myerson, "Lines Shift in Border War for Mexican Shopper," *New York Times*, April 25, 1994, pp. D1, D7; Myerson, "The Booming, Bulging Tex-Mex Border," *New York Times*, August 7, 1994, sec. 3, pp. 1, 6. Data from U.S. Commerce Department.

[5]John Tagliabue, "Coca-Cola Reaches into Impoverished Albania," *New York Times*, May 20, 1994, pp. D1, D3; Joseph B. Treaster, "Kellog Seeks to Reset Latvia's Breakfast Tables," *New York Times*, May 19, 1994, pp. D1, D8.

[6]Brenton R. Schlender et al., "Special Report/Pacific Rim: The Battle for Asia," *Fortune*, November 1, 1993, pp. 126–156; Philip Shenon, "Missing Out on a Glittering Market," *New York Times*, September 12, 1993, sec. 3, pp. 1, 6; Steven Greenhouse, "New Tally of World's Economies Catapults China into Third Place," *New York Times*, May 20, 1993, pp. A1, A8.

[7]Michael Porter, "Why Nations Triumph," *Fortune*, March 12, 1990, pp. 94–108.

[8]Jeffery Taylor and Neil Behrmann, "Coffee Prices Surge After Frost Hits Brazil," *Wall Street Journal*, June 28, 1994, pp. C1, C16; Dori Jones Yang with Bill Hinchberger, "Trouble Brewing at the Coffee Bar," *Business Week*, August 1, 1994, p. 62; "Coffee Surges on New Worries About Cold Weather in Brazil," *New York Times*, May 18, 1995.

[9]James Bennet, "A Stronger Yen Is Hurting Sales of Japan's Cars," *New York Times*, November 5, 1993, pp. A1, D2.

[10]John Rossant and Julia Flynn, "The Yanks Are Buying, the Yanks Are Buying," *Business Week*, October 11, 1993, p. 51.

[11]Rob Norton, "Strategies for the New Export Boom," *Fortune*, August 22, 1994, pp. 124–127.

[12]John Rockwell, "The New Colossus: American Culture as Power Export," *New York Times*, January 30, 1994, sec. 2, pp. 1, 30; Roger Cohen, "The French, Disneyed and Jurrasick, Fear Erosion," *New York Times*, November 21, 1993, sec. 4, p. 2; Sallie Hofmeister, "Used American Jeans Power a Thriving Industry Abroad," *New York Times*, August 22, 1994, pp. A1, D3.

[13]Anthony DePalma, "G.M. Gives Mexico Its Own 'Chevy'." *New York Times*, May 12, 1994, pp. D1, D6; Data from James B. Treece et al., "New Worlds to Conquer," *Business Week*, February 28, 1994, p. 51.

[14]Jeremy Main, "How to Go Global—and Why," *Fortune*, December 17, 1990, pp. 70–73.

[15]Norton, "Strategies for the New Export Boom," pp. 124–126, 130.

[16]Main, "How to Go Global," p. 72.

[17]Jeremy Main, "Making Global Alliances Work," *Fortune*, December 17, 1990, pp. 121–126.

[18]Norton, "Strategies for the New Export Boom," pp. 127, 129.

[19]David Woodruff and John Templeton, "Why Mercedes Is Alabama Bound," *Business Week*, October 11, 1993, pp. 138–39; David C. Holt, *Management: Principles and Practices*, 3d ed. (Englewood Cliffs, NJ: Prentice-Hall, 1993), pp. 70, 79.

[20]Tim Smart et al., "GE's Brave New World," *Business Week*, November 8, 1993, pp. 64–70; Emily Thorton, "Thailand: Japan vs. the U.S.," *Fortune*, November 1, 1993, pp. 145–146; Joyce Barnathan et al., "Behind the Great Wall," *Business Week*, October 25, 1993, pp. 42–43.

[21]Louis Uchitelle, "U.S. Corporations Expanding Abroad at a Quicker Pace," *New York Times*, July 25, 1994, pp. A1, D2. Data from the U.S. Commerce Department, Bureau of Economic Analysis.

[22]Clifford J. Levy, "A Wary Reply to South Africa's Call," *New York Times*, October 21, 1993, pp. D1, D20; Keith L. Alexander, "Mandela's Welcome Mat Starts Drawing Investors," *Business Week*, October 11, 1993, p. 54; Seth Faison, "Investors Wary, Despite Mandela," *New York Times*, October 8, 1994, pp. 39, 50.

[23]Jane Perlez, "In Poland, Gerber Learns Lessons of Tradition," *New York Times*, November 8, 1993, pp. A1, D3.

[24]Joyce Barnathan et al., "Behind the Great Wall," pp. 42–43; Barnathan et al., "China: The Emerging Economic Powerhouse of the 21st Century," *Business Week*, May 17, 1993, pp. 54–69; Barnathan et al., "China: Birth of a New

Economy," *Business Week*, January 31, 1994, pp. 42–43; Pete Engardio, "Motorola in China: A Great Leap Forward," *Business Week*, May 17, 1993, pp. 58–59; John J. Curran, "China's Investment Boom," *Fortune*, March 7, 1994, pp. 116–118, 120–124.

[25]Elaine Sciolino, "U.S. Will Allow Computer Sale to China," *New York Times*, November 19, 1993, pp. A1, A5.

[26]Geri Smith, "NAFTA: A Green Light for Red Tape," *Business Week*, July 25, 1994, p. 48.

[27]Henry R. Cheeseman, *Business Law: The Legal, Ethical, and International Environment*, 2nd ed. (Englewood Cliffs, NJ: Prentice Hall, 1994), p. 1282.

Chapter 4

[1]"Polartec," *Ad Age*, June 30, 1997, p. 36.

[2]Barbara Heger, "What's Behind Business' Sudden Fervor for Ethics," *Business Week*, September 23, 1991, p. 65.

[3]Frank B. Cross and Roger LeRoy Miller, *West's Legal Environment of Business: Text, Cases, Ethical and Regulatory Issues* (St. Paul, MN: West, 1992), p. 86.

[4]"Critics Confront a CEO Dedicated to Human Rights," *Wall Street Journal*, February 24, 1997, pp. B1, B7.

[5]Kenneth R. Andrews, "Ethics in Practice," *Harvard Business Review*, September–October, 1989, pp. 99–104.

[6]"Static in Cincinnati," *Business Week*, November 6, 1995, pp. 170–172.

[7]Archie Carroll, *Business and Society: Ethics and Stakeholder Management* (Cincinnati: Southwestern, 1989).

[8]John Holusha, "Paper Maker Turns a Cleaner Page," *New York Times*, October 20, 1993, pp. D1, D5.

[9]Timothy Egan, "Montana's Sky and Its Hopes Are Left Bare After Logging," *New York Times*, October 19, 1993, pp. A1, A26.

[10]John Holusha, "Recycled Material Is Finding a New and Lucrative Market," *New York Times*, October 8, 1994, pp. 1, 41. Data from Browning-Ferris Industries.

[11]John H. Cushman, Jr, "Administration Plans Revision to Ease Toxic Cleanup Criteria," *New York Times*, January 31, 1994, pp. A1, A14; Cushman, "Congress Forgoes Its Bid to Hasten Cleanup of Dumps," *New York Times*, October 6, 1994, pp. A1, A22.

[12]Phillip J. Hilts, "Manufacturer Admits Selling Untested Devices for Hearts," *New York Times*, October 16, 1993, pp. 1, 9.

[13]"Illegal Price-Fixing Charged in Danbury Hospital Lawsuit," *New York Times*, September 14, 1995, p. B6.

[14]"Hey Kid, Buy This!" *Business Week*, June 30, 1997, pp. 62–69.

[15]"Indonesian Nike Factory Closed," Associated Press news release as published in the *Bryan–College Station Eagle*, April 27, 1997, p. A18.

[16]Calvin Sims, "Trying to Mute the Whistle-Blowers," *New York Times*, April 11, 1994, pp. D1, D8.

[17]"Sex, Lies, and Home Improvements?" *Business Week*, March 31, 1997, p. 40.

[18]See Dan G. Stone, *April Fools: An Insider's Account of the Rise and Fall of Drexel Burnham* (New York: Warner 1991); James B. Stewart, *Den of Thieves* (New York: Simon & Schuster, 1991).

[19]John Tierney, "Recycling Is Garbage," *New York Times Magazine*, June 30, 1966, pp. 24–53.

Chapter 5

[1]"David Kirkpatrick, "Fast Times at Compaq," *Fortune*, April 1, 1996, pp. 121–123; "As Cheaper PCs Trip Up Rivals, Compaq Scores," *Wall Street Journal*, October 17, 1997, p. B1.

[2]Patricia Sellers, "Women, Sex, and Power," *Fortune*, August 5, 1996, pp. 42–46.

[3]"The Right Place, the Right Time," *Business Week*, May 27, 1996, pp. 42–46.

[4]Marc Gunther, "How GE Made NBC No. 1," *Fortune*, February 3, 1997, pp. 92–100.

[5]Charles W. L. Hill and Gareth Jones, *Strategic Management: An Analytical View*, 4th ed. (Boston: Houghton Mifflin, 1998).

[6]Gary Hamel, "Killer Strategies," *Fortune*, June 23, 1997, pp. 70–84.

[7]Amy Barrett, "Dial Succeeds by Stepping in Bigger Footsteps," *Business Week*, June 13, 1994, pp. 82–83.

[8]"Cruise-Ship Delays Leave Guests High and Dry," *Wall Street Journal*, October 24, 1997, pp. B1, B10.

[9]"Executive Pay," *Business Week*, April 21, 1997, pp. 58–102.

[10]Eric Calonius, "How Top Managers Manage Their Time," *Fortune*, June 4, 1990, pp. 250–262.

[11]Thomas A. Stewart, "Managing in a Wired Company," *Fortune*, July 11, 1994, pp. 44–47.

[12]Terrance Deal and Allen Kennedy, *Corporate Cultures: The Rites and Rituals of Corporate Life* (Reading, MA: Addison-Wesley, 1982). See also "Corporate Culture," *Inc.*, November 1996, pp. 42–53.

[13]"Egalitarianism Invades a Shrine of V.I.P. Privilege," *New York Times*, May 17, 1996, B1, B6.

[14]Bill Saporito, "A Week Aboard the Wal-Mart Express," *Fortune*, August 24, 1992, pp. 77–81.

Chapter 6

[1]Richard Daft, *Organizational Theory and Design*, 6th ed. (St. Paul, MN: West, 1998).

[2]Kathleen Kerwin et al., "Can Jack Smith Fix GM?" *Business Week*, November 1, 1993, pp. 126–131; Alex Taylor III, "GM Gets a Tune-Up," *Fortune*, November 29, 1993, pp. 54–58.

[3]Tim Smart, "UTC Gets a Lift from Its Smaller Engines," *Business Week*, December 20, 1993, pp. 109–110.

[4]Brian Dumaine, "Payoff from the New Management," *Fortune*, December 13, 1993, pp. 103–104.

[5]Patrick Oster and John Rossant, "Call It Worldpool," *Business Week*, November 28, 1994, pp. 98–99.

[6]John A. Byrne, "The Horizontal Corporation," *Business Week*, December 20, 1993, p. 79.

[7]Thomas J. Peters and Robert H. Waterman, Jr., *In Search of Excellence* (New York: Harper & Row, 1982).

[8]Mark Llewyn, "Fun: It's Fundamental," *Business Week*, 1993, p. 197.

Chapter 7

[1]Dianne Moller, "Russia—The Ultimate Emerging Market," *Forbes*, February 14, 1994, pp. 88–94; Joyce Barnathan et al., "Destination Vietnam," *Business Week*, February 14, 1994, pp. 26–27.

[2]This section is based on Sylvia Nasar, "Myth: Small Business as Job Engine," *New York Times*, March 25, 1994, pp. D1, D2. Data from listed companies.

[3]John Labate, "Companies to Watch: Maxim Integrated Products," *Fortune*, December 13, 1993, p. 172.

[4]Stephanie Losee et al., "Fortune Checks Out 26 Cool Companies," *Fortune*, July 11, 1994, p. 130.

[5]Gary Putka, "Small Companies Thrive by Taking Over Some Specialized Tasks for Big Concerns," *Wall Street Journal*, September 11, 1991, pp. B1, B2.

[6]"Hot Growth Companies," *Business Week*, May 27, 1996, pp. 113–114.

[7]John Labate, "Companies to Watch: Central Garden & Pet," *Fortune*, February 7, 1994, p. 137.

[8]Michael Oneal, "Just What Is an Entrepreneur?" *Business Week*, Enterprise 1993, pp. 104–105.

[9]Oneal, "Just What Is an Entrepreneur?" p. 105; Wilton Woods, "Products to Watch: Heavy Artillery," *Fortune*, May 30, 1994, p. 163; David Whitford, "Opposite Attractions," *Inc.*, December 1994, pp. 60–64.

[10]William Echikson, "Young Americans Go Abroad to Strike It Rich," *Fortune*, October 17, 1994, pp. 185–194.

[11]Wendy Zellner et al., "Women Entrepreneurs," *Business Week*, April 18, 1994, pp. 34–40.

[12]Echikson, "Young Americans Go Abroad to Strike It Rich," pp. 185–194.

[13]David H. Holt, *Entrepreneurship: New*

Venture Creation (Englewood Cliffs, NJ: Prentice Hall, 1992), p. 432.

[14]Holt, *Entrepreneurship*, pp. 443–444.

[15]Karl H. Vesper, *New Venture Mechanics* (Englewood Cliffs, NJ: Prentice Hall, 1993), p. 112.

[16]Barbara Presley Noble, "A Few Thousand Women, Networking," *New York Times*, March 27, 1994, sec. 3, p. 43.

[17]Kirk Johnson, "Franchise Stores Lure Corporate Refugees," *New York Times*, May 13, 1994, pp. A1, B5.

Chapter 8

[1]For a recent review of the field of human resource management, see C. D. Fisher et al., *Personnel/Human Resource Management*, 4th ed. (Boston: Houghton Mifflin, 1999).

[2]"Recruiters Work Hard to Showcase Fun Side of Job," *USA Today*, December 29, 1997, p. 5B.

[3]Keneth W. Thornicraft, "The War on Drugs Goes to Work: Employer Drug Testing and the Law," *Ohio Northern University Law Review*, 17 (1991), 771–789.

[4]Justin Martin, "So, You Want to Work for the Best," *Fortune*, January 12, 1998, pp. 77–78.

[5]"Corporate America Goes to School," *Business Week*, October 20, 1997, pp. 66–72.

[6]"Firms Laying Off," Associated Press wire story as reported in the *Bryan–College Station Eagle*, September 20, 1997, p. A13.

[7]Shawn Tully, "Your Paycheck Gets Exciting," *Fortune*, November 1, 1993, pp. 83–84; Howard Gleckman et al., "Bonus Pay: Buzzword or Bonanza," *Business Week*, November 14, 1994, pp. 62–64; Wendy Zellner et al., "Go-Go Goliaths," *Business Week*, February 13, 1995, pp. 64–70.

[8]"Perking Up Employees," *USA Today*, October 8, 1997, pp. 1B, 2B.

[9]Robert N. Corley et al., *The Legal and Regulatory Environment of Business*, 9th ed. (New York: McGraw-Hill, 1993), p. 483.

[10]Joan S. Lublin, "Companies Try a Variety of Approaches to Sexual Harassment on the Job," *Wall Street Journal*, October 11, 1991, pp. B1, B5; Linda Greenhouse, "Court, 9–0, Makes Sex Harassment Easier to Prove," *New York Times*, November 10, 1993, pp. A1, A22.

[11]Catherine S. Manegold, "Reich Talks of 'Glass Ceiling' Pervading the Business World," *New York Times*, September 27, 1994, p. B9; Peter T. Kilborn, "Women and Minorities Still Face 'Glass Ceiling,'" *New York Times*, March 16, 1995, p. A22; Kilborn, "White Males and Management," *New York Times*, March 17, 1995.

[12]Tamar Lewis, "Working Women Say Bias Persists," *New York Times*, October 15, 1994, p. 9. Data from the Department of Labor.

[13]Corley et al., *The Legal and Regulatory Environment of Business*, p. 442.

[14]Michele Galen and Ann Therese Palmer, "White, Male and Worried," *Business Week*, January 31, 1994, pp. 50–55. Data from U.S. Trust Corp. and Bureau of Labor Statistics.

[15]Russell Mitchell and Michael Oneal, "Managing by Values," *Business Week*, August 1, 1994, pp. 46–52.

[16]This section is based on Faye Rice, "How to Make Diversity Pay," *Fortune*, August 8, 1994, pp. 78–80.

[17]Kathleen Murray, "The Unfortunate Side Effects of 'Diversity Training,'" *New York Times*, August 1, 1995, p. 37.

[18]Rice, "How to Make Diversity Pay," p. 84.

[19]This section is based on Jaclyn Fierman, "The Contingency Work Force," *Fortune*, January 24, 1994, pp. 30–36; Barnaby J. Feder, "Bigger Roles for Suppliers of Temporary Workers," *New York Times*, April 1, 1995, p. 37.

[20]Fierman, "The Contingency Work Force," pp. 32–33. Data from the National Association of Temporary Services.

Chapter 9

[1]Udayan Gupta, "Keeping the Faith," *Wall Street Journal*, November 22, 1991, p. R16; Greg Moorhead and Ricky W. Griffin, *Organizational Behavior*, 5th ed. (Boston: Houghton Mifflin, 1998).

[2]Linda Grant, "Happy Workers, High Returns," *Fortune*, January 12, 1998, p. 81.

[3]Jeffery L. Seglin, "The Happiest Workers in the World," *Inc.*, The State of Small Business 1996, pp. 62–64.

[4]David Cay Johnston, "Nabisco to Eliminate 4,200 Jobs and Trim Product Line by 14%," *New York Times*, June 25, 1996, pp. D1, D20; Lawrence M. Fisher, "Apple Plans 1,300 Layoffs and Takes Losses," *New York Times*, January 18, 1996, p. D1, D10; Edmund L. Andrews, "Job Cuts at AT&T Will Total 40,000, 13% of Its Staff," *New York Times*, January 3, 1996, pp. A1, D2; Catherine Arnst, "The Bloodletting at AT&T Is Just the Beginning," *Business Week*, January 15, 1996, p. 30; Andrews, "Don't Go Away Mad, Just Go Away," *New York Times*, February 13, 1996, pp. D1, D6; Louis Uchitelle and N. R. Kleinfeld, "On the Battlefields of Business, Millions of Casualties," *New York Times*, March 3, 1996, sec. 1, pp. 1, 26.

[5]Robert Hanley, "New Jersey Hit Hard in Wave of Layoffs at AT&T," *New York Times*, January 17, 1996, pp. B1, B5; Brian O'Reilly, "Ma Bell's Orphans," *Fortune*, April 1, 1996, pp. 88–90.

[6]Anne B. Fisher, "Morale Crisis," *Fortune*, November 18, 1991, pp. 70–80.

[7]Fredrick W. Taylor, *Principles of Scientific Management* (New York: Harper & Brothers, 1911).

[8]See Robert Kanigel, *The One Best Way* (New York: Viking, 1997) for a recent assessment of Taylor's work and its impact on modern business.

[9]Elton Mayo, *The Human Problems of an Industrial Civilization* (Cambridge, MA: Harvard University Press, 1933).

[10]Douglas McGregor, *The Human Side of Enterprise* (New York: McGraw-Hill, 1960).

[11]Abraham Maslow, "A Theory of Human Motivation," *Psychological Review*, July 1943, pp. 370–396.

[12]Frederick Herzberg, Bernard Mausner, and Barbara Bloch Snyderman, *The Motivation to Work* (New York: Wiley, 1959).

[13]Victor Vroom, *Work and Motivation* (New York: Wiley, 1964); Craig Pinder, *Work Motivation* (Glenview, IL: Scott, Foresman, 1984).

[14]J. Stacy Adams, "Towards an Understanding of Inequity," *Journal of Abnormal and Social Psychology*, 75, no. 5 (1963), pp. 422–436.

[15]Kevin Kelly, "The New Soul of John Deere," *Business Week*, January 31, 1994, pp. 64–65.

[16]Stephen J. Carroll and Henry L. Tosi, *Management by Objectives* (New York: Macmillan, 1973).

[17]Briane Dumaine, "The Trouble with Teams," *Fortune*, September 5, 1994, pp. 86–88.

[18]Aimee L. Stern, "Managing by Team Is Not Always as Easy as It Looks," *New York Times*, July 18, 1993, sec. 3, p. 5.

[19]J. Richard Hackman and Greg Oldham, *Work Redesign* (Reading, MA: Addison-Wesley, 1980).

[20]Patricia Sellers, "Keeping the Buyers You Already Have," *Fortune*, Autumn–Winter 1993, pp. 56–58.

[21]Larry Armstrong and Julie Tilsner, "The Office Is a Terrible Place to Work," *Business Week*, December 27, 1993, p. 46D; Phil Patton, "The Virtual Office Becomes Reality," *New York Times*, October 28, 1993, pp. C1, C6; Kirk Johnson, "New Breed of High-Tech Nomads," *New York Times*, February 8, 1994, pp. B1, B5.

[22]Samuel Greengard, "Making the Virtual Office a Reality," *Personnel Journal*, September 1994, pp. 66–68.

[23]Lynne S. Dumas, "Home Work: The Telecommuting Option," *Working Mother*, July 1994, p. 22; Patricia Sharpe,

"Workforce Revolution," *Self*, February 1994, p. 82; Sue Schellenbarger, "Some Thrive, but Many Wilt Working at Home," *Wall Street Journal*, December 14, 1993, pp. 54–58.

[24]Brian S. Moskal, "Smith Freshens GM's Stale Air," *Industry Week*, October 4, 1993, pp. 19–22; Joseph B. White, "GM's Overhaul of Corporate Culture Brings Results but Still Faces Hurdles," *Wall Street Journal*, January 13, 1993, pp. A3, A4; White, "Metamorphosis at GM, in Style and Substance, May Be Taking Hold," *Wall Street Journal*, February 19, 1993, pp. A1, A11; Alex Taylor III, "GM Gets a Tune-Up," *Fortune*, November 29, 1993, pp. 54–58.

[25]Gregory Moorhead and Ricky W. Griffin, *Organizational Behavior*, 5th ed. (Boston: Houghton Mifflin, 1998).

Chapter 10

[1]Randall S. Schuler, *Managing Human Resources*, 4th ed. (St. Paul, MN: West, 1992).

[2]This section is based in part on Robert L. Sauer and Keith E. Voelker, *Labor Relations: Structure and Process*, 2nd ed. (New York: Macmillan, 1993), pp. 24–42.

[3]Sauer and Voelker, *Labor Relations*, pp. 73, 91, 456.

[4]Aaron Bernstein, "Why America Needs Unions—but Not the Kind It Has Now," *Business Week*, May 23, 1994, pp. 70–71.

[5]Barbara Presley Noble,"Big Union Win in the South," *New York Times*, September 11, 1994, sec. 3, p. 21.

[6]James Thacker, "Commitment to the Union: A Comparison of United States and Canadian Workers, " *Journal of Organizational Behavior*, June 1991, pp. 63–71.

[7]James Bennet, "For Ford, a New Contract but Little Ground," *New York Times*, September 17, 1993, pp. D1, D4.

[8]Bernstein, "Why America Needs Unions," p. 70.

[9]Steven Greenhouse, "Unions Recruit 10,000 People at US Airways," *New York Times*, September 30, 1997, p. 1; "Beer, Sandwiches and Statistics," *Economist*, July 12, 1997, p. 70; Aaron Bernstein, "Big Labor Invites a Few Friends Over," *Business Week*, April 21, 1997, p. 44; Justin Fox, "Big Labor Flexes Its Muscles," *Fortune*, June 10, 1996, pp. 24–26; Aaron Bernstein, "Sweeney's Blitz," *Business Week*, February 17, 1997, pp. 56–62.

[10]Kevin Kelly and Aaron Bernstein, "Labor Deals That Offer a Break from 'Us vs. Them,'" *Business Week*, August 2, 1993, p. 30.

[11]John Holusha, "LTV's Weld of Worker and Manager," *New York Times*, August 2, 1994, pp. D1, D17.

[12]Kelly and Bernstein, "Labor Deals That Offer a Break," p. 30; Bernstein, "Why America Needs Unions," p. 71.

[13]"Workers Docked over T-Shirts," *Bergen* (New Jersey) *Record*, November 26, 1994, p. A16.

[14]David Moberg, "Like Business, Unions Must Go Global," *New York Times*, December 19, 1993, sec. 3, p. 13.

[15]Louis Uchitelle, "Workers Said to Concede Manager's Power," *New York Times*, December 5, 1994, pp. D1, D10.

[16]Sauer and Voelker, *Labor Relations*, p. 93.

[17]Sauer and Voelker, *Labor Relations*, p. 174.

[18]Stephen Bluen and Vanessa Jubiler-Lurie, "Some Consequences of Labor-Management Negotiations: Laboratory and Field Studies," *Journal of Organizational Behavior*, September 1990, pp. 105–111.

[19]Calvin Sims, "After the Layoffs, Checks in the Mail," *New York Times*, November 18, 1993, pp. D1, D6.

[20]Peter T. Kilborn, "Overtime Is Money, but G.M. Assembly Workers Say They've Had Enough," *New York Times*, November 22, 1994, p. A16.

Chapter 11

[1]"AMA Board Approves New Marketing Definition," *Marketing News*, March 31, 1985, p. 1.

[2]*Harley-Davidson Inc.: 1995 Annual Report* (Milwaukee: Harley-Davidson, 1995), p. 33. See Philip Kotler, *Marketing Management: Analysis, Planning, Implementation, and Control*, 9th ed. (Upper Saddle River, NJ: Prentice Hall, 1997), pp. 12–13, 48–51.

[3]Ricardo Sookdeo, "Golfing Wear for Women," *Fortune*, November 14, 1994, p. 257.

[4]Tim Stevens, "Internet-Aided Design," *Industry Week*, June 23, 1997, pp. 50–54.

[5]"BarnesandNoble.com Goes Live on the World Wide Web," News release, Barnes & Noble, Inc., and Direct Report Corporation, May 13, 1997; "Barnes & Noble, Inc. Announces Initiative to Launch World's Largest Bookseller Online," News release, Barnes & Noble, Inc., and Direct Report Corporation, January 28, 1997; Myron Magnet, "Let's Go for Growth," *Fortune*, March 7, 1994, pp. 68, 70.

[6]*Standard & Poor's NASDAQ Stock Reports*, February 9, 1997, p. 5683K; David Griesing, "Quality: How to Make it Pay," *Business Week*, August 8, 1994, p. 58.

[7]*Standard & Poor's NASDAQ Stock Reports*, December 23, 1996, p. 3657P; John Labate, "Companies to Watch: Daka International," *Fortune*, November 14, 1994, p. 258.

[8]Glenn Collins, "Updating an Icon, Carefully," *New York Times*, November 17, 1995, pp. D1, D4.

[9]David Kirkpatrick, "Now Everyone in PCs Wants to Be Like Mike," *Fortune*, September 8, 1997, pp. 91–92.

[10]Lucette Lagnado, Anita Sharpe, and Greg Jaffe, "How Columbia/HCA Changed Health Care, for Better or for Worse," *Wall Street Journal*, August 1, 1997, pp. A1, A4; Kurt Eichenwald, "Whistle-Blower Lawsuits Aim at Big Provider of Health Care," *New York Times*, August 19, 1997, pp. C1, C8.

[11]Robin Pogrebin, "A Magazine Only a Mother Could Love?" *New York Times*, July 22, 1996 pp. D1, D8.

[12]Philip Kotler, *Marketing Management: Analysis, Planning, Implementation and Control*, 9th ed. (Upper Saddle River, NJ: Prentice Hall, 1997), pp. 294–301.

[13]Patricia Sellers, "How Coke is Kicking Pepsi's Can," *Fortune*, October 28, 1996, pp. 70–75.

[14]Pogrebin, "A Magazine Only a Mother Could Love?" pp. D1, D8.

[15]Jay Finegan, "Bicycle Built for You," *Inc.*, April 1996, pp. 80–89.

[16]Erick Schonfeld, "Betting on the Boomers," *Fortune*, December 25, 1995, pp. 78–80.

[17]David Fischer, "Let the Good Times Roll," *U.S. News & World Report*, July 1, 1996, pp. 51–52; David Leonhardt, "Like Totally Big Spenders," *Business Week*, June 3, 1996, p. 8; Shawn Tully, "Teens: The Most Global Market of All," *Fortune*, May 16, 1994, pp. 90–94; Laura Zinn, "Teens: Here Comes the Biggest Wave Yet," *Business Week*, April 11, 1994, pp. 76–79; John Greenwald, "Will Teens Buy It?" *Time*, May 30, 1994, pp. 50–52; Jane L. Levere, "Advertising: A New Survey Charts the Habits of Teen-Agers Around the World," *New York Times*, June 11, 1996, p. D8; Roger Ricklefs, "Marketers Seek Out Today's Coolest Kids to Plug into Tomorrow's Mall Trends," *Wall Street Journal*, July 11, 1996, pp. B1, B2.

[18]Dori Jones Yang, "The Starbucks Enterprise Shifts into Warp Speed," *Business Week*, October 24, 1994, pp. 76–78; Alex Witchell, "By Way of Canarsie, One Large Hot Cup of Business Strategy," *New York Times*, December 14, 1994, pp. C1, C8.

[19]Jane Perlez, "A Bourgeoisie Blooms and Goes Shopping," *New York Times*, May 14, 1996, pp. D1, D6.

[20]Marjorie Sorge, "Good-Bye World Cars; Honda Boosts Local Engineering," *Automotive Industries*, April 1996, p. 29.

[21]Kate Button, "Cashing In on Delivery," *Computer Weekly*, February 20, 1997, p. 50; David Griesing, "Quality: How to

Make It Pay," *Business Week*, August 8, 1994, p. 58.

[22]Elliot Aronson, *The Social Animal*, 7th ed. (New York: W.H. Freeman, 1988).

[23]*Fortune*, September 8, 1997, pp. 87–90.

[24]Terence P. Pare, "How to Find Out What They Want," *Fortune*, Autumn–Winter 1993, pp. 39–41.

[25]*Statistical Abstract of the United States* (Washington, DC: U.S. Department of Commerce, 1996), pp. 533, 736.

[26]*Statistical Abstract of the United States* (Washington, DC: U.S. Department of Commerce, 1996), pp. 765, 773.

[27]*Statistical Abstract of the United States* (Washington, DC: U.S. Department of Commerce, 1996), p. 298.

[28]John Labate, "Companies to Watch: EA Engineering Science & Technology," *Fortune*, December 12, 1994, p. 243.

[29]Zachary Schiller, Greg Burns, and Karen Lowry Miller, "Make it Simple," *Business Week*, September 9, 1996, pp. 96–99.

[30]John Rockwell, "The New Colossus: American Culture as Power Export," *New York Times*, January 30, 1994, sec. 2, pp. 1, 30.

[31]Sharon Nelton, "A Scrappy Entrepreneur," *Nation's Business*, June 1997, pp. 12, 14.

[32]Donna Fenn, "Leader of the Pack," *Inc.*, February 1996, pp. 30–32.

Chapter 12

[1]Jon Auerbach, "DEC Cuts Prices by Up to 47% on Its Line of Alpha-Based Servers, Workstations," *Wall Street Journal*, January 10, 1997, p. B16.

[2]"To Market, to Market. . . . It's a Simple Rhyme but the Reality Is That Getting an Ingredient to Market is Costly and Time Consuming," *Beverage Industry*, December 1996, pp. 43–46.

[3]David Castle, "New Improved American Dream," *Grocer*, January 18, 1997, p. 15; Cyndee Miller, "Little Relief Seen for New Product Failure Rate," *Marketing News*, June 21, 1993, p. 1; Nancy J. Kim, "Back to the Drawing Board," *The Bergen* (New Jersey) *Record*, December 4, 1994, pp. B1, B4.

[4]Bill McDowell, "Miller Continues on Downward Path: Lit Offers Glimmer of Good News as Sales Slip for Other Beer Brands," *Advertising Age*, October 28, 1996, p. 54; Michael J. McCarthy, "Bud Fight: In Texas Beer Brawl, Anheuser and Miller Aren't Pulling Punches; Barroom Blitzes, Price Wars Are Some of the Tactics Brewers Use to Conquer; Staying King of the Bubbas," *Wall Street Journal*, December 5, 1996, p. A1.

[5]James A. Dilworth, *Operations Management*, 2nd ed. (New York: McGraw Hill, 1996), pp. 652–653.

[6]Leonard E. Berry, A. Parasuraman, and Valerie A. Zeithaml, "Improving Service Quality in America," *Academy of Management Executives*, 8, no. 2 (1994), 37–38.

[7]James R. Evans and William M. Lindsay, *The Management and Control of Quality*, 3rd ed. (Minneapolis: West Publishing Co., 1996), pp. 175–176; James R. Evans, *Production/Operations Management*, 5th ed. (Minneapolis: West Publishing Co., 1997), pp. 132–133.

[8]Philip Kotler and Gary Armstrong, *Principles of Marketing*, 7th ed. (Englewood Cliffs, NJ: Prentice Hall, 1996), pp. 326–332.

[9]Larry Holyoke and Larry Armstrong, "Video Warfare: How Toshiba Took the High Ground," *Business Week*, February 20, 1995, pp. 64–66.

[10]G. L. Gordon, R. J. Calantone, and C. A. DiBenedetto, "Mature Markets and Revitalization Strategies: An American Fable," *Business Horizons*, May–June 1991, pp. 39–50.

[11]Betsy Morris, "The Brand's the Thing" *Fortune*, March 4, 1996, p. 72.

[12]Adrian Room, *Dictionary of Trade Name Origins* (London: Routledge & Kegan Paul, 1982), p. 7; Larry Kretchmar, "East Rates West," *Fortune*, January 28, 1991, p. 14.

[13]Bradley Johnson, "IBM's New PC Ads Tout 'Solutions,' Not the Product," *Advertising Age*, May 19, 1997, p. 82.

[14]Cathy Bond, "A Licence to Thrill," *Marketing*, March 28, 1996, p. 30.

[15]Peter Passell, "Ferrari's Road to Success Is Its Name," *New York Times*, July 5, 1997, pp. 35, 36.

[16]"Plan Offered to Make Store Labels Stick," *Supermarket News*, April 7, 1997, p. 38.

[17]Jonathan Berry et al., "Attack of the Fighting Brands," *Business Week*, May 2, 1994, p. 125.

[18]William C. Symonds and Paula Dwyer, "A Third Front in the Cola Wars," *Business Week*, December 2, 1994, pp. 66–68; Myron Love, "Private Label Drives Retail Engine," *Quick Frozen Foods International*, April 1996, pp. 106–108.

[19]Matthew L. Wald, "Corporate Designers Enroll in the 'Less is More' School," *New York Times*, May 5, 1994, p. D4; Bob Heitzman, "Ecology Concerns Spur Economic Benefits," *Packaging Digest*, March 1997, p. 12.

[20]Clare Collins, "Labeling the Toys That Could Choke," *New York Times*, October 27, 1994, p. C2.

[21]Sharon Nelton, "Cleaning Up by Cleaning Up," *Nation's Business*, January 1995, pp. 14–15.

[22]Lauran Neergaard, "Powerful New AIDS Drug Gets Quick Approval from FDA," *Detroit News*, March 2, 1996; Julia Flynn and John Carey, "Wellcome's AZT Faces Attacks on Two Fronts," *Business Week*, July 26, 1993, p. 36; Richard W. Stevenson, "Rocky Road Lies Ahead for Wellcome," *New York Times*, December 11, 1994, sec. 3, p. 4.

[23]Stewart A. Washburn, "Establishing Strategy and Determining Cost in the Pricing Decision," *Business Marketing*, July 1985, pp. 64–78.

[24]Alan Pearce, "Wireless Would Grow if Pricing Changed, Fell," *America's Network*, June 1, 1996, p. 54.

[25]Keith Bradsher, "Sticker Shock: Car Buyers Miss Haggling Ritual," *New York Times*, June 13, 1996, pp. D1, D23; Bradley J. Fikes, "Haggling Over Price Is No Longer Automatic," *San Diego Business Journal*, October 3, 1994, pp. 17–18.

[26]Bill Saporito, "Behind the Tumult at P&G," *Fortune*, March 17, 1994, pp. 74–76.

Chapter 13

[1]Stuart Elliott, "Disney and McDonald's as Double Feature," *New York Times*, May 24, 1996, pp. D1, D6; Michael McCarthy, "BK, 'LK' to Roar at X-Mas," *Brandweek*, September 1, 1994, p. 1; Ron Ruggless, "Burger King Scores TKO with Pocahontas Tie-In," *Nation's Restaurant News*, November 1994, p. 14.

[2]Ronald Henkoff, "Service is Everybody's Business," *Fortune*, June 27, 1994, p. 52.

[3]R. Craig Endicott, "Top Marketers Invest $47.3 Billion in '95 Ads," *Advertising Age*, September 30, 1996, p. s3.

[4]R. Craig Endicott, "Top Marketers Invest $47.3 Billion in '95 Ads," *Advertising Age*, September 30, 1996, p. s54.

[5]Stuart Elliott, "Big, Bold, Outside and In Fashion," *New York Times*, July 11, 1996, pp. D1, D6.

[6]Mary Kuntz, "Burma Shave Signs on the I-Way," *Business Week*, April 17, 1995, pp. 102, 104; Ken Gofton, "Welcome to My Web," *Marketing*, April 11, 1996, p. xviii; Peter C. Elsworth, "Internet Advertising Growing Slowly," *New York Times*, February 24, 1997, p. D5; Reuters, "Online Ad Spending Seen at $7.7 Bil in 2002," August 14, 1997.

[7]*Wall Street Journal*, September 16, 1997, p. A8.

[8]Carolyn M. Brown, "Acquisitional Growth: Many Fast-Growing Firms Are Buying Up the Competition," *Black Enterprise*, August 1996, p. 32; William Wells, John Burnett, and Sandra Moriarty, *Advertising: Principles, and Practice*, 3rd ed. (Englewood Cliffs, NJ: Prentice Hall, 1995), pp. 129–130.

[9]Alice Z. Cuneo, "Starbucks Breaks Largest Ad Blitz," *Advertising Age*, May 19, 1997, pp. 3, 84.

[10]Michael D. Hutt and Thomas W. Speh, *Business Marketing Management*, 6th ed. (New York: Dryden Press, 1998), pp. 504–505.

[11]Michael D. Hutt and Thomas W. Speh, *Business Marketing Management*, 6th ed. (New York: Dryden Press, 1998), p. 502.

[12]John F. Yarbrough, "Dialing for Dollar$," *Sales & Marketing Management*, January 1997, p. 60.

[13]Ira Sager and Amy Cortese, "IBM: Why Good News Isn't Enough," *Business Week*, January 23, 1995, p. 72; Craig Stedman, "Users Laud IBM Reorganization—For Now," *Computerworld*, January 30, 1995, p. 57.

[14]This section is based on Ronald B. Marks, *Personal Selling: An Innovative Approach*, 5th ed. (Boston: Allyn & Bacon, 1994), pp. 10–11.

[15]Bart Ziegler and Don Clark, "Chip Shot: Computer Giants' War Over Flaw in Pentium Jolts the PC Industry," *Wall Street Journal*, December 13, 1994, pp. A1, A8; James G. Kimball, "Jury Split on Pentium Fallout," *Advertising Age*, December 5, 1994, p. 39; Robert D. Hof, "Intel Takes a Bullet—And Barely Breaks Stride," *Business Week*, January 30, 1995, pp. 38, 39; John Markoff, "In About-Face, Intel Will Swap Its Flawed Chip," *New York Times*, December 21, 1994, pp. A1, D1.

[16]See Fraser P. Seitel, *The Practice of Public Relations*, 6th ed. (Englewood Cliffs, NJ: Prentice Hall, 1995), pp. 4–8.

[17]Matthew L. Wald, "Southwest Is Changing Black Boxes," *New York Times*, August 17, 1996, p. D6.

[18]Constance L. Hays, "Even Titles Are Flexible as U.S. Magazines Adapt to Foreign Ways," *New York Times*, August 4, 1997, p. D9.

[19]Glenn Collins, "Moves by Campbell Soup Send Shares Surging to Reach a High," *New York Times*, September 6, 1996, p. D1.

[20]Alan T. Shao and John S. Hill, "Advertising Sensitive Products in Magazines: Legal and Social Restrictions," *Multinational Business Review*, vol. 2, no. 2 (Fall 1994), pp. 16–24.

[21]Hays, "Even Titles Are Flexible," p. D9.

[22]"Does the 'Special Relationship' Include Ketchup and Cola?" *Adweek*, December 13, 1993, p. 17.

[23]Jean Halliday, "Chrysler Takes Corporate Branding to Asia-Pacific," *Advertising Age*, May 19, 1997, p. 83.

[24]Jean Halliday, Penny Warneford, "Going Global," *Adweek*, November 24, 1994, pp. 1–5.

[25]Michael Barrier, "A Global Reach for Small Firms," *Nation's Business*, April 1994, p. 66.

[26]Michael Barrier, "Ties That Bind," *Nation's Business*, August 1997, p. 12.

Chapter 14

[1]Stephanie Anderson Forest, "The Education of Michael Dell," *Business Week*, March 22, 1993, pp. 82–86; Peter Burrows, "The Computer Is in the Mail—Really," *Business Week*, January 23, 1995, pp. 76–77; Jennifer Steinhauer, "PC Shoppers Prove to Have Fickle Hearts," *New York Times*, January 8, 1997, pp. D1, D2; Scott McCartney, "Michael Dell—and His Company—Grow Up," *Wall Street Journal*, January 31, 1994, pp. B1, B2.

[2]Teri Lammers Prior, "Channel Surfers," *Inc.*, February 1995, pp. 65–68.

[3]Peter H. Lewis, "On-Line Middleman Opens for Business," *New York Times*, October 2, 1995, p. D5.

[4]Zachary Schiller and Wendy Zellner, "Making the Middleman an Endangered Species," *Business Week*, June 6, 1994, pp. 114–115.

[5]Ronald Henkoff, "Delivering the Goods," *Fortune*, November 28, 1994, pp. 64–66; Gene Bylinsky, "The Digital Factory," *Fortune*, November 14, 1994, pp. 92–95.

[6]Mary Kuntz, et al., "Reinventing the Store," *Business Week*, November 7, 1995, pp. 84–89; Jennifer Steinhauer, "Just Another Retail Bankruptcy? Maybe Not," *New York Times*, July 9, 1997, pp. D1, D4; William J. Holstein and Kerry Hannon, "They Drop Till You Shop," *U.S. News & World Report*, July 21, 1997, pp. 51–52.

[7]Mary Kuntz, et al., "Reinventing the Store," *Business Week*, November 7, 1995, pp. 84–89.

[8]Susan Caminiti, "Will Old Navy Fill the Gap?" *Fortune*, March 18, 1996, pp. 59–62.

[9]Karen Lowry Miller, Kevin Kelly, and Heidi Dawley, "Otto the Great Rules in Germany," *Business Week*, January 31, 1994, pp. 70J, 70K.

[10]John Huey, "Waking Up to the New Economy," *Fortune*, June 27, 1994, pp. 36–38.

[11]Edith Hill Updike and Mary Kunz, "Japan Is Dialing 1-800-BuyAmerica," *Business Week*, June 12, 1995, pp. 61, 64.

[12]Laura Zinn et al., "Retailing Will Never Be the Same," *Business Week*, July 26, 1993, pp. 54–60; Huey, "Waking Up," pp. 36–38.

[13]John F. Yarbrough, "Dialing for Dollar$," *Sales & Marketing Management*, January 1997, p. 60.

[14]Suein L. Hwang, "Ding Dong: Updating Avon Means Respecting History Without Repeating It," *Wall Street Journal*, April 4, 1994, pp. A1, A4; Claudia H. Deutsch, "Relighting the Fires at Avon Products," *New York Times*, April 3, 1994, sec. 3, p. 5; James Brooke, "Who Braves Piranha Waters? Your Avon Lady!," *New York Times*, July 7, 1995, p. A4.

[15]Gregory L. Miles, "Marriages of Convenience," *International Business*, January 1995, pp. 32–36.

[16]Ronald Henkoff, "Delivering the Goods," *Fortune*, November 28, 1994, pp. 64–66, 76, 78.

[17]Ronald Henkoff, "Delivering the Goods," *Fortune*, November 28, 1994, pp. 64–65.

[18]Henkoff, "Delivering the Goods," pp. 76–78.

Chapter 15

[1]Gene Bylinsky, "The Digital Factory," *Fortune*, November 14, 1994, pp. 92–96.

[2]Christopher Farrell, "A Wellspring of Innovation," *Business Week*, Enterprise 1993, pp. 57–62.

[3]Bylinsky, "The Digital Factory," p. 93.

[4]*Monthly Labor Review* (Washington, DC: U.S. Department of Labor), October 1994, p. 87.

[5]Ronald Henkoff, "Service Is Everybody's Business," *Fortune*, June 27, 1994, pp. 48–50, 56, 60; Ronald Henkoff, "Finding, Training, and Keeping the Best Service Workers," *Fortune*, October 3, 1994, pp. 110–113.

[6]Steven A. Melnyk and David R. Denzler, *Operations Management: A Value-Driven Approach* (Chicago: Irwin, 1996), Chapter 1.

[7]Patricia Sellers, "Companies That Serve You Best," *Fortune*, May 31, 1993, pp. 75, 85.

[8]Melnyk Denzler, *Operations Management*, p. 773.

[9]Jeffrey A. Tannenbaum, "Food Franchisers Expand by Pursuing Customers into Every Nook and Cranny," *Wall Street Journal*, October 26, 1994, p. B1.

[10]David Woodruff and John Templeton, "Why Mercedes Is Alabama Bound," *Business Week*, October 11, 1993, pp. 138–139; Bill Vlasic, "In Alabama, the Soul of a New Mercedes?" *Business Week*, March 31, 1997, pp. 70, 71.

[11]James D. Dilworth, *Operations Management*, 2nd ed. (New York: McGraw, 1996), pp. 250–251.

[12]Joseph S. Martinich, *Production and Operations Management* (New York: Wiley, 1997), pp. 335–340.

[13]Roger W. Schmenner, *Service Operations Management* (Englewood Cliffs, NJ: Prentice Hall, 1995), pp. 37–49.

[14]Dale H. Besterfield, *Quality Control*, 3rd ed. (Englewood Cliffs, NJ: Prentice Hall, 1990), p. 1.

[15]*Perrigo: 1996 Annual Report* (Allegan, MI: Perrigo, 1996).

[16]Myron Magnet, "Good News for the Service Economy," *Fortune*, May 3, 1993, pp. 50–51.

[17]Robert Fade, "Untying the Scheduling and Control Knot," *APICS: The Performance Advantage*, October, 1994, pp. 75–77.

[18]Henkoff, "Service Is Everybody's Business," p. 52.

[19]Henkoff, "Finding, Training, and Keeping the Best Service Workers," p. 113.

[20]Henkoff, "Finding, Training, and Keeping the Best Service Workers," p. 114.

[21]Martinich, *Production and Operations Management*, pp. 750–781.

[22]Richard A. Melcher, "Tune-Up Time for Harley," *Business Week*, April 8, 1996, pp. 90–91; Harley-Davidson Inc., *1996 Annual Report* (Milwaukee: Harley-Davidson, 1996); Gina Imperato, "Harley Shifts Gears," *Fast Company*, June–July 1997, pp. 104, 105, 113.

Chapter 16

[1]Sylvia Nasar, "More Signs of a Productive U.S.," *New York Times*, October 22, 1993, pp. D1, D6; *Monthly Labor Review* (Washington, DC: U.S. Dept. of Labor, February 1997), pp. 27, 29.

[2]Scott Thurm, "In California, Higher Productivity Leads to Low Unemployment and Inflation," *Knight-Ridder/ Tribune Business News*, March 17, 1997, p. 317B.

[3]Estimated from *Survey of Current Business* (Washington, DC: U.S. Dept. of Commerce, August 1997), p. 42; *Monthly Labor Review* (Washington, DC: U.S. Dept. of Labor, August 1997), p. 76; Carl G. Thor, *Perspectives '94* (Houston: American Productivity and Quality Center, 1994), p. 17.

[4]Thor, *Perspectives '94*, p. 17.

[5]*Monthly Labor Review* (Washington, DC: U.S. Dept. of Labor, May 1997), p. 76.

[6]Estimated from *Survey of Current Business* (Washington DC: U.S. Dept. of Commerce, September 1997), p. D3; *Monthly Labor Review*, August 1997, p. 76.

[7]*Monthly Labor Review* (Washington, DC: U.S. Dept. of Labor, July 1997), p. 99.

[8]Stephen Baker, "The Bridges Steel Is Building," *Business Week*, June 2, 1997, p. 39; Wendy Zellner et al., "Go-Go Goliaths," *Fortune*, February 13, 1995, pp. 64–70; John Holusha, "Why American Steel Is Big Again," *New York Times*, July 21, 1994, pp. D1, D6; Stephen Baker, "The Odd Couple of Steel," *Business Week*, November 7, 1994, pp. 106, 108.

[9]Duff McDonald, "Productivity Can Pump Up These Sturdy Profit Makers," *Money*, September 1997, p. 53.

[10]Joel Kurtzman, "Is Your Company Off Course? Now You Can Find Out Why," *Fortune*, February 17, 1997, p. 133.

[11]Internet Web site (http://www.quality.nist.gov/docs/winners/96win/custom.htm).

[12]James R. Evans and William M. Lindsay, *The Management and Control of Quality*, 3rd ed. (Minneapolis/St.Paul: West, 1996), pp. 186–187; David Woodruff, "Bug Control at Chrysler," *Business Week*, August 22, 1994, p. 26.

[13]Geoffrey Smith et al., "The Rules of the Game in the New World of Work," *Business Week*, October 17, 1994, pp. 94–100.

[14]David Greising, "Quality: How to Make It Pay," *Business Week*, August 8, 1994, pp. 54–59.

[15]Justin Martin, "Are You as Good as You Think You Are?" *Fortune*, September 30, 1996, pp. 146, 147.

[16]Stuart F. Brown, "Detroit to Suppliers: Quality or Else," *Fortune: Industrial Management & Technology*, September 30, 1996, p. 134; Ronald Henkoff, "The Hot New Seal of Quality," *Fortune*, June 28, 1993, pp. 116–120; Otis Port, "More Than a Passport to European Business," *Business Week*, November 1993, pp. 146H, 146J.

[17]"The Mobil Survey: More Than 127,000 ISO 9000 Certificates," *ISO 9000 News*, November/December 1996.

[18]Michael Hammer and James Champy, "The Promise of Reengineering," *Fortune*, May 3, 1993, pp. 41–48.

[19]David Greising, "Quality: How to Make It Pay," *Business Week*, August 8, 1994, pp. 54–59.

[20]Gene Bylinsky, "Five Heroes of U.S. Manufacturing," *Fortune: Industrial Management & Technology*, May 26, 1997, pp. 104A–104H.

[21]Bethany McLean, "Need Electricity? Call Your Broker," *Fortune*, September 29, 1997, pp. 153–156.

[22]Internet Web site (http://www.motorola.com), November 1997.

[23]Internet Web site (http://www.quality.nist.gov/docs/winners/96win/custom.htm), November 1997.

[24]David Greising, "Quality: How to Make It Pay," pp. 56–57.

[25]John Benson et al., "Self-Directed Work Teams," *Production and Inventory Management Journal*, First Quarter 1994, pp. 79–82.

[26]Leonard L. Berry, A. Parasuraman, and Valerie A. Zeithaml, "Improving Service Quality in America: Lessons Learned," *Academy of Management Executive*, 8, no. 2 (1994), pp. 32–45.

[27]Justin Martin, "Are You as Good as You Think You Are?" *Fortune*, September ber 30, 1996, pp. 142–144; Roberta Maynard, "Tailoring Products for a Niche of One," *Nation's Business*, November 1993, p. 43.

Chapter 17

[1]Edward O. Welles, "Burning Down the House," *Inc.*, August 1997, pp. 67–73.

[2]Sarah Schafer, "Caffeine Fix," *Inc. Technology*, no. 3, 1997, pp. 76–77.

[3]"Philips' TV Forecasts," *TV Digest*, July 8, 1996, p. 12; John Markoff, "Approaching a Digital Milestone," *New York Times*, January 7, 1995, pp. 39, 50; data from Electronic Industries Association.

[4]"Brøderbund Product Display," www.broderbund.com (Web site), December 13, 1997.

[5]Richard Behar, "Who's Reading Your E-Mail?" *Fortune*, February 3, 1997, pp. 57–70.

[6]William M. Bulkeley, "Stop, Thief!" *Wall Street Journal*, September 11, 1997, p. R14.

[7]Peter H. Lewis, "Security Is Lost in Cyberspace," *New York Times*, February 22, 1995, pp. D1, D19.

[8]"PC Sales Growth Slowed," *Television Digest*, June 2, 1997, p. 17.

[9]David Kirkpatrick, "How PCs Will Take Over Your Home," *Fortune*, February 21, 1994, pp. 100–104.

[10]G. B. Shelly, T. J. Cashman, G. A. Waggoner, and W.C . Waggoner, *Using Computers: The Gateway to Information* (New York: Boyd & Fraser, 1995), Chapter 1.

[11]Otis Port, "Speed Gets a Whole New Meaning," *Business Week*, April 29, 1996, pp. 90–91.

[12]Larry Long and Nancy Long, *Computers*, 3rd ed. (Englewood Cliffs, NJ: Prentice Hall, 1993), p. 219.

[13]*Tele Danmark Annual Report 1996* (Copenhagen: 1996), p. 23.

[14]Peter Nulty, "When to Murder Your Mainframe," *Fortune*, November 1, 1993, pp. 109–110.

[15]Brent Schlender, "A Conversation with the Lords of Wintel," *Fortune*, July 8, 1996, pp. 42–44.

[16]Peter Burroughs, Geoffrey Smith, and Steven V. Brull, "HP Pictures the Future," *Business Week*, July 7, 1997, pp. 100–103; Richard Brandt, "Bill Gates's Vision," *Business Week*, June 27, 1994, pp. 56–62; G. Christian Hill, "The Spoils of War," *Wall Street Journal*, September 11, 1997, pp. R1, R2.

[17]Kenneth C. Laudon and Jane Price Laudon, *Management Information Systems: Organization and Technology*, 4th ed. (Upper Saddle River, NJ: Prentice Hall, 1996), pp. 646–651.

[18]*GE 1996 Annual Report* (Fairfield, CT: General Electric Company, 1996), p. 8.

[19]Joshua Macht, "The Ultimate Head Trip," *Inc. Technology*, no. 3, 1997, p. 77.

[20]*GE 1996 Annual Report*, p. 9.

[21]Mary J. Cronin, "Using the Web to Push Key Data to Decision Makers," *Fortune*, September 29, 1997, p. 254; Schlender, "A Conversation with the Lords of Wintel," pp. 42–44.

[22]Amy Cortese, "The Software Revolution," *Business Week*, December 4, 1995, pp. 78–83; John W. Verity, "Everyone's Rushing the Net," *Business Week*, June 5, 1995, pp. 116, 118; Peter Coy, Robert D. Hof, and Paul C. Judge, "Has the Net Finally Reached the Wall?" *Business Week*, August 26, 1996, pp. 62–66.

[23]Robert D. Hoff, Kathy Rebello, and John W. Verity, "Java's Cup Runneth Over," *Business Week*, May 20, 1996, pp. 103–104.

[24]Phaedra Hise, "Getting Smart On-Line," *Inc. Technology*, no. 1, 1996, pp. 59–60.

[25]Stephen D. Solomon, "Staking a Claim on the Internet," *Inc. Technology*, March 1995, pp. 87–90.

[26]John W. Verity, "What Hath Yahoo Wrought?" *Business Week*, February 12, 1996, pp. 88–90.

[27]Amy Cortese, "Here Comes the Intranet," *Business Week*, February 26, 1996, pp. 76–79; Alison Sprout, "The Internet Inside Your Company," *Fortune*, November 27, 1995, pp. 161–162.

[28]Robert D. Hof, Seanna Browder, and Peter Elstrom, "Internet Communities," *Business Week*, May 5, 1997, pp. 64–76, 70, 74, 76, 78.

[29]*GE 1996 Annual Report*, p. 8.

[30]Schlender, "A Conversation with the Lords of Wintel," pp. 42–44; Andrew Kupfer, "Craig McCaw Sees an Internet in the Sky," *Fortune*, May 27, 1996, pp. 62–72.

[31]Brandt, "Bill Gates's Vision," pp. 56–62.

Chapter 18

[1]B. E. Needles, Jr., H. R. Anderson, and J. C. Caldwell, *Principles of Accounting*, 6th ed. (Boston: Houghton Mifflin, 1996), Chapter 1.

[2]Mark Heinzl, "Noranda to Shed Interests in Forestry and Energy, Refocusing on Mining," *Wall Street Journal*, November 19, 1997, pp. A3, A6.

[3]Needles, Anderson, and Caldwell, *Principles of Accounting*, pp. 25–26.

[4]Jill Andresky, "How Many Accountants Does It Take to Change an Industry?" *Inc.*, April 1997, pp. 63–69.

[5]"Audit Raises Flag at Baby Superstore," *New York Times*, February 27, 1996, p. D10.

[6]Needles, Anderson, and Caldwell, *Principles of Accounting*, p. 26; Phillip L.

Zweig and Dean Foust, "Corporate America Is Fed Up with FASB," *Business Week*, April 21, 1997, pp. 108, 110.

[7]Needles, Anderson, and Caldwell, *Principles of Accounting*, Chapter 20.

[8]Needles, Anderson, and Caldwell, *Principles of Accounting*, Chapter 25.

[9]Douglas Lavin, "GM Would Have to Cut 20,000 Workers to Match Ford Efficiency, Report Says," *Wall Street Journal*, June 24, 1994, p. C22.

[10]Needles, Anderson, and Caldwell, *Principles of Accounting*, pp. 410, 787.

[11]Stephen Barr, "Adidas on the Rebound," *CFO*, September 1991, p. 54.

[12]Stanley Reed, Larry Holyoke, and Douglas Harbrecht, "Here Comes the Great Global Tax War," *Business Week*, May 30, 1994, pp. 55–56; Chris Carroll, "IRS Targets Local Company in 'Transfer Pricing' Case," *Houston Business Journal*, January 31, 1997, p. 1A.

Chapter 19

[1]*Federal Reserve Bulletin* (Washington, DC: Board of Governors of the Federal Reserve System, November 1997), p. A12.

[2]Sylvia Nasar, "Older Americans Cited in Studies of National Savings Rate Slump," *New York Times*, February 2, 1995, pp. C1, C9; Susan Mitchell and Maxine Wilkie, "How Boomers Save," *American Demographics*, September 1994, pp. 22–29; Christopher Farrell, "The Economics of Aging," *Business Week*, September 12, 1994, pp. 60–64; "Economy 2000," *Financial World*, June 23, 1992, pp. 44–46.

[3]*Standard & Poor's NYSE Stock Reports* (New York: McGraw-Hill, August 12, 1997), p. 537M.

[4]*1996 Statistical Abstract of the United States* (Washington, DC: U.S. Department of Commerce, 1996), p. 517.

[5]Mickey Meece, "Nonbanks Now Five of Top 10 Credit Card Issuers," *American Banker*, February 5, 1996; "The Cutting Edge," *The Economist*, July 27, 1996, pp. 63–64.

[6]Richard L. Holman, "Korea Curbs Credit Cards," *Wall Street Journal*, December 22, 1994, p. A10.

[7]Richard W. Stevenson, "In New Economy, Russians Cannot Rely on Their Banks," *New York Times*, September 12, 1995, pp. A1, A10.

[8]*Fortune*, August 4, 1997, pp. F2–F11, F16–F18; *1996 Statistical Abstract of the United States*, p. 511.

[9]Terence P. Pare, "Clueless Bankers," *Fortune*, November 27, 1996, pp. 151–152.

[10]Terence P. Pare, "Clueless Bankers," *Fortune*, November 27, 1996, pp. 151.

[11]Saul Hansell, "A New Chase Tries to

Lead," *New York Times*, March 29, 1996, pp. D1, D4; Stephanie Strom, "King-Pin of the Big-Time Loan," *New York Times*, August 11, 1995, pp. D1, D4; Saul Hansell, "Merger-Hungry Banks Find the Pickings Slim," *New York Times*, January 2, 1997, pp. C22; *Standard & Poor's NYSE Stock Reports* (New York: McGraw-Hill, August 22, 1997), p. 275.

[12]Kathleen Morris, "Out of the S&L Ashes," *Business Week*, March 24, 1997, p. 192.

[13]*1996 Statistical Abstract of the United States*, p. 513.

[14]John W. Wright, ed., *The Universal Almanac* (Kansas City, MO: Andrews and McMeel, 1996), p. 254.

[15]*1996 Statistical Abstract of the United States*, p. 513.

[16]*1996 Statistical Abstract of the United States*, p. 507.

[17]*1996 Statistical Abstract of the United States*, p. 506.

[18]*Federal Reserve Bulletin* (Washington, DC: Board of Governors of the Federal Reserve System, November 1997), p. A33.

[19]*1996 Statistical Abstract of the United States*, p. 506.

[20]Charles Keenan, "EDS Is Testing Commercials on Teller Machines," *American Banker*, December 12, 1997, p. 11; Walter A. Dods, Jr., "ATMs—A Solution, Not the Problem," *ABA Banking Journal*, August 1997, p. 11.

[21]Saul Hansell, "The Ante Rises in East Asia," *New York Times*, July 14, 1996, sec. 3, pp. 1, 12; Terence P. Pare, "Clueless Bankers," *Fortune*, November 27, 1996, p. 158.

[22]Keith Bradsher, "Federal Reserve Trims a Key Rate; First Cut Since '92," *New York Times*, July 7, 1995, A1, D1, D4.

[23]Peter Rose, *Commercial Bank Management*, 3rd ed. (Chicago: Irwin, 1996), pp. 370–371.

[24]Steve Chocheo, "Interstate Banking Law Gets a Low-Key Sendoff," *ABA Banking Journal*, November 1994, pp. 7, 10; Olad DeSenerpont Domis, "Loophole in Interstate Law Benefits Branching in '95," *American Banker*, December 14, 1994, p. 24.

[25]Daniel Kaplan, "Interstate Branching Isn't a Done Deal Yet," *American Banker*, December 14, 1994, p. 24.

[26]David J. Morrow, "Handy? Surely, but Debit Card Has Risks, Too," *New York Times*, July 13, 1997, pp. 1, 16.

[27]Russell Mitchell, "The Smart Money Is on Smart Cards," *Business Week*, August 14, 1995, pp. 68–69; Nikhil Deogun, "The Smart Money Is on 'Smart Cards,' but Electronic Cash Seems Dumb to Some," *Wall Street Journal*, August 5, 1996, pp. B1, B8.

[28]Kelly Holland and Greg Burns, "Plastic Talks," *Business Week*, February 14, 1994, pp. 105–107; Saul Hansell, "An End to the 'Nightmare' of Cash," *New York Times*, September 6, 1994, pp. D1, D5; Thomas McCarroll, "No Checks. No Cash. No Fuss?" *Time*, May 9, 1994, pp. 60–62; Marla Matzer, "Plastic Mania," *Forbes*, October 24, 1994, pp. 281–282.

[29]Kelly Holland and Amy Cortese, "The Future of Money," *Business Week*, June 12, 1995, pp. 66–72.

[30]*Federal Reserve Bulletin* (Washington, DC: Board of Governors of the Federal Reserve System, November 1997), p. A51, A72.

[31]*Fortune*, August 4, 1997, pp. F-2, F-4, F-17.

[32]Robert J. Carbaugh, *International Economics*, 5th ed. (Cincinnati: South-Western, 1995), Chapter 11.

Chapter 20

[1]*Federal Reserve Bulletin* (Washington, DC: Board of Governors of the Federal Reserve System), November 1997, p. A31.

[2]*Federal Reserve Bulletin*, p. A31.

[3]*Prospectus: Rayovac® Common Stock* (Madison, WI: Rayovac), November 20, 1997.

[4]Mark Landler, "AT&T Warns of a Drop in Earnings and Its Stock Plunges," *New York Times*, September 25, 1996, D1, D3; Mark Landler, "Loss at AT&T Computer Unit Was $1 Billion Over Estimates," *New York Times*, September 27, 1996, D1, D7; *The Wall Street Journal Index* (Ann Arbor, MI: UMI, July–September, 1996), p. 23; Carol J. Loomis, "AT&T Has No Clothes," *Fortune*, February 5, 1996, pp. 78–80; Andrew Kupfer, "AT&T: Ready to Run, Nowhere to Hide," *Fortune*, April 29, 1996, pp. 116–118.

[5]*Prospectus: Rayovac® Common Stock*, November 20, 1997.

[6]*The Value Line Investment Survey*, January 28, 1994, p. 1095; *Standard & Poor's NYSE Stock Reports*, August 1996, p. 1210M; Irs Sager, "How IBM Became a Growth Company Again," *Business Week*, December 9, 1996, pp. 154–158; Laurence Zuckerman, "I.B.M. Earnings Top Forecasts, but Stir Doubt on Stock Price," *New York Times*, January 2, 1997, pp. D1, D9.

[7]*Standard & Poor's NYSE Stock Reports*, October 18, 1997, p. 1986F.

[8]You can visit the Web sites to examine online investing services at www.etrade.com and www.schwab.com.

[9]Russell Mitchell, "The Schwab Revolution," *Business Week*, December 18, 1994, pp. 88–91; Ellyn E. Spragins, "Is Bigger Better?" *Business Week*, July 4, 1994, pp. 54–55.

[10]New York Stock Exchange Web site, www.nyse.com, January 2, 1998.

[11]Michael Schroeder, "Babysitting the World's Emerging Bourses," *Business Week*, November 1, 1993, pp. 112–114; William Glasgall and Dave Lindorff, "The Global Investor," *Business Week*, September 19, 1994, pp. 96–102.

[12]*Federal Reserve Bulletin*, November 1997, pp. A27, A28, A31, A37.

[13]*Federal Reserve Bulletin*, November 1997, p. A31.

[14]*Moody's Bond Survey*, July 4, 1994, p. 4932, and July 18, 1994, p. 4712.

[15]Charles Gasparino and Michael Moss, "What Happened When a Small Town Trusted Local Financial Wizard," *Wall Street Journal*, December 26, 1997, pp. A1, A2; Sarah Lubman and John R. Emshwiller, "Before the Fall: Hubris and Ambition in Orange County: Robert Citron's Story," *Wall Street Journal*, January 18, 1995, pp. A1, A10; Laura Jereski, "But No Cigar; How a Rescue Mission Failed, Just Barely, in Orange County," *Wall Street Journal*, December 8, 1994, pp. A1, A12; Floyd Norris, "Bonds Roiled by Orange County Failure," *New York Times*, December 8, 1994, pp. D1, D17; Sallie Hofmeister, "Orange County's Battered Fund to Be Sold in Effort to Limit Loss," *New York Times*, December 14, 1994, pp. A1, D6; "Local Heroes: Public Finance Chiefs Are Often Very Boring; That's the Good News," *Wall Street Journal*, December 8, 1994, pp. A1, A8; Nanette Byrnes and Leah Nathans, "The Phantom of Orange County," *Business Week*, January 16, 1995, p. 70.

[16]*Moody's Bond Survey*, July 11, 1994, p. 4811.

[17]*Moody's Bond Survey*, April 26, 1993, p. 5884.

[18]*Wiesenberger Mutual Funds Update* (Rockville, MD: CDA Investment Technologies, June 30, 1997), p. iii.

[19]*Mutual Fund Fact Book* (Washington, DC: Investment Company Institute, 1995).

[20]U.S. Department of Commerce, *Statistical Abstract of the United States* (Washington, DC: Bureau of the Census, 1996), p. 527.

[21]Amey Stone, "Futures: Dare You Defy the Odds?" *Business Week*, February 28, 1994, pp. 12–13.

[22]Susan E. Kuhn, "How Crazy Is This Market?" *Fortune*, April 15, 1996, pp. 78–83; David Barboza, "Stocks Race Past New Milestone as Dow Breaks 7,000 Barrier," *New York Times*, February 14, 1997, pp. A1, D6.

[23]This illustration is based on Bill Alpert, "The Times Are Risky, the Game Is Dangerous," *New York Times*, August 27, 1995, sec. 3, p. 3.

[24]Jeffrey M. Laderman, "The Prospectus Tries Plain Speaking," *Business Week*, August 14, 1995, p. 72.

[25]Michael Schroeder and Amy Barrett, "A Bigger Stick Against Inside Traders," *Business Week*, May 27, 1996, pp. 34–35.

Chapter 21

[1]*The Coca-Cola Company 1996 Annual Report*.

[2]Shawn Tully, "Raiding a Company's Hidden Cash," *Fortune*, August 22, 1994, pp. 82–87.

[3]*Gucci Group n.v. Annual Report 1996*.

[4]*Moody's Bond Survey*, June 1991.

[5]Linda Himelstein, Kathy Rebello, and Leah Nathans Spiro, "Silicon Valley Seeds Itself," *Business Week*, March 11, 1996, pp. 74–75.

[6]Stephen E. Frank, Matt Murray, Michael Schuman, Namju Cho, and Christopher Rhoads, "Divisions Emerge Among Bankers Over Korea," *Wall Street Journal*, January 2, 1998, p. 5; David Wessel, "Korean Bailout Raises Tough Questions," *Wall Street Journal*, December 26, 1997, p. A2; Michael Shuman, David Wessel, and Jathon Sapsford, "Korea to Get Quick Release of $10 Billion in Aid," *Wall Street Journal*, December 26, 1997, pp. A5, A6.

[7]*Financial World*, February 28, 1995, p. 60; *Mutual Fund Profiles* (New York: Standard & Poor's, February 1994), p. ix; *Stock Reports Index* (New York: Standard & Poor's, November 1994), p. ix.

[8]John McQueen, "The Failure Roll-Call," *Accountancy*, June 1997, p. 40.

[9]J. W. Duncan, *D&B Reports*, September–October 1991, p. 8.

[10]Susan Hodges, "One Giant Step Toward a Loan," *Nation's Business*, August 1997, pp. 34, 36.

[11]Thomas P. Fitch, *Dictionary of Banking Terms*, 2nd ed. (Hauppauge, NY: Barron's, 1993), p. 531.

[12]Phillip L. Zweig et al., "Managing Risk," *Fortune*, October 31, 1994, pp. 86–90.

Appendix 1

[1]See S. S. Huebner, Kenneth Black, Jr., and Bernard L. Webb, *Property and Liability Insurance*, 4th ed. (Upper Saddle River, NJ: Prentice Hall 1996), pp. 369–372.

[2]Michael Quint, "Crackdown on Job Injury Costs," *New York Times*, March 16, 1995, D1, D7; see also Huebner, Black, and Webb, *Property and Liability Insurance*, pp. 432–437.

[3]Quint, "Crackdown."

[4]U.S. Dept. of Commerce, *Statistical Abstract of the United States* (Washington, DC: Bureau of the Census, 1997), p. 224.

[5]See Huebner, Black, and Webb, *Property and Liability Insurance*, pp. 260–263.

[6]*1997 Life Insurance Fact Book* (Washington, DC: American Council of Life Insurance), pp. 37, 43.

[7]*Los Angeles Business Times*, September 15, 1997, p. 11.

[8]Stephen Blakely, "Increases for the Year May Exceed Projections," *Nation's Business*, January 1998, p. 30; Allison Bell, "Rising Costs Will Rattle Health Plans for Next Year," *National Underwriter Life and Health*, December 22, 1997, pp. 2–3; *Statistical Abstract of the United States* (1997), p. 112.

[9]*Statistical Abstract of the United States* (1997), p. 115.

[10]Ibid., p. 117.

[11]Roberta Maynard, "The Power of Pooling," *Nation's Business*, March 1995, pp. 16–22.

Source Notes for Chapter-Opening Vignettes, Box Features, End-of-Chapter Cases, Tables, and Figures

Part 1

Beanie Baby Business Joseph Berger, "Goodbye, Tickle Me Elmo; Hello, Beanie Babies," *New York Times*, March 14, 1997, p. B1; William L. Hamilton, "The Short, Sweet Life of Peanut the Elephant," *New York Times*, October 30, 1997, p. F1; David Leonhardt, "Hey Kid, Buy This," *Business Week*, June 30, 1997, p. 62; Gary Samuels, "Mystique Marketing," *Forbes*, October 21, 1996, p. 276; Joanna Sullivan, "Bank Offers Hot Investment: Teeny Beanie Babies," *American Banker*, May 19, 1997, p. 17; Rod Taylor et al., "The Beanie Factor," *Brandweek*, June 16, 1997, p. 22; Randy Weston, "Beanie Babies Blitz IS," *Computerworld*, April 28, 1997, p. 1.

Chapter 1

America Online Meets Supply and Demand Peter H. Lewis, "An 'All You Can Eat' Price is Clogging Internet Access," *New York Times*, Dec. 17, 1996; Steve Lohr, "Pushed by States, America Online Plans Refunds to Customers," *New York Times*, Jan. 30, 1977; Edward Baig, "AOL Isn't the Only Connection in Town," *Business Week*, Feb. 24, 1997, p. 144. ***Can Privatization Save Our National Parks*** Michael Satchell, "Parks in Peril," *U.S. News and World Report*, July 21, 1997, p. 24; Timothy Egan, "Adapting to Fees for Enjoying Public Lands," *New York Times*, August 21, 1997, pp. A1, A28. ***Wages Are Rising But Whose?*** Kim Clark, "These *Are* the Good Old Days," *Fortune*, June 9, 1997, pp. 74–86; Aaron Bernstein, "Is American Becoming More of a Class Society?" *Business Week*, February 26, 1996, pp. 86–91; Michael Mandel et al., "How Long Can This Last?" *Business Week*, May 19, 1997, pp. 30–35; C.

Robert D. Hershey, Jr., "Fed Survey Says Higher Pay Mostly Eludes Workers," *New York Times*, March 13, 1997, p. D4. ***Dinner and a Movie? Just Click Here*** Amy Cortese, "Where the Action Is: Your Hometown," *Business Week*, April 14, 1997, pp. 95, 98; Edward C. Baig, "Previewing on the Web: A Night on the Town," *Business Week*, September 29, 1997, p. 147.

Chapter 2

When Gorillas Dance Jane Levere, "Microsoft–American Express Pact Shakes the U.S. Travel Industry," *New York Times*, August 3, 1996; "American Express and Microsoft Unveil Online Travel Reservations System for Corporations," *Online Money News*, July 14, 1997. ***Coping with Foreign Competition*** Joan Warner, "Clinging to the Safety Net," *Business Week*, March 11, 1996, p. 62; Alan Cowell, "In Germany, Workers Fear the Miracle Is Over," *New York Times*, July 30, 1997. ***Working At Home*** Melanie Warner, "Working at Home: The Right Way to Be a Star in Your Bunny Slippers," *Fortune*, March 3, 1997, pp. 165–166; "Bulletin Board: Growth Areas on the Internet," *Inc. Tech*, 1997, No. 2, p. 20; Susan J. Wells, "For Stay-Home Workers, Speed Bumps on the Telecommute," *New York Times*, August 17, 1997, section 3, p. 14. ***The Gee Whiz Company Stumbles*** Lawrence M. Fisher, "Silicon Graphics Shares Fall as Earnings Go Up," *New York Times*, August 5, 1996; John Diamond, "Officials Say Supercomputer Sale to Russia May Have Violated Law," *New York Times*, April 15, 1997; Robert D. Hof et al., "The Sad Saga of Silicon Graphics," *Business Week*, August 4, 1997, pp. 66–72.

Chapter 3

Understanding the Global Context of Business Mark L. Clifford et al., "Coke Pours into Asia," *Business Week*, July 28, 1997. ***A Kind of Equality*** Andrew Pollack, "Opportunity at a Price," *New York Times*, July 8, 1997, pp. D1, D4. ***An International Partnership*** David Woodruff and William C. Symonds, "The Hottest Thing in 'Green' Wheels," *Business Week*, April 28, 1997, p. 42; "Toyota Sports the Green," *Business Week*, February 16, 1998, p. 58; Anthony DePalma, "The Great Green Hope," *New York Times*, October 8, 1997, p. D6. ***Toyota Expands Its Reach*** Brian Bremner et al., "Toyota's Crusade," *Business Week*, April 7, 1997, pp. 104–114.

Chapter 4

Denny's Tries an About-Face Nicole Harris, "A New Denny's—Diner by Diner," *Business Week*, March 25, 1996, pp. 166, 168; Faye Rice, "Denny's

Changes Its Spots," *Fortune*, May 13, 1996, pp. 133–142, special advertising section, *Fortune*, June 23, 1997; David M. Herszenhorn, "Punitive Actions Are Advised in Discrimination at Denny's," *New York Times*, August 15, 1997, p. B4. ***How Ethical Are You?*** Henry Fountain, "Of White Lies and Yellow Pads," *New York Times*, July 6, 1997, p. F7. ***The Harder Side of Sears*** Barnaby J. Feder, "The Harder Side of Sears," *New York Times*, July 20, 1997, sec. 3, pp. 1, 3; Susan Chandler, "The Harder Side of Sears," *Business Week*, April 28, 1997, p. 48. ***The Case Against Recycling*** John Tierney, "Recycling Is Garbage," *New York Times Magazine*, June 30, 1996, pp. 24–53. **Table 4.1** *Taft Corporate Giving Directory*, 18th Ed.

Part 2

Cape Cod Revival Dale D. Buss, "Hello, Mr. Chips," *Income Opportunities*, August 1997; Cape Cod Potato Chip Press Releases, "As Potato Chip Companies Try to Gain an edge in the Snack Food Industry, Cape Cod Looks to the Russet," "Cape Cod Potato Chips' Success Wasn't Just By Accident," and "Just as Eaters Seem to Have Given Up Hope in the Taste of Low Fat Foods, Cape Cod Potato Chips Finds the Answer"; Linda Grant, "A Passion for Potato Chips," *Fortune*, August 18, 1997, p. 228; Dan McGraw, "Salting Away the Competition: Frito-Lay Launches a Powerful Snack Attack and Crunches the Competition," *U.S. News & World Report*, September 16, 1996, p. 71; Bernard Pacyniak, "Cape Cod Redux," *Snack & Bakery Foods*, March 1997, p. 33.

Chapter 5

Delta Clips Its Own Wings Adam Bryant, "What Price Efficiency?" *New York Times*, July 25, 1997, pp. D1, D6. ***Scandic Hotels Turn Green*** Ann Goodman, "Rooms with a View," *Fast Company*, June–July 1997, pp. 52–54. ***Dilbert Goes Establishment*** Barbara Whitaker, "If You Can't Dodge Dilbert, Hire Him," *New York Times*, June 26, 1997, sec. 3, p. 12; Adam Bryant, "Managing Dilbert, Inc." *New York Times*, September 7, 1997, sec. 3, pp. 1, 13.

Chapter 6

Firms Find Strength Claudia H. Deutsch, "Clearing Out the Kitchen Sink," *New York Times*, July 29, 1997, p. D1. ***How Is Your Doctor's Stock Today*** Erick Schonfeld, "Doctors Unite," *Fortune*, March 3, 1997, p. 200; Mike McNamee et al., "Health-Care Inflation: It's Baaack!" *Business Week*, March 24, 1997, pp. 28–30; Anthony Bianco and Eric Schine, "Doctors, Inc.," *Business Week*, March 24, 1997, pp. 204–210. ***Pepsico Sends Its Restaurants Out into the Cold*** Glenn Collins, "Pepsico to Spin Off Its Fast-Food Business," *New York Times*, January 24, 1997, p. D1–D2; Glenn Collins, "Left Alone at the Food Fight," *New York Times*, July 16, 1997, pp. D1, D4; Richard Gibson, "Fast-Food Spinoff Enters Pepsi-Free Era," *Wall Street Journal*, October 7, 1997, pp. B1–B2; Constance L. Hays, "Pizza Hut Sets a Revamping at a $425 Million Cost to New Owner," *New York Times*, December 10, 1997, pp. D1, D8. ***Hi-Tech Teamwork Pays Off*** William R. Pape, "Group Insurance: Mastering Business in a Networked World," *Inc. Tech 1997*, no. 2, pp. 29–31. ***Building Your Business Skills*** Amy Harmon, "Software Jobs Go Begging, Threatening Technology Boom," *New York Times*, January 13, 1998, p. A1.

Chapter 7

Advice for Nonprofits Heather McLeod, "Crossover: The Social Entrepreneur," *Inc.*, May 20, 1997, pp. 100–105. ***Go Home and Stay There*** David Whitford, "Never Too Small to Manage," *Inc.*, February 1997, pp. 56, 61. ***Location, Location, Location*** Joel Kotkin, "The 4 Best Small-Business Neighborhoods in America," *Inc.*, May 20, 1997, pp. 58–72; Elyse M. Friedman, ed., "Almanac: The New Economy," *Inc.*, May 20, 1997, pp. 108–121. ***If You Build It, Will They Come?*** John Grossman, "Running Out of Time," *Inc.*, February 1997, pp. 62–73. **Figure 7.4** *1996 Facts on Women-Owned Businesses*, © The National Foundation for Women Business Owners.

Part 3

The Wacky World of Southwest Airlines Ann Bruce, "Southwest: Back to the FUNdamentals," *HR Focus*, March 1997, p. 11; Anne Fisher, "The 100 Best Companies to Work for in America," *Fortune*, January 12, 1998, p. 69; Kristin Dunlap Godsey, "Slow Climb to New Heights; Combine Strict Discipline with Goofy Antics and Make Billions," *Success*, October 1996, p. 20; Polly LaBarre, "Lighten Up! Blurring the Line Between Fun and Work Not Only Humanizes Organizations but Strengthens the Bottom Line," *Industry Week*, February 5, 1996, p. 53; Robert Levering and Milton Moskowitz, "The 100 Best Companies to Work for in America," *Fortune*, January 12, 1998, p. 84; Ronald B. Lieber, "Why Employees Love These Companies," *Fortune*, January 12, 1998, p. 72; Justin Martin, "So, You Want to Work for the Best," *Fortune*, January 12, 1998, p. 77; Allen R. Myer-

son, "Air Herb," *New York Times Magazine*," November 9, 1997, p. 36; Donald J. McNerney, "Employee Motivation: Creating a Motivated Workforce," *HR Focus*, August 1996, p. 1; Dan Reed, "Flying Like a Madman," *Sales & Marketing Management*, October 1997, p. 92.

Chapter 8

Diversity Reigns Bruce Felton, "Technologies That Enable the Disabled," *New York Times*, September 14, 1997, sec. 3, pp. 1, 10–11. ***Is There a Job*** Abby Goodnough, "For Women, a Thin Blue Line," *New York Times, August 7, 1997, pp. B1–B6;* "Wanted: Liberal Arts Grads," *Fortune*, May 12, 1997, p. 151; Alan Farnham, "Where Have All the Secretaries Gone?" *Fortune*, May 12, 1997, pp. 152–154; Hal Plotkin, "Hollywood Lures High School Animators with Sweet Deals," *Inc.*, January 1997, p. 20; Shelly Branch, "MBAs Are Hot Again—and They Know It," *Fortune*, April 14, 1997, pp. 155–157; Ann Marsh, "Animadness," *Forbes*, May 5, 1997, p. 47; Rachelle Garbarine, "Goal Line to Bottom Line: Degrees in Sports Management," *New York Times*, September 28, 1997, Business p. 12. ***Downsizing's Pros and Cons*** Gene Koretz, "Big Payoffs from Layoffs," *Business Week*, February 24, 1997, p. 30; Gene Koretz, "The Downside of Downsizing," *Business Week*, April 28, 1997, p. 26; Peter Coy, "Lean May Not Be So Mean," *Business Week*, September 8, 1997, p. 26. ***It May Be Obnoxious*** Jennifer Steinhuaer, "If the Boss Is Out of Line, What's the Legal Boundary?" *New York Times*, March 27, 1997, pp. D1–D4.

Chapter 9

An Unusual Group Barnaby J. Feder, "Harvest of Shares," *New York Times*, June 26, 1997, pp. D1–D5. ***Work and Family*** Keith H. Hammonds, "Balancing Work and Family," *Business Week*, September 16, 1996, pp. 74–80; Keith H. Hammonds et al., "Work and Family," *Business Week*, September 15, 1997, pp. 96–99; Betsy Morris, "Is Your Family Wrecking Your Career (and Vice Versa)?" *Fortune*, March 17, 1997, pp. 71–90. ***Power Gets a New Look*** Thomas A. Stewart, "Get with the New Power Game," *Fortune*, January 13, 1997, pp. 58–62. ***Has Levi's Lost Its Touch*** Stratford Sherman, "Levi's: As Ye Sew, So Shall Ye Reap," *Fortune*, May 12, 1997, pp. 104–116.

Chapter 10

Union Takes Up Her Cause Aaron Bernstein, "This Union Suit Could Really Scratch," *Business Week*, March 10, 1997, p. 37. ***Is Union Membership in Your Future*** Keith Bradsher, "G.M. Strikers Fear

Threat to Way of Life," *New York Times*, March 21, 1996, pp. D1, D8; Bradsher, "General Motors and Union Agree to End Walkout," *New York Times*, March 22, 1996, pp. A1, D4; Bill Vlasic, "The Saginaw Solution," *Business Week*, July 15, 1996, pp. 76–77; Bradsher, "Hurt by Strike, G.M.'s Profits Are Off by Half," *New York Times*, April 23, 1996, pp. D1, D4. ***Union as Management Consultant*** Aaron Bernstein, "Look Who's Pushing Productivity," *Business Week*, April 17, 1997, pp. 72–74. ***A Tale of Two Cities*** Bruce Weber, "Big Opening Is At Risk in Chicago," *New York Times*, October 4, 1997; Phaedra Hise, "Labor-Union Disharmony Silences Symphony," *Inc.* May 1997, p. 28.

Part 4

Off to the Races Interview with M. J. Castelo, Sponsorship Manager, Texaco/Havoline Motorsports Program, October 9, 1996; Al Heller, "Motorsports Mania," *Inside Media*, June 26, 1996, p. 30; Tony Molla, "Motorsports Marketing: Race on Sunday, Sell on Monday," *Motor Age*, March 1997, p. 52; "NASCAR Is Becoming a Leader in Motorsports Entertainment," *Aftermarket Business*, November 1, 1996, p. 70; Texaco/Havoline 1996 marketing materials; Bill Vlasic, "Speedways Without Smoke," *Business Week*, July 21, 1997; Lee Walczak, "Speed Sells," *Business Week*, August 11, 1997.

Chapter 11

What Do Girls Really Want David Leonhardt and Kathleen Kerwin, "Is Madison Avenue Taking 'Get 'em While They're Young' Too Far?" *Business Week*, June 30, 1997; J. C. Herz, "Puzzling Over the Allure of Virtual Barbie," *New York Times*, March 19, 1998, G4; Tim Race, "Building Girls Cyber Rooms of Their Own," *New York Times*, March 5, 1998, G3; Steve Lohr, "It Takes a Child to Raze a Village," *New York Times*, March 5, 1998, G1, G7. ***Drug Companies Go Right to the Source*** Abigail Zuger, "Drug Companies' Sales Pitch: 'Ask Your Doctor,'" *New York Times*, August 5, 1997, p. C1; Thomas M. Burton and Yumiko Ono, "Campaign for Prozac Targets Consumers," *Wall Street Journal*, July 1, 1997, p. B1; "Soon, Drugmakers Can Pitch Doctors via Live Video," *Business Week*, March 10, 1997, p. 106I; David Stout, "Drug Makers Get Leeway on TV Ads," *New York Times*, August 9, 1997, p. 35. ***After the Suit and Tie*** Linda Himelstein and Nancy Walser, "Levi's vs. the Dress Code," *Business Week*, April 1, 1996, pp. 57–58; David Barboza, "Casual Friday on Wall Street," *New York Times*, September 27, 1997, p. B3. ***Playing***

to Win at Toys Я Us Jeanne Dugan, "Can Toys Я Us Get on Top of Its Game?" *Business Week*, April 7, 1997, pp. 124–128.

Chapter 12

When Your New Product Is a Blockbuster Bernard Weinraub, "New Wave of Hollywood Directors Break with Past Styles," *New York Times*, June 9, 1997; Bernard Weinraub, "Hollywood Studios Vie for Choice Summer Weekends," *New York Times*, April 7, 1997; Ronald Grover, "Movie Crazy on Wall Street," *Business Week*, August 11, 1997, pp. 60–61; Ron Grover, "Can't Wait Till Summer? Neither Can Hollywood," *Business Week*, March 24, 1997, p. 42; Ronald Grover, "Lights, Camera, Less Action," *Business Week*, July 1, 1996, p. 50. *Where Green Products Yield Green Dollars* Linda Grant, "Monsanto's Bet: There's Gold in Going Green," *Fortune*, April 14, 1997, pp. 116–118. *You'll Never Get Lost Again* Rik Paul, "BMW On-Board Navigation System," *MotorTrend*, August 1997, p. 130; "The Digital Driveway," *San Francisco Examiner*, August 6, 1997; Michelle Krebs, "Cars that Tell You Where to Go," *New York Times*, December 15, 1996; Larry Armstrong, "So This Is Utopia," *Business Week*, August 4, 1997, p. 16; Amy Gamerman, "Look, Ma, No Hands: A Car That Drives Itself," *Wall Street Journal*, October 23, 1997, p. A17. *It's Clean, It's Cheap* Joan O. Hamilton, "A Gene to Make Greener Blue Jeans," *Business Week*, March 31, 1997, pp. 82–83.

Chapter 13

Tiger, Tiger, Burning Bright Ron Stodghill II et al., "Tiger, Inc." *Business Week*, April 28, 1997, p. 34; Kerry Capell et al., "Tiger May Drive Asia's Golf Nuts Even Wilder," *Business Week*, April 28, 1997, p. 37; "Tiger Woods," by Jeff Jensen, *Advertising Age*, June 30, 1997, p. 52; Roy S. Johnson, "Tiger!" *Fortune*, May 12, 1997, p. 74. *"Shut Up and Buy It"* Joshua Wolf Shenk, "The New Anti-Ad," *U.S. News & World Report*, October 20, 1997, p. 80; Thomas Bartlett, "Two for Me, None for You," *Business Week*, August 11, 1997, p. 35. *Neither Rain, Nor Snow* Paul M. Eng, "Keeping the Junk Out of E-Mailboxes," *Business Week*, February 24, 1997, p. 104; Sheree R. Curry, "Stop the E-Mail Madness," *Fortune*, May 26, 1997, p. 165; "Make That Junk E-Mail Disappear," *Business Week*, February 10, 1997, p. 108E; "Lost in Space," *Inc. Tech*, 1997, no. 2, p. 26; J. William Gurley, "E-Mail Gets Rich," *Fortune*, February 17, 1997; Rajiv Chandrasekaran, "Group Blocks Posting of UUNet Customers," *Washington Post*, August 5, 1997, p. C1; Daniel Greenberg, "Spam Hater, Net Services," *Washington Post*, August 8, 1997, p. N62. *Spike Lee Takes a Lease* "Spike Lee: Madison Ave.'s Gotta Have Him," *Fortune*, April 14, 1997, pp. 84–86; Stuart Elliott, "Spike DDB Is Off to a Fast Start," *New York Times*, July 9, 1997, p. D2; "A-B Enlists Spike Lee for Bud Ads," *Advertising Age*, June 23, 1997. **Table 13.1** R. Craig Endicott, "Top Marketers Invest $47.3 Billion in '95 Ads," *Advertising Age*, September 30, 1996, p. s54.

Chapter 14

Welcome to the Cyberspace Mall Stephen H. Wildstrom, "Service with a Click," *Business Week*, March 24, 1997, p. 19; Amy Dunkin, "Going Once, Going Twice. Cybersold!" *Business Week*, August 11, 1997, pp. 98–99; Fred Hapgood, "Foreign Exchange," *Inc. Tech* 1997, no. 2, pp. 85–88; Paul Judge, "From Computers to Croissants," *Business Week*, February 10, 1997, p. 108H; Leonard Weiner, "On-Line Tax Bite," *U.S. News & World Report*, July 21, 1997, p. 62; Gina Imperato, "Let's Go Cyber-Shopping," *Fast Company*, June–July 1997, pp. 197–207; Ian Fisher, "From Phones to Floating Eagles," *New York Times*, April 1, 1997, pp. B1, B8. *It's Your Business: Sears* Jennifer Steinhauer, "A Minority Market with Major Sales," *New York Times*, July 2, 1997, pp. D1, D3. *Faster Than a Speeding Bullet* Claudia H. Deutsch, "Riding the Rails of Technology," *New York Times*, August 1, 1997, pp. D1, D3. *Bookselling Goes Electronic, Twice* Charles C. Mann, "Volume Business," *Inc. Tech*, 1997, no. 2, pp. 54–61.

Part 5

The Millennium Bomb Danna K. Henderson, "To Meet the Millennium, Airlines Are Taking Steps to Deal with Computer Complications Accompanying the Approaching Year 2000," *Air Transport World*, September 1997, p. 96; Kris Hunter, "Getting Ready for the Big One: Business Prepares for 'Millennium Bug,'" *Memphis Business Journal*, August 26, 1996, p. 1; "Millennium Blues," *Chain Store Age Executive with Shopping Center Age*, October 1997, p. 8B; "Millennium Dilemma Could Cause Big Problems as Early as 1999, Fitch CPAs Say," *Software Industry Report*, March 3, 1997, p. 1; Paul Minkin and Adrienne Guistwite, "Are You Ready for the Next Millennium?" *Telephony*, June 24, 1996, p. 72; Ruth Morris, "Labor Shortage Looms over Year 2000 Problem," *Reuters*, January 26, 1998; Tariq K. Muhammad, "The 2000 Year Glitch: Will Your Computer Be Able to Usher in the New Millennium?" *Black Enterprise*, May 1997, p. 38; Andrea Rock and Tripp Reynolds, "The Year 2000 Bug," *Money*, February 1998, p. 49.

Chapter 15

Send in the Clowns Lisa W. Foderaro, "F.A.O. Schwarz Expands, with Visions of Briefer Waits," *New York Times*, August 26, 1997, p. B3. *How Clean Is Clean Enough?* "Clearing the Air: Is Our Air Clean Enough?" *Consumer Reports*, August 1997, pp. 36–38; John Carey, "Tiny Particles, Big Dilemma," *Business Week*, August 4, 1997, pp. 82–83; Mary Beth Regan and Amy Borrus, "Global Warming: The Heat's on Bill," *Business Week*, July 7, 1997, p. 39; Mary Beth Regan, "The Dustup over Fine Air Pollutants," *Business Week*, March 24, 1997, p. 203. *Better Service for You* Neil Gross, "New Tricks for Help Lines," *Business Week*, April 29, 1996, pp. 97–98. *Honda's "Global" Accord* Valerie Reitman, "Honda Sees Performance and Profits from New Accord," *Wall Street Journal*, August 27, 1997, p. B4; Keith Naughton et al., "Can Honda Build a World Car?" *Business Week*, September 8, 1997, pp. 100–108. **Figure 15.1** *Monthly Labor Review* (Washington, DC: U.S. Department of Labor), August 13, 1993, p. 68, and July 1996, p. 67. **Figure 15.2** *Survey of Current Business* (Washington, DC: U.S. Department of Commerce), July 1993, p. 10; *Survey of Current Business* (Washington, DC: U.S. Department of Commerce), January/February 1996, p. 37; *Survey of Current Business* (Washington, DC: U.S. Department of Commerce), July 1996, p. 21.

Chapter 16

Dell Speeds Its Way to Quality Gary McWilliams, "Whirlwind on the Web," *Business Week*, April 7, 1997, pp. 132–136; Andrew E. Serwer, "Michael Dell Turns the PC World Inside Out," *Fortune*, September 8, 1997, pp. 76–86; David Kirkpatrick, "Now Everyone in PCs Wants to Be Like Mike," *Fortune*, September 8, 1997, pp. 91–92; Stephanie Anderson Forest et al., "And Give Me an Extra-Fast Modem with That, Please," *Business Week*, September 29, 1997, p. 38. *Outsourcing* John A. Byrne, "Has Outsourcing Gone Too Far?" *Business Week*, April 1, 1996, pp. 26–28; "Fast Facts About Outsourcing," *Purchasing Today*, August 1997; Edmund O. Welles, "Outsourcery," *Inc.*, April 1997, pp. 54–60; "What—Me, Outsource?" *Inc.*, October 1997, p. 112. *The Skies Are Getting Friendlier Again* Wendy Zellner, "Coffee, Tea—and On-Time Arrival," *Business Week*, January 20, 1997, p. 30.

Samsung Takes to the Road Louis Kraar, "Behind Samsung's High-Stakes Push into Cars," *Fortune*, May 12, 1997, pp. 119–120. **Figure 16.4** http://www.adaclabs.com/ about/quality.html

Chapter 17

Area Codes Go Global Andy Reinhardt et al., "Zooming Down the I-Way," *Business Week*, April 7, 1997, pp. 76–87; John W. Verity, "Try Beating These Long-Distance Rates," *Business Week*, April 22, 1996, pp. 131–132. ***"Your CEO Wears Combat Boots"*** Daniel H. Pink, "Hey, Your CEO Wears Combat Boots!" *Fast Company*, June–July 1997, pp. 46–48. ***How Much Is Information Worth?*** Iver Peterson, "Public Information, Business Rates," *New York Times*, July 14, 1997, pp. D1, D10. ***Is Your Computer a Television?*** Joel Brinkley, "PC Makers Challenge Broadcasters over Format for Digital Television," *New York Times*, April 8, 1997; Joel Brinkley, "Who Will Build Your Next TV? Industries Fight for $150 Billion Prize," *New York Times*, March 28, 1997; Neil Gross, "Defending the Living Room: How TV Makers Intend to Fend Off Cyberlopers," *Business Week*, June 24, 1996, pp. 96–98; Frank Rose, "The End of TV As We Know It," *Fortune*, December 23, 1996, pp. 58–68; Robert D. Hof and Gary McWilliams, "Digital TV: What Will It Be?" *Business Week*, April 21, 1997; Kyle Pope and Mark Robichaux, "Waiting for HDTV? Don't Go Dumping Your Old Set Just Yet," *Wall Street Journal*, September 12, 1997, p. 1; David Bank, "Changing Picture," *Wall Street Journal*, September 11, 1997, p. R15.

Chapter 18

Too Shady Even for an Audit? Mark Maremont, "Bean Counters Get an Early Warning System," *Business Week*, December 9, 1996, pp. 68–69. ***Closing the Gender Gap in Accounting*** Gene Koretz, "Accounting's Big Gender Switch," *Business Week*, January 20, 1997; Keith Hammonds and Gabrielle Saveri, "Accountants Have Lives, Too, You Know," *Business Week*, February 23, 1998, pp. 89–90. ***Psst! Want a New Credit Card?*** Mike McNamee and Richard A. Melcher, "Message from the Mall," *Business Week*, March 24, 1997, pp. 30–32; Joseph Weber and Alison Rea, "A Hard Blow for Easy Credit," *Business Week*, March 31, 1997, p. 39; Gene Koretz, "Who's Afraid of Credit Cards?" *Business Week*, March 3, 1997, p. 26; "Consumers: 'Rainy Day'?" *Inc.*, January 97, p. 58; Herb Greenberg, "The Trouble with Credit Cards," *Fortune*, May 26, 1997, pp. 28–29; "Why

More Nasty Card Tricks Are on the Way," *Money*, May 1997, p. 47; Halimah Abdullah, "Credit Lures College Students Down Path to Onerous Debt," *New York Times*, August 24, 1997, p. 20. ***The Food Was All Right*** Nelson D. Schwartz, "The Boston Chicken Problem," *Fortune*, July 7, 1997; Dottie Enrico, "Boston Market Spoofs Klein," *USA Today*, June 30, 1997; Eric Schine, "Coming Home to Roost," *Business Week*, June 16, 1997; "Boston Chicken Realigns Top Management," *Reuters*, May 29, 1997; Eric Schine, "The Squawk Over Boston Chicken," *Business Week*, October 21, 1996, pp. 64–72. **Figure 18.8** *Standard & Poor's NYSE Stock Reports* (New York: McGraw-Hill, 1997), July 23, 1997, p. 802; Mark Maremont, "Kodak's New Focus," *Business Week*, January 30, 1995, p. 65.

Part 6

Lettuce and Loans Christine Blank, "Are Consumers Confused?" *Progressive Grocer*, July 1996, p. 14; Brett Chase, "Banks Race to Expand Chicago Supermarket Networks," *American Banker*, January 22, 1997, p. 5; Garey Gillam, "Supermarket Branches Ring Up Another Big Year," *American Banker*, January 8, 1997, p. 7; Julie Monahan, "The Branch Is Dead. Long Live the Branch!" *ABA Banking Journal*, April 1997, p. S2; Stephen Timewell, "Shopping for Money," *The Banker*, August 1996, p. 18; Jeffrey Zack, "National Commerce Points Way to Success in the Supermarkets," *American Banker*, May 6, 1996, p. 4A.

Chapter 19

Who Needs Cash Anyway? Kalyani Vittala, "Cashless Society Put to Test in Ontario Town," *New York Times*, September 30, 1997, p. D2; Stephen E. Frank, "At Dawn of Cashless Revolution, It's Smart to Carry Spare Change," *Wall Street Journal*, October 7, 1997, p. B1; David M. Halbfinger, "West Siders Testing a Plastic Substitute for Pocket Change," *New York Times*, October 7, 1997, p. B1. ***On-line Banking*** Stephen H. Wildstrom, "Do's and Don'ts of Cyberbanking," *Business Week*, September 29, 1997, p. 19; Lisa Reilly Cullen, "Finally, You Could Profit by Banking On-line," *Money*, September 1997, pp. 31–35; "Paying Bills by Computer: Time to Switch to Digital Checks?" *Consumer Reports*, August 1997, pp. 54–55. ***His Bank Pushed Him "Into the Pool"*** Joshua Macht, "The Accidental Automator," *Inc. Tech* 1997, no. 2, pp. 66–71. ***Competition Heats Up for Your Dollars*** Linda Greenhouse, "Banks Take

On Credit Unions Over the Limits of Membership," *New York Times*, October 7, 1997, p. A23. **Figure 19.1** *Federal Reserve Bulletin* (Washington, DC: Board of Governors of the Federal Reserve System, November 1997), p. A12. **Figure 19.2** *Survey of Current Business* (Washington, DC: U.S. Department of Commerce), November 1997, pp. D13, D45, D57. **Table 19.1** "Big MacCurrencies," *The Economist*, April 12–18, 1997, p. 71.

Chapter 20

Investing in a Team of Your Own Dennis Berman, "A Home Team of Your Very Own," *Business Week*, September 22, 1997, p. 120; Tim Carvell, "So You Want to Own a Team?" *Fortune*, November 11, 1996, pp. 46–47; Phaedra Hise, "Cubs Send Minor-League Owners to the Showers," *Inc.*, April 1997, p. 24.; Roy Furchgott, "Joy in Mudville: The Resale Value of Minor League Teams," *New York Times*, October 26, 1997, Business section, p. 11. ***An Unusual Investment in the Future*** Claudia H. Deutsch, "Goldman, Sachs Invests Time in City Schools," *New York Times*, October 14, 1997, p. B8. ***How Do You Put Your Money Where Your Mouth Is?*** Amy Dunkin, "Want to Put Your Money Where Your Conscience Is?" *Business Week*, September 8, 1997, pp. 134–135. ***Investment Clubs Come into Their Own*** Eileen Kinsella and Nichole M. Christian, "Investment Clubs Catch On With Blacks," *Wall Street Journal*, October 15, 1997, pp. C1, C17–18; Jim Frederick, "These High-Tech Services Deliver Timely Investing News Directly to Your Computer—For Free," *Money*, September 1997, p. 23–24. **Figure 20.9** Data from the *Wall Street Journal*. **Figure 20.10** Susan E. Kuhn, "How Crazy Is This Market?" *Fortune*, April 15, 1996, pp. 78–83. Data from Smith Barney.

Chapter 21

Financing a Recipe into an Empire Julie Flaherty, "Sailing on a Rising Tide of Juice," New York Times, September 17, 1997, pp. D1, D5. ***Lasers to Keep Publisher's Inventory Under Control*** Doreen Carvajal, "Holtzbrinck's New Word on U.S. Publishing," *New York Times*, September 11, 1997, pp. D1, D4. ***How to Write a Business Plan*** Susan Hodges, "One Giant Step Toward a Loan," *Nation's Business*, August 1997, pp. 34, 36. ***Business Plastic*** Rodney Ho, "Credit Card Use to Finance Business Is Soaring, Says Survey of Small Firms," *Wall Street Journal*, September 25, 1997, p. B2. **Figure 21.1** Carl Beidleman, *The Handbook of International Investing* (Chicago: Probus, 1987), p. 133.

Appendix 1

Look Before You Compete Hal Lancaster, "How to Loosen Grip of a Noncompete Pact After Your Breakup," *Wall Street Journal*, February 17, 1998, B1. ***As You Drive, So Shall You Pay*** Keith Bradsher, "Big Insurers Plan to Increase Rates on Large Vehicles," *New York Times*, October 17, 1997, 1, D7.

Photo and Cartoon Credits

Chapter 1

Pages 4–5: D. Young-Wolff/PhotoEdit; page 6: Leo Cullum © 1992 from The New Yorker Collection. All rights reserved; page 9: C.Bruce Forster/ Viewfinders page 10: Tobias Everke/ Gamma Liaison, Inc.; page 18: AP/Wide World Photos; page 22: AP/Wide World Photos; page 25: Ann States/SABA Press Photos, Inc.

Chapter 2

Pages 32–33: Frank Orel/Tony Stone Images; page 35: Carnegie Library of Pittsburgh; page 39: Courtesy of Sears, Roebuck and Co.; page 47: Richard Cline © 1991 from The New Yorker Collection. All rights reserved; page 48: Kevin Peterson/Parallel Productions, General Mills

Chapter 3

Pages 54–55: Jeffrey Aaronson/Network Aspen; page 59: Tomasz Tomaszewski/ Thomasz Tomaszewski Photography; page 64: Peter Seiner © 1980 from The New Yorker Collection. All rights reserved; page 65: Michele Burgess; page 73: Eric Bouvet/Agence Ernoult Features

Chapter 4

Pages 80–81: Mike Greenlar; page 86: Andrew Holbrooke/Matrix International; page 88: Steve Starr/SABA Press Photos, Inc.; page 91: Anne Cusack/ Los Angeles Times Syndicate; page 95: Stephen Ferry/Gamma Liaison, Inc.; page 95: John Chiasson, Gamma Liaison, Inc.; page 95: Bill Swersey/Gamma Liaison, Inc.; page 98: Jeff Greenberg/PhotoEdit

Chapter 5

Pages 108–109: Ann States/SABA Press Photos, Inc.; page 111: Daniel Simon/ Gamma Liaison, Inc.; page 112: Chris Corsmeier/Corsmeier Photography; page 114: Pam Francis/Pam Francis Photography; page 117: J.B. Handelsman © 1972 from The New Yorker Collection. All rights reserved; page 124: Marilynn K. Yee/New York Times Permissions; page 125: United Feature Syndicate. Reprinted by permission.

Chapter 6

Pages 132–133: Corning Incorporated; page 136: Louis Psihoyos/Matrix International; page 141: Silvia Otte; page 142: Kucine photo/Maine; page 144: John Abbott/John Abbott, Photography; page 146: © James Schnepf; page 148: Mike Greenlar

Chapter 7

Pages 154–155: Yunghi Kim; page 158: John Harding; page 160: Cathlyn Melloan/Tony Stone Images; page 164: Brian Leng/Brian Leng Photography

Chapter 8

Pages 182–183: David Carson/New York Times Permissions; page 185: Leo Cullum © 1993 from The New Yorker Collection. All rights reserved; page 194: John Nollendorfs; page 196: Frank Polich/AP/Wide World Photos; page 202: Vincent J. Musi; page 204: Ed Kashi

Chapter 9

Pages 210–211: Chris Corsemeier/New York Times Permissions; page 212: Photo courtesy of Hewlett-Packard Company; page 215: Tom Raymond/ Medichrome/The Stock Shop, Inc.; page 221: Peter Yates/ SABA Press Photos, Inc.; page 223: Steve Woit; page 227: Scott Montgomery Photography; page 228: Leo Cullum © 1991 from The New Yorker Collection. All rights reserved.

Chapter 10

Pages 238–239: Summer Productions; page 241: Stock Montage, Inc./Historical Pictures Collection; page 247: Leo Cullum © 1993 from The New Yorker Collection. All rights reserved; page 257: Lesser/Gamma Liaison, Inc.

Chapter 11

Pages 268–269: Darcy Padilla/New York Times Permissons; page 275: Michael L. Abramson Photography

Chapter 12

Pages 300–301: Miramax/Shooting Star; page 305: William Hamilton © 1996 from The New Yorker Collection. All rights reserved; page 321: Paulo Fridman/Sygma

Chapter 13

Pages 328–329: David Longstreath/AP Wide World Photos

Chapter 14

Pages 354–355: Frank LaBua/Simon & Schuster/PH College; page 359: Christopher Covey/Christopher Covey Photography; page 361: Will Crocker/Thomas Mann; page 367: Churchill & Klehr Photography; page 370: Gerhard Joren/Katz Rea/SABA Press Photos, Inc.

Chapter 15

Pages 386–387: Ferry/Gamma Liaison, Inc.; page 389: Bob Sacha/Bob Sacha Photography; page 391: Fritz Hoffman/ The Image Works

Chapter 16

Pages 414–415: Richard Drew/AP/ Wide World Photos; page 422: Ed Fisher © 1995 from The New Yorker Collection. All rights reserved; page 427: Chris Jones/The Stock Market; page 430: Frito-Lay, Inc.; page 434: Steve LaBadessa/Steve LaBadessa Photography; page 435: U.S. Department of Commerce

Chapter 17

Pages 444–445: Coneyl Jay/Tony Stone Images; page 458: Michael Newman/ PhotoEdit; page 463: Tracey Kroll; page 464: Mort Gerberg © 1998 from The Cartoon Bank. All rights reserved; page 465: Brownie Harris/Brownie Harris, Photographer; page 465: Jerry Mason/NewScientist/Science Photo Library/Photo Researchers, Inc.; page 468: Brownie Harris/Brownie Harris, Photographer

Chapter 18

Pages 476–477: SuperStock, Inc.; page 480: Toys "R" Us, Inc.; page 495: Jack Ziegler © 1998 from The Cartoon Bank. All rights reserved; page 498: Mark

Richards/PhotoEdit

Chapter 19
Pages 512–513: Dave Caulkin/AP/Wide World Photos; page 514: Robert Mankoff © 1998 from The Cartoon Bank. All rights reserved; page 525: Peter Korniss; page 534: Richard B. Levine/Frances M. Roberts

Chapter 20
Pages 544–545: David Bergman/Miami Herald Publishing Co.; page 564: Dean Victor © 1998 from The Cartoon Bank.

All rights reserved; page 567: Reuters/Peter Morgan/Archive Photos

Chapter 21
Pages 576–577: Bob Benchley/New York Times Permissions; page 585: Carole

Subject Index

Multimedia communication systems, 467–68
Multinational firms, 69
    accounting system used by, 498
Multiple product lines, 304–5
Municipal bonds, 554–56
    in Orange County, California, 555–56
    in Tyrone, Pennsylvania, 554–55
Mutual funds, 557–58
    money market, 516
    quotations on, 562–63
Mutual insurance companies, 610
Mutual savings banks, 522

NAFTA. *See* **North American Free Trade Agreement (NAFTA)**
NARB. *See* National Advertising Review Board (NARB)
NASCAR, marketing by, 264–67
NASD. *See* National Association of Securities Dealers (NASD)
NASDAQ Composite Index, 553
NASDAQ (National Association of Securities Dealers Automated Quotation) system, 552–53
National Advertising Review Board (NARB), 340
National Alliance of Business, 91
National Association for the Advancement of Colored People (NAACP), 78
National Association of Investment Clubs, 572
National Association of Securities Dealers (NASD), 552
    on supermarket investment centers, 510
National banks, 520
National brands, 311
National Center for Social Entrepreneurs, 154
National Credit Union Administration, 542
National debt, 24
National Defense University (NDU), 453
National Education Association, 243
National Federation of Independent Businesses (NFIB), 168, 170
National Flood Insurance Association, 610
National Foundation for Women Business Owners (NFWBO), 163
Nationality, as demographic variable, 280
National Labor Relations Act (Wagner Act). *See* Wagner Act (1935)
National Labor Relations Board (NLRB), 250

National markets, small business promotion and, 347
National Park Service, privatization and, 11
National Tax Administration Agency (Japan), 498
National teachers' retirement system (TIAA-CREF), 49
National Trades Union, 241
National Typographical Union, 241
Natural laws, 35
Natural monopolies, 17
Natural resources, 7
Needs model. *See* Hierarchy of human needs model
Negligence torts, 604
Negotiation
    labor and, 245
    of prices, 320–21
Net. *See* Internet
Net earnings. *See* Net income
Net income, 490
Net profit. *See* Net income
Net profit margin. *See* Return on sales
Networking, 170, 189
Networks
    computer, 460–61
    data communication, 465
New products
    sales of, 325
    Samsung automobiles as, 441
    Web sites for, 326–27
New Social Entrepreneurs, The, 154
Newspapers, 38
    online services and, 29
    value of information to, 456
New York (state), privatization in, 10
New York Stock Exchange (NYSE), 41, 551, 552
    automatic trading suspension by, 567–68
Nigeria, 17
No-fault auto insurance, 612
No-load funds, 557
Noncertified public accountants, 482
Nondeposit institutions, 522–24
    insurance companies, 522–23
    pension funds, 522
    securities dealers, 523–24
Nonproductive facilities, 400
Nonprofit organizations (nonprofits), entrepreneurship in, 154–55
Nonstore retailing, 368–70
Norris-LaGuardia Act (1932), 250
North America, marketplaces in, 59–60
North American Free Trade Agreement (NAFTA), 608
    global marketing and, 273
    union cooperation and, 248
North Korea, 8

NOW accounts, 515
NYSE. *See* New York Stock Exchange (NYSE)

Objections, in personal selling, 343
Observation, in market research, 284
Occupational Safety and Health Act (1970), 199
Occupational Safety and Health Administration (OSHA), 199, 601
Ocean marine insurance, 612
Odd-even pricing, 320
Odd lot, 566
Office information technologies, 463–64
Office products industry, distribution in, 359
Office-to-office direct selling, 370
Off-price stores, 367
"Off the clock" labor, 238–39
Off-the-job training, 188
Oil industry, U.S. embargoes and, 75
Oligopoly, 15, 16–17
On-air time, SNI and managing of, V7–V8
On-line broker, 363, 364
On-line city guides, 29
On-line services, 467
On-line shopping, 354–55
On-line travel reservation system, American Express/Microsoft joint effort, 32–33
On-the-job training, 188
OPEC. *See* Organization of Petroleum Exporting Countries (OPEC)
Open-book credit, 582
Open-market operations, of Fed, 531
Open promotion system, 187
Operating expenditures. *See* Short-term (operating) expenditures
Operating expenses, 490
Operating income, 490
Operational plans, 115
Operations control, 404–8
    material management in, 405
    tools for, 405–7
Operations information systems, 464–65
Operations (production) management, 392
Operations managers, 120
Operations personnel, for computers, 453
Operations process, 394–95
Operations, 120
Operations management, 504
    Year 2000 problems and, 382–84
Operations planning, 397–403
Order cycle times, 375
Order processing, 342, 375
Organizational analysis, 114